ARCHITECTURAL ARTS & SCULPTURE

THE GUILD®

Kraus Sikes Inc.
Madison, Wisconsin
USA

Published by:
Kraus Sikes Inc.
228 State Street
Madison, WI 53703-2215
TEL 800-969-1556
TEL 608-256-1990
FAX 608-256-1938

Administration:
Toni Fountain Sikes, President
James F. Black, Jr., Vice President
Susan K. Evans, Vice President of Sales
Raymond Goydon, Consultant
Theresa Ace, Business Manager
Debbie Lovelace, Operations Manager
Emily Lovelace, Administrative Assistant
Kristen Syreini, Administrative Assistant

Production, Design, Editorial:
Cheryll Mellenthin, Production Manager
Kathlyn Williams, Production Assistant
Marcia LaCour-Little, Production Assistant

Katie Kazan, Editorial Manager
Theodora Zehner, Editorial Assistant
Christopher M. Herzig, Intern
Joseph R. Kultgen, Intern
Tia Michelle Simoni, Intern

Susan Troller, Writer • Jan Hersey, Writer
Natalee S. Morse, Writer

DNP America, Inc., Printer

Publisher's Representatives:
Susan K. Evans
Tom Christensen • Martha Johnson
Diane Nelson • Sharon Marquis
Bastien Atterbury • Karen O. Brown
Kimberly McKnight

Worldwide Distribution:
Hearst Books International
1350 Avenue of the Americas
New York, NY 10019

THE GUILD

ISBN (softback) 1-880140-18-7   ISBN (hardback) 1-880140-17-9
Printed in Hong Kong

Special thanks to our 1996 Review Committee:
Ann Ayres, Ayres Steinmetz Ltd.
David Philippart, Environment & Art Letter
Robert Shipley, Bowen Williamson Zimmermann

Cover Art:
Power Play by Erick C. Johnson, painted steel,
plexiglass and neon, 60' x 80' x 20' (atrium size),
photo by Kimball Hall. See page 135.

NOTHING LESS

I know, I know, it's a beautiful book. But it's so much more.

We get hundreds of letters; people tell us how much they love it, how it inspires and stimulates them. Patricia Harvey, **FASID**, writes, "When it arrives, I feel great! When I open it, I look — or try to look — at everything at once. The quality of work is magnificent."

The words of praise, the phone calls, the faxes from around the world make us feel good. After all, we work hard to put all of these resources under one cover.

But our efforts would be for naught if it weren't for you. For our mission is only accomplished when someone calls an artist for more information, or takes this book along to a client meeting, or even sits with it, dreaming of all the possibilities.

Therefore, as we enter our second decade of playing matchmaker to artists and those who work with them, we dedicate this edition of *The Architect's Sourcebook* to the people who help us accomplish our mission. Interspersed throughout these pages are interviews with design professionals and other individuals who put **THE GUILD** to its intended use, with marvelous results.

We salute them, and the countless others who embrace architectural art for the places where we live and work. They show us, time and time again, that it is possible to make buildings and spaces worthy of the public's interest and delight.

And, I think, nothing less will do.

Toni Fountain Sikes
Publisher

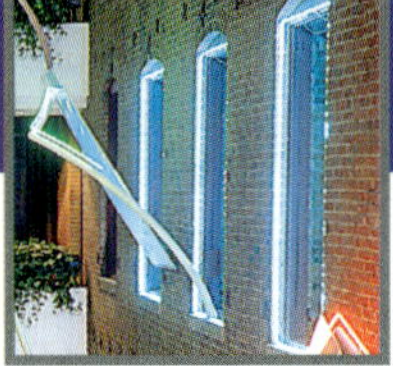

TABLE OF CONTENTS

FEATURES

Commissioned Artwork in the Mid-1990s 9
A report from our most recent survey of design professionals
suggests a healthy market for art in the built environment.

The Commissioning Process 13
The path to site-specific installations can be full of twists and turns. Our roadmap will
keep you headed in the right direction—and enjoying the scenic view.

A Collection by Committee 14
Designer Debra Woodward worked with a committee of employees at Amercian
Family Insurance to build a stellar collection of commissisoned artwork.

Profiles of GUILD *Users*
Interviews with design professionals who use THE GUILD to commission
art for their architectural projects.

RESOURCES

Ten Great Ways to Use The Architect's Sourcebook 8
A tour of the book's features and possibilities.

Working With an Art Consultant 305
Art consultants provide a specialized—and sometimes indispensable—service.

Listing of Art Consultants 308
Our state-by-state directory includes client lists and business descriptions.

National Organizations 316
A selected list of organizations devoted to the architectural arts.

Selected Publications 317
Periodicals featuring artist profiles and news about the architectural arts.

Index of Artists by State 320

Index of Artists and Companies 322

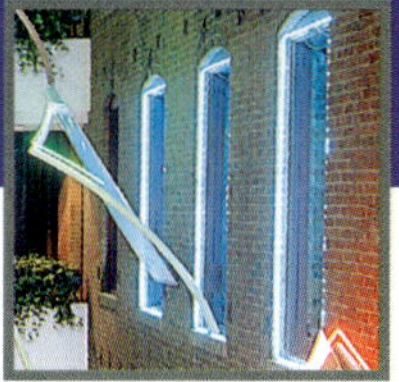

TABLE OF CONTENTS

ARTISTS

Artists by Section
Turn the page for a listing of featured artists.

THE GUILD REGISTERS®
Concise product and pricing information, as well as addresses and phones,
for artists working in four important areas.

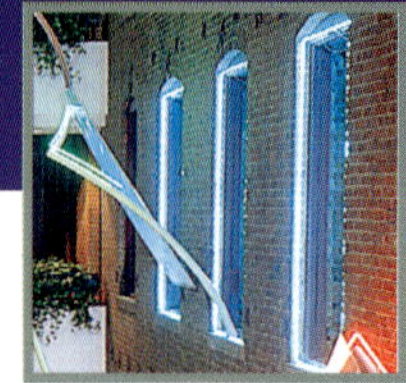

ARTISTS BY SECTION

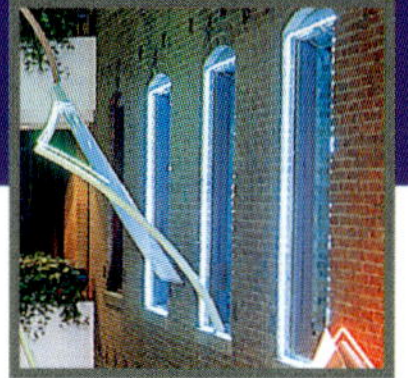

ARTISTS BY SECTION

1 QUALITY CONTROL. This book begins with an assurance: these artists are reliable and professional. Featured artists in GUILD sourcebooks have been juried in on the basis of experience, quality of work, and a solid reputation for working with architects and designers.

2 MOTIVATION. *The Architect's Sourcebook* is a great resource for client meetings. Clients have been known to reach levels of extreme excitement upon viewing the artistic possibilities showcased here.

3 GO AHEAD AND CALL. If something intrigues you while perusing *The Architect's Sourcebook*—a shape, a form, an exotic use of the commonplace—please, give the artist a call. Serendipity often leads to a wonderful creation.

4 HOW IT'S DONE. A wise guide is a great thing. Look throughout this volume for interviews with design professionals who have commissioned artwork with the help of THE GUILD. Their advice is insightful; their experiences inspiring.

5 MORE IS BETTER. We're always delighted to hear about firms that commission work from a GUILD artist. The American Family Insurance Company practically filled their new corporate headquarters with work by artists from THE GUILD. Look for the story—and photos of the artwork—beginning on page 14.

6 MORE ARTISTS … AND MORE. The right artist, the right media, the right region, and the right price. That's a lot of information, and we've got it. THE GUILD REGISTERS, beginning on page 226, list contact, product and pricing information for hundreds of artists working in architectural glass, metal and restoration, as well as public art.

7 CARING FOR THE OLD. Our newest resource, THE GUILD REGISTER of Architectural Restoration, uses a two-part format to direct you toward experienced artisans for your specific need. Start with the "Summary of Restoration Services," beginning on page 286, to identify areas of expertise. Continue your research with the detailed company listings that follow.

8 DESKTOP DIRECTORY. *The Architect's Sourcebook 11* is designed for quick reference, as well as leisurely browsing. The "Index of Artists and Companies" includes artists listed in THE GUILD REGISTERS, as well as those featured in the full-color pages, so finding a current phone number or checking product information is easily done. The information in your rolodex may grow stale; *The Architect's Sourcebook* is fresh each year.

9 ARTISTS THEN AND NOW. Many of the artists whose work you see here are also represented in earlier GUILD publications; look for references on artists' pages. You can order most of these early volumes through our main office; call 1-800-969-1556 for order information.

10 LET US HEAR FROM YOU. This volume of *The Architect's Sourcebook* is filled with stories about design professionals who use THE GUILD. We love hearing these stories and we love passing them on through the pages of our sourcebooks. Let us know about *your* project … perhaps we'll feature it in next year's edition.

THE GUILD's second in-depth survey on the commissioning process sheds new light on the people, steps and goals involved in commissioned artwork. One hundred and sixty-one surveys were distributed to design professionals who actively commission artwork through THE GUILD. A response rate of 32 percent included twenty-four interior designers, fifteen architects, eight art consultants, three developers and two art brokers.

Survey questions focused on two areas. Part one involved specific projects generated through use of GUILD sourcebooks; part two asked about characteristics of the respondent's firm, including its overall history of commissioning artwork and the various ways it uses THE GUILD. Responses to both sections are summarized on the following pages. In addition, descriptions of GUILD-generated projects can be found throughout this book in a series of interviews with survey respondents.

For us, it was particularly heartening to read —over and over again—about successful collaborations between design professionals and GUILD artists. Almost without exception, respondents reported both a positive working relationship and an exceptional aesthetic outcome. "The artist was extremely responsive and intuitive as to the needs of the client and the space," said one respondent. "A wonderful team experience," wrote another.

A grateful thanks to all who participated in the survey.

SURVEY RESULTS

What were the goals of including artwork in the project?

Create a more beautiful environment	52%
Enhance company image	27%
Public relations	5%
Increase property value	5%
Enhance employee morale	5%
Build client's art collection	5%
Reach a broader audience	1%

Who initiated including artwork in the project?

Interior designer	55%
Architect	21%
Art consultant	18%
Developer	3%
Client	3%

What were the most important factors in selecting the artist?

Quality of the artist's portfolio	43%
Artist's track record with similar jobs	16%
Strength of proposal for this project	13%
Personal chemistry with the artist	11%
Artist's prominence	10%
Artist's unique style	4%
Low cost of proposal	2%
Artist's location	1%

Overall, was this project a positive experience for you and your client?

Yes	97%
No	3%

FINDING: Increased property value is seldom the top goal of site-specific commissions.

To our surprise, only 5 percent of respondents ranked increased property value as the priority outcome for the project described. The variety of goals listed reflect a wide range of opinions about the value of art. But over half of respondents chose 'creating a more beautiful environment' as the primary goal for including artwork, clearly emphasizing the aesthetic and spiritual qualities of art much more than its financial worth.

FINDING: The client is seldom the first to suggest incorporating artwork in a project.

Real or perceived obstacles—including cost, time, and difficulty in accomplishing the task—may lead a client to believe that artwork is not feasible within a given budget or schedule. As a result, the design professional must often persuade the client that including artwork is both possible and desirable. Many respondents reported that the completed projects shown in GUILD sourcebooks were motivating to clients. And of course the pride of ownership, once all is said and done, is shared by all; 97 percent of respondents reported that the art component of the project was ultimately rewarding, both for themselves and their client.

FINDING: Low cost alone is not a significant factor in the choice of artist for a project.

Survey respondents indicate that previous work, as evidenced by a portfolio and track record with similar projects, is most helpful in selecting an artist. They also want a clear idea of what working with the artist will be like, based on the proposal and the initial collaborative chemistry. Interestingly, for the projects described, location and cost were not determining factors in the choice of artist.

CHARACTERISTICS OF SURVEY RESPONDENTS

The second part of the survey focused on general information about the respondent's firm and its history of commissioning artwork.

FINDING: Firms of every size, budget and focus commission artwork.

Firms working in every area of the design industry use THE GUILD to commission artwork. Surveys were returned by professionals specializing in areas as diverse as luxury hotels, landscape construction, liturgical design, and homes.

Almost 70 percent of survey responses were from firms employing just one to five design professionals, a range consistent with the average size of North American design and architecture firms. However, despite the small size of most firms, three of every four report annual income over $400,000; one in four have revenue over $3 million.

What is your firm's primary design focus?

Commercial/office	29%
Residential	22%
Interior architecture	11%
Medical/health care	9%
Renovation/restoration	7%
Retail	6%
Hospitality/recreational	5%
Liturgical	4%
Educational	3%
Municipal/government	3%
Industrial/warehouse	1%

How many design professionals are employed by your firm?

1 - 5	69%
6 - 10	4%
11 - 20	10%
21 - 50	4%
51 - 99	8%
100+	4%

What is your firm's annual dollar volume?

Under $200,000	6%
$200,000 - $399,000	19%
$400,000 - $999,999	21%
$1,000,000 - $2,999,999	27%
$3,000,000 - $4,999,999	10%
Over $5,000,000	17%

How are GUILD sourcebooks used by your firm?

Generate ideas and see what's available	96%
Identify artists for projects, using color pages	88%
Motivate clients to include artwork in a project	63%
Identify artists for projects, using B&W listings	29%
Loan to clients, for calling artists directly	25%
Display in the reception area	21%

What types of artwork have you or your firm commissioned?

Architectural glass	75%
Furniture	67%
Work for the wall	65%
Painted finishes/murals	65%
Architectural metal	63%
Textiles/floor coverings	58%
Architectural wood	58%
Sculpture (large standing)	52%
Architectural ceramics	50%
Sculptural objects	50%
Sculpture (atrium)	40%
Accessories	42%

Do you expect to increase the amount of artwork you commission in the coming years?

Yes	67%
No	6%
Unsure	27%

FINDING: Design professionals use THE GUILD in many ways to include a broad range of artworks in their projects.

Surveys confirmed that professionals use THE GUILD in all the ways we intend—and highlighted some additional benefits. Interior designer Carol Kodis likes GUILD sourcebooks because, "They show installations and give us a context. They help us think early on about how to include the artist's work in a project."

Across the board, respondents reported commissioning several types of artwork. Architectural glass and furniture lead the way with 75 and 67 percent respectively. But over half also commission work for the wall; painted finishes or murals; architectural metal, wood, or ceramics; textiles or floor coverings; and sculpture.

FINDING: Professionals predict continued good health for the architectural arts.

Our survey indicates that companies will commission more artwork in the coming years, with only 6 percent of respondents forecasting a decrease. This optimism might be explained by the observation of one respondent, an interior designer, who stated, "In my own community, people are becoming more aware of—and interested in—the arts each day."

Because THE GUILD operates as a kind of matchmaker between artists and design professionals, we have considerable interest in how the matches that begin here turn out. We want to help these relationships work by doing everything we can to make the contact between architect and artist satisfying and profitable.

We also want to make it easier for architects to create new professional alliances with artists. And we'd especially like to reassure those who have been reluctant to try such collaboration because of their concerns about how the process works.

Successful projects result when architects and artists form good relationships with each other, relationships founded on mutual understanding of expectations, clear communication and a willingness of both parties to accept their responsibilities for making a good project.

This article is a how-to guide of the commissioning process ... how it comes about, who is involved, the steps to take and when to take them, what to prepare for, and how to avoid problems. We hope it answers some questions and offers encouragement to design professionals seeking to work directly with artists and artisans.

By far the most important part of getting great work is choosing a great artist—or at least the right artist for your particular project and pocketbook. This choice is the decision from which all others will flow, so it's worth investing time and energy in the selection process and seasoning the process with both wild artistic hopes and hard-nosed realism. The right choices at this early stage will make things go easier later on.

Some clients will be very interested in helping select the artist, and working closely with him or her once the choice is made. Others will want only minimal involvement, leaving most of the decision-making to the design team.

Whoever is making the decision, there are several ways to find the right artist. Obviously, we recommend browsing through GUILD sourcebooks. Not only do they show a wide range of some of the top work available, they also have the advantage of weeding out people who may not really want to work with designers and architects on commissioned pieces. Every GUILD artist is looking for collaborative work—that's why they're here. And many already have a strong track record of working with designers, architects and their clients. You will gain from their professionalism and experience.

FINDING YOUR ARTIST

If you don't find exactly what you want through THE GUILD, or you want to know who else may be available, there are a number of other routes to take in the selection process.

You may see work you like at a gallery or craft fair. Ask for artists' names and business cards. Design magazines often feature artist profiles, along with contact information. Your own colleagues may offer more names. And if the project is a large one, you may go through a request-for-proposal process that will draw responses from all over the continent.

A qualified art consultant will also have a wide network of artists to choose from. If the complexity of your project warrants using an art consultant in the selection process, make sure the consultant is sophisticated and experienced enough to provide real guidance in working with the artist. This means the ability to help negotiate the technical details of a very specific contract, including issues like installation, insurance, storage, transportation and possible engineering costs.

Your first contact with an artist sets the tone for the relationship to follow. With that contact, via telephone or letter, be prepared to provide information about the size and scope of your project, the budget, the deadlines, and even the details about the building site. This will help the artist tailor his or her response more specifically, giving you a better sense of whether this is the right person for your project.

Make your initial selection on the basis of what you like about an artist's past work. Most experienced artists will be pleased to provide a portfolio—usually on slides, but sometimes printed. Don't, however, expect to see the exact piece you're looking for in a portfolio. Remember, you're choosing an artist at this point, not a piece of art. Look for creativity, command of the materials or technology, and how the work fits the specific environment.

EXPECT PROFESSIONALISM

Once you've made a tentative selection based on a portfolio and the artist's past experience and reputation, it's time to get serious. Even though some designers and architects still believe artists are too 'unbusinesslike' to worry much about such things as building codes, lighting specifications, deadlines and budgets, the great majority of artists who seek commissioned work will be conversant with

A COLLECTION BY COMMITTEE

This is the first of several 'user' interviews in this edition of *The Architect's Sourcebook*. Each of the design professionals we spoke with has used GUILD sourcebooks to commission original artwork.

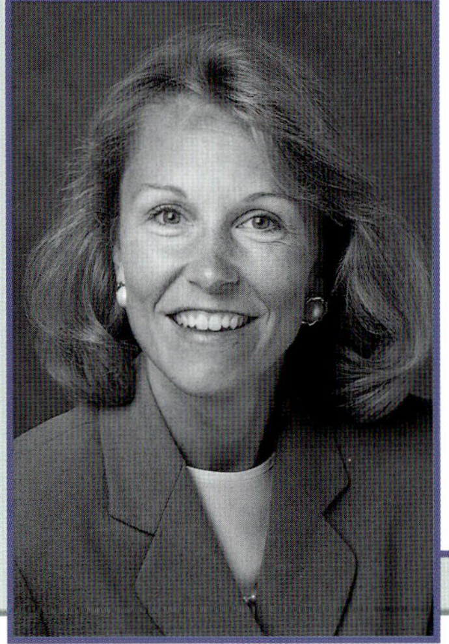

Debra Alton Woodward, design and planning supervisor at American Family Insurance, worked with a committee of employees to plan art for the company's new corporate headquarters. The results are exceptional, and because several GUILD artists are included, we decided to feature their work in the following pages.

Debra Alton Woodward   Steven Schumacher

these and other contract details. Most designers find that the artist's professionalism and knowledge of subject, materials, and details of code, safety and engineering is both complete and reassuring.

MEETING FACE-TO-FACE

Before making your final choice of artist, it's important to set up an initial, no-obligation meeting.

The purpose of this meeting is to find out if the chemistry is right—whether you have the basis to build a working relationship. It's also the time to confirm that the artist has the necessary skills to undertake your project. Be thorough and specific when asking questions. Ask what the artist sees as the important issues or considerations in the project. Evaluate his or her interest. Will your needs be a major or minor concern? Do the artist's style, approach and personality suit the project?

If it feels like you might have trouble working together, it's wise to heed these early warning signs. But if all goes well and you decide to move ahead with the artist, your second meeting will be to agree on a budget and timetable, and sign a contract.

At this second meeting, be resolved that silence is not golden and ignorance not bliss! Be frank. Tell the artist what you expect. Now is the time for possible misunderstandings to be brought up and resolved, not later, after the work is half done and deadlines loom.

A COLLABORATIVE ATMOSPHERE

Bring the artist into the process at the earliest possible stage—at about the same time you hire the general contractor. This is a wise investment for several reasons. From the very beginning, the space is designed with the art in mind, and the art is created to enhance the space. As a result, there are no unpleasant surprises about size or suitability of the artwork to the space. Furthermore, when art is planned for early on, it's far less likely to be cut at the end of the project, when money may be running low.

Early inclusion of the artist also helps ensure that the collaborative effort will go smoothly throughout all phases of the project. If the artist is respected as part of the team, his work can benefit the project's overall design.

onventional wisdom claims fine art can't co-exist with a committee selection process. But when the American Family Insurance Company built its new world headquarters in Madison, Wisconsin, it made a commitment to include major works of art selected by a committee of employees. The result is art that not only looks great, but also enjoys the enthusiastic support of the people who work for the company. Furthermore, the entire process—from the presentation of the earliest proposals to the selection of the artists to the final installation—has helped define and build American Family's corporate culture.

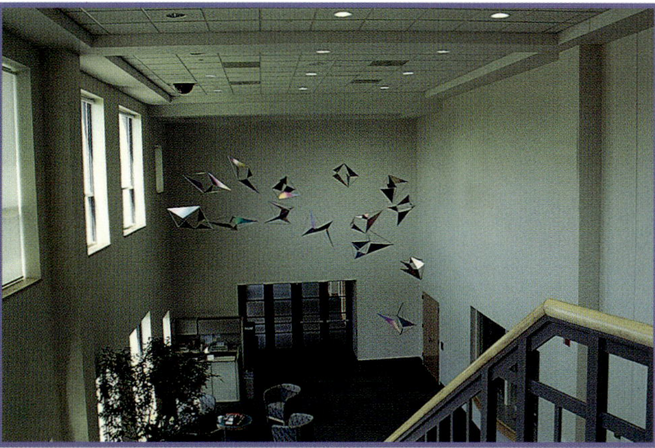

Unity, atrium sculpture by Robert Pfitzenmeier

For six years, designer Debra Alton Woodward was intimately involved with the design decisions that shaped the new headquarters of American Family, one of the nation's largest insurance carriers. Already a company veteran with a dozen years of experience running the in-house design department, Woodward became the liaison between art consultants, outside design team professionals, artists, and the committee of employees

Naturally, the scope of the project will determine the number of players to be involved with the artist. How will decisions be made? Will a single person sign off on recommendations? Are committees necessary? If so, it's a good idea to designate one person to serve as liaison with the artist to avoid mixed signals.

SEEK TWO-WAY UNDERSTANDING

Be sure the artist understands the technical requirements of the job, including traffic flow in the space, the intended use of the space, the building structure, maintenance, lighting and environmental concerns. By doing this, you ensure that the artist's knowledge, experience and skill become part of the project.

Keep the artist appraised of any changes you make that will affect the work in progress. Did you find a certain material you specified unavailable and replace it with something else? Did the available space become bigger or smaller? These may seem like small changes to you, but they could have a profound impact on an artist's planning and work.

At the same time, the artist should let you know of any special requirements his or her work will place on the space. Is it especially heavy? Does it need to be mounted in a specific way? Must it be protected from theft or vandalism? What kind of lighting is best? You may want to set aside a contingency budget to fund design changes or omissions once the project begins.

Most artists experienced with commissioned work factor the notion of a continuing design dialog into their

fee. There is an unfortunate belief—harbored by some architects, designers and, yes, artists too—that a willingness to change and compromise somehow indicates a lack of commitment or creativity. On the contrary. The ability to compromise on execution, without compromising on artistic quality, is a mark of professionalism. We recommend that you look for this quality in the artist you choose, and respect it by treating the artist as a partner in decisions made affecting his or her work.

Of course, part of working together is making clear who is responsible for what. Since few designers and architects—and even fewer contractors—are used to working with artists, the relationship is custom-made for misunderstanding. Without a firm understanding from the outset—nurtured by constant communication—things can easily fall through the cracks.

from many departments who were delegated to choose art for the new building.

"At least two really good things came out of the committee process," Woodward recalls. "First, it helped people buy into the decisions that were made. And second, in the process of educating themselves about artists and creativity, the committee also educated others in the organization. The Art Review Committee took its mission very seriously, and the art that was created fits and reflects our culture and the values of the company. It was a fascinating experience."

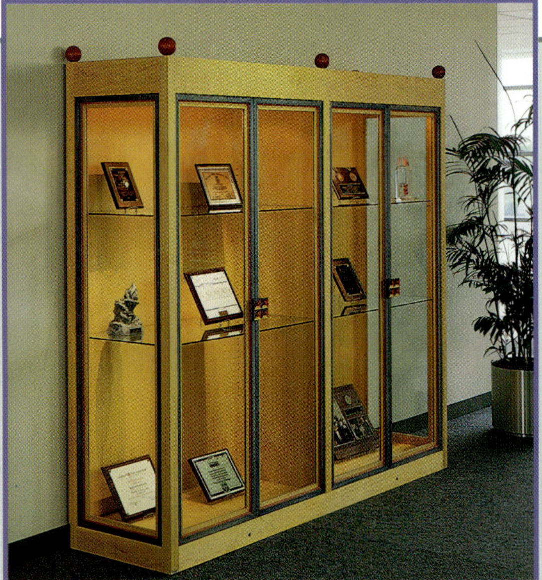

Display case by Woodfellows

Skot Weidemann

Working with Merrill Chase Galleries, a large Chicago-based art consulting firm, and charged with selecting artwork that reflected some aspect of American Family's heritage in its 13-state operational area, the committee reviewed a great number of proposals. Ultimately, several GUILD artists were among those chosen to produce work for the project. Robert Pfitzenmeier's hanging metal atrium sculpture is light reactive, creating a stunning, constantly changing pattern of shapes and colors. Glass artist Larry Zgoda adapted the circle-and-square motif of the entire

PUT IT
IN WRITING

It is a truism in any kind of business that it is much cheaper to get the lawyers involved at the beginning of a process than after something goes wrong. A contract or letter of agreement will assure you and the client that the artist will complete his or her work on time and to specifications. It will also assure the artist that he or she will get paid the right amount at the right time. That just about eliminates the biggest conflicts that can arise.

Contracts should be specific to the job. Customarily, artists are responsible for design, production, shipping and installation. If someone else is to be responsible for installation, be sure you specify who will coordinate it and who will pay for it—if it is not the artist, it usually is the client. With a large project, it is helpful to identify the tasks that, if held up for any reason, would delay completion of the project. They should be discussed up front to assure that both parties agree on requirements and expectations.

Most architects recognize that adequate compensation for the artist is in their best interest as it assures the type and level of service needed to fulfill their expectations. The more skill you need and the more complex the project, the more you should budget for the artist's work and services.

PAYMENT SCHEDULE

Payments are usually tied to specific points in the process. These serve as check points to make sure the work is progressing in a satisfactory manner, on time and on budget. Payment is customarily made in three stages, although this certainly depends on the circumstances, scope and complexity of the project.

The first payment is usually made when the contract is signed. It covers the artist's time and creativity in developing a design specific to your needs. You can expect to go through several rounds of trial and error in the design process, but at the end of this stage you will have detailed drawings and, for three-dimensional work, a maquette (model) that everyone agrees upon. The artist usually charges a fee to cover the costs of the maquette and design time.

The second payment is generally set for a mid-way point in the project and is for work done to date. If the materials are expensive, the client may be asked to advance money at this stage to cover materials' costs. If the commission is cancelled during this period,

---

project for a playful interior window of cut and stained glass. Ceramic artist Bruce Howdle created a massive wall installation, over 20 feet long and 11 1/2 feet tall. And finally, Woodfellows, a company producing fine architectural woodwork, collaborated with Woodward to design a series of superb, playful display cases.

Howdle's clay mural provided a very personal learning experience for numerous employees on the selection committee. "Lots of American Family people visited Bruce's stu-dio," Woodward says. "They watched the work develop and came to have a great appreciation for his level of craftsmanship and the sheer amount of time and energy involved in creating a piece on this scale." She adds that the wall, with its many references to elements that play a role in the company's history, has become a favorite stopping place for both locally-based employees and agents visiting the headquarters from out-of-town.

Woodward says the response to all of the artwork has been enthusiastic.

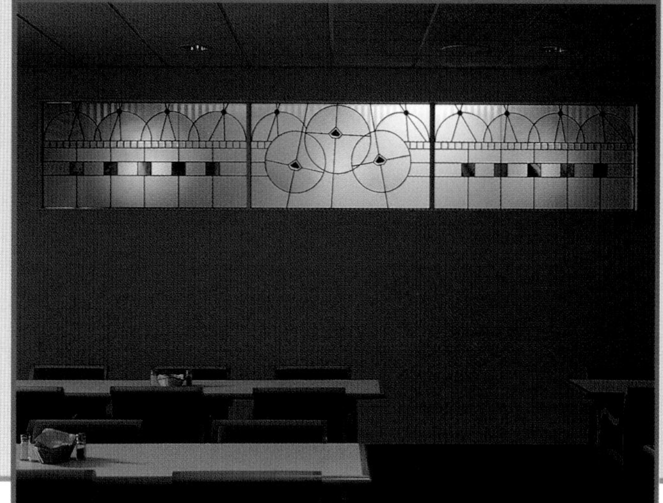

Architectural glass panels by Larry Zgoda

Harper Fritsch

the artist keeps the money already paid for work performed.

Final payment is usually due when the work is installed. If the piece is finished on time but the building or project is delayed, the artist is customarily paid on delivery, but still has the obligation to oversee installation.

You will find that most artists keep tabs on the project budget. Be sure that the project scope does not deviate from what was agreed at the outset. If the scope changes, amend the agreement accordingly.

FORGING A PARTNERSHIP

The partnership between artists and designers is an old and honorable one. Many venerable blueprints will indicate, for example, an architect's detail for a ceiling with the scrawled note, "Finish ceiling in this manner." The assumption, of course, is that the artisan working on the ceiling has both the technical mastery and aesthetic skill to create a whole expanse of space from a detail that comes from the mind and pen of the architect.

We believe today's new breed of artist is capable of such relationships, and we're delighted to see increasing numbers of design professionals including artists on their teams. After too many years of the arts being separated from architectural design, we're happy to be a part of a renewed interest in collaboration.

"The process allowed American Family employees to develop a real sense of ownership. Committee members focused on the company's values—the things it tries to stress as it reaches into the communities it serves—and looked for art that would reinforce those values.

"The company prides itself on being approachable, strong, vigorous, friendly and resourceful. The committee saw how hard the artists worked, and developed a great appreciation for American craftsmanship and know-how. There is a real connection between the people who work at American Family and this artwork."

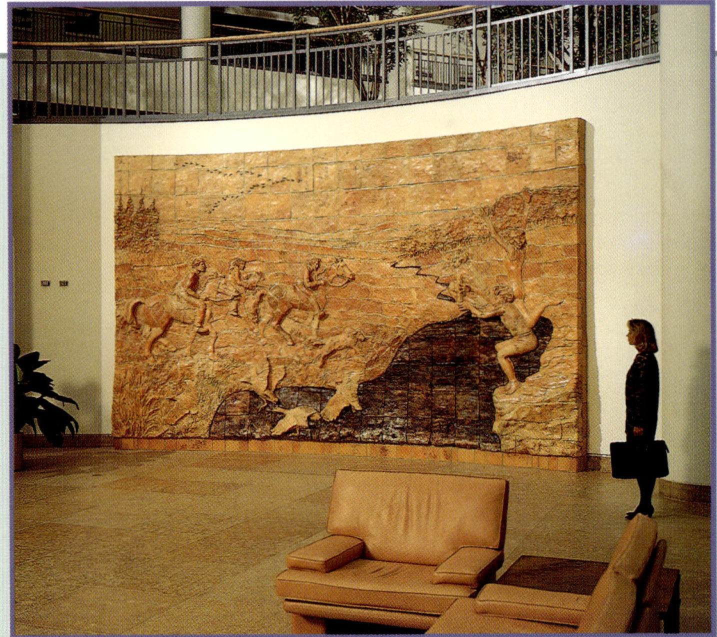

Debra Alton Woodward with Bruce Howdle's ceramic relief mural, titled *Exploration*   Skot Weidemann

ARCHITECTURAL METAL

Michael M. Amescua

3802 Cesar Chavez Avenue
Los Angeles, CA 90063
FAX 213-881-6447
TEL   213-268-0595

Michael M. Amescua has been producing free-standing sculpture and unique fences, gates, windows and chairs for public spaces and private individuals since 1985.

His public commissions have included the Los Angeles Metro Transit Authority, the California Highway Patrol, and the Los Angeles Department of Water and Power. His next scheduled private project includes window guards, a fence and a gate for a Craftsman-style home in the Silver Lake area of Los Angeles.

A *Moonlight Becomes You*, 1994,
steel, 10'H x 8'W x $^3/_8$"D

B *Guardian of the Rail*, 1995,
aluminum, 40'H x 8'W x $^3/_8$"D

C *Discussing the Cure*, 1993,
steel, 48"H x 12'L x $^1/_4$"D

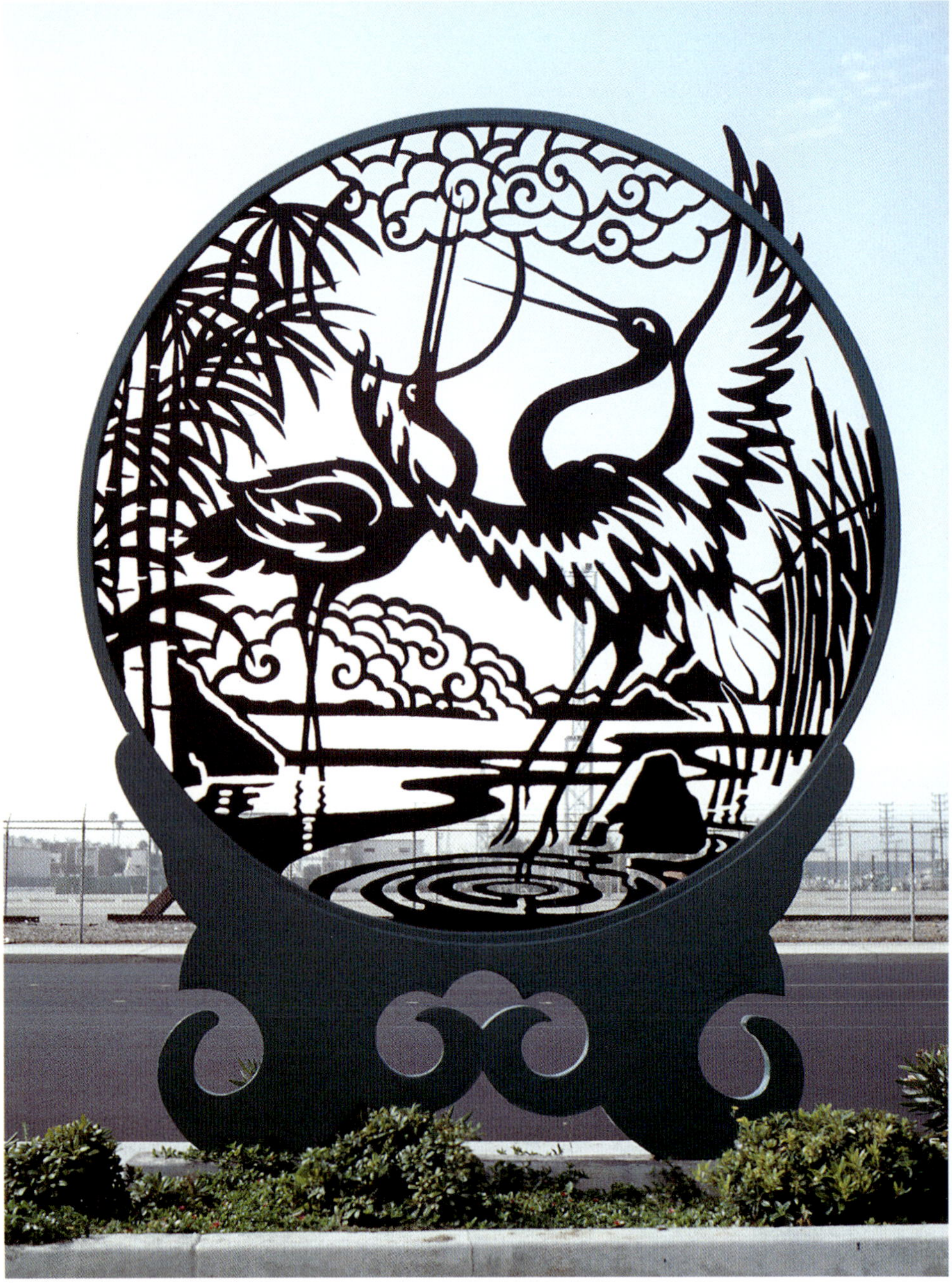

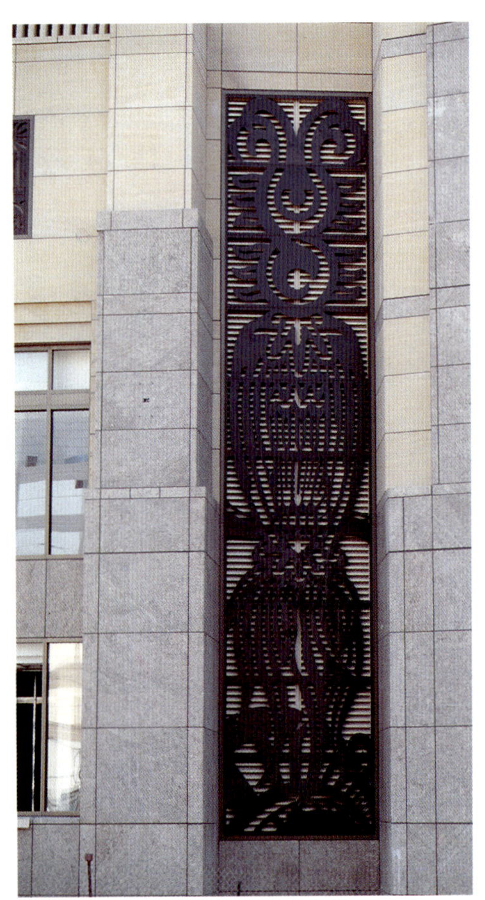

A

B

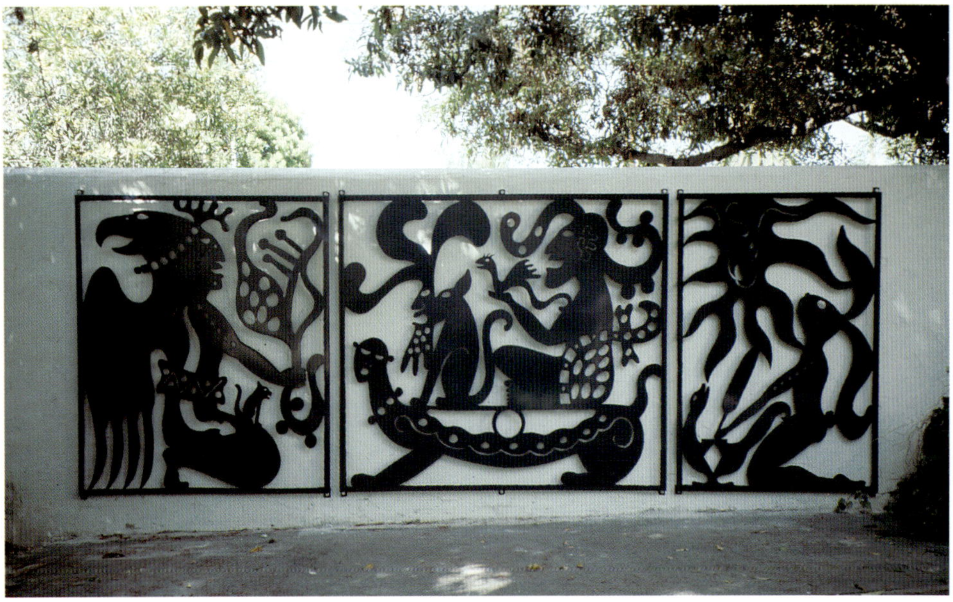

C

Michael Bondi

Michael Bondi Metal Design, Inc.
2801 Giant Road
Richmond, CA 94806
FAX 510-236-2615
TEL 510-236-2607

Michael Bondi Metal Design specializes in architectural and interior wrought metal, creating contemporary and classic designs in copper, bronze, monel, stainless, aluminum and iron. The studio works collaboratively or independently to develop unique solutions for architects, designers or individuals.

Commissions are undertaken worldwide for clients including Disney World, Disneyland, Euro Disney, Grand Hyatt Wailea, Donald Trump, Hendrix and Allardyce, Wolfgang Puck's Postrio Restaurant and Alice Waters' Chez Panisse.

Michael Bondi Metal Design has been honored with awards for excellence in design, technical detail and finish. The studio takes pride in thorough attention to detail, from the design phase through installation of the project.

Also see these GUILD publications:
Architect's Edition: 10
Designer's Edition: 6, 9

A Railing section, 1994, forged bronze and monel with copper caprail

B Main stair, 1994, forged steel with forged bronze caprail, bronze and stainless steel details, painted and patinated

C Interior staircase, 1995, venetian style rolling scrolls with three styles of forged leaves in steel and bronze with bronze caprail, painted and patinated

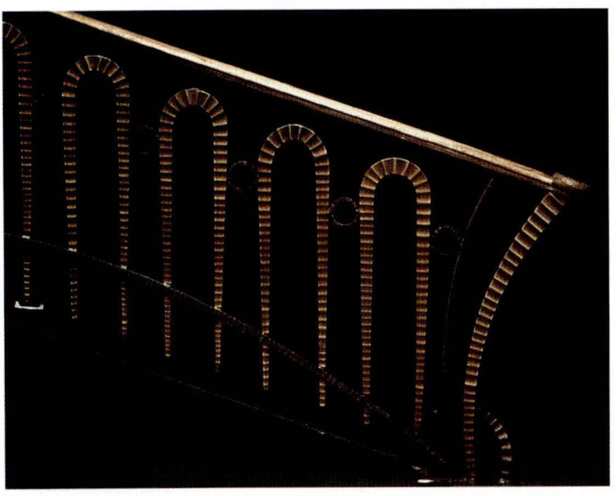

A

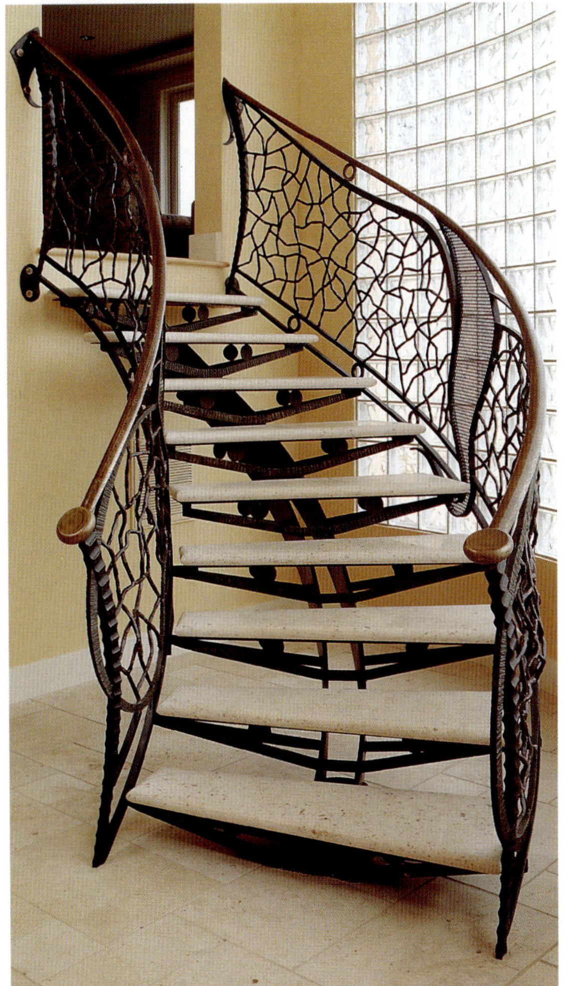

B

Colin McRae

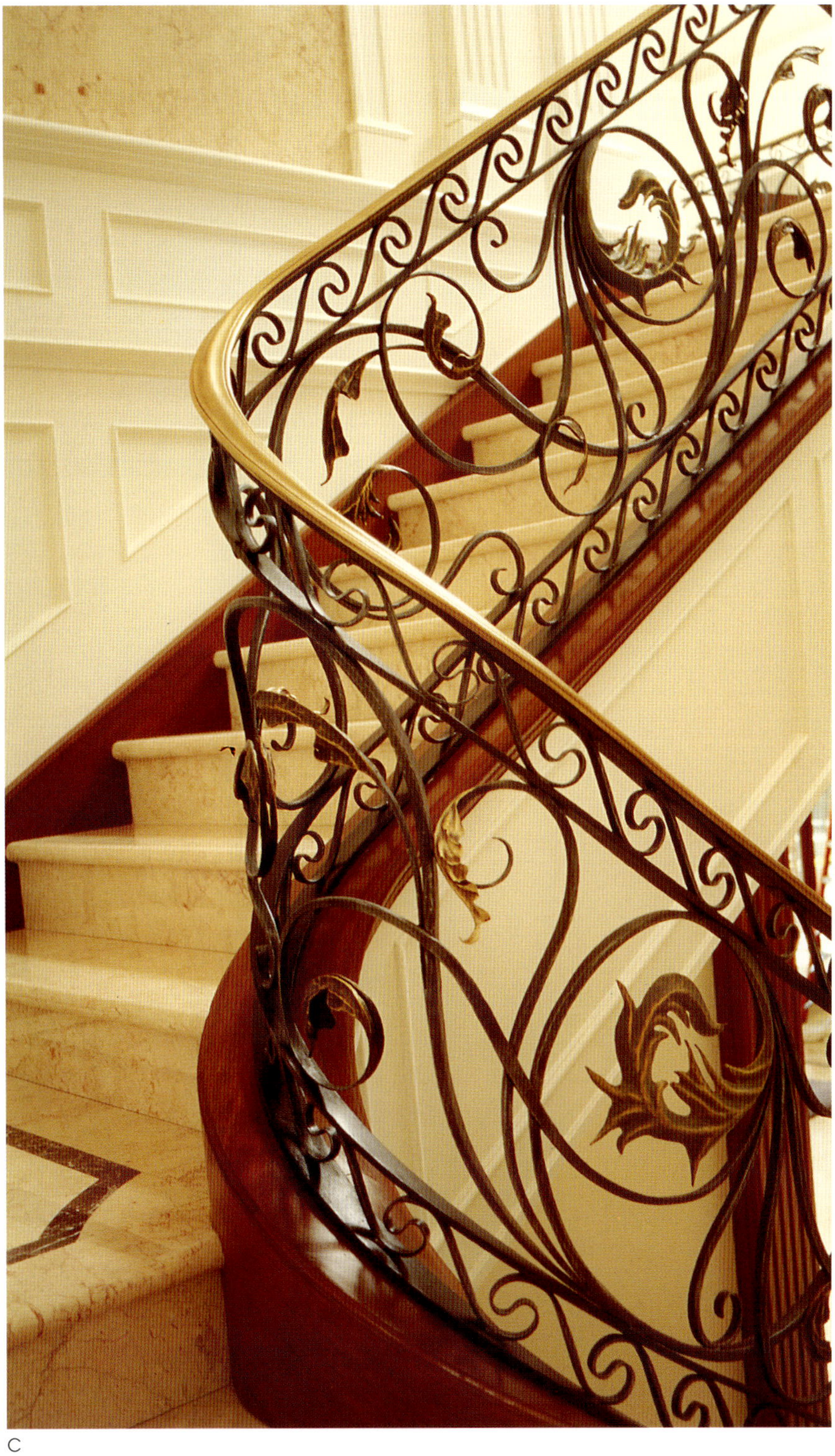

C

Nicholas Brumder

Brumder Ornamental Iron, Inc.
Formerly Liberty Forge
40128 Industrial Park
Georgetown, TX 78626
TEL 512-869-2830

Since 1972, Nicholas Brumder has been designing and producing the finest quality hand-wrought ornamental and sculptural metalwork. Working in collaboration with clients, architects, designers, and artists from a variety of disciplines, Brumder brings felicitous harmony between craft and setting.

Hot forging produces fluid forms, infusing life into rigid materials like steel, bronze, and aluminum. Brumder combines traditional methods with contemporary technology for a fresh interpretation of period style as well as contemporary work.

Projects range in scale from monumental and architectural to house jewelry, lighting and furniture. Brochure available on request.

A Cancer survivors memorial, Houston, TX, in collaboration with Thomas Studios, architect: Milosev Cekic

B & C Collumbarium gate for the Church of the Good Shepherd, Corpus Christi, TX, architect: Morgan Spear

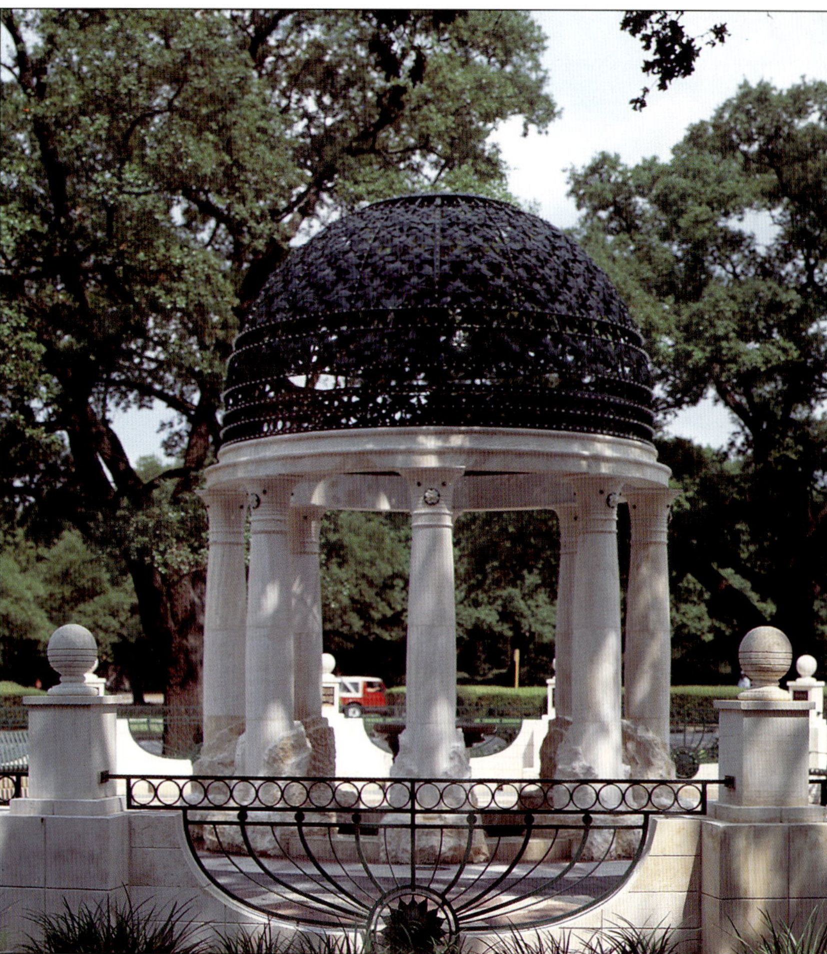

A

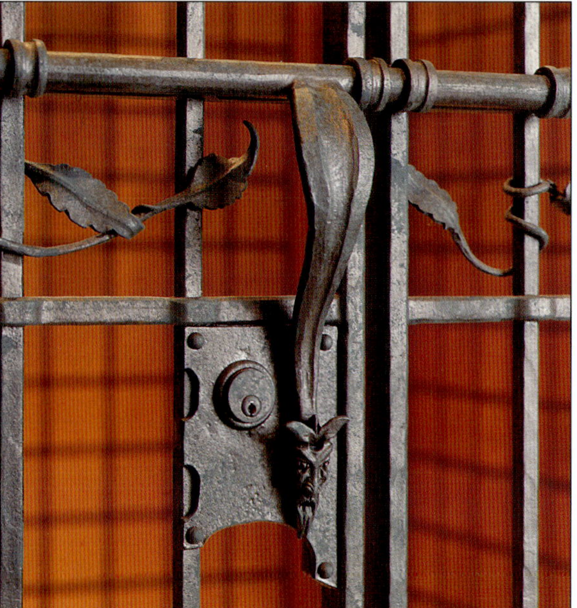

B

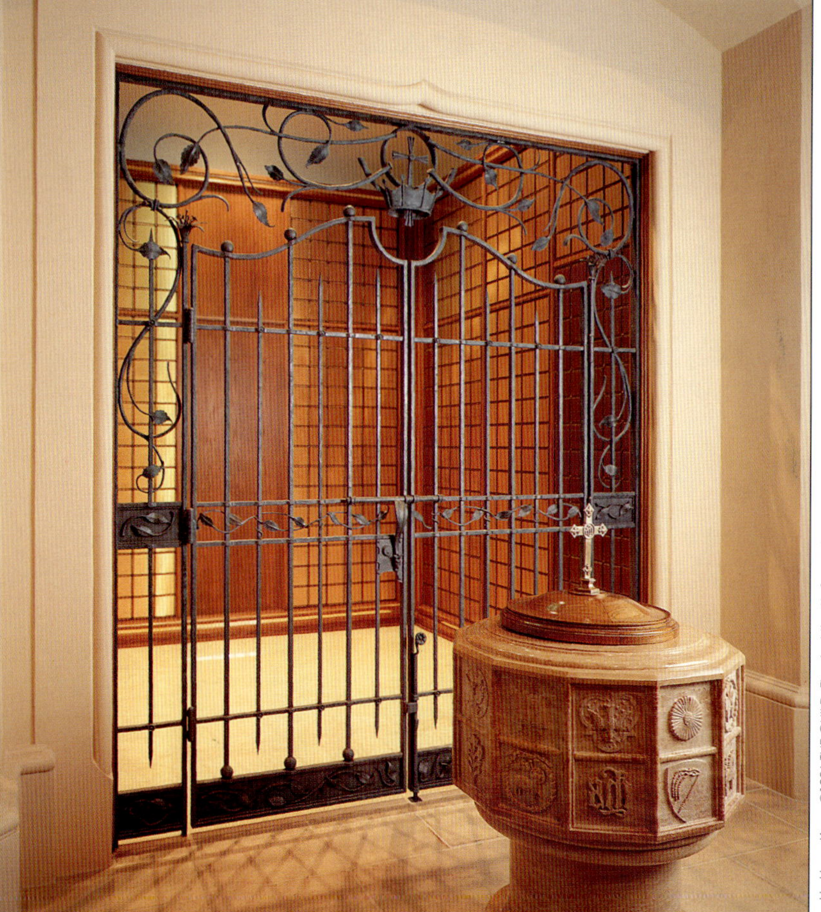

C

Bruce Paul Fink

90 Pole Bridge Road
Woodstock, CT 06281
FAX 203-974-0130
TEL   203-974-0130

Since the early `60s, the private foundry-studio of Bruce Paul Fink has seen the emergence of over 850 of his personal, unique sculptures that now reside in collections around the globe. These have ranged in size from hand-held to several stories high, and usually border on the edges of abstracted realism, with nature being his main subject.

Site-specific, open commissions and unique collaborations with designers and architects are welcomed. Inquiries invited.

Also see these GUILD publications:
Architect's Edition: 8, 9

A   Fox Estate communication, postal, lighting and
    lock entry receptacle, 1995, bronze, 9'H x 32"Dia

B   Fox sanctuary habitat entry gates, 1995, bronze,
    13'W x 8'H x 22"D

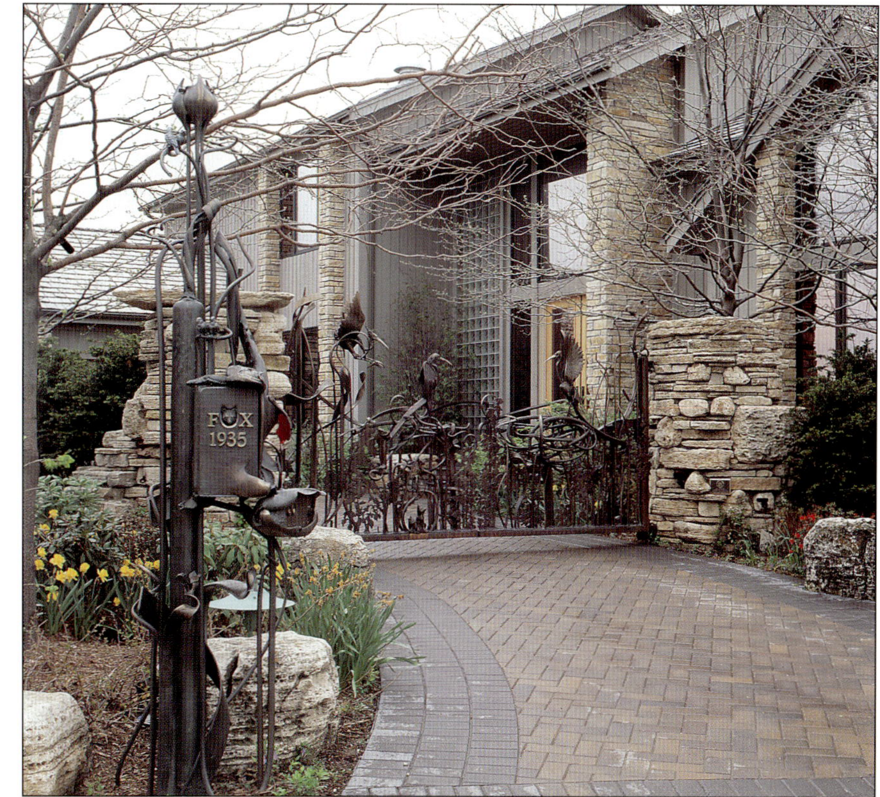

A

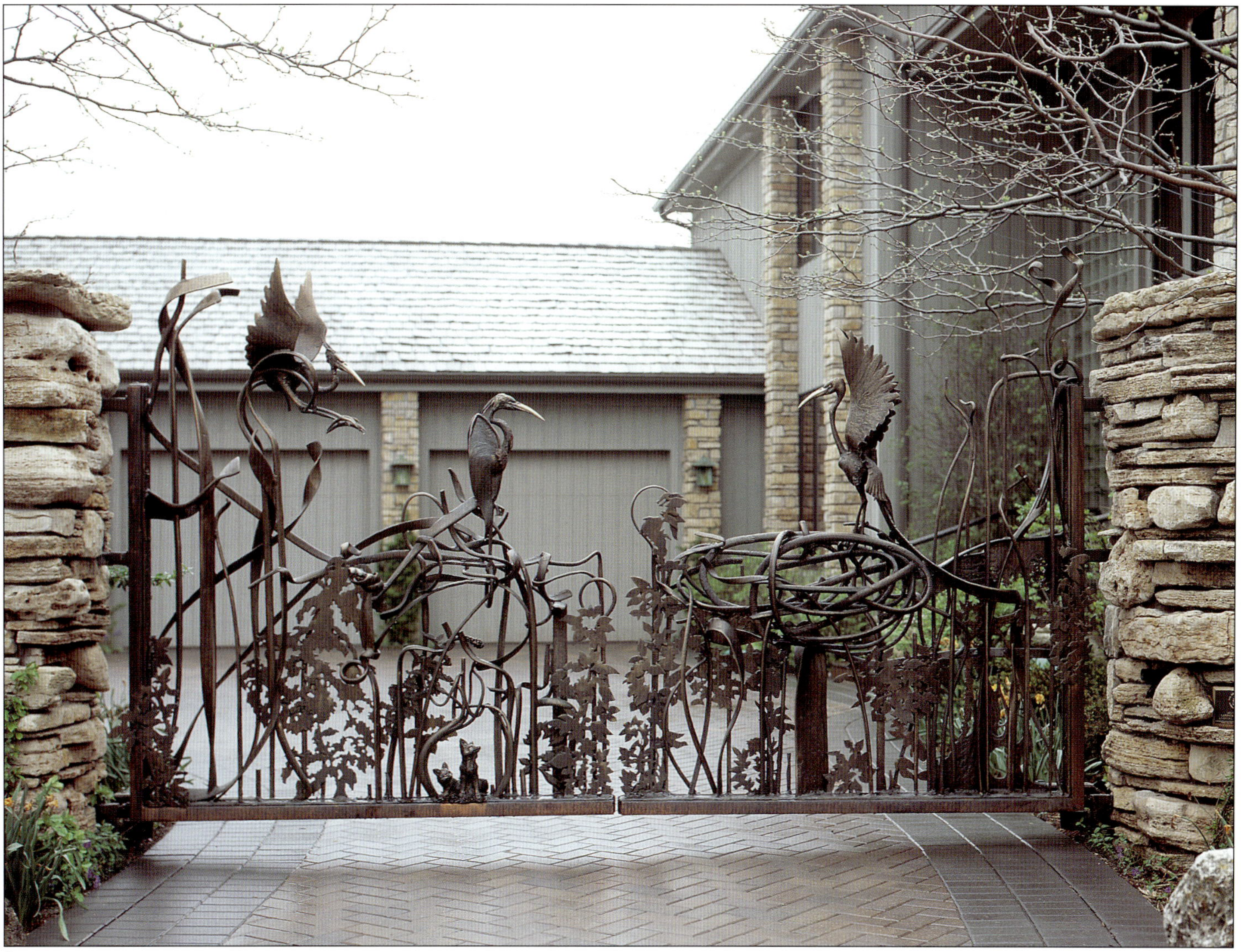

B

Historical Arts & Casting, Inc.

5580 West Bagley Park Road
West Jordan, UT 84088
FAX 801-280-2493
TEL 801-280-2400

Historical Arts and Casting, Inc. is a unique corporation dedicated to the design, manufacture and installation of architectural cast metal ornamentation. Having been in business for over 21 years, the company's reputation and services are well known and widely used by some of America's most respected architects and preservationists.

Skilled craftsmen specialize in the restoration and replication of many architectural details, including custom-built light fixtures, railing, gates, fountains, grilles, facades, canopies, elaborate store fronts and furniture. HACI offers castings in bronze alloys, aluminum and iron, with a variety of finishes.

The experienced staff will assist with product information, design and engineering services, shop drawings, manufacturing, and installation. For more information, please call 1-800-225-1414.

Commissions include:
Los Angeles Central Library, CA
Grand Central Terminal, NY
Ritz-Carlton Kappalua Hotel, HI
Saks Fifth Avenue, NY
D.O. Mills, Sacramento, CA
Westmoreland County Courthouse, PA
Governor's Mansion, MD
Beverly Hills Hotel, CA
Various private residences

A Fountain, Governor's Mansion, Annapolis, MD

B Grand staircase, D.O. Mills, Sacramento, CA

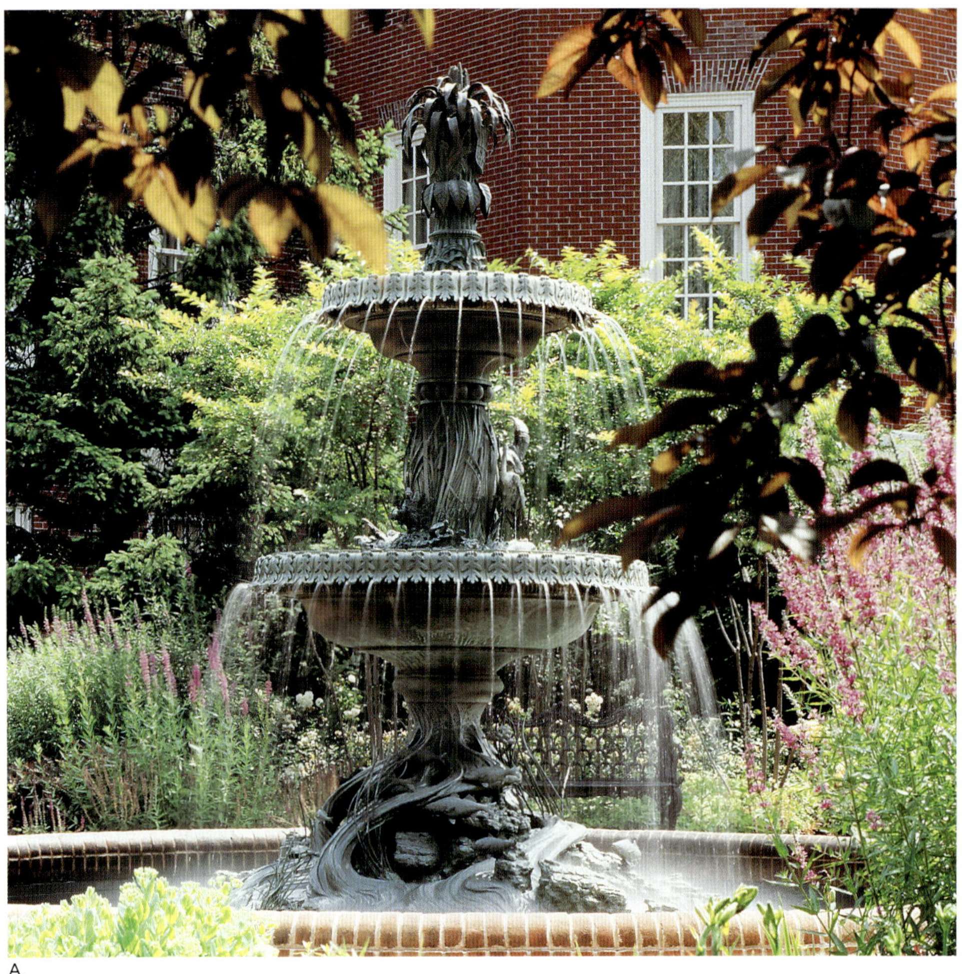

A

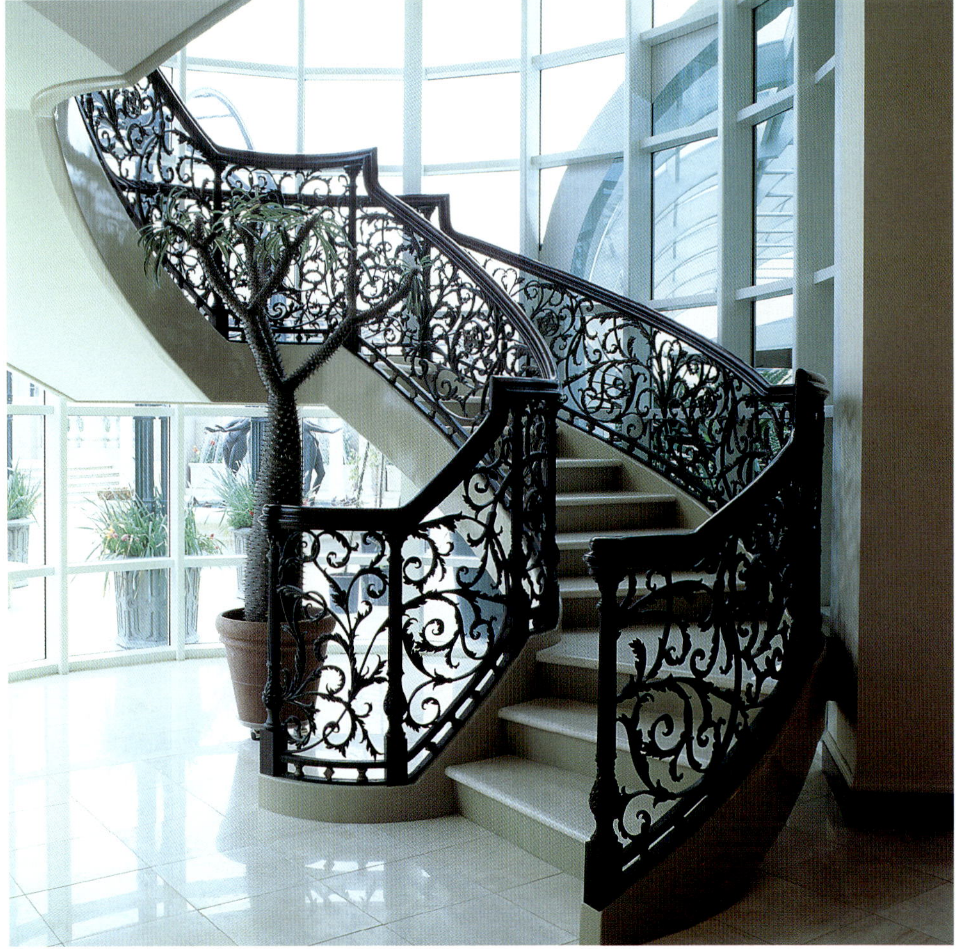

B

J. Dub's

Jerry W. Bement
1041 Bumpy Lane
Ellensburg, WA 98926
FAX 509-962-6070
TEL   509-925-9401

Jerry W. Bement has been creating true-to-life, two-dimensional silhouettes with a three-dimensional feel since 1980. Jerry torch cuts his images by hand from mild plate steel, then incorporates these images into functional items such as structural and non-structural signs, weathervanes, furniture, and chandeliers. However, the possible uses for these images are unlimited.

Also see this GUILD publication:
Designer's Edition: 8

A   *Cattle Drive*, 1994, Two Rivers Gallery,
     Steamboat, CO, 16' x 4'

B   *Elk in Trees*, 1993, Dan & Dee Stevens
     house, 10' x 2'

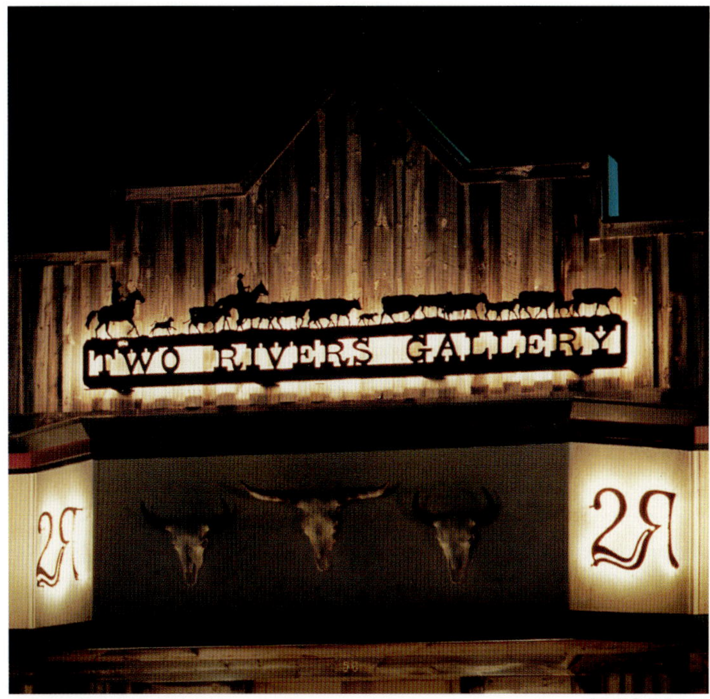

A

David C. Holloway

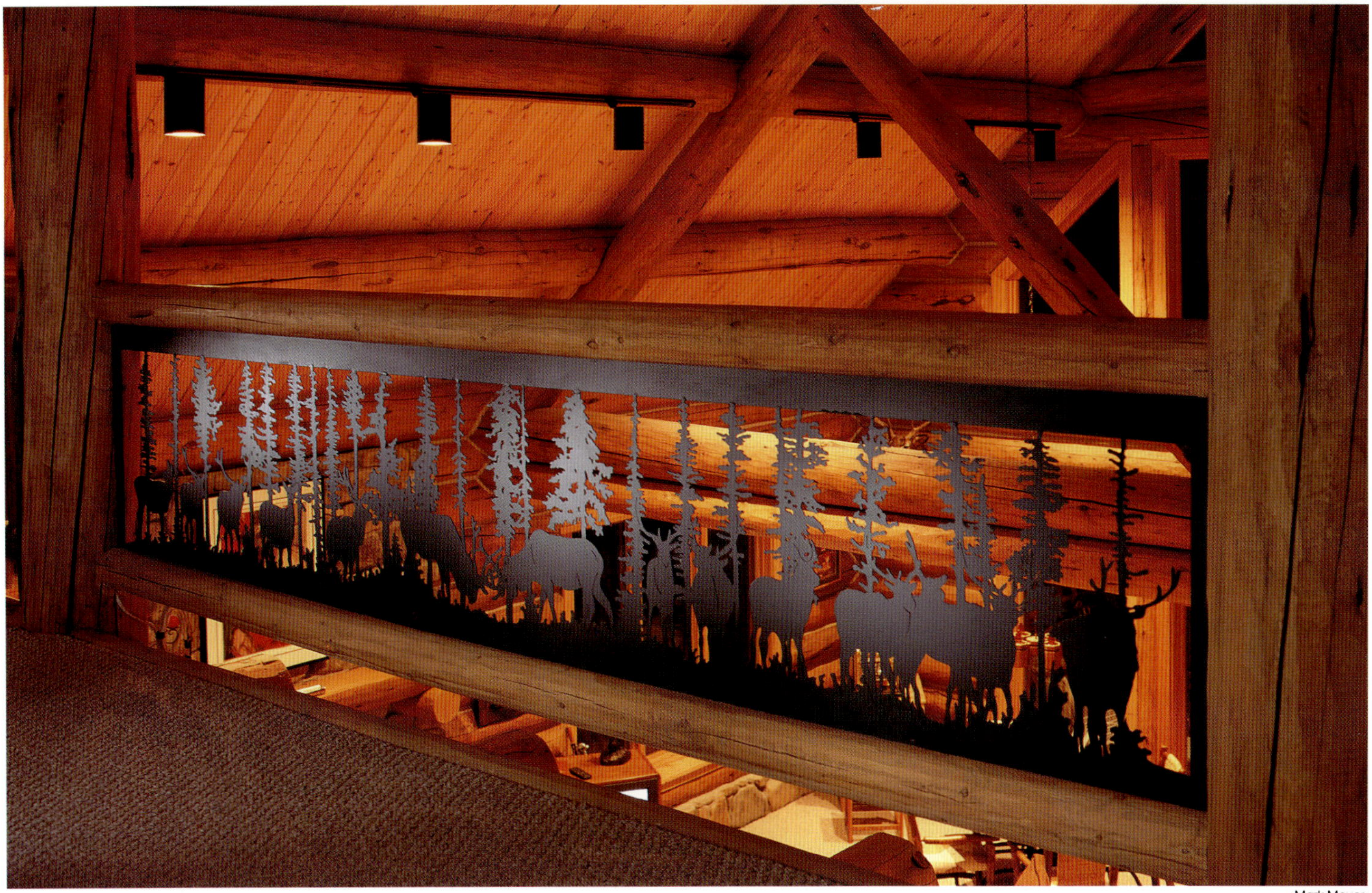

B

Mark Meyer

Leavitt Studios

Gregory Leavitt, Camille Leavitt, Lydia Leavitt
476 Valleybrook Road
Wawa, PA 19063-5614
FAX 610-358-1766
TEL 610-358-1766

Gregory Leavitt creates architectural and free-standing sculpture using mild steel, Cor-Ten steel, copper and bronze. His use of the ancient blacksmithing process combined with modern techniques provides for a full spectrum of styles, from 15th century to contemporary, large and small, interior or exterior. Leavitt works with his clients on a commission, site-specific basis to assure a good aesthetic and environmental fit. All projects are forged and/or constructed in-house.

Also see these GUILD publications:
Architect's Edition: 9, 10
Gallery Edition: 2

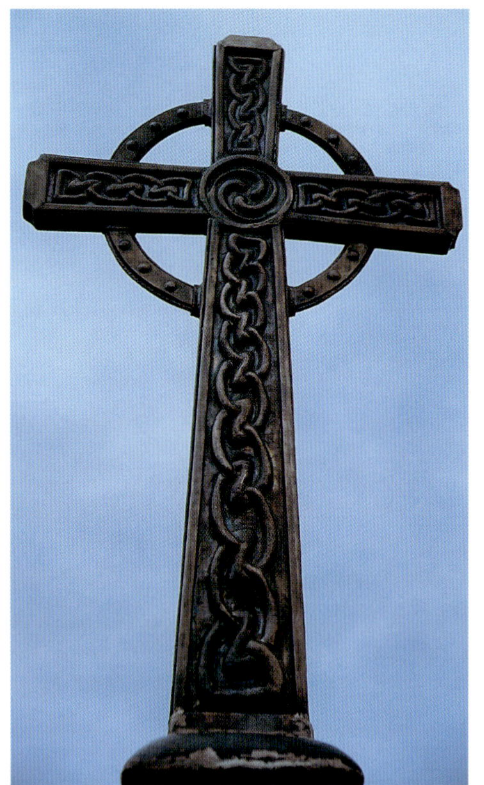

Celtic Cross, copper repoussé, Swarthmore Presbyterian Church, 4'H

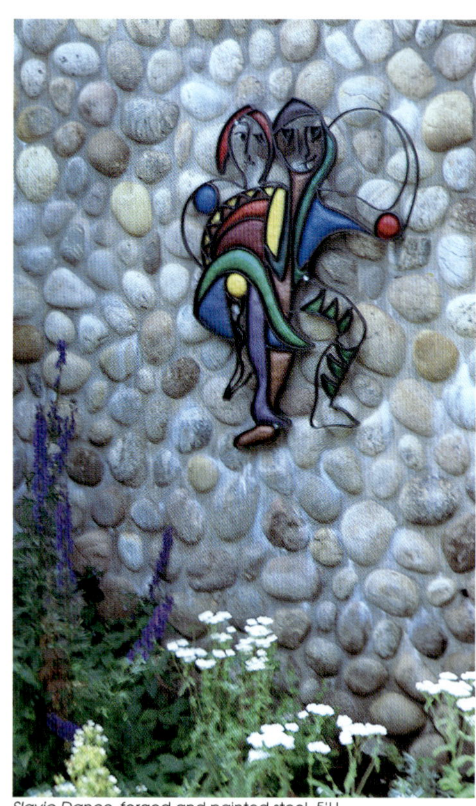

Slavic Dance, forged and painted steel, 5'H

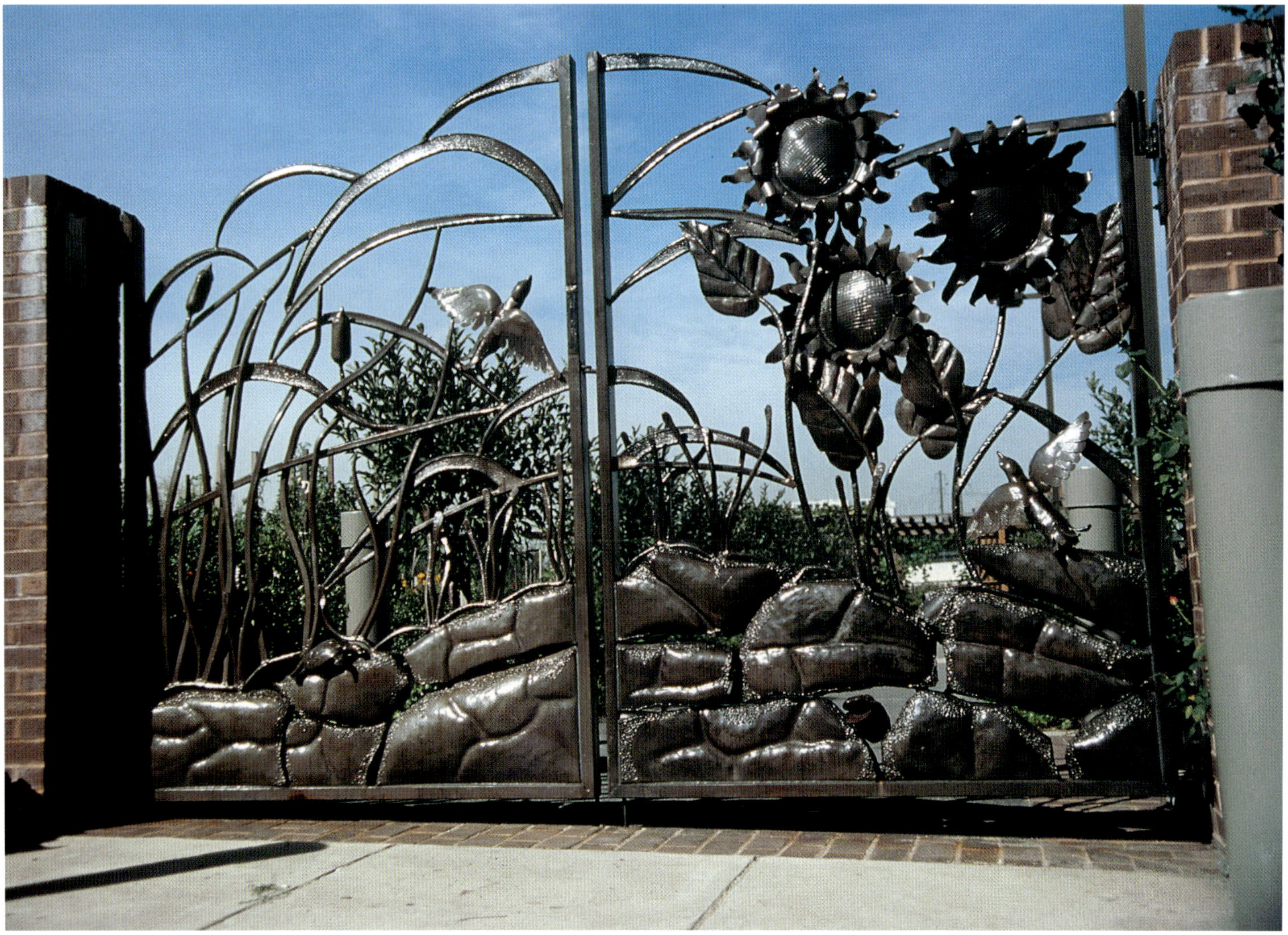

Entrance gate, forged steel, Schuylkill River Park, 7' x 11'

Dieter K. Muller-Stach

1959 Port Cardiff Place
Newport Beach, CA 92660
FAX 310-985-1650
TEL 714-644-5197

Dieter Muller-Stach has 30 years experience creating large art objects in metal for specific architectural sites. His work explores the functional object as sculpture and unique focal element within architecture. His work in private and corporate collections and churches in Europe, Africa and the U.S. includes wrought iron and hand-sculpted bronze driveway and entrance gates; a 17 foot tall bronze fireplace sculpture; pilaster light fixtures with laminated glass; liturgical implements in silver, niobium and bronze; and table sculptures in steel with enamel, and cast and laminated glass.

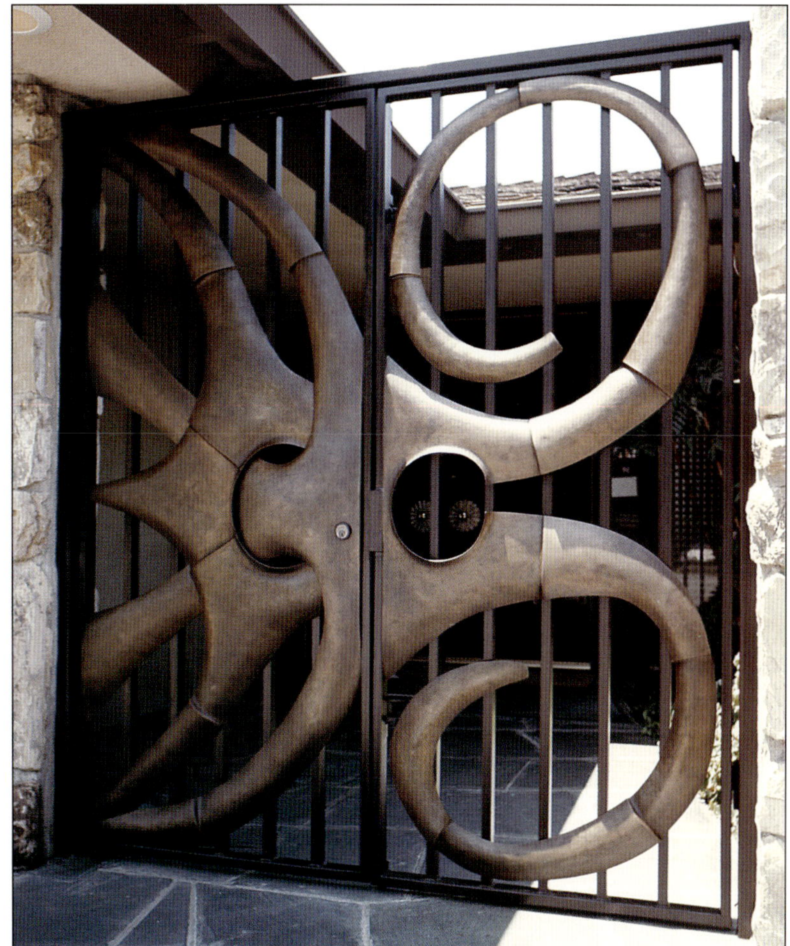

Entrance gate, bronze, steel, 6' x 6', private residence, Beverly Hills, CA

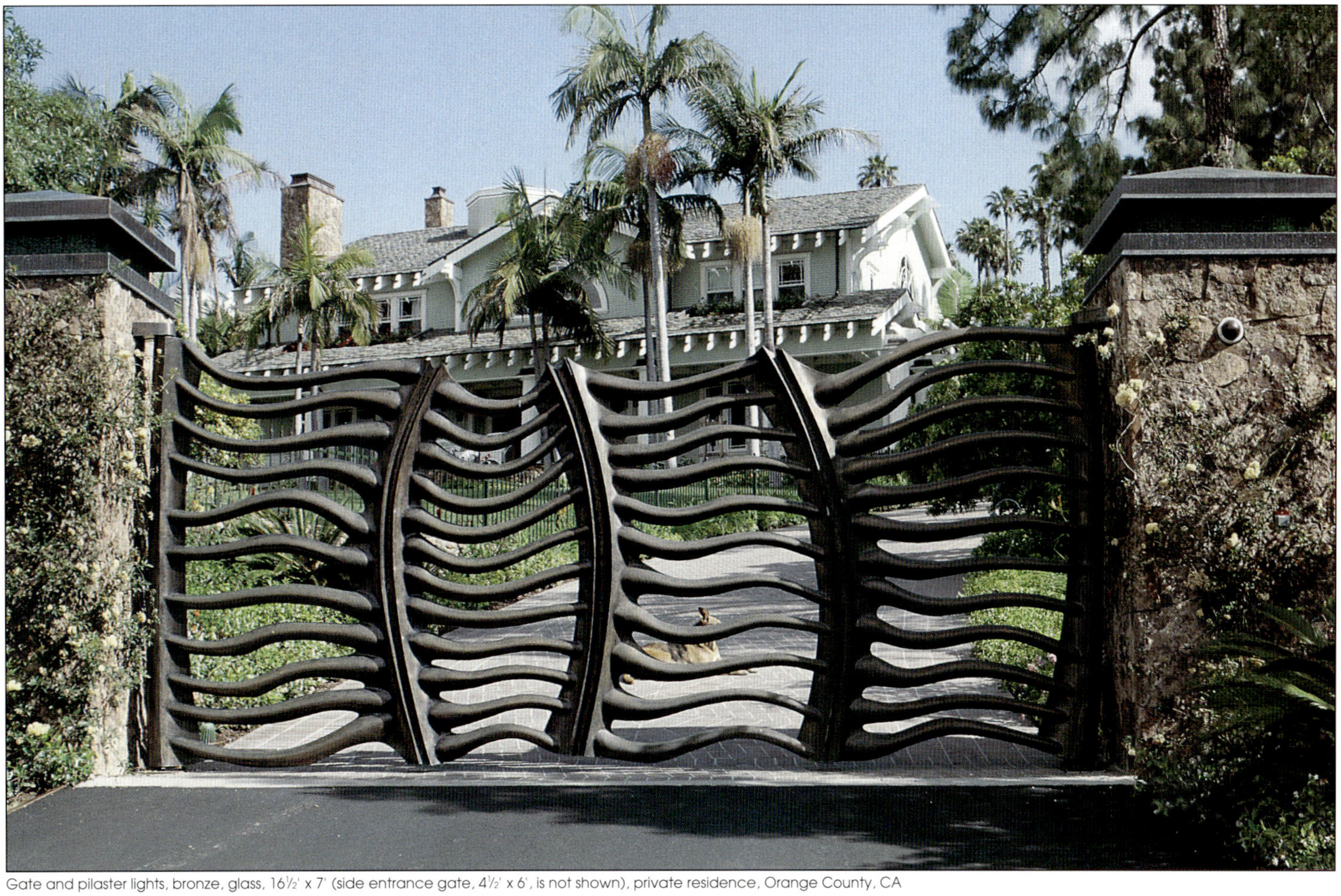

Gate and pilaster lights, bronze, glass, 16½' x 7' (side entrance gate, 4½' x 6', is not shown), private residence, Orange County, CA

Nol Putnam

White Oak Forge, Ltd.
PO Box 341, 45 Main Street
The Plains, VA 22171
FAX 540-253-5173
TEL 540-253-5269

Putnam creates hot-forged ironwork for public
and private clients; work varies in scale from
'house jewelry' to architectural.

He has been an artist-blacksmith for over 20
years, is the recipient of several national
awards, and has work throughout the United
States.

Also see these GUILD publications:
THE GUILD: 2, 4, 5
Architect's Edition: 8, 9, 10

SHOWN: *Rousseau Gate*, 1994, private client,
forged steel, brass, copper, 6' x 14'

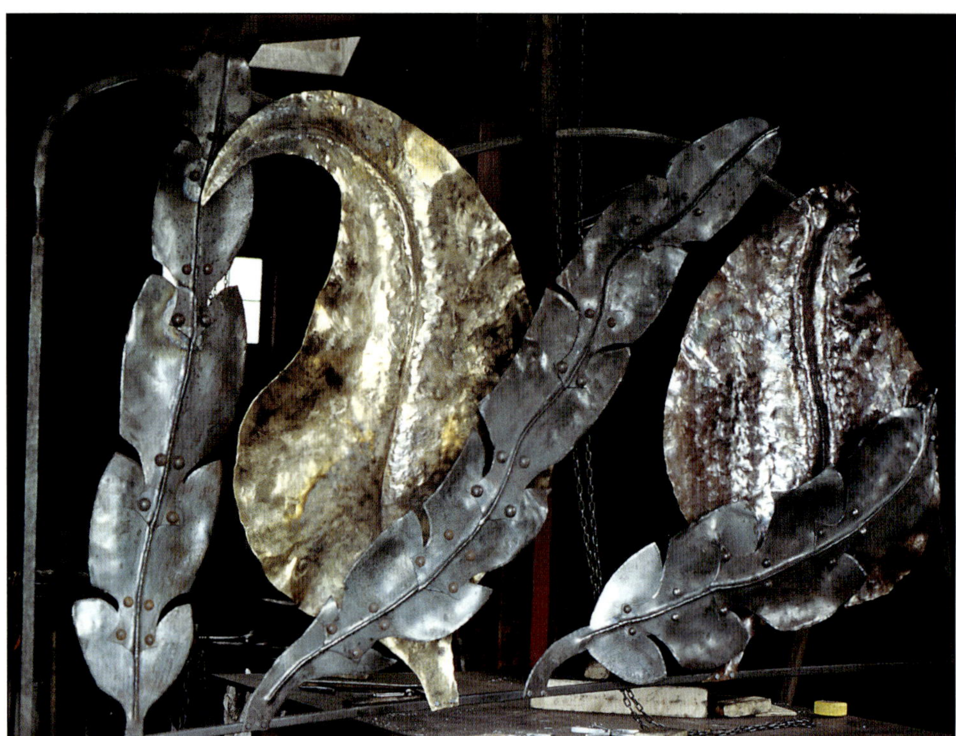

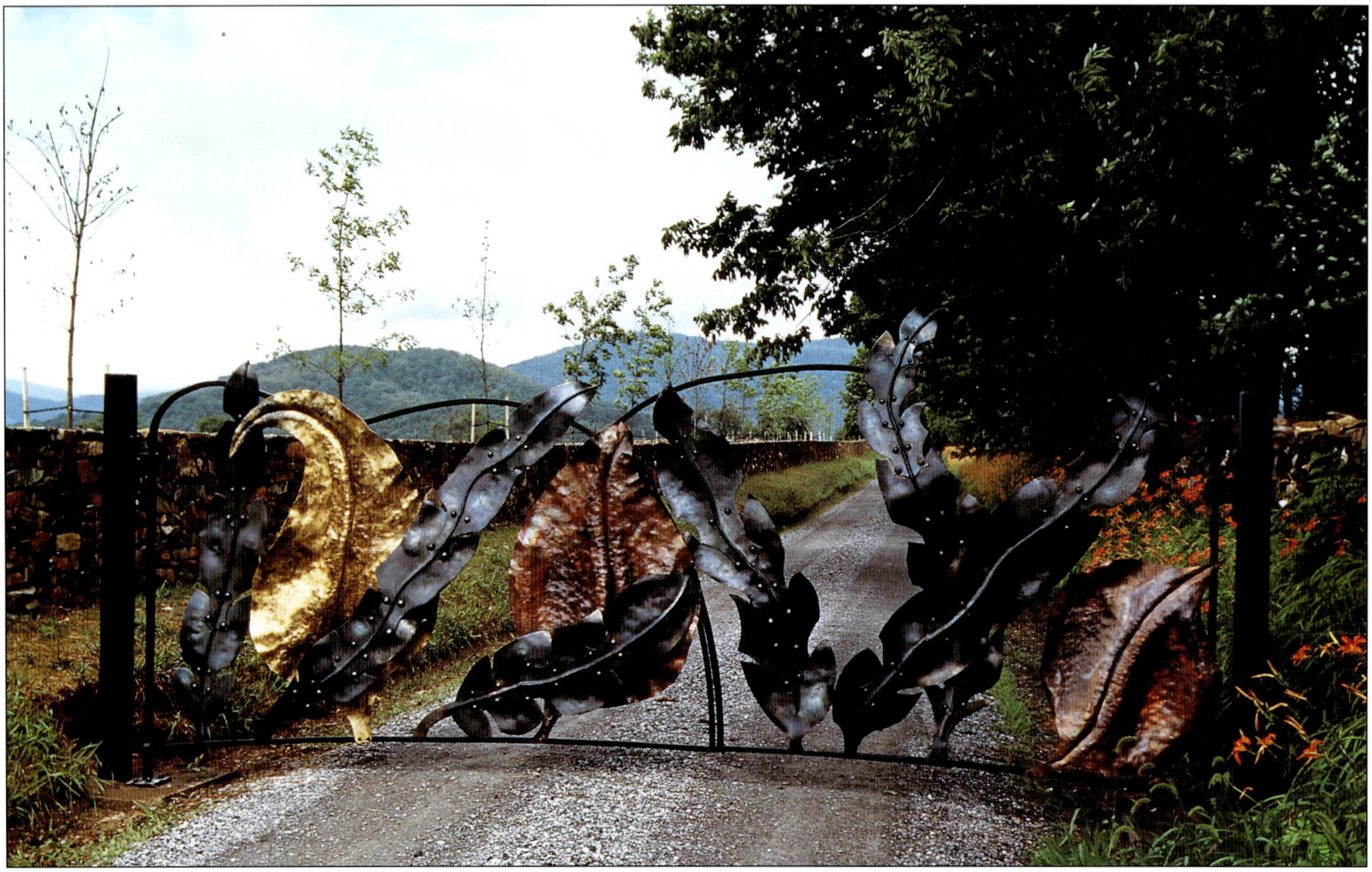

Henry Eastwood

Waylan Smithy

Toby Hickman
6030 Roblar Road
Petaluma, CA 94952
FAX 707-664-1691
TEL 707-664-8910
E-Mail: myriadgrp@aol.com

Since 1975, Waylan Smithy has fulfilled many large residential and commercial commissions, as well as numerous individual pieces of architectural detail and furniture, and limited runs of forged parts for custom and production fabricators. What differentiates Waylan Smithy is Hickman's collaborative focus: interfacing with designers of various disciplines to produce unique pieces. Through his control of texture and form, he can help a project transcend its concept, so that it achieves fullness and depth.

Clients include:
Joseph Phelps House, St. Helena, CA
Dolby House, San Francisco, CA
Chez Panisse, Berkeley, CA
Kuleto Residences, Sausalito and St. Helena, CA
Papago's Restaurant, Chicago, IL
Los Altos Hills Golf & Country Club,
   Los Altos Hills, CA
Boulevard Restaurant, San Francisco, CA

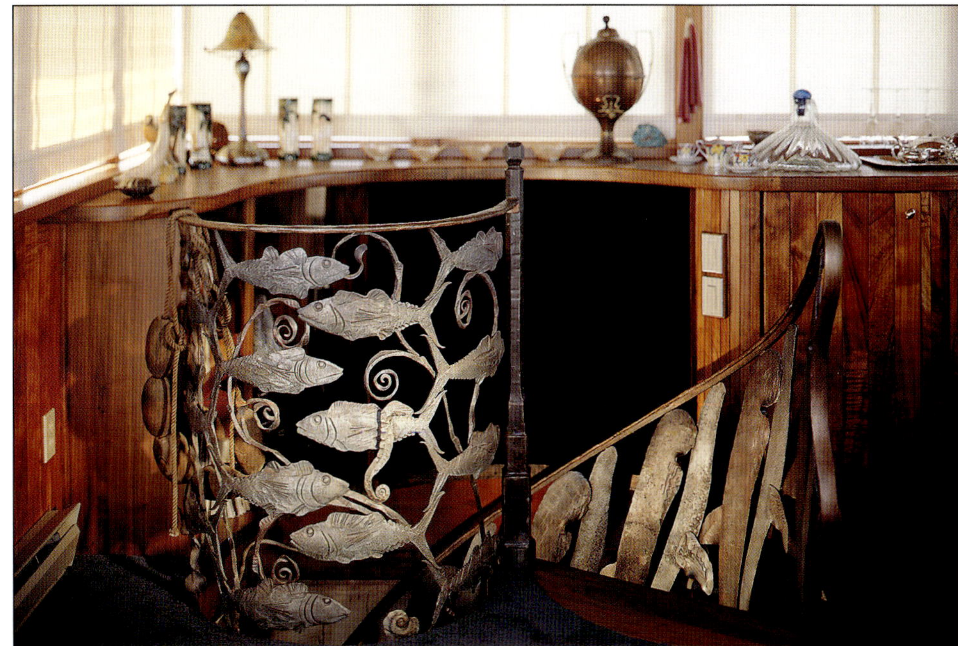

Railing, Kuleto houseboat, 1993. polychromed steel

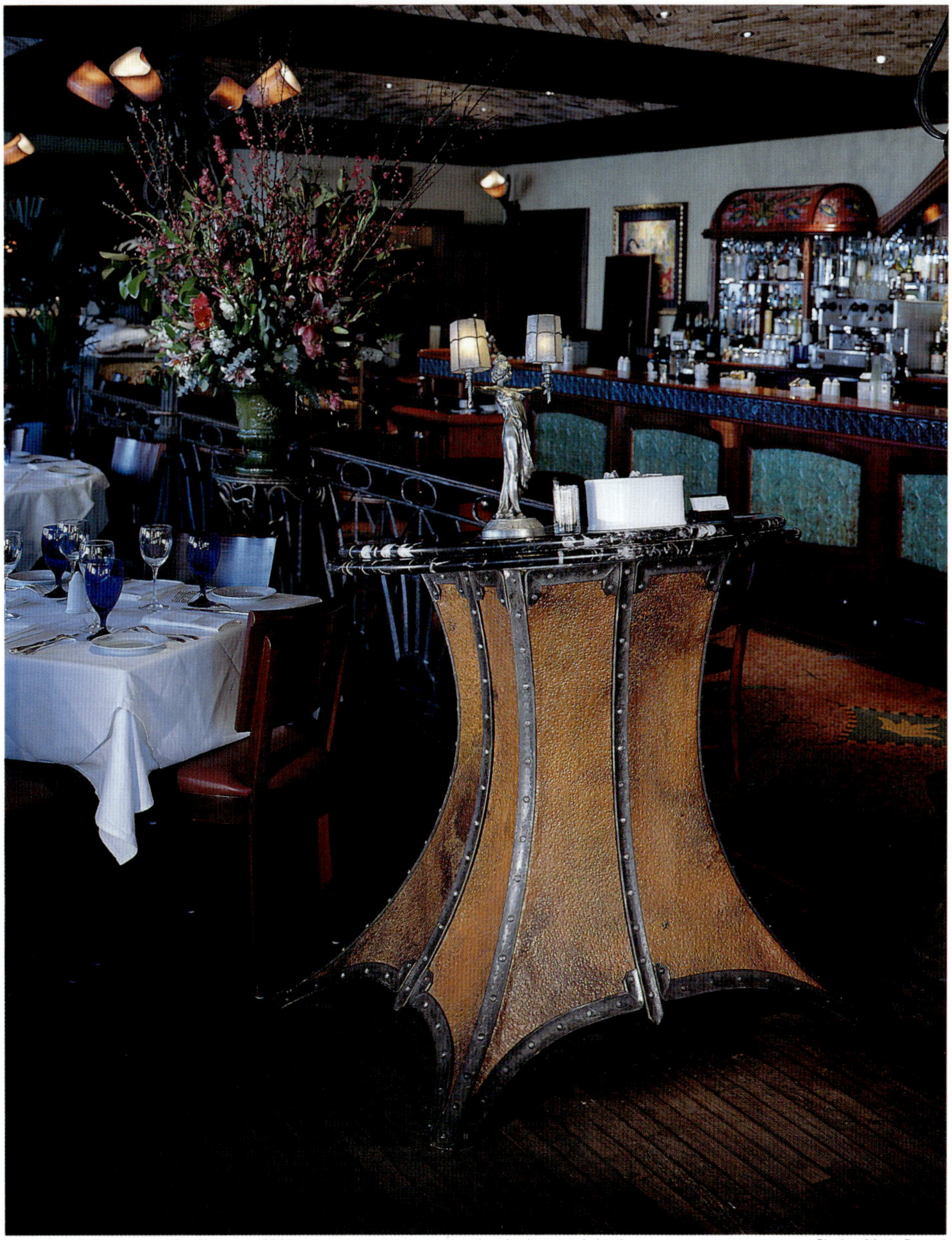

Host stand, Boulevard Restaurant, 1993, hammered copper and polychromed steel

Photos: Mario Parnell

Frederic Jean Zimmer

Artdoor Inc.
515 B. Kuwili Street
Honolulu, HI 96817
FAX 808-533-0623
TEL   808-955-5281

With a degree in art from Ecole des Beaux Art in Strasbourg, France, Frederic Zimmer has specialized in hand-carved, museum-quality portals, murals, sculptures and furniture. He works in copper, bronze, iron, stainless steel, aluminum, glass and stone, the first in the Islands to perform this particular type of work.

His work is recognized across the U.S., most notably in the Hawaiian Islands. Examples are also in France and in Saudi Arabia, where the artist's work can be seen gracing commercial buildings, resorts, luxury homes and palaces.

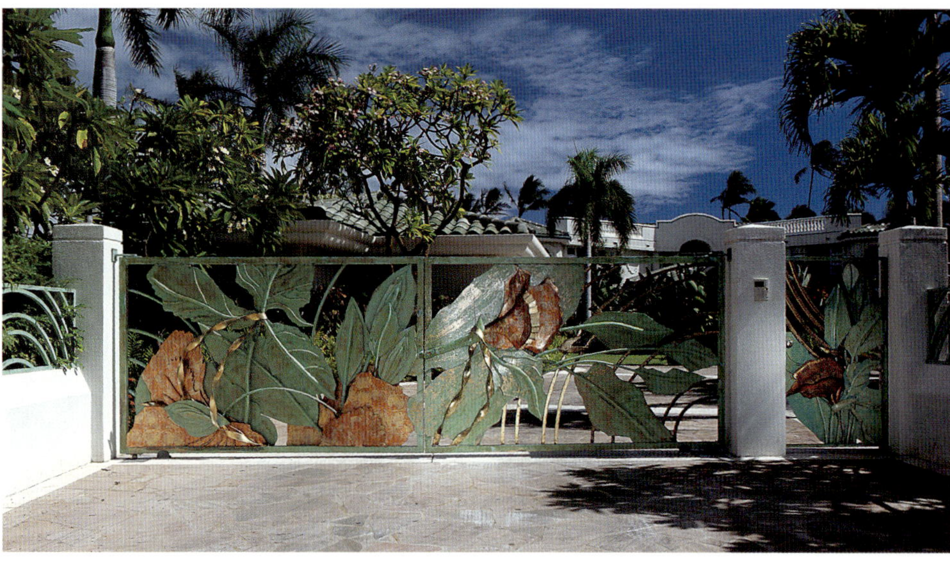

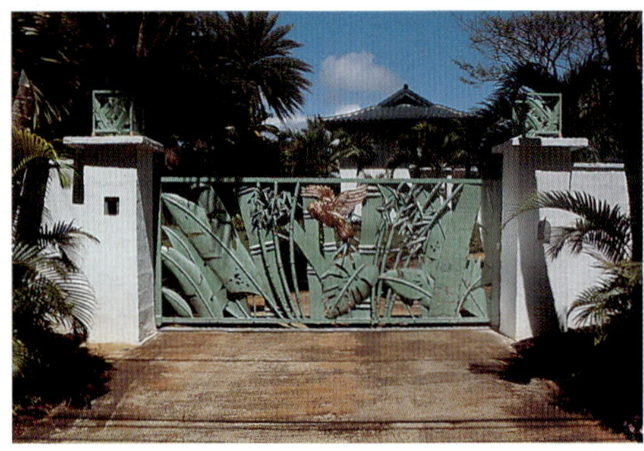

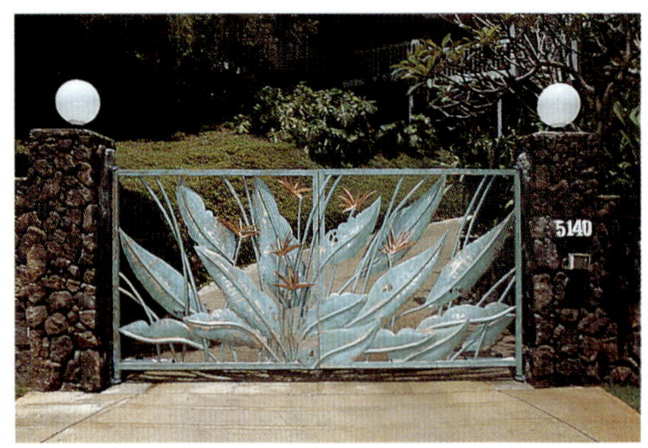

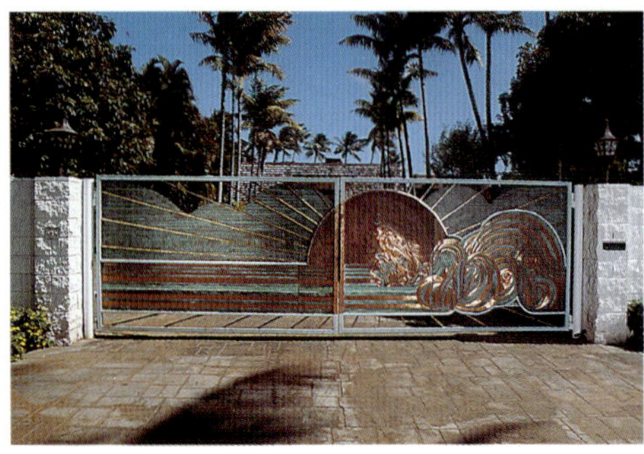

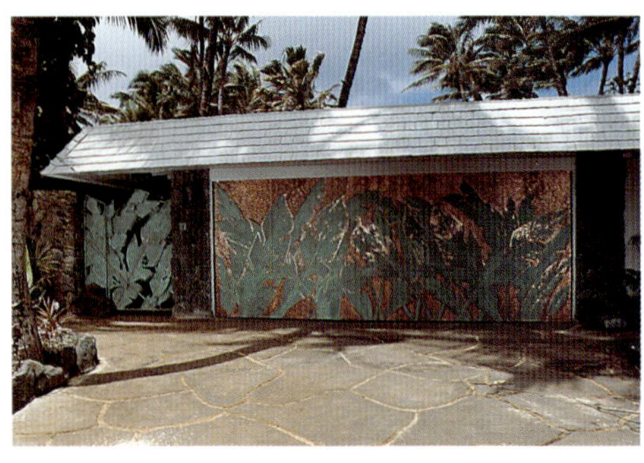

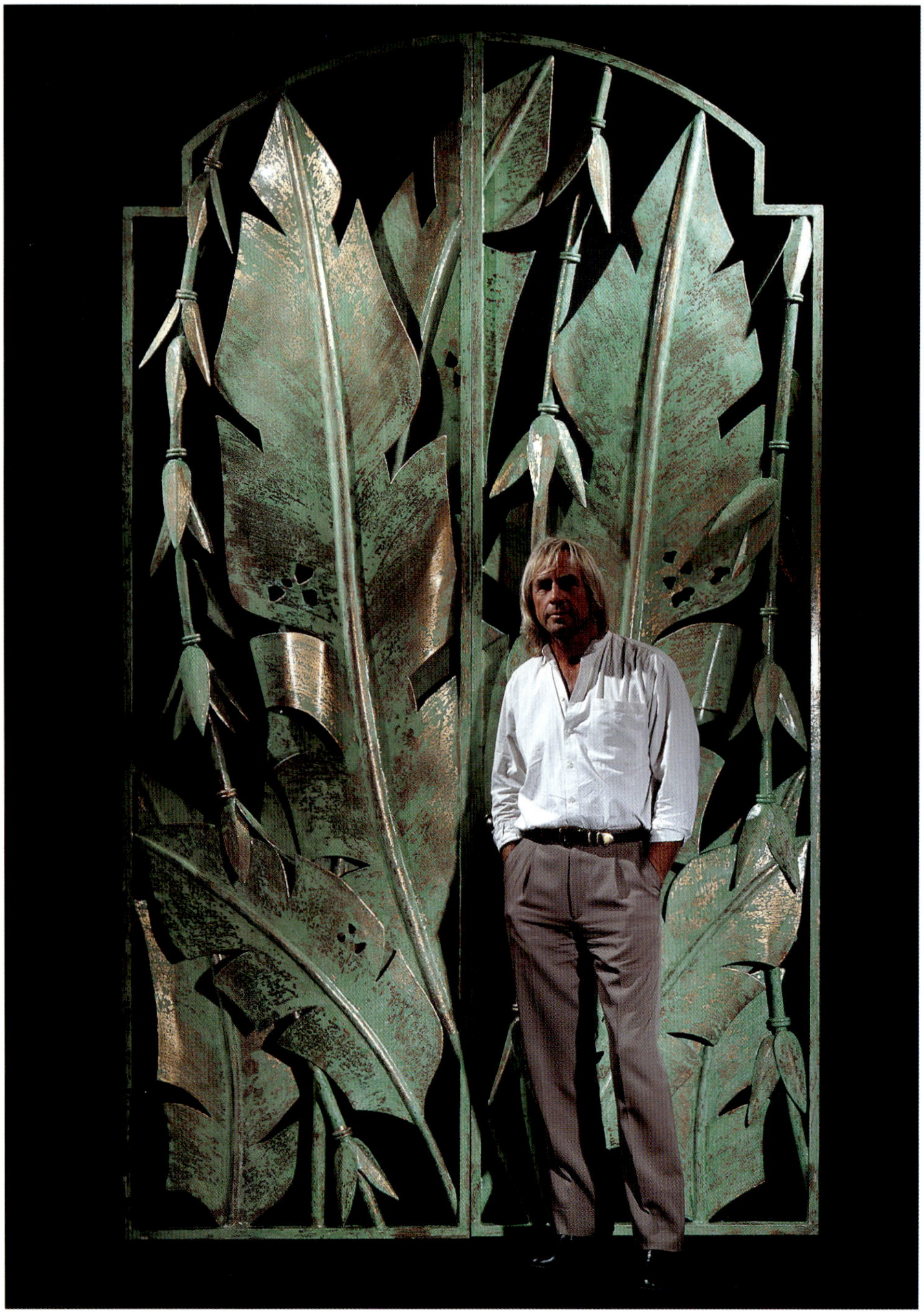

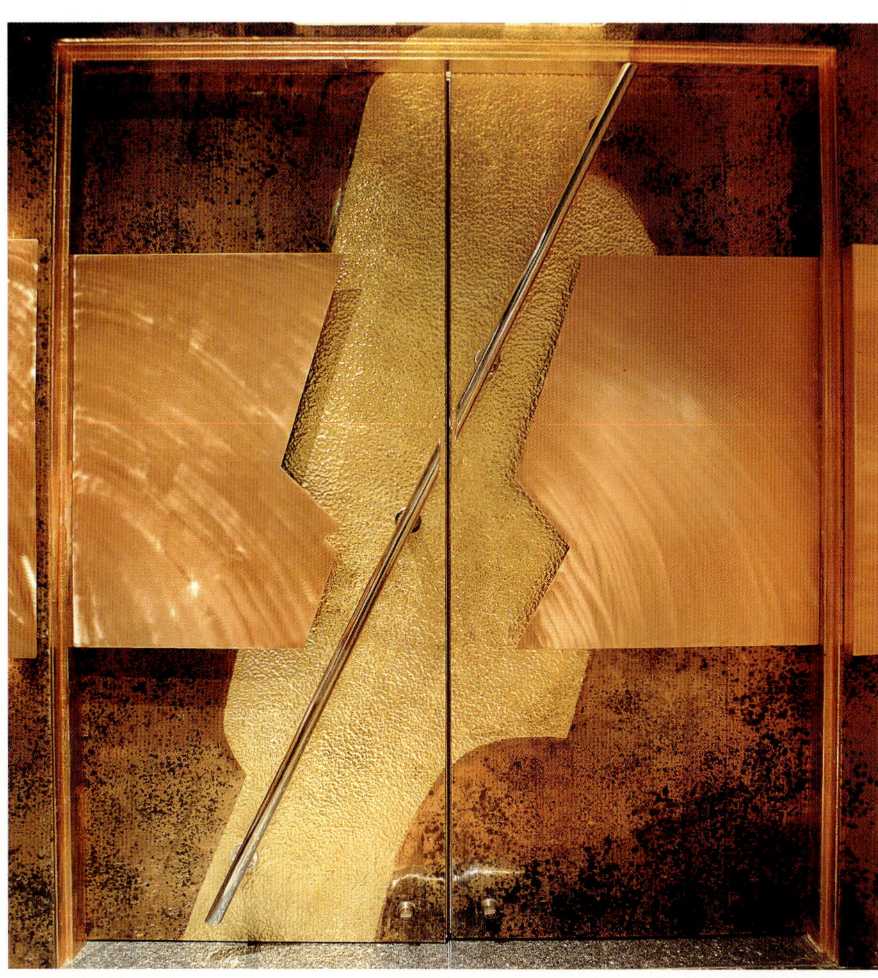

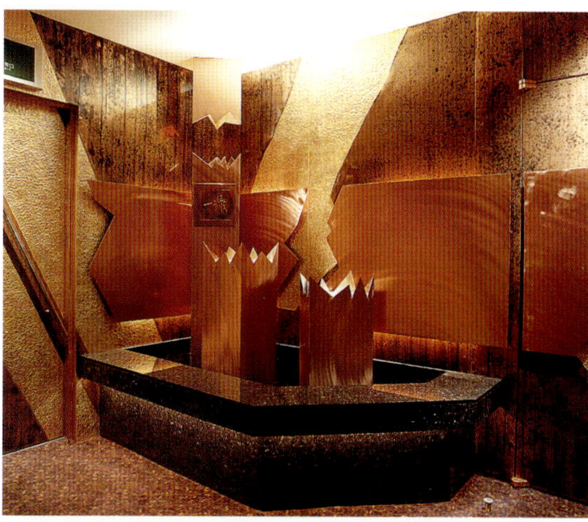

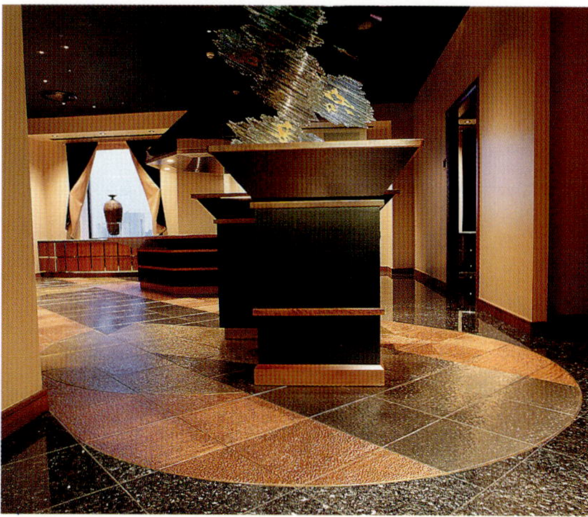

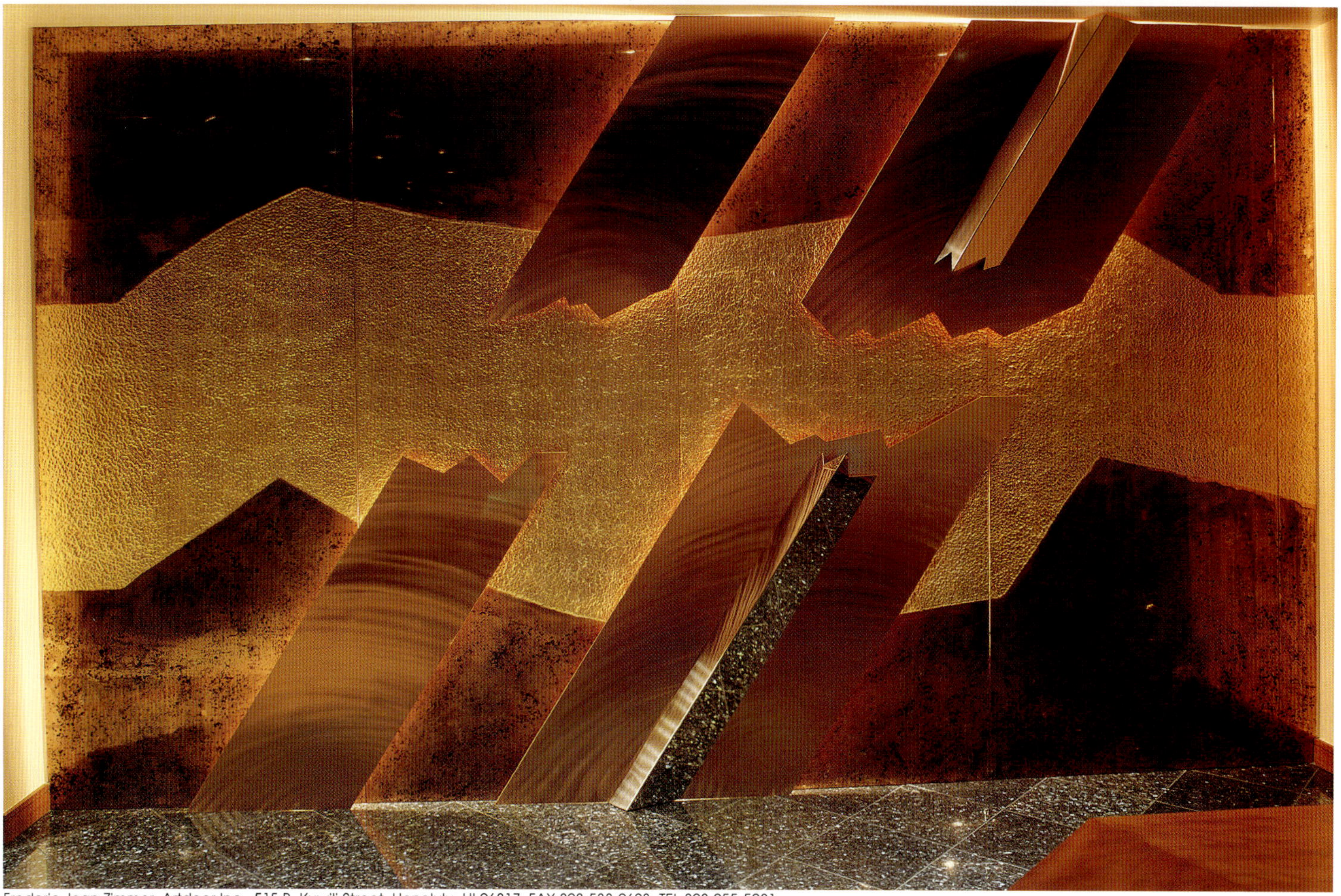

Frederic Jean Zimmer, Artdoor Inc., 515 B. Kuwili Street, Honolulu, HI 96817, FAX 808-533-0623, TEL 808-955-5281

ARCHITECTURAL GLASS

Acacia Art Glass Studios

Lucinda Shaw
3000 Chestnut Avenue #336
Baltimore, MD 21211
FAX 410-366-6446
TEL   410-467-4038

Lucinda Shaw, owner of Acacia Art Glass Studios, works with architects, designers, church committees and private clients to design site-specific glass that relates to the environment and the needs of the client. Works produced range from very traditional to modern.

Her work is represented in a 1% for Art project— a wall of glass—for the City of Honolulu, Hawaii (see page 251 of *Architect's Edition 10*); the City of Baltimore, MD; and two windows for a museum in England. Other windows and related works of art are in public and private collections throughout the United States and the world.

Commissions include:
1st Baptist Church, Birmingham, MI, 1995
St. Thomas à Becket, eight windows,
    Morgantown, WV, 1994
Ascension Lutheran, four windows,
    Towson, MD, 1994
Beth El Congregation, six windows,
    Baltimore, MD, 1992

Also see this GUILD publication:
Architect's Edition: 10

A Howard County General Hospital,
    Columbia, MD

B St. Thomas à Becket, 1994,
    Morgantown, WV, 8'Dia

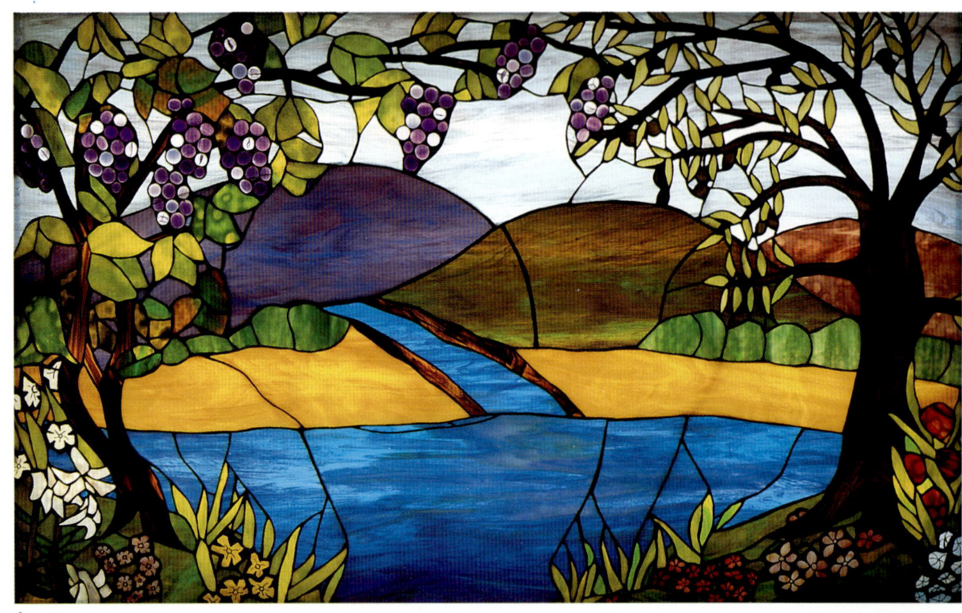

A

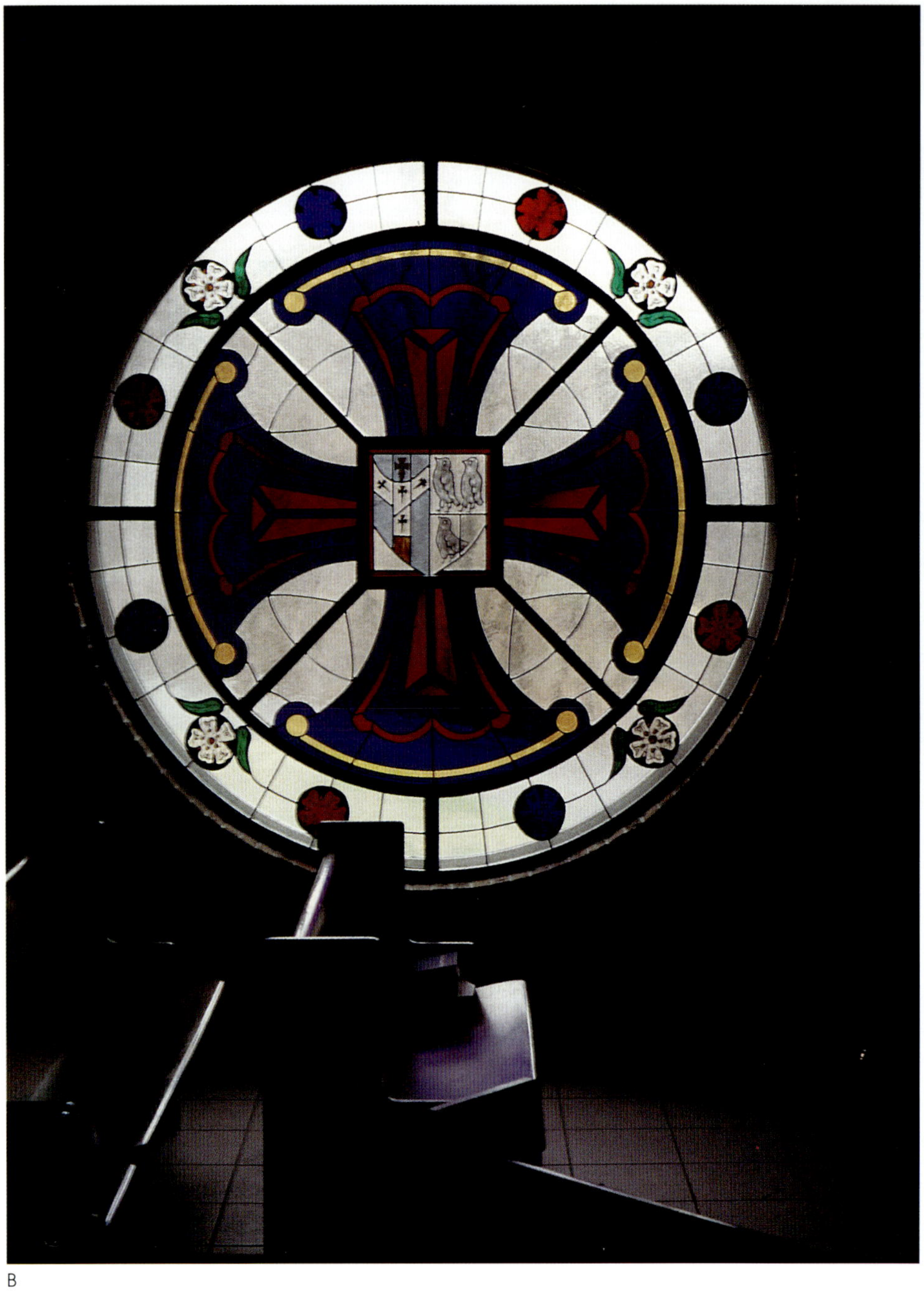

B

Architectural Glass Art, Inc.

Kenneth F. vonRoenn, Jr.
1110 Baxter Avenue
Louisville, KY 40204
FAX 502-585-2808
TEL   502-585-5421

Architectural Glass Art, Inc. is a unique glass studio, recognized for its innovative application of new technologies and traditional techniques in expanding the potential and application of glass as a contemporary architectural art.

Kenneth vonRoenn, the president of AGA, is an architect (Yale University, M. Arch.) and a renowned glass artist. His work has been published in numerous books and every major architecture magazine, and was recently featured in *Architecture* magazine (January 1992). He has received many awards, including three American Craft Awards.

VonRoenn is recognized for the sympathetic integration of his work into architecture, which is achieved by his ability to work in a diversity of styles to address the specific aesthetic concerns of each project. His work is also noted for subtle use of color and sophisticated application of the natural textures of blown clear glass, as well as the refractive qualities of beveled, engraved and prismatic glasses.

Because of his training as an architect, vonRoenn is especially concerned with sympathetic integration of his work with the architecture of which it is a part. This background is also of value in the administration and implementation of a project.

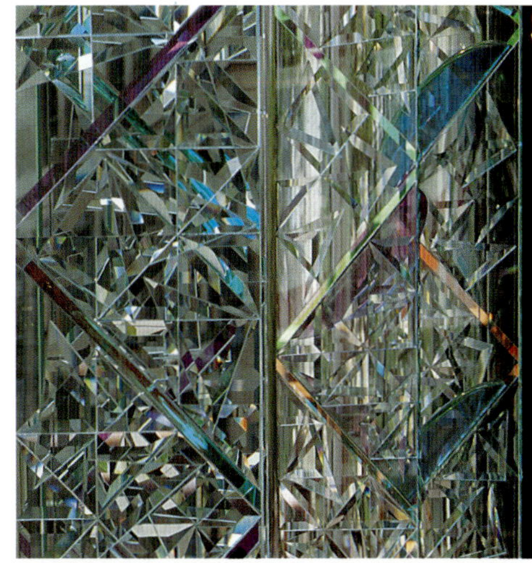

Indiana Power & Light Company Headquarters, Indianapolis, IN, 1995

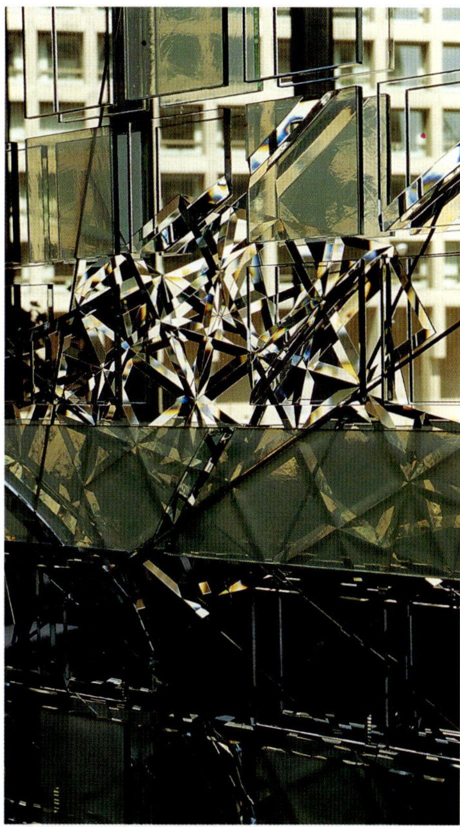

International Monetary Fund, Washington, DC, prototype detail, 1995-1997

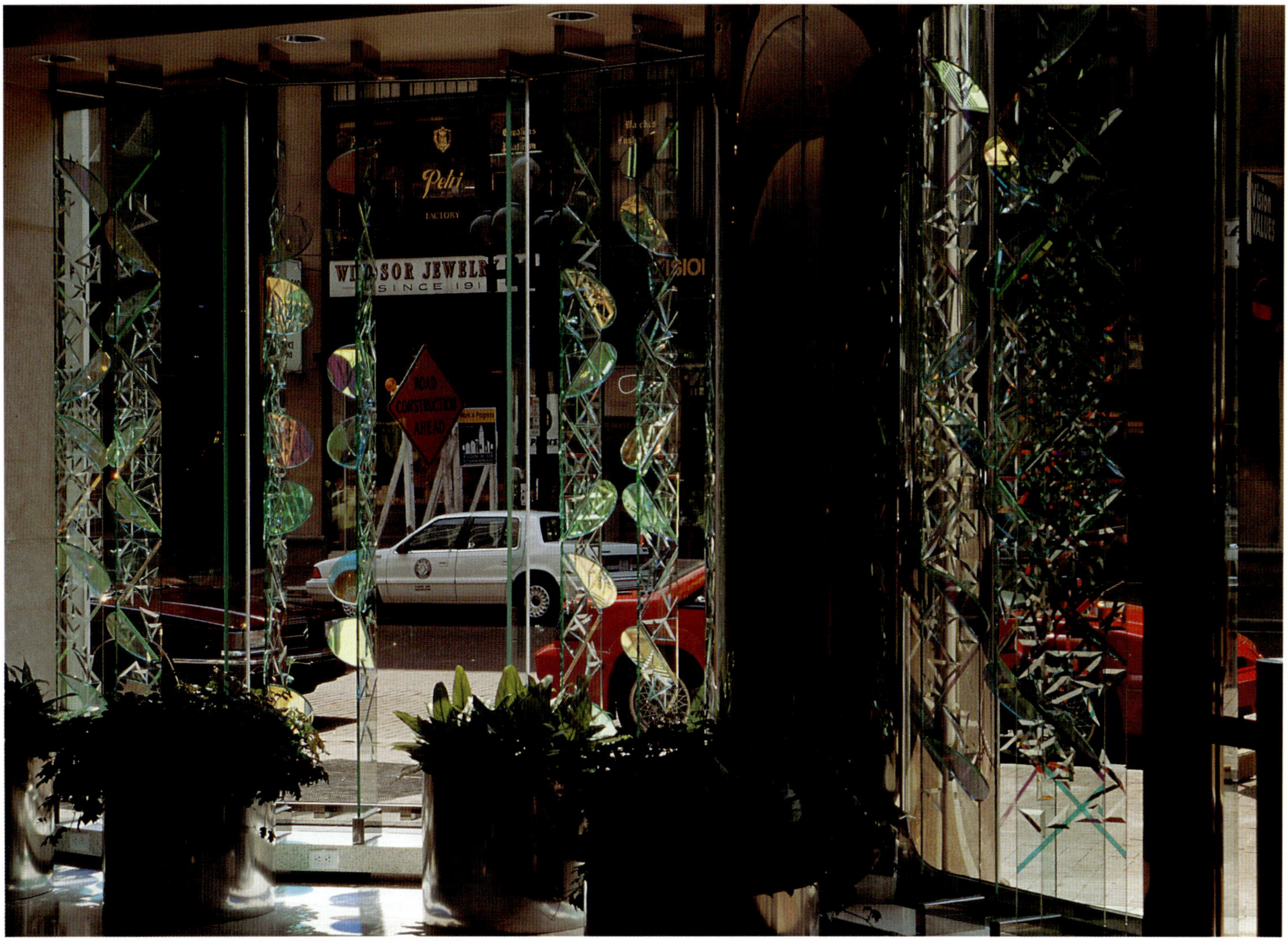

Indiana Power & Light Company Headquarters, Indianapolis, IN, 1995

Art Glass Environments, Inc.

Bill Klug, President
1865 NW Boca Raton Boulevard
Boca Raton, FL 33432
FAX 407-391-8447
TEL   407-391-7310 (Shop/Showroom)

Since 1973, A.G.E., Inc. has produced art glass projects for commercial and residential environments throughout the U.S.A., Central and South America.

As founder of A.G.E., Inc., Klug has surrounded himself with highly skilled artists/craftsmen who remain committed to excellence in their craft. Collaborating with architects and designers, they strive to achieve the highest quality design, fabrication and installation for their clients.

Commissions include complete entryways, windows, screens, furniture and sculptures in carved or leaded glass. Brochures and quotations upon request.

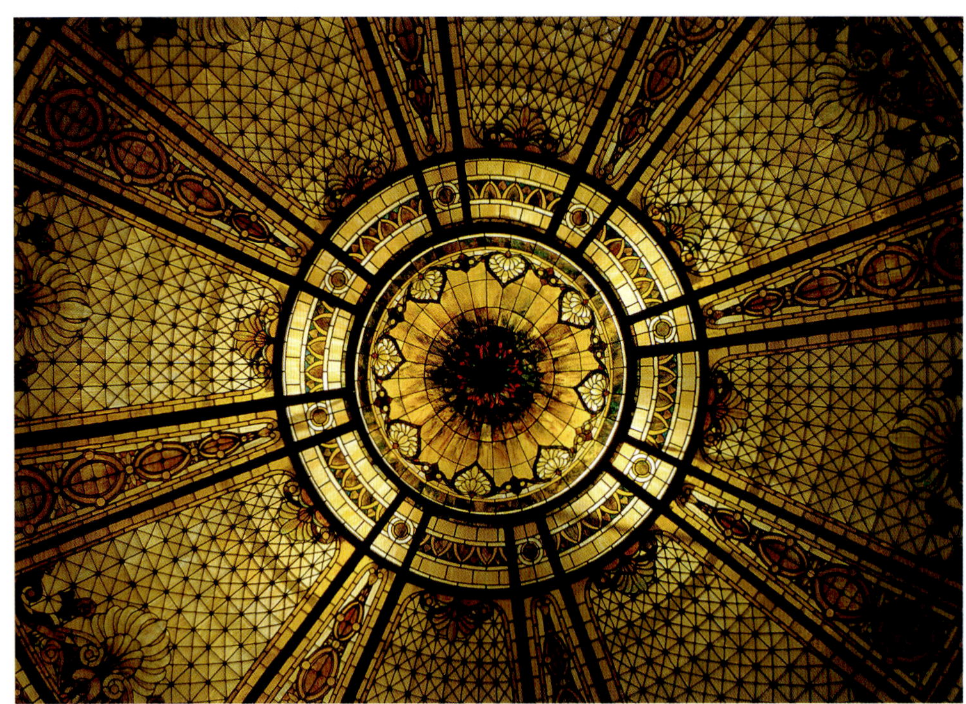

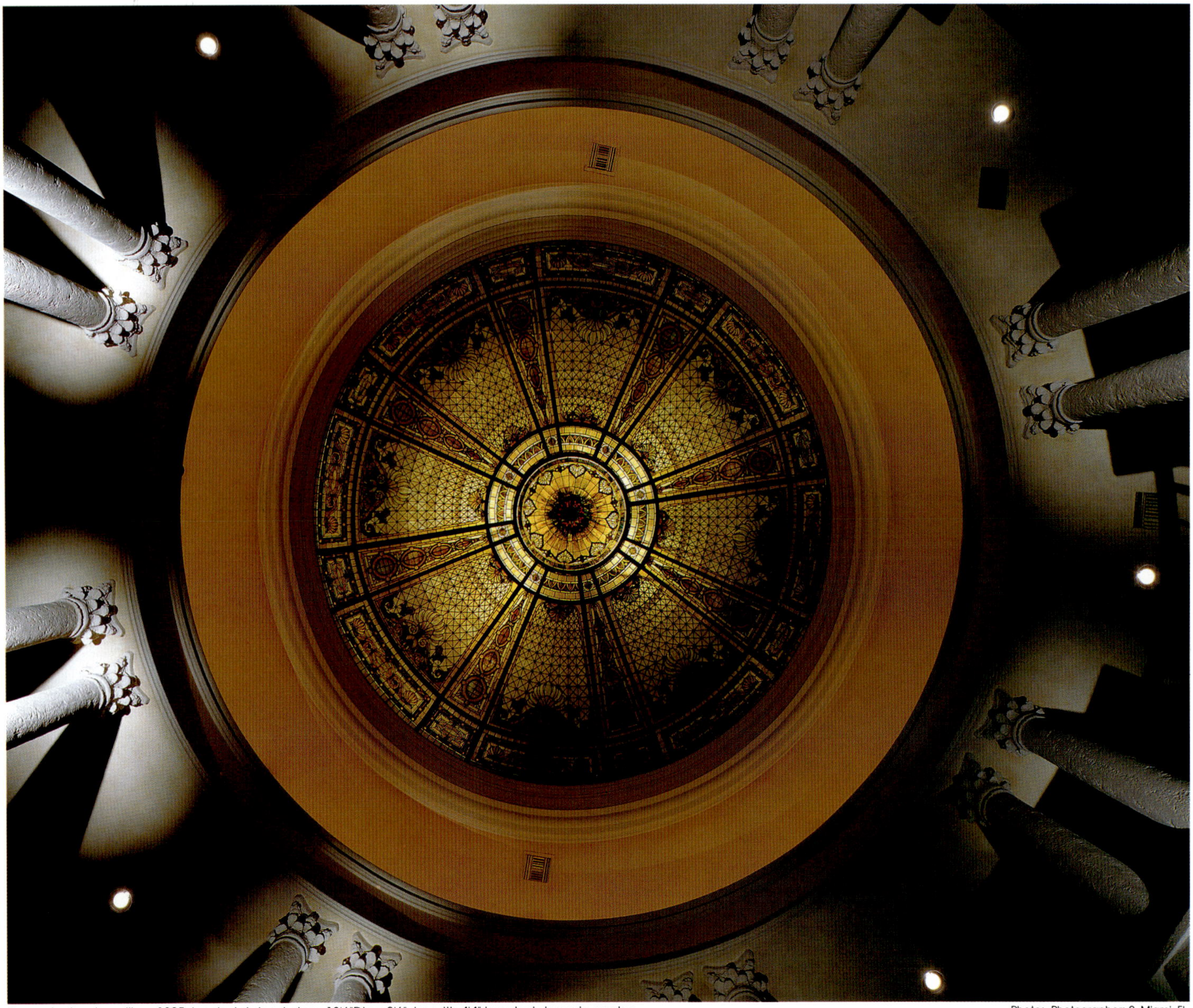

Domed rotunda ceiling, 1995, leaded stained glass, 18'6"Dia x 2'6" rise with 4'4" inverted dome in center

Sandra C.Q. Bergér

Quintal Unlimited
100 El Camino Real #202
Burlingame, CA 94010
FAX 415-340-0198
TEL   415-348-0310

Texture, dimension and depth … in glass!

Installation at right measures 4' x 6' 2". Durable construction of laminated safety glass enhanced with additional textured glass panes and crystal bevels.

Glass art installations include: wall reliefs, murals, entrances, window treatments, leaded glass panels and luminous sculptures.

Experienced. Professional. International. Worldwide service. Delivery three to six months.

Commissions include:
Cancer Research Center, Honolulu, HI
Minot State University, Minot, ND
Tanforan Business Center,
   So. San Francisco, CA
Sunnyvale Convalescent Hospital,
   Sunnyvale, CA
Pronto Restaurant, Redwood City, CA
Residential Services

Also see these GUILD publications:
THE GUILD: 1, 2, 3, 4, 5
Architect's Edition: 6, 7, 8, 10
Designer's Edition: 8
Gallery Edition: 2

Photography by William A. Porter

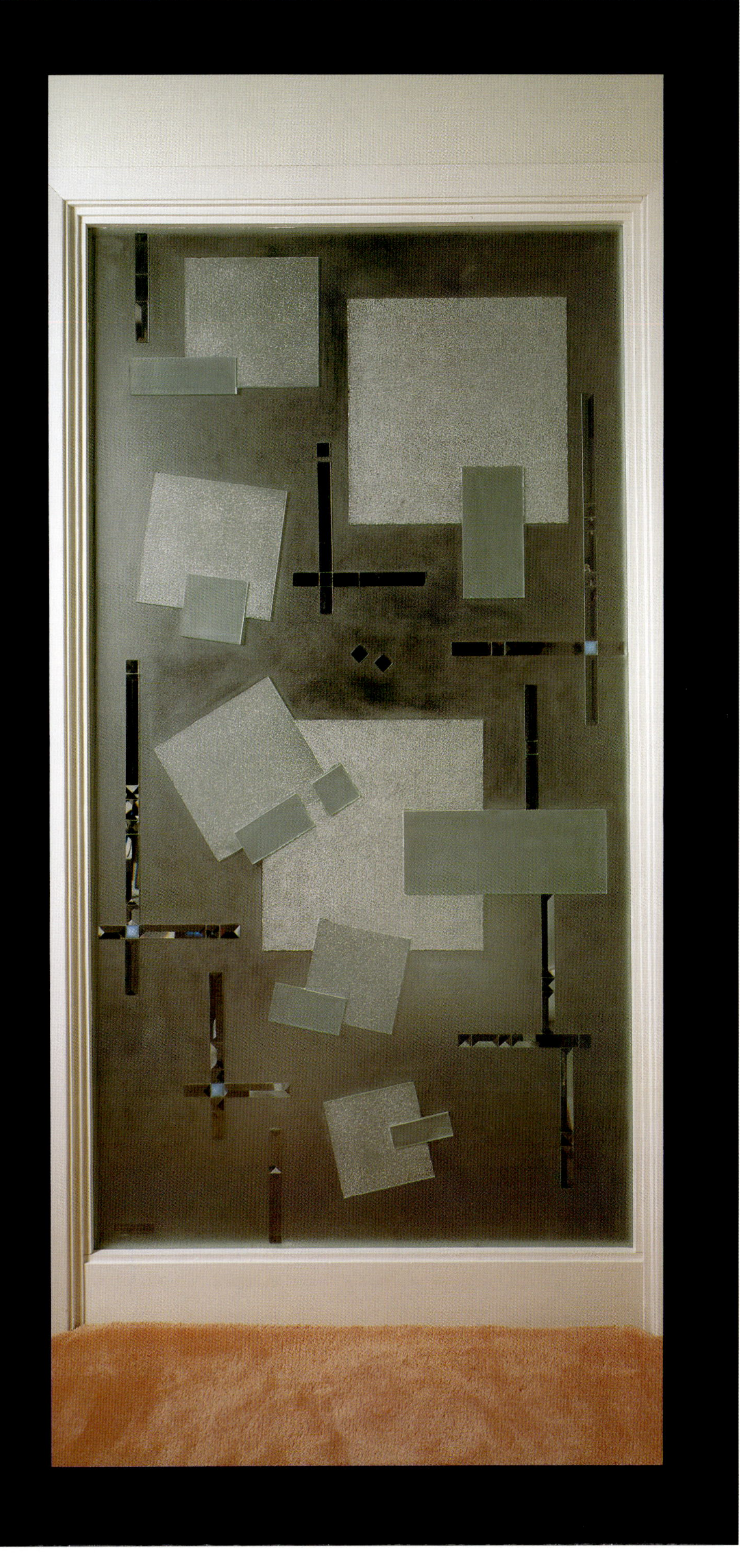

Beyer Stained Glass

Joseph K. Beyer
9511 Germantown Avenue
Philadelphia, PA 19118
FAX 215-848-3535
TEL   215-848-3502

The unique nature of the medium of architectural stained glass requires that the artists be willing to work as team players. Staffed by eight BFA graduates with a solid foundation of many diverse projects, Beyer Stained Glass is well suited for projects that require close coordination between an architect, general contractor and artist.

Services include consultation on framing, stained and leading glass window design, fabrication and installation. Special techniques such as acid etching and kiln-fired glass painting and staining are often employed. Special emphasis is placed on the long-term survivability of the window.

SHOWN: The Beasley Building, 1993, 19th century gothic revival building renovated for law offices, 12th and Walnut Streets, Philadelphia; architects: SRK Architects

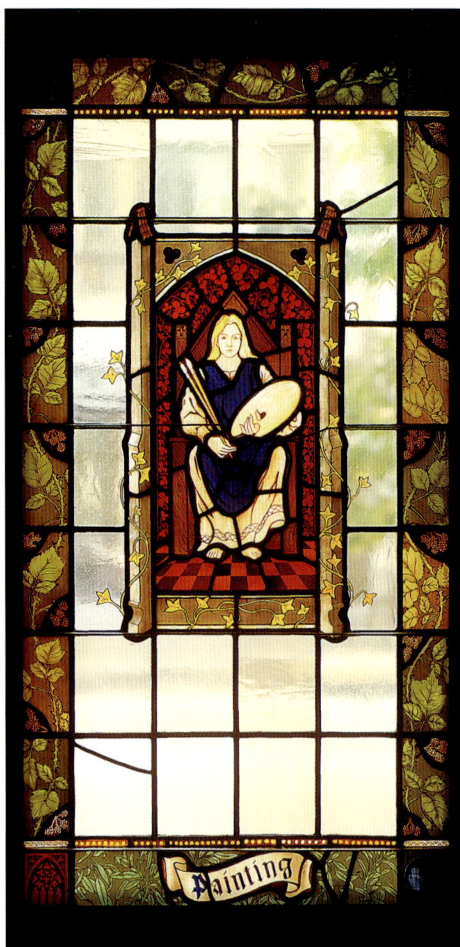

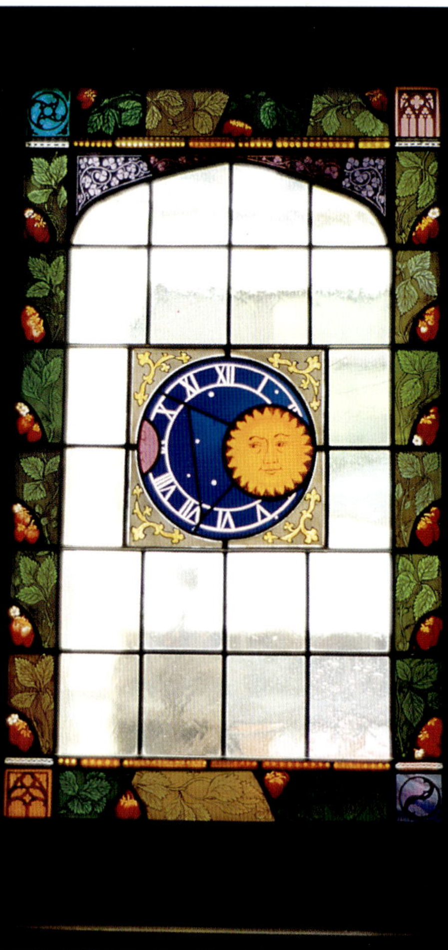

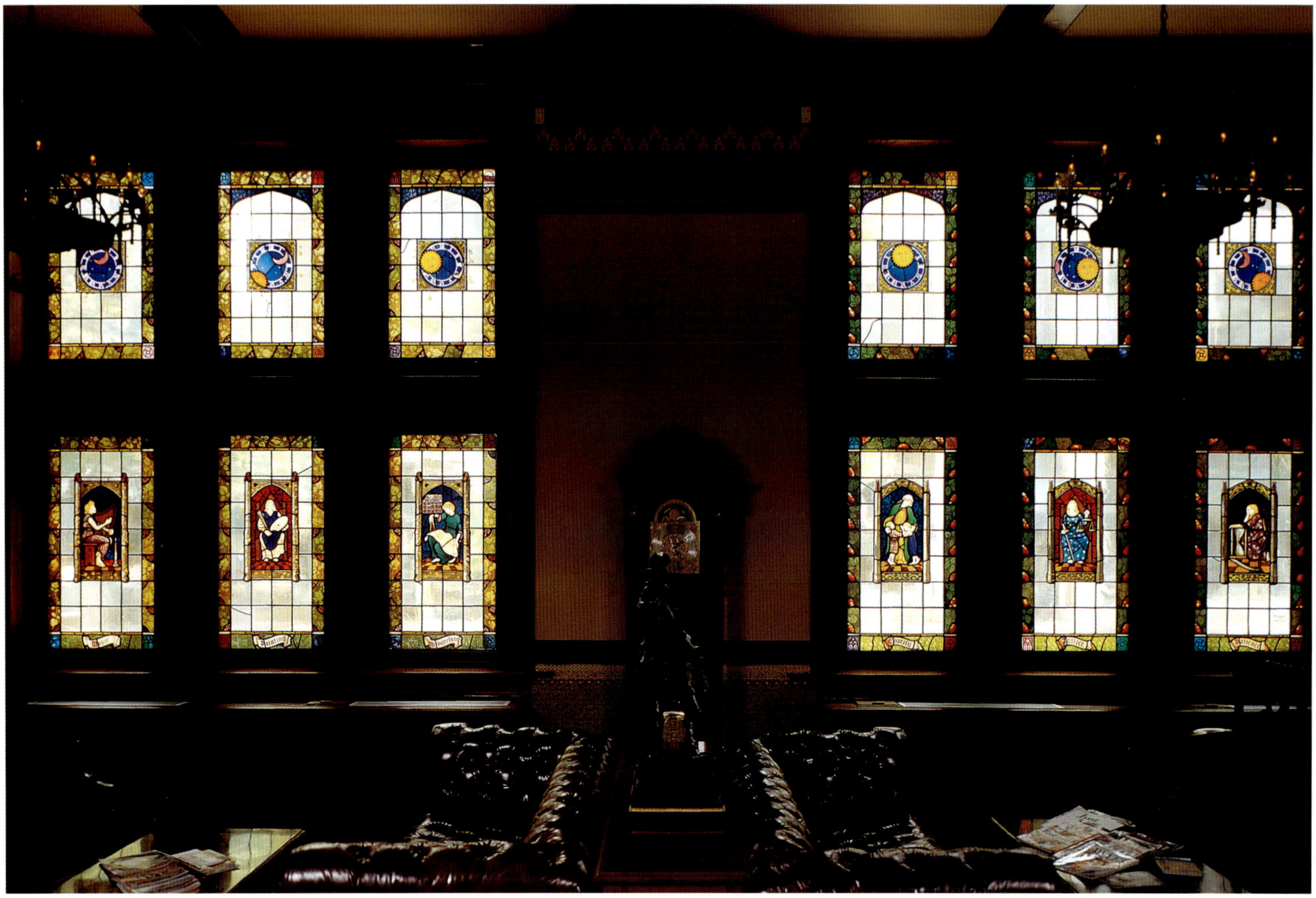

Beyer Stained Glass

Joseph K. Beyer
9511 Germantown Avenue
Philadelphia, PA 19118
FAX 215-848-3535
TEL 215-848-3502

Over the past 15 years, Joseph K. Beyer has acquired a reputation for innovative design solutions for business, medical and worship environments. Often the best visual concepts result from demanding circumstances. Physical and budgetary constraints are considered equally with the use and purpose of a particular space. This design philosophy has yielded a broad range of solutions from traditional interpretations to unique contemporary statements.

Prices ranging from $150 to $550 per sq. ft.

Additional information available upon request.

SHOWN: Church of the Lord Jesus Christ, Philadelphia, 1994, hand-blown glass, silver nitrate stain, ten windows, each measuring 8' x 30'

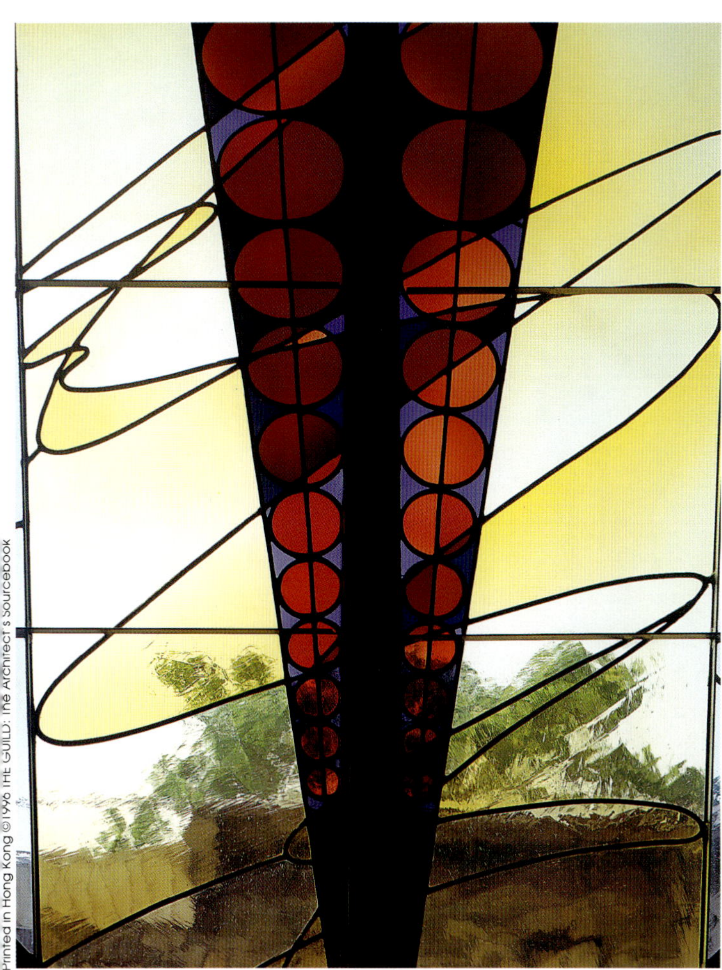

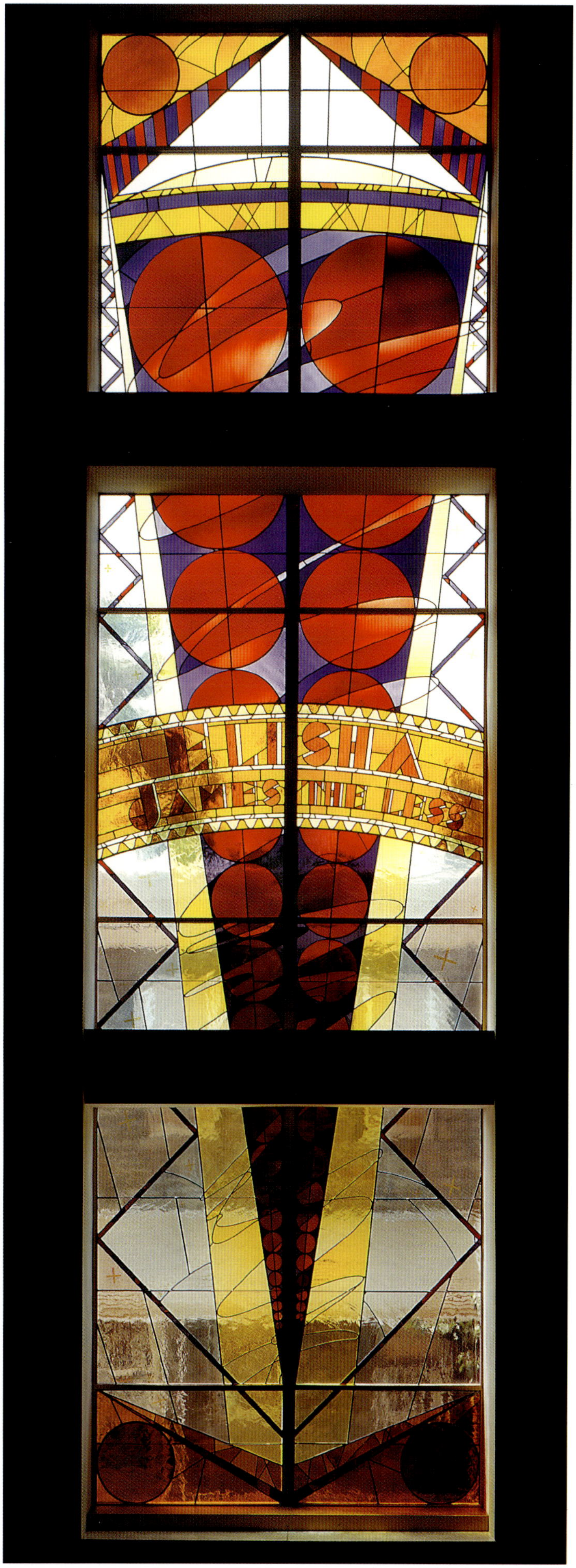

Joel Berman

Joel Berman Glass Studios Ltd.
1-1244 Cartwright Street
Vancouver, BC V6H 3R8
Canada
FAX 604-684-8373
TEL 604-684-8332

Joel Berman specializes in the design and fabrication of successful, site-specific architectural glass art for commercial interior space, with emphasis on corporate offices and building lobbies. The studio's work includes most forms of flat and curved glass, including kiln-cast glass in sheet form up to 72" x 125". Kiln-cast glass is also available in tempered and recycled glass.

Also see these GUILD publications:
Architect's Edition: 6, 7, 8, 9, 10

A Canada Free Trade Centre. Mexico City, kiln-cast reception wall, 20' x 8¹/₂', interior design: Bradley Stuike, Dept. of External Affairs, Government of Canada

B & C Wall Center Garden Hotel, Vancouver, BC, Onda kiln-cast restaurant wall and detail, 600' x 5', interior design: Chris Doray/Charlotte Wall

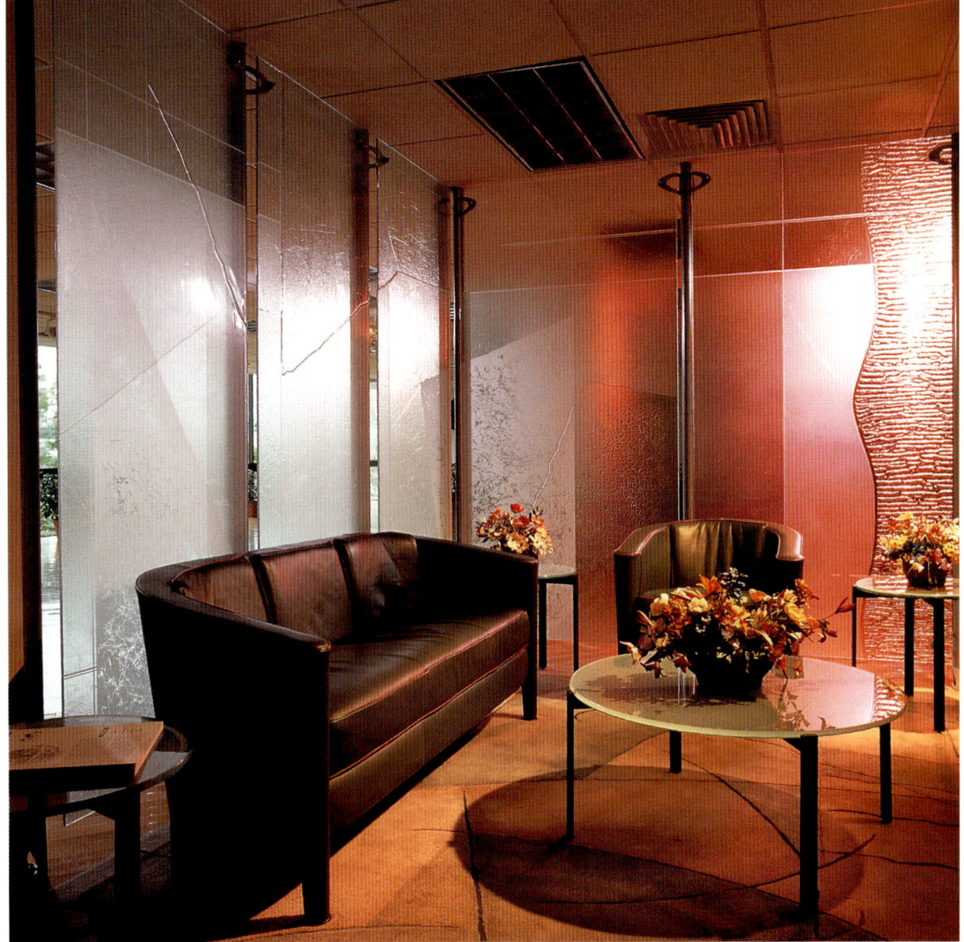

Yvonne Belanger

A

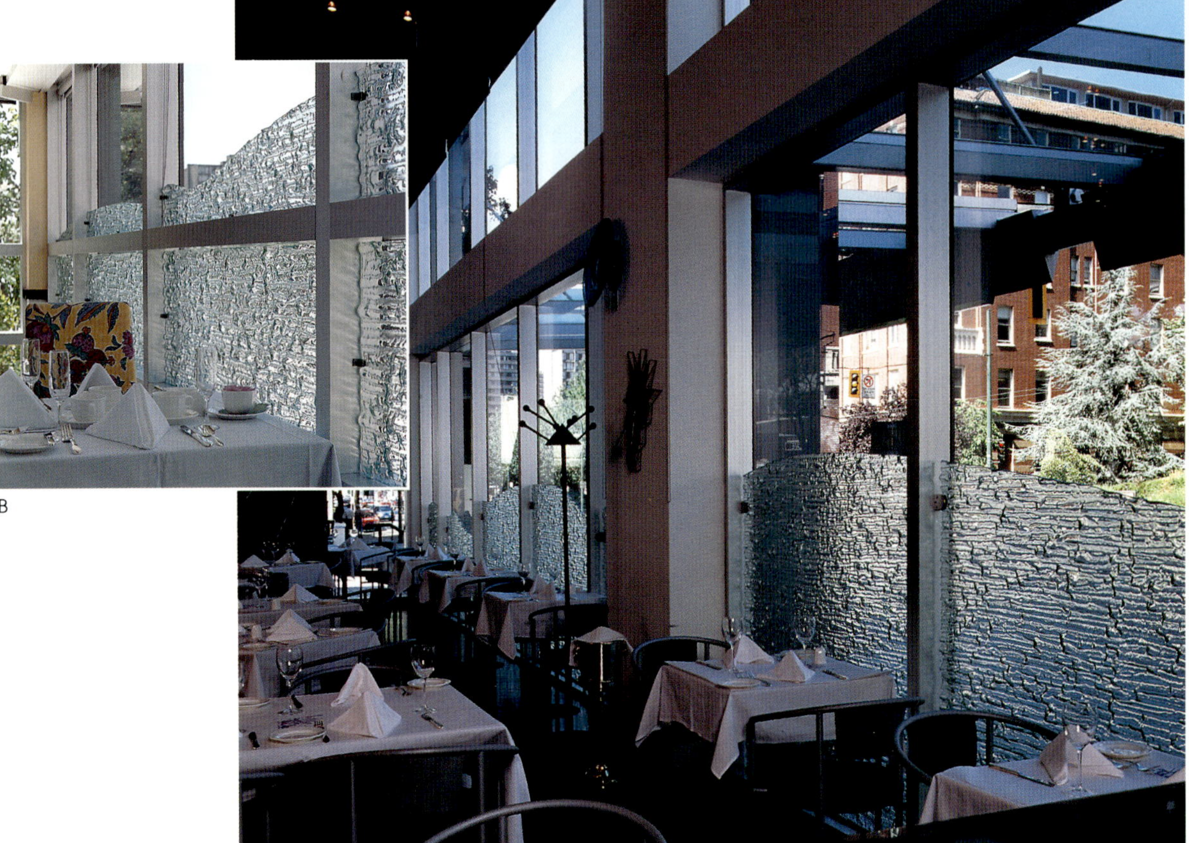

B

C

Dan Heringa

Rich Buswell

Stained Glass Artist
Route 4 Box 129
Lynchburg, VA 24503
FAX 804-525-6168 (East Coast)
TEL   800-237-6161 (East Coast)
FAX 417-667-8185 (MidWest)
TEL   800-525-8442 (MidWest)

Since 1976, the artist has been working primarily on site-specific liturgical commissions. He works closely with the architect and church representatives, interpreting the needs of his clients, using a creative mix of traditional elements and contemporary designs that harmonize in a variety of settings. Fabrication and restoration facilities in both Virginia and Missouri.

Member: Stained Glass Association of America

Also see this GUILD publication:
Architect's Edition: 10

A *Sorrow*, St. Bernadett's, Appleton, WI, 1 of 80 windows, Alan Birschbach, AIA

B St. Raphael's Catholic Church, Springdale, AR, 21' x 12', 1 of 2 window walls, Ed Drimmel, AIA

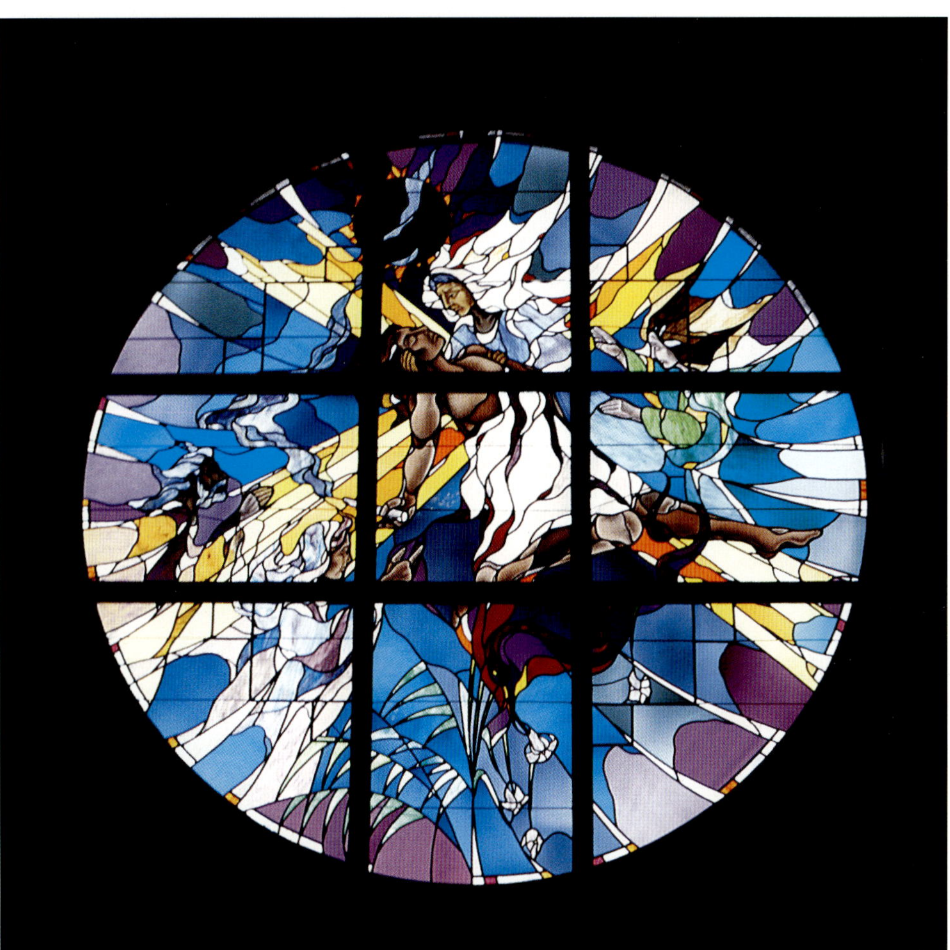

A

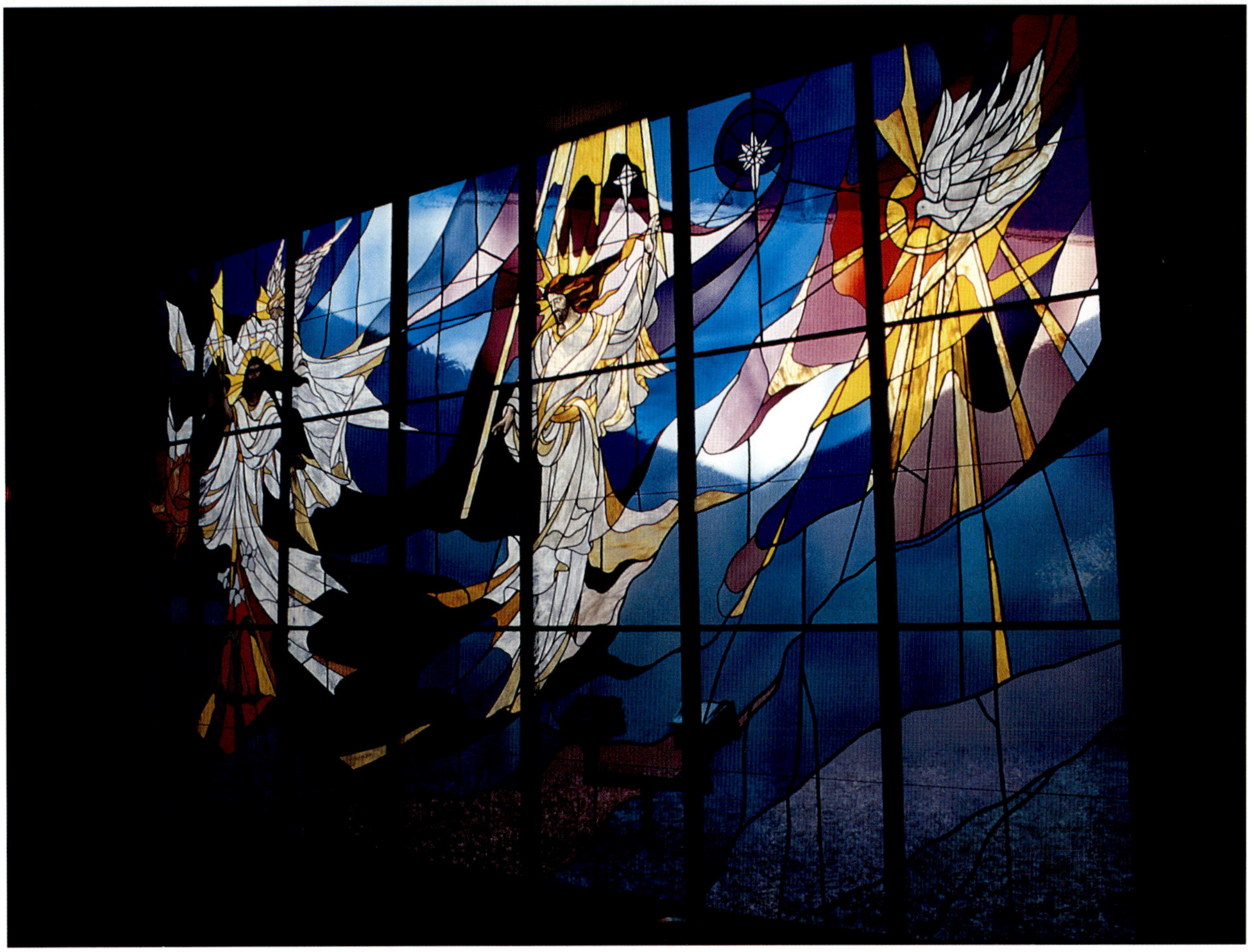

B

J. Gorsuch Collins

J. Gorsuch Collins Architectural Glass
8283 West Iliff Lane
Lakewood, CO 80227
FAX 303-980-0692
TEL   303-985-8081

The work of J. Gorsuch Collins exudes originality
and compatibility with the architectural setting.
Preferring to work in collaboration with the
architect, designer or client, Collins uses a wide
range of glass techniques, often in combination
with other materials or with other artists, to
accommodate the space. Any project may
be a complete departure from previous work.

Custom blown, etched, fused and beveled
glass allow maximum versatility of texture and
color, and permit Collins to also create small
architectural accessories to complement her
installations.

Delivery and installation are possible both
nationally and internationally. Prices range
widely according to technique, materials
and scale.

Also see these GUILD publications:
THE GUILD: 4, 5
Architect's Edition: 6, 7, 8, 9, 10

SHOWN: Leaded glass ceiling, 1994, custom-blown
glass, beveled glass, brilliant cut, carved, 12'Dia

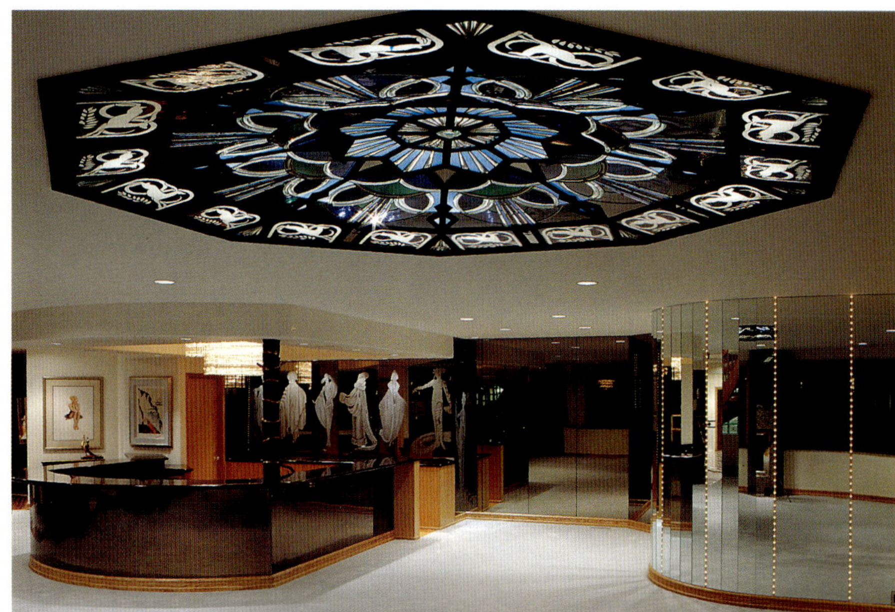

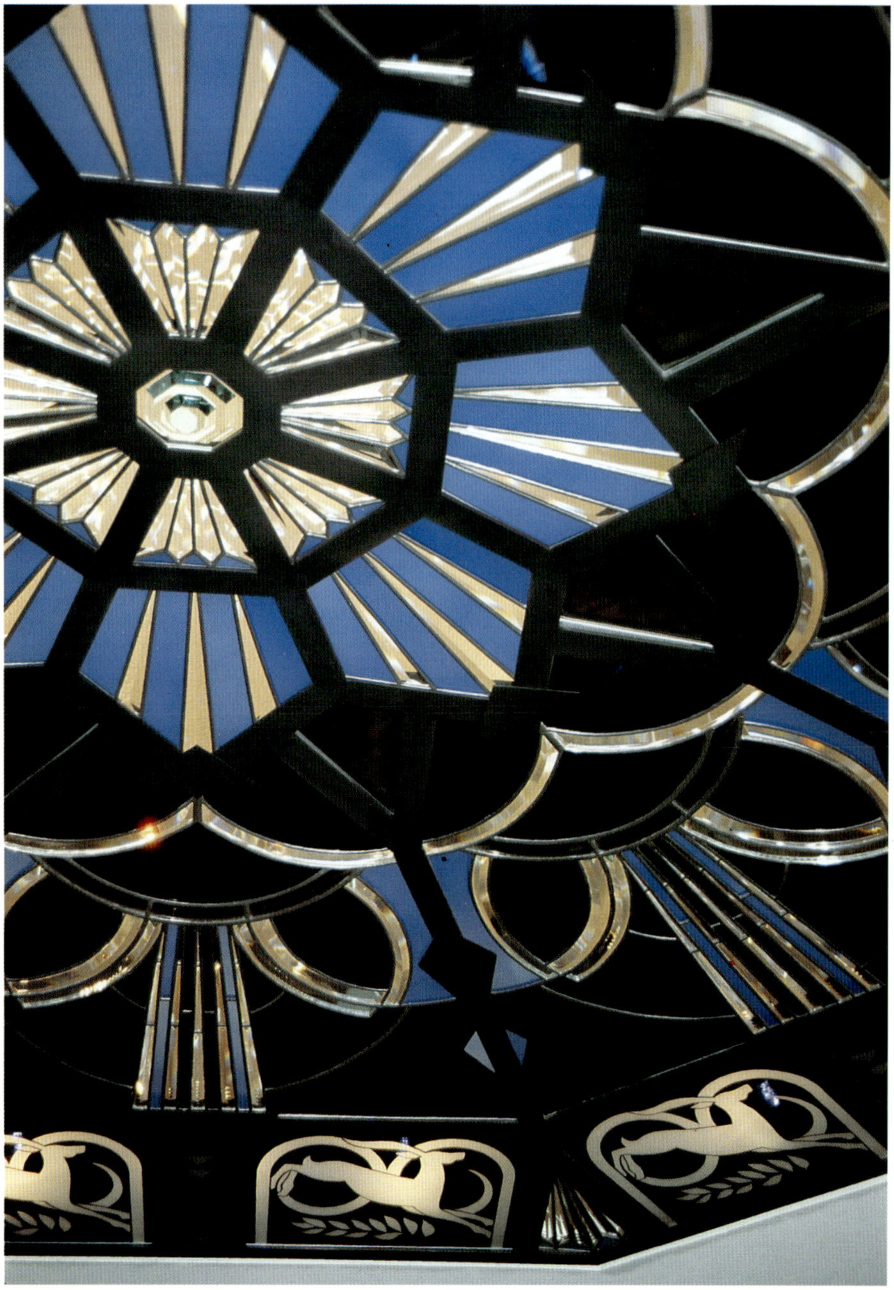

Photos: Ron Ruscio

Ellen Mandelbaum
Glass Art

Ellen Mandelbaum
39-49 46 Street
Long Island City, NY 11104-1407
FAX 718-361-8154
TEL 718-361-8154

Ellen Mandelbaum specializes in painted glass, which helps to create light and beautiful spaces. Landscape is a favorite subject. Panels complement architectural detailing, can help improve views, protect privacy, create a retreat from the tensions of the city, warm an impersonal lobby, or bring light to a holy space. Panels can be built in or suspended in front of existing light sources.

Mandelbaum collaborates with architects, interior designers and clients. An important artist listed in *Who's Who in American Art,* her works have been featured in international exhibitions and publications.

Glass is fired for permanence at 1200°F. Prices vary. Inquiries are welcomed. Reliable service since 1981.

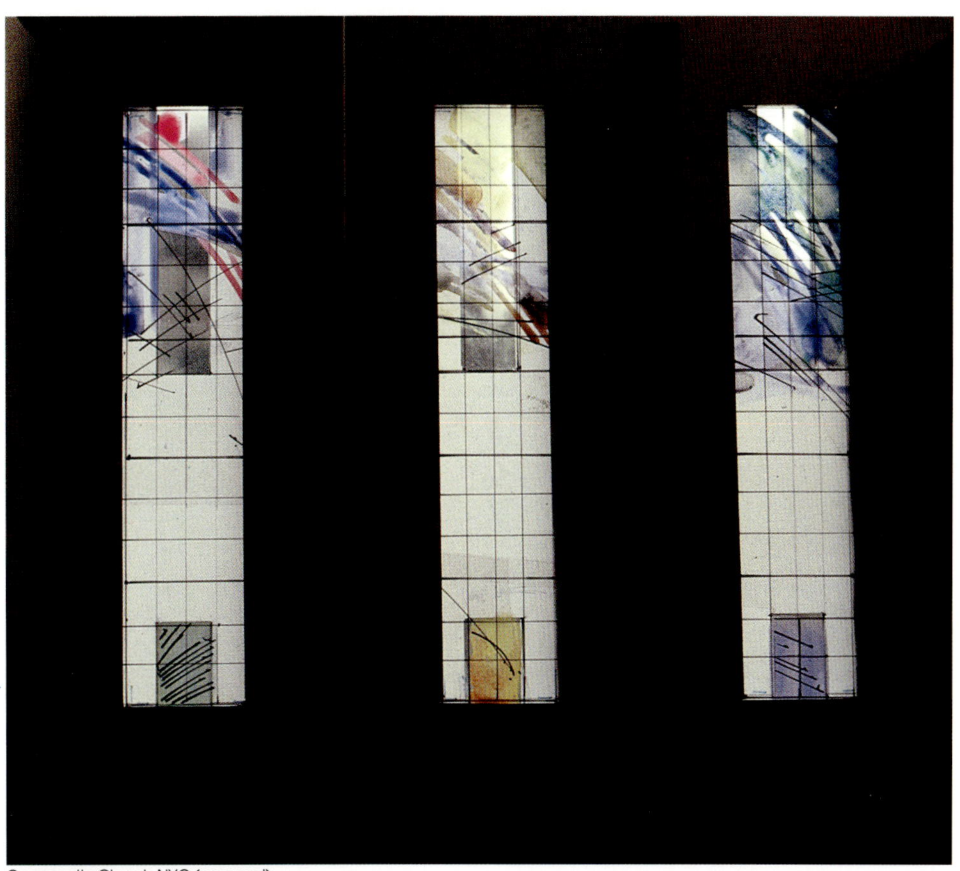

Community Church NYC (proposal)

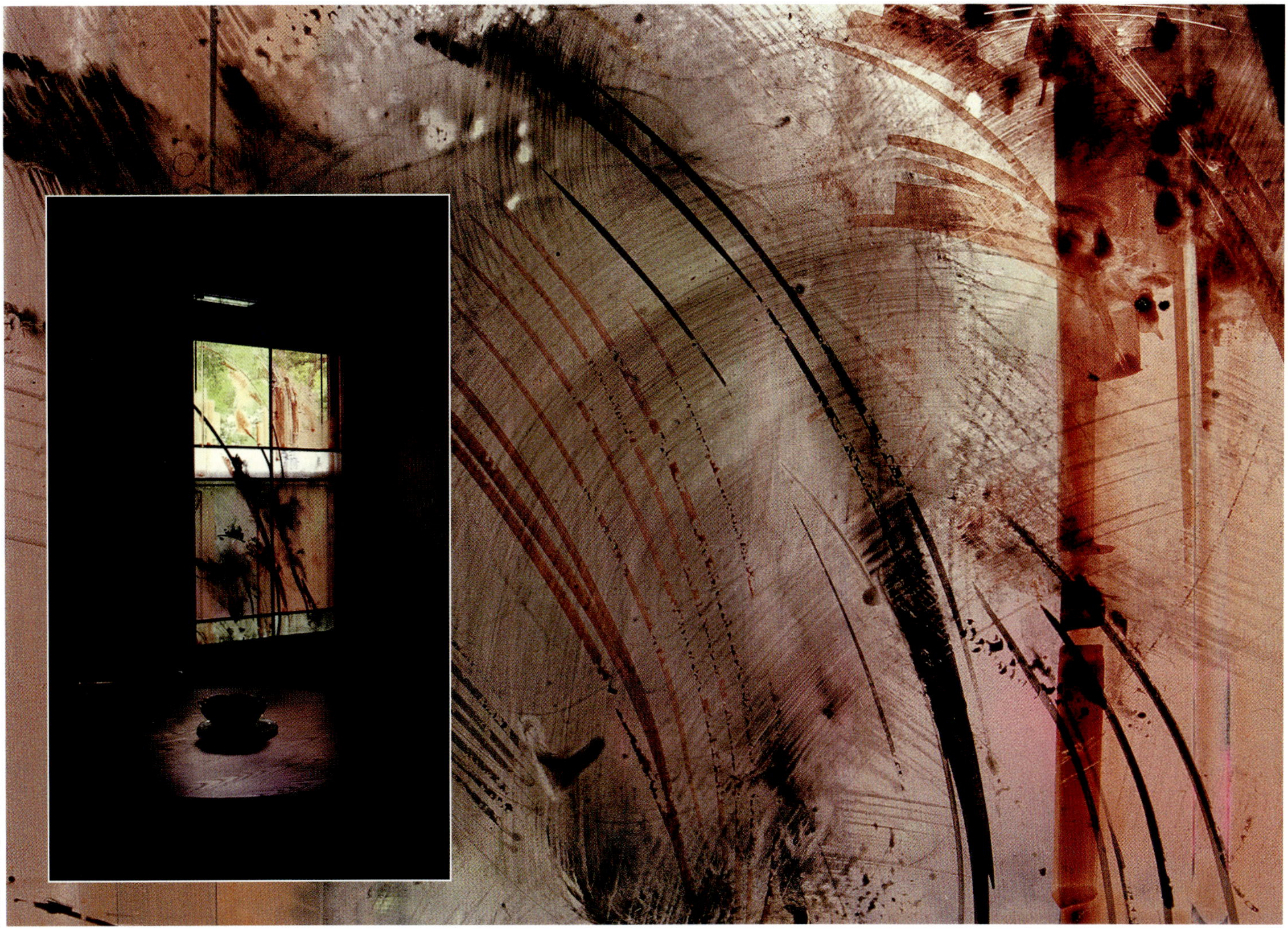

Mark Eric Gulsrud

Architectural Glass and Clay
3309 Tahoma Place West
Tacoma, WA 98466
TEL 206-566-1720

Primarily site-specific, commissions range internationally and include public, private, corporate and liturgical settings. Media include custom hand-blown and leaded glass, dalle de verre, sand-carved, laminated and cast glass. Encouraging professional collaboration, the artist is personally involved in all phases of design, fabrication and installation, and is primarily concerned with a sympathetic integration of artwork with environment.

Also see these GUILD publications:
THE GUILD: 3, 4
Architect's Edition: 7, 8, 9, 10

SHOWN: *Descending Dove*, St. John Fisher Catholic Church, Portland, OR, copper, stainless steel, laminated crystal prisms with hand-blown color, 8' x 16'

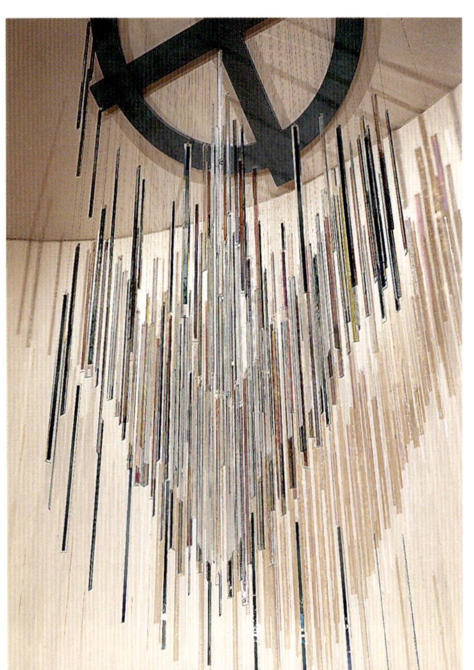

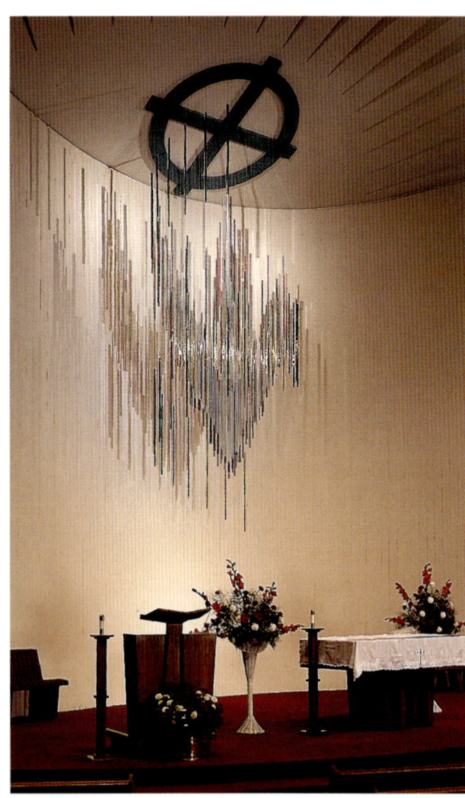

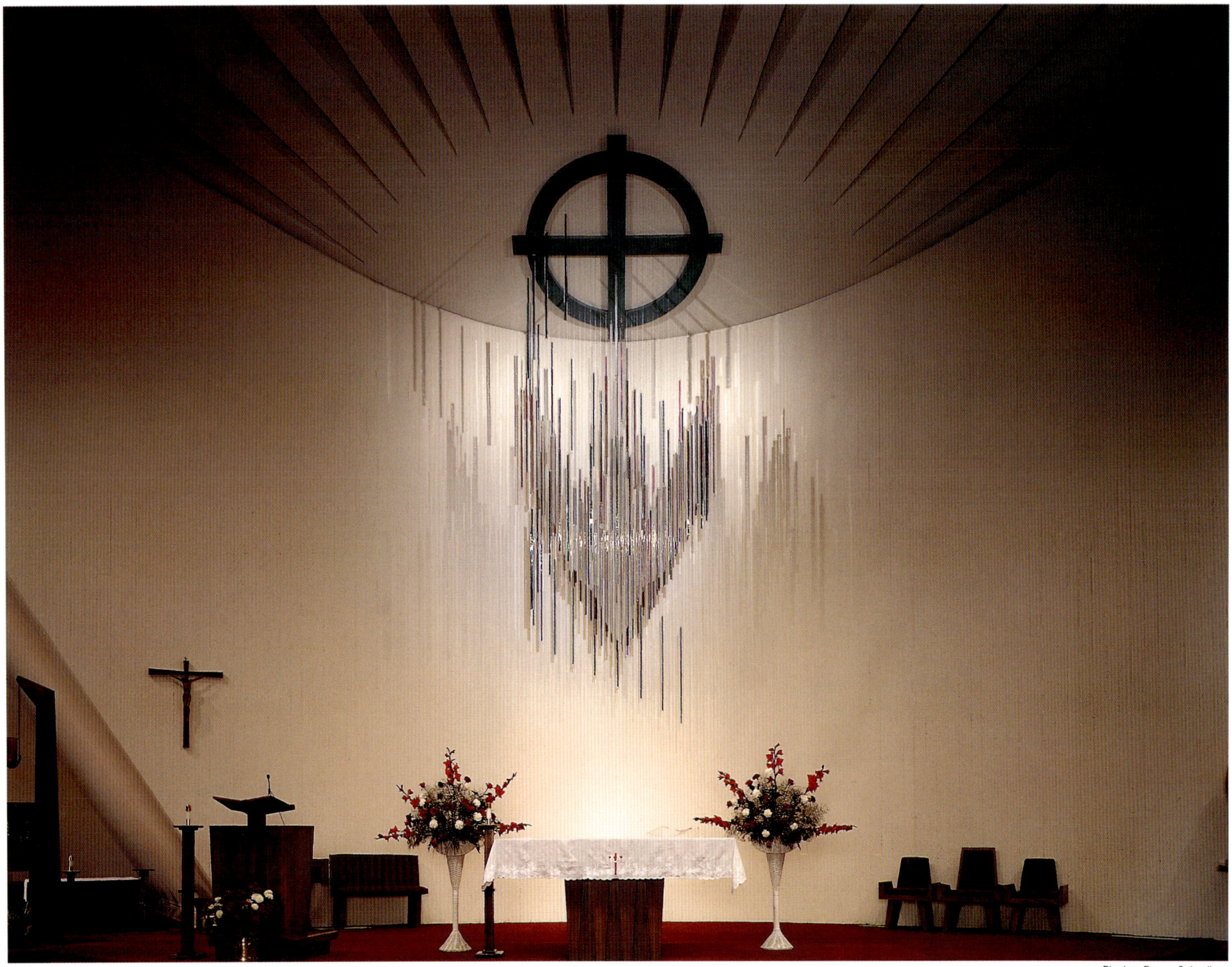

Mark Hall

Hallmark Art Glass
201 N. Rice POB 366
Kasota, MN 56050
TEL 507-931-9489

Collective ideas create the vision. Mark Hall utilizes 20 years experience and a full production studio that transforms vision into reality. The studio's capability is limited only by the imagination.

A *Two Nations, Under God, Indivisible,* fused, slumped, and leaded glass; speaks of our heritage, recalls promises made outlining our on-going responsibilities

B *Window of Hope,* wall murals at Immanuel St. Joseph's Hospital, Mankato, MN; this community art project focuses discussion on the HIV epidemic in rural Minnesota; each tile represents a person or a thought

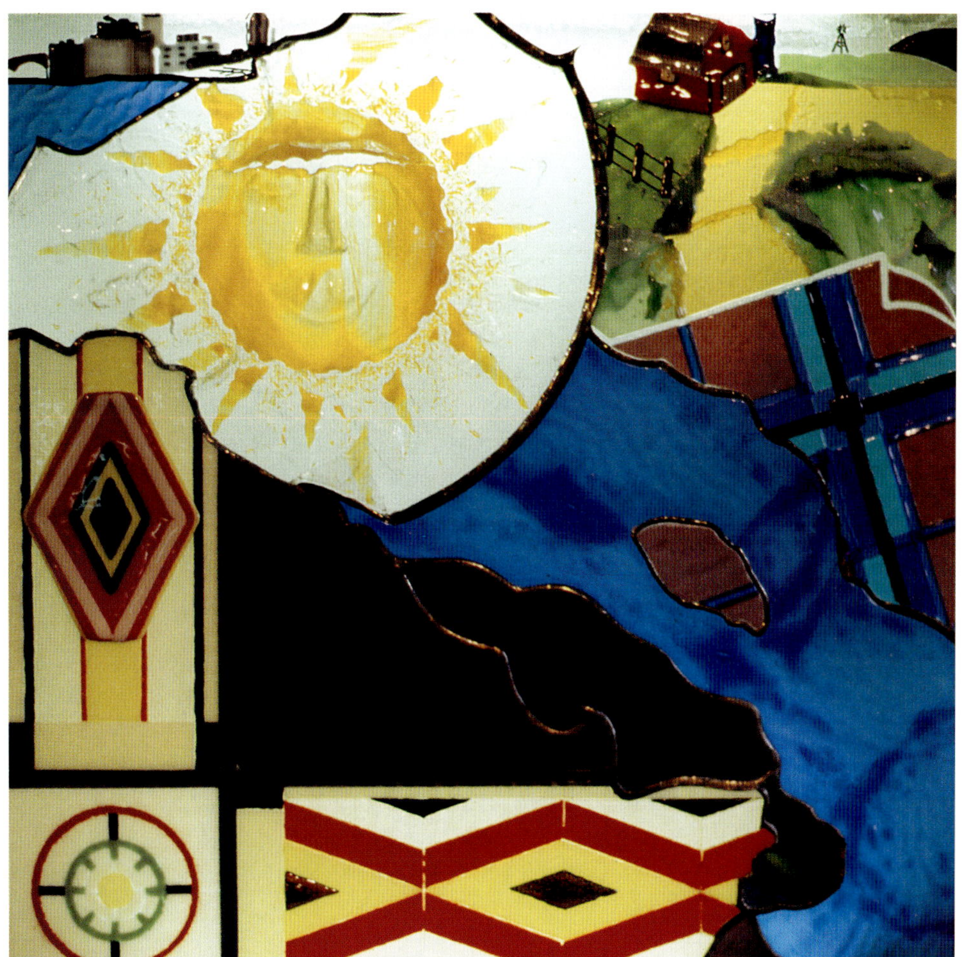

A

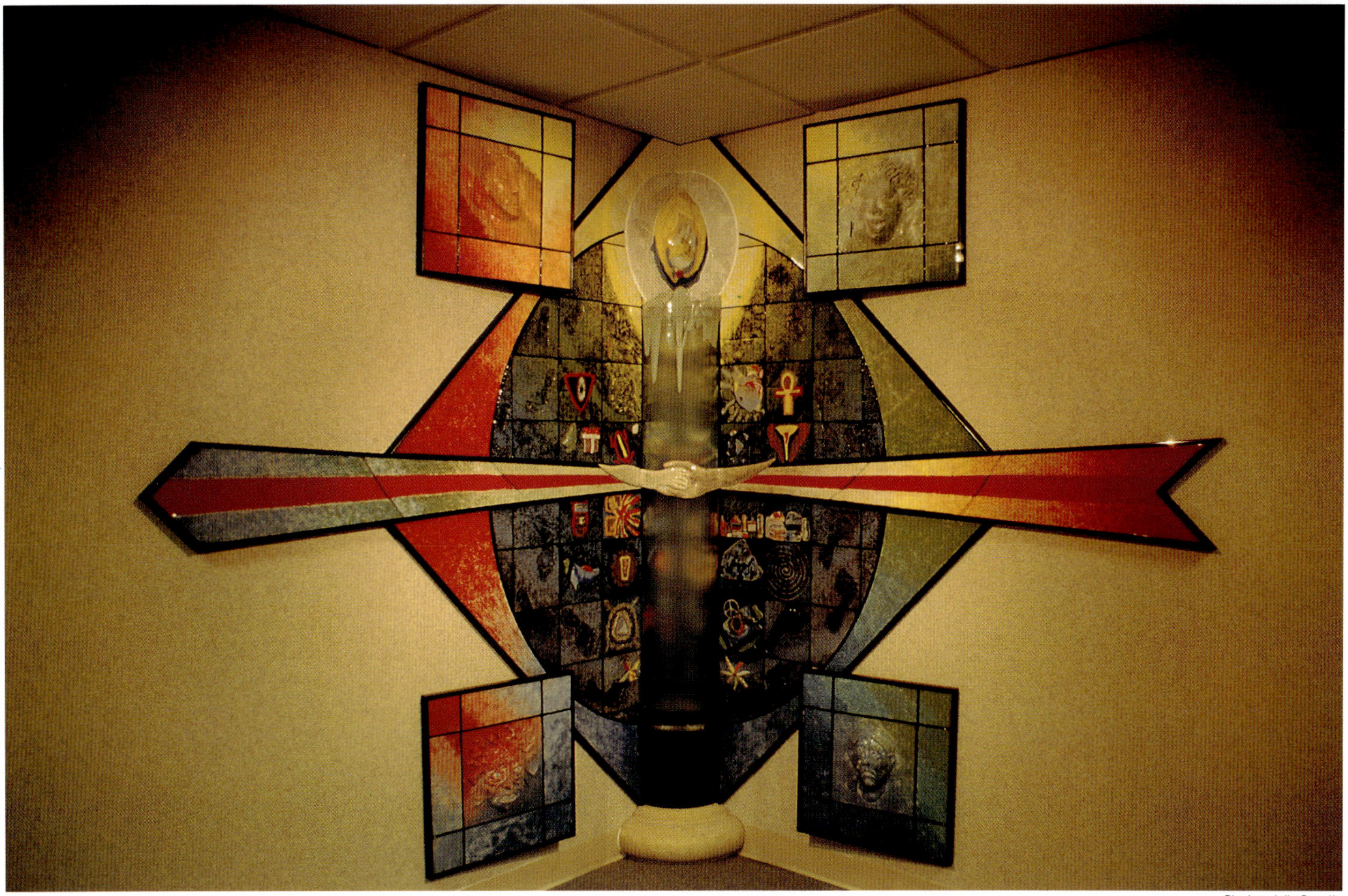

B

Photos: Julie Boertje

Paul Housberg

Glass Project, Inc.
59 Tingley Street
Providence, RI 02903
FAX 401-831-4881
TEL 401-831-4880

Paul Housberg creates site-specific works in glass. Central to his work is the use of light, texture and the power of glass to shape and define a space. Housberg is a graduate of Rhode Island School of Design and the recipient of a Fulbright Scholarship for architectural glass.

THIS PAGE: Charged with creating a contemplative space for employees at Pfizer Central Research in Groton, CT, Housberg used pixilated images of the seasons to make a 'forest clearing of glass.' Four walls of cast, cut and colored glass are located at the four compass points within a rotunda that serves as the employee dining room. The sun rises in the *Spring* (east) wall, is brightest in the *Summer* (south) wall, and sets in the *Autumn* (west) wall. Each wall measures 11'W x 12'H x 4"D and consists of 2,500 segments of glass. Architect: CUH2A, Inc., Princeton, NJ.

A *Winter* (north) wall with diffused light from skylights and clerestory windows

B Surface light reveals texture suggesting an outcropping of rock

C View of the rotunda showing *Summer* and *Autumn* walls

Also see interview with designer John Mudgett of CUH2A in this volume of the *Architect's Edition*.

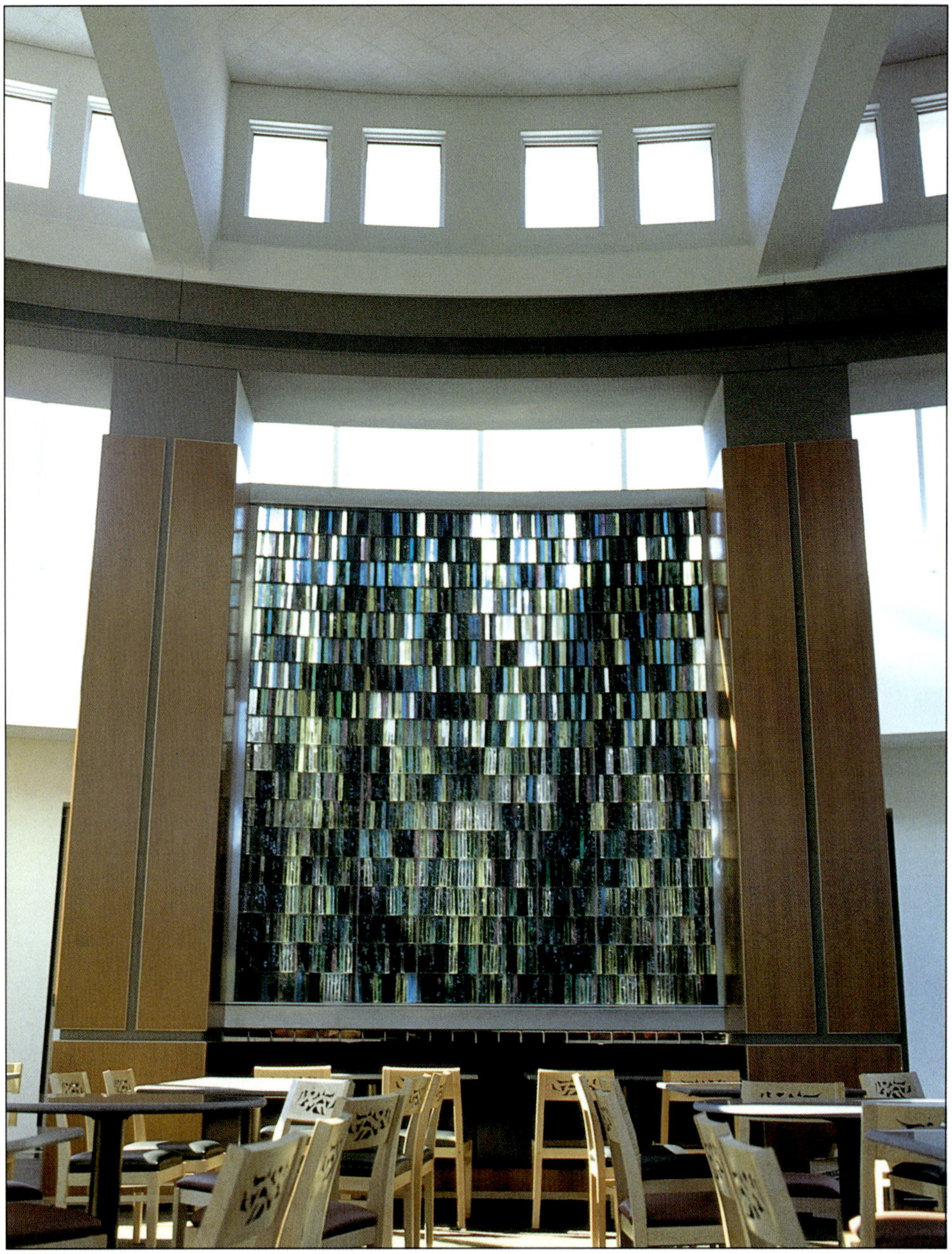

A

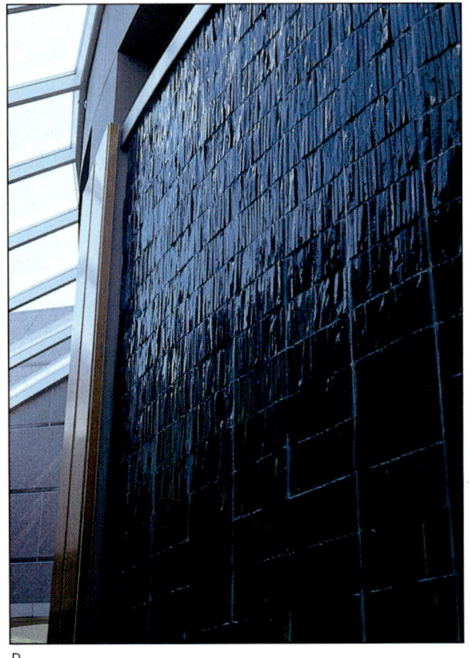

B

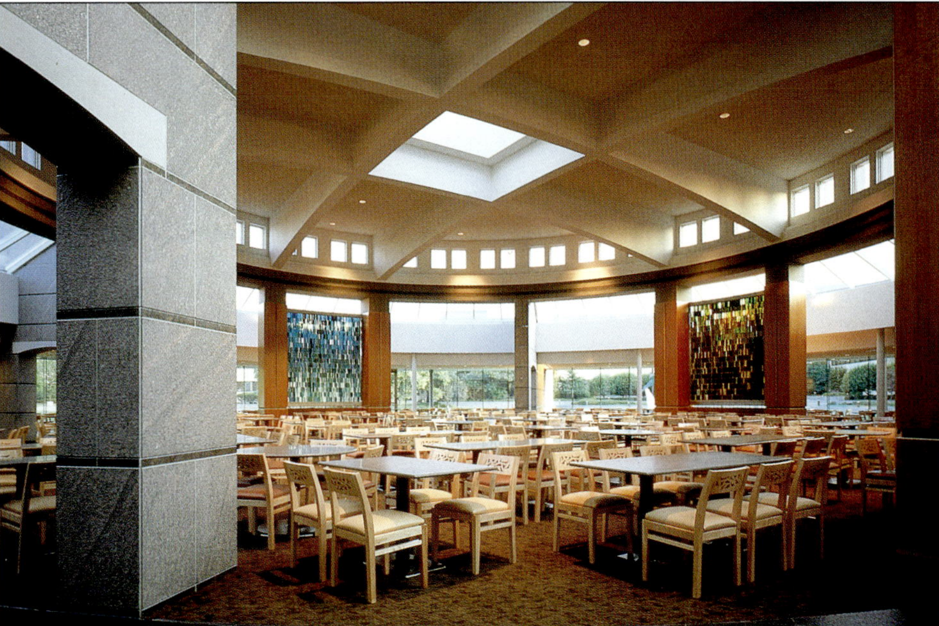

C

D Alpenglow Elementary School, Eagle River, AK. This 8' x 20' mural, entitled *Dream of the Arctic Flier*, is made of kiln-formed glass tiles which change color according to the angle of the sun. Located at the intersection of two main corridors and directly below a skylight, it shimmers in the profuse summer light. During dark Alaskan winters, the mural collects the scant ambient and artificial light and reflects it back into the school. Commissioned by the Municipality of Anchorage 1% for Art program.

E Housberg created this stained glass window—one of a pair—based on a photomicrograph of a butterfly wing. It refers to the client's residence which, with two wings extending at angles from a central foyer, resembles, in plan, a butterfly.

F This curved glass wall forms one side of a shower enclosure. The waterfall effect is the result of the thousands of black and clear glass marbles stacked in tubes and sandwiched between layers of bent glass. The wall provides both light and privacy.

The artist welcomes inquires regarding any aspect of a planned or contemplated project.

Also see these GUILD publications:
THE GUILD: 4, 5
Architect's Edition: 6, 7, 8, 9, 10

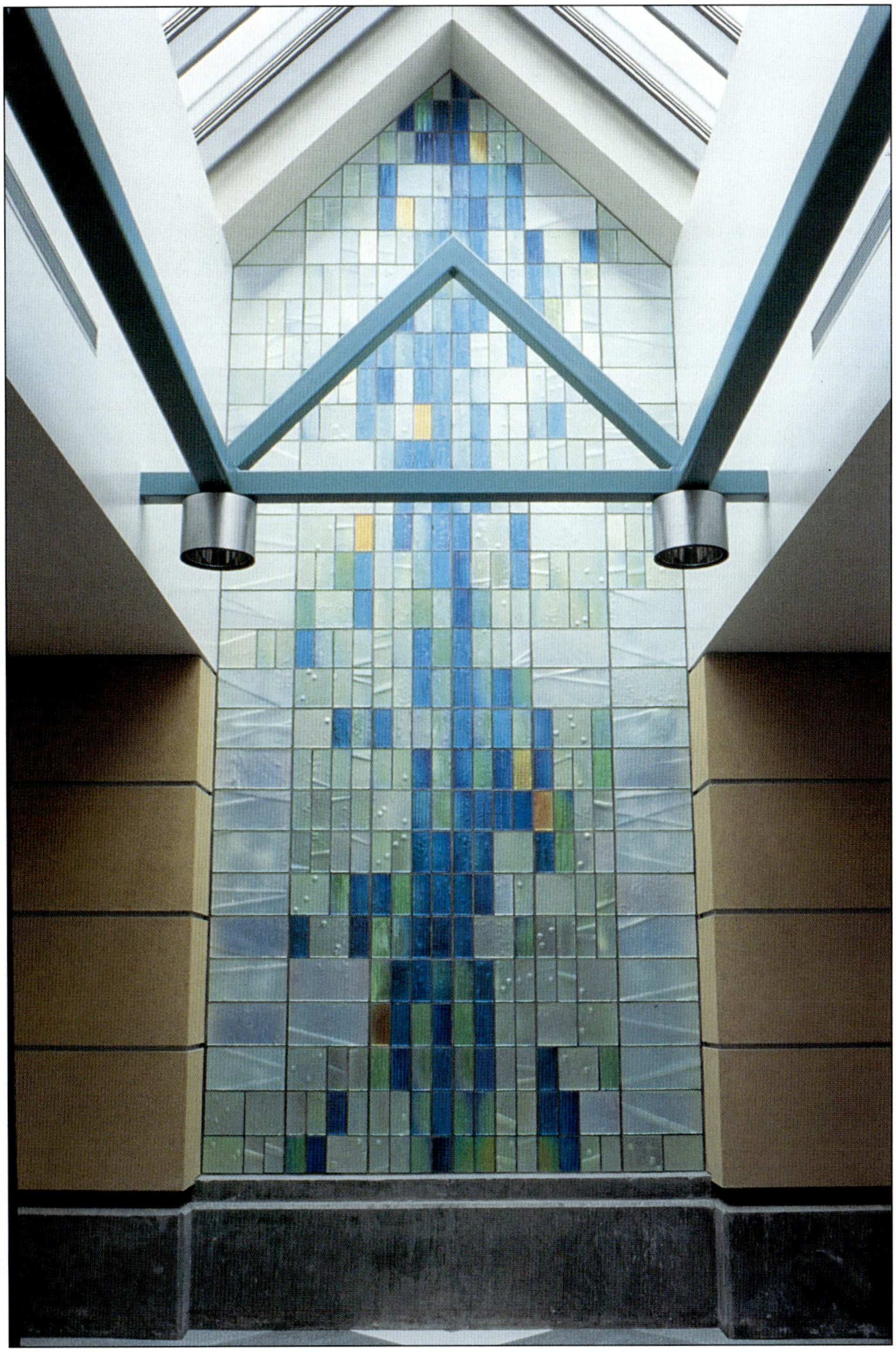

D

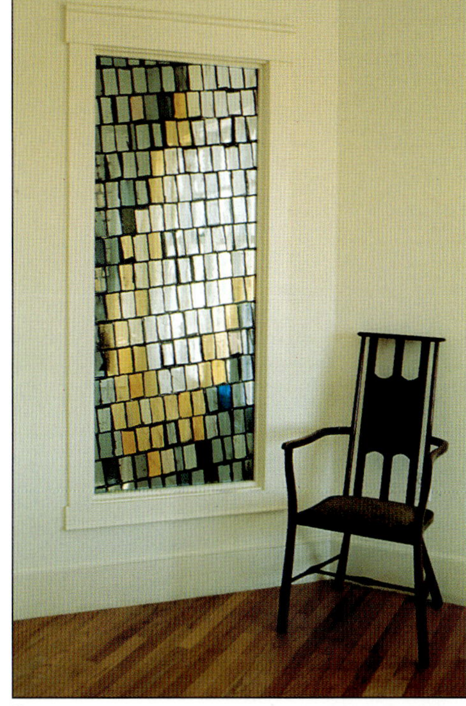

E

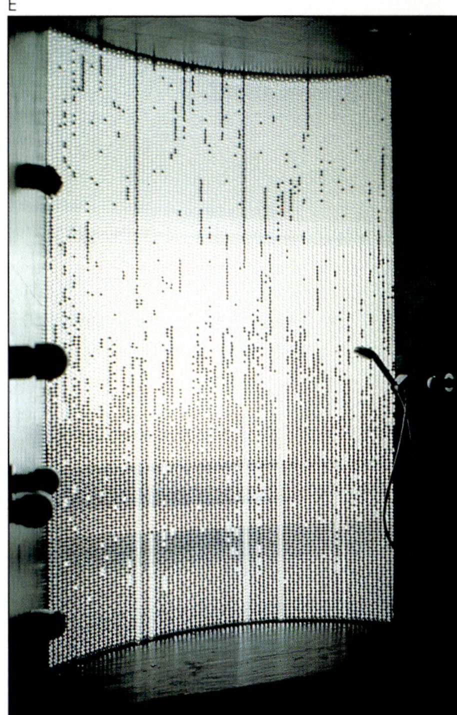

F

Guy Kemper

Kemper Studio
190 North Broadway
Lexington, KY 40507
FAX 606-254-3507
TEL 606-254-3507

Guy Kemper has exhibited nationally and inter-nationally, and has been featured in *The New York Times.* He has completed hundreds of com-missions—private, corporate and liturgical—with a history of meeting deadlines and budgets. His work is in collections in the U.S. and abroad.

Kemper transforms lightspaces with designs that reflect the room's spirit, the client's desires, and the architect's recommendations. He strives for a design of harmonious essentials that will out-last fashion.

His three-dimensional constructions combine layers of glass rods and laminated glass that shimmer and change with the movement of the viewer.

Also see these GUILD publications:
Architect's Edition: 9, 10

SHOWN: Jewish Hospital, Louisville, KY, 53' x 2', architect: Arrasmith Judd Rapp, Inc.

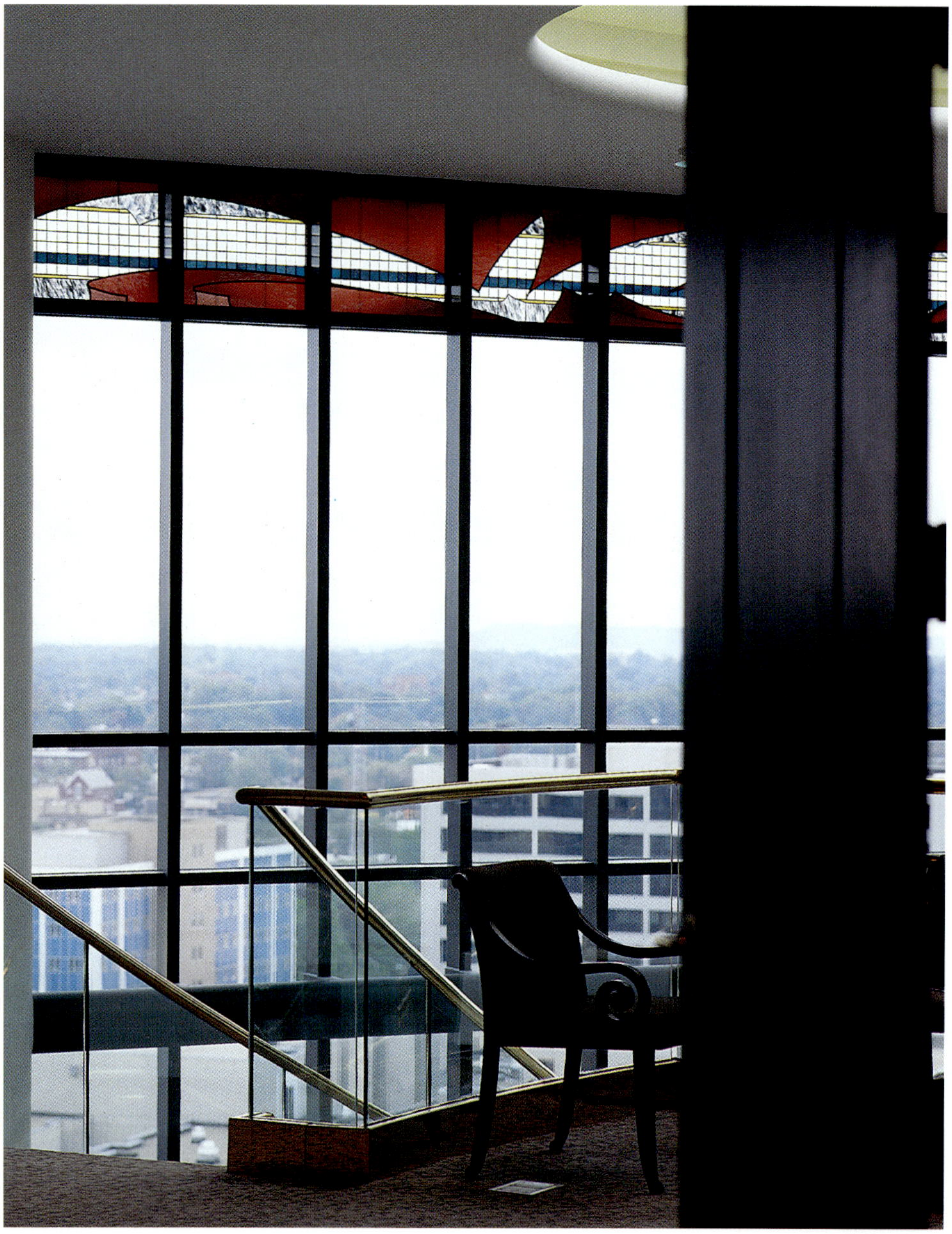

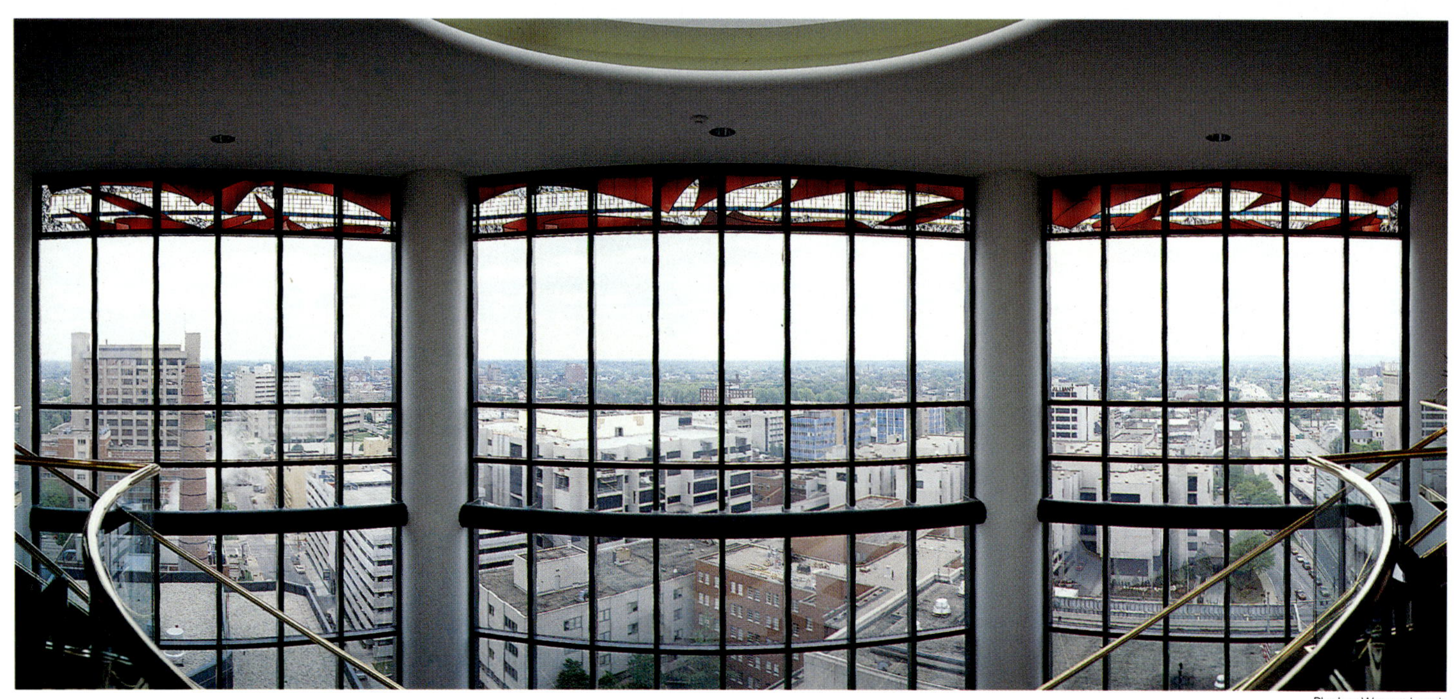

Photos: Warren Lynch

Stephen Knapp

74 Commodore Road
Worcester, MA 01602-2792
FAX 508-797-3228
TEL 508-757-2507

Stephen Knapp has collaborated with designers and architects on integrated architectural commissions for over 20 years, for both national and international clients. He is the author of "A Guide to Architectural Art Glass" in *Architectural Record* (May 1995) and "Architectural Art Glass" in *Glass Magazine* (May 1995).

With his innovative techniques in kiln-formed glass, he has created architectural art glass walls, doors, windows, and screens, and has combined steel and glass for furniture, sculpture and lighting.

Also see these GUILD publications:
Architect's Edition: 8, 9, 10

A Detail, kiln-formed glass window, with dichroics

B Tempered, kiln-formed glass doors, cast bronze handles

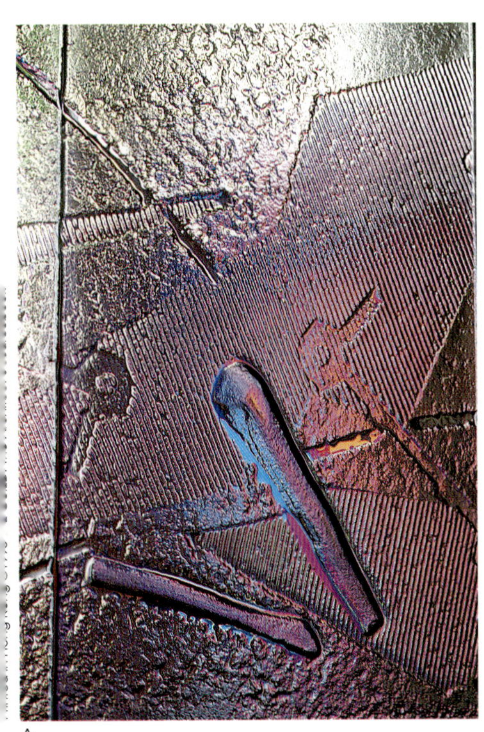

A

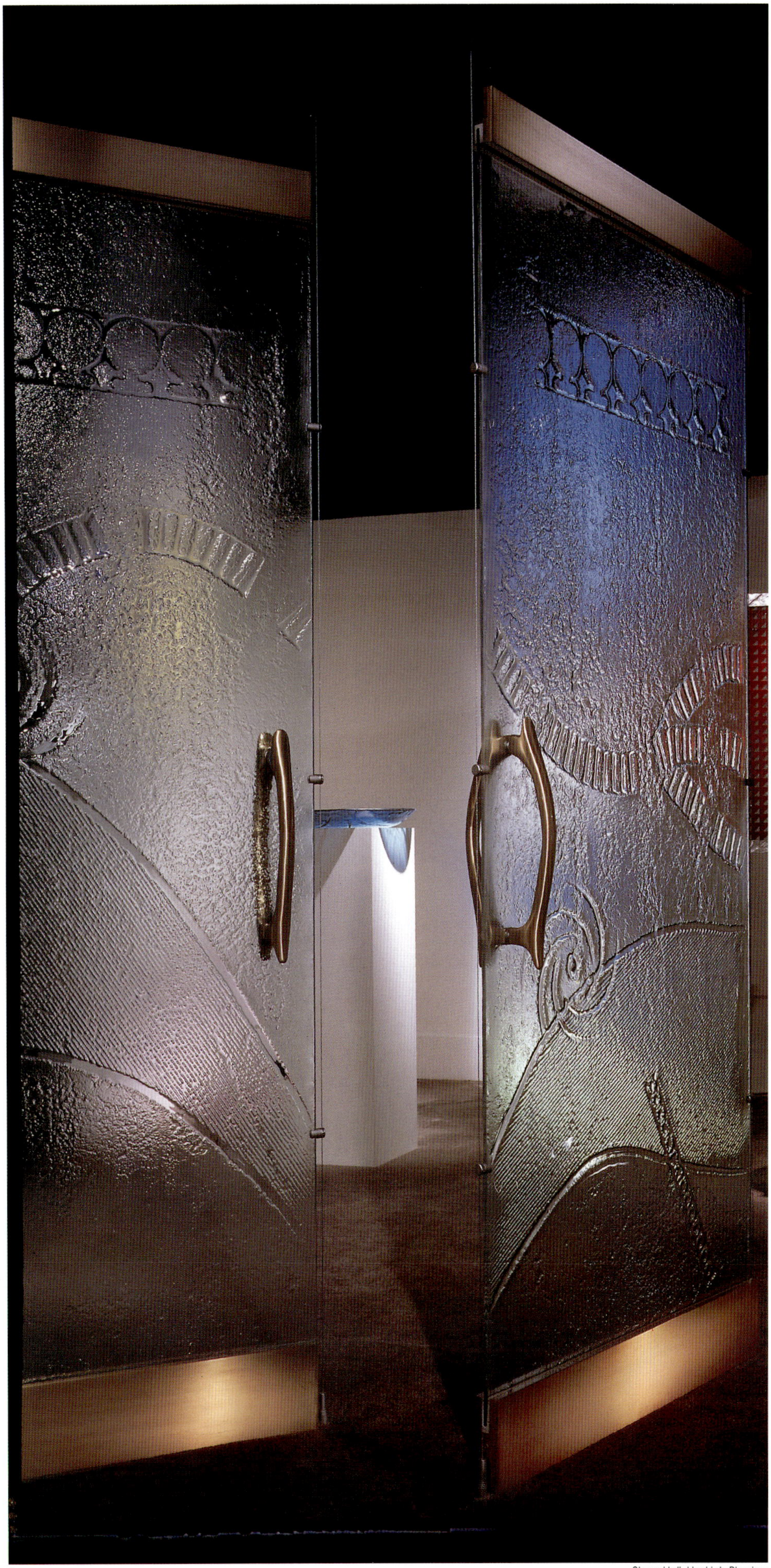

B

Leone McNeil

Lead & Light Works
PO Box 552
45131 Little Lake Street
Mendocino, CA 95460
FAX 707-937-5227
TEL 707-937-5227

Commissioned works for new and existing architecture have been created over the past 20 years for church and residential spaces by Leone McNeil. Great consideration is given to sensitive integration of architecture and interior design, as well as the ambience created by personalities occupying the space.

Leone finds addressing a diversity of styles challenging. Her broad foundation in painting, drawing and design earned her an M.F.A. from Otis Art Institute, Los Angeles, in 1965.

A new dimension has been added to McNeil's experience. Recently she worked in collaboration with 16 other stained glass designers under the broad hand of Prof. Johannes Schreiter of Germany on the *Life Center* project in San Francisco for AIDS, HIV. Each artist is represented in the large quilt-like window.

Leone's studio is small, with close supervision of the artists who work for her.

Also see these GUILD publications:
Architect's Edition: 8, 9, 10

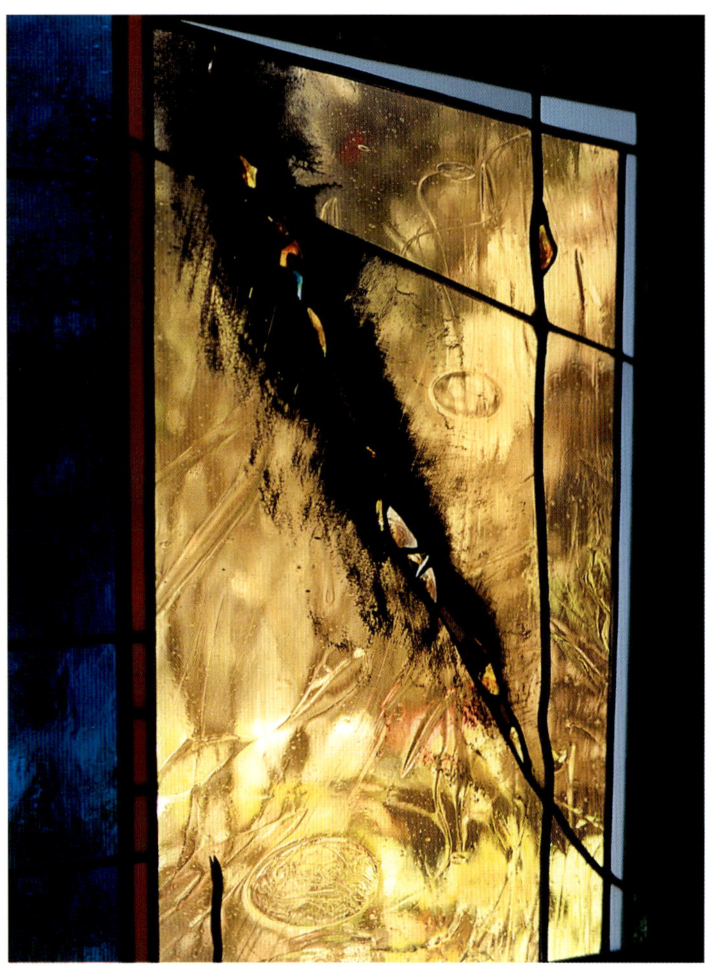

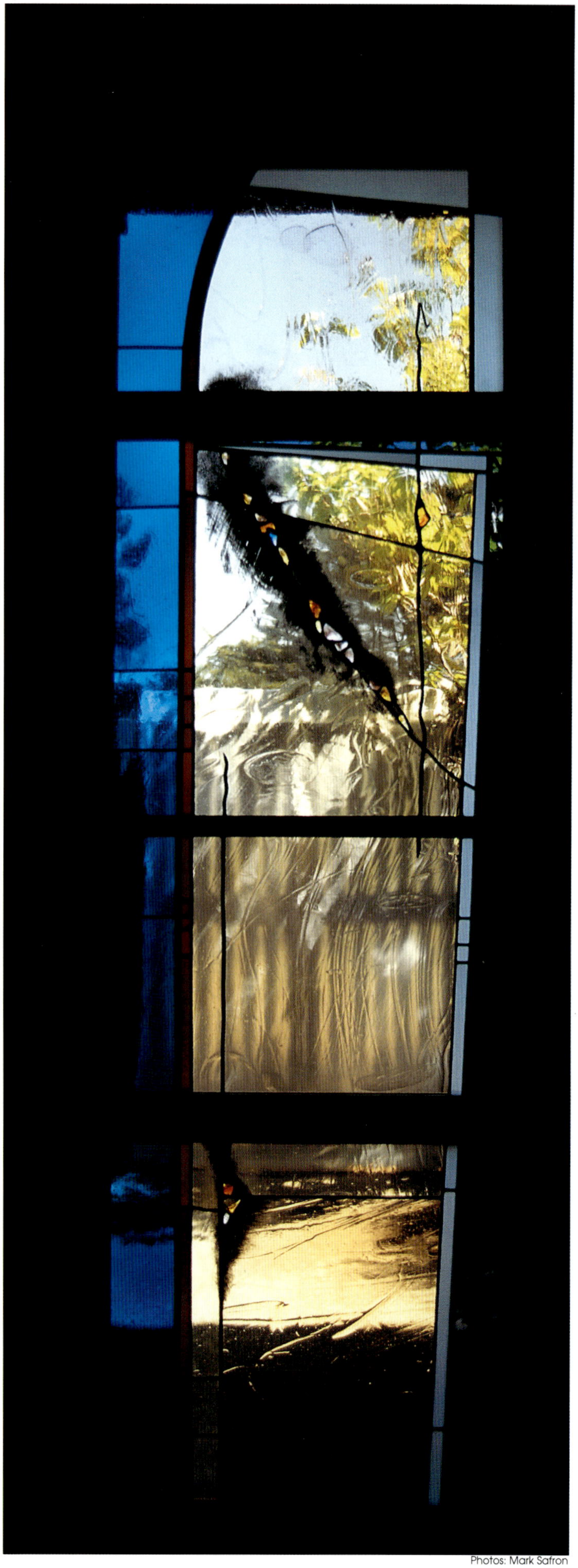

Photos: Mark Safron

Carl Powell

1610 Ninth Street
Berkeley, CA 94710
FAX 510-526-2637
TEL 510-526-2637

National Endowment for the Arts recipient, Corning Museum of Glass, *New Glass Review*, *Americans in Glass* national exhibition.

Since 1973, Carl Powell has been responding to the needs of architects and designers with his refreshing approach to stained glass. From residential projects to complete glass environ-ments for public buildings, Powell's hand-ground and polished thick, clear glass inserts have transformed the art of glass into a visually kinetic experience. These unique, multi-faceted shapes form prismatic optical illusions of movement, surprising the viewer with an invitation for a closer inspection.

Large commissions and collections include:
The International Olympic Committee
Cities of Atlanta, GA; and Oakland, CA
The Clock Tower, San Francisco, CA
Several art museum collections

Also see this GUILD publication:
Architect's Edition: 7

A Glass environment, Community Center, (detail), Oakland, CA, 21' x 7'

B Private residence (detail), 7' x 5½'

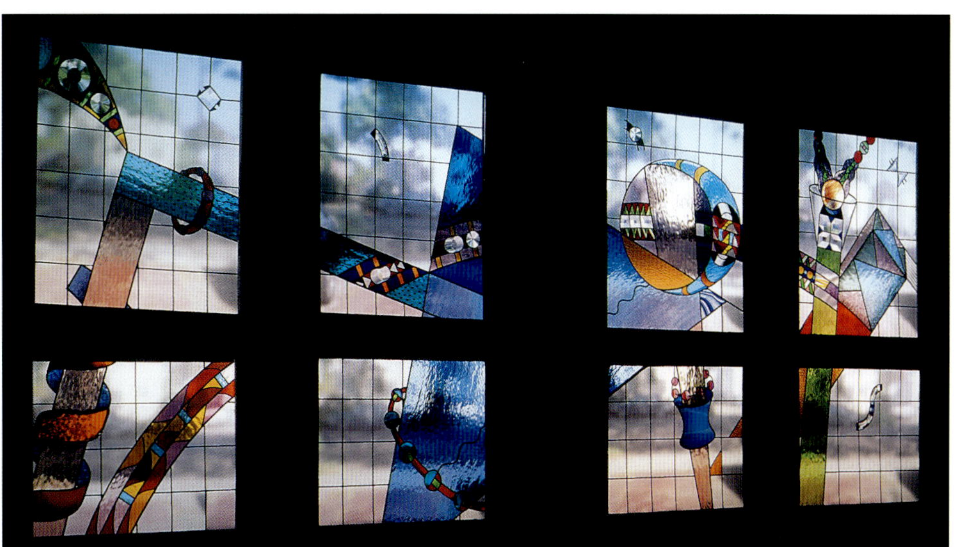

A

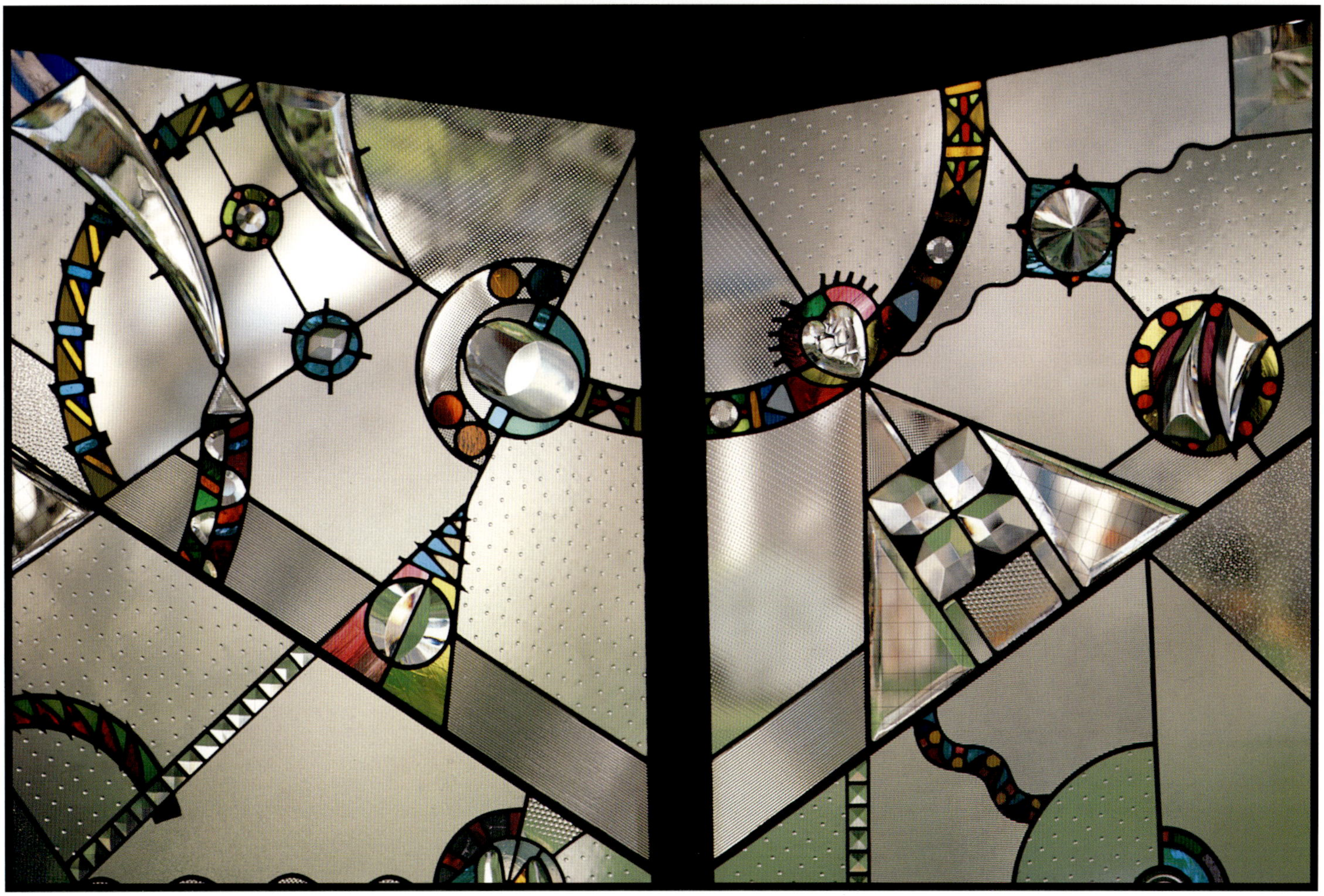

B

Bev Precious

Precious Design Studios, Inc.
950 N. Alabama Street
Indianapolis, IN 46202
FAX 317-631-6560
TEL 317-631-6560

The artist's use of clear textures in an architectural format creates privacy while maximizing light. Bev's knowledge of design and construction allows her to also work three-dimensionally, creating large public art sculpture.

Also see these GUILD publications:
Architect's Edition: 8, 9, 10

SHOWN: *For Endless Trees*, 1994, Evanston (Illinois) Public Library, Percent for Art Commission, Evanston Arts Council, $25,000, 8'H x 25'W, architect: Joseph Powell, AIA, Philadelphia

Media: architectural, carved and dichroic glass; Prairie House zinc came; laminated glass constructions; laser-cut stainless steel plate; and hand-forged iron

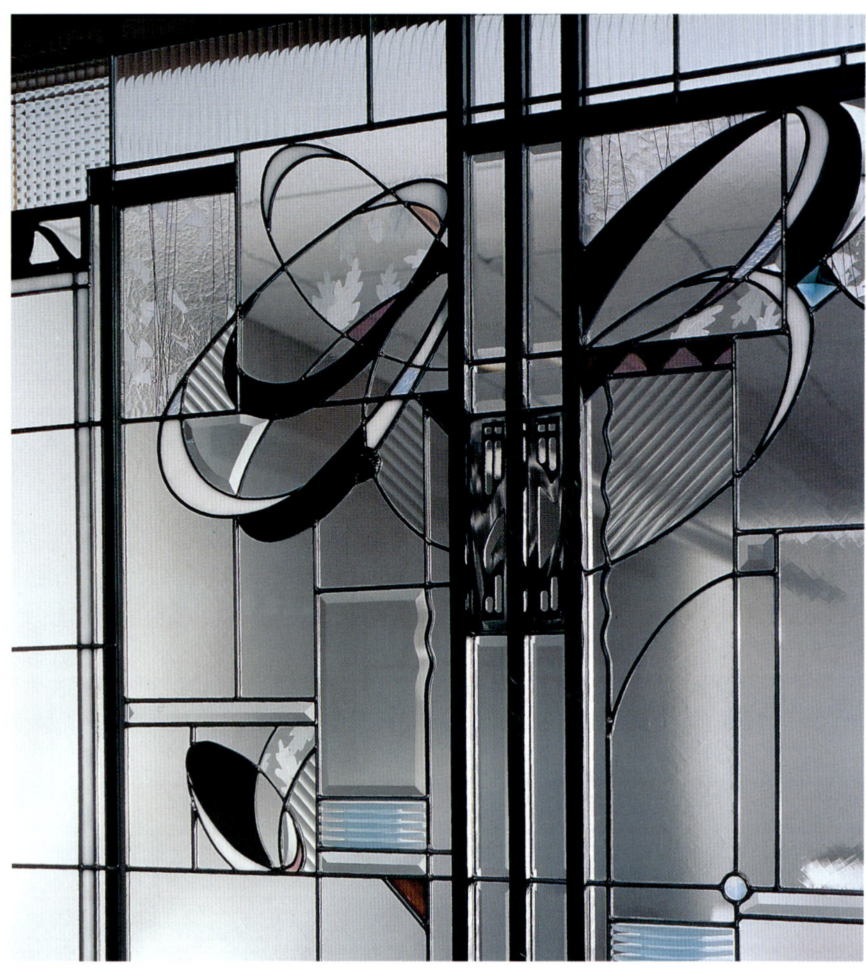

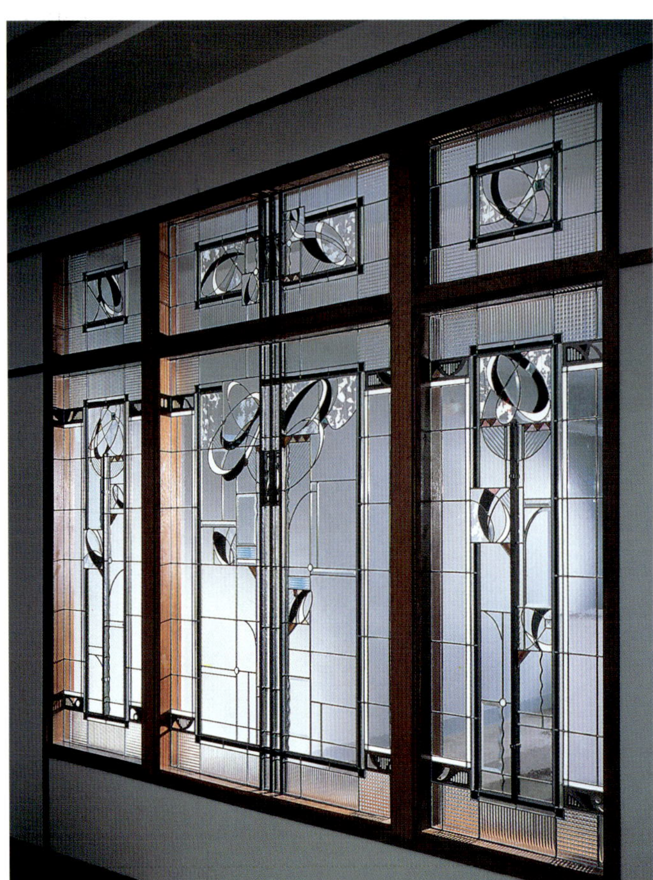

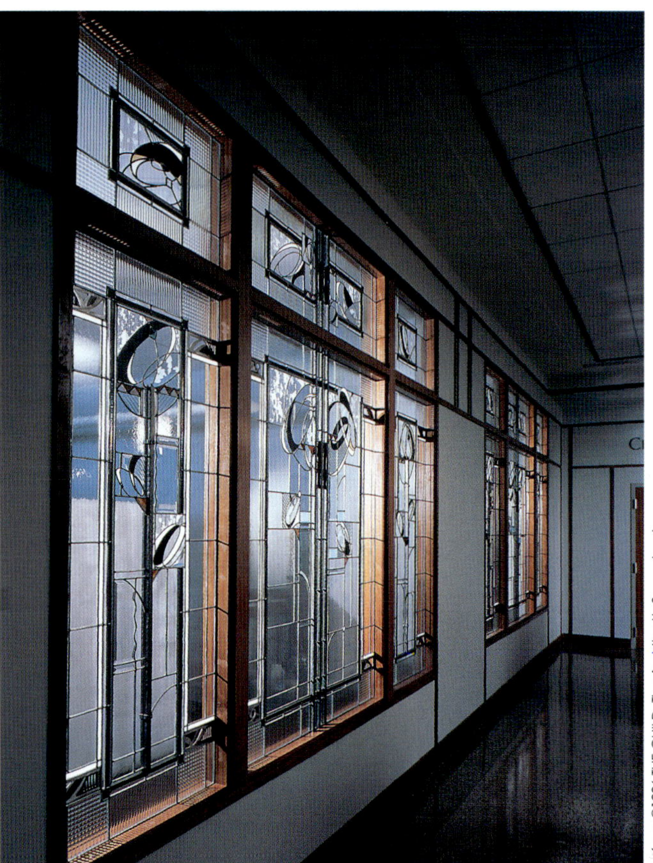

Photos: Greg Murphey

Maya Radoczy

Contemporary Art Glass
PO Box 31422
Seattle, WA 98103
FAX 206-524-9226
TEL   206-527-5022

Maya Radoczy creates work for site-specific corporate, public and residential projects. She is known for creating unusual surfaces in glass, developing fused glass collages and molded relief images through an application of fused, hand-blown and cast glass techniques.

She exhibits internationally and is featured in numerous publications and collections.

Selected installations include: Trump Plaza, NYC; Intrex, Inc., NYC; Linpro Co., Wilmington, DE; U.S. Bank, Seattle, WA; Bogle & Gates Law Office, Seattle, WA; I.M. Pei-Architect, specific installations, NYC; Colville School, Colville, WA; Lynnwood Library, Lynnwood, WA; University Hospital, Seattle, WA.

Also see these GUILD publications:
THE GUILD: 2, 3, 4, 5
Architect's Edition: 6, 7, 8, 9, 10
Designer's Edition: 7, 9

SHOWN: *Barrier-non-Barrier*, free-standing kiln-cast glass screen for office complex lobby, 6' x 12' (proposed photo); detail of type of kiln-cast glass used in screen

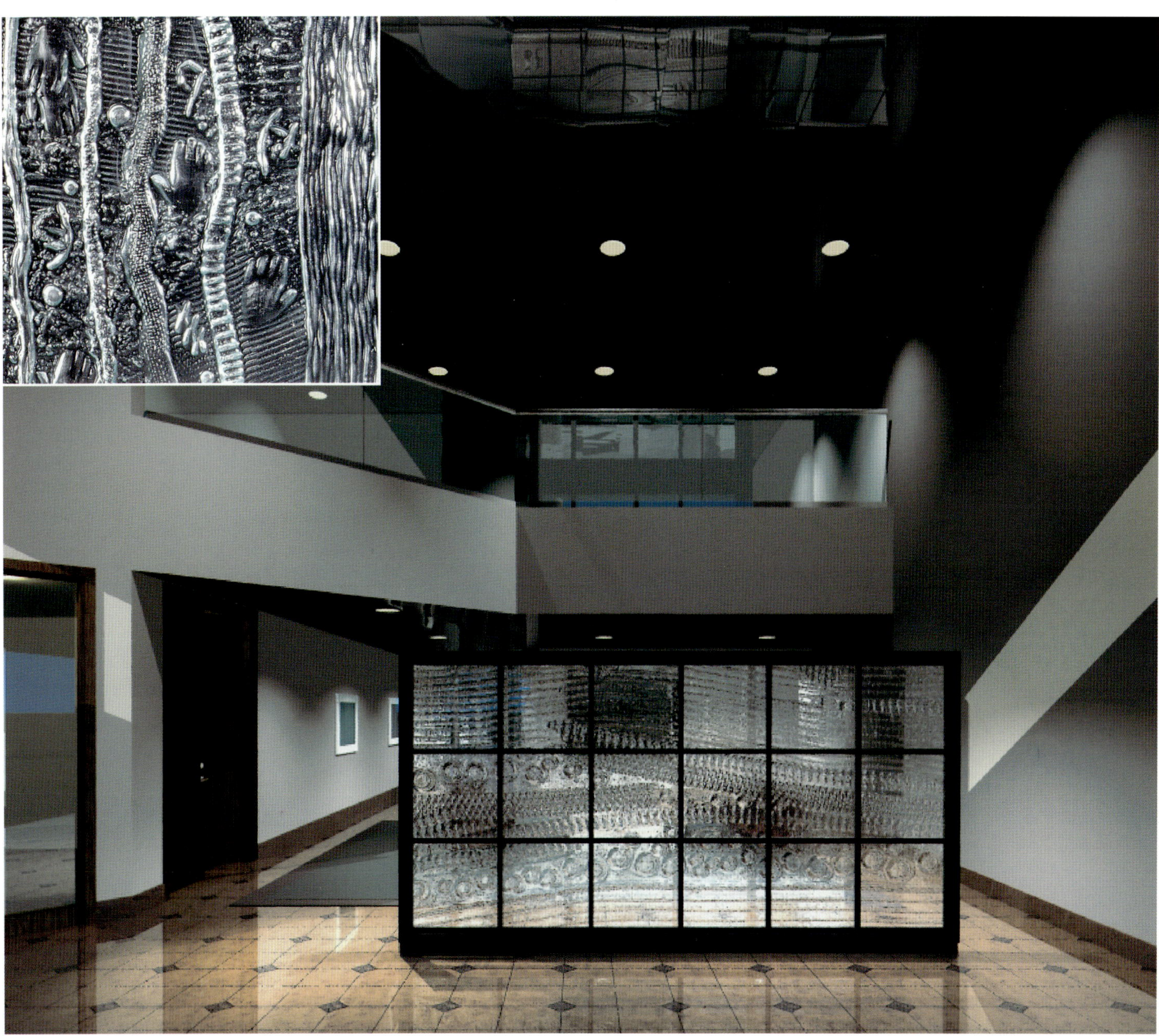

JOHN MUDGETT

Industrial Designer/Interior Space Designer

When John Mudgett plans space for the very large, very complex projects his firm designs and builds, he is always keenly aware of the need to humanize the environment. "We are one of only a handful of design firms in the country that specializes in large scientific complexes. Given the nature of our projects, we have a special challenge to make the environment appealing and hospitable."

Trained as an industrial designer, Mudgett runs his firm's interior design group, and advocates using artists as part of the professional design team. "We encourage clients to use original art both on a monumental scale and in more modest ways," he explains. "When art is woven throughout a space, it adds tremendously to the environment."

A recent project involved glass artist Paul Housberg's vision for the new cafeteria building at Pfizer Central Research in Groton, Connecticut. The cafeteria was located in what had been an employee walkway through a grove of trees.

"We wanted to capture the spirit of changing light and seasons and movement," Mudgett recalls. "Without being literal, we wanted the large dining area to feel as much like a forest as possible.

"I looked through THE GUILD and was immediately impressed by Paul's work. I felt this person could work with the kind of gesture we had in mind. And he did. His idea—to create four large walls of glass at the compass points and attach a season to each—was sheer brilliance."

Both the collaborative process and the final result are everything Mudgett could have hoped for. "Each panel is 11 feet wide by 12 feet high and weighs about 5,000 pounds. The space is spectacular, the art and artist were an integral part of creating it, and the client loves it. In fact, they've published a little booklet to hand out to people who ask about it. It's been a great success."

Photo by Cliff Moore

Karen Sepanski

2827 John R
Detroit, MI 48201
TEL 313-832-4941

For over 15 years, Karen Sepanski has executed numerous residential, public and corporate commissions. Her distinctive bas-relief panels of slumped and fused glass have been used in lighting, skylights, signage and doors.

Sepanski's latest work reveals a new level of expertise and visual splendor, a departure from her more familiar, understated designs. She continues to explore the medium and encourages collaboration in all phases of project development.

Commissions include:
Ingham Co. Correctional Facility, MI; National Steel, PA; Sheraton Torrey Pines Hotel, CA; Little Caesar's Enterprises, MI; Royal Caribbean Cruise Lines: Sun Viking, Song of Norway

Resume and slides AOR.

Also see these GUILD publications:
THE GUILD: 2, 3
Architect's Edition: 6, 7, 9

SHOWN: *Spacial Relations*, 1995, two murals for theater, *Legend of the Seas*; RCCL, fused, laminated, lustered glass, 60" x 132" x $^1/_2$"

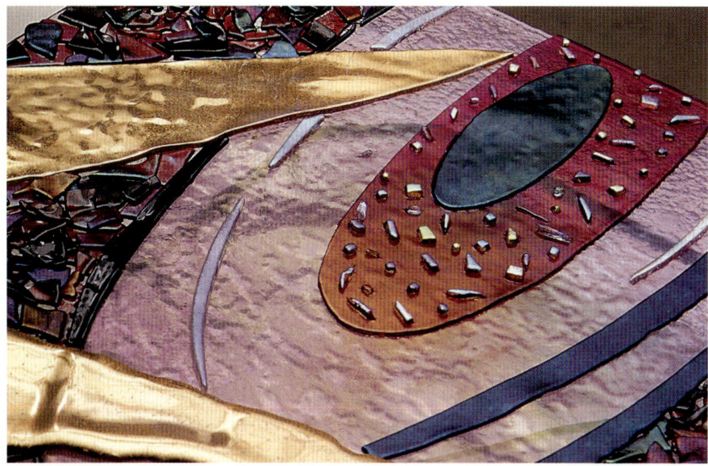

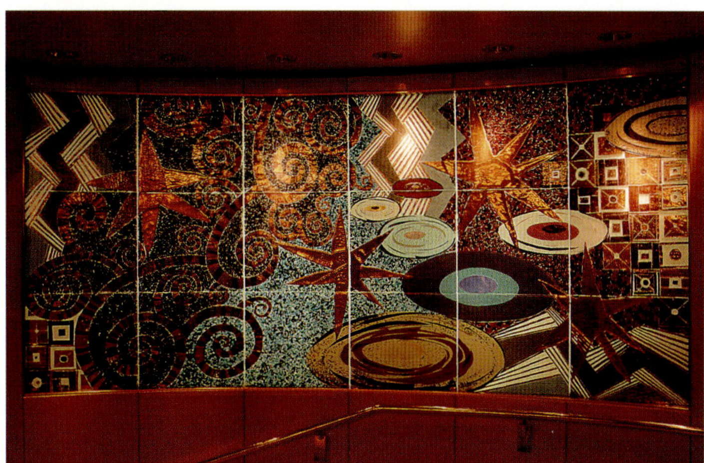

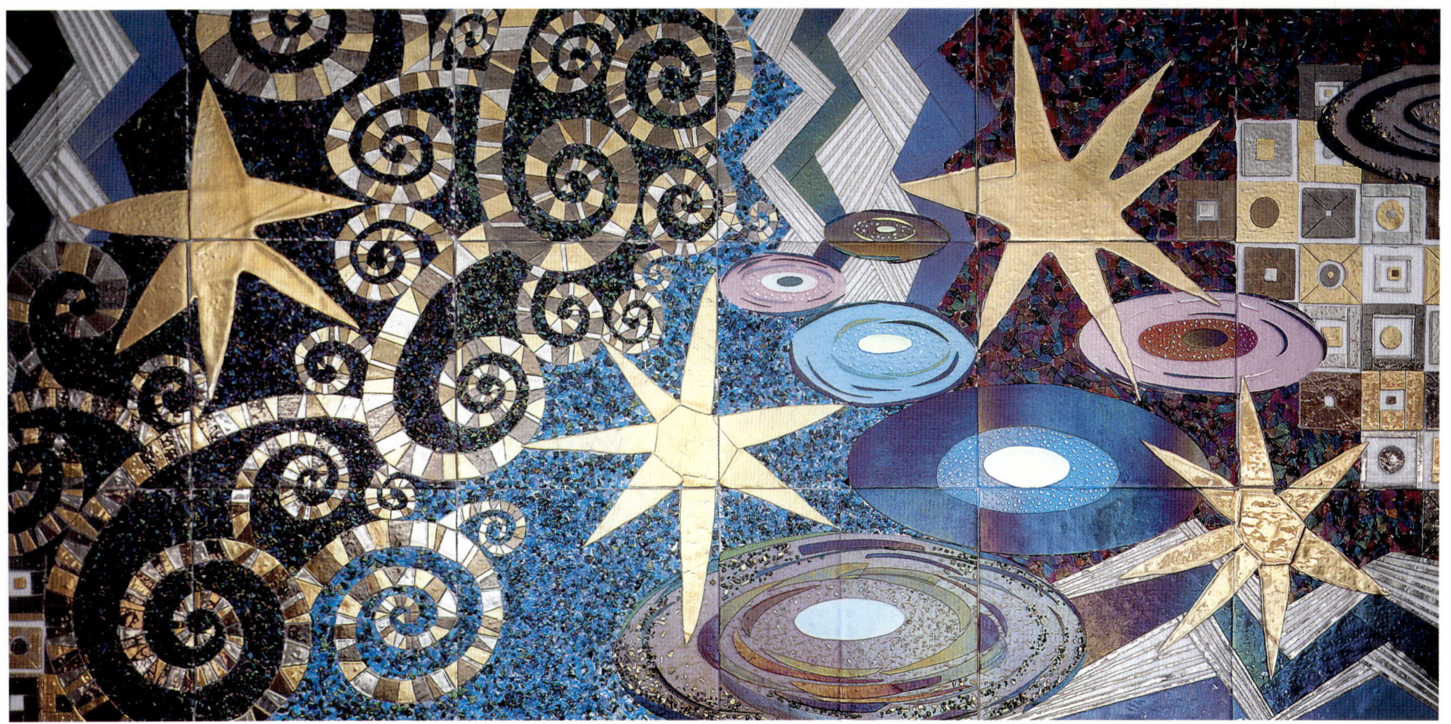

Dennis Chobot

Skyline Design

2653 W. Chicago Avenue
Chicago, IL 60622
FAX 312-278-3548
TEL 312-278-4660

Since 1982, Skyline Design has been providing
commercial and art glass to the design community. Our patented Skyline Etch Sealer, which
keeps sandblasted glass free of dirt and finger-
prints, has enhanced installations from
Chicago's Sears Tower to the Northern Trust
Bank of Toronto. Catalog and sealer sample
available upon request.

Also see these GUILD publications:
Architect's Edition: 7, 8, 9, 10

A Deep-carved, surface-etched logo panel,
shaded and sealed front and back sides, with
cable mount
Richard D. Irwin
Environmental Graphic Designer: Plancom, Inc.
Photo: Marc Stegen

B Some of Skyline's sample designs ranging from
the architecturally inspired to the whimsical,
surface-etched and sealed, deep-etched and
painted on one or both sides of glass
Photo: Marc Stegen

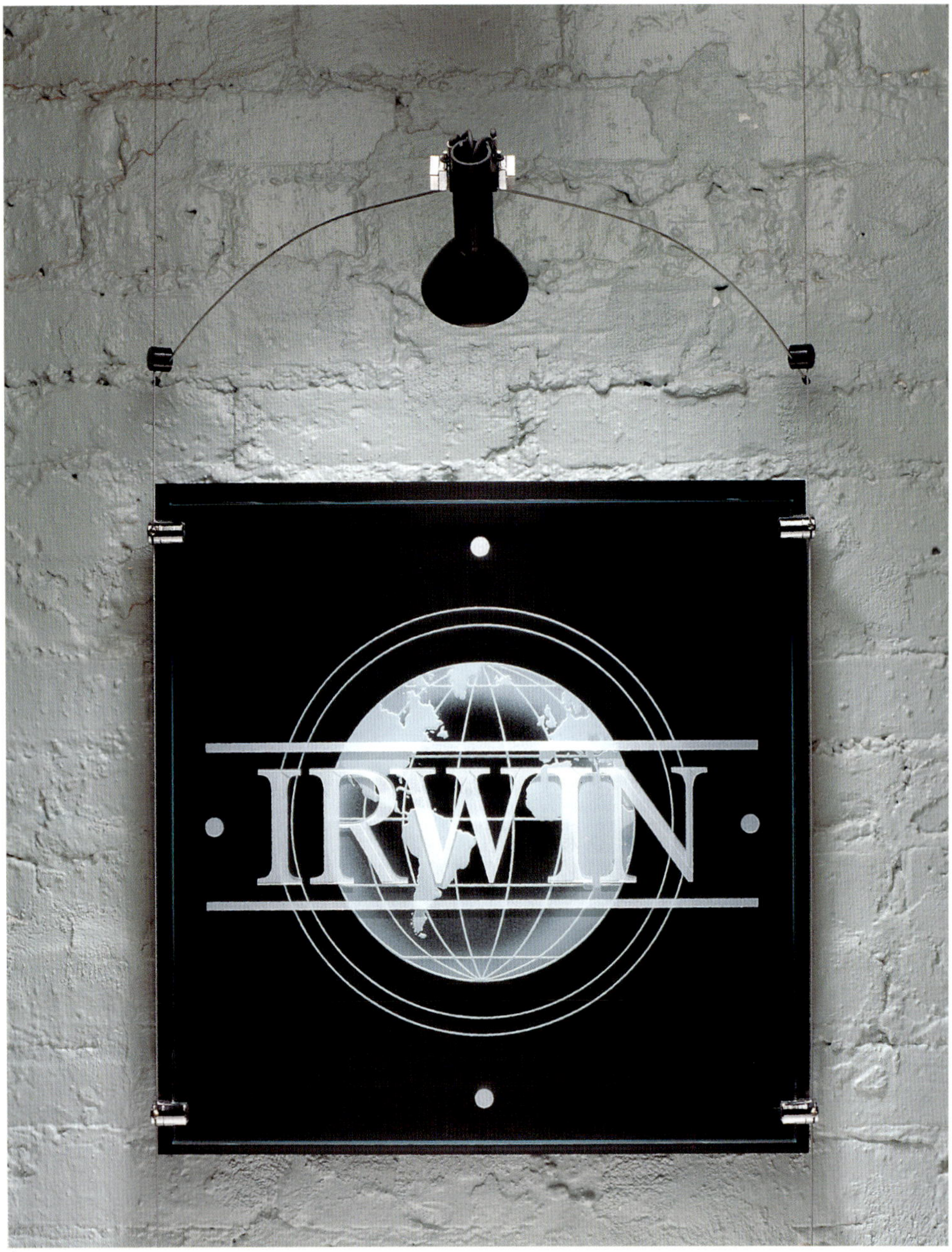

A

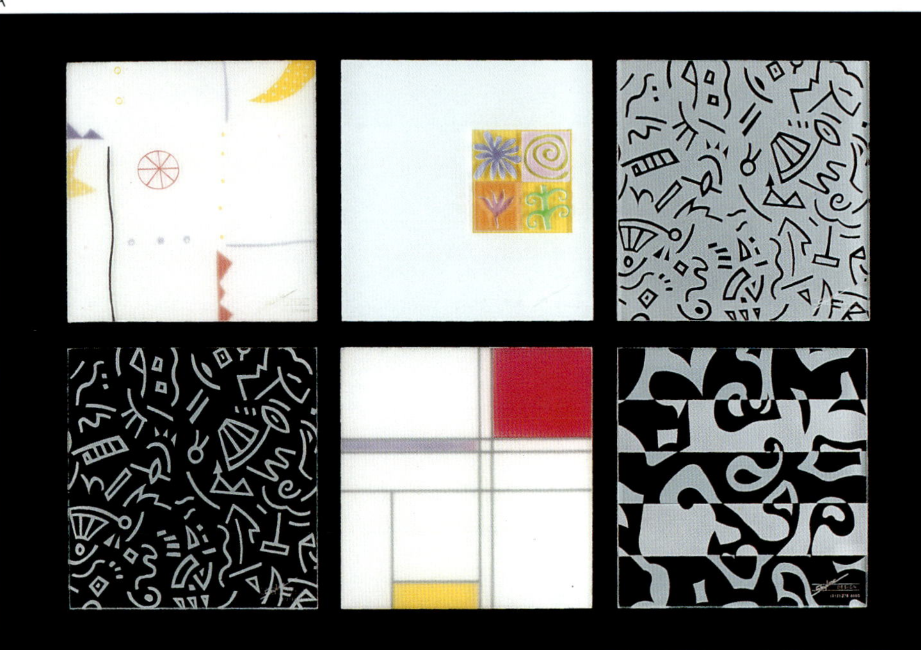

B

C Logo panel, surface-etched on front and back
   sides and sealed
   Spots BME, Inc.
   Photo: Marc Stegen

D Doors and side lights for restored interior jazz
   lounge, deep-carved glass with gold infill
   The Green Orchid Room
   The Bismarck Hotel
   Designer: Anderson Miller
   Photo: Marc Stegen

E Detail of North America from world map
   SAP American, Inc.
   Designer: R.C. Dannon
   Photo: Marc Stegen

F World map and logo, deep-carved, surface-
   etched glass, shaded and sealed on front and
   back sides
   SAP American, Inc.
   Designer: R.C. Dannon
   Photo: Marc Stegen

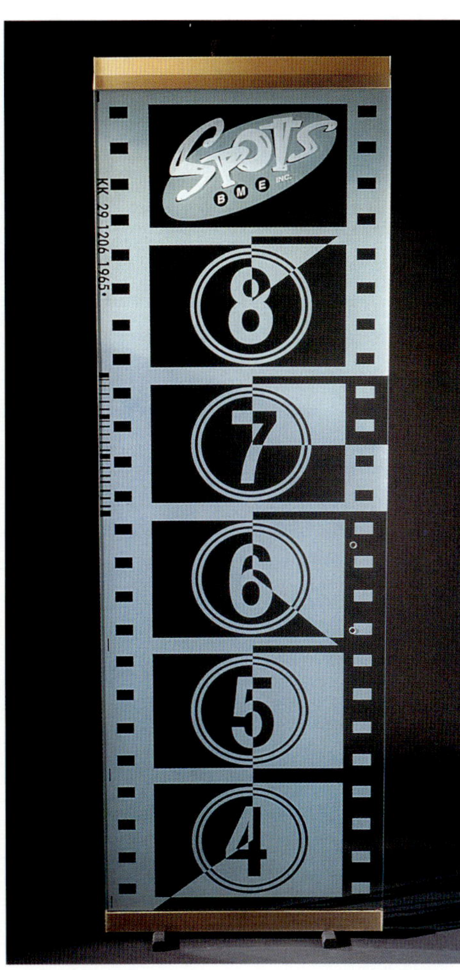

C

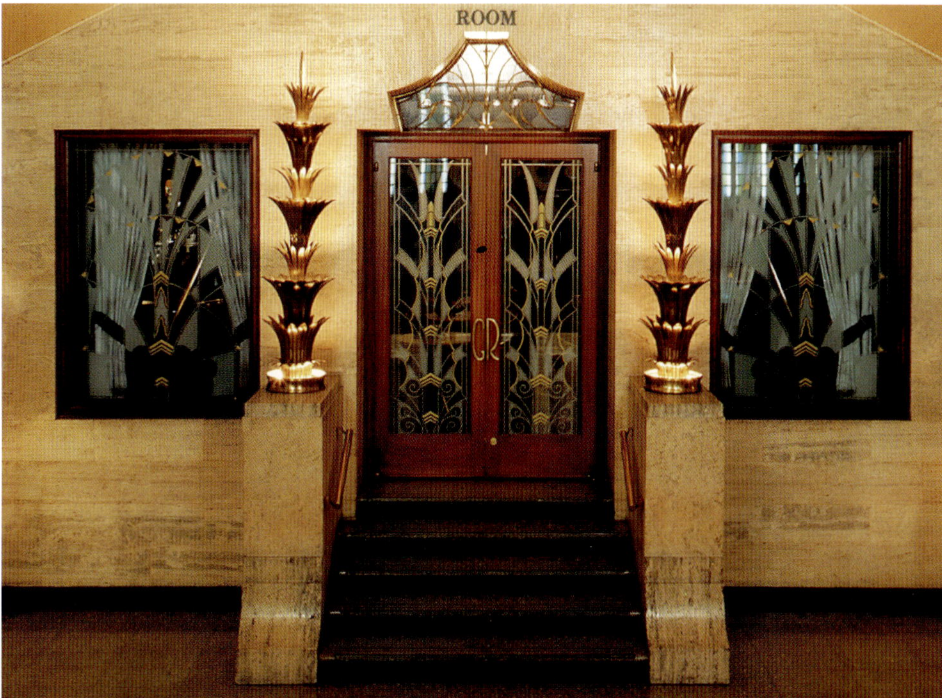

D

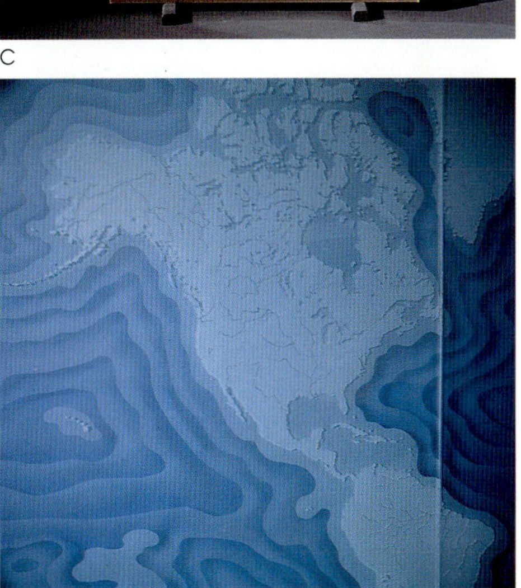

E

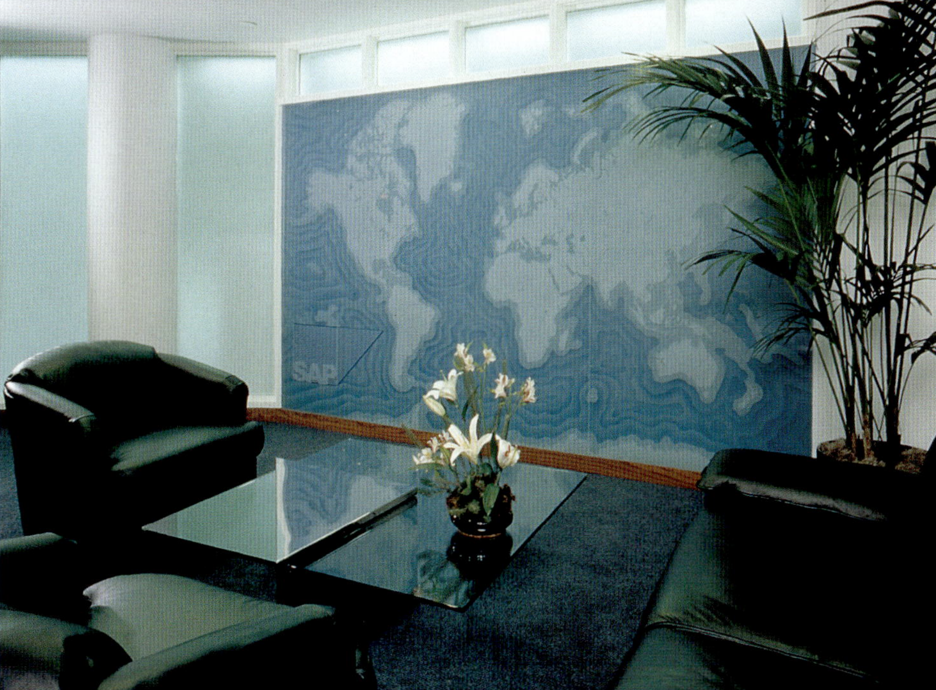

F

Arthur Stern

Arthur Stern Studios/Architectural Glass
1075 Jackson Street
Benicia, CA 94510
TEL 707-745-8480

Arthur Stern Studios specializes in producing custom glass and wood detailing to enhance architectural and interior design. By working closely with the shapes, rhythms, proportions and materials of the building, Stern creates doors and windows that become an integral part of the environment. The studio builds leaded glass panels as well as custom doors and window frames. Installations can be found all over the United States.

Pictured below are a ten-foot-tall stair landing window and double entrance doors from a residential project. These installations are part of a family of leaded glass designs that are variations on a theme. These variations are decorative as well as functional, preserving privacy in some cases and embellishing expansive vistas in others. This project called for a palette of clears, whites and grays, combined with beveled glass jewels and iridescent glass.

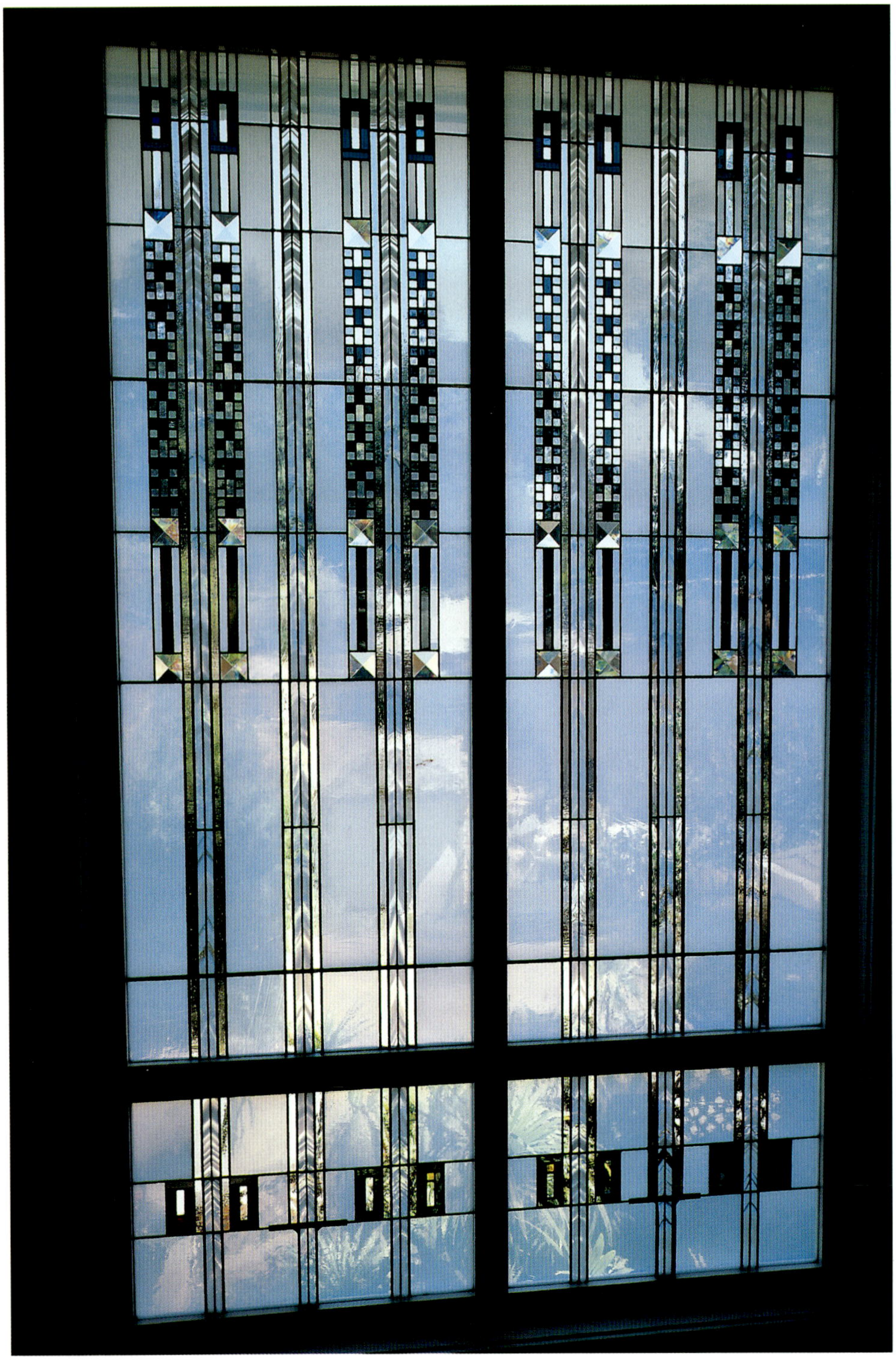

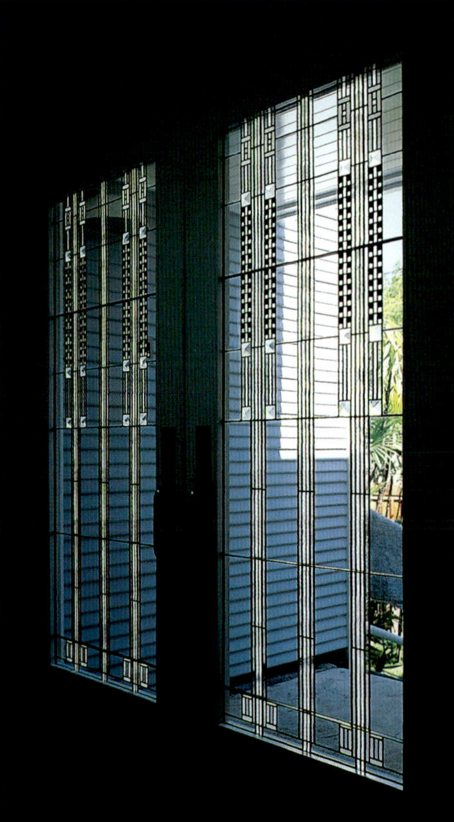

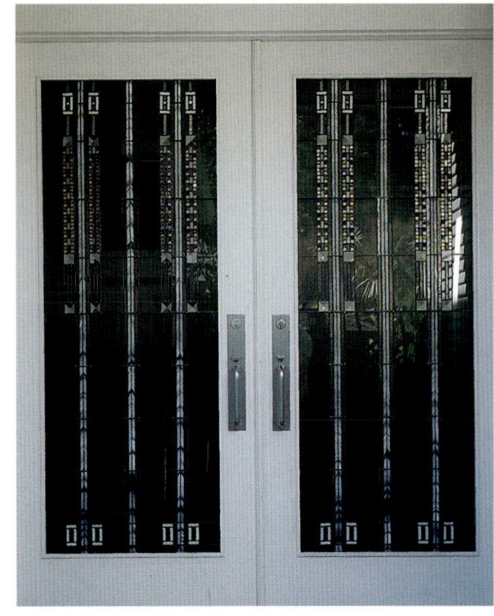

Arthur Stern

Arthur Stern Studios/Architectural Glass
1075 Jackson Street
Benicia, CA 94510
TEL 707-745-8480

Glass can be used creatively in many applications other than those traditionally associated with it. Its unique qualities of transparency, reflection and iridescence offer a sparkle matched by no other medium, giving it an ever-shifting personality as it interacts with available light.

Arthur Stern Studios designs and fabricates bas-relief wood and glass sculptures. These wall-mounted pieces combine various hardwoods with mirrored, iridescent, dichroic, and opaque glasses chosen for their light-reflective qualities.

Pictured below is a lobby sculpture at the new Federal Courthouse in Baton Rouge, LA. This is a national G.S.A. Percent for the Arts project. To the right are three 18" tall figures, installed in the lobby of Imperial Bancorp, Oakland, CA.

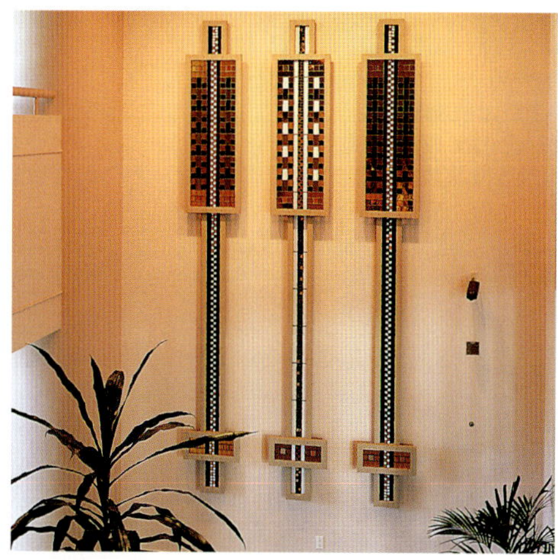

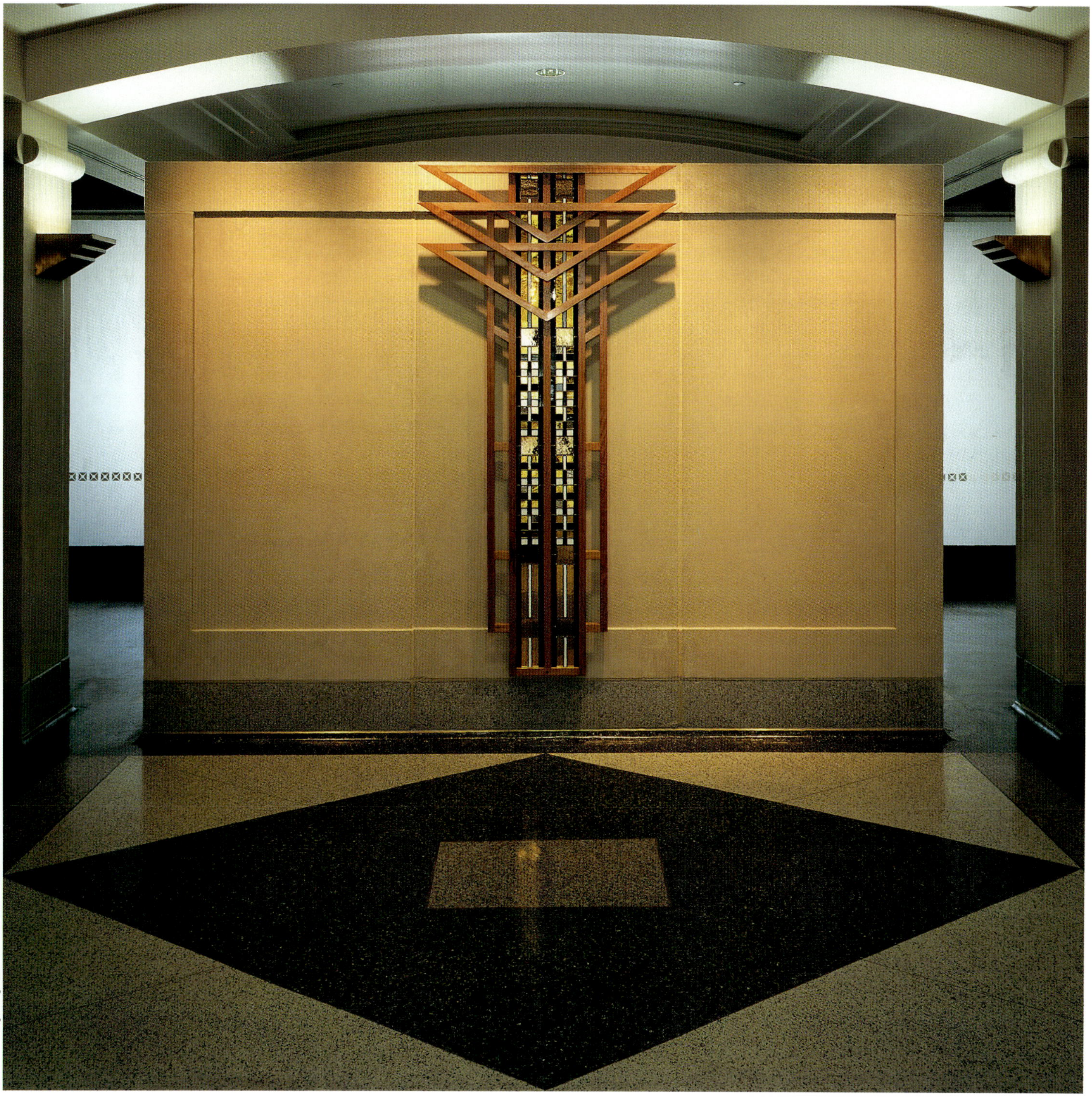

Jeff G. Smith

Architectural Stained Glass, Inc.
PO Box 9092
Dallas, TX 75209
FAX 214-827-5000
TEL 214-352-5050
E-Mail: Jeff_G_Smith@acd.org

By not limiting himself to the two-dimensional picture-plane of windows, Jeff Smith uses glass and light to create incredible and fully three-dimensional experiences within architectural spaces.

Raven: Sun Thief (shown) was inspired by native Athabaskan myths of Raven's theft of sunlight from the gods. Gray, fluttering 'feathers' symbolize Raven, while amber bands of 'stolen sunlight' are tugged outward. Concentric arcs around the central 'Sun/Moon' recall the paths traced by stars wheeling around Polaris. The night sky acknowledges the extreme variation of day and night at this latitude.

Smith provides a complete sequence of services from collaborative design through installation.

Please call for introductory information, pricing, slides and other support materials.

Also see these GUILD publications:
THE GUILD: 4
Architect's Edition: 6, 7, 8, 9, 10

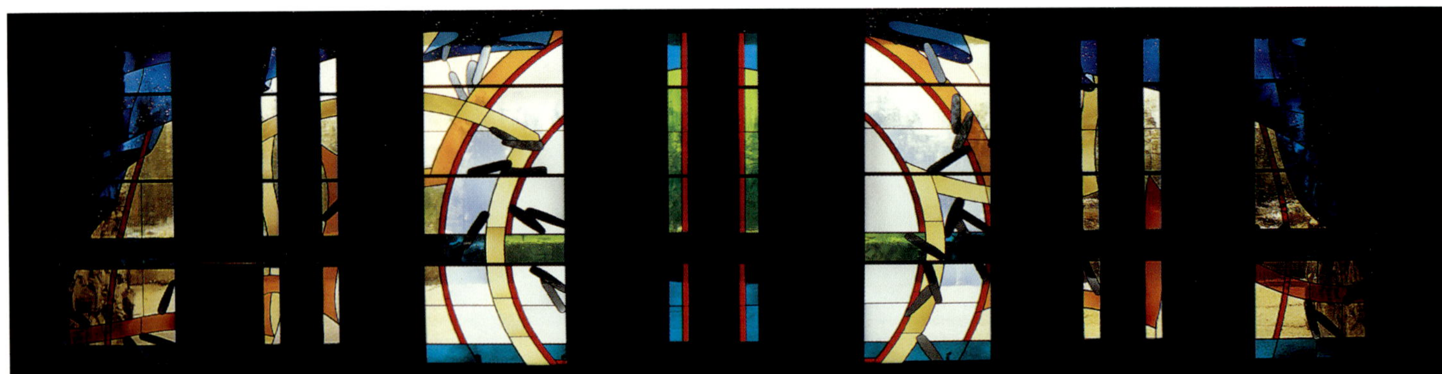

Raven: Sun Thief, University of Alaska, Fairbanks, design competition sponsored by the Alaska Arts Council, 31.75' x 8.83' overall

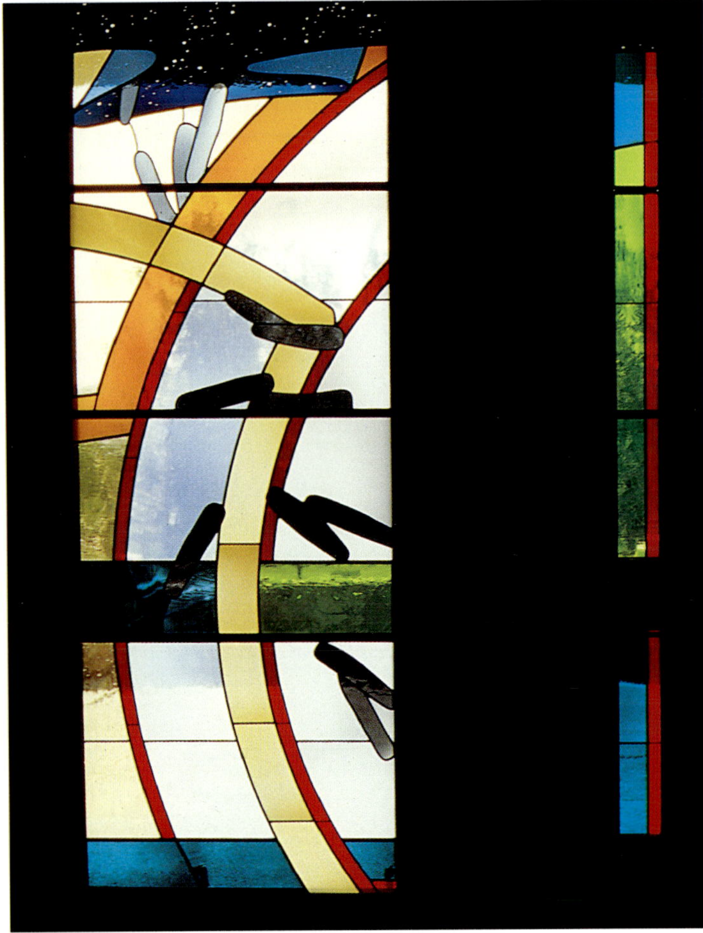

Raven: Sun Thief (detail), center panel

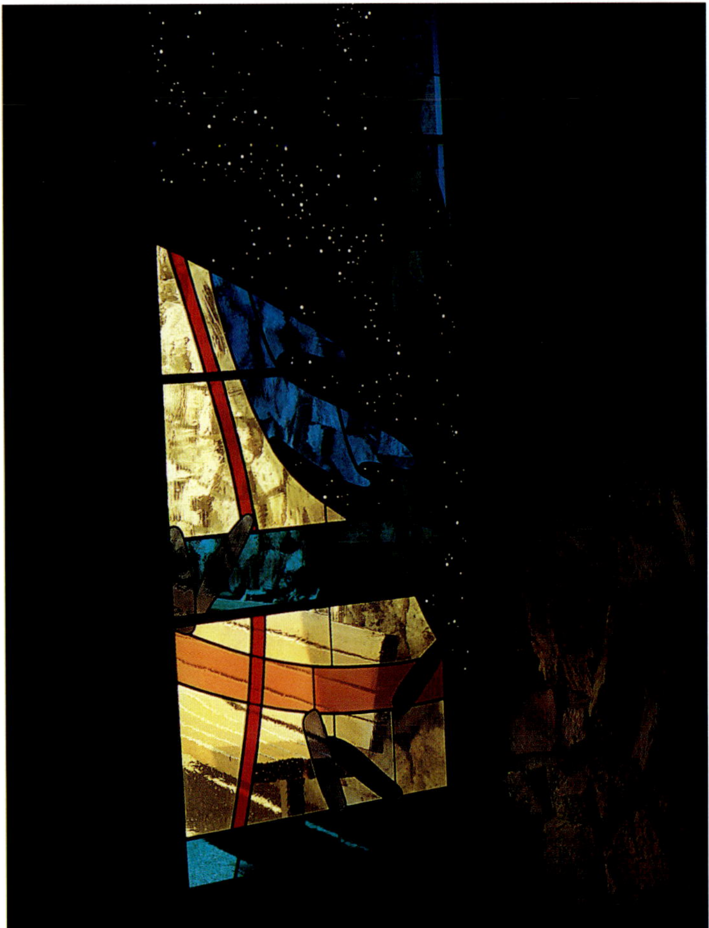

Raven: Sun Thief (detail), right panel

Thomas Meyers Studio

Thomas Meyers
163 Old Hancock Road
Antrim, NH 03440
FAX 603-588-2596
TEL 603-588-2596

Thomas Meyers has been a professional artist, designer, and craftsman for 20 years in leaded glass, mosaic glass and paper collage. His innovative architectural glass art fuses traditional glass methods with modern technology. Recent collaborations with Conrad Szymkowicz, Inc. Woodworkers has expanded the studio's capacities to include fine architectural wood components and furnishings.

This mahogany and glass panel—shown here in contrasting lighting—features random areas of transparent glasses illuminated from behind, set in a field of reflective mosaic glasses which respond to variations in the ambient light of its intended setting.

Also see these GUILD publications:
THE GUILD: 1, 2

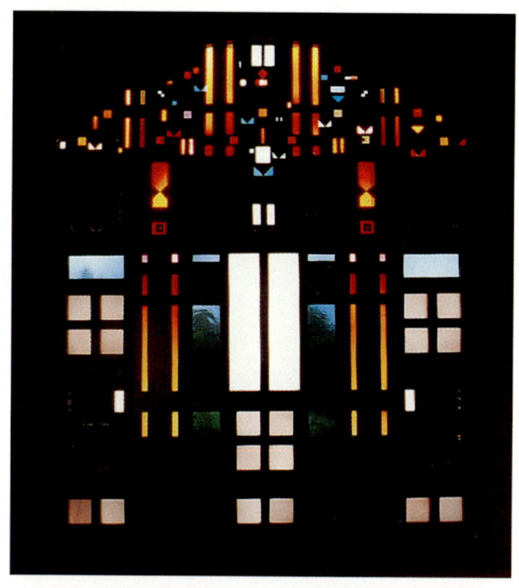

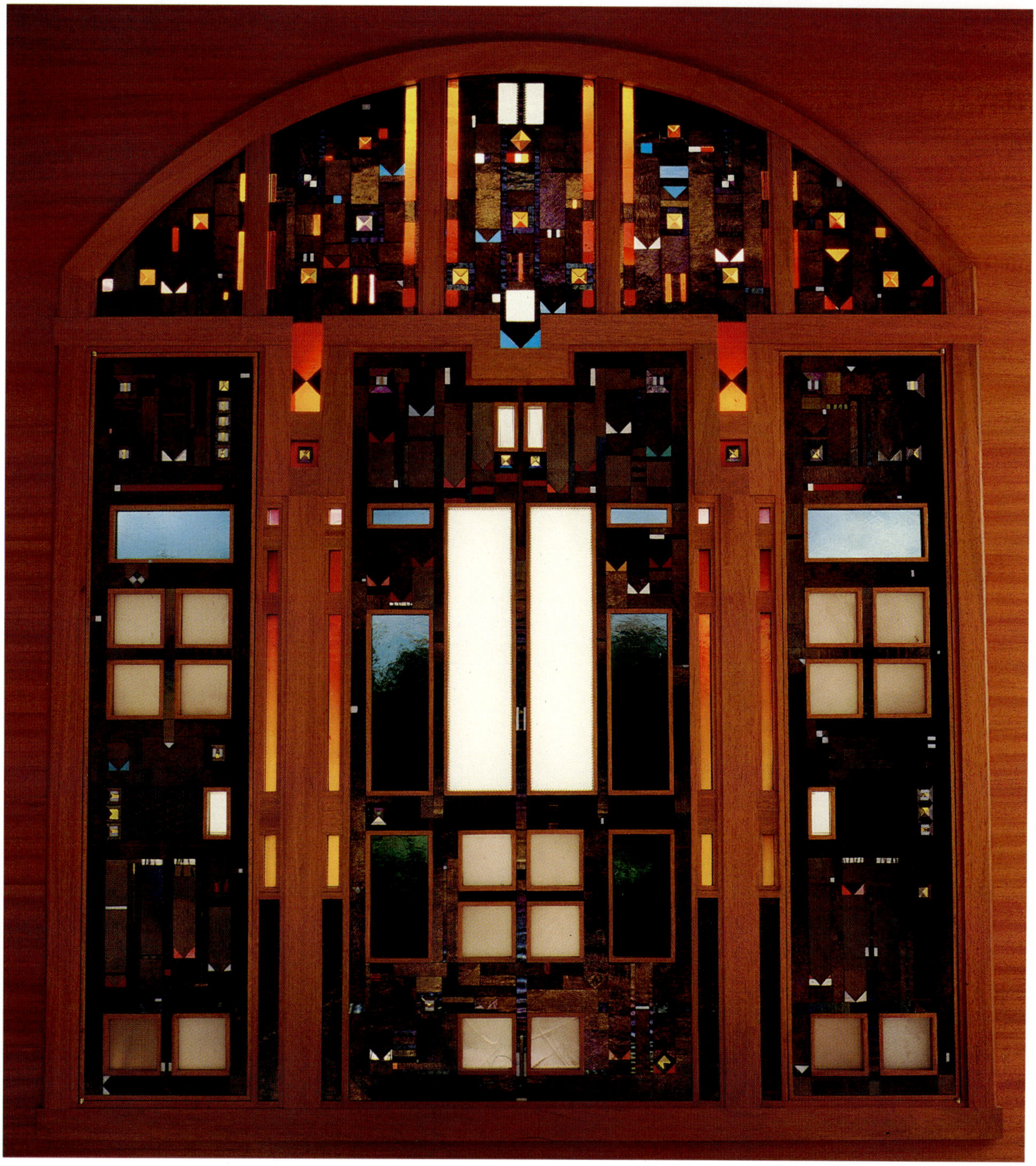

Yves Trudeau

Studio One Glass Art Ltd.
341 West 6th Avenue
Vancouver, BC V5Y 1L1
Canada
FAX 604-875-0601
TEL 604-875-0696

Yves Trudeau is a site-specific commissioned-glass sculptor. For 18 years, he has been creating for an exclusive local and international clientele.

Trudeau's work responds to the architectural, social and cultural environment in which it is located.

His approach is not committed to any one school or style but, more importantly, becomes a synthesis of space, his client's requirements, and a continual exploration of the medium.

Also see these GUILD publications:
Architect's Edition: 9, 10

SHOWN: *The Way of the Cross* (details), 1994, Good Shepherd Church, $^3/_4$" abrasive carved glass, kiln-fused copper, silver and gold leaf, 20" x 24", collaboration: Yves Trudeau, Thomas Bourns, François Cormier

A *Carrying the Cross*

B *Death on the Cross*

C *Mary and John*

D *Women of Jerusalem*

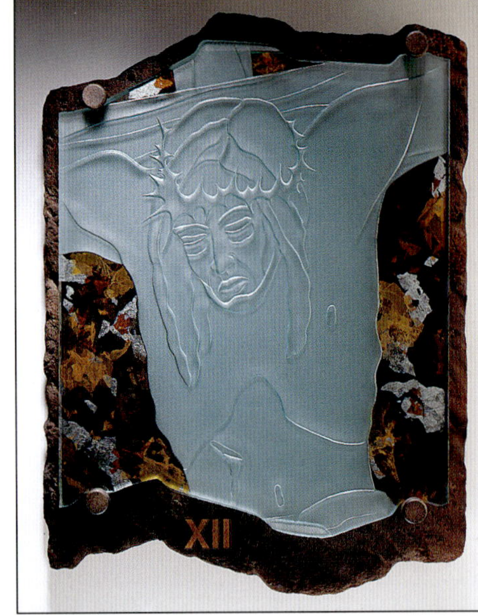

B

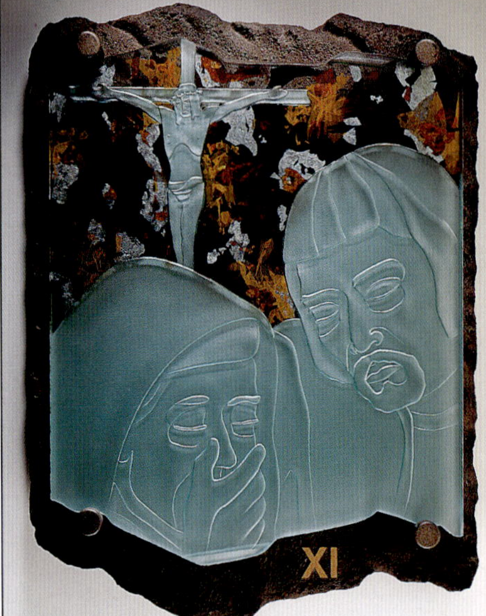

C

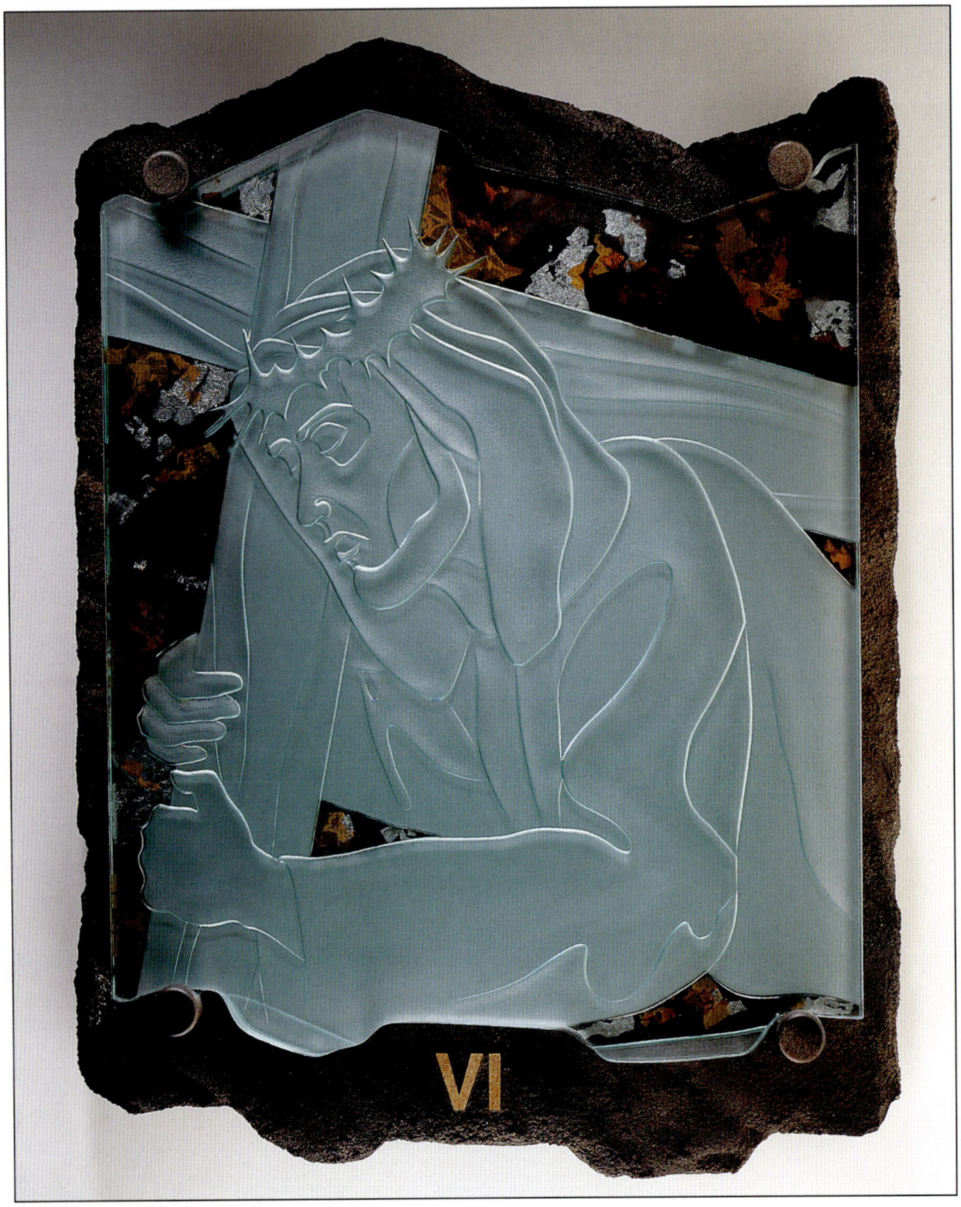

A

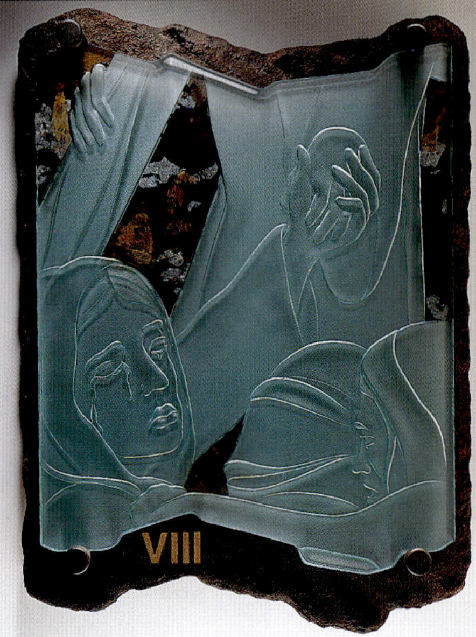

D

David Wilson

David Wilson Design
RD 2, Box 121A
South New Berlin, NY 13843
FAX 607-334-7065
TEL   607-334-3015

David Wilson has been integrating art with
architecture in public, corporate, private and
religious buildings since 1963. His design process
involves extensive collaboration with the client
and architect. His sensitivity to particular needs,
and commitment to aesthetics and function,
guide the development of each project from
design to fabrication and installation.

Recent commissions include:
Le Moyne College Chapel, Syracuse, NY,
    architects: QPK
Leeway, Inc, New Haven, CT,
    architect: Joseph Simeone
Methodist Medical Center, Oakridge, TN,
    designer: Terry Byrd Eason
Beth David Reform Congregation, Gladwyne,
    PA; architects: Shapiro, Petrauskas, Gelber
RLDS World Headquarters, Independence, MO,
    architects: HOK

Also see these GUILD publications:
THE GUILD: 1, 2, 3, 4, 5
Architect's Edition: 6, 7, 8

SHOWN: Merck & Co., Inc, world headquarters
lobby, Whitehouse Station, NJ, architects: Kevin
Roche John Dinkeloo and Associates

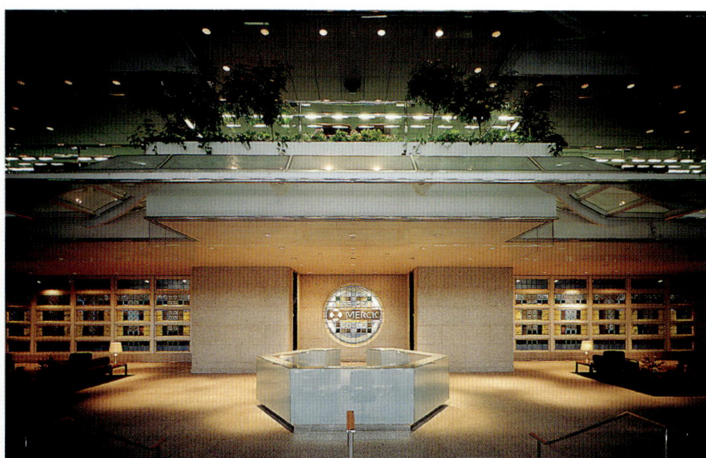

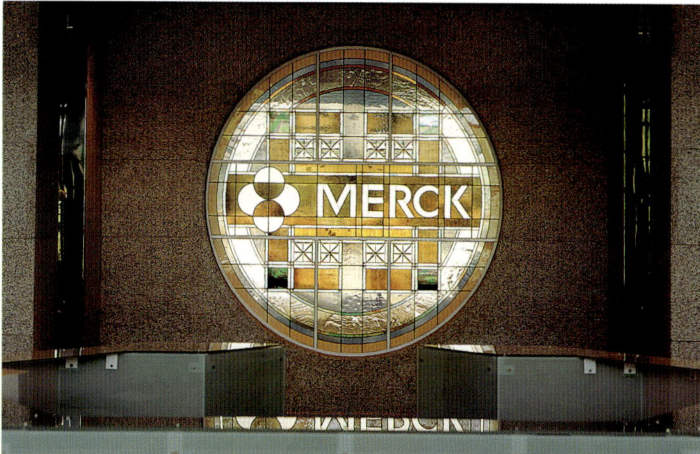

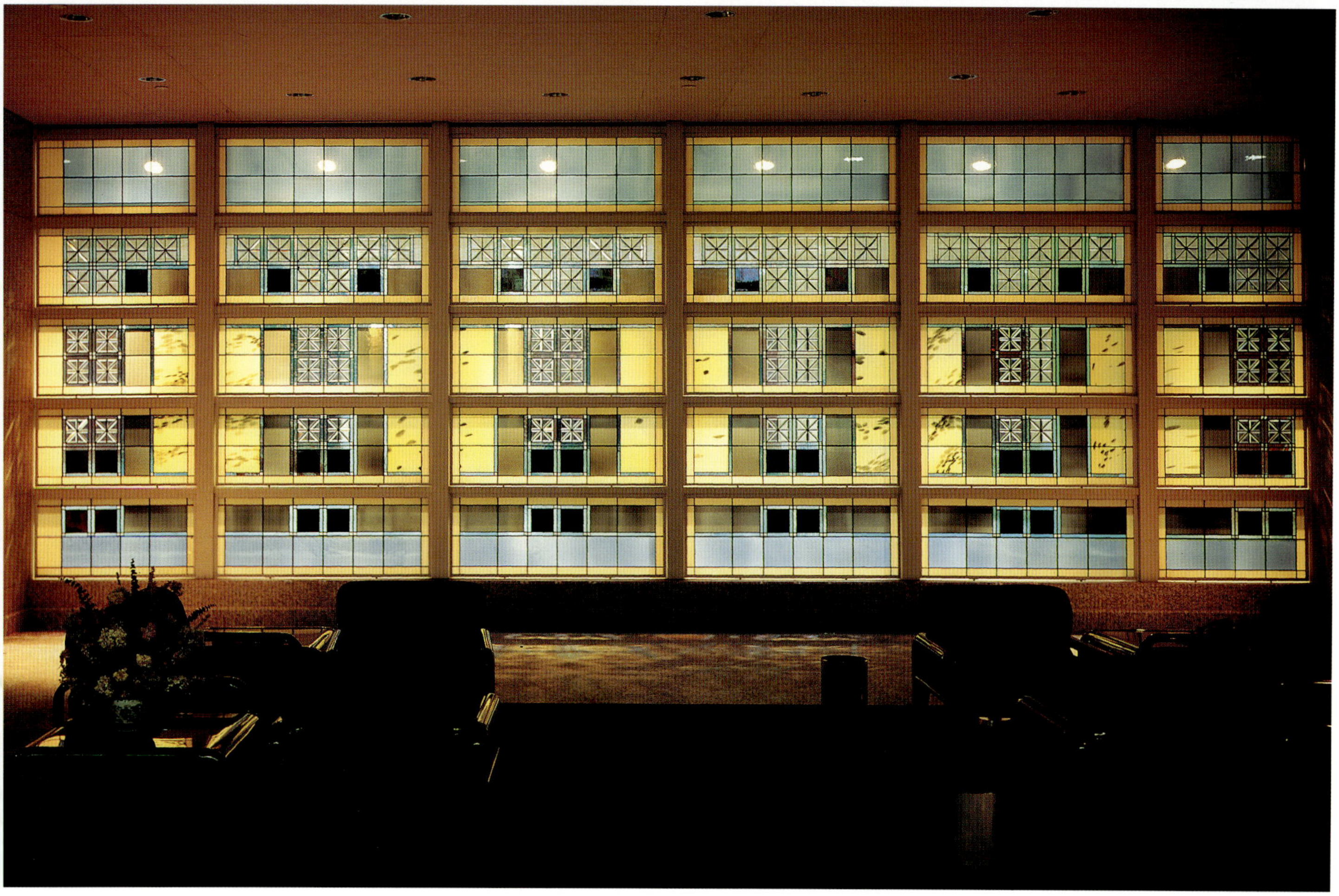

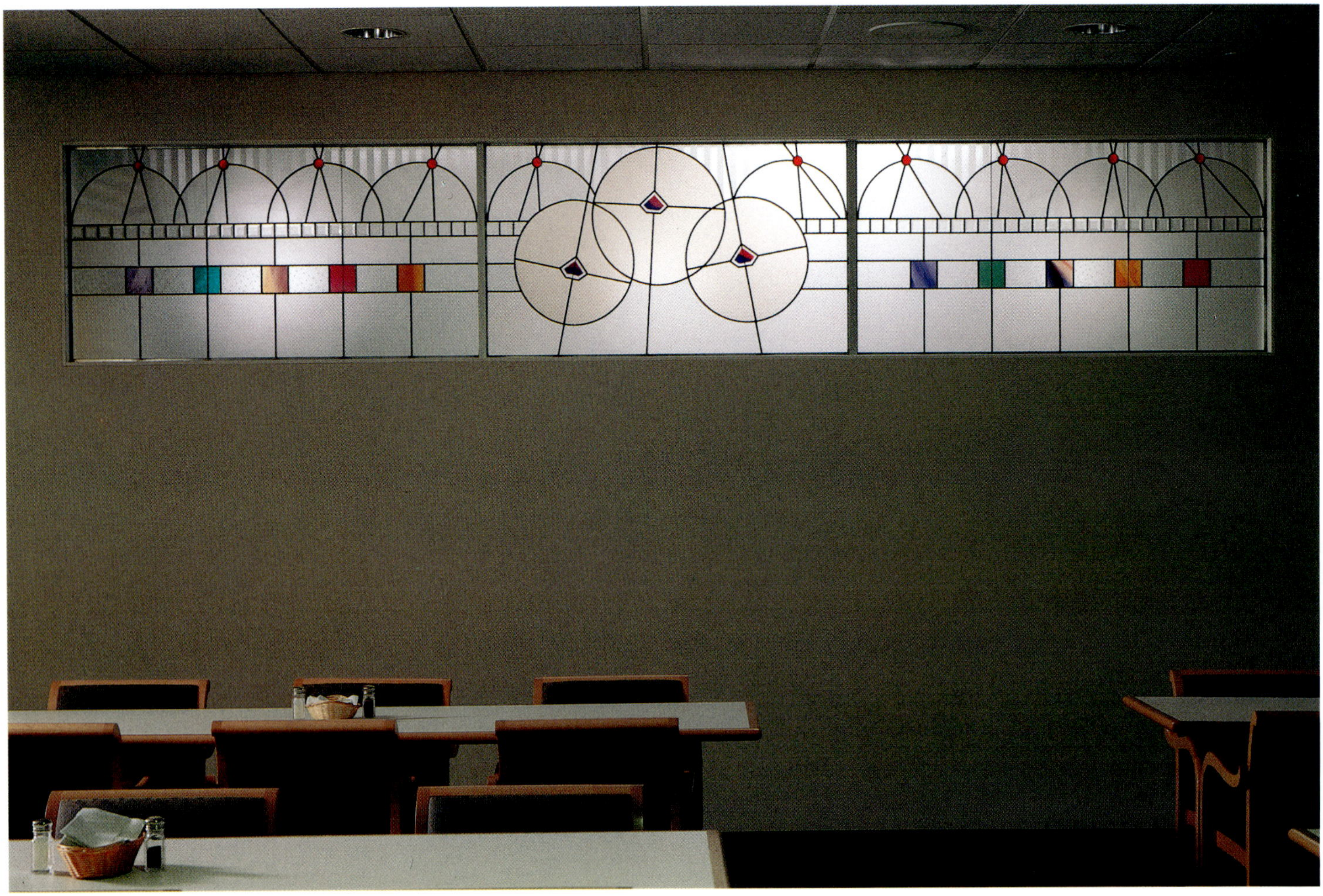

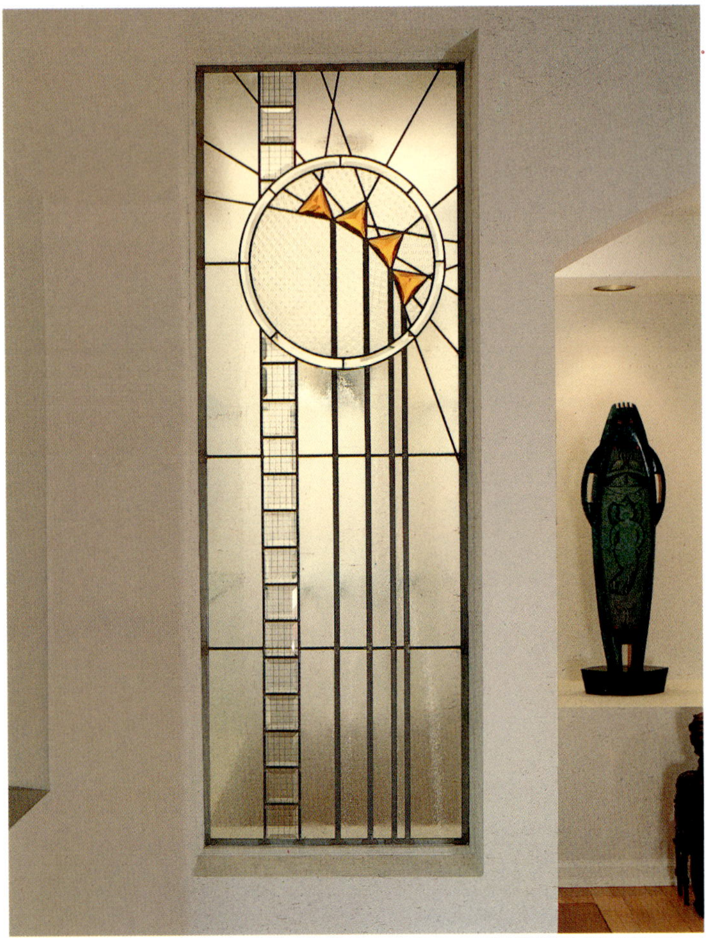

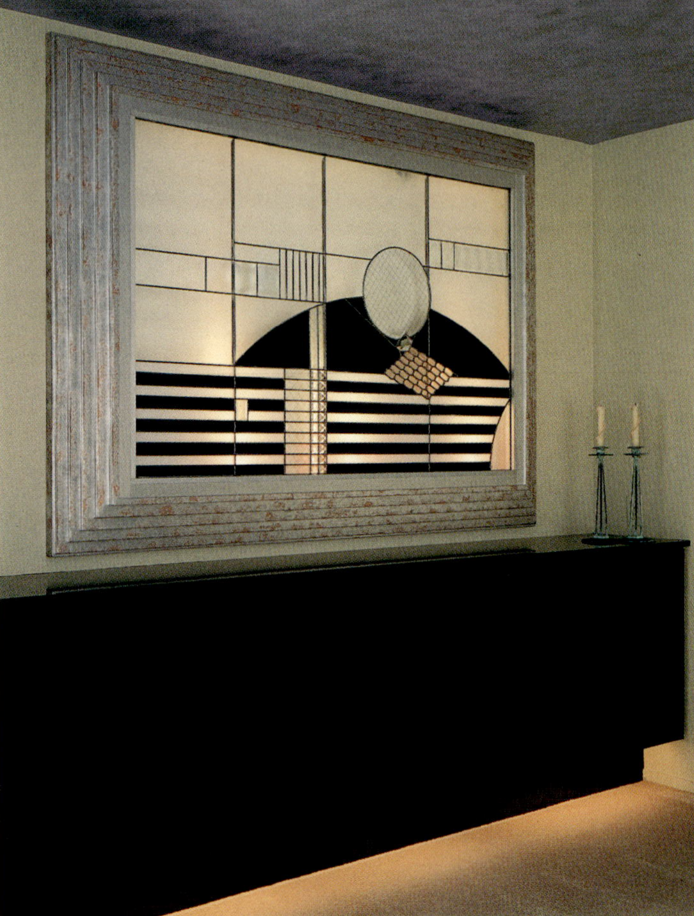

Larry Zgoda, Larry Zgoda Studio, 415 W. North Avenue, Chicago, IL 60610, TEL 312-943-9978

Larry Zgoda

Larry Zgoda Studio
415 W. North Avenue
Chicago, IL 60610
FAX 312-943-9987
TEL   312-943-9978

Larry Zgoda considers his work in stained glass as an ongoing exercise in architectural ornament. His understated color palette and imaginative application of patterned, textured and beveled glass qualify his designs for integration into an immense variety of architectural and interior settings. His works are visually compelling and have been well received by a host of public, corporate and private patrons.

Inquiries are welcome regarding brochure and project fees.

Also see these GUILD publications:
THE GUILD: 1, 2, 3, 4, 5
Architect's Edition: 6, 7, 8, 9, 10
Gallery Edition: 2

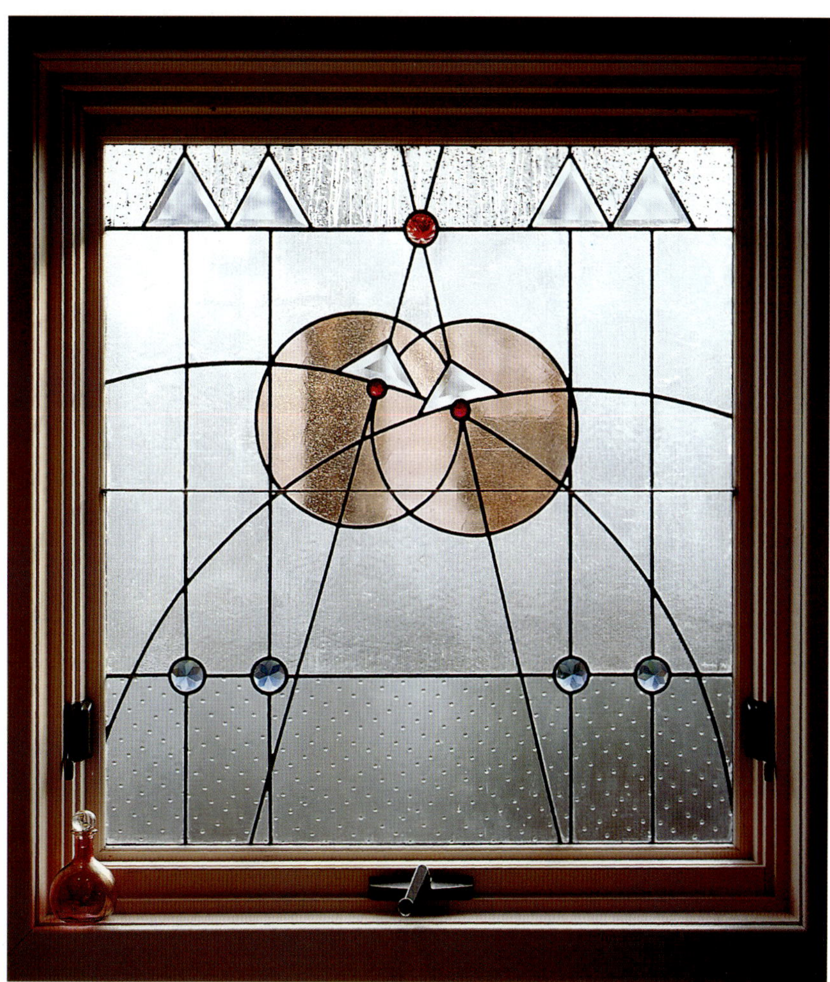

Harper Fritsch

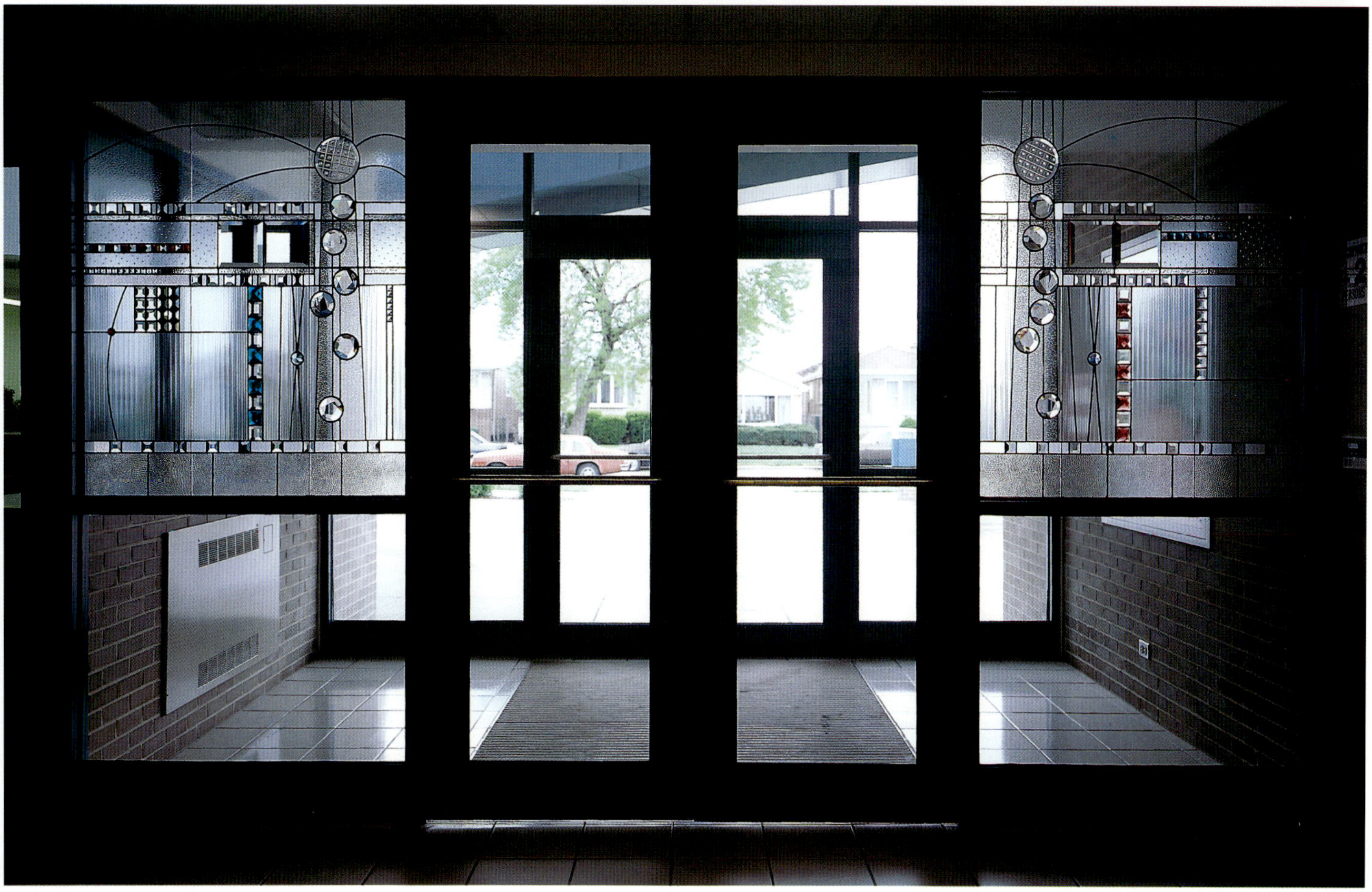

Wayne Cable

ARCHITECTURAL CERAMICS,
MOSAICS AND WALL RELIEFS

Art on Tiles

Rita Paul
32 Washington Square West
New York, NY 10011
FAX 212-979-8373
TEL ' 212-674-6388

Rita Paul creates sensuous paintings on tile. Her solid experience working with large-scale figural paintings, both in watercolor and oil, has given her the technical mastery with which to transmute any great painting onto tile. She has equal facility with abstract, contemporary or realistic subjects. Fitting the subject to the space involved is a challenge she prefers to resolve by working closely with the architect or designer on a conceptual level.

Shown at right: ceramic fireplace, stoneware, with ruffled edge framing unfinished oil painting. A ten-foot video screen is concealed directly over the fireplace, integrating today's technology with art. No wires are exposed, since they are hidden in the stoneware framework of the painting.

Also see this GUILD publication:
Designer's Edition: 10

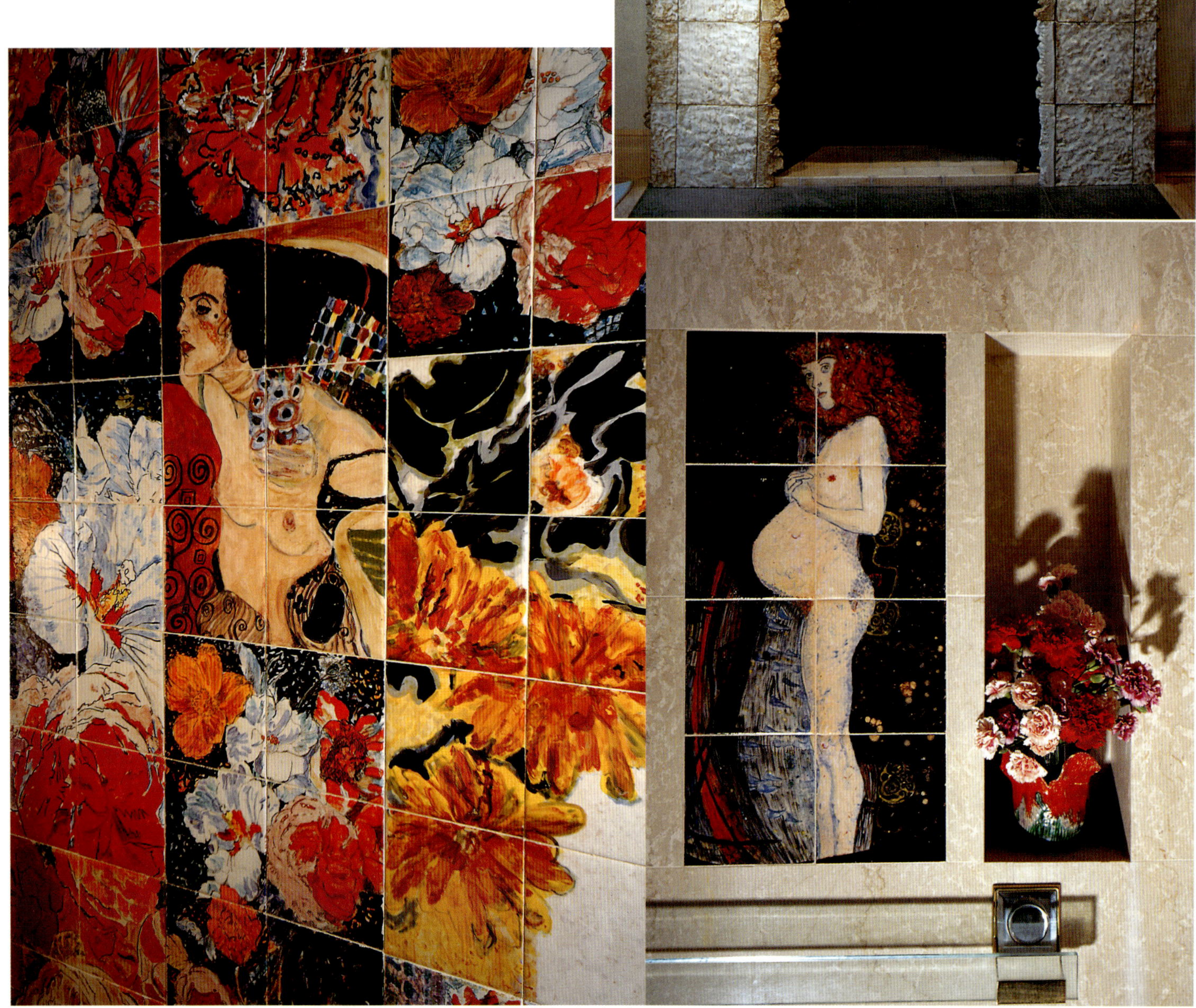

Beige marble bathroom, private residence, New York City, tile mural on one wall and tile inset on back wall of stall shower

Marty Heitner

Byzantium Mosaic Workshop

Luciano Franchi de Alfaro III
Master Designer/Principal
7255 SW 48th Street
Miami, FL 33155
FAX 305-669-1839
TEL   305-669-1670

The Byzantium Mosaic Workshop was created in 1990. Its emphasis and directions are of an artist's studio using a variety of media, primarily marble and glass tesserae. All work executed is based on commissions; the mosaics are custom and strictly one-of-a-kind. Our client's guarantee is to be unique.

Mosaics require little maintenance. Our color palette consists of over 1,000 shades. Special colors can be developed to meet clients' specific needs, however a minimum square footage is required.

Mosaic art pieces are currently at Steinbaum and Krauss gallery, NYC. Recent commission work ranges from Gianni Versace Shops in south Florida to Emilio and Gloria Estefan urns. Our workshop is represented in numerous corporate and private collections.

Guidelines upon request.

A *Bandana*, Byzantine glass, 23K gold

B *Peace Banner: World Silence* (VII), Byzantine glass, accents of sterling silver and 23K gold

C *Peace Banner: Recycle Faith* (III), Byzantine glass, 23K gold and silver accents; center: miniature glass work

D *Peace Banner: Home Sweet Home* (V), all in Byzantine glass

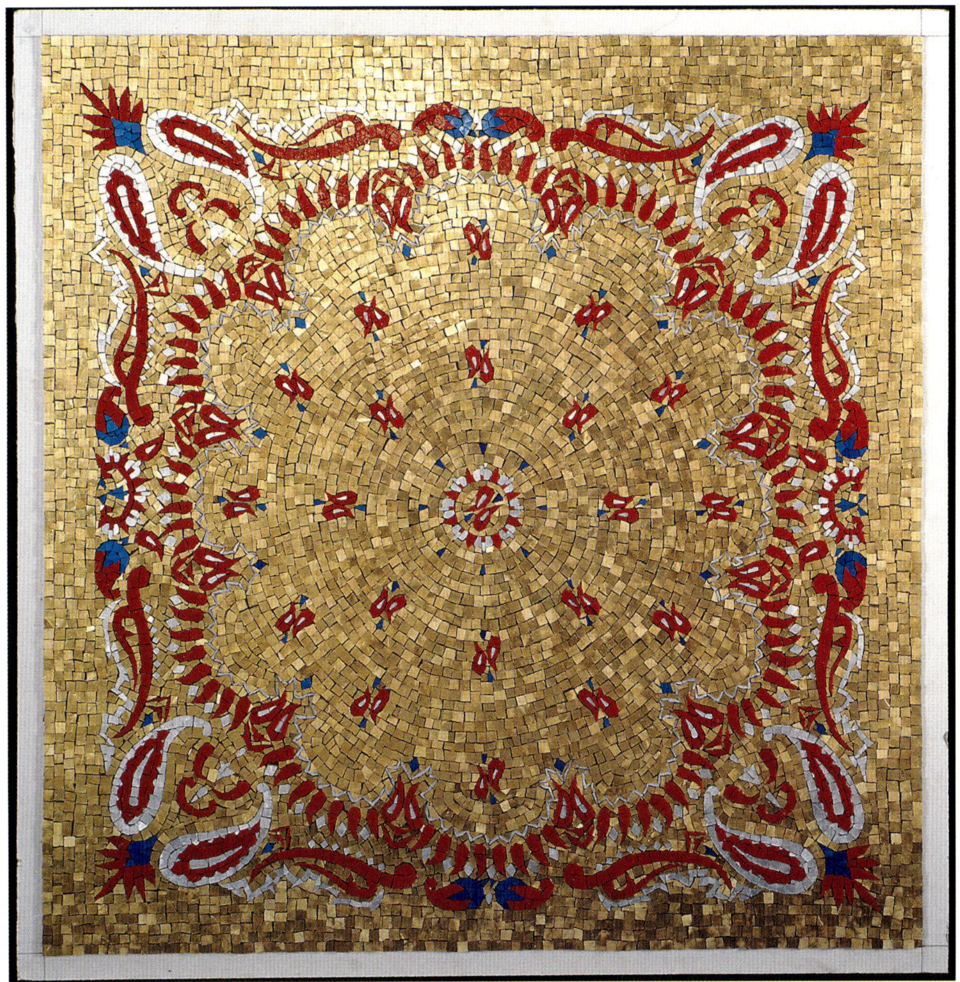

A

Photos: Patty Fisher

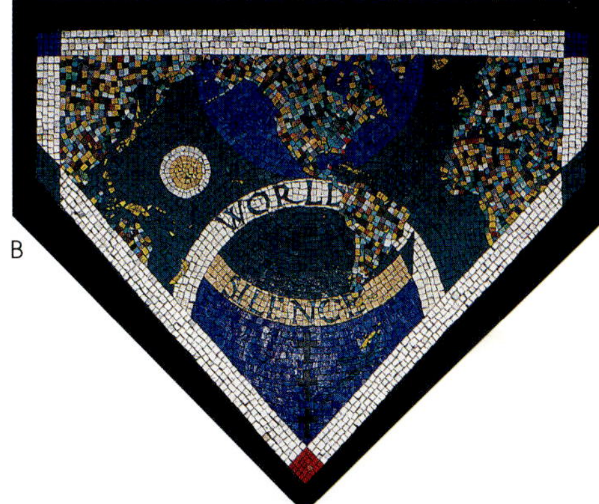

B

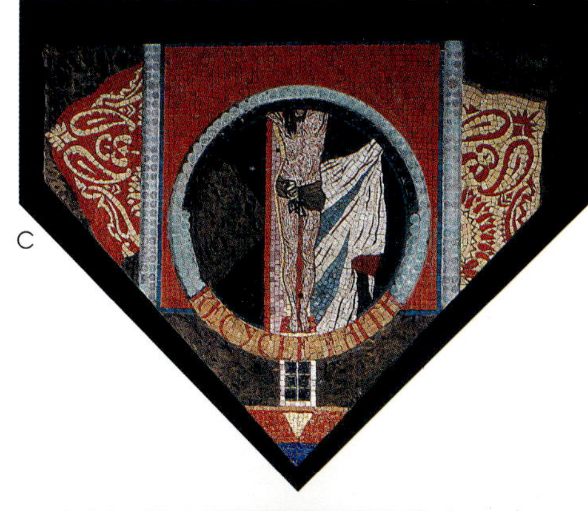

C

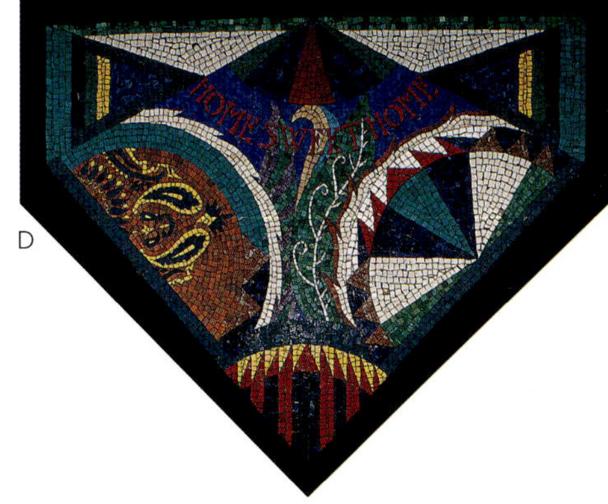

D

Donna L. Dobberfuhl

Sculptural Designs
202 Fir Dale, Suite 104
Converse, TX 78109-1340
TEL 210-659-7250
TEL 800-397-1452

A member of the National Sculpture Society, Donna holds her M.F.A. degree from the New York Academy of Art. Recent exhibits include Los Angeles' Museum of Natural History, Florida's Cypress Gardens and New York's Manhattan Towers. Current commissions include a Florida theater project, zoo installations, and the Order of Daedalians National Founders Memorial.

Each architectural setting for Donna's sculpted brick projects is one-of-a-kind, giving them a special presence that people remember so well. Each brick sculpture exists only in one place—people know and appreciate that it 'belongs there.'

Also see these GUILD publications:
Architect's Edition: 8, 9, 10

A *Pongo* ©, Cypress Gardens, FL, bronze, 50" x 78" x 52"

B *Way of the Cross* © (detail), St. Thomas Church, Staten Island, NY, brick, 6½' x 78' x 5"

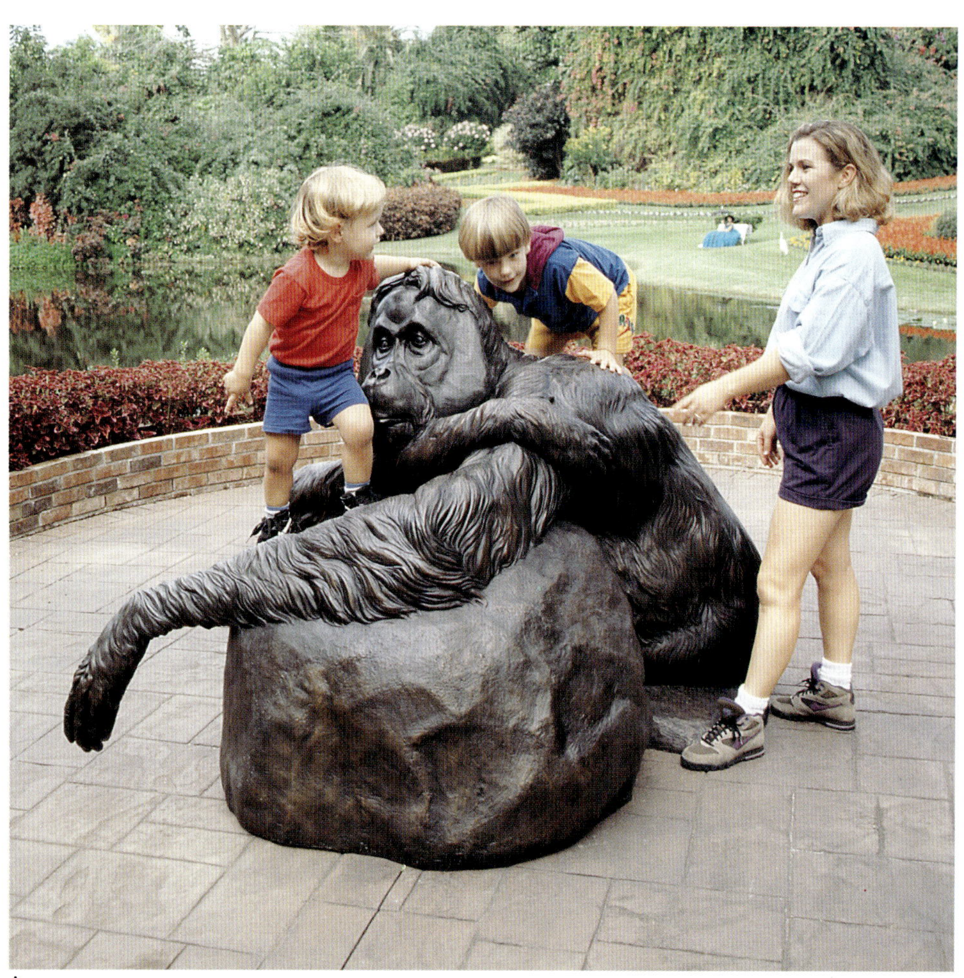

A

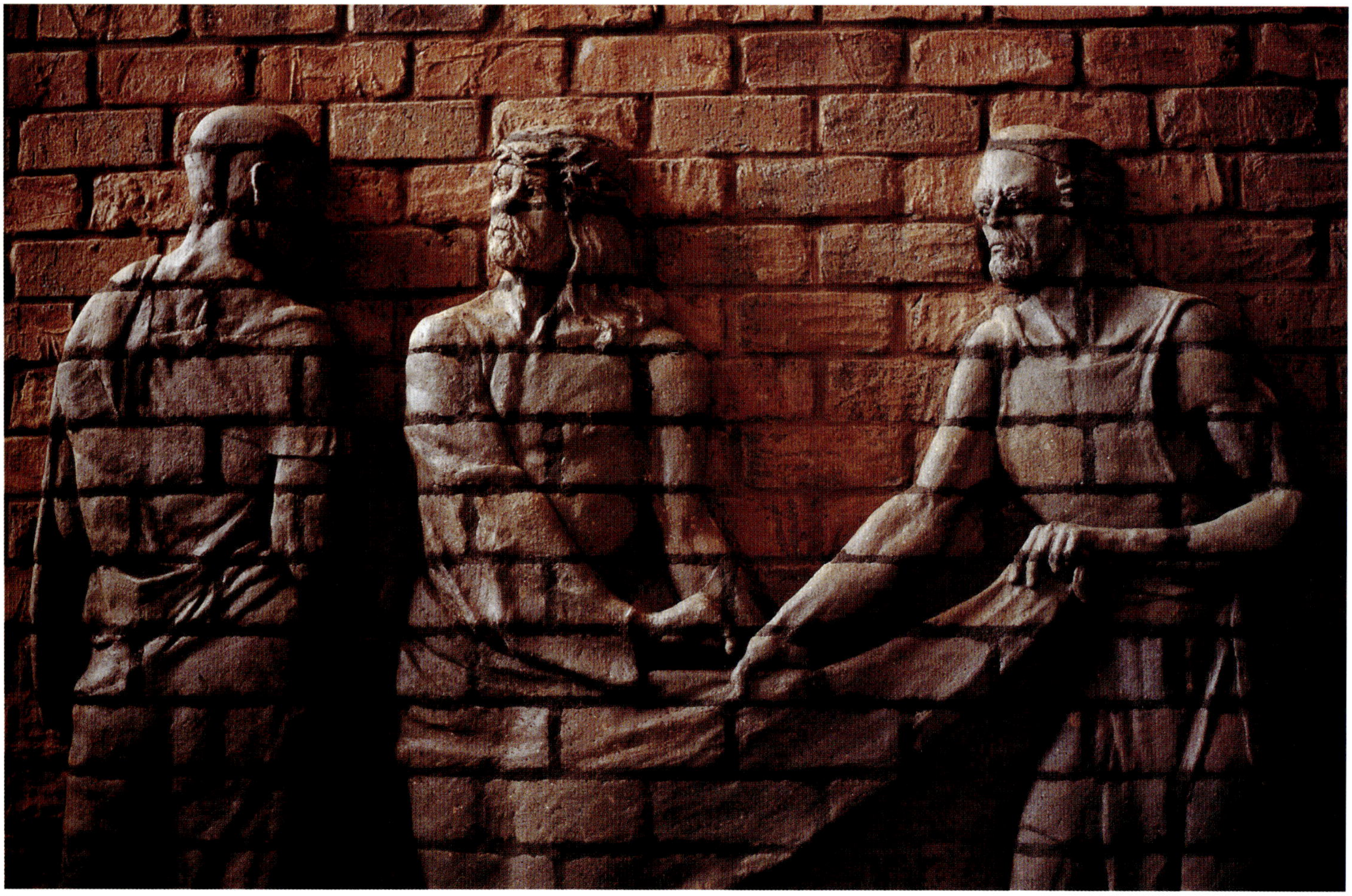

B

Bruce Howdle

225 Commerce Street
Mineral Point, WI 53565
608-987-3590

Bruce has been a ceramic sculptor since 1976. He has produced work ranging from thrown forms up to six feet in height to thirty foot relief murals utilizing nine tons of clay.

Bruce fires with a sodium process that melts the clay surface, preserving the integrity of the media and creating a very durable piece.

His work is suitable for free-standing or installed wall locations; pieces are in large public institutions, banks, corporations, private offices, and homes. Prices range from $1,500 to $60,000. Bruce collaborates closely with his clients and provides detailed drawings of proposed projects.

A *The Cycle of Life*, Dubuque Internal Medicine, 5'

B Relief mural, American Family Insurance National Headquarters, Madison, WI, sculpting stage prior to disassembly, hollowing and firing before installation, 21' x 11'6"

C *The West Begins*, Epply Airfield, Omaha, NE, 8' x 30'

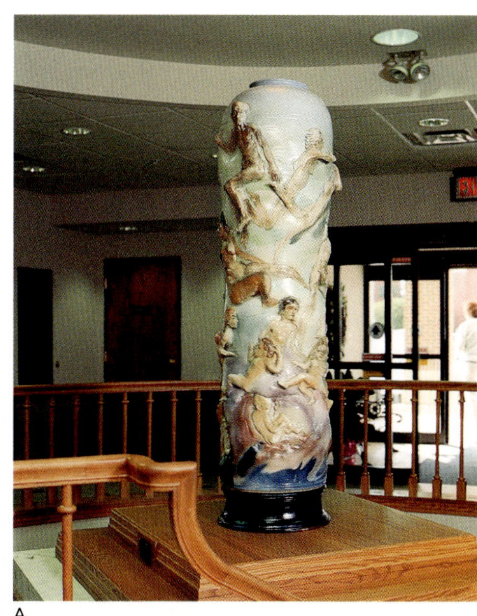

A

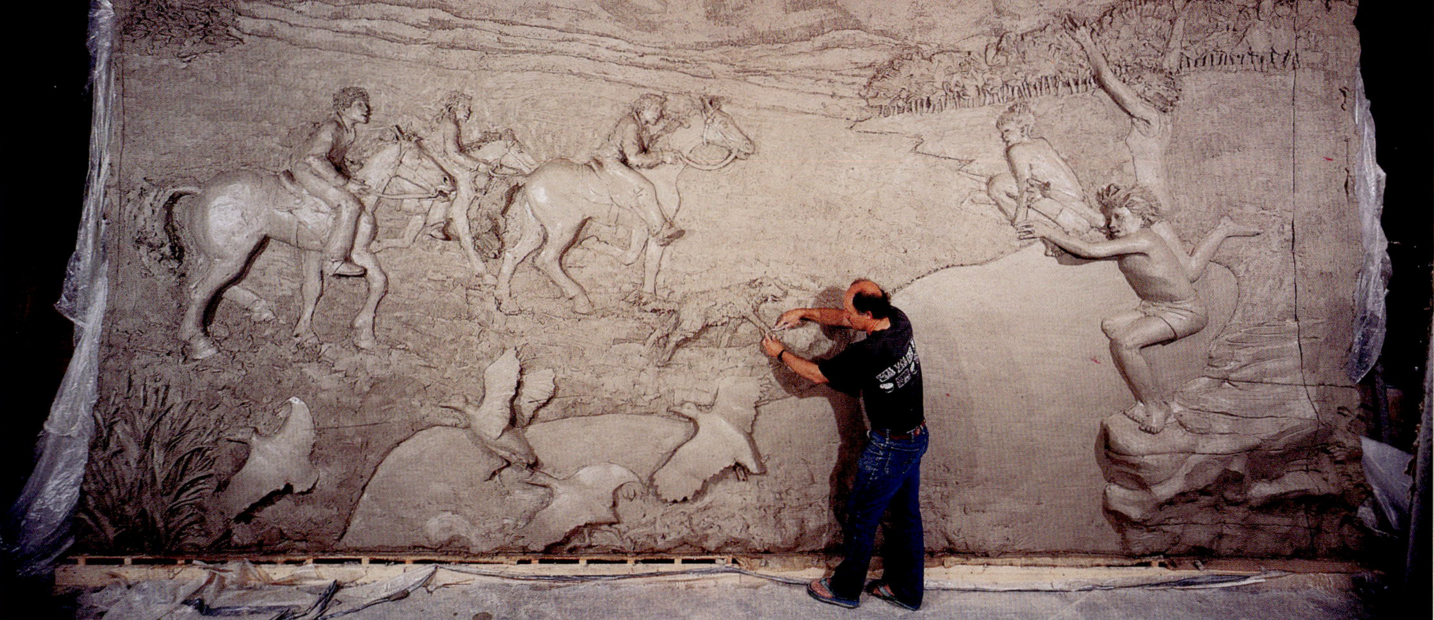

B

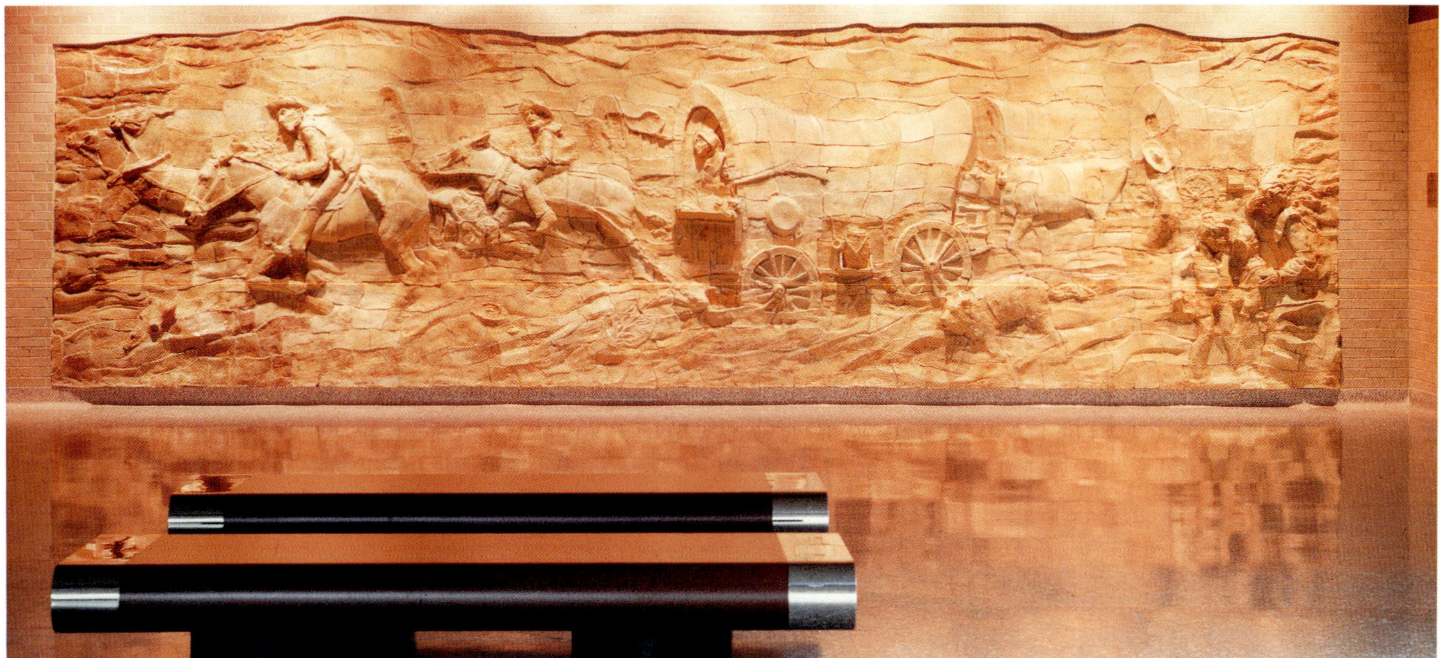

C

Elle Terry Leonard

Architectural Ceramics
910 Alameda Lane
Sarasota, FL 34234
FAX 941-952-0463
TEL 941-952-0463

Elle Terry Leonard specializes in site-specific
commissions in clay for corporate and residential clients. Studio specialties include relief
murals, architectural details, furniture and tile.
Complete studio services range from concept
and consultation through production, shipping
and installation. Installations are suitable for
both interior and exterior spaces. Prices and
portfolio upon request.

Clients include:
Arvida Corporation
Chamber of Commerce, Sarasota, FL
City of Venice, FL
Worldgate Marriott Hotels
Worldgate Athletic Club
Kaiser Permanente
Johns Hopkins Hospital

Also see these *GUILD* publications:
THE GUILD: 1, 2, 3, 4, 5
Architect's Edition: 6, 8, 9, 10

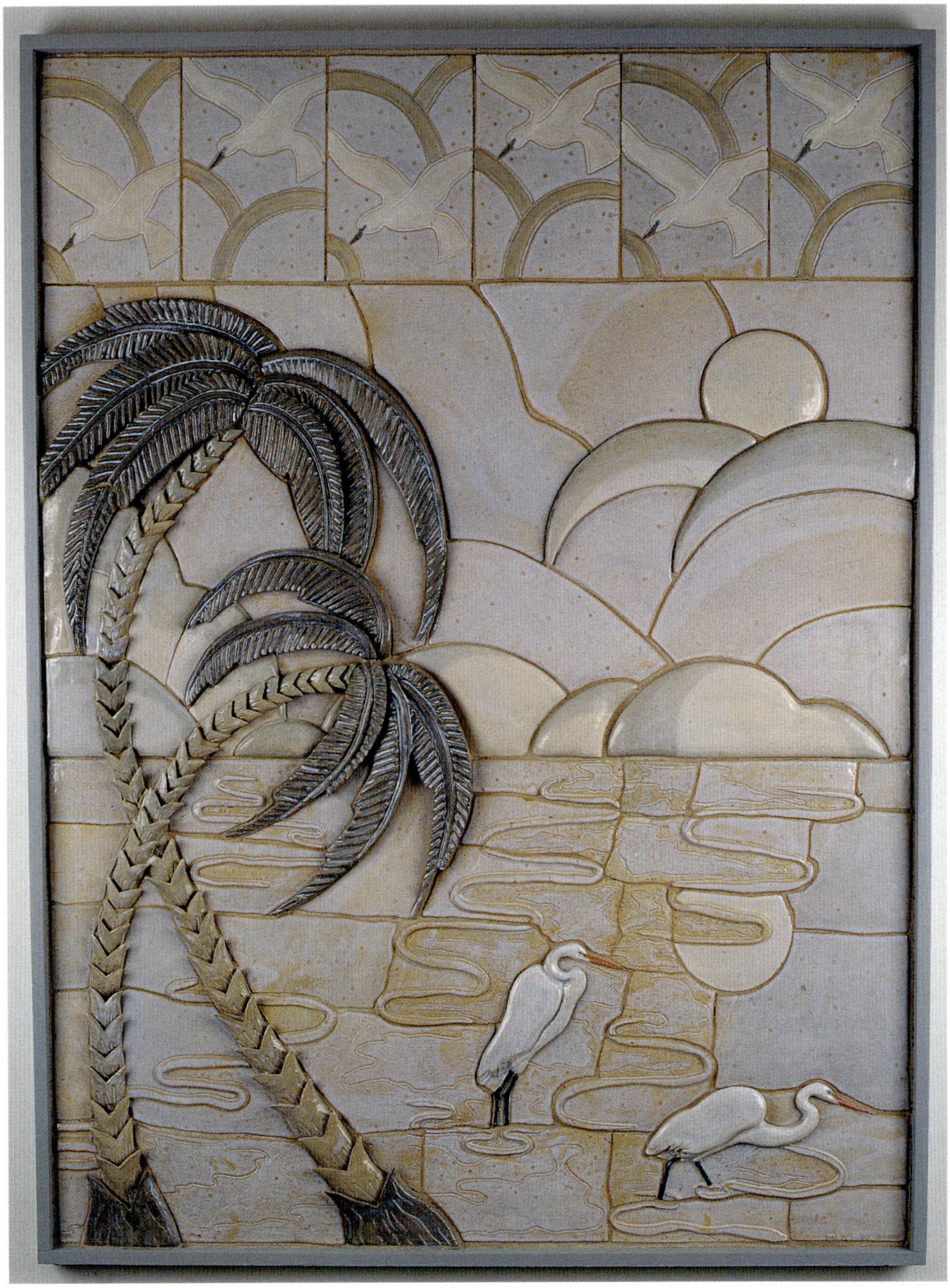

SHOWN: *La Luna Dulce*, relief mural,
private residence, 4' x 6'

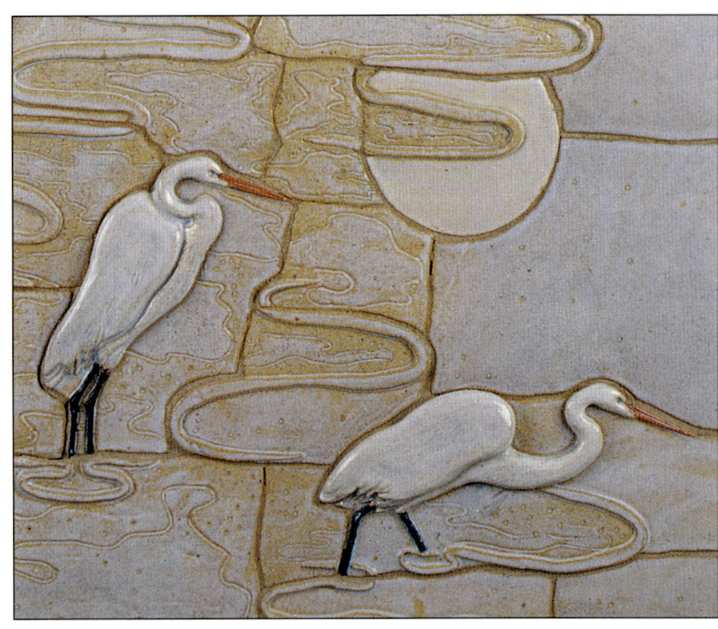

Elizabeth MacDonald

Box 186
Bridgewater, CT 06752
FAX 203-350-4052
TEL   203-354-0594

Elizabeth MacDonald produces tile paintings by layering ceramic powders on thin pieces of textured clay that have been torn into squares. The resulting surfaces suggest the patinas of age. After firing, these tiles are assembled into images, merging the organic into the formality of a grid. The compositions are suitable for either in- or out-of-doors and they take the form of free-standing columns, wall panels or architectural installations.

Commissions include Conrad International Hotel, Hong Kong; St. Luke's Hospital, Denver; ITT Hartford, for the City of Hartford, CT; the Department of Environmental Protection, Hartford, CT (% for Art); Miliken, Spartanburg, SC; University of Maryland Medical Center; U.S. Trust, Stamford, CT; Chubb and Sons; Pitney Bowes; the Aetna Life Insurance Company; Miles Pharmaceutical; and IBM.

Also see these GUILD publications:
THE GUILD: 1, 2, 3, 4, 5
Architect's Edition: 6, 8, 9, 10
Designer's Edition: 6, 7, 8, 9, 10

SHOWN: Nobu Restaurant, New York, NY

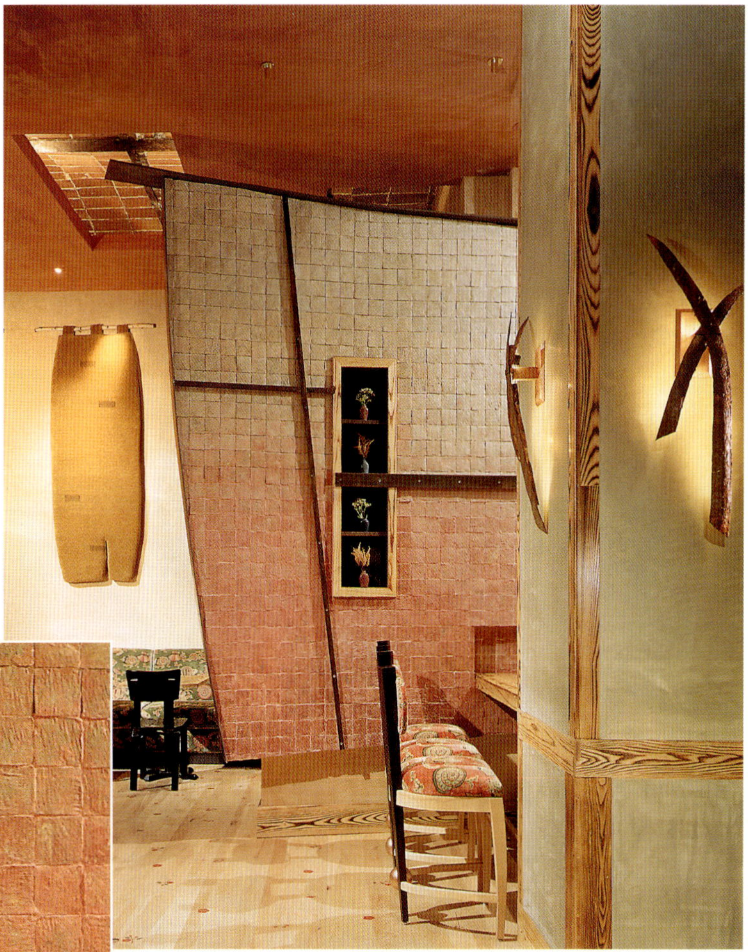

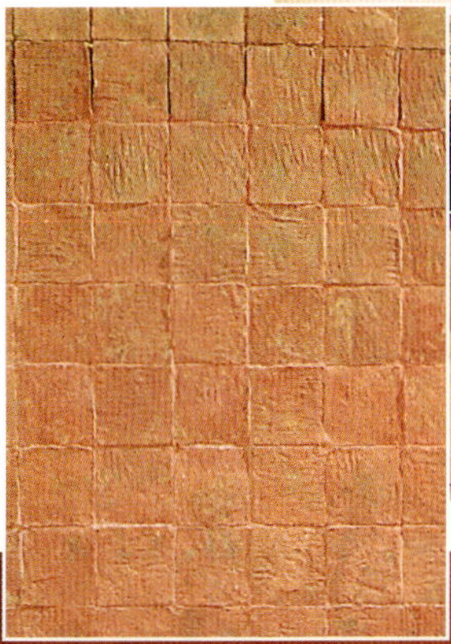

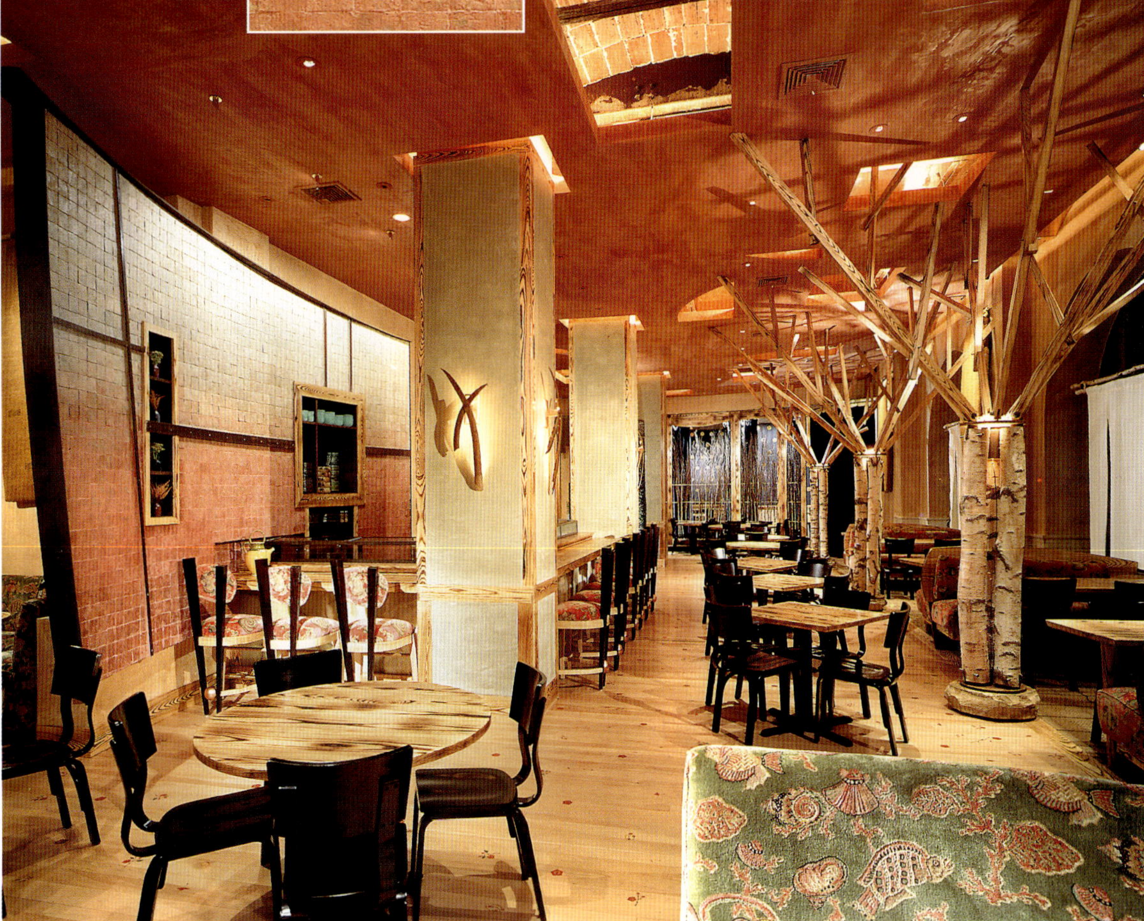

Laurel Neff

PO Box 3341
Madison, WI 53704
TEL 608-255-0056

Laurel Neff specializes in mixed media mosaic installations, both residential and commercial, interior and exterior.

She utilizes a wide variety of materials to achieve differing effects that are unique, durable and work well in any environment.

Her work runs the gamut from classical to eclectic, abstract to representational, and adorns floors, walls, counters, ceilings, walkways and free-standing objects.

Laurel works closely with clients to accommodate specific needs and budgets, while creatively bringing a client's vision to life.

Also see this previous GUILD publication:
Designer's Edition: 10

A Detail, Mother Fools' Coffeehouse, 1994, mixed media, 15" x 10"

B Exterior sign, Savory Thymes restaurant, 1994, ceramic tile, 8' x 4'

C Detail, Hair Unlimited, 1994, mirror and ceramic tile, 3' x 2'

D Private residence, 1993, broken china, 24 sq. ft.

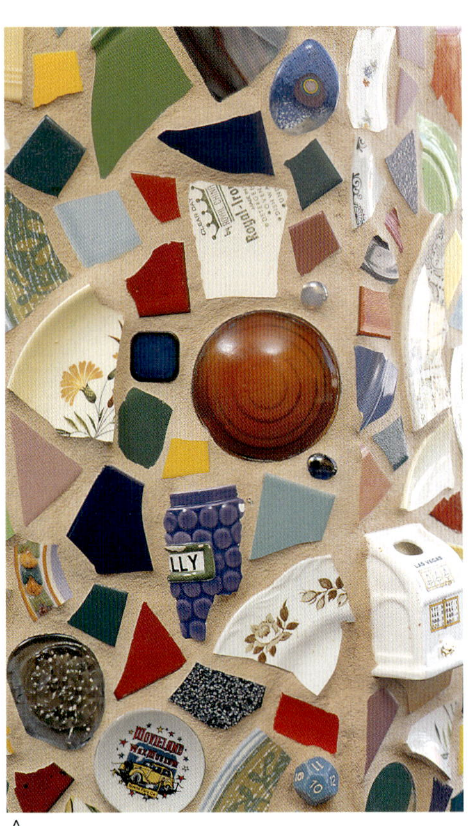

A

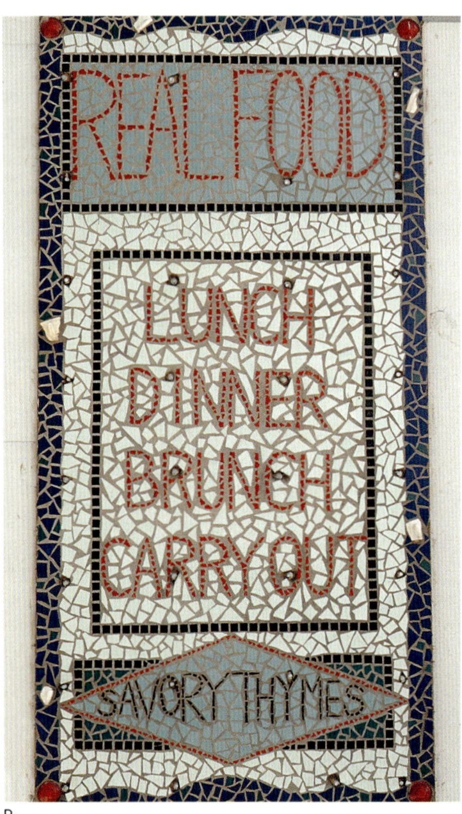

B

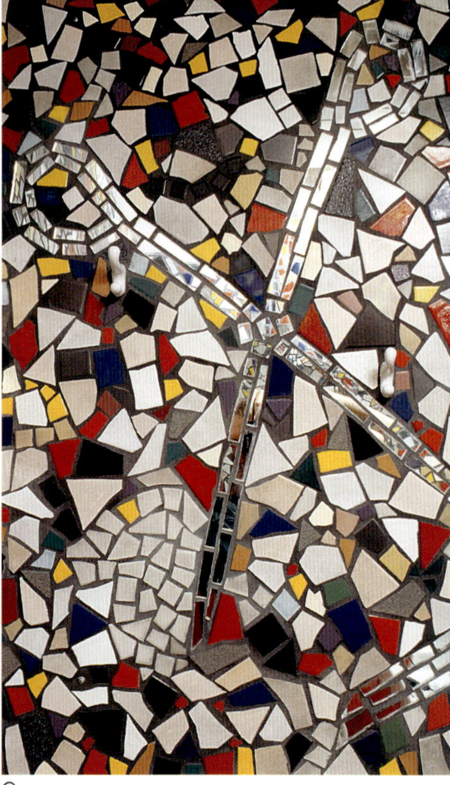

C

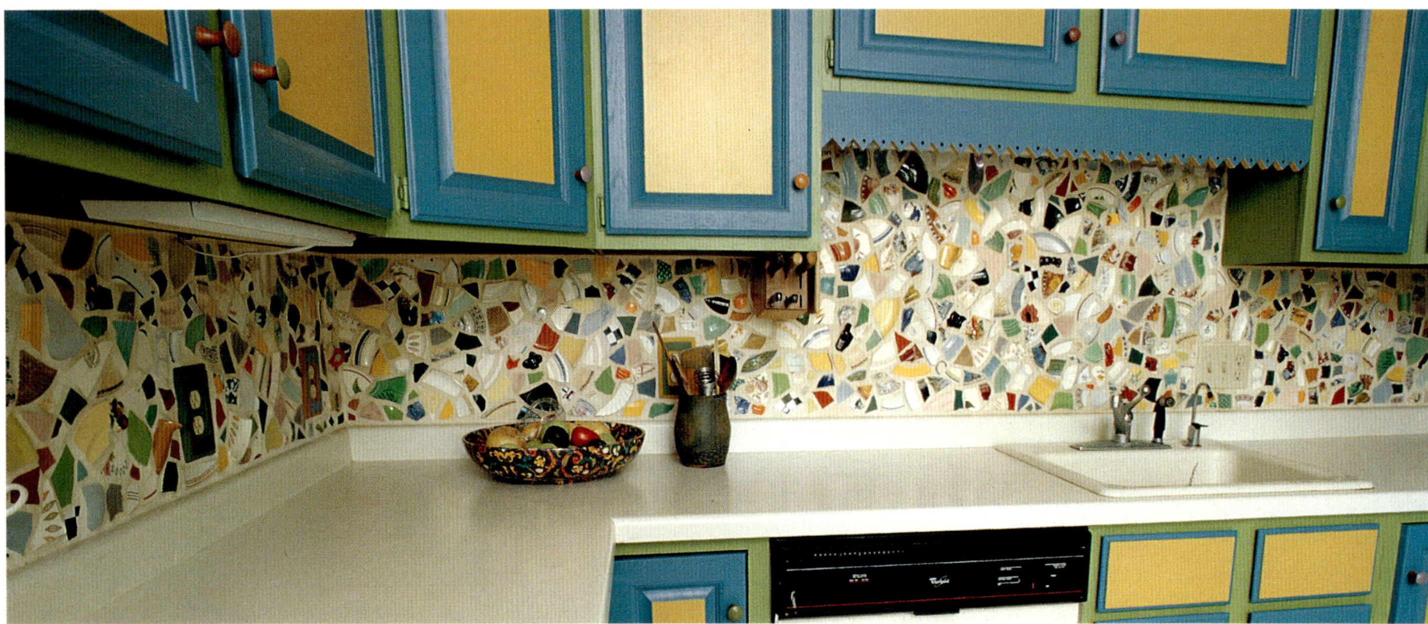

D

Hester C. Nelson

Architectural Ceramics
1779 Lanier Place NW
Washington, DC 20009
TEL 301-588-6533
TEL 202-462-1186

Hester Nelson is a ceramic artist whose work embraces the architectural environment, from public park settings to private homes and gardens. She uses a classical language of architectural forms combined with elaborate relief carving, and builds works which contain a myriad of references, layered like fragments, speaking of the history of ceramics and architecture. Nelson exhibits work in galleries and accepts a wide range of commissions. She often works with architects and designers to help clients achieve their goals. Her work includes all types of ceramic tiles, murals, walkways, tables and seating, as well as columns and fireplaces. Nelson received her B.F.A. degree from the Kansas City Art Institute.

A, B & C Fireplaces, 1991-1993, private commission, individually carved, hand-rolled tiles, low-fire to high-fire stoneware, raw clay to ornately glazed

D *Gazebo*, 1990, private commission, four hand-thrown, hand-carved columns of unglazed, high-fire stoneware, 8^1/$_2$'H; redwood trellis, 14'W x 9'D

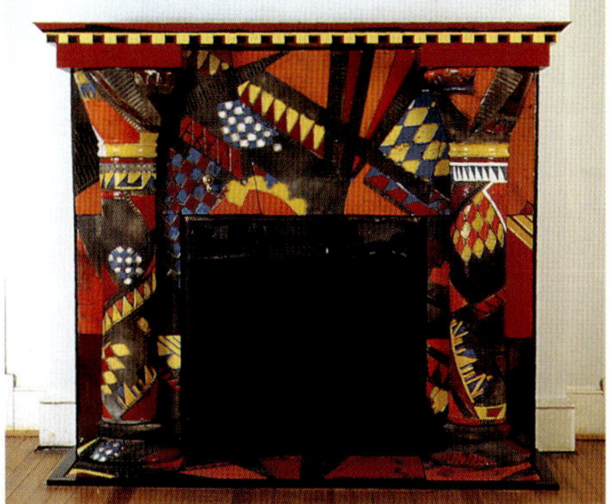

A

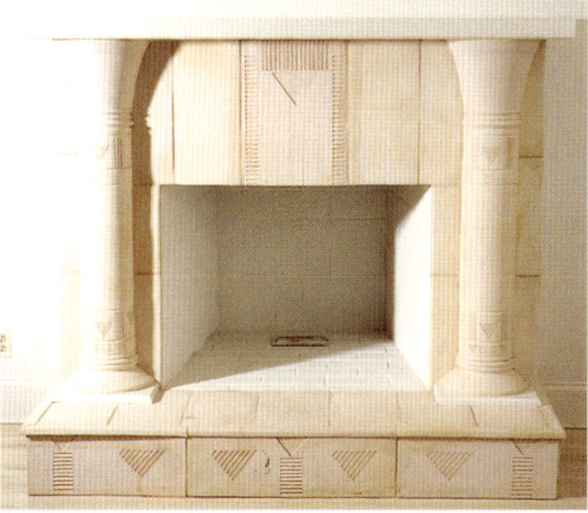

B

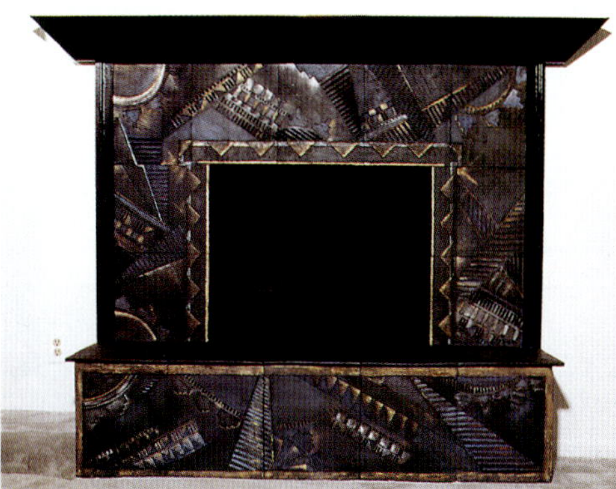

C

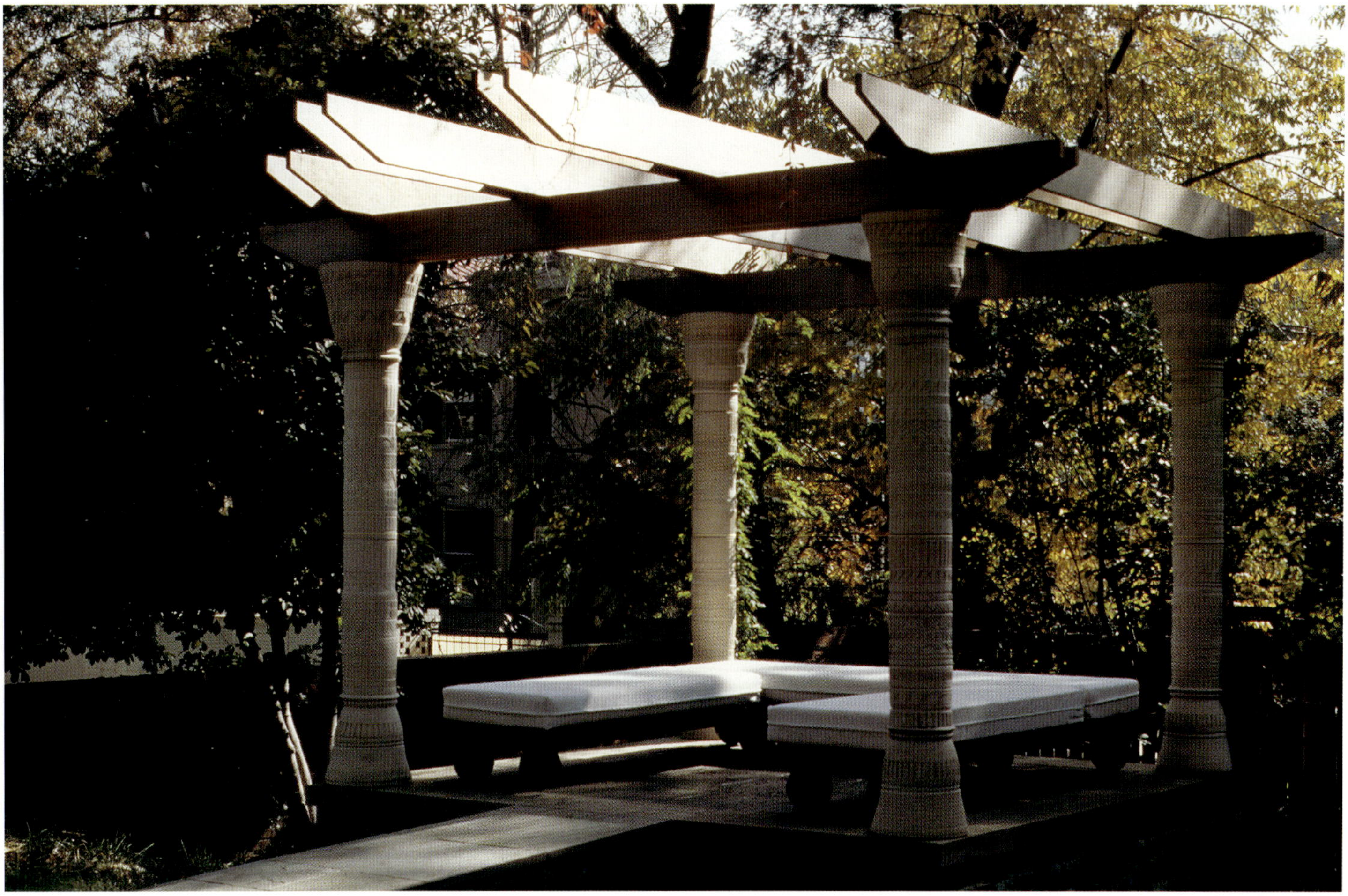

D

Terra Studios, Inc.

12103 Hazel Valley Road
Fayetteville, AR 72701
FAX 501-643-3356
TEL 501-643-3314

Leo Ward
Rita Ward
Trent Tally
Ron Mynatt
Bryan Gott
  Artists

Terra Studios, Inc. has over 20 years experience in hot glass and ceramic design and production.

Their multi-media artists and support staff offer the client unique design possibilities in exterior and interior murals, large urns and planters, and ceramic sculpture. Terra will work with clients on design concepts in a wide range of media.

A *Our Tribute to Nature*, 1993, stoneware, 6' x 27', by Trent Tally, Marty Jerkins, and Sharon Kilpartrick

B *Fireplace*, 1989, stoneware, 9' x 12', by Leo Ward

C *Mesa Verde Cliff Dwelling*, 1994, stoneware, 7' x 17', by Trent Tally

D *Thomas Hart Benton Study*, 1994, stoneware, 4' x 8', by Trent Tally

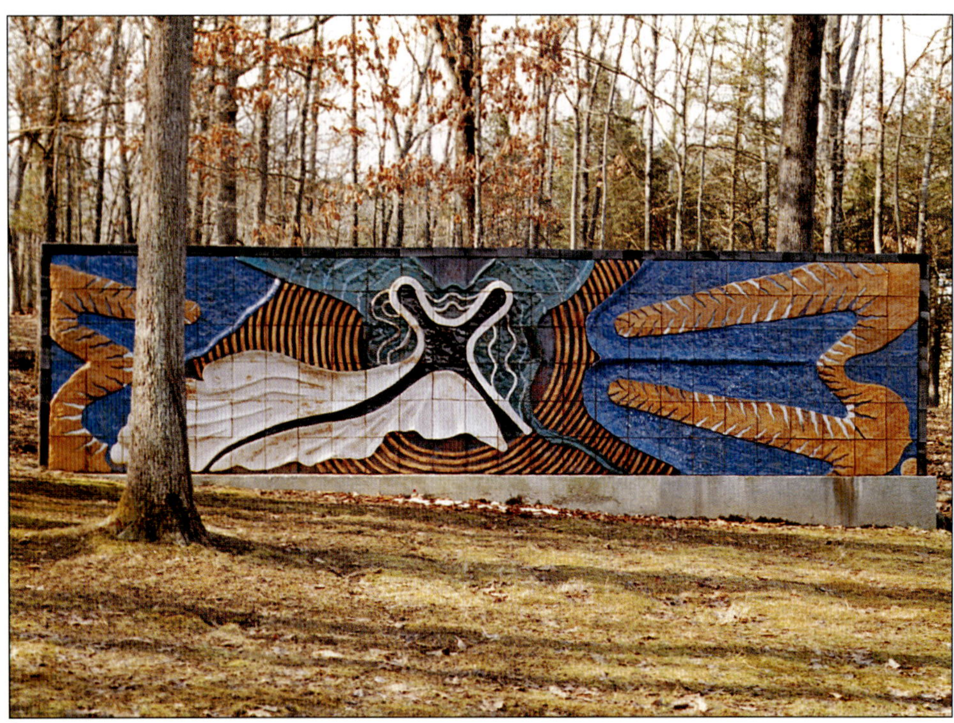

A

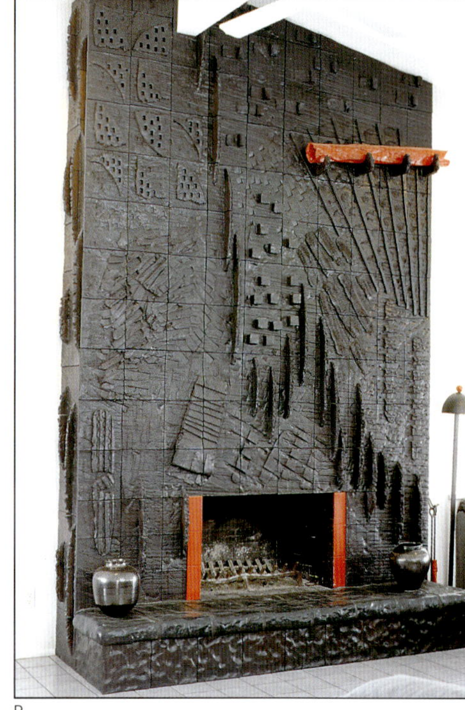

B

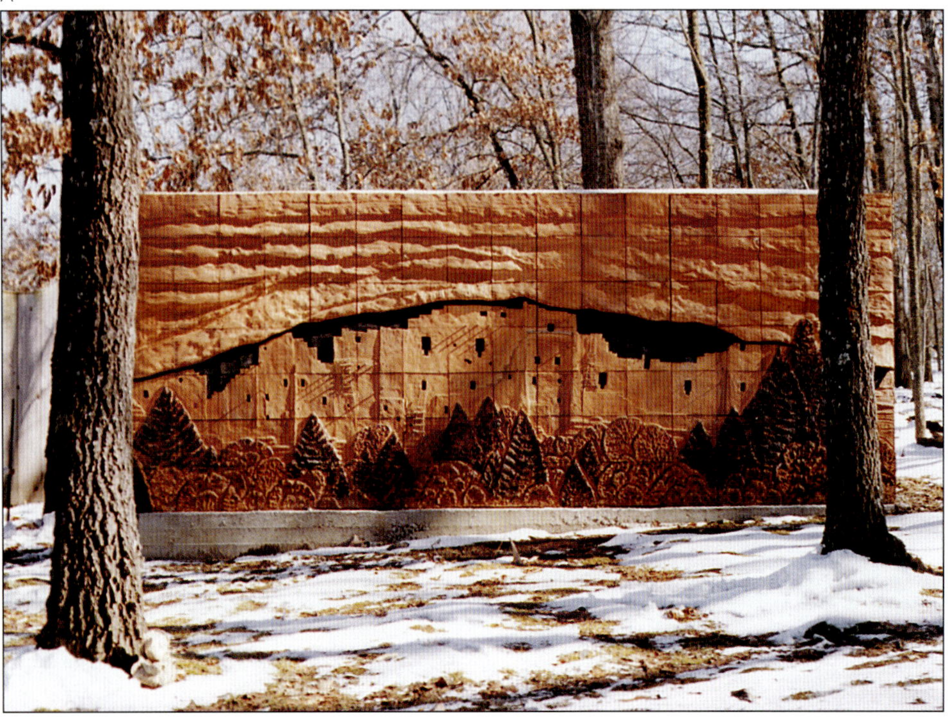

C

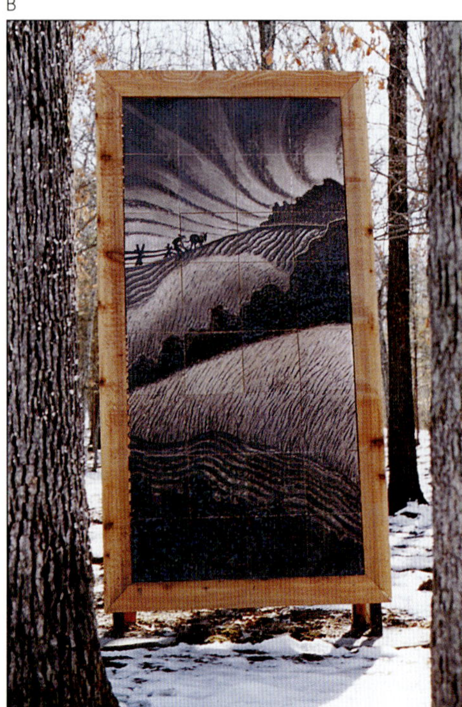

D

Peter Colombo
Artistic Mosaics

Peter Colombo
281 Phillips Avenue
South Hackensack, NJ 07606
FAX 201-641-5884
TEL 201-641-7964

Peter Colombo is a graduate of the School of Visual Arts in New York City. The artist uses materials of diverse origins, including marble, granite, handmade ceramic tile and colored glass to create custom artistic mosaics. This medium combines durability and low maintenance, while allowing full color and flexibility in design and style. A variety of textures is achieved through different setting techniques. The studio offers original or collaborative designs, fabrications from drawings and on-site installations.

Also see these GUILD publications:
Architect's Edition: 9, 10

A Marble and glass mosaic floor, 1995, residence, Atlanta, GA, Apropos Designs

B Ceramic tile and glass, 1994, Nick and Toni's, East Hampton, NY, original art by Eric Fischl

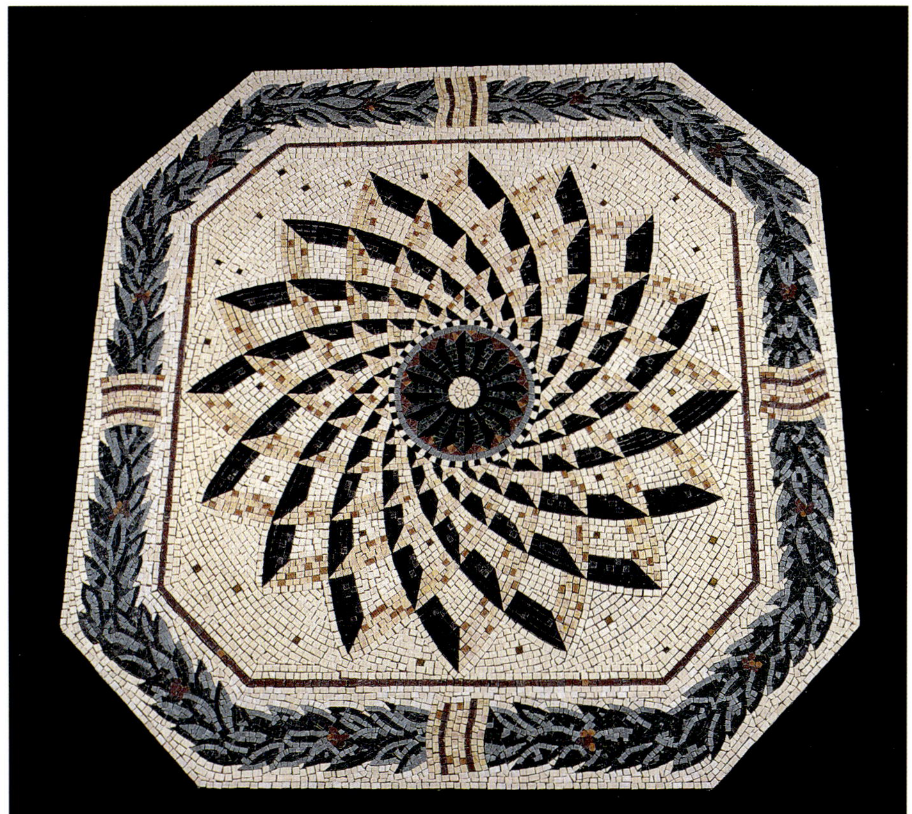

A

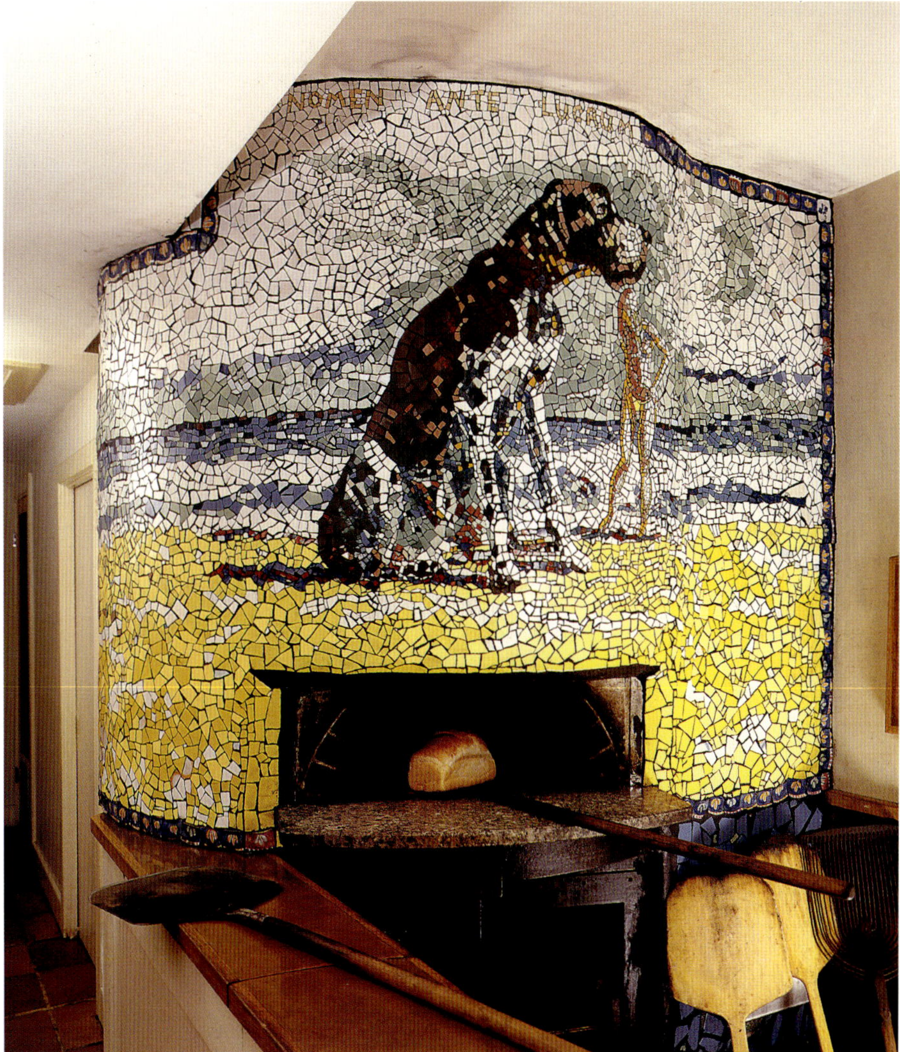

B

Photos: Robert Vance Blosser, New York, NY

Mara Smith
Kris King

Architectural Murals in Brick
339 NW 82nd Street
Seattle, WA 98117-4033
FAX 206-784-5118
TEL   206-789-2838

Texas A&M commissioned Mara and Kris for this massive 800+ square foot project in the new Student Development Center at Tarleton State University. This 30,000 pound project was carved and shipped from their studio, near Seattle, to its installation site in Stephenville, TX.

The murals depict some of the history, traditions and educational activities relative to TSU. Wall design and mural subjects were collaborated between the artists, architects, A&M facilities planners, masons, general contractor, students and faculty.

Mara and Kris share 30 years of carving and project experience, successfully completing over 325 public and private commissions.

Also see these GUILD publications:
Architect's Edition: 8, 9, 10

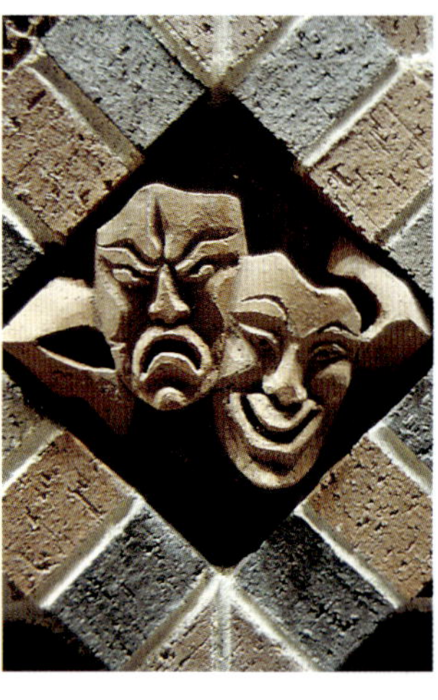

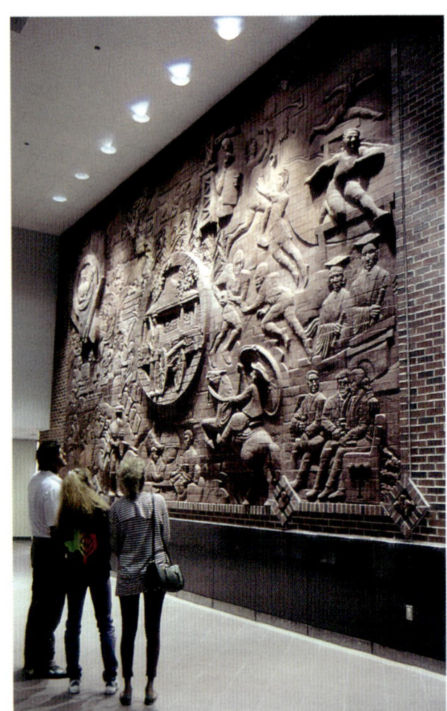

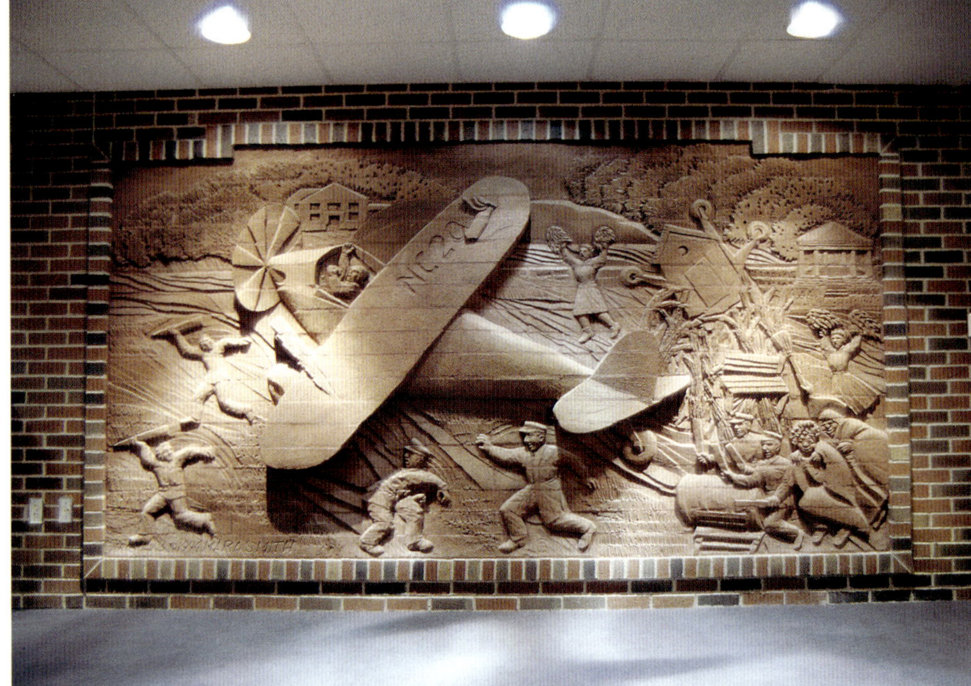

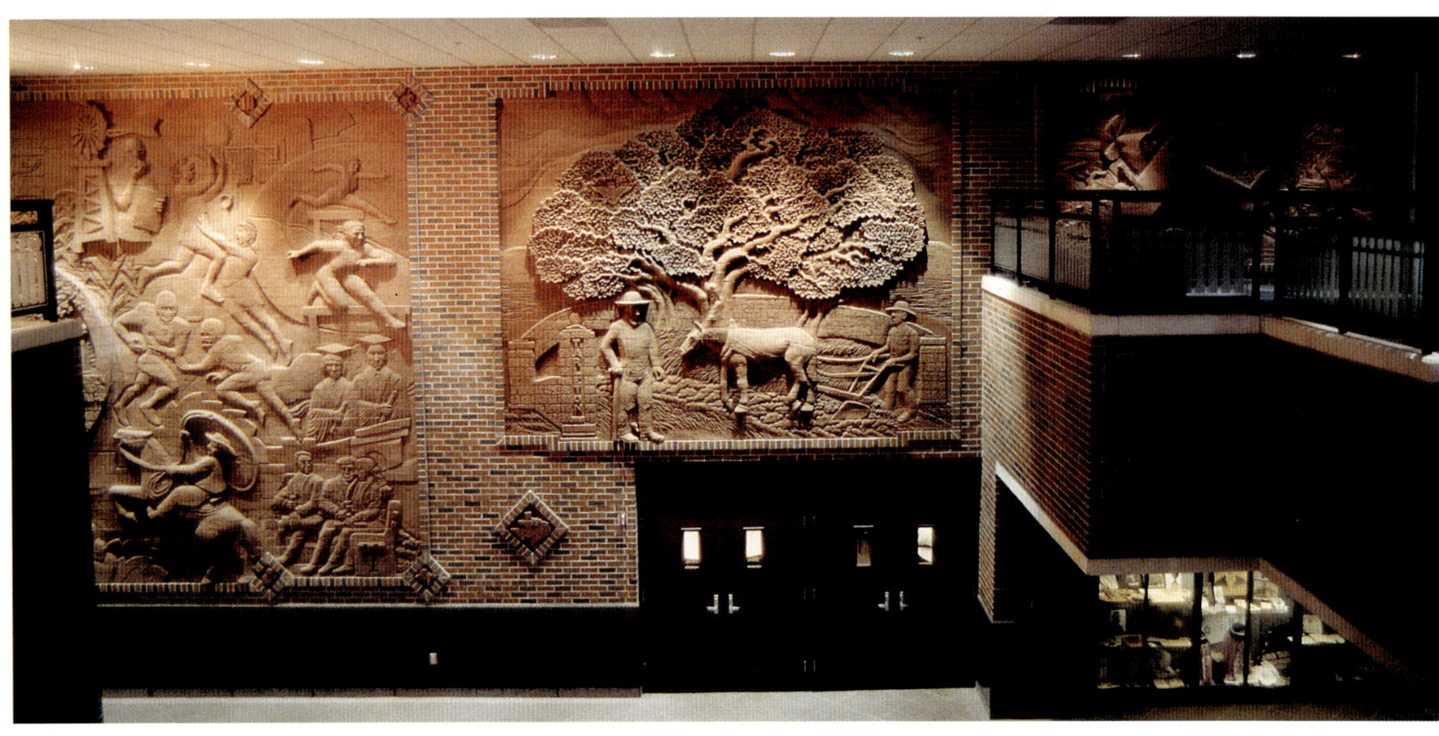

Suzanne M. Young

Suzanne M. Young Studio
2968 Phillips
Berkley, MI 48072
TEL 810 398-3837

The need for art is unique to each circumstance, building or community. It is with this in mind that Suzanne creates original sculpture based on individual requirements: function, size, color and the necessity for the art to communicate and inspire. Excellence in quality is provided at affordable prices.

Pieces are wrought from clay, cast resin and bronze. Suzanne is experienced in church, hospital, school and private commissions.

A *Last Supper* (in situ), 1994, wall relief, fired clay with raku glaze, St. Michael the Archangel Catholic Church, Aurora, CO, 5' x 8'

B *Christ*, 1994, suspended relief, fired clay with raku glaze, St. Michael the Archangel Catholic Church, Aurora, CO, 5' x 3'

C *Last Supper*

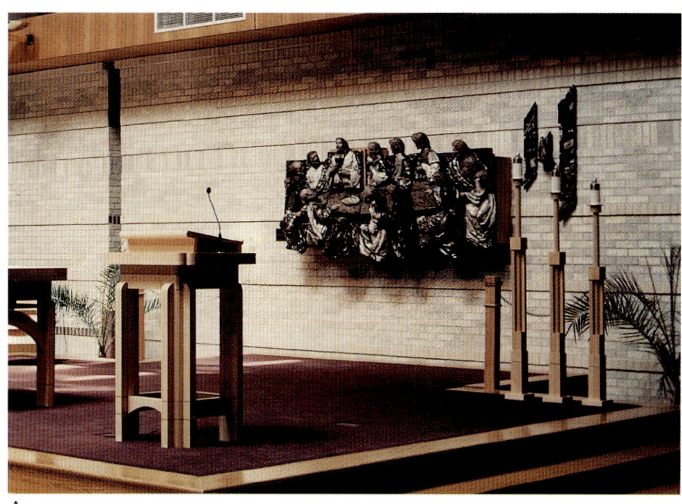

A

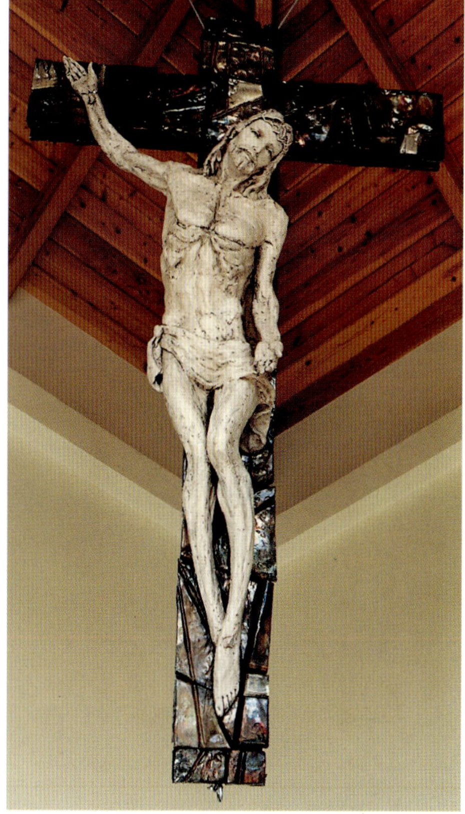

B

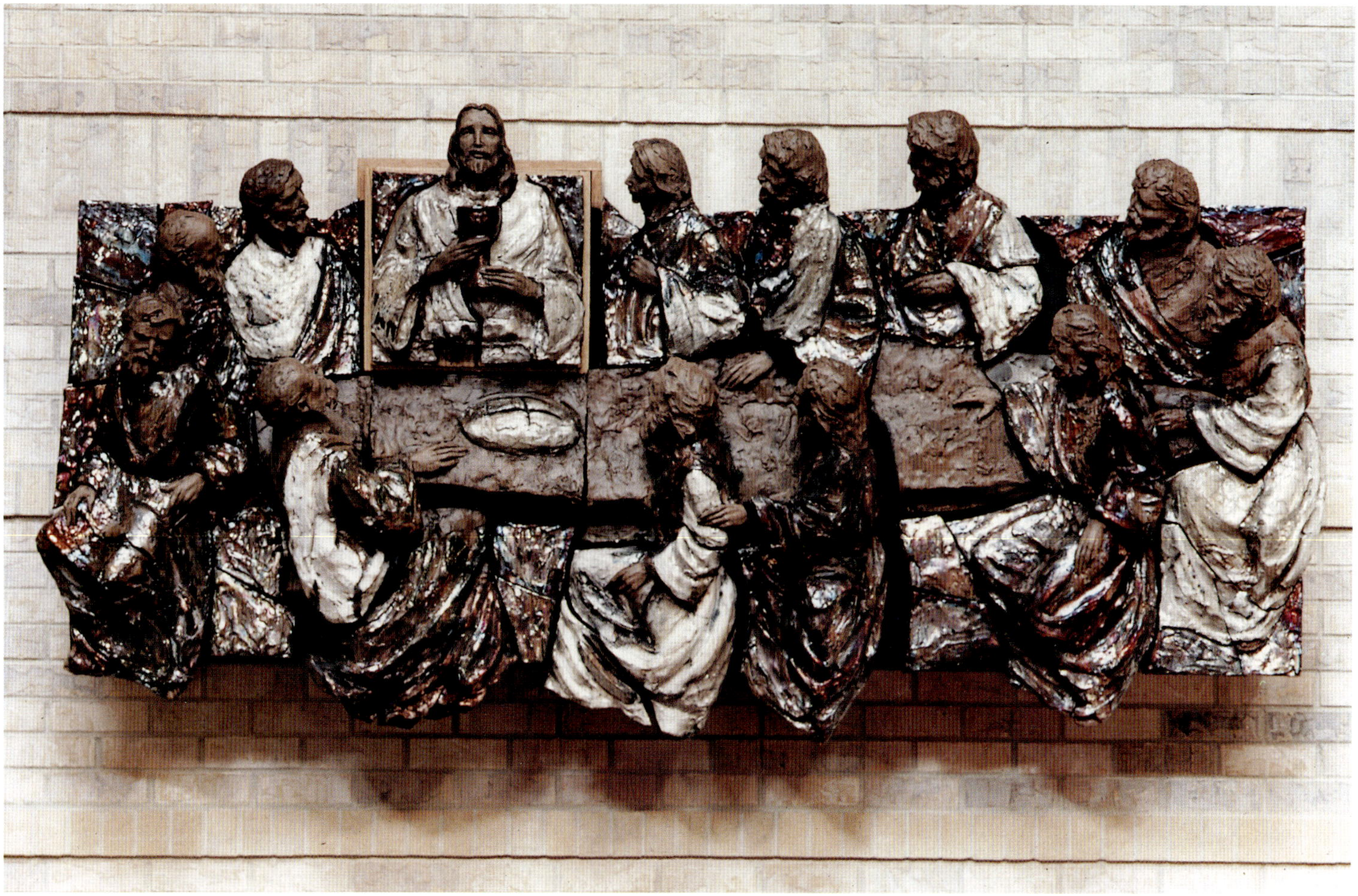

C

ARCHITECTURAL WOOD

Nathan P. Jackson

5972 Roosevelt Drive S.
Ketchikan, AK 99901
TEL 907-225-3431

Nathan Jackson, a Tlingit Indian, has been working as an artist since 1967. He works in the traditional style of Northwest Coast Indian art, primarily carving panels and totem poles in red cedar. He has artwork in the public and private sectors (see the *Architect's Edition 8*, pages 244-5, and the *Architect's Edition 10*, page 209). Please contact the artist for more information and prices.

Commissions include:
Horniman Museum, London, England, 1985
    (eagle/bear totem pole)
University of Alaska Southeast (library),
    Juneau, AK, 1990 (raven panel, eagle panel)
Ketchikan High School (auditorium), Ketchikan,
    AK, 1993 (killerwhale and king salmon panels)
Shedd Aquarium, Chicago, IL, 1994
    (eagle/killerwhale totem pole)
National Bank of Alaska (Shoreline), Ketchikan,
    AK, 1995 (*Eagle Holding Tinah*, panel)

SHOWN: Chief and Two Nephews, totem pole, 1994, Little Switzerland store, Ketchikan, AK

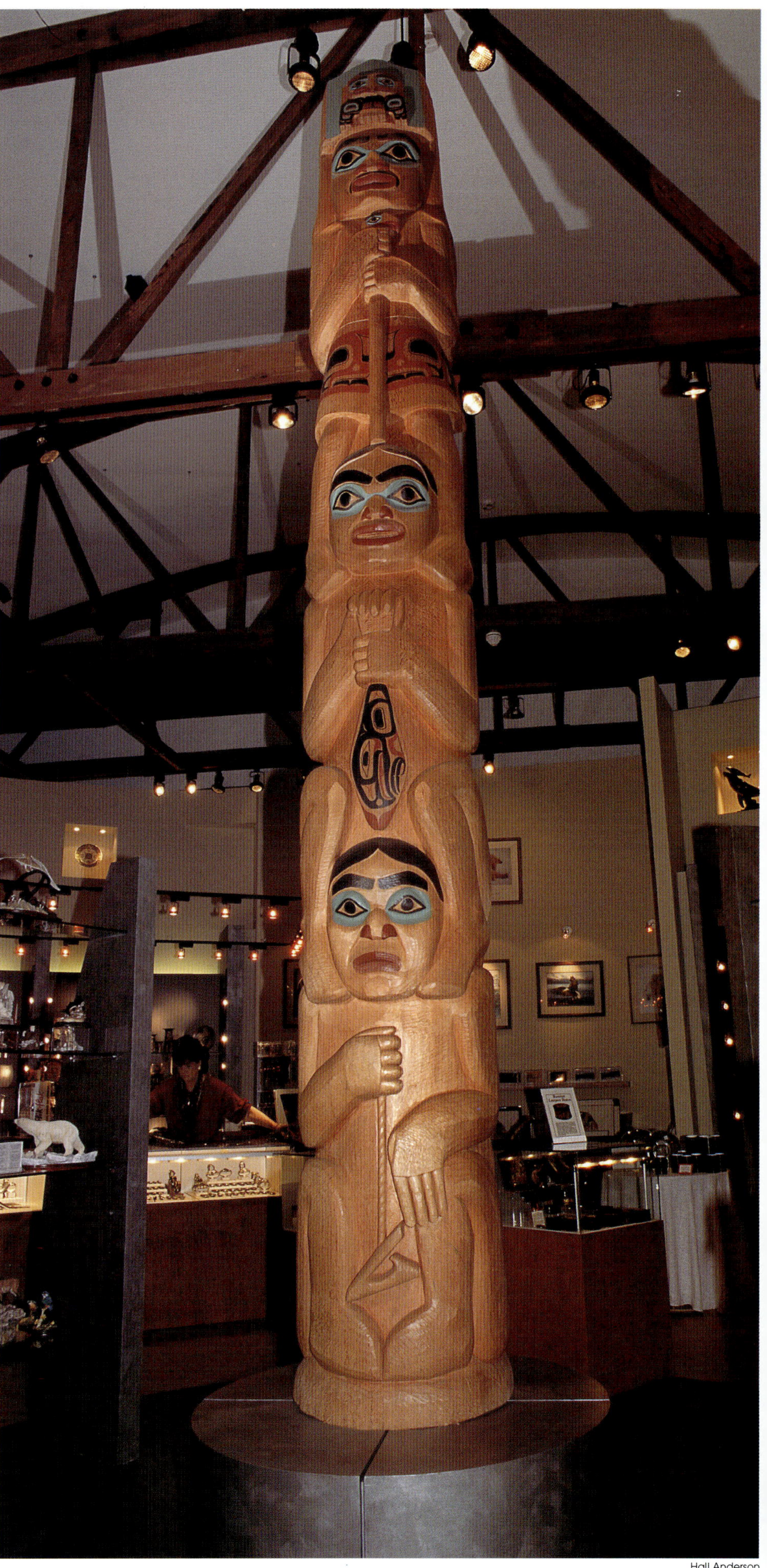

Hall Anderson

LepoWorks, Inc.

David Lepo, Robert Lepo
4640 Allentown Road
Lima, OH 45807
FAX 419-331-2787
TEL 419-331-5376

LepoWorks is a family of artists whose individual talents create with a one-of-a-kind philosophy. The basis of their success is a concern for detail and quality of the highest standards.

They design private, public and corporate art and collaborate with architects and designers. They enhance existing interior and exterior architectural elements and spaces. They offer solutions for aesthetic and technical demands, meeting budgets and deadlines. They handle all shipping and installation.

David and Robert Lepo express their distinct aesthetic approaches in a multitude of materials used in traditional as well as contemporary styles.

A brochure is available upon request.

Also see these GUILD publications:
Architect's Edition: 8, 9, 10

SHOWN: Custom, hand-carved, solid-hardwood furnishings

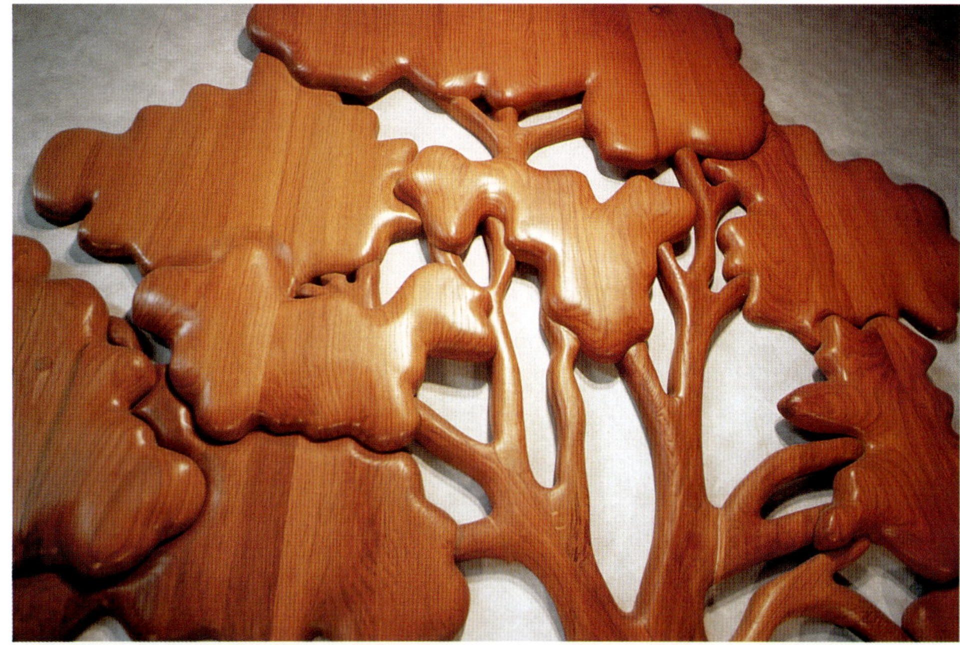

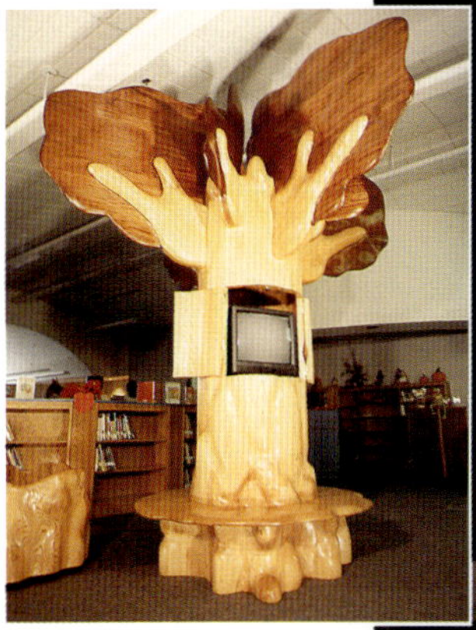

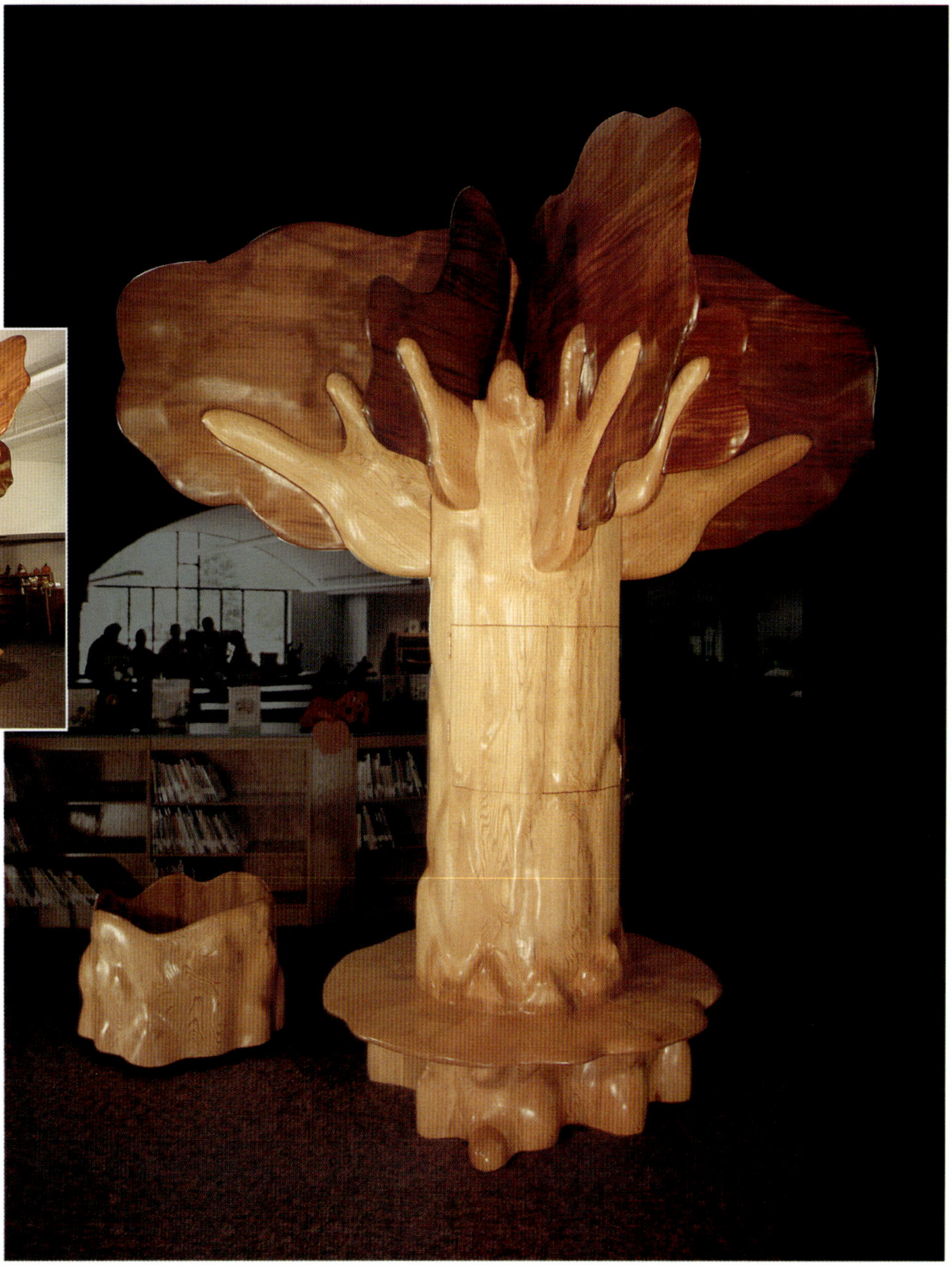

Randall Rosenthal

37 Fort Pond Boulevard
East Hampton, NY 11937
TEL 516-324-5618

Randall Rosenthal works primarily in wood, fabricating wall sculpture and architectural elements. His work is reductive, carved from a solid mass.

He has collaborated with architects on award-winning residential, corporate and liturgical projects, and shown in numerous gallery and museum exhibits.

Recent clients include:
Merck Pharmaceutical, Philadelphia, PA
St. James Cathedral, Seattle, WA
Gates of the Grove Synagogue,
  East Hampton, NY
Dearborn Construction, Huntington Beach, CA

Further information and brochure available upon request.

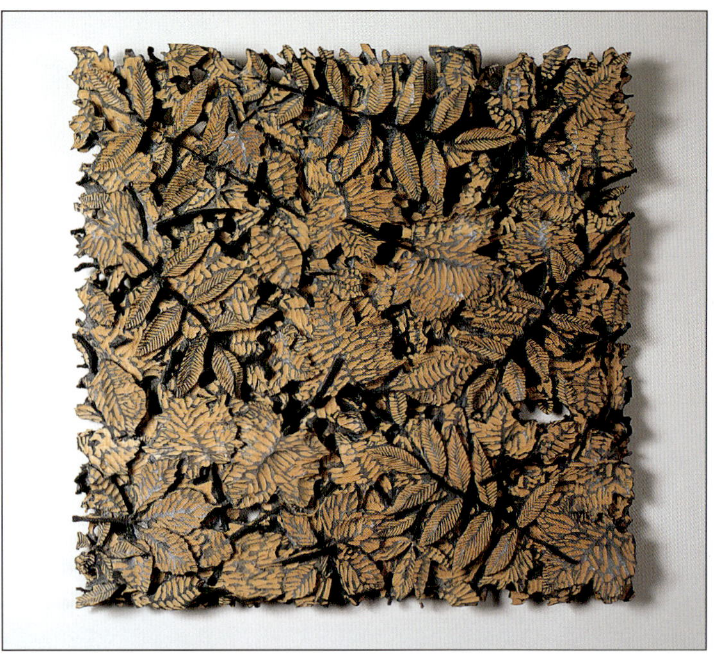

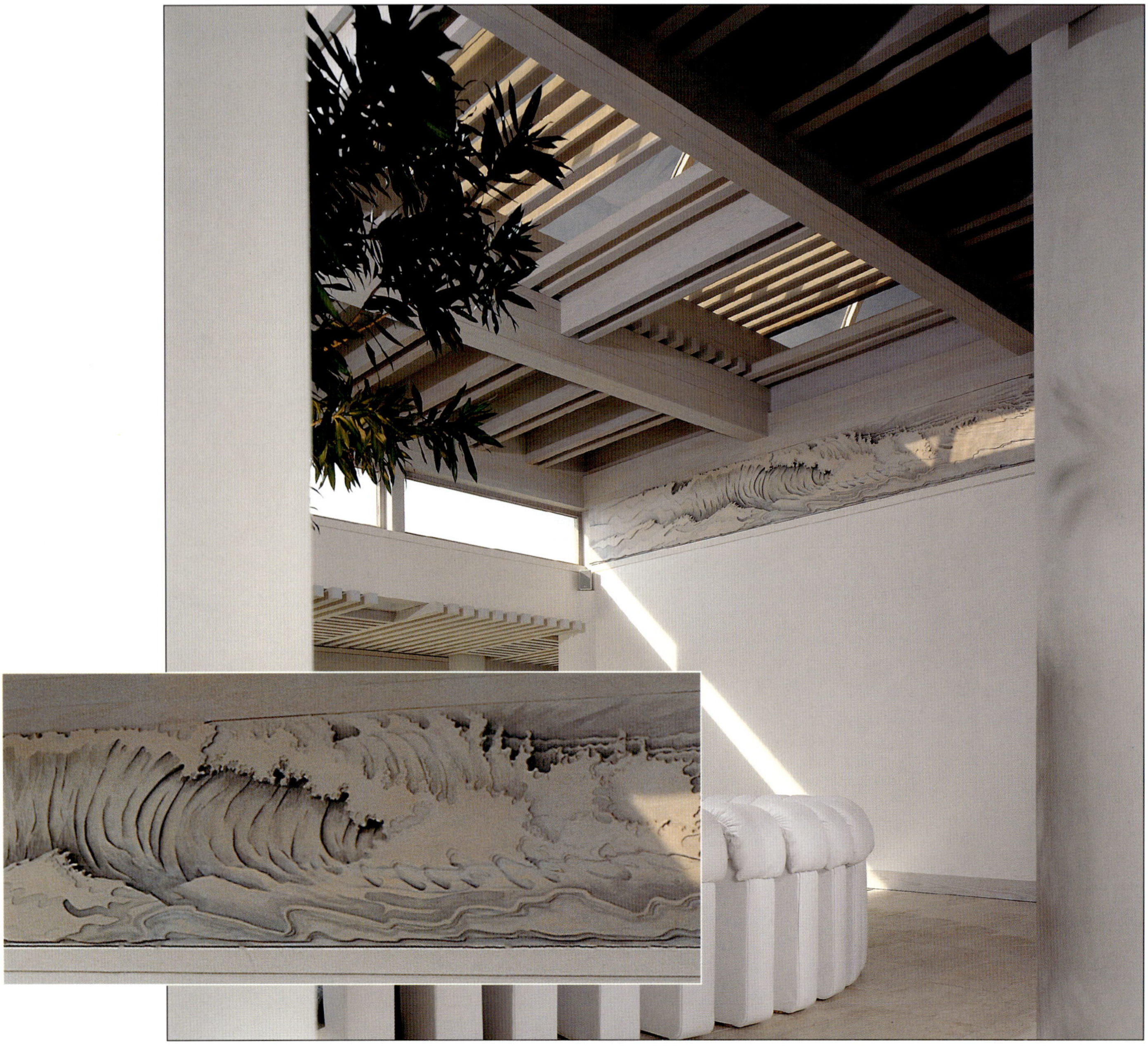

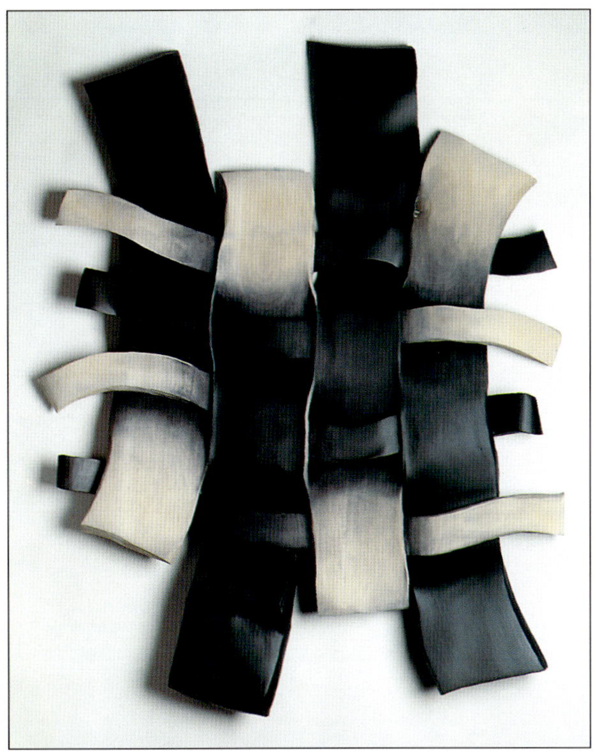

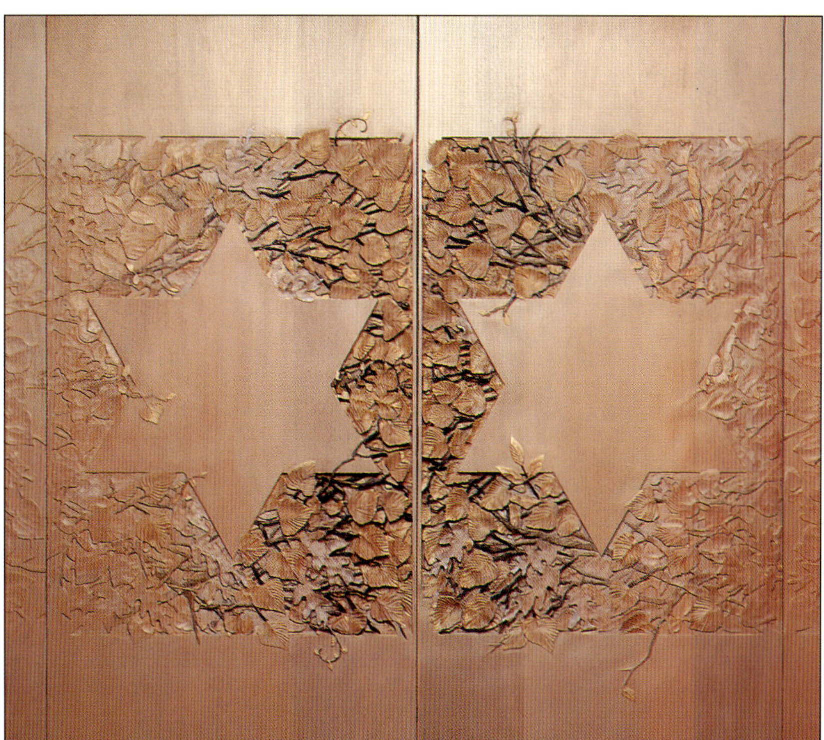

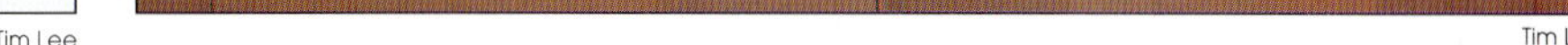

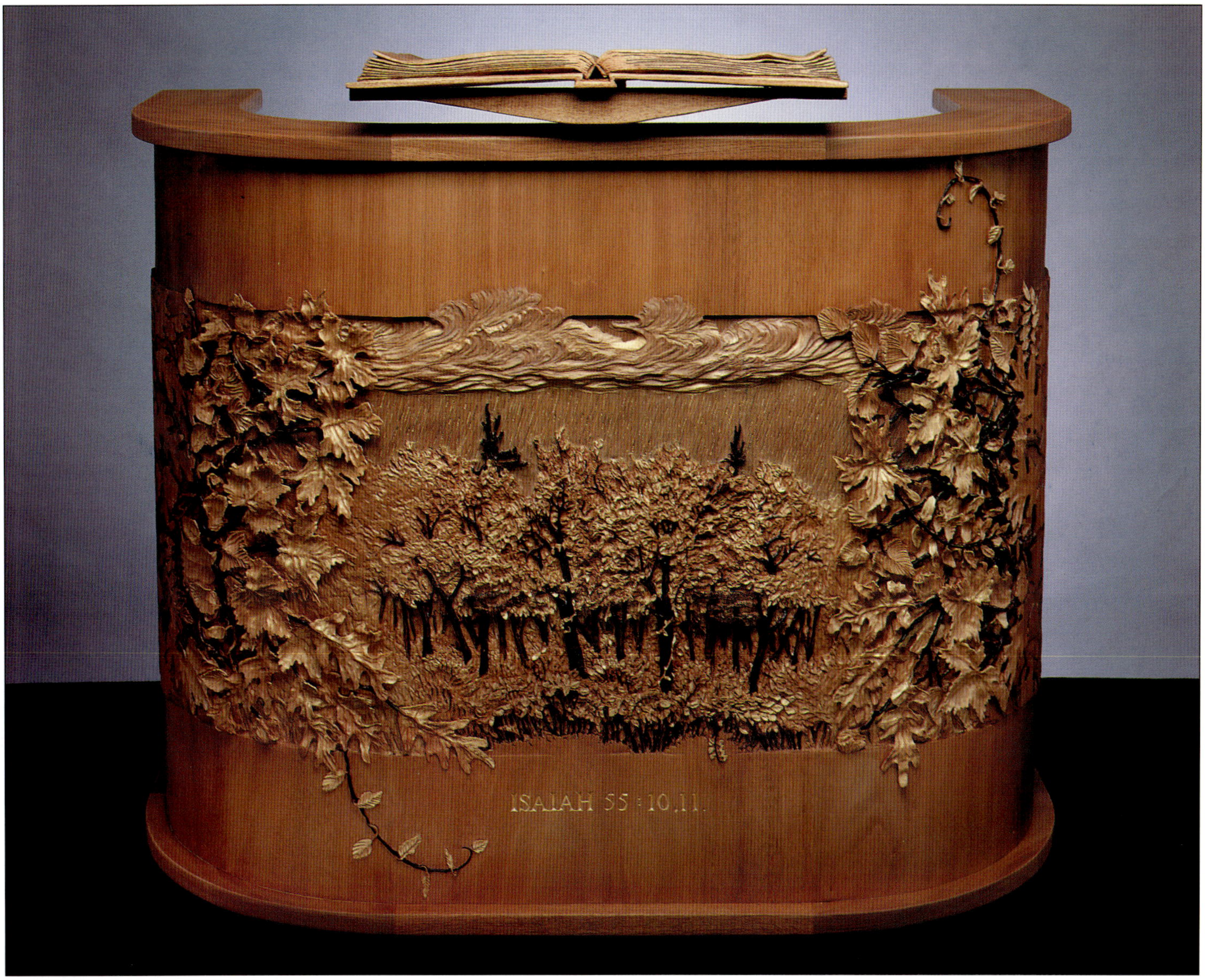

Randall Rosenthal, 37 Fort Pond Boulevard, East Hampton, NY 11937, 516-324-5618

Thomas D. Osborn

Mosaic Hardwood Floors
Thomas D. Osborn, Frances G. Welson
1421 Northampton Street
Holyoke, MA 01040
TEL 413-532-9034

Thomas D. Osborn specializes in the custom design, fabrication and installation of marquet and inlaid floors. Commissioned designs are developed in close collaboration with the architect, designer or client. Designs may be dramatic or subtle, accenting aesthetic and architectural features and complementing the shape and use of space.

The floors are a graceful and sensually elegant play of light and texture, form and color. By bringing out the natural beauty of the wood through a blend of traditional and modern flooring techniques, Osborn and Welson create a mosaic with the richness and vibrant warmth of a fine oriental carpet.

Full ¾-inch hardwood is used throughout. Extensive research has resulted in an increased palette of both native and sustainable-yield exotic woods; clients may choose from the natural color and luminous hues of over 80 species.

Brochure available upon request. Consultation early in the planning stages is highly recommended. Inquiries welcome.

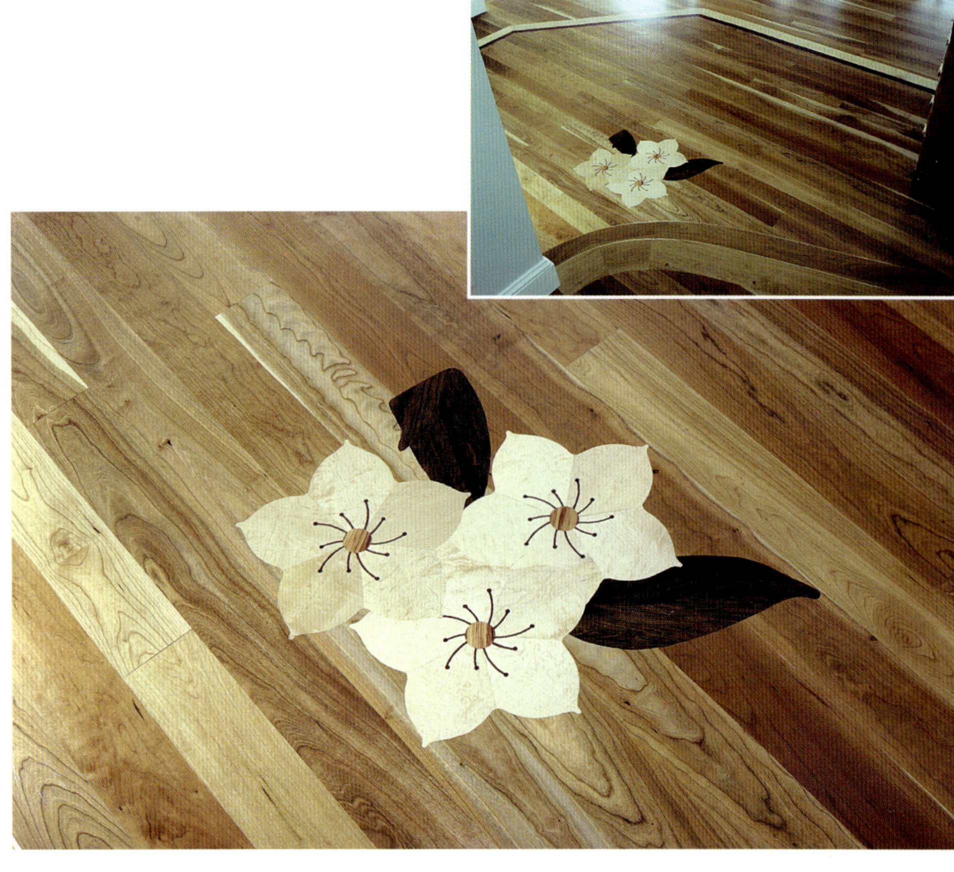

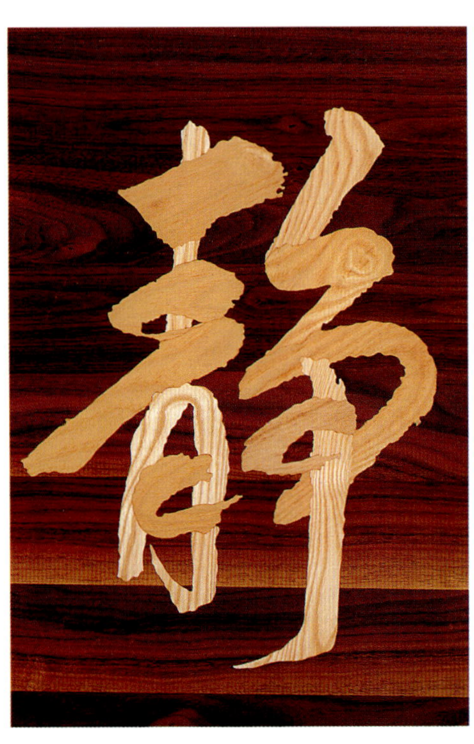

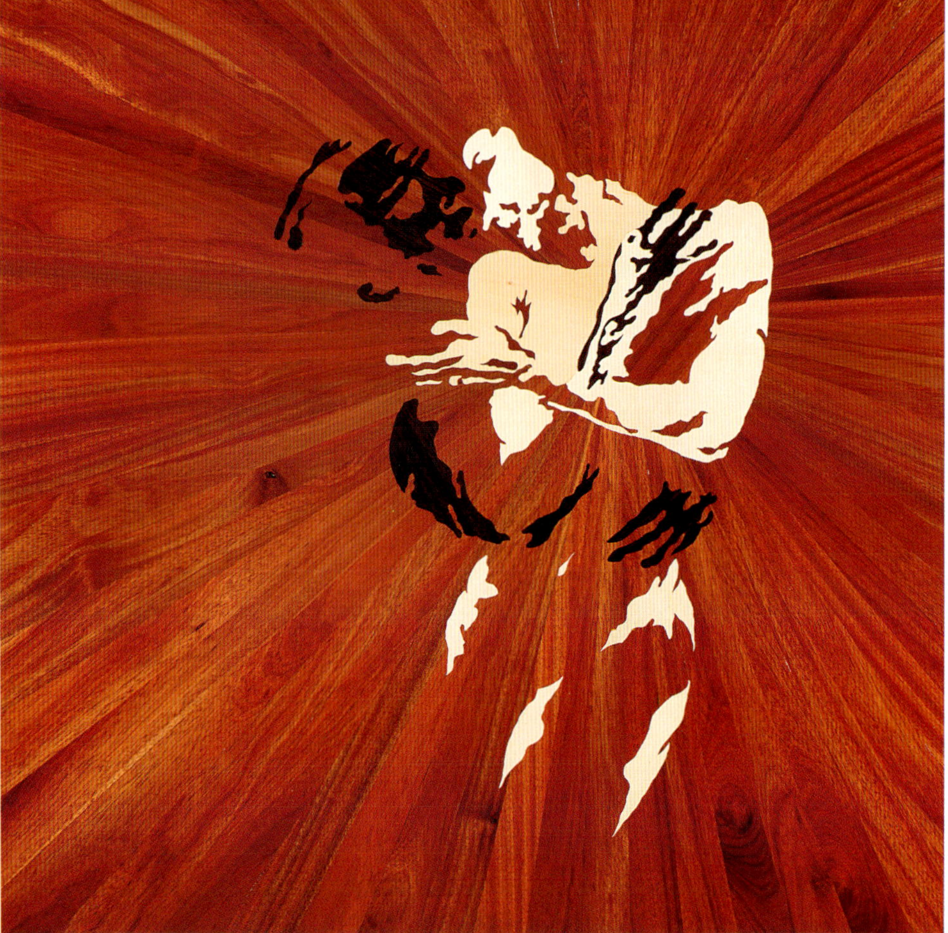

Woodfellows

Jean Wagner
8512 Fairway Place
Middleton, WI 53562
FAX 608-836-6514
TEL   608-831-9337

These projects demonstrate the diversity in design, detail in execution, and expertise in finishing as produced by Woodfellows. Whether working directly with a client, or through an architect or designer, Woodfellows' innovative approaches and value engineering continue to meet and exceed expectations.

Woodfellows' success comes from personal attention in delivering premium products and specialized services.

Also see these GUILD publications:
Architect's Edition: 8
Designer's Edition: 7

A Reception desk, cherry and marble, designed
by Woodfellows

B & C Altar furniture and architectural millwork for
sanctuary, designed by Ross Potter

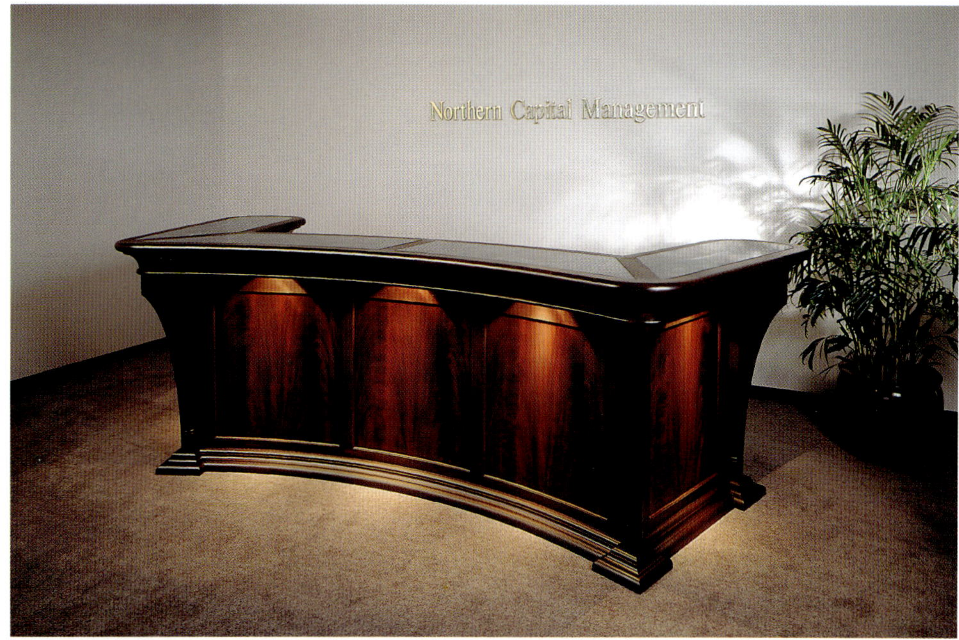

A

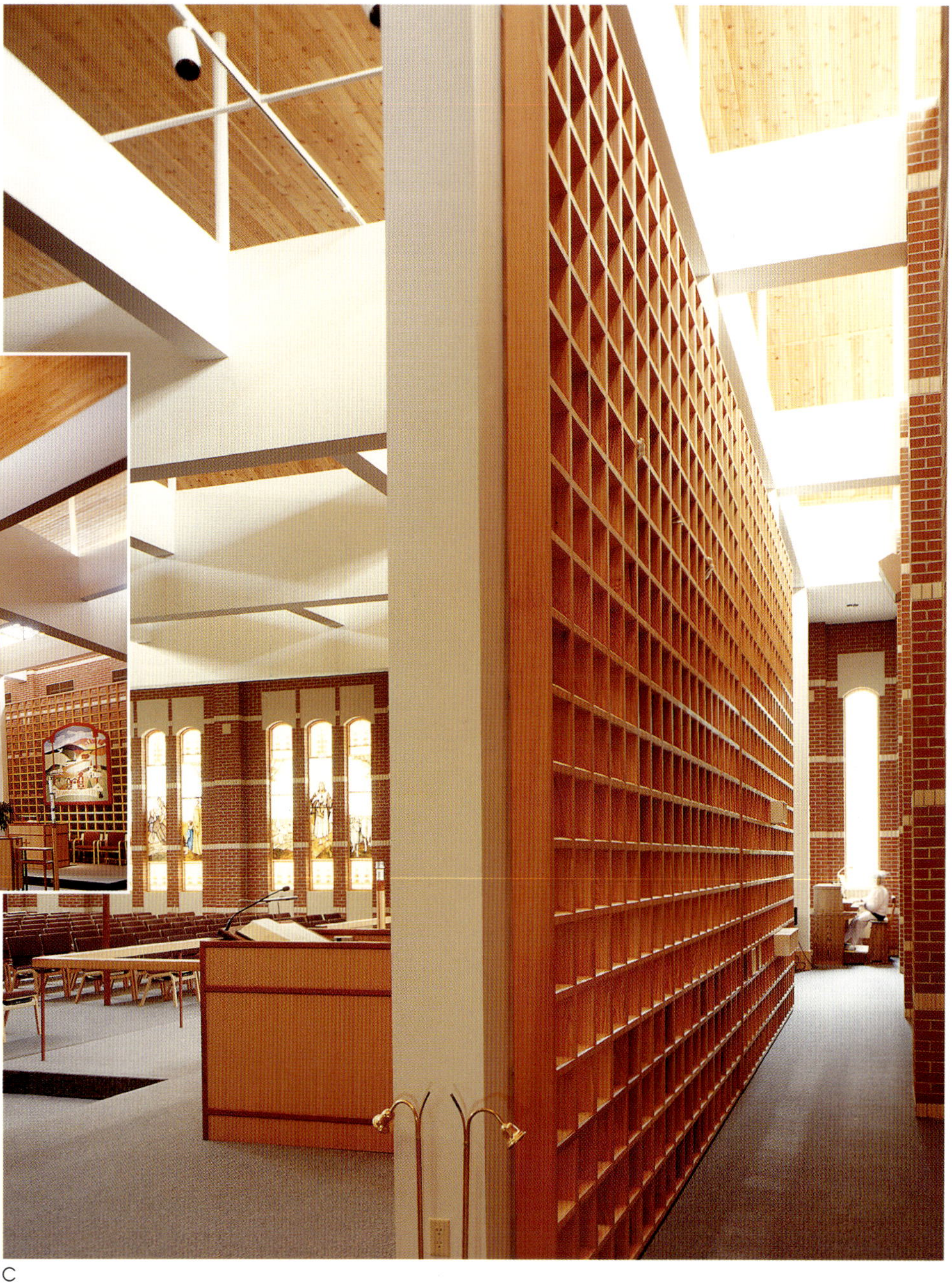

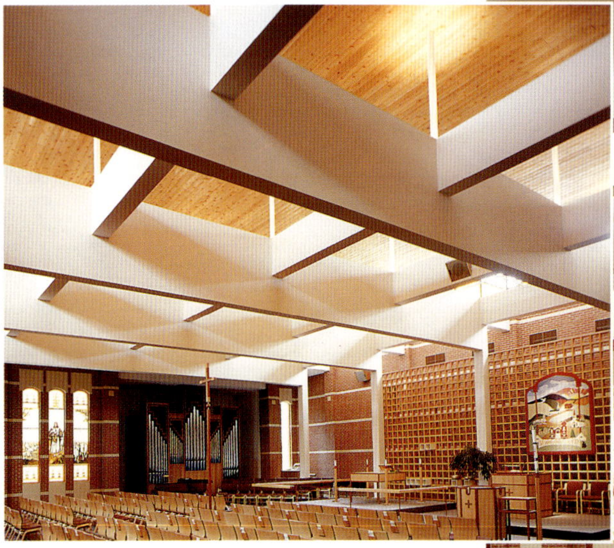

B

C

ARCHITECTURAL ELEMENTS AND RESTORATION

art i fax

Robert D. Fallon
Pfeiffer Ridge #9
Big Sur, CA 93920
FAX 408-667-2908
TEL   408-667-2754
E-Mail: BIGSUR BOB@aol.com

WELDED STEEL
STAINLESS STEEL
ENAMELED STEEL
GLASS
NEON
ALUMINUM

Custom Furniture and Fixtures
Architectural Panels
Low-Relief Sculpture
Residential and Commercial

Metals are available in a variety of finishes, natural and enameled. Vitreous enamels are naturally weather and graffiti resistant. Enameled pieces from ancient Egypt and Rome are as bright and colorful today as when they were made.

Drawing inspiration from … nature as the Creator intended it to be,' the studio makes things that glow, using diverse talents to shape plain and polychrome metals, and light colored by glass.

Also see this GUILD publication:
Architect's Edition: 10

A Store fixtures, 1994, Streetlight Records, upper Market Street, San Francisco

B Neon table, 1995, private residence

C Desk, 1995, private residence

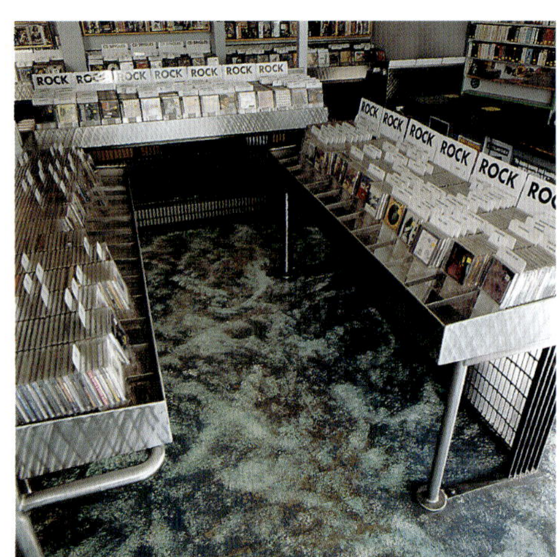

A

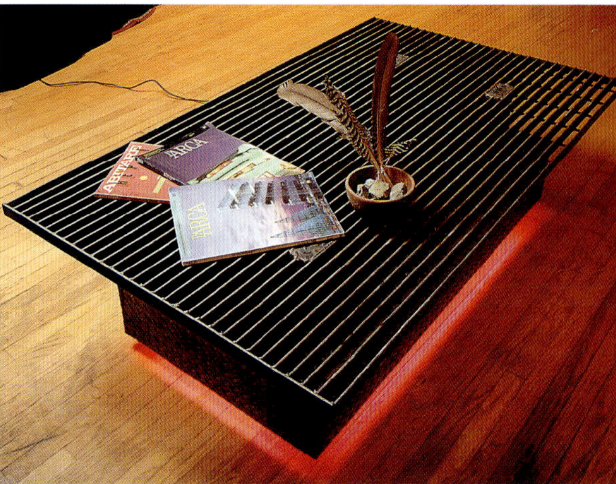

B

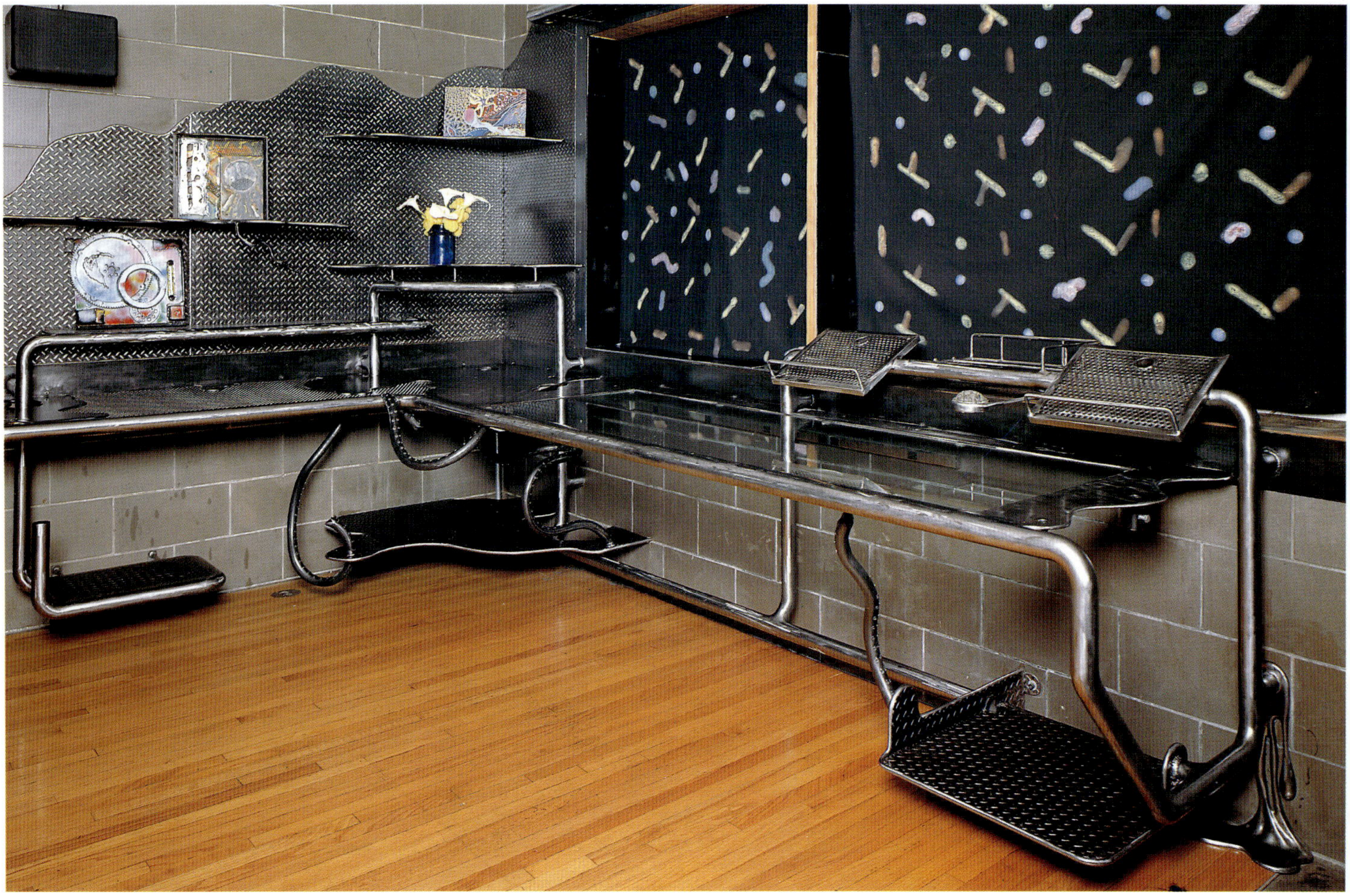

C

Pamela Joseph

MA Nose Studios
407 Aspen Oak Drive
Aspen, CO 81611
FAX 970-920-2242
TEL 970-920-4098
TEL 970-920-6820 (Studio)

For 20 years, Pamela Joseph focused on Public Art projects. Her current work is focused in the studio and on collaborating with other artists.

The contoured cabinets are the product of working with industrial designer Susan Farricielli. Pamela sketched the view from her kitchen of Independence Pass. Using rolls of carbon fiber and epoxy resin, they created an artwork that is impervious, lightweight and functional.

The staircase was created with computer artist Kurosh ValaNejad. Because of the interactive nature of this medium, many variations were tested before construction. The bent lamination support is made of oak, as are the treds and floor inlays. Cherry and walnut woods are alternated to give the impression of ever-descending space.

Both projects were created in Joseph's workshop and studio.

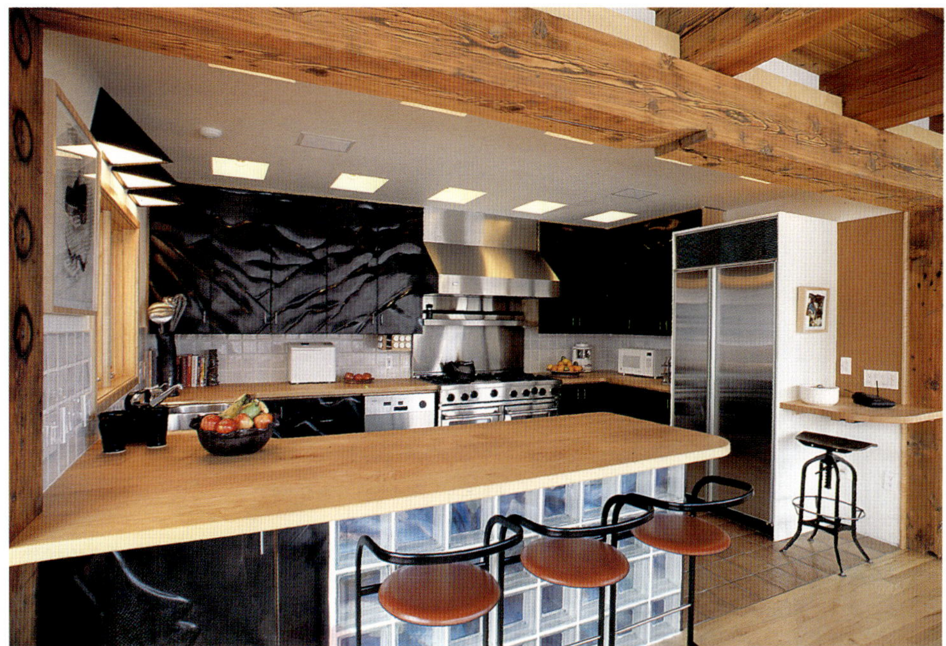

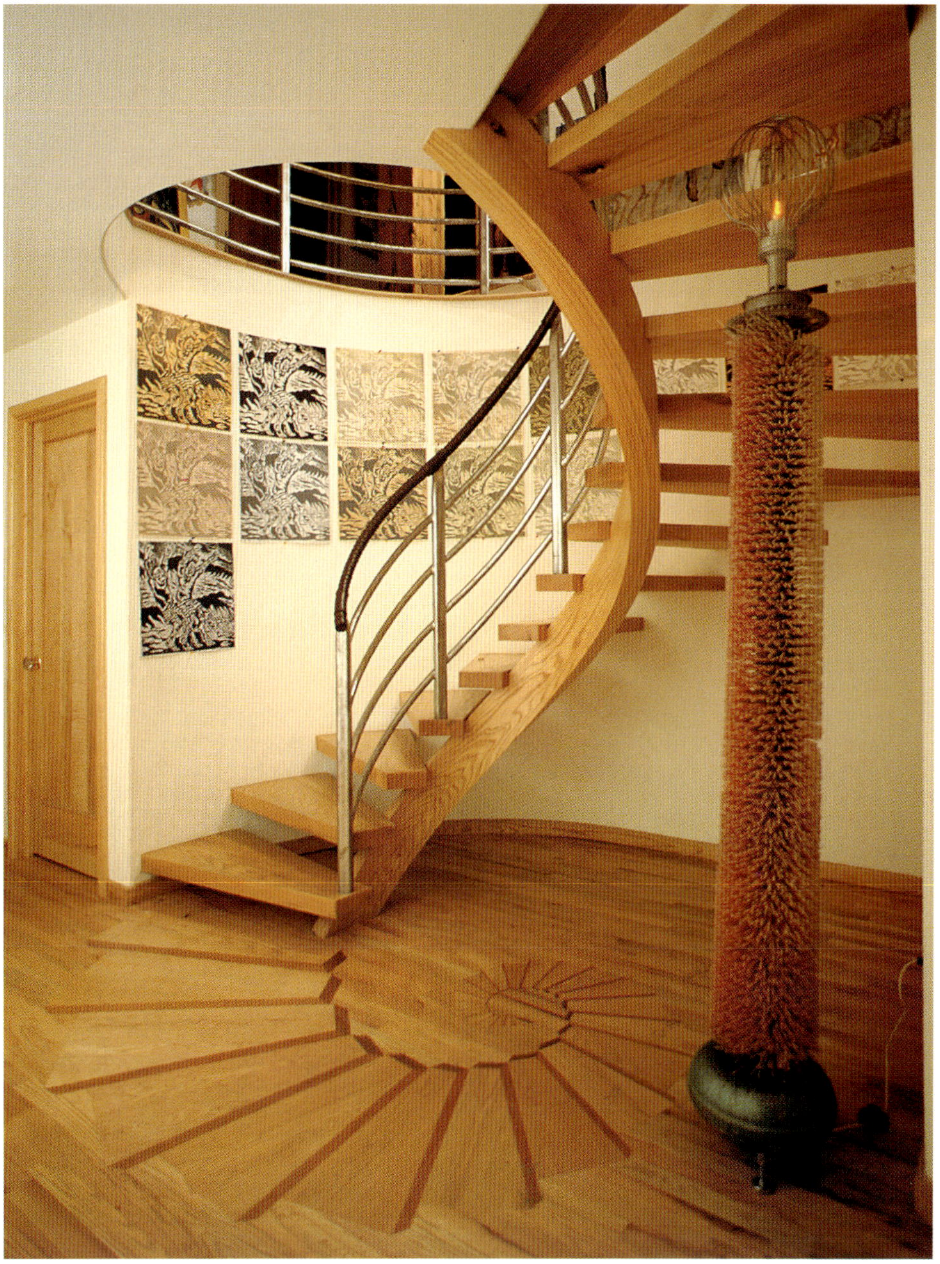

Ellen Miret-Jayson

25 Deer Trail
Ramsey, NJ 07446
FAX 201-934-0136 (call first)
TEL   201-934-0136
E-Mail: elmj@aol.com

Ellen Miret-Jayson specializes in architectural glass and sculptural furnishings. She works closely with clients from project conception to the final installation. Specializing in (but not limited to) ecclesiastical art, her work can be seen throughout the country.

Commissions include:
Iona College, New Rochelle, NY
Temple Emanuel, Cherry Hill, NJ
U.S. Naval Base, Reykjavik, Iceland
Ferncliff Mausoleum, Hartsdale, NY
Temple Beth-Orr, Coral Springs, FL
St. Charles Borromeo, Arlington, VA
St. Mary's Church, Portland, CT
Christ Church, Bronxville, NY
Beth El Zedeck, Indianapolis, IN
St. Joan of Arc, Toledo, OH
St. Mary's Church, Richmond Tnsp, PA

A Lamberts Glass Factory, Waldsassen, Germany

B Ner Tamid, copper, gold leaf, Temple Beth Israel, Euchland, PA

C Bima, Temple Beth Israel

D Arc (detail), copper, dichroic glass, Temple Beth Israel

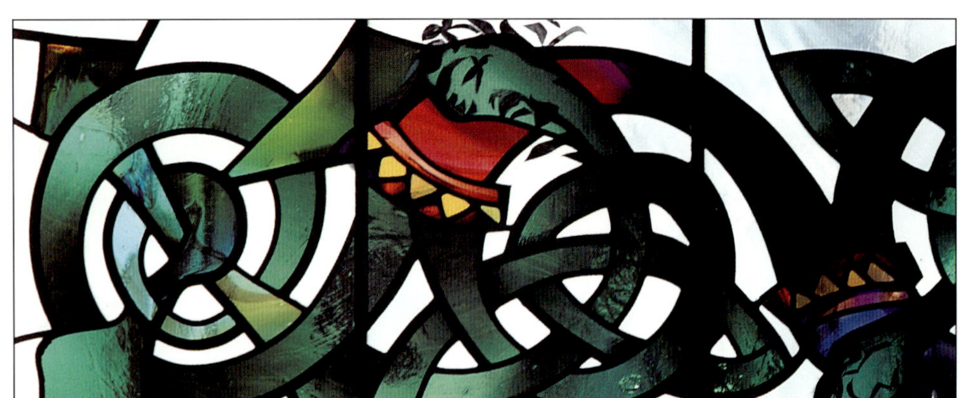

A

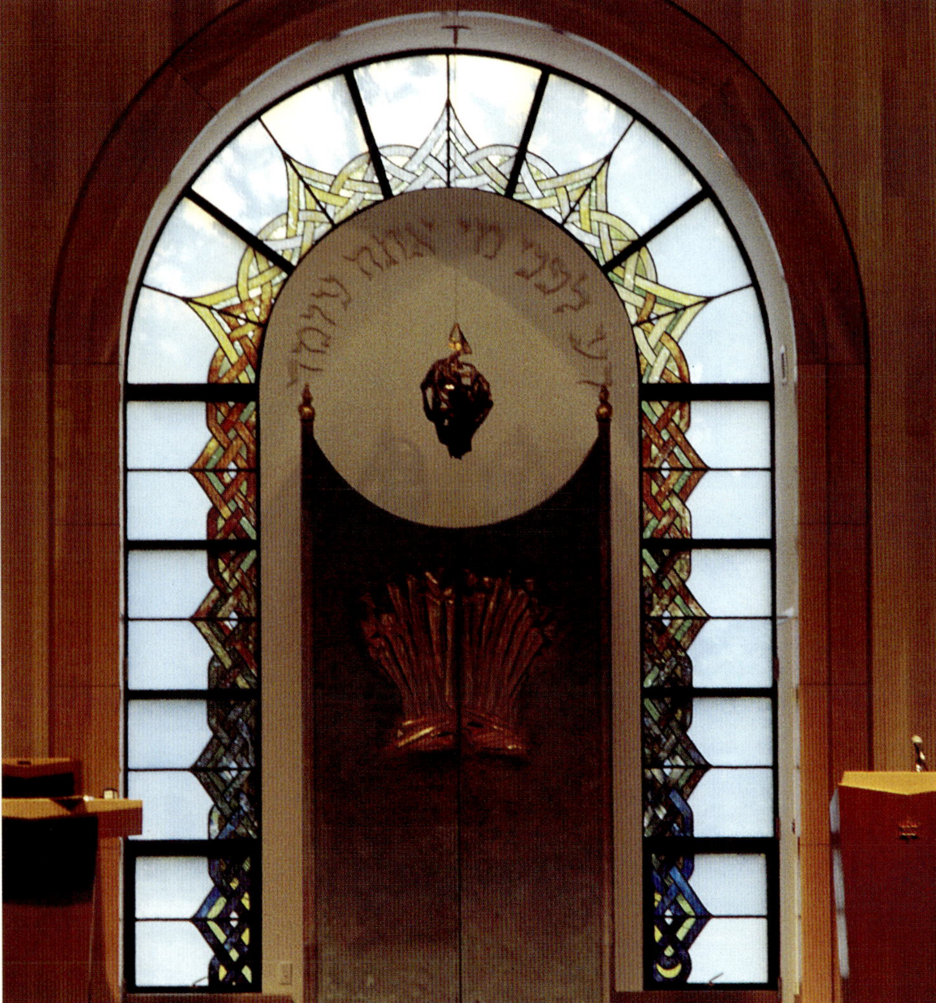

C

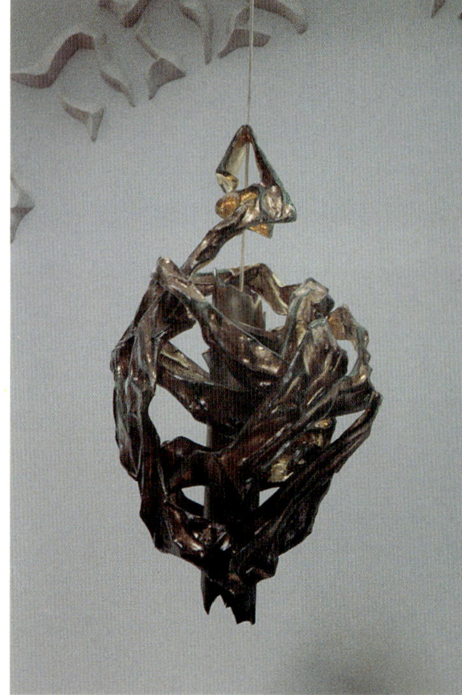

B

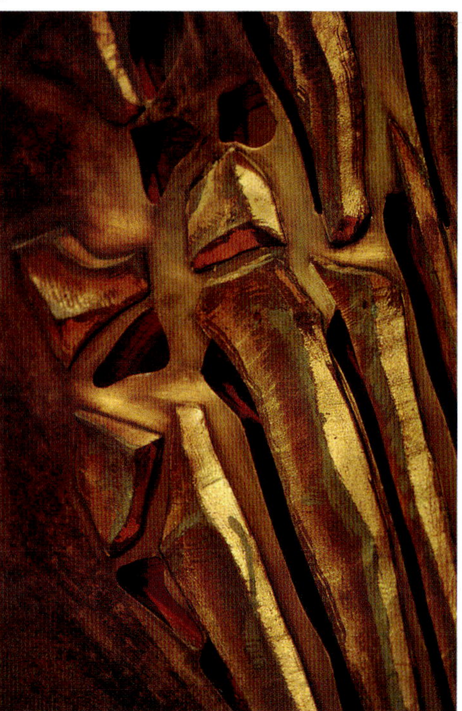

D

Louise Pezzi

L. Pezzi, Blacksmith
PO Box 40163
Philadelphia, PA 19106
FAX 215-336-4422
TEL 215-336-6023

The great malleability of hot forged iron remains a continuing source of inspiration for Louise Pezzi. A professional malleability has likewise inspired fruitful collaborations with architects and designers for nearly a decade.

Pezzi enjoys the engagement of distinctive custom projects and is sensitive to a full range of historical styles. Her acute attention to finishing detail has developed a specialization in hardware and interior pieces.

A Door handle, 1990, Di Nardo's Restaurant, Philadelphia, PA, iron and bronze, 22" x 15"

B Door handle, 1993, Jake's Restaurant, Philadelphia, PA, forged iron, 20"L

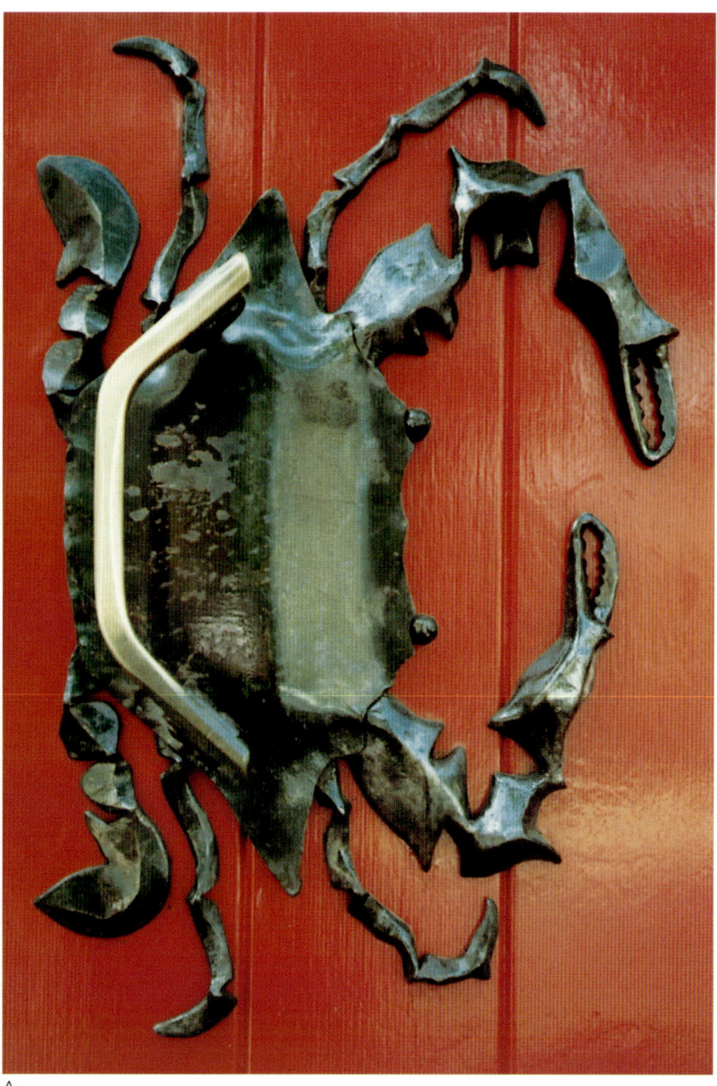

A

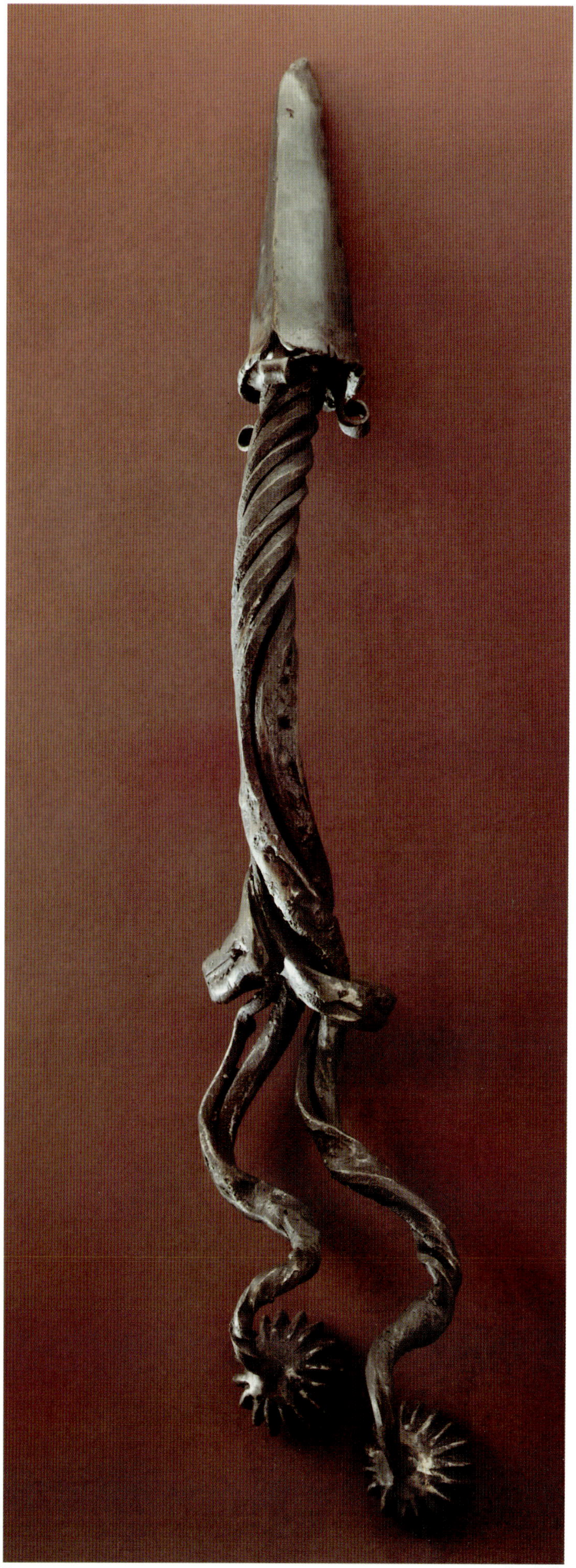

B

Barry Halkin

Robert W. Boucher
& Associates
Concrete Designs Inc.

Robert Boucher
10906 E. Hereford Road
Hereford, AZ 85615
FAX 520-366-0406
TEL 520-366-5769
TEL 800-279-2278

Robert Boucher & Associates offers custom design and sculpting services ranging from large architectural facades to architectonic furniture and murals in cast stone, GFRC and glazed terracotta.

The studio is committed to signature-quality work, and is not bound to one stylistic vocabulary. Commissions have ranged from original designs to collaborations with architects and interior designers for state agencies, private residences, churches and commerical projects, as well as award-winning commisssions for historic preservation.

Portfolio available upon request.

Also see these GUILD publications:
Architect's Edition: 8, 10

A & B Column capitals, Penninsula Hotel,
   Hong Kong, GFRC, architect: Rocco Design,
   designer: Orlando Diaz-Azcuy

C Clay patterns in studio prior to moldmaking

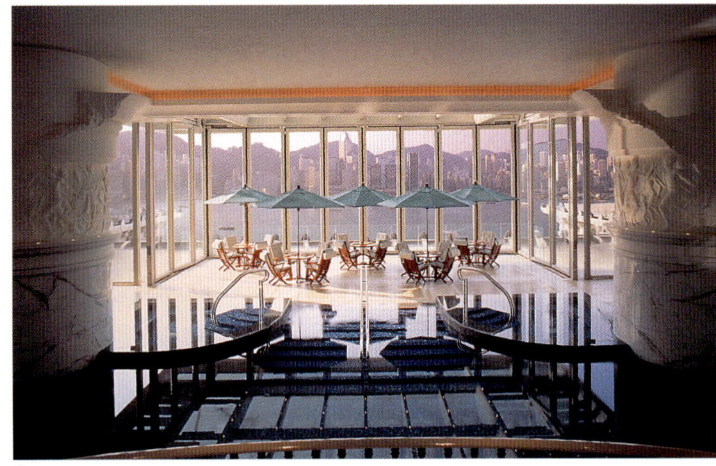

A

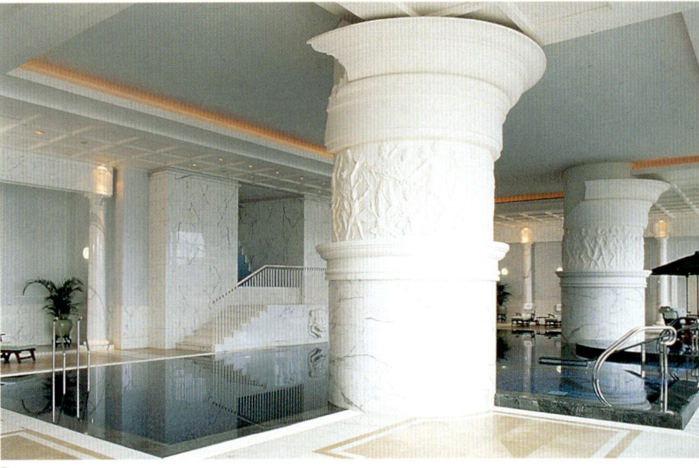

B

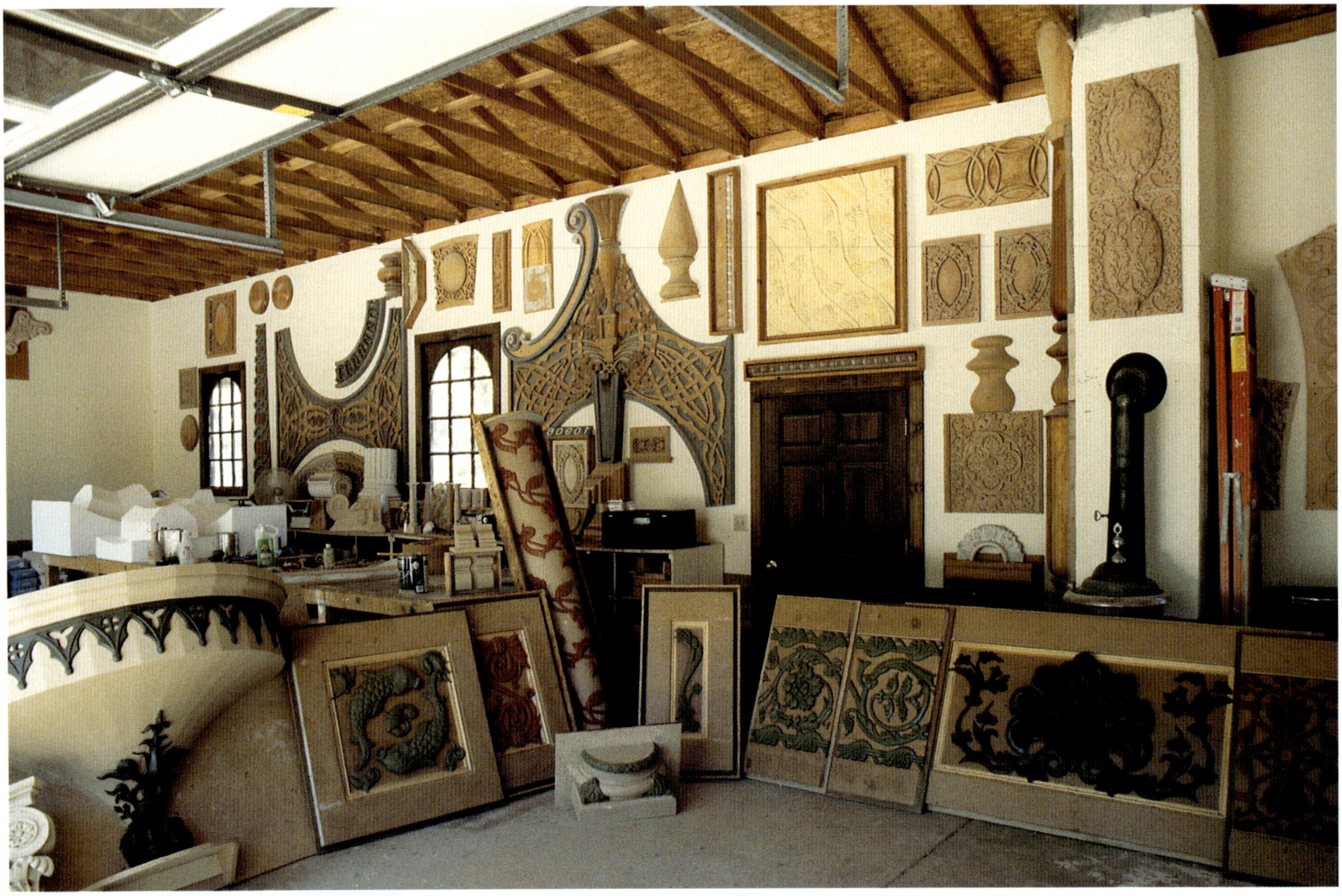

C

Frederic Jean Zimmer

Art de France Inc.
515 B. Kuwili Street
Honolulu, HI 96817
FAX 808-533-0623
TEL 808-523-7761

With a degree in art from Ecole des Beaux Art in Strasbourg, France, Frederic Zimmer has specialized in hand-carved, museum-quality portals, murals, sculptures and furniture. He works in copper, bronze, iron, stainless steel, aluminum, glass and stone, the first in the Islands to perform this particular type of work.

His work is recognized across the U.S., most notably in the Hawaiian Islands. Examples are also in France and in Saudi Arabia, where the artist's work can be seen gracing commercial buildings, resorts, luxury homes and palaces.

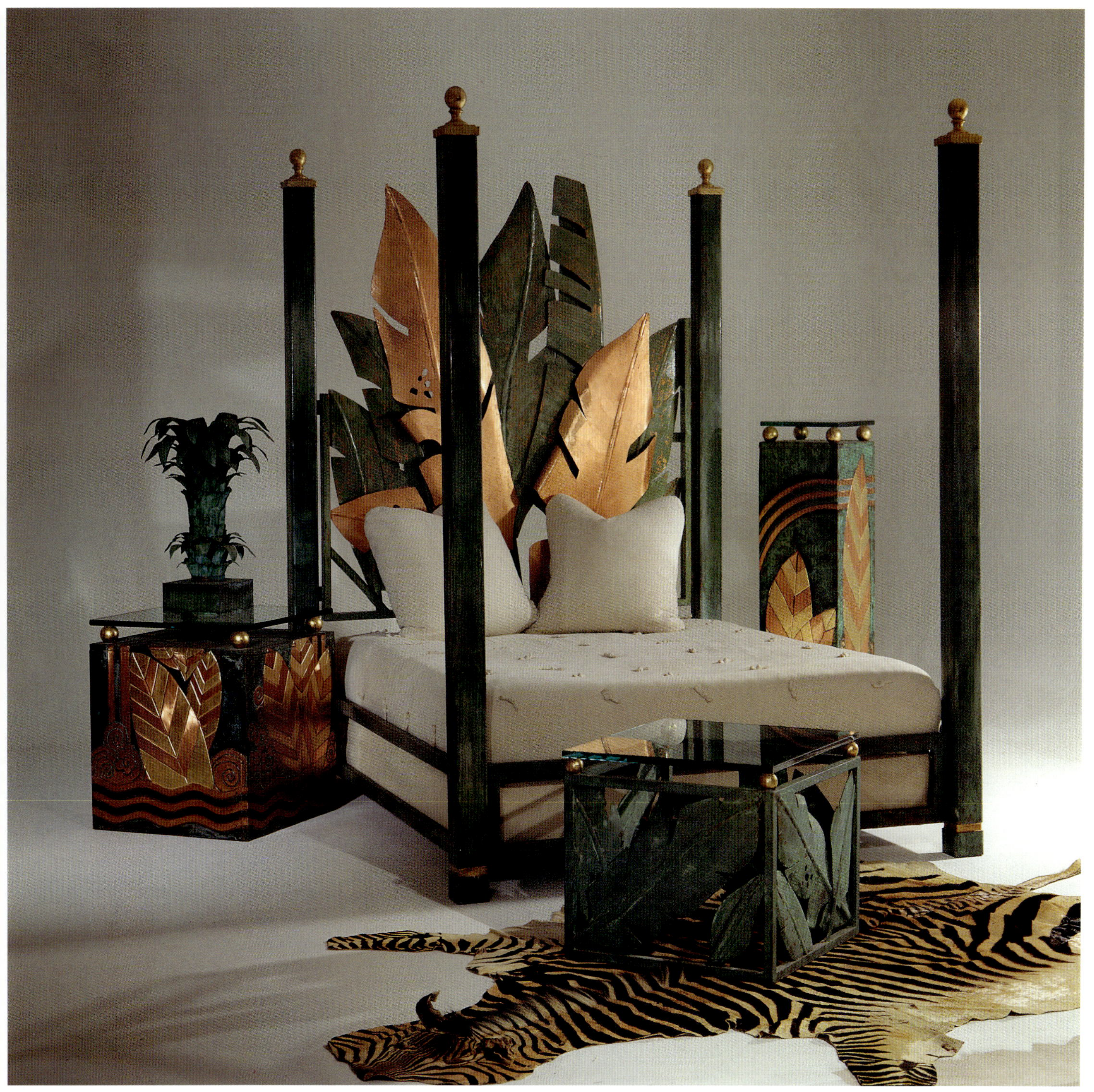

Conrad Schmitt Studios, Inc.

2405 S. 162nd Street
New Berlin, WI 53151
FAX 414-786-9036
TEL 414-786-3030
TEL 800-969-3033

Since 1889, the Conrad Schmitt Studios, Inc. has restored and decorated hundreds of interiors across the country. Their scope of work includes the investigation and documentation of original decorative schemes, the restoration of those schemes through the application of various decorating techniques including gilding, glazing, marbleizing, stencilling, trompe l'oeil painting, graining, as well as the conservation, restoration and replication of murals and stained glass.

Clients include:
The Hawaii Theatre, Honolulu, HI
Cathedral of the Assumption, Louisville, KY
The Wang Center for the Performing Arts,
  Boston, MA
Union Station, St. Louis, MO
The Waldorf-Astoria Hotel, New York, NY
The White House Visitor's Center,
  Washington, DC

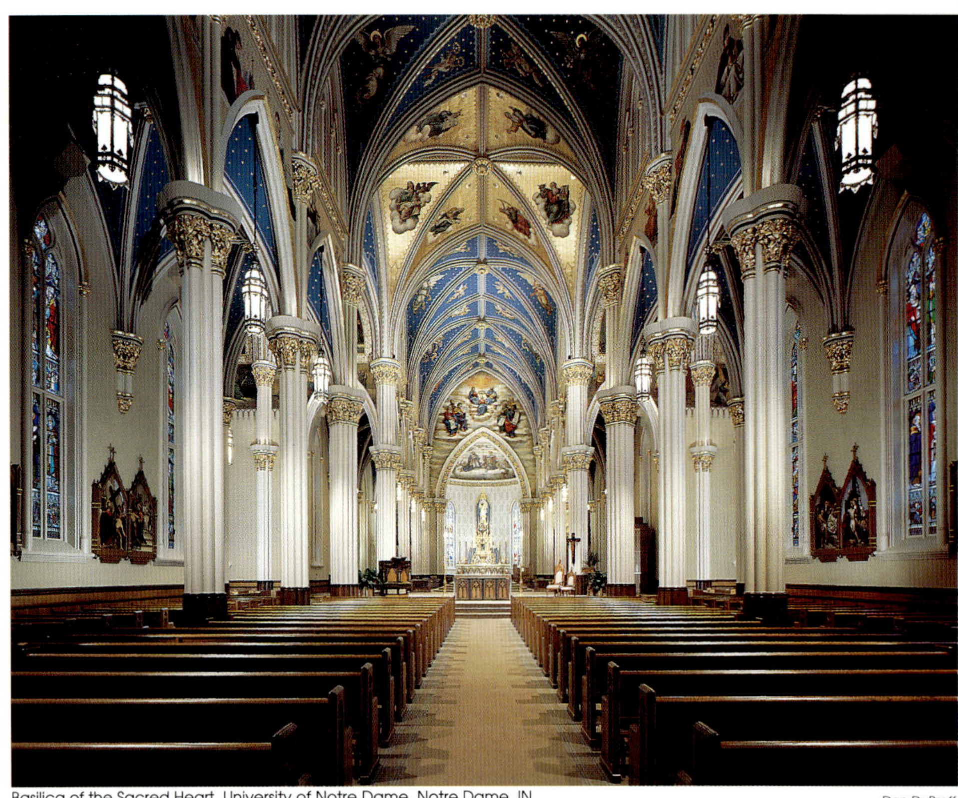

Basilica of the Sacred Heart, University of Notre Dame, Notre Dame, IN

Don DuBroff

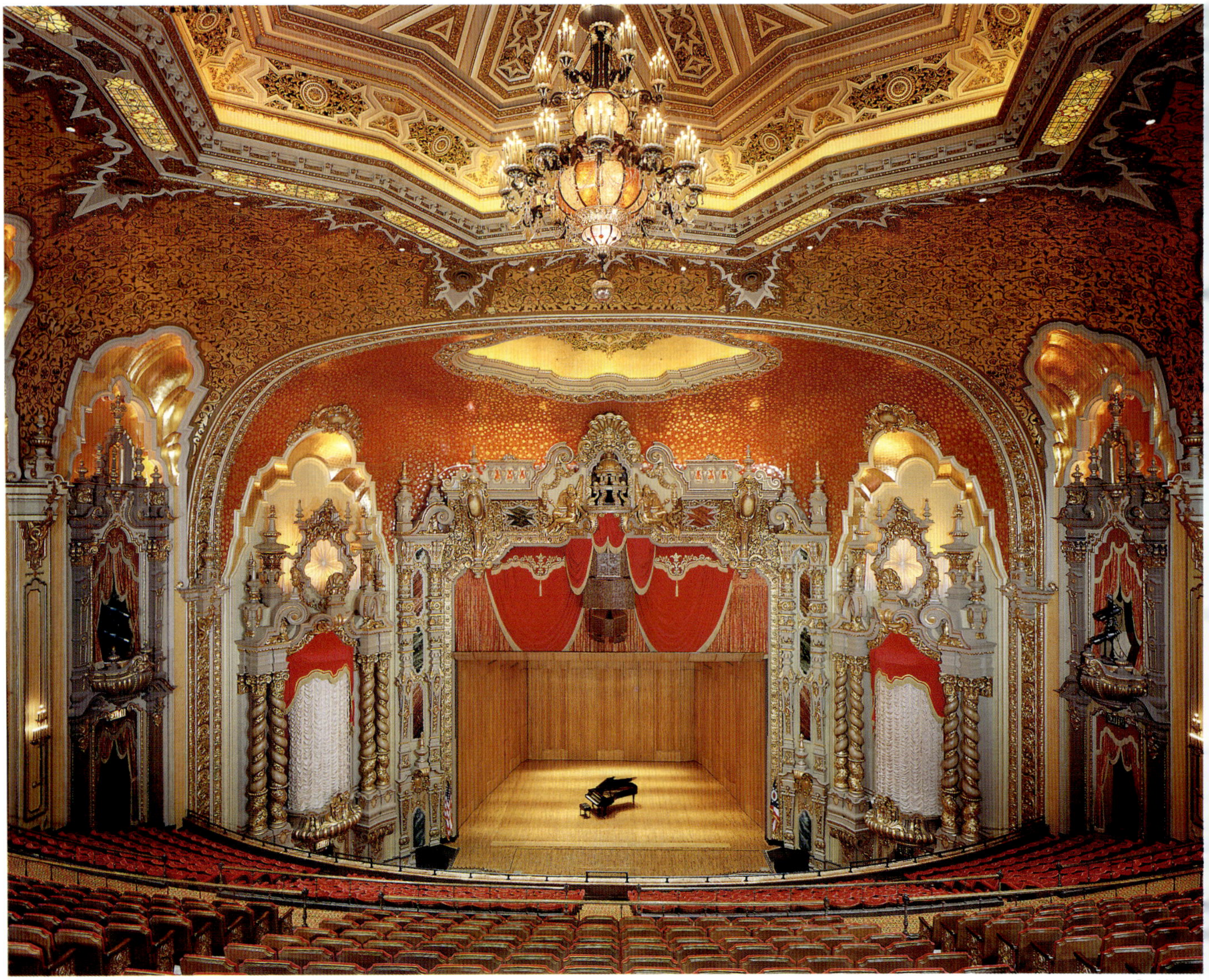

Ohio Theatre, Columbus, OH

David Lamb

International Fine Art Conservation Studios, Inc.

Geoffrey M. Steward
PO Box 180098
Atlanta, GA 30318
FAX 404-794-6229
TEL   404-794-6142

IFACS undertakes all aspects of conservation and restoration of easel paintings, murals, frescoes, ornamental plasterwork, interior and exterior decorative painting, and the execution of modern interior designs. They can provide surveys, scientific and technical analysis, and budget costs for conservation or restoration projects, and are happy to prepare estimates and time schedules.

Clients include the state capitols of Ohio, Pennsylvania, Alabama and Tennessee; Biltmore House, NC; Flagler College, FL; Georgia Trust for Historic Preservation; and in London, England: Buckingham and Kensington palaces; the House of Parliament; and The Foreign Office.

Recipient of Award for Excellence in Design by the Art Commission of the City of New York, January 1995.

A Old library ceiling, Tennessee State Capitol

B Foreign Office, London, England

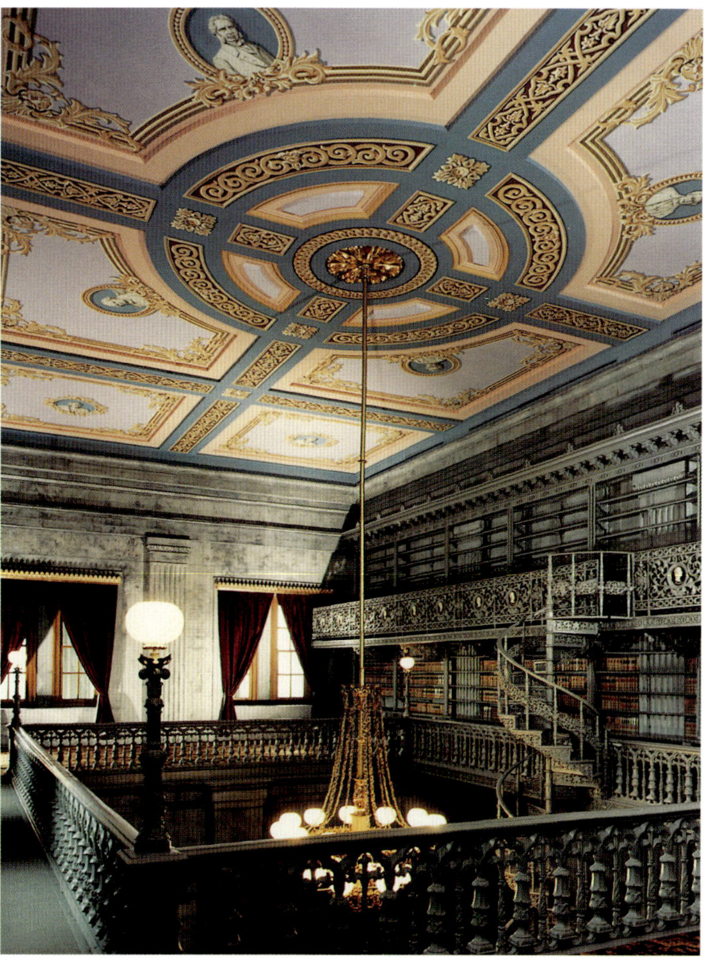

A

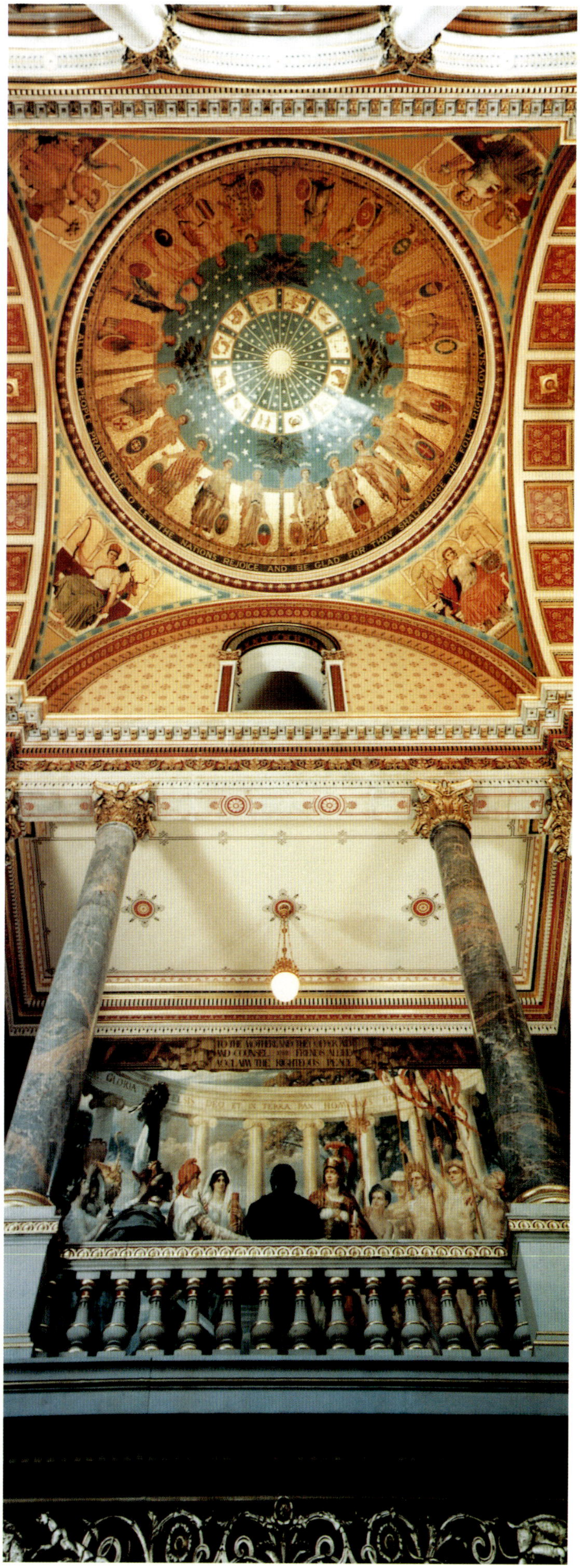

B

MURALS AND TROMPE L'OEIL

Otto de Souza Aguiar

901 Cypress Grove Drive, Suite 201
Pompano Beach, FL 33069
FAX 954-969-5072
TEL 954-973-5620

Otto Aguiar has successfully combined his vast fashion and theatrical background with the charm and romance of his native Brazil to create paintings and murals characterized by the portrayal of elegance and grace. With its sumptuous color, texture and gilding, his work is a dramatic embellishment for residences, institutions and corporate settings on several continents.

The artist delights in commissions and collaborations to achieve the ultimate work of art for every environment and specification.

Inquires are welcome.

Clients include the City Hall of Miami Beach; Graycliff Inn "Relais and Chateaux," Nassau, Bahamas; Florida State Legislature; Fedora Restaurants, Kansas City, MO, and Washington, DC; American White Cross, New Rochelle, NY.

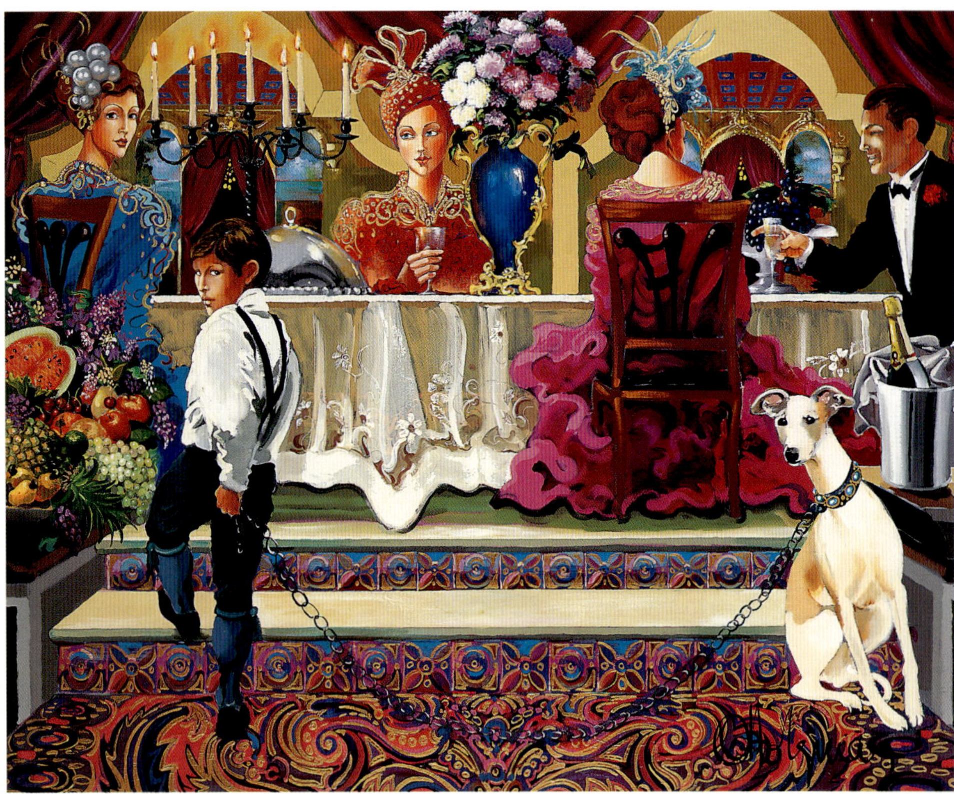

L'Art de Vivre, 1993, acrylic on canvas, 66" x 84"

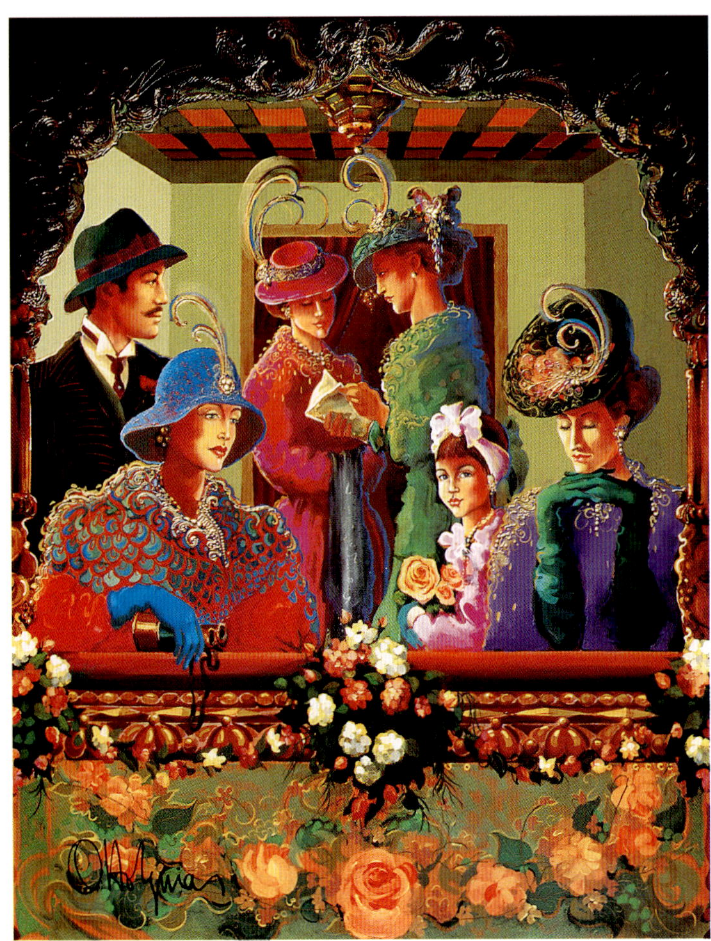

Teatro Amazonas, 1994, acrylic on canvas, 84" x 66"

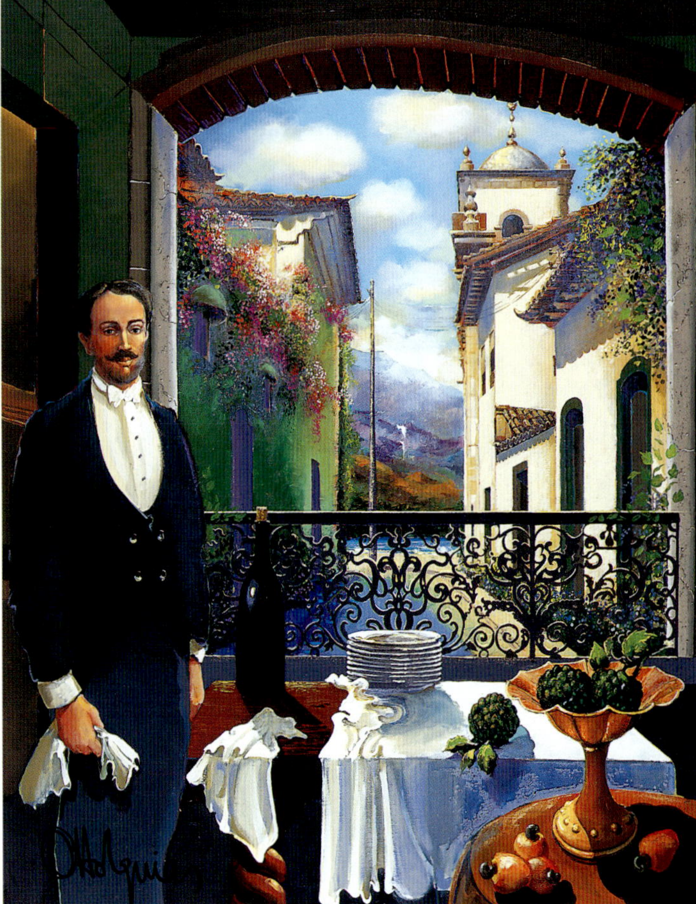

Parati, 1995, acrylic on canvas, 64" x 52"

Albert Michaels Gallery

William W. Tull, General Manager
1116 North 3rd Street
Harrisburg, PA 17102
FAX 717-234-0311
TEL 717-232-9592

Environments: murals and decorative painting.

Focal points: mural designs accenting without overpowering your space.

Integration: complete interior and exterior designs merge artwork and decorative treatment or meld with existing environment.

Permanence: artists and craftsmen with backgrounds in art and architectural conservation using traditional and time-tested techniques and materials. Interiors: oils on canvas painted *in situ*. Exteriors: acrylics for durability, final coating UV stabilizing varnish for ultimate protection in harsh environments.

Clients include:
Department of General Services, Harrisburg, PA
Capitol Preservation Committee, State Capital
  Building, Harrisburg, PA
Black Mansion, Hammonton, NJ
Immaculate Conception Church, Johnstown, PA
Indiana University of Pennsylvania, Indiana, PA

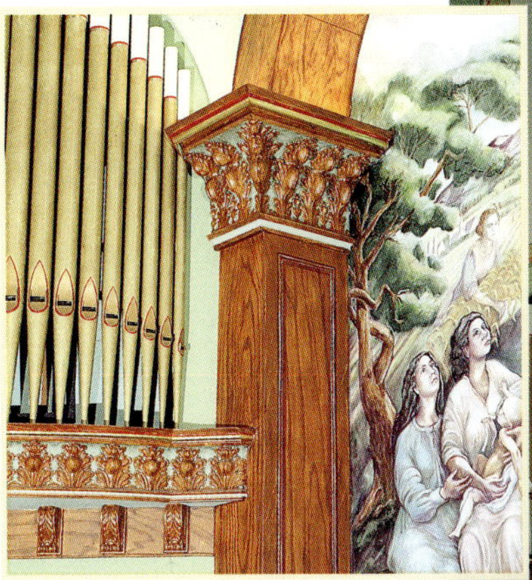

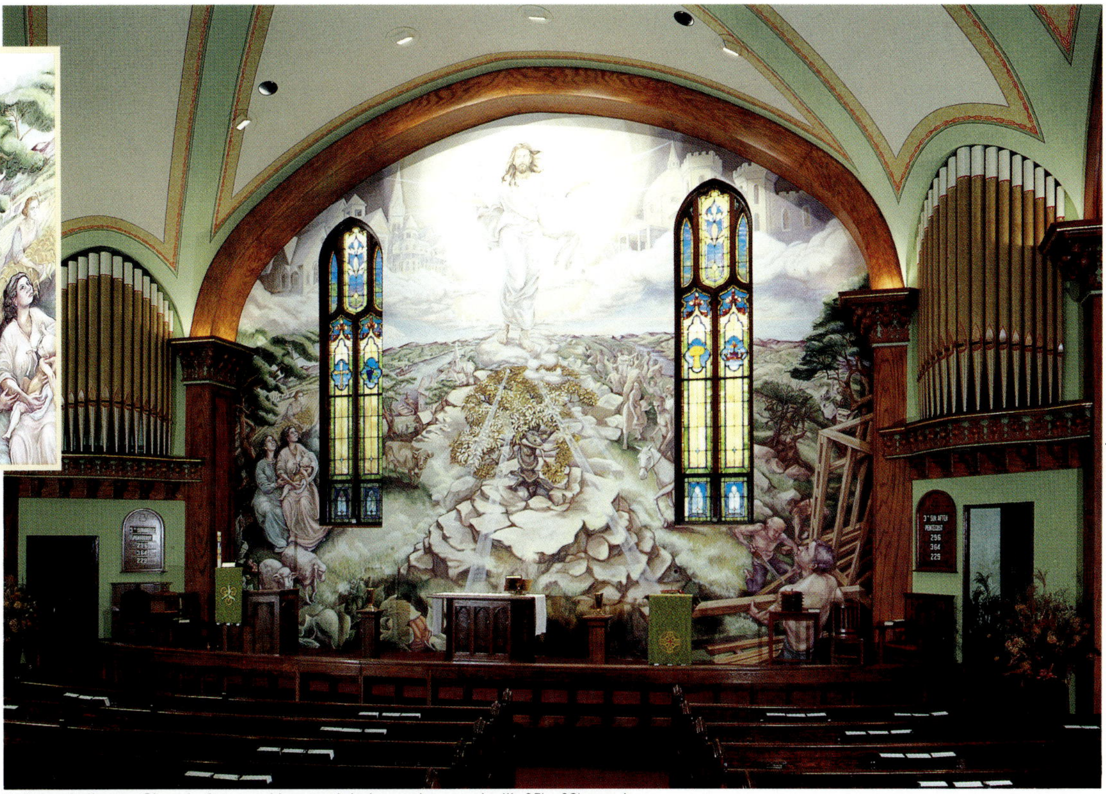

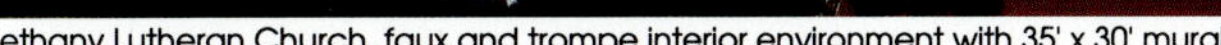

Bethany Lutheran Church, faux and trompe interior environment with 35' x 30' mural

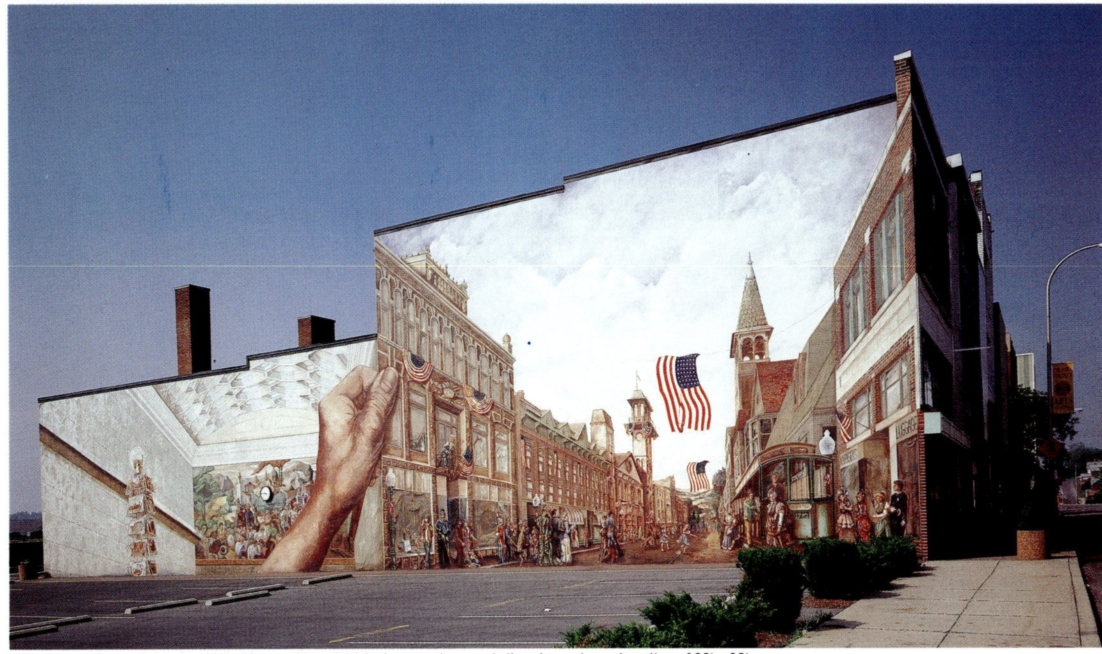

Altoona … Something to Write Home About, historic mural completing facade restoration, 120' x 30'

Andrea M. Biggs
Timothy G. Biggs

279 Sterling Place
Brooklyn, NY 11238
FAX 718-857-4018
TEL 718-857-9034

Andrea and Timothy Biggs are muralists collaborating to produce site-specific, custom works of art for residential and commercial sites. Painting can be done either on location or in their studio, on canvas, ready for shipping and installation at the site.

Andrea Biggs holds an M.F.A. degree from Bard College, and Timothy studied architectural design and painting at Parsons School of Design. The Biggses have been commissioned to paint murals and specialized finishes for apartment and hotel lobbies, restaurants in New York and Asia, fashion showrooms, and many private residences. Their clients range from architects and interior designers to home owners and connoisseurs.

Also see these GUILD publications:
THE GUILD: 2, 3, 4, 5
Architect's Edition: 6, 7, 8, 9, 10
Designer's Edition: 7, 9, 10

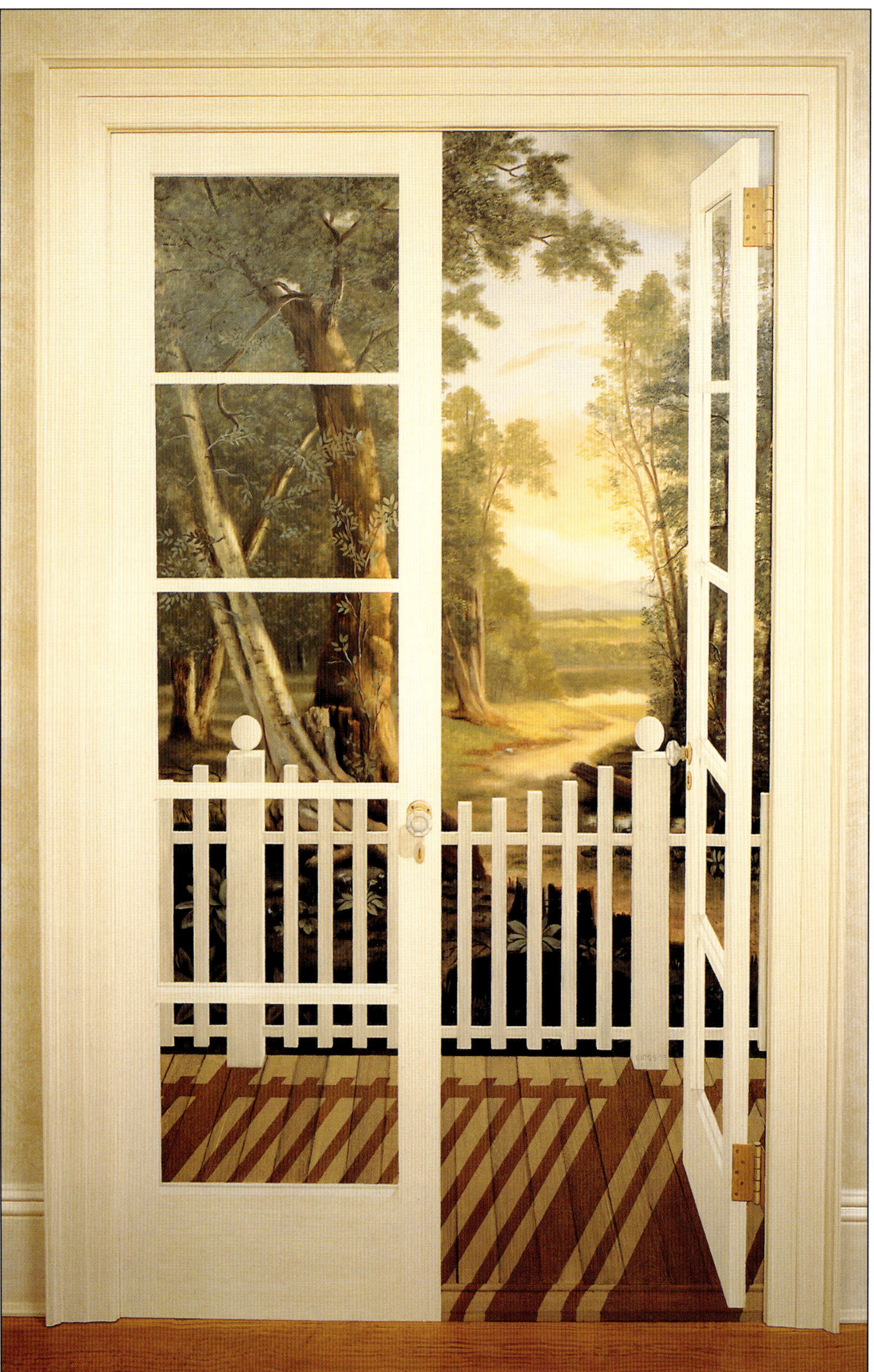

Oleg March

Bill Gibbons Studio

368 Broadway #203
New York, NY 10013-3936
FAX 212-227-0039
TEL 212-227-0039

Bill Gibbons is a painter with over ten years of experience designing and painting murals in a wide range of styles. The paintings shown here are from a series of four murals which decorate the Public Banquet Room in Masonic Hall, New York City, NY.

Also see these GUILD publications:
Architect's Edition: 10
Designer's Edition: 10

A Mural, 5' x 16', Public Banquet Room, Masonic Hall, New York, NY, interior design: Bonsignore & Mazzotta, P.C.

B Mural (detail), Masonic Hall, New York, NY

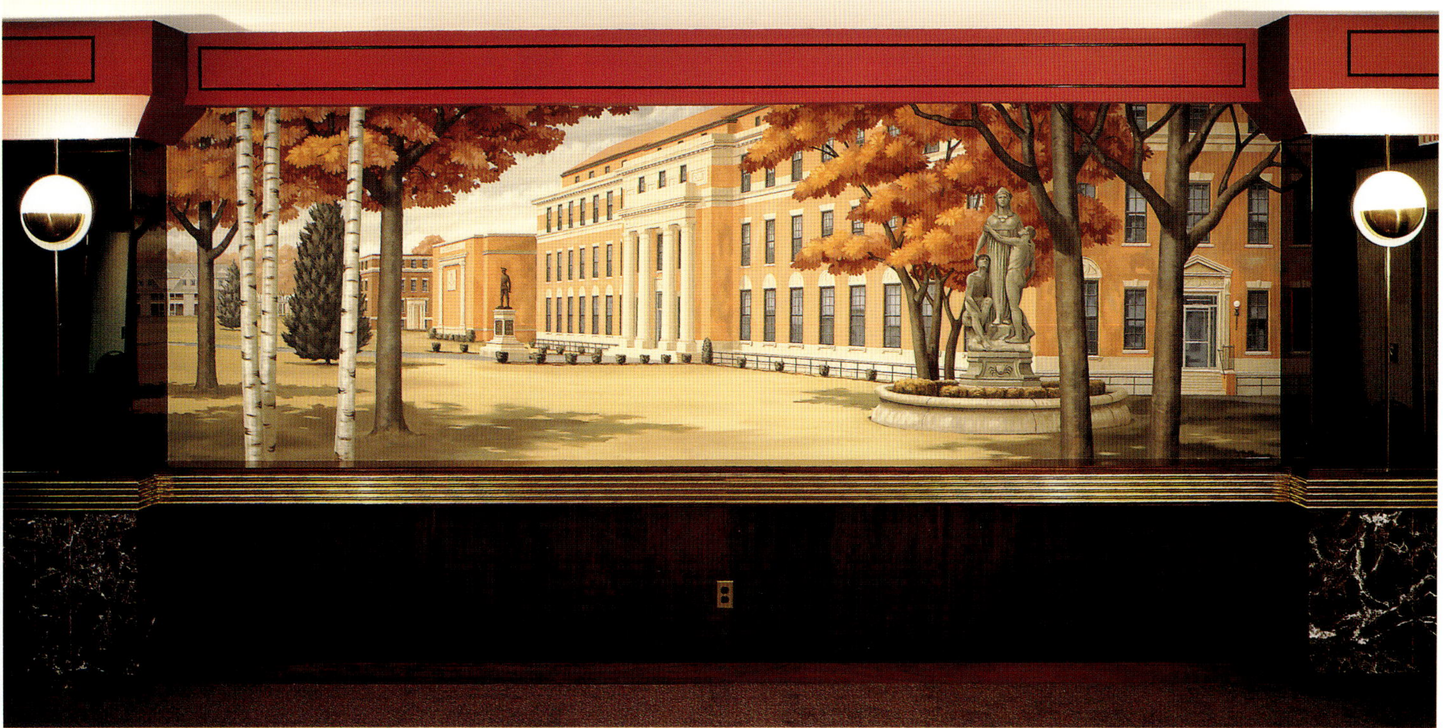

A

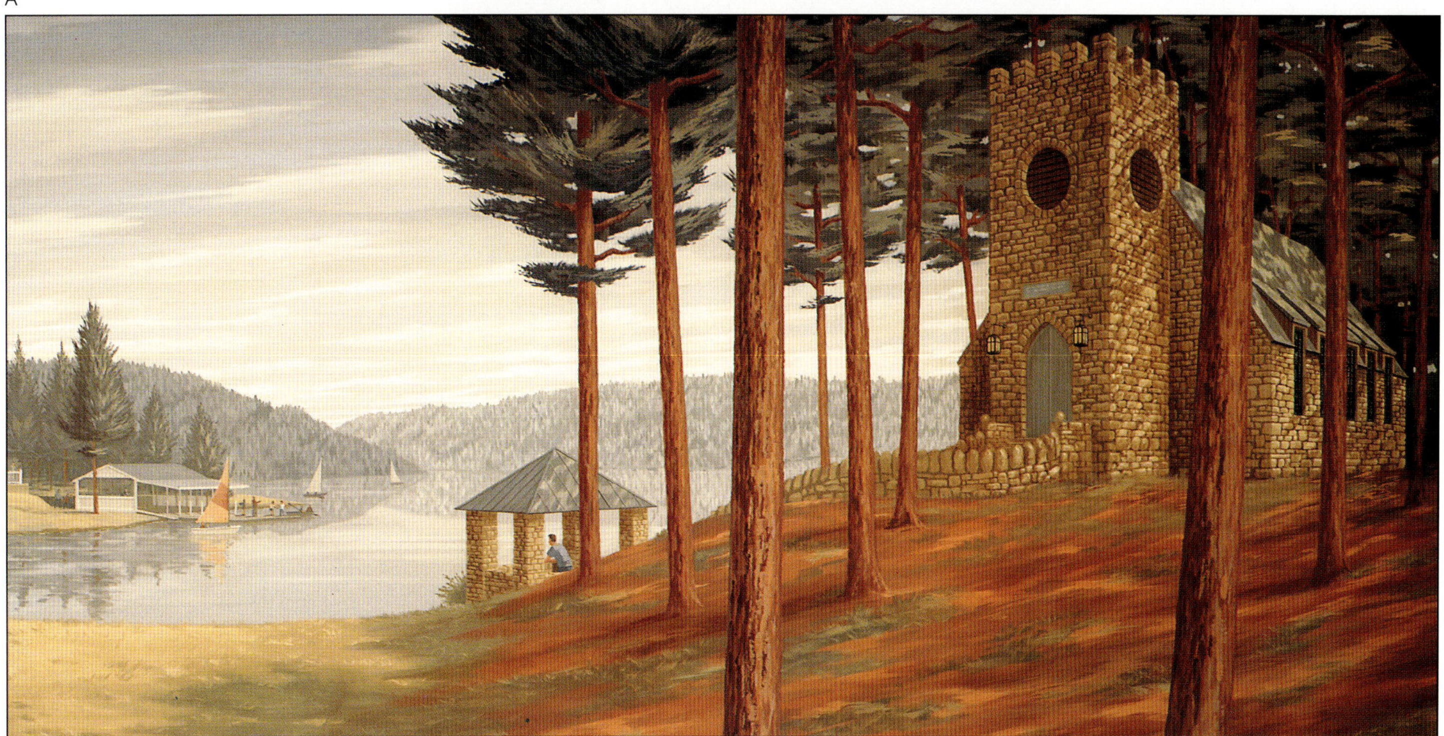

B

Photos: Michael Imlay

JERRY MACNEIL

Architect

Jerry MacNeil, president of Jerry MacNeil Architects Ltd. in Halifax, Nova Scotia, and a Fellow of the Royal Architectural Institute of Canada, is a passionate advocate for including art in architectural projects. "When art is integrated into an architectural design from the beginning, it plays a crucial and irreplaceable role in animating the space. It often makes a client more excited about a project and encourages people to experience the space in a more active, intelligent and engaged way."

MacNeil specializes in designing institutional buildings, especially churches, and says he'd encourage a client to leave a portion of a building unfinished rather than save money by cutting the art out of the budget. He reasons that, "They'll always eventually raise the money to finish construction, but they might not raise the money to pay for the art, and that would be a terrible loss."

MacNeil uses artists from all over North America on his projects. "Sometimes it's better to use an outside artist rather than someone local," he says. "An outsider brings a different vision that can be exciting and surprising."

According to MacNeil, distance is not a problem as long as the architect and artist share a vision and a professional attitude. To facilitate that trust and understanding, MacNeil sent one of his architects to the States to work for over three weeks with GUILD glass artist Steve Melahn. The result of that international collaboration has been four architectural glass projects—including one in MacNeil's home.

"Working with Steve is a great pleasure," says MacNeil. "We know how he and his staff work, and what we need to provide in terms of schedules and guidelines. And he is well aware of the flexibility an artist must have when working with buildings. It's an excellent situation for all of us."

Photo by Robert F. Calnen, Calnen of Canada Ltd.

EYECON, Inc.

Chris Arnold, Jeff Garrison
1915 West Colorado Boulevard
Dallas, TX 75208
TEL 214-871-3535

EYECON, Inc. is a custom murals and design firm founded by artists Chris Arnold and Jeff Garrison. Both have worked with architects, designers and individuals to produce site-specific works of art for the corporate, public and private sector. Arnold and Garrison have the unique ability to translate conceptual ideas into monumental-scale creations, making a profound impact on their audience. Portfolio and complete client list available upon request.

Also see this GUILD publication:
Designer's Edition: 10

A Untitled, 8' x 9', interior mural for Hethorn
   Photography, Dallas, TX

B *Mass Transit*, 214' x 121', outdoor mural for the
   Downtown Improvement District, Dallas, TX

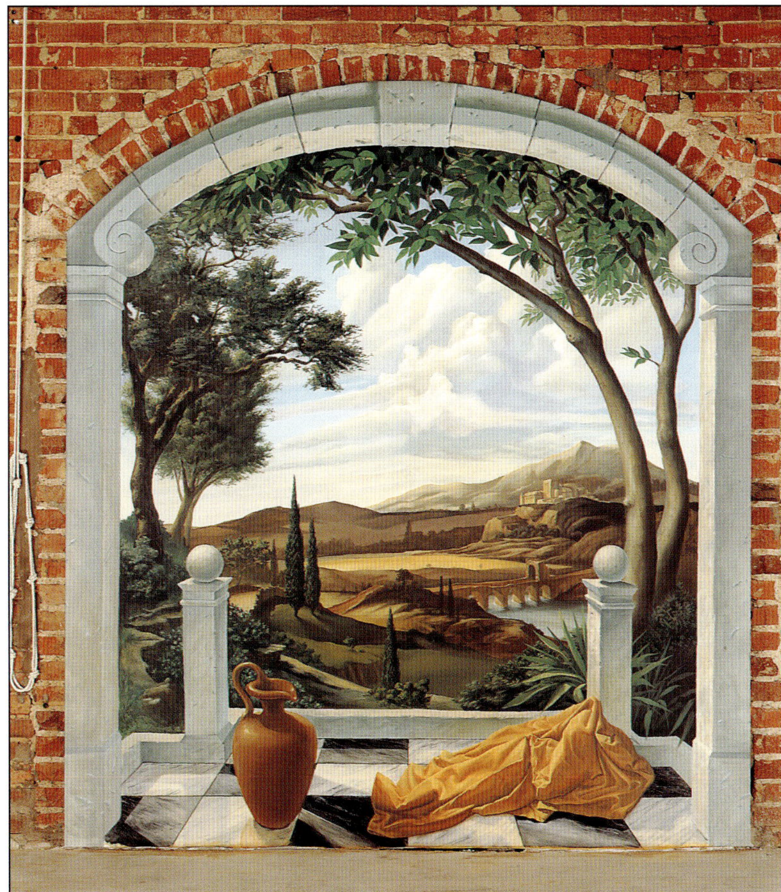

A

John Hethorn

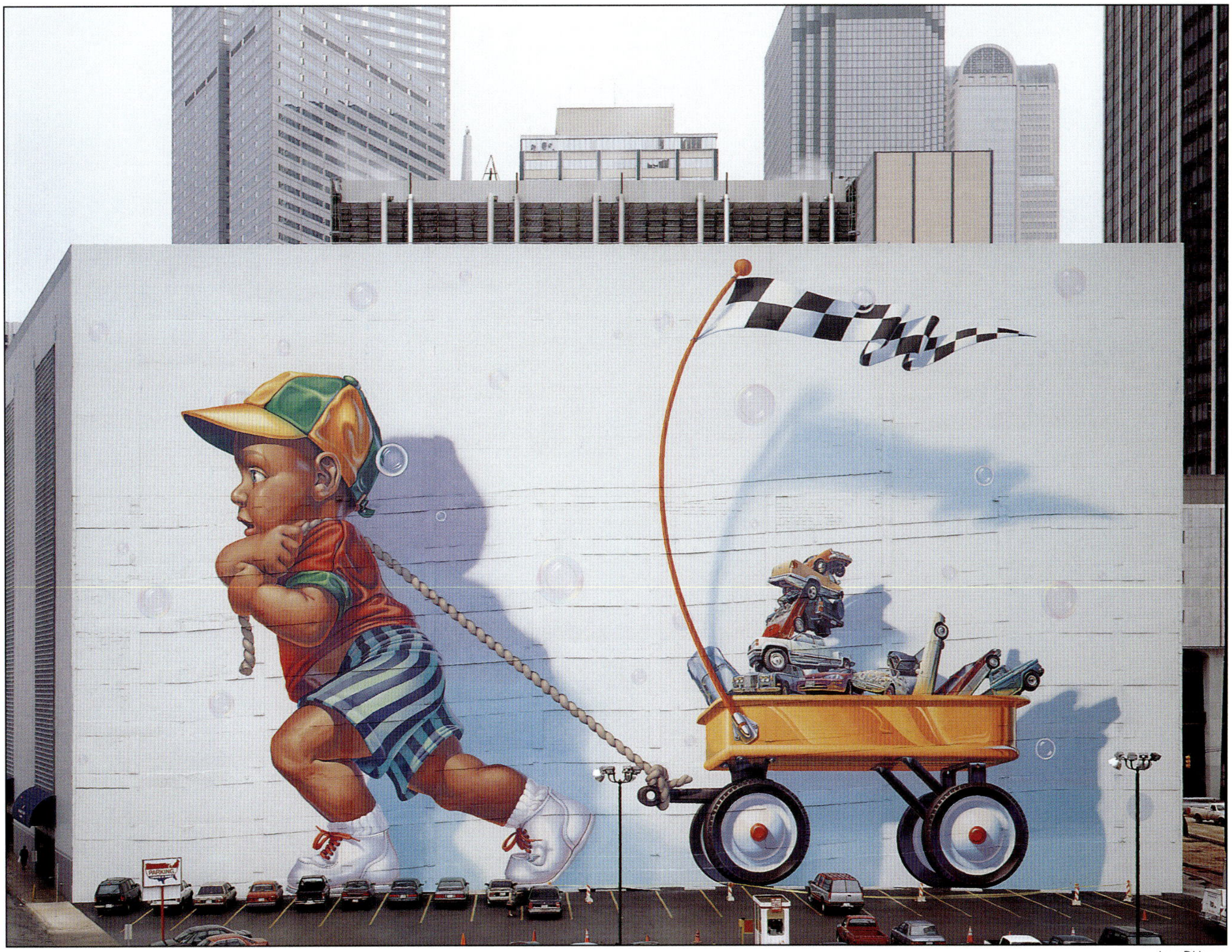

B

Lee Dirksen

Khuzami Studio

Vicki Khuzami
552 Broadway 3rd Floor
New York, NY 10012
FAX 212-941-6054
TEL   212-941-6054

Vicki Khuzami has concentrated on mural painting for the last decade. Much of her experience was gained as head designer and lead painter for Evergreene Painting Studios in New York City. There she worked with many talented artists, architects, and interior designers on exciting projects, from Trump's Taj Mahal Casinos to new murals for the United States Capitol Building in Washington, DC.

Khuzami started her own company in 1994, and her projects have expanded to include film and theater sets. Since then, her work has taken her on projects across the U.S. and to Japan.

A Double Rainbow Bakery,
   Albuquerque, NM, 40' x 8'

B Study for dining room,
   Marla Weinhoff Studio, NYC

C Sumie-inspired washes and
   brush strokes, NYC, 19' x 6'

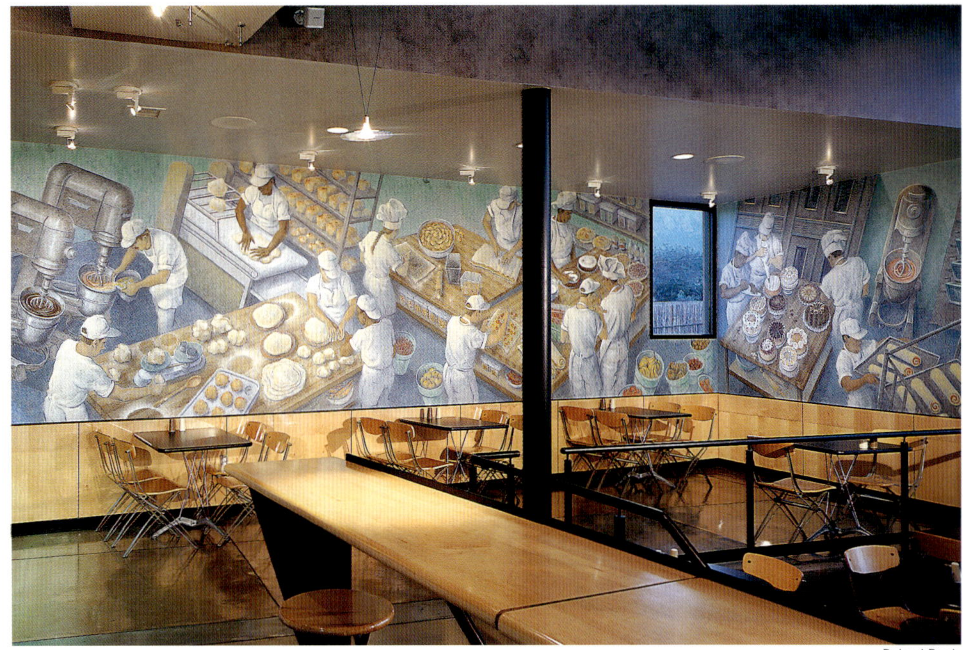

A

Robert Reck

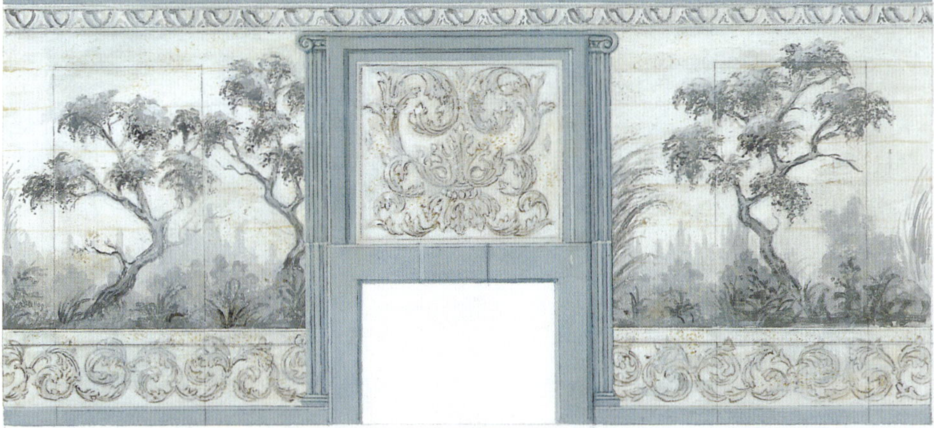

B

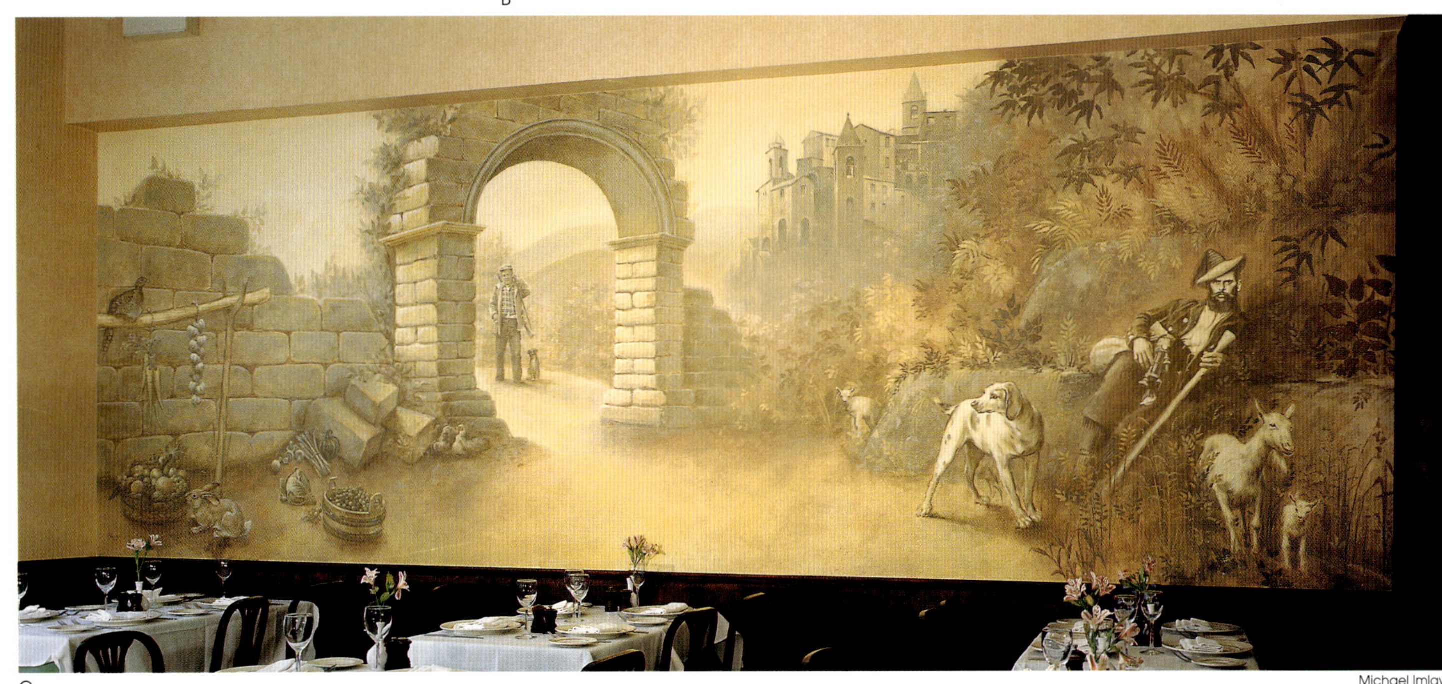

C

Michael Imlay

Khuzami Studio

Vicki Khuzami
552 Broadway 3rd Floor
New York, NY 10012
FAX   212-941-6054
TEL   212-941-6054

Unlike fine art painting, mural painting is a group effort. A unique vision is created by artist, architect, interior designer and client. Art history provides strong foundations of classical forms, while contemporary man's imagination can project him into any visual mind scape he wishes to illustrate. This journey has been shared throughout every century within the simple confines of a room, inspired, then transformed.

Vicki Khuzami previously worked as head designer for Evergreene Painting Studios. While there, clients included United States Capitol Murals, Euro Disney, Loews Corp., Trump Taj Mahal, New England Telephone, and I Magnin.

A Private residence, Saskia Weinstien Ltd., NYC

B Kirin Beer, Tokyo, Japan, Moo Mural Painting

C United States Capitol House Murals, 1993-94, Evergreene Studios

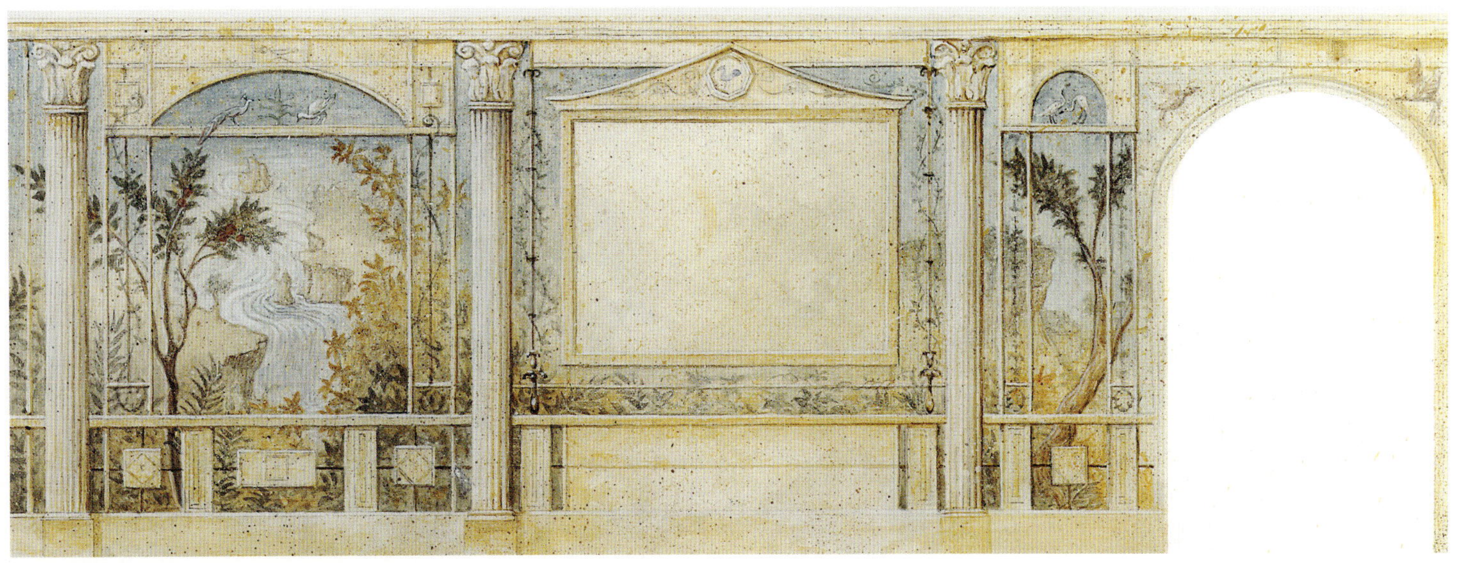

A

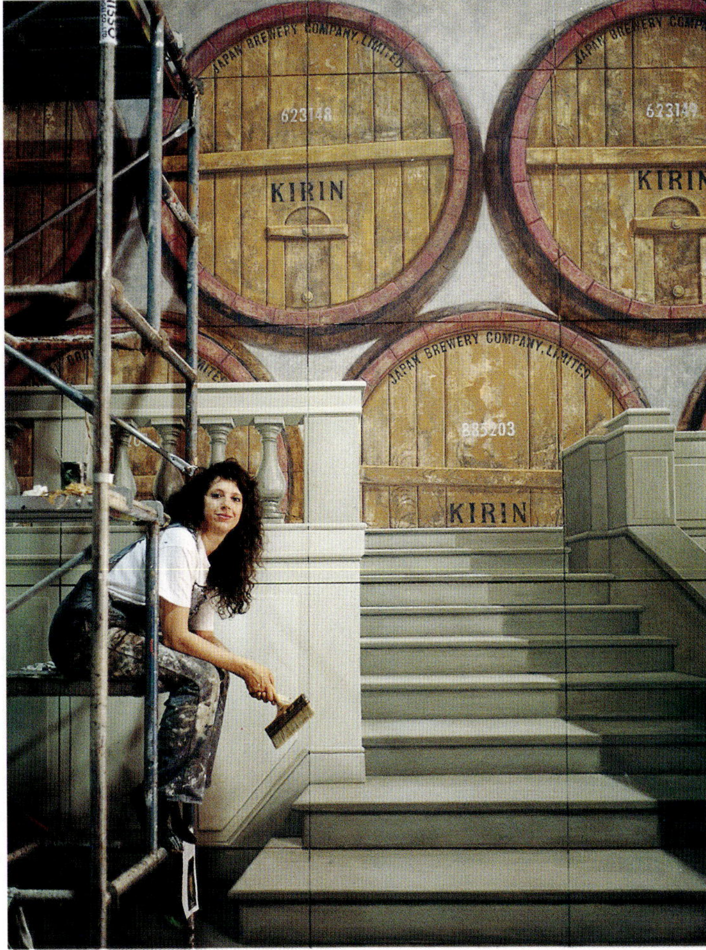

B

Mutsumi Saito

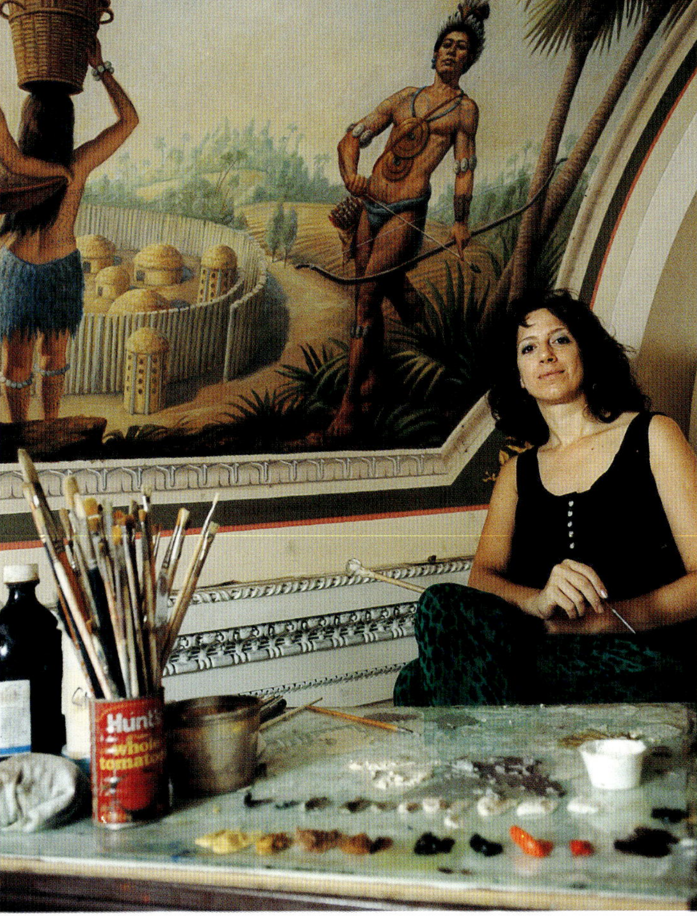

C

Tim Finch

Joel W.B. Heathcote

Limitless Light Studios
449 Santa Fe Drive #332
Encinitas, CA 92024
FAX 619-931-8609
TEL 619-931-8689
E-Mail: JHeathcote 75734,46
  @compuserve.com

This innovative light artist uses fiber optics to recreate the exact night sky for any date, past or future. His computer astronomy programs depict precise positions of planets, stars and constellations.

This vision of the firmament is reproduced as fiber optic panels covering as large a portion of the ceiling as desired. A concealed illuminator box causes the stars to twinkle, change colors, even produce random 'shooting stars' trailing across the sky.

For 20 years, Heathcote has created sophisticated, durable, kinetic light and laser sculptures for both public works and private collections worldwide. He enjoys co-creating with architects and designers.

Recently, custom *NightSky* ceilings averaged $100 per square foot.

SHOWN: *Birth of Augustus, August 23, 68 B.C.,* Caesars Palace Fantasy Suites

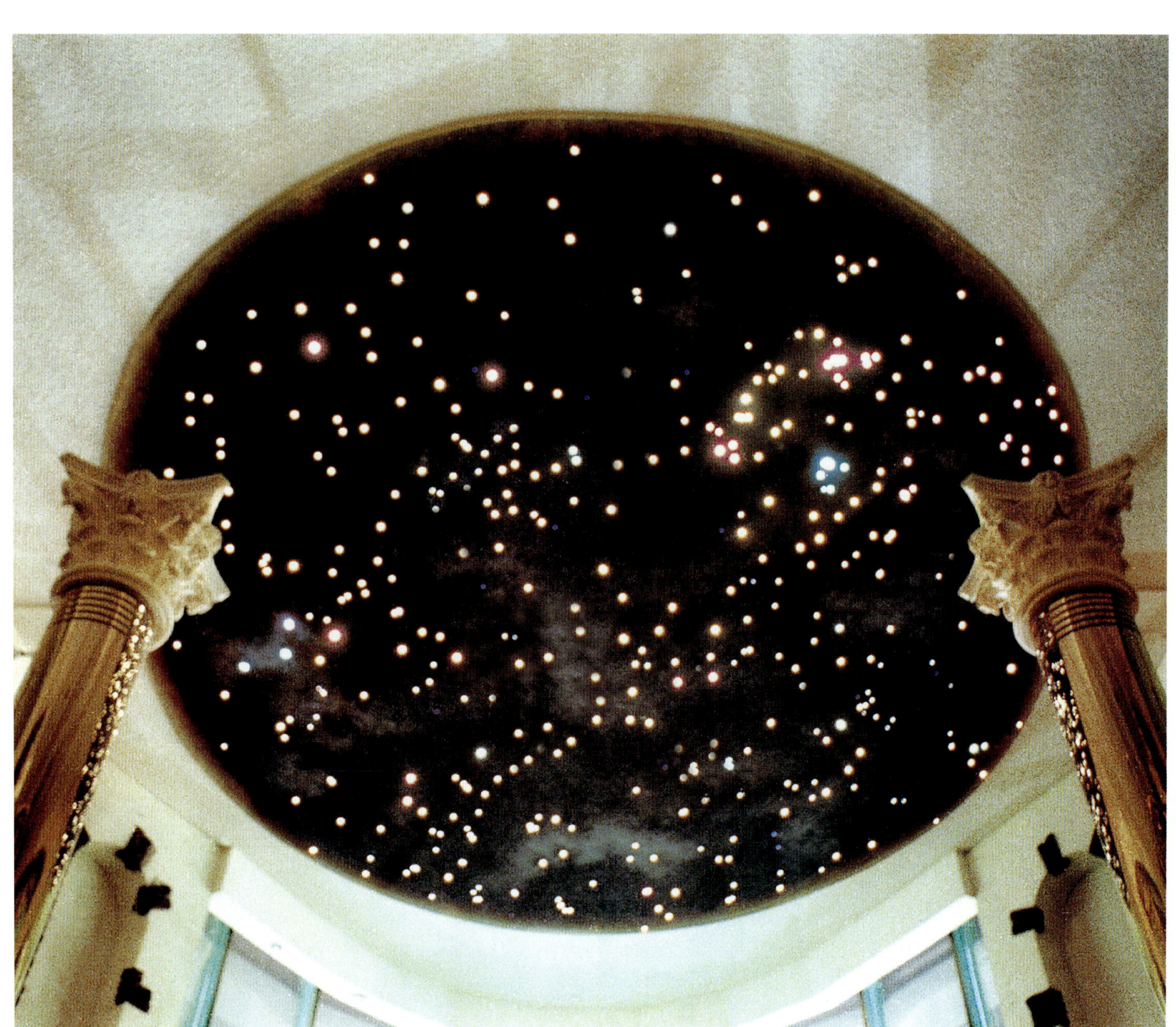

Trena McNabb

McNabb Studio
PO Box 327
Bethania, NC 27010
FAX 910-759-0641
TEL 910-924-6053

"You are the easiest person to work with ...
from your previous work and reputation, we
knew the painting would be good ... now
we also know you can work with business
executives having no art knowledge ...."

"Very professional! You really capture
the spirit of our employees and company ...
stayed within budget parameters ...
perfect example of art for public spaces ...."

Site-specific artwork. Commissions include industrial, medical and corporate sites in the U.S. and
Europe. Unusual materials like plexiglass used to
special effect with canvas and paint. Flexible
and always interesting, Trena's work will embrace
your theme and story in a unique blend of shapes,
colors and textures to form an allegorical depiction specific to your site and subject.

Also see these GUILD publications:
Architect's Edition: 6, 7, 8, 9, 10
Designer's Edition: 8

SHOWN: *Good Fortune Alliance,*
Japan Tobacco, Inc., Tokyo, Japan

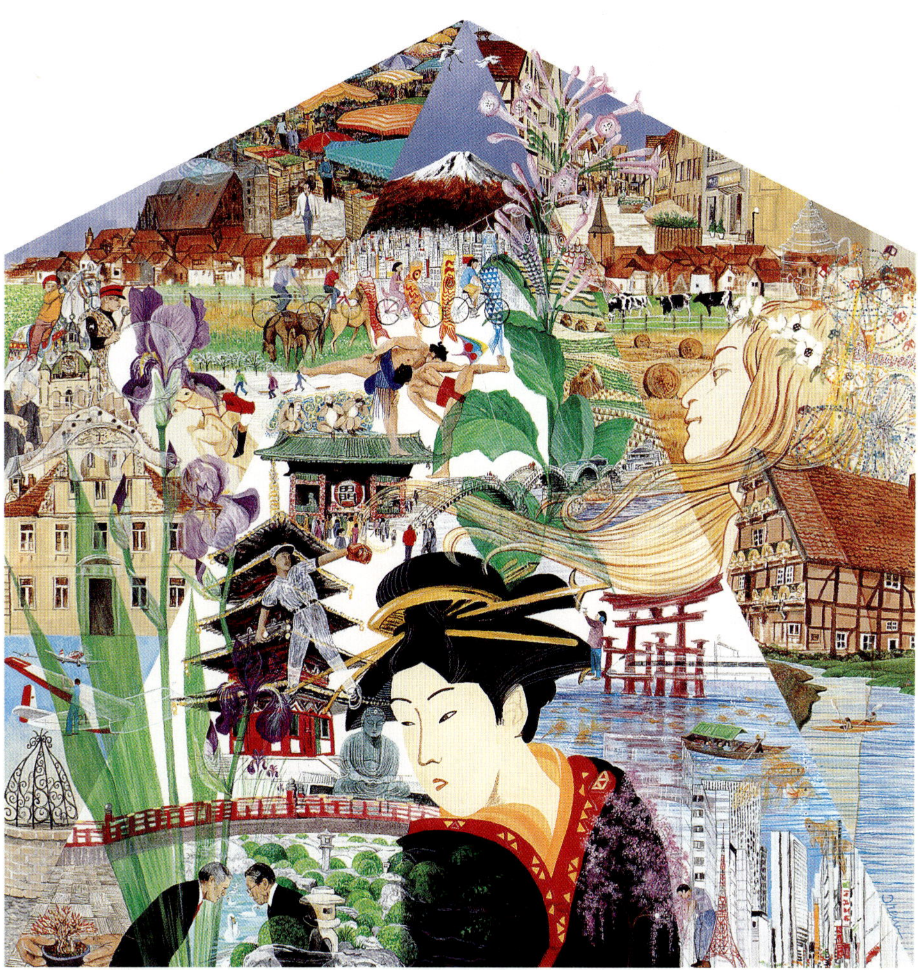

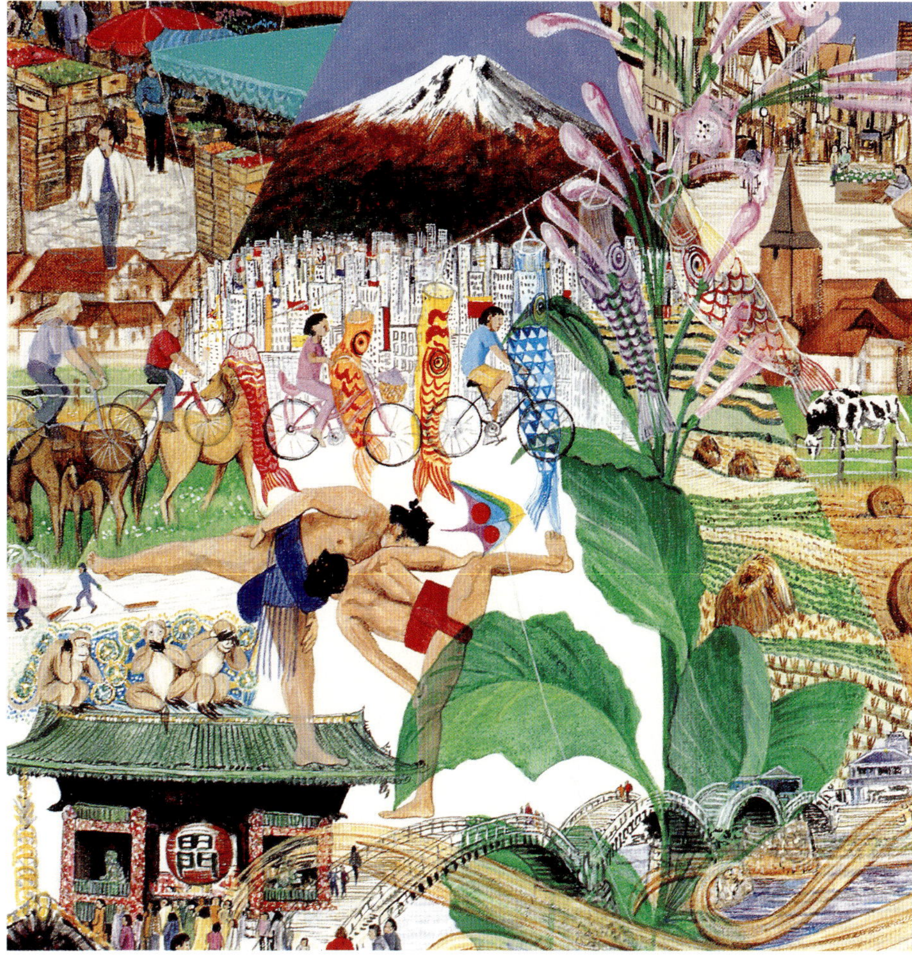

Karl-Heinz Meschbach

Karl-Heinz Meschbach & Friends
4901 106th Avenue N.E.
Circle Pines, MN 55014
FAX 612-784-9201
TEL 612-785-2533

TThe illusion of trompe l'oeil, the whimsicality of painted furniture, the luxurious look of faux mabre or tortoise shell … European decorative art has long been admired but has rarely been available in the United States because of the scarcity of trained artisans who can create the magic designs and are skilled masters of these techniques.

Only a very few traditionally trained artisans reside in the United States. One such artisan is Karl-Heinz Meschbach.

Meschbach began his career as a decorative painter and artist over 35 years ago, after completing rigorous European apprenticeship training under the masters of the Berlin Painters Guild.

Works by Karl-Heinz Meschbach have been featured in art galleries, commercial environments and many private homes.

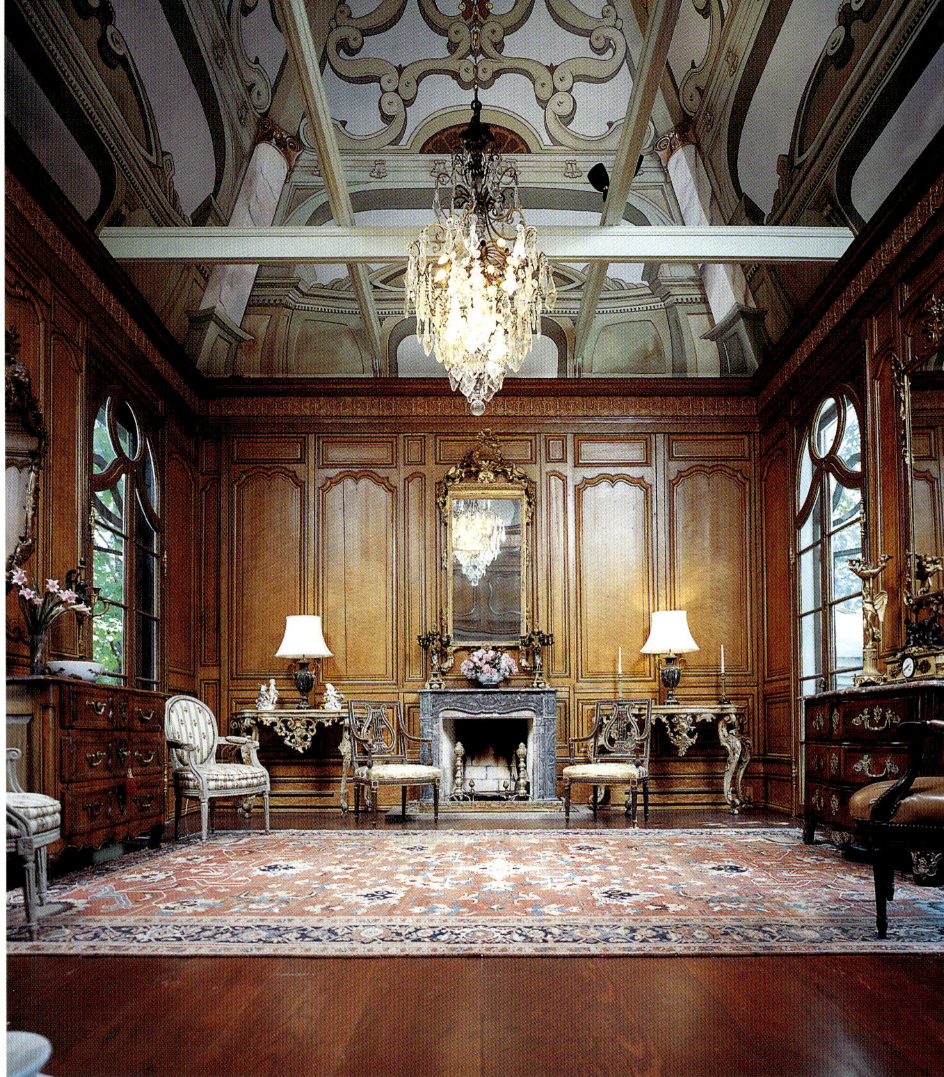

Trompe l'oeil ceiling, faux bois paneling, 16' x 16' x 16', 1991 PIPP award

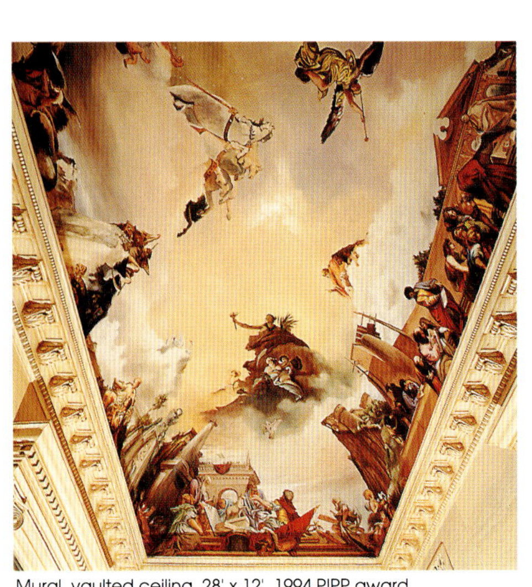

Mural, vaulted ceiling, 28' x 12', 1994 PIPP award

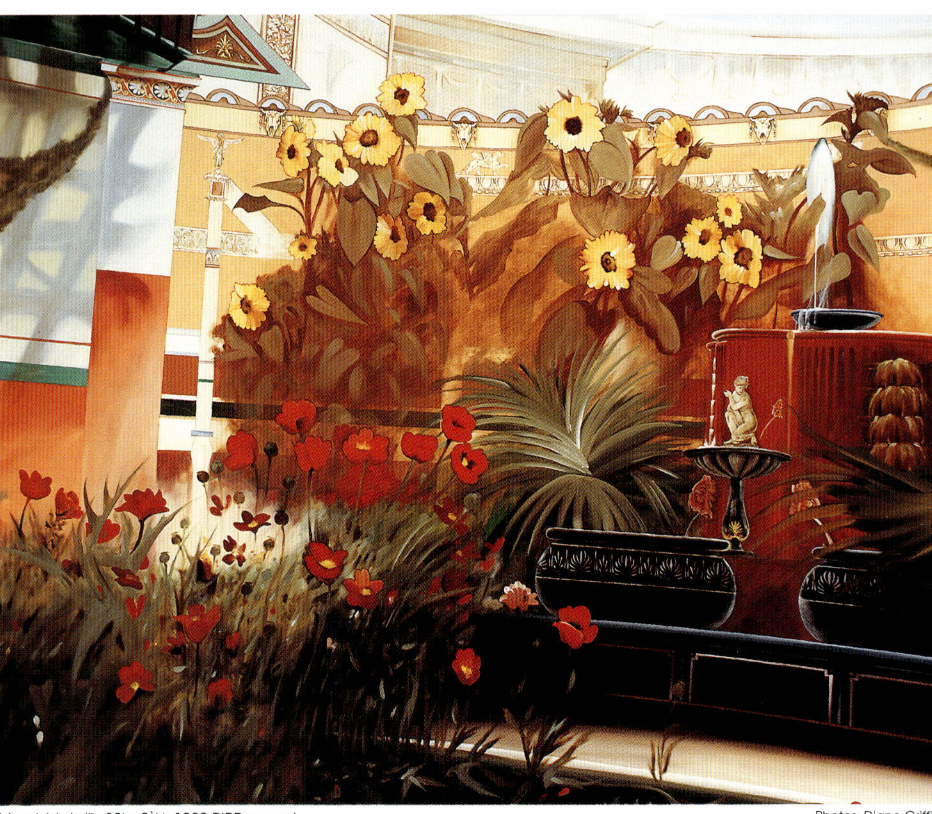

Mural (detail), 30' x 9½', 1992 PIPP award

Photos: Diane Griffin

Igor Naskalov

Roslyn Manor House, Inc.
87-B Cuttermill Road
Great Neck, NY 11021
FAX 516-466-7403
TEL 516-621-8824
TEL 609-921-9369 (Studio)

A combination of the Old Master's traditions and techniques with his personal talents and creativity makes Igor Naskalov an outstanding and unique artist, capable of creating high-quality works in different decorative styles, genres and techniques.

His deep knowledge of world art and his versatility helped him to acquire the reputation of a world-class artist for whom each image is unique.

Since 1986, he has been working with architects, designers and homeowners, assisting them to create necessary space effects by way of unique multi-figured frescos, murals and trompe l'oeil.

His highly creative works of art have been exhibited nationally, as well as in Italy, France, Russia and Japan.

Portfolio and video are available.

Also see these GUILD publications:
Architect's Edition: 10
Designer's Edition: 10

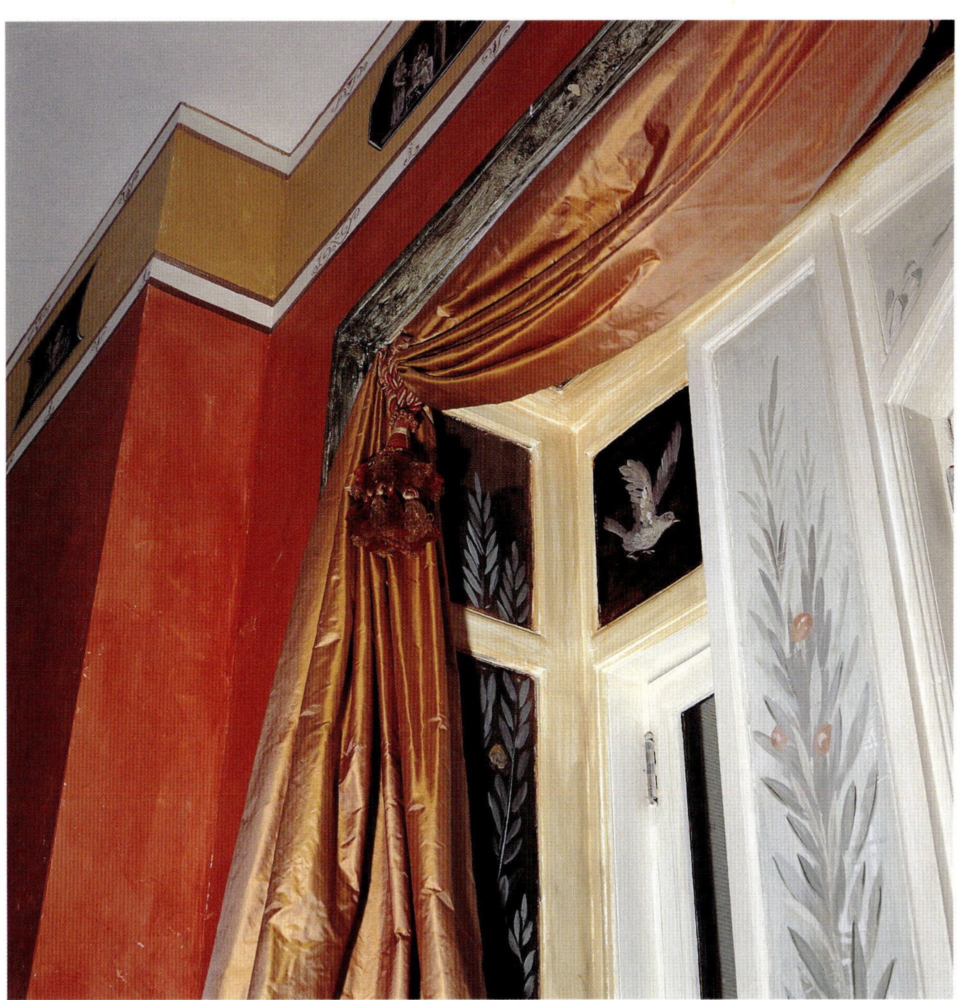

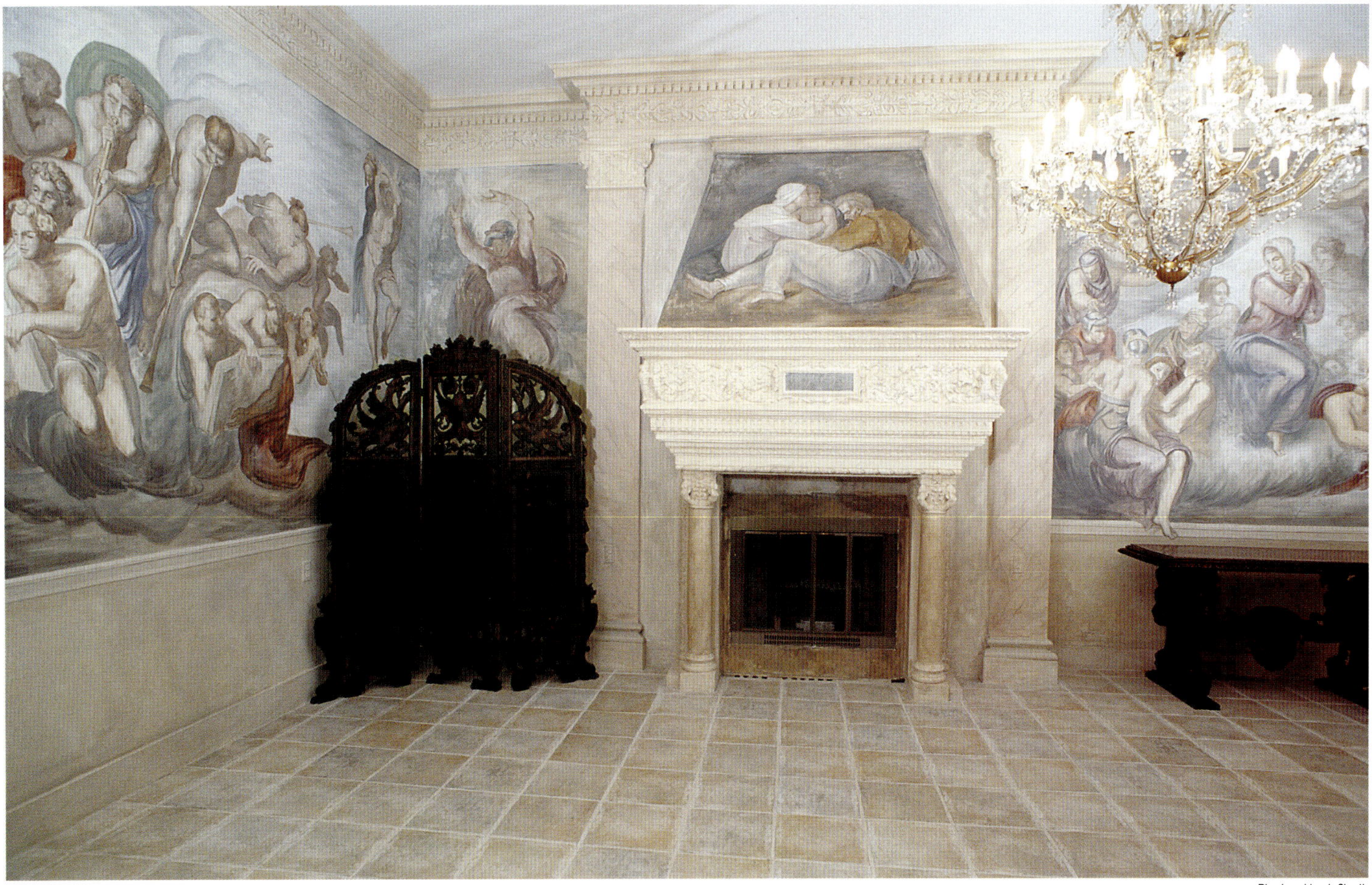

Photos: Hank Shull

NY Decorative Arts Studio

Michael Glickman
537 East 87th Street, Suite 1E
New York, NY 10028
FAX 212-570-9373
TEL 212-570-9373

Painting from a classical European art education, Michael Glickman and NY Decorative Arts Studio collaborate with architects and designers to create artworks for corporate, retail and residential clientele. They can bring you expertise in the fields of murals, frescos, trompe l'oeil, faux finishes, gilding, Italian encaustic, and restoration. Works can be painted on-site or on canvas for installation.

Commissions include:
The Barbizon Hotel, NY
Interiors by Royale, NY
Howard/Charczuk Architects, NY
Twenty-First Century McDonald's Corp., NJ
National Library of Russia, St. Petersburg, Russia
National Bank, St. Petersburg, Russia
Euton Architects, Brussels, Belgium

Also see this GUILD publication:
Architect's Edition: 10

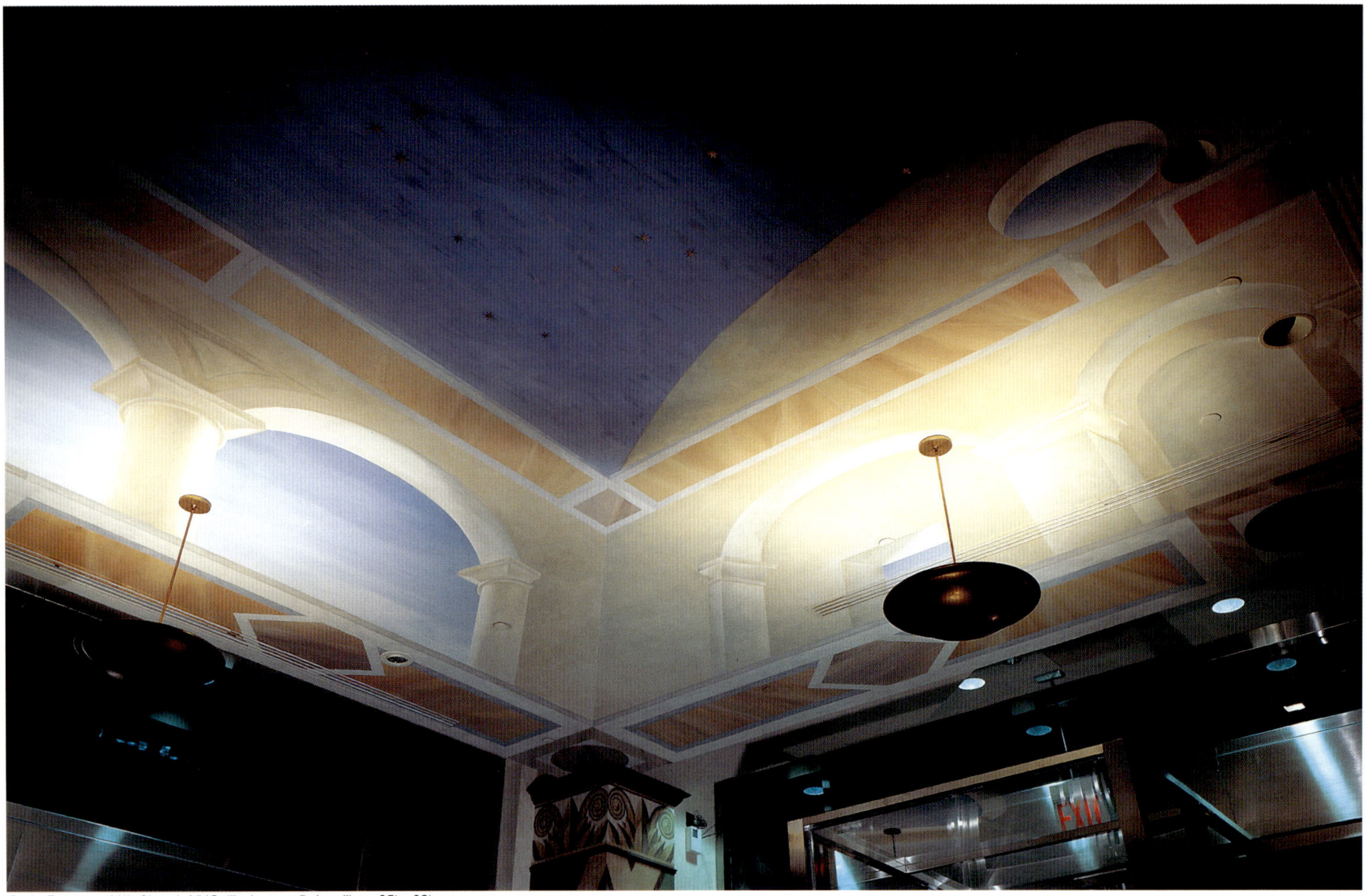

Cafe Europa, 46th Street, NYC, illusion on flat ceiling, 25' x 80'

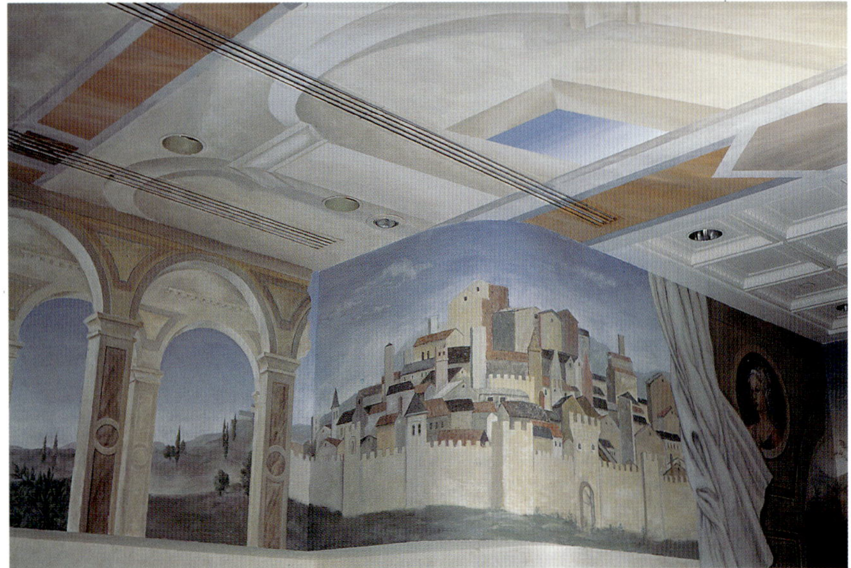

Cafe Europa, 46th Street, NYC, fresco, 10'H x 100'W

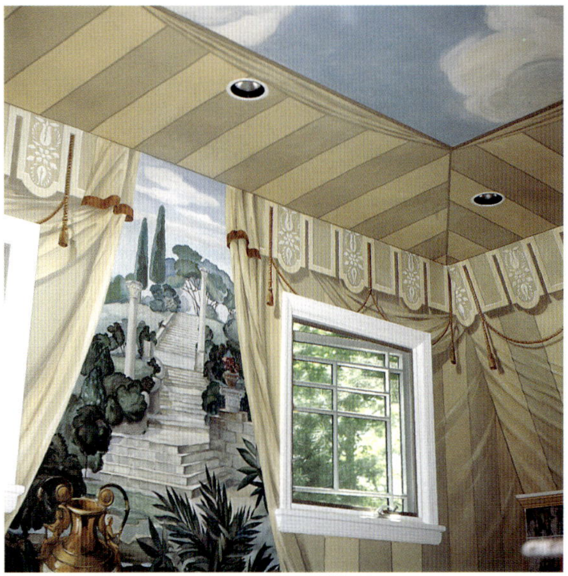

Trompe l'oeil for private residence, 8'H x 10'W

G. Byron Peck

G. Byron Peck Studios
1857 Lamont Street NW
Washington, DC 20010
FAX 202-986-1662
TEL 202-986-1662

For over 19 years, the G. Byron Peck Studios
have produced artwork for a variety of projects,
ranging from five-story-high exterior murals
and public art to complete corporate and
residential installations.

Works on this page (clockwise from top left)
were created for the National Endowment
for the Arts, Washington, DC; Nuclear Regulatory Commission, Bethesda, MD; DC Fine Arts
Commission, Washington, DC.

Commissions include:
American Embassy, Crete, Guyana, Chile
Bloomingdales, Georgetown Park
DC Fine Arts Commission
John F. Kennedy Center for the Performing Arts
Washington Metro Subway Main Terminal
Marriott Corp.
Union Station
U.S. Nuclear Regulatory Commission

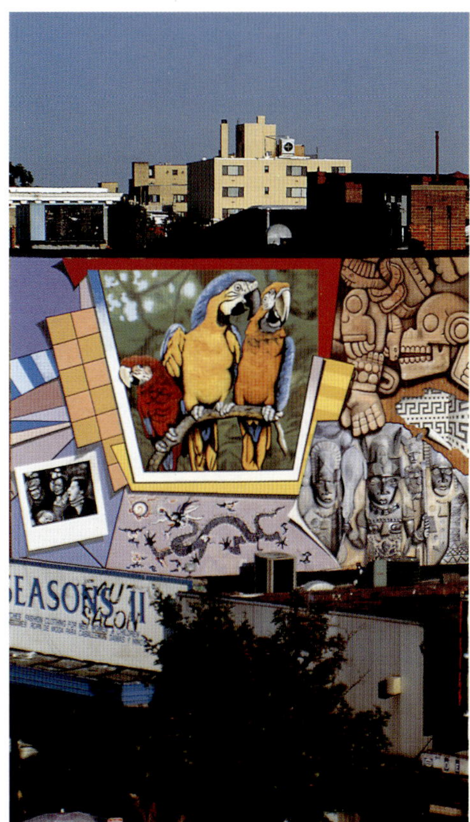
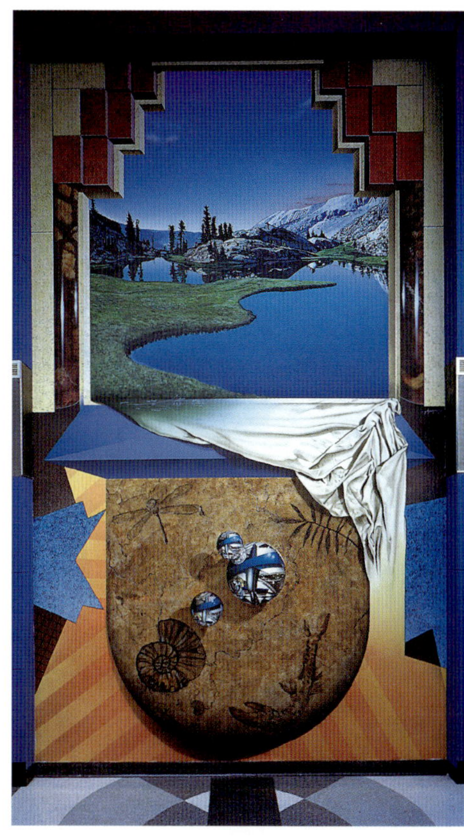

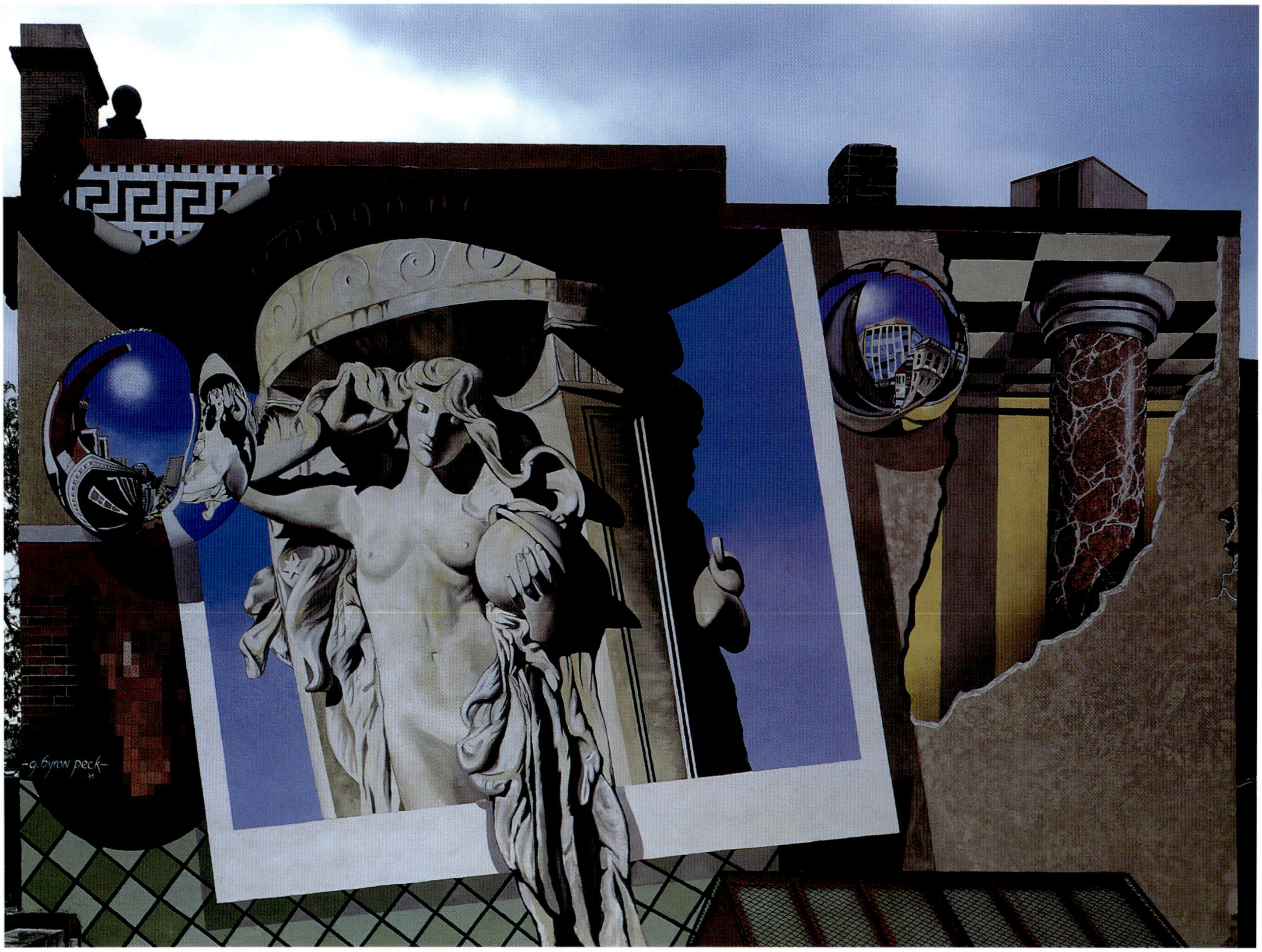

MARK SIMON

Architect

"Architects need to include elements that give richness and meaning to people's lives," says Mark Simon, "and among the most important of these elements are fine arts and crafts. They mark an environment with finger and thumb prints, and show human care in a way that nothing else can."

Simon, one of five partners with Centerbrook Architects, is an enthusiastic advocate for using original art in the built environment. For years he's encouraged his clients to use artists as collaborators with the design team as a way to create spaces that win not only awards, but raves from those who live and work there.

He recalls working on a private lodge with special fondness. "We started with the flavor of an Adirondacks Great Camp, but from the beginning I wanted to integrate artwork as a way to enrich the texture and provide a signature." As a result, every room in the house is rich in exquisitely-executed arts and craft details, including works by two GUILD metal artists. Joel Schwartz created custom-designed door hardware and Ira DeKoven contributed an intricate, one-of-a-kind fireplace screen. "It was a wonderful, fascinating project," says Simon, "and best of all, the client absolutely loves the place."

Simon encourages other architects to use artists, and to interview them carefully. "You need to be clear about deadlines and contractual responsibilities. And listen to artists carefully, because they often have wonderful suggestions. Most of all, be ready to collaborate.

"We need to remember to design environments that invite habitation, places we want to be," he says. "When we live with arts and crafts, it's very much like living with silent friends. We feel accompanied—less alone. This feeling should be protected, nurtured and appreciated."

John Pugh

PO Box 1332
Los Gatos, CA 95031
FAX 408-353-3370
TEL 408-353-3370

Imagine rounding a path to find an old, mossy sculpture niche or an ancient and mysterious colonnade, only then to realize these are painted illusions. Pugh is a master of architectural tromp l'oeil; he deceives and delights viewers by combining detailed imaginary space with planned or existing architecture.

Internationally recognized, John Pugh has worked with architects, businesses and private clients to create murals for public, corporate and private sites, both indoors and out.

Cost is relative to size and complexity and all inquiries are invited.

Also see these GUILD publications:
Architect's Edition: 7, 8, 9

A *Colonnade*, Los Gatos, CA 17' x 17'

B, C & D *Secret Garden Series I, III & II* panels,
    5'6" x 3'6"

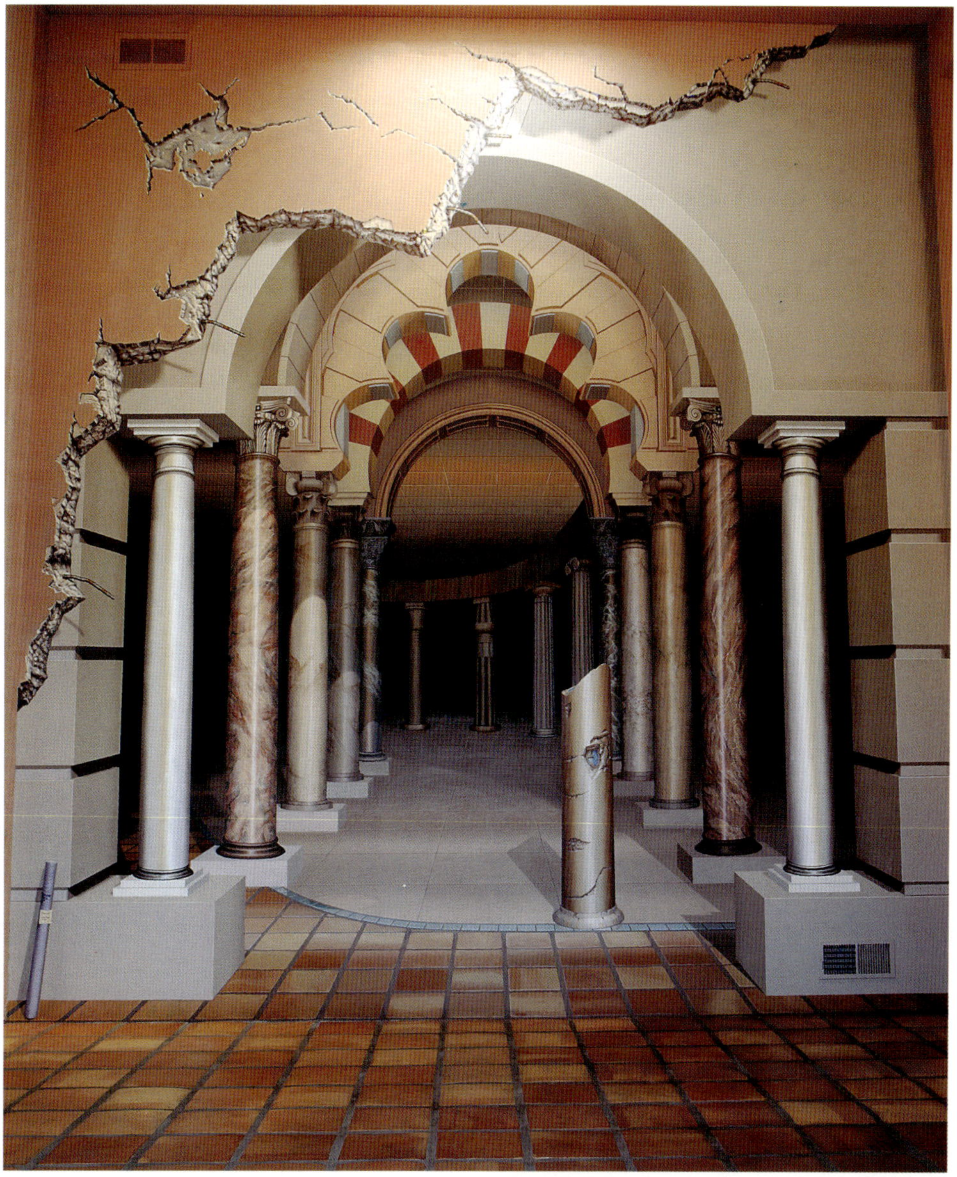

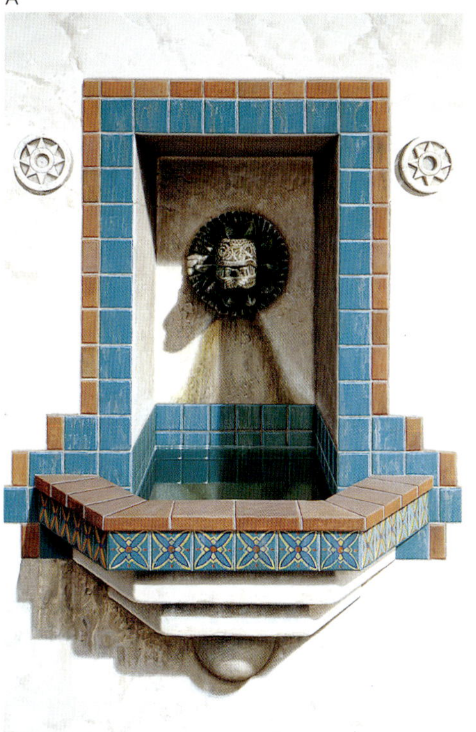

A

Mike Johnston

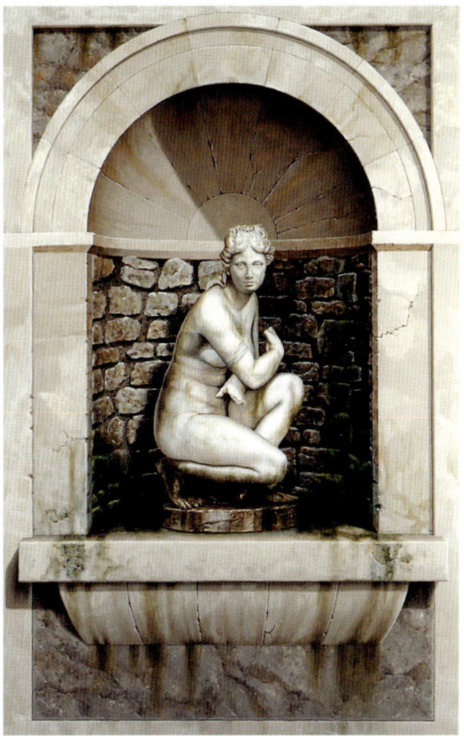

B

Erik DuBouys

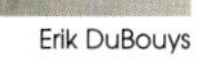

C

Erik DuBouys

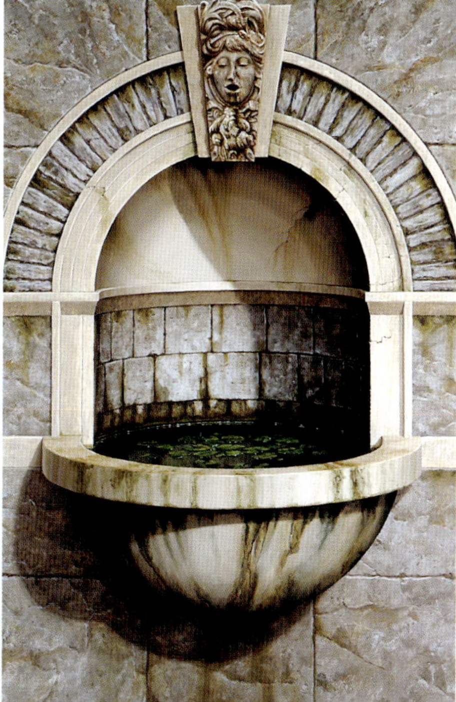

D

Erik DuBouys

Ralph Irwin Studio

Ralph C. Irwin
627 Main Street
Van Buren, AR 72956
TEL 501-474-4114

Born in Long Beach, California, in 1942, Ralph Irwin received his degrees in art from California State University. In 1972, he and his wife Nancy moved to western Arkansas and in 1982 they founded Art Form Galleries and Ralph Irwin Studio in historic Van Buren, Arkansas.

Irwin's artistic contributions span a career of 30 years and are represented nationally and internationally in museums, corporate offices, hospitals, restaurants, churches and private collections.

Meticulously hand-cut clearheart redwood with sand-carved surfaces are overlaid with various grades of sand and rendered with oil-base paints to produce murals that can depict scenes of epic proportions.

Irwin is both craftsman and visionary. With 30 years of art experience, he has proven to be an invaluable team member for not only large corporate clients, but also individuals striving to preserve part of their heritage.

Working in nearly 25 different mediums, including glass, exotic woods, copper, bronze, marble, oil, acrylic, watercolor and fabric, his skills and versatility stand unrivaled.

Irwin's long and diverse background makes him a creative resource for major architectural and interior design firms. Early involvement of the artist allows flexibility in design and ensures timely execution.

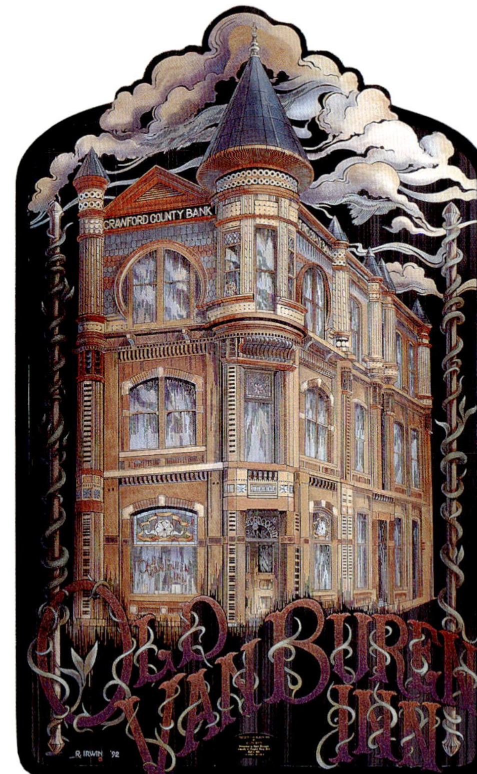

Old Van Buren Inn, 1992, sand-carved wood mural, 55"W x 6'6"H

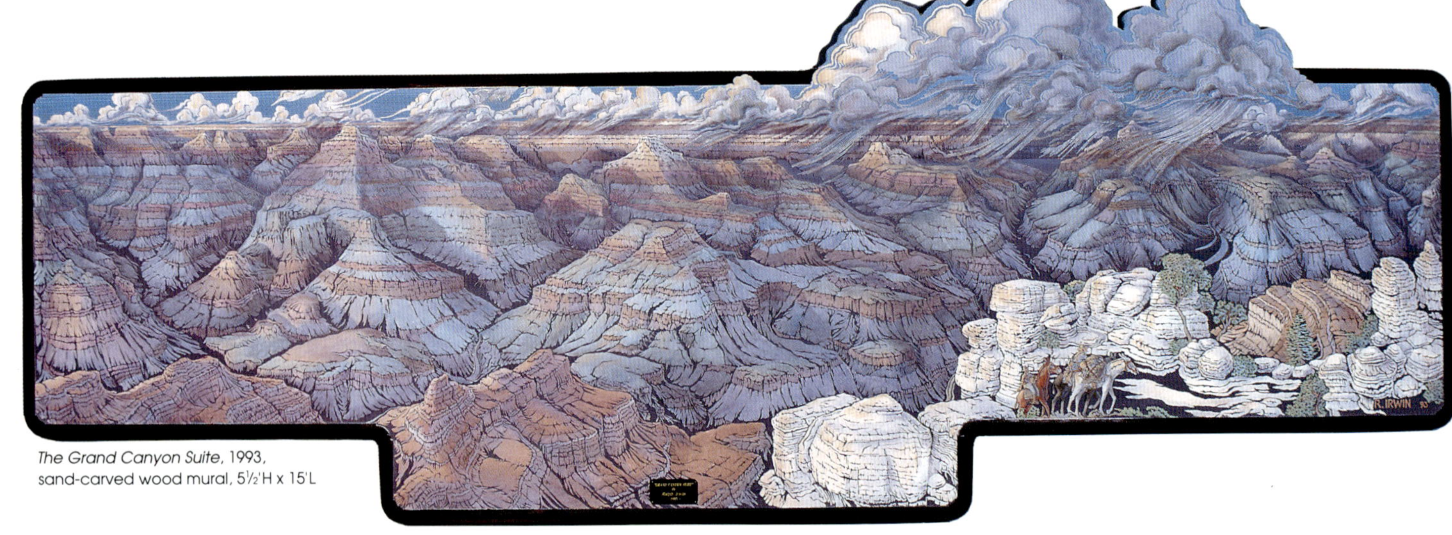

The Grand Canyon Suite, 1993,
sand-carved wood mural, 5½'H x 15'L

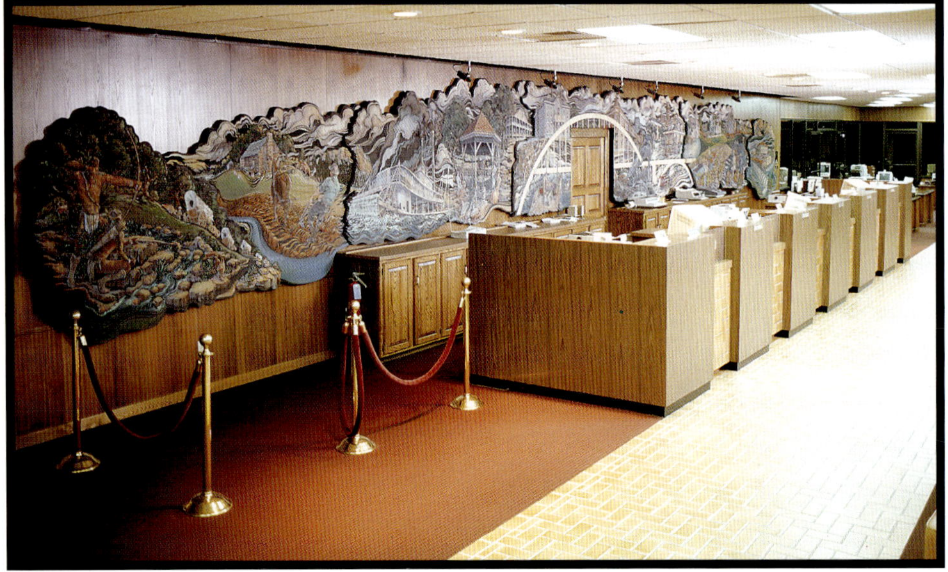

The Originial Ozark, 1992, sand-carved wood mural, 6'H x 56'L

Photos: Martin Duckworth, Van Buren, AR

Bonnie Siracusa

160 Middle Neck Road #4H
Great Neck, NY 11021
FAX 516-482-3349
TEL 516-482-3349

Bonnie Siracusa's murals have enchanted the walls of catering halls, restaurants, post offices, doctors' offices, stores and private residences. Her murals can also advertise a company's products and services, describe the historical background of a place and even eliminate a graffiti problem on outside walls.

The artist collaborates with designers and architects, and then produces a small-scale painting, which must meet their approval. Her murals can be painted either on site, or onto canvases ready for shipping and installation at the site. Call or write for prices and brochure.

Also see these GUILD publications:
THE GUILD: 5
Architect's Edition: 6, 7, 8, 9, 10

A *Southwestern Desert*, living room, private
   residence, Roslyn, NY

B *The Brooklyn Dodgers in Ebbets Field*,
   Ryder Retail Post Office lobby, Brooklyn, NY

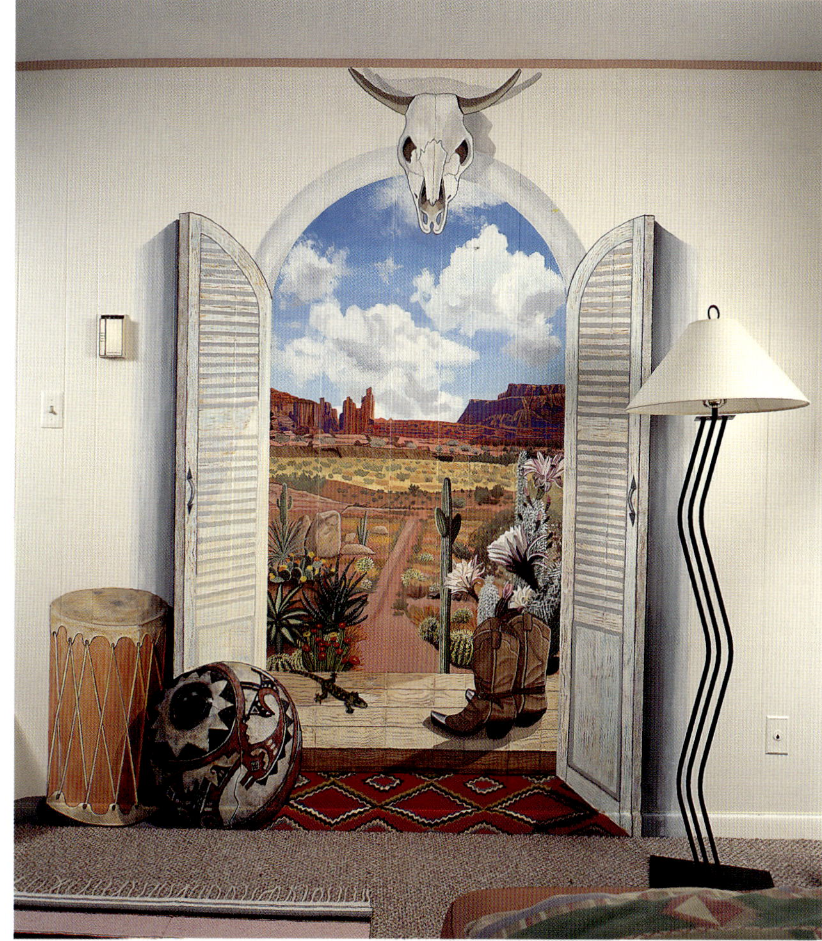

A

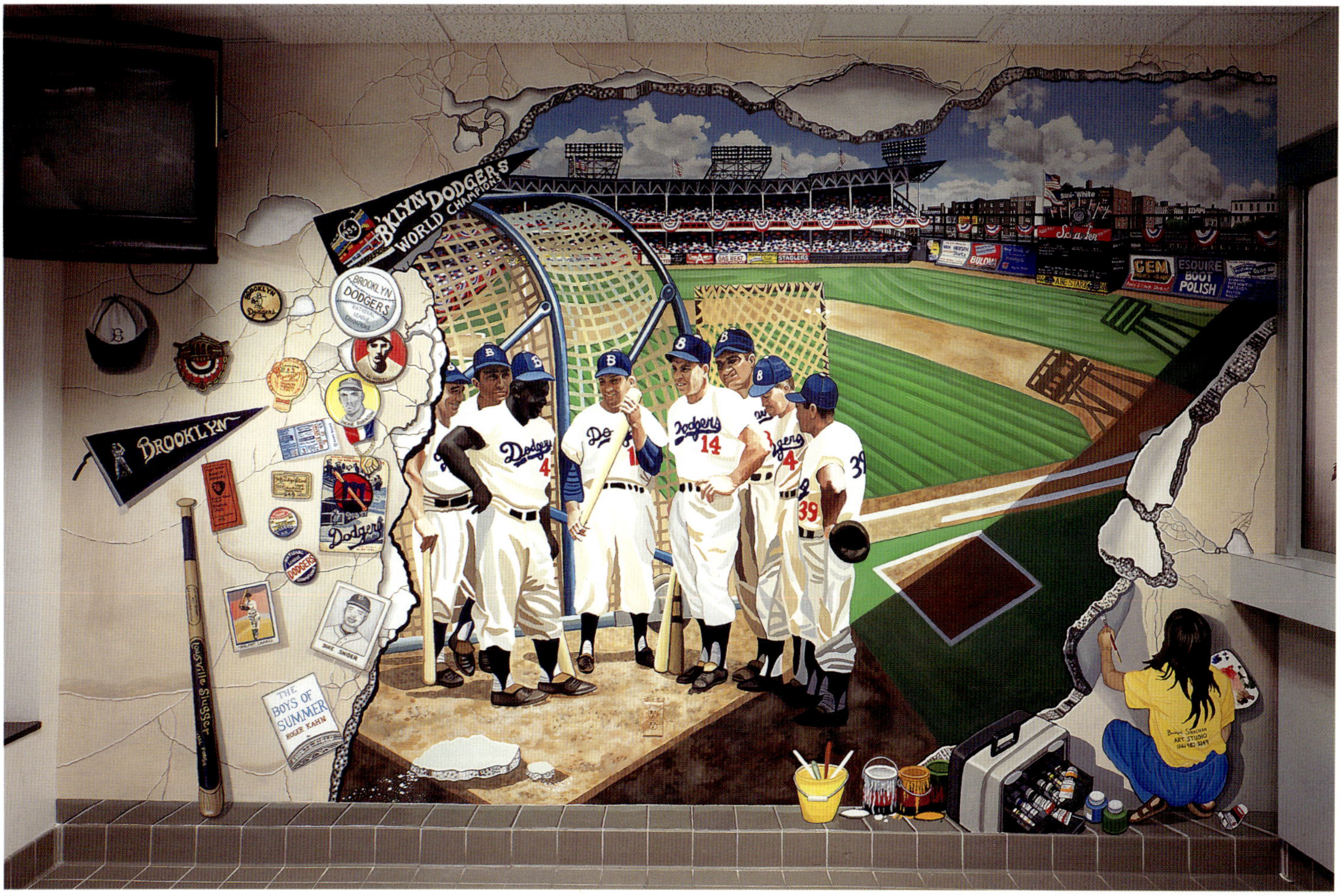

B

Photos: Bill Rothschild

Unique Editions™

Bonny Lhotka
5658 Cascade Place
Boulder, CO 80303
FAX 303-494-3472
TEL   303-494-5631
E-Mail: BonnyL5658@aol.com

Dorothy Simpson Krause
32 Nathaniel Way, PO Box 421
Marshfield Hills, MA 02051
FAX 617-837-1682 (Call first)
TEL   617-837-1682
E-Mail: DotKrause@aol.com

Unique Editions™ is an association of independent artists combining digital technologies with traditional materials. The artists each have two decades of experience working with corporate clients. Using digital media enables them to produce mural-sized work for virtually any site. Paintings are installed as wall murals or hung as translucent scrims and tapestries. The client is supplied with a scaled version in exact materials and colors. Limited-edition prints are available for the hospitality industry. The artists' work is in the collections of United Airlines, Johnson Space Center, AT&T, National Conference of State Legislators, Jansen Pharmaceuticals, the DeCordova Museum, and the Zimmerlie Museum at Rutgers University.

Also see these GUILD publications:
THE GUILD: 5
Designer's Edition: 6, 7, 8, 9

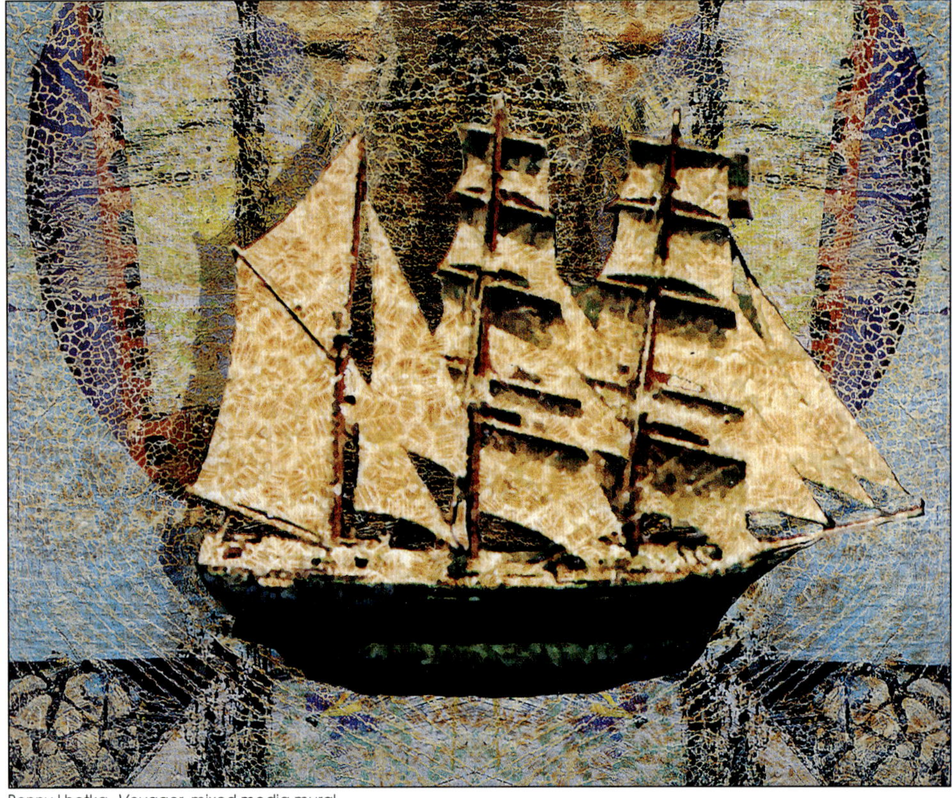

Bonny Lhotka, *Voyager*, mixed media mural

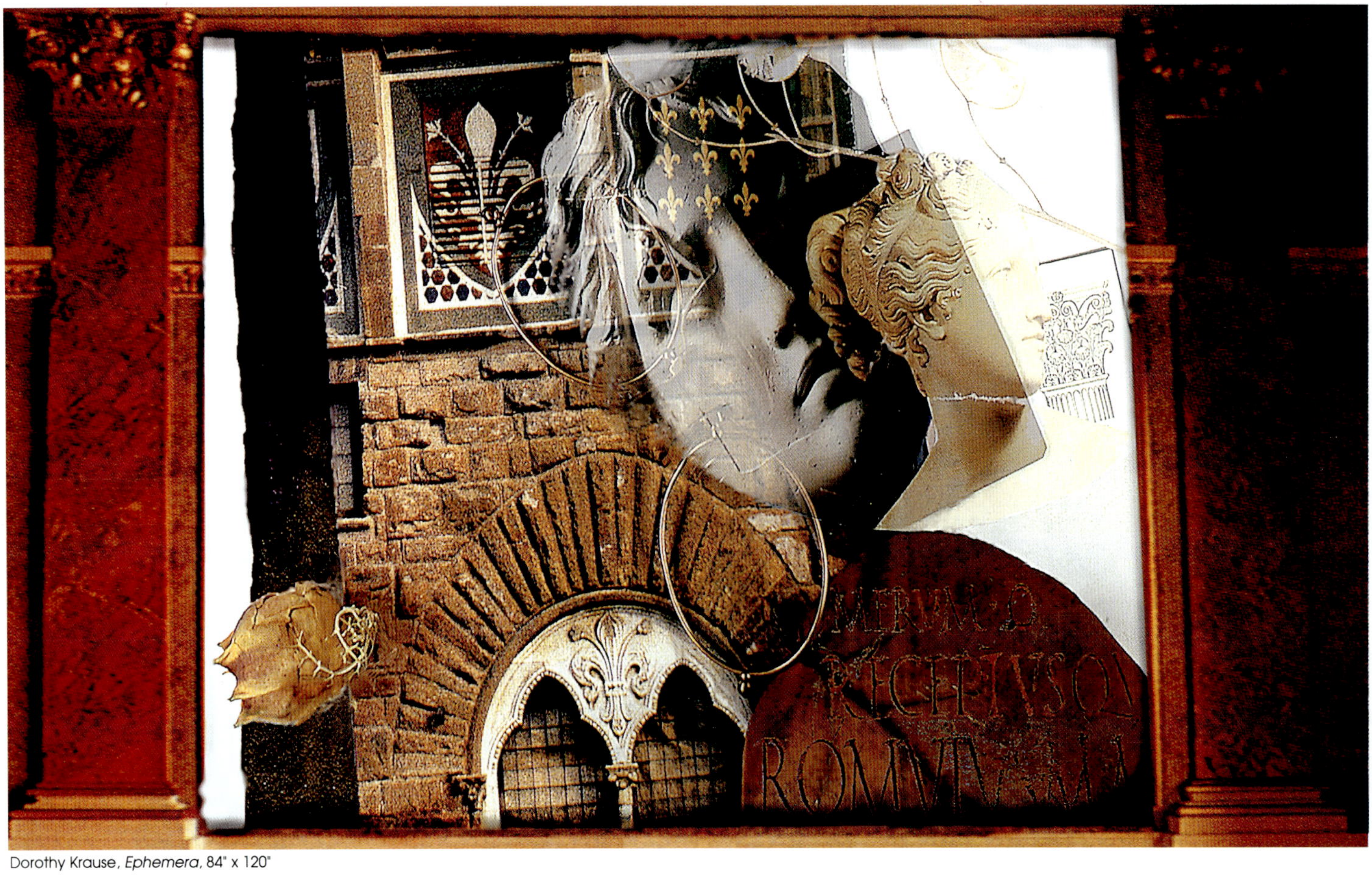

Dorothy Krause, *Ephemera*, 84" x 120"

Nicola VIGINI

Vigini and Associates
619 Western Avenue, Box 15
Seattle, WA 98104
TEL 206-682-4868

Nicola VIGINI produces the highest standard of art exacted by traditional Italian craftsmen. He has had extensive fine and decorative arts training at the *Liceo Artistico* in Rome and at the *Institut Supérieur de Peinture Décorative* of Paris. His background in classical drawing and painting and his fascination with artists such as Piranesi, led to his specialization in the centuries- old painting technique of architectural trompe l'oeil.

Trompe l'oeil is appreciated for its wit and style, and can also provide an ideal architectural solution for space where the actual material desired is either too costly or structurally unfeasible. Nicola VIGINI creates such trompe l'oeil subjects as domes, columns, bas-relief, moldings and vaulted ceilings.

Also see these GUILD publications:
Designer's Edition: 9, 10

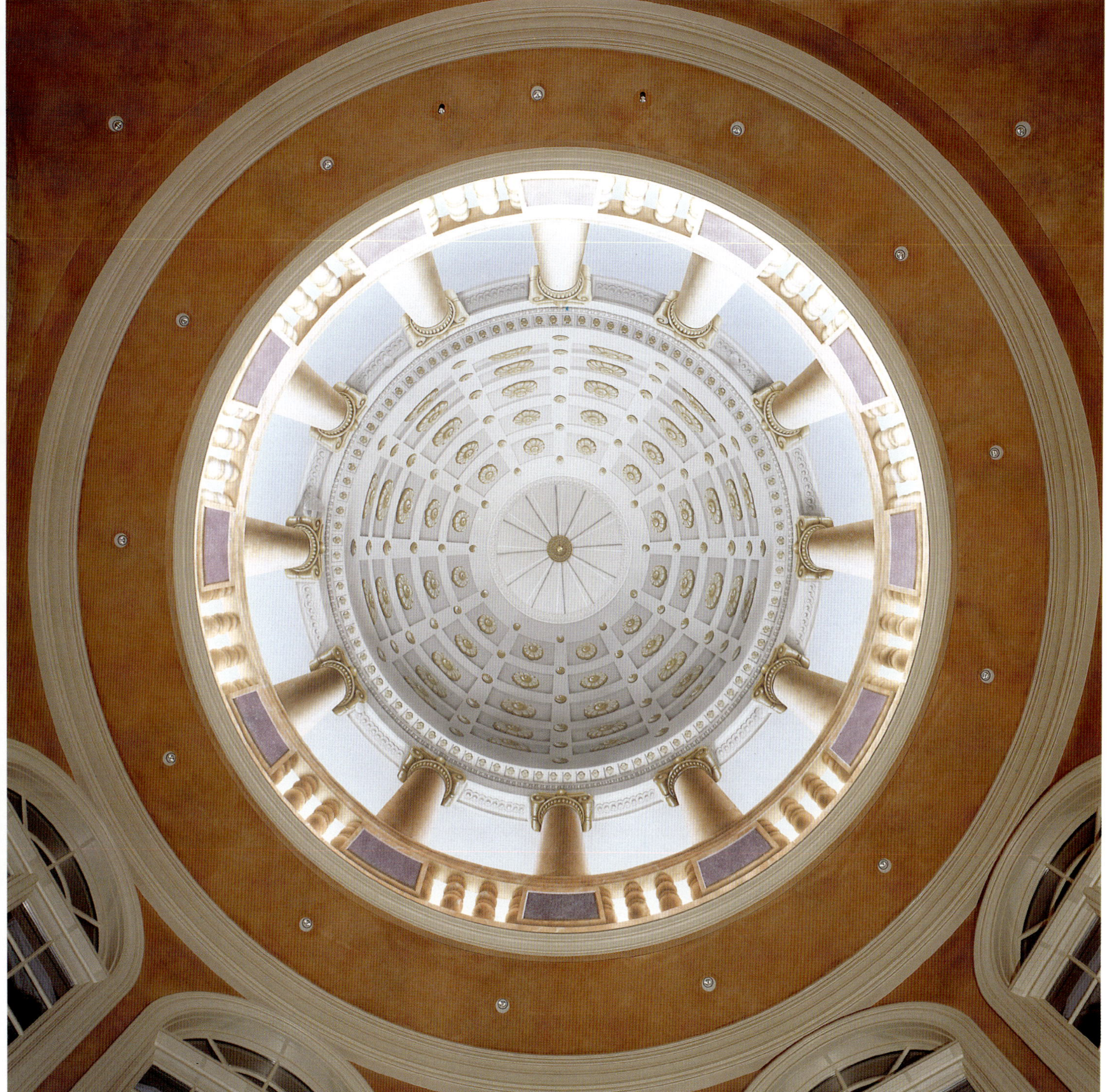

Dome, 1995, 20'Dia, 8'D, residential project

David Story

ATRIUM SCULPTURE

CAROL KODIS

Interior Designer

For Carol Kodis of Kodis Associates, art is not something that stands apart from architecture or design. Kodis brings art and artists into her plans from the very beginning of a project. Her Massachusetts space planning and interior design firm works primarily with commercial and corporate office design accounts, with a sprinkling of residential projects.

"I prefer to incorporate art work into the basic design of the space," she says, "to add imagination and support the image the client wants to develop. It's best to do that right from the start."

Kodis's design for the new corporate headquarters of Pegasystems, in Cambridge, is a case in point. Her challenge was to develop an office environment suitably creative for this fast-growing, high-tech software firm, while also enhancing Pegasystems' image with clients, including some of the world's largest banks.

The centerpiece of her award-winning design was a reception area featuring acid-etched glass by GUILD artist Duncan Laurie of Degnan/Laurie Studios. Large glass panels, set into two arched doorways, highlight a striking promenade leading from the reception area. "We did many things throughout the space that were distinctly Pegasystems," Kodis recalled. "Artwork is an elegant, sophisticated way for a corporate client to develop a unique identity."

Kodis uses GUILD sourcebooks to find both artists and inspiration. "As a resource, they are particularly helpful," she says, "because they show installations and give us a context. This is often more useful than seeing individual pieces in a gallery. It helps us think early on about how to incorporate the artist's work into a project.

"I urge designers and architects to explore working relationships with a variety of artists. The interplay of ideas between the client, designer and artist expands and enriches the dimensions of a project."

Photo by Yoke Wong

David Adams

6679 West Sunflower
Highland, UT 84003
FAX 801-756-5467
TEL 801-756-1167

David Adams works with architects and designers to provide site-specific commissioned works for corporate and private clients. He creates works for free-standing, wall-hung, and suspended presentations.

Mr. Adams' pieces are frequently composed of multiple forms which interact to animate the given space. The polychrome, graduated finishes utilize a wide range of colors, resulting in vibrant, engaging works for exterior and interior staging. He works in aluminum, bronze, stone, stainless, Cor-ten and mild steels, in any scale.

A *T.L. Imposed Order w/Points + Spark*, 1992, private residence, fabricated painted aluminum and stainless steel, 7'6" x 13' x 6"

B *Cyphered Moments, Prairie Dream Cycle w/Guides*, 1994, Bryan Memorial Hospital Medical Plaza

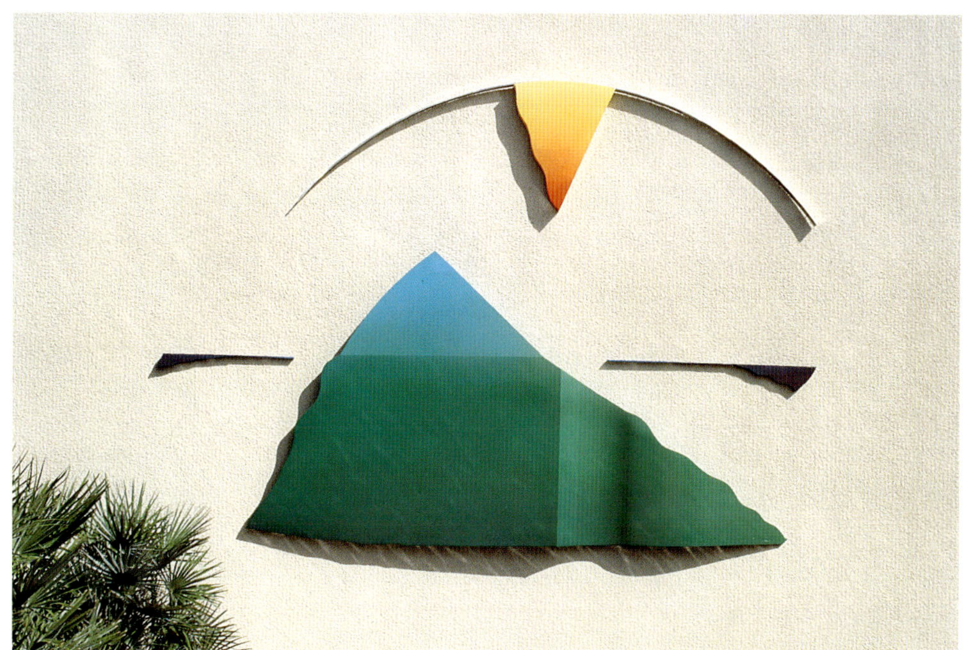

A

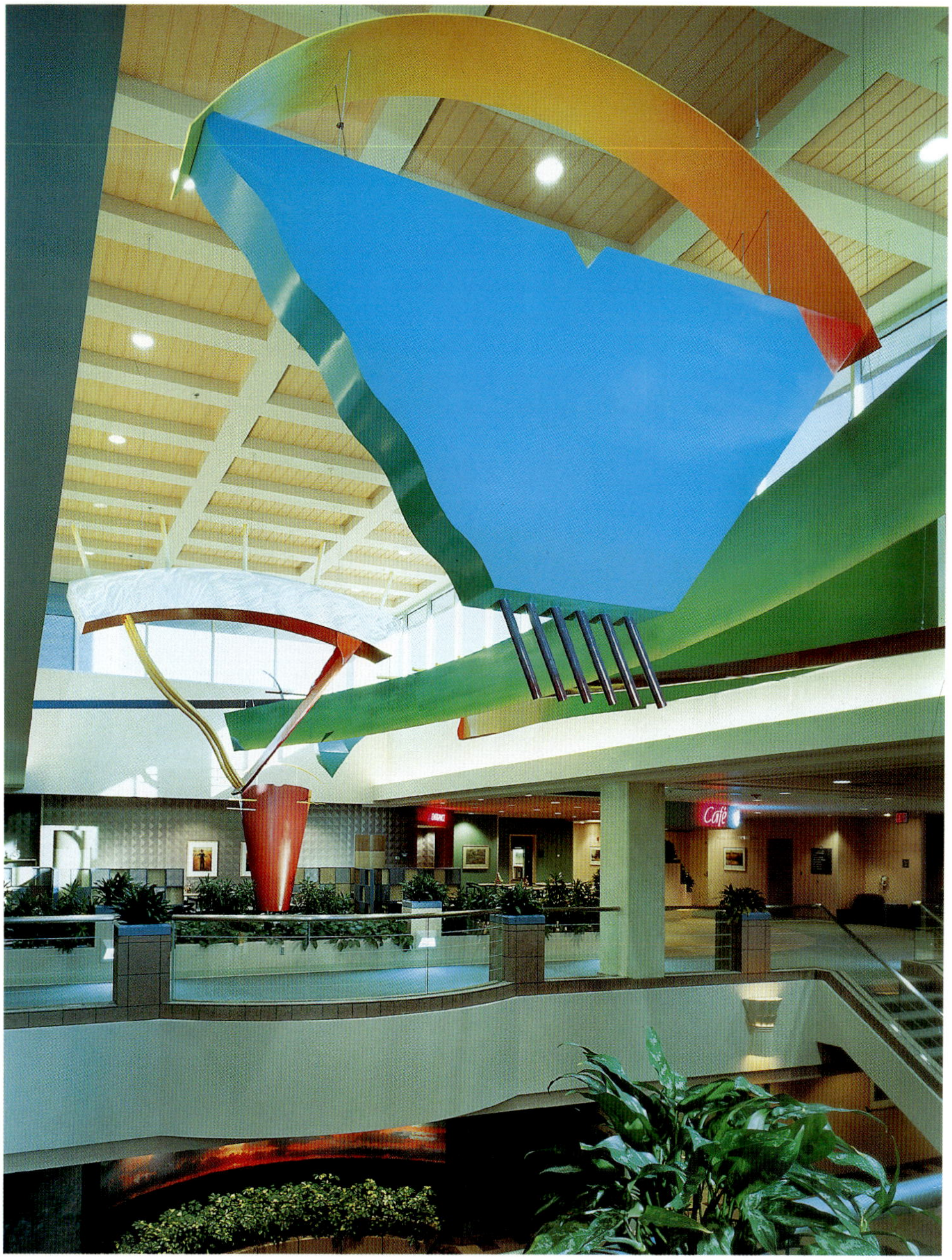

B

Peter Paige

Jill Casty

494 Alvarado Street, Suite D
Monterey, CA 93940
FAX 408-649-0713
TEL 408-649-0923

Jill Casty's exuberant aerial pieces—rhythmic, flowing and colorful—enhance not only public places, but the public's experience of these places.

She also creates abstract standing sculptures, unique lamps, wall-mounted constructions and innovative banners—sometimes merging genres.

Her work, while inventive and distinctive, is always sensitive to the site and to the vision of architect and client.

A *Light Sculpture*, seven curved acrylic panels, dyed images, 10'Dia

B *Atrium Medley* (detail), mobiles and fabric murals, atrium size: 38' x 24'/

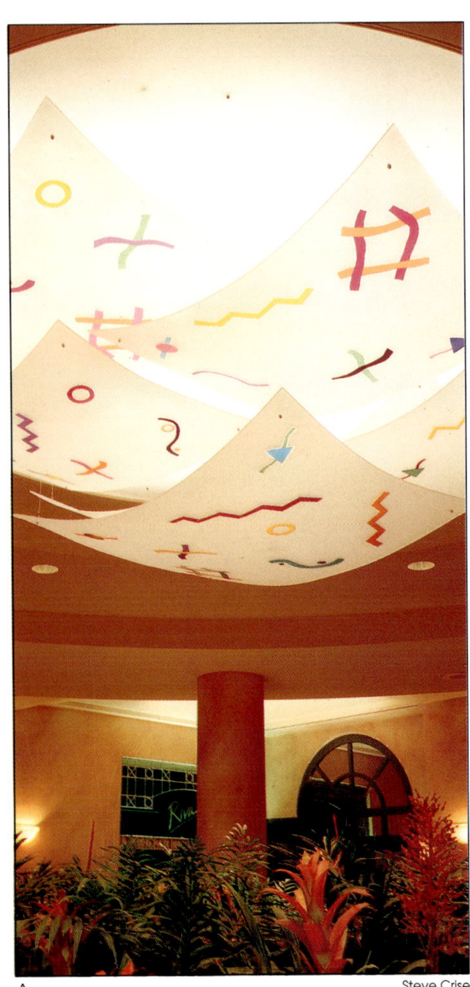

A

Steve Crise

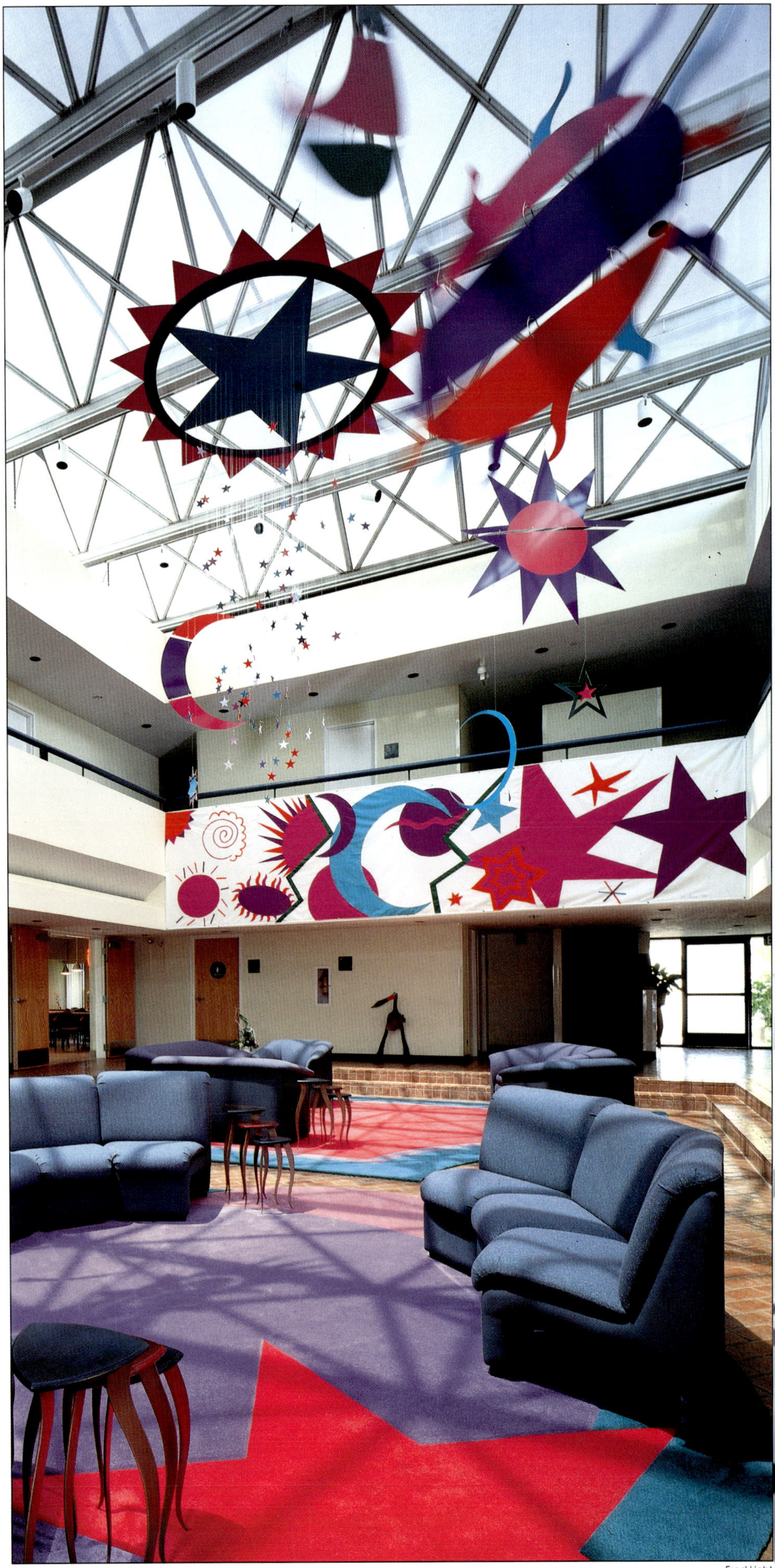

B

Fred Licht

Jonathan Clowes

RR 1, Box 486, March Hill
Walpole, NH 03608
FAX 603-756-9505
TEL 603-756-9505

Jonathan Clowes' hanging sculptures engage the viewer's spirit, giving it the opportunity to move beyond the bounds of daily existence. Each commissioned piece is unique, being designed and fabricated to suit either corporate or private clients and their spaces. Native hardwood elements may be combined with handwrought metals, fabric, stone, paper, and blown glass, contrasting strengths and textures in a fluid, balanced whole.

Since 1974, Jonathan has been a designer and sculptor, collaborating with both clients and fellow artists to create one-of-a-kind three-dimensional works. He welcomes inquiries, and studio visits by appointment.

Also see these GUILD publications:
THE GUILD: 2, 3, 4, 5
Architect's Edition: 6, 7, 8, 9, 10

SHOWN: *Luminia*, 1994, for Monadnock Paper Mills, mahogany and filter paper, 12'H x 6'W

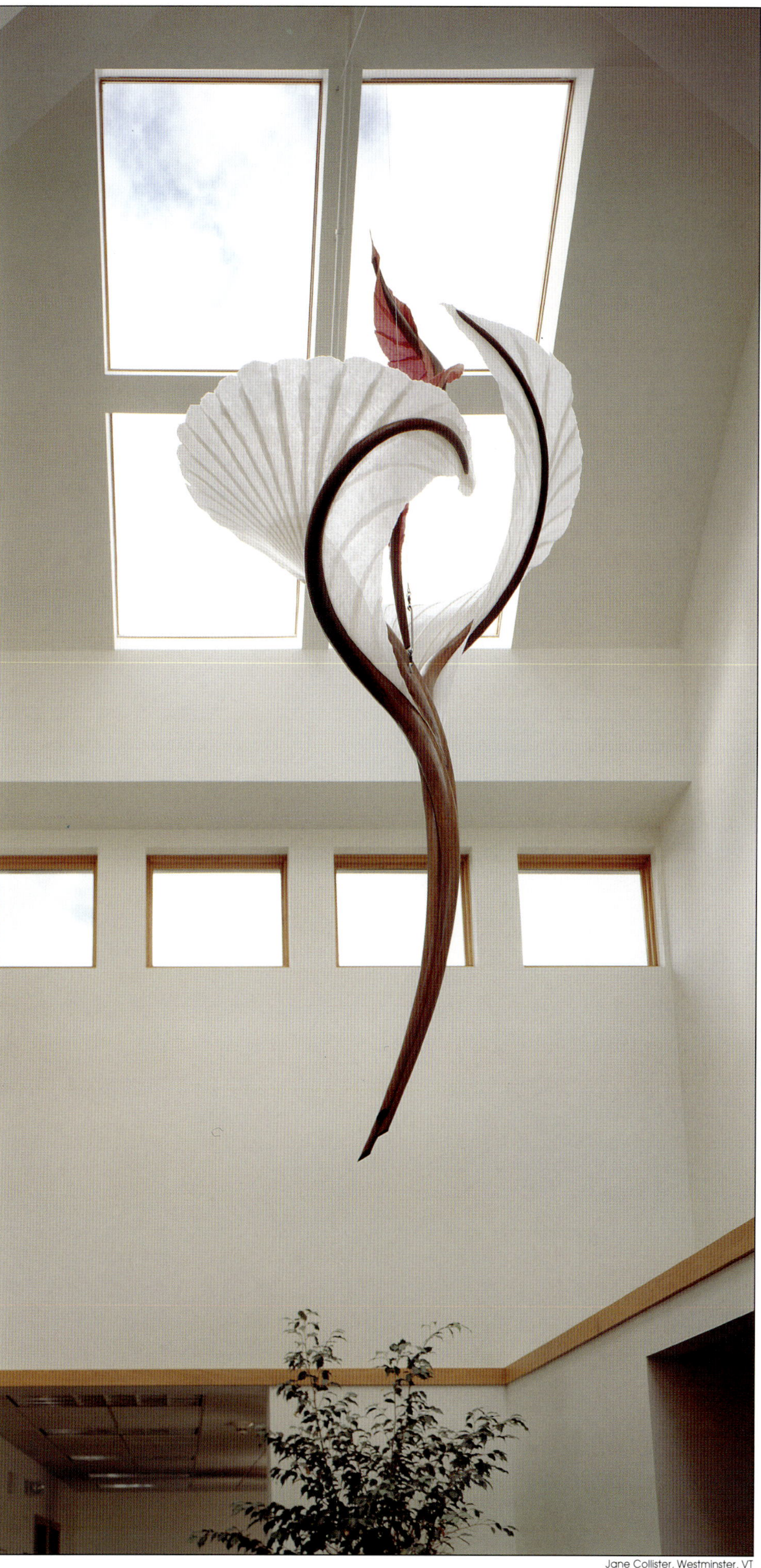

Jane Collister, Westminster, VT

Charles Fager
Joan Marmarellis

Marmarellis-Fager Studio
804 South Newport Avenue
Tampa, FL 33606
FAX 813-254-4028
TEL 813-254-4028

Charles and Joan have produced over 25 public art commissions. Their multiple talents and experience in the fields of art, architecture and education suit them to collaborate with art consultants, planners, architects and engineers.

Their site-sensitive projects are diverse in form and material, ranging from free-standing sculptures, relief walls, and suspended works to atrium pieces.

Also see these GUILD publications:
Architect's Edition: 7, 9, 10

A & B *Origami* (details), double-curtain hanging sculpture, reflective stainless steel with enamel color, suspended at Temple Terrace Family Recreation Complex, FL, each curtain 7' x 12'

C *Cubic Mosaic*, reflective stainless steel with enamel color, three-story lobby, Opus South Corporation, Tampa, FL, 120' x 50'

D *Hyperbolic-Paraboloidal Suspension*, polyester fabric, stainless steel cable, five-story lobby, The Paragon at Southpoint Office Complex, Jacksonville, FL, 120' x 60'

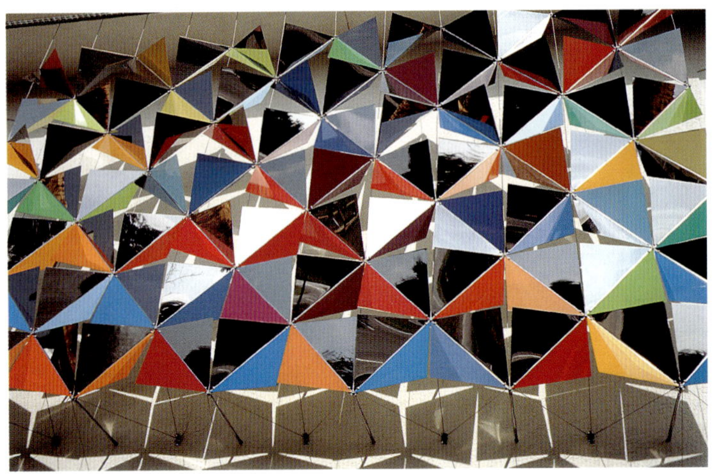

A

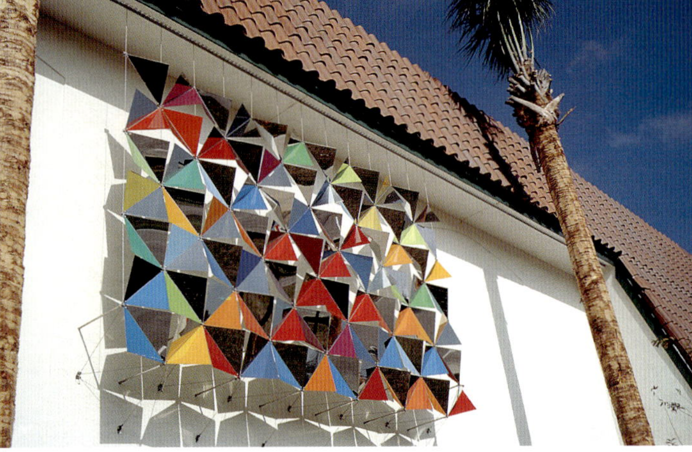

B

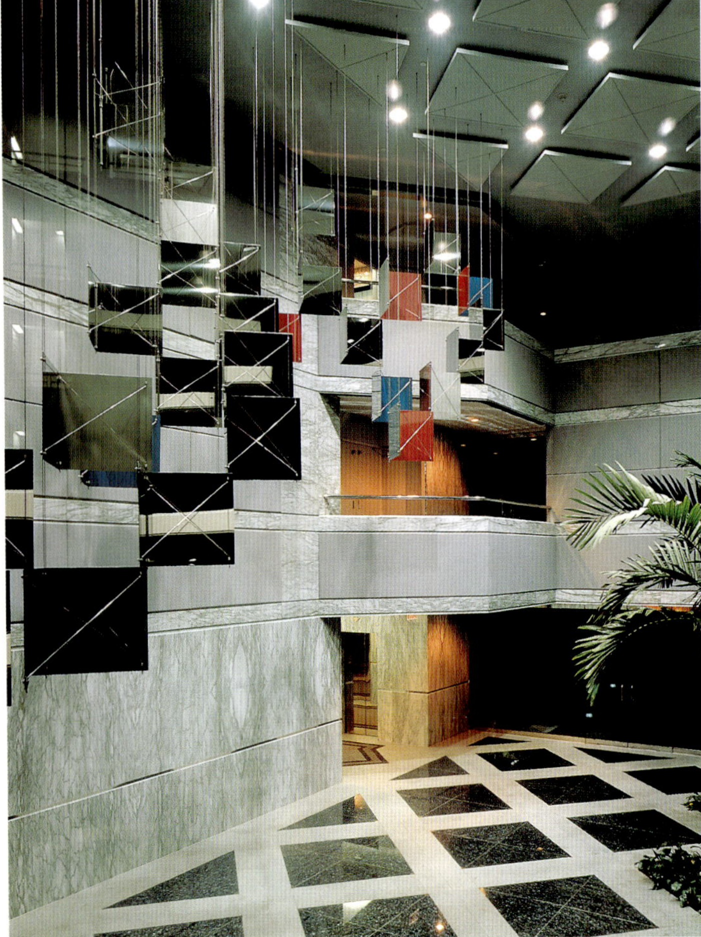

C

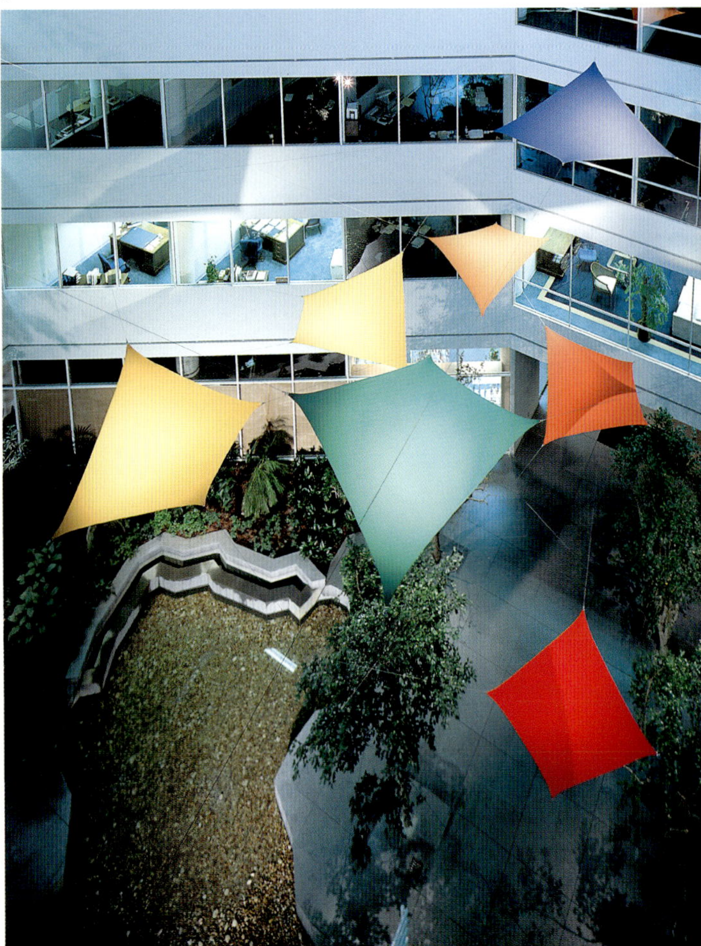

D

Rob Fisher

Environmental Sculpture
228 North Allegheny Street
Bellefonte, PA 16823
FAX 814-353-9060
TEL 814-355-1458
E-Mail: rnf1@andrew.emu.edu

Over the past 25 years, Rob Fisher has established an international reputation as a sculptor, author and lecturer. His monumental suspended sculptures of aluminum and stainless steel are installed in major public spaces including office buildings, hotels, banks, malls, city centers, medical centers and private residences.

A pioneer in the art/technology movement, Rob Fisher creates playful organic sculptures based on natural forms and fabricated with high-tech materials and processes. He collaborates with architects and lighting designers in the production of his artwork.

Clients include:
The Georgetown Company, NY
New England Development
DeBartolo Corporation
Westcor Partners, AZ
City of Hamamatsu, Japan
Osaka Hilton International, Japan
Kingdom of Saudi Arabia
Mellon Bank
Trump Corporation
Playboy Corporation
Ball-Unimark Corporation
Carnegie Science Center, PA

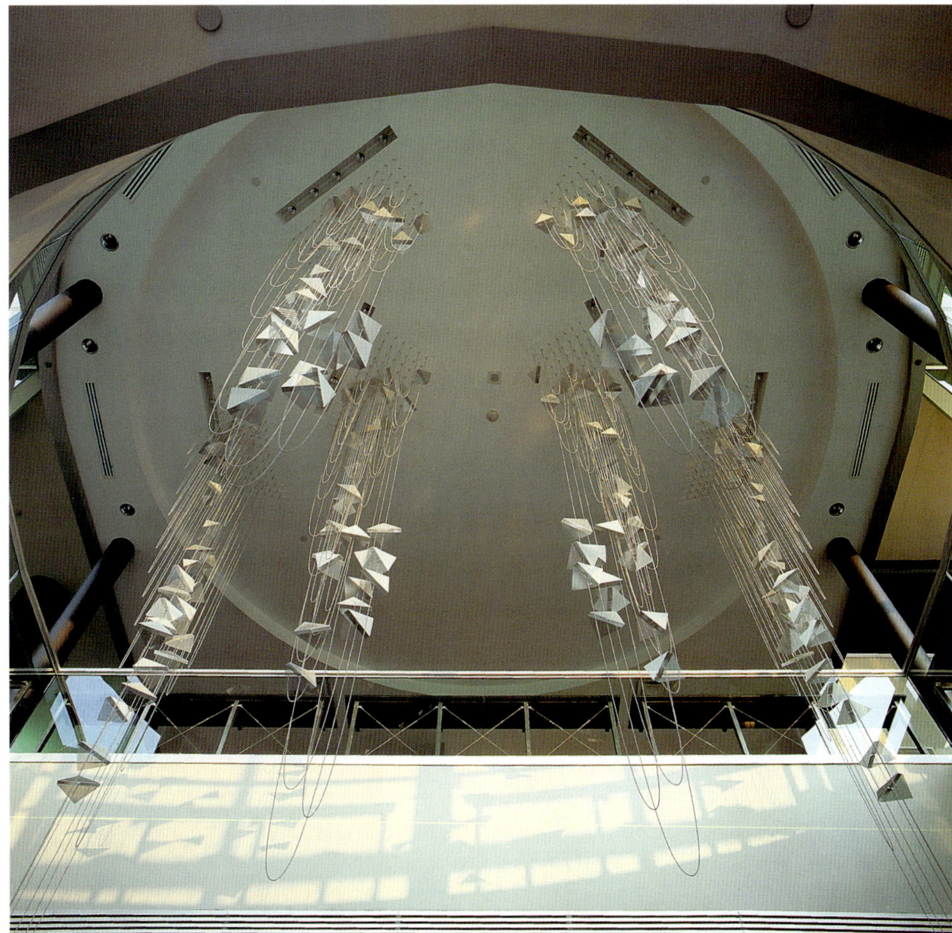

Aviary, 1995, aluminum and stainless steel, 30'H x 32'W x 16'D

Alan Schindler

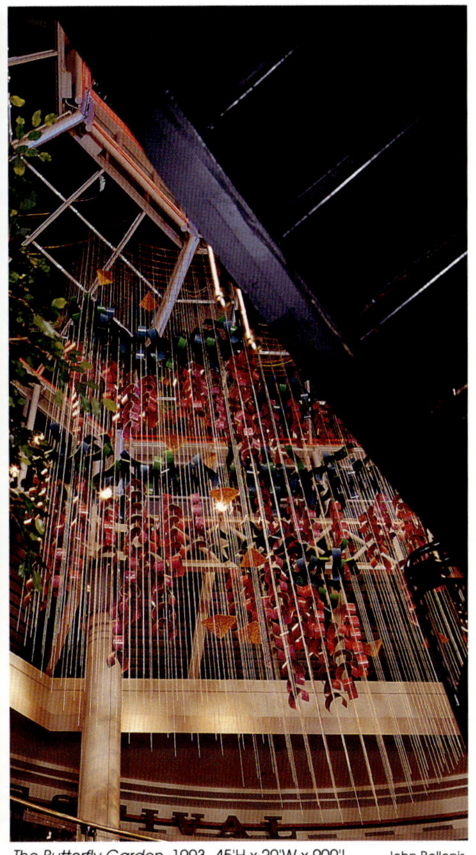

The Butterfly Garden, 1993, 45'H x 20'W x 900'L

John Bellenis

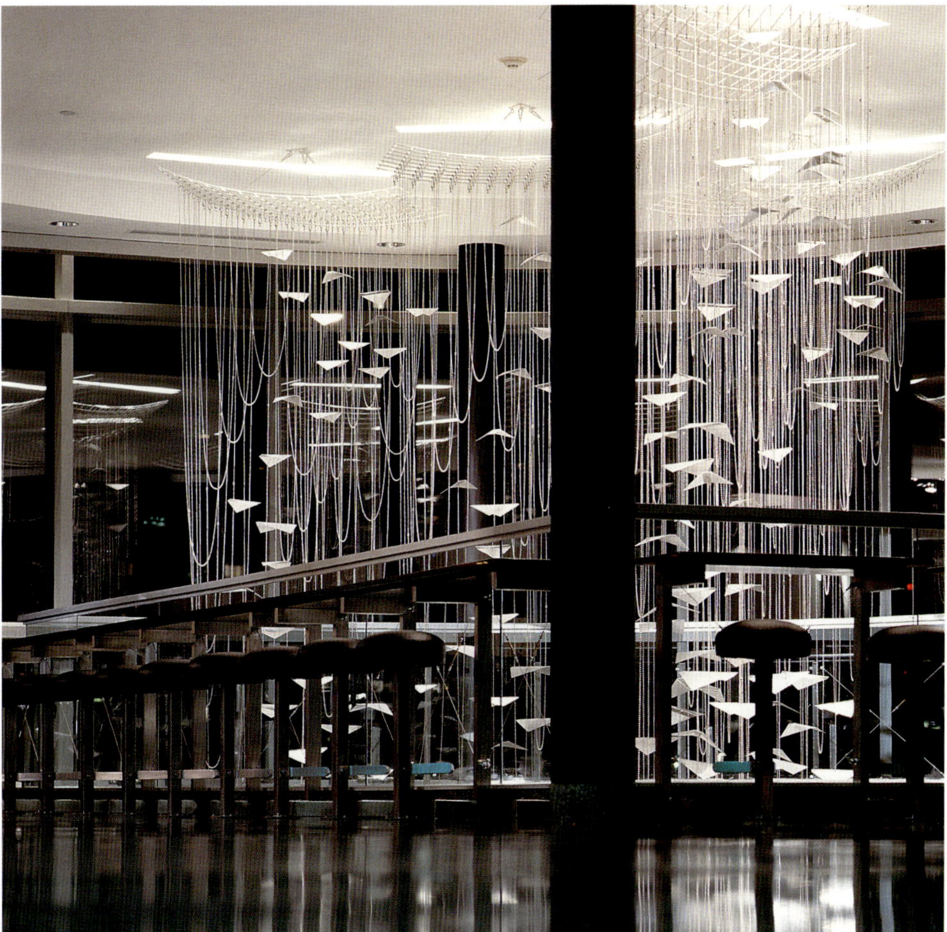

Aviary, 1995, aluminum and stainless steel, 30'H x 32'W x 16'D

Alan Schindler

Daniel Goldstein

224 Guerrero
San Francisco, CA 94103
FAX 415-648-4076
TEL 415-621-5761

Daniel Goldstein has collaborated with architects and designers for over 15 years on corporate and private commissions. His work is in the collections of major museums such as the Brooklyn, Carnegie and Chicago Art institute.

His kinetic sculptures, made of light and durable anodized aluminum, move gracefully through space, needing only a light breeze to propel them.

A *Heaven and Earth,* 1992, Good Samaritan Hospital, 58" x 58" x 58"

B *The Light Above The Stairs,* 1991, Kaiser Hospital, 16' x 14' x 12'

C *Wings,* 1993, Synoptics, 16' x 14' x 14'

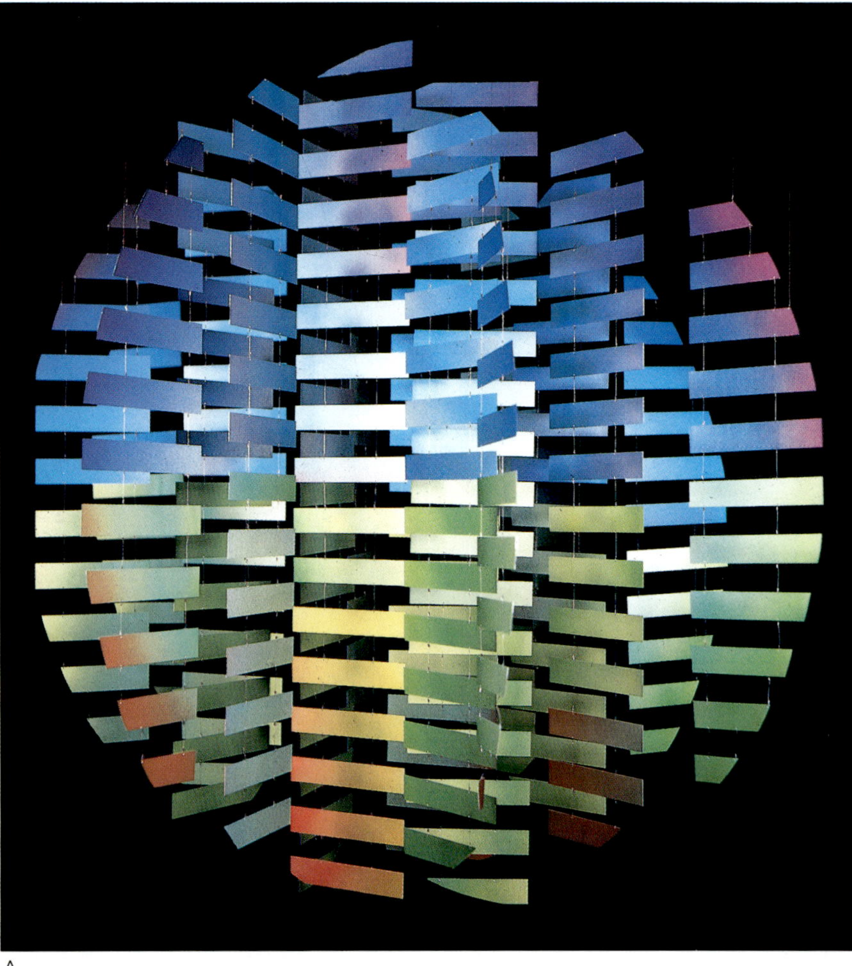

A

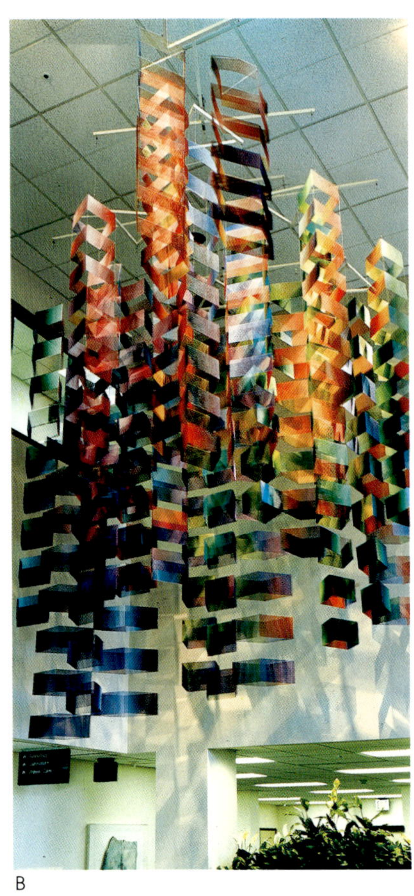

B

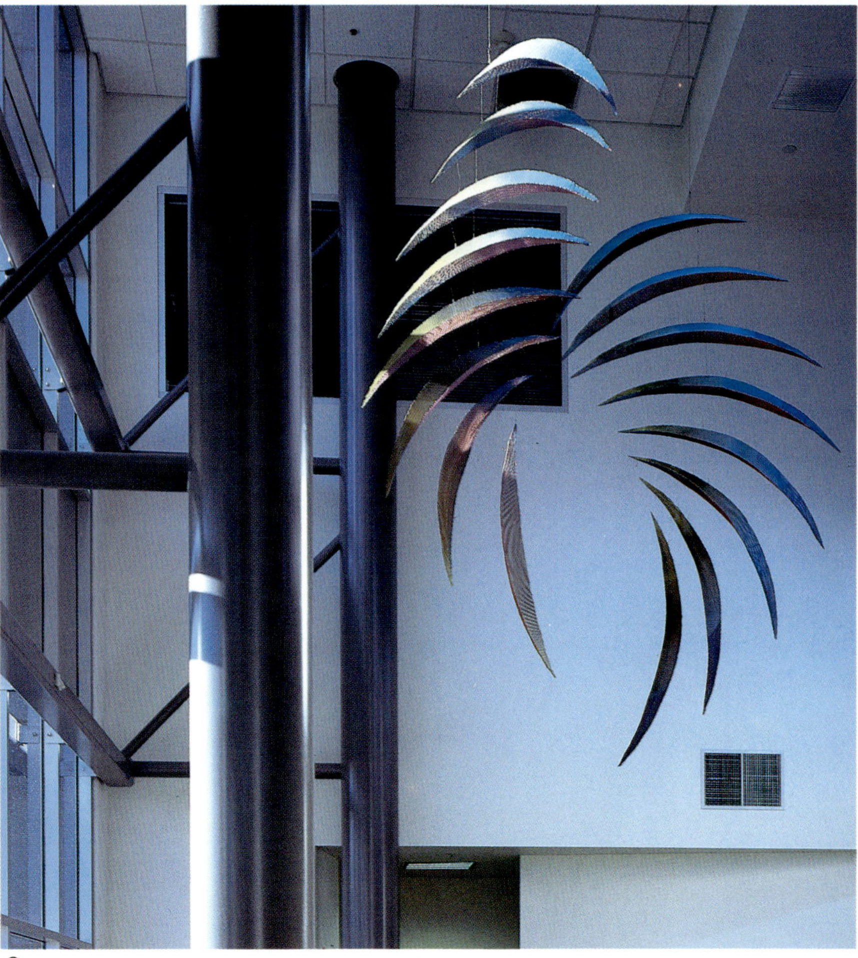

C

Walter Gordinier
Alice Van Leunen

Gordinier/Van Leunen Collaborations
3608 SE Milwaukie Avenue
Portland, OR 97202
FAX 503-234-1083 (Gordinier)
TEL 503-234-1083 (Gordinier)
FAX 503-636-0787 (Van Leunen)
TEL 503-636-0787 (Van Leunen)

Gordinier and Van Leunen work as a team, both within their own group and with the architects, designers, and community representatives designated by the client. They have the imagination and technical ability to create significant artworks that harmonize with the architectural site as well as express its purpose. Their goal is to produce work that is engaging, meaningful, accessible and enduring. The artists are versatile in their approach and in their use of a spectrum of traditional and innovative techniques and materials.

The engineering of each project is carefully planned and the artists are available to supervise installation.

Commissions include:
National High Magnetic Field Laboratory,
  Florida State University, Tallahassee, FL
Minnesota High Security Hospital, St. Peter, MN
Mulia Bank Tower, Djakarta, Indonesia

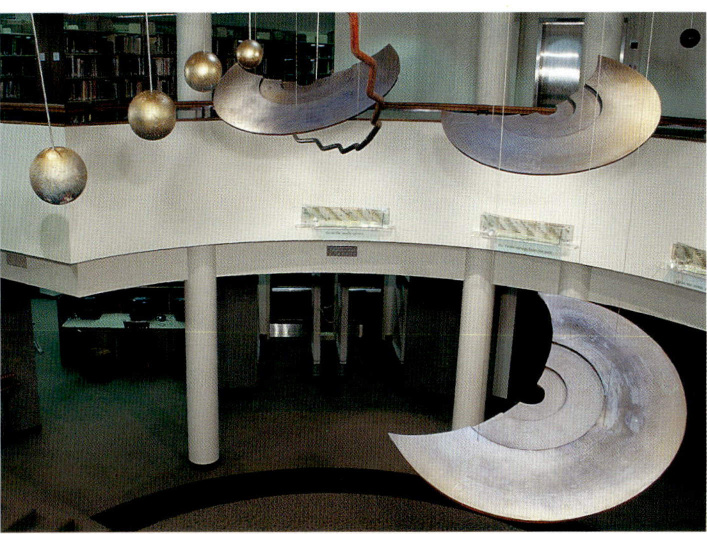

Passages (detail), 1995, glass, acrylic, metal, text, 15' x 25'Dia

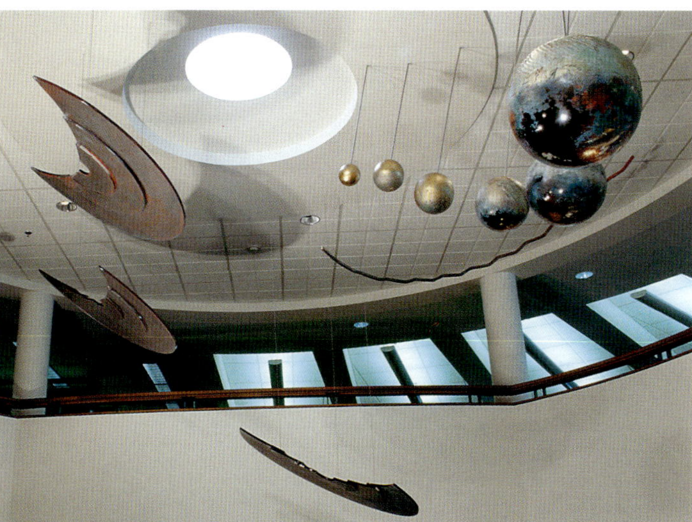

Passages (detail), commission for Portland Community College library rotunda

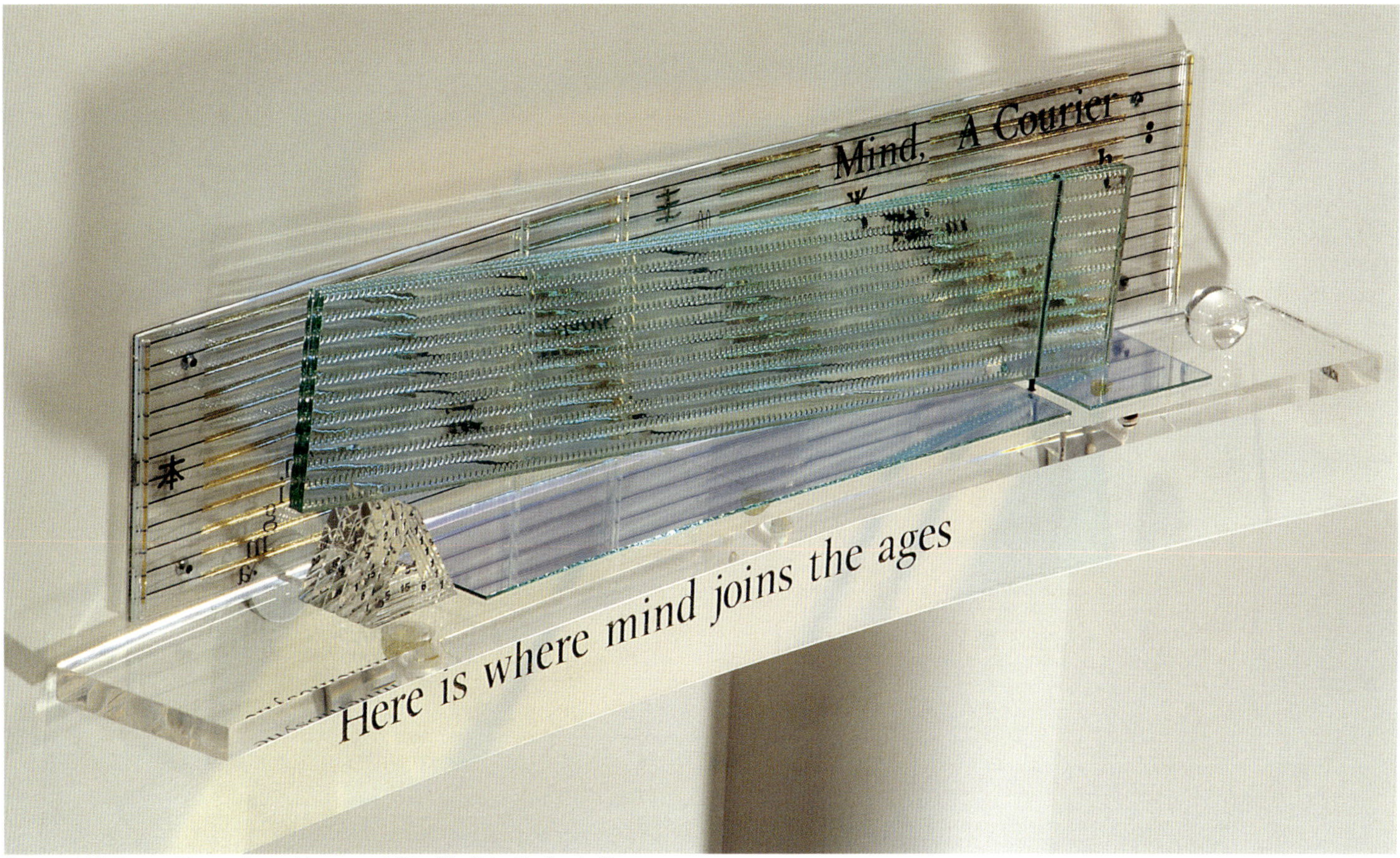

Passages (detail), one of four wall assemblages, each 15" x 48" x 6", text by Sandra Stone

Charles Gray

architectural artist
14425 N. 42nd Place
Phoenix, AZ 85032
FAX 602-996-2319
TEL   602-996-2319
E-Mail: golfart@mary.iia.org

Twenty years committed to fulfilling the artistic needs of architects and designers has resulted in a diverse portfolio of site-specific solutions by artist Charles Gray. Light, defracted by holography or excited by UV, is a specialty.

Commissioned atrium mobile sculptures may be seen at Walt Disney World's *Pleasure Island*; the '96 Olympic Infirmary, Atlanta; The Grand, Dallas, Texas; and AMC, Woodland Hills, California.

A *Burbank Blues*, commissioned prototype

B *Southern Lights*, AMC Phipp's Plaza, Atlanta, GA

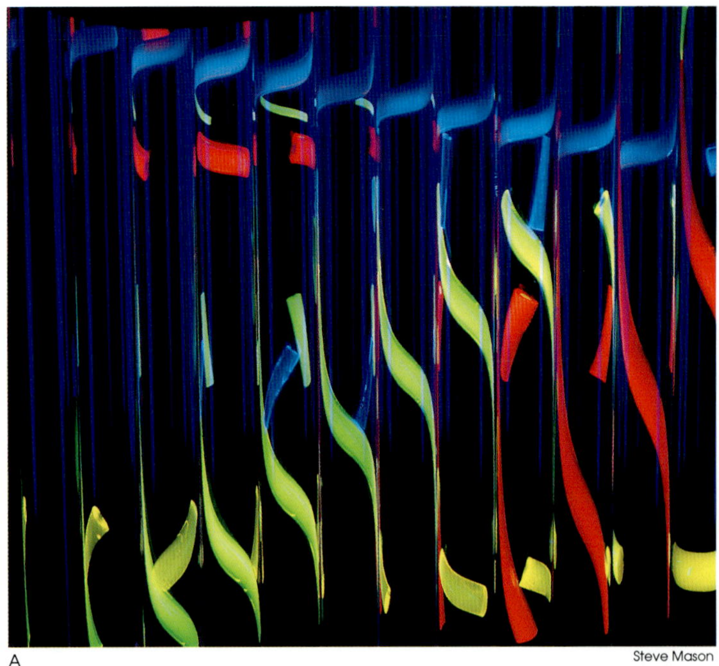

A

Steve Mason

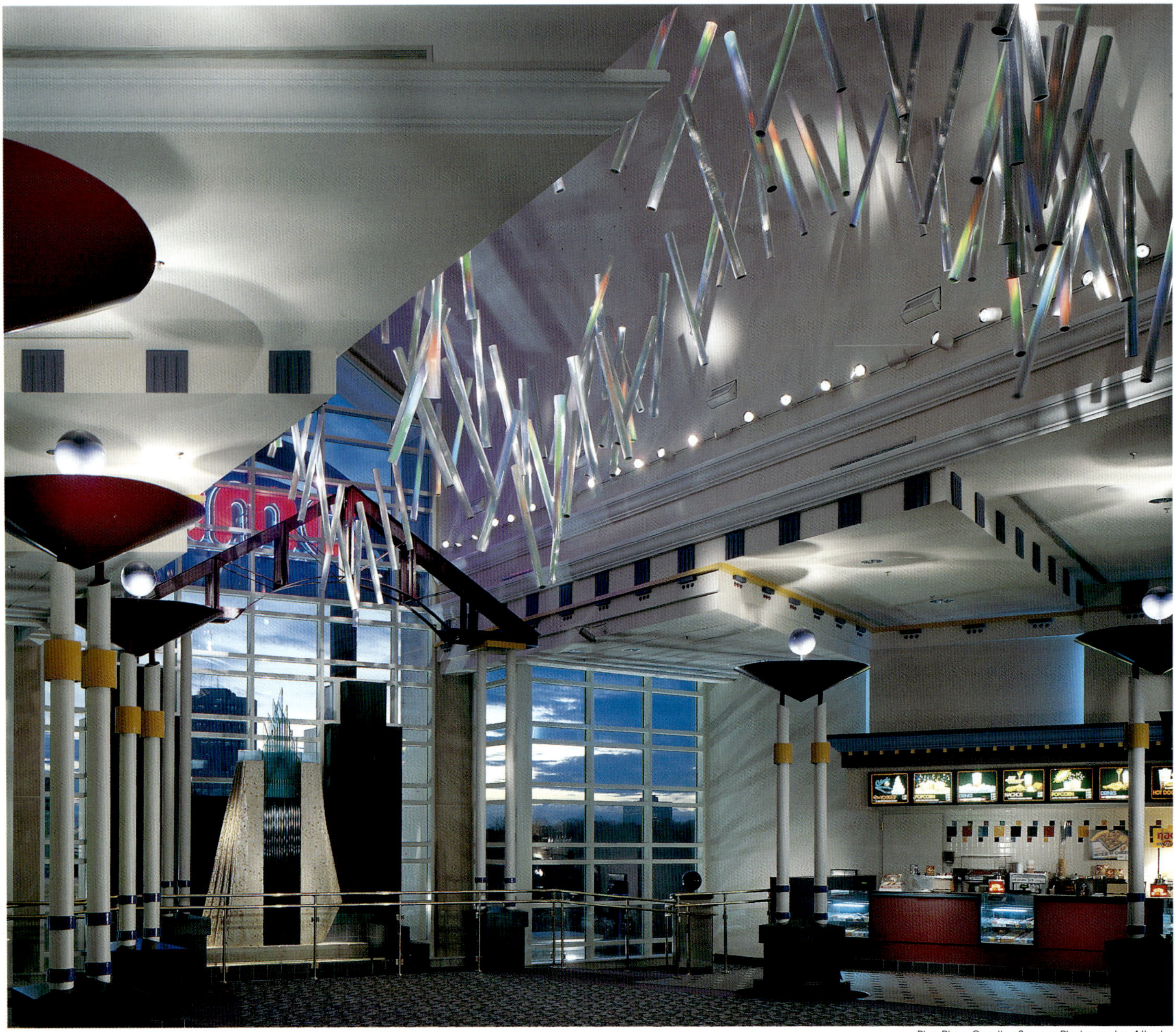

B

Rion Rizzo, Creative Sources Photography, Atlanta

Roland Hockett

361 Greenwood Circle
Panama City Beach, FL 32407
TEL 904-235-2011

Roland Hockett has produced works for numerous collections, including the *Liberty* mural in Juan Santa Maria International Airport in Costa Rica; the Panama City, Florida, international airport; the U.S. Embassy in Costa Rica (Centro Cultural); the Florida Supreme Court; and many other corporate and private collections in the United States and Costa Rica.

Active for over 30 years, he has accomplished works in welded copper, acrylic and carving. His works are rich in texture, relatively lightweight, and easily maintained. Projects range from large site-specific works to smaller individual sculptures and paintings.

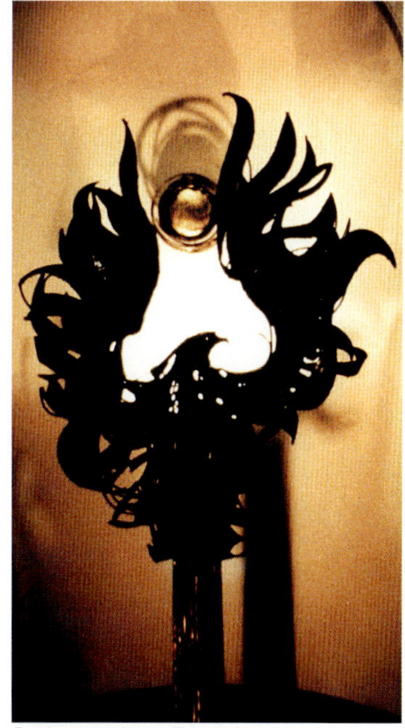

Eagle, one of two, Florida Supreme Court, copper, 7'

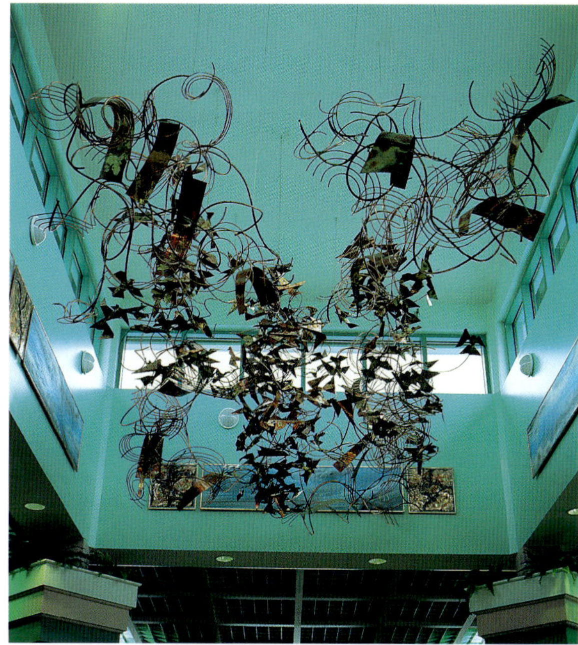

SKYscape, Panama City International Airport, copper and acrylic, 27' x 16'

Tim Allen

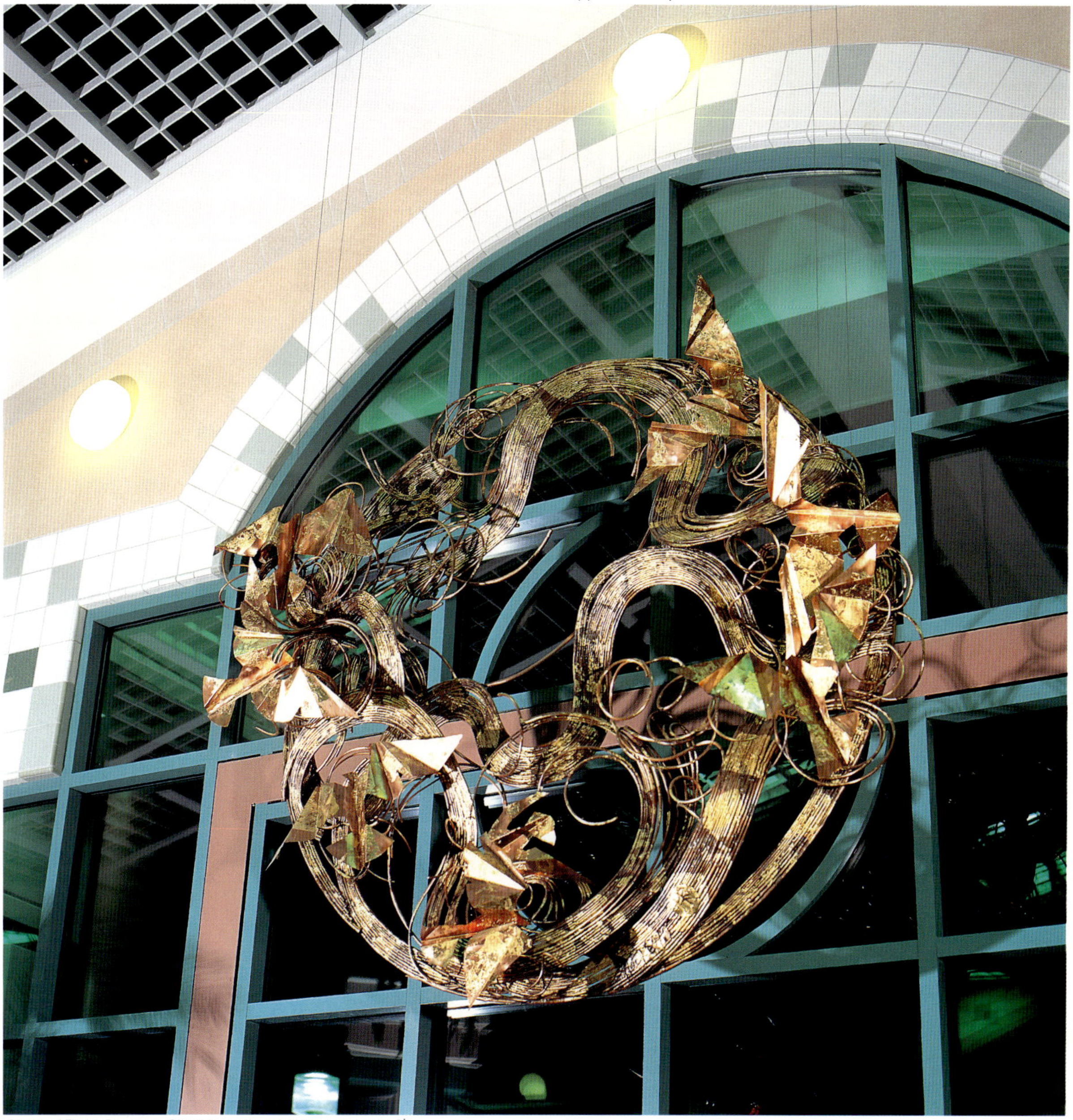

Circle of Flight, Panama City International Airport, copper, 8'

Tim Allen

EVA ZERVOS

Art Advisor

As a corporate art advisor, Eva Zervos values creativity and artistic excellence highly. However, she is quick to point out that her first role in working with clients is to provide information and guidance to help them feel confident about their artistic choices.

"I've worked with both public institutions and corporations in the Boston area for over 12 years," Zervos explains. "Most of my clients come from the Northeast, but the resources I use are nationwide. THE GUILD helps trigger my memory of what's available, and I often recommend GUILD artists for projects because they have the professionalism and experience that helps me do my job better."

Her firm is a full-service consulting business, which means she typically works through every stage of a project, from earliest contact with the artist to proposals, creation, installation and any services thereafter.

Zervos says that when a client selects or commissions original, site-specific art, they are often saying yes to something they haven't seen. "That requires a significant level of trust and comfort, and as a result, education is a large part of my job. The art has to be presented in a way that is both eloquent and accessible."

She cites her experience working with GUILD artist Robert Pfitzenmeier as a perfect example of the kind of professionalism that makes her job both easier and more rewarding. The project involved an atrium sculpture for a Boston health care center. "In the most successful projects, the client has a strong feeling of participation, and someone like Bob really helps keep the lines of communication open. His ideas were fascinating, his track record excellent and his presentation materials—from photographs to video to models of the sculpture—were superb. These are the tools that really help the client get excited.

"The completed sculpture is extraordinarily beautiful as you watch it move and the colors change. People absolutely love it."

Photo by Cecilia Hirsh

Erick C. Johnson

E.J. Sculpture Works
3300 Wolff Street
Denver, CO 80212
TEL 303-433-6334

Over the past 25 years, Erick C. Johnson has created many public and private commissions. Mr. Johnson has a unique ability to generate work that blends well with its host environment. Mr. Johnson understands and utilizes a wide variety of materials (i.e. wood, metal, plastics, neon and laser light). His diverse choice of media creates distinct results that are full of energy. Mr. Johnson invites architects and designers for prospective interior or exterior site-specific commissions.

Commissions include:
Coors Field, Denver Baseball District
  Commission
Colorado Convention Center, Denver
  Commission on Cultural Affairs
Colorado University in Colorado Springs,
  Colorado Council for the Arts and Humanities

A *Calculated Risk*, stainless steel
  and neon, 13'Dia

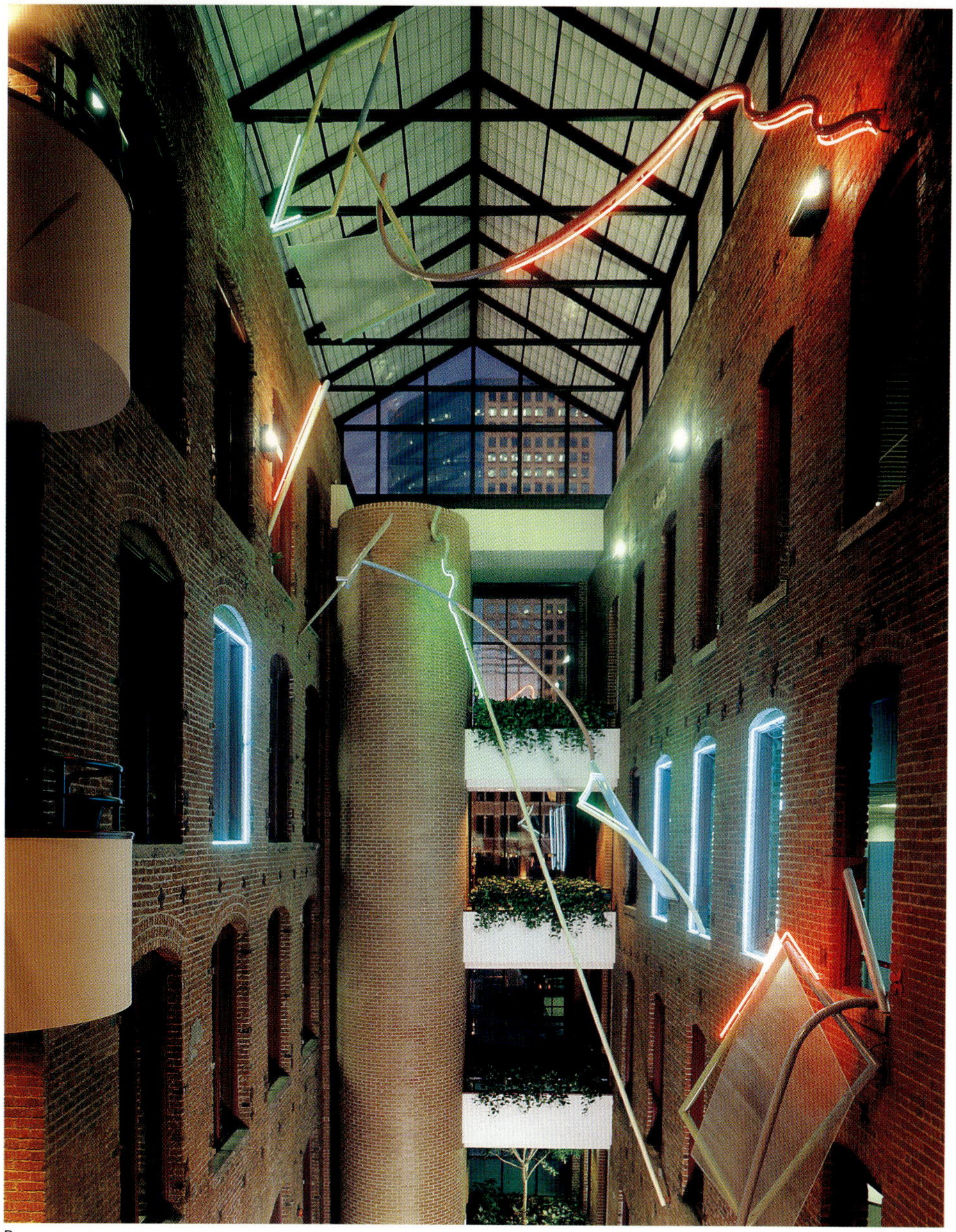

B *Power Play*, painted steel, plexiglass
  and neon, 60' x 80' x 20' (atrium size)

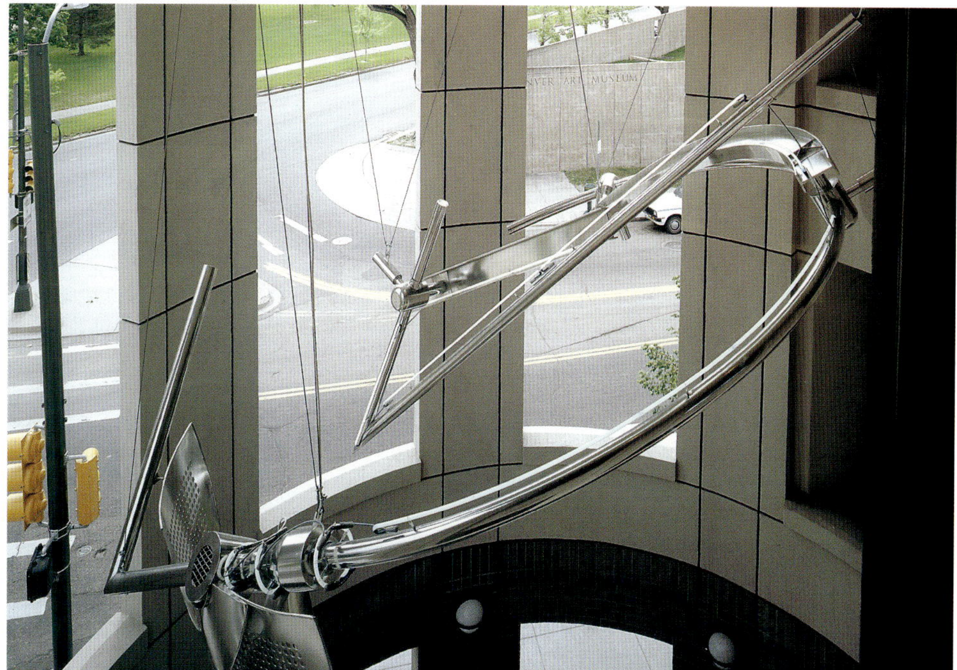

A

Heidi Bishop-LyVere

B

Kimbal Hall

Carolyn Kaneshiro

40325 Pageant Place
Hemet, CA 92544
FAX 909-925-0244
TEL 909-925-2504

Using light-but-durable sheet copper, Carolyn Kaneshiro shapes and textures the metal for light refraction. Heat is used to color the rich copper with additional natural hues including silver, blues and magenta, giving each panel a unique color combination. Fiber is dyed to match the colors created on the copper panels.

These kinetic sculptures enhance both stairwells and lobby areas, where air currents keep them in motion. The artist can adapt shapes and fiber colors to specific archtectural spaces.

Services include design, production and installation.

A *Lights, Action* (detail)

B *Lights, Action*, six panels, copper, cotton chenille tape, each panel 13'H x 30"

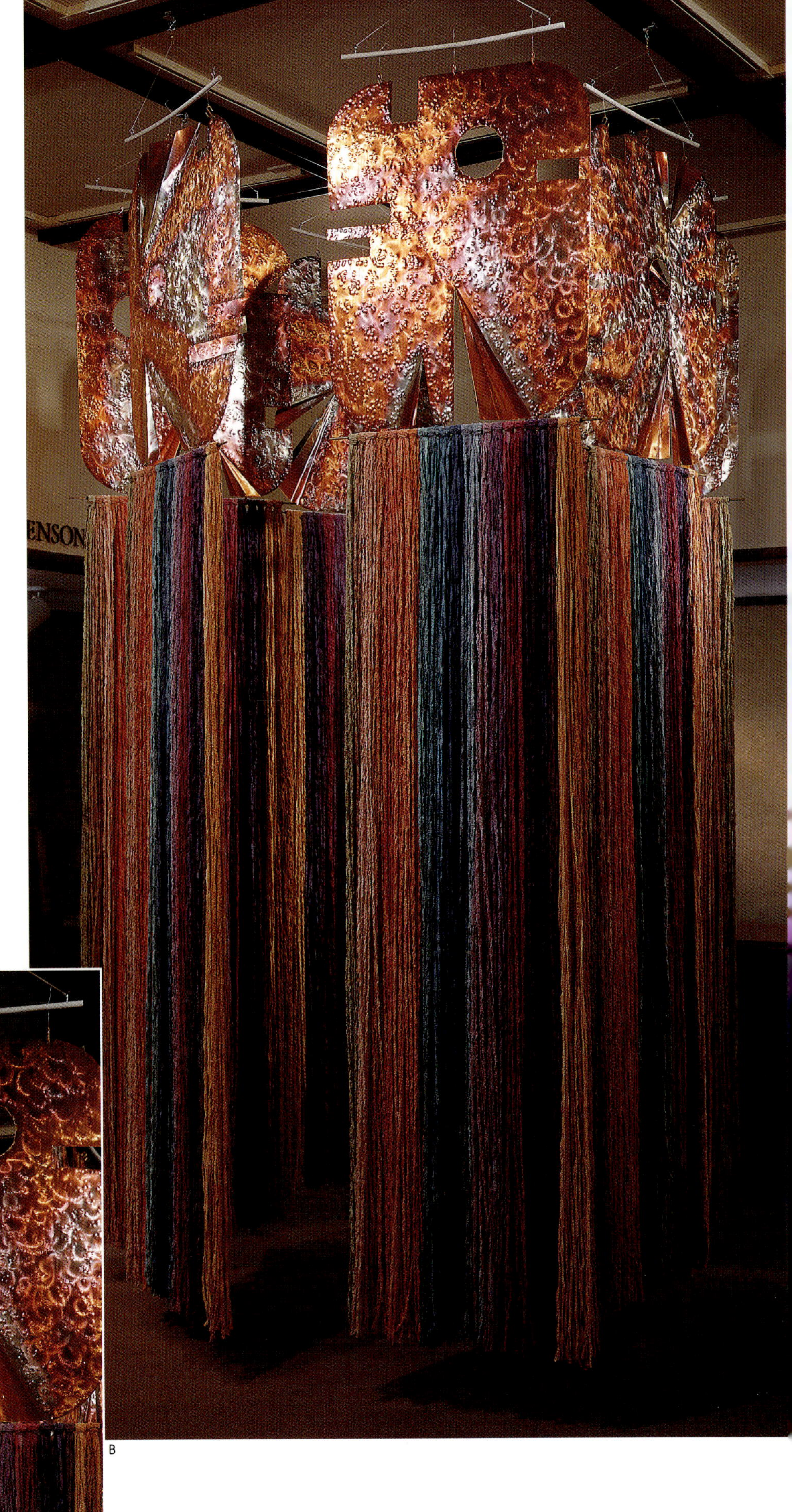

A

B

Joseph Anthony McDonnell

Cold Spring Atelier
11 Peekskill Road
Cold Spring, NY 10516
TEL 914-265-9249

Using gleaming stainless steel, glowing glass, and rich fabrics, Joe McDonnell has energized atriums of major corporations and public spaces throughtout the country.

These aerial gems float, turning ever so gently, in the architectural spaces they enhance.

Commissions include:
Fountain, Silver Spring, MD, 1988
Dulles Office Park, Fairfax, VA, 1988
1050 Washington Blvd., Stamford, CT, 1989
IBM, East Fishkill, NY, 1989
General Electric Hdqrs., Fairfield, CT, 1989
Station Plaza, Trenton, NJ, 1990
733 Third Avenue, New York, NY, 1991
140 Grand Street, White Plains, NY, 1992

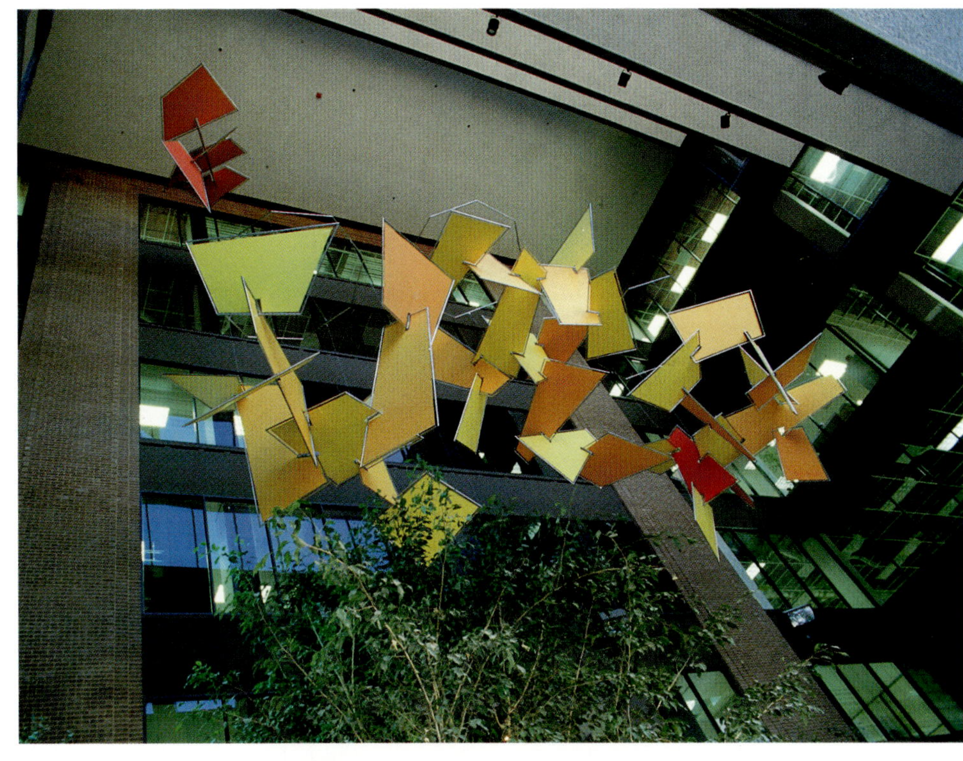

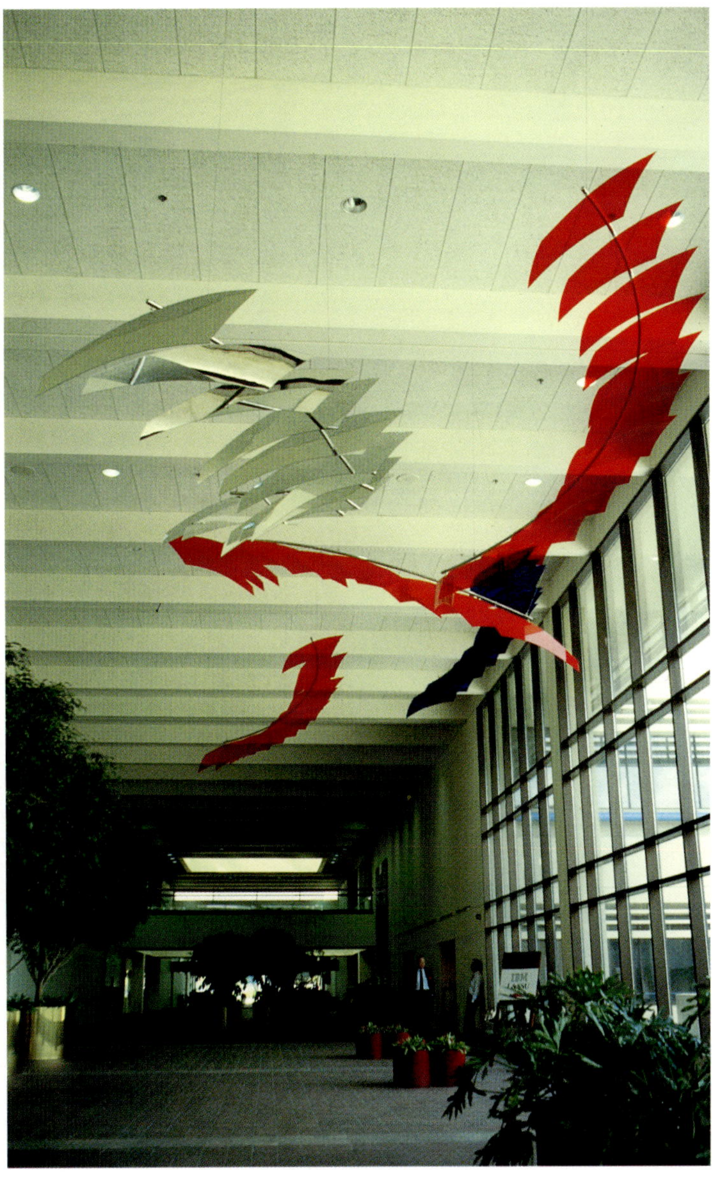

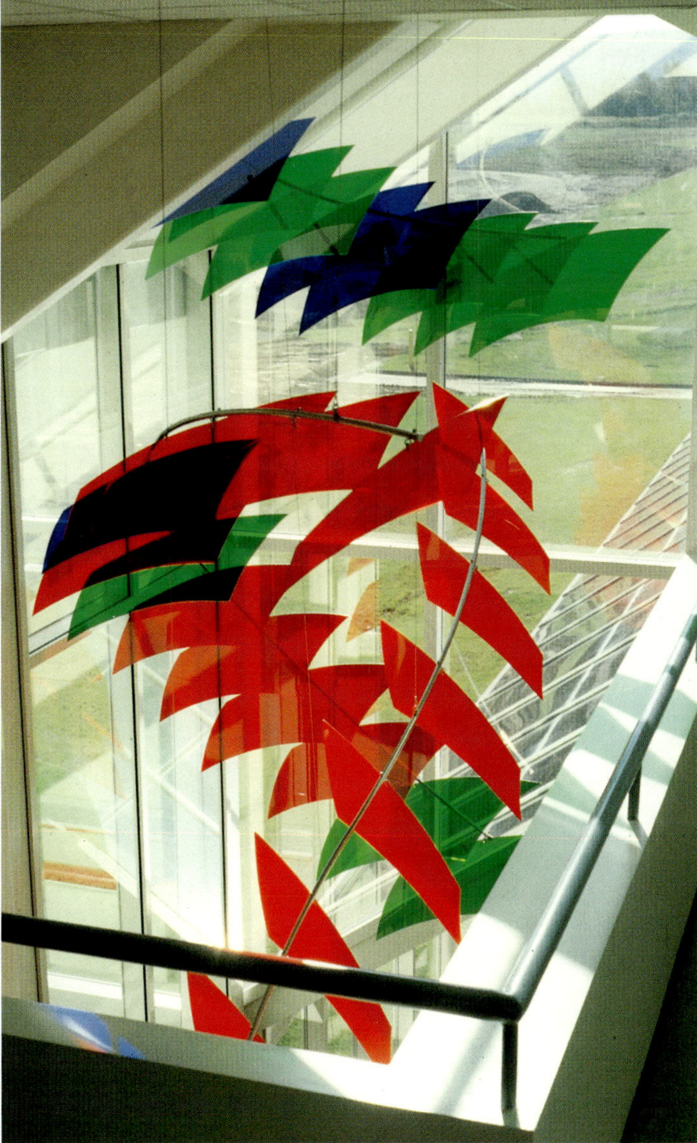

Robert Pfitzenmeier

111 First Street #1-3A
Jersey City, NJ 07302
FAX 201-659-4203
TEL 201-659-7629

Pfitz's light reactive sculptures bring an exciting, uplifting spirit to any environment. The color is a result of light refracted on the surface of the anodized niobium and zirconium. Utilizing the full spectrum of extraordinary color, Pfitz creates work that reacts to light, as well as air movement. Activated by air movement, a fluid kinetic dynamic ripples through each *Feather-Leaf*. The delicate appearance of these forms reflects the vulnerable state of our natural environment. These sculptures adapt well to large expansive areas as well as intimate sites.

Also see these GUILD publications:
THE GUILD: 5
Architect's Edition: 6, 9, 10
Gallery Edition: 1

A *Feather - Leaf III*, anodized niobium, stainless steel frame, 24"H x 50"W x 156"L

B *Feather/Leaf*, anodized niobium, stainless steel, 82"H x 28"W x 40"D

C *Fleeting Images*, anodized zirconium, stainless steel, 15'H x 16'W x 16'D, General Aviation Building, JFK International Airport

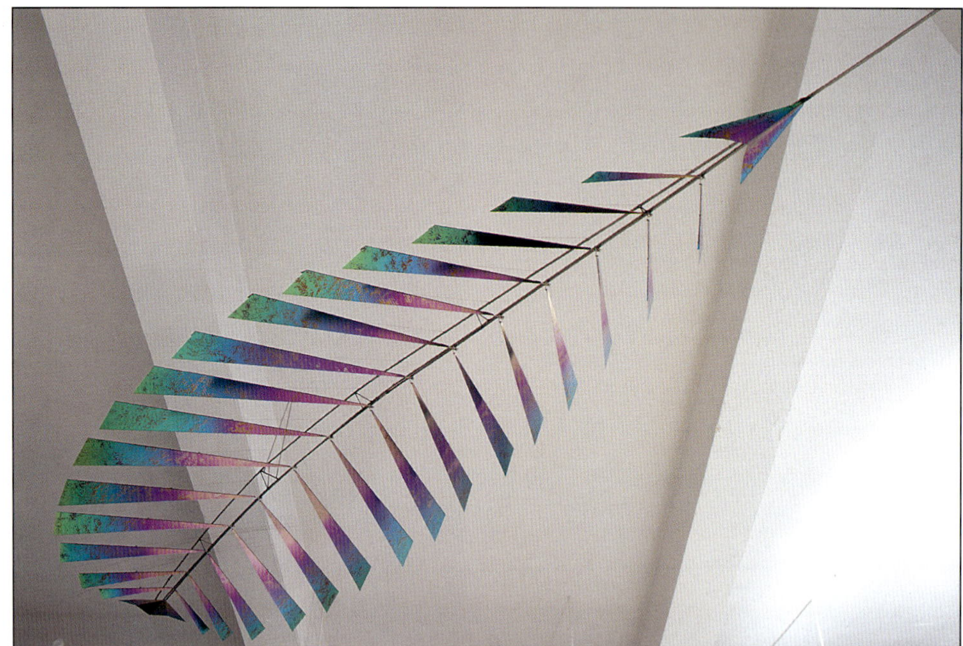

A

E. J. Carr

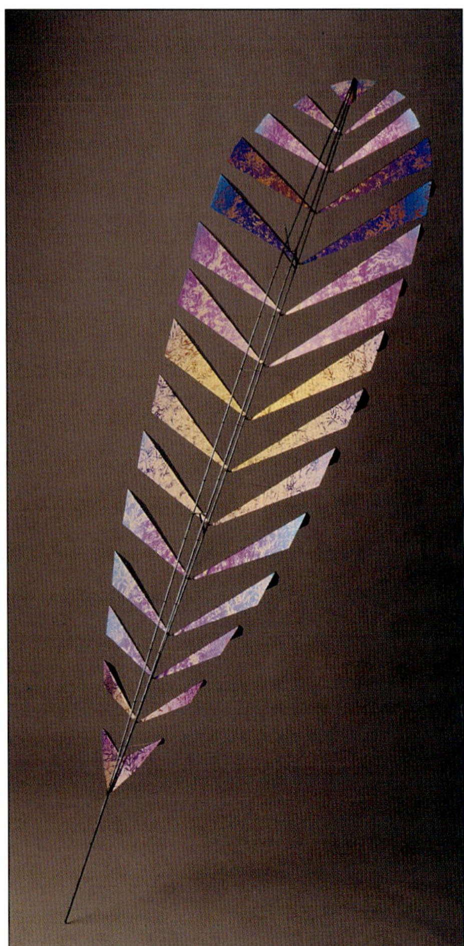

B

Carol Seitz

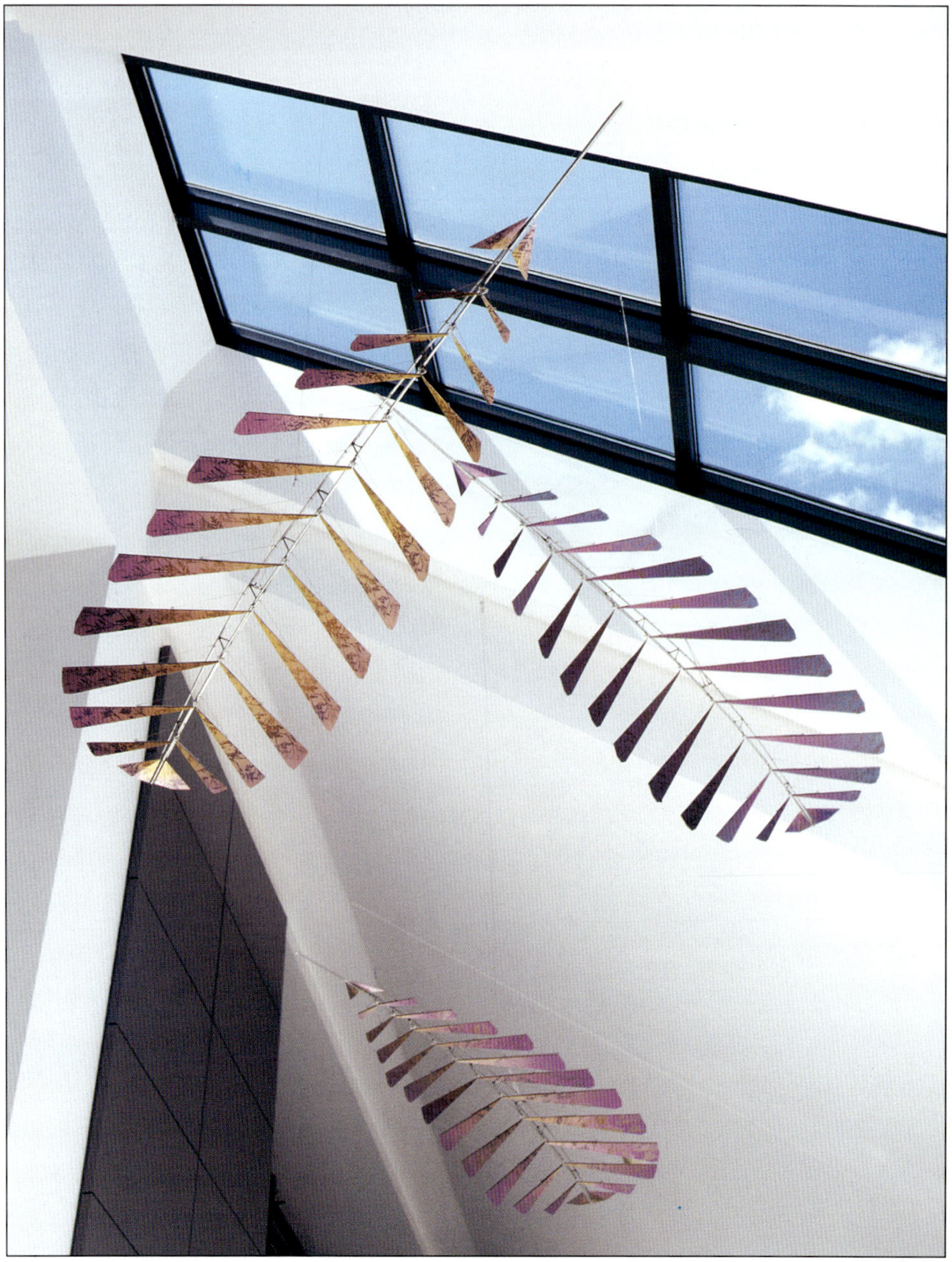

C

Peter Bodtke

Patricia Ravarra

1045 Leavenworth Street #5
San Francisco, CA 94109-5048
FAX 415-673-1907
TEL   415-673-9654
E-Mail: 756-6062@mcimail.com

Patricia Ravarra now includes anodized aluminum wire in her materials repertoire, along with nylon monofilament fibers. She weaves this lightweight and durable material before manipulating it into three-dimensional constructions. The wire, available in Pantone® colors, provides a dramatic, light-enhancing effect, ideal for atrium areas and wall treatments in more confined areas.

Commissions include:
Kaiser Permanente; Howe Street Medical Office Building, Oakland, CA; California Department of Transportation, Oakland, CA; Oakland City Hall, Oakland, CA; Green Gables Elementary School, Federal Way, WA.

Also see these GUILD publications:
Architect's Edition: 8, 10

SHOWN: *Scales of the Rainbow Dragon* (installation and details), multi-element, woven anodized aluminum wire

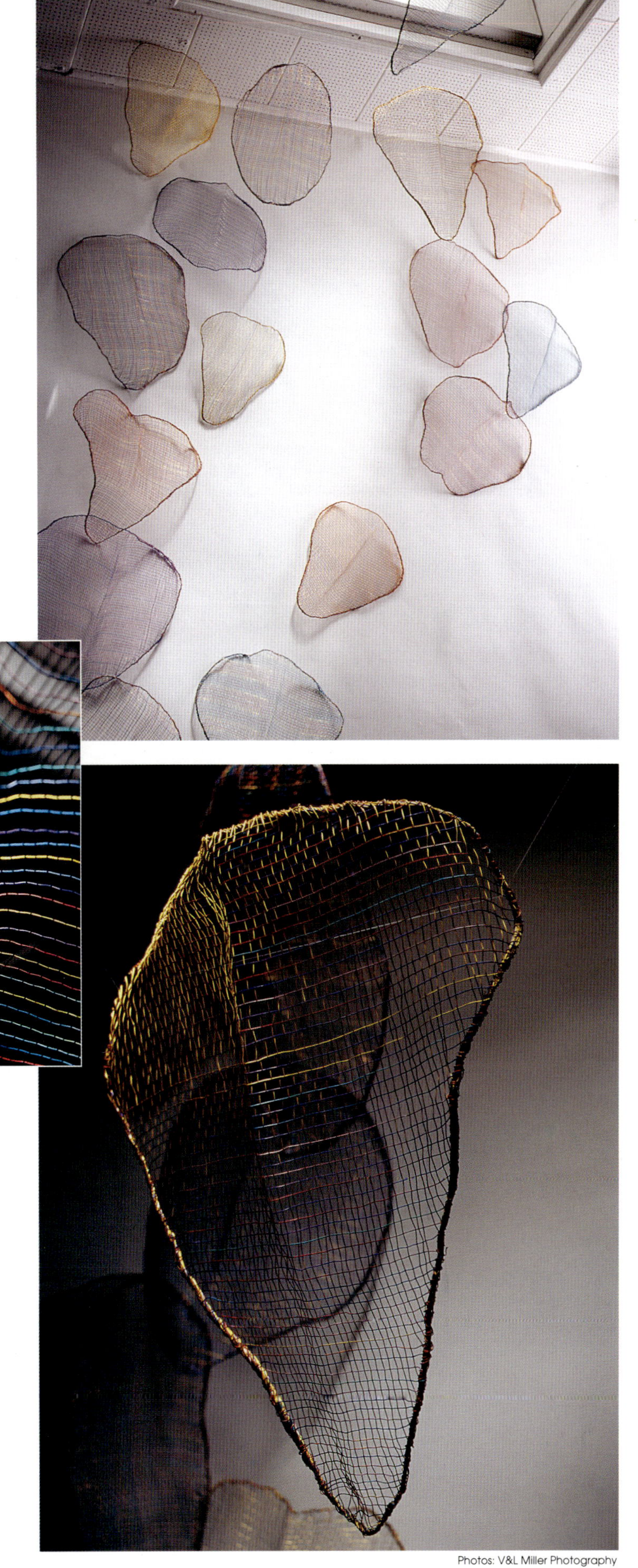

Photos: V&L Miller Photography

Sable Studios

Paul Sable
287 Gilchrist Lane
Watsonville, CA 95076
FAX 408-475-4012
TEL   800-233-7309
TEL   408-761-1766
E-Mail: azsimsab@cruzio.com

Paul Sable has collaborated successfully with architects and designers for over 25 years. His kinetic acrylic mobiles integrate color, light and movement to create a multidimensional experience. His custom-designed sculptures have harmonized into private, corporate and public spaces such as the Berklee Performance Center in Boston, MA; the Syntex Corporate Headquarters in Palo Alto, CA; and the Metro Plaza building in San Jose, CA.

A *Golden Spiral*, computer-generated proposal for Peoria, IL, civic center, illustrating Sable's ability to collaborate with clients to create custom designs and large-scale, three-dimensional presentations, 40' x 60' x 120'

B *Sky Ballet*, installation, Metropolitan Life, San Jose, CA, 4' x 6' x 17'

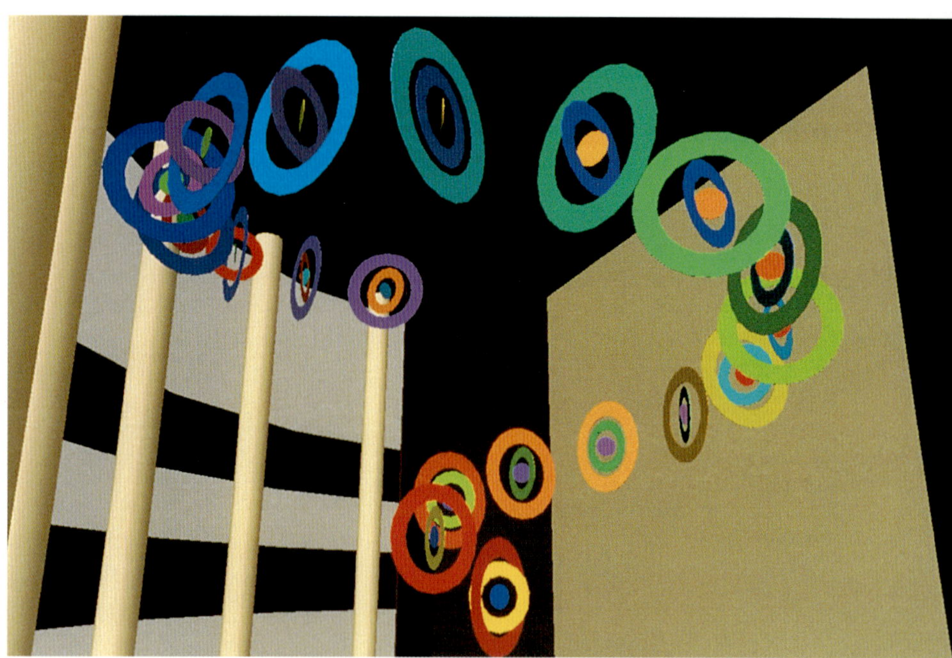

A

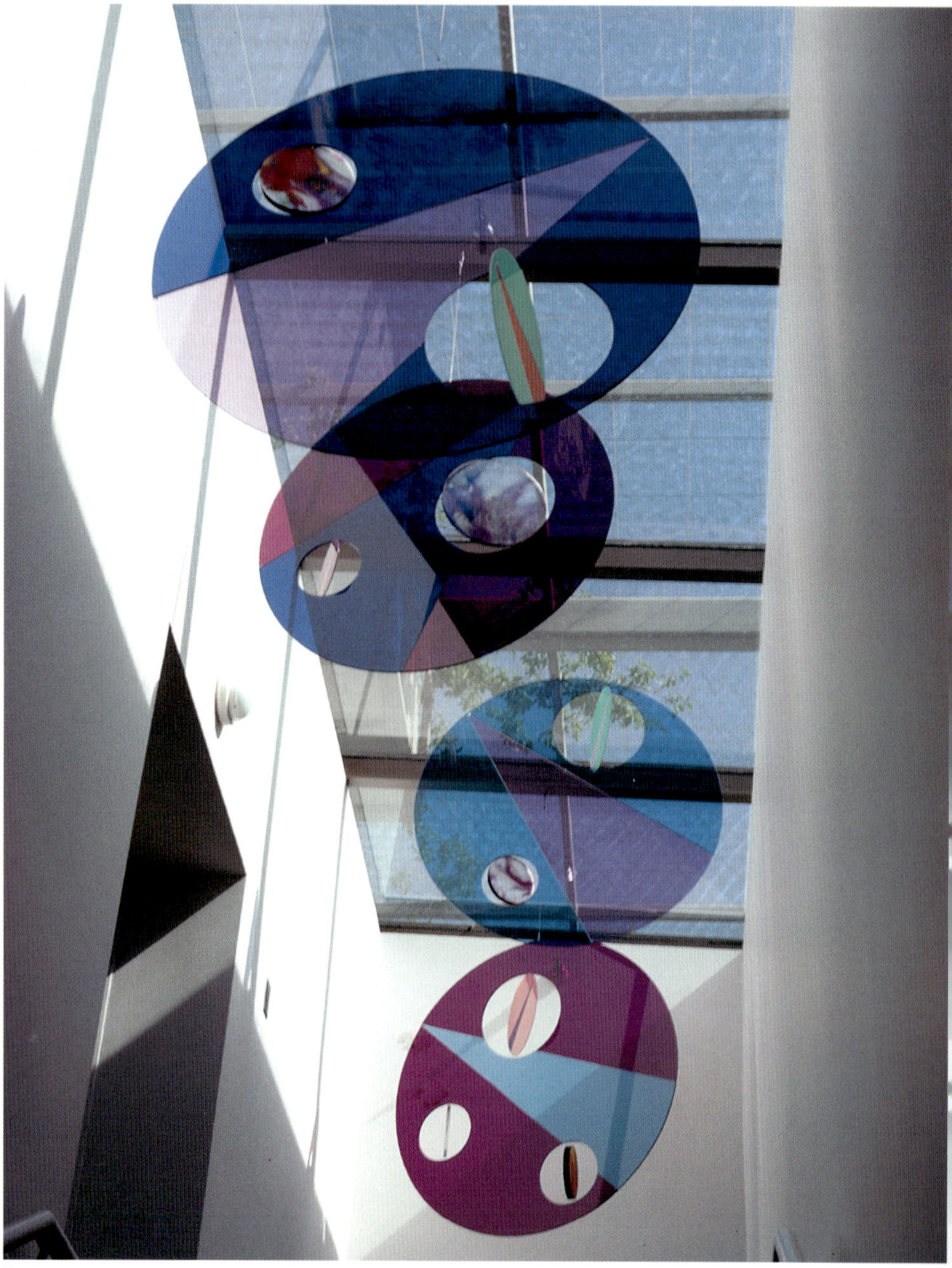

B

Wasserman Studios

Myron Wasserman
1817 N. 5th Street
Philadelphia, PA 19122
FAX 215-739-5448
TEL 215-739-5558

Wasserman Studios, under the direction of Myron Wasserman, has designed, created and orchestrated art commissions for more than three decades. In the past five years, the studio has expanded the scope of its work to include kinetic sculpture, sculptural elements, mobiles, stabiles, and *Whirly-Wassers* (contemporary weathervanes and stabiles). All work focuses on harmony and balance.

Materials encompass a myriad of metals with an array of natural and chemical patinas, suiting both interior and exterior applications.

Wasserman Studios is committed to creative solutions and enjoys collaborating with other design professionals. Inquiries, studio visits, and requests for additional information are welcome. "The greater the challenge, the more creative the solution."

Also see this GUILD publication:
Designer's Edition: 8

A Atrium mobile, 30' x 7'

B *Whirly-Wasser,* roof top, 15' x 7'

C *Stabile-Wasser,* 8' x 3'

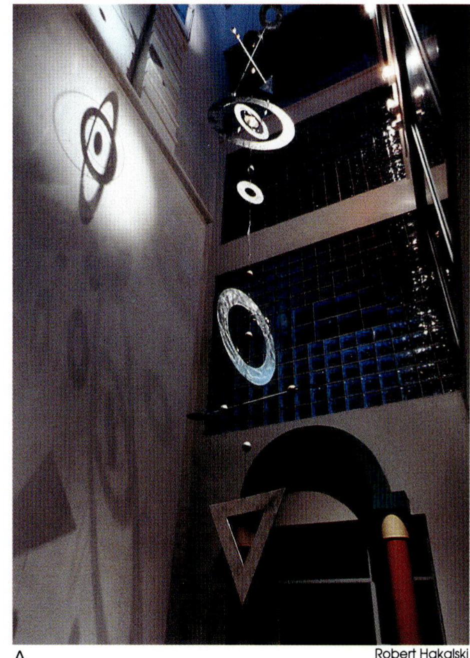

A

Robert Hakalski

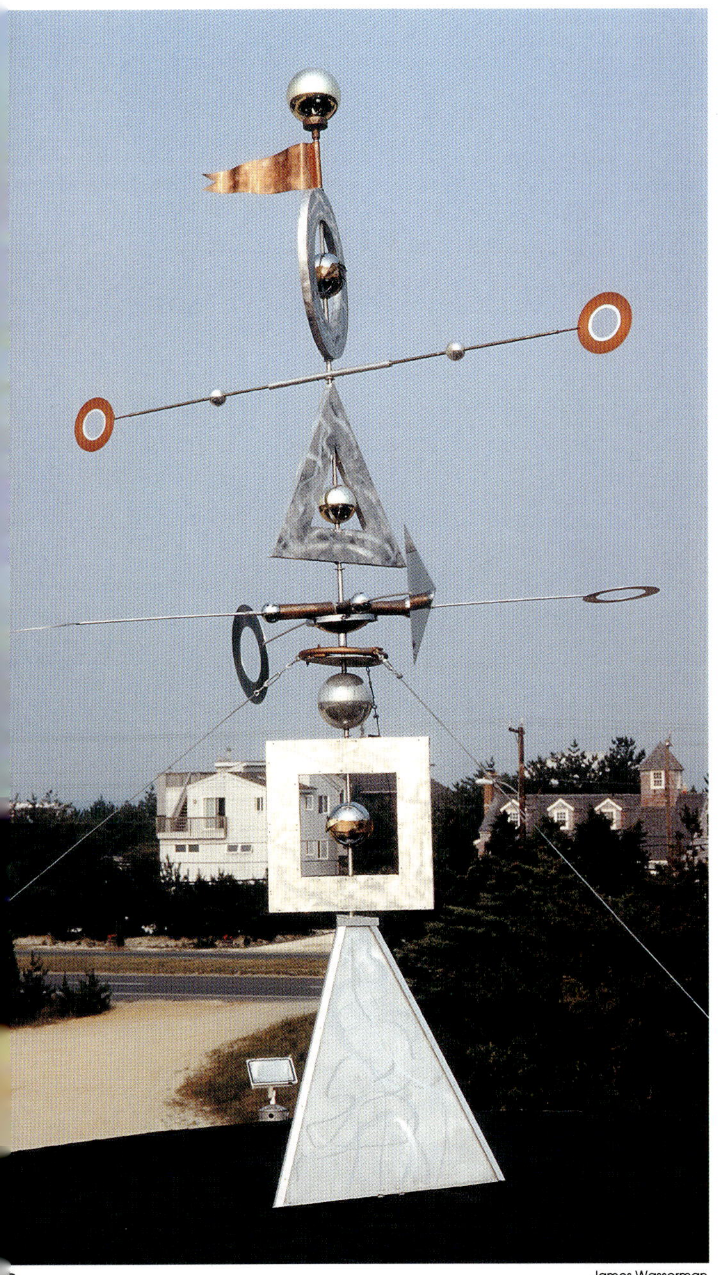

B

James Wasserman

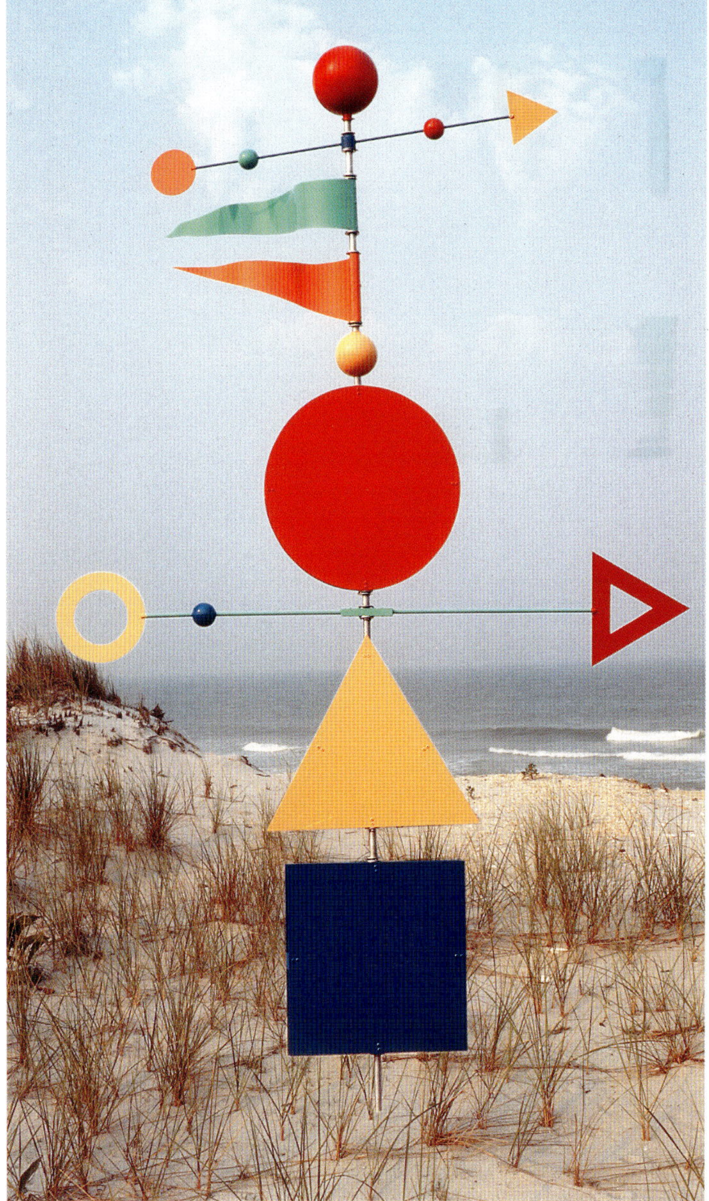

C

James Wasserman

LANDSCAPE ELEMENTS

Walter Einsel

Naiad & Walter Einsel Designs
26 Morningside Drive South
Westport, CT 06880
TEL 203-226-0709

Walter Einsel, known over the years as a kinetic sculptor, illustrator and graphic designer, has recently created a series of unique wind-driven sculptures and weathervanes, fashioned of copper, edged with brass, with verdigris patina, anchored in a cement pedestal of Victorian grace. Designs include birds, butterflies, grasshoppers, statues of liberty and mythological figures. Scale models and wallhangings are also available. Sizes range from 57" to 96"H, including base.

Einsel's work has been displayed at the Hudson River Museum, NY; EXPO Montreal; GE headquarters, Fairfield, CT; XEROX headquarters, Stamford, CT; and is on permanent exhibit in the AT&T building at EPCOT and the Barnum Museum, Bridgeport, CT. He has shown at many galleries throughout the country.

Photos and prices available.

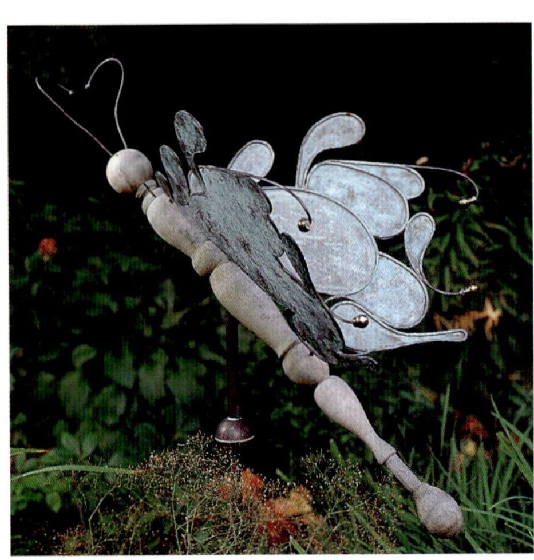

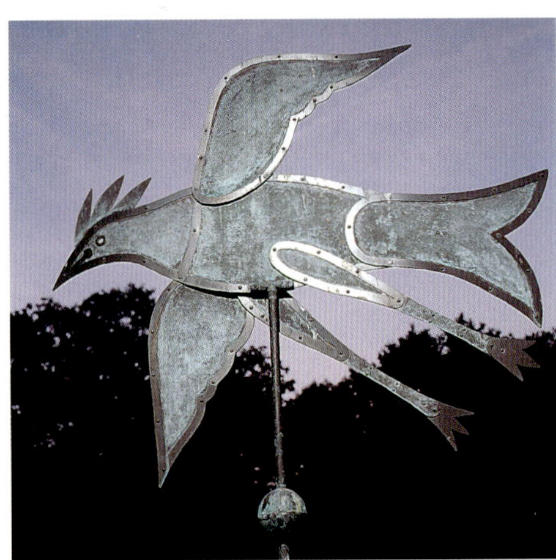

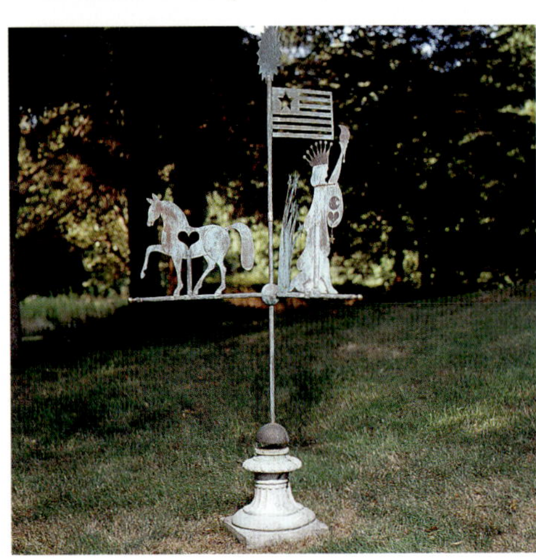

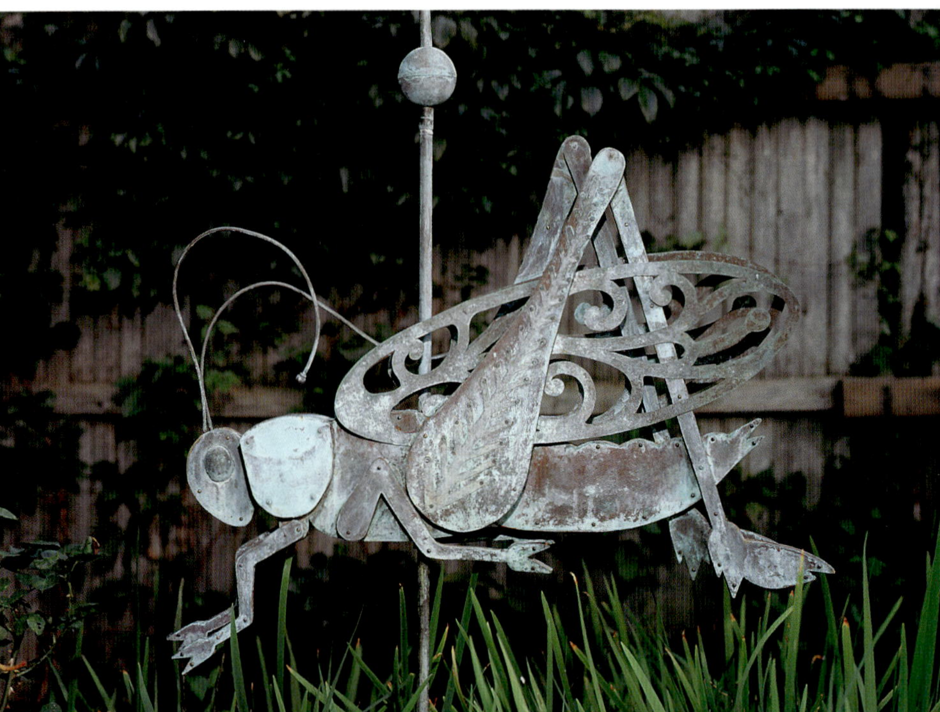

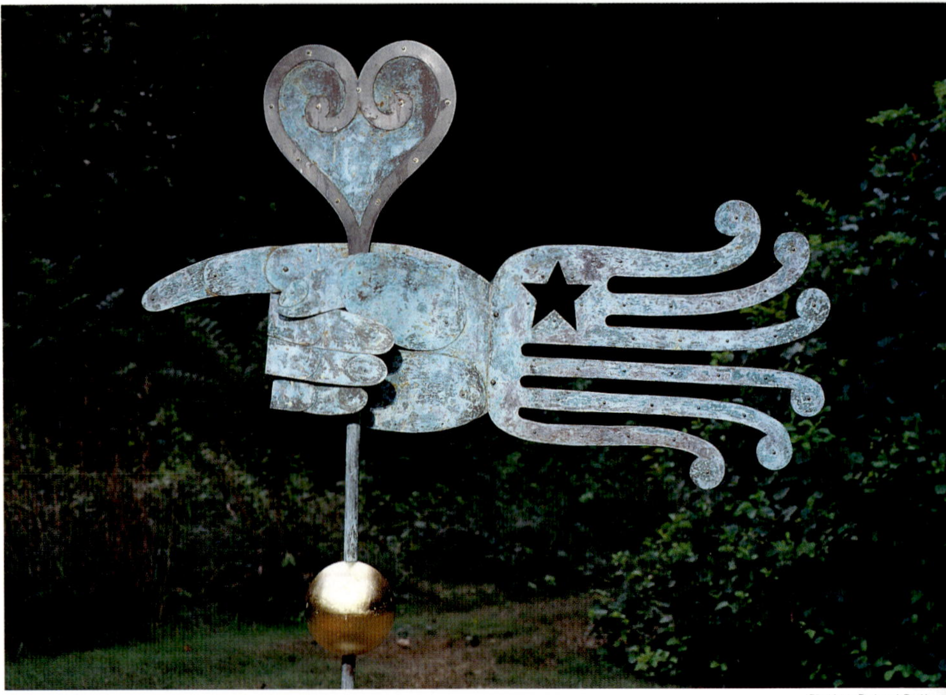

Photos: Robert Rattner

Harmony Wind Harps

R. Sundhara Barrable
PO Box 3039
Pagosa Springs, CO 81147
FAX 970-264-2962
TEL 970-264-2962

Eco-artist and musician Sundhara Barrable has designed and built stringed instruments for the past 18 years and is now creating acoustic sculptures that play music when the wind blows.

Constructed of titanium and bronze, these sleek, contemporary designs unite science, art and music with nature to create a sacred space within any outdoor setting.

Clients include:
City of Denver
Dallas Arboretum
Abu Dhabi Equestrian Club

Also see these GUILD publications:
Architect's Edition: 9, 10

A *Odyssey,* © 1990, silicone, bronze, stainless, amethyst sphere, 7'H

B *Infiniti II,* © 1995, titanium, steel, 8'H

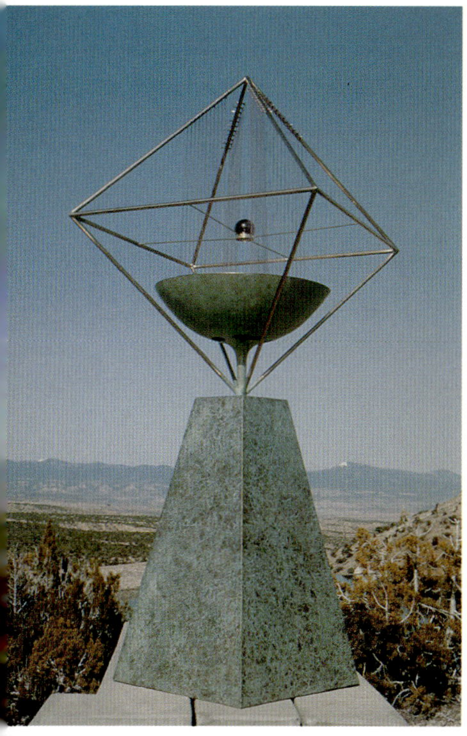

A

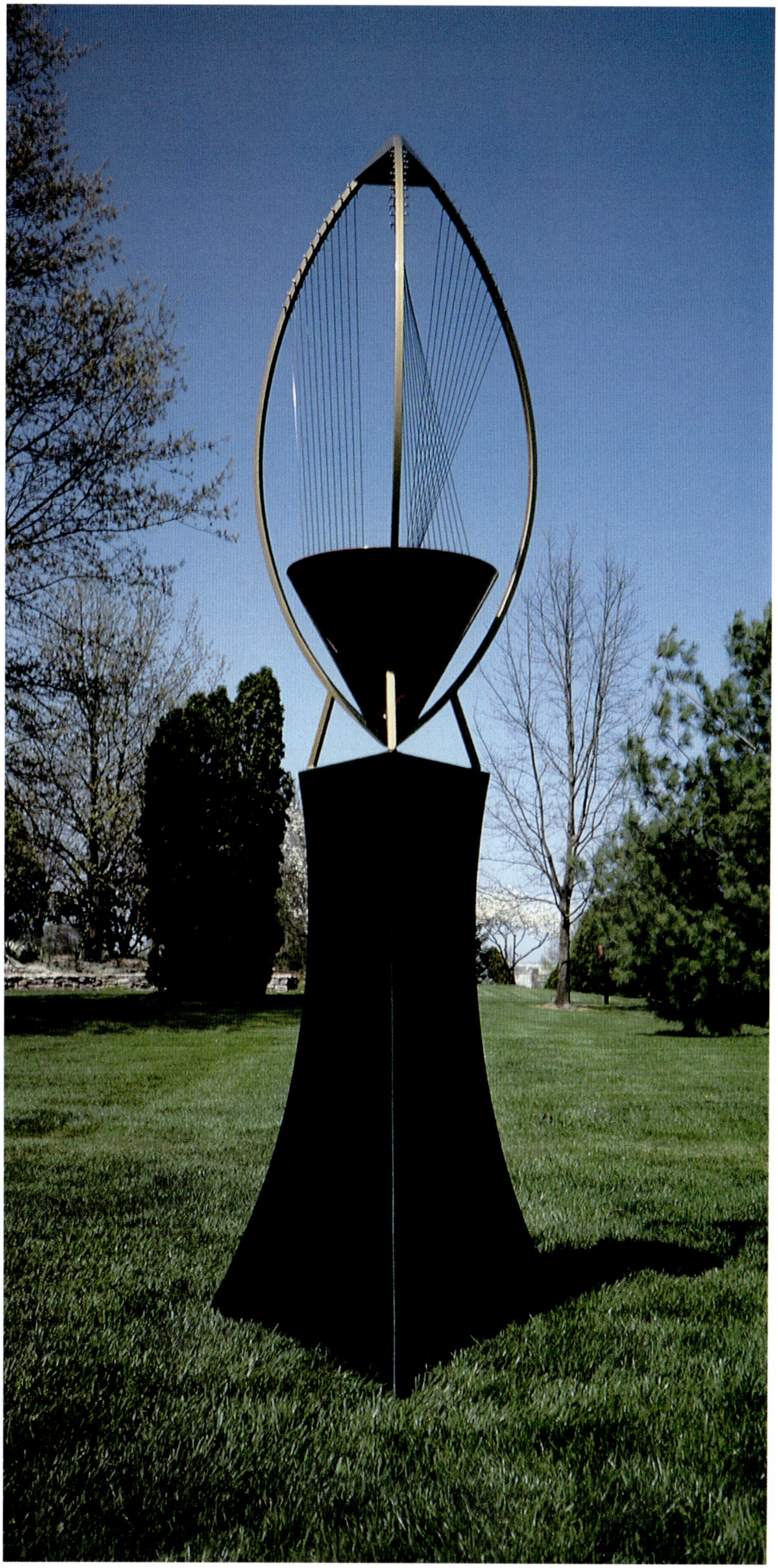

B

Tom Torrens
Sculpture Design

PO Box 1819
Gig Harbor, WA 98335
FAX 206-265-2404
TEL 206-857-5831
TEL 800-786-7736

Using strong, simple forms and familiar materials, Tom Torrens fashions works of uncommon strength and character. For the past 20 years, Mr. Torrens has designed and produced high-quality, functional works of art from recycled and industrial materials.

Mr. Torrens received his M.F.A degree in Sculpture from Washington University at St. Louis, and taught sculpture at the university level for 15 years. Mr. Torrens maintains a full-time design studio in Washington state, where he lives with his wife and son.

Functional sculptures from the Torrens collection include fountains, bells, gongs, birdfeeders, birdbaths, indoor and outdoor lighting, tables, candleholders and gates. Commissioned works are also available. Materials used are Corten and mild steel, copper, cedar and stainless steel.

Free catalog available.

Also see this GUILD publication:
THE GUILD: 1

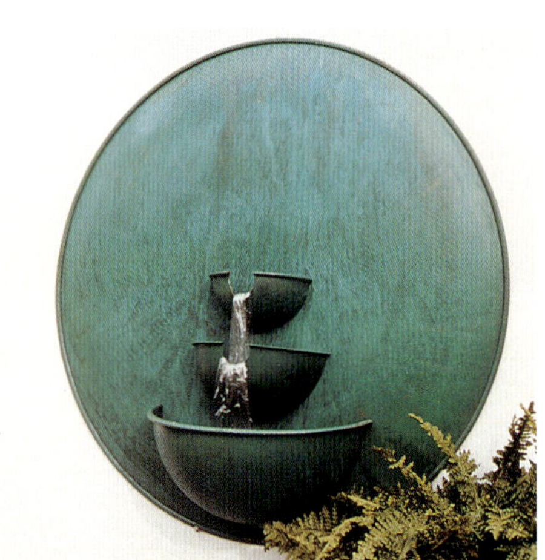

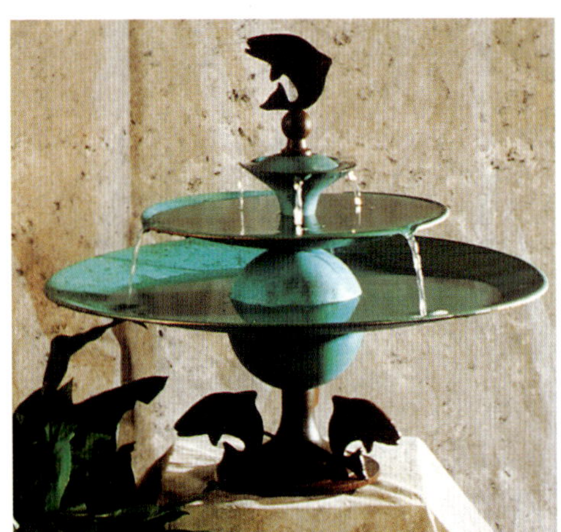

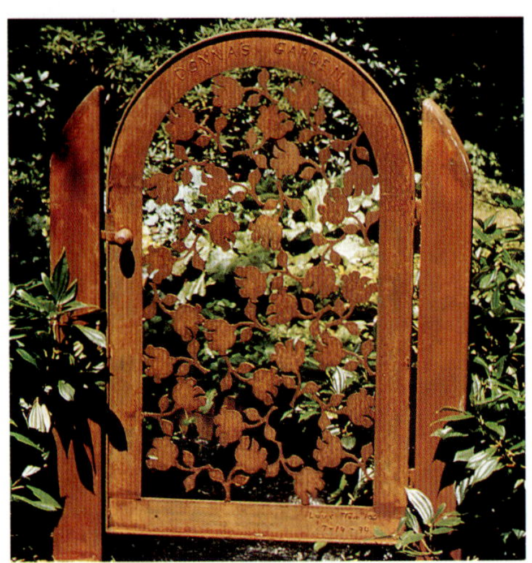

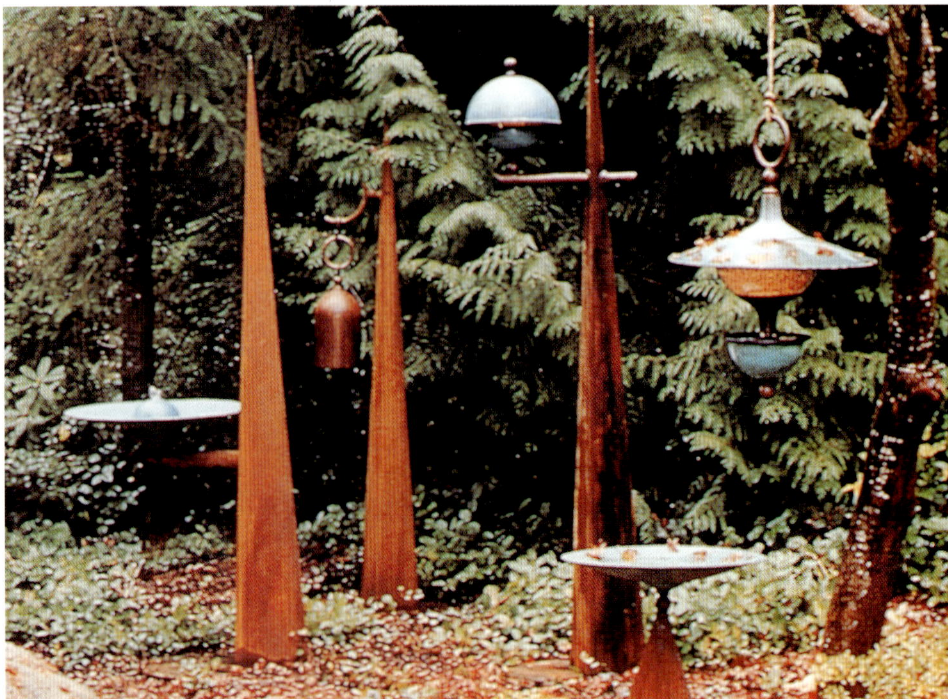

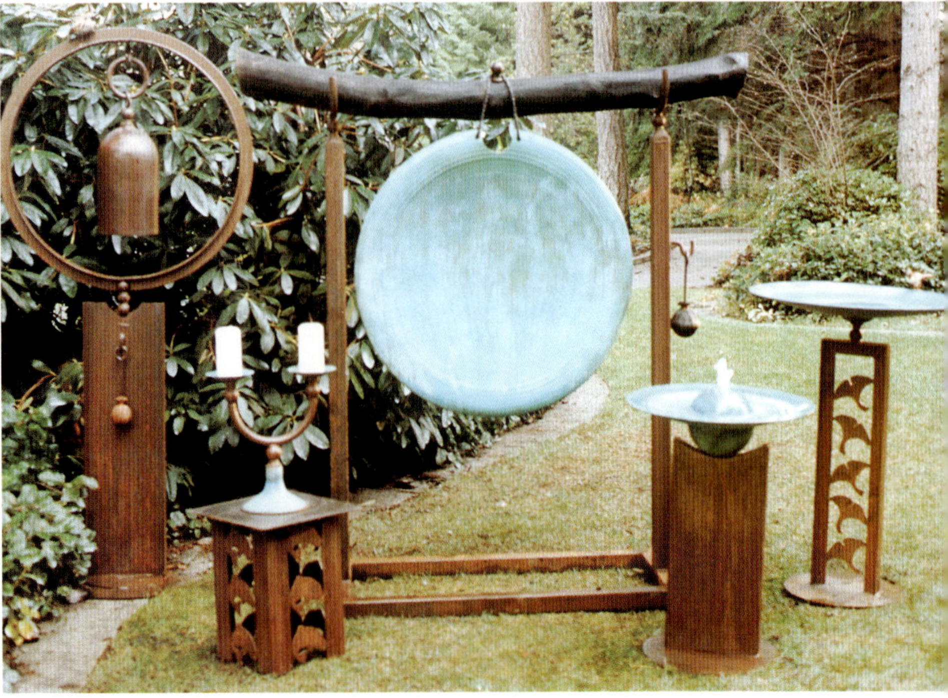

David Torgoff

Sculptor's Garden
1305 S. Cedar #402
Lansing, MI 48910
TEL 517-484-6578

Holding degrees in fine art and landscape architecture, David Torgoff is highly qualified and experienced in the creation of sculpture for garden, courtyard and landscape settings.

The pieces incorporate juxtapositions of conceptual and real elements that will continually intrigue and satisfy the viewer.

The pieces shown are made using steel, ferrocement, and various surface treatments. The screens can be adapted for use as gates and wall pieces. A series of fountains is planned for the future.

A *Zen Vessel* screen, 70"H x 17"W x 1 1/2"D

B Detail: inside of bird bath bowl

C Bird bath sculpture, 39"H x 32"W x 21"D

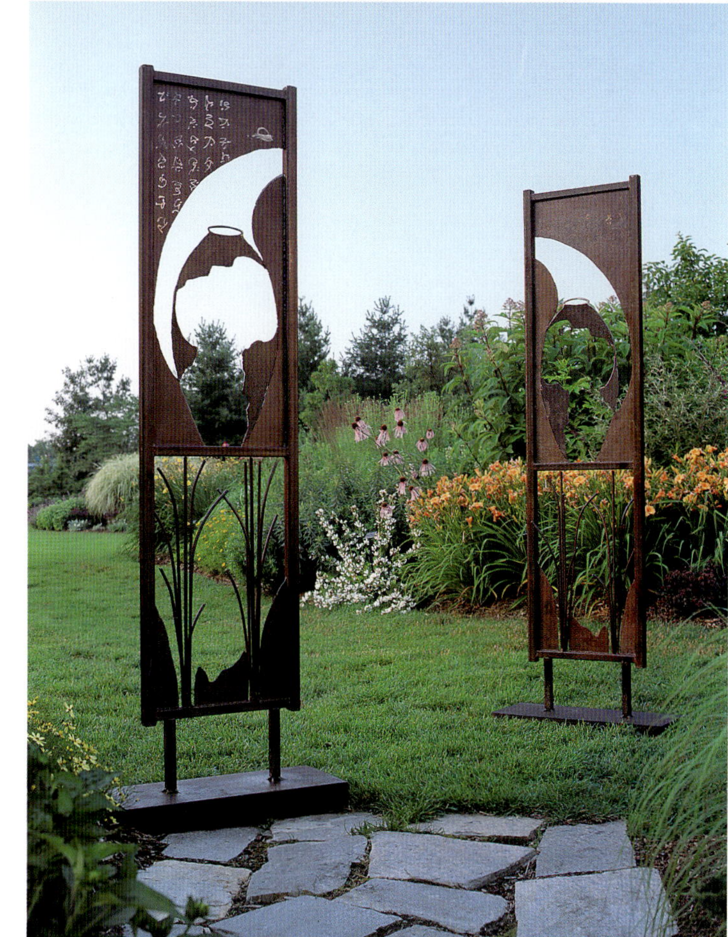

A

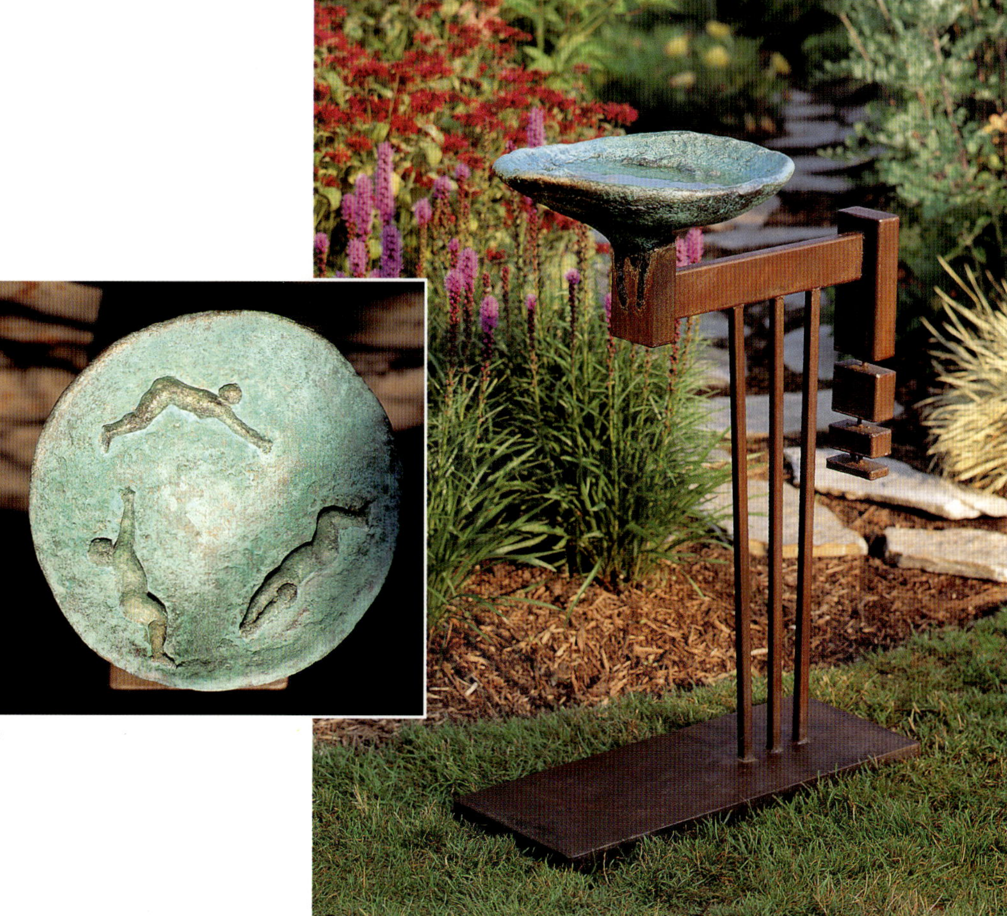

B

C

BOB PETERSON

Architect

A door can be just a door, or it can be a magical entry into another world created by the careful collaboration of architect, artist and client. Robert Peterson, the principal of Peterson Architects, a 12-person firm in Menlo Park, California, had the latter purpose in mind when he commissioned GUILD artist Al Garvey to create a doorway for a family room expansion.

Peterson's client was a wine connoisseur with a very substantial collection. Garvey gave substance to that interest by creating an imposing, 8-foot-high, 44-inch-wide, arch-topped doorway executed in bird's-eye maple. The antique-appearing doorway invites the visitor from the family living space into the wine cellar. "The earthy, slate floor and the very rich materials of the doorway beckon you into the new area and prepare you for a different experience from the rest of the house," Peterson explains. "This door provides excellent enrichment to the architectural design."

Since his teaching days at Stanford, and through decades of involvement with residential, commercial and civic design projects, Peterson has encouraged clients to use original art to enhance the architectural statement. He recalls one of his early projects from the 1960s, a psychiatrist's office that was done in bold, vibrant colors. For artwork, Peterson recommended a series of black-and-white photographs by Ansel Adams. Not only did the photography enrich the space and delight those who passed through, it's also proven to be the best investment the client ever made.

"People don't realize they can get something custom—something that's just for them—and it can be in their price range," Peterson says. "That's part of the pleasure of recommending original art."

Travis Tuck

Travis Tuck, Inc., Metal Sculptor
PO Box 1832-10, 89 Main Street
Martha's Vineyard, MA 02568
FAX 508-693-3914
TEL   508-693-3914

Travis Tuck has designed original commissioned pieces in 40 states and 11 countries over a period of 29 years.

Although best known for the finest custom weathervanes, themes can also be executed as wall or free-standing sculptures. Each heirloom-quality piece is a three-dimensional sculpture, constructed in the traditional pre-1800s repoussé method from copper and 23K gold leaf.

Tuck works with architects and designers, or directly with clients, to complement any architectural style and depict any personal interest, business symbol or logo.

Prices from $3,000. Brochure available.

Clients include:
President and Mrs. Clinton
Beverly Sills
James Taylor
Carly Simon
City of Hamburg, Germany
Bloomingdale's, 59th Street, NYC
Gainsborough Farms, Woodford County, KY
Universal Studios, Hollywood
American Booksellers Association, Tarrytown, NY

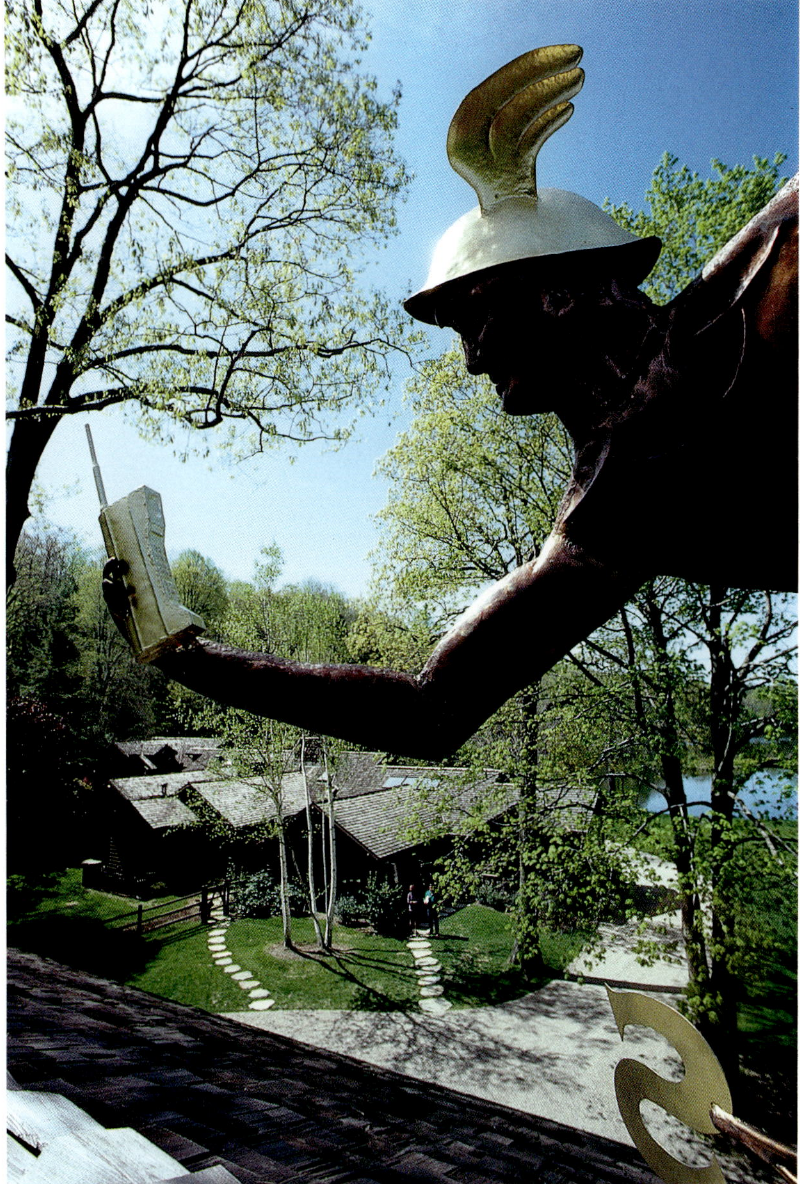

Mercury With Cellular Phone (detail), private collection, 7'6"

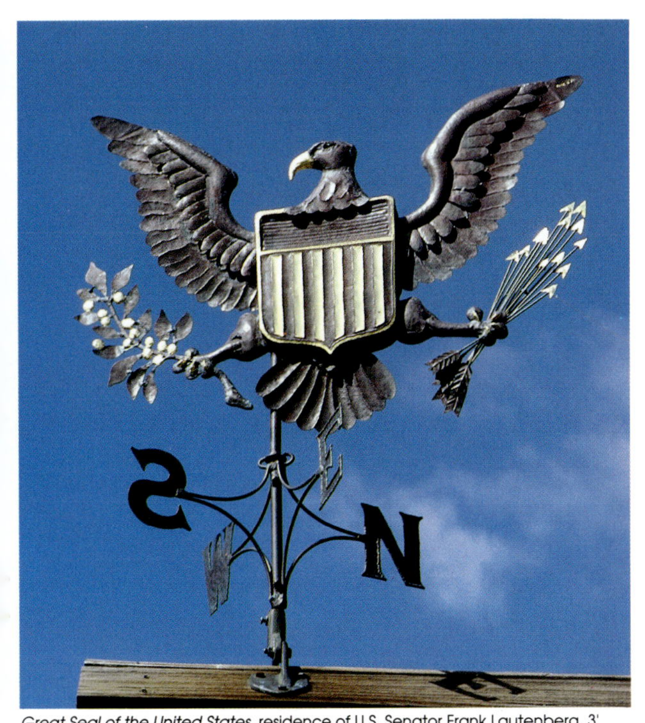

Great Seal of the United States, residence of U.S. Senator Frank Lautenberg, 3'

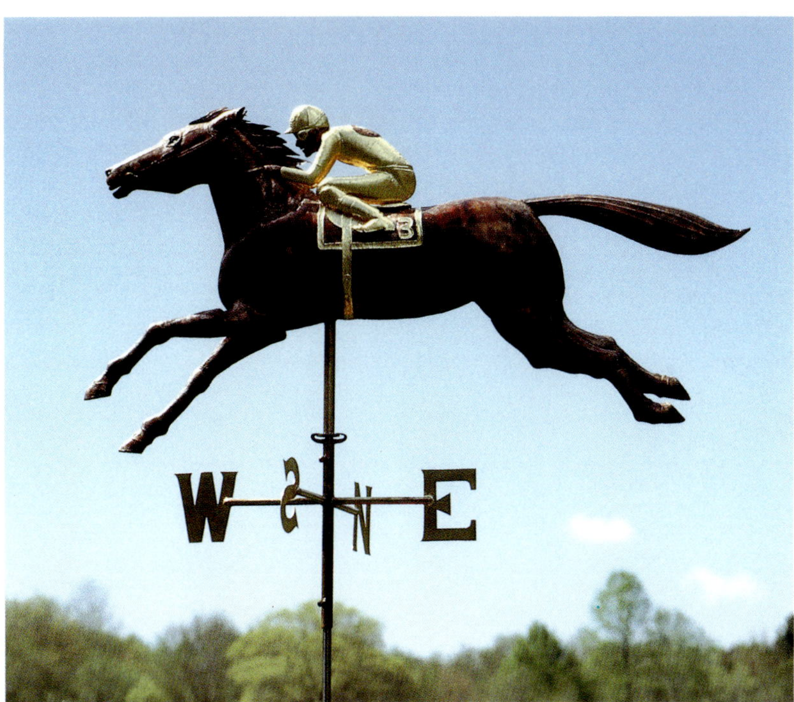

Thoroughbred With Jockey, Buttonwood Farm, Rhinebeck, NY, 5'

Photos: Mark Lennihan/Betsy Corsiglia

REPRESENTATIONAL SCULPTURE

Warren Archer

Archer Design
275 West 400 North
Salt Lake City, UT 84103
FAX 801-328-9150
TEL 801-328-1325
TEL 801-326-4337 (Foundry)

Warren Archer loves the human form and its ability to touch our hearts—from moments of inner reflection to explosive expressions of joy. Striving to capture poetic movement and visual grace, he sculpts figurative bronze to communicate the rich culture and physical diversity of humankind.

Archer enjoys working with people. He welcomes collaborations with architects, landscape architects, and designers. Satisfied clients are his priority. He encourages team effort in creating successful projects that are site appropriate, completed on time, and delivered within budget. Archer operates his own foundry to ensure the quality of each sculpture, from small interior pieces through monumental outdoor works. Feel free to call and discuss your project or to request more information.

A *Ring Dancer*, bronze

B *Gezel*, bronze

C *Under the Waterfall*, bronze

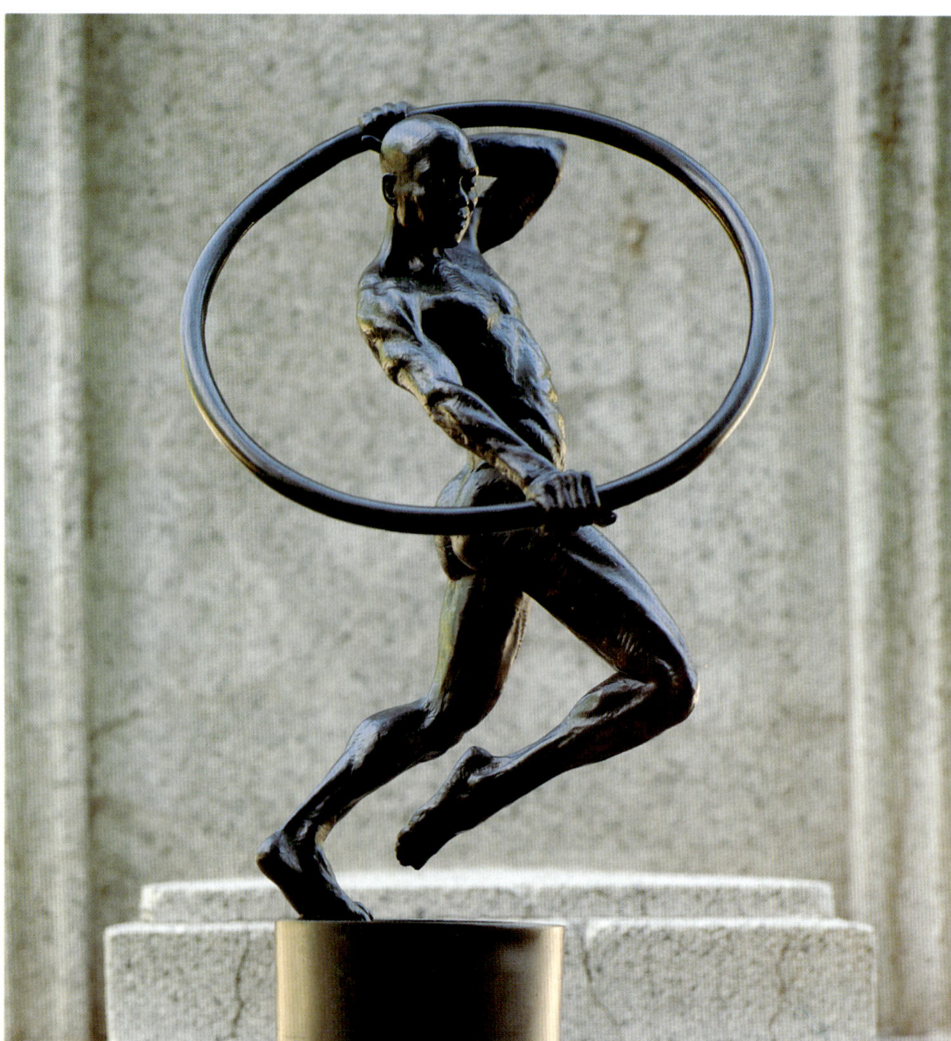

A

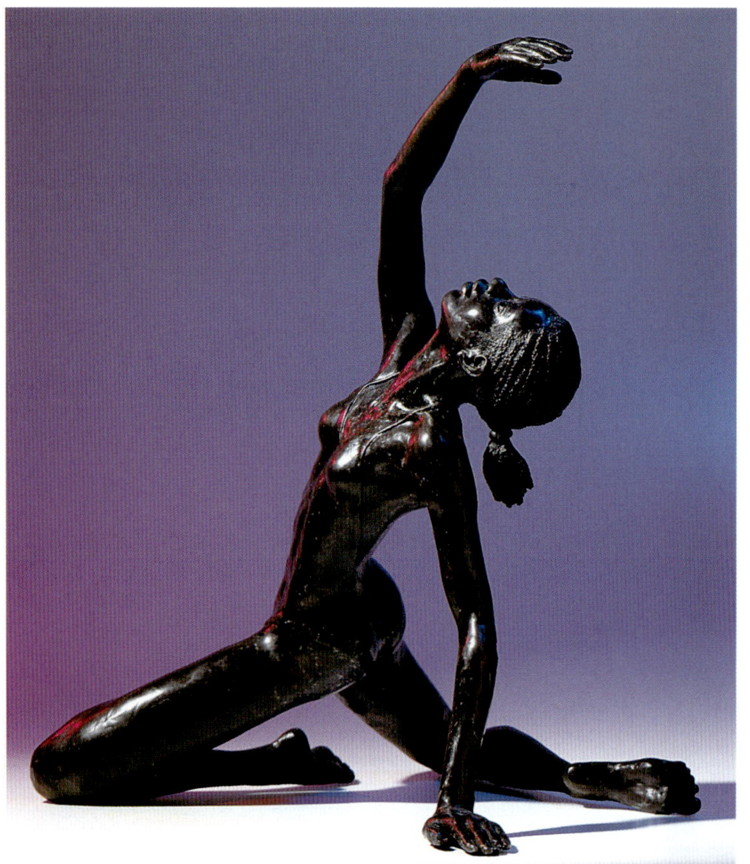

B

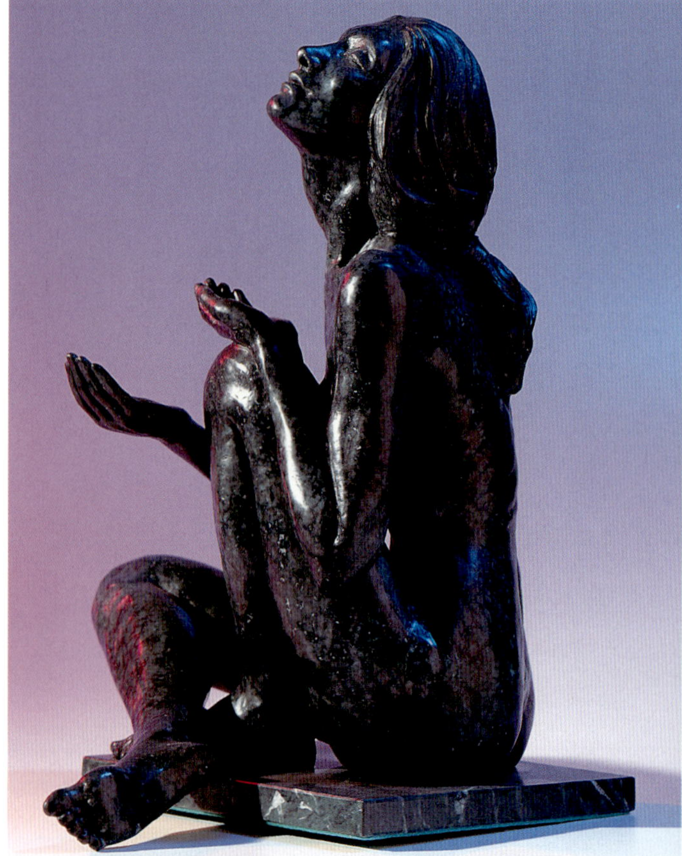

C

James Barnhill

206 S. Chapman Street
Greensboro, NC 27403
TEL 910- 275-7135

James Barnhill works from the live model, sculpting both fully in the round as well as in relief. Works range in size from tabletop to monumental. He has successfully executed work for corporate, public, liturgical and garden settings.

More than a mere copy of the human body, James Barnhill's work seeks to marry the abstract principles of design and composition to the natural form of the figure. His work is both engaging and inviting.

Professionally, his goal is to enhance a variety of settings with site-specific, figurative sculpture. Inquiries are welcome.

Also see these GUILD publications:
Architect's Edition: 7, 8

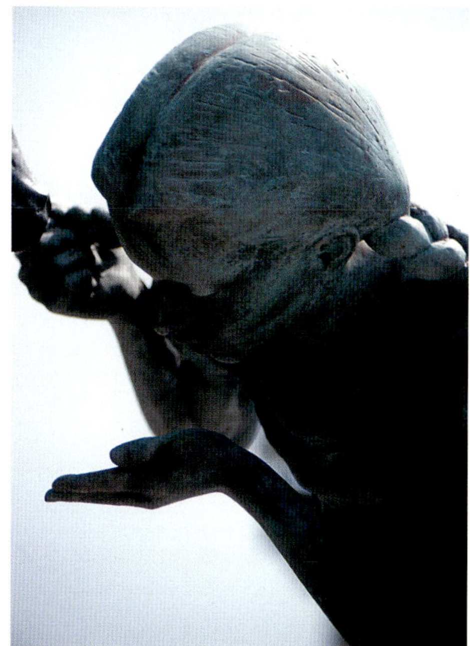

SHOWN: *Little Sipper*, 1995, bronze, commissioned for the City of Asheville, NC, 48" x 30" x 18"

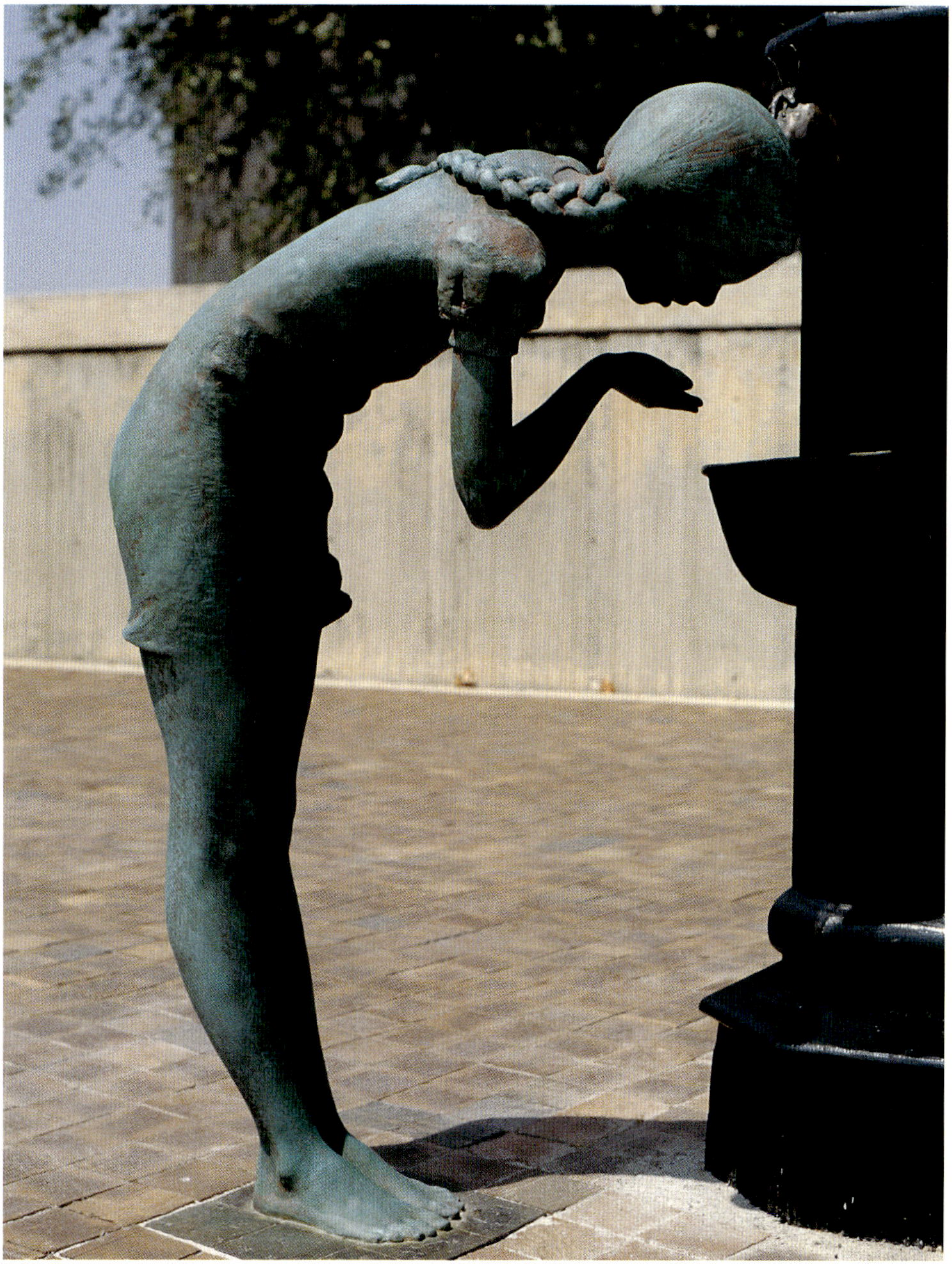

Barrett DeBusk Sculpture

Barrett DeBusk
3813 North Commerce
Ft. Worth, TX 76106
FAX 817-625-8476
TEL   817-625-8476

Barrett DeBusk, a Texas sculptor, illustrates his view of the world in uncomplicated steel-line drawings, as well as innovative furniture and large-scale outdoor pieces.

DeBusk's three-dimensional, pictorial stories are made from cold-rolled, hand-bent steel rod. After being welded together and framed, the images are coated with flat black Rustoleum paint, which makes maintenance easy. Not only do the built-in legs make hanging effortless, but they also enable you to see shadowy recreations of the images on the wall behind.

DeBusk is internationally known and represented world-wide. *Globe* (shown) was commissioned by the 1994 World Cup Soccer tournament.

A *Night of the Iguana*, 48" x 72" x 5"

B *Globe*, 1994 World Cup, stainless steel and neon

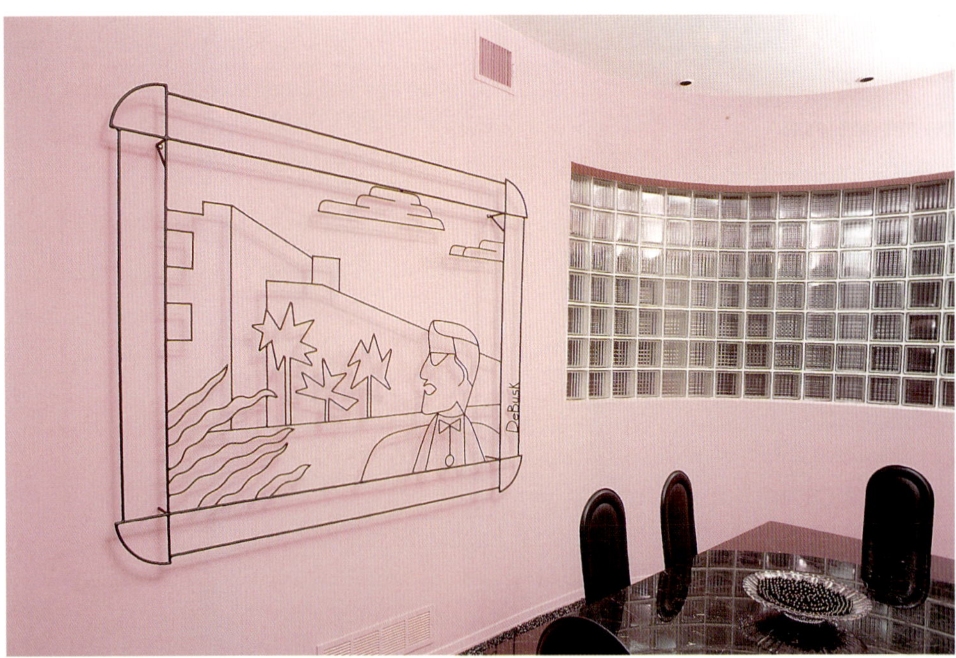

A

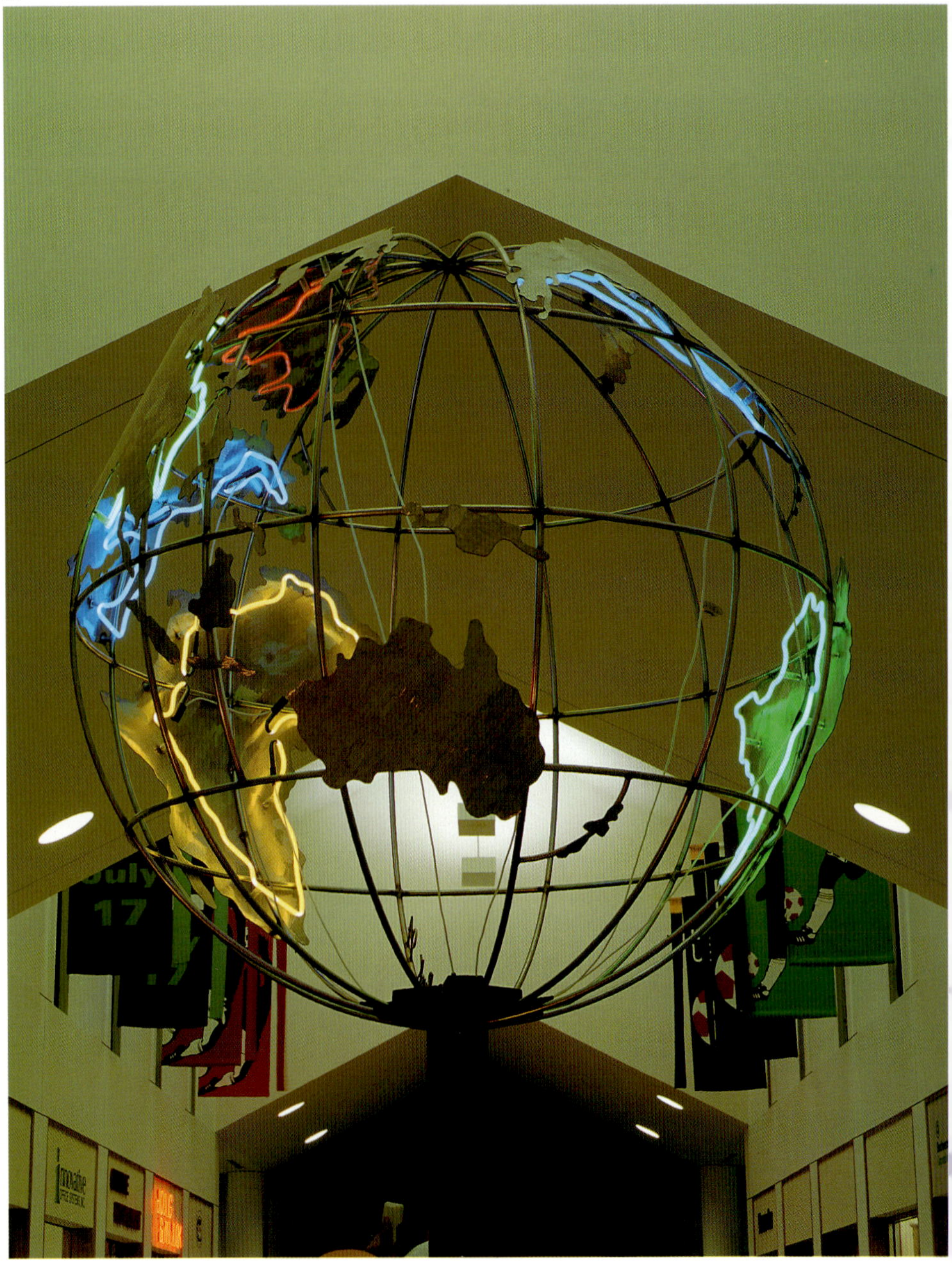

B

Ed Dwight Studios, Inc.

3824 Dahlia Street
Denver, CO 80207
FAX 303-322-9669
TEL   303-329-9040

Ed Dwight is internationally renown for his bronze series *The Evolution of Jazz*. For Ed, a former Air Force Test Pilot and America's first African American astronaut trainee, art has been a life-long passion. In 1975, he developed his series *Black Frontier Spirit in the American West*, depicting black contributions to the opening of the West for the State of Colorado.

Since then, Ed has created many large-scale works for federal, state and city governments; public/private organizations; and individual collectors. His vast body of work provides the viewer with unique, powerful images that evoke strong emotional response. His many large-scale installations include the *Underground Railroad Memorial, Black Patriots Memorial, Hank Aaron*, and *Martin Luther King, Jr.*

A *Underground Railroad Memorial,* installed at Kellogg Foundation, Battle Creek, MI, bronze, 28' x 14'

B *Everything You Wanted To Know About Sax, But Were Afraid To Ask,* bronze, 32" x 34"

C *Miles Davis,* bronze, 7'4" x 32"

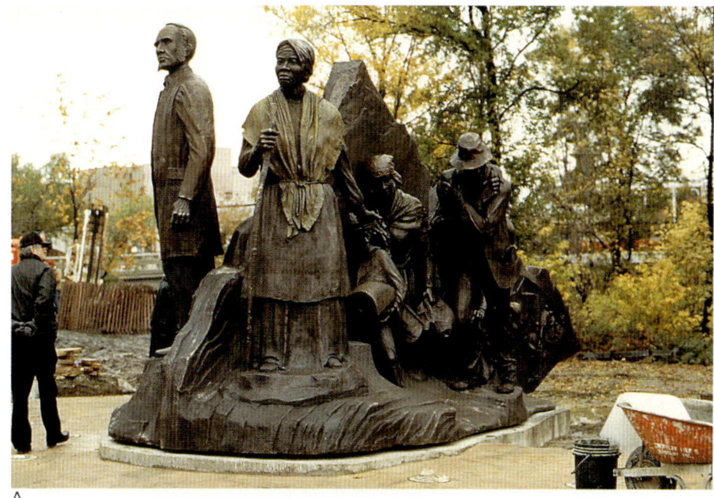

A

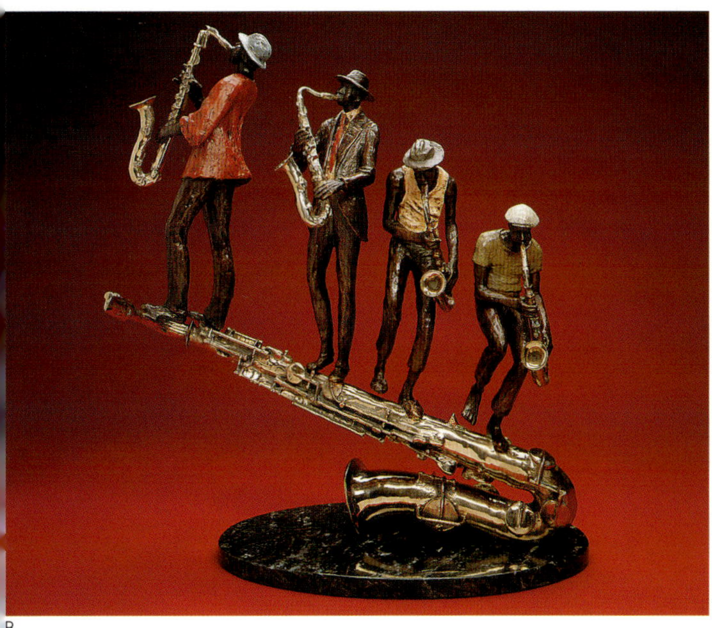

B

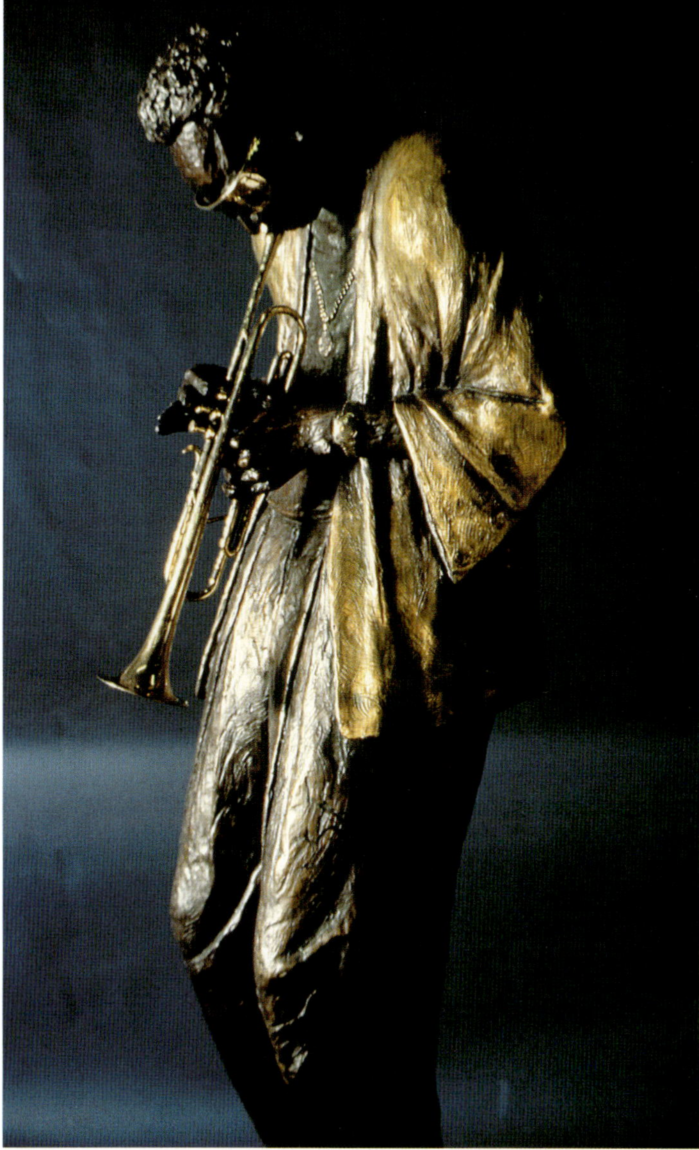

C

Foot's Artworks

Foot Young
2697 Som. Jack Road
Somerville, OH 45064
FAX 513-726-5537
TEL 513-726-5537
E-Mail: Comp 100242,346

PO Box 54
Hamilton Island
Queensland 4803
Australia
FAX 61-79-468-682
TEL 61-79-468-308

Foot Young works primarily in Australia, using marble and bronze. His work is shown in his own gallery on Hamilton Island, and in over 30 galleries worldwide. He has sculpted commissioned work for over 20 years, the most recent being for the Singapore World Trade Center. Marine themes are a favorite, but he also enjoys doing realistic human figures and busts.

SHOWN: *Humpback Breaching* (prototype), cold-cast bronze, 10' x 10' x 10', edition of ten in hot cast

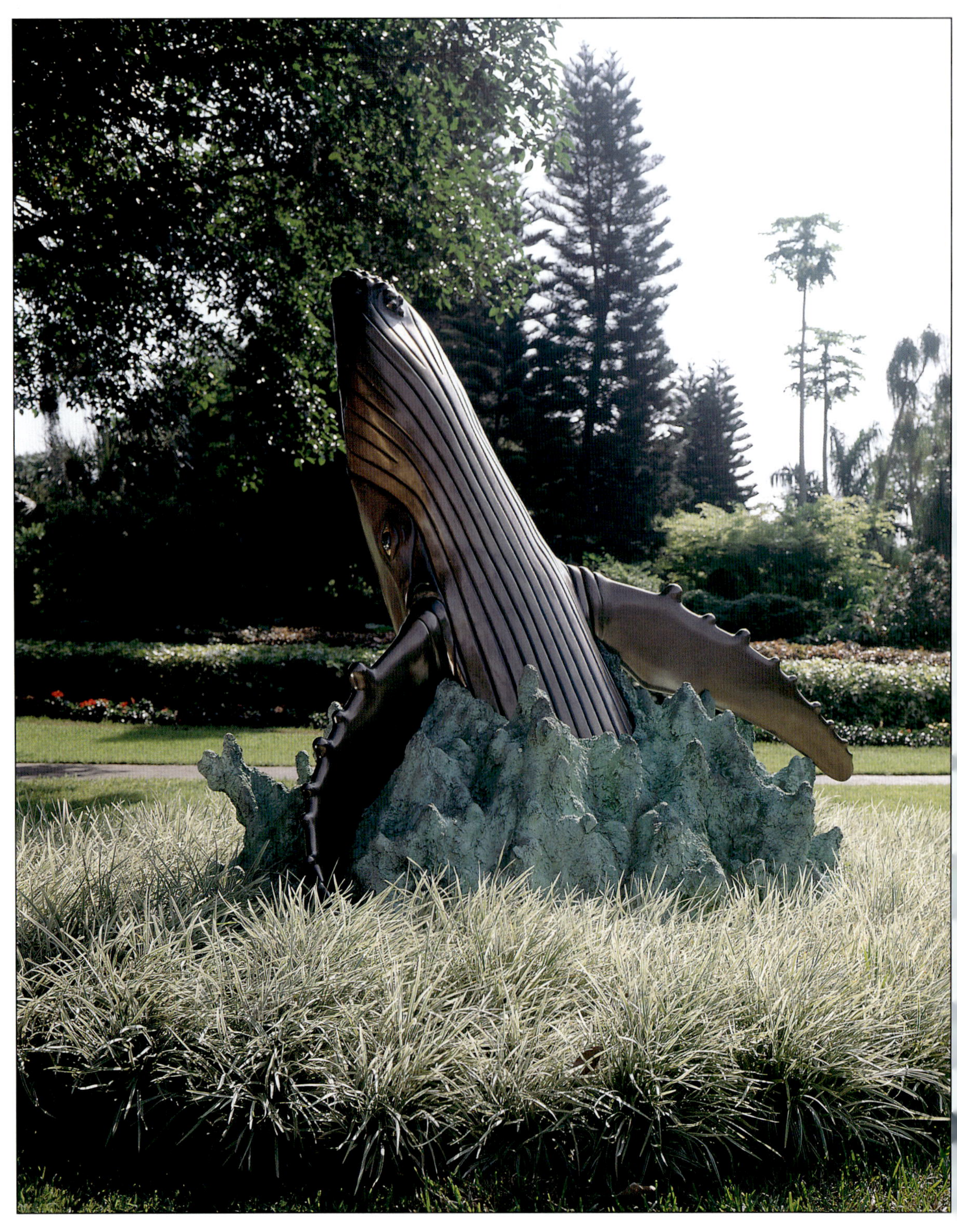

Bill GirarD

GirarD Studio
1628 Sagebrush Trail, SE
Albuquerque, NM 87123
TEL 505-298-1629

Bill GirarD's sculptures have become highly collectible across the nation. Mainly known for his colorful dancing warriors, Bill does equally well with wildlife and graceful nudes, from miniature to life-size, realism to impressionism.

Although his main volume of work has been in bronze, he's recently been working in stoneware and other water-based clays and is constantly experimenting with new casting materials.

Bill is open to commissions of all sizes and is a willing team participant with figurative or abstract monumental work.

Also see this GUILD publication:
Architect's Edition: 10

A *Feathered Friends*, bronze edition

B *War Dancer*, bronze edition

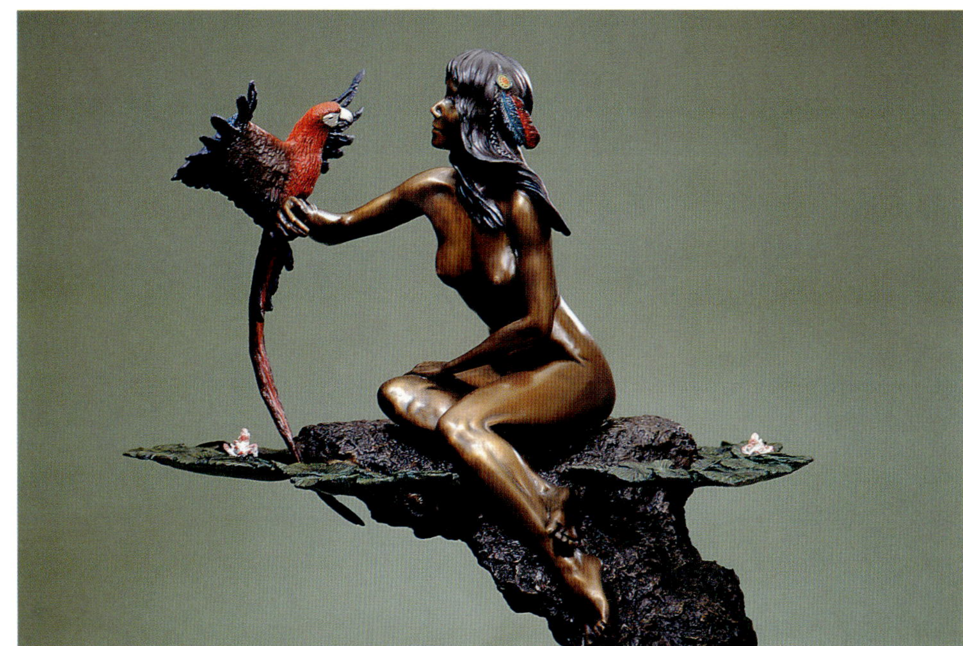
A

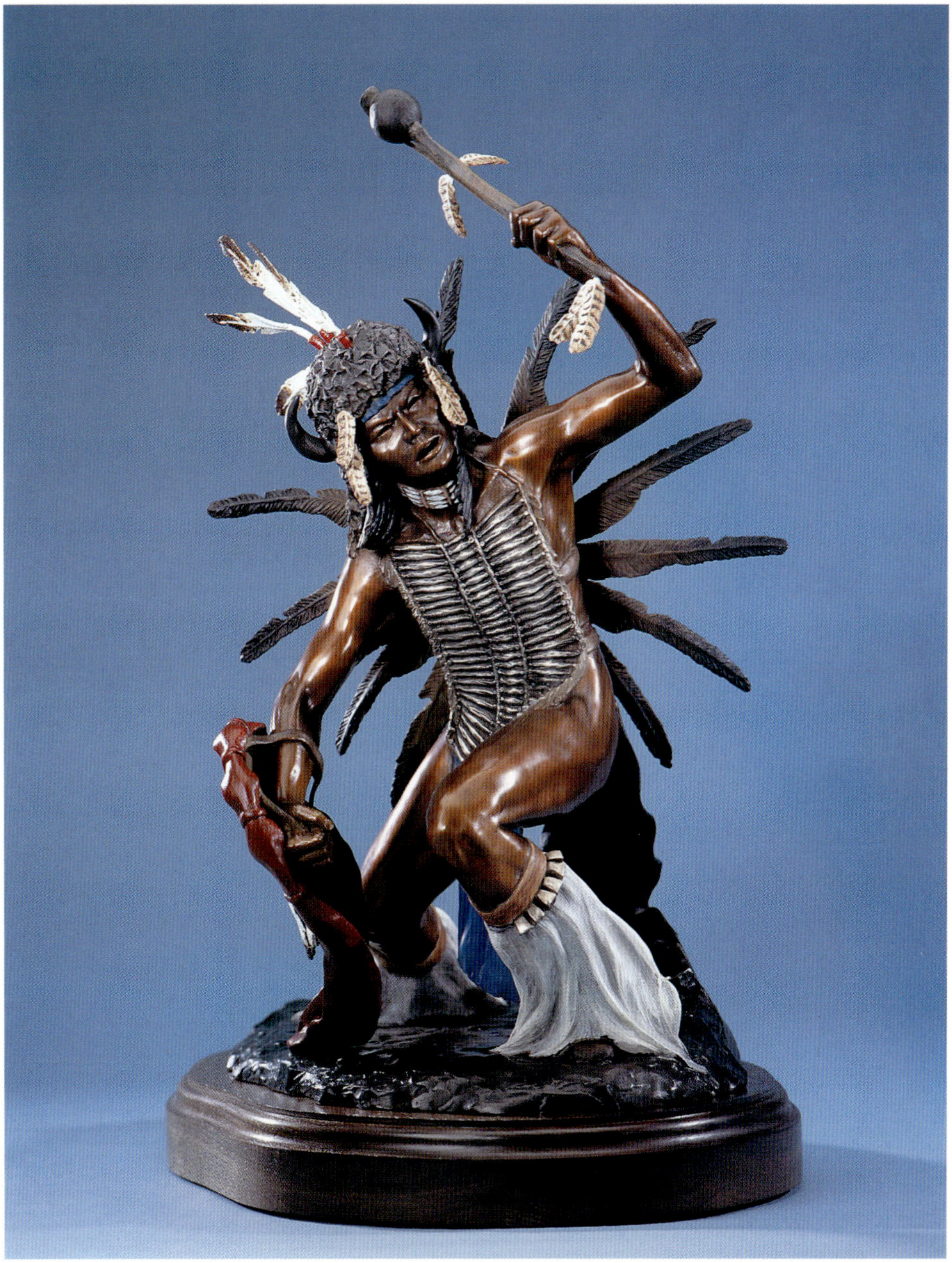

B

Bill Hopen

Hopen Studio
268 North Hill Road
Sutton, WV 26601
FAX 800-872-8578
TEL 800-872-8578

SCULPTOR OF THE FIGURE
BRONZE, STAINLESS STEEL
PORTRAITURE
MONUMENTS
LITURGICAL WORKS
SCULPTURE FOR GARDEN SETTINGS
FOUNTAIN WORKS
SMALLER SCALE INTERIOR WORKS

Bill Hopen is a noted sculptor of the human figure.
He has received many major bronze commissions
in the eastern United States. His personal work is
widely collected, and exhibited in one-man
museum and gallery shows.

Commissioned works generally require six months
to a year; smaller works for garden and interior
are available immediately.

Call to chat informally about your project and to
obtain a video brochure.

Also see these GUILD publications:
Architect's Edition: 9,10

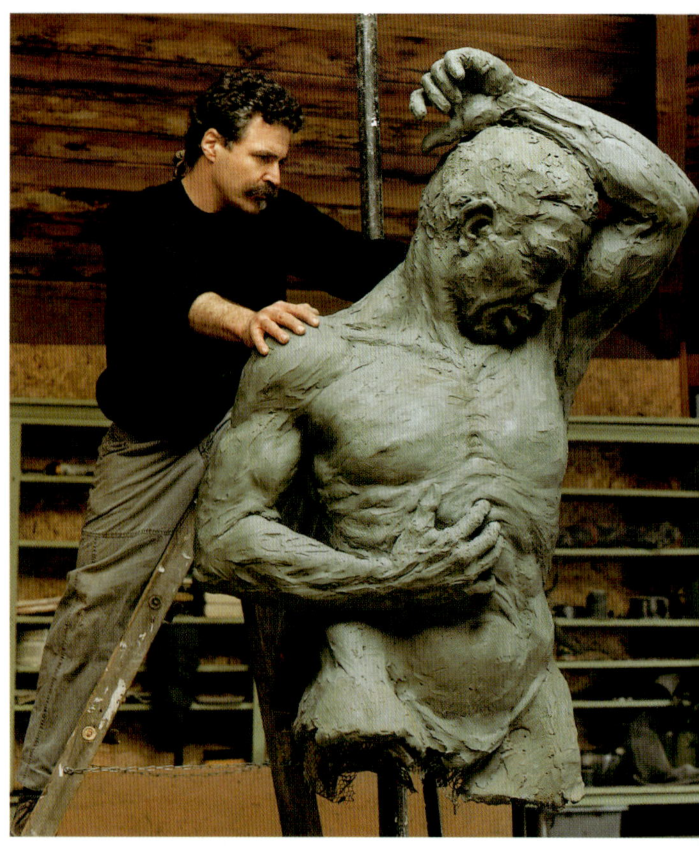

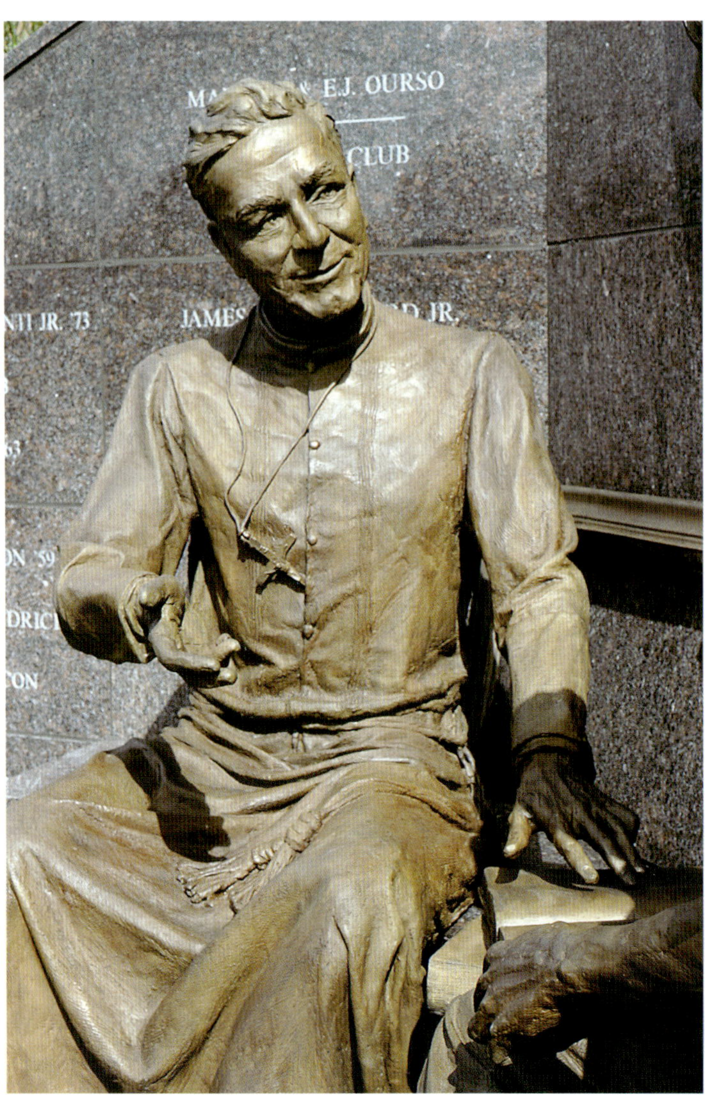

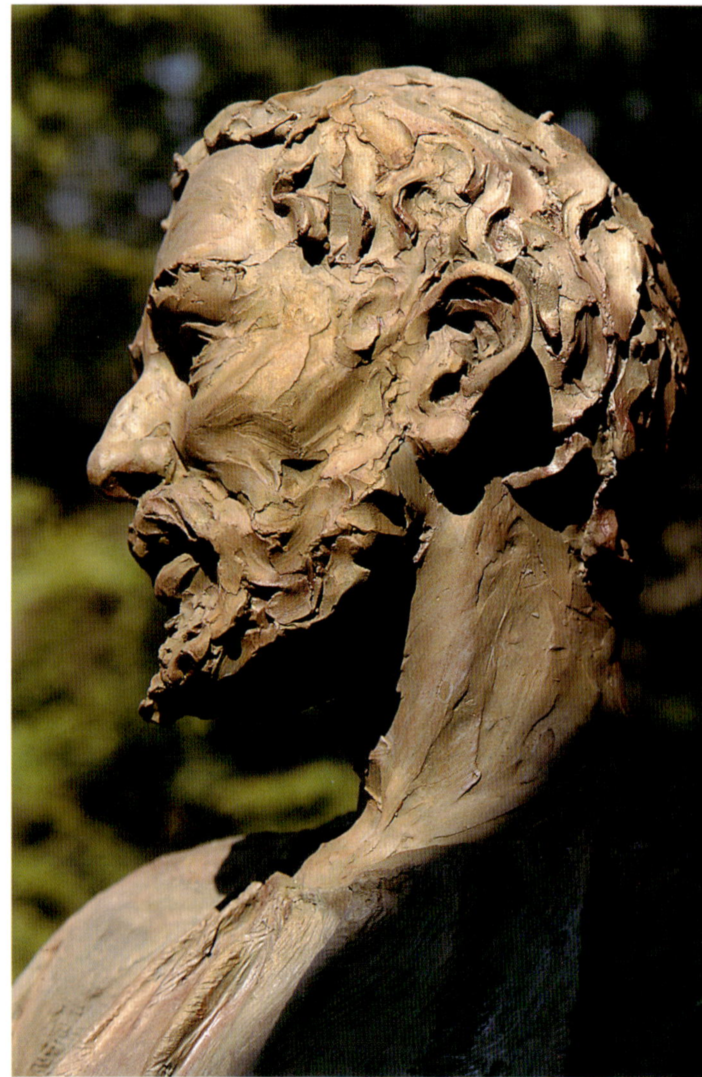

C. Kelly Lohr

The Lohr Studio
604 Hill Street
Churdan, IA 50050
FAX 515-389-3401
TEL 515-389-3210

C. Kelly Lohr, a professional artist for 25 years, incorporates the serenity of the Iowa prairie into life-size or larger sculptures. Lohr's unparalleled versatility is exemplified in both stylized and representational work. The artist creates one-of-a-kind 'direct' sculpture in stone and originals in clay for all types of cast materials.

Lohr is an environmental designer who guarantees timely delivery, integrity, and the flexibility required by a team approach. Projects include Mt. St. Helens National Volcanic Area, the Oregon Dunes National Recreation Area and the Roman Center in Germany.

Lohr invites inquirers to call, write or just stop in for a visit at the studio.

A *Sleeping Woman*, marble on wood, 48"H

B *I Feel Fifteen*, life-size ceramic, available in bronze

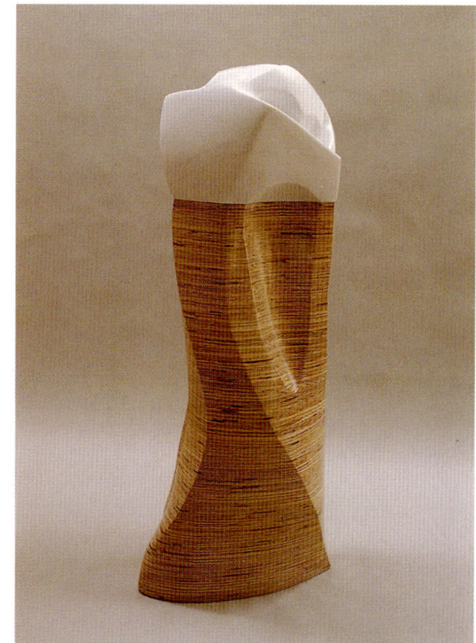

A

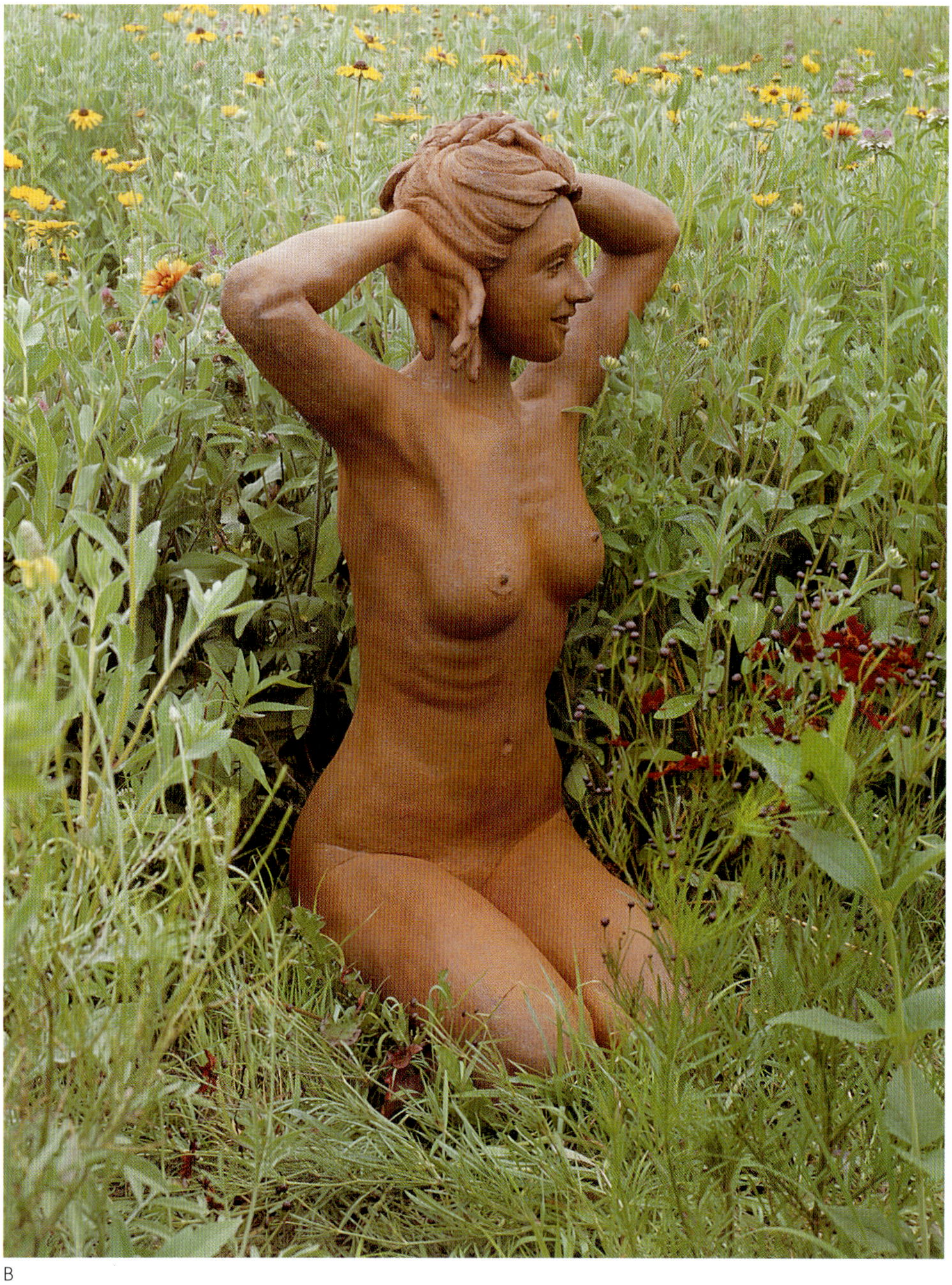

B

Sharon A. Loper

Loper Studio
5876 Tuxedo Terrace
Los Angeles, CA 90068
FAX 213-462-5134
TEL   213-462-5134

Sharon A. Loper lives and works in Los Angeles. Her sculpture is highly textured and communicates a strong visual impact to the viewer. The artist produces bronze animal and figurative sculpture, as well as one-of-a-kind commissioned works.

Sharon Loper has exhibited in many solo and group shows throughout the United States. Her work has appeared in numerous publications and has been collected here and abroad. Collections include the Museum Katten Kabinet, Amsterdam, Holland; San Diego Wild Animal Park; Children's Hospital, San Diego; and the Los Angeles Zoo.

Also see these GUILD publications:
Architect's Edition: 8, 10

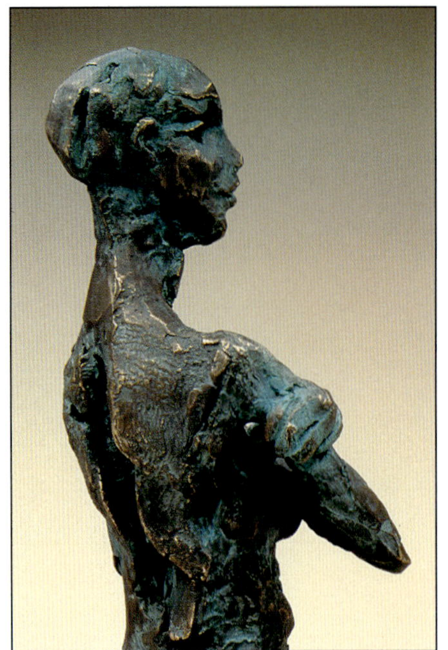

Female figure, 1994, detail

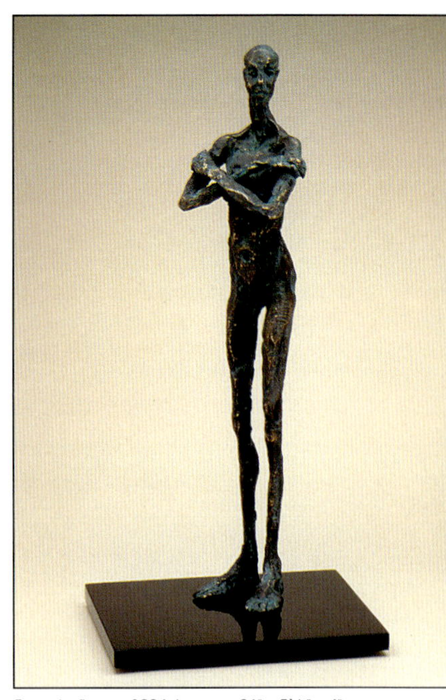

Female figure, 1994, bronze, 26" x 5¹/₂" x 4"

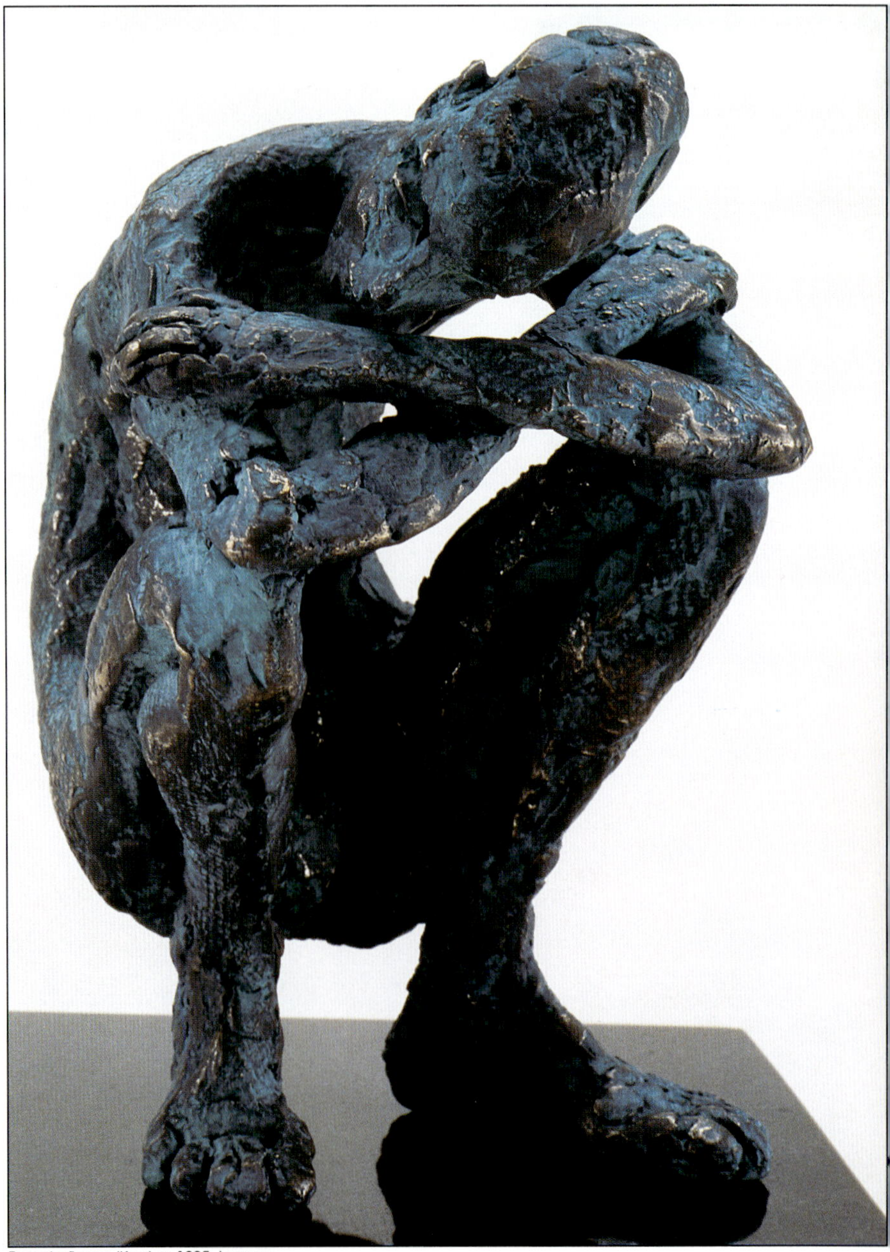

Female figure, life-size, 1995, bronze

Walter T. Matia

Curlew Castings
18601 Darnestown Road
Poolesville, MD 20837
TEL 301-349-2330

Matia specializes in limited-edition bronze fountains and garden sculpture. He is a member of the National Academy of Western Artists and the Society of Animal Artists. Commissions accepted.

Commissions include:
Blair House, the president's guest house, Washington, DC
Richard King Mellon Foundation, Pittsburgh, PA
Leigh Yawkey Woodson Art Museum, Wausau, WI
Benson Park Sculpture Garden, Loveland, CO
Wichita Botanical Garden, Wichita, KS
Deerwood Office Park, Jacksonville, FL

A *Rabbit Run*, eagle, 94" x 97" x 54"

B *Marshmaster*, heron, 55" x 26" x 14"

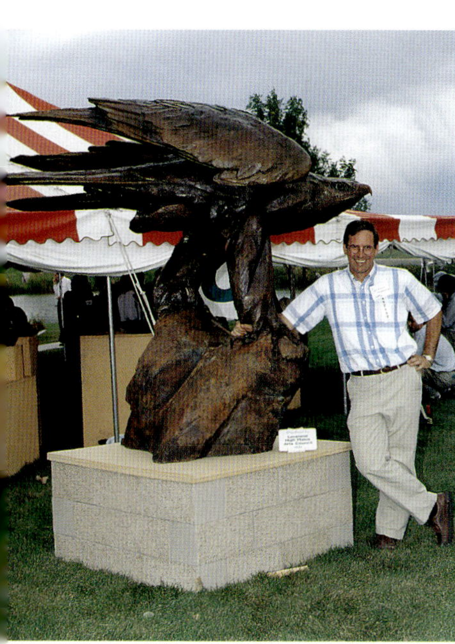

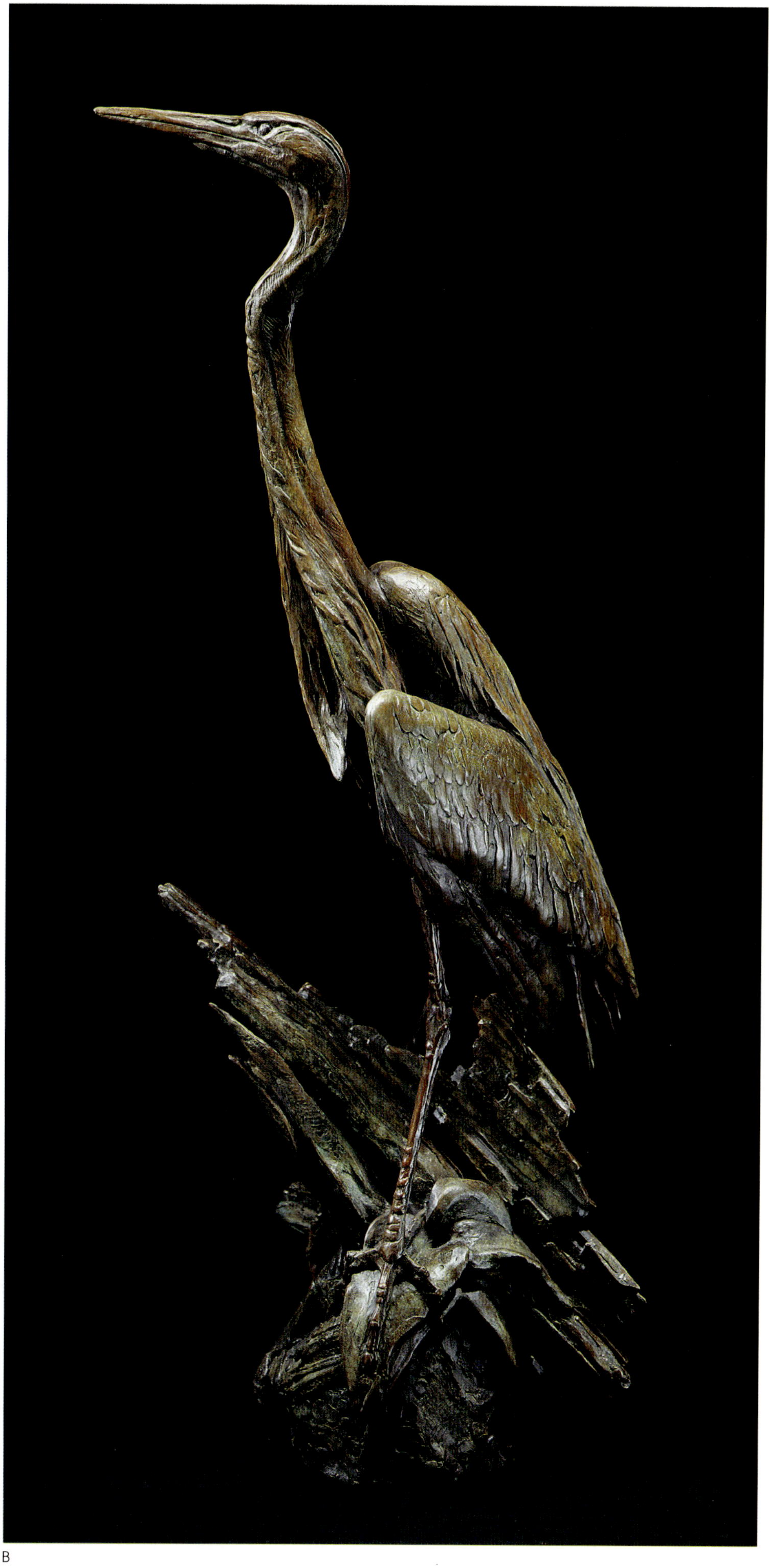

National Sculptors' Guild

2683 North Taft Avenue
Loveland, CO 80538
FAX 970-667-2068
TEL 970-667-2015

Dee Clements
Sculptor

Dee Clements dedicated his monumental, seven-figure, eleven-bas-relief *Desert Holocaust Memorial* in Palm Desert, California, on the 50th anniversary of the liberation of the camps. A long-favorite sculptor for commissions by America's major corporations, Clements has placed works in private, corporate and public collections throughout the world. His most recent commission is a 6'7" tall Shakespearean actor for a theater.

Videos with current work are available upon request. Collaborations welcome.

Also see these GUILD publications:
Architect's Edition: 9, 10
Designer's Edition: 10

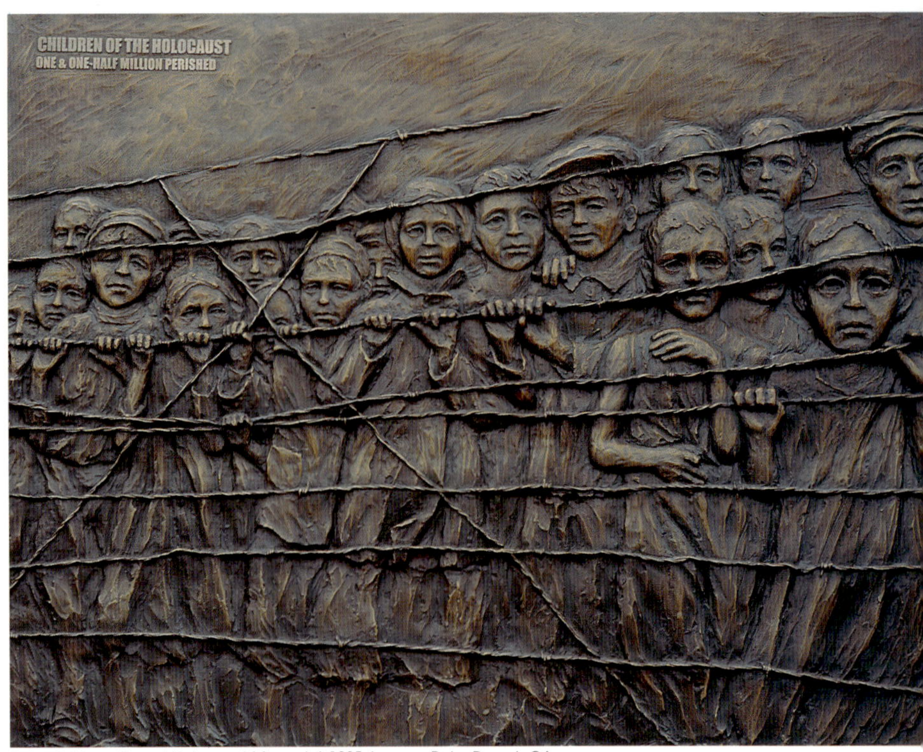

Bas-relief from *Desert Holocaust Memorial*, 1995, bronze, Palm Desert, CA

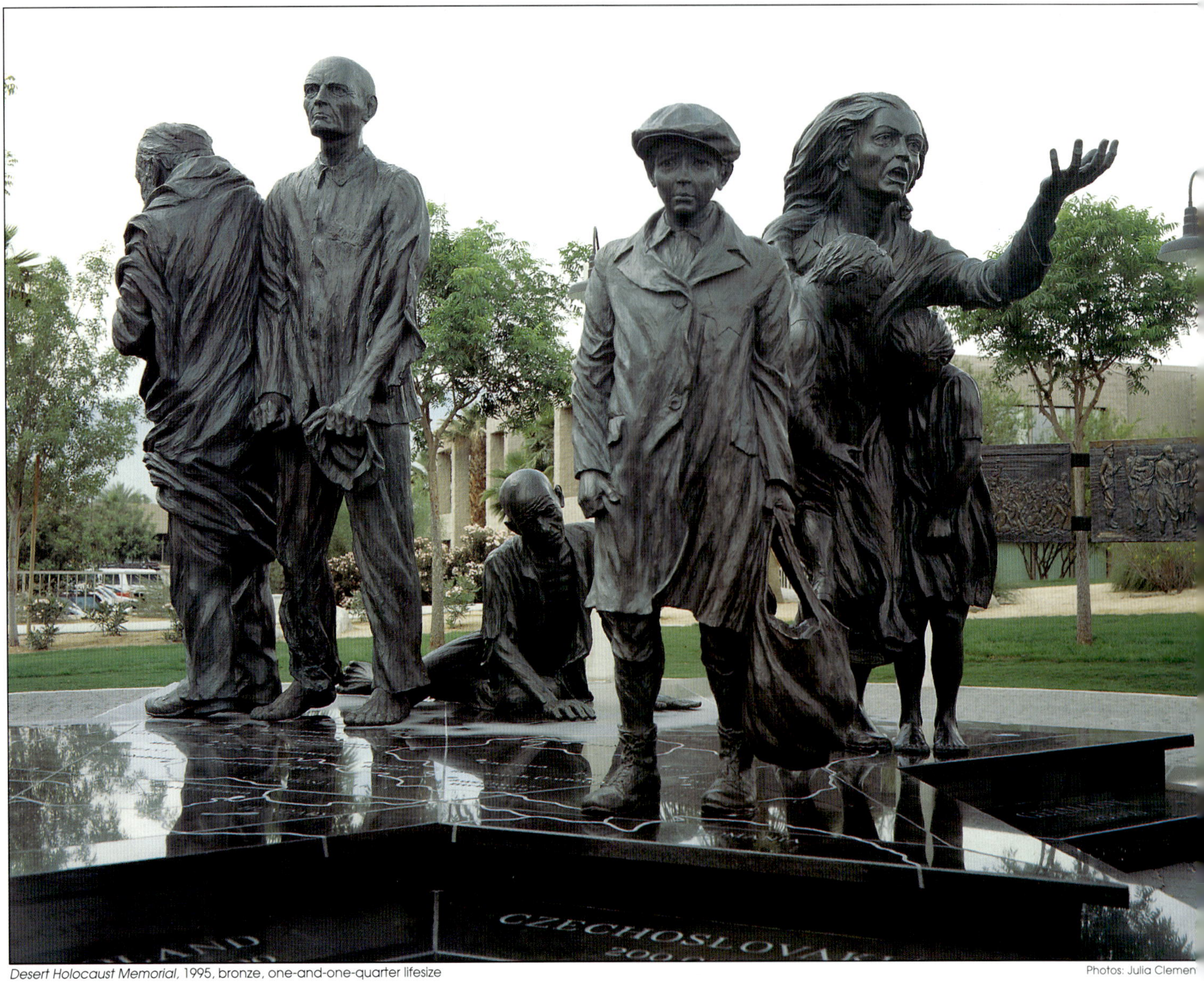

Desert Holocaust Memorial, 1995, bronze, one-and-one-quarter lifesize

Photos: Julia Clemen

National Sculptors' Guild

2683 North Taft Avenue
Loveland, CO 80538
FAX 970-667-2068
TEL 970-667-2015

Jane DeDecker
Sculptor

Jane DeDecker works predominantly with people as a theme, and imbues her figures with unmistakable personalities that spark recognition and humor in the viewer. She blends an evocative looseness of interpretation with insightful details that continue to bring her work recognition.

Commissions include the White House, Mayo Clinic, and Michael Jackson.

Videos with current work are available upon request. Collaborations welcome.

Also see these GUILD publications:
Architect's Edition: 9, 10
Designer's Edition: 10

A *Karen,* 1995, bronze, 28" x 21" x 13", edition of 31

Shortcut, 1995, bronze, 72" x 118" x 40", edition of 17

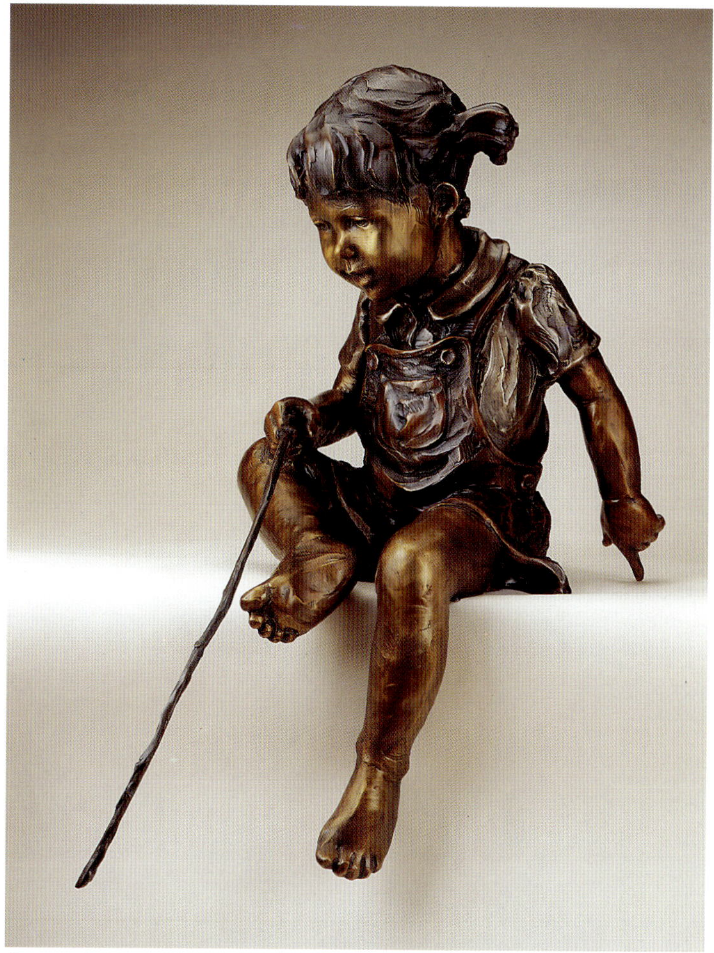

A

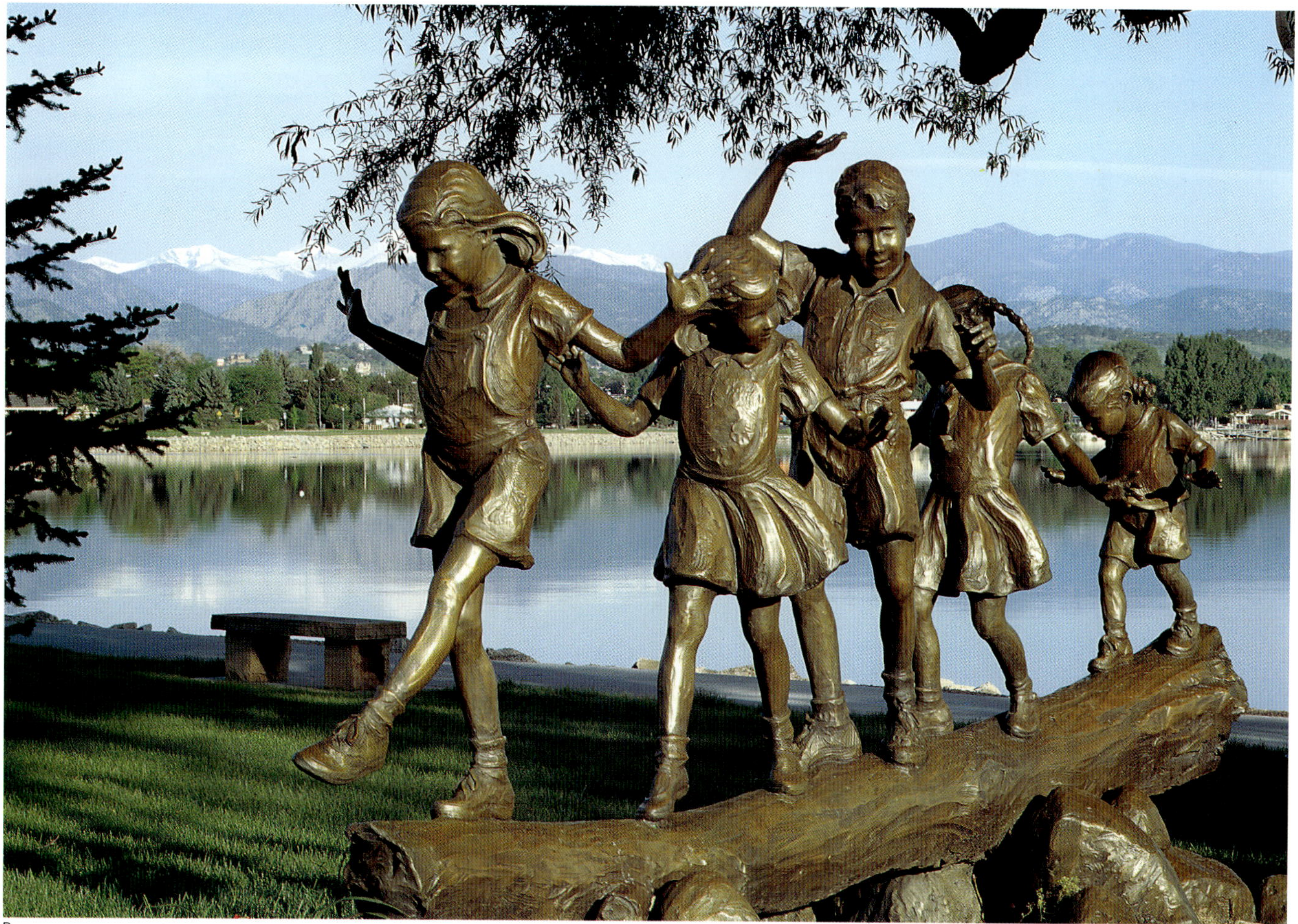

B

National Sculptors' Guild

2683 North Taft Avenue
Loveland, CO 80538
FAX 970-667-2068
TEL 970-667-2015

Sandy Scott
Sculptor

Sandy Scott received her formal art training at the Kansas City Art Institute and later worked as an animation background artist for the motion picture industry. Her earlier work led her to etching and printmaking in the 1970s and to sculpture in the next decade. She is now considered one of the United States' top wildlife sculptors, with commissions placed around the world.

Her eagle and horse sculptures range in size from tabletop to 22 feet. Her list of awards includes the Ellin P. Speyer Prize at the National Academy of Design, and the Gold Medal for Sculpture at the National Academy of Western Art. She maintains studios in both the United States and Canada.

Videos with current work are available upon request. Collaborations welcome.

Also see these GUILD publications:
Architect's Edition: 9, 10
Designer's Edition: 10

A *Fountain of Peace*, bronze, 84"H, edition of 12

B *Above It All*, 1995, bronze, 8¹/₂' wing span, edition of 35

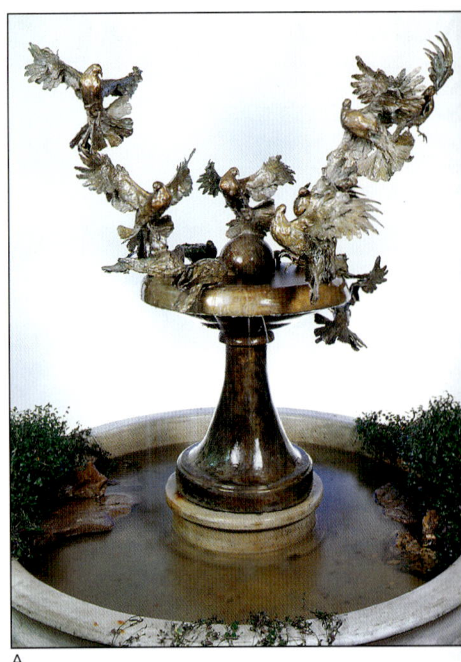

A

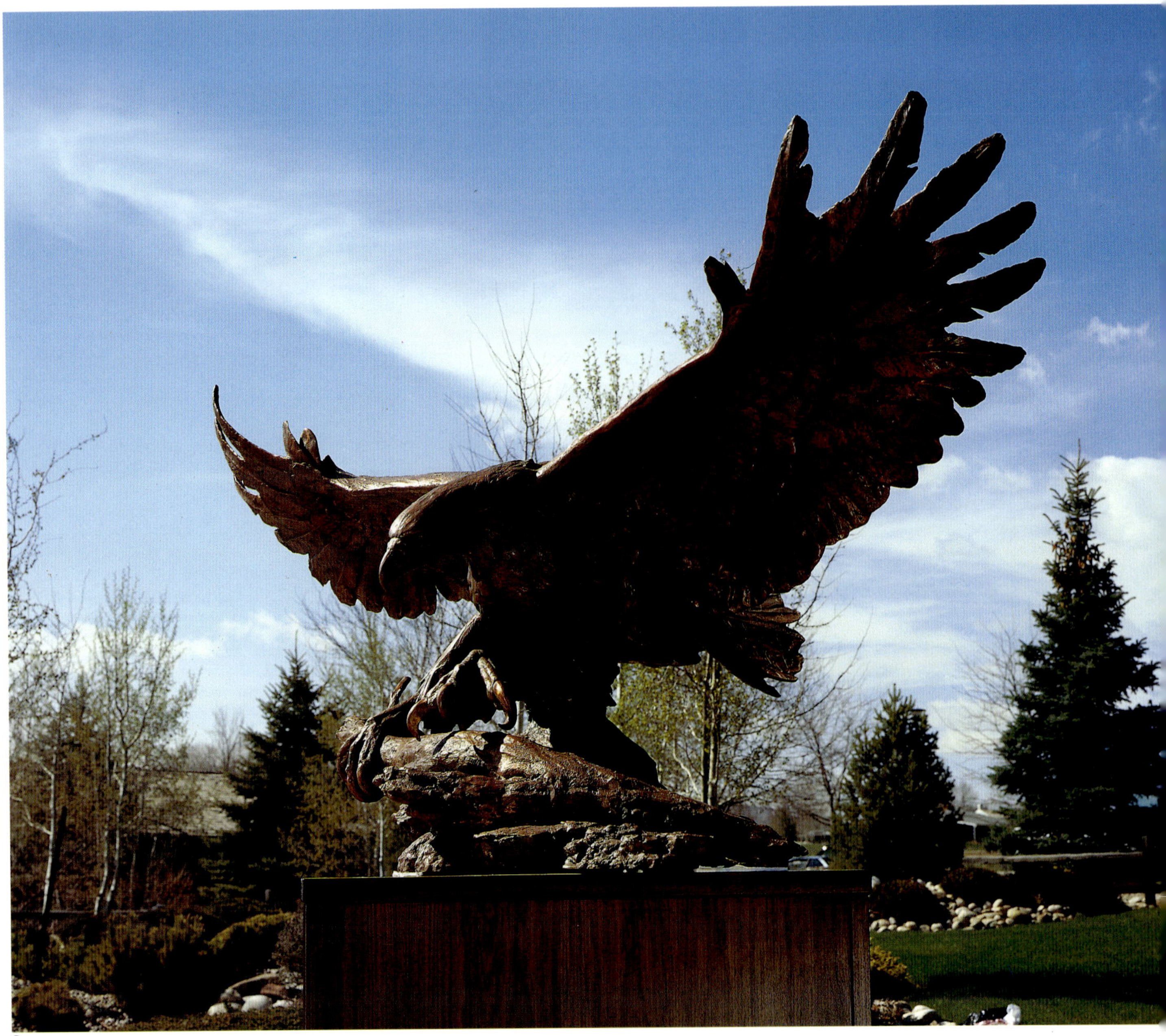

B

National Sculptors' Guild

2683 North Taft Avenue
Loveland, CO 80538
FAX 970-667-2068
TEL 970-667-2015

Bart Walter
Sculptor

At any moment his work looks as though it might leap down from its pedestal and approach you. Such is the power and prirnal force evident in the bronze sculptures of Bart Walter. He combines the experience of the artist and the naturalist to produce forceful, yet subtle, images of the animal kingdom. Creatures both great and small are fixed immutably in bronze.

The works are not limited to the world of animals, but excel in the whole domain of sculpture with the predilection for animal forms—his chosen field. A sampling of the artist's recent accomplishments include a sculpture of three gamboling otters at the Baltimore Zoo and work in the Jane Goodall Institute in Tucson, Arizona.

Videos with current work are available upon request. Collaborations welcome.

Also see these GUILD publications:
Architect's Edition: 9, 10
Designer's Edition: 10

A *Mountain Landscape,* 1991, bronze,
   78" x 41"x 48", edition of three

B *Otter Rocks,* 1993, bronze and concrete,
   72" x 78"x 72", edition of three

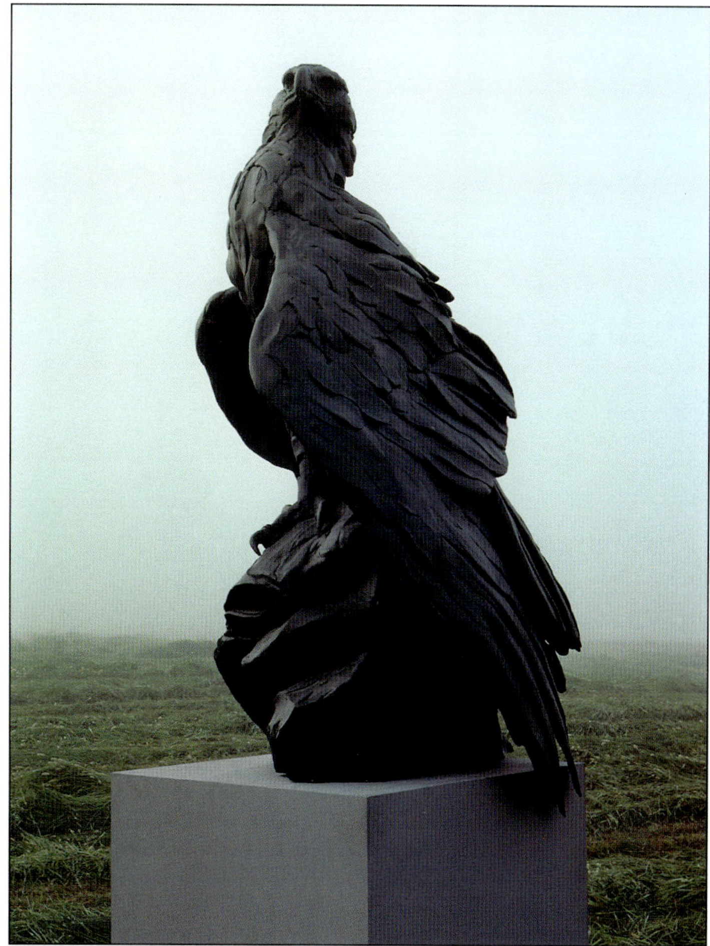

A

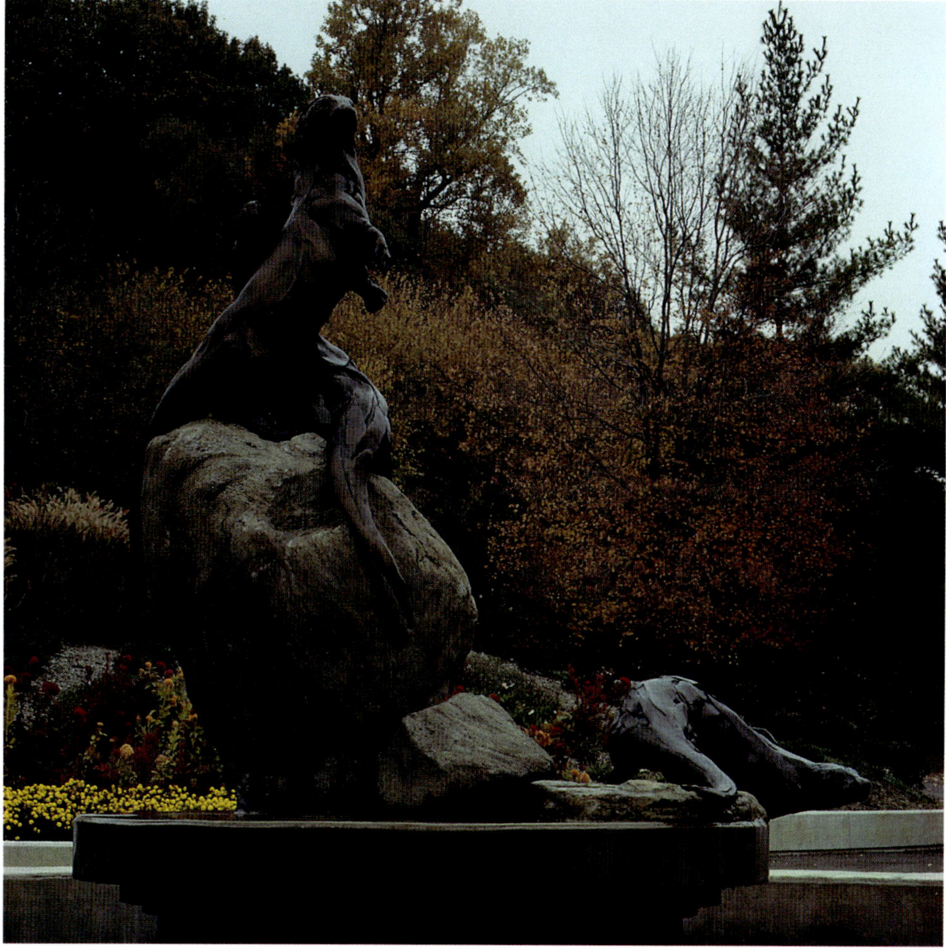

B

Jo Schneider

Art/Architecture
1007 Winding Way
Baltimore, MD 21210
TEL 410-323-2764

Jo Schneider, artist and licensed architect, has created works of art in public places throughout the country. She has exhibited her sculptures nationally in numerous museums and juried exhibitions. Artworks and their architecturally designed environments are created to be site-specific in a variety of media.

Commissions include:
JMB Retail Properties, RTKL Associates
City of Evanston, IL, Art at the Viaduct
Pleasantview Housing Project, Washington, DC
Children's Cloisters Museum, MD
Rouse Company headquarters, Columbia, MD

A *Lizards*, 1995, Brandon Town Center, FL, bronze, moving jaw, waterjets in tail. 10' x 9' x 9'

B *Manatee*, 1995, Brandon Town Center, FL, bronze, moving tail and flippers, 7'6" x 6' x 4'

(All movement created by waterwheels.)

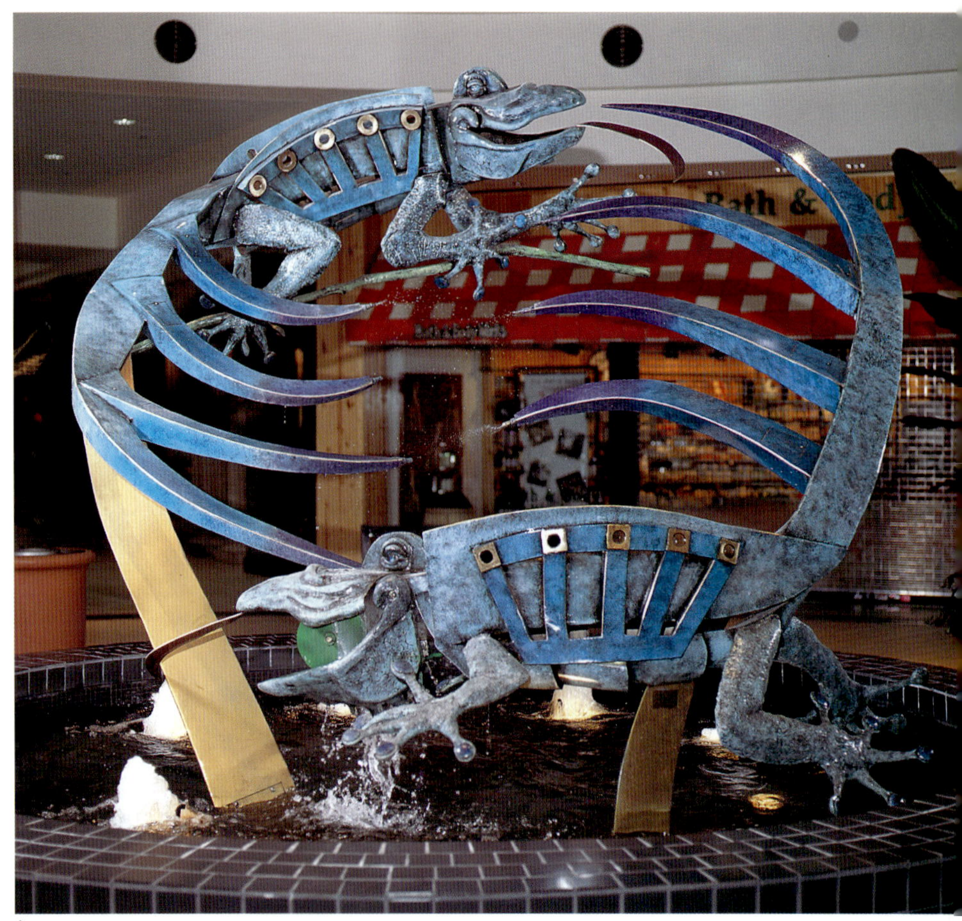

A

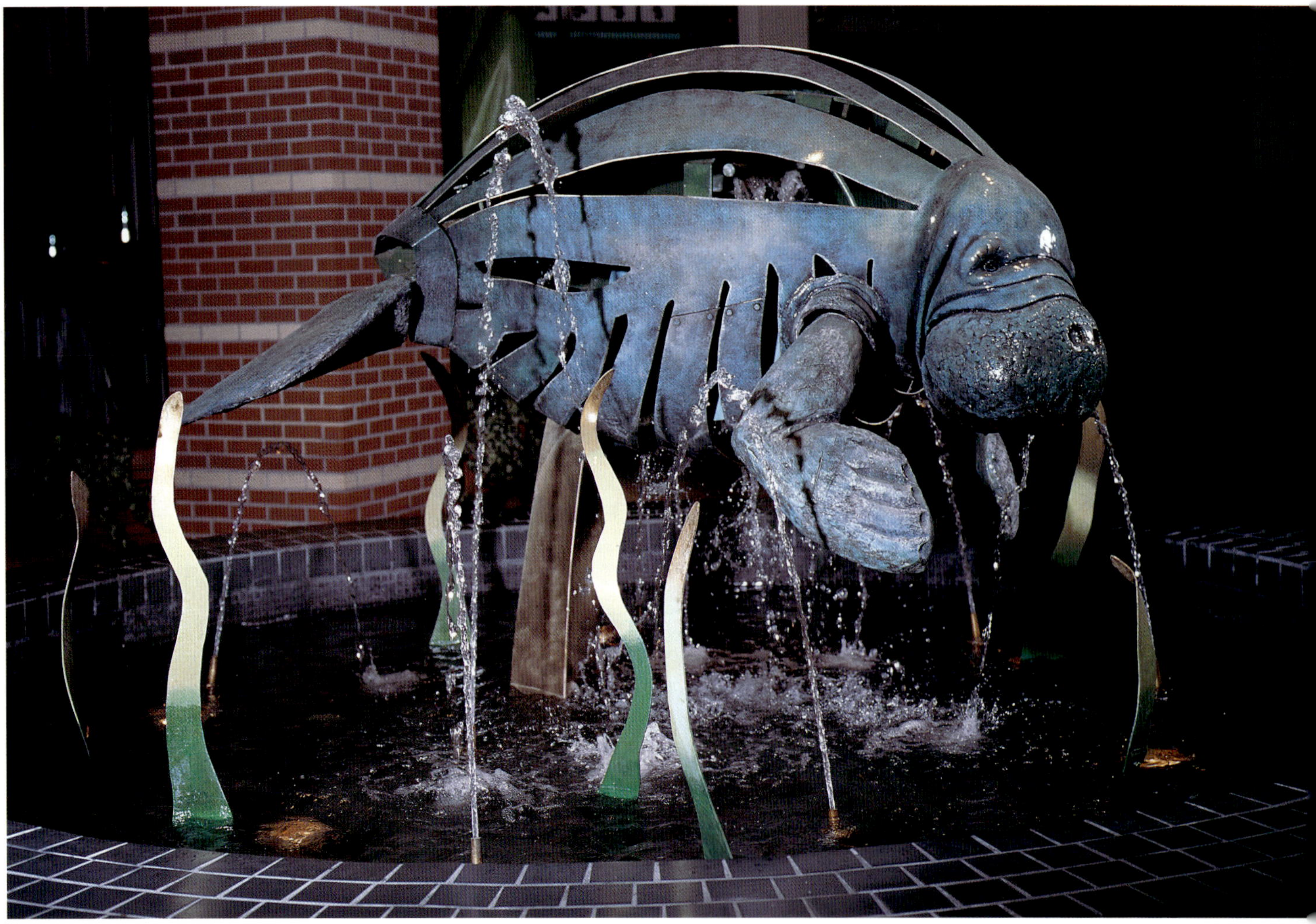

B

Beverly Steigerwald

782 South Emporia
Denver, CO 80231
TEL 303-364-8498

Bev Steigerwald creates contemporary sculpture with a classic look. People are her subject and her bronzes are fresh and full of life. Projects include many portraits, free-standing sculptures, relief walls, and sensitive solutions to site-specific needs. The work is in small to large scale for both exterior and interior areas.

Bev has worked well with architects and committees, always on time and within budget. Where color or relief work are appropriate, Bev displays a fine touch. Her sculptures are figurative and deeply spiritual. They are in private residences, churches, gardens, hospitals and museums, and have been recognized with numerous national and international awards.

Also see this GUILD publication:
Architect's Edition: 9

A *Spirit of Air* (with inset), 1995, bronze,
   30"H x 12" x 17"

B *Mary at Cana*, plaster wall, 8' x 15';
   bronze sculpture, 6'H

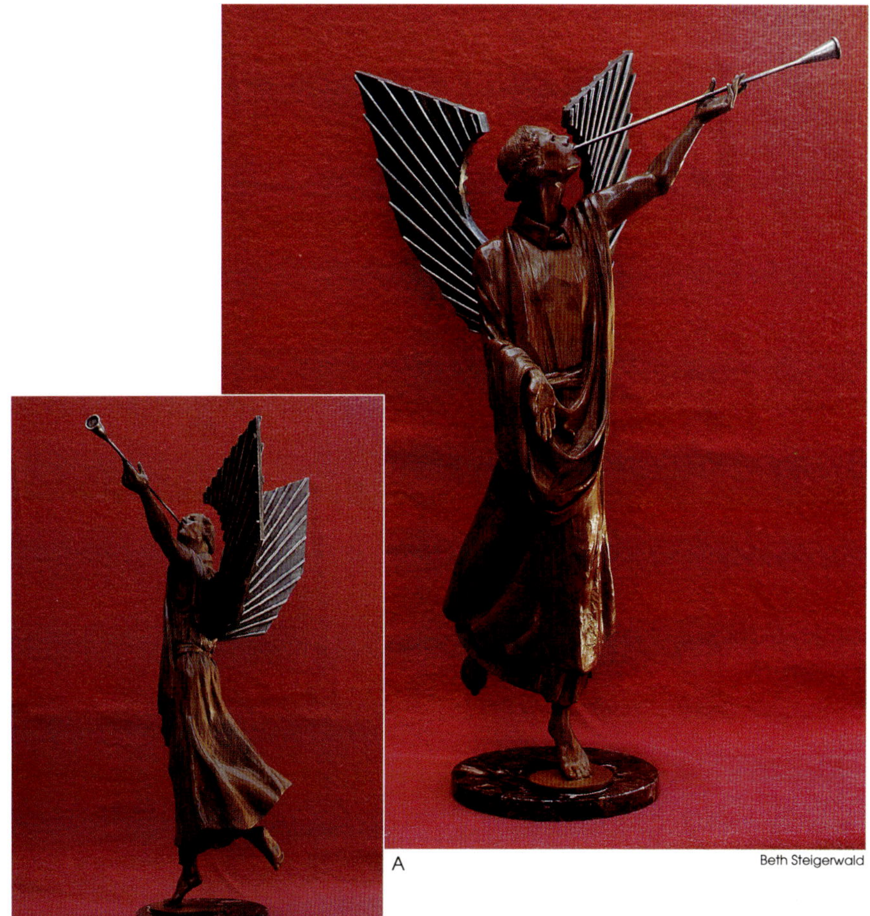

A

Beth Steigerwald

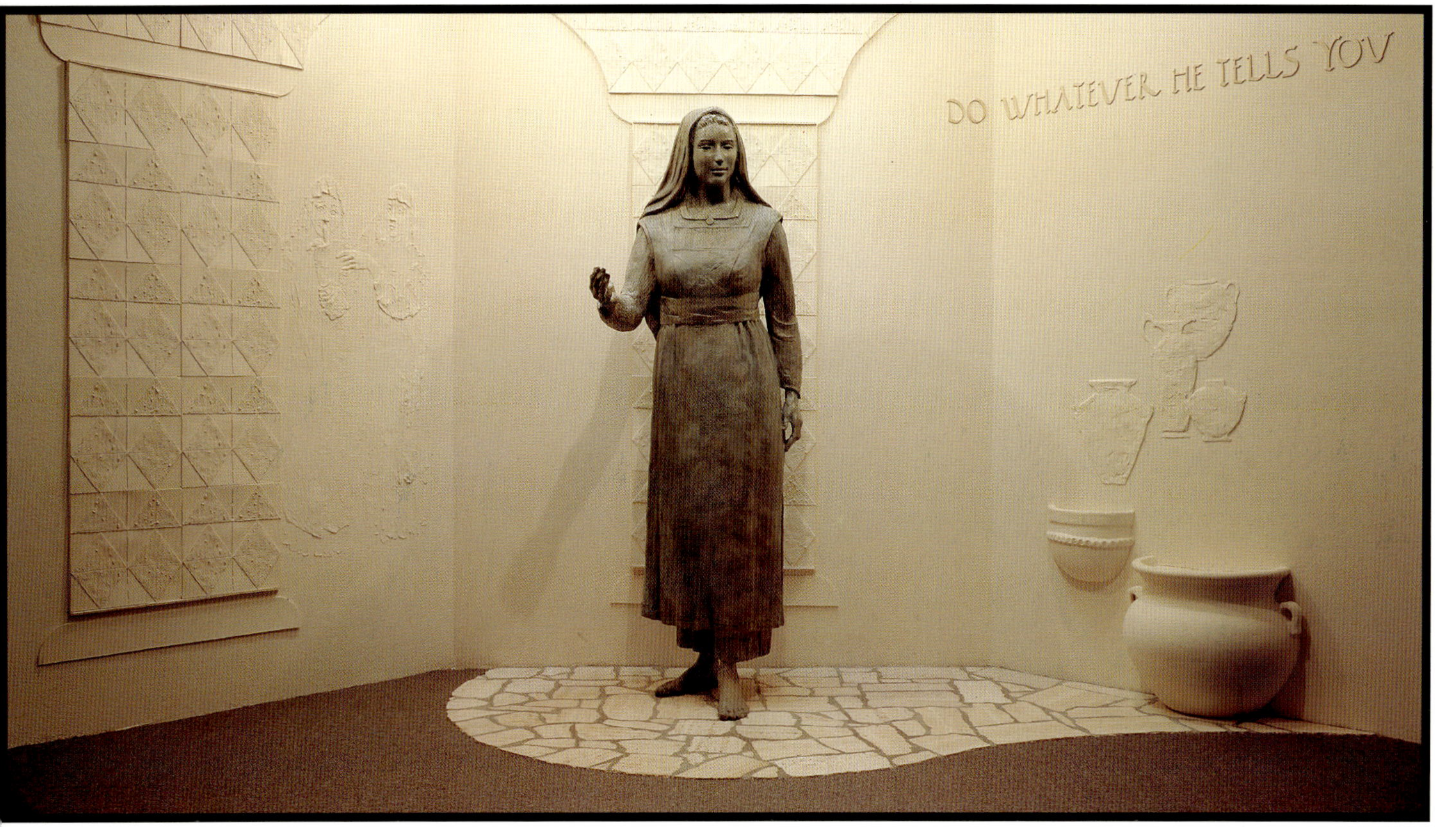

B

Warren Blanc

Márton Váró

2 Charity
Irvine, CA 92715
FAX 714-856-2943
TEL   714-856-0249

Equally known for his draped female figures and cubes with drapery fragments, Márton Váró carves directly in marble or stone. His understanding of materials and their integration with architecture make these works suitable for major public projects. The sculptor has generated great interest through educational programs involving on-site carving and community participation.

Commissions include:
Forum Hotel, Budapest, Hungary
Congress Center, Budapest, Hungary
Volos, Greece
City of Brea, CA
Peace Memorial, Palm Desert, CA
Plaza of the Americas, Dallas, TX
Art Institute of California, Laguna Beach, CA
Tustin Ranch Marketplace
Performing Arts Hall, Fort Worth, TX

A *Breaking Free*, 1994, red Persian travertine, Art Institute of Southern California, Laguna Beach, 7' x 2^1/$_2$' x 2'

B Congress Center, Budapest, Hungary, 1984, limestone, 25' x 9'

C *Primavera*, 1995, carrara statuario marble, Tustin Ranch Marketplace, Tustin, CA, 5' x 1' x 1'

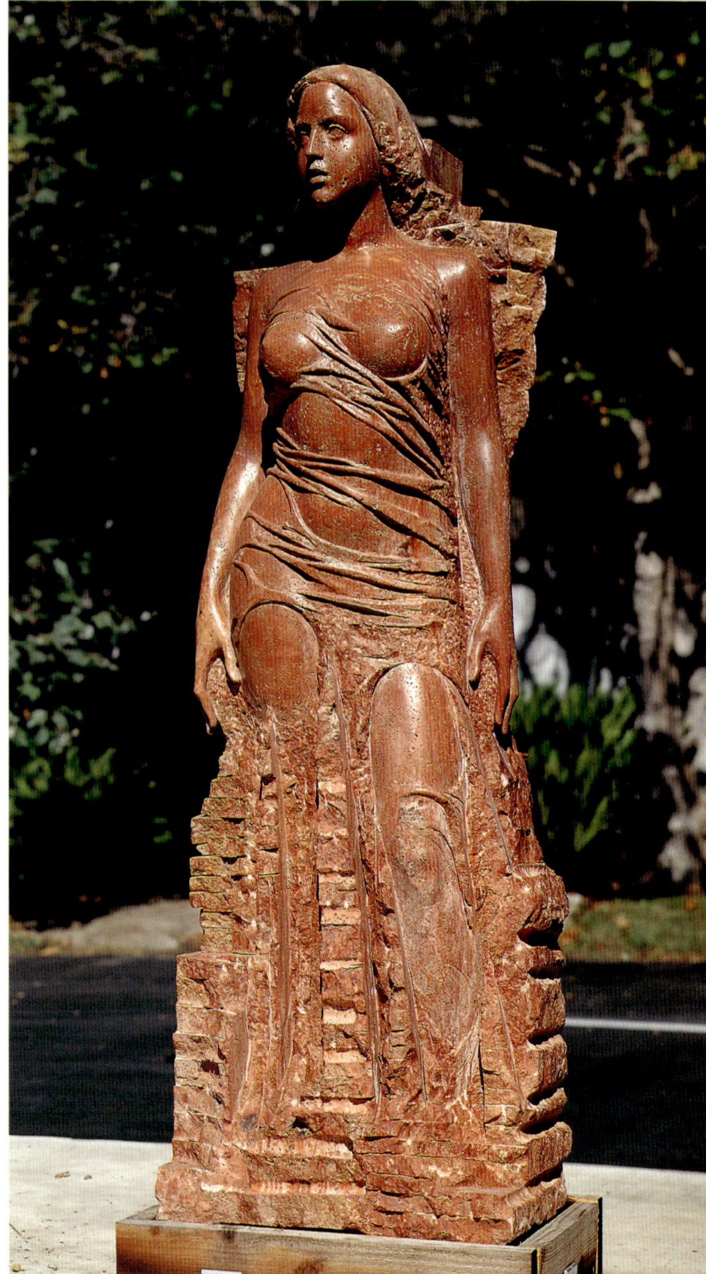

A

Kevin Wright

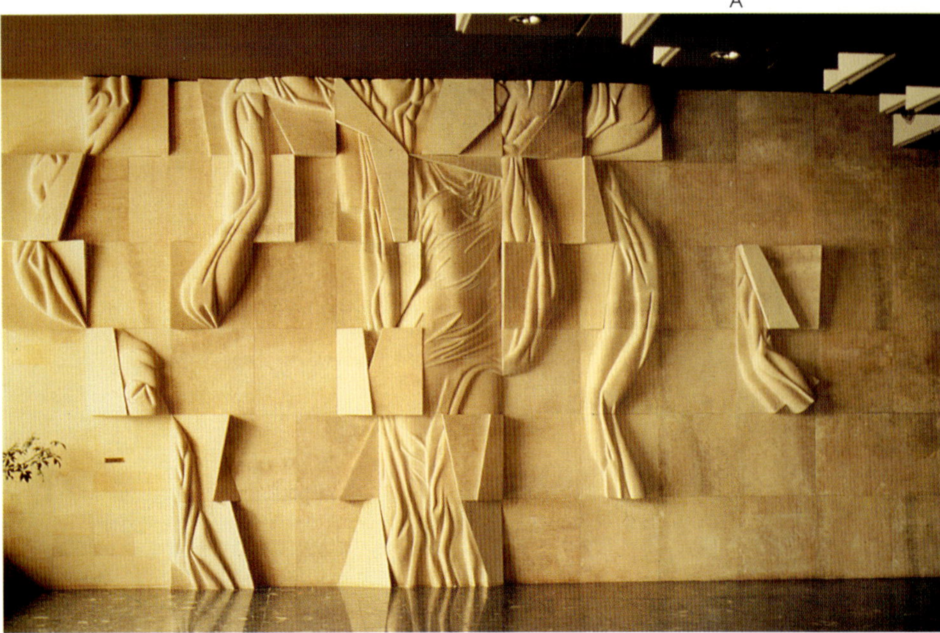

B

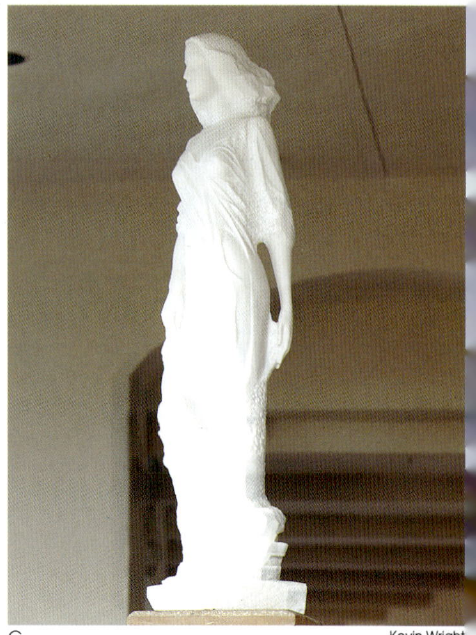

C

Kevin Wright

Visual Art Access

Michael S. Bell, Curator
Box 2880
Santa Fe, NM 87504-2880

Louise Lieber
Buck McCain
James N. Muir
Lee Roy Champagne
Artists

"And I could touch them with my hand, Almost,
I thought, from where I stand,"
Edna St. Vincent Millay

A Louise Lieber
The Angel Who Weeps, 1989, acrylic on
wood and sheet metal, 84" x 144" x 36",
private collection, #415-285-5582

B Buck McCain
Spirit, 1990, cast bronze, 168" x 240" x 120",
collection of the Fleischer Museum,
#602-743-7465

C James N. Muir
... And Justice For All, 1994, cast bronze,
96" x 48" x 36", collection of W.W. Steel and
Aspey, Watkins & Diesel, Attorneys, #520-284-1154

D Lee Roy Champagne
The Grail (Chalice of Light), 1988, neon, glass
block, steel, 480" x 120" x 24", collection of the
City and County of San Francisco, #707-747-6167

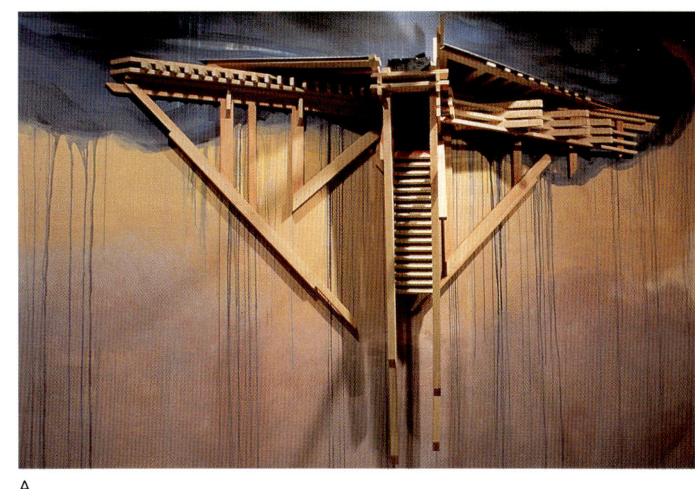

A

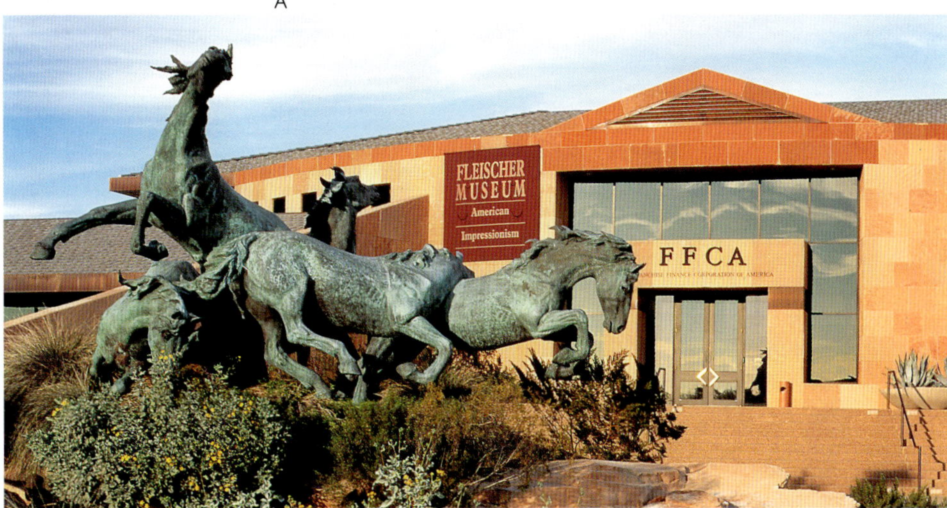

The Fleischer Museum

B

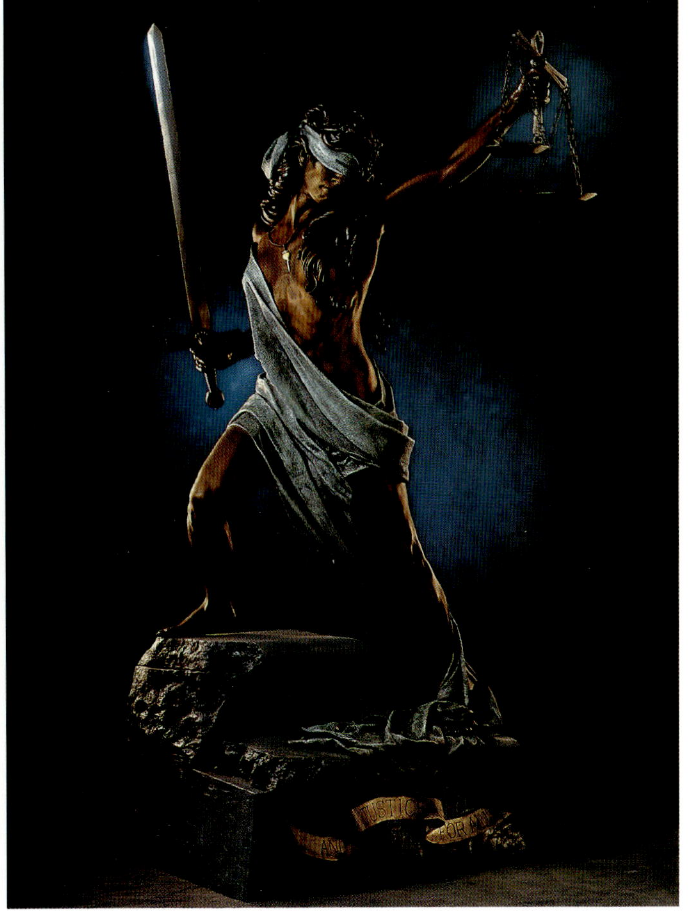

C

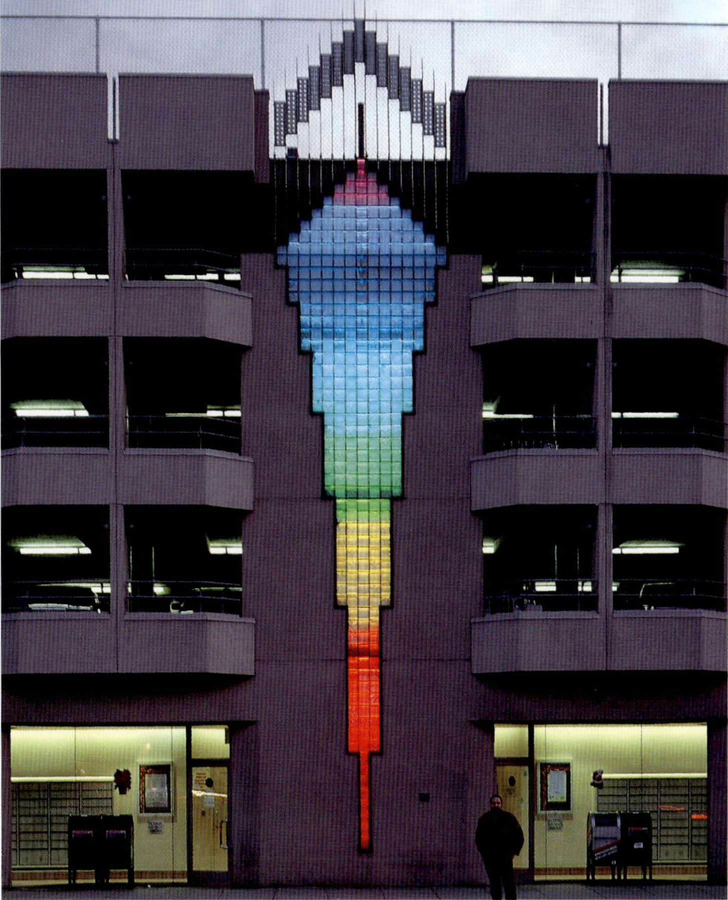

D

Orlando Santiago

Dawn Weimer

Western Dawn Studio
1125 Centennial Road
Fort Collins, CO 80525-2373
FAX 970-282-4351
TEL 800-858-4920

Since completing her first bronze in 1991, Dawn Weimer has garnered numerous awards nationally and attracted collectors internationally.

Her style is expressive yet realistic, maintaining exceptional quality. New York City awards include: *Pen & Brush Annual Sculpture Exhibit*, *American Artists Professional League Exhibition*, and *Catharine Lorillard Wolfe Exhibition*, among others. She has been recently commissioned to do a monumental bronze for Colorado State University.

A *Taking Stalk*, maquette, 16"H x 13"L x 7"W, edition of 20

B *Taking Stalk*, lifesize, edition of 5

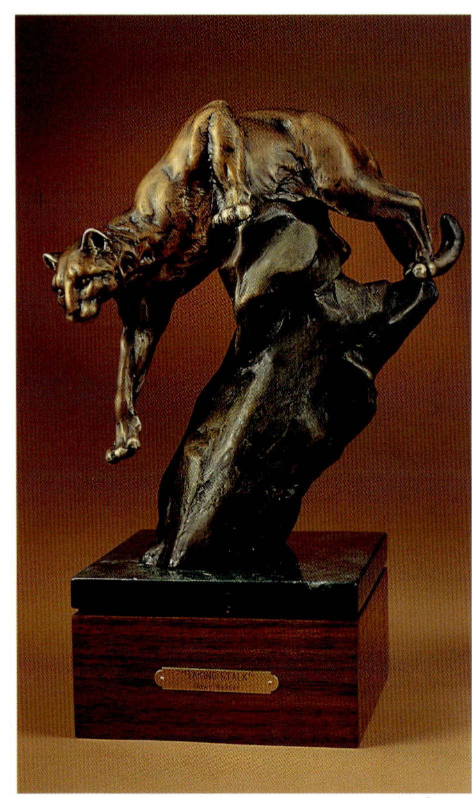
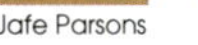

A   Jafe Parsons

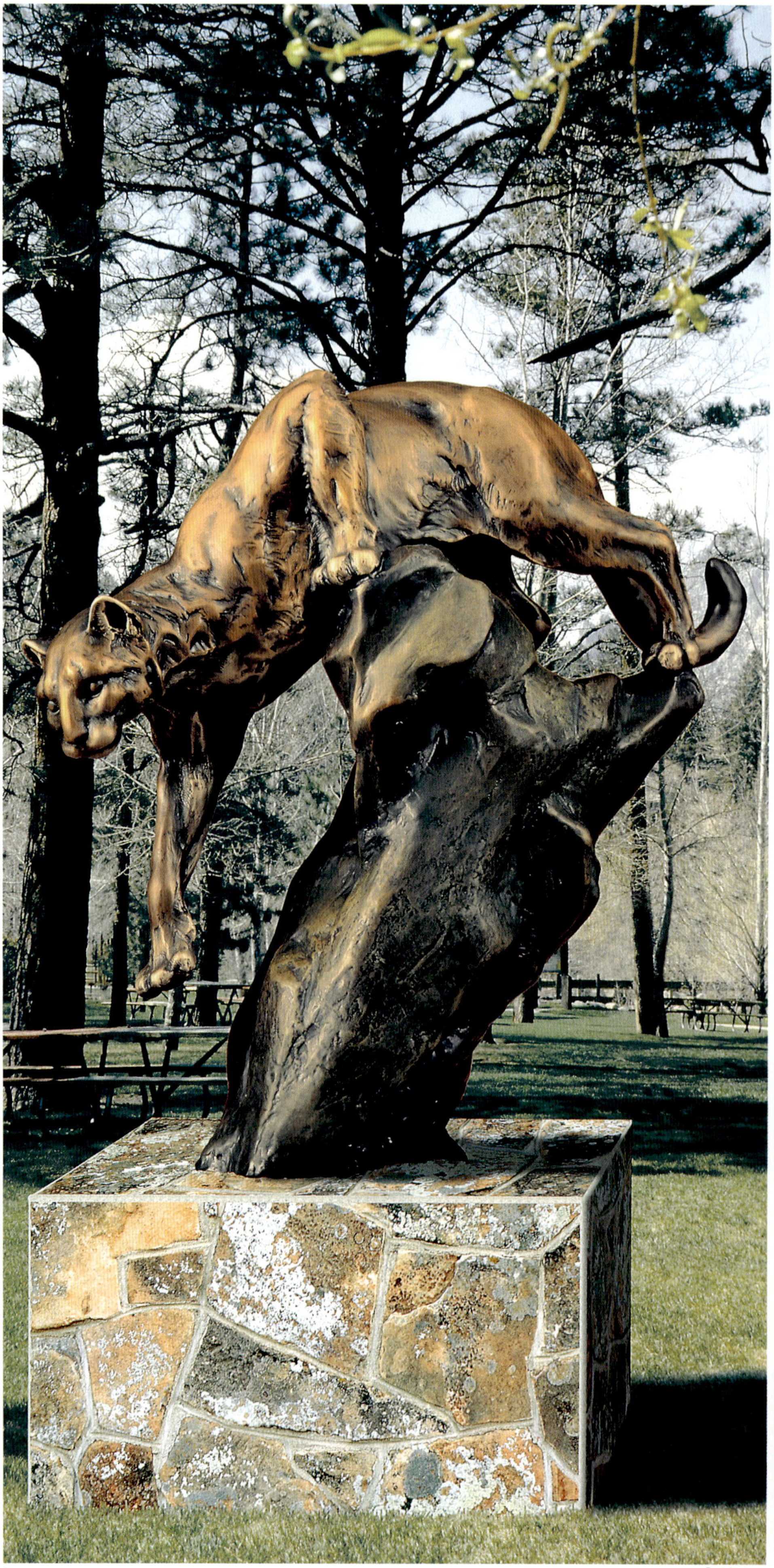

B   Dan Looper

Esther Wertheimer

7064 Siena Court
Boca Raton, FL 33433
FAX 407-392-0065
TEL   407-392-3503

Esther Wertheimer began her art career in 1958. For more than ten years, she has created monumental sculptures, specializing in those of bronze and steel which often depict themes of motherhood, freedom and new beginnings.

Her sculptures reflect the grace of dancers, the tenderness of poetry and the rhythm of classical music. She is able to transform bronze into lyrical expressions of kinetic energy.

Wertheimer is presently working on a nine-foot version of *Seven Dancers* for the Okaloosa-Walton Community College; two outdoor sculptures, *Grace* and *Paolo and Francesca*, are being installed at the Upper Iowa University. Her sculptures are displayed around the globe and have received international honors. From 1991-95 she completed thirteen large commissions in Japan and Singapore.

Also see this GUILD publication:
Architect's Edition: 8

A *Invictus*

B *Ascendence*

C *Seven Dancers*

D *Paolo and Francesca*

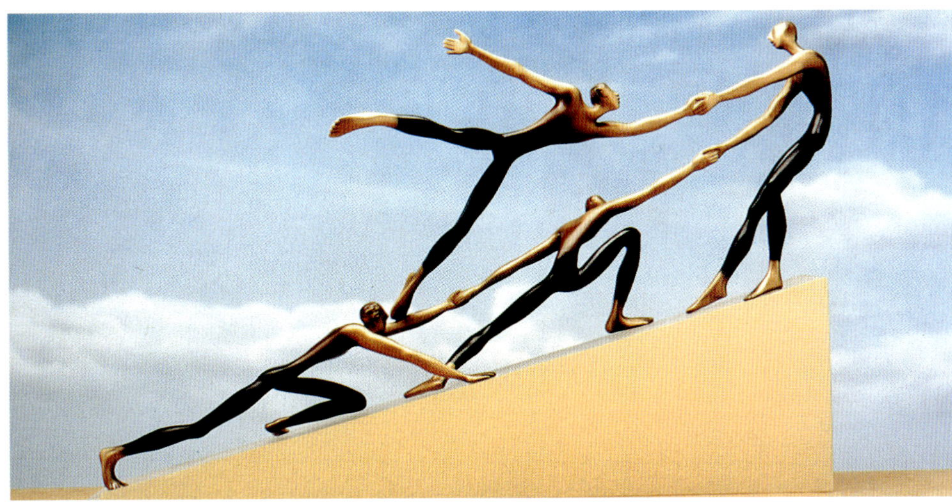

A

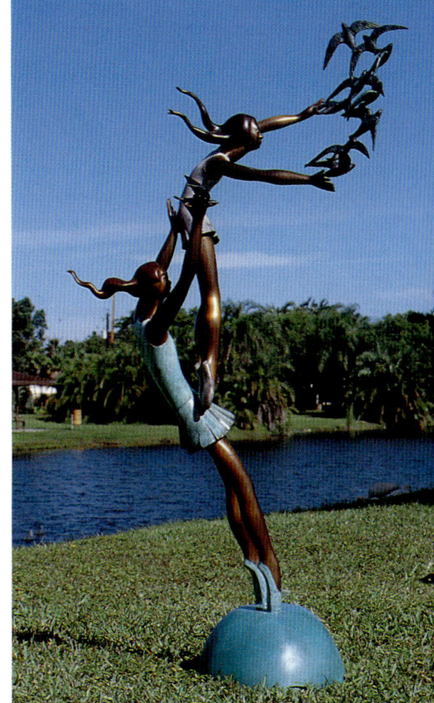

B

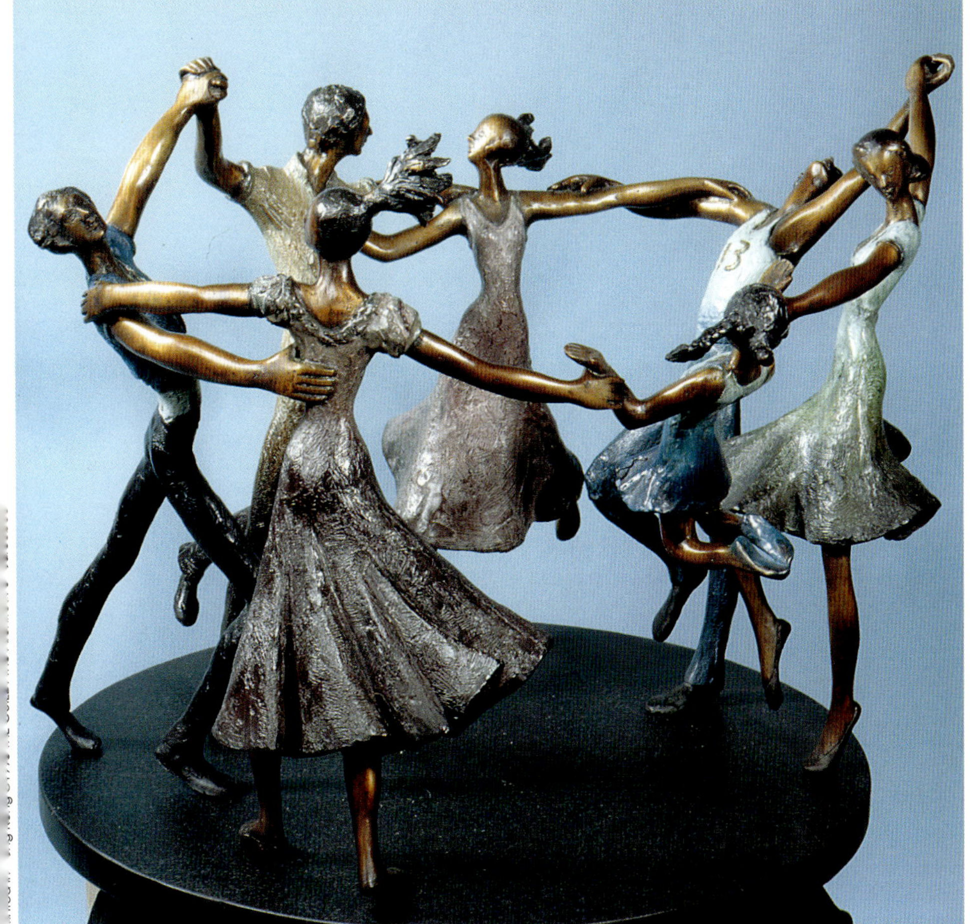

C

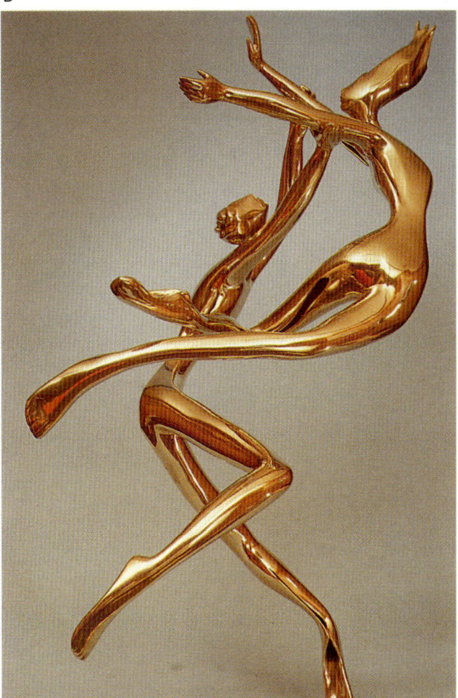

D

Russell Whiting

139 Decal Street
Lafayette, LA 70508
TEL 318-233-6173

Russell Whiting uses techniques that are rare and innovative to achieve sculpture that is both graceful and energetic.

Whiting's style (modern classism) is executed in bronze, stainless steel, aluminum and Cor-ten steel. The pieces are hammered, torch-carved and welded, directly in the metals, no casting.

A *Helen*, 1994, commissioned for Dr. Dennis and Anna Cuendet, hammered sheet bronze, 78" x 54" x 18"

B *Icarus*, 1994, commissioned for a private retreat and sculpture garden, hammered sheet bronze, 14' x 14' x 12'

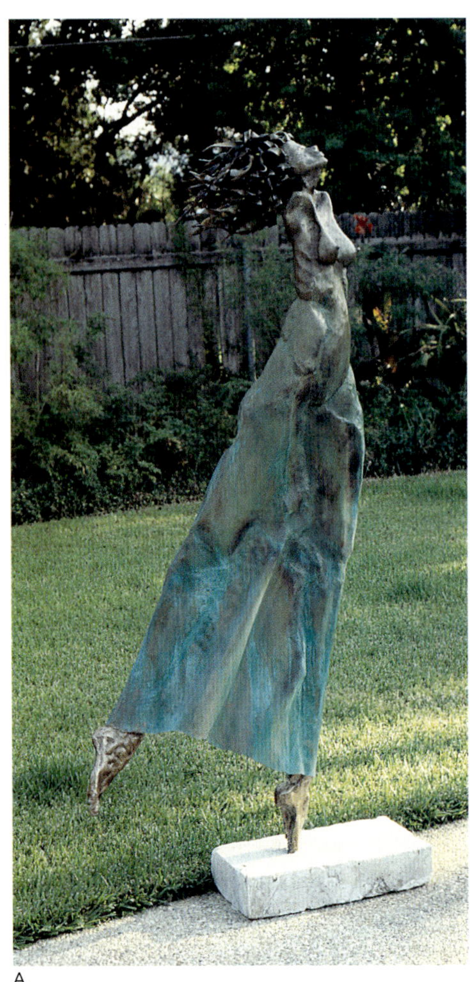

A

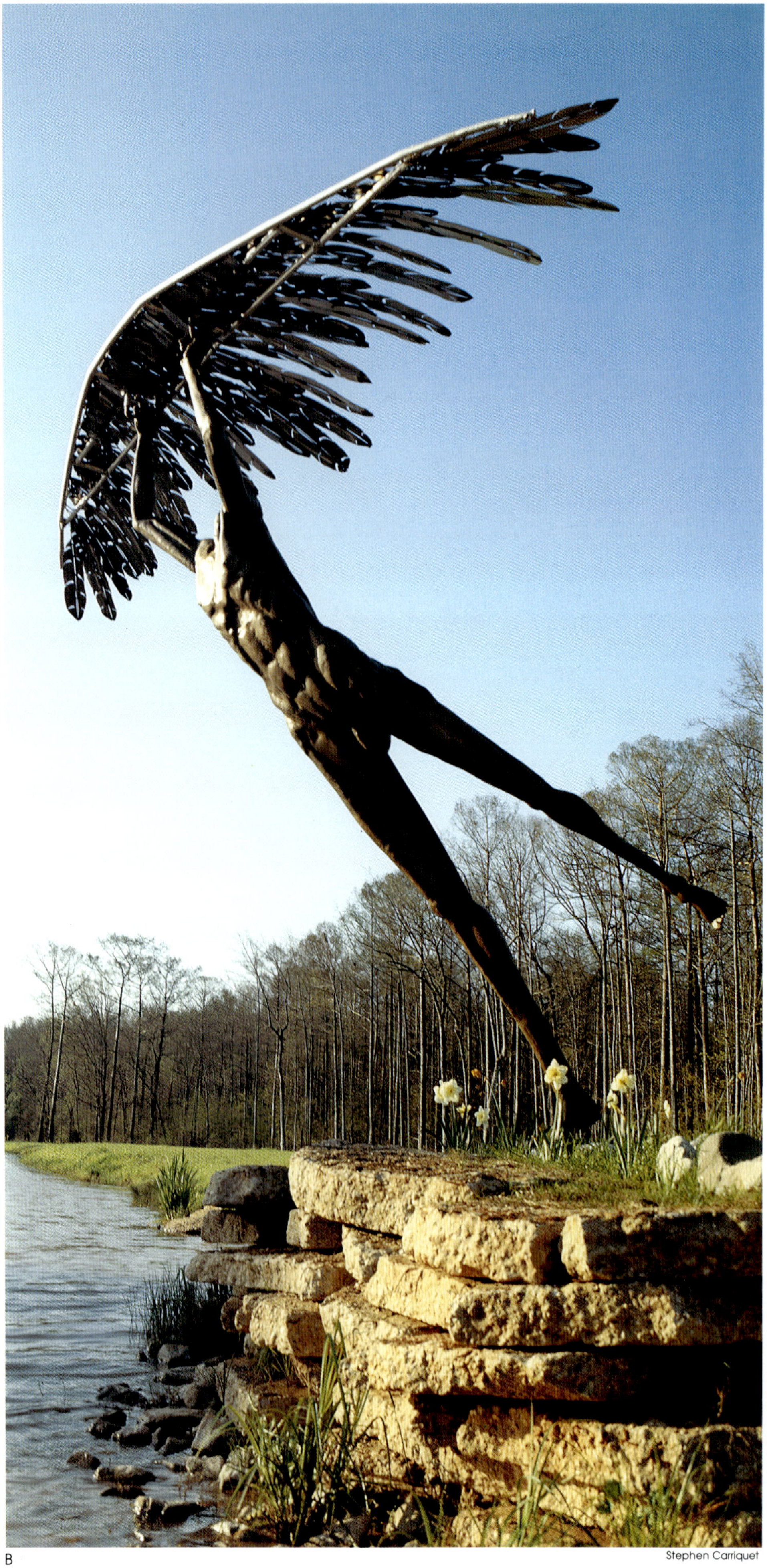

B

Stephen Carriquet

Bruce Wolfe

206 El Cerrito Avenue
Piedmont, CA 94611
FAX 510-601-7200
TEL 510-655-7871

Bruce Wolfe creates contemporary sculpture with a classic look. His bronzes are fresh and full of life, reflecting his enjoyment of the people he works with and the whole creative process.

Clients include: Chevron, Hewlett Packard, Levi Strauss, NASA, St. Marys College, San Francisco Opera, Sierra Club, Southwest Texas University, Stanford University, University of Chicago, and University of Oklahoma.

Please call or fax for more information and a complimentary color brochure.

A *Pugilist* (work in progress), 29"H; *The Rugged Individualist,* bronze with marble base, black patina, 15"H

B *Essence,* original lost wax bronze with bronze base, antique patina, 31"H, limited to an edition of 30

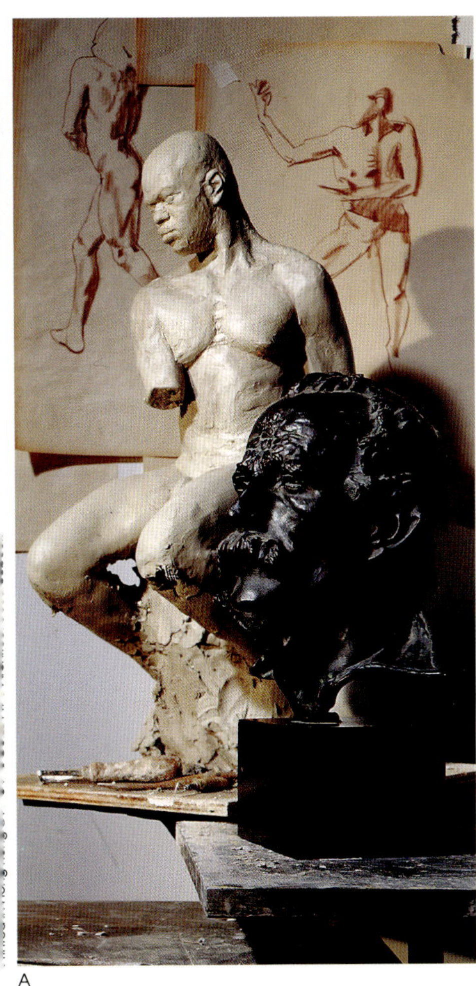

A

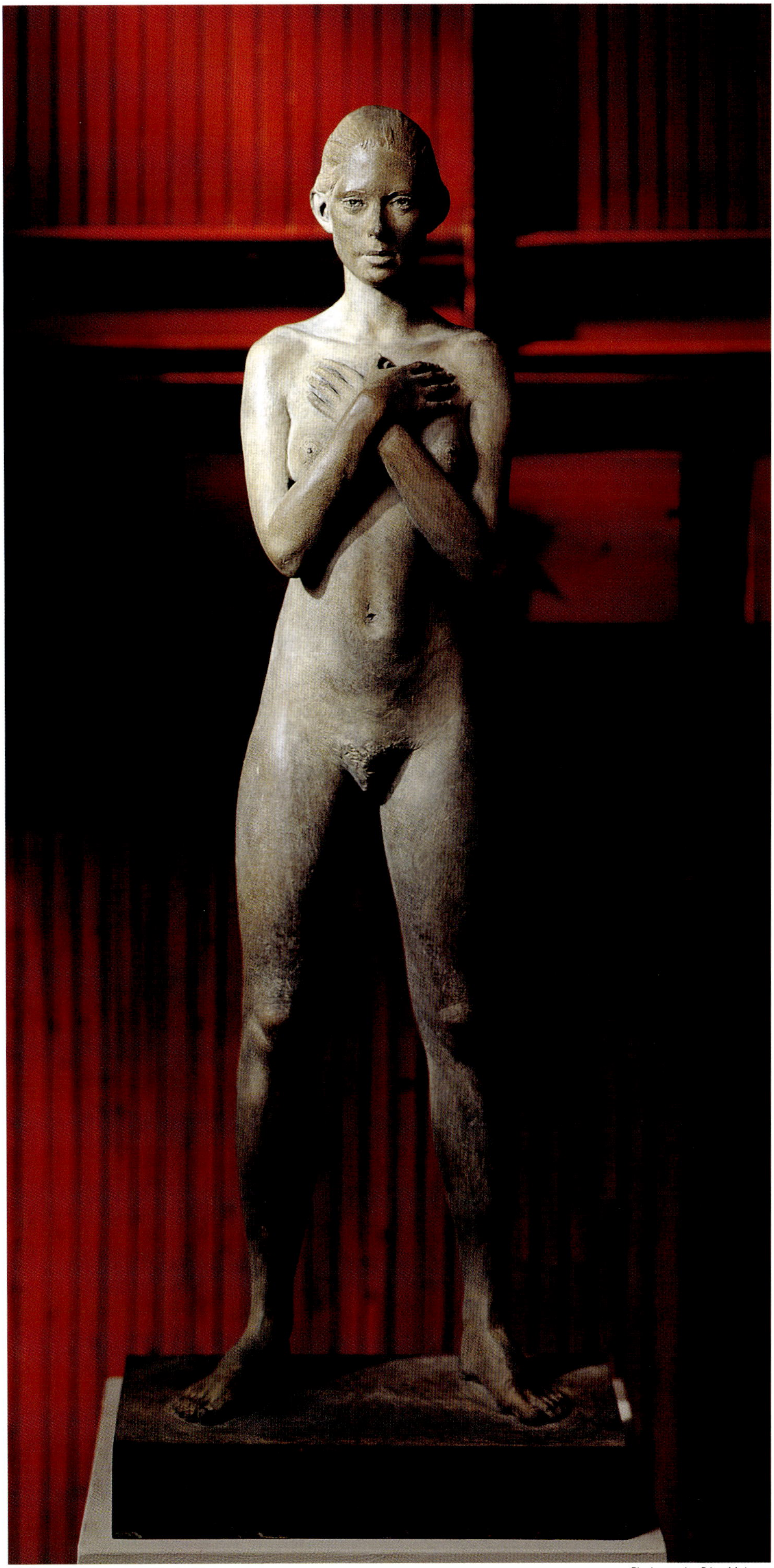

B

NON-REPRESENTATIONAL SCULPTURE

Michael Anderson

5121 N. 13th Place
Phoenix, AZ 85014
FAX 602-279-6105 (Call first)
TEL 602-279-6105

Michael Anderson has created sculpture in different media since the early 70s, but is most recognized for his gracefully sweeping works in steel. His use of bold colors and shapes attract the attention of the passerby and create exciting contrasts to the existing environment.

Michael Anderson's works are in public and private collections across the United States and around the world in Canada, Mexico, Switzerland, United Arab Emirates, Australia and Africa.

Commissions include:
City of Palm Desert, Palm Desert, CA
Superstition Springs Mall, Meza, AZ
Carlsbad Research Center, Carlsbad, CA
Lionshead, Vail, CO
Phoenix Sky Harbor International Airport,
  Phoenix, AZ
Scottsdale Center for the Arts, Scottsdale, AZ

A *Homeboy*, 1988, 72" x 40" x 30"

B *Loose Ends*, 1994, 24" x 14" x 6"

C *Desert Dessert*, 1991, 20' x 75' x 20'

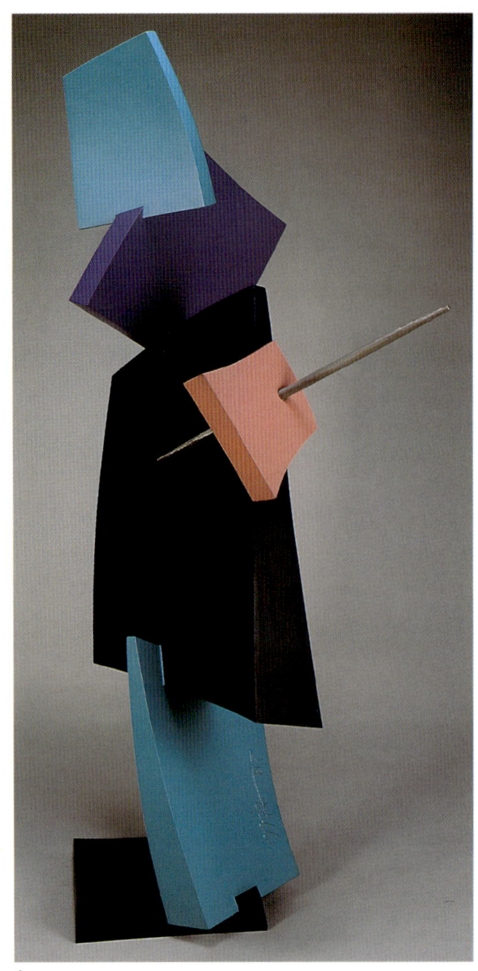

A

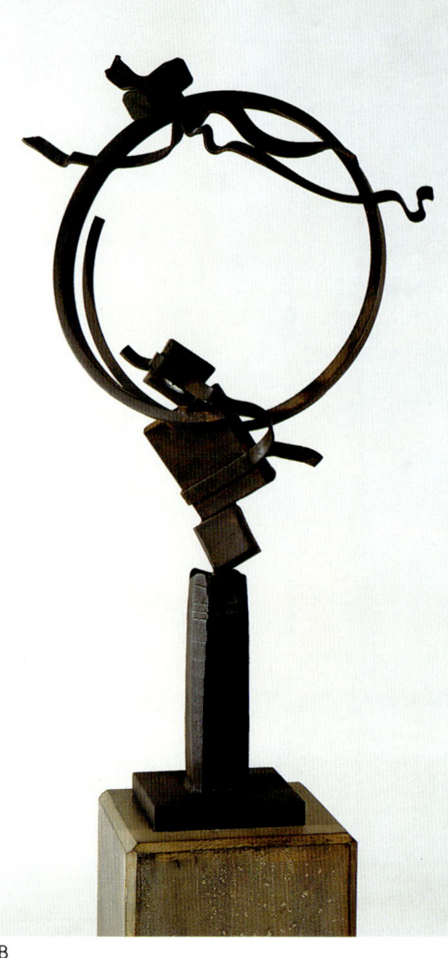

B

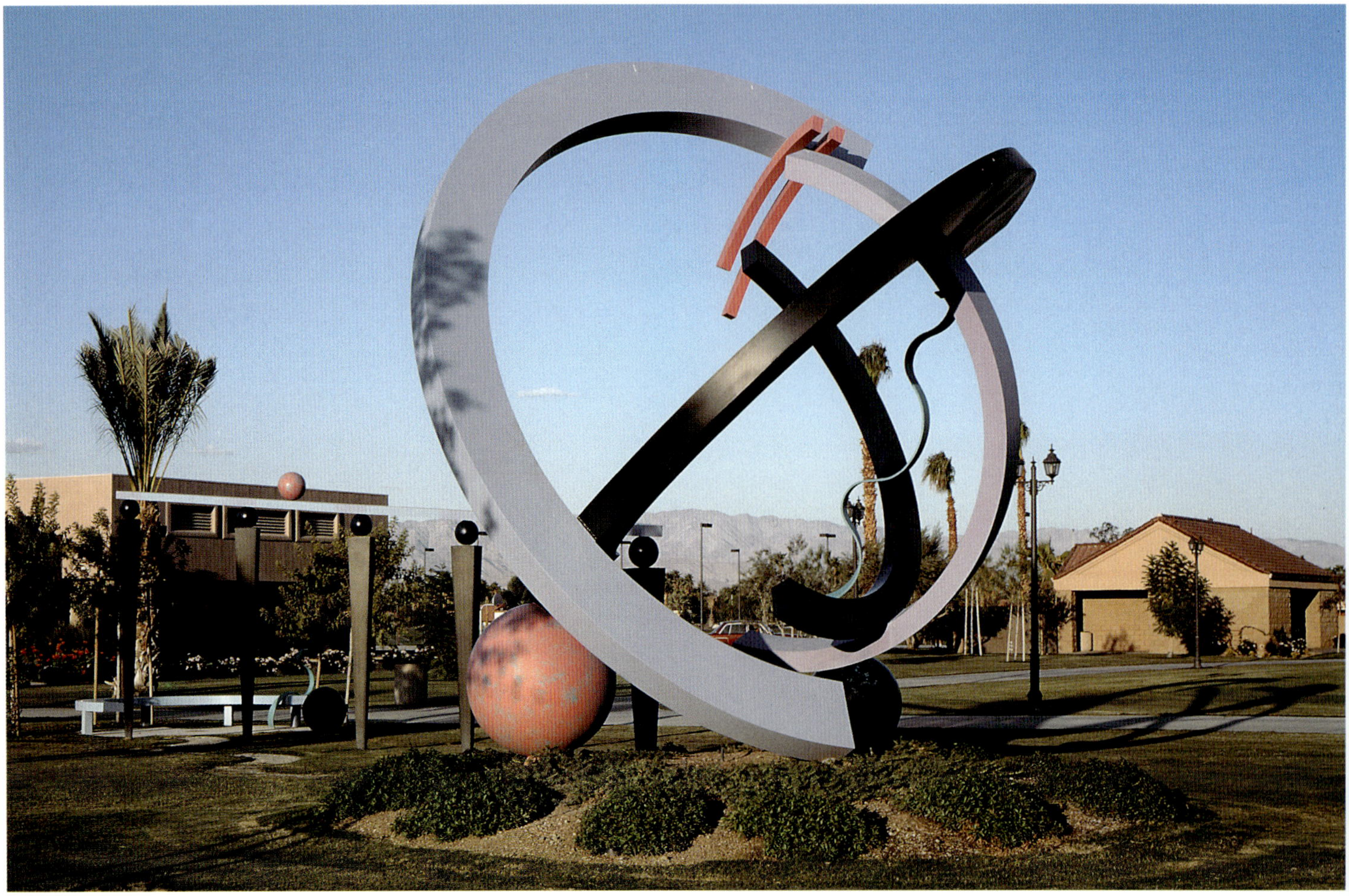

C

Sean K.L. Browne

2965 Robert Place
Honolulu, HI 96816-1732
FAX 808-732-1824
TEL 808-732-1824

Sean Browne has been doing commissioned sculpture for 20 years. He works in a variety of sculptural mediums, including metal and stone.

Sean has studied in Italy and Japan and in 1985 he received a Fulbright Fellowship to study under the guidance of sculptor Isamu Noguchi. He has exhibited internationally and his work is included in various public, private and corporate collections in the U.S. and abroad.

The work shown here is a result of Sean's collaboration with architects and other professionals in designing and executing site-specific artwork.

A *Healing Hand,* Hawaii State Hospital, Hawaii, terrazzo, 24' x 30'

B *Sculpture Fountain,* Pali Momi Medical Center, Hawaii, granite tile, 24' x 24'

C *Life of the Land,* Wailuku Judiciary Complex, Hawaii, Carrara marble, 8' x 20' x 16'

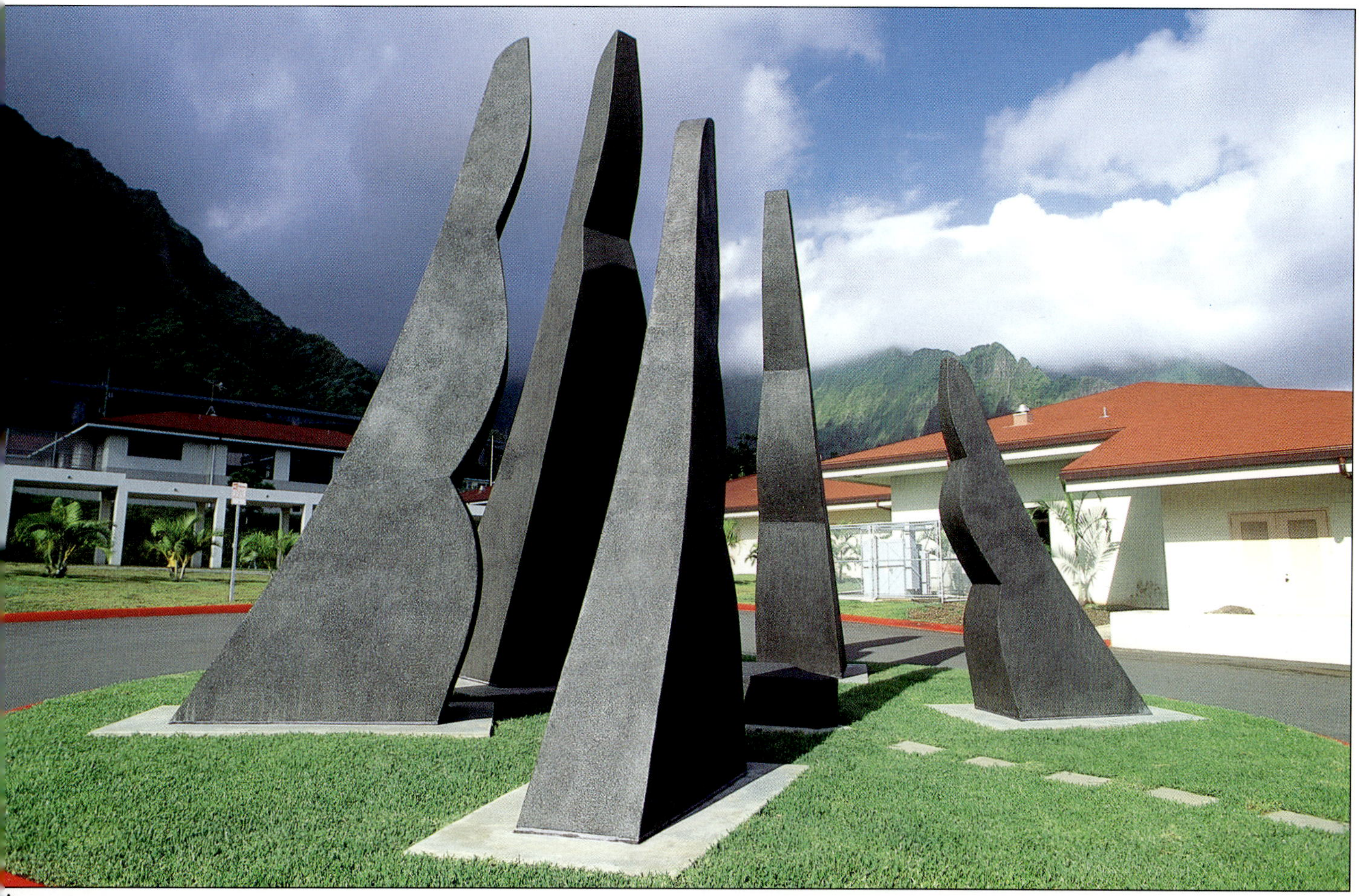

A

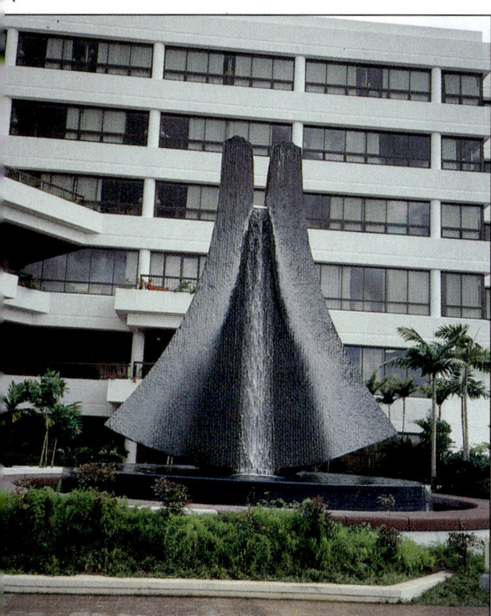

B

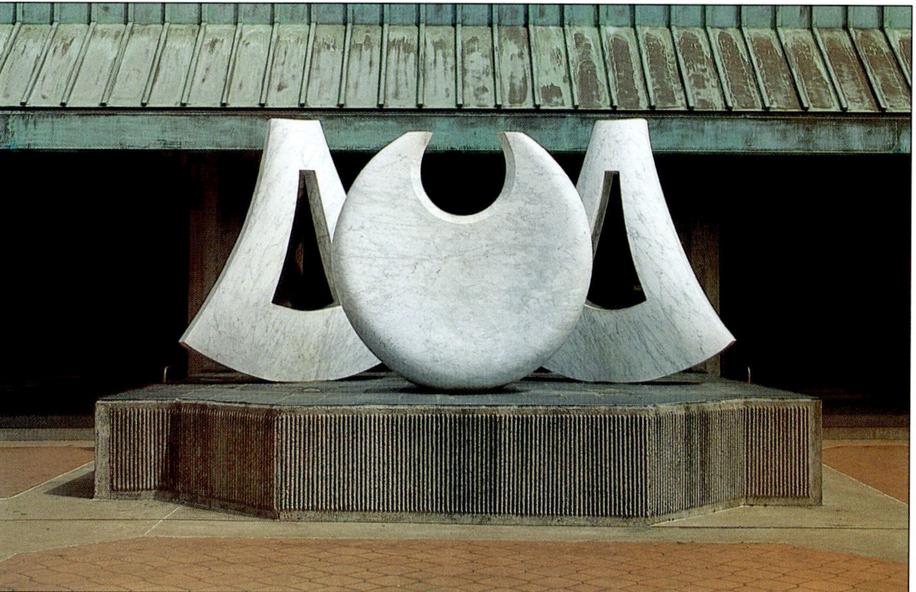

C

Susana Arias

Susana Arias Artist Studios
2523-A Mission Street
Santa Cruz, CA 95060
FAX 408-475-4756
TEL   408-423-7910

Susana Arias' cacti series is inspired by the saguaro, majestically reaching for the sky.

Both examples shown are made in clay and fired in primitive organic pit fires to achieve their coloration. Works in clay are available up to 15 feet high. The artist also creates works in this series in bronze and in colored cement with laminated wood, in any scale.

Arias has created many pieces using this basic form, and is pleased to adapt designs for both interior and exterior sites. Pieces in this series are elegant, sturdy and weather resistant.

Selected commissions and collections include the Santa Cruz County Arts Commission (clay mural); the Santa Cruz County Parks and Recreation Department (painted mural); the Deutsch-Sudamericanische Bank of Panama (bronze sculpture); and the Museum of Modern Art of Latin America in Washington, DC (earth sculpture).

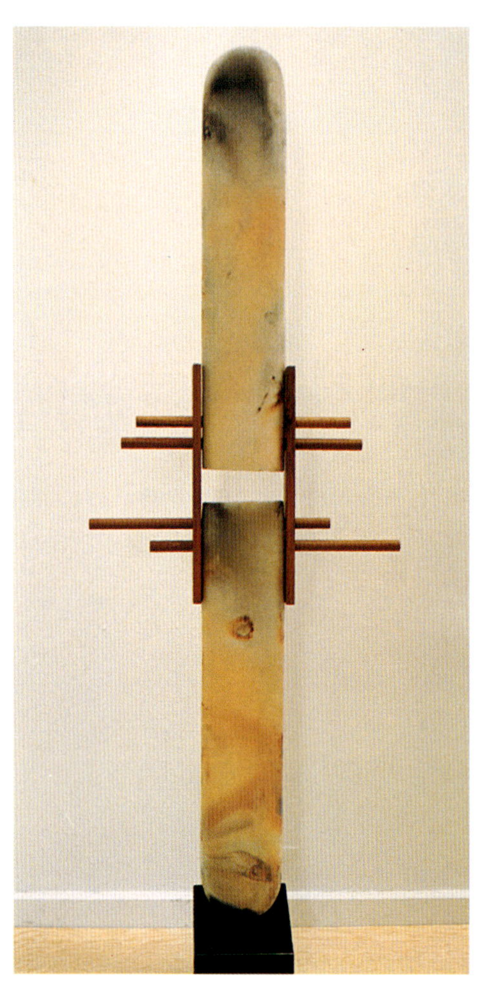

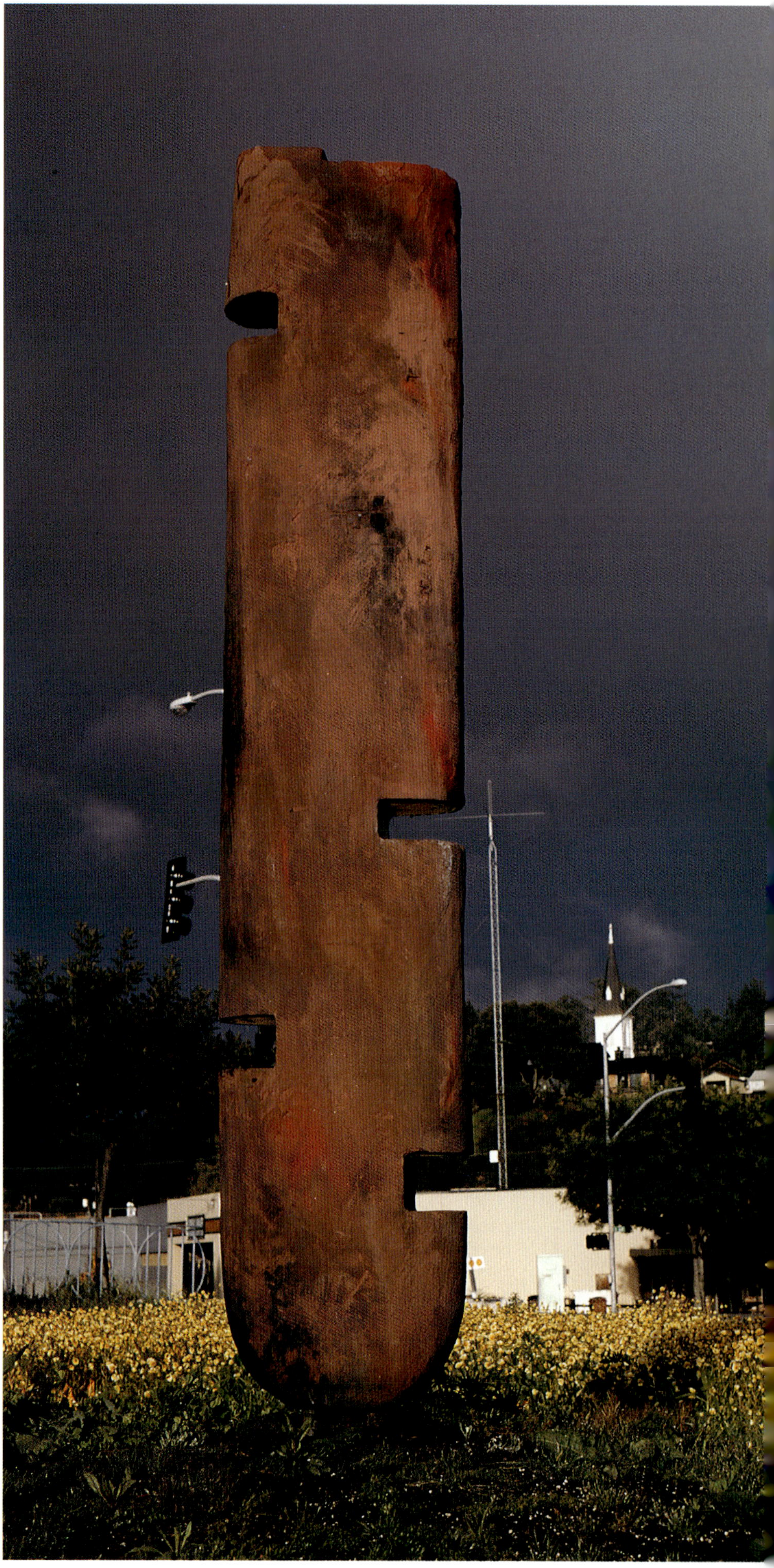

Warren Carther

Carther Studio, Inc.
464 Hargrave Street
Winnipeg, MB R3A 0X5
Canada
FAX 204-942-1434
TEL 204-956-1615

Award-winning artist Warren Carther has received considerable recognition in Canada and abroad for his numerous public and corporate commissions.

Utilizing heavy glass as a structural material, Carther is able to create new forms on almost any scale. Deeply carved and employing various color techniques, his glass is translucent bas-relief.

The sculpture shown here, titled *Prairie Boy's Dream*, possibly the tallest free-standing glass sculpture in the world, consists of two 35-foot towers of glass. Stainless steel columns flank each tower, supporting 17 spans of curved, carved and colored glass, each measuring ten feet long, two feet high and ¾-inch thick.

Clients include:
Investor's Group, Winnipeg
Legislative Assembly Building, N.W.T.
Canadian Embassy, Tokyo, Japan
Regional Municipality of Ottawa,
    Carlton, Ottawa
Musée Des Arts Decoratifs, Lucerne, Switzerland

Also see these GUILD publications:
Architect's Edition: 6, 7, 9, 10

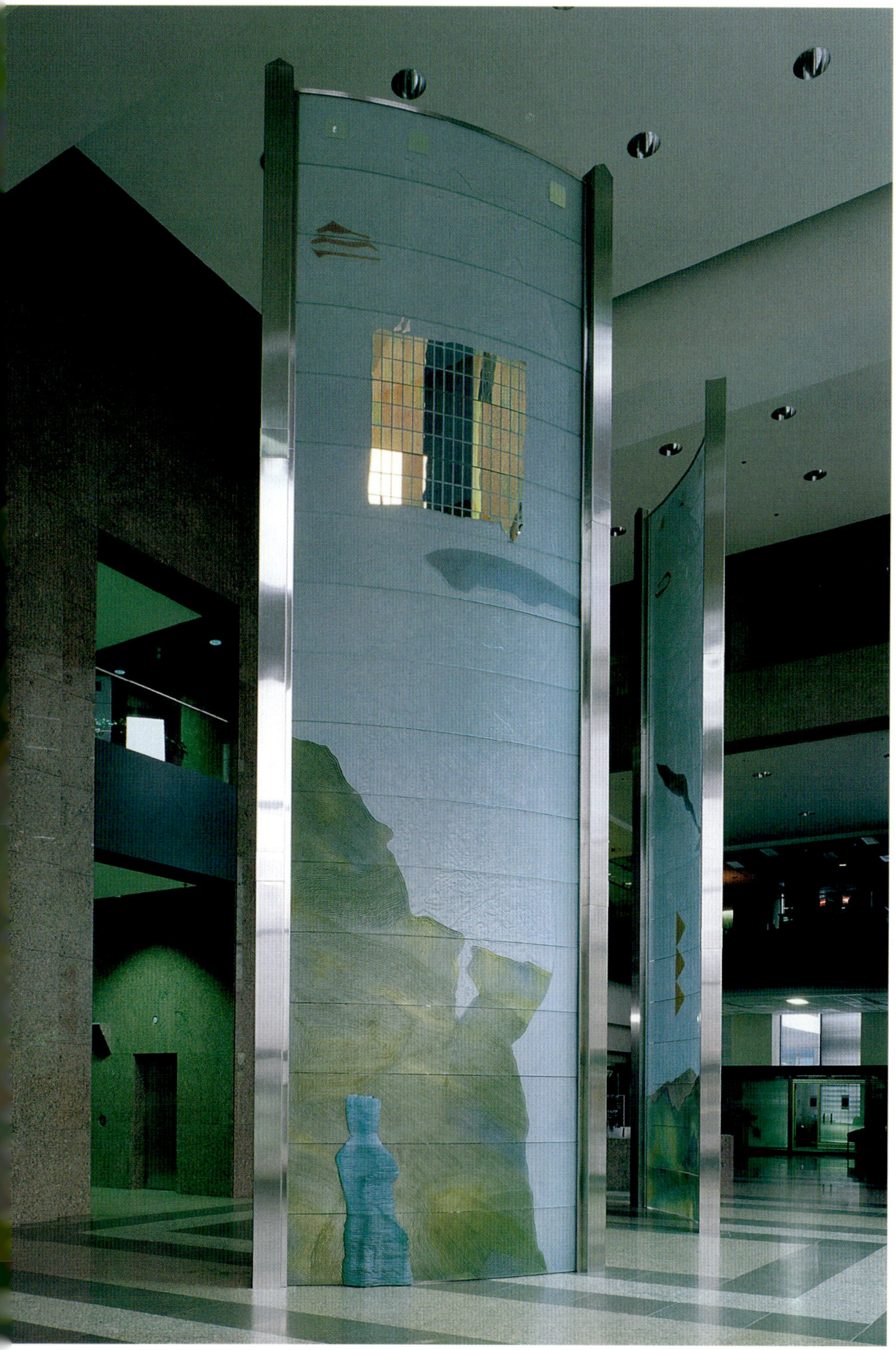

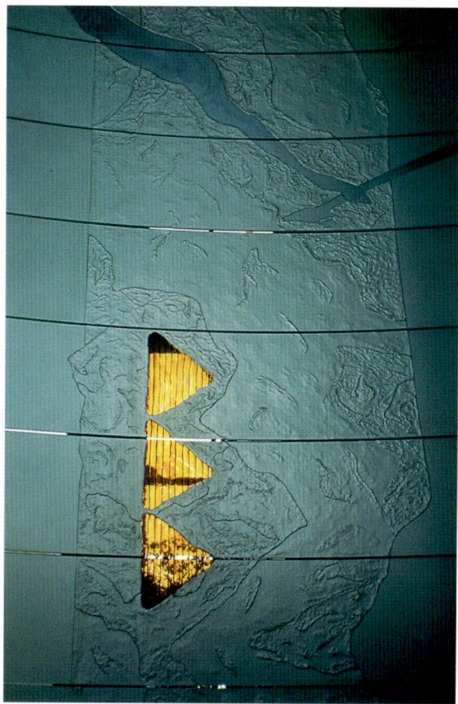

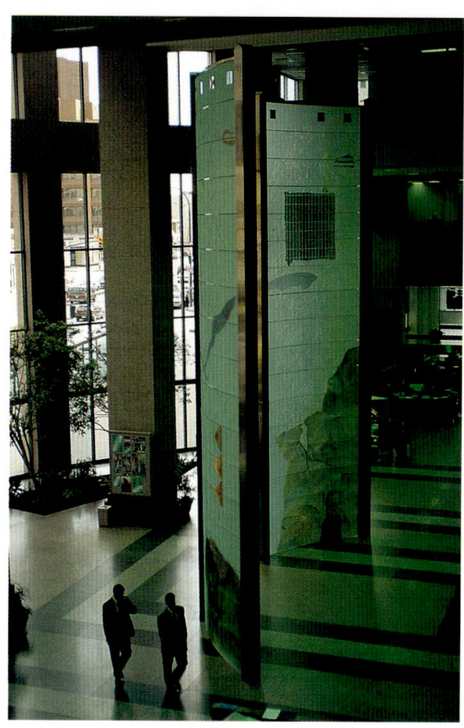

Henry Kalen

D'Alessandro Sculpture Studio

Sara D'Alessandro
108 Woodhull Avenue
Riverhead, NY 11901
TEL 516-727-8457

Organic columns rising from the earth toward the sky. Teeming movement, texture, color, shadow and light shift constantly with sun, weather, and viewer location. Each column is a sculpted unique, a distinct individual with character. Meaning arises from arrangement: pairs, clusters, surrounds, colonnades, individuals. Best installation fosters interplay among sculpture, architecture, site elements, and observer. Light creates visual impact: natural shifting daylight, applied dramatic light, or both. Terra cotta shown.

Available in terra cotta and metal, uniques only.
Height: 5' to 8' terra cotta; 5' to 12' metal
Site-adaptable and interactive.
Exterior, interior suitability.
Straight forward installation.
Collaboration for on-site placement and installation.

For further information, please contact Sara D'Alessandro.

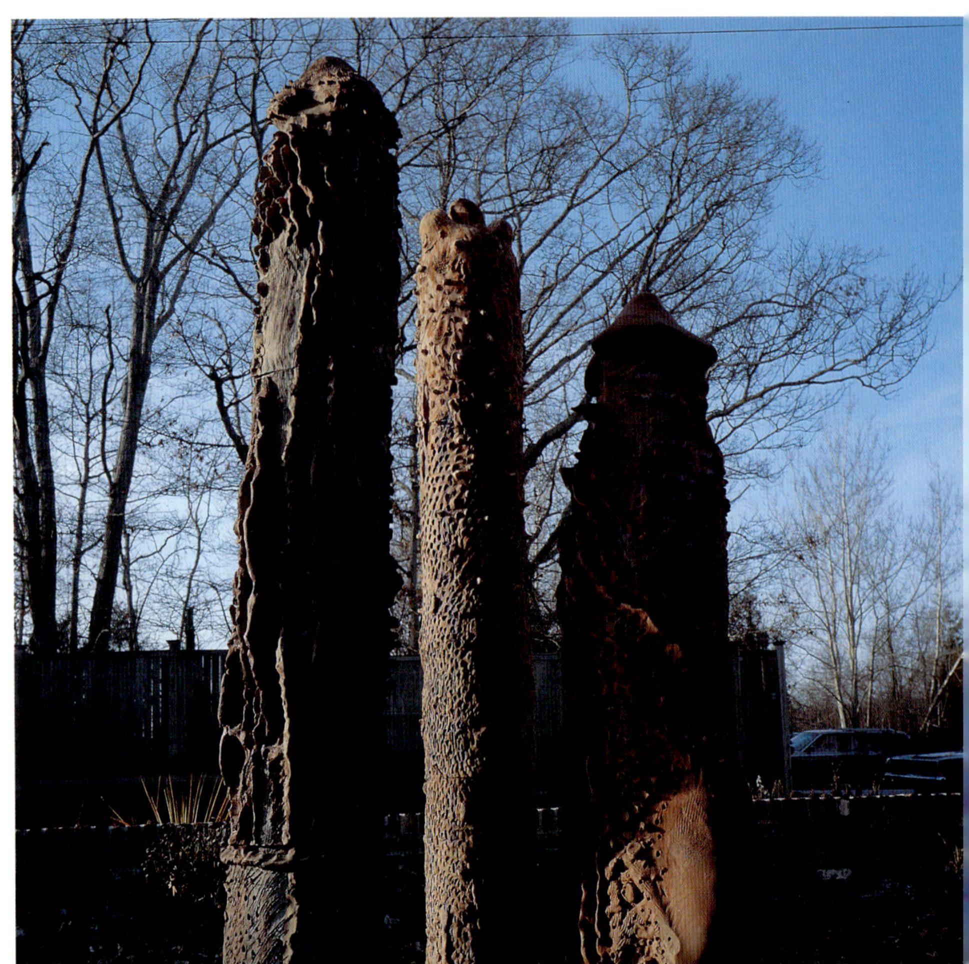

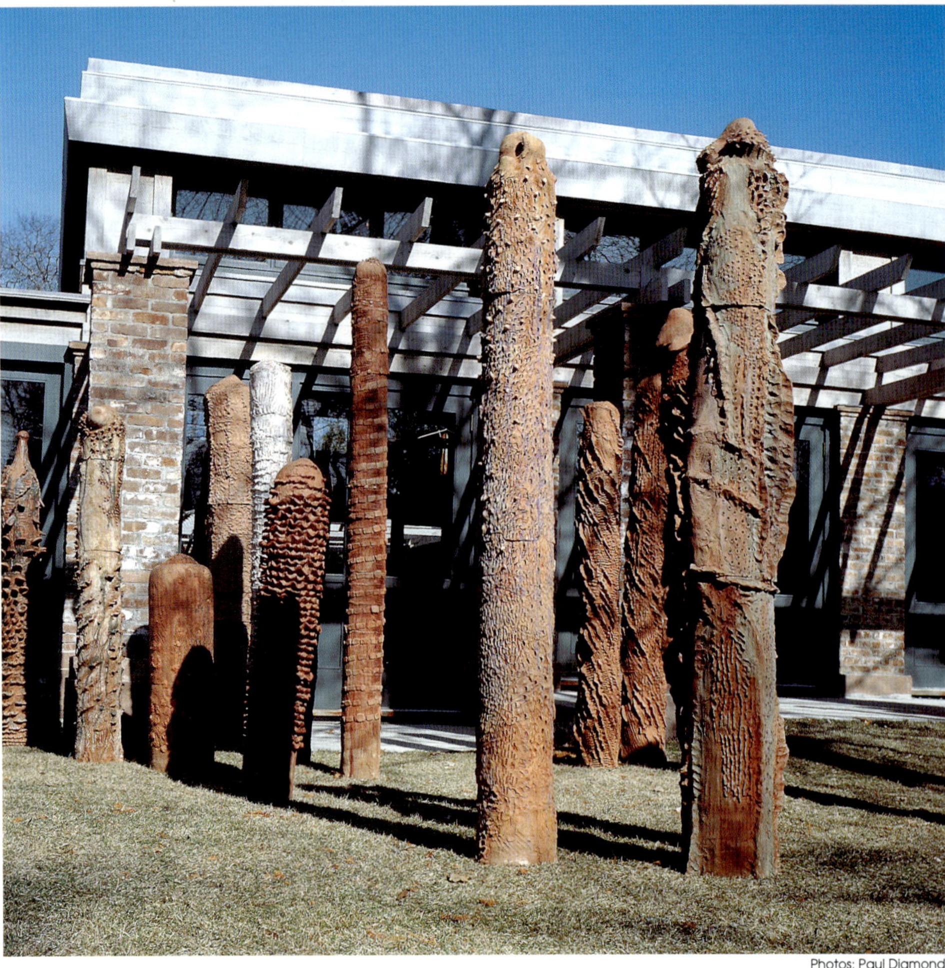

Photos: Paul Diamond

Edward Falkenberg

Falkenberg Studio
RR 5
Claremont, ON L1Y 1A2
Canada
FAX 905-649-2444
TEL 905-649-2444

From Toronto, Canada, to Riyadh, Saudi Arabia, Falkenberg's sculptures have enhanced the corporate and private world. For the past 30 years, architects and designers have worked successfully with this Canadian artist.

Commissions include:
Bell Canada
Cadillac Fairview Corp.
Canada Post
Cluny Property Management
Government of Canada
Government of Ontario
Imperial Oil
Marathon Security

A *Entrée*, 1991, main entrance, private residence, Pickering, ON, Canada, ash, stain, 3'W x 6'8"H

B *Leaf*, 1992, Ontario Forestry Research, Sault Ste. Marie, ON, Canada, stainless steel, 10'W x 12'H x 4'D

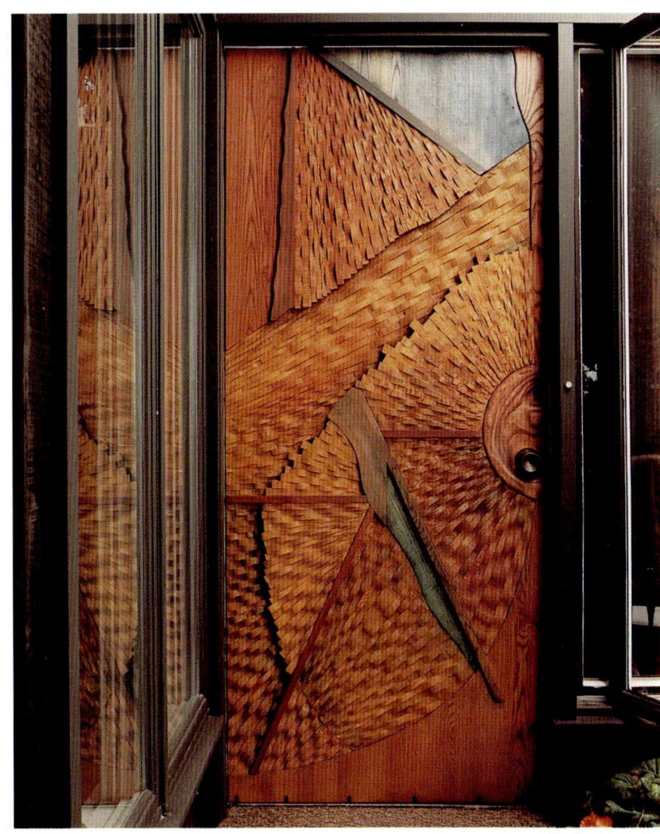

A

Ajay Photographic

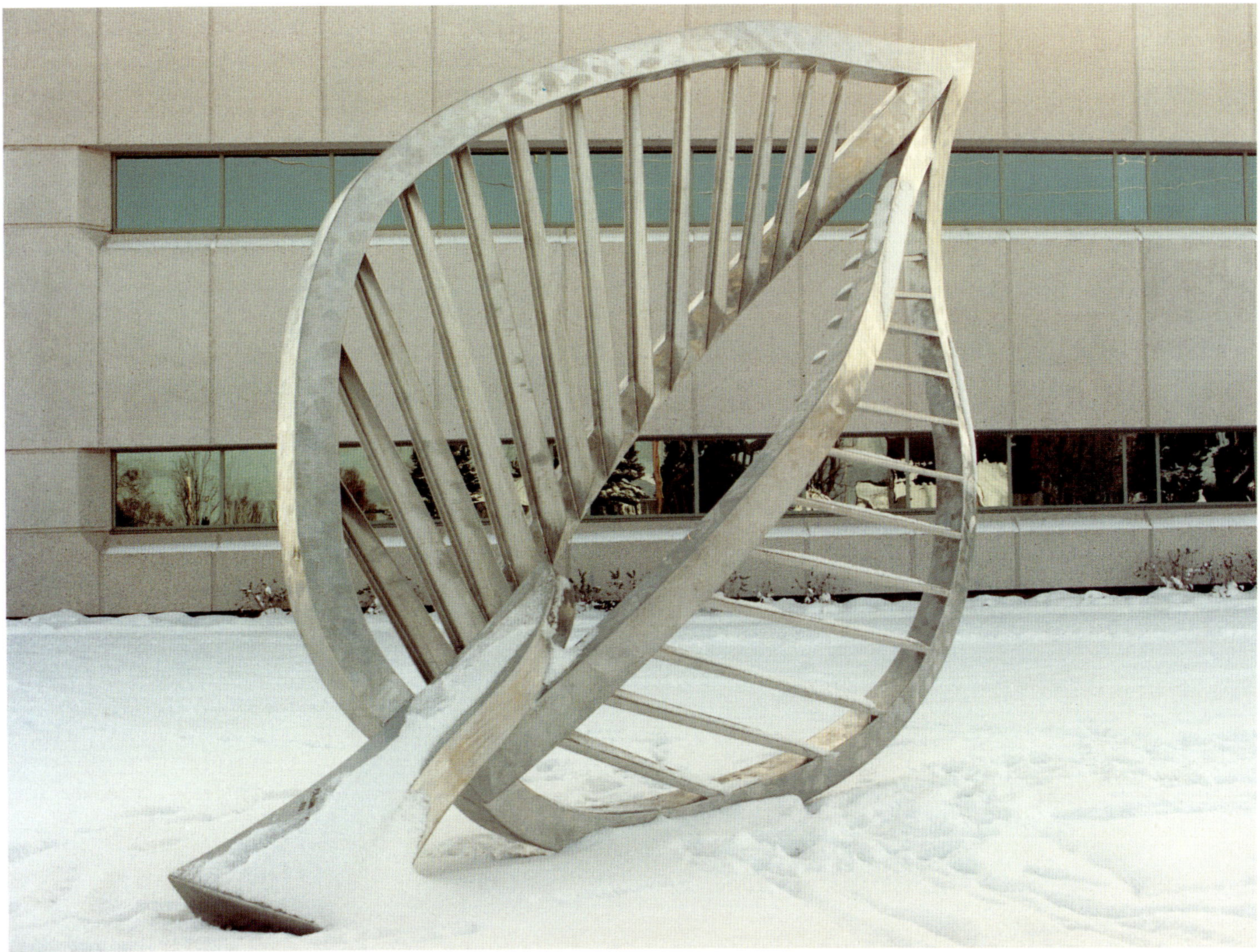

B

Douglas O. Freeman

Douglas Freeman Sculpture Studio
310 North Second Street
Minneapolis, MN 55401
FAX 612-339-5201
TEL 612-339-7150

Doug Freeman creates sculpture and designs spaces—fountains, plazas, memorials—that invite the viewer to participate, to play and to imagine. Works range from small sculptural focal points to large groupings with custom lighting. Freeman often collaborates with landscape architects and other design profesionals and enjoys the expanded range of possibilities a design team provides. Projects are delivered within budget, and quality craftsmanship is guaranteed.

SHOWN: *The Fountain of the Wind*, a major civic fountain created for Canal Park in Duluth, MN

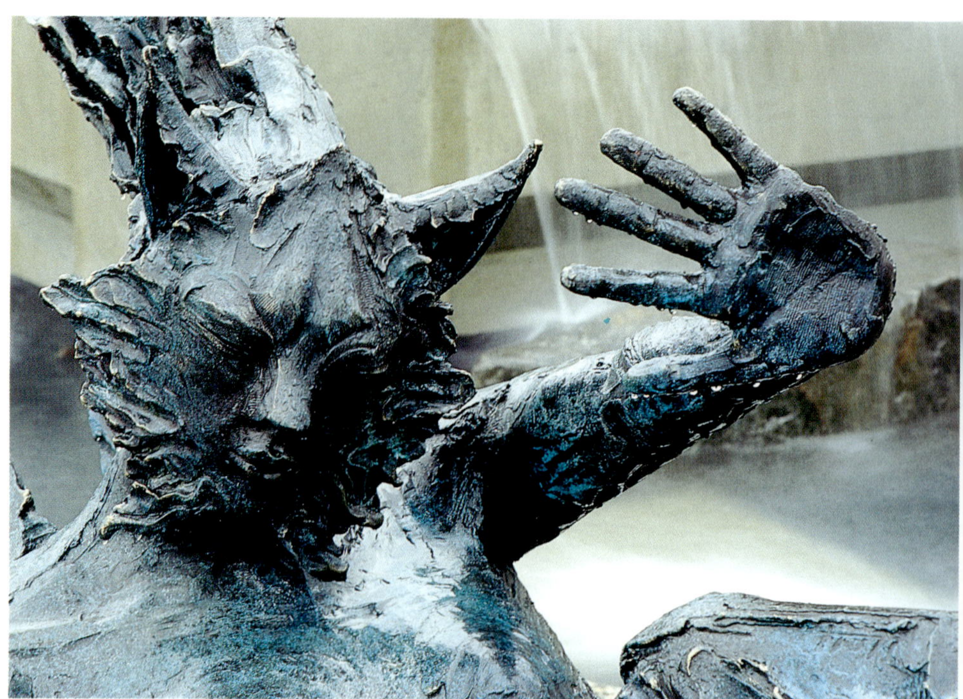

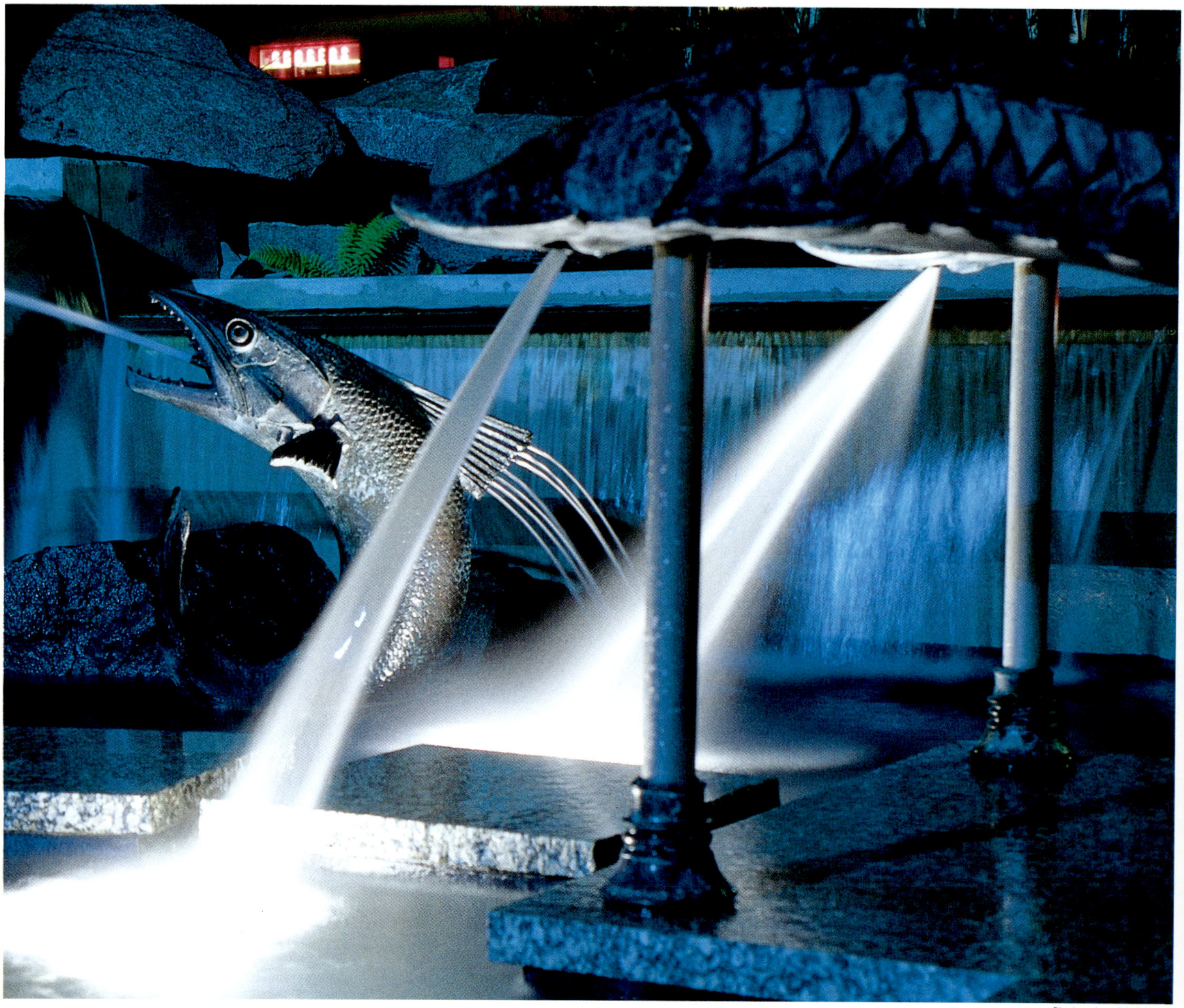

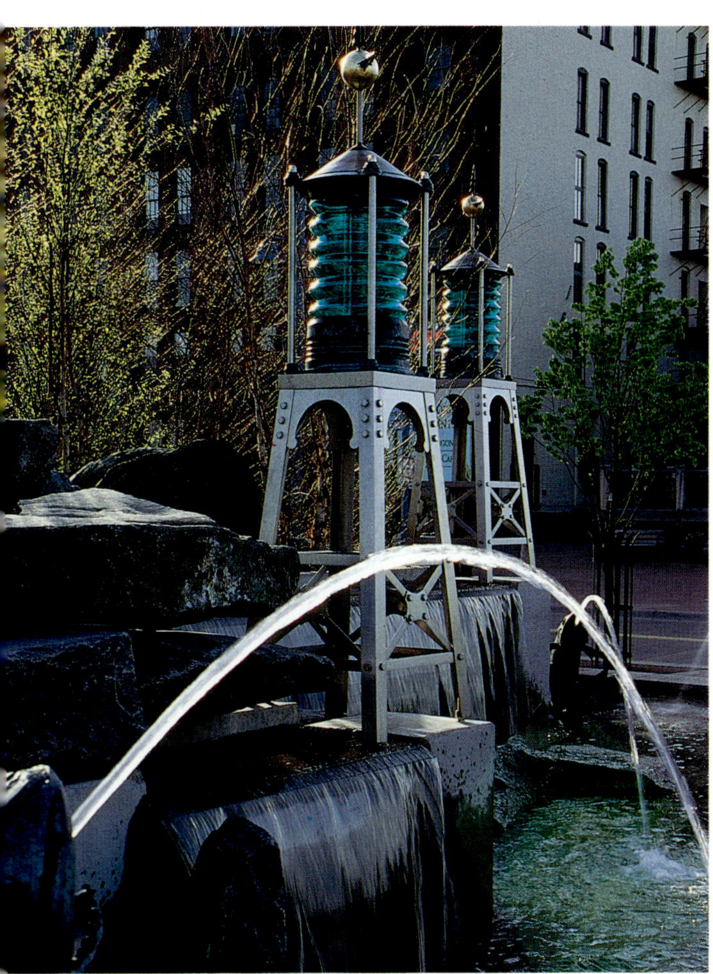
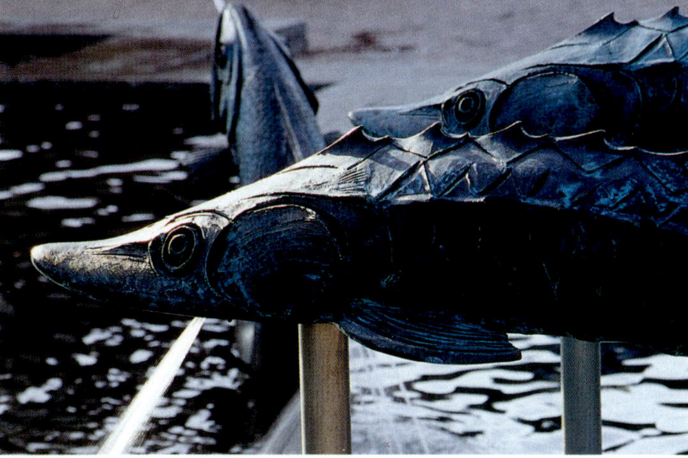
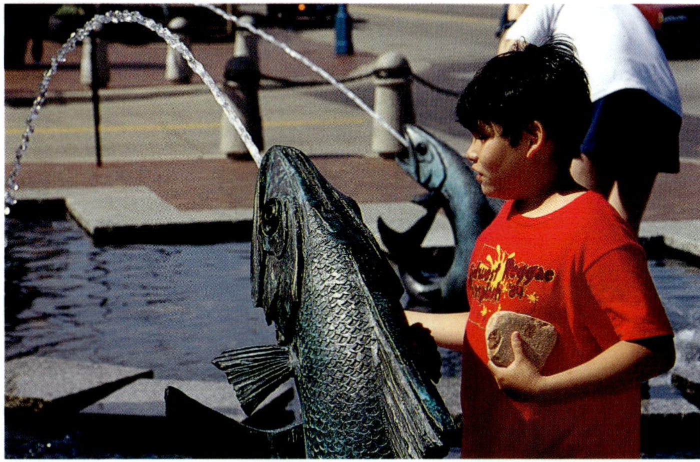

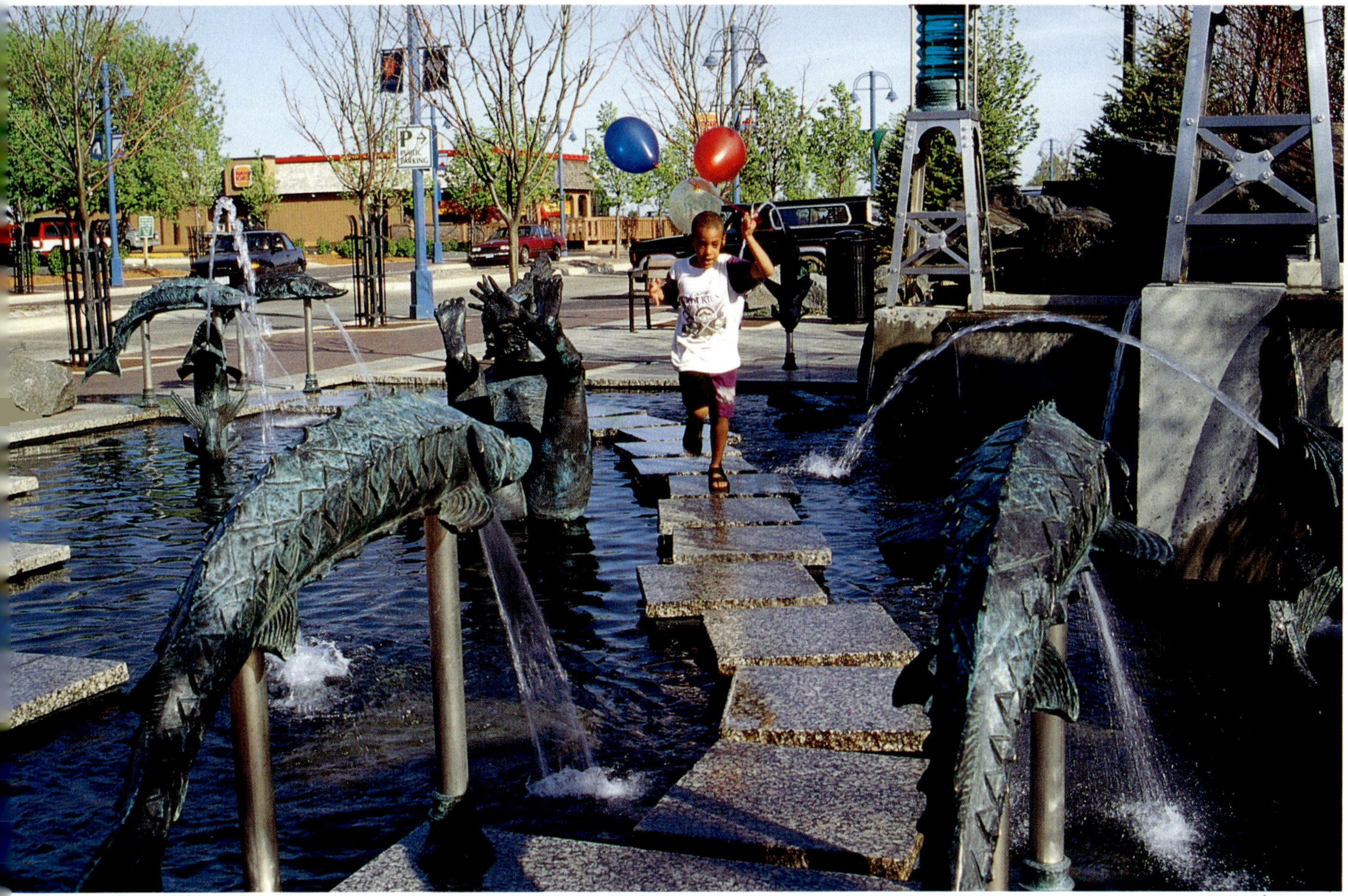

The Fountain of the Wind, Canal Park, Duluth, Minnesota, sculptor: Douglas O. Freeman (612) 339-7150

Rick Harry
(Xwa Lack Tun)
Marina Papais

169 Whonoak Street
North Vancouver, BC V7P 3R1
Canada
TEL 604-990-9464
TEL 604-521-7887

Xwa Lack Tun, a Squamish Nations artist, sculpts in cedar, stone, bronze, gold and glass. His public and architectural works are extensive throughout the Coast Salish territories. Award-winning artist Marina Papais' works are rich with mythical, spiritual and modern allusions. Her commissions include architectural, sculptural, carved, fused and stained glass for residential and corporate environments. Both Rick's and Marina's works have been shown internationally and are in corporate and private collections throughout the world. Their designs weave together mythological figures from Papais' Venetian roots with traditional Native American culture in fascinating visual collaborations.

A *Introspections and Illusions*, carved cedar and glass

B *Spirit Quest*, carved cedar and layered glass, kiln elements, dichroic glass, 22K gold and color

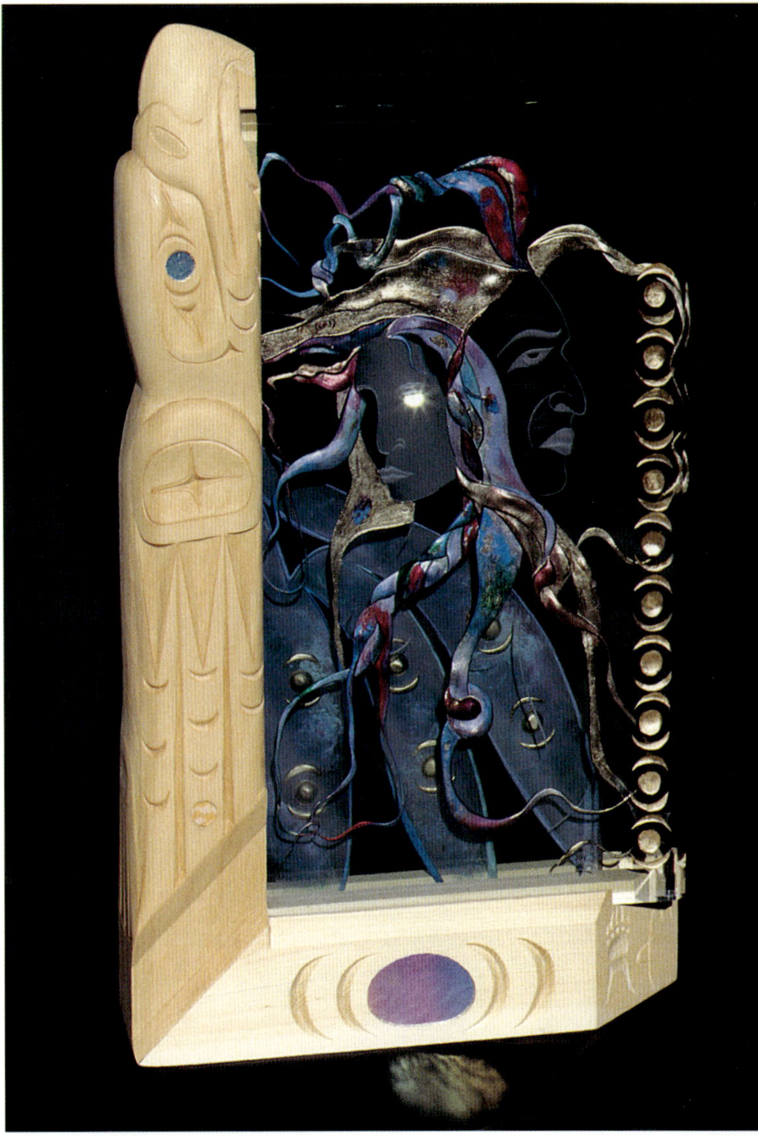

A

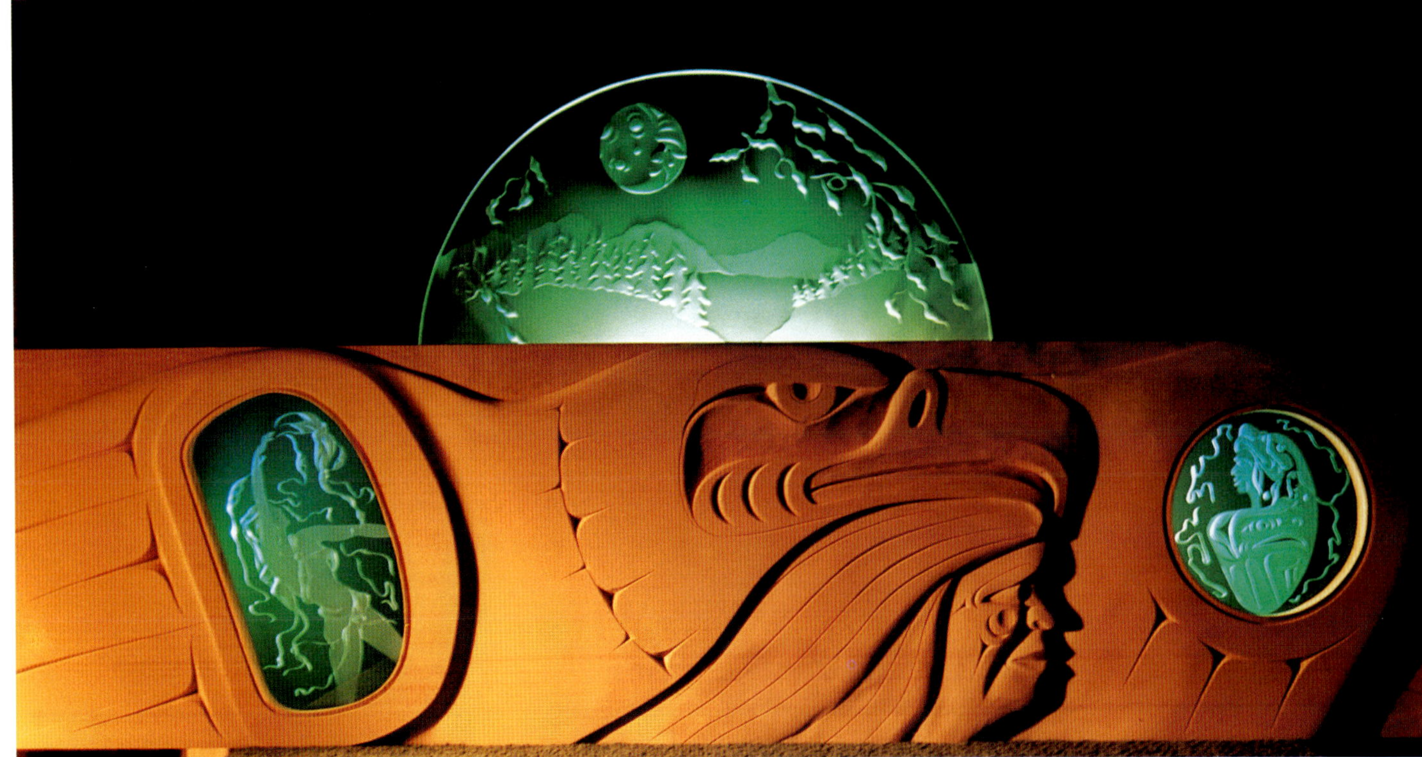

B

Robert Holmes

270 Pilot Reach, Box 244
The Sea Ranch, CA 95497
TEL 707-785-2934 (Studio)
TEL 707-829-5480 (Foundry)

Robert Holmes is represented in fine art galleries nationally. His semi-abstract, figurative cast bronze sculptures (small to monumental scale) are in collections throughout the world. To ensure quality, Holmes established his own foundry, Bronze +, Inc., in Sebastopol, California.

Please contact artist for more information.

Also see these GUILD publications:
Architect's Edition: 7, 8, 9, 10

A *Ascending Dancer*, 20" x 13" x 3", edition of 12

B *Strolling Woman*, 78" x 30" x 21", edition of 5

C *Cici*, 61" x 61" x 27", edition of 5

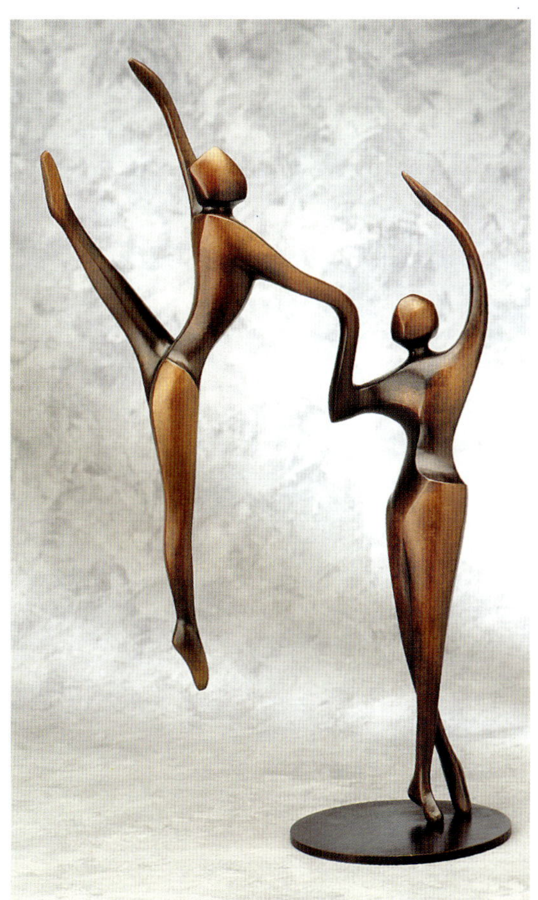

A

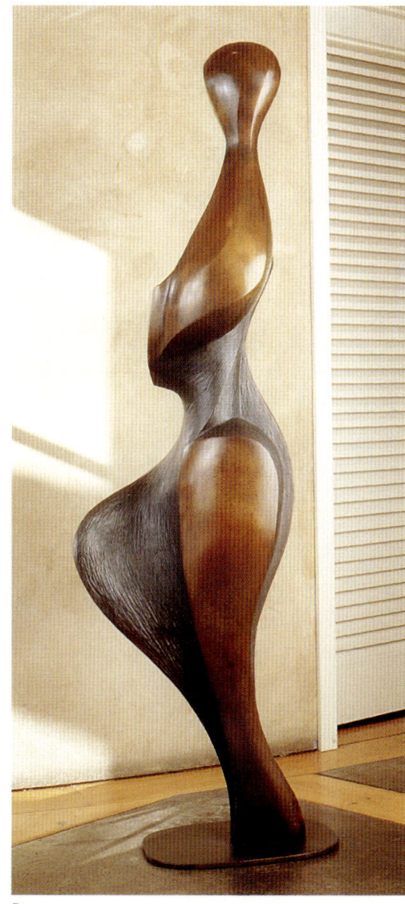

B

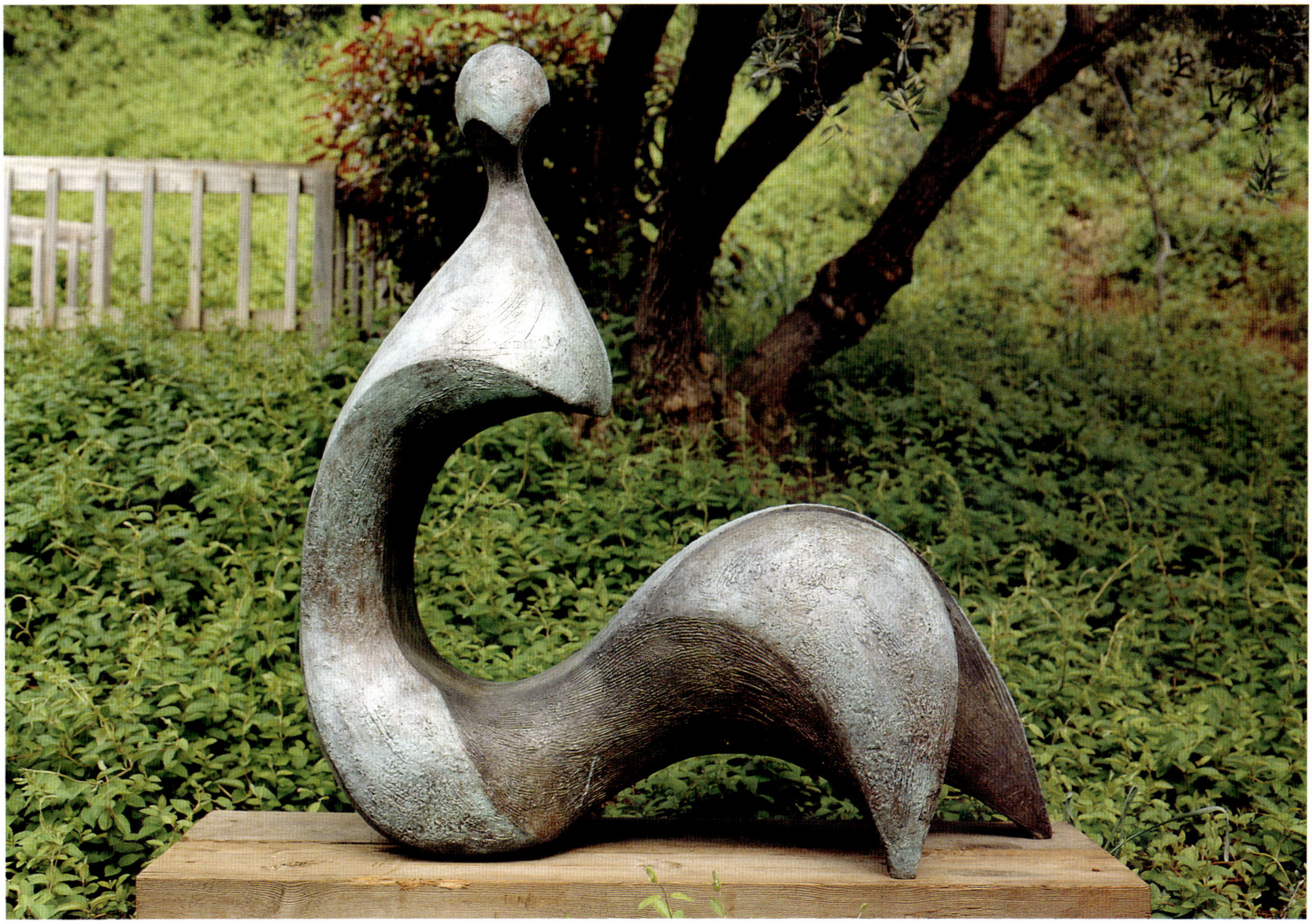

C

Rodger Lang

1655 Hoyt Street
Denver, CO 80215
TEL 303-237-8538
E-Mail: LangR@ZENO.MSCD.EDU

For 30 years, Rodger Lang's sculptures have been widely exhibited and have won numerous awards.

The sculptures presented here are among the most recent in Lang's *Cryptic Vestige* series, a series which Lang began in 1986. All of these sculptures were executed in cast bronze or fired stoneware.

Lang continues to investigate images drawn from his interest in the earliest development of cultures and civilizations.

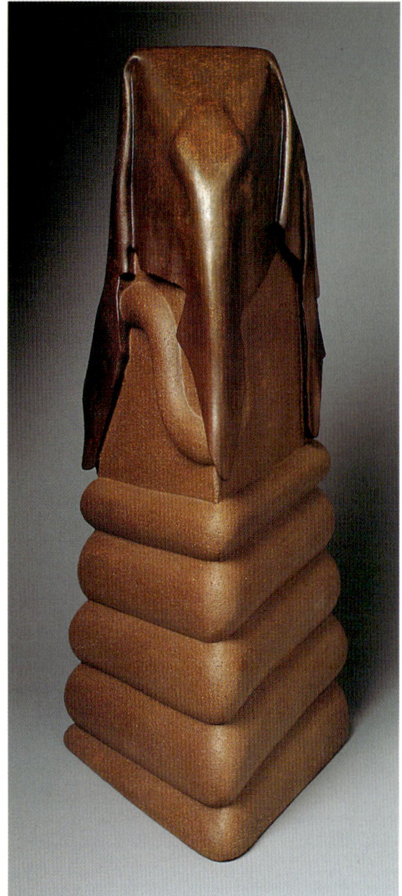

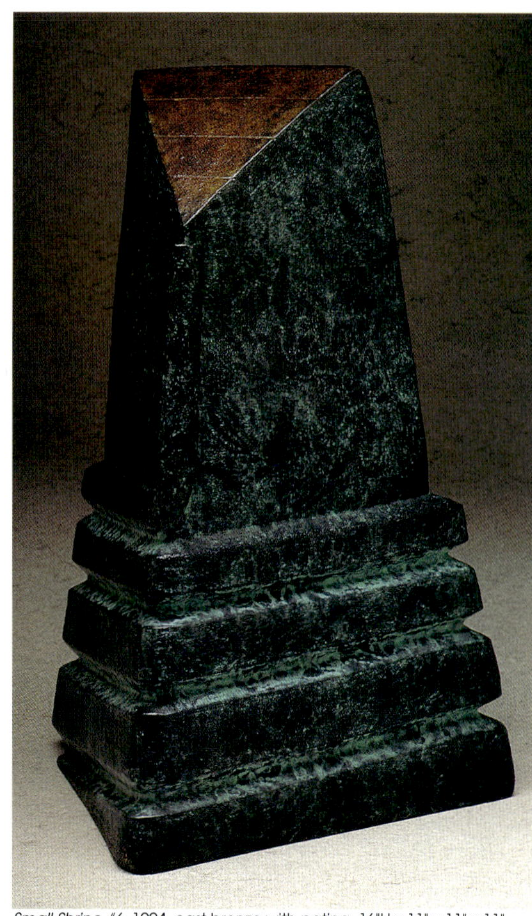

Cryptic Vestige #2: Draped, 1994, fired stoneware, 30"H x 15" x 15" x 15"

Small Shrine #6, 1994, cast bronze with patina, 16"H x 11" x 11" x 11"

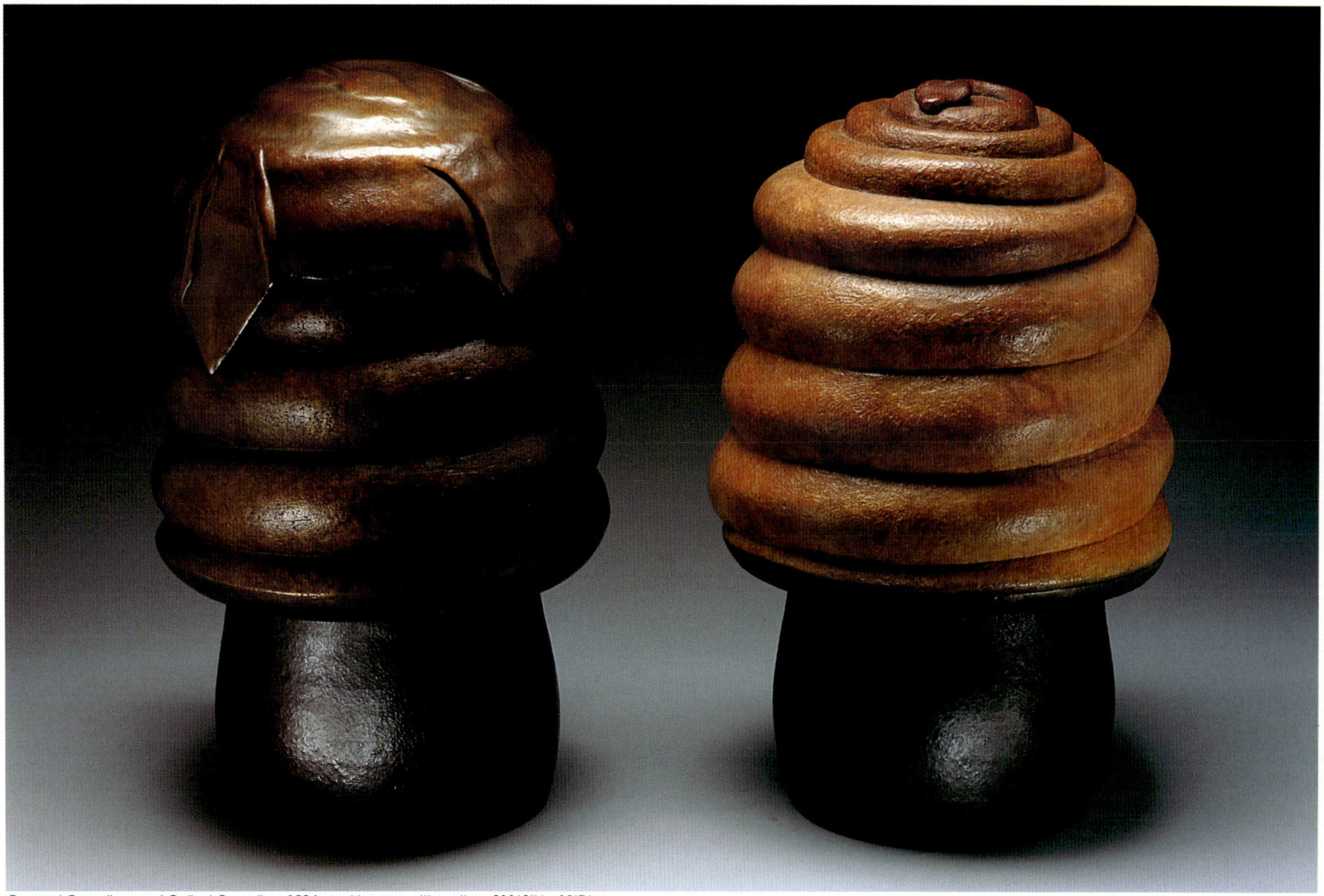

Draped Guardian and Coiled Guardian, 1994, cast bronze with patina, 21 1/2"H x 13"Dia

James Mitchell

4564 West Mission Boulevard
Ontario, CA 91762
FAX 909-628-9923
TEL 909-625-2048

Fabricated from a variety of materials and in a wide range of scales, Mitchell's sculpture is a visual delight. These are masterful works which attract and encourage physical and visual interaction. The careful blend of material and design creates a work of enduring quality to be enjoyed for generations.

Mitchell's sculpture is displayed across the United States in both public and private collections. His work is available from galleries and art consultants with commissions for site-specific installations of fountains and other sculptural designs being accepted by the artist.

Photos, prices and references are available from the artist.

Also see this GUILD publication:
Architect's Edition: 8

A *Abstract Muse*, 1993, 18'H, painted aluminum commission, Coopers & Lybrand, Los Angeles, CA

B *Circular Illusions*, 1995, 10'H, copper and aluminum commission, Allstate Plaza, Glendale, CA

C *Abstract Agenda*, 1994, 6'H, painted aluminum private collector, TX

D *Abstract Projections III*, 1994, 3'H, painted aluminum, private collector, ID

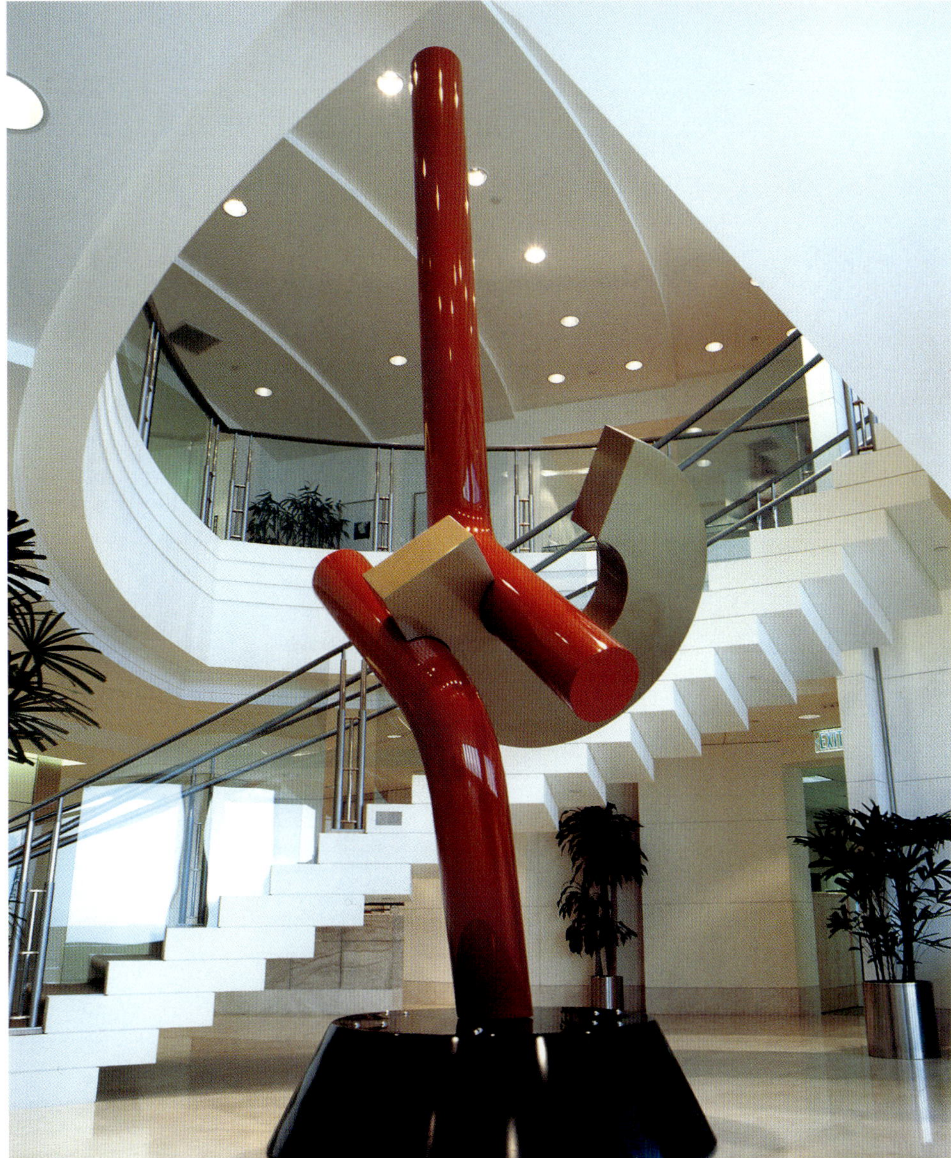

A

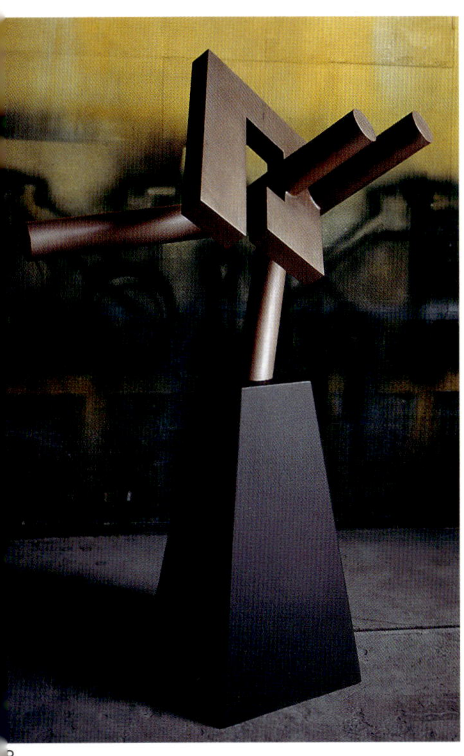

B

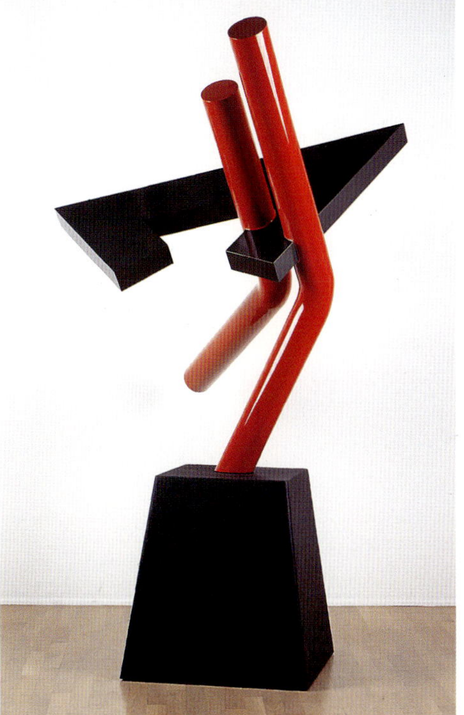

C

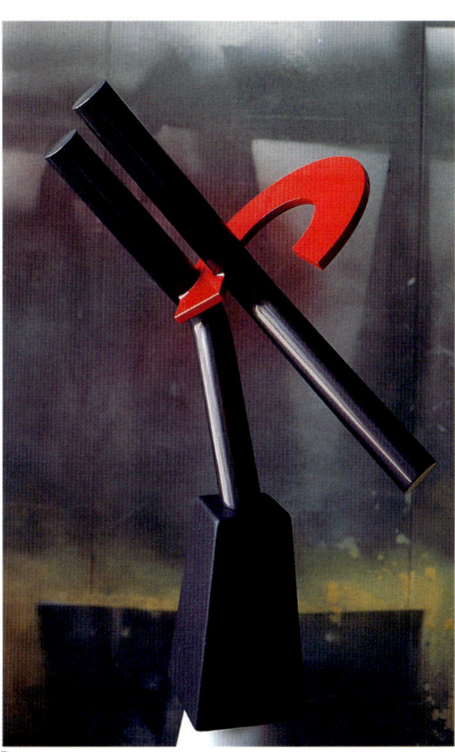

D

SUZY LOCKE

Art Consultant

Suzy Locke has been a professional art consultant in the San Francisco area for 18 years, serving corporate, civic and private clients. But, despite her thorough knowledge of the field and the rich selection of artists of all kinds available in her part of the world, Locke often turns to THE GUILD to search out exactly the right artists for her demanding and sophisticated clients.

"We have a long and excellent craft tradition here in the Bay area, but I use THE GUILD to remind myself of the range of work available throughout the country," she says. "As I look at art for clients, I'm considering everything from tabletop sculpture to monumental works."

Recently, Locke found just the right bronze sculpture by GUILD artist James Barnhill of Greensboro, North Carolina, for a client with an extensive art collection. "They were looking for a full-size bronze of a standing nude female for a specific site, but fell in love with a smaller, bronze nymph James had made. They were completely satisfied with the work, and the nymph seems right at home on a rock ledge overlooking a gorgeous indoor swimming pool. I can't tell you how thoroughly thrilled my clients were.

"It was a delight to work with James. He was prompt about sending the slides and collateral material we asked for, and he was thoroughly professional in every way, from consulting about the patina on the piece, to the shipping arrangements. Commissioning art over the phone and through correspondence is not a problem when you're dealing with artists of this caliber and experience."

Locke also recommends using the glossy tear sheets THE GUILD makes available to its artists. She uses them as leave-behinds, a very professional, very persuasive marketing tool.

Photo by Douglas Keister

James C. Myford

James C. Myford
20 Cranberry Road
Grove City, PA 16127
TEL 412-458-9672

James C. Myford's sculptures are found in corporate, museum, university, public and private collections throughout the United States. His works are also in collections in Japan, Sweden, Venezuela, Australia and Brazil.

Myford's cast and fabricated aluminum sculptures, though often outwardly abstract, are closely linked to nature and reality. The energy and vitality expressed in his compositions reflect a subtle inner strength and spirit that expand and interact gracefully with space.

Myford's sculpture ranges in size from smaller indoor works to major outdoor, site-specific commissions. Indoor works start at $1,000; outdoor works range from $8,000 to $80,000. A large selection of unique works for indoors and out can be viewed, by appointment, at the sculptor's residence.

Also see these GUILD publications:
Architect's Edition: 9, 10

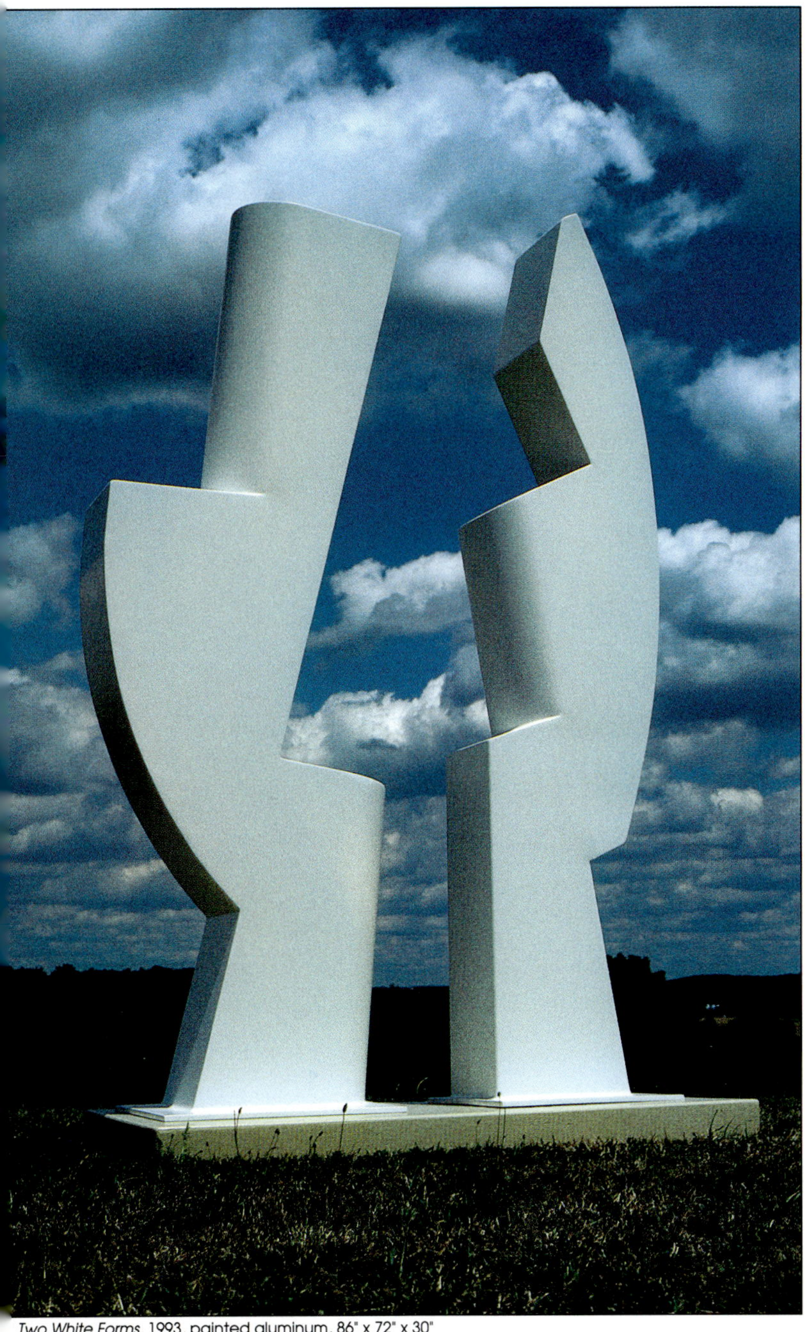

Two White Forms, 1993, painted aluminum, 86" x 72" x 30"

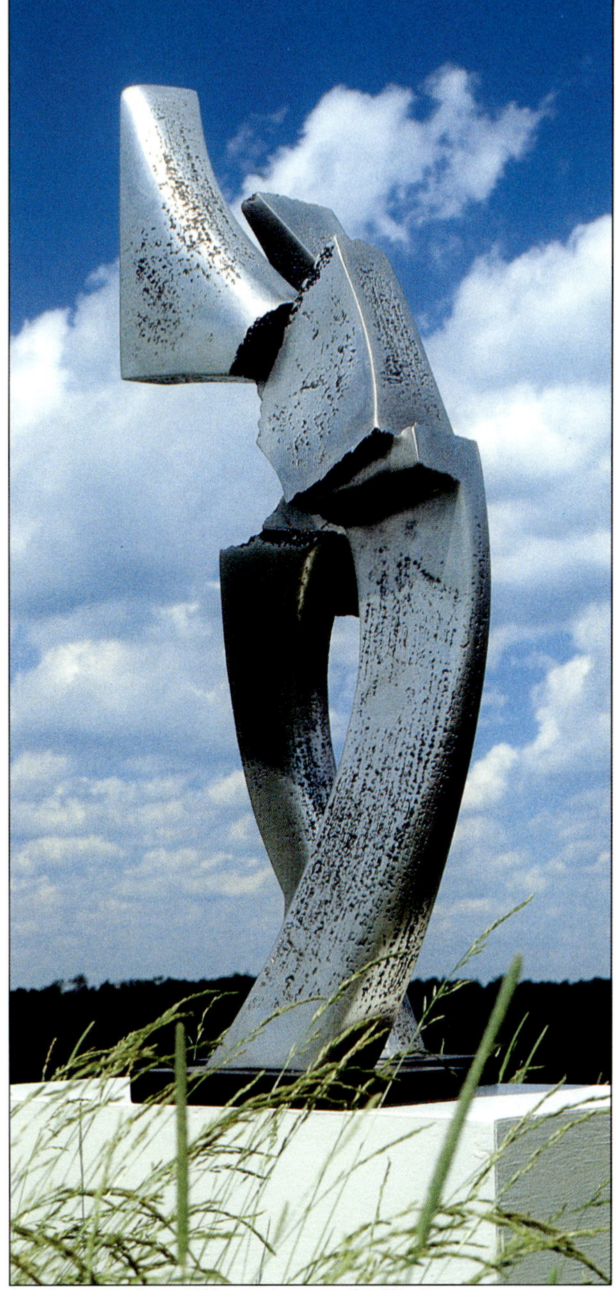

Two Compatible Forms, 1989, cast aluminum, 42" x 20" x 17"

Keiko Nelson

Art Studio
2604 3rd Street
San Francisco, CA 94107
FAX 510-527-4822
TEL   415-824-1545

Keiko Nelson is an artist of extraordinary versatility. Her expressive sculptures are abstract in presentation, yet resemble nature's peaceful and organic formations. Her pieces are timeless and fabricate out of diverse materials. Varying from very large corporate commissions to intimate garden and indoor pieces, her work has been exhibited in America, Japan and all over the world.

Keiko Nelson's architectural projects combine stained glass, relief, mosaic tile, ceramic and bronze to produce spectacular sculptural pieces that enhance atria and architectural spaces. Pursuing her 20-year commitment to art, Keiko lives and works in San Francisco.

Clients include:
Hotel Nikko, San Francisco, CA
Kaiser Medical Center, Epcot, FL
NTT International, Tokyo
Maxray Co., Osaka
Cairo University Children's Hospital
Cairo Opera House

Portfolio and pricing available upon request.

A Installation of standing sculpture, cast paper,
    stone, cement, branches, wood panel

B Installation of bronze casting sculpture, indoor
    and outdoor, varying sizes

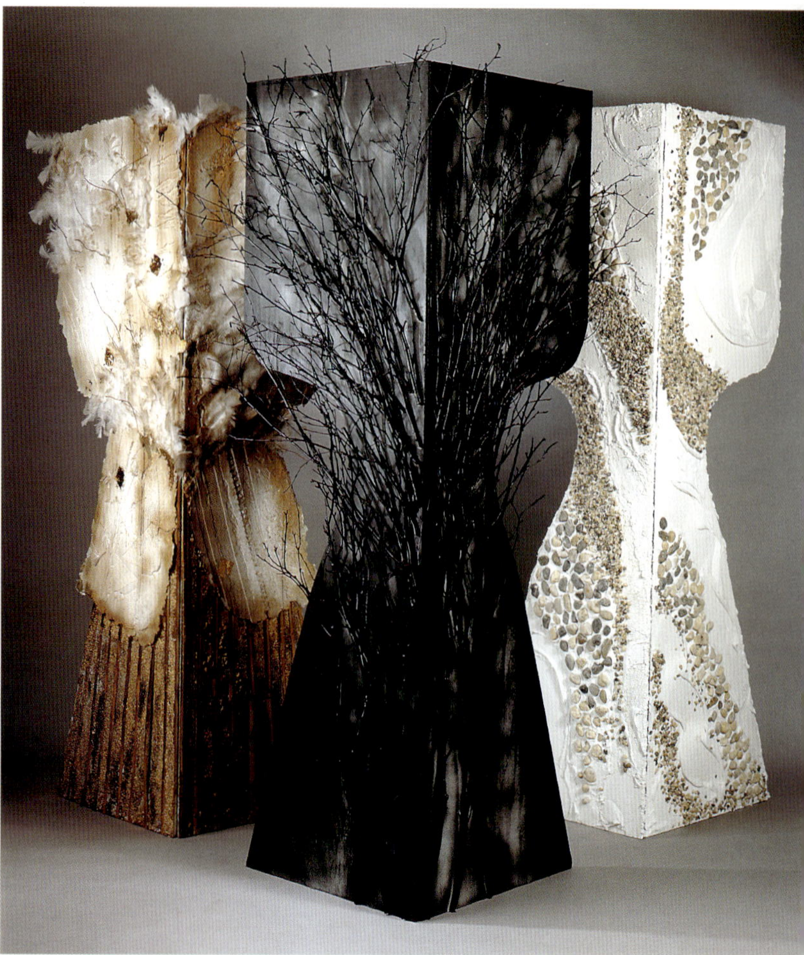

A

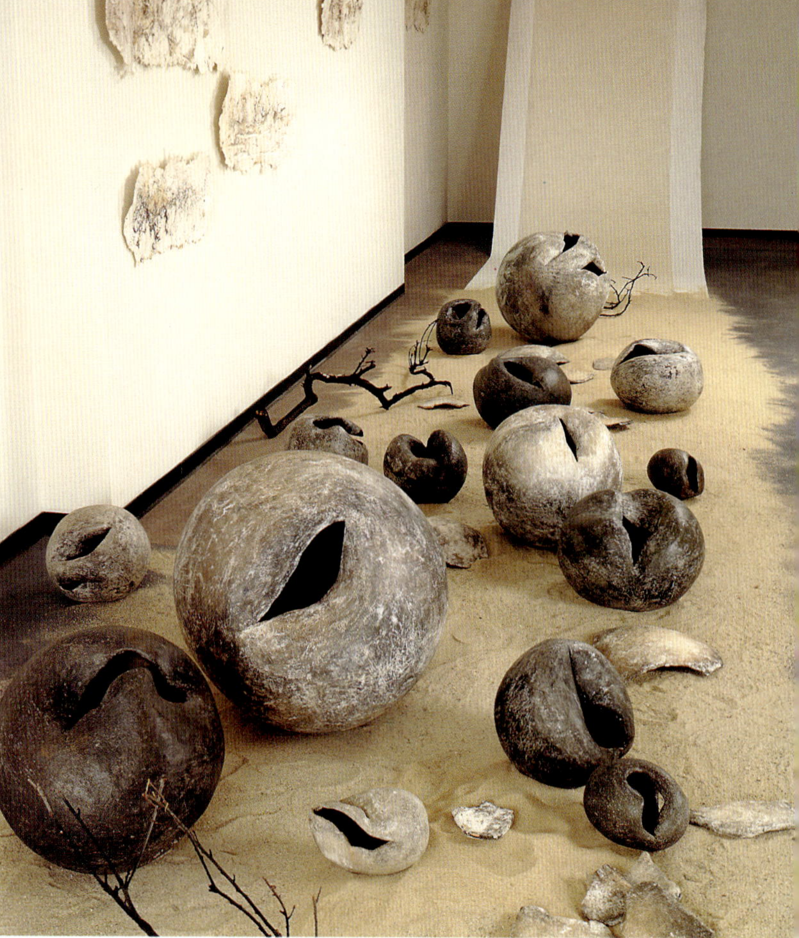

B

Bruce A. Niemi

24444 Petite Lake Road
Lake Villa, IL 60046
TEL 708-249-8480
TEL 708-356-0356

With over 20 years experience, Niemi creates sculptures finished with a burnished surface or painted with bright colors. Stainless steel, aluminum and bronze are his primary materials. Bruce's work ranges from small interior pieces and sculptural furniture to large-scale public sculptures.

Also see these GUILD publications:
Architect's Edition: 9, 10

A *Interim III*, 1995, 304 stainless steel, 7' x 7' x 5'

B *Praise*, 1994, 304 stainless steel, 17' x 8' x 5', Phelps Tool and Die, Kansas City, MO

C *Essence of Dance*, 1995, 304 stainless steel, 12' x 5' x 6'

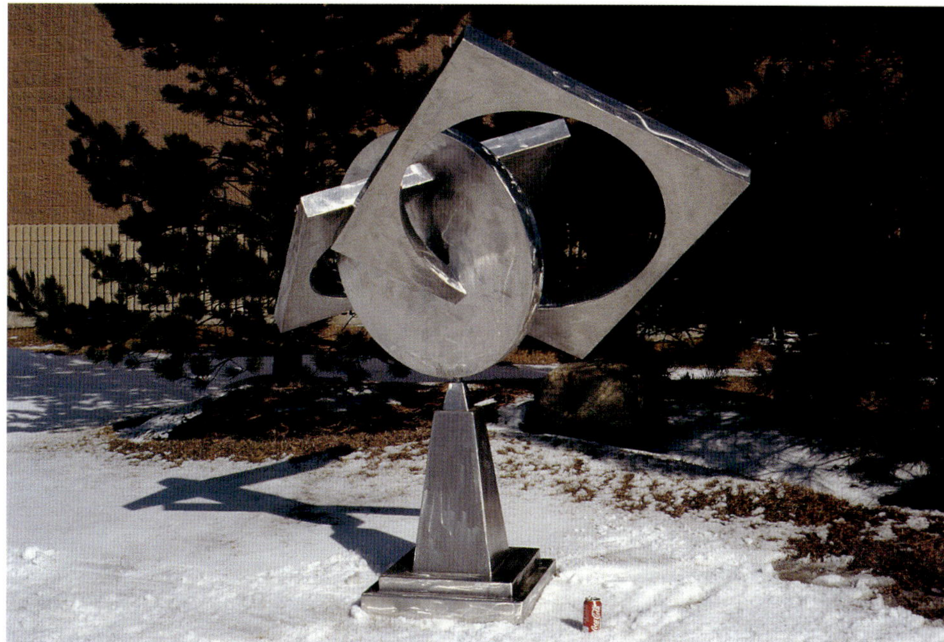

A

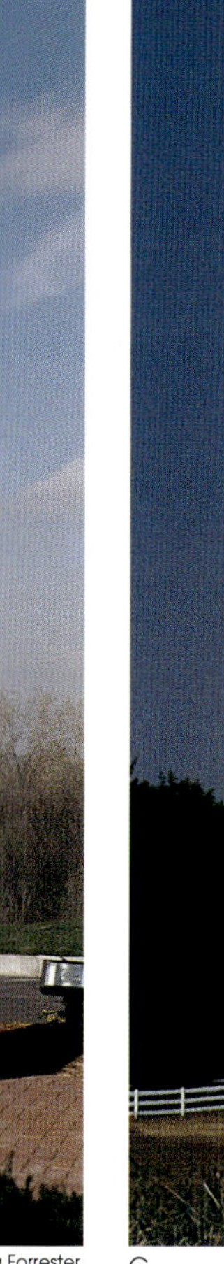

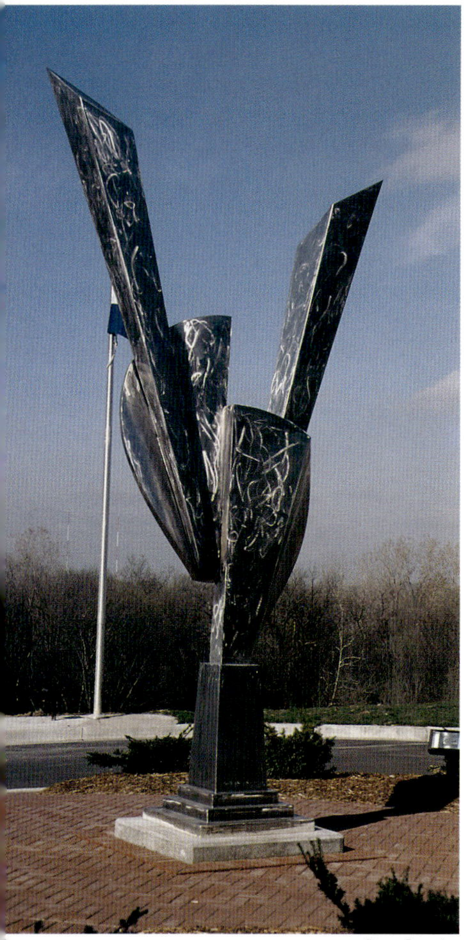

B
Dana Forrester

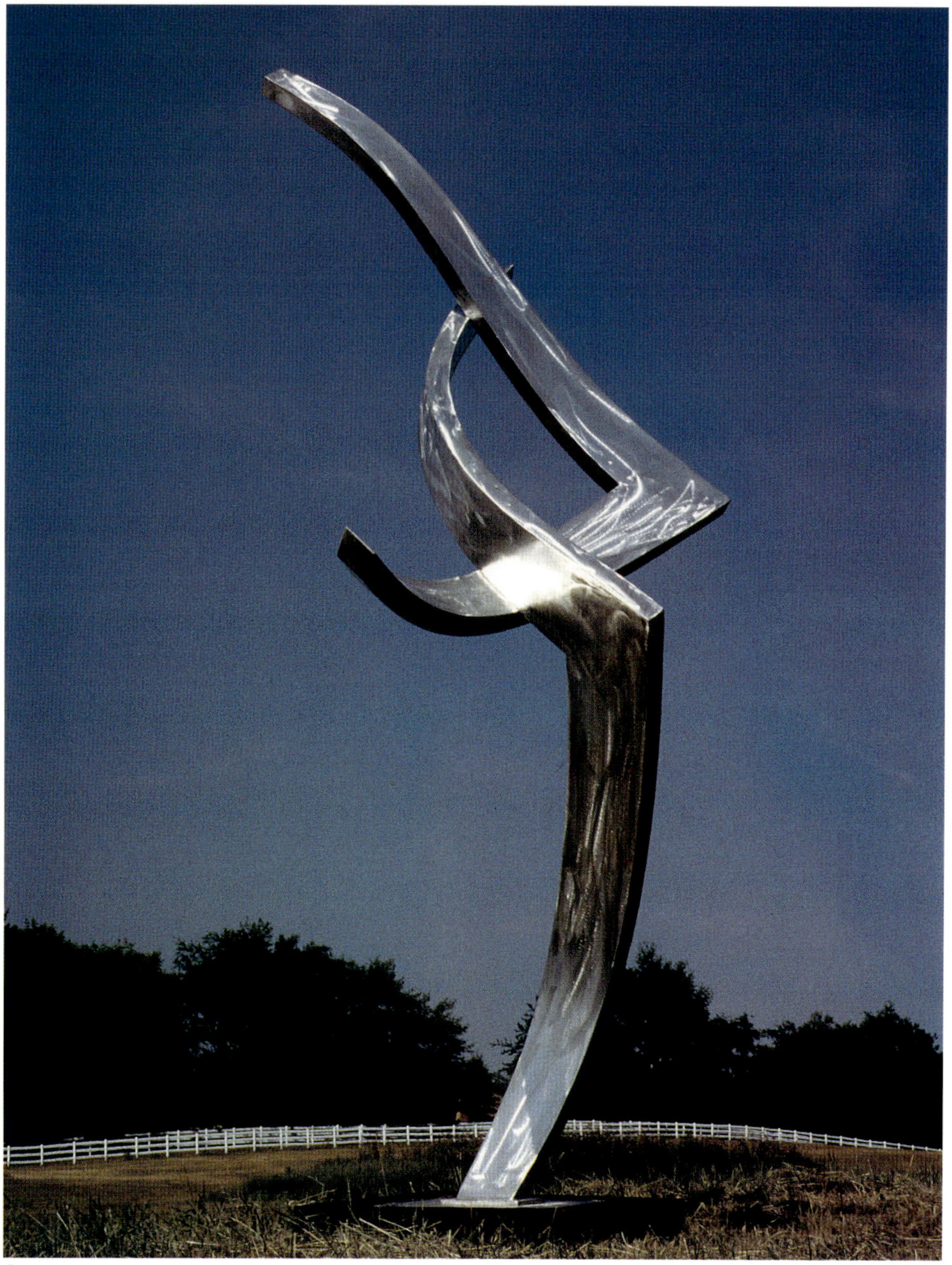

C

Mihai Popa

The Ark Project, Inc.
30 Millstone Road
Water Mill, NY 11976
FAX 516-537-0061
TEL 516-537-0061

545 8th Avenue
New York, NY 10018
TEL 212-695-1740

Mihai is known for his 'Integral Art,' combining painting and sculpture with architecture. His murals, bas-relief, sculptural compositions and paintings are throughout Europe and in six museums world-wide. Feature articles have appeared in *The New York Times, New York Newsday, Southampton Press,* and *The Independent.*

Mihai's public art seeks to reach the power of ancient Mayans and Egyptians in simplified forms of our modern age. People stare a lot at his art, excited, as if standing on a bridge between humans and cosmos.

The Species represents a reconciliation between humans, vegetation and animals of planet earth. A modern Noah and wife stand near a 15-foot Tree of Life, surrounded by animals. *The Ocean and the Land* integrates painting and sculpture. *Orion* talks about the constellations and our human expansion outward to space.

Mihai cooperates closely on projects with architects and other artists. Feel free to contact him or visit his art complex in Bridgehampton, NY.

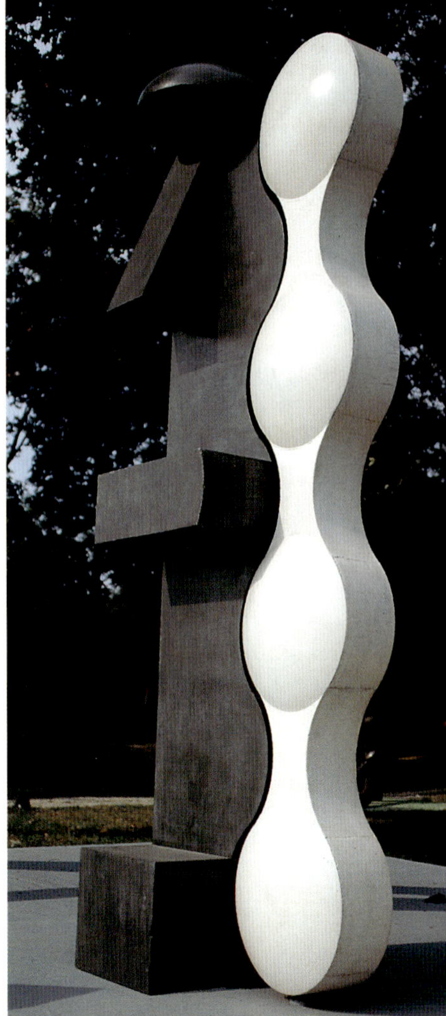

Tundra Wolf

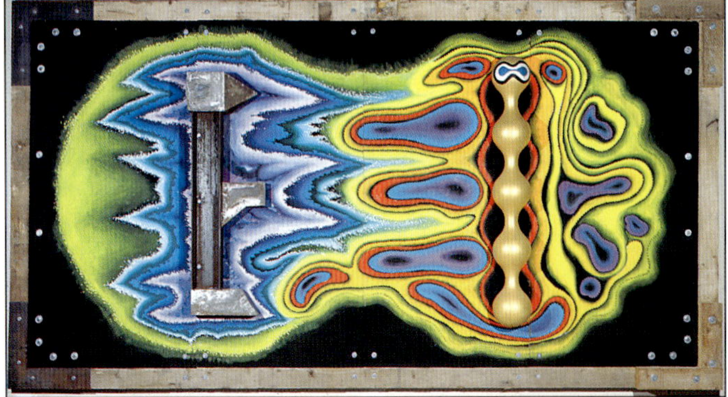

The Ocean and the Land, steel, wood, acrylic, 10' x 20'

Gary Bartoloni

The Species: Noah and Wife (detail), colored concrete, 10'H

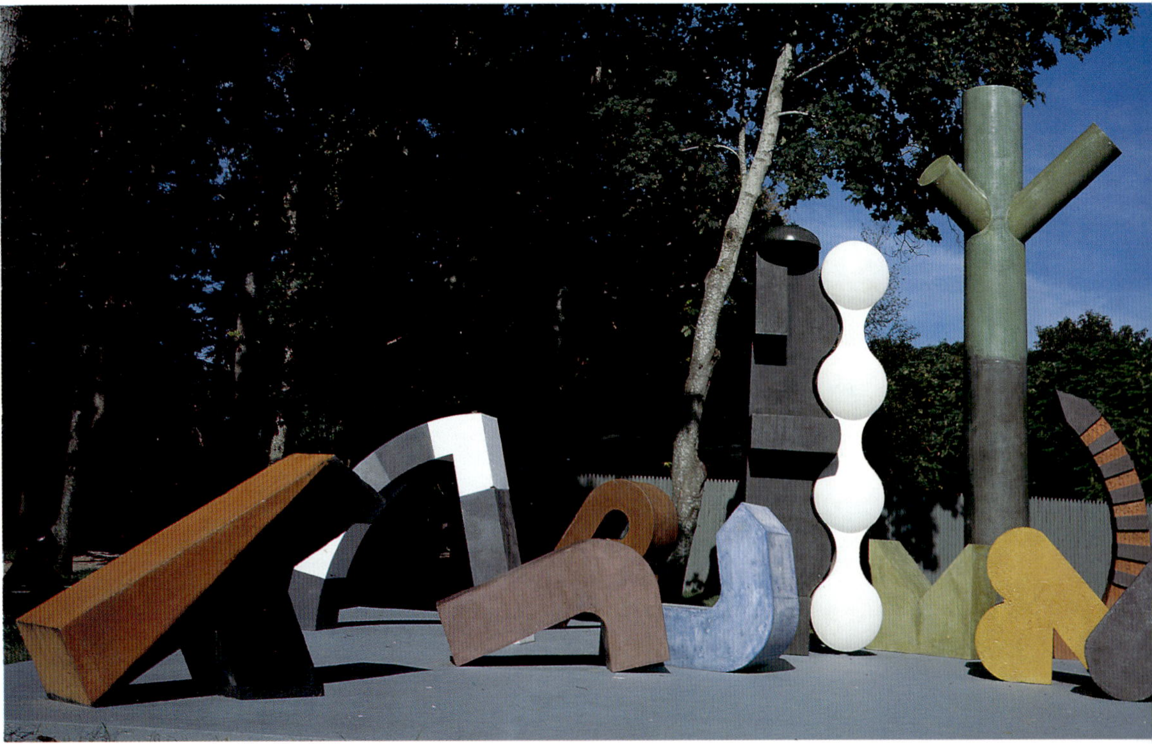

The Species, colored concrete, 40' x 30' x 15'H

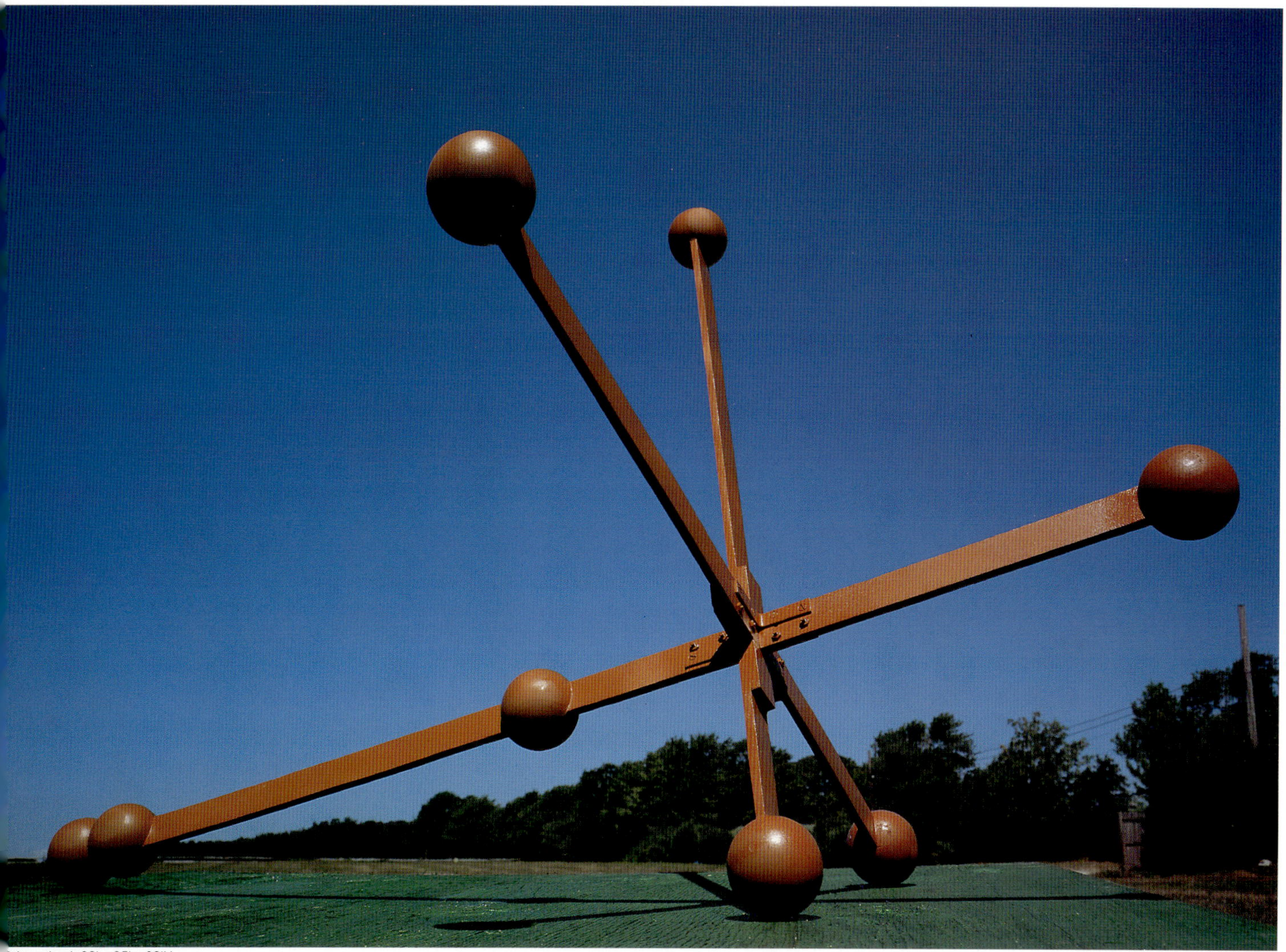

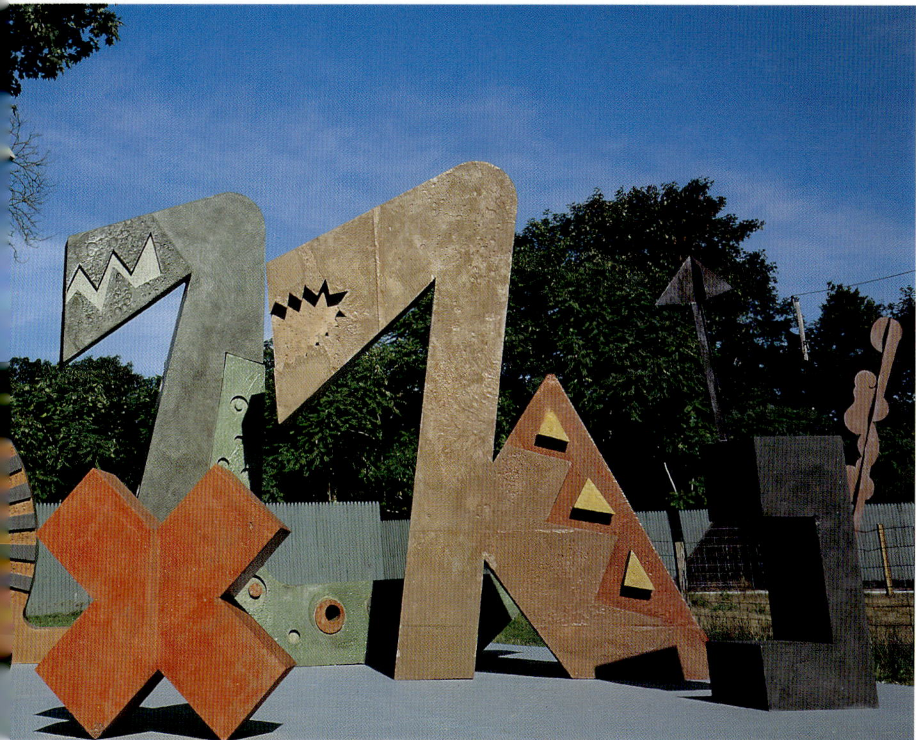

Orion, steel, 30' x 35' x 30'H   Gary Bartoloni

Gary Bartoloni

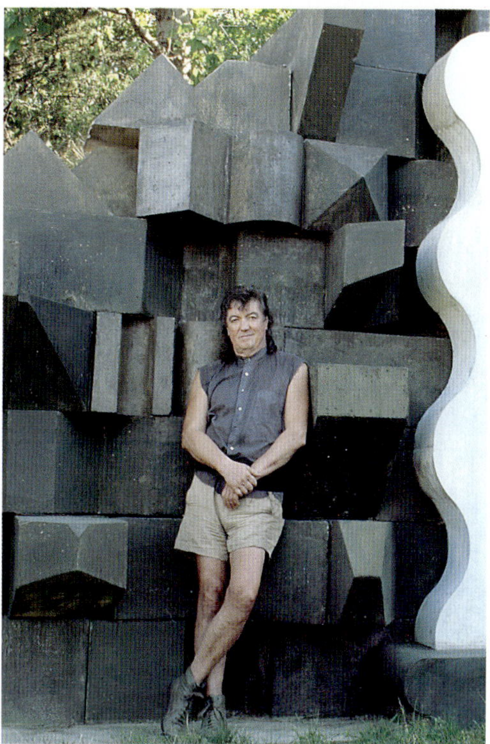

Manole's Legend: The Wall, colored cement,   Tundra Wolf
13'H x 25'W

Russ Rubert

1101 S. Fremont Avenue
Springfield, MO 65804
FAX 417-864-7988
TEL   417-862-3760 (Office)
TEL   417-864-7985 (Studio)

Russ Rubert creates site-specific sculpture for indoor and outdoor public areas. His work draws on figurative and organic imagery and often incorporates pathways, seating, and kinetic elements such as moving parts or water.

From conception to installation, Rubert works well with other professionals and successfully meets time schedules. His talent and enthusiasm for working with people and public spaces enable him to create art that elevates and inspires communities and organizations.

Clients include:
Internal Medicine Inc.
Letco Incorporated
Mid America Cancer Center
St. John's Regional Health Center
Southwest Missouri State University
Walt Disney Children's Arts Festival

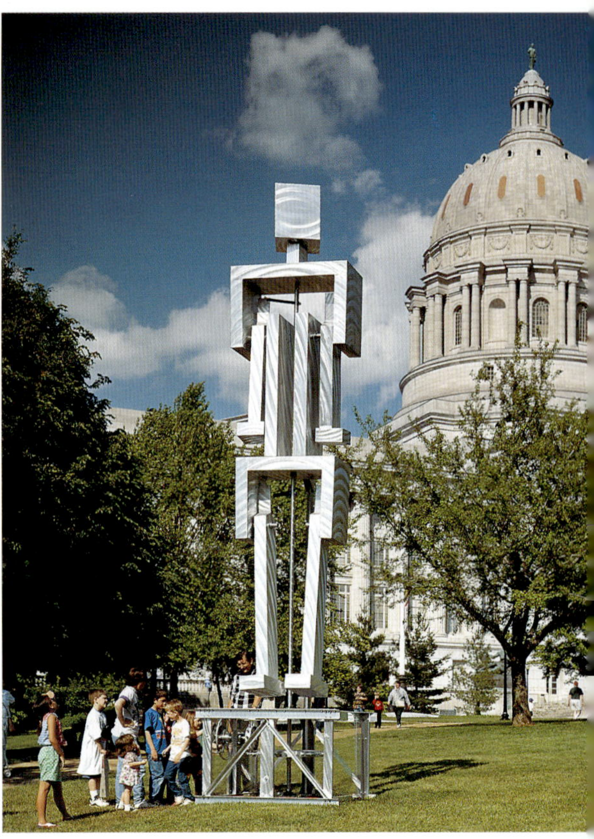

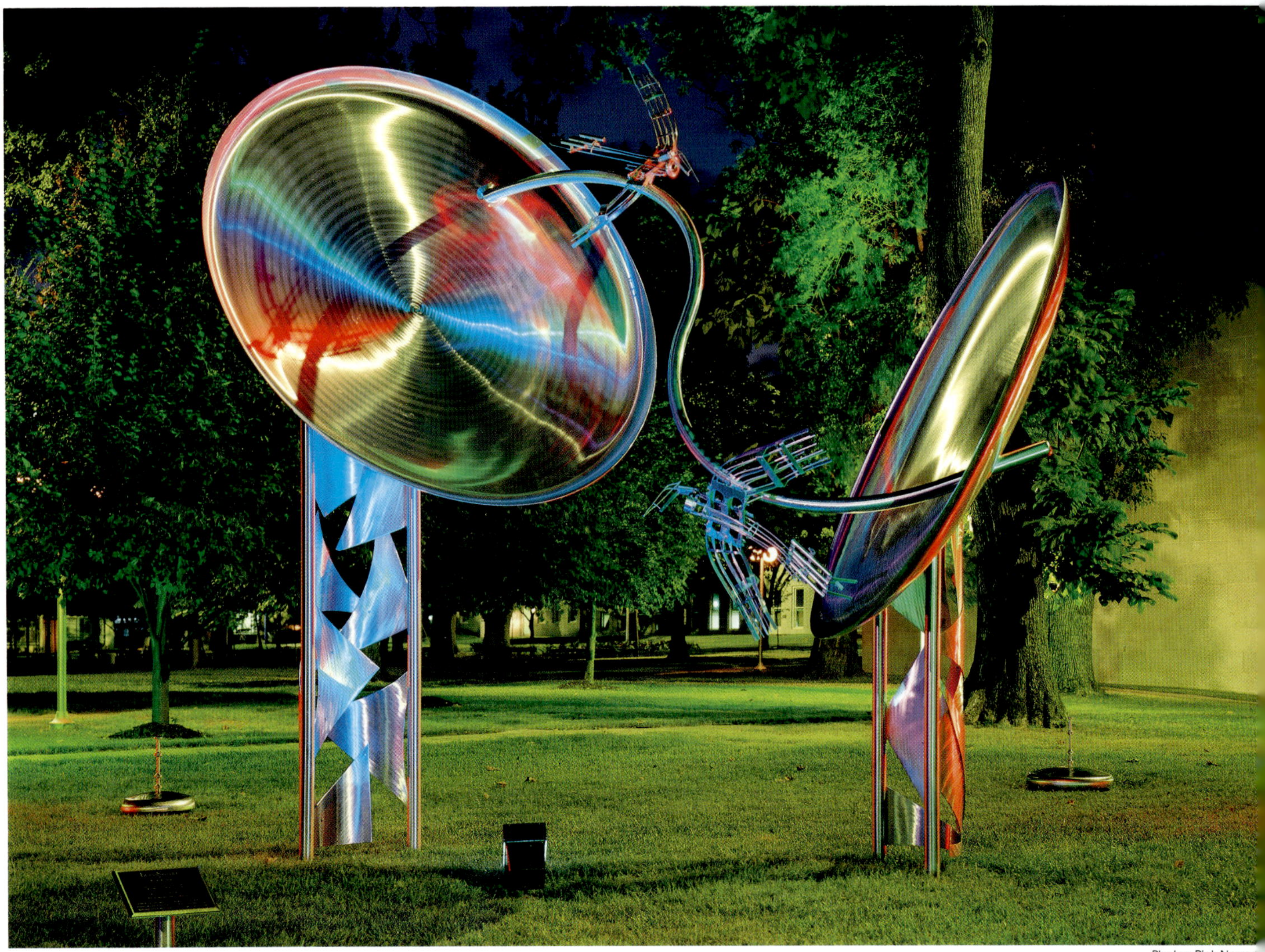

Photos: Rick Norma

John E. Simms

John E. Simms Studio
PO Box 517
Jackson, WY 83001
FAX 307-733-1190
TEL 307-733-2277

John's creative process couples a vivid imagination with rigorous engineering in a unique artistic synthesis. Often working on location, he views each site and designs a number of sculptural options around it. This process is driven by client desires, as well as aesthetic concerns.

Ultimately, each finished piece is supported by a detailed Autocad® drawing as an assurance of structural integrity and site-specific base design.

John enjoys the challenge of commission work and speaks the language of both architect and client.

A *Linear Dog and Man*, 1994, steel, life-size

B *Aspen Leaf*, 1994, bronze, 10'H x 6'W x 4'D

C *Bison of = Radii*, 1992, steel, 16'H x 24'W x 6"D

D *Exclamation Point*, 1993, stainless steel, 9'H x 2'W x 16"D

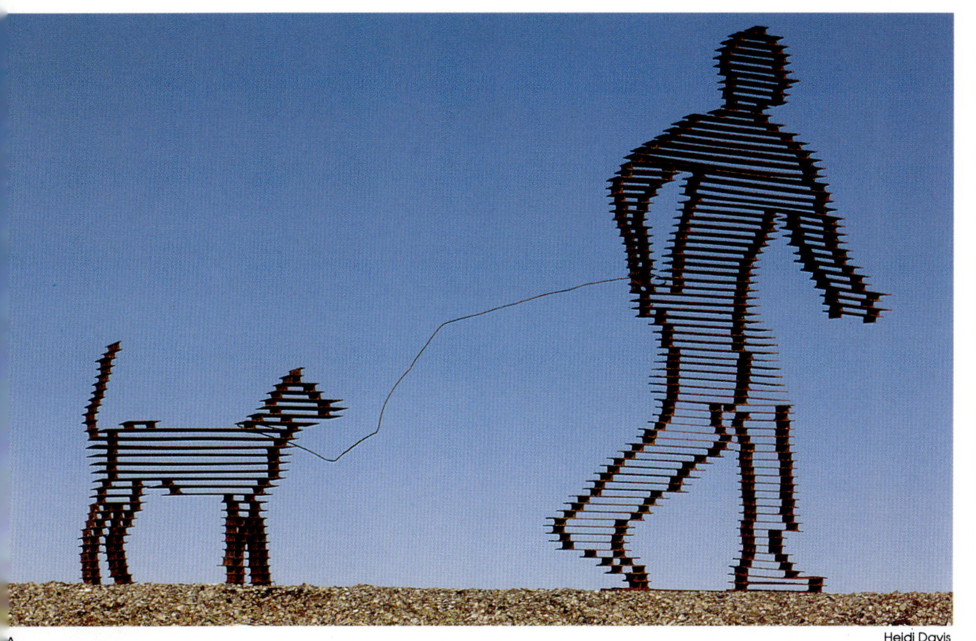

A

Heidi Davis

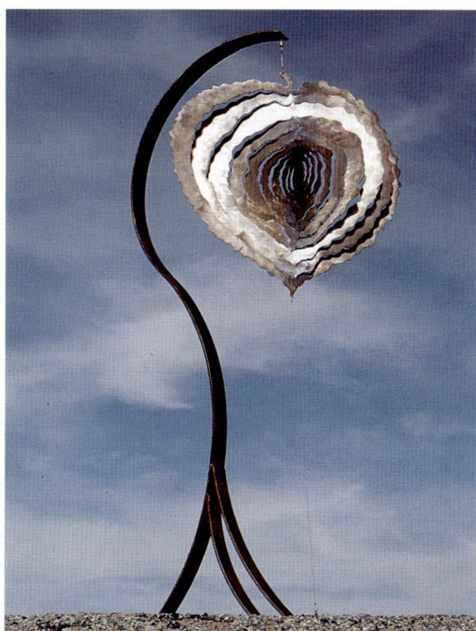

B

T.K. Hill

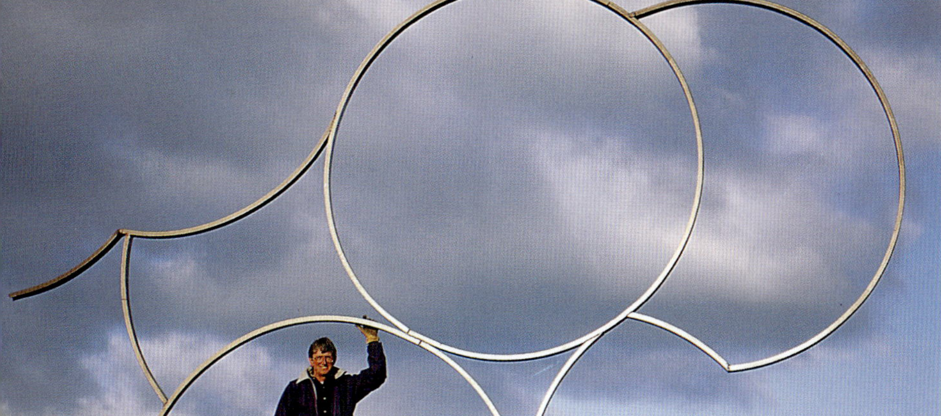

C

Tom Montgomery

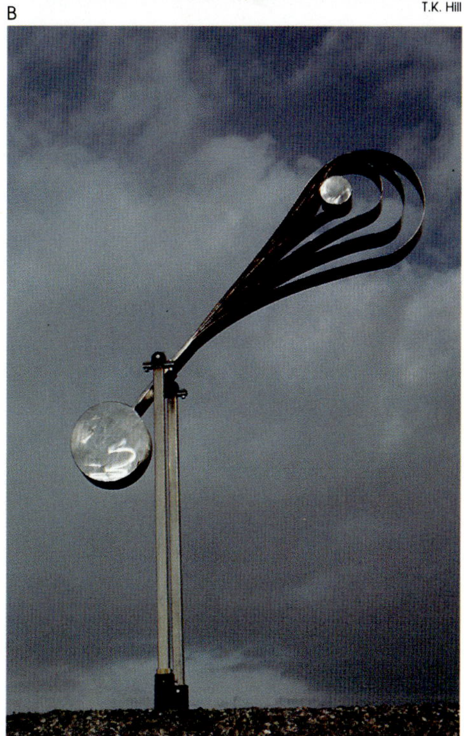

D

S. Gallina Simpson

Simpson Sculpture Studios
67-31 Cooper Avenue
Glendale, NY 11385
TEL 718-456-6155

Marta S. Hurwitz, Representative
TEL 619-689-8407

S. Gallina Simpson carves stone into movement and figurative imagery. A dozen years of carving. Three decades of professional experience.

Site-specific. Intimate. Monumental. Waterworks.

The *Movement Series* is a progression of direct carved limestone sculpture exploring the illusion of movement: vertical, horizontal, spiral. Twisting, flowing, compelling organic sculptures with tactile pleasures and sunlight performances in public and private landscapes.

A *Two Figures Merge In Flame*, 2'H carved limestone maquette for 9'H sculpture, 1994

B *Movement #33* and *#34*, a pair of 7'H limestone columns, illusionary figurative and organic imagery, 1993

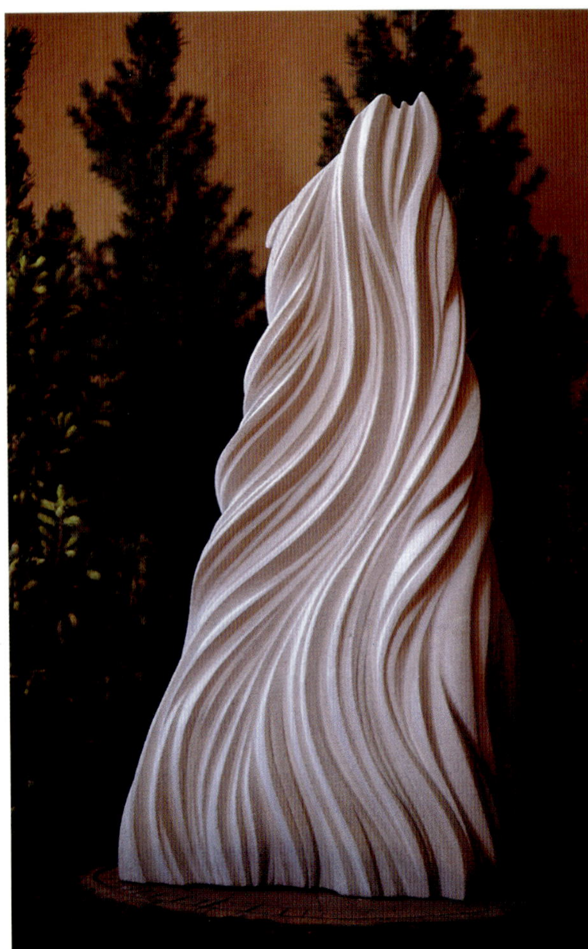

A

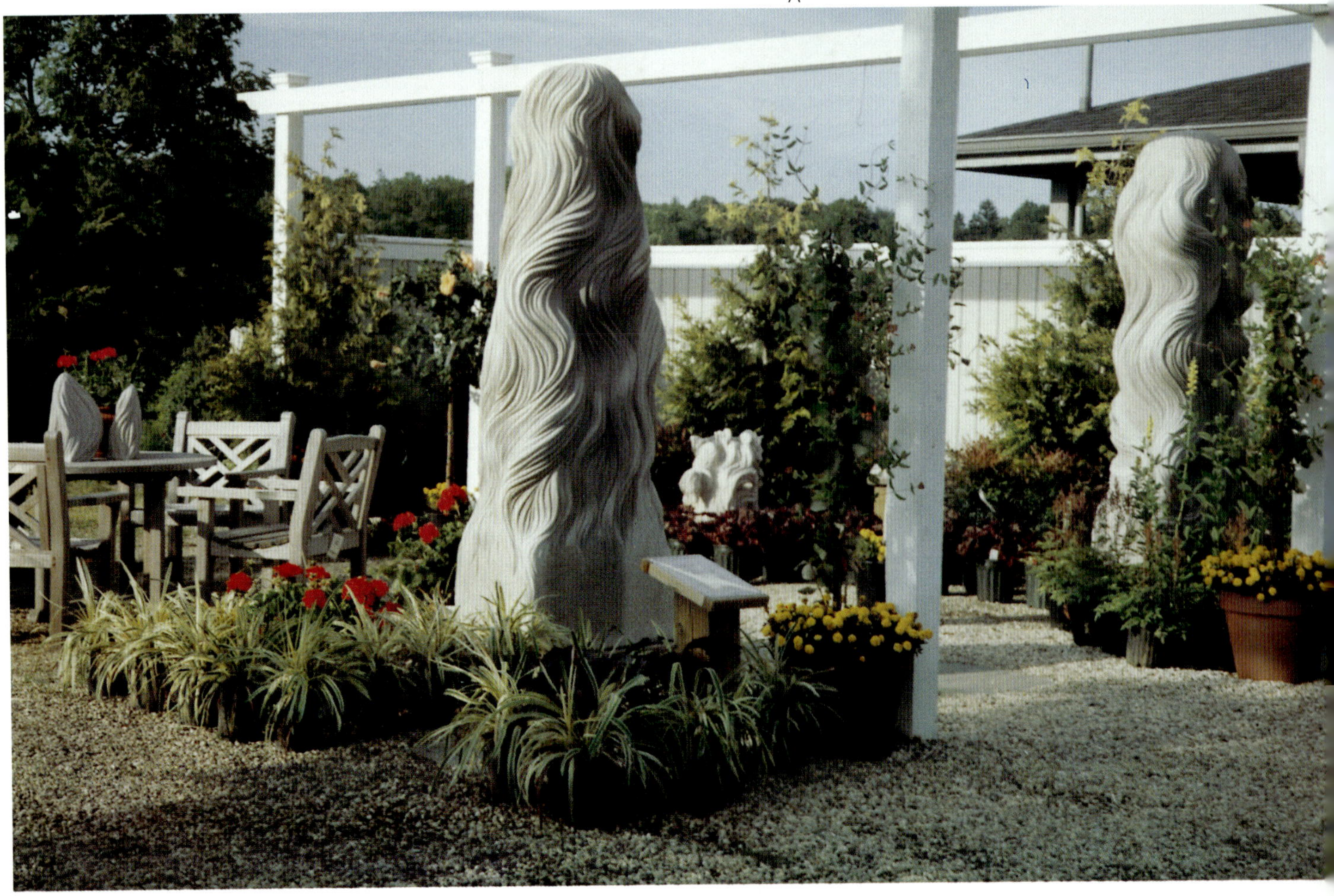

B

Cordell Taylor

Cordell Taylor, Inc.
250 South 200 West
Salt Lake City, UT 84101
TEL 801-580-1746

The work of Cordell Taylor is deeply rooted in his personal ideals and philosophy. Through his work, Taylor constructs universal relations into personal statements about life, society and culture. His works relate a sophisticated degree of technical skills and understanding, which give his sculpture the purity and originality necessary to achieve international recognition.

Working with architects and designers daily, Taylor creates site-specific commissioned works; one can also draw from his portfolio of original pieces.

A *Four Worlds*, 1994, wood, steel, wire

B *Probe*, 1994, wood, steel, wire

C *Two Gods of a Distorted World*, 1994, Sandler Commission, Deer Valley, UT, steel, wood, wire, stone

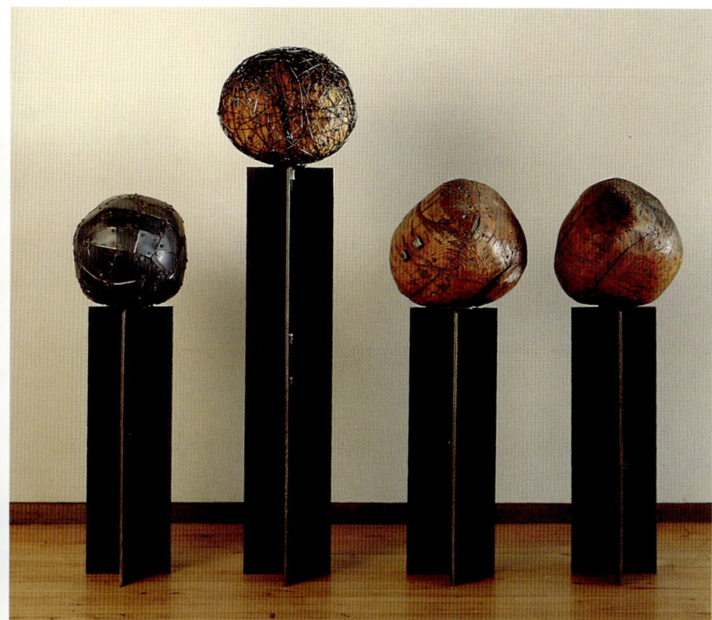

A

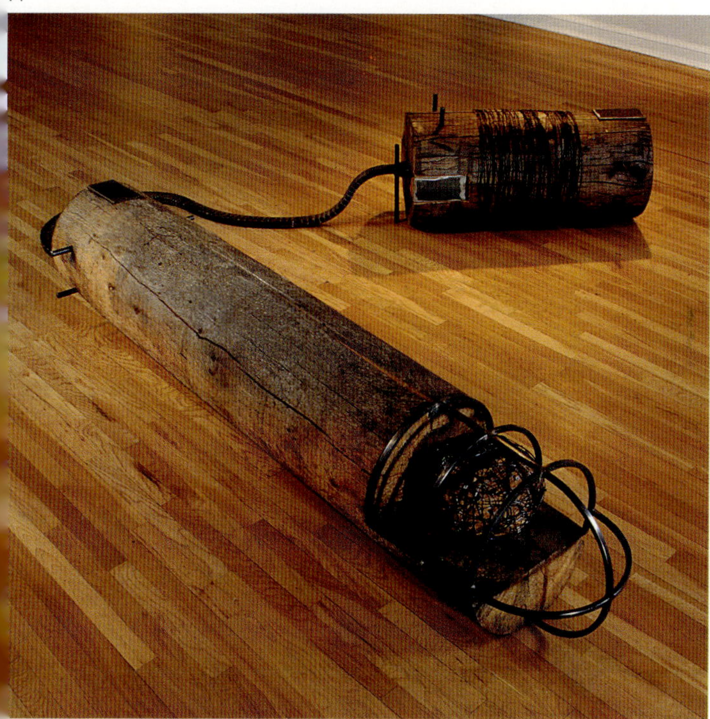

B

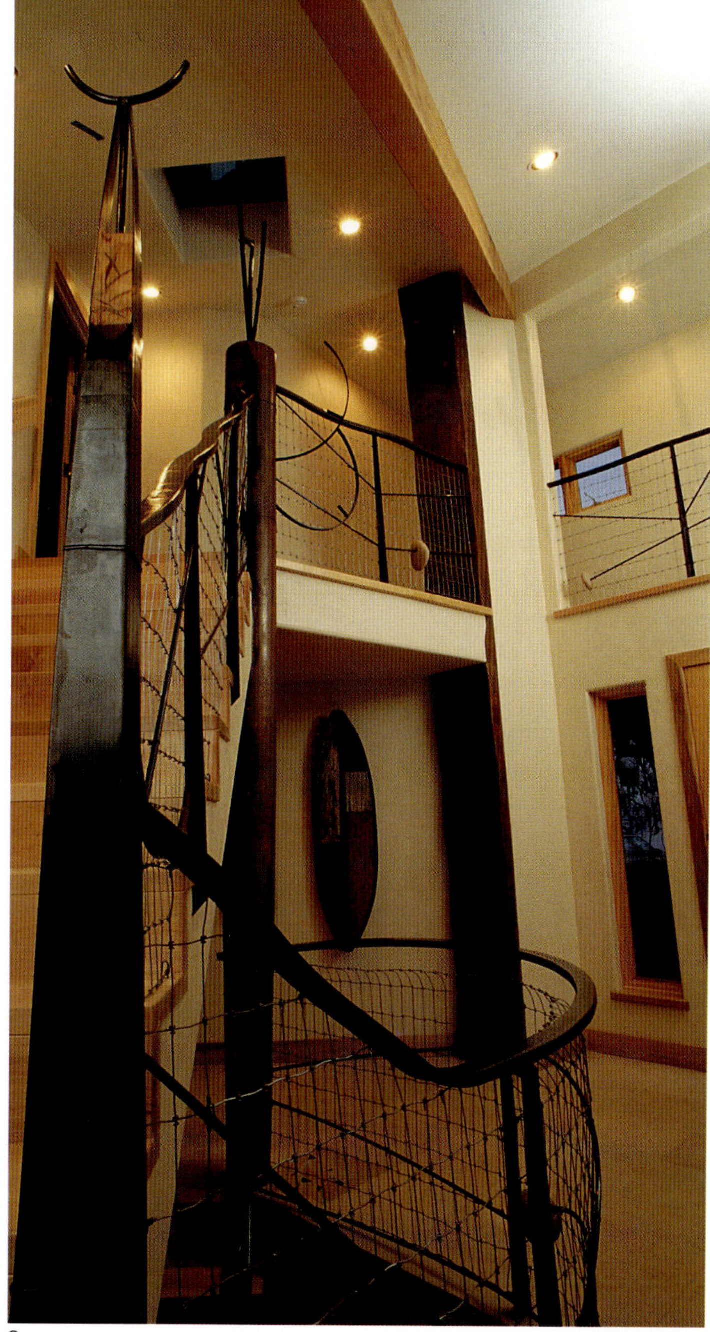

C

Photos: André Ramjoué

Terry A. Thommes

Thommes Studio
Route 1, Box 515T
Big Pine Key, FL 33043
FAX 305-872-9909
TEL 305-872-9689

Terry Thommes welcomes commissions and collaborations for his work from his studio in the Florida Keys. His sculpture, which is suitable for outdoor placement, also includes works in marble and stone. He recently completed an 8'H carved black marble fish piece for a private residence near Key West, and has recently installed works in the new Marathon Regional Airport in Marathon, Florida.

Thommes' hanging trap-like pieces and caged figures, developed from years of building underwater environmental sculptures, are in public and private collections worldwide. His works can be fabricated up to 20'H for large public placements in atriums, courtyards and lobbies, and are fabricated of durable, permanent materials. He also welcomes commissions and purchases of smaller sculpture.

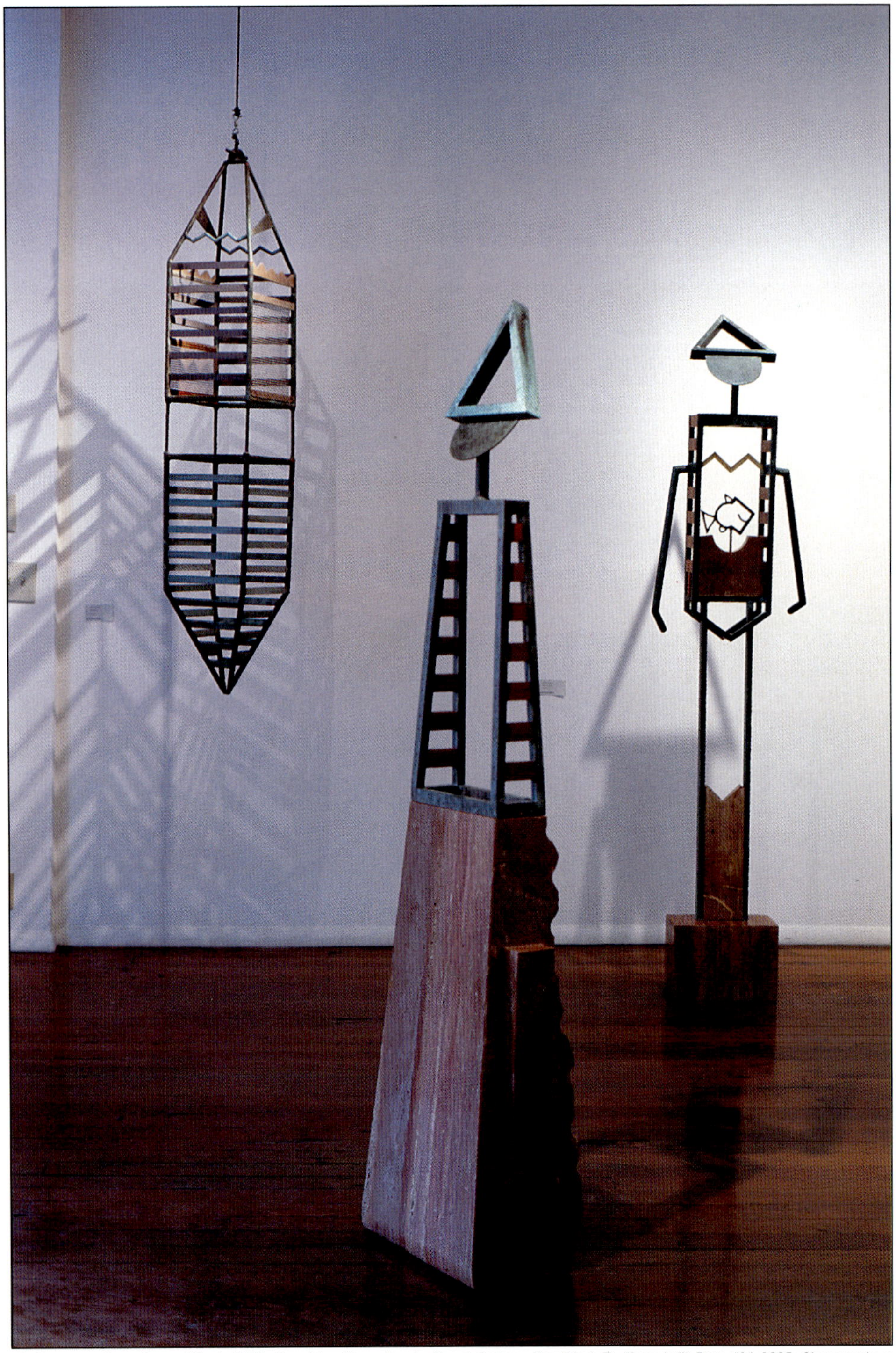

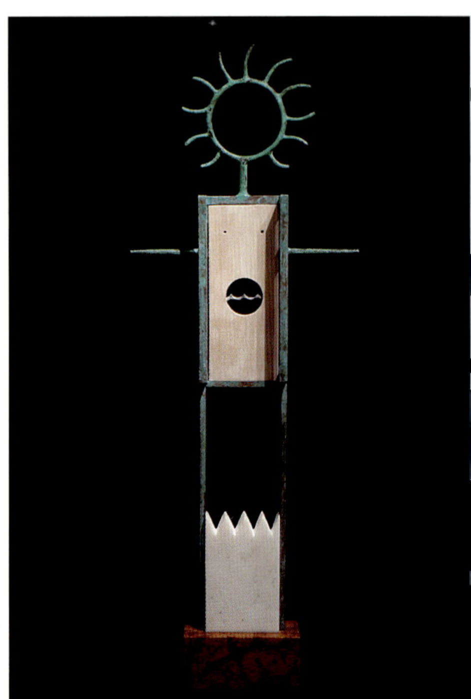

Aquasol, 1994, bronze, marble, wood, 74" x 28" x 6"

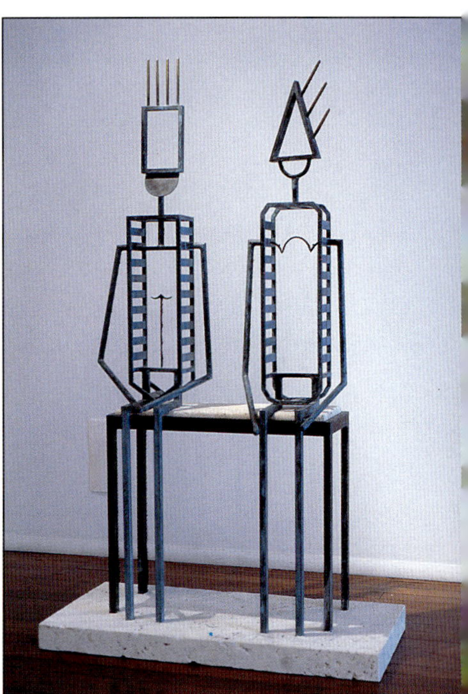

Fundamentalists, 1995, bronze, coral, teak, 69" x 41" x 20"

Gallery overview, *Caged Souls*, 1995, One-Man Show, Lucky Street Gallery, Key West, FL, (from left) *Trap #16*, 1995; *Stranger in a Strange Land*, 1995, Persian travertine, bronze, teak; *Self Portrait*, 1995, bronze, Persian travertine, teak

Ken Valimaki

8580 Woodlands Court
Pickerington, OH 43147
TEL 614-866-1851

As a sculptor, Ken Valimaki has a commitment to design that contributes to the identity of buildings and architectural spaces. Valimaki's sculptures are not limited to his own creation, but are intended to create a dialogue in which both the viewer and artist come away from each piece with a new way of looking at the world.

Valimaki has worked and collaborated with architects and clients for 20 years on corporate, public and private commissions.

Valimaki's work consists of concept, design, fabrication and installation. His works are created in bronze, stainless steel, Cor-ten steel, aluminum, neon, and fiber optics. Projects range from $10,000 to $300,000.

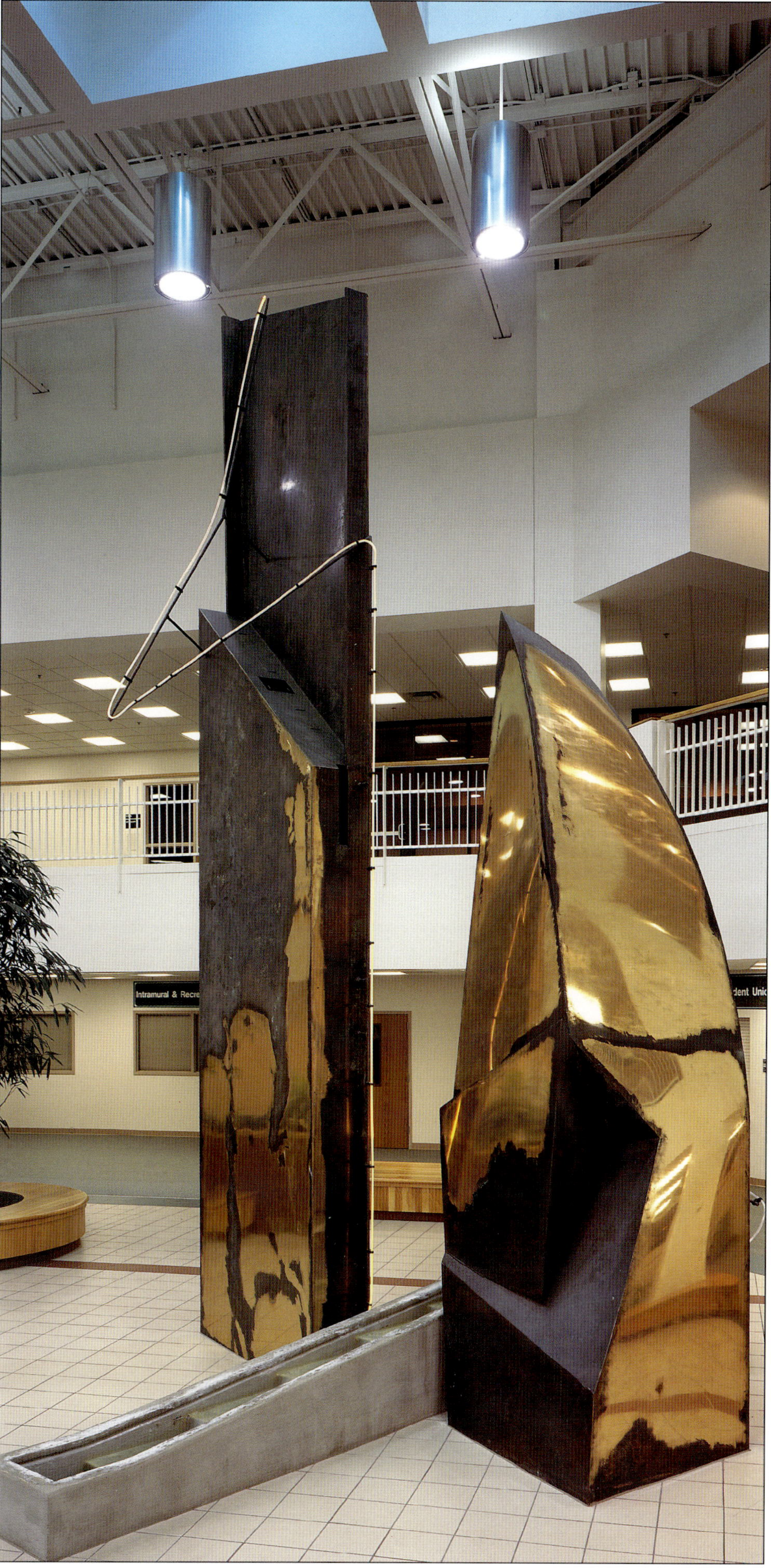

Scenario, 1994, bronze, fiber optics, Wright State University, Dayton, Ohio, 24' x 11' x 6'

Jennifer Dunlap

Hans Van de Bovenkamp

661 Springtown Road
Tillson, NY 12486
FAX 914-658-8888
TEL   914-658-8363

Hans Van de Bovenkamp is an architect and a sculptor. He has earned an international reputation over the past 35 years for designing, fabricating, installing and maintaining unique sculptures and fountains in collaboration with architects and designers. His works can be seen in public, civic, corporate and private collections. He has executed over 100 commissions.

Clients include:
  Private:
Beverly Sills
Edward Albee
Estate of Nelson Rockefeller
Barbara Walters

  Architects:
John C. Portman
Edward Durrell Stone
Lanthrop Douglas
Matthew Warshauer

  Municipalities:
Oklahoma City
State of Nebraska

Stony Brook University
State Capital, Lansing, MI
Lowe Museum
Texas A&M University
University of Missouri

  Corporations:
Bloomingdales, Neiman Marcus,
Phellps Dodge, Cargill,
Tiffany's, Delaware Trust Company

  Awards:
Emily Lowe Award
American Institute of Arts & Letters
Nebraska Bicentennial Competition

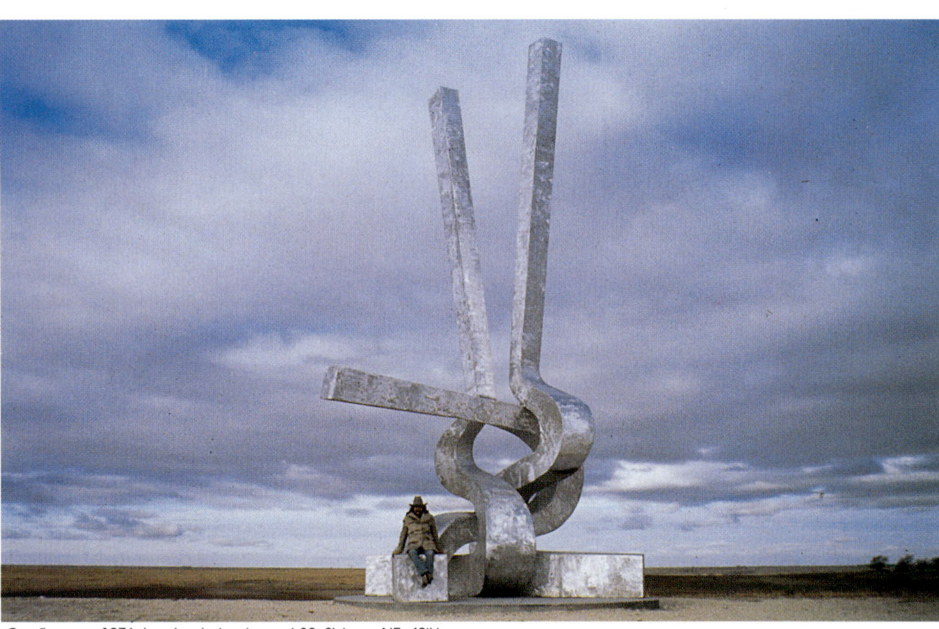

Confluence, 1976, brushed aluminum, I-80, Sidney, NE, 40'H

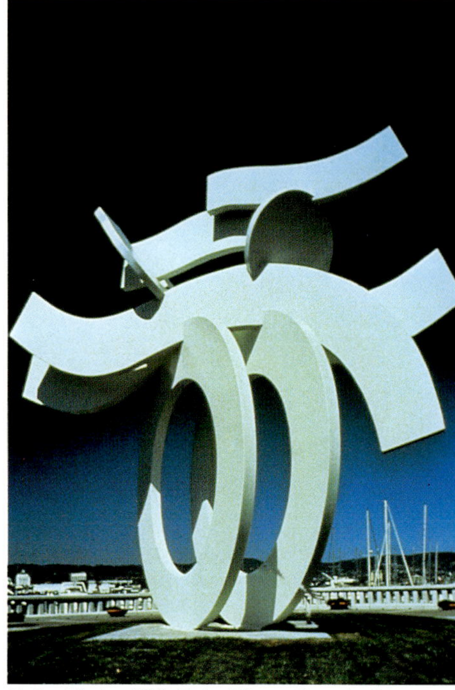

Marina Window, 1990, Marina Village, Alemeda, CA, painted steel, 35'H

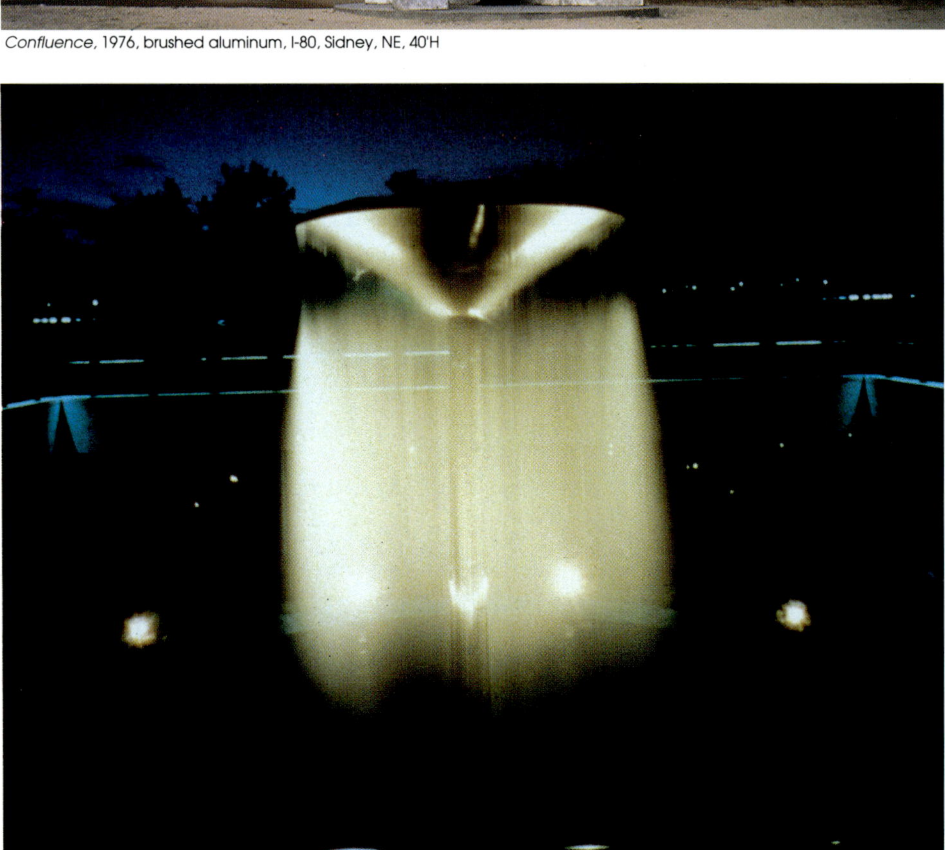

Ottawa Falls, 1983, stainless steel, State Capitol Plaza, Lansing, MI, 24' x 14', architect/designer: Sigmund Blum

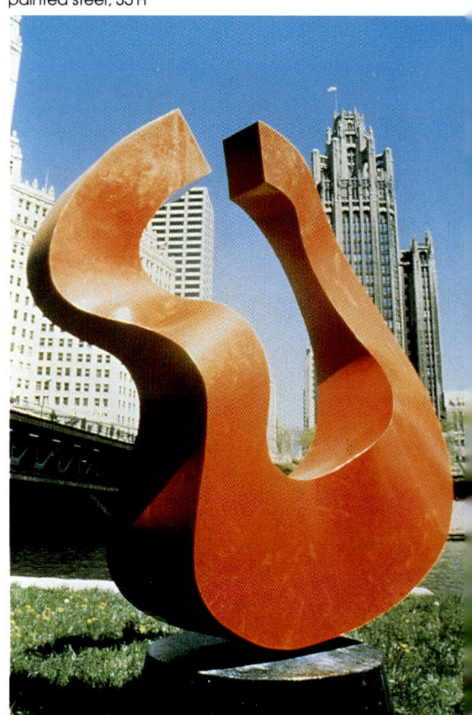

Gateway, 1993, red painted aluminum, Myriad Gardens, Oklahoma City, OK, 14'H x 14'W x 5'D

Mark West

2144 Rollin Road
St. Pascal de Baylon, ON K0A 3N0
Canada
FAX 613-488-3880
TEL 613-488-2829

Mark West's reinforced concrete sculptures and structures are a unique marriage of art and building technology. Reinforced concrete is reborn through his use of fabric formwork techniques that produce an immaculate surface finish and striking sculptural forms. His work may be used as full-scale structures (columns, walls, beams, slabs, etc.) or as free-standing sculpture in both pre-cast and poured-in-place applications.

Landscape installations and public art commissions have been done in Ottawa, Ontario; Bar Harbor, Maine; Tallahassee, Florida; and New York City. Mr. West's work has been shown in galleries across the U.S. and Canada, and has received public attention and critical acclaim in numerous architectural, artistic, and academic publications, including a *Progressive Architecture* research award.

A Columns at Bar Harbor, ME, 1991, poured-in-place reinforced concrete, 12' to 14'H x 12" to 18"Dia

B Small columns, pre-cast sculptural columns, 1992, reinforced concrete, 8'H x 6" to 9"Dia

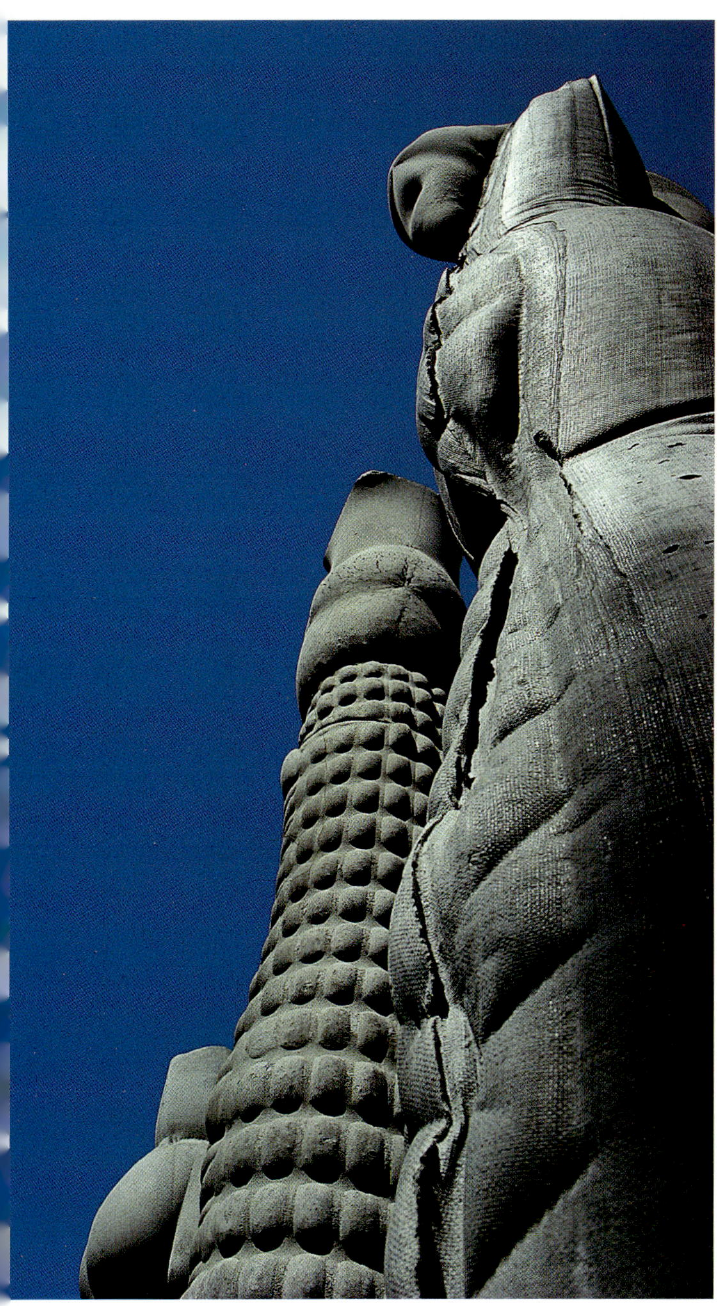

A

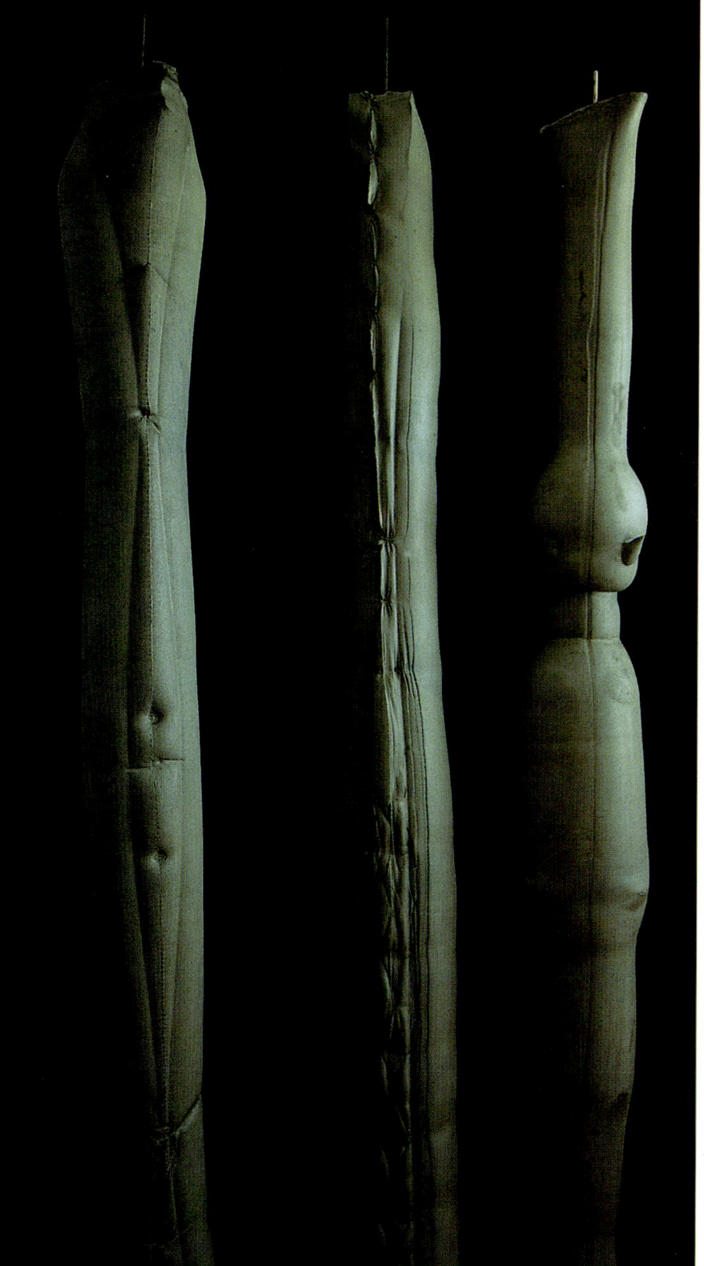

B

Nancy Metz White

Nancy Metz White/Sculpture
3038 N. Shepard Avenue
Milwaukee, WI 53211
FAX 414-671-2499
TEL 414-332-9358

Nancy Metz White's environmental installations link people, sculpture and architecture into a harmonizing whole. The site sculpture *Portals* exemplifies her approach. *Portals* invites participation by creating a series of doorways for people to move through. At the opening of *Sculpture on the Plaza–92*, a national exhibition, White presented a modern dance troupe interacting with her sculpture.

The artist's work has been exhibited in museums and galleries in the Midwest, including the Milwaukee Art Museum, Lawrence University, and the University of Chicago. The sculpture, made of stainless or painted steel pipe and duct, is suitable for indoor or outdoor settings. Prices range from $5,000 to $75,000.

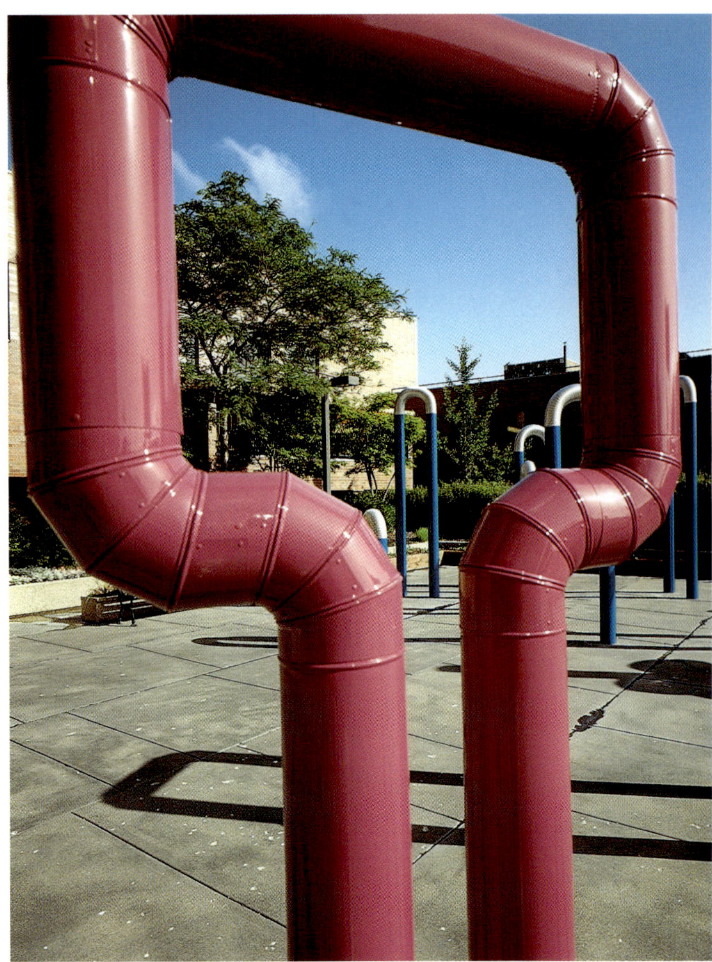

Fuchsia Portal (detail), painted steel pipe, 11'H x 4'W x 7"Dia

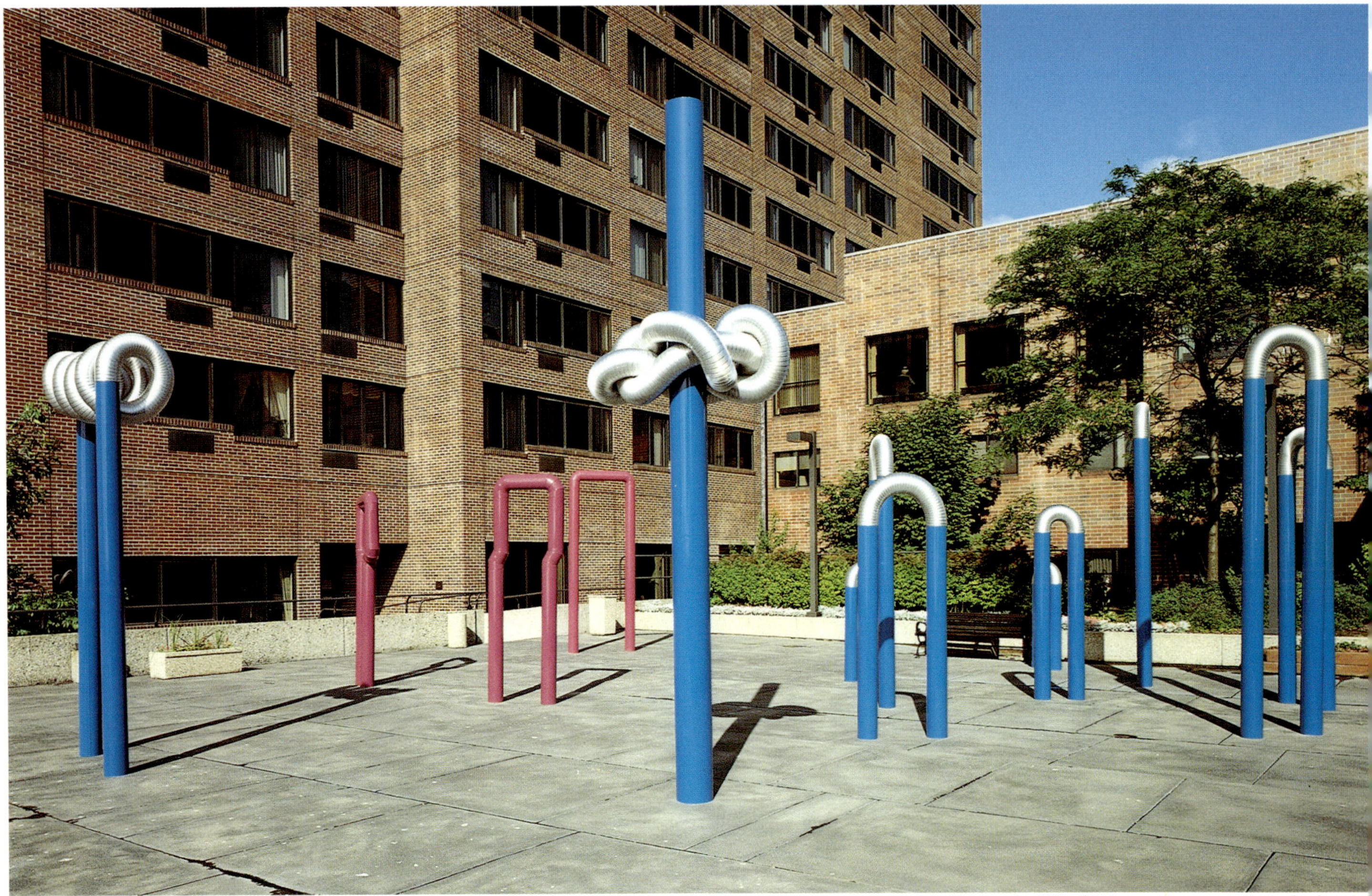

The site sculpture *Portals*, painted steel pipeand aluminum duct, St. John's Tower, Milwaukee, WI, site area 30' x 80'; center element, *Blue Rondo*, 15'H x 10"Dia

Photos: Eric Oxendorf

Jean Woodham

Jean Woodham/Sculpture
26 Pin Oak Court
Westport, CT 06880
TEL 203-226-9372

Jean Woodham works in welded metals and has over 150 sculptures in public and private collections.

Award-winning work by this sculptor has been exhibited in museums and galleries throughout the United States and in England, Japan, Belgium, Bulgaria, Mexico, Argentina, Chile and Brazil.

Woodham has the creative ability, training, experience and temperament to create large-scale sculptures relating to the human spirit and the environment. Woodham also works successfully with other professionals and the public.

Clients include:
World Bank
New York City Board of Education
Connecticut State Art Commission
NYNEX Corporation
General Electric Credit Corporation
Texas Eastern Transmission
Auburn University
GTE Corporation
Westport Temple Israel

Slides and prices on request

SHOWN: *Western Tori I: Sungate*

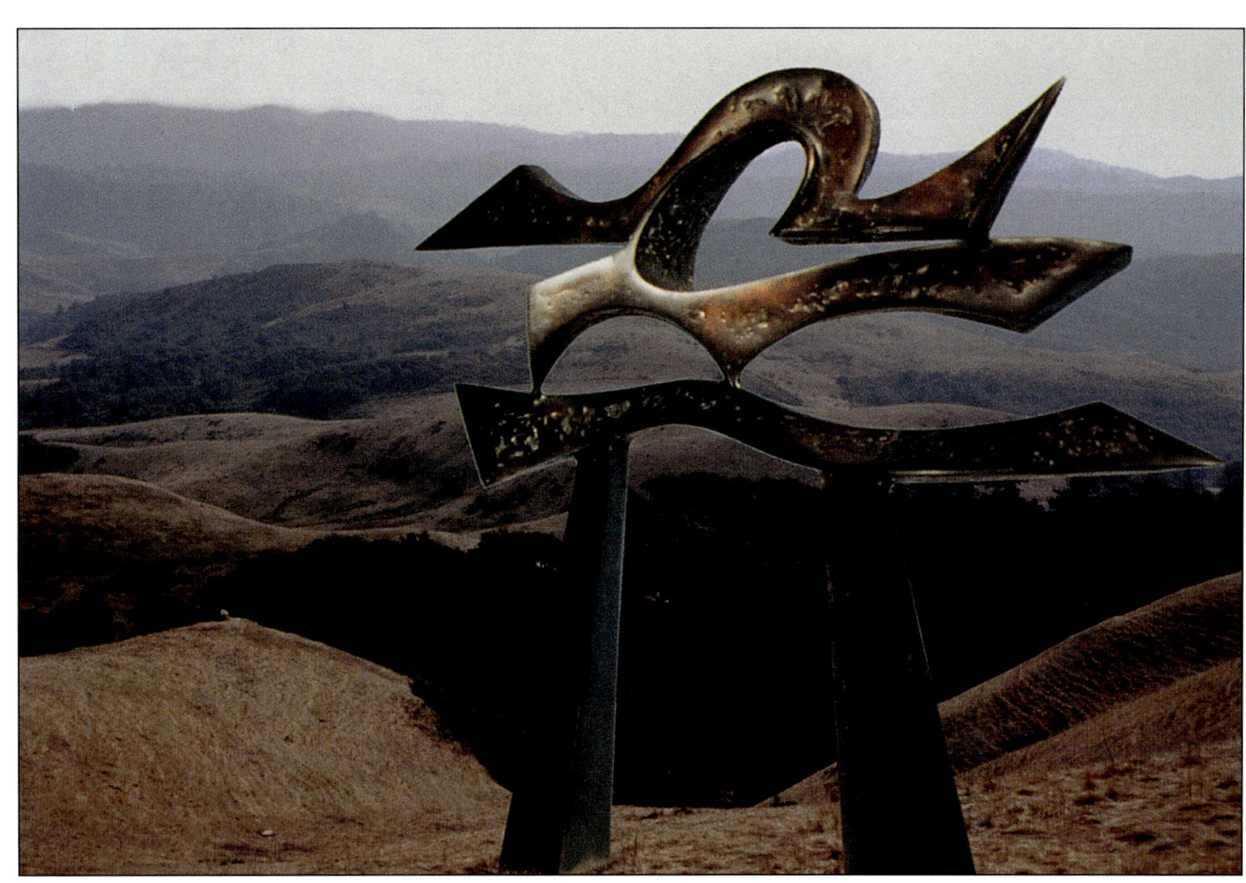

PUBLIC ART

William C. Culbertson

32 Warren Avenue
North Smithfield, RI 02896
FAX 401-766-6256
TEL 401-766-6256

As a sculptor and former corporate Director of Sculpture filling the needs of the toy industry, the artist brings to his fine art a commitment to quality in design and execution. He has extensive experience working with architects, engineers and designers, from initial concept to project completion. Having worked in a variety of media and styles, the artist can work successfully with clients to meet and exceed their sculptural needs.

Clients include:
Children's Television Workshop
The Walt Disney Company
Hasbro, Inc.
Tyco

A Spirit of Garland, 1994, Garland, TX, Granite Thoro System Granstone Finish, 30' x 4' x 4'

B Time Piece, 1994, Garland, TX, Granite Thoro System Granstone Finish, 20' x 4' x 4'

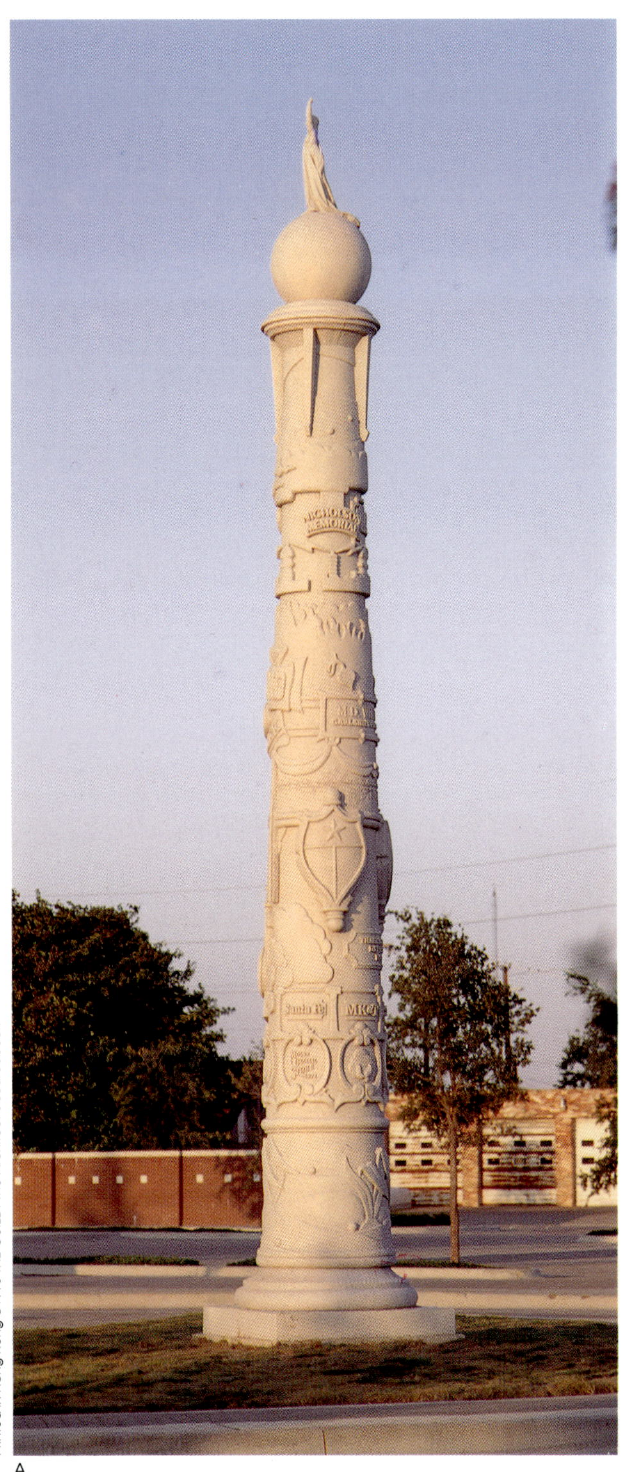

A

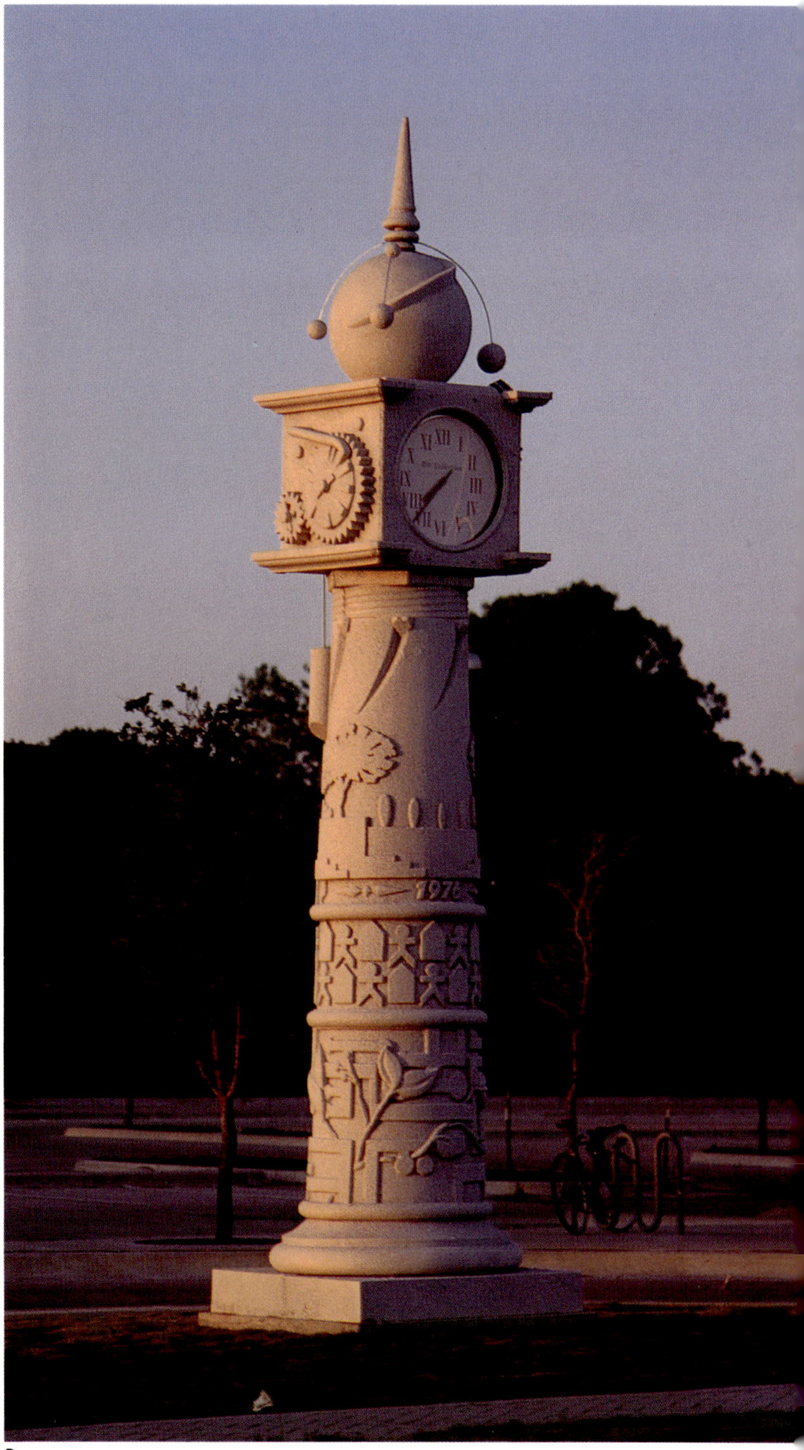

B

Kevin Earley

1231 E. Wilson Street
Madison, WI 53703
FAX 608-256-5171
TEL 608-256-5171

Kevin Earley has been designing furniture on commission since 1971, and still enjoys the challenge of balancing a design functionally and aesthetically, as well as meeting the goals of the individual project. His work is designed through discussions with the client, with models, samples and prototypes used to convey the final concept. Materials are chosen to mediate between the design and the architecture and construction is carried out to the standards of the finest furniture.

Also see these GUILD publications:
Designer's Edition: 6, 7, 8, 9

SHOWN: *Cumulonimbus, Mama,* 1994. Library Services desk, white oak, 4' x 30' x 11'; mosaic by James S. Watrous

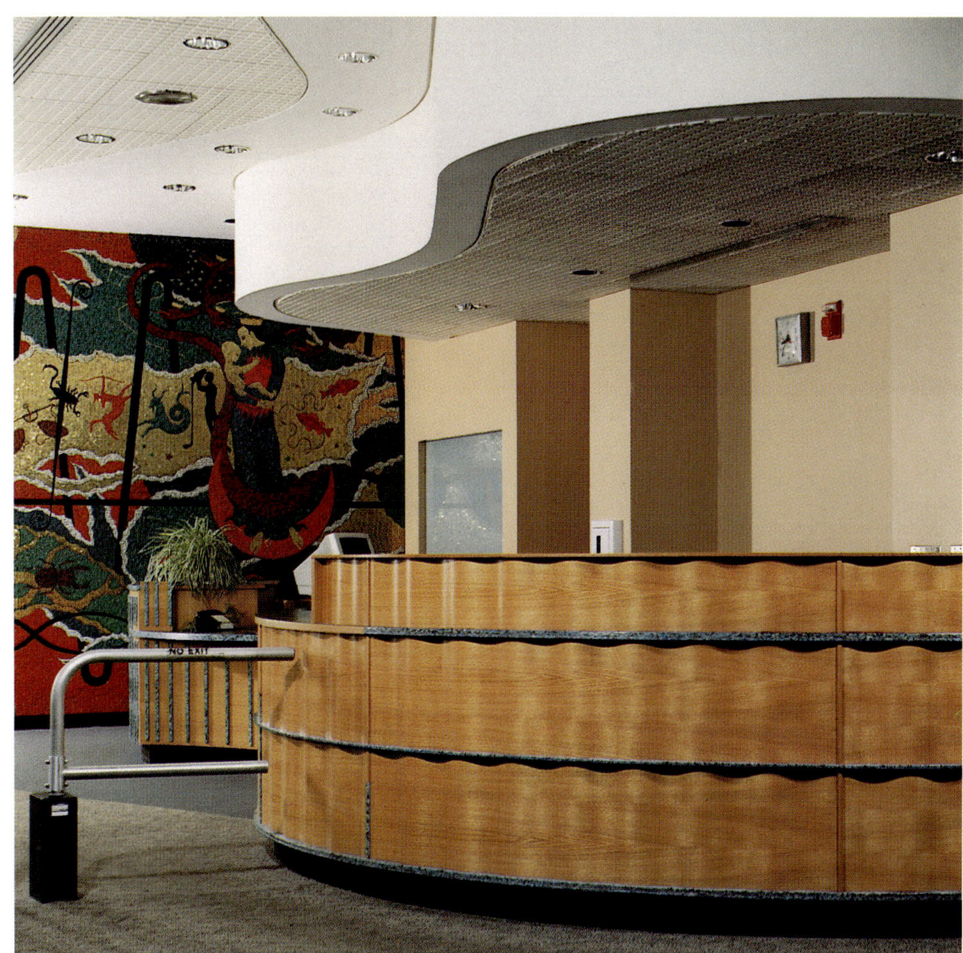

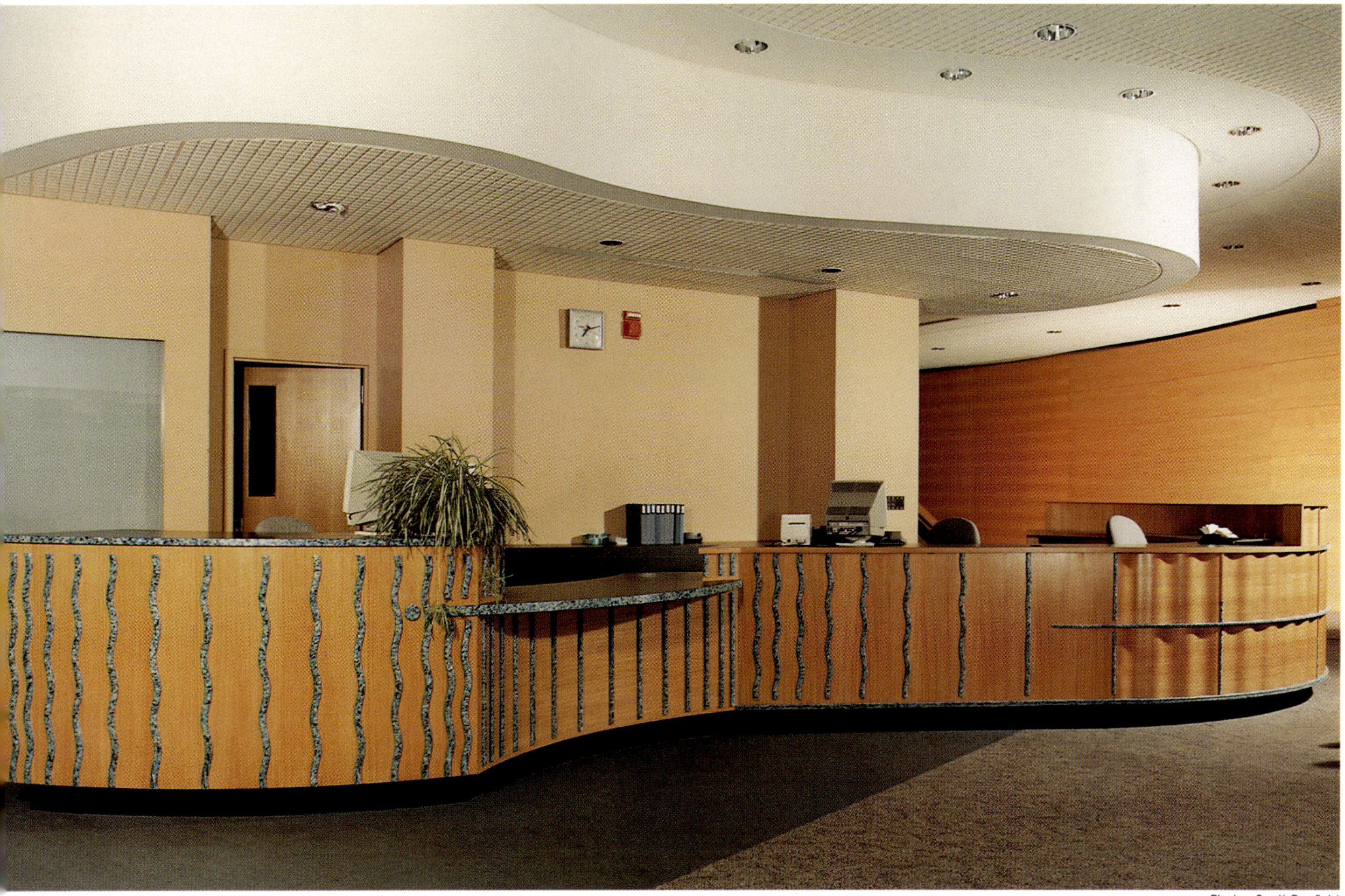

Photos: Scott Canfield

Blayney Foster

Foster Studio
PO Box 10
Morgan Hill, CA 95037
TEL 408-534-1322

Blayney Foster creates site-specific environments using natural phenomena to enhance the architectural qualities of a space. By incorporating shadows, light, time and distance, Foster draws in the viewer and encourages users to both enjoy and speculate about the space.

Foster uses materials appropriate to the space, often incorporating natural elements such as rock and wood.

SHOWN: *Central Park Cafe Patio Mural and Circular Windows*, 1994, Applied Materials, Inc., CA, 6'H x 80'W x 8"D

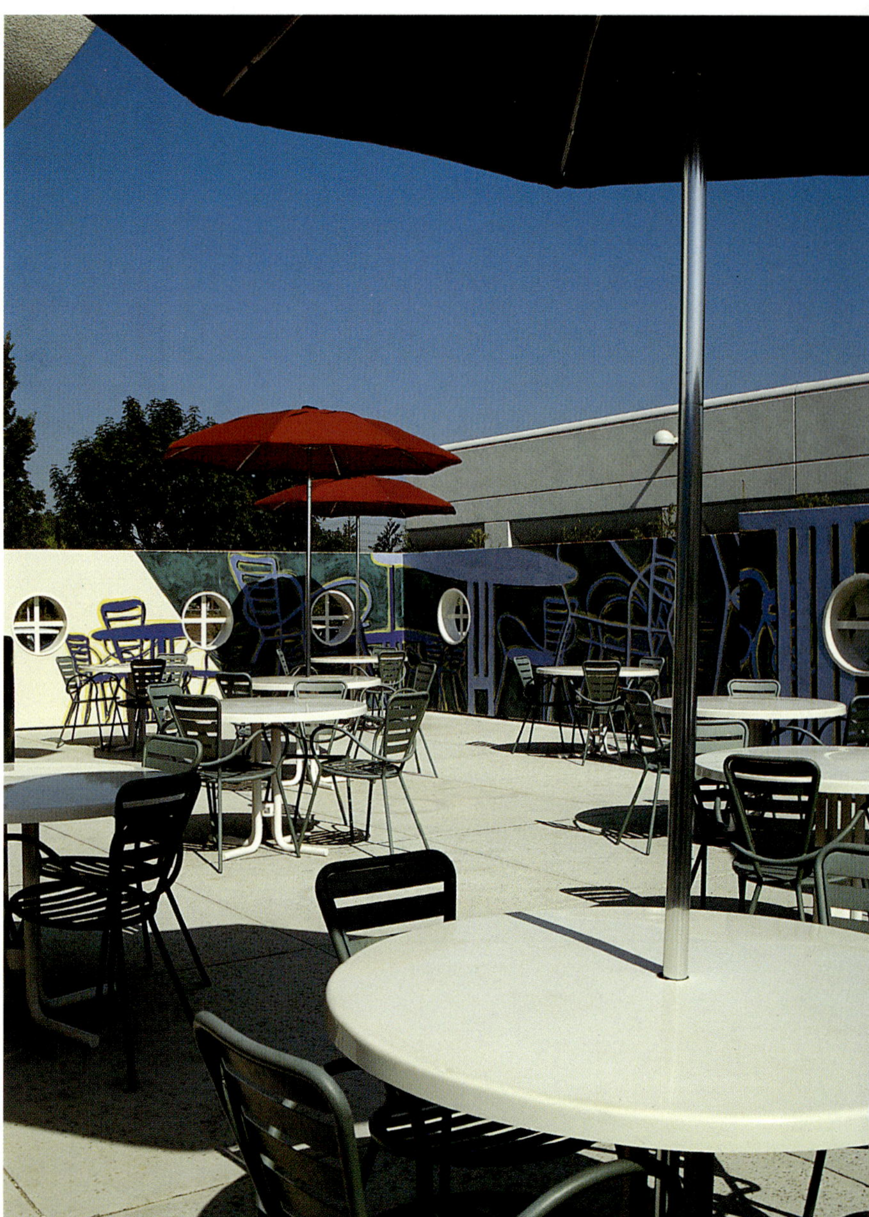

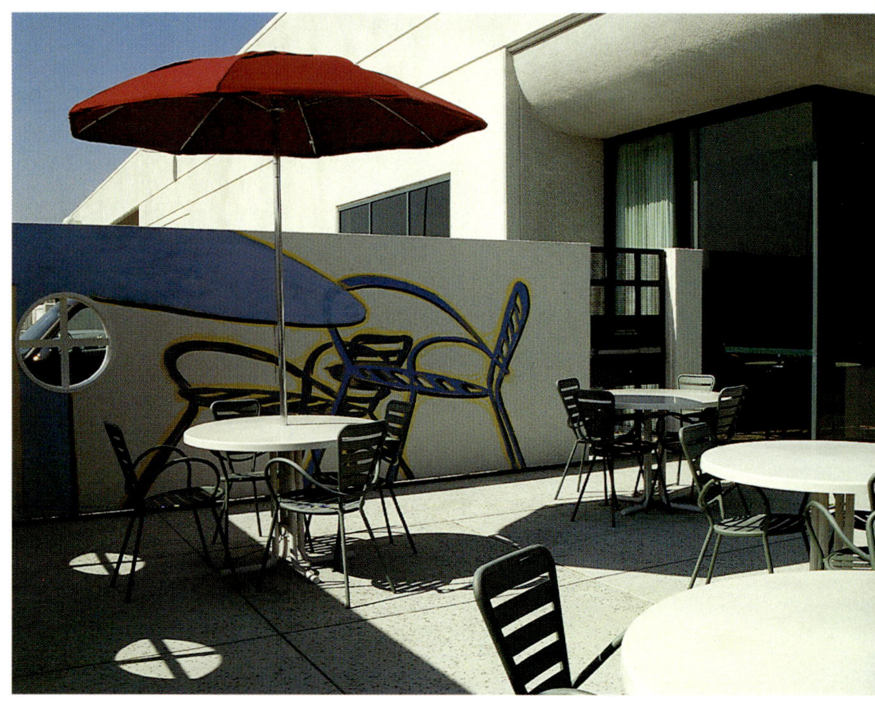

Dan George

195 North 5th Street
Brooklyn, NY 11211
FAX 718-388-2587
TEL 718-782-2409

Dan George brings 15 years of experience in site-specific installations to your project. His studio fabricates in all metals and installs the work under his personal supervision. These installations are highly durable and require little, if any, maintenance.

George has collaborated with architects, designers and public officials in developing plans for public art projects. He has served as a consultant to state arts councils and organizations and is available to discuss your planning or to serve on your design team for collaborative projects.

Commissions include:
Massachusetts Bay Transit Authority, Boston
Metropolitan Transit Authority, New York City
New Jersey State Department of Motor
    Vehicle Services
Bi-State Development Authority, St. Louis

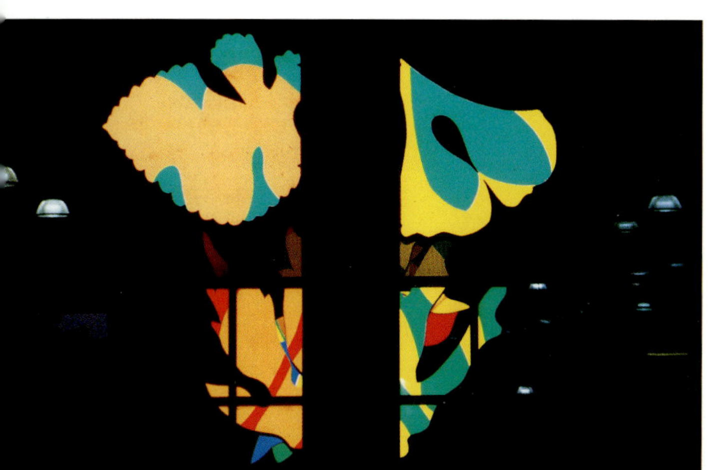

Transcendental Greens, 1991, MBTA, Boston, nine units, aluminum and reflective, 14' x 12' x 200'

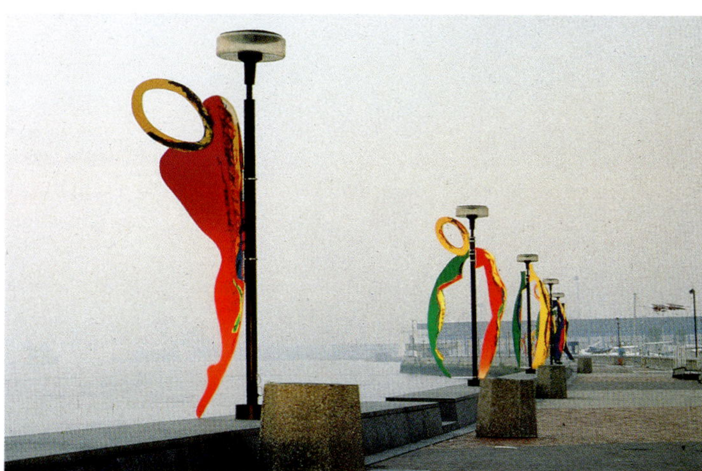

Chrysalis, 1985, Port of Philadelphia, 11 units, aluminum and color reflective, 12' x 6' x 250'

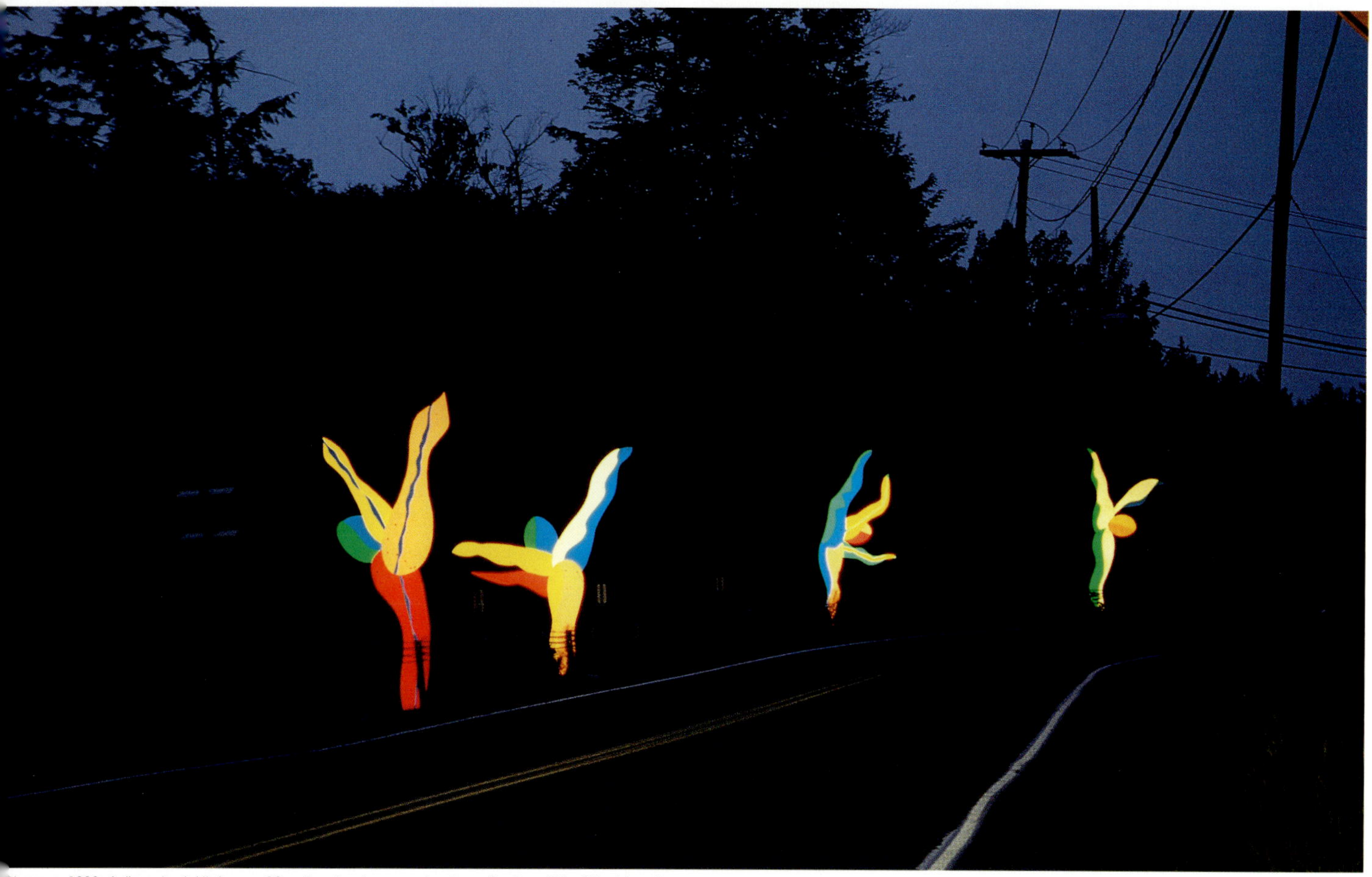

Riverrun, 1988, Adirondack Highway, 12 units, aluminum and color reflective, 12' x 28' x $^{1}/_{10}$ mile

CARY FERNANDEZ

Interior Designer

Designer Cary Fernandez believes the right original artwork can be the element that lifts a design from 'attractive' to truly exceptional. "I really believe the decision to use original art in a design can make or break a project," she says.

A designer with the Diane Joyce Design Group in Miami, Florida, she and 15 other architects and interior designers plan space for both corporate clients and individuals. "We do a great deal of design for the hospitality industry—hotels, resorts and restaurants, as well as high-end residential work," she explains. Her firm, she adds, is always seeking particularly unique and exciting design solutions for customers that include Disney and the Sandals Resorts located throughout the Caribbean.

A recent project that was especially successful used architectural glass designed by Kenneth vonRoenn of Architectural Glass Art, Inc. (AGA). Trained as an architect himself, and with a wealth of experience in creating and installing very significant architectural elements in major projects, vonRoenn has precisely the skills and creative sensibilities Fernandez was seeking when she began the design for a Japanese restaurant at the Sandals Resort in Antigua. "I couldn't find what I wanted from artists in our local area," she recalls, "so I turned to THE GUILD, and was immediately struck by Ken vonRoenn's work. I called him up and discussed what we had in mind via phone and FAX. The presentation we got from AGA was fantastic—and incredibly professional. The glass samples were unbelievably beautiful and exciting, and the photographs of his completed projects were thoroughly impressive.

"Ken created wood-framed glass screens for our space and they are very, very important elements in the architectural design. He was wonderful to work with from day one, and a real source of inspiration for our team. The restaurant is fabulous, the client is ecstatic and, needless to say, we're thrilled."

Photo by Elizabeth Cerejido

Lisa Kaslow

Lisa Kaslow, Inc.
2313-15 Essex Street
Baltimore, MD 21224
FAX 410-276-8330
TEL 410-276-3810

With 36 public art commissions completed since 1978, Lisa Kaslow's work projects community identity and architectural compatibility. She collaborates with architects, landscape architects and design teams. Kaslow designs site-specific environments for public agencies, developers and corporations. Her commissions include benches and seating, shelters and porticos, gazebos, pergolas, gateways and arbors. All works are fabricated from durable, low-maintenance materials such as coated structural steel, non-ferrous metals, fiberglass and concrete. Her work is collected by states, municipalities, corporations and institutions.

Clients include:
Amway Corporation, Peter Island Resort, B.V.I.
City of Baltimore
Bergen County Department of Parks and
    Recreation, NJ
Giant Food Stores, Washington, DC
Insignia Realty Co., Washington, DC
Michigan State University
Montgomery County Government, MD
North Carolina Arts Commission

A   *Imagination Arbor*, 1992, steel, coatings,
    10'H x 20'W x 10'D, collection of Michigan
    State University

B   *Harmony Gate,* 1994, steel, coatings, 13'H x 11'W,
    collection of Bergen County, NJ, Dept. of Parks

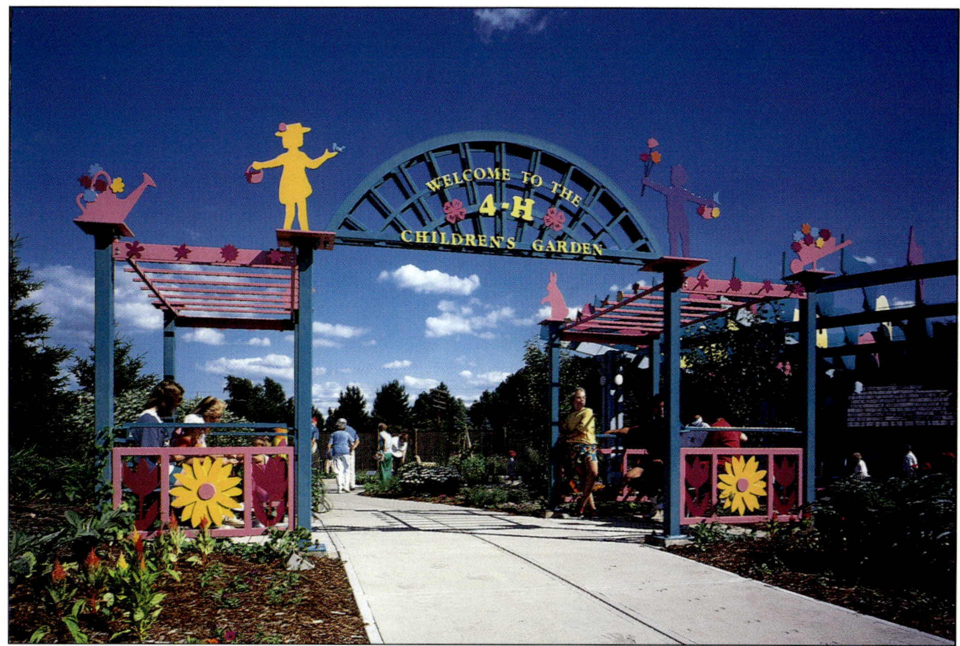

A
J.D. Small, Okemos, MI

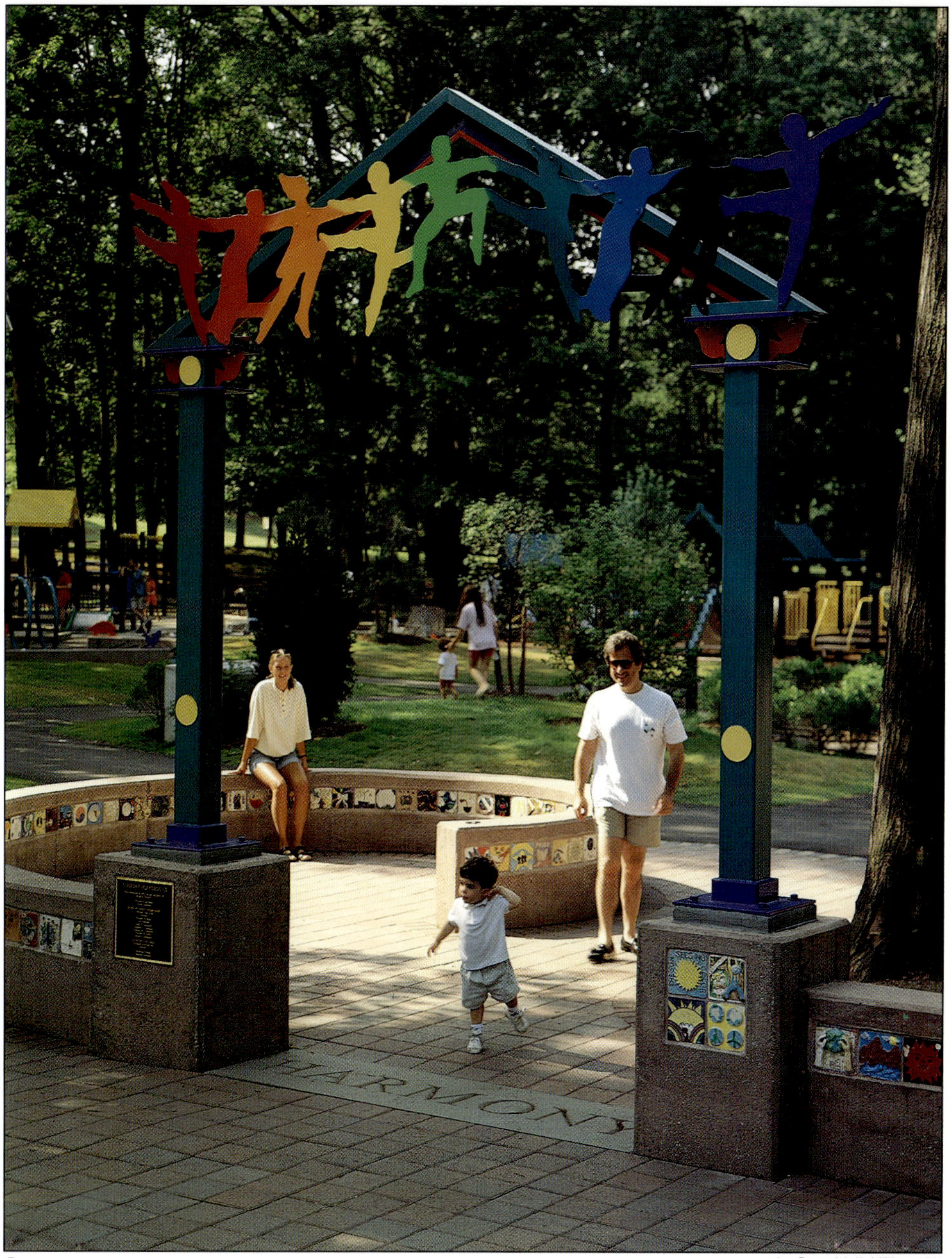

B
Jay Rosenblatt, Millburn, NJ

Rockne Krebs

1428 "U" Street NW
Washington, DC 20009
FAX 202-265-8045
TEL 202-265-4808

Rockne Krebs pioneered the use of the laser in art. He was granted a patent on the system he used to create the first 3D laser beam structures. He employed this system to create the first city-scale laser art works, and he produced the first work of art with a digital memory that created imagery based on laser scanning. Krebs found that he could create assemblages of light in the serendipity of the urban night, giving it a new order and context. In the course of creating works of art based on the urban environment, Krebs came to believe that bridges are often the cities' most interesting structures, and in the 1980s, began a series of neon bridges.

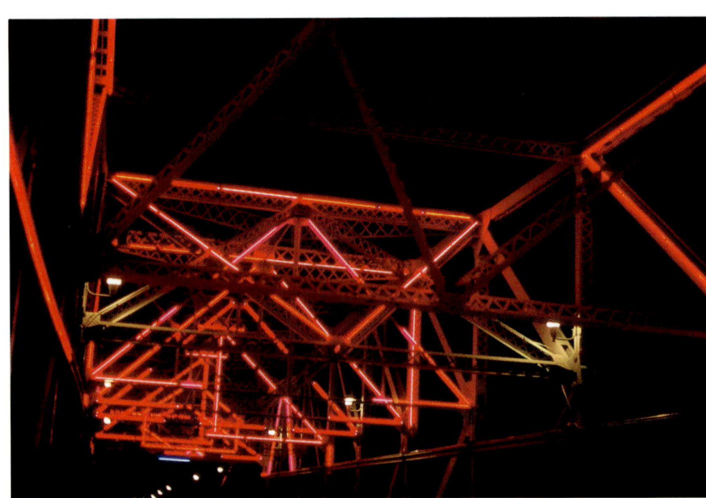

The Red River Bridge, 1993

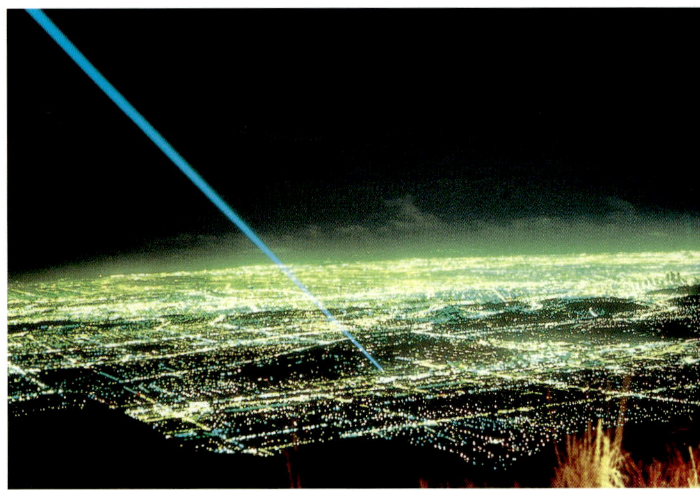

The Green Hypotenuse, 1983, Mt. Wilson to Caltech campus, laser and L.A. basin

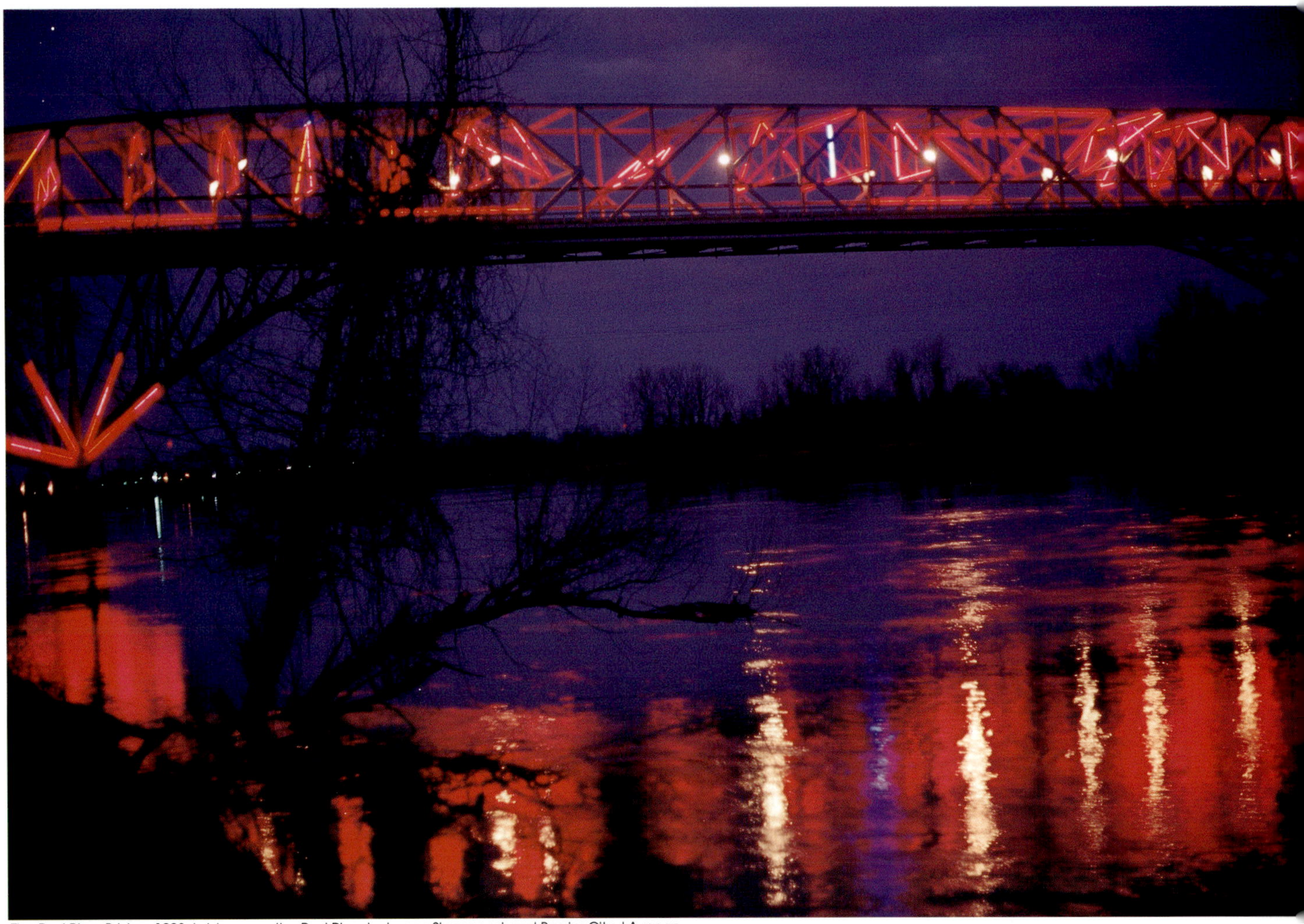

The Red River Bridge, 1993, bridge over the Red River between Shreveport and Bossier City, LA, neon

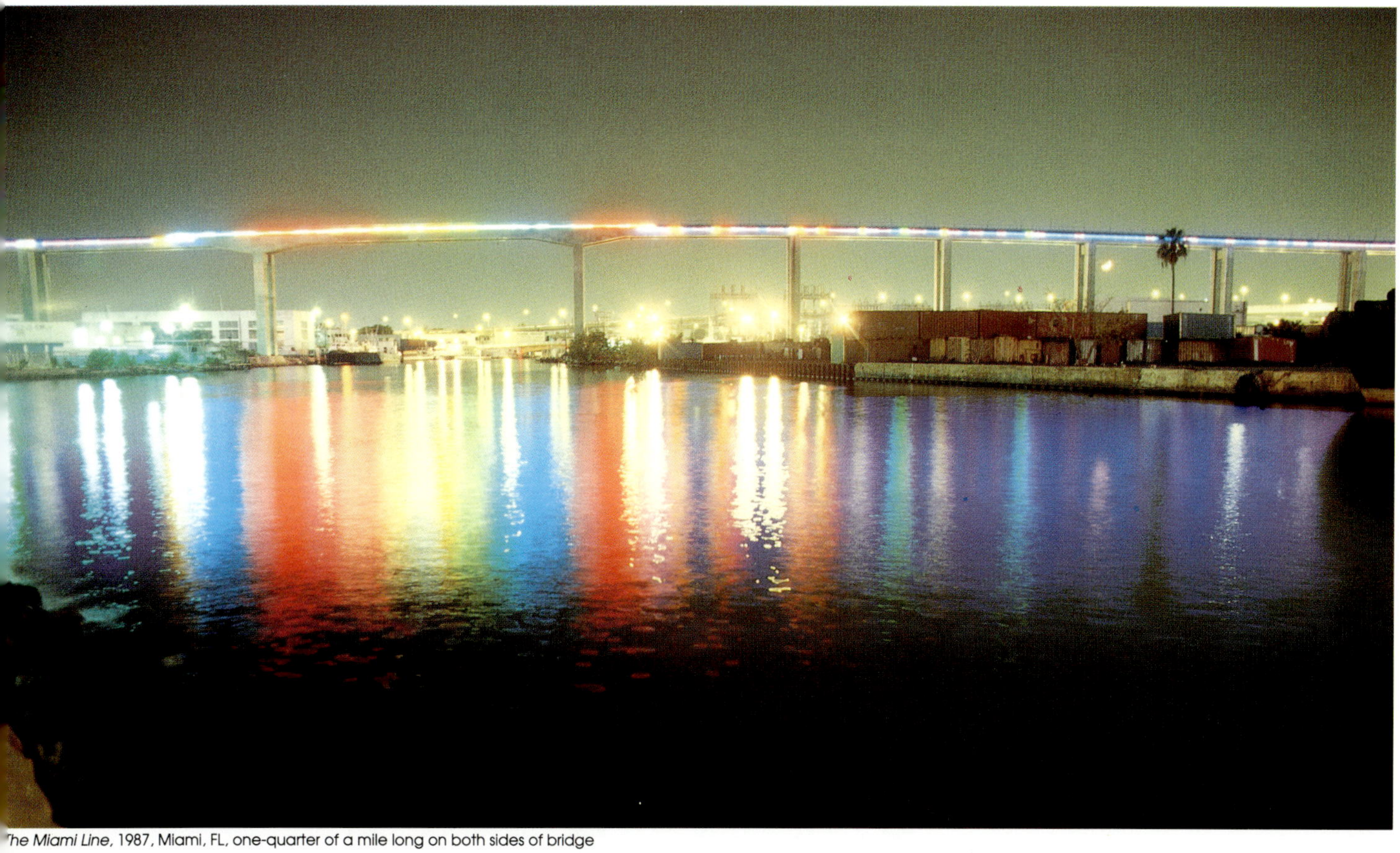

The Miami Line, 1987, Miami, FL, one-quarter of a mile long on both sides of bridge

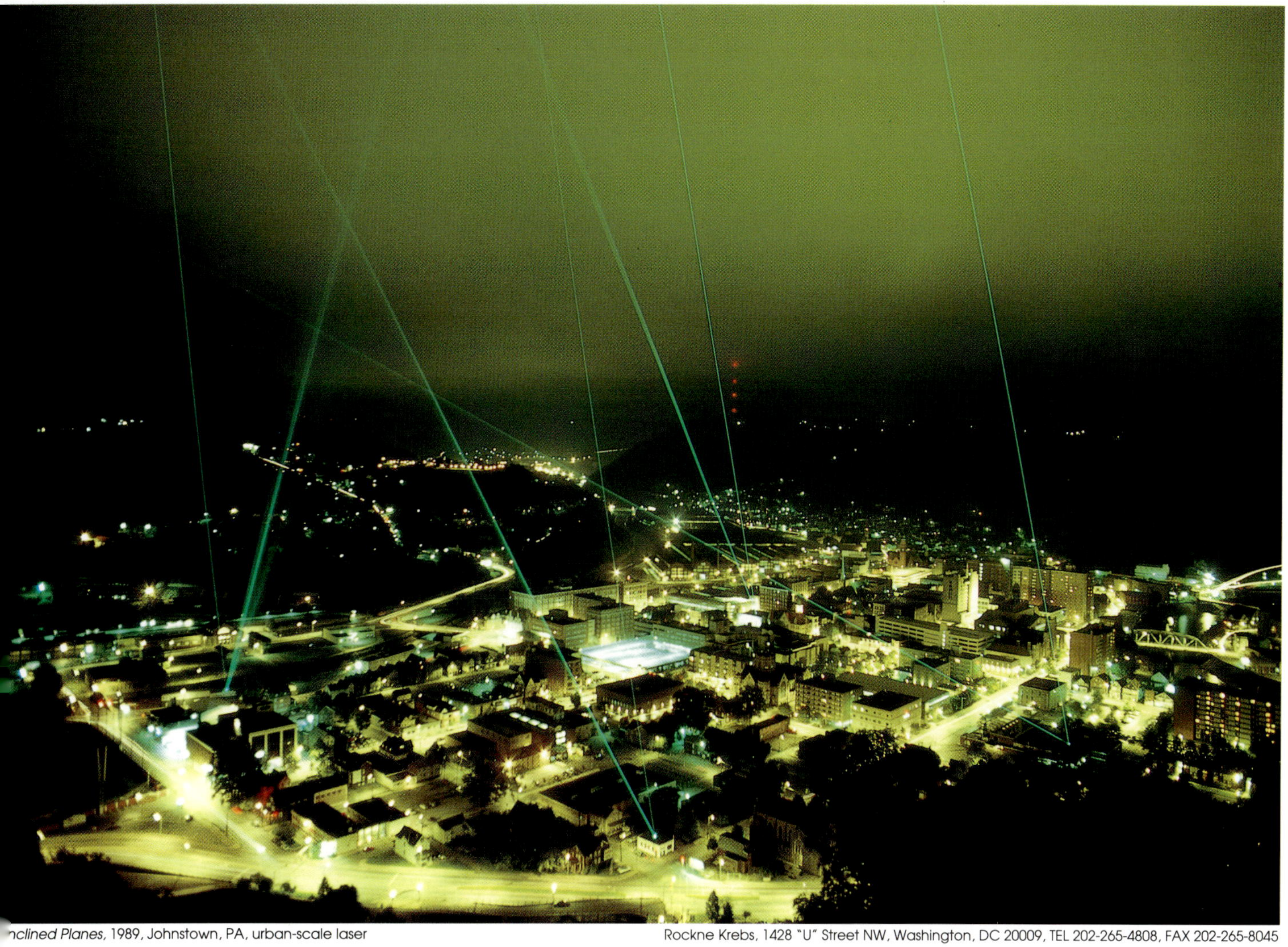

Inclined Planes, 1989, Johnstown, PA, urban-scale laser

Rockne Krebs, 1428 "U" Street NW, Washington, DC 20009, TEL 202-265-4808, FAX 202-265-8045

JIM CARLEY

Developer

Art in public spaces too often becomes a lightening rod for criticism and controversy. But when art is carefully integrated into a project, it can serve as a highly visible and very effective selling point. Such was the experience of Jim Carley, chair of the commission created to build an expanded exposition center for Dane County, Wisconsin. The space incorporates two works on a grand scale by artists found through THE GUILD.

For the large lobby and mezzanine area, artist Michele Oka Doner has created a terrazzo floor incorporating more than 1,000 bronze castings, each reflecting some aspect of the county's history. Cork Marcheschi's 600-linear-foot neon sculpture brings the center's lobby to life with an ever-changing sequence of moving lights.

Carley describes the process of working with both artists as "a wonderful experience. They are professionals in their art and our architects were thoroughly impressed." So, too, were prospective users of the meeting facility. One exhibitor was so excited by the work-in-progress that he actually made a significant contribution toward funding the art work. Another brought his stockholders together in the unfinished space for their annual meeting.

Naturally, this kind of enthusiasm and support is extremely satisfying to Carley, a strong supporter of the arts, both private and public.

For the Dane County project, a selection committee sifted through a list of more than 200 artists. Nine finalists were asked to submit site-specific proposals, for which they were paid. Carley believes that having a knowledgeable selection committee and a rigorous selection process greatly aided public support for the work. Despite the scale and the highly visible nature of the art, there has been only enthusiastic support from county officials, exhibitors and the public.

Carley's advice to other developers is to build broad support for art early on and to choose work that fits the project. "If appropriate art is chosen," he says, "it can't help but sell the building."

Artwork by Jerome Ferretti

Ulrika Leander

Contemporary Tapestry Weaving
107 Westoverlook Drive
Oak Ridge, TN 37830
FAX 423-483-7911
TEL 423-482-6849

Ulrika Leander has established a reputation for superb craftsmanship and a remarkable range of creative and imaginative designs. With 25 years of experience in this field, Leander has installed more than 150 tapestries commissioned for public, commercial and private settings in the United States and her native Scandinavia. Using 100% natural fibers, she produces single pieces measuring up to 12 feet by 30 feet.

Additional information upon request.

Also see these GUILD publications:
Designer's Edition: 8, 9, 10

A *On Duty—Our Bounty*, 1988, University of Tennessee College of Veterinary Medicine, Knoxville, TN, 12' x 30'

B *Healing Flight*, 1994, St. Michael Hospital, Texarkana, TX, 5' x 12'

C *Skyline*, 1989, private collection, New York, NY, 1' x 8'

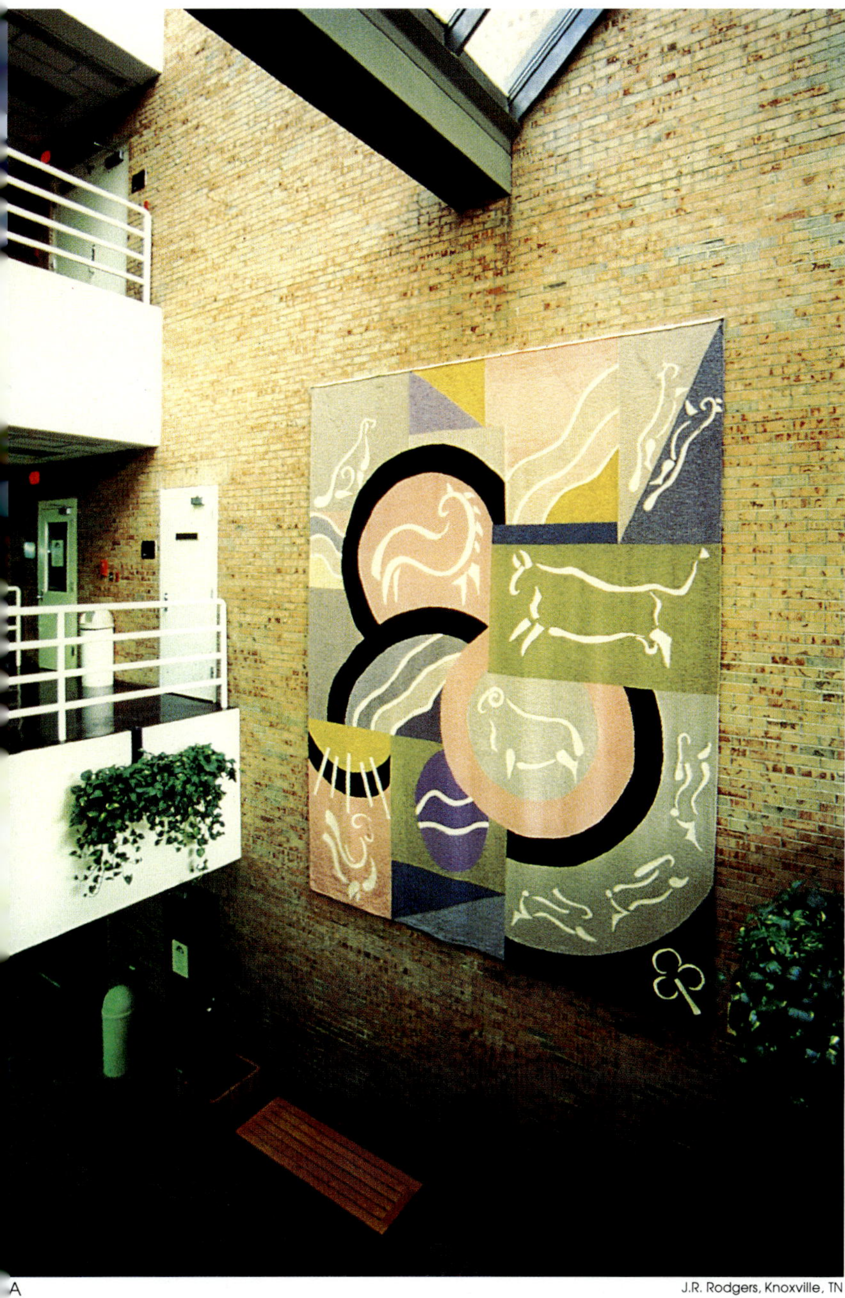

A
J.R. Rodgers, Knoxville, TN

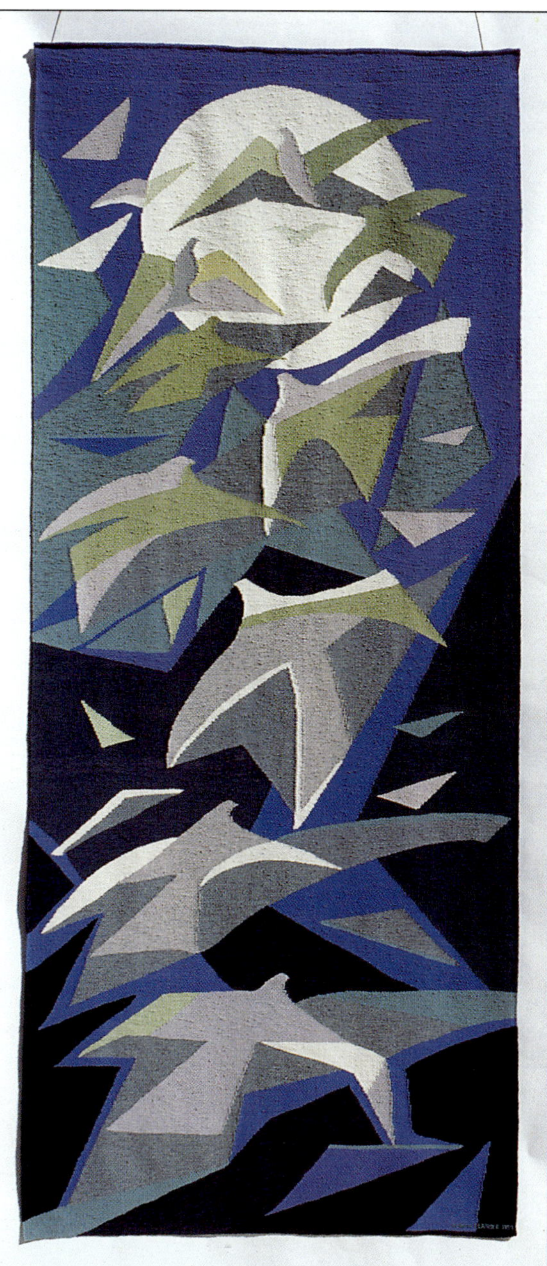

B
J.W. Nave

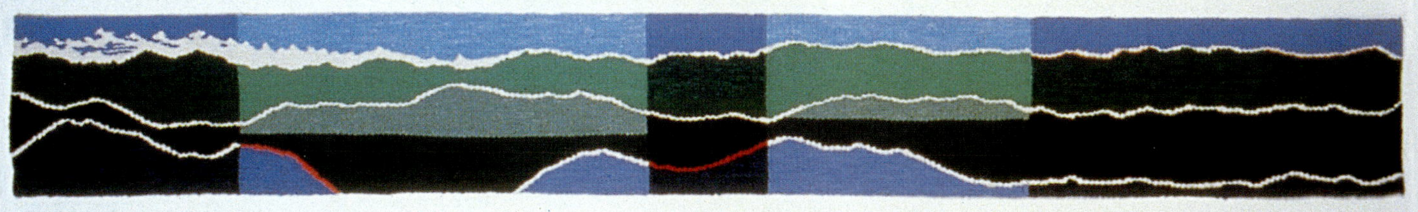

C
J.W. Nave

Joyce P. Lopez

Joyce Lopez Studio
1147 W. Ohio Street #304
Chicago, IL 60622-5874
FAX 312-243-5033
TEL 312-243-5033

Joyce P. Lopez has successfully collaborated with architects, designers and consultants for over 18 years on corporate and private commissions. Her work is included in the collections of Sony of America, Michael Reese Hospital, State of Washington, State of Illinois, Bank of America, etc.

Lopez's sculptures, made from steel tubes hand wrapped with vibrantly colored thread chosen from a palette of over 350 colors, are easily maintained and are Scotch-Guarded for protection.

Prices start at $3,000. Call or FAX for a brochure.

Also see these GUILD editions:
THE GUILD: 1, 2, 3, 4, 5
Designer's Edition: 6, 7, 8, 9, 10

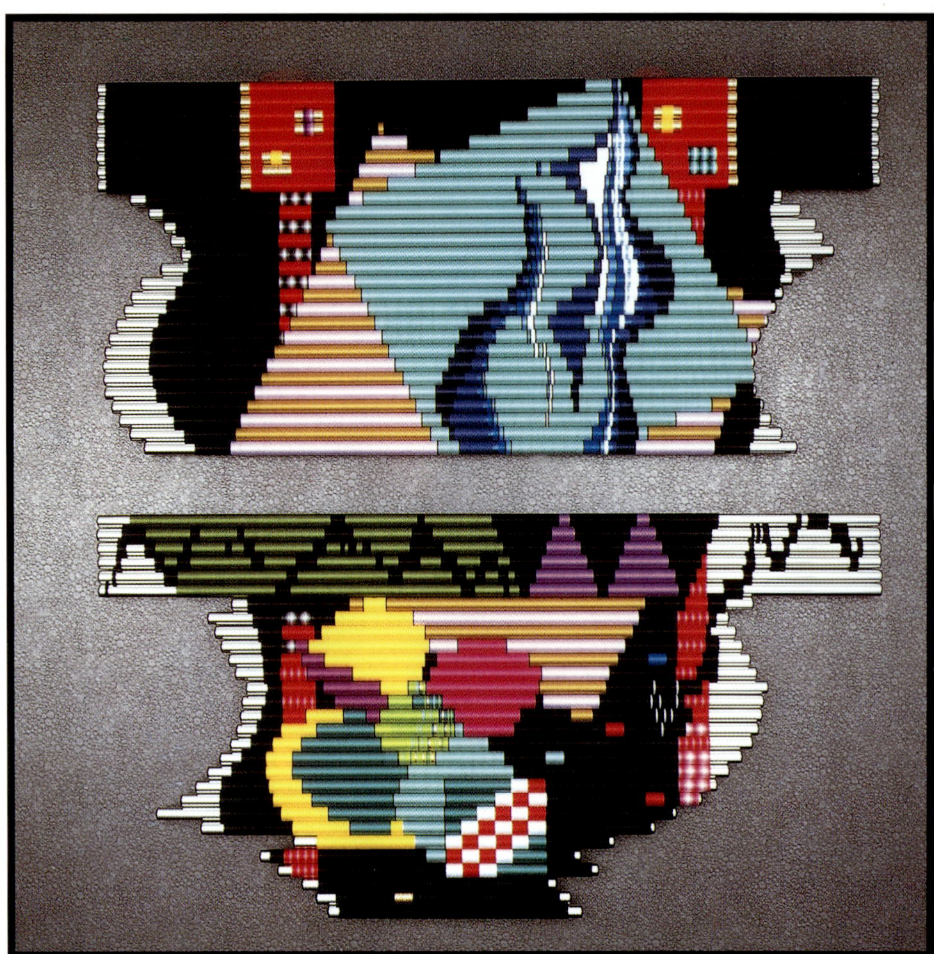

Pearl River Gardens, steel and thread sculpture, 48" x 46" x 2"

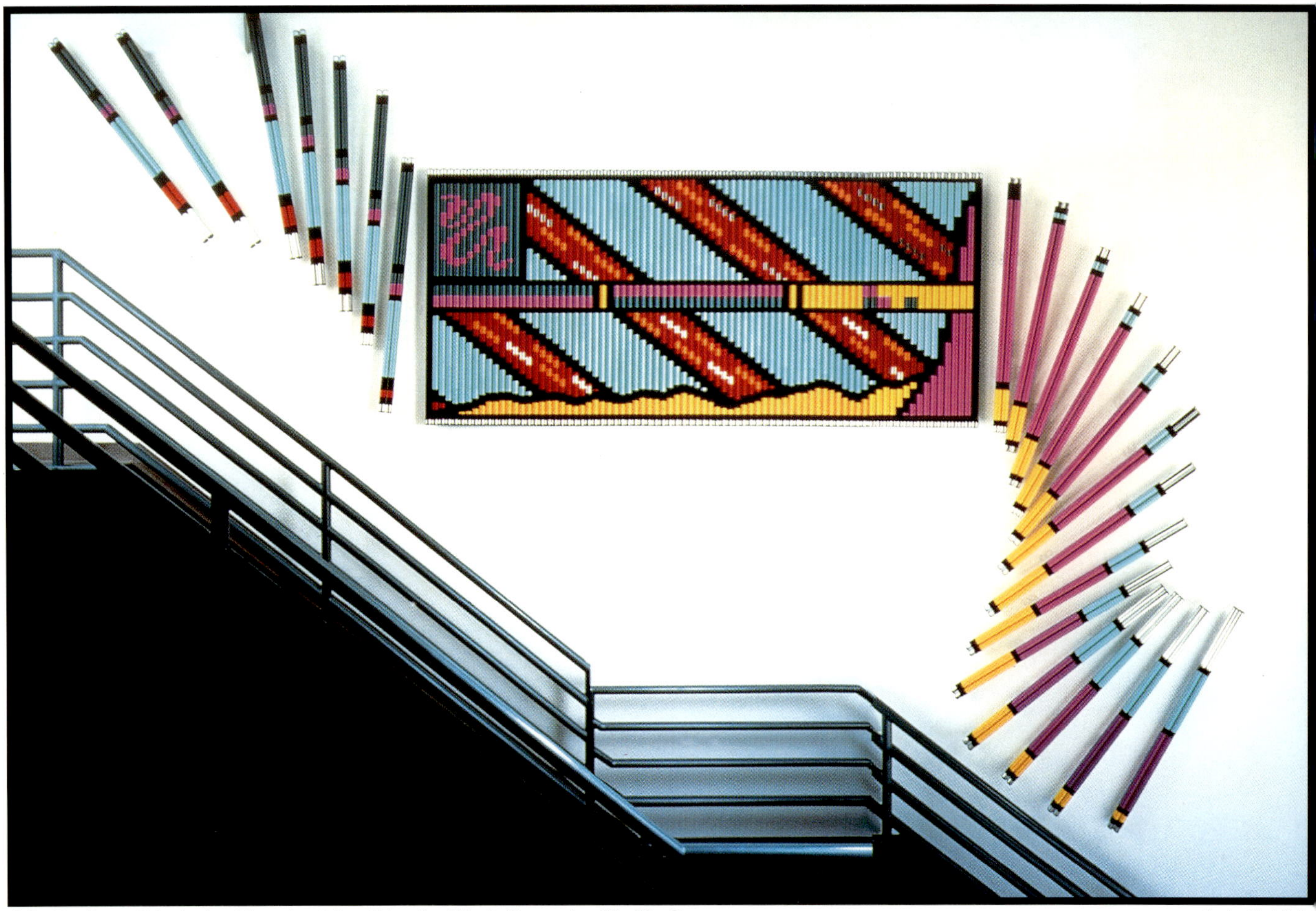

A Pre/Cautionary Tale, steel and thread sculpture, University of Illinois, Champaign, 20' x 30' x 2"

Photos: Mark Belter

Cork Marcheschi

192 Connecticut Street
San Francisco, CA 94107
FAX 415-621-2096
TEL 415-621-3981

Over the past 28 years, Cork Marcheschi has created a number of large- and small-scale works for public, as well as private, collections throughout the world. Cork's sculptures are often internally illuminated and gently animated with the use of neon tubing and custom fade units. Other materials, such as aluminum and plastic, give the work a daytime as well as nighttime, presence.

Price range is from $20,000 to $500,000.

A *Please Lose My Suitcase Full of Blues*, 1994, Ft. Lauderdale Airport, FL, 6' x 400' x 3'

B *Too Many Notes*, 1993, Victoria Peak, Hong Kong, 20' x 36' x 11'

C *Return to Grovers Mill*, 1994, Rowen College, NJ, 18' x 18' x 18' x 16'

D *Iowa Cycle*, 1994, University of Northern Iowa, Cedar Rapids, 60" x 40" x 20'

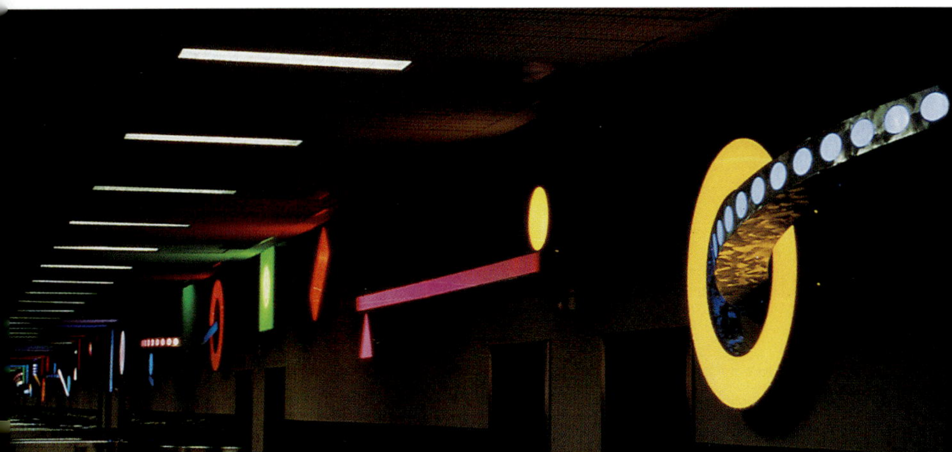

A

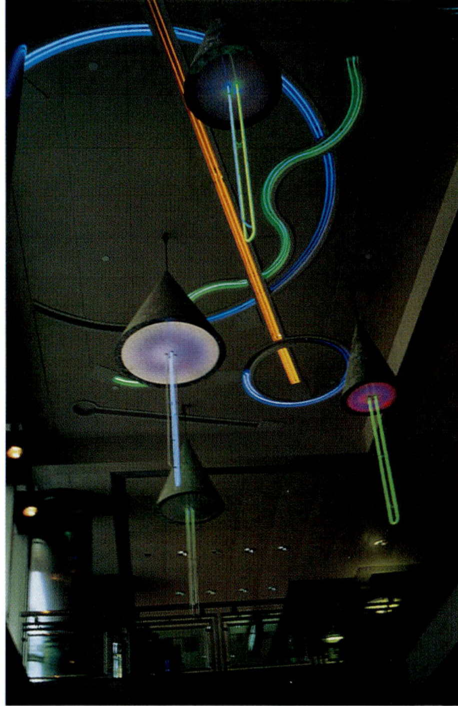

B

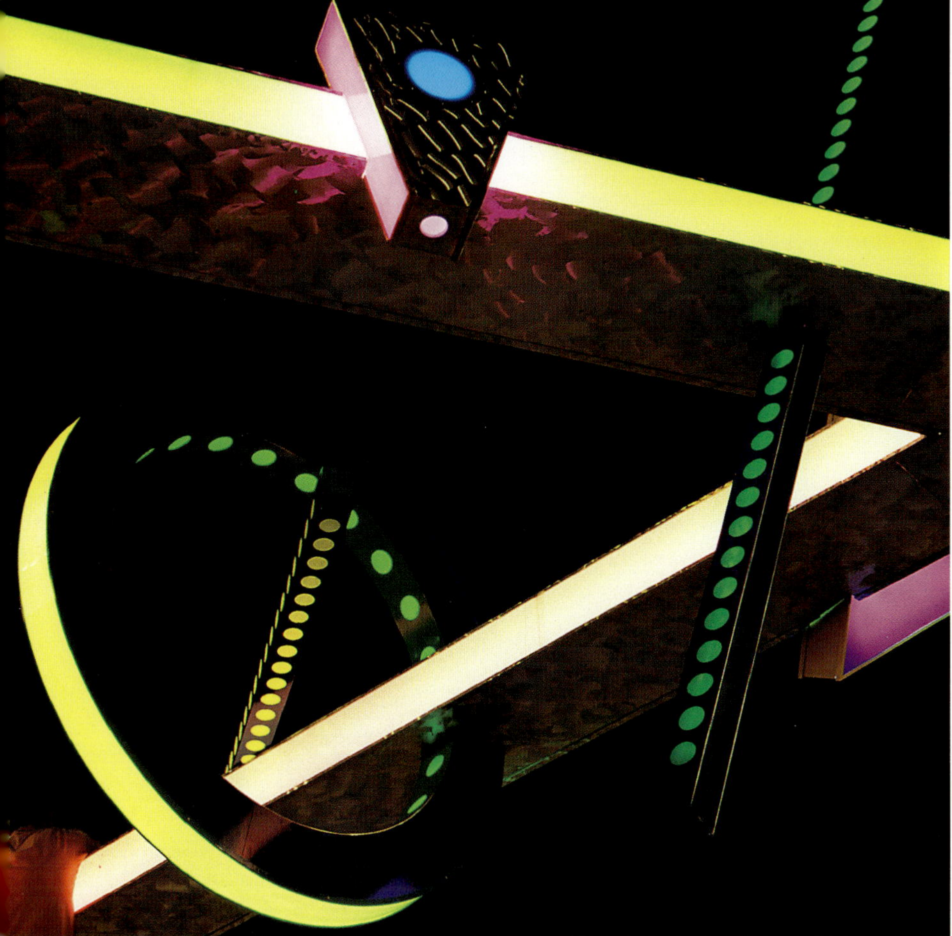

C

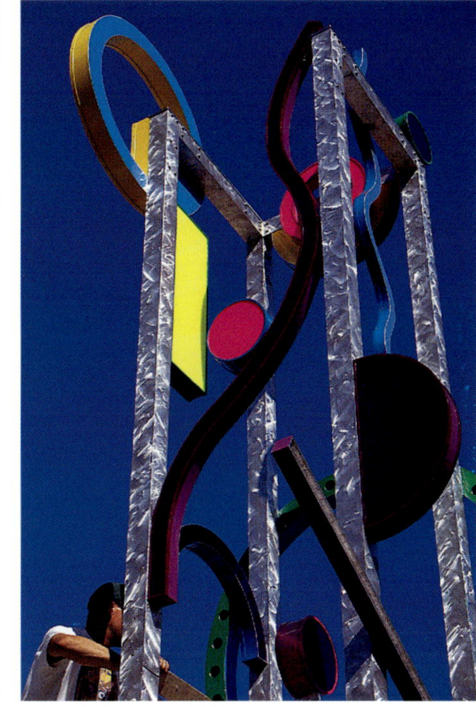

D

Howard Meehan
Kathleen Meehan

Firefly Studio
2511 NW Upshur
Portland, OR 97210
TEL 503-274-0865

Howard and Kathleen Meehan conduct extensive research for each project, focusing on site relevance, history, geology, topography, and architecture. Materials vary depending upon project site and need.

Experience includes 14 public art projects and numerous corporate commissions, always completed within budget and on time.

The artists are accustomed to working with architects, structural engineers, facilities people, and committees, and welcome the opportunity to share ideas and information.

Also see these GUILD publications:
Architect's Edition: 7, 8, 9, 10

A & B *Shade Sculpture*, inspired by Cahuilla Indian basketry, Civic Center Rose Garden, Palm Desert CA, 28' x 12'. Phase II will include seating, trash receptacles and mosaic paths etched with rose poetry.

C & D *Voices of the Columbia*, Clark College, Vancouver, WA, 8' x 9' x 10', glass, aluminum, brass, and copper. Design inspired by the people who have lived along the Columbia River.

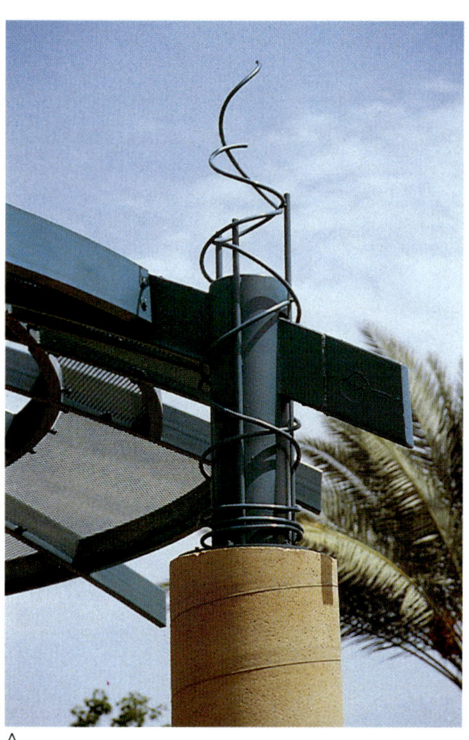

A

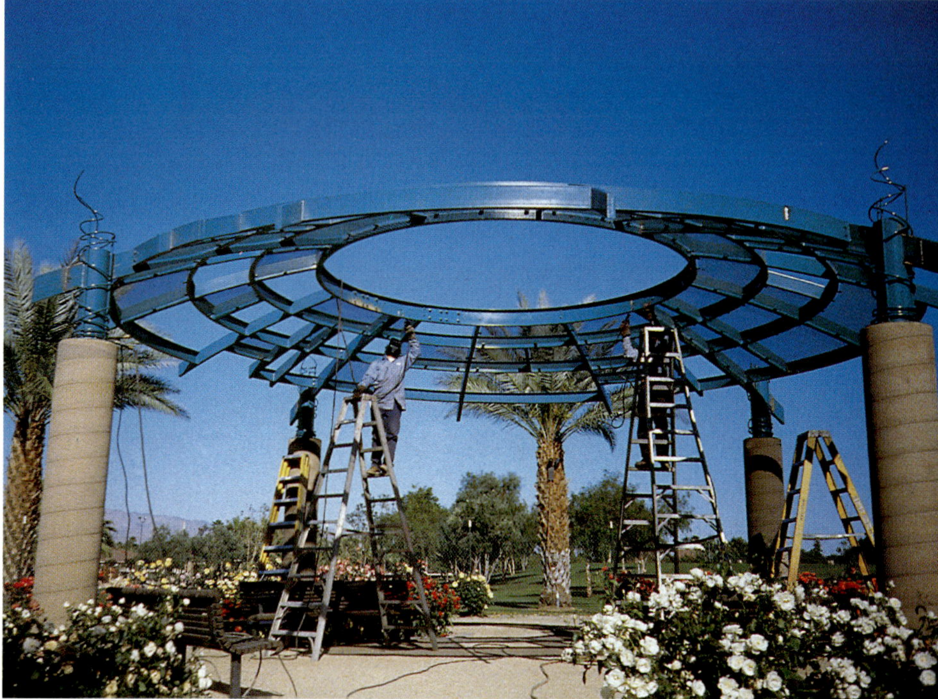

B

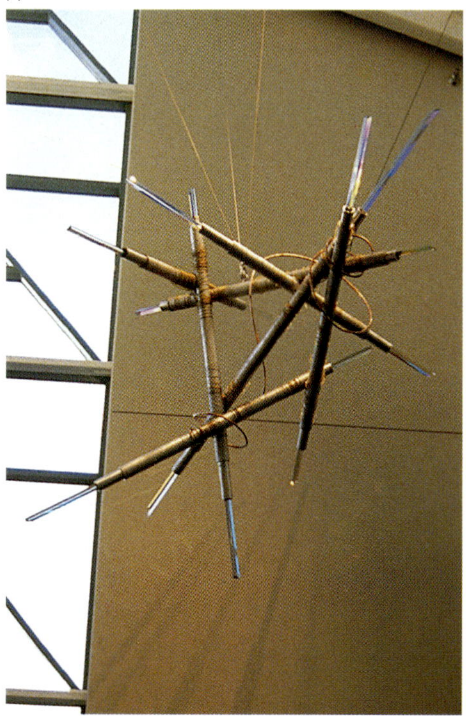

C

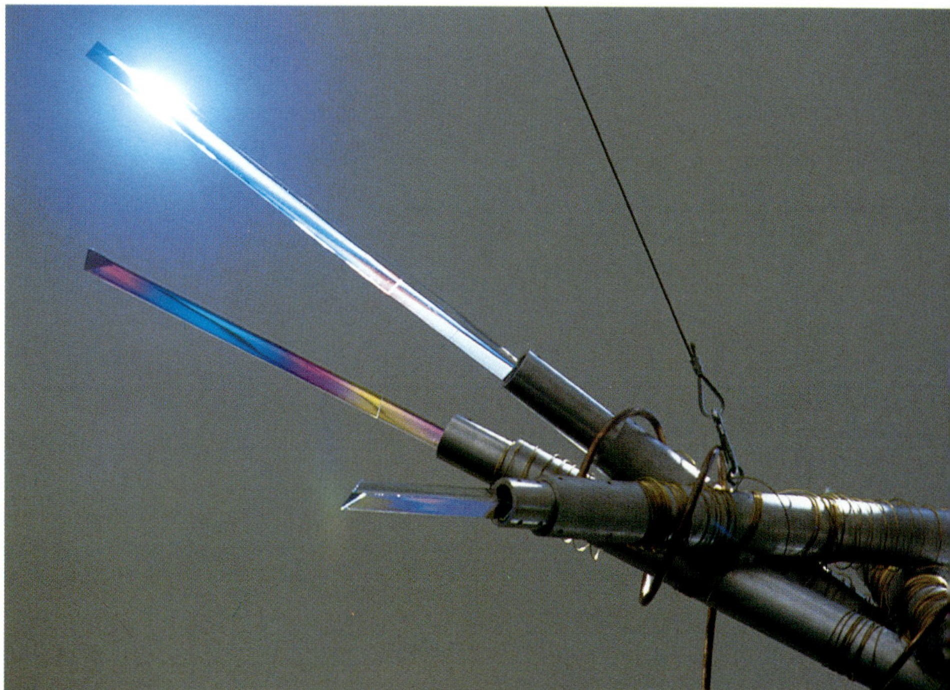

D

Konried Muench

2222 E Hawthorne Street
Tucson, AZ 85719
TEL 520-325-6767

Human- to monumental-scale, site-sensitive
sculpture from proposal to unveiling. Emphasis
is placed on positive client/community interest
and understanding.

B.F.A., School of the Art Institute, Chicago;
M.F.A., University of Arizona. The artist has
completed four major public works.

For additional photographs, information, or
portfolio review, call or write above number
or address for a prompt reply.

All sculpture © Konried Muench, 1995.

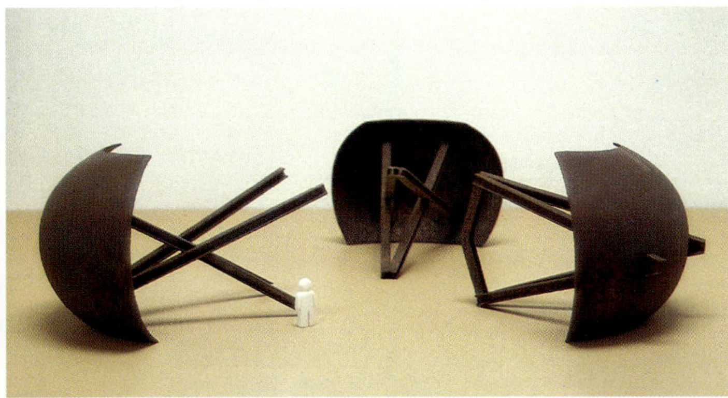

Water Tower Project, 1985, proposal, bronze

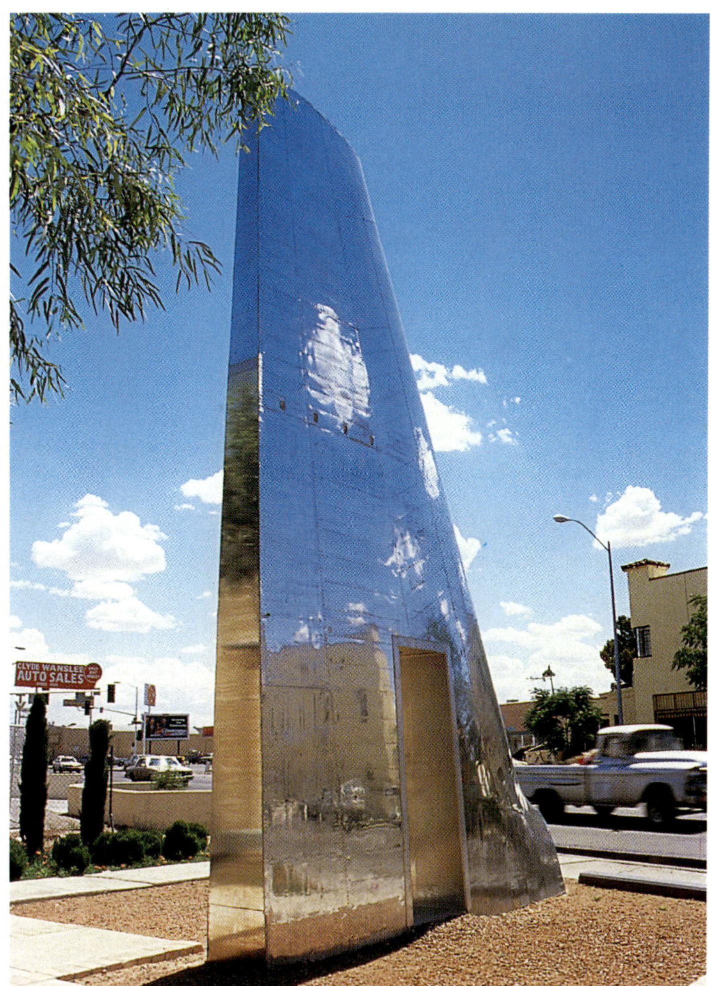

Vertical Wing w/Doorway, 1988-89, aluminum, cement, steel, 16' x 15' x 3'

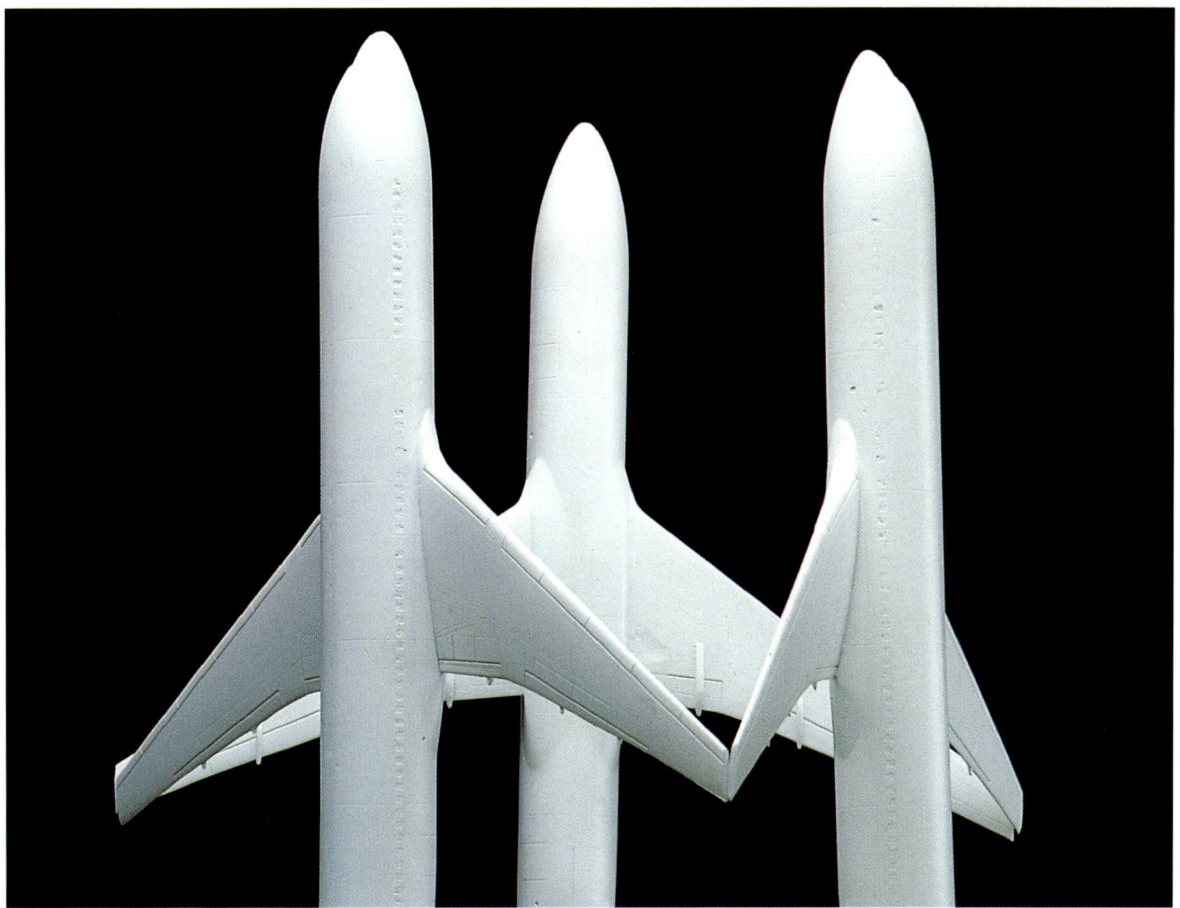

Three Graces, proposal, 1992, project for 707's

Mary Findyz Studios

Juan Navarrete
Patricia Navarrete

Navarrete Studio
PO Box 2251
Taos, NM 87571
TEL 505-776-2942

Since 1980, the Navarretes, sculptors in varied mediums, have drawn national acclaim for their diverse approach to the integration of bas-relief with architectural environments. The Navarrete Studio is recognized for its innovative application of new technologies and traditional techniques in expanding the application of plasters, cements, concrete and synthetics that respond to new solutions for technical problems of specific projects.

Research into history of the location becomes a source of inspiration, resulting in work unique to its environment. The petroglyph symbols (see below) give reference to the adjacent mountain range and petroglyphs of the area.

Each symbol is associated with a distinct building and has become a component to the signage system. With their commitment to excellence throughout all phases of this public venture, the Navarretes, as part of the design team, created a unifying visual aesthetic that was integrated with the entire project.

Clients include:
Carlsbad Department of Labor, Carlsbad, NM
Los Lunas Senior Center, Los Lunas, NM
Central Avenue Beautification Project, Phoenix, AZ
Embassy Suites Resort, Maui, HI
Coyote Cafe, Santa Fe, NM
Salt River Project, Phoenix, AZ

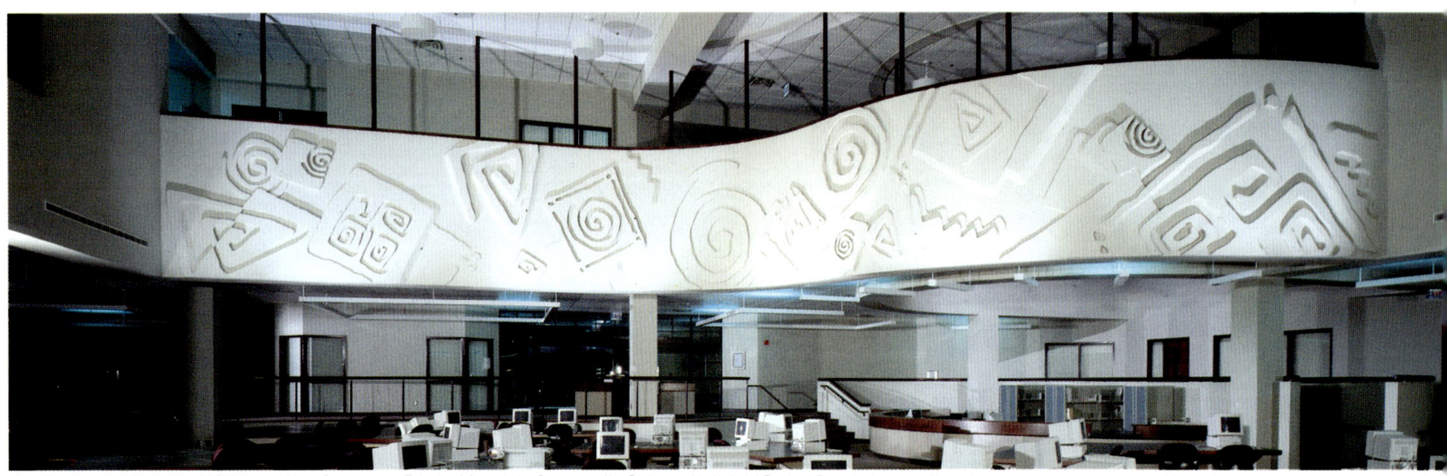

The Continuous Source, 1992, Information Commons, Estrella Mountain Community College, Licthfield Park, AZ, polystyrene, fiberglass mesh, acrylic stucco, 10'H x 76'W x 3"D

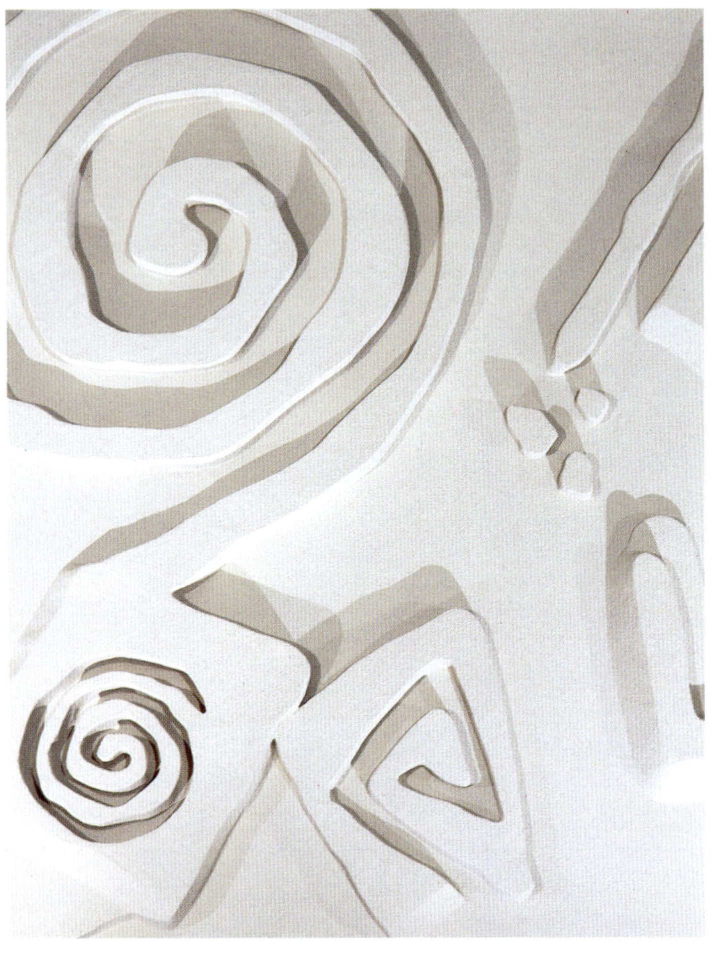

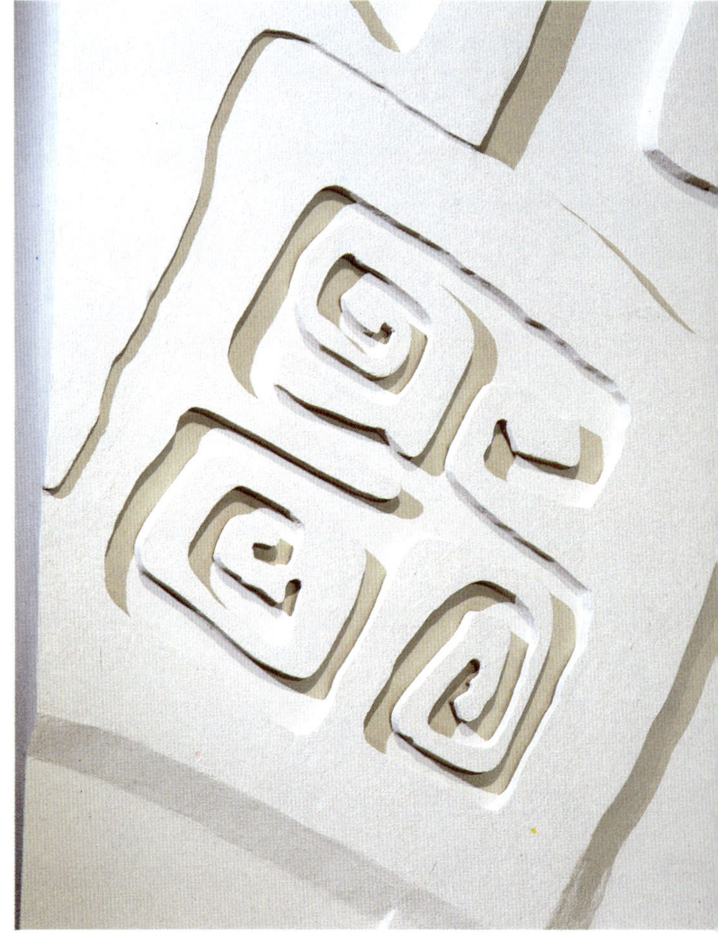

Fluffy Palmer

638 Kater Street
Philadelphia, PA 19147
TEL 215-928-1313

Palmer's LIGHTSCAPES capture a feeling of daylight and space, and are of particular value in light-deprived areas. Her public art in Fairbanks, Alaska, has 'brought sparkle to our lives and made our winter seem shorter,' as shown below.

The artist works with architects, planners and engineers to design site-specific pieces incorporating painting, lighting, glass blocks and other diverse materials. LIGHTSCAPES can be created for healthcare facilities, corporate spaces, or homes, to provide a heightened illusion of daylight and nature. Works shown range from 42" x 54" to 9' x 16'.

Clients include:
Environmental Compliance Services
Rhone Poulenc Rorer Intl. Headquarters
Chagai-Upjohn
E.I. DuPont de Nemours
Unisys Corporation
Hunt Manufacturing Co.

'What a pleasure it is to gaze at one of Fluffy Palmer's LIGHTSCAPES on a dreary winter day. Highly recommended.'

Norman Rosenthal, MD
National Institute of Mental Health

'Palmer's work gives us the feeling of outdoors in our lobby and in the middle of winter it is a great release.'

Theodore Fuller, President
Johnson & Higgens, PA

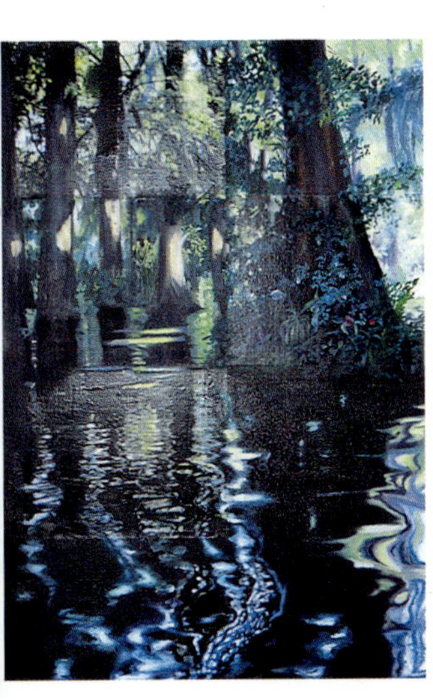
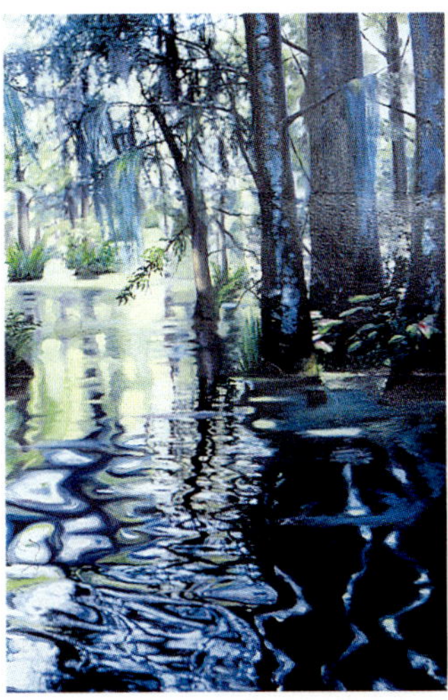
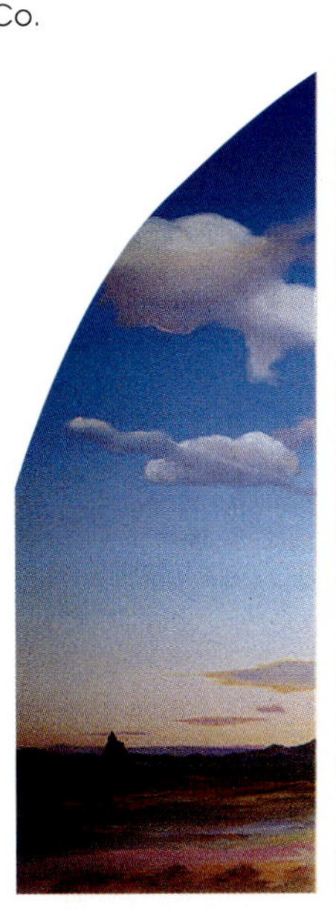
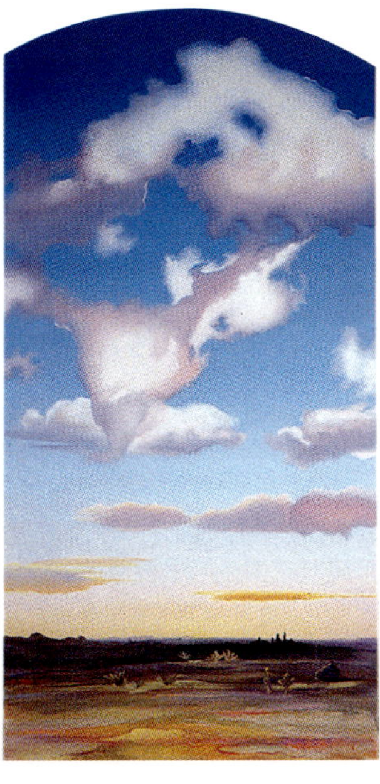
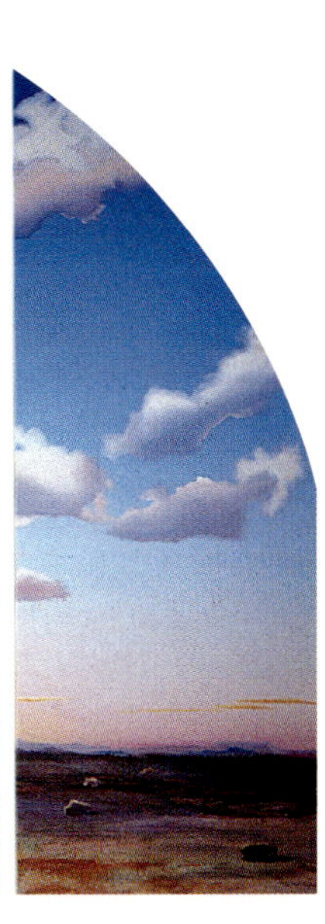

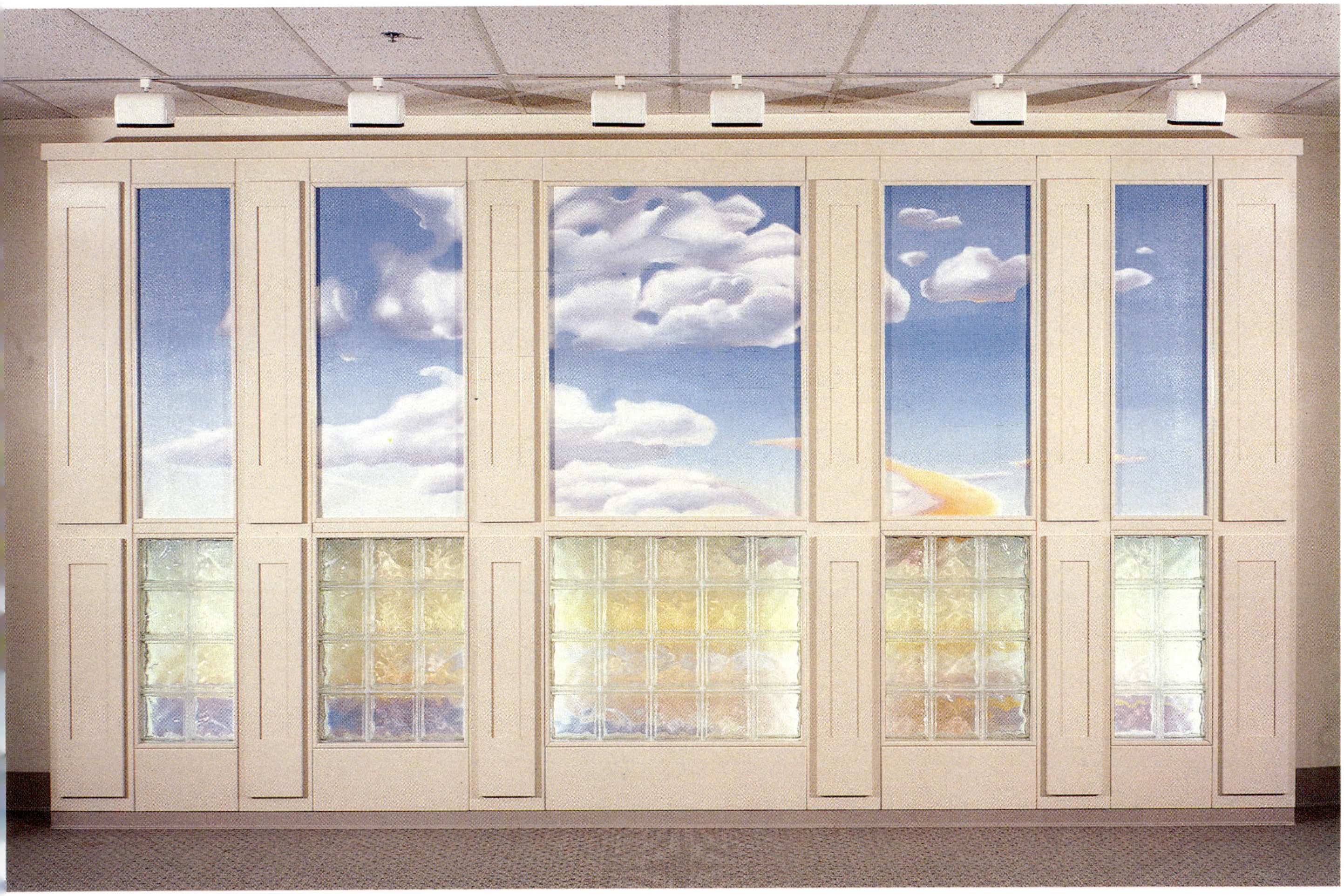

Benson Shaw

4136 Meridian N
Seattle, WA 98103
FAX 206-632-1363
TEL 206-632-3552

Benson Shaw creates site-specific, architecturally integrated work for public and private projects. His work includes fine art sculpture, contemporary architectural sculpture, architectural elements for restoration of historic register buildings, site design, and installation. Shaw also provides fabrication and technical support for other design professionals. He produces castings in concrete, terrazzo, glass, metals, plastics and plaster.

A Site plan with layout of *Bromeliad* and location of *City River* at the new Downtown Olympia Transit Center, Olympia, WA

B *Bromeliad*, detail of pedestrian island pavement, color-hardened concrete, 80' x 280'

C *City River*, stained glass glued into voids of clerestory thermal window panels; map image shows corridor through central Olympia, 5' x 65'

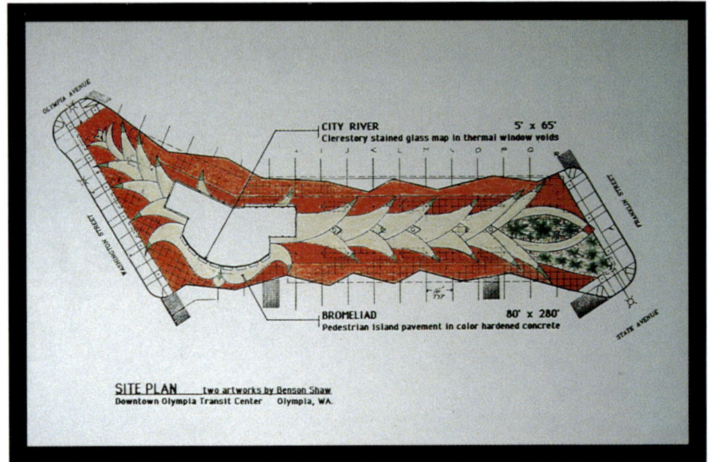

A

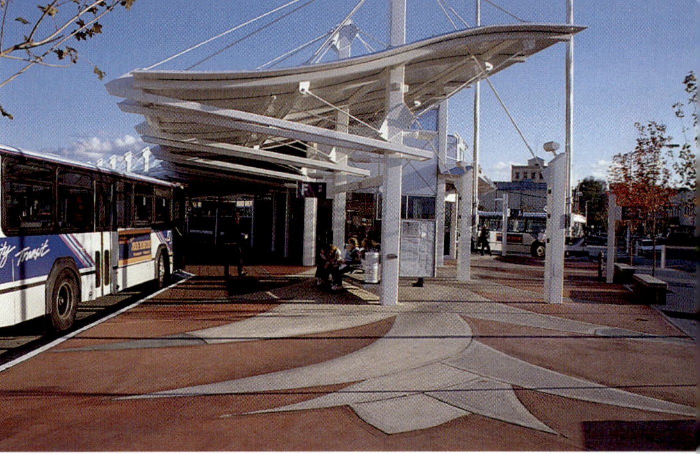

B

S. Vento

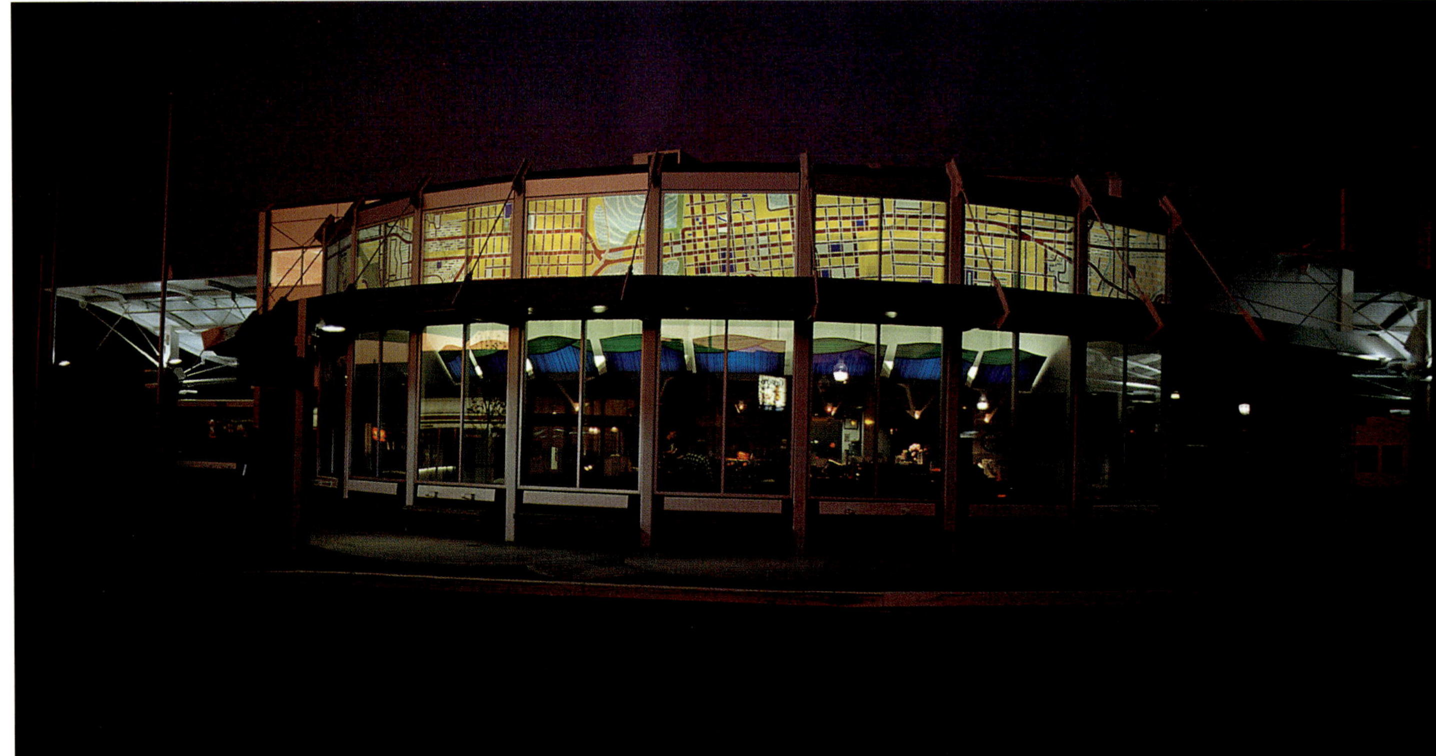

C

S. Vento

Michael Watling

The Watling Company
51 Alpine Village
Mountain Center, CA 92561
FAX 619-349-8502
TEL 619-349-3292

Michael Watling make sculpture, earthworks and gardens in many materials including bronze, steel, stone, soil, plants and water. Site-specific works are a speciality, incorporating local terrain, architecture and cultural heritage. His works—ranging from free-standing sculptures to earthworks of several acres—are in public and private collections from California to Boston. He works well with committees and collaborators and is known for delivering on time and on budget.

Commissions include:
City of Palm Desert, CA
The Grossman Co., Boston, MA
Downey Savings Development Corp.,
 Newport Beach, CA
City of Indio, CA

A *Spathe*, Palm Desert, CA, bronze, 7'H

B *Mother and Child*, Palm Desert, CA,
 sandstone, 8' x 4' x 4'

C *Cahuilla Baskets*, Palm Desert, CA,
 steel and water, 18' x 12' x 12'

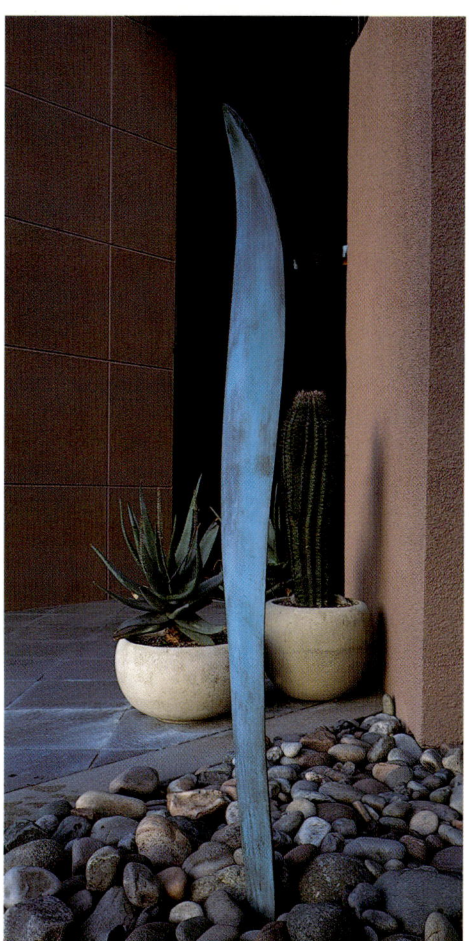

A

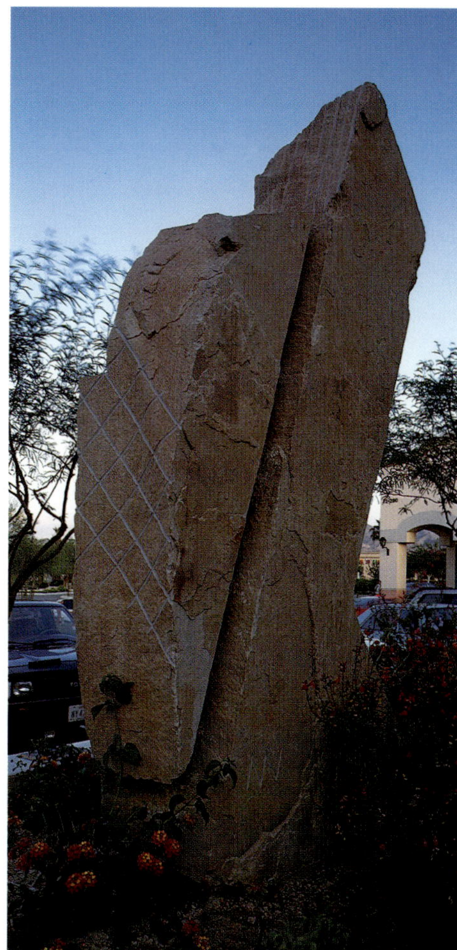

B

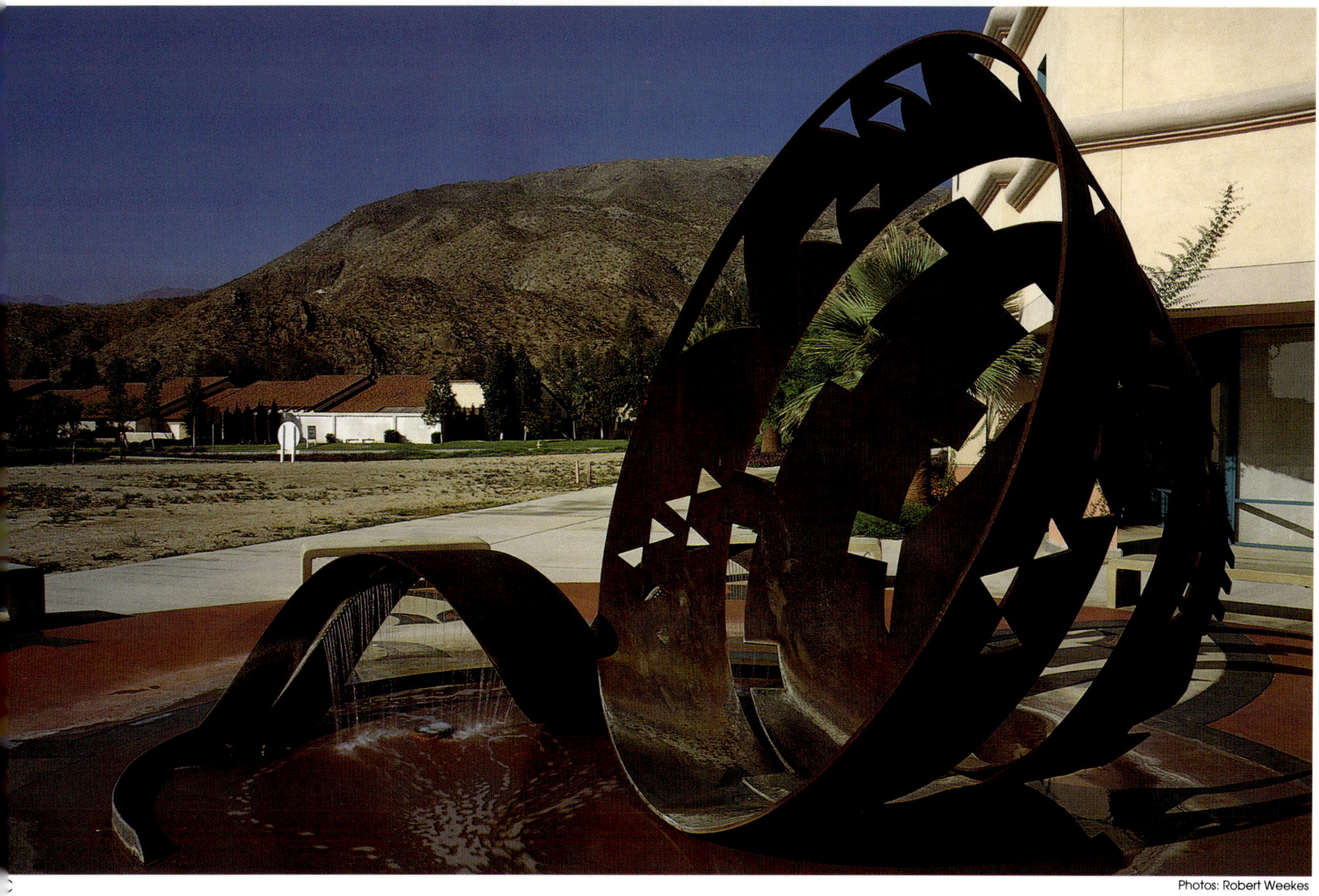

Photos: Robert Weekes

Mary Boone
Wellington

88 Boston Post Road
Amherst NH 03031
FAX 603-673-2311
TEL 603-673-2311
E-Mail: mryboone@aol.com

Mary Boone Wellington has completed many public and corporate commissions in her 20 years as a sculptor. She works in collaboration with architects, community representatives, designers and contractors to create works of art on time and within budget, while satisfying aesthetic and safety criteria.

Known for an economy of form, rich surfaces, and colorful patinas, Wellington's work in steel, aluminum and bronze combines powerful universal images with a lightness of spirit. Her sculptures create a timeless moment that resonates in the heart.

A & B *Taking Off*, 1994, Manchester, NH, airport, commissioned by the City of Manchester, aluminum, 12' x 65' x 35'

C *Mt. Meru*, 1995, Rockingham County Courthouse, Brentwood, NH, commissioned by the State of New Hampshire, Cor-ten steel, 12' x 20' x 10'

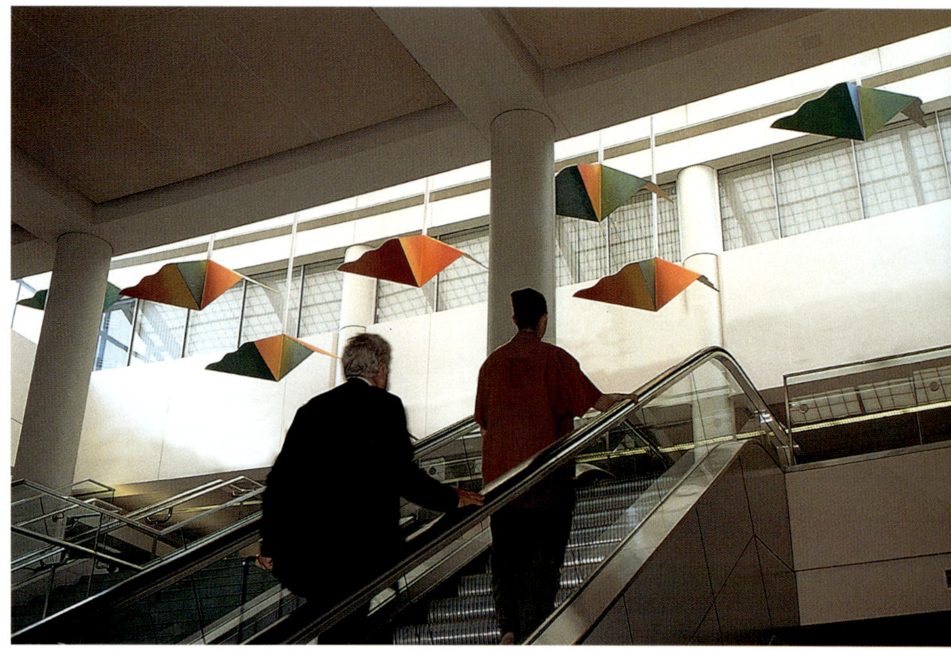
A

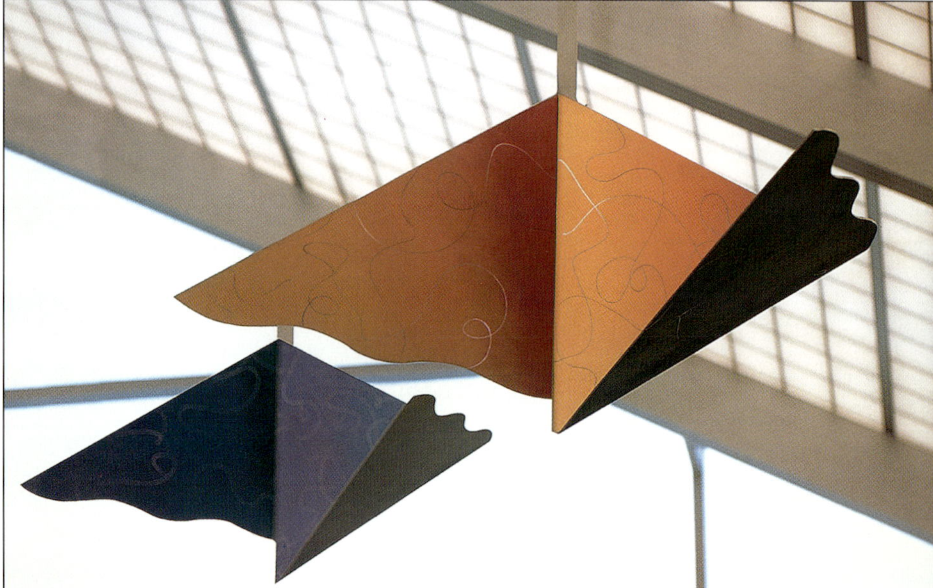
B

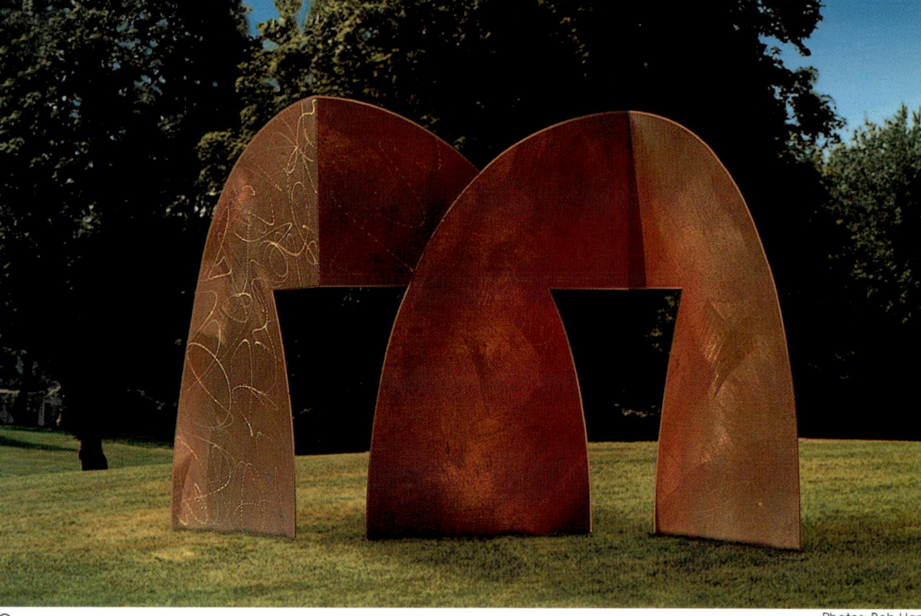
C

Photos: Bob Hamc

"

REGISTERS AND RESOURCES

This year's GUILD REGISTERS include almost 800 listings for artists working in architectural glass and metal, public art, and architectural restoration. In each instance, the artist provided new or revised information, thereby ensuring up-to-date addresses, phones and product descriptions.

In the case of THE GUILD REGISTER of Public Art, administrators of public art agencies throughout the country are asked to suggest artists for inclusion in the register each year. With their help, we present a reliable directory of artists who have competed and succeeded in the public art process.

Only experienced, professional artists are invited to be listed in THE GUILD REGISTERS. However, please note that inclusion does not constitute a referral from THE GUILD. We urge you to contact references from similar, previous projects, as you would when seeking any other professional service.

THE GUILD REGISTER®

THE GUILD RESOURCES

THE GUILD REGISTER®
of Public Art

KIM ABELES

2401 SANTA FE AVE #100
LOS ANGELES, CA 90058-1138
TEL 213-587-4652
Work: sculpture (free standing)
Media: mixed, paint
Special Concerns: historical/documentary issues, environmental issues
Commission Amounts: $1,500 - $25,000
Agencies: California Arts Council; California Bureau of Automotive Repair; Los Angeles Cultural Affairs Department; Metropolitan Transportation Authority
Recent Project: Artwork integration into the architecture for Panorama City Public Library (1992-95)

LARRY ULAAQ AHVAKANA

AHVAKANA FINE ARTS
PO BOX 1052
SUQUAMISH, WA 98392-1052
TEL 360-598-3552
Work: sculpture (free standing and wall relief), architectural elements, temporary installations, neon, wood, bronze casting
Media: metal, concrete, stone, wood, bronze casting
Special Concerns: collaborative design teams, multicultural issues, environmental issues
Commission Amounts: $4,500 - $100,000
Agencies: WA State Arts Commission
Recent Project: Retrospective/new work, one-person show, Anchorage Museum of History and Art, Anchorage, AK

ALIAH SAGE STUDIO & GALLERY

ALIAH SAGE
24 LEDOUX ST PO BOX 2888
TAOS, NM 87571
FAX 505-758-9564
TEL 505-758-9564
Work: collaborative site design, mosaic flooring and ground plane, architectural tile
Media: metal, ceramics
Special Concerns: collaborative design teams, historical and documentary issues
Commission Amounts: $21,000 and up
Agencies: Art in Public Places, Program of the New Mexico Arts Division of the Office of Cultural Affairs
Recent Project: Mosaic and tile floor for Luna Vo-Tech, Las Vegas, NM

JANE INGRAM ALLEN

37 MILFORD ST PO BOX 153
HAMILTON, NY 13346-0153
FAX 315-824-1619
TEL 315-824-1619
Work: sculpture (atrium and wall relief), other work for interior walls, temporary installations
Media: metal, paint, paper
Special Concerns: community involvement, environmental issues, science and teaching related
Commission Amounts: $5,000 - $20,000
Agencies: Federal Reserve Bank of New York Operations Center, E. Rutherford, NJ; MTA, Arts for Transit, NYC, Creative Stations, grant award, NY
Recent Project: *High Five*, a suspended, painted, handmade paper and string sculpture of five hands for New York City subway station

MARIA ALQUILAR

703 DARWIN ST
SANTA CRUZ, CA 95062-2208
TEL 408-423-2490
Work: sculpture (free standing and wall relief), collaborative site design, viewer interrelated
Media: metal, ceramics, mixed
Special Concerns: collaborative design teams, community involvement, site-specific
Commission Amounts: $30,000 - $160,000
Agencies: U.S. General Services Administration; Sacramento (CA) Metropolitan Arts Commission; Phoenix Arts Commission; Denver Arts Commission
Recent Project: Nine ceramic murals, Fairbairn water treatment plant, Sacramento, CA

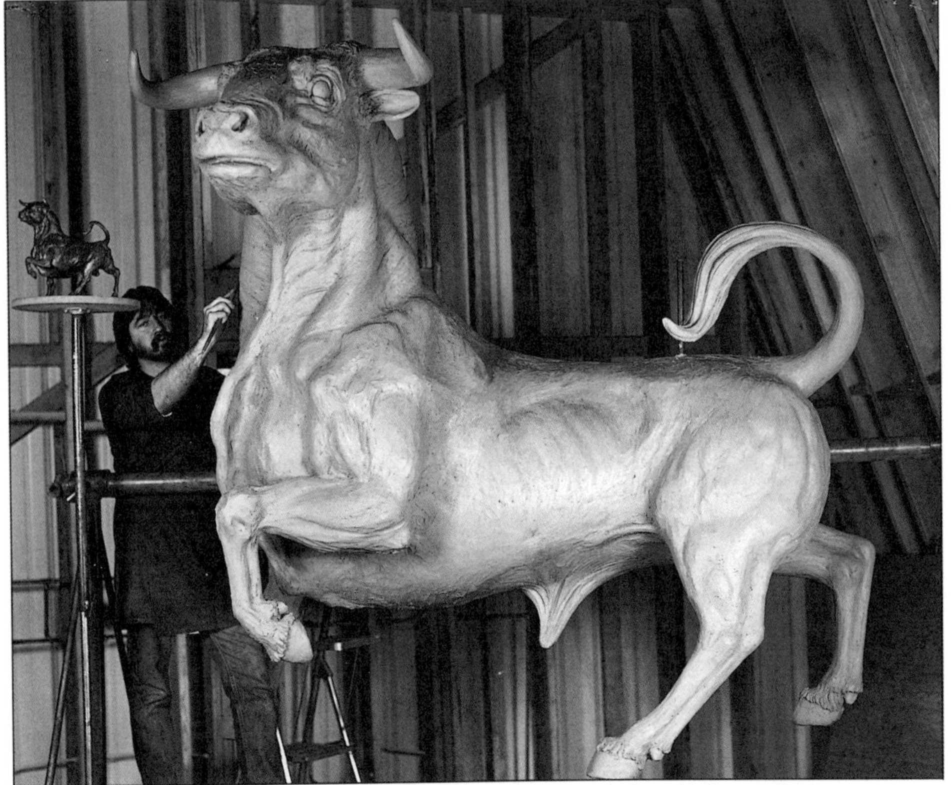

Todd Andrews, *El Toro*, clay for bronze, Holiday Inn, Solvang/Buellton, CA, photo: Anita Rossovich Photography

GARY ALSUM

NATIONAL SCULPTORS' GUILD
2683 N TAFT AVE
LOVELAND, CO 80538
FAX 970-667-2068
TEL 970-667-2015
Work: sculpture (free standing and pedestal), collaborative site design
Media: metal
Special Concerns: collaborative design teams
Commission Amounts: $50,000
Agencies: Carnegie Art Museum, Oxnard, CA; City of Palm Desert, CA (1995)
Recent Project: Commercial commission and installation, three-figure sculpture of grandfather and two children, 1 1/4% life-size (1994)

AMERICAN STONECRAFTERS, INC.

JOHN KRONBERG
488 WASHINGTON ST
WALLLINGFORD, CT 06492
FAX 203-269-7471
TEL 203-294-0422
Work: sculpture (free standing), fountains, furniture
Media: mixed, stone
Special Concerns: historical and documentary issues
Commission Amounts: $80,000
Agencies: City of New Haven, CT
Recent Project: Replication of eight hand-carved fireplaces for the restoration of City Hall

B. AMORE
WOODY DORSEY

KOKORO CARVERS
ROOT POND RD BOX 191
BENSON, VT 05731
FAX 802-273-3402
TEL 802-537-4727
Work: stone environments
Media: metal, stone, wood
Commission Amounts: $20,000 and up
Agencies: Lion and the Lamb Peace Arts Center; Earth Promise Foundation
Recent Project: *Ark of Promise*, stone sculpture and park for Fossil Rim Wildlife Center (1995)

MARTA AMUNDSON

GOOSE KNOB GLASS AND FIBER
85 GOOSE KNOB DR
RIVERTON, WY 82501-8306
FAX 307-856-5176
TEL 307-856-3373
Work: architectural glass, fiber work for interior walls
Media: glass, fiber
Special Concerns: environmental issues
Commission Amounts: $1,400 - $15,000
Agencies: Wyoming Arts Council
Recent Project: Commerative quilt for the National Museum of Wildlife Art, Jackson, WY (1995)

CELIA CARL ANDERSON

BY SITE
PO BOX 1331
SOLDOTUA, AK 99669
TEL 907-283-7962
Work: sculpture (atrium), mosaics, fiber work for interior walls
Media: metal, mixed, fiber
Special Concerns: historical/documentary issues, multicultural issues, science and teaching related
Commission Amounts: $5,000 - $30,000
Agencies: Municipality of Anchorage 1% for Art Program. Anchorage, AK; State of Alaska 1% for Art Program
Recent Project: Suspended installation of painted stainless steel mesh units

JUAN L. ANDREU

JUAN ANDREU STUDIO
280 UPPER GRASSY HILL
WOODBURY, CT 06798
FAX 203-263-0910
TEL 203-263-0910
Work: sculpture (wall relief)
Media: metal
Special Concerns: community involvement, historical and documentary issues, multicultural issues
science and teaching related
Commission Amounts: $15,000 - $48,000
Agencies: Connecticut State Commission on the Arts; Hartford Board of Education, CT; House of Puerto Rico

★ TODD ANDREWS

TASCO
16311 INDIAN SPRINGS RANCH
GRASS VALLEY, CA 95949-8776
FAX 916-272-7612
TEL 916-272-7612
Work: sculpture (free standing)
Media: metal, concrete, stone
Special Concerns: community involvement, historical/documentary issues, environmental issues
Commission Amounts: $18,000 - $500,000
Agencies: San Jose Redevelopment Agency; Historical Landmarks, Inc.; Roseville Parks and Recreation
Recent Project: Six 22'L, bronze panthers for the Carolina's Stadium Corporation, Charlotte, NC

See photograph page 226.

JACK ARCHIBALD

REVISIONARY GLASSWORKS
3465 SW CAMANO DR
CAMANO ISLAND, WA 98292-7065
TEL 360-387-9395
Work: architectural glass, murals
Media: metal, wood, glass, light boxes
Special Concerns: collaborative design teams, community involvement
Commission Amounts: $6,500 - $40,000
Agencies: Washington State Arts Commission, Percent for the Arts
Recent Project: *Quixote's Comet*, 70' x 20' curved glass mural, Combined Transportation Center, Tacoma, WA

★ ARCHITECTURAL CERAMICS

ELLE TERRY LEONARD
910 ALAMEDA LN
SARASOTA, FL 34234-7315
FAX 941-952-0463
TEL 941-952-0463
Work: sculpture (wall relief)
Media: ceramics
Special Concerns: environmental issues
Commission Amounts: $12,000
Agencies: City of Venice

See page 74 for photographs and additional information.

★ ARCHITECTURAL STAINED GLASS, INC.

JEFF G. SMITH
PO BOX 9092
DALLAS, TX 75209-9092
FAX 214-827-5000
TEL 214-352-5050
Work: architectural glass, other work for interior walls, including 'wall windows'
Media: metal, glass, mirror
Special Concerns: collaborative design teams, community involvement, environmental issues
Commission Amounts: $35,000 - $175,000
Agencies: Alaska State Council on the Arts; Utah Arts Council Percent for Art; Texas State Department of Corrections
Recent Project: 'Nine Muses Suite' at Florida Atlantic University

As project artist, Jeff Smith not only contributes his widely acclaimed and unique creativity, but also brings a familiarity with the language and needs of the many professionals that collaborate during a public art project. He has the ability to recognize essential characteristics of a space and the needs of those who will use it. By combining his communicative, technical and analytical skills with his inventive, thoughtful artistry, Smith is able to produce wonderfully appropriate works of art.

See page 62 for photographs and additional information.

WARREN ARNOLD

5876 LONE PINE RD
SEBASTOPOL, CA 95472
TEL 707-823-1373
Work: sculpture (free standing and pedestal), fountains
Media: stone, earth and plants
Special Concerns: collaborative design teams, environmental issues
Commission Amounts: $5,000 - $50,000
Agencies: Marin General Hospital, Ross, CA; City of Sausalito, CA
Recent Project: Marble fountain and garden, *Meditation Garden*, Marin General Hospital, Ross, CA

ANDREA ARROYO

509 CATHEDRAL PKY #3H
NEW YORK, NY 10025-2078
FAX 212-316-1645
TEL 212-864-6648
Work: sculpture (wall relief), painted finishes and murals, polychrome relief
Media: paint, mixed, fiberglass
Special Concerns: multicultural issues, environmental issues, science and teaching related
Commission Amounts: $6,000 - $85,000
Agencies: New York City Percent For Art; School Construction Authority
Recent Project: *Harmony*, two monumental-scale relief murals for a public school, Bronx, NY

ART & METAL LTD.

MICHAEL DE STEFANO
232 JUPITER ST
JUPITER, FL 33458
FAX 407-745-9403
TEL 407-745-9403
Work: sculpture (free standing), fountains, architectural metal
Media: metal, stone, glass
Special Concerns: collaborative design teams, historical and documentary issues, environmental issues
Commission Amounts: $10,000 - $500,000
Agencies: General Services Administration; Lakewood Art Council; Southern Society of the Arts
Recent Project: Large copper fountains with iron architectural elements

ART IN ARCHITECTURE

A.H. SHAMIR
275 W 231 ST RIVERDALE #1119
NEW YORK, NY 10463
FAX 718-884-6875
TEL 212-695-5378
Work: sculpture (free standing), architectural glass
Media: paint, concrete, glass, painted finishes
Special Concerns: collaborative design teams, historical and documentary issues
Commission Amounts: $30,000 - $200,000
Agencies: New York City Commission on the Arts
Recent Project: Memorial to the Holocaust, cast concrete, fountain and plaza design, Civic Center, Tucson, AZ

ARTSHOP

ABBIGAIL SCHERMESSER
570 E TURKEYFOOT LAKE RD
AKRON, OH 44319-4108
TEL 216-896-9258

Work: sculpture (free standing and wall relief), painted finishes and murals, 2D work, paintings
Media: paint, wood, ceramics, stucco reliefs
Special Concerns: collaborative design teams, historical and documentary issues, environmental issues
Commission Amounts: $2,000 - $10,000
Agencies: Akron/Summit Counties Public Libraries, Akron, OH; Children's Center & Medical Hospital, OH; Akron Medical Center
Recent Project: 25' x 9' acrylic painted skyscape three-dimensionalized by sculpted paper-pulp kites

ART STUDIO WEST

ANNA KARESH
PO BOX 900528
SAN DIEGO, CA 92190-0528
FAX 916-565-1161
TEL 619-258-0766

Work: sculpture (wall relief), other work for interior walls, paper wood
Media: wood, mixed, paper
Special Concerns: collaborative design teams
Commission Amounts: $26,000
Agencies: C.P.W. Corporate and Service Headquarters for Municipal Water Supply, Charleston, SC
Recent Project: Four wall sculptures designed to float in separate, recessed, lighted spaces

AURORA GLASS STUDIO

SANDRA D. EISMIN
634 MAIN ST
LAFAYETTE, IN 47901-1451
FAX 317-742-2721
TEL 317-742-7387

Work: sculpture (pedestal), architectural glass, lighting
Media: glass
Special Concerns: collaborative design teams, community involvement, participatory works
Commission Amounts: $1,000 - $6,000
Agencies: Indiana Arts Commission; Tippacanoe Arts Federation; Frankfort Public Library
Recent Project: Architectural glass entrance for elementary school

DOUGLAS BAKER

NORMAN B. STUDIO
2990 NANAIMO ST
VANCOUVER, BC V5N 5G3
CANADA
FAX 604-436-2805
TEL 604-451-1100

Work: architectural glass, architectural elements, other work for interior walls
Media: metal, wood, glass
Special Concerns: community involvement, science and teaching related, health issues
Commission Amounts: $100,000
Agencies: Vancouver General Hospital and Health Sciences Foundation Centre
Recent Project: A water-form movement captured in a glass wall, 33'W x 10'H

PAULA BARR

PAULA BARR PRODUCTIONS
195 HUDSON ST PH
NEW YORK, NY 10013-1813
FAX 212-226-5414
TEL 212-226-5275

Work: architectural glass, 2D work
Media: glass, photography
Special Concerns: seeing anew
Commission Amounts: $12,000 - $125,000
Agencies: Port Authority of New York and New Jersey
Recent Project: Photo mural composed of 185 glass tiles, each 2' x 2'

BILL BARRETT

WORTH STREET STUDIOS
11 WORTH ST
NEW YORK, NY 10013-2922
FAX 212-431-5591
TEL 212-431-5591

Work: sculpture (free standing, atrium and wall relief)
Media: metal
Special Concerns: collaborative design teams, community involvement
Commission Amounts: $45,000 - $300,000
Agencies: Connecticut Commission on the Arts; Percent for Art, City of New York, New Dorp High School
Recent Project: *L.A. Family Baroque*, Los Angeles, CA, fabricated bronze, 13'H

BRIAN BAXTER
MARKIAN OLYNYK

OLYNYK/BAXTER COLLABORATIVE
2776 W 10TH AVE
VANCOUVER, BC V6K 2J9
CANADA
FAX 604-738-9722
TEL 604-738-9791

Work: sculpture (free standing and atrium), architectural glass
Media: glass
Special Concerns: collaborative design teams, community involvement, historical/documentary issues
Commission Amounts: $15,000 minimum
Agencies: Museum of Civilizations, Hull, QB; Renfrew Library, Vancouver, B.C.; Surrey Memorial Hospital, BC; Vancouver International Airport, BC

BRUCE BEASLEY

322 LEWIS ST
OAKLAND, CA 94607-1236
FAX 510-763-4431
TEL 510-836-1414

Work: sculpture (free standing, atrium and pedestal)
Media: metal, stone
Commission Amounts: $25,000 - $150,000
Agencies: San Francisco Arts Commission; U.S. General Services Administration; California Arts Commission
Recent Project: 18' vertical abstract bronze sculpture for the Federal Home Loan Bank, San Francisco (1992)

ROSS PALMER BEECHER

4719 WHITMAN AVE N
SEATTLE, WA 98103-6650
TEL 206-634-0643

Work: sculpture (free standing), other work for interior walls
Media: paint, mixed, soda and beer cans
Special Concerns: environmental issues
Commission Amounts: $12,000 - $30,000
Agencies: King County Arts Commission, Seattle, WA; Seattle Arts Commission, WA
Recent Project: A wall relief of recyclable cans depicting traditional quilts and flags

FRED BENDHEIM

160 UNDERHILL AVE
BROOKLYN, NY 11238-4404
TEL 718-638-0219

Work: fountains, 2D work
Media: concrete, stone, water
Special Concerns: collaborative design teams, community involvement, environmental issues
Commission Amounts: $15,000
Agencies: New York City Dept. of Parks; Polish National Theatre
Recent Project: Paintings for NYC Dept. of Parks Headquarters (1992)

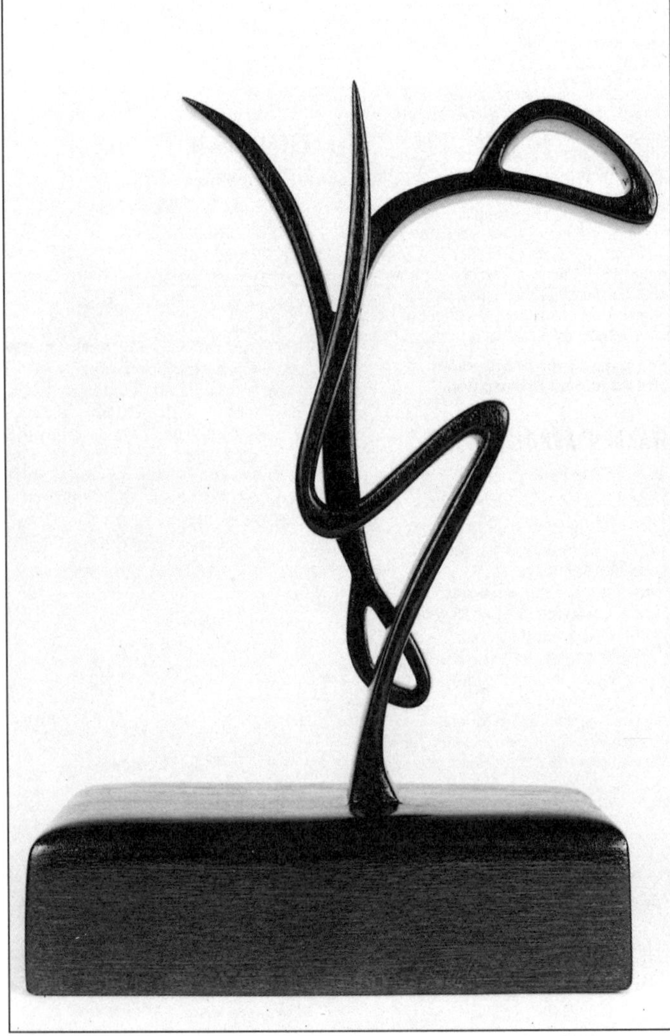

Rita Blitt, *Jazz* (maquette), 1994, laminated, cut, stained poplar, 15"H x 6"D x 10"W, available in many materials and sizes

LYNDA BENGLIS

222 BOWERY
NEW YORK, NY 10012-4216
TEL 212-226-7979
Work: sculpture (wall reliefs), fiber work for interior walls, fountains
Media: metal, ceramics, fiber
Commission Amounts: $50,000 - $200,000
Agencies: General Services Administration Art in Architecture; Hartsfield Atlanta International Airport; First City Center, Dallas
Recent Project: Leo W. O'Brien Federal Building, Albany, NY

BILLY AL BENGSTON

BILLY'S STUDIO & DESIGN
805 HAMPTON DR
VENICE, CA 90291
FAX 310-450-3211
TEL 310-822-2201
Work: painted finishes and murals, 2D work, furniture
Media: metal, paint, wood
Commission Amounts: $12,000 - $200,000
Agencies: Los Angeles Public Arts Program; California Arts Commission; City of Pasadena
Recent Project: Entry sculpture and fountain for mixed-use development apartments, City of Pasadena, CA

ZIGI BEN-HAIM

ZIGI STUDIO
94 MERCER ST
NEW YORK, NY 10012-4425
FAX 212-966-0551
TEL 212-431-4689
Work: sculpture (free standing, pedestal and wall relief), collaborative site design, outdoor furniture and equipment, 2D work, furniture
Media: metal, paint, concrete, wood, mixed, paper
Commission Amounts: $10,000 - $300,000
Agencies: Tel-Aviv Foundation
Recent Project: 100'H hanging sculpture in atrium of a public space

MEREDITH G. BERGMANN

400 E 77TH ST #14D
NEW YORK, NY 10021-2337
FAX 212-861-2768
TEL 212-861-2768
Work: sculpture (free standing and wall relief)
Media: cast stone, cement
Special Concerns: community involvement, multicultural issues, issues related to disabilities
Commission Amounts: $4,000 - $30,000
Agencies: New York City Parks Department; Port Authority of New York and New Jersey; Bronx Council on the Arts; Dallas Area Rapid Transit
Recent Project: Memorial to poet Countee Cullen, Bronx Council on the Arts (1995)

JULIE BERNER

29953 FOX HOLLOW RD
EUGENE, OR 97405-9436
TEL 503-484-9220
Work: fiber work for interior walls
Media: fabric
Special Concerns: collaborative design teams, historical and documentary issues, multicultural issues
Commission Amounts: $5,000 - $10,000
Agencies: Dept. of General Services, Salem, OR; State of Oregon Board of Higher Education; City of Everett, WA
Recent Project: Photo-silkscreen on cotton, pieced, stitched, Oregon State Archives Building (1991)

BERTOIA STUDIO

MR. VAL BERTOIA
PO BOX 383
BALLY, PA 19503-0383
FAX 610-845-7128 (Call first)
TEL 610-845-7096
Work: sculpture (free standing and pedestal), fountains
Media: metal, concrete
Special Concerns: community involvement, environmental issues
Commission Amounts: $10,000 - $30,000
Agencies: Reading Redevelopment Authority
Recent Project: *Notte Tree: Rebirth of Ecology*, climb-able aluminum sculpture, 10' x 12' x 6' (1993)

BERYL SOLLA, INC.

BERYL SOLLA
1222 NW 83RD AVE
CORAL SPRINGS, FL 33071
TEL 305-345-8588
Work: sculpture (wall relief), mosaics, flooring and ground plane
Media: ceramics
Special Concerns: collaborative design teams, community involvement, multicultural issues
Commission Amounts: $10,000 - $100,000
Agencies: Dade County Art in Public Places, Miami, FL; Broward County Art in Public Places, Ft. Lauderdale, FL; State of Florida, Tallahassee, FL
Recent Project: 1,000 sq. ft. patio and fountain project using brightly glazed, handmade tiles

DAVID BLACK

1066 LINCOLN RD
COLUMBUS, OH 43212-3234
TEL 614-486-5153
Work: sculpture (free standing and atrium) architectural metal
Media: metal, brick
Special Concerns: collaborative design teams, historical/documentary issues
Commission Amounts: $35,000 - $365,000
Agencies: Tucson-Pima (AZ) Arts Council; Greater Toledo (OH) Arts Commission; Michigan Commission on the Arts
Recent Project: *Ottawa Gate*, sculpture pavilion for Ottawa Park Entrance, 25' x 40' x 50'

AL BLANKSCHIEN

AL BLANKSCHIEN STUDIO
3205 N BREMEN ST
MILWAUKEE, WI 53212-2276
TEL 414-264-3644
Work: neon/laser/light related
Media: neon
Special Concerns: environmental issues, science or teaching related
Commission Amounts: $5,000 - $15,000
Agencies: Wisconsin Percent for Art; Arizona Arts Commission; New Mexico Arts Division
Recent Project: *Acadamia: A Terminal for Life's Journey*, neon (1993)

★ RITA BLITT

RITA BLITT, INC.
8900 STATE LINE #333
LEAWOOD, KS 66206
FAX 913-381-5624
TEL 913-381-3840
Work: sculpture (pedestal and wall relief)
Media: metal, paint, wood
Commission Amounts: $15,000/project
Agencies: City of Los Angeles, Sherman Oaks
Recent Project: *Dancing*, 6' bronze sculpture

Rita Blitt's public and garden sculptures bring joy to spaces they occupy. Working closely with architects and owners, Blitt creates site-specific commissioned works from aluminum, wood, bronze, corten, stainless and painted steel. Blitt's sculptures up to sixty feet tall are included in private and museum collections in United States, Israel and Singapore.

See photograph page 228.

SONJA BLOMDAHL

1211 ALOHA ST
SEATTLE, WA 98109-4401
TEL 206-622-1404
Work: sculpture (pedestal), architectural glass, other work for interior walls
Media: glass
Commission Amounts: $10,000 - $50,000
Agencies: Cultural Commission, Everett, WA
Recent Project: Eight large leaded glass panels of all color, hand blown rondels

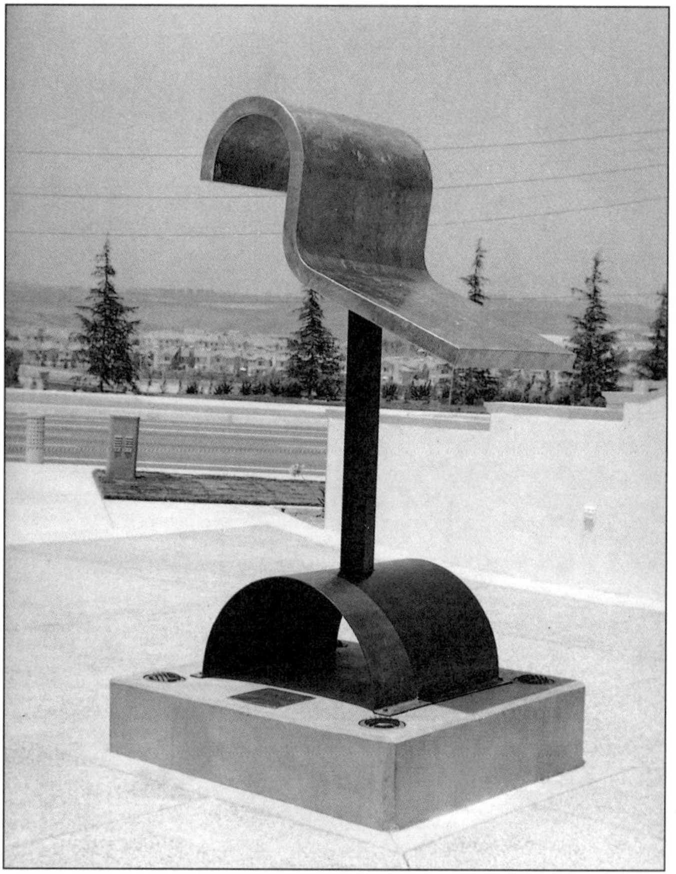

Susan Boomhouwer, *Your House is My House*, 1995, steel, The Marketplace, Laguna Niguel, CA, 8'H x 3'D x 4'W

BILL BOND

NATIONAL SCULPTORS' GUILD
2683 N TAFT AVE
LOVELAND, CO 80538
FAX 970-667-2068
TEL 970-667-2015
Work: sculpture (free standing and pedestal), collaborative site design
Media: metal
Special Concerns: historical and documentary issues
Commission Amounts: $52,000
Agencies: City of Westminister, CO
Recent Project: Golfing monument of historic design (1992)

★ SUSAN BOOMHOUWER

**24035 CORMORANT LN
LAGUNA NIGUEL, CA 92677
TEL 714-326-3595**
Work: sculpture (free standing), painted finishes and murals, 2D work
Media: metal, wood, mixed
Special Concerns: collaborative design teams, historical and documentary issues, multicultural issues
Commission Amounts: $1,500 - $32,000
Agencies: Municipal Arts Commission, Kansas City, MO; California State University, Fullerton, CA; Cultural Arts Depiction Program, Laguna Niguel, CA
Recent Project: One steel sculpture and 14 tile murals

My work emphasizes historical issues and symbolic images combined with contemporary concerns. I design my work to give access to a broad and/or varied public. I find mutual ground between the parties involved to bring ideas to a resolution in a design that works successfully with the site while meeting the needs of the community.

See photograph page 229.

LOUISE BOURNE

RR 1 BOX 90
SURRY, ME 04684
TEL 207-667-6614
Work: sculpture (free standing), 2D work, ceramic tile murals
Media: paint, mixed, ceramics
Special Concerns: participatory works, geographical, cultural
Commission Amounts: $7,000 - $35,000
Agencies: Percent for Arts Program, Maine Arts Commission
Recent Project: Narrative ceramic tile mural with individually shaped tiles converging into a frieze

DANA BOUSSARD

2 HEART CREEK RT 1
ARLEE, MT 59821
FAX 406-726-4136
TEL 406-726-3357
Work: architectural glass, fiber work for interior walls
Media: paint, fiber
Special Concerns: historical/documentary issues, environmental issues
Commission Amounts: $6,000 - $75,000
Agencies: Idaho Commission on the Arts; Alaska State Arts Council; Washington State Arts Commission; Oregon Arts Commission
Recent Project: Statehouse murals, six pieces, 9' x 80', capitol rotunda, Boise, ID (1994)

CAROLYN BRAAKSMA

PO BOX 12203
DENVER, CO 80212-0203
FAX 303-477-5520
TEL 303-477-5520
Work: sculpture (wall relief), collaborative site design, flooring and ground plane
Media: metal, concrete, stone
Special Concerns: collaborative design teams, historical and documentary issues
Commission Amounts: $25,000 - $500,000
Agencies: Denver International Airport Public Art Program
Recent Project: Denver Airport, floor depicting fossils, dinosaurs, Native Americans

GORDON BRADT

KINETICO, INC.
RR 2 BOX 470
EUREKA SPRINGS, AR 72632-9579
FAX 501-253-9098
TEL 501-253-9114
Work: sculpture (free standing and pedestal), kinetic sculpture clocks
Media: metal, mixed
Special Concerns: science or teaching related
Commission Amounts: $5,000 - $150,000
Agencies: King County Arts Commission, Seattle, WA; Toronto (Canada) International Airport
Recent Project: *Seven Man Kinetic Tower Clock*, 15'H, chrome, Seattle's Pacific Science Center (1994)

KEITH S. BRAMER

PARROT STUDIOS/UHU DESIGNS
820 EMORY ST
SAN JOSE, CA 95126-1818
TEL 408-294-4494
Work: sculpture (free standing and pedestal), architectural glass
Media: stone, glass, wood
Special Concerns: historical and documentary issues
Commission Amounts: $2,000 - $36,000
Agencies: Snoopy Museum
Recent Project: Set of exterior french doors with stained and leaded glass.

BRANDELL STUDIOS, INC.

KIM BRANDELL
1718 BAY RD
MIAMI BEACH, FL 33139-1414
FAX 305-532-7446
TEL 305-531-3499
Work: sculpture (free standing), architectural metal, outdoor furniture and equipment
Media: metal, paint
Special Concerns: collaborative design teams, community involvement, environmental issues
Commission Amounts: $10,000 - $25,000
Agencies: Dade County, FL; Coconut Grove Arts Festival, FL
Recent Project: Stainless steel bench with free-standing stainless palm tree.

DAVID BREEDEN

BISCUIT RUN STUDIOS, LTD.
981 OLD LYNCHBURG RD
CHARLOTTESVILLE, VA 22903-9705
FAX 804-977-5411
TEL 804-977-5411
Work: sculpture (free standing and pedestal), collaborative site design, architectural glass, mosaics
Media: metal, stone, glass
Special Concerns: collaborative design teams, community involvement, participatory works
Commission Amounts: $5,000 - $175,000
Agencies: Roanoke Arts Council
Recent Project: *Out of Many One*, three 14'H soapstone sculptures, 30 tons, Negril, Jamaica

NIZETTE BRENNAN

NIZETTE BRENNAN, SCULPTOR
1428 U ST NW
WASHINGTON, DC 20009
FAX 202-265-8045
TEL 202-265-4808
Work: sculpture (wall), collaborative site design, architectural elements, sculpture
Media: brick, stone, earth and plants
Special Concerns: historical and documentary issues, science and teaching related, environmental issues
Commission Amounts: $5,000 - $500,000
Agencies: GSA Art In Architecture; City of Rockville, Percent for Art; Art in the Parks, Montgomery County, MD
Recent Project: Free-standing American flag, monumental, stone, GSA commission

BRIDGE STAINED GLASS

BRIGITTE PASTERNAK
301 RIVER RD
NYACK, NY 10960-5003
TEL 914-359-2884
Work: architectural glass
Media: glass
Special Concerns: intelligible to the public
Commission Amounts: $3,300 - $13,600
Agencies: Public Libraries, Valley Cottage, NY, and Spring Valley, NY
Recent Project: Stained glass windows, 6'2"H x 25'W, for public library, Spring Valley, NY

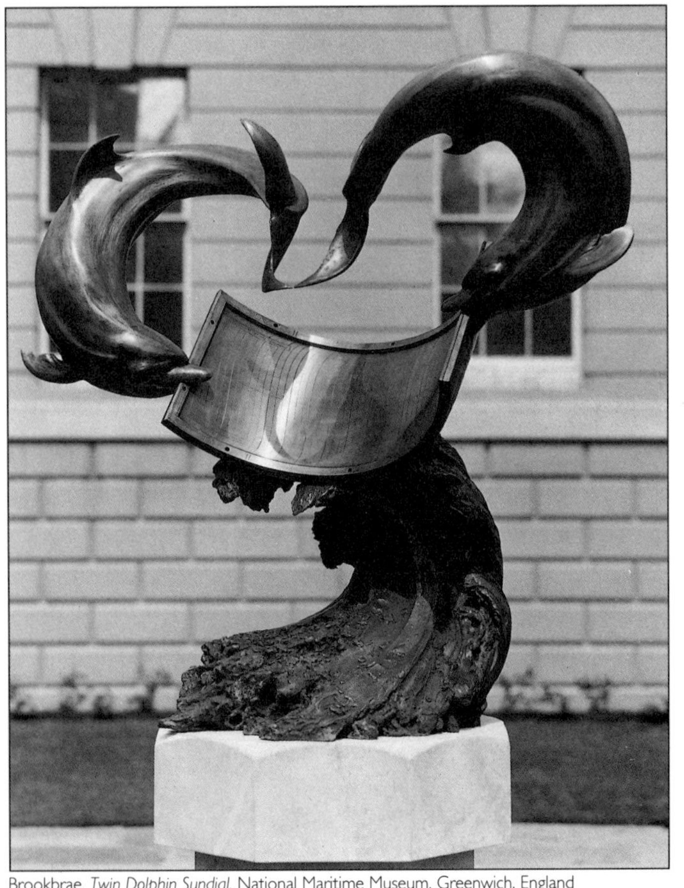

Brookbrae, *Twin Dolphin Sundial*, National Maritime Museum, Greenwich, England

★ BROOKBRAE

OLIVER GERO
10 FRESCENIUS RD
WESTPORT, CT 06880-3820
FAX 203-221-9195
TEL 203-454-2754

Work: sculpture (free standing),
fountains, clocks
Media: metal, mixed, stone
Special Concerns: collaborative design
teams, historical/documentary issues,
science or teaching related
Commission Amounts: $10,000 - $360,000
Agencies: London Underground; City
of London Corporation; Public Services
Administration (for National Maritime
Museum)

Brookbrae are a group of established
British artists working on site-specific
commissions. Internationally known
for sculptural feature clocks, including
sundials and armillary spheres, many
creations combine advanced science
with art. Materials and methods used
include modelling and casting into bronze;
fabrication in stainless steel, aluminum
and brass; stone carving (granite, marble
and slate); G.R.P. acrylic and glass;
painting and gilding. Clients range from
private individuals to corporate and institutional. No limit to versatility, size and
complexity.

See photograph page 230.

CAROL K. BROWN

101 W DILIDO DR
MIAMI, FL 33139
FAX 305-448-1326
TEL 305-899-9800

Work: sculpture (free standing and
pedestal), other media for interior walls
Media: metal, mixed
Agencies: Dade County Art in Public
Places; Florida State Division of Cultural
Affairs; City of Orlando Art in Public
Places
Recent Project: Free-standing aluminum
sculpture, four elements, University of
Florida

DAVID LEE BROWN

621 SPRINGS FIREPLACE RD
EAST HAMPTON, NY 11937-1732
FAX 516-324-0187
TEL 516-324-0187

Work: sculpture (free standing, atrium
and pedestal)
Media: metal, concrete, mixed
Special Concerns: collaborative design
teams, science and teaching related
Commission Amounts: $40,000 - $250,000
Agencies: Tulsa Public Arts Commission;
Art in Public Places, Fort Lauderdale, FL
Recent Project: Six-ton, mirror-polished,
stainless steel sculpture, Ft. Lauderdale
Airport (1989)

★ SEAN K.L. BROWNE

2965 ROBERT PL
HONOLULU, HI 96816-1732
FAX 808-732-1824
TEL 808-732-1824

Work: sculpture (free standing and
pedestal), fountains
Media: metal, earth and plants, stone
Special Concerns: collaborative design
teams, community involvement, multi-
cultural issues
Commission Amounts: $10,000 - $200,000
Agencies: Hawaii State Foundation on
Culture and the Arts
Recent Project: *Healing Hand*, monu-
mental, abstract, free-standing sculpture,
terrazzo

**See page 177 for photographs
and additional information.**

JEANNE BRUCE

JEANNE BRUCE SCULPTURE
PO BOX 579
TEMPLE, ME 04984-0579
TEL 207-778-9447

Work: ceramics, wall reliefs
Media: ceramics, wood, papier mache
Commission Amounts: $10,000 - $22,000
Agencies: Maine Arts Commission
Recent Project: Animals, skeletons, relief
6' x 22' x 1 1/2' (1993)

BRURIA FINKEL, ART

1225 HILL ST
SANTA MONICA, CA 90405-4707
FAX 310-396-0887
TEL 310-396-0887

Work: sculpture,(free standing, atrium,
pedestal, wall), collaborative site design,
fountains, architectural glass, terrazzo
Media: metal, painted, mixed, stone,
paper, water
Special Concerns: collaborative
design teams, environmental issues
Commission Amounts: $20,000 - $500,000
Agencies: Nes Park Natural Elements
Sculpture Park, Santa Monica, CA;
Step up on Second (an institution for
mentally ill adults)
Recent Project: *New Hope* apartments
for residents with HIV and AIDS,
Santa Monica, CA

PAUL BUCKNER

2332 ROCKWOOD ST
EUGENE, OR 97405-1413
TEL 503-342-6982

Work: sculpture (free standing and
pedestal)
Media: metal, concrete, wood
Special Concerns: historical/documentary
issues, multicultural issues, environmental
issues
Agencies: Oregon Arts Commission
Recent Project: *Mother and Child*,
figurative life-size bronze, Albany,
Oregon General Hospital (1992)

BILL BURGESS

BURGESS STUDIO
1005 EAGLE ROCK RD
COLORADO SPRINGS, CO 80918
TEL 719-599-7773

Work: sculpture (free standing and
wall relief)
Media: metal, paint, concrete
Special Concerns: historical and
documentary issues
Commission Amounts: $26,000 - $30,000
Agencies: Mayor's Office of Art, Culture
& Film, Denver, CO; Colorado Council
on the Arts & Humanities, Denver, CO;
Percent for the Arts, Rockville, MO

JOYCE MARQUESS CAREY

913 HARRISON ST
MADISON, WI 53711-2104
TEL 608-256-1537

Work: fiber work for interior walls
Media: fiber
Commission Amounts: $3,500 - $10,900
Agencies: Wisconsin Arts Board; Min-
nesota Arts Board; Florida Cultural Af-
fairs; Dane County Cultural Affairs
Commission, WI; Madison CitiArts
Recent Project: Four pieces for women's/
children's shelters, Madison, WI (1994)

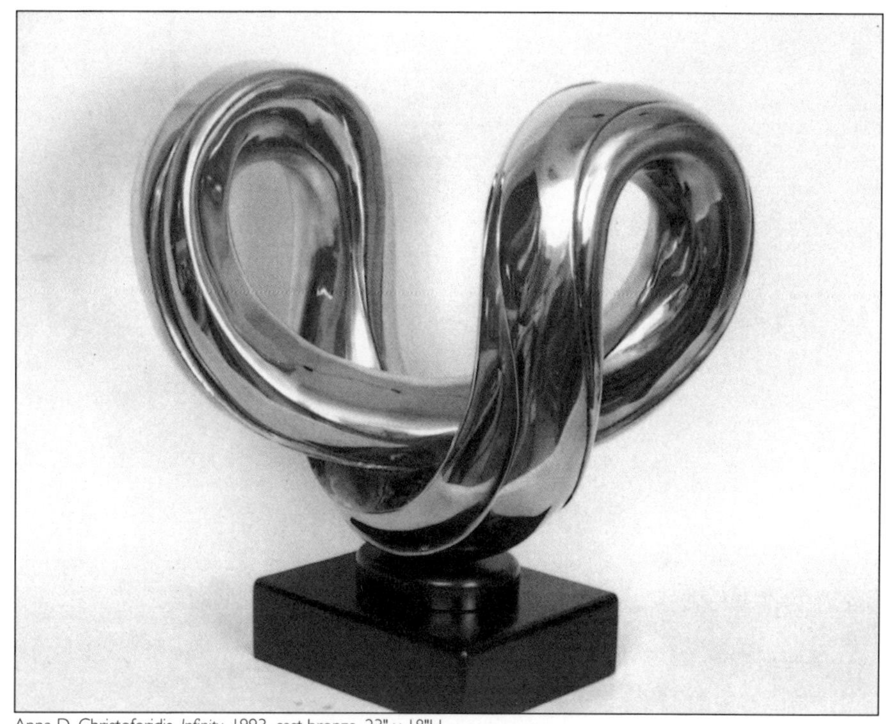

Anna D. Christoforidis, *Infinity*, 1993, cast bronze, 23" x 18"H

PUBLIC ART

ED CARPENTER

1812 NW 24ND AVE
PORTLAND, OR 97210-2538
FAX 503-224-6729
TEL 503-224-6729

Work: architectural glass, fountains, sculpture, monuments, bridges
Media: metal, glass, mixed
Special Concerns: collaborative design teams, community involvement, historical/documentary issues
Commission Amounts: $50,000 minimum
Agencies: New York City Percent for Art; Miami Metro Dade Percent for Art; Minnesota State Cultural Affairs Dept.
Recent Project: Lobby glass, 2,300 sq. ft., for 1251 Rockefeller Center, NYC

MURIEL CASTANIS

444 AVENUE OF THE AMERICAS
NEW YORK, NY 10011-8424
FAX 212-477-0788
TEL 212-477-0787

Work: sculpture (free standing, pedestal and wall relief), fiber work for interior walls, hardened cloth
Media: metal, plastics
Special Concerns: classical references
Commission Amounts: $60,000 - $500,000
Agencies: Montgomery County, MD; Arizona State University, State of Oregon
Recent Project: Six large friezes for Flatbush Ave. Station, Metropolitan Transportation Authority

DARRON J. CHADWICK

CHADWICK STUDIOS
6116 KINGSLEY DR
INDIANAPOLIS, IN 46220
FAX 317-251-4050
TEL 317-251-4050

Work: sculpture (wall relief), architectural elements, 2D work
Media: paint, ceramics, plastics
Commission Amounts: $2,000 - $25,000
Agencies: Indianapolis Arts Center Art Reach

CARL CHENG

JOHN DOE COMPANY
1518 17TH ST
SANTA MONICA, CA 90404-3402
FAX 310-450-4242
TEL 310-828-2381

Work: sculpture (free standing), fountains, site-specific
Media: all permanent materials
Special Concerns: participatory works, environmental issues, historical and documentary issues
Commission Amounts: $40,000 - $1,500,000
Agencies: San Francisco Arts Commission; Santa Monica Arts Commission; Metropolitan Transit Authority of Los Angeles
Recent Project: Water Lens Tower, Kaiser Permanent Hospital, Los Angeles Community Redevelopment Agency

LOTTE CHERIN

ARCHITECTURAL SCULPTURE
PO BOX 786
MALIBU, CA 90265-0786
TEL 310-457-4819

Work: sculpture (pedestal), architectural metal, other media for interior walls
Media: metal, mixed, plastics
Special Concerns: collaborative design teams
Agencies: City of Long Beach, CA

WANDA W. CHIN

DRAGON WIND DESIGN
PO BOX 82148
FAIRBANKS, AK 99708-2148
TEL 907-479-0131

Work: sculpture (atrium), architectural metal, fiber work for interior walls
Media: metal, fiber, mixed
Special Concerns: collaborative design teams, multicultural issues
Commission Amounts: $10,000 to $50,000
Agencies: Anchorage Municipality; State of Alaska

CHRISTO AND JEANNE-CLAUDE

48 HOWARD ST
NEW YORK, NY 10013-2561
FAX 212-966-2891

Work: large-scale, temporary works in urban and rural environments
Media: includes works on paper and preparation drawings
Special Concerns: accept no sponsorship or commissions
Recent Project: *The Umbrellas*, U.S. and Japan (1984-1991)

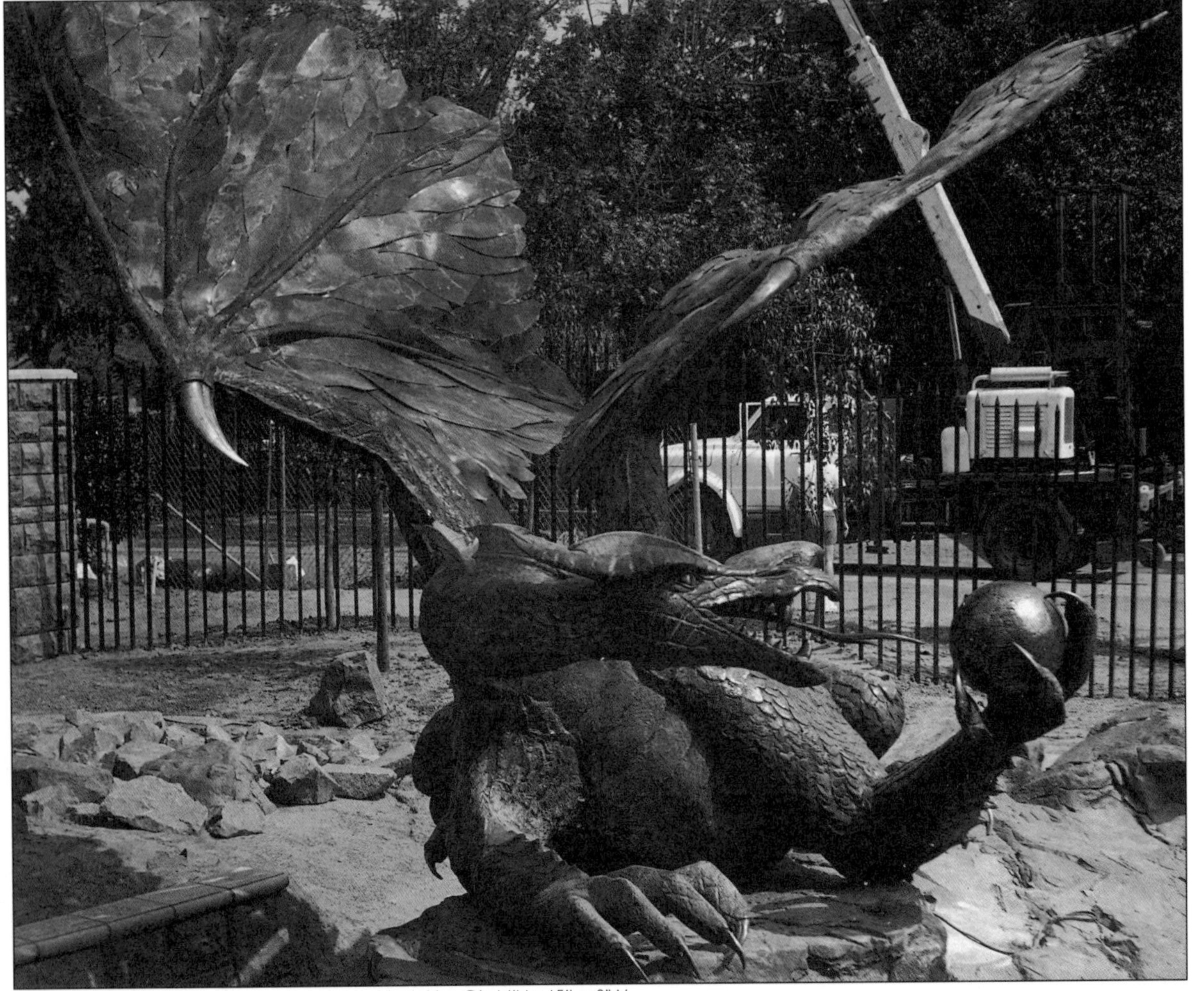

Gesso Cocteau, *The Dragon Aspasia*, private estate, Northridge, CA, 14'H x 15'L x 8'W

★ ANNA D. CHRISTOFORIDIS

2741 ABINGTON RD
COLUMBUS, OH 43221
FAX 614-481-0198
TEL 614-481-0198

Work: sculpture (pedestal and wall relief), architectural elements
Media: metal, plastics, plaster
Special Concerns: historical /documentary issues, science and teaching related, social, philosophical
Commission Amounts: $5,000 - $28,000
Agencies: State of Ohio

Art and Growth: I search for a point where the mechanics of life and living images meet, where geometric and biomorphic forms fuse together to create action within basic forms. The idea of metamorphosis is emphasized by a rhythmic motion which leads to constant play among positive and negative forms. In representing the human figure, I accentuate its abstract inner forces. When the human form is used as an element in repetition, it results in the creation of an animated unit as these elements interact. Portraits emphasize the character, as well as the likeness of the subject.

See photograph page 231.

★ DEE CLEMENTS

NATIONAL SCULPTORS' GUILD
2683 N TAFT AVE
LOVELAND, CO 80538
FAX 970-667-2068
TEL 970-667-2015

Work: sculpture (free standing and pedestal), collaborative site design
Media: metal
Special Concerns: collaborative design teams, historical and documentary issues, multicultural issues
Commission Amounts: $7,500 - $330,000
Agencies: City of Palm Desert, CA; City of Loveland, CO; Loveland Colorado Museum
Recent Project: *Monumental Desert Holocaust Memorial*, seven figures on two-tiered granite plinth surrounded by twelve bas-relief (1995)

Although Dee Clement's early interest and focus was abstract design, he learned that the added dimension of realism created a challenge that is both demanding and stimulating. A great deal of his inspiration comes from the development of his craft and its application to other arts, such as music, theater, landscape design and architecture. The idea, the motivation, the spirit, comes from his life experiences, the world and people around him and from his other sculptures in progress.

See page 162 for photographs and additional information.

★ JONATHAN CLOWES

CLOWES WOODWORKING
610 WASHINGTON ST
WALPOLE, NH 03608-0610
FAX 603-756-9505
TEL 603-756-9505

Work: sculpture (free standing and atrium), collaborative site design
Media: metal, wood, glass
Special Concerns: collaborative design teams, participatory works
Commission Amounts: $10,000 minimum
Agencies: New Hampshire Council on the Arts; Cultural Arts Committee, Visalia, CA; Grand Monadnock Arts Council
Recent Project: *Visalia Volandera*, hanging wooden sculpture at Visalia (CA) Convention Center (1992)

Jonathan Clowes designs and builds mobiles that speak of peace and serenity, while reflecting inspiration that comes from nature, spirituality, motion and shapes. Inviting and accessible, the art of Jonathan Clowes reflects a vulnerable, individual process that is his intuitive response to his surroundings. The artist welcomes inquiries, creative dialogue and the challenges of special commissions sized and priced to suit public and private requirements.

See page 127 for photographs and additional information.

★ GESSO COCTEAU

75310 DESERT PARK DR
INDIAN WELLS, CA 92210
TEL 619-568-0752

Work: sculpture (free standing)
Media: metal, bronze
Special Concerns: historical and documentary, mythological studies
Commission Amounts: $20,000 - $100,000
Agencies: Sylvia Deller Foundation for the Arts.
Recent Project: Life-size bronze dragon for private estate (1995)

For me, inspiration stems from many sources: the creatures of Mythology, the heroines of the Antiquities, and the diversity of the Humanities. Because art is the mediator that welds the mind to the senses, the chaotic to the orderly, and the passionate to the indifferent, I enjoy creating larger-than-life sculptures which demand a reaction and the release of emotions.

See photograph page 232.

★ J. GORSUCH COLLINS

J. GORSUCH COLLINS
ARCHITECTURAL GLASS
8283 W ILIFF LN
LAKEWOOD, CO 80227-3018
FAX 303-980-0692
TEL 303-985-8081

Work: architectural glass, architectural metal, furniture, hardware
Media: glass, metal
Special Concerns: collaborative design teams, participatory works
Commission Amounts: $200 - $500
Agencies: Colorado Council on the Arts and Humanities; City of Avon, CO
Recent Project: Avon Public Library, 9'H x 8'W textural and layered glass

J. Gorsuch Collins Architectural Glass specializes in innovative glass techniques, often incorporating other materials, accommodating many styles, welcoming the opportunity to collaborate with architects and designers from conception. Techniques include etched, deep-carved, fused, blown, leaded, copper foil, laminated, beveled, painted and cast glass. Custom-blown glass may be ordered for each project, allowing for total color control and flexibility.

See page 44 for photographs and additional information.

BRIGITTE SEKIRKA COOPER

BSC DESIGN
PO BOX 871840
WASILLA, AK 99687-1840
TEL 907-373-6067

Work: fiber work for interior walls, contemporary quilts
Media: fiber, mixed
Special Concerns: collaborative design teams, community involvement, multicultural issues
Commission Amounts: $4,000 - $62,000
Agencies: Alaska State Council on the Arts; Cannon Beach Arts Association; City of Anchorage Public Works
Recent Project: Contemporary quilted and painted hanging, 103"W x 48"H, University of Alaska, MSC, AK (1992)

GLORIA E. CROUSE

FIBER ARTS
4325 JOHN LUHR RD NE
OLYMPIA, WA 98516-2320
TEL 360-491-1980

Work: collaborative site design, fiber work for interior walls, outdoor furniture
Media: metal, mixed, fiber
Special Concerns: community involvement, historical and documentary issues, issues related to disabilities
Commission Amounts: $7,000 - $35,000
Agencies: Washington State Arts Commission Public Art Program; Seattle Arts Commission (Public Art Collection)
Recent Project: Mini-park consisting of four chairs, concrete pad, mosaic, lighting, five bird houses, Woodmoor Elementary, Bothell, WA (1995)

★ WILLIAM C. CULBERTSON

32 WARREN AVENUE
NORTH SMITHFIELD, RI 02896
FAX 401-766-6256
TEL 401-766-6256

See page 206 for photographs and additional information.

DAVID CULVER

DAVID CULVER STUDIO
661 N 5TH AVE #185
MINNEAPOLIS, MN 55405
TEL 612-339-5691

Work: sculpture (free standing), flooring and ground plane, landscape
Media: mixed, stone, earth and plants
Special Concerns: environmental issues, site improvement
Commission Amounts: $5,000 - $140,000
Agencies: Ohio State Arts Council; Minnesota State Arts Council; Dallas Area Rapid Transportation System, TX
Recent Project: *Wind Walls*, soil bermed, granite walls to control the wind

LINDA DABOUB

LINDA DABOUB/SCULPTOR
PO BOX 10126
ALBUQUERQUE, NM 87184-0126
FAX 505-898-2227
TEL 505-898-2227

Work: sculpture (free standing, pedestal, wall relief), collaborative site design, fountains, architectural glass, architectural elements
Media: metal, stone, glass
Special Concerns: collaborative design teams, community involvement, participatory works
Commission Amounts: $5,000 - $125,000
Agencies: New Mexico Percent For Art

DAN DAILEY

2 NORTH RD
KENSINGTON, NH 03833
FAX 603-778-1331
TEL 603-778-2303

Work: sculpture (pedestal), architectural glass, architectural metal
Media: glass, metal
Special Concerns: collaborative design teams, community involvement, historical and documentary issues
Commission Amounts: $60,000 - $350,000
Agencies: Town of Vail, Art in Public Places; Commonwealth of Mass.; Newburyport Court House
Recent Project: *Exuberance*, cast glass block mural, Vail Transportation Center

SUZANNE DALTON

12387 SCOTT RD
ELLSWORTH, MI 49729
FAX 616-599-2496
TEL 616-599-2496

Work: sculpture (atrium and wall relief), fiber work for interior walls, collaborative site design
Media: metal, plastics, fiber
Special Concerns: collaborative design teams
Commission Amounts: $3,000 - $45,000
Agencies: Commission on Art in Public Places, State of Michigan
Recent Project: Fiber sculpture, major interior piece for Western Michigan University

PUBLIC ART

DANNENFELSER SCULPTURE STUDIO & DANNENBECK TILE

SUSAN M. DANNENFELSER
PO BOX 1153
LAFAYETTE, CA 94549-1153
TEL 510-283-8875

Work: sculpture (free standing), architectural ceramics, mosaics, and wall relief, fountains
Media: metal, ceramics, concrete, natural stone
Special Concerns: collaborative design teams, environmental issues, specific to site and audience
Commission Amounts: $5,000 - $20,000
Agencies: Sacramento Metropolitan Arts Commission; Sacramemto Regional Transit
Recent Project: Five ceramic tile installations: mural, ground, wall and table, New Children's Hospital, Stanford, CA (1991)

JOAN DANZIGER

2909 BRANDYWINE ST NW
WASHINGTON, DC 20008-2139
FAX 202-659-0194
TEL 202-686-5285

Work: sculpture (free standing, atrium and pedestal)
Media: mixed, paint, fiberglass
Special Concerns: community involvement, historical/documentary issues, environmental issues
Commission Amounts: $15,000 - $125,000
Agencies: State of Maryland Percent for Art; DC Convention Center Art Committee; Governor's Office of Art and Culture, Maryland

★ DAVID E. DAVIS

12204 EUCLID AVE
CLEVELAND, OH 44106
TEL 216-721-1827

Work: sculpture (free standing and wall relief), fountains
Media: metal, paint, stone
Special Concerns: collaborative design teams, community involvement, historical and documentary issues
Commission Amounts: $18,000 - $90,000
Agencies: Florida Department of State, Art in State Buildings; Ohio Arts Council; Cuyahoga County Public Library, Beachwood Ohio Branch
Recent Project: A fountain with emphasis on the sound of water, like a mountain stream

David E. Davis has over 20 years experience in public art commissions and site-specific work, completing numerous projects throughout the U.S. He works in his own fabricating studio, using a variety of materials, including stainless steel, Cor-ten, aluminum and wood. As an abstract artist, he uses symbols to express the mission and interest of the client while creating work of the highest aesthetic quality.

Sound Tower A originated as a result of his recent interest in incorporating sound into sculpture. The tower is very sensitive to passing air currents and reacts by creating sound.

See photograph below.

★ JANE DeDECKER

NATIONAL SCULPTORS' GUILD
2683 N TAFT AVE
LOVELAND, CO 80538
FAX 970-667-2068
TEL 970-667-2015

Work: sculpture (free standing and pedestal), collaborative site design
Media: metal
Special Concerns: collaborative design teams, historical/documentary issues, multicultural issues
Commission Amounts: $10,000 - $100,000
Agencies: U.S. Parks Service; President's Committee for the Handicapped; Loveland Public Library, Loveland, CO
Recent Project: Three figures for Mayo Clinic, Glendale, AZ (1995)

Each of Jane DeDecker's sculptures is a point on the horizon. The spontaneous gestures and impressionistic quality of her work parallels the pace of the world in which we live, continuously describing the sensitivity and fragility of humanity as we speed by.

See page 163 for photographs and additional information.

DORA DE LARIOS

8560 VENICE BLVD
LOS ANGELES, CA 90034-2549
TEL 310-839-8305

Work: sculpture (free standing and wall relief), architectural metal
Media: metal, ceramics, concrete
Special Concerns: community involvement, historical and documentary issues
Commission Amounts: $25,000 - $125,000
Agencies: Los Angeles (CA) Community Redevelopment Agency; Pasadena (CA) Community Art Committee; Santa Fe Springs (CA) Community Art Committee
Recent Project: Trammell Crow Company commission of a free-standing sculpture

JOHN A. De MARCHI

3740 ROBLAR RD
PETALUMA, CA 94952-9787
TEL 707-795-5047

Work: sculpture (free standing and pedestal), collaborative site design
Media: metal, stone, wood
Special Concerns: collaborative design teams, science and teaching related, art and technology
Commission Amounts: $2,500 - $85,000
Agencies: City of Mountian View Art Commission; San Francisco Art Commission
Recent Project: Stainless steel sculpture, 14'H with seating, site specific, geometric

PAULA SCHILDHAUER DICKEY

CREATIVE HOUSING, INC.
PO BOX 2677
HOMER, AK 99603-2677
TEL 907-235-7953

Work: collaborative site design, mosaics, fiber work for interior walls
Media: ceramics, fiber
Special Concerns: collaborative design teams, historical and documentary issues
Commission Amounts: $5,000 - $30,000
Agencies: State of Alaska Percent for Art; Municipality of Anchorage Percent for Art
Recent Project: Fabric design for seating Anchorage Performing Arts Center, AK

ANTHONY DI MARCO

ANTHONY DI MARCO AGENCY
2948 1/2 GRAND RTE SAINT JOHN ST
NEW ORLEANS, LA 70119-3003
TEL 504-948-3128

Work: sculpture (free standing, pedestal and wall relief), collaborative site design, architectural elements, paintings, photographs (2-D), restoration of art
Media: mixed, wood, plastics, fiberglassed polyfoam
Special Concerns: collaborative design teams, community involvement, science or teaching related, religious
Commission Amounts: $5,000 - $30,000
Agencies: Contemporary Arts Center, New Orleans; Greater New Orleans Arts Council; Louisiana Nature and Science Center; LA Association for Conservation of Arts
Recent Project: Creation of realistic monarch butterfly sculpture for Audubon Institute, 6' x 5' x 5" (1995)

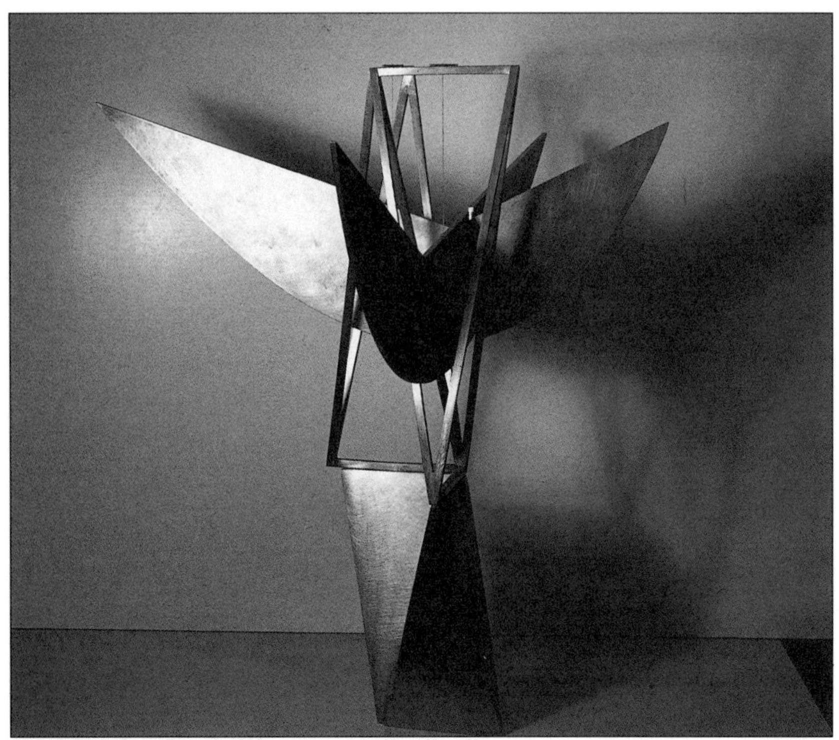

David E. Davis, *Sound Tower A*, 1993, stainless steel, 19" x 18" x 18"

★ DONNA L. DOBBERFUHL

SCULPTURAL DESIGNS
202 FIR DALE #104
CONVERSE, TX 78109-1340
TEL 800-397-1452

Work: sculpture (free standing), architectural ceramics, mosaics, and wall relief
Media: metal, brick
Special Concerns: historical and documentary issues
Commission Amounts: $30,000 - $175,000
Agencies: Connecticut Commission on the Arts; U.S. National Park Service; GSA Art-in-Architecture
Recent Project: *Biscayne National Park*, sculpted exterior brick, bronze, 8' × 200' (1994)

A National Sculpture Society member, Donna L. Dobberfuhl has earned national acclaim for unique historic and contemporary brick sculpture. Clients ranging from arts commissions in Ohio, Connecticut, Minnesota, Oklahoma and New York to NCR Corporation, Humana Hospitals and Busch Entertainment have discovered her remarkable enthusiasm matched by her technical command and artistic skills. Donna's design capabilities, complemented by her ability to listen to her client's needs, result in warm, inviting and exciting results.

See page 72 for photographs and additional information.

STAN DOLEGA

702 S PINE ST
LARAMIE, WY 82070-7064
TEL 307-745-7135

Work: sculpture (free standing), sited environmental
Media: concrete, wood, earth
Special Concerns: community involvement, participatory works, environmental issues
Commission Amounts: $5,000 - $150,000
Agencies: National Endowment for the Arts - Art in Public Places; Wyoming Council for the Arts; Montgomery County Arts Commission
Recent Project: Earthwork and concrete, mini-amphitheater (1988)

JESUS DOMINGUEZ
ELLEN PHILLIPS
MARY LYNN DOMINGUEZ

9180 SHIRLEY DR
LA MESA, CA 91941-4255
TEL 619-466-3867
TEL 619-463-0676

Work: sculpture (free standing and relief), temporary installations
Media: metal, stone, wood, tile
Special Concerns: community involvement, participatory works, historical and documentary issues
Commission Amounts: $14,000 - $80,000
Agencies: City of Phoenix (AZ) Arts Commission; Los Angeles Cultural Affairs Department
Recent Project: Participatory tile mural, bronze sculptural forms with moveable parts, San Diego Children's Hospital (1993)

SCOTT DONAHUE

1420 45TH ST #49
EMERYVILLE, CA 94608-2906
FAX 510-420-8455
TEL 510-658-5182

Work: sculpture (free standing), architectural ceramics, mosaics, and wall relief, fountains
Media: metal, ceramics, concrete
Special Concerns: historical/documentary issues, multicultural issues, science or teaching related
Commission Amounts: $2,000 - $85,000
Agencies: Cities of Denver (CO) and San Francisco (CA)
Recent Project: Exterior portrait, St. Dominic's Church, Benicia, CA (1995)

DONER STUDIO

MICHELE OKA DONER
94 MERCER ST
NEW YORK, NY 10012-4425
FAX 212-334-9236
TEL 212-334-9056

Work: architectural metal, architectural ceramics, mosaics, and wall relief, furniture, flooring
Media: metal, ceramics, concrete, terrazzo
Special Concerns: collaborative design teams, historical and documentary issues, science or teaching related
Commission Amounts: $50,000 - $350,000
Agencies: Miami/Dade (FL) Art in Public Places; Arts for Transit, Metropolitan Transit Authority, NY; City of Philadelphia (PA) Percent for Art
Recent Project: 2,000 flat bronze elements embedded in terrazzo, Miami International Airport (1992)

SEENA DONNESON

SEENA DONNESON STUDIO
4349 10TH ST
LONG ISLAND CITY, NY 11101-6923
TEL 718-706-1342

Work: sculpture (free standing), architectural ceramics, mosaics, and wall relief, fiber work for interior walls
Media: metal, concrete, paper
Special Concerns: community involvement, multicultural issues, environmental issues
Commission Amounts: up to $75,000
Agencies: New York (NY) Dept. of Parks; Artists Representing Environmental Art (AREA); New York (NY) Dept. of Cultural Affairs
Recent Project: Painted steel abstract sculpture, 10' × 5' × 5', for permanent outdoor installation at mall

CATHERINE COFFIN DOSS

7050 CRAWFORD ST
ANCHORAGE, AK 99502-2729
TEL 907-243-6843

Work: architectural glass, other media for interior walls, painted wood with fused glass
Media: glass, wood, paint
Special Concerns: science or teaching related
Commission Amounts: $1,200 - $22,000
Agencies: Municipality of Anchorage Percent for Art in Public Places
Recent Project: Painted wood panel with attached fused glass (1990)

DON DRUMM

DON DRUMM STUDIOS AND GALLERY
437 CROUSE ST
AKRON, OH 44311-1220
FAX 216-253-4014
TEL 216-253-6268

Work: sculpture (free standing and wall relief)
Media: metal, concrete
Special Concerns: site/client specific
Commission Amounts: $3,000 - $50,000
Agencies: City of Akron, OH; City of Baltimore, MD; US Department of State, Foreign Building Operations, American Embassy, Honduras
Recent Project: *The Golfer's Sun*, three wall relief sculptures for the NEC World Series of Golf (1993)

TIMOTHY DUFFIELD

1551 JOHNNYS WAY
WEST CHESTER, PA 19382-7851
TEL 610-430-8557

Work: sculpture (free standing), architectural elements, fountains
Media: metal, brick, earth and plants
Special Concerns: collaborative design teams, historical and documentary issues, garden art and artifacts
Commission Amounts: $12,000 - $150,000
Agencies: City of Wilmington, DE; Fairmount Park Art Commission, Philadelphia, PA; Redevelopment Authority, Philadelphia, PA
Recent Project: World War II Memorial, bronze, Wilmington, DE, 14'6"H

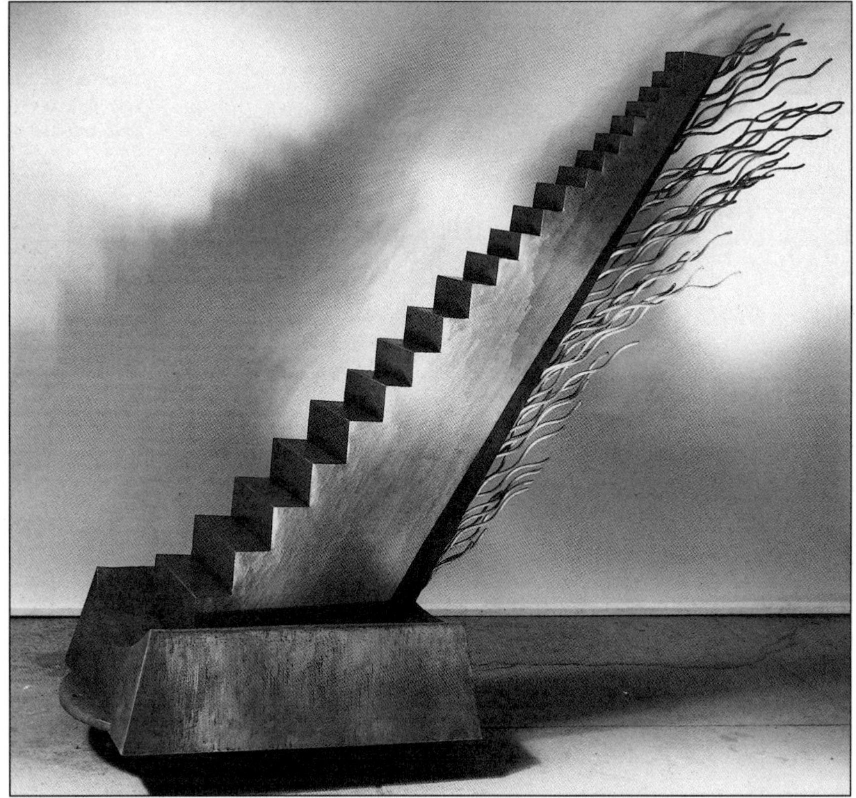

Bella Feldman, *Afloat*, 1987, steel, 56" × 62" × 20"

PUBLIC ART

PAT DURR

PAT DURR ARTS
167 FIRST AVE
OTTAWA, ON K1S 2G3
CANADA
TEL 613-232-8755

Work: sculpture (wall relief), painted finishes and murals, 2D work
Media: paint, wood, engraved glaze bloc
Special Concerns: collaborative design teams, science and teaching related
Commission Amounts: $16,000 - $45,000
Agencies: City of Ottawa Art & Public Places, 1% program; Regional Municipality of Ottawa/Carleton & OC Transpo; Ontario Ministry of Gov't Services, 1% program
Recent Project: *Linkages* dramatically unites the landscape and architecture with color and image

★ ED DWIGHT

ED DWIGHT STUDIOS, INC.
3824 DAHLIA ST
DENVER, CO 80207-1020
FAX 303-322-9669
TEL 303-329-9040

Work: sculpture (free standing, pedestal and wall relief), collaborative site design, fountains
Media: metal, mixed
Special Concerns: historical and documentary issues, multicultural issues
Commission Amounts: $10,000 - $4.5 million
Agencies: National Park Service; Ohio Arts Commission; State of Colorado
Recent Project: Underground Railroad Memorial monument, 30'L, installed in Battle Creek, MI

For Ed Dwight, internationally renown for his *Jazz: An American Art Form* series of bronzes, art has been a lifelong passion. In 1961, Ed detoured to become America's first African American astronaut trainee. By 1975, he realized his real passion for art, developing a series depicting the contributions of Blacks in the American Frontier West. In addition, Ed has created many large scale works, including Frederick Douglass, Hank Aaron, and Martin Luther King, Jr., and a memorial to the Underground Railroad.

See page 155 for photographs and additional information.

MICHAEL DWYER

EGG PRODUCTIONS
9 WOOD ST
HONESDALE, PA 18431
TEL 717-253-5874

Work: sculpture (wall relief), billboards
Media: metal, wood, plastics
Special Concerns: community involvement, participatory works, environmental issues
Commission Amounts: $10,000 - $25,000
Agencies: Cambridge Arts Council, MA; Dancing in the Streets, New York, NY; Lookout Sculpture Park, PA
Recent Project: *Birdboard*, a cross between a billboard and a bird feeder

★ KEVIN EARLEY

KEVIN EARLEY FURNITURE DESIGN
1231 E WILSON ST
MADISON, WI 53703-3759
FAX 608-256-5171
TEL 608-256-5171

Work: architectural elements, furniture, temporary installations
Media: wood, mixed, plastics
Special Concerns: collaborative design teams, historical and documentary issues, environmental issues
Commission Amounts: $8,000 - $26,000
Agencies: Wisconsin Arts Board
Recent Project: UW Library Lobby, 40' reception desk with abstract relief sculpture

After more than 20 years, I find that I still enjoy the challenge of balancing a design functionally and aesthetically as well as meeting the goals of the individual project. My work is designed on paper after discussion with the client. I also use models, samples and prototypes to convey the final design concept. Construction is carried out in my own studio and with the help of skilled workers whom I've dealt with for years.

See page 207 for photographs and additional information.

EAST LOS STREETSCAPERS

WAYNE HEALY
PO BOX 31460
LOS ANGELES, CA 90031-0460
FAX 818-571-6762
TEL 818-571-6761

Work: painted finishes and murals, architectural ceramics, mosaics, and wall relief, paintings, photographs (2-D), multimedia installations
Media: metal, ceramics, paint
Special Concerns: collaborative design teams, multicultural issues, environmental issues
Commission Amounts: $50,000 - $375,000
Agencies: City of Los Angeles Cultural Affairs Dept.; California Arts Council
Recent Project: Los Angeles Police Recruit Training Center Memorial (1994); El Pueblo San Jose de Guadalupe (1995); Union Station Gateway (1995)

GARTH EDWARDS

1602 10TH AVE W
SEATTLE, WA 98119-2925
TEL 206-789-9956

Work: architectural elements, architectural ceramics, mosaics, and wall relief, collaborative site design
Media: metal, glass, stone
Special Concerns: collaborative design teams
Commission Amounts: $15,000 - $150,000
Agencies: Seattle Arts Commission; Kansas City Art Commission; Anchorage Art Commission
Recent Project: Project Artist, Seattle Children's Theater, Seattle Center (1993)

ROBERT W. ELLISON

6480 EAGLE RIDGE RD
PENNGROVE, CA 94951
FAX 707-795-9775
TEL 707-795-9775

Work: sculpture (free standing), architectural metal, furniture
Media: metal, paint, concrete
Special Concerns: community involvement, issues related to disabilities, science and teaching related
Commission Amounts: $15,000 - $200,000
Agencies: Wisconsin Arts Board, Percent for Art Project; San Francisco Art Commission, Public Art Program; Municipality of Anchorage, Museum of History and Art
Recent Project: Heroic 18' abstract sculpture for Athletic Fieldhouse, University of Wisconsin

FREDERICK EVERSLEY

ENGINEERED AESTHETICS
29 MERCER ST
NEW YORK, NY 10013
FAX 212-431-3120
TEL 212-431-4222

Work: sculpture (free standing, atrium and pedestal)
Media: metal, concrete, plastics, fountains
Special Concerns: multicultural issues, environmental issues
Commission Amounts: $30,000 - $175,000
Agencies: Dade County Art in Public Places, Miami, FL; San Francisco Art Commission, San Francisco, CA; California Art Commission, Sacramento, CA
Recent Project: Large crystal-clear oil fountain, Expo 92, Seville, Spain

★ CHARLES FAGER
★ JOAN MARMARELLIS

MARMARELLIS-FAGER STUDIO
804 S NEWPORT AVE
TAMPA, FL 33606-2935
FAX 813-254-4028
TEL 813-254-4028

Work: sculpture (free standing, atrium and wall relief)
Media: metal, ceramics, concrete
Special Concerns: collaborative design teams, community involvement, science and teaching related
Commission Amounts: $9,000 - $100,000
Agencies: State of Florida Art in State Buildings; Jacksonville (FL) Department of Housing and Urban Development; St. Petersburg (FL) Percent for Art
Recent Project: *Art-Cistern*, water conservation collaboration for Hillsborough County Courthouse, FL

These artists combine their skills in art, craft and architecture to produce engaging public art. Projects include ceramic walls, brightly colored, reflective, metal sculptures, cast concrete sculptures, and atrium pieces in metal or fabric. Their current courthouse project involves collaboration with county officials, planners, engineers and landscape architects in an exciting water conservation project. They have designed the 'art-cistern,' garden seating, educational signage, and site plan which includes xeriscaping and accommodates two exsisting war memorials.

See page 128 for photographs and additional information.

M. ANNA FARIELLO

PO BOX 6965
RADFORD, VA 24142-6965
TEL 703-831-5754

Work: sculpture (free standing and wall relief), temporary installations, performances
Media: mixed
Special Concerns: participatory works, historical and documentary issues
Commission Amounts: $850 - $3,000
Agencies: Roanoke (VA) Arts Council; Hult Center, Eugene OR

MING FAY

MING FAY STUDIO
830 BROADWAY
NEW YORK, NY 10003
FAX 212-477-6508
TEL 212-477-6508

Work: sculpture (free standing, pedestal and wall relief), architectural metal
Media: metal, ceramics, glass
Special Concerns: multicultural issues, environmental issues
Commission Amounts: $60,000 - $180,000
Agencies: New York City Percent for Art; Philadelphia, PA Percent for Art
Recent Project: Sculpture using the treasures of the elm tree as an emblem, P.S.7 school in Elmhurst, Queens, NY

LONNIE FEATHER

LONNIE FEATHER STUDIO
733 NW EVERETT #24
PORTLAND, OR 97209
TEL 503-222-9773

Work: architectural glass
Media: mixed, glass
Special Concerns: community involvement, historical and documentary issues, environmental issues
Commission Amounts: $3,000 - $30,000
Agencies: Regional Arts & Culture Council, Percent for Art Program, Portland, OR
Recent Project: Metro Headquarters, 30 glass panels depicting livability of regional Portland (1993)

RANDY FEIN

MOUNTAIN STUDIO
4163 YOUNGTOWN RD
LINCOLNVILLE, ME 04843
TEL 207-763-3433

Work: ceramics, wall relief
Media: clay
Special Concerns: historical/documentary issues, environmental issues, nature, underwater life
Commission Amounts: $3,000 - $40,000
Agencies: Maine Arts Commission; University of Southern Maine
Recent Project: *If I Could See Beneath the Sea*, wall relief, Children's Hospital waiting room, 4' x 36' (1994)

★ BELLA FELDMAN

12 SUMMIT LN
BERKELEY, CA 94708-2213
FAX 510-843-2591
TEL 510-654-0968

Work: sculpture (free standing, atrium and pedestal)
Media: metal, wood, mixed
Special Concerns: collaborative design teams, participatory works, environmental issues
Commission Amounts: $15,000 - $107,000
Agencies: Worked directly for Federal Home Loan Bank of San Francisco; City of Richmond; Newport Harbor
Recent Project: Designed, built and installed a stainless steel sculpture fountain in lobby

See photograph page 235.

HELAMAN FERGUSON

HELAMAN FERGUSON, SCULPTOR
10512 PILLA TERRA CT
LAUREL, MD 20723-5728
FAX 301-776-0499
TEL 301-604-4270

Work: sculpture (free standing, atrium and pedestal)
Media: metal, stone
Special Concerns: science and teaching related
Commission Amounts: $5,000 - $45,000
Agencies: Utah Arts Commission; Ohio Arts Council
Recent Project: *Eight Fold Way*, marble, steel, serpentine

JACKIE FERRARA

121 PRINCE ST
NEW YORK, NY 10012-3162
FAX 212-673-2215
TEL 212-673-0625

Work: collaborative site design, courtyard, lobby
Media: concrete, wood, stone
Special Concerns: collaborative design teams, community involvement, architectural
Commission Amounts: $25,000 - $160,000
Agencies: Public Art St. Paul; Dormitory Authority, State of New York; City Transit Authority, NY
Recent Project: *Covered Walkway*, 110'L, concrete block structure, Lehman College, Bronx, NY

BARBARA FIELD

1637 ELECTRIC AVE
VENICE, CA 90291-4803
FAX 310-314-0096
TEL 310-396-4474

Work: sculpture (free-standing), murals, functional elements
Media: mosaic tile, others
Special Concerns: collaborative design teams, community involvement, historical and documentary issues
Commission Amounts: $7,000 - $58,000
Agencies: Public Art Visions for Environment (PAVE); Los Angeles Dept. of Cultural Affairs; City of Palm Desert
Recent Project: Installation of sculpture and functional elements for the John C. Fremont Library

★ BRUCE PAUL FINK

POLE BRIDGE STUDIO/FOUNDRY
90 POLE BRIDGE RD
WOODSTOCK, CT 06281-1202
FAX 203-974-0130
TEL 203-974-0130

Work: sculpture (free standing, pedestal and wall relief), architectural metal, fountains, functional sculpture
Media: metal, stone, plastics, metalized bronzes
Special Concerns: participatory works, issues related to disabilities
Commission Amounts: $3,000 - $40,000
Agencies: Connecticut Commission on the Arts; United Health Services of Dayville and Eastern CT
Recent Project: Sculptural works in conjunction with special-need families and community relations, converting their endeavors into bronze, etc.

See page 25 for photographs and additional information.

R.M. FISCHER

R.M. FISCHER ARTWORK, INC.
12 WARREN ST
NEW YORK, NY 10007-2238
FAX 212-619-1425
TEL 212-619-1425

Work: sculpture (free standing and atrium), lighting
Media: metal, mixed, stone
Special Concerns: community involvement, historical and documentary issues, environmental issues
Commission Amounts: $50,000 - $1,000,000
Agencies: Commitee for Public Art, Cleveland, OH; Municipal Art Commission, Kansas City, MO; New Jersey State Council on the Arts
Recent Project: *Gateway Columns-Sport Stacks*, 92'H and 80'H, illuminated plaza towers for ballpark and arena complex in Cleveland (1992-94)

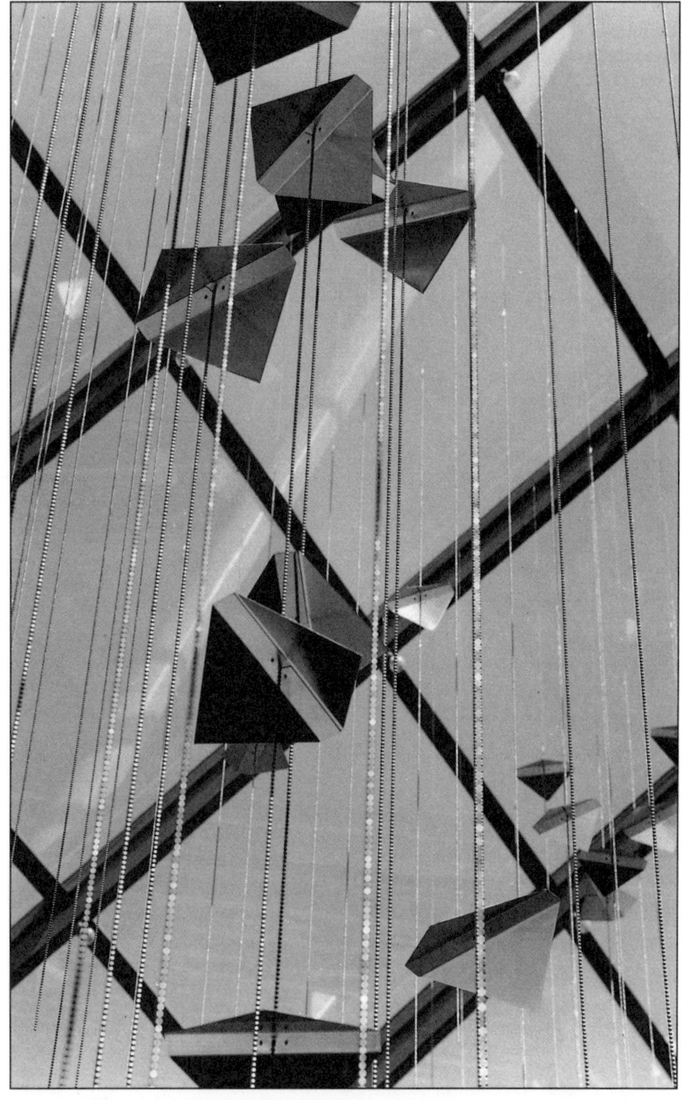

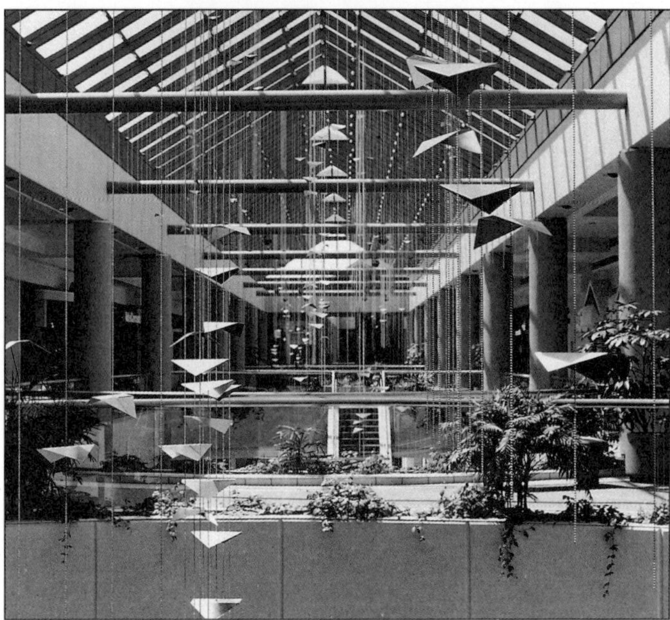

Rob Fisher, *Symphony of the Air*, 1991, Scottsdale, AZ, stainless steel, 20' x 46' x 800', photo: Al Payne

★ ROB FISHER

ENVIRONMENTAL SCULPTURE
228 N ALLEGHENY ST
BELLEFONTE, PA 16823-1630
FAX 814-353-9060
TEL 814-355-1458
Work: sculpture (atrium), fountains,
light related
Media: metal, paint, fiber optics
Special Concerns: science and teaching
related, nature
Commission Amounts: $50,000 - $180,000
Agencies: Scottsdale, Arizona Percent
for Art; City of Hamamatsu, Japan;
Philadelphia (PA) Percent for Art
Recent Project: Suspended stainless steel
sculpture, 800'L, Scottsdale, Arizona (1991)

Public art must address many issues, from
the functional and aesthetic character of
the site to the needs of the client, the
culture of the country or city, durability
of materials, economics, scheduling, installation procedures, and safety considerations. While maintaining an experienced perspective on these items, I endow
my artworks with a sense of place, an
evocation of nature, and a boldness of
scale and vision that has captured the
imagination and appreciation of viewers
worldwide.

See pages 129 and 237 for photo-
graphs and additional information.

BILL FITZGIBBONS

PO BOX 460852
SAN ANTONIO, TX 78246
FAX 210-826-0223
TEL 210-826-0223
Work: collaborative site design,
neon, laser, light related, plazas
Media: mixed, ceramics, neon
Special Concerns: collaborative design
teams, participatory works, environmental
issues
Commission Amounts: $7,000 - $200,000
Agencies: Rhode Island State Council
of the Arts; Alaska State Arts Council;
Hampshire Sculpture Trust, Hampshire,
England
Recent Project: Neon mural for the
Rhode Island Convention Center

DAN FONTES

2200 ADELINE ST #250
OAKLAND, CA 94607-2332
TEL 510-208-2942
Work: painted finishes and murals,
2D work
Media: paint
Special Concerns: collaborative design
teams, historical and documentary issues,
environmental issues
Commission Amounts: $20,000 - $100,000
Agencies: CALTRANS; City of Oakland
Cultural Arts Division; City of Concord
Art in Public Places
Recent Project: Exterior mural painting
for CALTRANS, Oakland, CA (1994)

SARA AUERBACH FOX

PO BOX 55
LAKE HELEN, FL 32744-0055
TEL 904-238-5899
Work: sculpture (free standing), painted
finishes and murals, temporary installations
Media: mixed
Special Concerns: historical and docu-
mentary issues, multicultural issues,
environmental issues
Commission Amounts: $45,000 - $100,000
Agencies: County of Deland, FL; County
of Daytona Beach, FL
Recent Project: Paintings of the Holo-
caust for Memorial and Education
Center, State of Michigan

MARY EDNA FRASER

PO BOX 12250
CHARLESTON, SC 29422-2250
FAX 803-723-1307
TEL 803-762-2594
Work: sculpture (atrium), collaborative
site design, fiber work for interior walls,
batik on silk
Media: fiber, silk
Special Concerns: collaborative design
teams, environmental issues, science and
teaching related
Commission Amounts: $500 - $20,000
Agencies: City of Charleston (SC) Visitor
Reception Center; Charleston (SC)
County Aviation Authority; American
Embassy of Thailand
Recent Project: One-woman exhibition,
National Air and Space Museum, Smith-
sonian Institute, Washington, DC

★ DOUGLAS OLMSTED FREEMAN

DOUG FREEMAN
SCULPTURE STUDIO
310 N 2ND ST
MINNEAPOLIS, MN 55401-1311
FAX 612-339-7150
TEL 612-339-7150
Work: sculpture (free standing),
fountains
Media: metal, glass, stone
Special Concerns: collaborative design
teams, participatory works, myth
Commission Amounts: $5,000 - $250,000
Agencies: Duluth Public Arts Commis-
sion; Minnesota Percent for Art
Recent Project: *Fountain of the Wind*,
a participatory fountain including ten
sculptures (1994)

Commissions evolve with a creative
response to site, context and the client's
goals for the project. Doug Freeman is
open to collaboration and is particularly
interested in projects that involve participation of the viewer, such as parks,
plazas, playgrounds, zoos, fountains or
memorials. Works have included figurative bronze, stainless steel, custom lighting and fountains. Please call or write
if your would like to discuss ideas or
project plans.

See pages 182-183 for photographs
and additional information.

FRESCO

RAYMOND PATLAN
& EDUARDO PINEDA
54 BALMY ST
SAN FRANCISCO, CA 94110-4111
FAX 415-863-1165
TEL 415-282-9076
Work: collaborative site design, painted
finishes, murals, temporary installations
Media: metal, ceramics, paint, mixed
Special Concerns: community involve-
ment, multicultural issues, issues related
to disabilities
Commission Amounts: $6,000 - $30,000
Agencies: San Francisco Arts Commission;
California Arts Council
Recent Project: Created indoor mural
environment for local restaurant and
alternative gallery

MARY FULLER

2955 SONOMA MOUNTAIN RD
PETALUMA, CA 94954-9559
TEL 707-795-4612
Work: sculpture (free standing and
wall relief), fountains
Media: concrete
Special Concerns: community involvement
multicultural issues
Commission Amounts: $15,000 - $90,000
Agencies: San Francisco Art Commission;
California Arts Council; Santa Cruz Art
Commission
Recent Project: Four new sculptures for
Portsmouth Square, SF Art Commission
(1994)

CLYDETTA FULMER

LONGVIEW STUDIO
RR 1 BOX 310
MONTGOMERY, AL 36105-9723
TEL 205-281-9485
Work: sculpture (free standing, pedestal
and wall relief), collaborative site design,
fountains, architectural metal
Media: metal, concrete
Special Concerns: collaborative design
teams, historical and documentary issues,
issues related to disabilities, religious
Commission Amounts: $7,500 - $33,000
Agencies: Montgomery (AL) County
Commission; State of Alabama;
U.S. Government
Recent Project: Life-sized bronze figure
of a newsboy for the free Lance-Star
Newspaper, Fredericksburg, VA

SUSAN FURINI

1417 S RITA LN
TEMPE, AZ 85281-5806
TEL 602-967-2385
Work: sculpture (free standing and wall
relief), temporary installations
Media: ceramics, glass, synthetic plaster
Special Concerns: community involve-
ment, historical and documentary issues,
functional
Agencies: Arizona Commission on the
Arts; Colorado Commission on the Arts
and Humanities; City of Corpus Christi
Recent Project: *Oasis*, relief wall mural,
8'H x 23'W x 8"D, Wickenburg Munici-
pal Center, Wickenburg, AZ

CHARLES EUGENE GAGNON

GAGNON STUDIO
PO BOX 4
ROCHESTER, MN 55903-0004
TEL 507-282-5202
Work: sculpture (free standing),
fountains
Media: metal, bronze
Special Concerns: community involve-
ment, historical and documentary issues
Agencies: City of Rochester, MN
Recent Project: *Peace Fountain*, bronze
sculpture, 12'H (1989)

GAIL

2105 SANBORN DR
SEDONA, AZ 86336-3250
TEL 602-282-2665
Work: sculpture (free standing, pedestal
and wall relief)
Media: metal, stone, brick
Special Concerns: community involve-
ment, historical and documentary issues,
multicultural issues
Commission Amounts: $20,000 - $120,000
Agencies: Prescott Community Art
Trust, Prescott AZ; Phoenix Commission
for the Arts, Phoenix, AZ
Recent Project: Tribute to Arizona's
smallest Native American tribe, over
80% larger than life, bronze

SUSAN GAMBLE

815 E MABEL ST
TUCSON, AZ 85719-4036
FAX 520-882-0868
TEL 520-623-1856
Work: sculpture (wall relief), collabora-
tive site design, fountains, mosaics, other
work for interior walls
Media: metal, ceramics, concrete
Special Concerns: collaborative design
teams, community involvement, historical/
documentary issues, multicultural issues
Commission Amounts: $5,000 - $95,000
Agencies: Tucson/Pima Arts Council;
Tucson Arts District Partnership;
Tempe Arts Council
Recent Project: Ceramic mosaic work
documenting multicultural/historic
development of Tucson City Center

ROBERT GEHRKE

613 N BARSTOW ST
EAU CLAIRE, WI 54703-3043
TEL 715-835-7076
Work: sculpture (free standing and
pedestal)
Media: metal, glass, wood
Special Concerns: historical and docu-
mentary issues
Commission Amounts: $2,000 - $16,000
Agencies: Maine Arts Commission; Wis-
consin Arts Board; Minnesota Arts Board
Recent Project: *Flyway*, birds in Cor-ten
steel, Winona (MN) State University
(1993)

★ DAN GEORGE

567 DRIGGS AVE
BROOKLYN, NY 11211-3205
FAX 718-388-2587
TEL 718-782-2409

Work: sculpture, collaborative site design, site-specific
Media: metal, reflective color
Special Concerns: collaborative design teams, community involvement, historical and documentary issues
Commission Amounts: $50,000 minimum
Agencies: Arts for Transit, Metropolitan Transit Authority, New York, NY; Urbanarts, Inc., MBTA, Boston; Arts Inclusion, NJSCA, NJ
Recent Project: Serial installation suspended from MTA tracks at Brighton Beach, New York City (1994)

See page 209 for photographs and additional information.

DIMITRI GERAKARIS

SCULPTURAL AND ARCHITECTURAL METALWORK
UPPER GATES RD PO BOX 928G
CANAAN, NH 03741
FAX 603-523-7366
TEL 603-523-7366

Work: architectural metal
Media: metal
Commission Amounts: $10,000 - $140,000
Agencies: City of Boston; New York, MTA
Recent Project: *Boylston Place Gateway*, award-winning entrance gate to Boston's Theater District

ANN GILLEN

62 GRAND ST
NEW YORK, NY 10013-2245
TEL 212-226-5288

Work: sculpture (free standing, atrium and wall relief)
Media: metal, stone, paint
Special Concerns: collaborative design teams, participatory works, environmental issues, use of solar energy
Commission Amounts: $10,000 - $1500,000
Agencies: New York City Percent for Art; New Jersey State Council on the Arts; Lincoln Center for the Performing Arts, NY
Recent Project: Murals, columns, stairwells, Lincoln Center for the Performing Arts, NY

GLASS ART STUDIO

LAURIE L. THAL
STAR RT 352-A
JACKSON, WY 83001
TEL 307-733-5096

Work: architectural glass
Media: glass
Agencies: Wyoming Arts Council
Recent Project: *Soaring Rays*, slumped plate glass forms portraying floating bird or sea forms, 3'W × 4'L (1990)

★ HELEN GLAZER

3413 NANCY ELLEN WAY
OWINGS MILLS, MD 21117
FAX 410-654-0077
TEL 410-654-0077

Work: painted finishes and murals, 2D work
Media: paint, cast plaster
Special Concerns: multicultural issues, issues related to disabilities, science or teaching related
Commission Amounts: $6,000 - $15,000
Agencies: Mayor's Advisory Committee on Art and Culture, Baltimore, MD; Department of Education, City of Baltimore, MD
Recent Project: 28' × 60' outdoor mural in an urban neighborhood

I am interested in the intersection of art and other areas of human inquiry - the theme of the mural pictured in this publication ecompasses comparative mytholyogy and astronomy. While my public art always has a solid intellectual underpinning, it is also accessible to a wide audience, visually appealing, and integrated with the architecture and function of the space where it is installed. I am currently creating a tactile mural for an elementary school serving the visually impaired.

See photograph below.

BETTY GOLD

1324 PACIFIC AVE
VENICE, CA 90291-3608
TEL 310-399-5205

Work: sculpture (free standing), fountains
Media: metal
Special Concerns: community involvement
Commission Amounts: $10,000 - $200,000
Agencies: Downey Museum of Art, Downey, CA; City of Stoughton, WI
Recent Project: South Texas Museum of Art, steel, geo design, permanent installation, 8' × 9¹/₂' × 5' (1995)

GOLDMAN ARTS, INC.

JONATHAN GOLDMAN
107 SOUTH ST #403
BOSTON, MA 02111-2811
FAX 617-423-6601
TEL 617-423-6606

Work: sculpture (free standing and atrium), collaborative site design, outdoor furniture and equipment, furniture, temporary installations
Media: fabric
Special Concerns: collaborative design teams, environmental issues, science or teaching related
Commission Amounts: $2,500 - $45,000
Agencies: Massachusetts Arts Lottery
Recent Project: Parade float for Clairmont, Monclair, NJ

PAUL MIRCEA GORE

MOUNTAIN VIEW SCULPTURE STUDIO
100 WOOD RD
LOS GATOS, CA 95030-6704
FAX 408-354-0163
TEL 408-354-0163
TEL 408-247-2023

Work: sculpture (free standing), sculptural fountains
Media: metal, stone
Special Concerns: hope of humanity for peace
Commission Amounts: $35,000 - $250,000
Agencies: Cities of Concord (CA), Los Gatos (CA) and Palo Alto (CA) Art in Public Places programs

JIM GREEN

720 16TH ST #314
DENVER, CO 80202
FAX 303-442-1508
TEL 303-629-7617

Work: collaborative site design, temporary installations, sound installations
Media: mixed, sound
Special Concerns: collaborative design teams, participatory works, humor issues
Commission Amounts: $3,000 - $120,000
Agencies: Denver Public Art Program; Port of Seattle Percent for Art Program; Miami Metro-Dade Art in Public Places
Recent Project: *Train Call*, musical chimes and voice messages for Denver International Airport train system

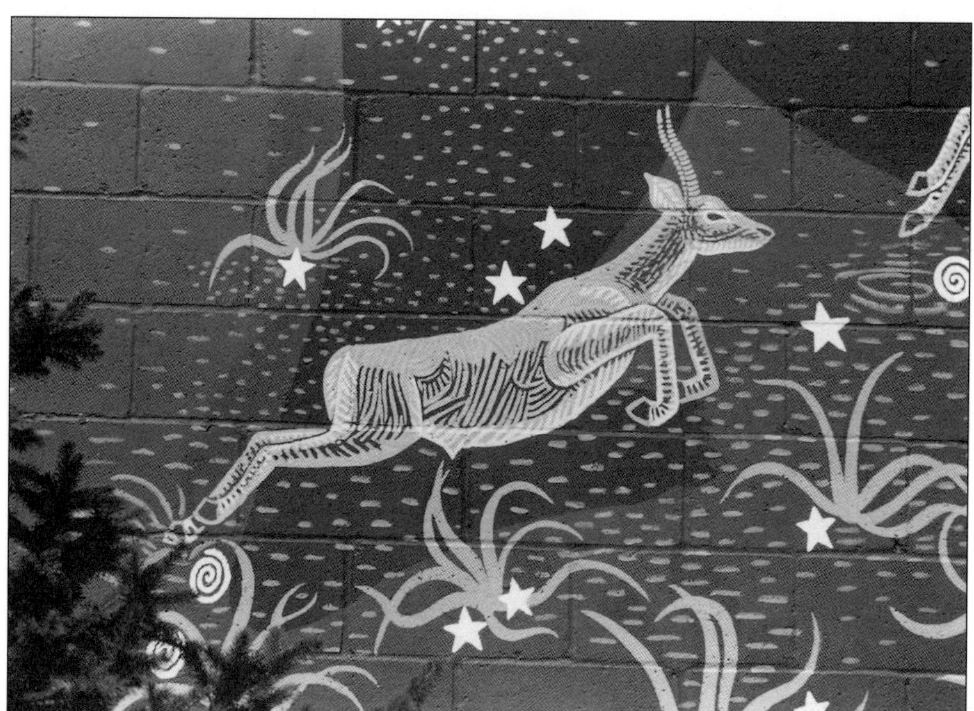

Helen Glazer, *Two Bears and Variations* (detail),1993, mural commissioned by the City of Baltimore, MD, exterior latex on cinderblock wall, 56" × 80" detail of 28' × 60' mural

PUBLIC ART

GEORGE MOSSMAN GREENAMYER

CARESWELL SCULPTURE AND
 IRON WORKS
994 CARESWELL ST
MARSHFIELD, MA 02050-5637
FAX 617-837-8242
TEL 617-834-9688
Work: sculpture (free standing), gateways
Media: metal, paint
Special Concerns: community involve-
ment, historical and documentary issues,
narrative
Commission Amounts: $40,000 - $80,000
Agencies: Longmont (CO) Art in Public
Places; Arizona Percent for Art; Oregon
Percent for Art
Recent Project: Outdoor narrative sculp-
ture, Clinical Academic Building, Univer-
sity of Medicine and Dentistry of New
Jersey, New Brunswick (1994)

BARBARA GRENELL

1132 HALLS CHAPPEL RD
BURNSVILLE, NC 28714-9760
TEL 704-675-4073
Work: fiber work for interior walls
Media: mixed, fiber, tapestry
Special Concerns: environmental issues,
the landscape
Commission Amounts: $5,000 - $20,000
Agencies: Wake Medical Center, Raleigh,
NC; North Carolina Arts Council
Recent Project: Three triangular
constructed tapestries, 8' x 18' overall

GREY DUN STUDIO

PATRICIA POWERS
 & DIANA HENRY
383 POOLES HILL RD
ANCRAM, NY 12502
FAX 518-589-3659
TEL 518-329-2671
Work: floor cloths, wall cloths
Media: paint, ceramics
Special Concerns: collaborative design
teams, science or teaching related, art
historical imagery
Commission Amounts: $1,000 - $300,000
Agencies: California Arts Council;
Dutchess County Arts Council (NY);
Greene County Arts Council (NY)
Recent Project: Mural on canvas,
120" x 216", horses and arches,
California Arts Council (1987)

DAVID GRIGGS

1229 S SHERMAN ST
DENVER, CO 80210-1512
FAX 303-744-2651
TEL 303-733-7945
Work: sculpture (free standing and
atrium), neon/laser/light related
Media: metal, mixed, wood
Special Concerns: collaborative design
teams, historical/documentary issues,
environmental issues
Commission Amounts: $10,000 - $400,000
Agencies: Washington State Arts Com-
mission; Denver Airport Arts Commission;
City of Albuquerque Arts Commission
Recent Project: *Dual Meridian*, the evolu-
tion of transportation at Denver's new
airport (1993)

ESTHER A. GRILLO

214 BEACH 120TH ST
BELLE HARBOR, NY 11694
TEL 718-945-3131
Work: sculpture (free standing), architec-
tural ceramics, mosaics, and wall relief,
temporary installations
Media: ceramics, concrete, mixed
Special Concerns: historical/documentary
issues, multicultural issues, environmental
issues
Commission Amounts: $10,000
Agencies: New York City Mass Trans-
portation Authority; Creative Arts
Recent Project: *In Search of Harmony
Bay*, 38' x 4' x 6' painted concrete
(1992)

JACK GRON

UNIVERSITY OF KENTUCKY
207 FINE ARTS BUILDING
LEXINGTON, KY 40506-0001
FAX 606-257-3042
TEL 606-257-8155
Work: sculpture (free standing),
architectural metal
Media: metal
Special Concerns: community involve-
ment, historical and documentary issues,
science and teaching related
Commission Amounts: $15,000 - $75,000
Agencies: City of Lexington, KY; Village
of Elmwood Park, IL
Recent Project: Cast bronze and welded
steel monument for the City of Lexington

BARBARA GRYGUTIS

135 S 6TH AVE #C
TUCSON, AZ 85701-2007
FAX 602-882-5572
TEL 602-882-5572
Work: sculpture (free standing), collabo-
rative site design, fountains
Media: concrete, ceramics, stone
Special Concerns: community involve-
ment, environmental issues, multicultural
issues, importance of place
Commission Amounts: $25,000 - $300,000
Agencies: Ohio Arts Council; Minnesota
Percent for Art in Public Places; General
Services Administration
Recent Project: Gateway to and from
Mexico at border station in South Texas

★ MARK ERIC GULSRUD

**ARCHITECTURAL GLASS
 AND CLAY
3309 TAHOMA PL W
TACOMA, WA 98466-1620
TEL 206-566-1720**
Work: sculpture (free standing), collabo-
rative site design, architectural glass
Media: metal, ceramics, glass
Special Concerns: collaborative design
teams, community involvement
Commission Amounts: $45,000 - $175,000
Agencies: Alaska State Arts Commission;
Hollywood Redevopment Agency; King
County (Seattle) Arts Commission

**See page 46 for photographs
and additional information.**

BARRY GUNDERSON

PO BOX 515
GAMBIER, OH 43022-0515
TEL 614-427-3770
Work: sculpture (free standing)
Media: metal, paint
Commission Amounts: $5,000 - $70,000
Agencies: Ohio Arts Council; Oregon
Arts Council; Washington Arts Council
Recent Project: *Understorms*, Franklin
Park Conservatory courtyard, Columbus,
OH (1992)

GRIGORY GUREVICH

282 BARROW ST
JERSEY CITY, NJ 07302-3502
TEL 201-451-4862
Work: sculpture (free standing and wall
relief), temporary installations, architec-
tural ceramics, mosaics, and wall relief
Media: mixed
Special Concerns: historical and docu-
mentary issues
Commission Amounts: $10,000 - $230,000
Agencies: New Jersey Transit
Recent Project: *Commuters*, seven life
size bronze sculpture tableau, circa 1935,
Newark Pennsylvania Station, NJ (1985)

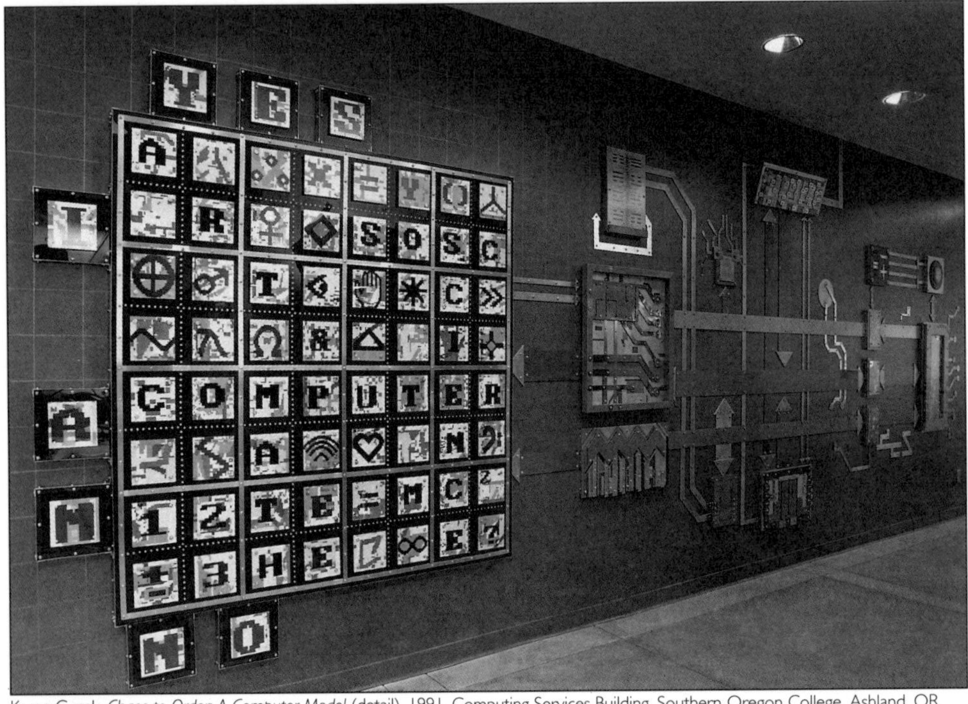

Karen Guzak, *Chaos to Order: A Computer Model* (detail), 1991, Computing Services Building, Southern Oregon College, Ashland, OR,
aluminum, plexiglass, L.E.D.'s, 14' x 65'

★ KAREN GUZAK

KAREN GUZAK, INC.
707 S SNOQUALMIE
SEATTLE, WA 98108
FAX 206-622-9878
TEL 206-343-0290

Work: sculpture (wall relief), painted finishes and murals, architectural elements
Media: metal, paint, glass
Special Concerns: collaborative design teams, science and teaching related
Commission Amounts: $16,000 - $45,000
Agencies: Oregon Arts Commission; Southern Oregon State College, Ashland, OR; Port of Seattle, Seatac Airport, Seattle WA
Recent Project: Team collaboration for design of four focal-point elevators at Seatac Airport, Seattle, WA

Karen Guzak is a multidisciplinary artist who is an innovator in combining traditional art-making techniques with computer assisted technology. She integrates architectural concerns and materials with artistic problem solving, often superimposing the mark of the machine and the mark of the hand to create lively, visual tapestries of the interface between art and science. Guzak's paintings and prints have been shown internationally, and her public sculpture commissions are in the Northwest.

See photograph page 240.

★ LLOYD HAMROL

LLOYD HAMROL STUDIO
PO BOX 861025
LOS ANGELES, CA 90086-1025
TEL 213-587-0945

Work: collaborative site design, site specific projects
Media: metal, concrete, stone, wood
Special Concerns: collaborative design teams, participatory works, environmental issues
Commission Amounts: $30,000 - $200,000
Agencies: Phoenix Arts Commission; Alaska State Arts Council; Seattle Arts Commission
Recent Project: Steel, stone and concrete elements for bridge over-wash, Phoenix, AZ (1995)

Over the past 20 years, the artist's primary interest has been audience interactive structures on a landscape scale. He favors stone masonry for its historical and cultural associations. Foremost among his concerns are to give the site a human scale, a memorable sense of place and a physical dimension through kinesthetic experience.

See photograph below.

PETER C. HARRIS

PO BOX 856
WEST DOVER, VT 05356
TEL 802-464-7187

Work: sculpture (free standing and wall relief), temporary installations
Media: metal, stone, plastics
Commission Amounts: $8,000 - $20,000
Agencies: Vermont Council on the Arts; Burlington City Arts Commission; Vermont Community Fund
Recent Project: Designed and fabricated water-sited temporary sculpture, Williamstown, MA

DENNY HASKEW

NATIONAL SCULPTORS' GUILD
2683 N TAFT AVE
LOVELAND, CO 80538
FAX 970-667-2068
TEL 970-667-2015

Work: sculpture (free standing and pedestal), collaborative site design
Media: metal, mixed
Special Concerns: collaborative design teams, historical and documentary issues, multicultural issues
Commission Amounts: $8,000 - $100,000
Agencies: City of Loveland, CO
Recent Project: Five bronze and stone monumental figures, Mariana Butte Golf Course, Loveland, CO (1995)

BROWER HATCHER

L.B. HATCHER & ASSOCIATES, INC.
PO BOX 41
DIAMOND POINT, NY 12824-0041
TEL 518-668-2662

Work: sculpture (free standing and wall relief), collaborative site design
Media: metal, stone, glass
Special Concerns: collaborative design teams, community involvement, environmental issues
Commission Amounts: $50,000 - $300,000
Agencies: Phoenix (AZ) Arts Commission; New York City Department of Cultural Affairs; City of Philadelphia Arts Commission
Recent Project: Stainless steel sculpture of 8' globe on 12' tree-form base, Thomas Jefferson Park, New York City

SARAH HAVILAND

SARAH HAVILAND STUDIO
906 SOUTH ST
PEEKSKILL, NY 10566-3427
TEL 914-734-4979

Work: sculpture (free standing and pedestal), fountains
Media: metal, concrete, earth and plants
Special Concerns: participatory works, multicultural issues
Commission Amounts: $3,000 - $20,000
Agencies: New York City Parks Department; The Dormitory Authority of New York, NY
Recent Project: *Queens Arch*, 10'H figure as archway, made of reinforced cement

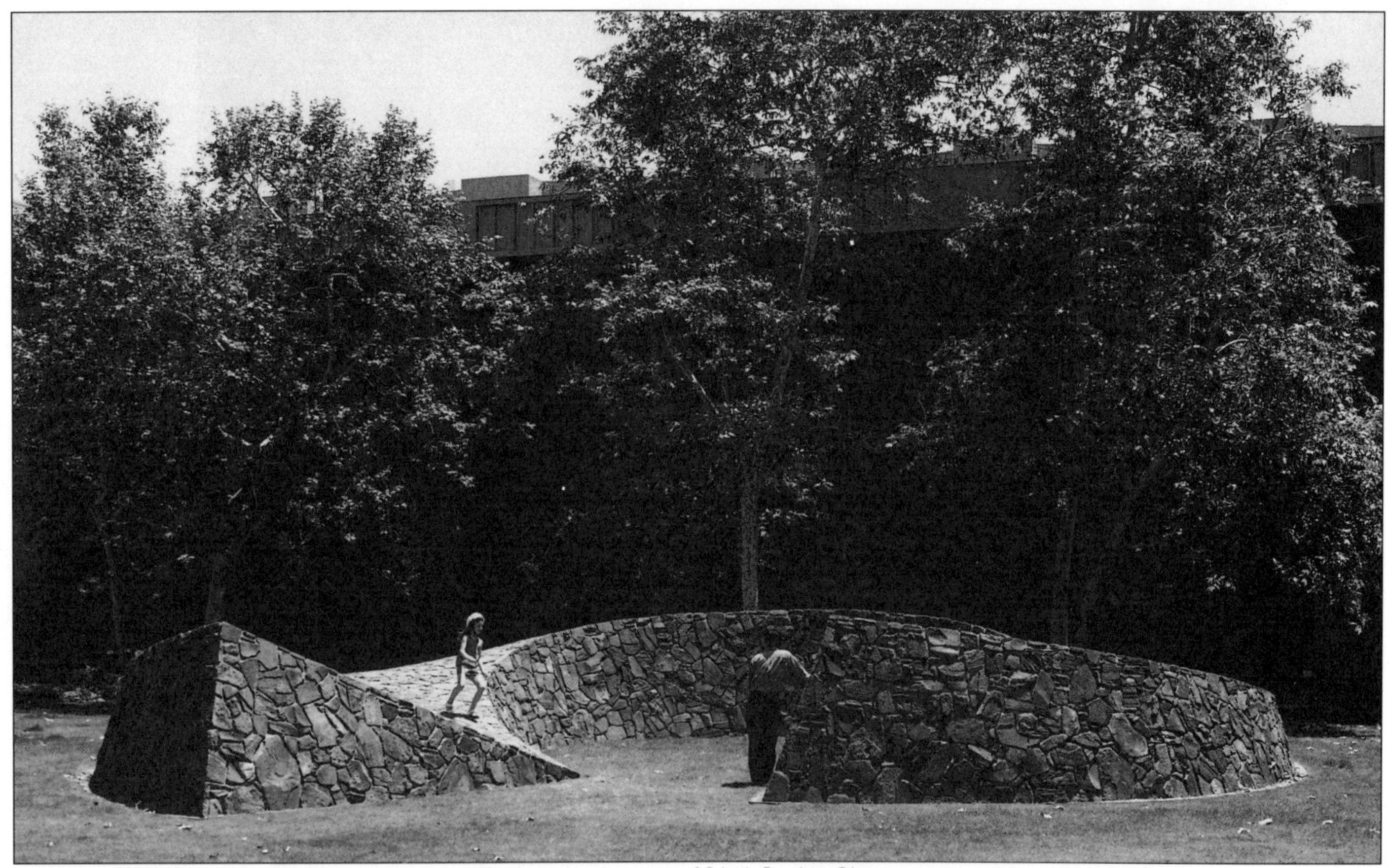

Lloyd Hamrol, *Moore's Stone Volute*, 1995, stone masonry, 6'H x 55'Dia, located on the campus of Caltech, Pasadena, CA

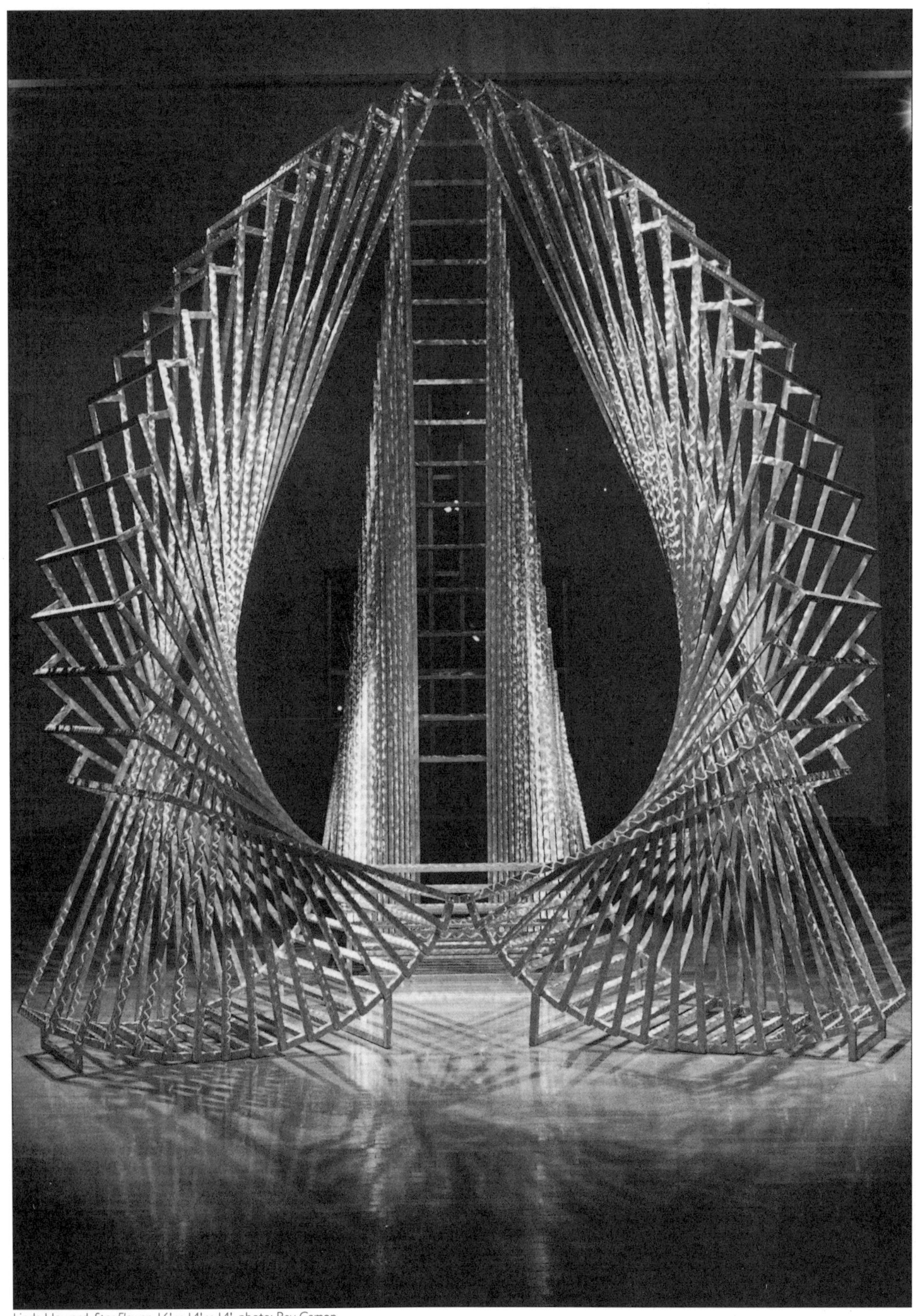

Linda Howard, *Star Flower*, 16' x 14' x 14', photo: Ray Carson

RALPH HELMICK

447 LOWELL AVE
NEWTON, MA 02160-2116
TEL 617-332-2433
Work: sculpture (free standing and atrium), collaborative site design
Media: metal, stone
Special Concerns: collaborative design teams, community involvement, art and technology
Commission Amounts: $45,000 - $250,000
Agencies: Austin (TX) Art in Public Places; Cambridge (MA) Arts Council; Evanston (IL) Arts Council
Recent Project: *Ghost Writer*, suspended sculpture for the Evanston (IL) Public Library

HOLLAND HOAGLAND HENEFIELD

95 PACKARDVILLE RD
PELHAM, MA 01002-9797
TEL 413-253-4212
Work: sculpture (free standing and wall relief), architectural elements
Media: wood, tree carvings
Special Concerns: community involvement, environmental issues, science and teaching related, wildlife art
Agencies: Massachusetts State Arts Council
Recent Project: *Eco-log*, wildlife tree carving; environmental art for a public school

DONNA HENES

279 STERLING PL
BROOKLYN, NY 11238-4400
TEL 718-857-5619
Work: performance art, temporary installations, public celebration
Media: fiber, energy
Special Concerns: participatory works multicultural issues, environmental issues
Commission Amounts: $5,000 - $20,000
Agencies: Port Authority of New York and New Jersey; Battery Park City Authority, NYC; Liberty Science Center
Recent Project: Temporary installation and public participatory celebration for spring equinox (1994); clock & weather tower, Tampa, FL

HERA

32 W 20TH ST
NEW YORK, NY 10011-4207
FAX 212-929-1969
TEL 212-924-4518
Work: collaborative site design, architectural elements, outdoor furniture and equipment, site specific
Media: metal, concrete, wood, earth/plants
Special Concerns: collaborative design teams, community involvement, historical and documentary issues, environmental issues
Commission Amounts: $5000 - $300,000
Agencies: Hillsborough Area Regional Transit; New York City Housing Authority; Laumeier Sculpture Park
Recent Project: Clock and weather tower for Hillsborough Area Transit, Tampa, FL (1990)

ARTHUR HIGGINS

OAK RUN STUDIOS
PO BOX 499
MOSIER, OR 97040-0509
FAX 503-478-2269
TEL 800-346-3451
Work: sculpture (wall relief)
Media: metal, mixed, wood
Special Concerns: site specific work
Commission Amounts: $8,000 - $40,000
Agencies: State of Alaska; Municipality of Anchorage, AK; North Star School District, Fairbanks, AK
Recent Project: 3' × 60' painted wood/mixed metals interior wall relief sculpture

BRUCE HIPPEL

DESIGNS & EXECUTIONS IN STAINED GLASS
218 W PACIFIC AVE
VILLAS, NJ 08251-2760
TEL 609-886-2206
Work: architectural glass
Media: glass, stained glass
Special Concerns: historical and documentary issues, historical and documentary issues
Commission Amounts: $7,500 - $11,500
Agencies: Cape May County Office of Cultural and Heritage
Recent Project: Large-scale architectural stained glass window for Cape May County Courthouse, NJ

DAVID J. HOLMES

WOLF'S CRAG SCULPTURE
RR BOX 2810
DETROIT, ME 04929
TEL 207-948-3742
Work: sculpture (free standing and wall relief)
Media: metal, wood, stone
Special Concerns: community involvement, multicultural issues, space/client concerns
Commission Amounts: $2,000 - $20,000
Agencies: Maine Arts Commission; State University, ME; Bureau of Public Improvements, ME
Recent Project: 3D mermaid riding life-sized dolphin; waves and dolphins in relief

NANCY HOLT

HOLT ARTWORKS INC.
HC 75 BOX 716
GALISTEO, NM 87540
FAX 505-466-4404
TEL 505-466-6820
Work: sculpture (free standing), fountains, environmental landscape
Media: metal, concrete, stone
Special Concerns: historical and documentary issues, environmental issues, science and teaching related
Commission Amounts: $100,000 - $1,000,000
Agencies: GSA Art in Architecture program; Arlington County Planning Commission, Arlington, VA; Connecticut Commission on the Arts
Recent Project: *Solar Rotary*, aluminum, bronze, concrete, meteorite, 20'H × 125' × 135', University of South Florida, Tampa, FL (1994)

THOMAS HOLZER

GLASS DESIGN STUDIOS
PO BOX 2278
BOULDER, CO 80306-2278
FAX 303-449-8745
TEL 303-449-2085
Work: architectural glass, architectural elements, architectural ceramics, mosaics, and wall relief
Media: ceramics, concrete, mixed, mosaic
Commission Amounts: $40,000 minimum
Agencies: Utah Art Council; Ohio Art Council; Nebraska Art Council

JOHN J. HOOVER

E-841 W STADIUM
GRAPEVIEW, WA 98546
TEL 360-275-3399
Work: sculpture (free standing, atrium and wall relief)
Media: metal, wood
Special Concerns: historical and documentary issues, multicultural issues, shamanism
Commission Amounts: $5,000 - $35,000
Agencies: Percent for Art programs, Cities of Anchorage, AK; Seattle, WA; and Portland, OR

★ LINDA HOWARD

LINDA HOWARD SCULPTURES, INC.
6451 19TH ST E BOX 235 #2, B6
SARASOTA, FL 34243
TEL 941-739-9228
Work: sculpture (free standing and atrium), architectural metal
Media: metal, aluminum
Special Concerns: collaborative design teams, community involvement, environmental issues
Commission Amounts: $18,000 - $150,000
Agencies: Federal Art in Architecture Program, Washington DC; Florida Art in Public Places; Alaska Art in Public Places
Recent Project: Federal Art in Architecture Program, Federal Courthouse, Urbana, IL (1994)

My sculpture is made up of geometric elements in progression, stacked and rotated. Straight linear elements form spiral curves in space, creating growth forms from nature. The use of large scale creates a transition space between human and architectural scale, allowing for personal interaction with the sculpture, the space around and thru it. Light is an important element. The surface is a ground finish of interlaced wavy lines. The patterning is like drawing on the metal surface and makes the sculpture shimmer in the light. Light appears to de-materialize the aluminum, changing matter into light/energy.

See photograph page 242.

JON BARLOW HUDSON

HUDSON SCULPTURE
PO BOX 710
YELLOW SPRINGS, OH 45387-0710
FAX 513-767-7766
TEL 513-767-7766
E-MAIL: jbhudson@aol.com
Work: sculpture (free standing and atrium), fountains
Media: metal, stone, bronze
Special Concerns: collaborative design teams, community involvement, participatory works
Commission Amounts: $10,000 - $300,000
Agencies: Metro-Dade Arts Council; Omaha Metro Arts Council; Partners of the Americas (USIA) Brazil
Recent Project: *Cloud Hands*, large-scale granite sculpture installed at Europos Parkas, Vilnias, Lithuania

HARRIET HYAMS

PO BOX 178
PALISADES, NY 10964-0178
FAX 914-359-0062
TEL 914-359-0061
Work: architectural glass, architectural ceramics, mosaics, and wall relief, sculpture
Media: metal, glass, stone, mosaic
Special Concerns: collaborative design teams, community involvement
Commission Amounts: $5,000 - $35,000
Agencies: New York Percent for Art
Recent Project: *The Seasons*, New Dorp High School, Staten Island, NY

★ NATHAN JACKSON

5972 ROOSEVELT DR S
KETCHIKAN, AK 99901-9716
TEL 907-225-3431
Work: sculpture (free standing), architectural ceramics, mosaics, and wall relief
Media: wood
Special Concerns: collaborative design teams, historical and documentary issues, multicultural issues
Commission Amounts: $3,000 - $30,000
Agencies: City of Ketchikan; Alaska State Council on the Arts; Ketchikan Gateway Borough
Recent Project: *Thundering Wings*, eagle sculpture, 9'H, red cedar, Ketchikan, AK (1991)

Nathan Jackson, a Tlingit Indian, has been working as an artist since 1967. He works in the traditional style of Northwest Coast Indian art, primarily carving panels and totem poles in red cedar. He has artwork in both the public and private sectors and enjoys the opportunity to work with architects. Artwork in different mediums have also been designed by Jackson, then subcontracted out. See the *Architect's Edition: 8* for a photograph of *Thundering Wings*. Please contact the artist for more information.

See page 84 for photographs and additional information.

PUBLIC ART

CHRISTOPHER JANNEY

PHENOMEN ARTS, INC.
75 KENDALL RD
LEXINGTON, MA 02173
FAX 617-862-6114
TEL 617-862-6413
Work: neon, laser, light related, sound, participatory
Media: sound
Special Concerns: participatory works
Commission Amounts: $25,000 - $600,000
Agencies: North Carolina Council for the Arts; New York City Arts-in-Transit Program
Recent Project: *Harmonic Runway*, interactive sound and light installation

LUIS JIMENEZ

PO BOX 75
HONDO, NM 88336-0175
FAX 505-653-4499
TEL 505-653-4211
Work: sculpture (free standing and pedestal)
Media: fiberglass, illumination
Special Concerns: historical and documentary issues, multicultural issues
Commission Amounts: $50,000 - $450,000
Agencies: NEA Art in Public Places, U.S. General Services Administration; Denver International Airport
Recent Project: Fiesta dancers sculpture for international crossing, Otay Mesa, CA (1991)

BRAD P. JIRKA

ST. ELMO'S INC.
2688 89TH COURT W
NORTHFIELD, MN 55057
FAX 612-338-5045
TEL 612-338-0926
Work: sculpture (free standing and wall relief), neon, laser, light related
Media: metal, wood, plastics
Special Concerns: participatory works, science and teaching related, experiential
Commission Amounts: $2,000 - $34,000
Agencies: Minnesota State Arts Board Percent for Art in Public Places
Recent Project: *Mechanicks of the Ether*, animated and illuminated aviation keystone installation

JOESAM.

PO BOX 883894
SAN FRANCISCO, CA 94188-3894
FAX 415-822-4045
TEL 415-822-7245
Work: sculpture (free standing, atrium and wall relief)
Media: metal, mixed, fiberglass
Special Concerns: collaborative design teams, community involvement, multicultural issues
Commission Amounts: $20,000 - $225,000
Agencies: San Francisco Art Commission; Los Angeles Cultural Affairs Department; Los Angeles County Metropolitan Transit Authority
Recent Project: *Hide 'n' Seek*, installation of 55 sculptures for Wilmington/Imperial Metro Rail Station, Los Angeles, CA

PATRICIA JOHANSON

RR 1 BOX 328
BUSKIRK, NY 12028-9611
FAX 518-753-4795
TEL 518-753-4795
Work: architectural elements, collaborative site design, ecological sculpture
Media: metal, concrete, plants and animals
Special Concerns: participatory works, environmental issues, science or teaching related
Commission Amounts: $24,000 - $30,000,000
Agencies: San Francisco Arts Commission; City of Dallas; Sacramento Arts Commission
Recent Project: One-third mile Baywalk, tidal sculpture, habitat gardens around San Francisco Bay (1987-1993)

★ ERICK C. JOHNSON

E.J. SCULPTURE WORKS
3300 WOLFF ST
DENVER, CO 80212-1824
TEL 303-433-6334
Work: sculpture (free standing and atrium), architectural metal, architectural elements, neon, laser, light related, other work for interior walls
Media: metal, paint, wood, plastics
Special Concerns: environmental issues, environmental issues, science and teaching related
Commission Amounts: $20,000 - $300,000
Agencies: Colorado Council for the Arts and Humanities; Denver Commission on Cultural Affairs; Denver Baseball Commission District
Recent Project: Coor's Baseball Park, aluminum and neon-animated base runner sliding into home plate

See page 135 for photographs and additional information.

RICHARD JOHNSTON

RICHARD JOHNSTON SCULPTURE
2266 WILD CANYON DR
COLTON, CA 92324-9624
FAX 909-880-5903
TEL 909-422-1956
Work: sculpture (free standing and pedestal), collaborative site design, architectural metal, outdoor furniture and equipment, furniture
Media: metal, concrete, earth and plants
Special Concerns: collaborative design teams, community involvement
Commission Amounts: $5,000 - $175,000
Agencies: Yasuda Educational Community, Hiroshima, Japan; Utah Arts Council; Salt Lake City Corporation
Recent Project: Yasuda University, Hiroshima, Japan (1993)

NAPOLEON JONES-HENDERSON

12 MORLEY ST
ROXBURY, MA 02119
FAX 617-445-5525
TEL 617-427-8325
Work: sculpture (free standing, atrium and wall relief), painted finishes and murals, mosaics, architectural elements, metal and enamel works
Media: metal, mixed, enamel, fiber
Special Concerns: collaborative design teams, historical and documentary issues, multicultural issues
Commission Amounts: $35,000 - $150,000
Agencies: Massachusetts Council on the Arts; Massachusetts Port Authority; Rhode Island Convention Center; Rhode Island Arts Council
Recent Project: An 8' x 26' enamel-on-copper wall for the Rhode Island Convention Center

★ TED JONSSON

805 NE NORTHLAKE WAY
SEATTLE, WA 98105-6431
TEL 206-547-4552
Work: sculpture (free standing), collaborative site design, fountains
Media: metal
Special Concerns: collaborative design teams, participatory works
Commission Amounts: $15,000 - $300,000
Agencies: Washington State Art Commission; Seattle Art Commission; Alaska Council on the Arts
Recent Project: Suite of three sculptures for Federal Reserve Bank of Seattle

See photograph below.

CONNIE JOST

20 SPRING GARDEN RD
MILLVILLE, NJ 08332-9602
TEL 609-825-0532
Work: sculpture (wall relief), 2D work, other media for interior walls
Media: mixed, paint, fiberglass
Special Concerns: environmental issues, marine biodiversity
Commission Amounts: $25,000 minimum
Agencies: New Jersey State Council of the Arts; Cape May County Cultural and Heritage Commission; Montana Council of the Arts
Recent Project: *Shelf Life*, interior wall sculpture depicting sea life (1993)

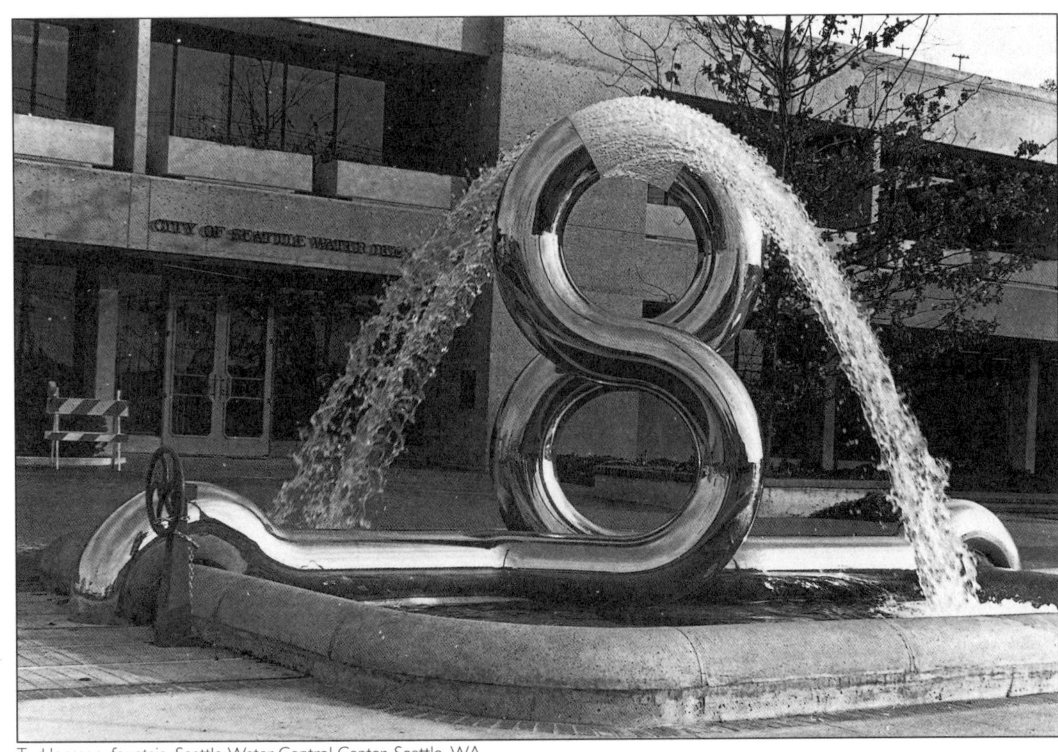

Ted Jonsson, fountain, Seattle Water Control Center, Seattle, WA

NED KAHN

1345 COLE ST
SAN FRANCISCO, CA 94117-4323
FAX 415-561-0380
TEL 415-564-2742
Work: sculpture (atrium), collaborative
site design, fountains
Media: metal, stone, water
Special Concerns: participatory works,
environmental issues, science or teaching
related
Commission Amounts: $50,000 - $450,000
Agencies: San Francisco Arts Commission; City of Ventura, CA; Washington
State Arts Commission
Recent Project: A bronze ocean wave-powered fountain for the Ventura Pier

JODI KANTER

CUSTOM DESIGNS IN WEAVING
5659 CHEROKEE DR
LYNDHURST, OH 44124-3047
TEL 216-449-7543
Work: sculpture (atrium), fiber work
for interior walls
Media: fiber
Commission Amounts: $2,500 - $90,000
Agencies: Connecticut Commission on
the Arts; U.S. Veteran's Administration
Recent Project: *Healing Waters & Sound
Growth*, a two-part mural representing
the healing process (1990)

SUSAN KAPROV

149 WILLOW ST
BROOKLYN HEIGHTS, NY 11201
TEL 718-624-2775
Work: collaborative site design, 2D
work, photo-collage murals
Media: photos on metal
Special Concerns: historical and documentary issues, multicultural issues, science, technology
Commission Amounts: $40,000 - $250,000
Agencies: Port Authority of New York
and New Jersey; National Aeronautics
and Space Administration; NYC Percent
for Art Program; The City University of
New York
Recent Project: Photo-collage mural for
the Liberty Science Center, Jersey City, NJ

COLLENE KARCHER

KARCHER STONECARVING STUDIO
40 N BETA RD
SYLVA, NC 28779
FAX 704-586-5274
TEL 704-586-4813
Work: sculpture (free standing), collaborative site design, figurative sculpture
Media: metal, wood, stone
Commission Amounts: $3,000 - $40,000
Agencies: North Carolina Center for the
Advancement of Teaching

ANNE MARIE KARLSEN

ARTIST
4637 MAYTIME LN
CULVER CITY, CA 90230-5070
TEL 310-815-8109
Work: 2D work, collages, jet-painted
murals
Media: ceramics, tile, relief
Special Concerns: collaborative design
teams, historical and documentary issues,
architectural relationship
Commission Amounts: $200,000
Agencies: Culver City Arts Commission
Art in Public Places
Recent Project: *Multiplicity*, six sculptural
wall structures 9'6"H x 28'W x 12'D,
handmade porcelain ceramic tile (1992)

★ LISA KASLOW

LISA KASLOW, INC.
2313-15 ESSEX ST
BALTIMORE, MD 21224-3616
FAX 410-276-8330
TEL 410-276-3810
Work: sculpture (free standing and wall
relief), outdoor furniture and equipment
Media: metal, mixed, earth and plants
Special Concerns: collaborative design
teams, community involvement, environmental issues
Commission Amounts: $10,000 - $180,000
Agencies: Montgomery County Art in
Architecture; Civic Design Commission
Percent for Art, Baltimore, MD; State
of Florida Art in Public Places
Recent Project: Gateway entrance
for Bergen County, Van Saun Park
Playground, NJ

With 36 public art commissions completed since 1978, Lisa Kaslow's work
projects community identity and architectural compatibility. She collaborates
with architects and landscape architects.
Kaslow designs site-specific environments
for developers and corporations. Her
commissions include benches, seating,
porticos, gazebos, pergolas, gateways
and arbors. All works are fabricated from
durable, low maintenance materials,
including coated structural steel, non-ferrous metals, fiberglass and concrete.
Her work is in the collections of states
municipalities, corporations and institutions.

**See page 211 for photographs
and additional information.**

MARTHA KEATING
BOB LUNA

ARTNIKS STUDIO
3729 LIPAN ST
DENVER, CO 80211
TEL 303-477-7909
Work: mosaics
Media: ceramics
Special Concerns: collaborative design
teams, community involvement, historical
and documentary issues
Commission Amounts: $12,500 - $120,000
Agencies: City of Denver, Mayor's
Council of Art, Culture and Film;
Longmont Arts Council
Recent Project: Ten tile mosaic murals
describing history of neighborhood,
3,500 sq.ft

JEFF KELLER

7 WALCOTT AVE
FALMOUTH, ME 04105
TEL 207-781-3858
Work: sculpture (free standing), collaborative site design, outdoor furniture and
equipment
Media: metal, wood, stone
Special Concerns: collaborative design
teams, community involvement, participatory works
Commission Amounts: $8,000 - $20,000
Agencies: Maine Arts Commission;
University of Maine
Recent Project: Interactive granite,
bronze and copper outdoor sculpture,
University of Maine

★ GUY KEMPER

KEMPER STUDIO
190 N BROADWAY
LEXINGTON, KY 40507
FAX 606-254-3507
TEL 606-254-3507
Work: collaborative site design,
architectural glass
Media: metal, glass, wood
Special Concerns: collaborative
design teams
Commission Amounts: $12,000 and up
Agencies: Kentucky Arts and Crafts
Foundation; Louisville Jewish Community
Foundation
Recent Project: 53' stained glass frieze
for Jewish Hospital, Louisville, KY

**See page 50 for photographs
and additional information.**

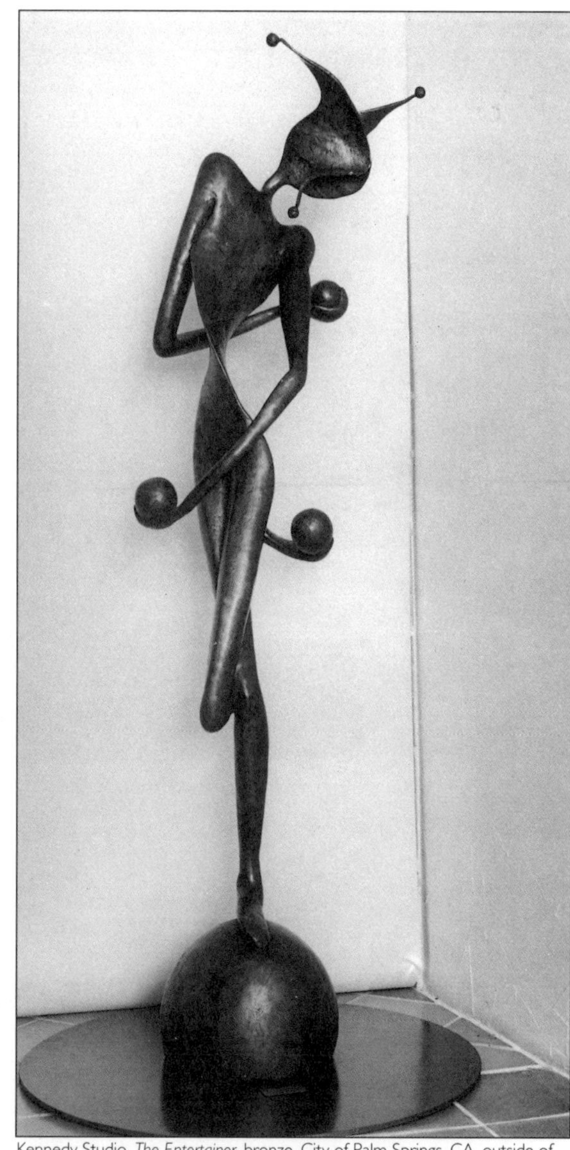

Kennedy Studio, *The Entertainer*, bronze, City of Palm Springs, CA, outside of
Plaza Theatre, Palm Canyon Drive, Palm Springs, 86" x 24"

★ KENNEDY STUDIO

JOHN KENNEDY
996 N TUXEDO CIR
PALM SPRINGS, CA 92262-4164
FAX 619-320-9516
TEL 619-320-9205

Work: sculpture (free standing)
Media: metal
Special Concerns: community relations
Commission Amounts: $40,000 - $200,000
Agencies: City of La Quinta, CA
Recent Project: *Spirit of Life*, bronze sculpture for a garden at Ogden School, Chicago, IL; 6 figures, 16' x 20' for State Fair College, Sedalia, MO

The interpretation of my work is a personal visual dialogue with the viewer, either collectively or individually. My simplified figuration is direct and embodies a spectrum of human relationships and communicating emotions. So my work could be described as 'Figurative Emotionalism.'

See photograph page 245.

JAMES PATRICK KENNEDY

NATIONAL SCULPTORS' GUILD
2683 N TAFT AVE
LOVELAND, CO 80538
FAX 970-667-2068
TEL 970-667-2015

Work: sculpture (free standing and pedestal), collaborative site design
Media: metal
Special Concerns: collaborative design teams, historical and documentary issues, environmental issues
Commission Amounts: $5,000 - $45,000
Agencies: Cheyenne (WY) Frontier Old West Museum; Millicent Rogers Museum, Taos, NM
Recent Project: Commission for Rocky Mountain Mall, two life-sized mule deer (1995)

LYMAN E. KIPP

375 21ST ST SW
NAPLES, FL 33964
FAX 813-455-8959
TEL 813-455-8959

Work: sculpture (free standing, pedestal and wall relief)
Media: metal, paint
Special Concerns: community involvement, environmental issues, science and teaching related
Commission Amounts: $18,000 - $75,000
Agencies: General Services Administration, Washington, DC; National Endowment for the Arts, Washington, DC; State of Florida, Art in Public Places
Recent Project: Five large-scale sculptures for Ft. Lauderdale Art Museum

JEROME KIRK

5648 BACON RD
OAKLAND, CA 94619
TEL 510-530-0410

Work: sculpture (free standing, pedestal and wall relief)
Media: metal
Special Concerns: kinetic by wind and touch
Commission Amounts: $20,000 - $200,000
Agencies: Palo Alto Cultural Center, CA; Civic Plaza, Phoenix, AZ; University of California, Berkley, CA
Recent Project: Outdoor kinetic sculpture, 12'H, painted aluminum and stainless steel

★ SUSAN KLEBANOFF

4208B HOWARD AVE
KENSINGTON, MD 20895
TEL 301-564-9164

Work: fiber work for interior walls
Media: fiber
Commission Amounts: $3,000 - $60,000
Agencies: U.S. State Department; Superior Court of the District of Columbia; National Rehabilitation Hospital

Internationally recognized for her multi-layered tapestries, Susan Klebanoff creates works to enhance the lobbies of major institutions such as IBM, TRW, Peat Marwick, British Petroleum, the State Department, various embassies, and many other public, corporate and private collections. She incorporates various rich textures, materials and images into these 3D reliefs. Her career has been documented by CNN TV-Broadcasting, CBC-TV- Japanese Broadcasting, and various other television and magazine articles. Videos, slides, catalogs and references available upon request.

See photograph this page.

M.A. KLEIN

M.A. KLEIN DESIGN
20 ARASTRADERO RD
PORTOLA VALLEY, CA 94028-8013
FAX 415-854-7815
TEL 415-854-7815
TEL 800-700-7815

Work: fiber work for interior walls, banners
Media: fiber, paper, paint
Special Concerns: multicultural issues, environmental issues, science and teaching related
Commission Amounts: $6,500 - $25,000
Agencies: Library of Congress, Washington D.C.
Recent Project: *A Most Unusual Watering Hole*, mixed media fiber collage, 3^1/$_2$'x 9'

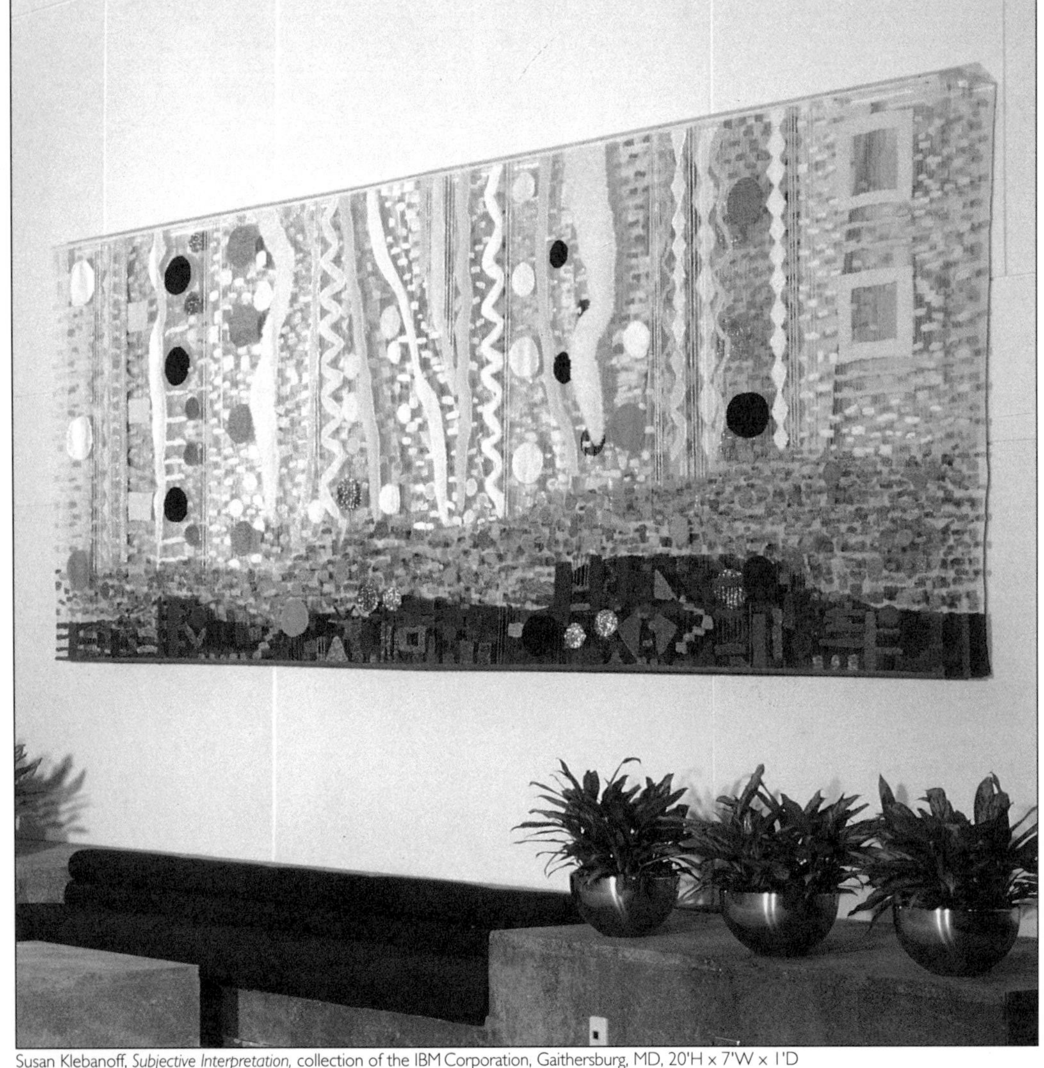

Susan Klebanoff, *Subjective Interpretation,* collection of the IBM Corporation, Gaithersburg, MD, 20'H x 7'W x 1'D

★ STEPHEN KNAPP

74 COMMODORE RD
WORCESTER, MA 01602-2727
FAX 508-797-3228
TEL 508-757-2507

Work: architectural glass, architectural metal, architectural ceramics, mosaics, and wall relief
Media: ceramics, glass, stone, metal
Special Concerns: collaborative design teams, historical and documentary issues
Commission Amounts: $55,000
Agencies: Hamilton County, OH
Recent Project: *Convergence*, 14' x 72' mural reflecting Hamilton Co, dyed, etched aluminum (1986)

Stephen Knapp has collaborated with architects and designers for 20 years and has been instrumental in developing new techniques and materials for public art. He is known for large-scale problem-solving, finding the right medium and solution for site-specific art works, using cast and kiln-formed glass, ceramic, etched and fabricated metal, and stone. He frequently writes and lectures on the collaborative process.

See page 51 for photographs and additional information.

KAREN KOBLITZ

2919 TILDEN AVE
LOS ANGELES, CA 90064-4013
FAX 310-477-1160
TEL 310-477-1937

Work: sculpture (free standing, pedestal and wall relief), collaborative site design, tile murals
Media: ceramics
Special Concerns: collaborative design teams, community involvement, historical and documentary issues
Commission Amounts: $28,000 - $45,000
Agencies: Community Redevelopment Agency of Los Angeles; Cultural Affairs Department of Los Angeles
Recent Project: Exterior bench of hand-painted tiles for the Sunland-Tujunga Public Library, CA, (1995)

MICHAEL BRUCE KOPRIVA

917 LANE 11
POWELL, WY 82435-9204
TEL 307-754-3658

Work: sculpture (free standing), painted finishes and murals, architectural metal
Media: metal, paint
Special Concerns: historical and documentary issues
Commission Amounts: $5,000 - $10,000
Agencies: Wyoming Council on the Arts; Montgomery County (MD) Art in Public Architecture
Recent Project: Life-size welded steel figure of an irrigator, exterior site (1991)

MICHIHIRO KOSUGE

THE LAURA RUSSO GALLERY, INC.
805 NW 21ST AVE
PORTLAND, OR 97209-1408
TEL 503-226-2754

Work: sculpture (free standing), outdoor furniture and equipment, site-specific design
Media: metal, mixed, stone, stainless steel
Commission Amounts: $20,000 - $70,000
Agencies: Oregon Arts Commission; City of Portland (OR) Percent for Art; Los Angeles (CA) Percent for Art
Recent Project: Four large sculptures of stone and stainless steel, Oregon Department of Transportation, Portland, OR

★ ROCKNE KREBS

1428 "U" STREET NW
WASHINGTON, DC 20009
FAX 202-265-8045
TEL 202-265-4808

See pages 212-213 for photographs and additional information.

KRISTENSEN STUDIO

GAIL KRISTENSEN
360 CATHEDRAL ROCK TR
SEDONA, AZ 86336-6843
TEL 602-282-2448

Work: sculpture (free standing), architectural elements, architectural ceramics, mosaics, and wall relief
Media: metal, ceramics, mixed
Special Concerns: environmental issues, religious
Commission Amounts: $3,000 - $40,000
Agencies: Arizona Commission for the Arts; Phoenix Art Commission
Recent Project: Fountain for Phoenix College, Phoenix, AZ, 10'10"H, through Percent for Art program (1993)

JANET KUEMMERLEIN

KUEMMERLEIN FIBER ART INC.
7701 CANTERBURY ST
PRAIRIE VILLAGE, KS 66208-3946
TEL 816-842-7049
TEL 913-649-8292

Work: sculpture (free standing and wall relief), fiber work for interior walls
Media: fiber, mixed
Commission Amounts: $10,000 - $58,370
Agencies: Municipality of Anchorage, AK; Richmond, CA; City of Wichita, KS
Recent Project: An abstract design for cast concrete tiles on seven walls

ZELJKO KUJUNDZIC

RR2 SITE 6 COMPARTMENT 9
OSOYOOS, BC V0H 1V0
CANADA
TEL 604-495-2913

Work: sculpture (free standing, pedestal and wall relief)
Media: metal, concrete, ceramics
Special Concerns: multicultural issues, environmental issues
Commission Amounts: $5,000 - $45,000
Agencies: City of Nelson, British Columbia

LDDK STUDIOS

LINDA DIXON & DREW KROUSE
5741 ERECT RD
RAMSEUR, NC 27316-8111
FAX 910-879-4200
TEL 910-879-4200

Work: fountains, mosaics, terra-cotta murals
Media: ceramics
Special Concerns: collaborative design teams, historical and documentary issues
Commission Amounts: $50,000 - $120,000
Agencies: Metropolitan Transportation Authority of New York, NY, Long Island Railroad
Recent Project: *Wings for IRT*, murals for Grand Army Plaza Subway Station, Brooklyn, NY

PETER LADOCHY

17 OCEAN FRONT
CAYUCOA, CA 93430
FAX 805-995-0118
TEL 805-995-3579

Work: sculpture (wall relief), mosaics architectural elements, other work for interior walls, furniture
Media: wood, stone, glass
Special Concerns: community involvement, historical and documentary issues, multicultural issues
Commission Amounts: $1,400 - $14,000
Agencies: San Luis Obispo County Arts Council; Palm Desert Percent for Arts Grant; Morro Bay City, State of California
Recent Project: A southwest-motif mural, relief, mosaic, tiles on cement board

TUCK LANGLAND

12632 ANDERSON RD
GRANGER, IN 46530-7619
FAX 219-272-2708
TEL 219-272-2708

Work: sculpture (free standing and pedestal), relief
Media: metal, bronze
Special Concerns: historical/documentary issues, multicultural issues
Commission Amounts: $3,000 - $30,000
Agencies: City of Portland, IN; City of Niles, MI; City of Dowagiac, MI; City of Fort Wayne, IN
Recent Project: Lifesize figure, Farr Park, Dowagiac, MI (1995)

GAIL LARNED

LARNED MARLOW
144 S MONROE AVE
COLUMBUS, OH 43205-1084
TEL 614-258-7239

Work: fiber work for interior walls
Media: fiber
Special Concerns: collaborative design teams, participatory works, environmental issues
Commission Amounts: $15,000 - $60,000
Agencies: Ohio Arts Council; Metropolitan Library of Columbus; Greater Columbus Arts Council
Recent Project: 5' x 15' knotted wall mural for Southeast Psychiatric Hospital, Athens, OH

TOM AND JEAN LATKA

LATKA STUDIOS
229 MIDWAY AVE
PUEBLO, CO 81004-1912

Work: sculpture (free standing and wall relief), fountains
Media: metal, concrete, ceramics
Special Concerns: collaborative design teams, historical and documentary issues, multicultural issues
Commission Amounts: $10,000 - $30,000
Agencies: Colorado Arts & Humanities; City of Pueblo
Recent Project: 10' x 10' outdoor ceramic relief depicting the history of Colorado

J. KENNETH LEAP

THE PAINTED WINDOW
43 LINDSEY AVE
RUNNEMEDE, NJ 08078-1732
FAX 609-939-5934
TEL 609-939-5934

Work: architectural glass
Media: glass
Special Concerns: historical and documentary issues
Commission Amounts: $118,000
Agencies: New Jersey State Council on the Arts
Recent Project: Pictorial stained glass skylight for NJ State House annex

JEANNE B. LEFFINGWELL

JEANNE LEFFINGWELL DESIGNS
835 N MOUNTAIN VIEW RD
MOSCOW, ID 83843-9234
TEL 208-882-7211

Work: sculpture (atrium and wall relief), fiber work for interior walls
Media: metal, glass
Special Concerns: science and teaching related
Commission Amounts: $10,000 - $70,000
Agencies: State of Alaska Percentage for Art Program; Municipality of Anchorge Percent for Art
Recent Project: *Beaded Sky Curtain*, made with over 5 million hand-strung glass beads, Egan Convention Center, Anchorage, AK

MARK S. LEICHLITER

NATIONAL SCULPTORS' GUILD
2683 N TAFT AVE
LOVELAND, CO 80538
FAX 970-667-2068
TEL 970-667-2015

Work: sculpture (free standing and pedestal), collaborative site design
Media: metal, stone, wood
Special Concerns: collaborative design teams
Agencies: City of Loveland, CO, Museum & Gallery
Recent Project: Sculpture garden placement in Oklahoma City (1993)

PUBLIC ART

★ LEPOWORKS, INC.

DAVID LEPO, ROBERT LEPO
4640 ALLENTOWN RD
LIMA, OH 45807-1928
FAX 419-331-2787
TEL 419-331-5376

Work: sculpture (free standing), painted finishes and murals, architectural elements
Media: metal, paint, wood
Special Concerns: collaborative design teams, community involvement, participatory works
Commission Amounts: $7,500 - $100,000
Agencies: Ohio Arts Council

Lepoworks is a family of artists whose individual talents create with a one-of-a-kind philosophy. The basis of their success is a concern for detail and quality of the highest standards. They design private, public, and corporate art and collaborate with architects and designers. Lepoworks express their diversity in a multitude of materials used in traditional as well as contemporary styles. A brochure is available upon request.

See page 85 for photographs and additional information.

ALAN LEQUIRE

1222 4TH AVE N
NASHVILLE, TN 37208-2714
TEL 615-242-5408

Work: sculpture (free standing and pedestal)
Media: metal, concrete, stone
Special Concerns: community involvement, historical and documentary issues, human figure
Commission Amounts: $85,000 - $200,000
Agencies: City of Nashville (TN) Board of Parks and Recreation
Recent Project: Re-creation of the colossal (42'H) *Athena Parthenos* for The Parthenon, Nashville (1990)

MARK LERE

1146 N CENTRAL AVE #181
GLENDALE, CA 91202
FAX 818-246-6690
TEL 818-246-5444

Work: sculpture (free standing), collaborative site design, flooring and ground plane
Media: metal, mixed
Special Concerns: collaborative design teams, historical and documentary issues, environmental issues
Commission Amounts: $25,000 - $250,000
Agencies: General Services Administration Washington, DC; Metro Transit Administration, Los Angeles, CA; Seattle Arts Commission, WA
Recent Project: Ocean front plaza for City of Ventura, CA

PHILLIP LEVINE

430 S 124ST ST
SEATTLE, WA 98168-2069
FAX 206-246-4698
TEL 206-244-7139

Work: sculpture (free standing and pedestal), fountains
Media: metal
Commission Amounts: $10,000 - $115,000
Agencies: Washington State Arts Commission; King County (WA) Arts Commission; Renton (WA) Arts Commission
Recent Project: Six 7' bronze figures for the Veterans' Memorial Arena, Spokane, WA

ROSS LEWIS

180 VARICK ST FL 16
NEW YORK, NY 10014-4606
FAX 212-633-2524
TEL 212-633-2506

Work: sculpture (free standing and wall relief), 2D work, multi-media installations
Media: metal, fiberglass, lucite
Special Concerns: community involvement, multicultural issues, environmental issues
Commission Amounts: $7,000 - $70,000
Agencies: Metropolitan Transportation Authority, New York City; City of New York Dept. of Parks and Recreation; City of Tampa Art in Public Places
Recent Project: *Fanscapes*, nine wind-activated, painted, nylon and steel fans, Belvedere Castle, Central Park, NYC (1993)

LIGHT SCULPTURE WORKS

RON DEWEY
1460 W 29TH ST
CLEVELAND, OH 44113-2961
TEL 216-566-0321

Work: sculpture (free standing, atrium and pedestal)
Media: metal, stone, cast stainless steel, bronze
Special Concerns: collaborative design teams, historical and documentary issues, multicultural issues
Commission Amounts: $12,000 - $35,000
Agencies: Ohio Arts Council Percent for Art; Cleveland Heights, University Heights Board of Education; Cleveland Clinic Foundation; University of Southern Calicornia
Recent Project: *Lauree P. Gearity Memorial*, life-size cast bronze figures, University Heights, Cleveland, OH

LIGHTWRITERS

JACOB FISHMAN
834 BACH ST
NORTHBROOK, IL 60062
FAX 708-291-6865
TEL 708-291-4160

Work: sculpture (free standing and wall relief), neon, laser, light related
Media: mixed, glass, neon
Special Concerns: historical and documentary issues, multicultural issues, science and teaching related
Commission Amounts: $500 - $80,000
Agencies: Cultural Center, City of Chicago, IL; Walker Art Center, MN; Smithsonian Institute, Washington, DC
Recent Project: Fabrication and installation at the Cultural Center, Chicago, IL

HUNG LIU

HUNG LIU & JEFF KELLEY
5500 LEONA ST
OAKLAND, CA 94605-1236
FAX 510-530-6013
TEL 510-530-3225

Work: collaborative site design, other work for interior walls, 2D work
Media: paint, mixed, ceramics
Special Concerns: community involvement, historical and documentary issues, multicultural issues
Commission Amounts: $10,000 - $200,000
Agencies: San Francisco Arts Commission
Recent Project: *Map No. 33*, historical installation, Moscone Convention Center, San Francisco

JANET LOFQUIST

2013 STEVENS AVE #1
MINNEAPOLIS, MN 55404-2515
TEL 612-872-1491

Work: sculpture (free standing), collaborative site design, sculptural environments
Media: metal, concrete, stone
Special Concerns: historical/documentary issues, environmental issues, science or teaching related
Commission Amounts: $10,000 - $135,000
Agencies: Minnesota State Arts Board Percent for Arts; Ohio Arts Council Percent for Arts; Art in City Buildings, Ames, IA
Recent Project: Sculptural environment for Trafton Science Center, Mankato State University, MN

★ JOYCE P. LOPEZ

JOYCE LOPEZ STUDIO
1147 W OHIO ST #304
CHICAGO, IL 60622-5874
FAX 312-243-5033
TEL 312-243-5033

Work: sculpture (pedestal and wall relief), fiber work for interior walls
Media: metal, fiber, mixed
Commission Amounts: $6,000 - $85,000
Agencies: Capital Development Board, Art in Architecture; State of Illinois
Recent Project: Steel and fiber sculpture sited at Seattle's Community College (1995)

See page 216 for photographs and additional information.

LUBEN

SCULPTURE BY LUBEN INC.
79 SPRINGDALE ST
SAINT JOHN'S, NF A1C 5B5
CANADA
FAX 709-754-0568
TEL 709-754-0568

Work: sculpture (free standing)
Media: cast bronze only
Special Concerns: community involvement, historical and documentary issues, environmental issues
Commission Amounts: $10,000 - $127,000
Recent Project: *Echos of Valor*, two figures, 9' × 8' × 6', bronze, for the Municipal Center, St. Lawrence, Newfoundland, Canada (1992)

GEERT MAAS

GEERT MAAS SCULPTURE GARDENS, GALLERY AND STUDIO
RR #1 250 REYNOLDS RD
KELOWNA, BC V1Y 7P9
CANADA
FAX 604-860-2697 (Attn: Geert Maas)
TEL 604-860-7012

Work: sculpture (free standing), architectural metal, other work for interior walls
Media: metal, mixed, ceramics
Special Concerns: collaborative design teams, community involvement, human related
Commission Amounts: $10,000 - $150,000
Agencies: Public Art Gallery of Richmond, BC, Canada
Recent Project: *War-Liberation Monument 1945-1995*, "Freedom" City of Vancouver, BC, Canada

★ ELIZABETH MacDONALD

PO BOX 186
BRIDGEWATER, CT 06752-0186
FAX 203-350-4052

TEL 203-354-0594

Work: sculpture (free standing and wall relief), ceramic tile
Media: ceramics
Special Concerns: collaborative design teams
Commission Amounts: $10,000 - $90,000
Agencies: Art commissions in New York and Connecticut
Recent Project: 700 sq. ft. area (11,000 tiles) for Connecticut Dept. of Environmental Protection; Nobu Restaurant, New York, NY

Elizabeth MacDonald produces tile paintings by layering ceramic powders on thin pieces of textured clay that have been torn into squares. She makes surfaces that suggest either nature's erosion or patinas of age and use. After firing, these tiles are assembled into images, merging the organic into the formality of a grid. Compositions are suitable for interior or exterior settings and take the form of free-standing columns, wall panels or architectural installations. MacDonald's work is represented in major public and private collections. Recent commissions include Conrad International Hotel, Hong Kong; St. Luke's Hospital, Denver; and ITT Hartford for the City of Hartford, CT.

See page 75 for photographs and additional information.

DAWN MacNUTT

DAWN MacNUTT,
   WEAVER/SCULPTOR
70 JACKSON RD
DARTMOUTH, NS B3A 4A6
CANADA
FAX 902-466-4792
TEL 902-466-4792
Work: sculpture (free standing), architectural metal, fiber work for interior walls
Media: metal, fiber
Commission Amounts: $1,000 - $100,000
Agencies: Federal government of Canada (Bedford Institute of Oceanography); Ukraine Community of Canada (Comwallis Park, Halifax)
Recent Project: Woven life-size figures cast in bronze, Dartmouth, NS, Canada

MICHAELA MAHADY

PEGASUS STUDIO, INC.
5155 BLOOMINGTON AVE
MINNEAPOLIS, MN 55417-1849
FAX 612-724-4563
TEL 612-724-4563
Work: sculpture (free standing), architectural glass
Media: metal, mixed, glass
Special Concerns: community involvement, participatory works, historical and documentary issues
Commission Amounts: $8,000 - $26,000
Agencies: Minnesota Percent for Art in Public Spaces; City of St. Paul, MN
Recent Project: Leaded glass wall at Cambridge Community College, Cambridge, MN

JANET MAHER

ARCILLA WORKS
125 BUENA VISTA SE
ALBUQUERQUE, NM 87106
TEL 505-843-9396
Work: sculpture (wall relief), ceramic tile
Media: ceramics, paint
Special Concerns: multicultural issues, science or teaching related
Agencies: New Mexico Arts Division, Santa Fe
Recent Project: Los Alamos, ceramic relief and tile, site-specific installation with scientific/mathematic theme (1991)

LIZ MAPELLI

MAPELLI STUDIO
PO BOX 3885
PORTLAND, OR 97208-3885
FAX 503-796-0221
TEL 503-796-0221
Work: sculpture (wall relief), architectural glass, flooring and ground plane
Media: glass, metal, glass and marble, terrazzo
Special Concerns: community involvement, historical and documentary issues, collaborative design teams, humor
Commission Amounts: $10,000 - $150,000
Agencies: Mayor's Office on Culture and the Arts, Honolulu, HI; Anchorage (AK) Arts Commission; Cambridge (MA) Arts Commission
Recent Project: Exterior four-story artwork for performing arts center and high school, dichroic and enameled glass with text, Sumner, WA

ANITA MARGRILL

670 SHOTWELL ST
SAN FRANCISCO, CA 94110-2624
FAX 415-826-0528
TEL 415-826-0528
Work: sculpture (free standing), fountains, outdoor furniture and equipment
Media: metal, concrete, water, solar
Special Concerns: community involvement, participatory works, environmental issues
Commission Amounts: $25,000 - $400,000
Agencies: City of Antioch, CA; City of Emeryville, CA; Washington State Arts Commission
Recent Project: Fountain celebrating the meeting of the Sacramento and San Joaquin Rivers, Antioch, CA

TOM MARIONI

657 HOWARD ST
SAN FRANCISCO, CA 94105-3902
FAX 415-495-3193
TEL 415-495-3193
Work: sculpture (free standing), architectural ceramics, mosaics and wall relief, performance art
Media: metal, concrete, mixed
Special Concerns: collaborative design teams, participatory works, environmental issues
Commission Amounts: $5,000 - $100,000
Agencies: Public Art Works, Marin County, CA; City of San Francisco
Recent Project: Observatory Bird, 40' mound with telescope, Marin Civic Center (1989)

MARK SWITLIK MURALS

MARK SWITLIK
502 W JACKSON
PHOENIX, AZ 85003
FAX 602-254-2248
TEL 602-254-7840
Work: painted finishes and murals, architectural elements, 2D work
Media: paint
Special Concerns: science and teaching related
Commission Amounts: $10,000 - $28,000
Agencies: Phoenix Art Museum; Arizona Museum of Science and Technology; Phoenix Sky Harbor Art Program
Recent Project: Sky Harbor Airport project, 9' x 12' mural for the NBA All-Star Weekend

MOLLY MASON

111 BEACH ST
PORT JEFFERSON, NY 11777-1306
TEL 516-473-7226
Work: sculpture (free standing and pedestal), collaborative site design
Media: metal, concrete, wood, cast concrete w/ceramic tile
Special Concerns: collaborative design teams, community involvement, participatory works
Commission Amounts: $5,000 - $50,000
Agencies: City of Albuquerque, NM; national sculpture parks of Hungary and Yugoslavia
Recent Project: 12' stainless steel and copper sculpture with fountain, Long Island Cultural Center, NY

MATIOSIAN STUDIO

PAMELA MATIOSIAN
1808 CENTRAL ST
EVANSTON, IL 60201-1317
TEL 708-475-5132
Work: other work for interior walls
Media: wood, mixed, paper
Special Concerns: historical and documentary issues
Commission Amounts: $30,000 - $62,000
Agencies: Ohio Arts Council, Percent for Art; City of Oaklawn, IL
Recent Project: A wall relief with subtle references depicting community development and architectural elements; curved-wall installation inspired by nature

DANAE MATTES

3681 17TH ST #6
SAN FRANCISCO, CA 94114
TEL 415-864-1452
Work: sculpture (free standing, pedestal and wall relief)
Media: mixed, ceramics, stone
Commission Amounts: $4,000 - $15,000
Agencies: Kiel Ministry of Culture, Schleswig-Holstein, Germany; City of Lavenburg/Elbe, Germany; Redwood City (CA) Public Library
Recent Project: Memorial exterior relief for the City of Molln, Germany (1994)

WILLIAM JACKSON MAXWELL

2590 WALNUT #5
BOULDER, CO 80302
FAX 303-938-8456
TEL 303-938-8456
Work: collaborative site design, fountains, neon, laser, light related, site specific
Media: mixed, plastics, water and light
Special Concerns: collaborative design teams, environmental issues, science and teaching related
Commission Amounts: $10,000 - $350,000
Agencies: Washington State Arts Commission; San Francisco Arts Commission; Florida State Arts Commission
Recent Project: Endangered, environmental fountains for University of West Florida, Pensacola, FL

ROSLYN MAZZILLI

PO BOX 609
MOSS BEACH, CA 94038-0609
TEL 415-728-1924
Work: sculpture (free standing), collaborative site design, fountains
Media: metal, paint, water
Special Concerns: collaborative design teams, community involvement, environmental issues
Commission Amounts: $10,000 - $95,000
Agencies: Bramelea Pacific, CA, Art in Public Places
Recent Project: Cuca Mona Lisa, fountain sculpture, Town Center, Rancho Cucamonga, CA

BARBARA McCARREN

1366 APPLETON WY
VENICE, CA 90291-2917
FAX 310-396-8782
TEL 310-396-8782
Work: sculpture (free standing), collaborative site design, architectural elements, 2D work
Media: metal, mixed, stone
Special Concerns: collaborative design teams, participatory works, historical and documentary issues
Commission Amounts: $50,000 - $280,000
Agencies: Los Angeles Community Redevelopment Agency; City of Culver City; City of Manhattan Beach
Recent Project: Panoramic and Quotation Courtyard artworks for the City Hall of Culver City, CA

DAVE McGARY

McGARY STUDIOS, INC.
PO BOX 1310
RUIDOSO, NM 88345
FAX 505-257-1004
TEL 505-257-1000
Work: sculpture (free standing and pedestal)
Media: metal
Special Concerns: historical/documentary issues, multicultural issues
Commission Amounts: $100,000 - $500,000
Agencies: Santa Fe Arts Commission
Recent Project: The Founding of Santa Fe, monument for the City of Santa Fe, NM

★ TRENA McNABB

McNABB STUDIO
PO BOX 357
BETHANIA, NC 27010-0357
FAX 910-759-0641
TEL 910-759-0640
Work: other media for interior walls
Media: mixed, paint, canvas, plexiglass
Commission Amounts: $10,000
Agencies: Cleveland Memorial Hospital Foundation
Recent Project: A Caring Tradition, colorful kaleidoscope of transparent images, 13'3" x 9' x 2"

Trena juxtaposes different images one over another to create a transparent montage effect. Each colorful kaleidoscope of images depicts a thematic story which enhances the site-specific work and personalizes it for the viewer. The use of unusual materials adds a variety of textures to many of her paintings. Trena is experienced in working to clients' expectations, staying within budget and schedule parameters. Her works range from small to large depending upon the site requirements.

See page 111 for photographs and additional information.

B. HUGH McPECK

GLACIER ART
8900 BASHER DR
ANCHORAGE, AK 99507-1202
TEL 907-338-0719

Work: sculpture (pedestal), collaborative
site design
Media: metal, concrete, wood, architec-
tural structures
Special Concerns: collaborative design
teams, community involvement, multicul-
tural issues
Commission Amounts: $5,000 - $40,000
Agencies: Municipality of Anchorage;
Anchorage School District
Recent Project: *RavenHouse*, cedar,
stainless, copper, glass, 13' x 12' x 12'

BRANKO MEDENICA

SCULPTURE SIGHT
417 25TH ST S
BIRMINGHAM, AL 35233-2501
FAX 205-323-6251
TEL 205-323-6251

Work: sculpture (free standing and
pedestal), other media for interior walls
Media: metal, concrete, mixed
Special Concerns: community involve-
ment, participatory works, historical and
documentary issues
Commission Amounts: $28,000 - $135,000
Agencies: National Endowment for the
Arts; Alabama State Council for the
Arts and Humanities; Birmingham Arts
Commission
Recent Project: A 10' bronze figure
honoring Olympic athlete, Jesse Owens
(1996)

★ HOWARD MEEHAN
★ KATHLEEN MEEHAN

FIREFLY STUDIO
2511 NW UPSHUR ST
PORTLAND, OR 97210-2549
TEL 503-274-0865

Work: fountains, architectural glass,
outdoor furniture and equipment
Media: metal, glass, concrete
Special Concerns: collaborative design
teams, science and teaching related,
historical and documentary issues
Commission Amounts: $10,000 - $275,000
Agencies: Oregon Art Commission;
Washington Arts Commission; City of
Palm Desert, CA
Recent Project: 28' diameter steel,
concrete *Shade Sculpture*, Palm Desert
Rose Garden, CA

Experience includes 14 completed public
art projects as well as numerous corporate commissions in a variety of materials, always on budget and on time.
Accustomed to working with architects,
structural engineers, facilities people, and
committees, we welcome the opportunity
to share ideas and information.

**See page 218 for photographs
and additional information.**

MELOTTE-MORSE
STAINED GLASS, INC.

STEVEN J. BROOKS
213 S 6TH ST
SPRINGFIELD, IL 62701-1502
FAX 217-789-9518
TEL 217-789-9515

Work: sculpture (atrium), architectural glass
Media: metal, glass, plastics
Special Concerns: site specific
Commission Amounts: $10,000 - $50,000
Agencies: Illinois Department of Revenue
Percent for Art; Illinois State Capitol
Building; Illinois State Preservation
Recent Project: Hanging sculpture
of acrylic and glass, two stories tall

GRAY MERCER

MERCER SCULPTURES
PO BOX 695
EL PRADO, NM 87529-0695
TEL 505-758-4977

Work: sculpture (free standing)
Media: metal, stone, wood
Special Concerns: environmental issues
Commission Amounts: $8,000 - $65,000
Agencies: City of Albuquerque
Recent Project: *Running Horses*, two
huge steel horses galloping toward
the West (1990)

MIKE ROY ART & DESIGN

MIKE ROY
1269 ELIZABETH ST
PASADENA, CA 91104
FAX 818-797-2159
TEL 818-797-1600

Work: collaborative site design,
2D work, temporary installations
Media: paint, wood, mixed
Special Concerns: collaborative
design teams
Commission Amounts: $2,500 - $250,000
Agencies: City of Los Angeles Community
Redevelopment Association; Rock Walk
Museum, Inc.; the Light Brinuer Project
Recent Project: Street mural celebrating
75th anniversary of the Grand Canyon
National Park

ROBERT MILLAR

PO BOX 515
MANHATTAN BEACH, CA 90267-0515
FAX 310-376-5313
TEL 310-376-5313

Work: collaborative site design
Media: all materials
Special Concerns: collaborative design
teams, environmental issues, planning
and design issues
Commission Amounts: $30,000 - $1,560,000
Agencies: San Diego Arts Commission;
Los Angeles County Transportation
Commission; California Arts Council

★ JIM MILLER
★ DIANNA THORNHILL MILLER

OMNI ART DESIGN
1716 W MAIN ST
FORT WAYNE, IN 46808-3355
FAX 219-422-3677
TEL 219-422-3677

Work: sculpture (atrium and wall relief),
fiber work for interior walls, leather
mosaic™ murals
Media: metal, wood, fiber, leather
Special Concerns: multicultural issues,
historical and documentary issues, collaborative design teams, thematic relevance
Commission Amounts: $10,000 - $50,000
Agencies: Fort Wayne Fine Arts Foundation; Fort Wayne Committee for Public
Art, Sister Cities International Cultural
Arts Exchange
Recent Project: Celebration, 30'H x 6'W x 8"D
pyramidal fiber relief warms castle-like
walls in Louis I. Kahn's great hall foyer

"The Millers are open-minded and free
in designing for environments … fitting
the appropriate materials to the means
of construction results in works which
are wonderfully adapted to their location
in scale, theme and purpose … and their
understanding of historic decoration and
knowledge of architectural antecedents
underlie a belief in the justification for
the interdependency of art and architecture. Sensitive to the classic clarity necessary to the aesthetic of many modern
buildings, the Millers are cognizant of the
need to preserve the integrity of the
architect's design, as evidenced in their
Celebration for Louis Kahn's Performing
Arts Center [Fort Wayne, IN]." William
E. Story, Director, Saginaw Art Museum,
Saginaw, MI.

**See the *Designer's Edition: 10* for pho-
tographs and additional information.**

ROSS MILLER

75 RICHDALE AVE #16
CAMBRIDGE, MA 02140
TEL 617-876-4987

Work: neon, laser, light related, conceptual
Media: metal, stone, light, steel, bronze
Special Concerns: collaborative design
teams, community involvement, environ-
mental issues
Commission Amounts: $12,000 - $150,000
Agencies: Cambridge Arts Council;
Metropolitan Boston Transit Authority;
Boston Park Department
Recent Project: Scientifically and culturally
based miniature golf course for Boston
Children's Museum (1992)

JAMES MOORE

BLACK OAK STUDIOS
PO BOX 2447
BERKELEY, CA 94702
FAX 415-898-2991
TEL 510-839-3886

Work: sculpture (free standing), cast
stone and metal
Media: metal, cast stone, gypsum cement
Special Concerns: multicultural issues
Commission Amounts: $15,000 - $125,000
Agencies: Gateway Center for Arts and
Social Change; Oakland Parks and
Recreation; City of Oakland
Recent Project: 150'L seating wall exe-
cuted in relief

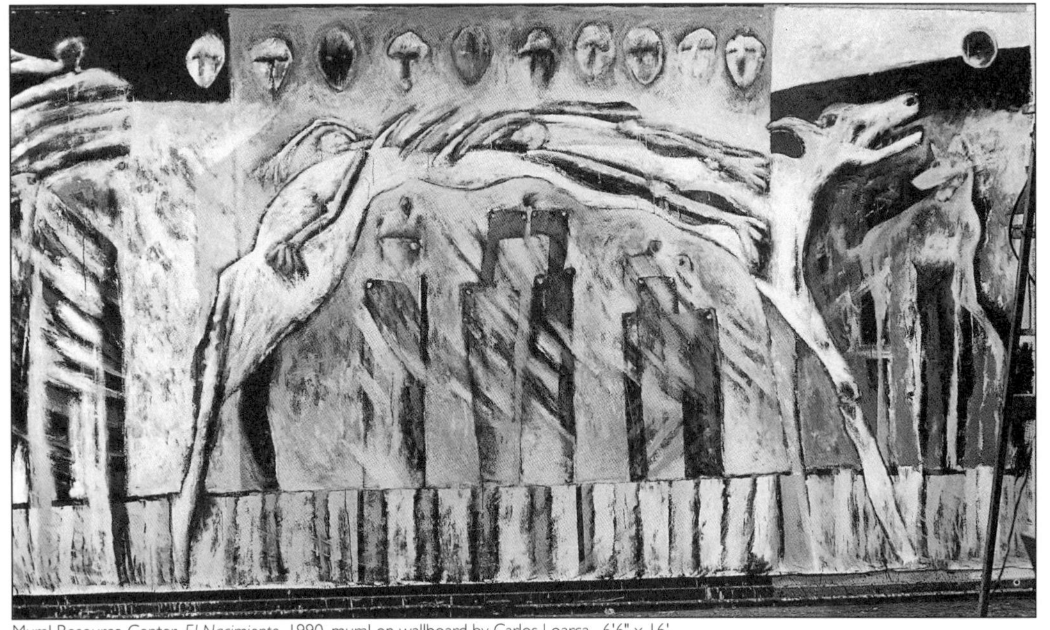

Mural Resource Center, *El Nacimiento*, 1990, mural on wallboard by Carlos Loarca, 6'6" x 16'

CARLA ERICKSON MOSS

NORTHERN STAR ENTERPRISES
186A BERESFORD CT
MILPITAS, CA 95035-4405
FAX 408-287-8412 (Please call first)
TEL 800-946-5974

Work: sculpture (free standing, pedestal and wall relief), fountains, architectural metal, outdoor furniture and equipment, 2D work
Media: metal, concrete, wood
Special Concerns: community involvement, historical and documentary issues, environmental issues
Commission Amounts: $10,000 - $50,000
Agencies: Anchorage, AK Percent for Art; Milpitas (CA) Cultural Arts
Recent Project: *The Flute Player*, life-size, City of Milpitas (CA) community center

WENDY MUELLER

40 LARCH ST
PROVIDENCE, RI 02906
TEL 401-331-3178

Work: fiber work for interior walls
Media: fiber, handmade wool felt
Commission Amounts: $47,000
Agencies: Rhode Island State Council on the Arts
Recent Project: Handmade wool felt tapestries for the Rhode Island Convention Center

KATHLEEN MULCAHY

260 WHITTENGALE RD
OAKDALE, PA 15071-3606
TEL 412-693-0758

Work: sculpture (free standing, pedestal and wall relief), collaborative site design, architectural metal, neon/laser/light related, glass, temporary installations
Media: metal, glass, mixed, wood
Special Concerns: collaborative design teams, community involvement, participatory works, historical and documentary issues
Commission Amounts: $1,000 - $30,000
Agencies: Port Authority of Pittsburg, PA; Chartiers Valley Arts Council, Carnegie, PA
Recent Project: Temple sitting room, painted walls, furniture, cast bronze, etched glass

★ MURAL RESOURCE CENTER

BETSIE MILLER-KUSZ
934 BRANNAN ST
SAN FRANCISCO, CA 94110
FAX 415-552-0136
TEL 415-552-2131

Work: collaborative site design, painted finishes and murals, temporary installations
Media: paint, concrete, ceramics
Special Concerns: collaborative design teams, community development, multicultural issues
Commission Amounts: $3,200 - $60,000
Agencies: Mayor's Office of Community Development; San Francisco Art Commission; Neighborhood Beautification Fund
Recent Project: Hospitality House community mural, artist working with homeless youth (1995)

The Mural Resource Center is celebrating 20 years of sponsoring mural projects, guiding them through city agencies, coordinating the permit process, consulting and advocating for public murals and muralists. As a program of SOMAR, the South of Market Cultural Center, our muralists reach out to the public in their communities, including them in the design and painting of mural walls, reflecting the multicultural diversity of San Francisco.

See photograph page 250.

MURASE ASSOCIATES, INC.

ROBERT K. MURASE
1300 NW NORTHRUP
PORTLAND, OR 97209
FAX 503-295-0942
TEL 503-242-1477

Work: fountains, architectural elements
Media: concrete, earth and plants, stone
Special Concerns: collaborative design teams, environmental issues
Commission Amounts: $35,000 - $1,000,000
Agencies: Oregon Arts Commission

★ JUAN & PATRICIA NAVARRETE

NAVARRETE STUDIO
PO BOX 2251
TAOS, NM 87571-2251
TEL 505-776-2942

Work: sculpture (wall relief)
Media: cementuous materials, metal
Special Concerns: concrete sitting area
Commission Amounts: $12,000 - $60,000
Agencies: Phoenix Arts Commission; New Mexico Arts Division; Gallup Arts Council
Recent Project: Metal relief wall sculpture, Tijeras Library, NM

See page 220 for photographs and additional information.

LENN NEFF

CONTEMPORARY LEADED GLASS AND ARCHITECTURAL ARTS
PO BOX 1931
SAINT PETERSBURG, FL 33731-1931
TEL 813-823-3919

Work: architectural glass, neon/laser/light related, lighting
Media: metal, glass, wood
Commission Amounts: $11,000 - $34,500
Agencies: Florida Arts Council Art in State Buildings; City of St. Petersburg Public Art Commission
Recent Project: *Place Settings*, glass and light construction in Shands Teaching Hospital, 8' x 16' 6" x 16" (1991)

WILL NETTLESHIP

526 PINEHURST AVE
PLACENTIA, CA 92670-4450
FAX 714-579-1239
TEL 714-579-3636

Work: sculpture (free standing), collaborative site design, outdoor paving
Media: concrete, brick, earth and plants
Special Concerns: community involvement, issues related to disabilities
Commission Amounts: $20,000 - $50,000
Agencies: California Arts Council (1994); Alameda County (CA) Art Commission (1993); NEA thru the Exploratorium, San Francisco, CA (1992)
Recent Project: Earth, concrete and stone landscape for a state park facility

SHEL NEYMARK

SHEL NEYMARK ARCHITECTURAL CERAMICS
PO BOX 25
EMBUDO, NM 87531-0125
FAX 505-579-4432
TEL 505-579-4432

Work: architectural ceramics, mosaics, and wall relief
Media: ceramics
Commission Amounts: $10,000 - $50,000
Agencies: City of White Rock, NM; City of Albuquerque
Recent Project: In progress: fountain for botanical garden under construction in Albuquerque

DONALD CLAUDE NOEL

THE OPEN SEA SCULPTURE STUDIO
1406 MAIN ST
GREEN BAY, WI 54302
TEL 414-433-0540

Work: sculpture (free standing and pedestal), mosaics
Media: metal, mixed, stone
Special Concerns: collaborative design teams, historical and documentary issues
Commission Amounts: $10,000 - $65,000
Recent Project: *Volunteer Fireman*, 7', bronze, City of Morris, IL

PHYLLIS NORDIN

DIMENSIONS UNLIMITED
4035 TAN TARA DR
TOLEDO, OH 43623-3311
TEL 419-841-9536

Work: sculpture (free standing, atrium and pedestal), collaborative site design, fountains
Media: metal, concrete, plastics
Special Concerns: collaborative design teams, historical and documentary issues, memorial/liturgical
Commission Amounts: $5,000 - $60,000
Agencies: Arts Commission of Greater Toledo; Toledo Botanical Gardens; City of Sylvania, OH
Recent Project: Bronze life-sized children for the New Kingston, TN, Library

JOSEPH NORMAN

1141 AQUIDNECK AVE #426
MIDDLETOWN, RI 02840
TEL 401-849-0594

Work: painted finishes and murals
Media: paint, wood, paper
Special Concerns: historical and documentary issues, multicultural issues
Commission Amounts: $150,000
Agencies: Rhode Island State Council for the Arts
Recent Project: 100' mural for the Rhode Island Convention Center

PATSY NORVELL

78 GREEN ST
NEW YORK, NY 10012
TEL 212-431-5341

Work: collaborative site design, architectural glass, architectural metal
Media: metal, mixed, glass, earth/plants
Special Concerns: collaborative design teams, historical and documentary issues, environmental issues
Commission Amounts: $20,000 - $275,000
Agencies: New York City Public Art Fund; General Services Administration, Washington, DC; Metropolitan Transit Authority Percent for Art, New York, NY
Recent Project: Two Brooklyn subway stations, fence, railing; sandblasted, image-laminated windows

LORI NOZICK

PO BOX 771
CROMPOND, NY 10517
TEL 914-528-2434

Work: sculpture (free standing, pedestal and wall relief), collaborative site design, architectural elements, murals
Media: concrete, wood, mixed
Special Concerns: collaborative design teams, community involvement, science and teaching related
Commission Amounts: $2,500 - $200,000
Agencies: New York State Council for the Arts; New York Foundation for the Arts; Percent for Arts, Public Art in Schools, New York, NY
Recent Project: Wall relief mural relating to community history, 96'L x 11'H, of wood, steel, paint for New York City public school auditorium (1995)

GENE OLSON

THE METTLE WORKS
8600 ODEAN AVE NE
ELK RIVER, MN 55330-7167
FAX 612-441-1563
TEL 612-441-1563

Work: sculpture (free standing and atrium), architectural metal
Media: metal, mixed, stone
Special Concerns: collaborative design teams, historical and documentary issues, science or teaching related
Commission Amounts: $8,000 - $100,000
Agencies: Wisconsin State Arts Board; Minneapolis Arts Commission

PATENAUDE/CLOSE STUDIO, INC.

FRANK CLOSE
115 GRAND ST
NEW YORK, NY 10013-2691
FAX 212-431-3211
TEL 212-925-1140
Work: sculpture (free standing and atrium), architectural glass
Media: metal, glass
Commission Amounts: $10,000 - $275,000
Agencies: Minnesota Percent for Art in Public Places
Recent Project: Suspended construction of steel, dichroic glass, Roche Carolina, Inc. (1994)

★ G. BYRON PECK

**G. BYRON PECK STUDIOS
1857 LAMONT ST NW
WASHINGTON, DC 20010-2603
FAX 202-887-6752
TEL 202-331-1966**
Work: painted finishes and murals, architectural ceramics, mosaics, and wall relief, paintings, photographs (2-D)
Media: concrete, paint, keim paint
Special Concerns: collaborative design teams, historical and documentary issues, multicultural issues
Commission Amounts: $5,000 - $49,000
Agencies: DC Arts Commission
Recent Project: U.S. State Department Embassy murals - Crete, Chile, Guyana; U.S. Nuclear Regulatory Commission mural; three-story mural at DuPont Circle (1994)
See page 115 for photographs and additional information.

ROBERT PERLESS

37 LANGHORNE LN
GREENWICH, CT 06831-2611
FAX 203-869-0718
TEL 203-869-0710
Work: sculpture (free standing, atrium and wall relief), fountains
Media: metal, polycarbonate prisms, water
Special Concerns: environmental issues, site-specific, science
Commission Amounts: $30,000 - $250,000
Agencies: Connecticut Commission on the Arts; Stamford Commission of the Arts; Palm Desert Cultural Council
Recent Project: Stainless steel and prism sculpture which alligns itself with the sun to create rainbows, University of Connecticut at Stoors

MELODY PETERS

1416 E 10TH ST
TUCSON, AZ 85719-5809
TEL 520-623-1331
Work: sculpture (free standing and wall relief), collaborative site design, painted finishes and murals, mosaics, neon, laser, light related
Media: metal, ceramics, earth and plants
Special Concerns: collaborative design teams, historical and documentary issues, environmental issues
Commission Amounts: $17,000 - $60,000
Agencies: General Services Administration, Tucson, AZ; General Services Administration, Pima County; City of Tucson, AZ
Recent Project: Collaborative ceramic mural with multicultural them for a prison

DAVID PHILLIPS

SCULPTOR'S WORKSHOP
88 WINSLOW AVE
SOMERVILLE, MA 02144-2573
TEL 617-623-5088
Work: collaborative site design, fountains, architectural elements, garden installations
Media: metal, paint, concrete, brick earth/plants, water
Special Concerns: collaborative design teams, participatory works, environmental issues
Commission Amounts: $50,000 - $300,000
Agencies: Connecticut Commission for the Arts; Utah Arts Commission Percent for Art; Cambridge Arts Council, Cambridge, MA
Recent Project: *City Square*, collaborative park design, Charlestown, MA

JODY PINTO

124 CHAMBERS ST
NEW YORK, NY 10007-1002
FAX 212-349-1648
TEL 212-349-4429
Work: collaborative site design, architectural elements, bridges, functional
Media: metal, stone, landscape materials
Special Concerns: collaborative design teams, participatory works, environmental issues
Commission Amounts: $150,000 - $500,000
Agencies: Phoenix Arts Commission; Miami-Dade Arts Commission; Washington State Percent For Art
Recent Project: *Papago Park*, collaborative desert-reclamation project using water-harvesting techniques

RICHARD POSNER

FREE ADVICE
PO BOX 1151
CULVER CITY, CA 90232-1151
FAX 310-838-9865
TEL 310-815-0248
Work: collaborative site design, architectural glass, public sculpture
Media: mixed, glass, earth and plants
Special Concerns: participatory works; historical and documentary issues, environmental issues; interactive involvement
Commission Amounts: $50,000 - $150,000
Agencies: GSA Art In Architecture program; Veterans' Administration Art in Public Places program; Washington State Arts Commission
Recent Project: 1992 GSA Design Excellence Award, U.S.F.D.A. Pacific NW Headquarters

LESLIE ANN POWERS

LESLIE ANN POWERS STUDIO
241 STATE ST
GUILFORD, CT 06437
FAX 203-453-6179
TEL 203-453-9583
Work: painted finishes and murals, faux carpets on floors
Media: paint
Special Concerns: collaborative design teams, historical and documentary issues
Commission Amounts: $2,000 - $20,000
Agencies: Madison Historical Society; Guilford Historic Society; Shoreline Alliance for the Handicapped
Recent Project: Transformed restaurant into a Black Forest German scene

PATRICIA POWERS

383 POOLES HILL RD
ANCRAM, NY 12502-5413
TEL 518-329-2671
Work: painting and murals, 2D work
Media: paint
Special Concerns: environmental issues
Commission Amounts: $3,500 - $100,000
Agencies: Washington State Arts Commission; California Arts Council; Columbia County Council on the Arts
Recent Project: *Hobson's Choice*, 10' x 18' three-panel oil-on-canvas life-size horses and architecture (1987)

★ BEV PRECIOUS

**PRECIOUS DESIGN STUDIOS INC.
950 N ALABAMA ST
INDIANAPOLIS, IN 46202-3350
TEL 317-631-6560**
Work: sculpture (free standing and atrium), architectural glass
Media: metal, concrete, glass
Commission Amounts: $25,000 - $138,000
Agencies: Ohio Arts Council; Evanston Arts Council
Recent Project: *Windward*, dichroic and carved wire glass, copper, stainless steel (1994)

As a glass artist, Beverly Precious is drawn to the medium by the drama of light and color. In large-scale public art pieces, the color is not only contained in the piece, but is reflected onto the surroundings, integrating the piece with the environment. Likewise, the mirror quality of glass reflects the movement of each passerby. This highly-kinetic result draws the viewer into the piece, the ultimate goal for public art.

See page 54 for photographs and additional information.

DAMIAN PRIOUR

DAMIAN PRIOUR STUDIO
17120 HAMILTON POOL RD
AUSTIN, TX 78738
FAX 512-264-2080
TEL 512-264-2008
Work: sculpture (free standing), fountains, architectural glass
Media: mixed, stone, glass
Special Concerns: community involvement, historical and documentary issues, environmental issues
Commission Amounts: $20,000 - $100,000
Agencies: Art in Public Places: Cities of Palm Springs (CA), Corpus Christi (TX), Austin (TX)
Recent Project: 20' sculpture of stone and glass depicting *Flight*, Palm Springs, CA

★ JOHN PUGH

**21590 MADRONE RD
LOS GATOS, CA 95030
FAX 301-353-3370
TEL 408-353-3370**
Work: murals
Media: paint
Special Concerns: community involvement, historical issues, environmental issues, multicultural issues
Commission Amounts: $21,000 - $62,000
Agencies: Sacramento Metropolitan Art Commission; Fremont Arts Commission; Palm Desert Arts Commission
Recent Project: Illusionary art work integrated into the architecture and area's cultural diversity, Sacramento, CA

See page 117 for photographs and additional information.

DAVE PUTNAM

DAVE PUTNAM, SCULPTOR
PO BOX 620358
WOODSIDE, CA 94062
TEL 415-851-8218

Work: sculpture (free standing)
Media: metal, paint, concrete
Special Concerns: environmental issues, science and teaching related
Commission Amounts: $5,000 - $20,000
Agencies: Antioch Art in Public Places, CA; Audobon Zoo, New Orleans, LA; International Wildlife Museum, Tucson, AZ
Recent Project: Life-size grizzly bears of stainless steel with wire fur

LIZ WHITNEY QUISGARD

145 READE ST
NEW YORK, NY 10013-3833
TEL 212-571-4283

Work: painted finishes and murals, 2D work, flooring and ground plane
Media: paint, wood, concrete
Commission Amounts: $15,000 - $50,000
Agencies: Bureau of Cultural Affairs and Arts Festival of Atlanta
Recent Project: 4' x 8' painting, Medical College of Virgina, Richmond, public art commission

JOHN RAIMONDI

JOHN RAIMONDI, SCULPTOR, INC.
165 SEMINOLE AVE
PALM BEACH, FL 33480-3732
FAX 407-659-4972
TEL 407-659-4971

Work: sculpture (free standing, atrium and pedestal)
Media: metal
Special Concerns: historical and documentary issues, environmental issues, spiritual
Commission Amounts: $35,000 - $500,000
Agencies: Omaha (NE) Airport Authority; National Endowment for the Arts; Southwest Florida International Airport
Recent Project: *Grace*, stainless steel sculpture for Lee County (FL) Port Authority

RAY KING STUDIO

RAY KING
835 N 3RD ST
PHILADELPHIA, PA 19123-2203
FAX 215-625-8421
TFI 215-627-5112

Work: sculpture (atrium), neon, laser, light related, architectural glass
Media: metal, glass, light
Special Concerns: collaborative design teams, light phenomenon
Commission Amounts: $53,000 - $524,000
Agencies: New Jersey State Council on the Arts; Minnesota State Arts Board, Percent For Art; General Services Administration, Washington, DC
Recent Project: Seven 6' steel and illuminated glass torches, lining college entranceway

JEFFREY REED

4701 SAN LEANDRO ST #10
OAKLAND, CA 94601-5138
FAX 510-261-9888
TEL 510-261-9888

Work: sculpture (free standing), furniture, lighting
Media: concrete, glass, earth
Special Concerns: environmental issues, function
Commission Amounts: $15,000 - $28,000
Agencies: Sacramento Metropolitan Arts Commission; City of Davis Art in Public Places

ZENAIDE REISS

STONE HOUSE STUDIO
10 MAPLE ST
MILFORD, NJ 08848-1313
TEL 908-995-9336

Work: fiber work for interior walls, textiles and floor coverings
Media: fiber, mixed, plastics/polymer
Commission Amounts: $4,000 - $32,000
Agencies: Georgia Council for the Arts; MARTA Arts Council
Recent Project: Polymer/plastic window decoration for 72' window wall, Atlanta Fulton County Library System (1992)

★ AMANDA RICHARDSON

PO BOX 2147
FRIDAY HARBOR, WA 98250-2147
TEL 360-378-4359

Work: fiber work for interior walls
Media: fiber
Special Concerns: environmental issues
Commission Amounts: $6,000 - $34,000
Agencies: Alaska Percent for Arts; Universities of Alaska and Washington
Recent Project: *San Juan Invertebrates*, fiber installation, 53" x 72", for marine laboratory (1993)

The rich, light-reflective tapestries of Amanda Richardson respond to their environment, the image varying with the angle and intensity of light, allowing the viewer to become actively involved in the artistic experience. The artist developed the technique of Richardson-tapestry, in which fabrics are hand-dyed, cut into intricate forms, and bonded together, layer on layer, to build up a rich and complex final image. These images give the impression of a great spatial depth, with a visual impact few art medium can equal. The artist enjoys working closely with the commissioning agent.

See the *Designer's Edition: 10* for photographs and additional information.

CHERYL RENEE RILEY

RIGHT ANGLE DESIGNS
829 SHRADER ST
SAN FRANCISCO, CA 94117-2723
FAX 415-386-7828
TEL 415-386-7828

Work: sculpture (wall relief), architectural glass, mosaics, architectural metal, lighting, furniture
Media: metal, concrete, mixed
Special Concerns: collaborative design teams, community involvement, multicultural issues
Commission Amounts: $40,000 - $200,000
Agencies: National Endowment for the Arts; San Francisco Art Commission; Sacramento Metropolitan Art Commission
Recent Project: Ndebele-inspired wall panels for the NEA and a San Francisco police station

RIK RITCHEY

667 11TH ST
OAKLAND, CA 94607
FAX 510-548-5431
TEL 510-763-8735

Work: sculpture (free standing and wall relief), educational
Media: metal, wood, glass
Special Concerns: collaborative design teams, participatory works, historical and documentary issues
Commission Amounts: $20,000 and up
Agencies: City of Pusan, Korea
Recent Project: Two sculptures of carved wood cast in bronze, 3 meters in height, Olympic Park, Pusan, Korea

BOB RIVERA

84 WITHERS ST
BROOKLYN, NY 11211-2247
FAX 718-389-0105
TEL 718-389-2161

Work: sculpture (free standing), other media for interior walls
Media: metal, paint, wood
Special Concerns: community involvement, multicultural issues
Commission Amounts: $5,000 - $350,000
Agencies: Chester County Art Association; New York State Dormitory Authority; New York City Percent for Art
Recent Project: *Open Voyage*, aluminum sculpture, 19' x 40' x 14', paint and powder coated (1992)

STEPHEN ROBIN

1910 N MARSHALL ST
PHILADELPHIA, PA 19122-2111
FAX 215-763-7167
TEL 215-763-7167

Work: sculpture (free standing, pedestal and wall relief)
Media: metal, concrete, stone
Special Concerns: collaborative design teams, historical and documentary issues
Commission Amounts: $13,000 - $110,000
Agencies: U.S. General Services Administration; PA Convention Center Authority, Philadelphia, PA
Recent Project: *Cornucopiae*, 13' plaza sculptures, M.L. King, Jr. Federal Building, Newark, NJ

URSULA ROEDENBERG

707A UNION ST
BROOKLYN, NY 11215
TEL 718-857-2394

Work: collaborative site design, painted finishes and murals
Media: paint
Special Concerns: collaborative design teams, community involvement, multicultural issues
Commission Amounts: $5,000 - $20,000
Agencies: Parks and Recreation Department, City of New York, NY; Bronx Council on the Arts, NY; HUD, City of Ottomwa, IA
Recent Project: Trompe l'oeil mural for a city park, 75' x 20', with neighborhood participation, New York, NY

JOHN ROLOFF

2020 LIVINGSTON ST
OAKLAND, CA 94606-5229
FAX 510-261-9196
TEL 510-261-9196

Work: sculpture (free standing), collaborative site design, flooring and ground plane
Media: mixed, glass, earth and plants
Special Concerns: collaborative design teams, environmental issues, science or teaching related
Commission Amounts: $30,000 - $140,00
Agencies: San Francisco Redevelopment Agency, CA ; California Department of Fish and Game, Moss Landing, CA; Sacramento Regional Transit, CA
Recent Project: Site-related sculpture, *Deep Gradient*, Yerba Buena Gardens, San Francisco, CA

RAMSEY ROSE

ART + ARCHITECTURE
109 14TH ST SW
ALBUQUERQUE, NM 87102-2821
TEL 505-247-8227

Work: sculpture (atrium), architectural metal, lighting, interior and exterior
Media: metal, mixed, fabrics
Special Concerns: collaborative design teams, environmental issues, architectural installations
Commission Amounts: $5,000 - $100,000
Agencies: Cities of Albuquerque (NM), Phoenix (AZ); Albany (NY)
Recent Project: Installation for the City of Albuquerque International Airport

EVELYN ROSENBERG

DETONOGRAPHICS
7770 GUADALUPE TRL NW
ALBUQUERQUE, NM 87107-6506
TEL 505-899-0017

Work: sculpture (free standing and wall relief)
Media: metal
Special Concerns: historical and documentary issues, science and teaching related, figurative and abstract
Commission Amounts: $15,000 - $150,000
Agencies: City of Albuquerque Percent for Art; Nebraska Percent for Art; City of Denver Percent for Art
Recent Project: Sonora Desert Museum, Tucson, AZ (1994); Planetarium lobby, Santa Fe, NM

ROSETTA

NATIONAL SCULPTORS' GUILD
2683 N TAFT AVE
LOVELAND, CO 80538
FAX 970-667-2068
TEL 970-667-2015

Work: sculpture (free standing and pedestal), collaborative site design
Media: metal, mixed
Special Concerns: collaborative design teams, environmental issues
Commission Amounts: $25,000
Agencies: City of Loveland Visual Arts Commission
Recent Project: Premiere sculpture for Homestate Bank sculpture garden (1993); Chapman University Commission (1994)

CHARLES ROSS

383 W BROADWAY
NEW YORK, NY 10012-4377
FAX 212-925-0341
TEL 212-925-0341

Work: sculpture (free standing, atrium and pedestal)
Media: metal, stone, plexiglass
Special Concerns: participatory works, environmental issues, science or teaching related
Commission Amounts: $60,000 - $400,000
Agencies: General Services Administration; Cities of San Francisco, Chicago, and San Diego, State of Connecticut
Recent Project: 20 large prisms in skylights, Harvard Business School Chapel, 1992

ROSSI METAL SCULPTURE

KAREN ROSSI
PO BOX 444
SOUTH WINDSOR, CT 06074-0444
FAX 203-528-2472
TEL 203-289-5180

Work: sculpture (free standing and atrium), fountains
Media: metal, mixed, paint
Special Concerns: collaborative design teams, community involvement, participatory works
Commission Amounts: $5,000 - $30,000
Agencies: Cities of New Haven and Stamford, CT
Recent Project: *Oyster Man*, cast bronze, for Fair Haven Harbor Park, New Haven, CT (1993)

CLAUDE ROUSSEL

905 AMIRAULT
DIEPPE, NB E1A 1E1
CANADA
TEL 506-855-5872

Work: sculpture (pedestal), architectural elements, other media for interior walls
Media: metal, stone, wood
Special Concerns: collaborative design teams, community involvement, historical and documentary issues
Commission Amounts: $2,000 - $350,000
Agencies: City of Kingston, Ontario; Seoul (Korea) Sculpture Garden; Moncton 100 Special Committee, Moncton, New Brunswick
Recent Project: *Moncton 100 Monument*, reflecting pool, bronze statue, stainless steel sails, granite and concrete (1991)

DEANNE SABECK

STUDIO 215
710 13TH ST STE 215
SAN DIEGO, CA 92101-7347
FAX 619-234-0814
TEL 619-234-0814

Work: architectural glass, architectural metal
Media: metal, glass, stone
Special Concerns: historical/documentary issues, environmental issues
Commission Amounts: $25,000 - $50,000
Agencies: San Diego Commission for Arts and Culture; Tucson Pima Arts Council
Recent Project: Glass and steel installation exploring the environmental impact of development on a pristine canyon

JILL SABLOSKY

PO BOX 1552
GLEN ROSE, TX 76043-1552
FAX 817-897-3785
TEL 817-897-4774

Work: sculpture (free standing), collaborative site design, functional
Media: concrete, stone, marble, slate
Special Concerns: collaborative design teams, community involvement, participatory works, environmental issues
Commission Amounts: $3,000 - $50,000
Agencies: GSA Art-in-Architecture Federal Program; Percent for Art Program, Redevolpment Authority of Philadelphia, PA
Recent Project: 11' free-standing, carved, functional sculpture with landscaped concrete walkways, General Services Administration Building, San Antonio, TX

PATRICK ST. GERMAIN

LAST COAST STUDIO
121 N FRONT ST
MARQUETTE, MI 49855-4300
TEL 906-226-8122

Work: painted finishes and murals, neon/laser/light related, paintings, photographs (2-D)
Media: mixed, paint, wood
Special Concerns: environmental issues
Commission Amounts: $1,000 - $38,000
Agencies: Michigan Commission on Art in Public Places, Wisconsin Arts Board
Recent Project: Four 8' x 11' paintings, Sports Dome, Marquette, MI

ELIZABETH SALTOS

120 CARMEL AVE
PACIFICA, CA 94044-2555
TEL 415-355-9248

Work: sculpture (atrium and wall relief), painted finishes and murals
Media: metal, paint, wood
Special Concerns: science and teaching related, geometric
Commission Amounts: $12,000 - $26,000
Agencies: Sacramento (CA) Metropolitan Arts Commission; San Francisco (CA) Art Commission
Recent Project: Relief sculpture for library, galvanized metal, polyurethanes, 90'L

ARTURO ALONZO SANDOVAL

HIGH TECH ART FORMS
PO BOX 237
LEXINGTON, KY 40584-0237
FAX 606-257-3042
TEL 606-273-8898

Work: fiber work for interior walls, other media for interior walls
Media: fiber, mixed
Special Concerns: community involvement, historical and documentary issues, multicultural issues
Commission Amounts: $6,000 - $25,000
Agencies: Kentucky Medical Services Foundation
Recent Project: *Sky Grid*, 30' x 40' linear abstraction, Kentucky Clinic, Lexington (1992)

CLAIRE JEANINE SATIN

ARTWORKS
101 SW 1ST ST
DANIA, FL 33004-3628
TEL 305-923-9117

Work: architectural metal, other work for interior walls, flooring and ground plane, handmade paper, artists' books
Media: metal, mixed, ceramics, handmade paper
Special Concerns: community involvement, participatory works
Commission Amounts: $5,000 - $60,000
Agencies: State of Alaska Percent For Art; Broward County (FL) Art in Public Places
Recent Project: *Chapman Chronicles*, mathematical notations, 12 powder-coated steel plates, $10^{1}/_{2}'$ x $9^{1}/_{2}'$, Fairbanks, AK (1992)

WILLIAM SCHAEFER STUDIO

15 BAY ST
CAMBRIDGE, MA 02139-3144
FAX 617-661-1857
TEL 617-661-7582

Work: 2D work
Media: photo collage
Special Concerns: collaborative design teams, community involvement, environmental issues
Commission Amounts: $4,000 - $12,000
Agencies: Massachusetts Bay Transportation Authority
Recent Project: *Musee Rodin, Paris*, laminated photos, 6' x 5,' Hale & Dore, Boston, MA (1995)

KENNY SCHNEIDER

409 W MATILIJA ST
OJAI, CA 93023-2550
FAX 805-640-1390
TEL 805-640-1390

Work: sculpture (free standing and pedestal), collaborative site design
Media: metal, mixed
Special Concerns: collaborative design teams, community involvement, humor
Commission Amounts: $10,000 - $80,000
Agencies: Community Redevelopment Agency, Los Angeles, CA; Seattle Arts Commission, Seattle, WA; Miami-Dade Art in Public Places
Recent Project: Community Redevopment Agency's Hollywood Boulevard Project, Los Angeles (1993), Noho Sculpture Project, N. Hollywood, CA (1994)

GLENN SCHWAIGER

224 W HADLEY AVE
LAS CRUCES, NM 88005-1807
TEL 505-525-1625
Work: sculpture (free standing), architectural glass, temporary installations
Media: mixed, ceramics, glass
Special Concerns: community involvement, participatory works, science and teaching related
Commission Amounts: $5,000 - $50,000
Agencies: New Mexico Arts in Public Places; City of Los Cruces Arts in Public Places
Recent Project: Composite, tiled mural, 8' x 10,' of images important to children, Clovis High School, Clovis, NM (1995)

LENI SCHWENDINGER

LIGHT PROJECTS
448 W 37TH ST #8G
NEW YORK, NY 10018-4017
FAX 212-947-6289
TEL 212-947-6282
Work: collaborative site design, lighting, temporary installations
Media: metal, light/shadow, reflective
Special Concerns: participatory works historical/documentary issues, vehicular viewer
Commission Amounts: $20,000 - $340,000
Agencies: Denver International Airport Art; Fairmount Park Art Association; Rhode Island State Council on the Arts
Recent Project: Large-scale light/sculpture environment for train tunnel, Denver, CO (1994)

★ SANDY SCOTT

NATIONAL SCULPTORS' GUILD
2683 N TAFT AVE
LOVELAND, CO 80538
FAX 970-667-2068
TEL 970-667-2015
Work: sculpture (free standing, pedestal and wall relief), fountains
Media: metal
Special Concerns: collaborative design teams
Commission Amounts: $1,000 - $300,000
Agencies: National Cowboy Hall of Fame, Oklahoma City 1% for the Arts; Fountain Commission, Albuquerque, NM; El Paso Zoo, TX; Ritz Carlton Hotel, Aspen, CO
Recent Project: Eagle sculpture, National Wildlife Art Museum, Jackson, WY

See page 164 for photographs and additional information.

VICKI SCURI

SITEWORKS
1066 NE 106TH ST
SEATTLE, WA 98125-7533
FAX 206-361-5964
TEL 206-361-5964
Work: collaborative site design, neon, laser, light related, architectural elements
Media: metal, concrete, earth and plants
Special Concerns: collaborative design teams, participatory works, environmental issues
Commission Amounts: $50,000 - $1,000,000
Agencies: San Francisco Arts Commission; Phoenix Arts Commission; Seattle Arts Commission
Recent Project: *Dreamy Draw*, pedestrian bridge, represents infrastructure as public art

SENIOR/OESTERLE ARCHITECTURE + ART

VIRGINIA SENIOR
 & JEFF OESTERLE
1230A E JACKSON ST
PHOENIX, AZ 85034
FAX 602-254-8178
TEL 602-256-2622
Work: sculpture (free standing), collaborative site design, furniture
Media: metal, concrete, mixed
Special Concerns: collaborative design teams, participatory works, environmental issues
Commission Amounts: $500 - $30,000
Agencies: Tempe Municipal Arts Commission; Tempe Arts Center
Recent Project: Decorative transit shelter, 12'H steel canopy and benches

SHARLES

NATIONAL SCULPTORS' GUILD
2683 N TAFT AVE
LOVELAND, CO 80538
FAX 970-667-2068
TEL 970-667-2015
Work: sculpture (free standing and pedestal), fountains
Media: metal
Special Concerns: collaborative design teams, environmental issues
Agencies: City of Loveland, CO
Recent Project: 101" wingspand eagle, Rocky Mountain Mall (1995)

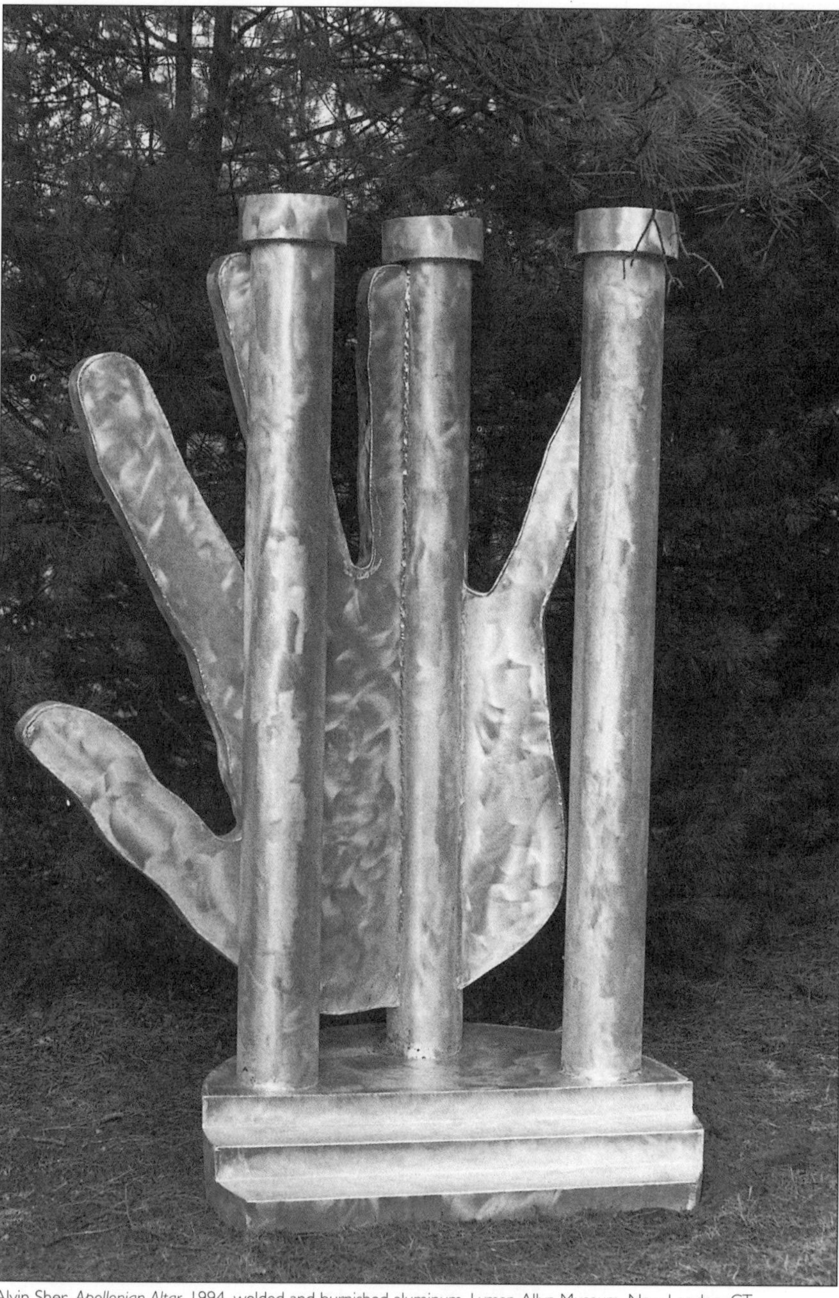

Alvin Sher, *Apollonian Altar*, 1994, welded and burnished aluminum, Lyman Allyn Museum, New London, CT, 8'H x 12'L x 8'W

★ BENSON SHAW

**4136 MERIDIAN AVE N
SEATTLE, WA 98103-8308
TEL 206-632-3552**

Work: architectural glass, architectural ceramics, mosaics, and wall relief, pavement
Media: ceramics, concrete, glass
Special Concerns: collaborative design teams, community involvement, historical and documentary issues
Commission Amounts: $3,000 - $80,000
Agencies: King County (WA) Arts Commission; Bainbridge Island (WA) Arts Committee; Olympia (WA) Arts Commission
Recent Project: 22 porcelain sidewalk mosaics giving historic Seattle street names

**See page 222 for photographs
and additional information.**

★ LUCINDA SHAW

**ACACIA ART GLASS STUDIOS
3000 CHESTNUT AVE STE 336
BALTIMORE, MD 21211-2751
FAX 410-366-6472
TEL 410-467-4038**

Work: architectural glass
Media: glass
Commission Amounts: $3,000 - $25,000
Agencies: Mayor's Council for Culture and the Arts, Honolulu, HI; Owen Brown Community Center, Columbia, MD

Lucinda Shaw produces site-specific glass, working with architects, designers, public art commissions, individuals and church groups. Each piece is designed as a component of the building's design. Stained glass, sandblasted and carved glass, fused glass enamel wall murals, fused glass sculptures and autonomous panels are some of the works produced. Shaw's pieces are included in museum collections; she has exhibited nationally and internationally and has work throughout the world.

**See page 36 for photographs
and additional information.**

ERNEST SHELTON

SHELTON SCULPTURE STUDIOS
1148 WILCOX PL
LOS ANGELES, CA 90038-1412
TEL 213-871-0677

Work: sculpture (free standing and pedestal), wall relief
Media: metal, concrete, stone
Special Concerns: historical/documentary issues, sports portraiture
Commission Amounts: $50,000 - $600,000
Agencies: Community Redevelopment Agency; City of Culver City Art in Public Places
Recent Project: Three life-size bronzes for Academy of Television, Arts and Sciences (1992)

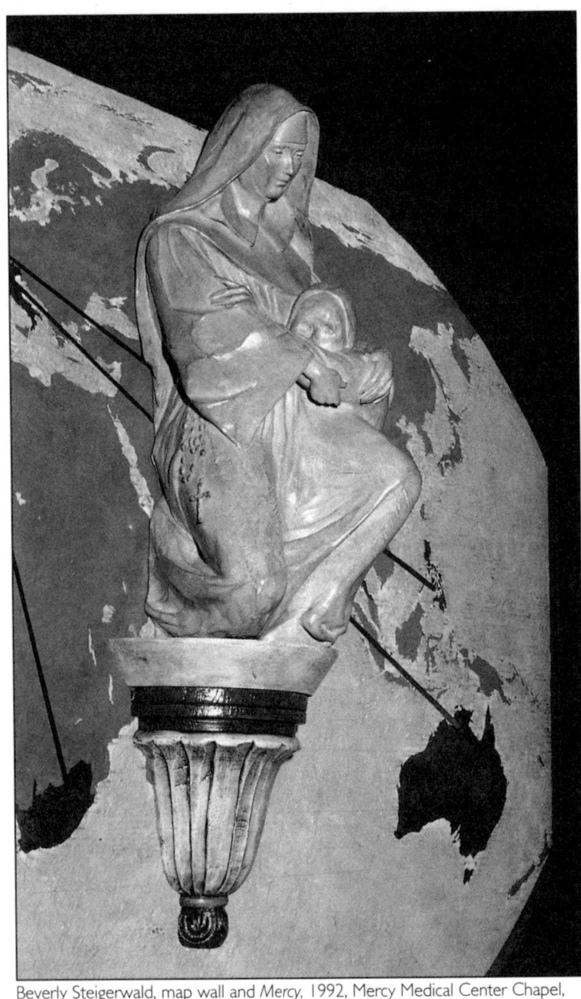

Beverly Steigerwald, map wall and *Mercy*, 1992, Mercy Medical Center Chapel, Denver, CO, map: 5' × 3'; bronze sculpture: 25" × 10" × 9", photo: Beth Steigerwald

★ ALVIN SHER

**4 N PINE ST
NIANTIC, CT 06357-2767
FAX 203-739-7288
TEL 203-739-7288**

Work: sculpture (free standing, atrium and wall relief)
Media: metal, concrete, stone
Special Concerns: historical/documentary issues, environmental issues, science or teaching related
Commission Amounts: $20,000
Agencies: College of Santa Fe, NM; City of New York Parks Department; Southern Vermont Arts Center
Recent Project: Sculptural bench/sundial for Roger Williams Park, Providence, RI (1994)

The works are an exploration of architectural forms that are both imaginary and possible. The structures are places and events used to express human longings and curiosity through symbolic forms such as temples, altars and observatories. These inventions are influenced by both modern and ancient works, executed using traditional materials such as bronze and contemporary media in the form of plasma-cut and heli-arc welded aluminum and stainless steel. Computer simulations are used to develop forms and explore functional astronomical/environmental and lighting situations. The works bridge time and ideas with a mixture of ancient and new materials and forms.

See photograph page 255.

PETER SHIRE

PETER SHIRE STUDIO
1930-32 ECHO PARK AVE
LOS ANGELES, CA 90026-1836
FAX 213-662-1218
TEL 213-662-5385

Work: sculpture (free standing and wall relief), painted tile
Media: metal, paint, ceramics
Special Concerns: collaborative design teams, historical and documentary issues, environmental issues
Commission Amounts: $20,000 - $250,000
Agencies: Los Angeles Community Redevelopment Agency; Phoenix Arts Commission; Los Angeles County Metropolitan Transit Authority
Recent Project: Atrium sculpture, 3½ stories in depth, Sapporo factory, Hokkaido, Japan

ARTHUR SILVERMAN

ARTHUR SILVERMAN INC.
3915 BARONNE ST
NEW ORLEANS, LA 70115-5312
TEL 504-891-2618

Work: sculpture (free standing and wall relief), furniture, fountains
Media: metal
Special Concerns: collaborative design teams, site/client specific
Commission Amounts: $50,000 - $200,000
Agencies: Art Council of New Orleans; Lee County Art in Public Places Board, City of Concord, CA
Recent Project: *Aluminum Attitudes*, six identical sculptures placed in differing attitudes

★ S. GALLINA SIMPSON

**SIMPSON SCULPTURE STUDIOS
67-31 COOPER AVE
GLENDALE, NY 11385
TEL 718-456-6155**

Work: sculpture (free standing)
Media: concrete, stone
Commission Amounts: $6,000 - $30,000
Agencies: Planting Fields Arboretum; Oyster Bay, NY; NY State Arboretum Park; Department of Parks, Harrisburg, PA
Recent Project: Group of storyteller and two children, movement forms realistic heads

**See page 196 for photographs
and additional information.**

JANE A. SKEETER

ULTRAGLAS INC.®/SKEETER STUDIOS, INC.
9186 INDEPENDENCE AVE
CHATSWORTH, CA 91311-5902
FAX 818-772-8231
TEL 818-772-7744

Work: sculpture (free standing), architectural glass, fountains
Media: glass, metal, mixed
Special Concerns: collaborative design teams, community involvement, environmental issues
Commission Amounts: $8,000 - $200,000
Agencies: California Home for the Aging; Beverly Hills City Hall
Recent Project: United States Geologic Service, Menlo Park, CA (1995)

PETER E. SMITH

PIETRO DESIGNS
962 ALEXANDER RD
PRINCETON JCT, NJ 08550-1024
FAX 609-799-0806
TEL 609-799-3714

Work: sculpture (free standing), architectural ceramics, mosaics, and wall relief, paintings, photographs (2-D)
Media: ceramics, stone, wood
Special Concerns: collaborative design teams, community involvement, historical and documentary issues
Commission Amounts: $2,000 - $83,000
Agencies: West Windsor Township Veteran's Monument Commission; USDA Forest Service
Recent Project: Limestone stele sculpture with gold leaf, 48", USDA Forest Service

ELIZABETH L. SOLOMON

1 COTTAGE ST #9
EASTHAMPTON, MA 01027
TEL 413-586-7179

Work: painted finishes and murals, architectural ceramics, mosaics, and wall relief
Media: concrete, paint
Special Concerns: historical/documentary issues, issues related to disabilities
Commission Amounts: $8,000 - $50,000
Agencies: Colorado Council on the Arts and Humanities; Northampton (MA) Public Art Council; Easthampton (MA) Arts Lottery Council
Recent Project: Polychromed cast concrete bas-relief panels, University of Colorado Theater Lobby (1991)

KENNETH SPEISER

KENNETH SPEISER SCULPTURE
131 ROCHAMBEAU AVE
PROVIDENCE, RI 02906
FAX 401-454-0184
TEL 401-521-9652
Work: sculpture (free standing), collaborative site design, architectural elements, flooring and ground plane, temporary installations
Media: metal, concrete, wood
Special Concerns: community involvement, historical and documentary issues, environmental issues
Commission Amounts: $54,000
Agencies: Rhode Island Percent for Arts Program
Recent Project: 30' outdoor plaza sculpture

LAURIE SPENCER

2511 E 17TH PL
TULSA, OK 74104-5110
TEL 918-742-8913
Work: sculpture (free standing), temporary installations
Media: metal, ceramics
Special Concerns: site-specific design
Commission Amounts: $8,000 - $40,000
Agencies: Arts Commission, City of Oklahoma City; Toledo Botanical Garden
Recent Project: Site-specific metal sculpture in a park setting

CHRISTOPHER SPROAT

PO BOX 2086
NEW YORK, NY 10013-0875
FAX 212-966-4917
TEL 212-966-4917
Work: sculpture (atrium),neon/laser/light related, lighting
Media: metal, stone, wood
Special Concerns: collaborative design teams
Commission Amounts: $20,000 - $150,000
Agencies: San Francisco Art Commission; Los Angeles County Transportation Commission; Massachusetts Bay Transportation Authority
Recent Project: 275' florescent, functional light sculpture, San Francisco (1993)

LARS A. STANLEY

ARCHITECTS & ARTISANS
PO BOX 3095
AUSTIN, TX 78764-3095
FAX 512-445-0444
TEL 512-445-0444
Work: sculpture (free standing), architectural metal, lighting
Media: metal, concrete, wood
Special Concerns: collaborative design teams, participatory works, multicultural issues
Commission Amounts: $8,000 - $50,000
Agencies: City of Austin, TX
Recent Project: Collaboration, main-entry gates for Zilker Botanical Gardens (1995)

★ PENELOPE COMFORT STARR

60 OLIVE AVE
SAN ANSELMO, CA 94960-2132
FAX 415-456-3698
TEL 415-456-9345
Work: architectural glass, neon, laser, light related
Media: stone, glass, lighting
Special Concerns: collaborative design teams, environmental issues, art that heals
Commission Amounts: $2,000 - $12,000
Agencies: U.S. Department of Defense; Department of the Army; Letterman Army Medical Center
Recent Project: 175 square-foot stained glass, Letterman Army Medical Center

See photograph page 273.

★ BEVERLY STEIGERWALD

782 S EMPORIA
DENVER, CO 80231
TEL 303-364-8498
Work: sculpture (free standing, pedestal and wall relief)
Media: metal, mixed
Special Concerns: collaborative design teams, multicultural issues, spiritual
Commission Amounts: $5,000 - $35,000
Agencies: Loveland Visual Arts Commission; Manitou Art Project
Recent Project: *Mercy*, honors the Sisters of Mercy, whose works are wordwide

See pages 167 and 256 for photographs and additional information.

★ ARTHUR STERN

ARTHUR STERN STUDIOS
 ARCHITECTURAL GLASS
1075 JACKSON ST
BENICIA, CA 94510
FAX 707-745-8480
TEL 707-745-8480
Work: sculpture (wall relief), architectural glass
Media: metal, wood, glass
Special Concerns: collaborative design teams, community involvement, site-specific installations
Commission Amounts: $70,000 - $500,000
Agencies: U.S. General Services Administration; California and Oregon Arts Commissions
Recent Project: Over 4,000 of stained glass windows for the Mormon Temple in Bountiful, Utah (1994)

See pages 60-61 for photographs and additional information.

STONE/PAPER/SCISSORS

GWENDOLYN GOMEZ, LYNN
 SUSHOLTZ, AIDA MANCILLAS
3505 28TH ST
SAN DIEGO, CA 92104-4102
FAX 619-291-0331
TEL 619-291-0054
Work: collaborative site design, architectural metal, ceramic tile, sculpture
Media: metal, concrete, mixed, ceramic, stone
Special Concerns: collaborative design teams, community involvement, multicultural issues
Commission Amounts: $40,000 - $200,000
Agencies: San Diego Commission for Arts and Culture; Escondido Percent for Art
Recent Project: Kinetic, colored aluminum outdoor, hanging sculptures, Escondido Medical Arts Center Plaza, CA

NANCY TAYLOR STONINGTON

N. TAYLOR STONINGTON, INC.
PO BOX 2269
VASHON, WA 98070-2469
FAX 206-463-6599
TEL 206-463-6588
Work: sculpture (wall relief), fiber work for interior walls, 2D work
Media: metal, paint, wood
Special Concerns: community involvement, historical and documentary issues
Commission Amounts: $10,000 - $45,000
Agencies: Anchorage Municipality; State of Alaska Division of Corrections; State of Alaska Department of Transportation
Recent Project: Watercolor paintings for the Alaska State Fisheries Research Institute (1993); 18' X 20' fiber mural, Grand Aleutian Hotel, Dutch Harbor, AK

ROBERT L. STOUT

TWIN DOLPHIN MOSAICS
808 WELLESLEY DR NE
ALBUQUERQUE, NM 87106-1937
TEL 505-266-2675
Work: mosaics
Media: ceramics, stone, smalti (glass tile)
Special Concerns: science and teaching related, imagery from the sciences
Commission Amounts: $4,500 - $99,360
Agencies: State of New Mexico 1% for Art; City of Albuquerque; Alaska State Council on the Arts
Recent Project: Contemplative fountain area, Sequoyah Adolescent Treatment Center, Albuquerque, NM

DAVID STROMEYER

COLD HOLLOW IRON WORKS
RR 2 BOX 3480
ENOSBURG FALLS, VT 05450-9318
TEL 802-933-2518
Work: sculpture (free standing and wall relief)
Media: metal, paint
Special Concerns: collaborative design teams, participatory works
Commission Amounts: $15,000 - $60,000
Agencies: State of Massachusetts; State of Connecticut; City of Charlotte, NC

JAMES SURLS

I.C. ART CO.
26041 MIDLINE RD
CLEVELAND, TX 77327-8501
FAX 713-592-4563
TEL 713-592-0425
Work: sculpture (free standing and atrium)
Media: metal, wood, stone
Special Concerns: collaborative design teams, community involvement, environmental issues
Commission Amounts: $100,000 - $200,000
Agencies: Mariposa Park, Corpus Christi, TX; Market Square Park, Houston, TX; Brazos Community Center, Bryan, TX
Recent Project: *Family*, installation piece in collaboration with Charmaine Locke, Mariposa Park, Corpus Christi, TX (1993)

★ SUSANA ARIAS ARTIST STUDIOS

SUSANA ARIAS
2523A MISSION ST
SANTA CRUZ, CA 95060
FAX 408-475-4756
TEL 408-423-7910
Work: sculpture (free standing), architectural ceramics, mosaics, and wall relief, temporary installations
Media: ceramics, concrete, paint, bronze
Special Concerns: collaborative design teams, community involvement, participatory works
Commission Amounts: $1,000 - $50,000
Agencies: Cultural Council of Santa Cruz, CA; Santa Cruz City Arts Commission
Recent Project: Relief sculpture, clay and stucco, two walls of underpass of Hwy 1, 110' x 15', Santa Cruz, CA

See page 178 for photographs and additional information.

JOHN EDWARD SVENSON

SVENSON ARTS
2480 VISTA DR
UPLAND, CA 91784-1111
FAX 909-981-1865
TEL 909-981-1865
Work: sculpture (free standing and wall relief)
Media: metal, concrete, wood
Special Concerns: collaborative design teams, historical and documentary issues, environmental issues
Commission Amounts: $35,000 - $150,000
Agencies: One Percent of Art, Brea, CA; City of Garden Grove, CA; School District of Skagway, AK
Recent Project: *California Song*, 37' sculpture, bronze and steel ecological monument, Orange County Park, CA

BRIAN SWANSON

BRIAN SWANSON ARTS
727 16TH AVE W
KIRKLAND, WA 98033-4824
TEL 206-827-0398
Work: architectural elements, outdoor
furniture and equipment, furniture
Media: metal, mixed, stone
Special Concerns: collaborative design
teams, historical and documentary issues
Commission Amounts: $3,500 - $20,000
Agencies: Port of Seattle, Seatac Airport;
Public Development Authority, Pike
Place Market, Seattle, WA
Recent Project: Public seating, three pieces,
Pike Place Public Market, Seattle, WA

MERYL TARADASH

503 BROADWAY #511
NEW YORK, NY 10012-4401
TEL 212-431-3509
Work: sculpture (free standing and
atrium) neon/laser/light related, wind-
driven sculpture
Media: metal, acrylic
Special Concerns: collaborative design
teams, participatory works, art based
on technology
Commission Amounts: $20,000 - $80,000
Agencies: NJ State Council on Arts, NJ
Division of Building and Construction
Recent Project: *Wind Dancing*, outdoor
wind-driven sculpture, aluminum, steel,
light, University of California/David
Bermant Foundation

JULIO TEICH

JULIO TEICH STUDIOS
4600 WAVERLY AVE
RICHMOND, VA 23231-1404
FAX 804-226-6121
TEL 804-226-8361
Work: sculpture (free standing and
atrium), architectural glass
Media: metal, glass, paint, mosaic
Special Concerns: multicultural issues,
playful, celebratory, environmental,
architectural
Commission Amounts: $7,000 - $100,000
Agencies: Montgomery County (MD)
Public Schools; Washington Suburban
Sanitary Commission (MD), City of
Honolulu, HI
Recent Project: Pedestrian bridge for
Ballston, Arlington, VA (1995) including
metal, glass sculptures, windows, ceramic
mosaics

WILLIAM J. THOMPSON

175 DEER RDG
ATHENS, GA 30605-4411
FAX 706-546-8417
TEL 706-548-7989
Work: sculpture (free standing, pedestal
and wall relief)
Media: metal, concrete, ceramics
Special Concerns: collaborative design
teams
Commission Amounts: $30,000 - $175,000
Agencies: State of Georgia; National
Park Service; City of Americus, GA
Recent Project: Bronze figure of Charles
Lindbergh as a young wing walker

VINCENT AND CAROLYN LEE TOLPO

55918 HWY 285 PO BOX 134
SHAWNEE, CO 80475
FAX 303-838-2351
TEL 303-670-1733
Work: sculpture (free standing and wall
relief), fiber work for interior walls
Media: metal, concrete, ceramics
Special Concerns: historical and docu-
mentary issues, environmental issues,
nonexploitive
Commission Amounts: $2,500 - $25,000
Agencies: Colorado Arts Council; Park
County Cultural Council
Recent Project: Steel, brass, ceramic
sculpture about books, pages, works
and phrases

MARK TOMLINSON

CERAMIC TILE & SCULPTURE
640 HAZEL ST
RIVER FALLS, WI 54022-2533
FAX 715-425-8828
TEL 715-425-6528
Work: sculpture (wall relief), fountains,
painted finishes and murals, swimming
pools, tile murals
Media: ceramic relief tile
Special Concerns: collaborative design
teams, environmental issues
Commission Amounts: $1,500 - $250,000
Agencies: State of Minnesota Percent
for Art; State of Montana Percent for
Art; Nat'l Wildflower Research Center,
Austin, TX
Recent Project: National Wildflower
Research Center, Austin, TX

SHARON TOWNSHEND

SAWYER STREET STUDIOS
131 SAWYER ST
SOUTH PORTLAND, ME 04106-2127
TEL 207-767-4394
Work: sculpture (wall relief)
Media: ceramics
Special Concerns: community involve-
ment, participatory works
Commission Amounts: $5,000 - $15,000
Agencies: Maine Arts Commission
Percent for Art
Recent Project: *River Journal: Rapids*, two
glazed terra cotta reliefs, ceiling to floor

IRA TROY

14 COLUMBIA RD
ARDSLEY, NY 10502
FAX 914-693-8774
TEL 914-693-1669
Work: sculpture (free standing, atrium
and pedestal), kinetic
Media: metal, paint, wood
Special Concerns: environmental issues
Commission Amounts: $8,000 - $16,000
Agencies: Town of Mamaroneck, NY;
United Geriatic Center, New Rochelle,
NY (1% for Art)

FREDA COFFING TSCHUMY

FREDA C. TSCHUMY, ARTIST
3610 BAYVIEW RD
MIAMI, FL 33133-6503
FAX 305-443-7748
TEL 305-444-2825
Work: sculpture (free standing and
pedestal)
Media: metal, plastics
Special Concerns: environmental issues,
science and teaching related, spiritual
Commission Amounts: $10,000 - $45,000
Agencies: Dade County (FL) Art in Public
Places
Recent Project: *Light Gate*, prismatic
entry sculpture for main library,
Melbourne, FL

KENT TWITCHELL

6480 LYONS RD
LAKEPORT, CA 95453-6410
TEL 707-263-1065
Work: painted finishes and murals,
2D work
Media: paint, mixed
Special Concerns: Americana
Commission Amounts: $20,000 - $250,000
Agencies: National Endowment for the
Arts; California Arts Council; California
Office of the State Architect
Recent Project: 8-story mural, Los Angeles
Chamber Orchestra, Citicorp Plaza (1994)

ALEXANDER TYLEVICH

896 CLEVELAND AVE #8
SAINT PAUL, MN 55116-1846
TEL 612-690-4117
Work: sculpture (free standing and
wall relief), site specific
Media: metal, mixed
Special Concerns: collaborative design
teams, historical and documentary issues,
science and teaching related
Commission Amounts: $37,280 - $1,300,000
Agencies: Minnesota Percent for Art;
Pillsbury Neighborhood Services;
Forecast Public Artworks
Recent Project: St. Mary's College,
Winona, MN: *Gateway to Belief*, 25'H
steel and bronze; sculptural bronze
and steel tryptic, 3' x 10'

DAVID VAN ARSDALE

NEON ART GROUP
3806 S FERDINAND ST
SEATTLE, WA 98118
FAX 206-722-6986
TEL 206-722-6986
Work: sculpture (free standing),
neon, laser, light related, lighting
Media: metal, concrete, glass
Special Concerns: historical and docu-
mentary issues, science and teaching
related
Commission Amounts: $13,000
Agencies: King County Art Commission,
Percent for Art Program
Recent Project: Outdoor sculptures for
the Covington Library, Covington, WA

★ HANS VAN DE BOVENKAMP

661 SPRINGTOWN RD
TILLSON, NY 12486
FAX 914-658-8888
TEL 914-658-8363
Work: sculpture (free standing and
wall relief), fountains
Media: metal, paint, concrete
Special Concerns: collaborative design
teams, community involvement, partici-
patory works
Commission Amounts: $20,000 - $215,000
Agencies: Nebraska Bicentennial Com-
petition; Texas A&M University; Okla-
homa City Percent for Art
Recent Project: Sculpture for public park
through international competition, Okla-
homa City, OK; Mayer Collection, CO

I find myself working towards an art which
includes a spiritual dimension. I have become increasingly aware of an art as a
dialogue between matter and spirit. In
recent works, I have emphasized myth,
symbol and dream to evoke an atmos-
phere in which the sculpture and its
environment speak to the subconscious
to make the observer aware of the
dreamlike nature of life, of which we
all are part.

**See page 200 for photographs
and additional information.**

★ MÁRTON VÁRÓ
2 CHARITY
IRVINE, CA 92715
FAX 714-856-2943
TEL 714-856-0249

Work: sculpture (free standing and wall relief), collaborative site design
Media: marble, stone, wood
Special Concerns: collaborative design teams, community involvement
Commission Amounts: $25,000 - $700,000
Agencies: Architectural Arts, Dallas, TX; City of Palm Desert, CA
Recent Project: Marble torso, 6', for the Pacific Design Center, Los Angeles, CA

Equally known for his draped female figures and cubes with drapery fragments, Váró carves directly in marble or stone. His understanding of materials and their integration with architecture made these works suitable for major public projects in Budapest, Hungary; Volos, Greece; Brea, California; the Palm Desert Peace Memorial, California; and the Plaza of the Americas, Dallas, TX. The sculptor has generated great interest through educational programs involving on-site carving and community participation.

See page 168 for photographs and additional information.

ENRIQUE VEGA
E. VEGA STUDIOS
505 LUTHER RD
APEX, NC 27502
FAX 919-362-0543
TEL 919-362-0543

Work: architectural glass, architectural metal, furniture
Media: metal, glass
Special Concerns: community involvement, historical and documentary issues
Commission Amounts: $24,000 - $50,000
Agencies: North Carolina Arts Council
Recent Project: Forged gates and etched glass panels for the John Umstead Hospital

JANTJE VISSCHER
1666 COFFMAN ST #208
SAINT PAUL, MN 55108-1339
TEL 612-332-3917

Work: sculpture (free standing), murals, bronze relief
Media: mixed
Special Concerns: science related
Commission Amounts: $10,000 - $40,000
Agencies: Wisconsin and Minnesota State Arts Boards Percent for Art programs
Recent Project: Entry areas, St. Paul Civic Center, St. Paul, MN (1995)

ANDREAS von HUENE
VON HUENE DESIGN
PO BOX 401
WOOLWICH, ME 04579-0401
TEL 207-442-7292

Work: sculpture (free standing and atrium), environmental
Media: mixed, stone, earth and plants
Special Concerns: historical and documentary issues, environmental issues, site-specific
Commission Amounts: $7,000 - $28,000
Agencies: Maine Arts Commission; Urban Arts, Boston, MA; Brewer Centennial Committee, Brewer, ME
Recent Project: Outdoor raised circular classroom of trees and carved stone seats

★ KENNETH F. von ROENN
ARCHITECTURAL GLASS ART
1110 BAXTER AVE
LOUISVILLE, KY 40204-1649
FAX 502-585-2808
TEL 502-585-5421

Work: architectural glass
Media: glass
Special Concerns: collaborative design teams
Commission Amounts: $5,000 - $1,000,000
Agencies: Connecticut Commission on the Arts; Alaska Council on Arts; Oregon Arts Commission
Recent Project: 7,000 sq. ft. glass for atrium, Mountain View (CA) City Hall (1990)

Architectural Glass Art, Inc. (AGA) is a unique glass studio recognized for its innovative use of new and traditional techniques in expanding the potential and application of glass as a contemporary architectural art. Kenneth vonRoenn, the president of AGA, is an architect (Yale University, M. Arch) and renowned glass artist. Because of his training as an architect, vonRoenn is especially concerned with the sympathetic integration of his work with the architecture of which it is a part. This background is also of value in the administration and implementation of a project.

See page 37 for photographs and additional information.

DAVID WALKER
WALKER DESIGN STUDIOS
PO BOX 388
BOONVILLE, CA 95415-0388
TEL 707-895-2144

Work: sculpture (free standing, pedestal and wall relief)
Media: stone, ceramics, metal
Special Concerns: community involvement, historical and documentary issues, multicultural issues
Commission Amounts: $5,000 - $75,000
Agencies: Cherry Creek North Arts Foundation, Denver, CO
Recent Project: Figurative, cubist, multi-sided, cast, granite, cut and polished, multi-colored

WILLIAM WALSH
WORK ON WALLS
45 BROADWAY
BROOKLYN, NY 11211
TEL 718-486-7357

Work: painted finishes and murals, neon, laser, light related, 2D work, temporary installations
Media: paint, ceramics, glass
Special Concerns: participatory works, multicultural issues, community involvement
Commission Amounts: $16,000 and up
Agencies: New York Foundation for the Arts, Cityarts Workshop, Inc.
Recent Project: Public murals in Germany

★ BART WALTER
NATIONAL SCULPTORS' GUILD
2683 N TAFT AVE
LOVELAND, CO 80538
FAX 970-667-2068
TEL 970-667-2015

Commission Amounts: $5,000 - $50,000
Agencies: Baltimore Zoo, MD; Automated Financial Service, Exon, PA; National Wildlife Visitors Center, MD; Bell Museum, Minneapolis, MN
Recent Project: Life-size, silver back gorilla for a university

See page 165 for photographs and additional information.

TIM WATKINS
40 HOYT ST
BROOKLYN, NY 11201-5848
FAX 718-852-0808
TEL 718-522-4786

Work: sculpture (atrium), neon/laser/light related, temporary installations
Media: metal, glass, mixed
Special Concerns: collaborative design teams, participatory works, environmental issues
Commission Amounts: $1,000 - $55,000
Agencies: Liberty Science Center, Jersey City, NJ; Staten Island Children's Museum; Glenhyrst Art Gallery of Brant, ON, Canada
Recent Project: *Giant Ear*, 600 sq. ft. educational interactive play area, Children's Museum of Manhattan

★ MICHAEL L. WATLING
THE WATLING COMPANY
51 ALPINE VILLAGE
MOUNTAIN CENTER, CA 92561
FAX 619-349-8502
TEL 619-349-3292

Work: sculpture (free standing), earthworks
Media: metal, stone, earth and plants
Special Concerns: community involvement, historical and documentary issues, environmental issues
Commission Amounts: $10,000 - $50,000
Agencies: City of Palm Desert, CA; City of Indio, CA; Bureau of Land Management, CA
Recent Project: Monumental stone work reflecting local Native American cultural heritage

See page 223 for photographs and additional information.

JOHN WEHRLE
775 LASSEN ST
RICHMOND, CA 94805-1459
FAX 510-234-0363
TEL 510-234-0645

Work: painted finishes and murals
Media: paint
Special Concerns: historical/documentary issues, environmental issues
Commission Amounts: $20,000 - $150,000
Agencies: Richmond (CA) Art Commission; Los Angeles Cultural Arts; San Francisco Art Commission
Recent Project: Public mural for the City of Richmond, CA

★ MARY BOONE WELLINGTON
88 BOSTON POST ROAD
AMHERST NH 03031
FAX 603-673-2311
TEL 603-673-2311
E-mail: mryboone@aol.com

See page 224 for photographs and additional information.

WALTER WHITE
WALTER A. WHITE INC.
1708 N 35TH ST
SEATTLE, WA 98103-9012
TEL 206-547-7317

Work: sculpture (free standing), neon, laser, light related, lighting, architectural metal, weathervanes
Media: metal, wood, glass
Special Concerns: historical and documentary issues, science and teaching related
Commission Amounts: $3,000 - $48,000
Agencies: Metropolitan Arts Commission, Portland, OR; Seattle (WA) Arts Commission; King County Library System (Percent for Art), Seattle, WA
Recent Project: Art lighting for Bellevue Regional Library, Bellevue, WA

JAY S. WILLIS
206 S SAN MARINO AVE
PASADENA, CA 91107-4015
FAX 818-796-1372
TEL 818-796-1372

Work: sculpture (free standing), collaborative site design, temporary installations
Media: metal, paint
Special Concerns: collaborative design teams, environmental issues, science and teaching related
Commission Amounts: $30,000 - $2,000,000
Agencies: City of Irvine, CA; City of Thousand Oaks, CA
Recent Project: Artist consultant for redesign of Hud Plaza in Washington, DC

PUBLIC ART

DOUGLAS E. WILSON

WILSON FORGE
PO BOX 225
DEER ISLE, ME 04627-0225
TEL 207-348-6871
Work: sculpture (free standing and wall relief), architectural metal, furniture
Media: metal, wood, stone
Special Concerns: community involvement, historical and documentary issues, environmental issues
Commission Amounts: $12,000 - $28,000
Agencies: Maine Arts Commission, Augusta; Bangor Chamber of Commerce, ME
Recent Project: Whale's tail and armillary sphere, Maine Maritime Academy, Castine, ME

ROY WILSON

PO BOX 156
PLYMOUTH MEETING, PA 19462-0156
FAX 215-825-6963
TEL 215-825-6963
Work: sculpture (free standing), architectural metal, temporary installations
Media: metal, wind (kinetic)
Special Concerns: environmental issues
Commission Amounts: $8,000 - $140,000
Agencies: Redevelopment Authority of Philadelphia; Pennsylvania Dept. of General Services; Arts Commission of Greater Toledo
Recent Project: *Susquehanna Dawn*, Department of Environmental Resources, with wind vanes, seating (1995)

JOSHUA C. WINER

ARCHITECTURAL MURALS
32 SCHOOL ST
ARLINGTON, MA 02174-6122
FAX 617-643-1980
TEL 617-643-3517
Work: painted finishes and murals, other work for interior walls, 2D work
Media: paint
Special Concerns: collaborative design teams, historical and documentary issues, science and teaching related
Commission Amounts: $10,000 - $150,000
Agencies: The Cambridge Arts Council, Cambridge, MA; Chesterwood Sculpture Park, Stockbridge, MA; Massachusetts Bay Transit Authority
Recent Project: one-quarter-mile-long, architectural mural along a freeway

BIA WINTER

POLAR BEAR STUDIO
3360 NORTH RD
MOUNT VERNON, ME 04352
TEL 207-293-2835
Work: sculpture (atrium)
Media: metal, fiberglass, light
Special Concerns: multicultural issues environmental issues, science or teaching related
Commission Amounts: $6,000 - $10,000
Agencies: Maine Arts Commission; Minnesota State Arts Board
Recent Project: Two large mobiles (11' and 15') for new Maine schools (1993)

WINTER SCULPTURE STUDIO

JOSEPH WINTER
207 W MEADE ST
PHILADELPHIA, PA 19118-3811
FAX 215-242-0243
TEL 215-248-2122
Work: sculpture (free standing and wall relief), fountains
Media: metal, concrete, ceramics
Special Concerns: historical and documentary issues, multicultural issues, environmental issues
Commission Amounts: $6,000 - $45,000
Agencies: Fairmount Park Art Commission, Philadelphia, PA; Housing and Urban Development; City of Salem, MA
Recent Project: Glazed ceramic outdoor wall sculpture of 75 one-square-foot. tiles

AL WONG

83 LAFAYETTE ST #3
SAN FRANCISCO, CA 94103
TEL 415-255-9402
Work: sculpture (free standing and atrium), fountains, lighting
Media: metal, wood, mixed
Special Concerns: historical and documentary issues, multicultural issues, science and teaching related
Commission Amounts: $10,000 - $200,000
Agencies: San Francisco Art Commission; California State Art Commission
Recent Project: *Light Clouds*, glass marquee, 42'L by 7'W, for San Francisco Fire Station #2 (1994)

RICK WRIGLEY

GATEHOUSE FURNITURE STUDIOS
GATEHOUSE RD
HOLYOKE, MA 01040
FAX 413-535-1389
TEL 413-536-2034
Work: architectural elements
Media: wood
Special Concerns: collaborative design teams, historical and documentary issues
Commission Amounts: $110,000
Agencies: Connecticut Commission on the Arts
Recent Project: 44 doors for the legislative office building, Hartford, CT

JOHN T. YOUNG

7334 RAVENNA AVE NE
SEATTLE, WA 98115
TEL 206-525-3380
Work: sculpture (free standing), collaborative site design, architectural elements
Media: metal, mixed, stone
Special Concerns: collaborative design teams, community involvement, environmental issues
Commission Amounts: $20,000
Agencies: Spokane Arts Commission, WA; Oregon Arts Commission; Steamboat Arts Council, Steamboat Springs, CO
Recent Project: Large-scale stone and steel environmental sculpture, surrounding pedestrian walkway

ZAGAMI FINE ART & DESIGN

SALVATORE ZAGAMI
515 SW 4TH AVE
FORT LAUDERDALE, FL 33315-1009
TEL 305-463-0014
Work: sculpture (free standing, atrium and pedestal)
Media: metal, mixed, plastic
Commission Amounts: $12,000
Agencies: Broward County Art in Public Places

VALDIS ZARINS

ZARINS STUDIO U.S.A.
17327 W LAKE DESIRE DR SE
RENTON, WA 98058-9525
FAX 206-228-5627
TEL 206-228-5672
Work: sculpture (free standing), fountains, wind-activated forms
Media: metal, concrete, mixed, water, wind-activated
Commission Amounts: $1,000 - $35,000
Agencies: King County Arts Commission; City of Edmonds Arts Commission; City of Kent Arts Commission
Recent Project: *Sentinel; Kent*, three stainless steel columns, 16" x 16" x 9'H, appear to float above reflecting pool in response to wind (1991)

★ LARRY ZGODA

LARRY ZGODA STUDIO
415 W NORTH AVE
CHICAGO, IL 60610-1117
FAX 312-943-9987
TEL 312-943-9978
Work: architectural glass
Media: glass, crystal
Commission Amounts: $14,000
Agencies: City of Chicago Dept. of Cultural Affairs
Recent Project: Clearing Branch of the Chicago Public Library, main entry

Larry Zgoda is self-taught. In the more than two decades in which he has studied, experimented with and worked in the field of stained glass, ZGODA has covered the bases of classical, contemporary and avant-garde design. Whether it is a clerestory for a corporate office structure, an entry for a library, or a transom for a Victorian townhome, the design considerations are weighed and focused. The result is stained glass that is an integral part of the architecture, as well as a unique LARRY ZGODA signature composition.

See pages 66-67 for photographs and additional information.

◆

**ELLEN ABBOTT
MARC LEVA**

CUSTOM ETCHED GLASS
1330 LAWRENCE ST
HOUSTON, TX 77008-3830
FAX 713-868-1227
TEL 713-864-4773
E-Mail: 71165.3412 @ compuserve.com
Est. 1976
Products: doors and entrances, murals or bas relief, room dividers or screens, walls, windows
Techniques: cast, laminated, sandcarved or etched, pate de verre
Price Range: $50 - $130 sq. ft.

★ ACACIA ART GLASS STUDIOS

**LUCINDA SHAW
3000 CHESTNUT AVE #336
BALTIMORE, MD 21211-2751
FAX 410-366-6472
TEL 410-467-4038**
Est. 1981
Products: autonomous panels, doors and entrances, room dividers or screens, windows, work for the wall
Techniques: bent, fused or kiln-formed, copper-foiled, leaded, painted or enameled, sandcarved or etched
Specialization: liturgical-public
Price Range: $100 - $250 sq. ft.

See page 36 for photographs and additional information.

ANCIENT ARTS

MARK SCHOEM
333 W 7TH ST
SAN PEDRO, CA 90731-3323
FAX 310-832-3891
TEL 310-832-7613
Est. 1980
Products: doors and entrances, windows, skylights, lamps
Techniques: beveled, copper-foiled, leaded, sandcarved or etched, painted
Specialization: liturgical, residential
Price Range: $75 - $300 sq. ft.

AVERY H. ANDERSON

ANDERSON GLASS WORKS
4 WESSON ST
NORTH GRAFTON, MA 01536-2008
FAX 508-839-4314
TEL 508-839-6095
Products: windows, doors and entrances, room dividers and screens, autonomous panels, work for the wall
Techniques: sandcarved or etched, copper-foiled, bent, fused or kiln-formed
Specialization: custom art glass
Price Range: $50 - $300 sq. ft.

ANN CUNNINGHAM STAINED GLASS STUDIO

ANN CUNNINGHAM
4916 UNDERWOOD AVE
OMAHA, NE 68132
TEL 402-551-0456
Products: windows, doors and entrances, room dividers and screens, autonomous panels, skylights and domes
Techniques: leaded, beveled, painted or enameled
Specialization: contemporary liturgical
Price Range: $100 - $250 sq. ft.

ANN WOLFF GLASS DESIGN

ANN WOLFF
1161 SAINT PAUL ST
DENVER, CO 80206-3347
FAX 303-388-8350
TEL 303-388-8350
Products: windows, doors and entrances, room dividers and screens, furniture
Techniques: leaded, beveled, painted or enameled, sandcarved or etched, dalle de verre
Price Range: $150 - $700 sq. ft.

APPLEBECK STUDIOS, LTD.

ROCKY APPLEBECK/JO APPLEBECK
100 S BALDWIN ST #202
MADISON, WI 53703-3001
TEL 608-284-1900
Est. 1983
Products: autonomous panels, doors and entrances, lamps or lighting fixtures, room dividers or screens, windows
Techniques: bent, fused or kiln-formed, copper-foiled, leaded, painted or enameled, verdigris patina
Specialization: opalescent glass
Price Range: $100 - $450 sq. ft.

JACK ARCHIBALD

REVISIONARY GLASSWORKS
3465 SW CAMANO DR
CAMANO ISLAND, WA 98292-7065
TEL 206-387-9395
Est. 1981
Products: autonomous panels, doors and entrances, skylights or domes, windows
Techniques: beveled, leaded
Price Range: $100 - $500 sq. ft.

ARCHITECTURAL ART GLASS

DOUG SOELBERG
410 W 1200 N
OREM, UT 84057-2947
FAX 801-223-9938
TEL 801-224-6646
Products: windows, doors and entrances, autonomous panels, sculpture, walls
Techniques: leaded, painted or enameled, dalle de verre
Specialization: contemporary design
Price Range: $75 - $250 sq. ft.

★ ARCHITECTURAL STAINED GLASS, INC.

**JEFF G. SMITH
PO BOX 9092
DALLAS, TX 75209-9092
FAX 214-827-5000
TEL 214-352-5050**
Est. 1977
Products: windows, doors and entrances, room dividers and screens, skylights and domes, false windows
Techniques: leaded, sandcarved or etched, mirror-lit
Specialization: commercial, liturgical, public
Price Range: $140 - $275 sq. ft.

See page 62 for photographs and additional information.

★ ART GLASS ENIVORNMENTS, INC.

**BILL KLUG
1865 NW BOCA RATON BLVD
BOCA RATON, FL 33432
FAX 407-391-8447
TEL 407-391-7310**
Est. 1973
Products: windows, doors and entrances, room dividers and screens, skylights and domes, sculpture
Techniques: leaded, sandcarved or etched, painted or enameled, bent, fused or kiln-formed, laminated, beveled
Specialization: custom entryways
Price Range: $75 - $300 sq. ft.

See page 38 for photographs and additional information.

ARTISTRY STAINED GLASS FIREPLACE DECOR

ROBERT VITERBO
904 N SCOTTSDALE RD
TEMPE, AZ 85281-1900
TEL 602-966-6167
Est. 1978
Products: autonomous panels, doors and entrances, lamps or lighting fixtures, windows, fireplace screens
Techniques: beveled, copper-foiled, leaded, sandcarved or etched, fused, kiln-formed, painted
Price Range: $75 - $300 sq. ft.

ASCALON ART STUDIOS, INC.

DAVID ASCALON
115 ATLANTIC AVE
BERLIN, NJ 08009-9300
FAX 609-768-3902
TEL 609-768-3779
Est. 1981
Products: windows, skylights and domes, sculpture, murals and bas relief, work for the wall
Techniques: leaded, sandcarved or etched, beveled, dalle de verre
Specialization: art for worship spaces
Price Range: $140 - $300 sq. ft.

AURORA GLASS STUDIO

SANDRA D. EISMIN - OWNER
634 MAIN ST
LAFAYETTE, IN 47901-1451
FAX 317-742-2721
TEL 317-742-7387
Est. 1980
Products: windows, doors and entrances, autonomous panels, lamps and lighting fixtures, work for the wall
Techniques: leaded, bent, fused or kiln-formed, dalle de verre, painted or enameled, sandcarved or etched
Specialization: restoration, liturgical
Price Range: $100 - $300 sq. ft.

RICHARD AVIDON

RICHARD AVIDON/ARCHITECTURAL GLASS
305 RIVERSIDE DR
NEW YORK, NY 10025-5286
TEL 212-866-1931
Est. 1969
Products: doors and entrances, skylights or domes, windows room dividers and screens
Techniques: beveled, leaded, sandcarved or etched dalle de verre
Price Range: $100 - $300 sq. ft.

PAULA BARR

PAULA BARR PRODUCTIONS
195 HUDSON ST PH
NEW YORK, NY 10013-1813
FAX   212-226-5414
TEL   212-226-5275
Est. 1973
Products: murals and bas relief, work for the wall, tiles
Techniques: laminated
Specialization: photo glass/tiles
Price Range: $250 - $350 sq. ft.

BAUT STUDIOS INC.

GERHARD F. BAUT
1095 MAIN ST
SWOYERSVILLE, PA 18704-1337
FAX 717-288-0380
TEL 717-288-1431
Est. 1927
Products: windows, doors and entrances, room dividers and screens, skylights and domes, lamps and lighting fixtures
Techniques: leaded, sandcarved or etched, painted or enameled, blown, structural stained glass
Specialization: liturgical restoration
Price Range: $75 - $200 sq. ft.

JACK BECKER

BETTER VISION STUDIO
2450 SEABURY
MINNEAPOLIS, MN 55406
FAX 612-641-0028
TEL 612-641-1128
Products: room dividers and screens, sculpture, murals and bas relief, abstract constructions
Techniques: beveled, laminated, water jet and polished
Specialization: contemporary
Price Range: $100 - $300 sq. ft.

BRENDA BELFIELD

BELFIELD STUDIO OF
   ARCHITECTURAL GLASS
2320 MILES WAY
PORT REPUBLIC, MD 20676-2304
FAX 410-586-3589
TEL 410-586-3589
Est. 1970
Products: autonomous panels, doors and entrances, room dividers or screens, walls, windows
Techniques: beveled, dalle de verre, leaded, painted or enameled, sandcarved or etched
Specialization: liturgical, corporate
Price Range: $100 - $250 sq. ft.

★ SANDRA C.Q. BERGÉR

QUINTAL UNLIMITED
100 EL CAMINO REAL #202
BURLINGAME, CA 94010-5225
FAX 415-340-0198
TEL 415-348-0310
Est. 1978
Products: windows, doors and entrances, room dividers and screens, skylights and domes, sculpture, work for the wall
Techniques: leaded, sandcarved or etched, copper-foiled, beveled, laminated, cast, neon, fused or kiln-formed
Specialization: contemporary
Price Range: $125 - $500 sq. ft.

**See page 39 for photographs
and additional information.**

BEVELED GLASS WORKS, INC.

REY CANO
23715 W MALIBU RD #351
MALIBU, CA 90265
FAX 310-456-2539
TEL 310-456-3201
Est. 1991
Products: windows, doors and entrances, room dividers and screens, autonomous panels, beveled leaded glass
Techniques: leaded, sandcarved or etched, beveled
Specialization: residential, commercial entrys
Price Range: $50 - $100 sq. ft.

★ JOSEPH K. BEYER

BEYER STAINED GLASS
9511 GERMANTOWN AVE
PHILADELPHIA, PA 19118
FAX 215-848-3535
TEL 215-848-3502
Est. 1980
Products: windows, doors and entrances, room dividers and screens, autonomous panels, skylights and domes
Techniques: leaded, painted or enameled
Specialization: architectural stained glass
Price Range: $100 - $550 sq. ft.

**See pages 40-41 for photographs
and additional information.**

LAURIE R. BIEZE

BIEZE'S CITY CENTER GALLERY
   AND STUDIOS
216 S BARSTOW ST
EAU CLAIRE, WI 54701
TEL 715-833-0007
Est. 1978
Products: windows, doors and entrances, room dividers or screens, sculpture, valences
Techniques: leaded, sandcarved or etched, copper-foiled, beveled
Specialization: restaurants
Price Range: $80 - $350 sq. ft.

WILFRED J. BISSONNETTE

STUDIO B
177 JERUSALEM RD
BRISTOL, VT 05443-9801
TEL 802-453-4254
Products: windows, doors and entrances
Techniques: leaded, sandcarved or etched, dalle de verre
Specialization: stained; etched wood entries
Price Range: $150 - $950 sq. ft.

MARJORIE BLAKE

MARJORIE BLAKE STAINED GLASS
2343 FERNDALE AVE
BATON ROUGE, LA 70808-2227
TEL 504-343-7850
Est. 1976
Products: autonomous panels, doors and entrances, room dividers or screens, walls, windows
Techniques: bent, fused or kiln-formed, dalle de verre, leaded, sandcarved or etched
Specialization: liturgical
Price Range: $100 - $250 sq. ft.

SONJA BLOMDAHL

1211 ALOHA ST
SEATTLE, WA 98109-4401
TEL 206-622-1404
Est. 1982
Products: windows, room dividers and screens
Techniques: blown, leaded
Specialization: custom-blown rondels
Price Range: $150 - $250 sq. ft.

BARBARA LILLIAN BOECK
GENE MILO

GB STUDIO INC.
711 BROADWAY
WESTWOOD, NJ 07675-1604
TEL 201-664-8686
Est. 1984
Products: doors and entrances, room dividers or screens, autonomous panels, work for the wall, fireplace facings
Techniques: sandcarved or etched, painted
Specialization: all architectural settings
Price Range: $75 - $300 sq. ft.

BOLHUIS STUDIO

LINDA BOLHUIS
941 FERNWOOD PACIFIC DR
TOPANGA, CA 90290-3219
FAX 310-455-1637
TEL 310-455-1689
Est. 1970
Products: windows, doors and entrances, room dividers and screens, skylights and domes, sculpture
Techniques: leaded, sandcarved or etched, copper-foiled, beveled, painted or enameled
Specialization: contemporary designs
Price Range: $100 - $500 sq. ft.

KATHY BRADFORD

NORTH STAR ART GLASS, INC.
142 WICHITA RD
LYONS, CO 80540-8232
TEL 303-823-6511
Est. 1974
Products: autonomous panels, doors and entrances, murals or bas relief, sculpture, tiles
Techniques: bent, fused or kiln-formed, cast, copper-foiled, sandcarved or etched
Specialization: sandcarved or etched
Price Range: $100 - $300 sq. ft.

KEITH S. BRAMER

PARROT STUDIOS
820 EMORY ST
SAN JOSE, CA 95126-1818
TEL 408-294-4494
Est. 1978
Products: doors and entrances, room dividers or screens, sculpture, windows, work for the wall, architectural tiles
Techniques: bent, fused or kiln-formed, cast, engraved, leaded, sandcarved or etched
Specialization: site-specific
Price Range: $75 - $450 sq. ft.

BOB BRASHEARS

NEW LIGHT STAINED GLASS
PO BOX 8145
REDLANDS, CA 92375
TEL 909-792-5840
Products: windows, doors and entrances, room dividers and screens, autonomous panels, sculpture
Techniques: leaded, sandcarved or etched, cast
Price Range: $50 - $500 sq. ft.

BRIDGE STAINED GLASS

BRIGITTE PASTERNAK
301 RIVER RD
NYACK, NY 10960-5003
TEL (914) 359-2884
Products: windows, doors and entrances, room dividers and screens, skylights or domes, autonomous panels
Techniques: leaded, sandcarved or etched, copper-foiled, painted or enameled, beveled
Specialization: custom work any size
Price Range: $100 - $300 sq. ft.

BRIER PATCH GLASSWORKS

JODY WILHITE
1724 S WESTERN ST
AMARILLO, TX 79106-5927
TEL 800-261-8288
Est. 1984
Products: windows, doors and entrances,
room dividers and screens, autonomous
panels
Techniques: sandcarved or etched,
beveled, mirror resilvering
Specialization: beveled and stained glass
Price Range: $150 - $500 sq. ft.

BONNIE BROWN

ETCHINGS: GLASS, METAL, MARBLE
45 STE 45D MITCHELL BLVD
SAN RAFAEL, CA 94903-2011
FAX 415-492-9321
TEL 415-492-8986
Est. 1986
Products: doors and entrances, room
dividers or screens, windows, mirrors,
tabletops, showers
Techniques: sandcarved or etched,
edge-lit
Price Range: $30 - $300 sq. ft.

WENDY SAXON BROWN

341 W SAUGERTIES RD
SAUGERTIES, NY 12477
TEL 914-246-4673
Products: autonomous panels, doors and
entrances, room dividers or screens,
windows, work for the wall
Techniques: painted or enameled,
sandcarved or etched
Specialization: sandblasted installations
Price Range: $50 - $100 sq. ft.

BURCHETTA HOTGLASS

JOHN AND KATHLEEN BURCHETTA
8A BELDEN RD
CARMEL, NY 10512
FAX 914-225-1430
TEL 914-225-1430
Est. 1985
Products: sculpture, lamps and lighting
fixtures, tiles
Techniques: leaded, sandcarved or
etched, copper-foiled, cast
Specialization: unique hand-blown glass
Price Range: $250 - $1,500 sq. ft.

★ RICHARD BUSWELL

BUZKO DESIGN STUDIO, INC.
RR 4 BOX 129
LYNCHBURG, VA 24503-9703
FAX 804-525-6168
TEL 804-525-6161
Products: windows, doors and entrances,
walls, skylights or domes, room dividers
and screens, tabernacles
Techniques: dalle de verre, leaded, paint-
ed or enameled, beveled, sandcarved
Specialization: custom-designed liturgical
Price Range: $40 - $325 sq. ft.

**See page 43 for photographs
and additional information.**

MARY ANN GALLAGHER BYRNE
KERRY BYRNE

DER GLASS WERKS ART GLASS
STUDIO
6055 N COLLEGE AVE
INDIANAPOLIS, IN 46220
FAX 317-257-7603
TEL 317-257-7603
Est. 1921
Products: windows, doors and entrances,
skylights and domes, sculpture, lamps
and lighting fixtures
Techniques: leaded, sandcarved or
etched, beveled, painted or enameled,
laminated
Specialization: site-specific art work
Price Range: $50 - $400 sq. ft.

GERALD CAMP

GLASS CASTLE
2746 CASTLE ROCK RD
DIAMOND BAR, CA 91765-3539
TEL 909-598-3162
Est. 1975
Products: doors and entrances, skylights
or domes, windows, work for the wall,
fireplace screens
Techniques: beveled, leaded, painted or
enameled, pate de verre, etch and glue
chip
Price Range: $40 - $400 sq. ft.

ED CARPENTER

1812 NW 24TH AVE
PORTLAND, OR 97210-2538
FAX 503-224-6729
TEL 503-224-6729
Est. 1971
Products: sculpture, skylights or domes,
stabiles or suspended sculpture,
windows
Techniques: bent, fused or kiln-formed,
laminated, leaded, painted or enameled,
sandcarved or etched
Specialization: architectural
Price Range: $100 - $500 sq. ft.

SYDNEY CASH

72 RESERVOIR RD
MARLBORO, NY 12542-5010
TEL 914-236-7032
Est. 1970
Products: windows, autonomous panels,
sculpture, murals and bas relief, work for
the wall
Techniques: painted or enameled, bent,
fused or kiln-formed
Specialization: high-tech optics
Price Range: $200 - $1,500 sq. ft.

CELINDER'S GLASS STUDIO

MARY ANN CELINDER
21341 FLEET LN
HUNTINGTON BEACH, CA 92646-
7220
FAX 714-963-1675
TEL 714-962-8361
Est. 1976
Products: windows, doors and entrances,
room dividers and screens, autonomous
panels, skylights and domes
Techniques: leaded, copper-foiled,
beveled, painted or enameled
Specialization: residential, public
Price Range: $65 - $450 sq. ft.

RAY CENTANNI

GREAT PANES ARCHITECTURAL
GLASS ART
3764 SILVERADO TRL
CALISTOGA, CA 94515-9613
TEL 707-963-9115
Est. 1973
Products: doors and entrances, skylights
or domes, walls, windows, glass/tile
mosaic
Techniques: dalle de verre, laminated,
leaded, painted or enameled, sandcarved
or etched
Specialization: liturgical and commercial
Price Range: $75 - $500 sq. ft.

CHATHAM GLASS WORKS

EMILY ZEITLIN/STUART HALL
5 MAPLE ST
EAST HAMPTON, CT 06424-1107
TEL 203-267-7679
Est. 1983
Products: autonomous panels, doors and
entrances, furniture, room dividers or
screens, windows
Techniques: bent, fused or kiln-formed,
copper-foiled, laminated, leaded, sand-
carved or etched
Price Range: $75 - $150 sq. ft.

CLASSIC STAINED
GLASS DESIGNS

DICK LAPADULA
86 E MOUNT AVE
ATLANTIC HIGHLANDS, NJ 07716
FAX 908-872-7061
TEL 908-291-5999
Est. 1987
Products: autonomous panels, doors and
entrances, room dividers or screens,
skylights or domes, windows
Techniques: beveled, copper-foiled,
leaded, sandcarved or etched
Price Range: $95 - $185 sq. ft.

FRANK CLOSE

PATENAUDE-CLOSE
115 GRAND ST
NEW YORK, NY 10013-2691
FAX 212-431-3211
TEL 212-925-1140
Est. 1976
Products: doors and entrances, room
dividers or screens, skylights or domes,
stabiles or suspended sculpture, windows
Techniques: beveled, leaded, sandcarved
or etched
Specialization: contemporary design
Price Range: $100 - $250 sq. ft.

★ J. GORSUCH COLLINS

**J. GORSUCH COLLINS
ARCHITECTURAL GLASS**
8283 W ILIFF LN
LAKEWOOD, CO 80227-3018
FAX 303-980-0692
TEL 303-985-8081
Est. 1978
Products: doors and entrances, murals
or bas relief, windows, walls, furniture
Techniques: bent, fused or kiln-formed,
leaded, cast
Specialization: public, corporate,
residential
Price Range: $225 - $500 sq. ft.

**See page 44 for photographs
and additional information.**

SAMUEL JOSEPH CORSO

DUFOUR/CORSO STUDIOS, LTD.
PO BOX 4272
BATON ROUGE, LA 70821-4272
TEL 504-344-4504
Est. 1963
Products: windows, doors and entrances,
autonomous panels, walls, mosaics
Techniques: leaded, sandcarved or
etched, copper-foiled, beveled
Specialization: liturgical, residential
Price Range: $250 - $500 sq. ft.

DON CROSS

D&C STAINED GLASS
614 TURNER BLVD
OMAHA, NE 68105-1423
TEL 402-342-8718
Est. 1977
Products: windows, doors and entrances,
room dividers and screens, autonomous
panels, lamps and lighting fixtures
Techniques: beveled, copper-foiled,
leaded, sandcarved or etched
Specialization: residential
Price Range: $40 - $150 sq. ft.

CRYSTAL GLASS STUDIO INC.

MARY MATCHAEL
50 WEANT BLVD
CARBONDALE, CO 81623-2040
FAX 970-963-0996
TEL 970-963-3227
Products: windows, doors and entrances,
room dividers and screens, lamps and
lighting fixtures, sculpture
Techniques: leaded, sandcarved or
etched, bent, fused or kiln-formed
Specialization: doors and entrances
Price Range: $150 - $500 sq. ft.

DORIS CULTRARO

DORIS CULTRARO STAINED GLASS
50 SYCAMORE AVE
MOUNT VERNON, NY 10553-1216
FAX 914-667-4619
TEL 914-667-4619
Est. 1975
Products: autonomous panels, doors and
entrances, room dividers or screens, sky-
lights or domes, windows, glass model
houses, lampshades
Techniques: copper-foiled, leaded, neon
Specialization: custom designs
Price Range: $125 - $300 sq. ft.

CUMMINGS STAINED GLASS STUDIO, INC.

H.W. CUMMINGS
182 E MAIN ST PO BOX 427
NORTH ADAMS, MA 01247-0427
FAX 413-664-6570
TEL 413-664-6578
Est. 1922
Products: windows, doors and entrances,
room dividers and screens, autonomous
panels, skylights and domes
Techniques: leaded, beveled, painted
or enameled, copper-foiled
Specialization: restoration
Price Range: $200 - $2,000 sq. ft.

ALAIN CUNEO

911 GENERAL TAYLOR ST
NEW ORLEANS, LA 70115
TEL 504-897-3754
Est. 1978
Products: windows, room dividers and
screens, autonomous panels, work for
the wall, furniture
Techniques: leaded, sandcarved or
etched, beveled
Specialization: contemporary designs
Price Range: $55 - $200 sq. ft.

BARBARA E. CUNHA

FLYING COLORS STAINED GLASS
PO BOX 97
ASSONET, MA 02702-0097
TEL 508-644-2433
Est. 1984
Products: windows, doors and entrances,
autonomous panels, meditation art glass
Techniques: leaded, sandcarved or
etched, copper-foiled
Specialization: sacred and healing spaces
Price Range: $125 - $500 sq. ft.

CURRAN GLASS & MIRROR

PATRICK CURRAN
30 N MAPLE ST #3
FLORENCE, MA 01060-1360
TEL 413-584-5761
Est. 1977
Products: windows, doors and entrances,
room dividers and screens, sculpture,
lamps and lighting fixtures
Techniques: bent, fused or kiln-formed,
beveled, copper-foiled, leaded, sand-
carved or etched
Specialization: custom-etched, stained glass
Price Range: $100 - $250 sq. ft.

DAHL GLASS

DUANE DAHL
3 SILER LN
SANTA FE, NM 87505-3118
FAX 505-474-7000
TEL 505-474-6000
Products: windows, doors and entrances,
lamps and lighting fixtures, murals and
bas relief, fountains
Techniques: sandcarved or etched, bent,
fused or kiln-formed, cast
Specialization: unique fabrications
Price Range: $80 - $250 sq. ft.

DAN DAILEY

2 NORTH RD
EXETER, NH 03833
FAX 603-778-1331
TEL 603-778-2303
Products: sculpture, lamps and lighting
fixtures, murals and bas relief, work for
the wall, furniture
Techniques: sandcarved or etched,
painted or enameled, cast, blown
Specialization: cast glass block murals
Price Range: $400 - $1,000 sq. ft.

D'ANDREA GLASS ETCHINGS

NORMA D'ANDREA M.F.A.
3671 TACOMA AVE
LOS ANGELES, CA 90065-1817
FAX 213-225-9920
TEL 213-223-7940
Products: windows, doors and entrances,
room dividers and screens, skylights and
domes, furniture
Techniques: sandcarved or etched
Specialization: fine art and small
production
Price Range: $60 - $200 sq. ft.

DANIEL MAHER STAINED GLASS

DANIEL MAHER
266 CONCORD AVE
CAMBRIDGE, MA 02138-1338
TEL 617-661-5771
Est. 1989
Products: windows, doors and entrances,
autonomous panels, computer-
generated imagery
Techniques: leaded, copper-foiled,
painted or enameled, multiple layered
Specialization: residential, architectural
Price Range: $200 - $2,000 sq. ft.

F.L. DECKER

PO BOX 13
BLANCHARD, WA 98232-0013
TEL 360-766-6530
Est. 1969
Products: autonomous panels, doors
and entrances, room dividers or screens,
skylights or domes, windows
Techniques: beveled, engraved, leaded,
painted or enameled, sandcarved or
etched
Specialization: fine art
Price Range: $100 - $2,500 sq. ft.

DEGNAN/LAURIE INC.

DUNCAN LAURIE
PO BOX 78
JAMESTOWN, RI 02835-0078
FAX 718-361-0651
TEL 401-423-3992
Est. 1972
Products: windows, doors and entrances,
room dividers and screens, autonomous
panels, sculpture, architectural glass. metal
Techniques: sandcarved or etched,
laminated
Specialization: sculpture
Price Range: $35 and up sq. ft.

JUDY DeSANDERS

4203 ABBOTT AVE
DALLAS, TX 75205-4342
TEL 214-522-1916
Est. 1965
Products: windows, autonomous panels,
doors and entrances
Techniques: leaded, painted or
enameled, bent, fused or kiln-formed
Specialization: all settings
Price Range: $300 - $600 sq. ft.

ELIZABETH DEVEREAUX

DEVEREAUX ARCHITECTURAL GLASS
2155 PARK AVE
CHICO, CA 95928-6702
FAX 916-342-2074
TEL 916-342-2074
Est. 1969
Products: windows, doors and entrances,
skylights and domes, work for the wall,
fused tiles
Techniques: leaded, sandcarved or
etched, beveled, painted or enameled
Specialization: liturgical, public art
Price Range: $100 - $500 sq. ft.

DON YOUNG GLASS STUDIO

DON YOUNG
PO BOX 470041
FORT WORTH, TX 76147-0041
TEL 817-731-2787
Est. 1973
Products: windows, doors and entrances,
sculpture, murals and bas relief, work for
the wall
Techniques: sandcarved or etched, paint-
ed or enameled, photographic etching
Specialization: photo-etching
Price Range: $100 and up sq. ft.

YOURIJ DONSKOJ

DONSKOJ & COMPANY
93 BROADWAY
KINGSTON, NY 12401-6017
TEL 914-338-8473
Est. 1972
Products: windows, doors and entrances,
autonomous panels
Techniques: leaded, copper-foiled,
painted or enameled
Specialization: panel restoration
Price Range: $100 and up sq. ft.

DAVID DUFF

CLASSICAL GLASS
1333 MAIN ST
CINCINNATI, OH 45210-2376
TEL 513-381-4334
Est. 1973
Products: autonomous panels, lamps or
lighting fixtures, room dividers or
screens, sculpture, work for the wall
Techniques: bent, fused or kiln-formed,
beveled, dalle de verre, leaded, painted
or enameled
Specialization: all leaded glass
Price Range: $20 - $500 sq. ft.

KARI DUNN

KARI A. DUNN, DESIGNER
4418 31ST AVE W
SEATTLE, WA 98199-1436
TEL 206-285-9426
Est. 1992
Products: windows, doors and entrances,
room dividers, screens, work for the wall
Techniques: sandcarved or etched,
painted or enameled, glue chipped
Specialization: illustrative
Price Range: $25 - $250 sq. ft.

JEROME R. DURR

THE JUST GLASS STUDIO
PO BOX 46
MOTTVILLE, NY 13119-0046
FAX 315-478-1767
TEL 315-428-1322
Est. 1973
Products: windows, doors and entrances,
room dividers and screens, sculpture, walls
Techniques: leaded, sandcarved or
etched, pate de verre
Price Range: $85 - $300 sq. ft.

JEAN-JACQUES DUVAL

DUVAL STUDIO
RIVER RD
SARANAC, NY 12981
FAX 518-293-7827
TEL 518-293-7827
Est. 1959
Products: doors and entrances, room
dividers or screens, walls, windows
Techniques: dalle de verre, leaded
Specialization: liturgical, secular
Price Range: $150 - $300 sq. ft.

DIANE C. EISSINGER

DIANE EISSINGER CUSTOM
  STAINED GLASS
44290 WILLIS RD
BELLEVILLE, MI 48111-8942
TEL 313-699-9344
Est. 1985
Products: windows, doors and entrances,
room dividers and screens, autonomous
panels, 3D altar crosses
Techniques: leaded, copper-foiled, painted
Specialization: liturgical
Price Range: $75 - $250 sq. ft.

★ ELLEN MANDELBAUM GLASS ART

ELLEN MANDELBAUM
3949 46TH ST
LONG ISLAND CITY, NY 11104-1407
FAX 718-361-8154
TEL 718-361-8154
Est. 1981
Products: autonomous panels, doors and entrances, room dividers or screens, windows, religious spaces, lobbies
Techniques: leaded, painted or enameled
Specialization: painted architectural
Price Range: $250 - $400 sq. ft.

See page 45 for photographs and additional information.

JAMES V. ERICKSON

68-234 AU ST
WAIALUA, HI 96791-9324
FAX 808-637-8934
TEL 808-637-8934
Est. 1971
Products: sculpture, murals or bas relief, windows
Techniques: laminated, leaded, sandcarved or etched
Price Range: $100 - $500 sq. ft.

ETCHINGS FANTASTIQUE

MARSHA HILL
99-412 FERNRIDGE PL
AIEA, HI 96701-3105
FAX 808-488-4845*
TEL 808-488-4845
Est. 1980
Products: autonomous panels, doors and entrances, murals or bas relief, room dividers or screens, windows
Techniques: engraved, neon, sandcarved or etched
Specialization: custom carved projects
Price Range: $50 - $250 sq. ft.

ETHEREAL GLASS ART

ALAN D. WEBB
PO BOX 1296
GREENVILLE, TX 75403-1296
TEL 903-455-1020
Est. 1980
Products: autonomous panels, doors and entrances, windows, large-scale installations
Techniques: copper-foiled, leaded, sandcarved or etched, bent, fused or kiln-formed
Price Range: $200 - $500 sq. ft.

TONY EVANS

EVANS DESIGNS/CALIFORNIA
PO BOX 1212
HEALDSBURG, CA 95448
FAX 707-433-9392
TEL 707-433-9392
Est. 1983
Products: work for the wall, tiles
Techniques: sandcarved or etched, painted or enameled, bent, fused or kiln-formed, engraved, blown
Price Range: $20 - $200 sq. ft.

LONNIE FEATHER

LONNIE FEATHER STUDIO
733 NW EVERETT #2Y
PORTLAND, OR 97209
TEL 503-222-9773
Products: windows, doors and entrances, room dividers and screens, work for the wall
Techniques: sandcarved or etched, painted or enameled
Specialization: corporate, public art
Price Range: $100 - $300 sq. ft.

FENTON GLASS STUDIO

DAN FENTON
4001 SAN LEANDRO ST STE 8
OAKLAND, CA 94601-4023
FAX 510-533-9983
TEL 510-533-5515
Est. 1969
Products: windows, autonomous panels, tiles, lighting fixtures
Techniques: leaded, sandcarved or etched, copper-foiled, painted or enameled, bent, fused or kiln-formed
Specialization: instruction and consulting
Price Range: $200 - $1,000 sq. ft.

JOHN HAWK FITCH

JOHN HAWK FITCH STUDIO
279 W COLLEGE ST
OBERLIN, OH 44074
TEL 216-774-1728
Est. 1990
Products: windows, doors and entrances, room dividers and screens, lamps and lighting fixtures, tiles
Techniques: bent, fused or kiln-formed
Price Range: $30 - $150 sq. ft.

JOHN FORBES

BONNY DOON ART GLASS
7258 EMPIRE GRADE
SANTA CRUZ, CA 95060-9605
TEL 408-426-5828
Est. 1968
Products: windows, skylights and domes, sculpture, lamps and lighting fixtures, murals and bas relief
Techniques: leaded, sandcarved or etched, copper-foiled, beveled, bent, fused or kiln-formed
Specialization: custom, large-scale work
Price Range: $100 - $1,000 sq. ft.

ROBERT FORMAN

ROBERT FORMAN
412 GRAND ST
HOBOKEN, NJ 07030-2703
TEL 201-659-7069
Est. 1978
Products: windows, skylights or domes, walls, murals and bas relief, tiles
Techniques: copper-foiled, leaded, mosaic
Specialization: synagogues
Price Range: $175 - $200 sq. ft.

FRANKLIN ART GLASS STUDIOS INC.

GARY L. HELF
222 E SYCAMORE ST
COLUMBUS, OH 43206-2144
FAX 614-221-5223
TEL 614-221-2972
Est. 1924
Products: windows, doors and entrances, room dividers and screens, autonomous panels, skylights and domes
Techniques: leaded, sandcarved or etched, copper-foiled, beveled, painted or enameled, dalle de verre
Specialization: liturgical and restoration
Price Range: $50 - $500 sq. ft.

PAUL H. FRIEND

PAUL FRIEND ARCHITECTURAL GLASS AND DESIGN INC.
216 LINCOLN AVE
HADDONFIELD, NJ 08033-1851
FAX 609-428-1199
TEL 609-428-9100
Est. 1974
Products: windows, doors and entrances, room dividers and screens, sculpture, furniture
Techniques: leaded, sandcarved or etched, painted or enameled, bent, fused or kiln-formed
Specialization: full-service studio
Price Range: $150 minimum sq. ft.

JAMES B. FURMAN

JAMES B. FURMAN GLASS STUDIO
PO BOX V
TRUMANSBURG, NY 14886-0722
TEL 607-387-4141
Est. 1975
Products: autonomous panels, doors and entrances, room dividers or screens, stabiles or suspended sculpture, windows
Techniques: bent, fused or kiln-formed, copper-foiled, laminated, leaded, painted or enameled
Specialization: liturgical
Price Range: $150 - $300 sq. ft.

SAARA GALLIN

142 SHERMAN AVE
WHITE PLAINS, NY 10607-2415
FAX 718-993-3712
TEL 914-592-6930
Est. 1974
Products: autonomous panels, doors and entrances, room dividers or screens, skylights or domes, windows
Techniques: bent, fused or kiln-formed, copper-foiled, laminated leaded
Specialization: work in relief
Price Range: $150 - $300 sq. ft.

GAYTEE STAINED GLASS

JOHN SALISBURY
2744 LYNDALE AVE S
MINNEAPOLIS, MN 55408-1395
FAX 612-872-4551
TEL 612-872-4550
Est. 1918
Products: doors and entrances, room dividers or screens, windows
Techniques: bent, fused or kiln-formed, dalle de verre, leaded, painted or enameled, sandcarved or etched
Price Range: $125 - $500 sq. ft.

JOHN GILVEY
MICHAEL BENZER

GILVEY STUDIO ART GLASS LTD.
RT 216
POUGHQUAG, NY 12570
FAX 914-724-3149
TEL 914-724-5088
Est. 1978
Products: sculpture, tiles, table tops
Techniques: cast
Price Range: $40 - $100 sq. ft.

GLASS ILLUMINATIONS, INC.

SCOTT HUNTER, VICE PRESIDENT
PO BOX 309
SUN VALLEY, CA 91352-0309
FAX 818-556-6778
TEL 818-556-6777
Est. 1993
Products: windows, room dividers and screens, lamps and lighting fixtures
Techniques: sandcarved or etched, painted or enameled, kiln-formed
Specialization: fiber-optic systems for glass

GLASS CRAFT STAINED GLASS STUDIO

FRED KOHLER
1809 LINCOLN WAY E
MASSILLON, OH 44646-6962
FAX 216-833-2565
TEL 800-336-2565
Est. 1971
Products: doors and entrances, room dividers or screens, windows
Techniques: copper-foiled, leaded, sandcarved or etched
Price Range: $50 - $150 sq. ft.

NANCY GONG

GONG GLASS WORKS
42 PARKVIEW DR
ROCHESTER, NY 14625-1034
FAX 716-288-2503
TEL 716-288-5520
Est. 1979
Products: fine art, architectural
Techniques: leaded, sandcarved or etched, chipped, hand-colored
Specialization: extraordinary glass art
Price Range: minimum $250 sq. ft.

ARCHITECTURAL GLASS

MICHAEL GREENWALD

CONTEMPORARY STAINED GLASS
 DESIGN
2240 MURRAY HILL #1
CLEVELAND, OH 44106
TEL 216-231-7200
Est. 1993
Products: windows, room dividers and
screens, autonomous panels, work for
the wall
Techniques: leaded, copper-foiled,
beveled
Specialization: contemporary design
Price Range: $50 - $200 sq. ft.

RAY GREGORY

ART GLASS RESPLENDENT, INC.
2708 WYOMING AVE
NORFOLK, VA 23513-4440
TEL 804-855-4312
Est. 1978
Products: autonomous panels, doors
and entrances, room dividers or screens,
skylights or domes, walls, windows
Techniques: bent, fused or kiln-formed,
beveled, leaded, painted or enameled,
sandcarved or etched
Price Range: $100 - $500 sq. ft.

★ MARK ERIC GULSRUD

**ARCHITECTURAL GLASS
 AND CLAY**
3309 TAHOMA PL W
TACOMA, WA 98466-1620
TEL 206-566-1720
Est. 1972
Products: windows, doors and entrances,
skylights and domes, sculpture, stabiles
and suspended sculpture
Techniques: bent, fused or kiln-formed,
leaded, laminated, dalle de verre, cast
Price Range: $100 - $350 sq. ft.

**See page 46 for photographs
and additional information.**

★ HALLMARK ART GLASS

MARK V. HALL
PO BOX 366
KASOTA, MN 56050-0366
TEL 507-931-9489
Est. 1988
Products: windows, doors and entrances,
murals and bas relief, work for the wall,
tiles
Techniques: leaded, painted or enameled,
bent, fused or kiln-formed, cast, pate de
verre
Specialization: collaborative work
Price Range: $150 - $500 sq. ft.

**See page 47 for photographs
and additional information.**

LUTZ HAUFSCHILD

1461 NELSON AVE
WEST VANCOUVER, BC V7T 2G9
CANADA
FAX 604-926-9452
TEL 604-926-8594
Est. 1970
Products: windows, doors and entrances,
room dividers and screens, autonomous
panels, skylights and domes, murals and
bas relief
Techniques: leaded, sandcarved or
etched, beveled, painted or enameled,
bent, fused or kiln-formed, laminated
Price Range: $150 - $400 sq. ft.

HEATHER GLASS

HEATHER ROBYN MATTHEWS
4401 STE B SOQUEL DR
SOQUEL, CA 95073-2120
FAX 408-462-2306
TEL 408-462-3231
Est. 1979
Products: doors and entrances room
dividers and screens, sculpture, walls,
furniture
Techniques: sandcarved or etched
Price Range: $125 - $400 sq. ft.

GENE HESTER

GENESIS ART GLASS STUDIO
2704 SACKETT ST
HOUSTON, TX 77098-1100
TEL 713-522-2950
Products: windows, doors and entrances,
room dividers or screens, autonomous
panels, plates and bowls
Techniques: leaded, beveled, bent, fused
or kiln-formed
Specialization: contemporary
Price Range: $65 - $250 sq. ft.

HIEROS GAMOS

JEFFREY WOROB
HC 29 BOX 447
PRESCOTT, AZ 86301
TEL 602-445-0008
Est. 1980
Products: windows, autonomous panels,
skylights and domes, sculpture, work for
the wall, 3D windows/sculpture
Techniques: leaded, copper-foiled, bent,
fused or kiln-formed, laminated, cast, form
building over molds
Specialization: "creating" objective artifacts
Price Range: $125 - $600 sq. ft.

PAMELA MENGERS HODGES

LAKEHOUSE STUDIOS
15589 ORCHARD SPRINGS RD
GRASS VALLEY, CA 95945
FAX 916-274-7777
TEL 916-274-7777
Est. 1979
Products: windows, doors and entrances,
room dividers and screens, autonomous
panels, skylights and domes
Techniques: leaded, sandcarved or
etched, copper-foiled, beveled, plating
Specialization: public reception areas
Price Range: $150 - $800 sq. ft.

THOMAS HOLZER

GLASS DESIGN STUDIOS
PO BOX 2278
BOULDER, CO 80306-2278
FAX 303-449-8745
TEL 303-449-2085
Est. 1986
Products: doors and entrances, murals
or bas relief, sculpture, walls, windows
Techniques: bent, fused or kiln-formed,
leaded, painted or enameled, glass/stone
mosaic
Price Range: $125 - $500 sq. ft.

HOPCROFT STAINED GLASS STUDIO, INC.

LEO GOETSCH
5810 QUINCY AVE
KANSAS CITY, MO 64130-4549
FAX 816-363-5812
TEL 816-363-5810
Est. 1914
Products: doors and entrances, room
dividers or screens, skylights or domes,
windows
Techniques: bent, fused or kiln-formed,
dalle de verre, leaded, painted or
enameled, sandcarved or etched
Specialization: liturgical
Price Range: $110 - $450 sq. ft.

★ PAUL HOUSBERG

GLASS PROJECT, INC.
59 TINGLEY ST
PROVIDENCE, RI 02903-1021
FAX 401-831-4881
TEL 401-831-4880
Est. 1979
Products: windows, doors and entrances,
room dividers and screens, murals and
bas relief, walls
Techniques: leaded, sandcarved or
etched, bent, fused or kiln-formed, cast
Price Range: $50 - $500 sq. ft.

**See pages 48-49 for photographs
and additional information.**

FRANK HOUTKAMP

HOUTKAMP ART GLASS STUDIO
120 N MAIN ST
ROCKFORD, IL 61101-1102
TEL 815-964-3785
Est. 1972
Products: doors and entrances, room
dividers or screens, windows
Techniques: beveled, leaded, sandcarved
or etched
Price Range: $75 - $250 sq. ft.

HUNT STAINED GLASS STUDIOS, INC.

NICHOLAS OR DAVID PARRENDO
1756 W CARSON ST
PITTSBURGH, PA 15219-1036
TEL 412-391-1796
Est. 1890
Products: doors and entrances, room
dividers or screens, sculpture, skylights
or domes, windows
Techniques: beveled, dalle de verre,
leaded, painted or enameled, sandcarved
or etched, cast
Specialization: liturgical
Price Range: $75 - $500 sq. ft.

HARRIET HYAMS

PO BOX 178
PALISADES, NY 10964-0178
FAX 914-359-0062
TEL 914-359-0061
Est. 1967
Products: autonomous panels, murals or
bas relief, sculpture, skylights or domes,
windows, others
Techniques: laminated, leaded,
sandcarved or etched
Specialization: all
Price Range: $100 - $350 sq. ft.

ILLUMINATIONS

MARGARET OLDMAN
71 DELANO AVE
SAN FRANCISCO, CA 94112-2519
FAX 415-469-9789
TEL 415-469-9789
Products: windows, doors and entrances,
room dividers and screens, skylights and
domes, sculpture
Techniques: sandcarved or etched
Specialization: intricate carved glass
Price Range: $60 - $400 sq. ft.

INDIANA ART GLASS

GREG THOMPSON
TIM LEVANDOSKI
1424 SAPLIER CIR E DR
INDIANAPOLIS, IN 46239
FAX 317-359-9630
TEL 317-353-6369
Products: windows, doors and entrances,
room dividers or screens, sculpture,
furniture
Techniques: sandcarved or etched, bent,
fused or kiln-formed, stainless steel
Price Range: $50 - $250 sq. ft.

IRON ORCHID

D. KEYES
107 N 8TH ST PO BOX 638
HENDERSON, MN 56044-0638
TEL 612-248-3353
Est. 1992
Products: windows, doors and entrances,
room dividers and screens, work for the
wall, portraits
Techniques: sandcarved or etched,
engraved, controlled glue chip
Specialization: 300 dpi photo-etched
glass
Price Range: $21.60 - $150 sq. ft.

JANE IRWIN
KATHRYN IRWIN
ART ZONE
592 MARKHAM ST
TORONTO, ON M6G 2L8
CANADA
FAX 416-534-1892
TEL 416-534-1892
Est. 1987
Products: windows, doors and entrances,
room dividers and screens, sculpture
Techniques: bent, fused or kiln-formed,
beveled, leaded, sandcarved or etched,
acid-etched
Specialization: site-specific contemporary
Price Range: $150 - $600 sq. ft.

JMB STUDIOS
JULIE MCDONOUGH B.
1012 N VERMONT AVE
ROYAL OAK, MI 48067-1410
TEL 313-547-0507
Products: autonomous panels, doors and
entrances, furniture, sculpture, work for
the wall
Techniques: bent, fused or kiln-formed,
laminated, leaded, neon, sandcarved or
etched
Specialization: innovative glass work
Price Range: $100 - $300 sq. ft.

THE JUDSON STUDIOS
WALTER & WILLIAM JUDSON
200 S AVENUE 66
LOS ANGELES, CA 90042-3632
FAX 213-255-8529
TEL 800-445-8376
Est. 1897
Products: windows, doors and entrances,
autonomous panels, skylights and domes,
stabiles and suspended sculpture
Techniques: leaded, sandcarved or
etched, beveled, painted or enameled,
bent, fused or kiln-formed, dalle de verre
Price Range: $125 - $1,200 sq. ft.

JURS ARCHITECTURAL GLASS
SHELLEY JURS
4167 WILSHIRE BLVD
OAKLAND, CA 94602-3423
FAX 510-531-6173
TEL 510-482-0225
Est. 1978
Products: doors and entrances, room
dividers or screens, skylights or domes,
windows, work for the wall, walls
Techniques: leaded, beveled
Specialization: hand-cast German jewels
Price Range: $190 - $300 sq. ft.

KARDELL STUDIO
ELLEN KARDELL
904 WESTMINSTER ST NW
WASHINGTON, DC 20001-4130
FAX 202-328-9309
TEL 202-462-4433
Est. 1976
Products: autonomous panels, doors
and entrances, room dividers or screens,
skylights or domes, windows
Techniques: copper-foiled, leaded,
sandcarved or etched
Specialization: traditional
Price Range: $65 - $650 sq. ft.

KATZ GLASSWORKS
IRA S. KATZ
12114 VELVET HILL DR
OWINGS MILLS, MD 2117
FAX 410-581-8596
TEL 410-581-8596
Est. 1989
Products: windows, doors and entrances,
room dividers and screens, autonomous
panels, work for the wall
Techniques: leaded, sandcarved or
etched, copper-foiled, beveled
Specialization: contemporary, abstract
Price Range: $75 - $225 sq. ft.

ROBERTA KATZ
PENTACLE STUDIO
PO BOX 202
CLINTON, AR 72031-0202
TEL 501-745-4589
Est. 1972
Products: autonomous panels, lamps
or lighting fixtures, windows
Techniques: copper-foiled, beveled, leaded
Price Range: $100 - $300 sq. ft.

KAZANJIAN ARCHITECTURAL GLASS
GARY KAZANJIAN
423 PIER AVE
HERMOSA BEACH, CA 90254-3820
FAX 310-374-7798
TEL 310-374-7798
Est. 1969
Products: autonomous panels, doors
and entrances, room dividers or screens,
skylights or domes, windows
Techniques: beveled, copper-foiled, leaded
Specialization: contemporary clear
textures
Price Range: $100 - $245 sq. ft.

KEBRLE STAINED GLASS STUDIO, INC.
JOHN KEBRLE
2829 BACHMAN DR
DALLAS, TX 75220-5854
FAX 214-357-5922
TEL 214-357-5922
Est. 1920
Products: autonomous panels, doors and
entrances, skylights or domes, windows
Techniques: dalle de verre, engraved,
laminated, painted or enameled,
sandcarved or etched, leaded
Specialization: liturgical secular
Price Range: $150 - $550 sq. ft.

KELLER ART GLASS
JERRY KELLER
2013 MURRAY HILL RD
CLEVELAND, OH 44106-2336
FAX 216-721-0314
TEL 216-721-0314
Est. 1973
Products: windows, doors and entrances,
autonomous panels, work for the wall,
furniture
Techniques: sandcarved or etched,
beveled, leaded, stained, computerized
photo carving
Price Range: $50 - $400 sq. ft.

★ GUY KEMPER
KEMPER STUDIO
190 N BROADWAY ST
LEXINGTON, KY 40507-1270
FAX 606-254-3507
TEL 606-254-3507
Est. 1983
Products: windows, doors and entrances,
sculpture, walls, stabiles and suspended
sculpture
Techniques: leaded, laminated, layered,
three-dimensional
Specialization: architectural, liturgical
Price Range: $75 - $250 sq. ft.

**See page 50 for photographs
and additional information.**

KENSINGTON GLASS ARTS, INC.
4213 HOWARD AVE
KENSINGTON, MD 20895-2419
FAX 301-897-8215
TEL 301-897-0057
Est. 1976
Products: autonomous panels, furniture,
room dividers or screens, skylights or
domes, windows
Techniques: beveled, copper-foiled,
engraved, leaded, sandcarved or etched
Specialization: architectural, commercial
Price Range: $100 - $400 sq. ft.

KERSEY'S GLASS WORKS
STEPHEN AND MARY KERSEY
23962 CLAWITER RD
HAYWARD, CA 94545-1811
FAX 510-782-2062
TEL 510-782-7813
Products: windows, doors and entrances,
room dividers and screens, sculpture,
lamps and lighting fixtures
Techniques: sandcarved or etched,
bent, fused or kiln-formed, laminated,
glue-chipped glass
Price Range: $75 - $700 sq. ft.

KESSLER STUDIOS
ROBERT KESSLER/CINDY KESSLER
273 E BROADWAY ST
LOVELAND, OH 45140-3121
FAX 513-683-7527
TEL 513-683-7500
Est. 1980
Products: windows, doors and entrances,
room dividers and screens, autonomous
panels, mosaics
Techniques: leaded, sandcarved or
etched, beveled
Specialization: contemporary
Price Range: $80 - $300 sq. ft.

KITTRELL/RIFFKIND ART GLASS
BARBARA KITTRELL
5100 BELTLINE RD #820
DALLAS, TX 75240
FAX 214-239-7998
TEL 214-239-7957
Est. 1979
Products: autonomous panels, doors and
entrances, sculpture, windows, work for
the wall
Techniques: bent, fused or kiln-formed,
beveled, leaded, painted or enameled,
sandcarved or etched
Price Range: $75 - $300 sq. ft.

SUSAN KLEIN
SUSAN KLEIN DESIGN
1100 BLOOMFIELD ST
HOBOKEN, NJ 07030-5304
TEL 201-420-7339
Est. 1978
Products: autonomous panels, doors
and entrances, room dividers or screens,
skylights or domes, windows
Techniques: beveled, copper-foiled, leaded,
painted or enameled, sandcarved or etched
Price Range: $50 - $200 sq. ft.

★ STEPHEN KNAPP
74 COMMODORE RD
WORCESTER, MA 01602-2727
FAX 508-797-3228
TEL 508-757-2507
Est. 1971
Products: windows, doors and entrances,
room dividers and screens, sculpture,
furniture
Techniques: sandcarved or etched, bent,
fused or kiln-formed, cast
Price Range: $100 - $700 sq. ft.

**See page 51 for photographs
and additional information.**

JERRY KRAUSKI
LITURGICAL ENVIRONMENTS CO.
RR 4 BOX 4344
HAYWARD, WI 54843-9183
FAX 715-462-3481
TEL 715-462-3097
TEL 800-449-8554
Est. 1962
Products: doors and entrances, room
dividers or screens, skylights or domes,
windows, work for the wall
Techniques: copper-foiled, beveled, leaded,
dalle de verre, sandcarved or etched
Price Range: $100 - $250 sq. ft.

ARCHITECTURAL GLASS

J & R LAMB STUDIOS, INC.

PO BOX 291
PHILMONT, NY 12565-0291
FAX 518-672-7597
TEL 518-672-7267
Est. 1857
Products: doors and entrances, murals
or bas relief, skylights or domes, walls,
windows, cast glass walls
Techniques: beveled, cast, copper-foiled,
dalle de verre, engraved, others
Specialization: restoration and new
Price Range: $100 - $400 sq. ft.

J. KENNETH LEAP

THE PAINTED WINDOW
12 WASHINGTON AVE
RUNNEMEDE, NJ 08078
FAX 609-939-5934
TEL 609-825-6800X2763
Est. 1987
Products: windows, doors and entrances,
room dividers or screens, autonomous
panels, skylights and domes
Techniques: leaded, beveled, painted or
enameled
Specialization: full-service studio
Price Range: $125 - $550 sq. ft.

LINDA LICHTMAN

17 TUDOR ST
CAMBRIDGE, MA 02139-4514
FAX 617-354-1119
TEL 617-876-4660
Est. 1978
Products: windows, doors and entrances,
room dividers and screens, autonomous
panels, glass paintings
Techniques: painted or enameled,
laminated, engraved, acid etched
Specialization: color, painting, light
Price Range: $200 - $600 sq. ft.

LINDEN STUDIO

JANET LINDEN
811 RIVERSIDE SW
ALBUQUERQUE, NM 87105-3969
TEL 505-877-6972
Est. 1982
Products: windows, doors and entrances,
room dividers and screens, autonomous
panels, lamps and lighting fixtures
Techniques: leaded, sandcarved or etched,
copper-foiled, painted or enameled, bent,
fused or kiln-formed
Price Range: $80 - $160 sq. ft.

WILLIAM R. LITTIG

WILLIAM R. LITTIG STAINED GLASS
333 PIERPONT AVE
SALT LAKE CITY, UT 84101-1712
TEL 801-531-7515
Est. 1970
Products: windows, doors and entrances,
autonomous panels, domes
Techniques: beveled, leaded, sandcarved
or etched bent, fused or kiln-formed
Specialization: contemporary
Price Range: minimum $100 sq. ft.

MICHAELA MAHADY

PEGASUS STUDIO, INC.
5155 BLOOMINGTON AVE
MINNEAPOLIS, MN 55417-1849
FAX 612-724-4563
TEL 612-724-4563
Est. 1976
Products: doors and entrances, lamps or
lighting fixtures, sculpture, room dividers
and screens, windows
Techniques: beveled, leaded, sandcarved
or etched
Price Range: $150 - $700 sq. ft.

PAUL MARIONI
ANN TROUTNER

"GLASS"
4136 MERIDIAN AVE N
SEATTLE, WA 98103-8308
FAX 206-632-1363
TEL 206-633-1901
Est. 1970
Products: autonomous panels, doors
and entrances, murals or bas relief, tiles,
windows
Techniques: blown, cast, leaded, painted
or enameled, sandcarved or etched
Specialization: cast glass
Price Range: $25 - $100 sq. ft.

MARTINO ART GLASS STUDIO

S. (NINO) MARTINO
839 ELLROSE AVE
WINDSOR, ON N8Y 3W6
CANADA
TEL 519-974-2780
Est. 1989
Products: windows, doors and entrances,
room dividers and screens, autonomous
panels
Techniques: leaded, sandcarved or
etched, painted or enameled
Specialization: liturgical and restoration
Price Range: $150 - $400 sq. ft.

CRAIG McCULLEN

WHOOJOO GLASS COMPANY
532 JEFFERSON ST
LAFAYETTE, LA 70501-6906
TEL 318-269-9310
Est. 1979
Products: autonomous panels, doors and
entrances, sculpture, windows, work for
the wall
Techniques: bent, fused or kiln-formed,
beveled, copper-foiled, dalle de verre,
leaded, painted or enameled
Specialization: architectural art glass
Price Range: $45 - $200 sq. ft.

MAUREEN McGUIRE

DESIGN ASSOCIATES, INC.
924 E BETHANY HOME RD
PHOENIX, AZ 85014-2147
FAX 602-277-0203
TEL 602-277-0167
Est. 1968
Products: windows, walls, doors and
entrances, room dividers and screens,
skylights and domes, woodcarved
sculpture
Techniques: leaded, painted or enameled,
sandcarved or etched, bent, fused or
kiln-formed
Specialization: all settings
Price Range: $130 - $200 sq. ft.

EDWARD McILVANE

ARTIST & DESIGNER IN GLASS
21 HOLDEN ST
PROVIDENCE, RI 02908-5754
TEL 401-274-6909
Est. 1978
Products: autonomous panels, doors
and entrances, room dividers or screens,
skylights or domes, windows
Techniques: blown, dalle de verre, leaded,
painted or enameled, sandcarved or
etched
Specialization: photo processes,
site-specific
Price Range: $100 - $350 sq. ft.

★ LEONE McNEIL

LEAD & LIGHT WORKS
45131 LITTLE LAKE ST
PO BOX 552
MENDOCINO, CA 95460-0552
FAX 707-937-5227
TEL 707-937-5227
Est. 1975
Products: autonomous panels, doors
and entrances, room dividers or screens,
skylights or domes, windows
Techniques: bent, fused or kiln-formed,
laminated, leaded, painted or enameled,
sandcarved or etched
Specialization: liturgical, residential
Price Range: $150 - $200 sq. ft.

**See page 52 for photographs
and additional information.**

★ HOWARD MEEHAN
★ KATHLEEN MEEHAN

FIREFLY STUDIO
2511 NW UPSHUR ST
PORTLAND, OR 97210-2549
TEL 503-274-0865
Est. 1975
Products: windows, room dividers and
screens, sculpture, suspended sculpture
Techniques: sandcarved or etched,
waterjet-cut, dichroic
Specialization: science and technology
Price Range: $75 - $500 sq. ft.

**See page 218 for photographs
and additional information.**

MELOTTE-MORSE STAINED GLASS, INC.

STEVEN J. BROOKS
213 S 6TH ST
SPRINGFIELD, IL 62701-1502
FAX 217-789-9518
TEL 217-789-9523
Est. 1978
Products: windows, doors and entrances,
autonomous panels, sculpture, skylights
or domes
Techniques: leaded, sandcarved or
etched, dalle de verre
Specialization: new work
Price Range: $60 - $500 sq. ft.

RACHEL MESRAHI

RACHEL MESRAHI STAINED GLASS
STUDIO
50 OAK KNOLL AVE
SAN ANSELMO, CA 94960-1868
FAX 415-721-0607
TEL 415-454-8537
Est. 1981
Products: autonomous panels, doors
and entrances, room dividers or screens,
skylights or domes, windows
Techniques: leaded, stained glass
Price Range: $150 - $300 sq. ft.

MIMI GELLMAN DESIGNS

MIMI GELLMAN
96 SPADINA AVE #809
TORONTO, ON M5V 2J6
CANADA
FAX 416-363-9706
TEL 416-363-9706
Est. 1984
Products: doors and entrances, room
dividers or screens, skylights or domes,
walls, windows
Techniques: beveled, leaded, painted or
enameled, sandcarved or etched, photo
silkscreen
Price Range: $150 - $350 sq. ft.

PETER MOLLICA

MOLLICA STAINED GLASS
1579 E 38TH ST
OAKLAND, CA 94602-1244
TEL 510-655-5736
Est. 1964
Products: autonomous panels, windows
Techniques: leaded
Specialization: windows and free-hanging
panel
Price Range: $200 - $250 sq. ft.

WILLIAM MORRIS

31321 3RD AVE NE
STANWOOD, WA 98292-9694
FAX 206-629-4564
TEL 206-629-4423
Products: sculpture
Techniques: blown
Price Range: $15,000 - $45,000 sq. ft.

MOSS STAINED GLASS

TED MOSS
2501 E 8TH ST
ANDERSON, IN 46012-4401
FAX 317-643-0439
TEL 800-782-7406
Est. 1946
Products: doors and entrances, skylights or domes, windows, autonomous panels, sculpture
Techniques: leaded, sandcarved or etched, beveled
Price Range: $40 - $350 sq. ft.

MICHAEL DAVID MYERS

18597 FOWLER RD
LAKE ANN, MI 49650-9606
FAX 616-275-7993
TEL 616-275-7498
Est. 1976
Products: autonomous panels, sculpture, work for the wall, mobiles, suspended sculpture
Techniques: copper-foiled, leaded
Specialization: contemporary abstract
Price Range: $100 - $400 sq. ft.

ROGER NACHMAN

ROGER NACHMAN ARCHI-
 TECTURAL FUSED GLASS STUDIO
1473 ELLIOTT AVE W
SEATTLE, WA 98119-3104
FAX 206-281-9406
TEL 206-281-9406
Est. 1977
Products: murals or bas relief, tiles, work for the wall table wear, sconces
Techniques: bent, fused or kiln-formed, blown, cast, painted or enameled, pate de verre
Price Range: $75 - $350 sq. ft.

NAUTILUS ART GLASS STUDIO

SHARON ANN WOOD
9438 S 29TH ST
FRANKLIN, WI 53132-9148
TEL 414-761-9233
Est. 1987
Products: windows, doors and entrances, room dividers and screens, sculpture, lamps and lighting fixtures
Techniques: leaded, sandcarved or etched, copper-foiled, bent, fused or kiln-formed, laminated
Specialization: fine art custom homes
Price Range: $60 - $150 sq. ft.

LENN NEFF

CONTEMPORARY LEADED GLASS
 & ARCHITECTURAL ARTS
PO BOX 1931
SAINT PETERSBURG, FL 33731-1931
TEL 813-823-3919
Est. 1973
Products: doors and entrances, lamps or lighting fixtures, room dividers or screens, windows, public installations
Techniques: beveled, dalle de verre, leaded, neon, pate de verre
Price Range: $120 - $250 sq. ft.

NEW ENGLAND STAINED GLASS

RAYMOND J. DORAZIO
5 CENTER RD
W STOCKBRIDGE, MA 01266
FAX 413-232-7181
TEL 413-232-7181
Est. 1968
Products: lamps or lighting fixtures, windows
Techniques: copper-foiled
Price Range: $100 - $400 sq. ft.

PATSY NORVELL

78 GREENE ST
NEW YORK, NY 10012-5100
TEL 212-334-1961
Est. 1979
Products: room dividers or screens, sculpture, windows, furniture
Techniques: laminated, sandcarved or etched, gold-leafed
Specialization: public art, space
Price Range: $75 - $500 sq. ft.

NOSTALGIC GLASS WORKS, INC.

ROGER R. RHODENBAUGH
1004 BRIOSO DR
COSTA MESA, CA 92627-4501
FAX 714-646-4173
TEL 714-646-7474
Est. 1974
Products: windows, doors and entrances, skylights or domes, room dividers or screens, windows
Techniques: beveled, sandcarved or etched, leaded
Specialization: residential entries
Price Range: $100 - $500 sq. ft.

OMNIBUS DESIGN INC.

RICHARD E. HANLEY
4245 OKEMOS RD
OKEMOS, MI 48864-2574
FAX 517-349-5028
TEL 517-349-5027
Products: windows, room dividers and screens, lamps and lighting fixtures
Techniques: leaded, sandcarved or etched, painted or enameled
Specialization: liturgical stained glass
Price Range: $145 - $650 sq. ft.

PALMER-POHLMANN STUDIO, INC.

MERRIDY L. POHLMANN
JED D. PALMER
2600 PLEASANTDALE RD STE 1
DORAVILLE, GA 30340-1542
FAX 404-448-8070
TEL 404-448-8400
Est. 1986
Products: doors and entrances, room dividers or screens, sculpture, walls, windows
Techniques: beveled, dalle de verre, laminated, leaded, sandcarved or etched
Specialization: sandcarved and laminated
Price Range: $75 -$350 sq. ft.

PATRICIA PATENAUDE

PATENAUDE/CLOSE STUDIO, INC.
115 GRAND ST
NEW YORK, NY 10013
FAX 212-431-3211
TEL 212-925-1140
Products: windows, doors and entrances, room dividers and screens, autonomous panels, stabiles and suspended sculpture
Techniques: leaded, sandcarved or etched, laminated
Specialization: contemporary design
Price Range: $100 - $200 sq. ft.

PATTIE WALKER STUDIO

PATTIE WALKER
290 CARLAW AVE #203
TORONTO, ON M4M 3L1
CANADA
FAX 416-465-8249
TEL 416-465-8249
Products: windows, doors and entrances, room dividers and screens, walls
Techniques: leaded, sandcarved or etched, painted or enameled, glass applique
Price Range: $175 - $450 sq. ft.

LESLIE PERLIS

LESLIE PERLIS STUDIO
4587 NIAGARA AVE
SAN DIEGO, CA 92107-2945
FAX 619-224-0587
TEL 619-222-8776
Est. 1972
Products: autonomous panels, doors and entrances, room dividers or screens, windows, work for the wall, furniture
Techniques: bent, fused or kiln-formed, leaded, painted or enameled, fused with titanium
Specialization: high-tech leaded and fused
Price Range: $100 - $200 sq. ft.

PERRY STAINED GLASS STUDIO

JAMES M. PERRY
470 FRONT ST N
ISSAQUAH, WA 98027-2914
FAX 206-391-7734
TEL 206-392-1600
Est. 1971
Products: doors and entrances, windows
Techniques: leaded, dalle de verre, sandcarved or etched, beveled, painted
Specialization: liturgical
Price Range: $85 - $300 sq. ft.

JIM PIERCEY

J. PIERCEY STUDIOS, INC.
1714 ACME ST
ORLANDO, FL 32805-3604
FAX 407-841-6444
TEL 800-368-9226
TEL 407-841-7594
Products: windows, walls, glass and stone mosaic
Techniques: leaded, beveled, painted or enameled
Specialization: public art
Price Range: $100 - $350 sq. ft.

MICHAEL F. PILLA

MONARCH STUDIOS, INC.
2242 UNIVERSITY AVE W STE 316
SAINT PAUL, MN 55114-1817
FAX 612-649-0456
TEL 612-644-7927
Est. 1976
Products: doors and entrances, room dividers or screens, skylights or domes, windows, work for the wall
Techniques: beveled, copper-foiled, leaded copper channel/clips
Price Range: minimum $300 sq. ft.

POREMBA STAINED GLASS STUDIO, INC.

FRED M. POREMBA, SR.
20806 AURORA RD
BEDFORD, OH 44146-1006
FAX 513-662-8361
TEL 513-662-8360
Est. 1943
Products: doors and entrances, lamps or lighting fixtures, skylights or domes, windows, table tops
Techniques: beveled, copper-foiled, leaded, painted or enameled, sandcarved or etched, laminated
Specialization: churches, homes and restaurants
Price Range: $60 - $300 sq. ft.

RICHARD POSNER

CHANCE BROS. GLASS WORKS
PO BOX 1151
CULVER CITY, CA 90232-1151
FAX 310-838-9865
TEL 310-815-0248
Products: windows, doors and entrances, autonomous panels, sculpture, lamps and lighting fixtures, cast, blown glass components
Techniques: sandcarved or etched, laminated, cast
Specialization: public, private commissions
Price Range: $750 - $2,100 sq. ft.

★ CARL POWELL

CARL POWELL GLASS
1610 9TH ST
BERKELEY, CA 94710-1815
TEL 510-526-2637
Est. 1973
Products: autonomous panels, doors and entrances, room dividers or screens, skylights or domes, windows
Techniques: beveled, engraved, leaded, painted or enameled, sandcarved or etched
Specialization: architectural
Price Range: $125 - $500 sq. ft.

See page 53 for photographs and additional information.

ARCHITECTURAL GLASS

★ BEV PRECIOUS

PRECIOUS DESIGN STUDIOS, INC.
950 N ALABAMA ST
INDIANAPOLIS, IN 46202-3350
TEL 317-631-6560
Est. 1984
Products: room dividers or screens, sculpture, windows, work for the wall
Techniques: bent, fused or kiln-formed, laminated, leaded, painted or enameled, sandcarved or etched
Price Range: $125 - $250 sq. ft.

See page 54 for photographs and additional information.

PRESTON STUDIOS

JERRY D. PRESTON
JOHN C. EMERY, SR.
552 S MAGNOLIA AVE
MELBOURNE, FL 32935-6438
TEL 407-259-0044
Est. 1976
Products: autonomous panels, doors and entrances, lamps or lighting fixtures, room dividers and screens, windows
Techniques: copper-foiled
Specialization: entrances, nature, lamps
Price Range: $200 - $450 sq. ft.

ELIZABETH QUANTOCK

QUANTOCK DESIGNERS
50 JERSEY ST
MARBLEHEAD, MA 01945-2452
TEL 617-631-8761
Est. 1970
Products: windows, doors and entrances, room dividers and screens, autonomous panels, work for the wall, painting/collage
Techniques: leaded, sandcarved or etched, painted or enameled, laminated, dalle de verre
Specialization: free hanging, painted
Price Range: $150 - $500 sq. ft.

★ MAYA RADOCZY

CONTEMPORARY ART GLASS
PO BOX 31422
SEATTLE, WA 98103-1422
FAX 206-524-9226
TEL 206-527-5022
Est. 1982
Products: doors and entrances, stabiles or suspended sculpture, walls, windows, work for the wall
Techniques: bent, fused or kiln-formed, blown, cast, leaded, pate de verre
Price Range: $200 - $300 sq. ft.

See page 55 for photographs and additional information.

RAMAZZINI ART GLASS

JUDITH RAMAZZINI
5252 N BAY RIDGE AVE
MILWAUKEE, WI 53217-5101
TEL 414-332-0710
Est. 1972
Products: windows, doors and entrances, sculpture, lamps and lighting fixtures, work for the wall
Techniques: copper-foiled, blown
Specialization: abstract lamps
Price Range: $100 - $500 sq. ft.

REFLECTIONS

DIANE TOOROIAN
7225 E SYLVANE DR
TUCSON, AZ 85710-5526
TEL 520-886-4063
Est. 1994
Products: windows, doors and entrances, gift items
Techniques: leaded, sandcarved or etched, copper-foiled, bent, fused or kiln-formed
Specialization: Southwest designs
Price Range: $65 - $300 sq. ft.

CATHY RICHARDSON

NATURE'S IMAGE STUDIO
1201 AIRPORT RD BLDG D
AMES, IA 50010-8289
TEL 515-232-4529
Est. 1986
Products: autonomous panels, doors and entrances, lamps or lighting fixtures, room dividers or screens, windows
Techniques: bent, fused or kiln-formed, beveled, copper-foiled, leaded, sandcarved or etched
Specialization: residential
Price Range: $80 - $300 sq. ft.

GUNDAR ROBEZ

GUNDAR ROBEZ STUDIOS
17837 HORSESHOE HILL RD
CALEDON, ON L0N 1C0
CANADA
FAX 905-660-7638
TEL 519-927-9396
Est. 1976
Products: autonomous panels, doors and entrances, skylights or domes, stabiles or suspended sculpture, windows
Techniques: beveled, laminated, leaded, neon, sandcarved or etched
Specialization: site-specific design
Price Range: $100 - $300 sq. ft.

ROHLF'S STAINED & LEADED GLASS STUDIO, INC.

PETER A. ROHLF
783 S 3RD AVE
MOUNT VERNON, NY 10550-4946
FAX 914-699-7091
TEL 800-969-4106
Est. 1920
Products: windows, doors and entrances, room dividers and screens, autonomous panels, skylights and domes
Techniques: leaded, sandcarved or etched, painted or enameled, dalle de verre, stained
Specialization: new design, restoration
Price Range: $50 - $500 sq. ft.

JOHN ROSE

ROSE DESIGN STUDIOS
1168 W 2ND AVE
EUGENE, OR 97402-4921
FAX 503-484-0325
TEL 503-342-6872
Est. 1974
Products: doors and entrances, lamps or lighting fixtures, tiles, windows, murals and bas relief
Techniques: bent, fused or kiln-formed, painted or enameled, leaded
Specialization: exquisite details
Price Range: $225/sq. ft.

ROWE STUDIOS ART GLASS, INC.

BRIAN ROWE
4768 SW 72ND AVE
MIAMI, FL 33155-4518
FAX 305-666-7212
TEL 305-666-5164
Est. 1973
Products: autonomous panels, doors and entrances, lamps or lighting fixtures, room dividers or screens, windows
Techniques: beveled, leaded, painted or enameled, sandcarved or etched, bent, fused or kiln-formed
Specialization: exotic beveling
Price Range: $200 - $800 sq. ft.

THE RUDY GLASS STUDIO

STEPHEN E. MITCHELL
15 E PHILADELPHIA ST
YORK, PA 17401-1131
FAX 717-846-1011
TEL 717-843-3345
Est. 1892
Products: autonomous panels, doors and entrances, furniture, lamps or lighting fixtures, others
Techniques: bent, fused or kiln-formed, beveled, copper-foiled, dalle de verre, laminated, others
Specialization: laminated art glass
Price Range: $10 - $200 sq. ft.

DAVID RUTH

GLASS SCULPTURE STUDIO
1122 57TH AVE
OAKLAND, CA 94621-4428
FAX 510-533-3102
TEL 510-533-8528
E-Mail: druth@holonet.net
Est. 1989
Products: room dividers and screens, autonomous panels, sculpture, walls, tables
Techniques: cast, bent, fused or kiln-formed
Specialization: cast-glass sculpture, panels
Price Range: $150 - $500 sq. ft.

JOHN ROSE

BARBARA SAULL

CREATIVE STAINED GLASS STUDIO
85 S UNION BLVD STE C
LAKEWOOD, CO 80228-2207
FAX 303-985-2668
TEL 303-988-0444
Est. 1973
Products: doors and entrances, lamps or lighting fixtures, room dividers or screens, tiles, windows
Techniques: bent, fused or kiln-formed, beveled, dalle de verre, leaded, sandcarved or etched
Price Range: $75 - $250 sq. ft.

ARNOLD SCHWARZBART

STUDIO OF ARNOLD SCHWARZBART
5200 BUCKHEAD TR
KNOXVILLE, TN 37919-8983
FAX 423-584-4181
TEL 423-588-6111
Est. 1981
Products: lamps and lighting fixtures
Techniques: sandcarved or etched, beveled
Specialization: Judaica

THE SEA PARROT

BOB & SUE RIOUX
PO BOX 1216
KENNEBUNKPORT, ME 04046-1216
TEL 207-967-5393
Est. 1978
Products: doors and entrances, room dividers or screens, windows
Techniques: bent, fused or kiln-formed, copper-foiled
Price Range: $150 - $500 sq. ft.

RANDY SEWELL

SEWELL STAINED GLASS
38 MUSCOGEE AVE NW
ATLANTA, GA 30305-3541
FAX 404-239-9045
TEL 404-239-9130
Est. 1975
Products: doors and entrances, room dividers or screens, windows, walls
Techniques: copper-foiled, laminated, leaded
Specialization: public commissions
Price Range: $100 - $300 sq. ft.

★ SHADETREE STUDIO

JOHN BOWE & PENNY KRISTO
417 HOWARD ST
PETOSKEY, MI 49770
FAX 616-347-4826
TEL 616-347-1011
Est. 1975
Products: autonomous room dividers, screen panels, lamps, sconces, doors, sidelights, skylights
Techniques: copper foil, leaded, painted, sandcarved, etched, bent, fused, beveled
Specialization: award-winning designs for churches, businesses, private residences
Price Range: $150 - $5,000 sq. ft.

See photograph page 271.

GLENN SHALAN

ARCHITECTURAL STAINED GLASS
54 HIGHWOOD TER
WEEHAWKEN, NJ 07087
TEL 201-392-9160
Est. 1982
Products: windows, doors and entrances, room dividers and screens, autonomous panels, skylights and domes
Techniques: leaded, sandcarved or etched, copper-foiled
Price Range: $100 - $300 sq. ft.

SHENANDOAH STUDIOS

1602 STRASBURG RD
FRONT ROYAL, VA 22630-1468
FAX 703-636-2413
TEL 800-950-1415
Est. 1980
Products: windows, room dividers and screens, autonomous panels, skylights and domes, tiles
Techniques: leaded, sandcarved or etched, beveled, painted or enameled, dalle de verre
Specialization: liturgical/restoration
Price Range: $40 and up sq. ft.

SHERICK, INC.

SHERRY & RICK MECH
12551 W 159TH ST
LOCKPORT, IL 60441-7845
FAX 708-301-2801
TEL 708-301-2800
Est. 1980
Products: windows, doors and entrances, autonomous panels, skylights and domes, walls
Techniques: leaded, sandcarved or etched, copper-foiled, beveled, painted or enameled
Specialization: carved, beveled, stained glass
Price Range: $60 - $400 sq. ft.

SIGSTEDT STUDIO

VAL SIGSTEDT
7433 FERRY RD
POINT PLEASANT, PA 18950-0263
FAX 215-297-8682
TEL 215-297-5924
Est. 1961
Products: windows, skylights and domes, lamps and lighting fixtures, murals and bas relief, ceilings
Techniques: leaded, copper-foiled, painted or enameled, pressed glass
Specialization: ceiling joins to murals
Price Range: $150 -$1,800 sq. ft.

JANE A. SKEETER

ULTRAGLAS® INC. & SKEETER STUDIOS INC.
9186 INDEPENDENCE AVE
CHATSWORTH, CA 91311-5902
FAX 818-772-8231
TEL 818-772-7744
Est. 1971
Products: doors and entrances, murals or bas relief, room dividers or screens, skylights or domes, windows, floors, sculpture
Techniques: bent, fused or kiln-formed, cast, sandcarved or etched, leaded
Price Range: $60 - $1,000 sq. ft.

★ SKYLINE DESIGN

CHARLES RIZZO
2653 W CHICAGO AVE
CHICAGO, IL 60622-4519
FAX 312-278-3548
TEL 312-278-4660
Est. 1982
Products: doors and entrances, room dividers or screens, sculpture, walls, windows
Techniques: sandcarved or etched, leaded, painted or enameled
Price Range: $5 - $150 sq. ft.

See pages 58-59 for photographs and additional information.

MARIE SNELL

14201 HART ST
OAK PARK, MI 48237-1179
TEL 810-399-8224
Est. 1977
Products: windows, doors and entrances, room dividers and screens, autonomous panels
Techniques: copper-foiled
Specialization: portraits
Price Range: $150 - $1,000 sq. ft.

TONI SOMMA-CAVALUZZI

BARDOT
599 ARMSTRONG AVE
STATEN ISLAND, NY 10308-1947
TEL 718-967-6777
Est. 1983
Products: windows, room dividers and screens, autonomous panels, work for the wall
Techniques: leaded, sandcarved or etched, copper-foiled, beveled
Price Range: $75 - $300 sq. ft.

SPARE MOMENTS STAINED GLASS

LISA MYERS
RR 1 BOX 100
SAINT AGATHA, ME 04772-9719
TEL 207-543-6150
Est. 1989
Products: autonomous panels, doors and entrances, lamps or lighting fixtures, windows, work for the wall
Techniques: bent, fused or kiln-formed, copper-foiled, leaded
Specialization: unique lighting
Price Range: $75 - $200 sq. ft.

★ MARIANNE SPOTTSWOOD

MAGUS
272 GLEN FARM RD
PORTSMOUTH, RI 02871
FAX 401-849-8741
TEL 401-849-6887
Est. 1980
Products: room dividers and screens, sculpture, lamps and lighting fixtures, murals and bas relief, furniture, light sculpture
Techniques: sandcarved or etched, painted or enameled, bent, fused or kiln-formed, cast, pate de verre, fusing metal in glass
Specialization: mobiles, fountains
Price Range: $100 - $2,000 sq. ft.

See photograph page 272.

STAIN IN THE GLASS

KEN DE ANGELIS
3180 NE MAPLE AVE
JENSEN BEACH, FL 34957-7277
FAX 407-225-6167
TEL 800-293-8920
Est. 1985
Products: autonomous panels, doors and entrances, room dividers or screens, skylights or domes, windows
Techniques: bent, fused or kiln-formed, beveled, copper-foiled, leaded, sandcarved or etched
Price Range: $35 - $250 sq. ft.

STAN HANSEN & ASSOCIATES

STANLEY C. HANSEN
42251 6TH ST
TEMECULA, CA 92590-1829
TEL 909-694-5507
Est. 1969
Products: doors and entrances, room dividers or screens, windows
Techniques: beveled, leaded, painted or enameled
Specialization: restoration
Price Range: $50 - $350 sq. ft.

★ PENELOPE COMFORT STARR

60 OLIVE AVE
SAN ANSELMO, CA 94960-2132
FAX 415-456-3698
TEL 415-456-9345
Est. 1967
Products: sculpture, fountains with lighting
Techniques: bent, fused or kiln-formed, beveled, sandcarved or etched, laminated, airbrushed
Specialization: fountains with lighting
Price Range: $100 - $400 sq. ft.

See photograph page 273.

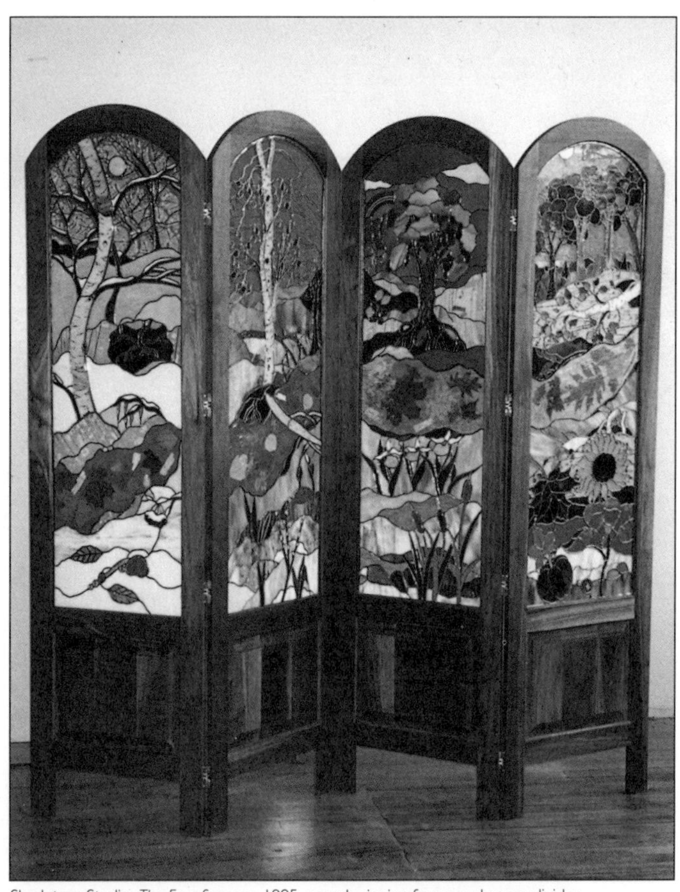

Shadetree Studio, *The Four Seasons*, 1995, award-winning four-panel room divider, 80"W x 72"H

ARCHITECTURAL GLASS

★ ARTHUR STERN

**ARTHUR STERN STUDIOS
ARCHITECTURAL GLASS
1075 JACKSON ST
BENICIA< CA 94510
TEL 707-745-8480**
Est. 1978
Products: doors and entrances, murals
or bas relief, room dividers or screens,
skylights and domes, windows
Techniques: leaded, beveled, engraved
Specialization: site-specific glass art
Price Range: $100 - $200 sq. ft.

**See pages 60-61 for photographs
and additional information.**

SUSAN STINSMUEHLEN-AMEND

IMPRESA, INC.
291 AVENIDA DEL RECREO
OJAI, CA 93023-9607
FAX 805-640-8313
TEL 805-640-0078
Est. 1973
Products: doors and entrances, room
dividers or screens, windows, work
for the wall, murals or bas relief
Techniques: leaded, painted or
enameled, mosaic
Specialization: versatile, original design
Price Range: minimum $250 sq. ft.

STUDIO ARTS & GLASS INC.

ROBERT L. JOLIET
1132 30TH ST NW
CANTON, OH 44709-2921
FAX 216-492-7751
TEL 216-492-7326
Est. 1982
Products: doors and entrances, skylights
or domes, walls, windows, ceilings
Techniques: bent, fused or kiln-formed,
beveled, leaded, sandcarved or etched,
painted
Specialization: custom designed leaded
Price Range: $50 - $500 sq. ft.

★ STUDIO ONE GLASS ART LTD.

**YVES TRUDEAU
341 W 6TH AVE
VANCOUVER, BC V5Y 1L1
CANADA
FAX 604-875-0601
TEL 604-875-0696**
Est. 1981
Products: doors and entrances, murals
or bas relief, sculpture, stabiles or
suspended sculpture, fountains
Techniques: bent, fused or kiln-formed,
dalle de verre, laminated, leaded,
sandcarved or etched
Price Range: $100 - $1,000 sq. ft.

**See page 64 for photographs
and additional information.**

SULLIVAN STAINED
GLASS STUDIO

JOHN SULLIVAN
3827 MAGAZINE ST
NEW ORLEANS, LA 70115-2638
TEL 504-895-6720
Est. 1978
Products: autonomous panels, lamps and
lighting fixtures, work for the wall, furni-
ture, stabiles and suspended sculpture
Techniques: beveled, leaded, sandcarved
or etched, copper-foiled, laminated
Price Range: $55 - $200 sq. ft.

NICK AND SANDRA SWEETMAN

THE GLASS ARTISAN
RR #2 MORRISON POINT RD
MILFORD, ON K0K 2P0
CANADA
TEL 613-476-7113
Est. 1978
Products: autonomous panels, doors
and entrances, lamps or lighting fixtures,
room dividers or screens, windows
Techniques: bent, fused or kiln-formed,
beveled, copper-foiled, laminated,
sandcarved or etched
Price Range: $150 - $250 sq. ft.

MIMI LAYNE TAWES

FIRELIGHT GLASS ART
201 2ND ST NW
CHARLOTTESVILLE, VA 22902-5012
TEL 804-295-7973
Est. 1979
Products: autonomous panels, doors
and entrances, lamps or lighting fixtures,
windows, room dividers
Techniques: bent, fused or kiln-formed,
beveled, copper-foiled, leaded, painted
or enameled
Price Range: $70 - $150 sq. ft.

VINCENT TAYLOR

VINCENT TAYLOR
ARCHITECTURAL ART GLASS
PO BOX 608
SONOMA, CA 95476-0608
TEL 707-996-8300
Est. 1970
Products: autonomous panels, doors
and entrances, furniture, room dividers
or screens, windows
Techniques: beveled, copper-foiled,
leaded, sandcarved or etched
Price Range: $150 - $350 sq. ft.

JULIO TEICH

4600 WAVERLY AVE
RICHMOND, VA 23231-1404
FAX 804-226-6121
TEL 804-226-8361
Est. 1955
Products: furniture, sculpture, stabiles or
suspended sculpture, walls, windows
Techniques: cast, glass blocks with metals
Price Range: $100 - $400 sq. ft.

ANA THIEL

COLEGIO MILITAR #1
SAN MIGUEL DE ALLENDE
GUANAJUATO, 37710
MEXICO
FAX 011-52-565-71092
TEL 011-52-415-23979
Est. 1981
Products: murals and bas relief, sculpture,
windows, fountains
Techniques: bent, fused or kiln-formed,
cast, sandcarved or etched, lamp worked
Specialization: architectural glass
Price Range: $100 - $500 sq. ft.

THOMAS MEYERS STUDIO

THOMAS MEYERS
163 OLD HANCOCK RD
ANTRIM, NH 03440-9705
TEL 603-588-2596
Est. 1975
Products: autonomous panels, doors and
entrances, windows, work for the wall,
murals
Techniques: laminated, leaded, reflective
mosaic
Specialization: custom architectural works
Price Range: $90 - $250 sq. ft.

STEPHANA TOOMEY, OP

EFHARISTO STUDIO, INC.
4900 WETHEREDSVILLE RD
BALTIMORE, MD 21207-6625
FAX 410-448-1711
TEL 410-448-1711
Est. 1989
Products: windows, doors and entrances,
room dividers and screens, autonomous
panels, murals and bas relief, work for
the wall
Techniques: leaded, copper-foiled,
beveled, dalle de verre
Specialization: liturgical, residential
Price Range: $150 and up sq. ft.

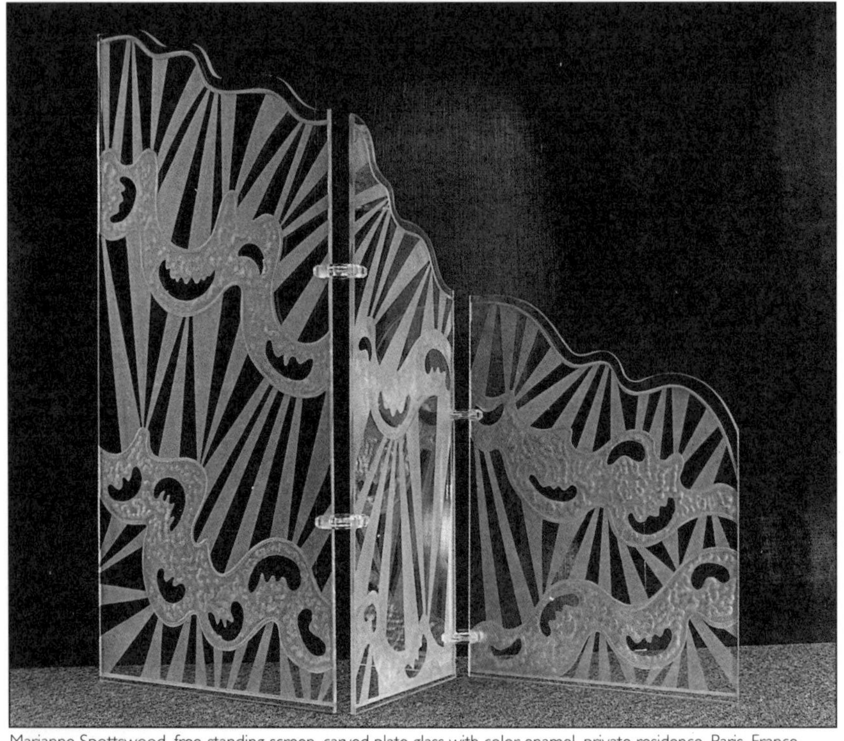

Marianne Spottswood, free-standing screen, carved plate glass with color enamel, private residence, Paris, France,
6'H x 10'W

INGE PAPE TRAMPLER

INGE PAPE STUDIO
23 DEL REY DR
MOUNT VERNON, NY 10552-1305
TEL 914-699-8616
Est. 1974
Products: autonomous panels, doors and entrances, sculpture, skylights or domes, windows
Techniques: leaded, copper-foiled, painted or enameled, laminated, dalle de verre
Specialization: liturgical, restoration
Price Range: $125 - $425 sq. ft.

ANGELIKA TRAYLOR

100 POINCIANA DR
INDIAN HARBOUR BEACH, FL 32937-4437
FAX 407-779-3612
TEL 407-773-7640
Est. 1980
Products: autonomous panels, doors and entrances, lamps or lighting fixtures, skylights or domes, windows
Techniques: copper-foiled, leaded, painted or enameled
Specialization: residential one-of-a-kind
Price Range: $250 - $1250 sq. ft.

UTOPIAN ARTS, INC.

NOEL LAUE
16261 WOODS VALLEY RD
VALLEY CENTER, CA 92082
TEL 619-749-7590
Products: doors and entrances, room dividers and screens, skylights and domes, windows, lamps and lighting fixtures
Techniques: leaded, sandcarved or etched, copper-foiled, cast, blown
Specialization: hot-worked elements
Price Range: $50 - $750 sq. ft.

★ KENNETH F. vonROENN, JR.

ARCHITECTURAL GLASS ART, INC.
1110 BAXTER AVE
LOUISVILLE, KY 40204-1649
FAX 502-585-2808
TEL 502-585-5421
Est. 1892
Products: doors and entrances, lamps or lighting fixtures, skylights or domes, walls, windows
Techniques: bent, fused or kiln-formed, beveled, laminated, leaded, sandcarved or etched
Specialization: custom design
Price Range: $100 - $250 sq. ft.

See page 37 for photographs and additional information.

DICK WEISS

CIRCLE W STAINED GLASS
811 N 36TH ST
SEATTLE, WA 98103-8806
TEL 206-632-8873
Est. 1975
Products: windows, doors and entrances, room dividers and screens, autonomous panels, sculpture
Techniques: leaded, painted or enameled, blown
Specialization: stained glass
Price Range: $125 - $600 sq. ft.

WENDY GORDON GLASS STUDIO

WENDY GORDON
PO BOX 878
STEVENSVILLE, MD 21666-0878
FAX 410-643-1493
TEL 410-643-1123
Est. 1980
Products: doors and entrances, murals or bas relief, room dividers or screens, windows, work for the wall
Techniques: bent, fused or kiln-formed, beveled, leaded, neon, sandcarved or etched
Price Range: $75 - $300 sq. ft.

ROBBI WHIPP

ROBBI WHIPP DESIGNS
2335 SKYLINE BLVD
RENO, NV 89509-5162
TEL 702-826-5275
Est. 1983
Products: autonomous panels, doors and entrances, windows
Techniques: bent, fused or kiln-formed, laminated, leaded, painted or enameled
Specialization: residential
Price Range: $85 - $250 sq. ft.

MARY BAYARD WHITE

MARY WHITE DESIGN
1793 12 ST
OAKLAND, CA 94607-1437
FAX 510-832-7002
TEL 510-832-7002
Products: windows, doors and entrances, room dividers and screens, sculpture
Techniques: sandcarved or etched, painted or enameled, bent, fused or kiln-formed
Specialization: representational images
Price Range: $80 - $200 sq. ft.

DAVID WILDE

SMITH & WILDE GLASS STUDIO
RR#2
HOLSTEIN, ON N0G 2A0
CANADA
FAX 519-334-3195
TEL 519-334-3119
Est. 1980
Products: windows, doors and entrances, room dividers and screens, autonomous panels, sculpture
Techniques: leaded, sandcarved or etched, painted or enameled
Specialization: vanguard designs
Price Range: $150 - $500 sq. ft.

WILLIAMS ART GLASS STUDIO, INC.

RICHARD WILLIAMS
KAREN WILLIAMS
22 N WASHINGTON ST
OXFORD, MI 48371-4665
FAX 810-628-5238
TEL 810-628-1111
Est. 1981
Products: windows, doors and entrances, autonomous panels, skylights and domes, free-standings carvings
Techniques: leaded, sandcarved or etched, beveled, neon, zinc
Specialization: original design
Price Range: $100 - $600 sq. ft.

WILMARK STUDIOS, INC.

MARK LIEBOWITZ
177 S MAIN ST
PEARL RIVER, NY 10965-2446
FAX 914-735-0172
TEL 914-735-7443
Est. 1979
Products: doors and entrances, room dividers or screens, skylights or domes, windows, fabrication facility
Techniques: dalle de verre, leaded, painted or enameled, etched
Specialization: repairs and restoration
Price Range: $75 - $350 sq. ft.

★ DAVID WILSON

DAVID WILSON DESIGN
RR 2 BOX 121A
SOUTH NEW BERLIN, NY 13843-9508
FAX 607-334-7065
TEL 607-334-3015
Est. 1979
Products: doors and entrances, room dividers or screens, skylights or domes, windows
Techniques: beveled, laminated, leaded, painted or enameled, sandcarved or etched
Price Range: $150 - $250 sq. ft.

See page 65 for photographs and additional information.

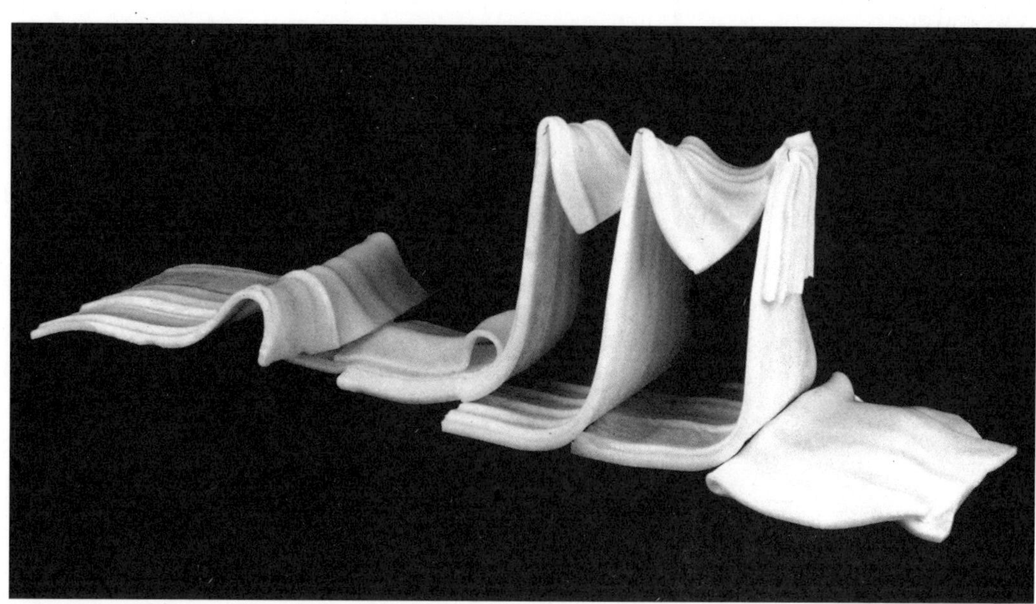

Penelope Comfort Starr, maquette for proposed sculpture in performing arts center, resin, fiberglass, concrete, finished size 6' x 15' x 4', photo: Jay Graham

BARNEY ZEITZ

BARNEY ZEITZ STAINED GLASS
RFD 595A
VINEYARD HAVEN, MA 02568
TEL 508-693-9421
Est. 1972
Products: windows, doors and entrances,
room dividers and screens, autonomous
panels, lamps and lighting fixtures
Techniques: leaded, bent, fused or
kiln-formed, laminated
Specialization: liturgical, fused, bonded
Price Range: $200 - $1,000 sq. ft.

★ **LARRY ZGODA**

LARRY ZGODA STUDIO
415 W NORTH AVE
CHICAGO, IL 60610-1117
FAX 312-943-9987
TEL 312-943-9978
Est. 1978
Products: windows, doors and entrances,
room dividers or screens, sculpture,
furniture inserts
Techniques: beveled, leaded
Specialization: stained glass design
Price Range: $150 - $400 sq. ft.

**See pages 66-67 for photographs
and additional information.**

FRANK ZIKA

ZIKA ARCHITECTURAL GLASS
141 CUESTA DR
SAN LUIS OBISPO, CA 93405
TEL 805-549-8125
Est. 1992
Products: windows, doors and entrances,
room dividers and screens, autonomous
panels, sculpture, walls
Techniques: bent, fused or kiln-formed,
insulated
Specialization: large-tempered panels
Price Range: $65 - $180 sq. ft.

ZSIBA SMOLOVER

MAURA SMOLOVER
10 STERLING PL
NEW MILFORD, CT 06776
FAX 203-354-9294
TEL   203-354-5221
Est. 1982
Products: windows, doors and entrances,
skylights and domes, murals and bas
relief, tiles
Techniques: sandcarved or etched,
beveled, painted or enameled, bent,
fused or kiln-formed, laminated, cast
Price Range: $85 - $375 sq. ft.

GLOSSARY OF TERMS

THIS GLOSSARY DEFINES TERMS AS THEY ARE COMMONLY USED TODAY.
THIS IS NOT ALWAYS CONSISTENT WITH THE HISTORICAL DEFINITION.

Antique Glass — glass which is mouth blown into a cylinder, scored along its length, reheated and allowed to flatten into a sheet. The term 'antique' describes the method by which the glass was made, not its age.

Beveled Glass — plate glass that has had its perimeter ground and polished at an angle.

Came — the extruded H-shaped channel which is fitted around individual pieces of glass so that they can be assembled into a panel. Came can be made of lead, zinc, brass or copper. Pronounced like 'name.'

Carved Glass — glass that has been deeply sandblasted to different depths. Also called 'stage blasted.'

Cathedral Glass — glass which is composed of the same ingredients as antique glass, but is rolled or formed in a machine to a uniform texture.

Cast Glass — glass, molten, that has been poured into a mold and allowed to anneal as a shaped form.

Copper Foil Method — a process whereby each piece of glass is wrapped on all edges with strips of copper foil (similar to tin foil). The edges are butted and a bead of solder is laid down on both sides of the piece forming a rigid H channel. This is a process most often used in lamp shades.

Dalle de Verre — a process of assembling panels in which very thick shaped pieces of glass are held together by pouring epoxy resin or cement around the individual pieces. Sometimes called slab glass or faceted glass.

Etched Glass — the process of abrading the surface of glass either with hydrofluoric acid or by sandblasting, resulting in a frosted look.

Fused Glass — glass that has been heated in a kiln to the point where two separate pieces are permanently joined as one without losing their individual color.

Kiln-Formed Glass — flat glass that has been heated enough to cause it to slump or sag over a mold, giving it a sculptural, bas-relief effect. Also called 'slumped' or 'bent' glass.

Leaded Glass — panels composed of individual pieces of glass cut to conform to a pattern (cartoon) and assembled with came.

Laminated — multiple layers of glass permanently bonded to each other.

Painted Glass — glass that has been painted with special paints and then fired so that the paint becomes a permanent part of the glass.

Pate de Verre — a type of cast glass utilizing a glass 'paste' that is mixed, heated, poured into a mold, annealed or cooled, and ultimately freed from the mold. Similar to cast sculpture.

Wheel Engraving — glass that has had 'gouges' carved into its face by holding it against assorted vertical wheels. Cut glass decanters or stemware are wheel engraved. Also called "brilliant cutting."

LEONARDO ACOSTA

BAJA WEST
180 MACE ST STE C10
CHULA VISTA, CA 91911-5878
FAX 619-476-9146
TEL 619-422-9081
TEL 619-427-2624
Est. 1979
Products: furniture, lighting and candelabras, gates, beds, drapery rods
Process: casting, hand forging, hand carving
Media: iron, bronze, aluminum
Specialization: aluminum furniture
Price Range/Horiz. Ft.: $100 - $300
Item Price Range: $100 - $500 for lamps

★ LUCI ALLEN

LUCI ALLEN COPPER SCULPTURE
1 S BARN HILL RD
BLOOMFIELD, CT 06002
TEL 203-242-8001
Est. 1983
Products: sculpture, wall pieces, masks, sculpted watering cans
Process: fabricating, repoussé, brazed constuction
Media: brass
Specialization: detailed garden vanes
Item Price Range: $200 - $26,000 for garden weathervanes

See photograph this page.

ALI AMERCUPAN

GLEN CANYON FORGE
390 GLEN CANYON RD
SANTA CRUZ, CA 95060
FAX 408-459-7542
TEL 408-459-7542
Est. 1987
Products: furniture, lighting and candelabras, sculpture, wall pieces, weathervanes, wrought iron tables
Process: hand forging, fabricating, machining, repoussé
Media: iron, stainless steel, brass
Specialization: sculpture
Price Range/Horiz. Ft.: $75 - $150
Item Price Range: $1,000 to $5,000 for forged iron tables with marble tops

AMERICAN ART FORGE

THOMAS SHEETS
161 MANGUM ST SW #400
ATLANTA, GA 30313
TEL 404-584-9979
Est. 1971
Products: gates and railings, sculpture, furniture, furnishings
Process: hand forging, fabricating, machine forging
Media: iron
Specialization: forged, wrought goods
Price Range/Horiz. Ft.: $100 - $1,000
Item Price Range: $350 - $8,000 for custom tables and furnishings

ARCHITECTURAL IRONWORKS

STANLEY WINKLER
175 S THIRD ST
SAINT GENEVIEVE, MO 63670
TEL 314-883-7670
FAX 314-883-7670
Est. 1980
Products: gates and railings, furniture, lighting and candelabras, grilles and screens, fences
Process: hand forging, fabricating, machining
Media: bronze, mild steel, copper
Price Range/Horiz. Ft.: $100 - $750
Item Price Range: $2,500 - $10,000 for gates

★ STEVE AUSTIN

AUSTIN'S IRON WORKS
44 NE 69 HWY
KANSAS CITY, MO 64119
FAX 816-454-2680
TEL 816-454-7736
Est. 1973
Products: gates and railings, grilles and screens, fences, motorized-drive gates
Process: hand forging, fabricating, machining
Media: iron, mild steel, bronze
Specialization: drive gate, fence packages
Price Range/Horiz. Ft.: $120 - $1,500
Item Price Range: $300 - $1,200 for motorized drive gates

See photograph page 276.

CHRIS AXELSSON

AXELSSON METALSMITH
PO BOX 222598
CARMEL, CA 93922-2598
FAX 408-624-3940
TEL 408-624-3909
Est. 1979
Products: gates and railings, furniture, lighting and candelabras, sculpture, grilles and screens
Process: fabricating, hand forging
Media: bronze, copper, iron
Specialization: traditional and contemporary
Price Range/Horiz. Ft.: $150 - $950
Item Price Range: $2,500 average for tables, walk gates

BLACK ROSE FORGE

GREG CAMPBELL
12615 VEIRS MILL RD
ROCKVILLE, MD 20853-3534
FAX 301-946-4605
TEL 301-946-4605
Est. 1981
Products: furniture, gates and railings, sculpture, wall pieces lighting and chandeliers
Process: fabricating, hand forging, casting
Media: bronze, copper, mild steel
Price Range/Horiz. Ft.: $200 - $700

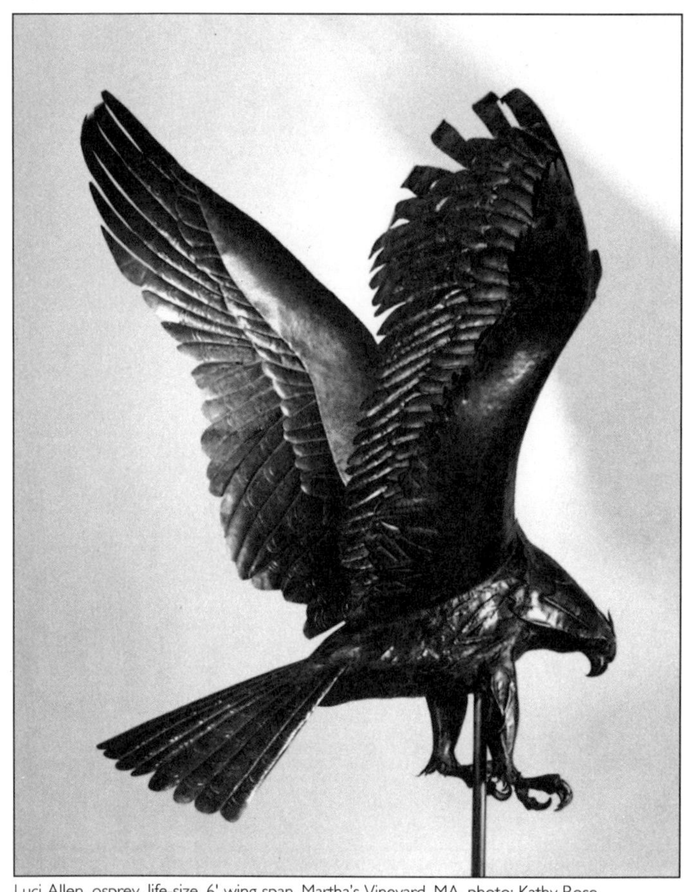

Luci Allen, osprey, life-size, 6' wing span, Martha's Vineyard, MA, photo: Kathy Rose

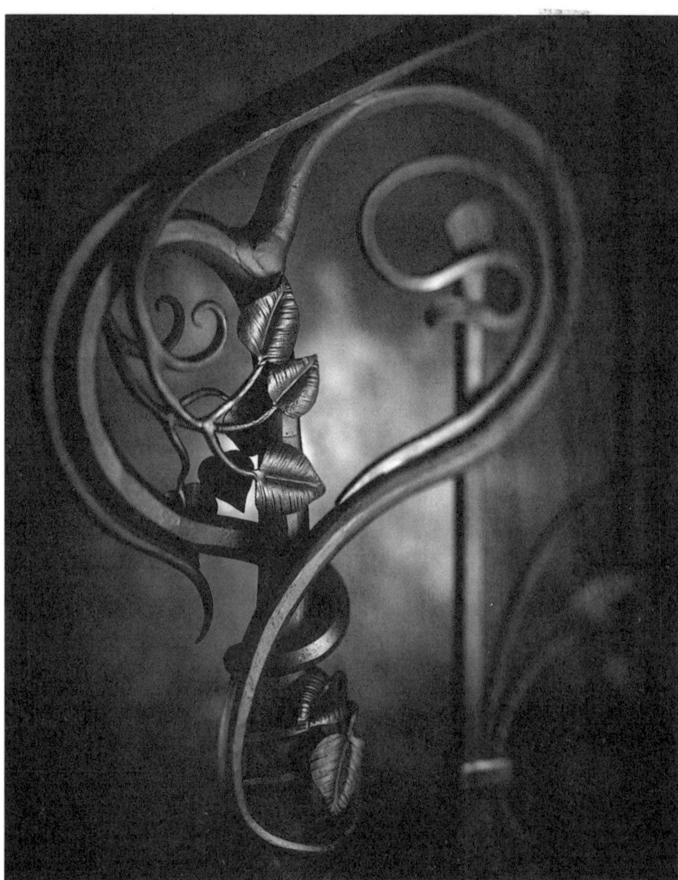

Steve Austin, nouveau railing terminal post, 1995, acid-washed finish over mild steel, forged and fabricated assembly, top frame is triangular bundling of three pieces of ¾" round bar

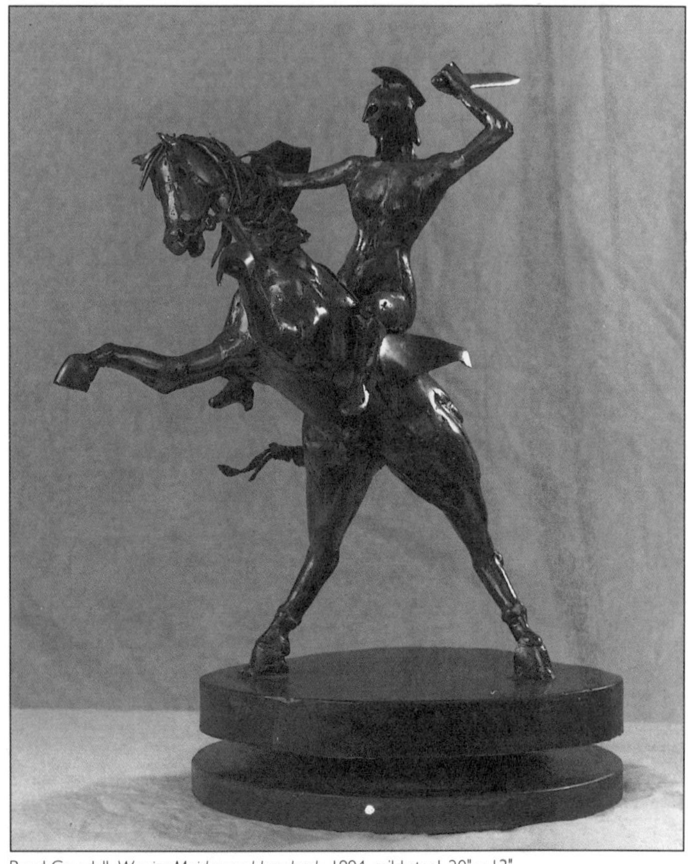

Reed Crandall, *Warrior Maiden on Horseback*, 1994, mild steel, 20" x 13"

BOB'S ORNAMENTAL IRON STUDIO, INC.

BOB FOUST
734 SOUTHWEST BLVD
KANSAS CITY, KS 66103-1924
FAX 913-236-5320
TEL 913-236-4444
Est. 1954
Products: furniture, gates and railings, grilles and screens, lighting and candelabras, fences
Process: fabricating, hand forging, repoussé
Media: iron, brass, aluminum
Specialization: custom designed metal work
Price Range/Horiz. Ft.: $225 - $800

MARK BOKENKAMP

BOKENKAMP'S FORGE
10132 LIBERTY RD S
POWELL, OH 43065-9302
TEL 614-889-0819
Est. 1974
Products: architectural hardware, gates and railings, grilles and screens
Process: fabricating, hand forging
Media: brass, copper, iron
Price Range/Horiz. Ft.: $250 - $1,000

★ MICHAEL BONDI

MICHAEL BONDI METAL DESIGN
2801 GIANT RD
RICHMOND, CA 94806-2246
FAX 510-236-2615
TEL 510-236-2607
Est. 1980
Products: gates and railings, grilles and screens, architectural hardware, doors, stairs
Process: hand forging, fabricating, repoussé
Media: iron, bronze, monel, copper
Specialization: contemporary forgings
Price Range/Horiz. Ft.: $200 - $1,200
Item Price Range: $500 - $50,000 for doors

See page 23 for photographs and additional information.

JOSEPH A. BONIFAS

BLACK OAK FORGE
9090 SPENCERVILLE RD
SPENCERVILLE, OH 45887
TEL 419-647-6598
Est. 1980
Products: furniture, gates and railings, wall pieces, lighting and candelabras, sculpture
Process: fabricating, hand forging, repoussé
Media: bronze, mild steel, stainless steel
Specialization: site-specific pieces
Price Range/Horiz. Ft.: $200 - $1,200

BRADLEY METAL DESIGN, INC.

BRAD SILBERBERG
9172B BROOKVILLE RD
SILVER SPRING, MD 20910-1808
FAX 301-589-1575
TEL 301-589-7828
Est. 1986
Products: fireplace hardware, furniture, gates and railings, grilles and screens, lighting and candelabras
Process: fabricating, hand forging, machining
Media: brass, iron, stainless steel
Specialization: forged plant forms
Price Range/Horiz. Ft.: $250 - $1,000

BRANDELL STUDIOS, INC.

KIM BRANDELL
1718 BAY RD
MIAMI BEACH, FL 33139-1414
FAX 305-532-7446
TEL 305-531-3499
Est. 1974
Products: gates and railings, lighting and candelabras, sculpture, wall pieces, doors
Process: fabricating, hand forging, repoussé
Media: aluminum, brass, copper, stainless steel, iron
Specialization: casino, restaurant, commercial
Price Range/Horiz. Ft.: $500 - $1,500

JACK BRUBAKER

BRUBAKER DESIGNS
2900 S SHEPHERD RD
NASHVILLE, IN 47448-9086
FAX 812-988-7830
TEL 812-988-7830
Est. 1970
Products: furniture, lighting and candelabras, sculpture, architectural hardware, wall pieces
Process: hand forging, fabricating
Media: iron, brass, bronze, aluminum
Specialization: creative accessories

★ NICHOLAS B. BRUMDER

BRUMDER ORNAMENTAL IRON, INC.
40128 INDUSTRIAL PARK CIR
GEORGETOWN, TX 78626-4707
FAX 512-869-0140
TEL 512-869-2830
Est. 1979
Products: gates and railings, lighting and candelabras, grilles and screens, architectural hardware, wineracks
Process: hand forging, fabricating, repoussé
Media: iron, brass, copper
Specialization: European Techniques
Price Range/Horiz. Ft.: $125 - $800

See page 24 for photographs and additional information.

KATE BURKE

KATE BURKE STUDIO
767 LEESBURG STATION
VOLANT, PA 16156
FAX 412-533-5546
TEL 412-533-5546
Products: wall pieces, plaques, manhole covers
Process: casting
Media: iron, bronze
Specialization: manhole covers
Item Price Range: $1,000 - $5,000 for manhole cover

PETER CASSIDY

CASSIDY BROS. FORGE, INC.
U.S. Route One
ROWLEY, MA 01969
FAX 508-948-7629
TEL 508-948-7303
Est. 1967
Products: fences, gates and railings, grilles and screens
Process: fabricating, hand forging
Media: aluminum, bronze, cast and forged iron
Price Range/Horiz. Ft.: $100 - $400

LOWELL CHAPUT

LOWELL CHAPUT METALSMITH
5677 REDWOOD DR #E
ROHNERT PARK, CA 94928
FAX 707-586-0438
TEL 707-586-1324
Est. 1981
Products: gates and railings, lighting and candelabras, architectural hardware, doors, furnishings
Process: hand forging, fabricating
Media: iron, bronze, copper
Specialization: classical to contemporary
Price Range/Horiz. Ft.: $200 - $1,000

E.A. CHASE

201 FERN ST
SANTA CRUZ, CA 95060-2119
TEL 408-423-3188
Products: gates and railings, furniture, sculpture, grilles and screens, architectural hardware
Process: hand forging
Media: iron, stainless steel, bronze copper, brass, monel
Price Range/Horiz. Ft.: $300 - $1,000
Item Price Range: $8,000 - $100,000 for gates

CHRISTOPHER T. RAY STUDIOS

CHRISTOPHER T. RAY
PO BOX 44128
PHILADELPHIA, PA 19144-0428
FAX 215-438-3477
TEL 215-438-7129
Est. 1960
Products: furniture, gates and railings, sculpture
Process: fabricating, hand forging, machining
Media: bronze, iron, aluminum
Specialization: sculpture and gates
Price Range/Horiz. Ft.: $350 - $900

JIM COLLINS

JIM COLLINS STUDIO
201 N PALISADES DR
SIGNAL MT, TN 37377
TEL 615-886-3340
Est. 1983
Products: gates and railings, furniture, sculpture, doors, weathervanes
Process: casting, fabricating
Media: stainless steel, bronze, aluminum
Specialization: figurative sculpture
Item Price Range: $3,000 - $48,000 for sculpture

★ REED CRANDALL

CRANDALL'S CREATIONS
RT 2 BOX 2211
CLARKESVILLE, GA 30523
FAX 706-754-7003
TEL 706-754-9123
Est. 1993
Products: gates and railings, furniture, sculpture, weathervanes
Process: fabricating, welding
Media: stainless steel, bronze, mild steel
Specialization: kinetic sculpture
Item Price Range: $2,500 - $38,000 for sculpture

See photograph page 276.

CRISTOFER'S CREATIONS

CRISTOFER AVEN, MS - METALSMITH
659 MORVA CT
HAYWOOD, CA 94541-1826
FAX 510-278-4941
TEL 510-278-4941
Est. 1984
Products: sculpture, architectural hardware, custom designs
Process: casting
Media: brass, silver/gold plated
Specialization: sculpted faces
Item Price Range: $250 - $500 for small shrines, drawer pulls

CUSTOM DESIGN METAL ARTS

BILL ROBERTS
3740 NE 40TH PL #C
OCALA, FL 34479-2229
FAX 904-351-5512
TEL 904-351-5512
Est. 1984
Products: gates and railings, furniture, lighting and candelabras, sculpture, wall pieces, functional art
Process: hand forging, casting, repoussé
Media: bronze, mild steel, aluminum
Specialization: beds w/ mixed metals, lighting
Item Price Range: $750 - $4,000 for headboards, 4-posters

DAN SIGLAR, BLACKSMITH

ARCHITECTURAL METALWORK
315 LAWN AVE
KANSAS CITY, MO 64124-2113
TEL 816-231-6633
Est. 1987
Products: doors, gates and railings, grilles and screens, lighting and candelabras, custom furniture
Process: fabricating, hand forging, repoussé
Media: bronze, copper, iron
Specialization: interior handrails
Price Range/Horiz. Ft.: $100 - $2,000

DONNA DENNIS

TUNNELS & TOWERS, INC.
131 DUANE ST
NEW YORK, NY 10013-3850
FAX 212-233-0605
TEL 212-233-0605
Est. 1985
Products: gates and railings, grilles and screens, architectural hardware, fences
Process: fabricating
Media: iron, stainless steel
Specialization: public art fences

★ PAUL DiFRANCESCO

LIGHTNING FORGE
229 W 4885 S
MURRAY, UT 84107
FAX 801-268-1869
TEL 801-268-1838
Est. 1980
Products: gates and railings, lighting and candelabras, architectural hardware, fences, furnishings
Process: hand forging, casting, fabricating
Media: stainless steel, mild steel, aluminum
Specialization: unique railings, furnishings
Price Range/Horiz. Ft.: $75 - $400

See photograph below.

ROBERT DONNOE

504 SPRING MEADOWS
VINCENNES, IN 47591
FAX 812-882-1351
TEL 812-882-1351
Est. 1971
Products: sculpture
Process: fabricating
Media: stainless steel, mild steel
Specialization: abstract constructivism
Item Price Range: $7,000 - $30,000 for large outdoor sculpture

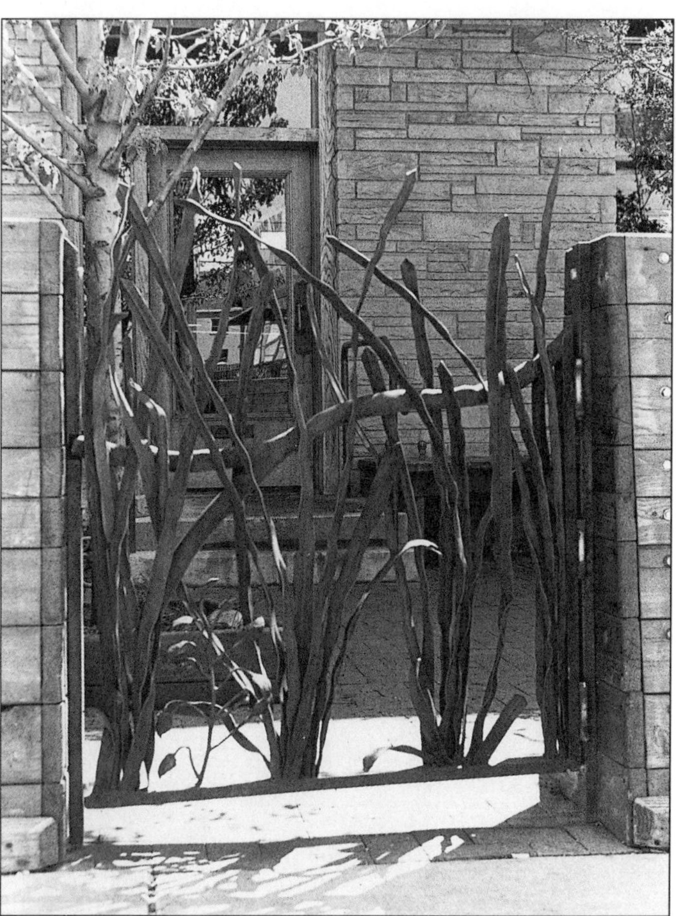

Paul Di Francesco, *Tall Grass Gate*, entrance to garden dining area, Salt Lake Roasting Co., hot and cold forged steel

ARCHITECTURAL METAL

EUROPEAN IRON WORKS

JEAN-PIERRE MASBANJI
420 CAMINO DEL REMEDIO
SANTA BARBARA, CA 93110-1345
TEL 805-967-8076
Est. 1986
Products: gates and railings, grilles and
screens, lighting and candelabras, doors,
furniture
Process: fabricating, hand forging,
repoussé
Media: brass, bronze, iron
Specialization: hand-forged arch. interior
Price Range/Horiz. Ft.: $300 - $1,500

★ PETER M. FILLERUP

WILD WEST DESIGNS
PO BOX 286
HEBER CITY, UT 84032
FAX 801-654-1653
TEL 801-654-4151
Products: gates and railings, lighting
and candelabras, sculpture, grilles and
screens, architectural hardware
Process: casting, fabricating, machining
Media: bronze, aluminum
Specialization: sculpture lighting
Item Price Range: $900 - $25,000
for chandeliers, sculptures

See photograph below.

FINE ARCHITECTURAL METALSMITHS

ED MACK/RHODA WEBER MACK
PO BOX 30
CHESTER, NY 10918-0030
FAX 914-651-7857
TEL 914-651-7550
Est. 1978
Products: fences, furniture, gates and
railings, grilles and screens, entrance
doors
Process: fabricating, hand forging,
repoussé
Media: iron, bronze, copper
Specialization: forged driveway gates
Price Range/Horiz. Ft.: $250 - $1,200

★ BRUCE PAUL FINK

SCULPTURE STUDIO/FOUNDRY
90 POLE BRIDGE RD
WOODSTOCK, CT 06281
FAX 203-474-0130
TEL 203-474-0130
Est. 1961
Products: sculpture, wall pieces,
functional sculpture
Process: casting, fabricating, spray
metalizing
Media: bronze, aluminum, resin-bonded
marble
Specialization: general sculpture

**See page 25 for photographs
and additional information.**

FISCHER ARTWORKS

BRIAN FISCHER
6530 S WINDERMERE ST
LITTLETON, CO 80120-3202
FAX 303-795-8805
TEL 303-798-4841
Products: weathervanes, finials, lightning
rods
Process: fabricating, casting, spinning
Media: copper, bronze
Specialization: roof ornamentation
Price Range/Horiz. Ft.: $14 - $44, roof
cresting
Item Price Range: $100 - $520 for finials
& spires, custom design service

DAVID FLAHARTY

1064 MAGAZINE RD
GREEN LANE, PA 18054-2232
FAX 215-234-8242
TEL 215-234-8242
Products: gates and railings, sculpture,
grilles and screens, wall pieces, doors
Process: casting, fabricating, machining
Media: iron, bronze, aluminum
Specialization: ornamental metals
Price Range/Horiz. Ft.: $300 - $750

DOUGLAS OLMSTED FREEMAN

**DOUG FREEMAN SCULPTURE
  STUDIO**
310 N 2ND ST
MINNEAPOLIS, MN 55401-1311
FAX 612-339-7150
TEL 612-339-7150
Products: sculpture, grilles and screens,
architectural hardware, lighting, archi-
tectural bronze
Process: casting, fabricating
Media: stainless steel, bronze
Specialization: cast bronze

**See pages 182-183 for photographs
and additional information.**

JEFFREY FUNK

SCULPTURE IN FORGED
  METALS/RIVER BEND FORGE
280 RIVER BEND RD
BIG FORK, MT 59911
TEL 406-837-4208
Products: gates and railings, sculpture,
fireplace hardware, public sculpture
Process: hand forging, fabricating,
repoussé
Media: iron, stainless steel, bronze
Specialization: public sculpture on
commission
Item Price Range: $3,000 - $50,000
for sculpture and gates

DIMITRI GERAKARIS

SCULPTURAL & ARCHITECTURAL
  METALWORK
BOX 928G
CANAAN, NH 03741
TEL 603-523-7366
Est. 1971
Products: grilles and screens, sculpture,
wall pieces
Process: fabricating, hand forging
Media: bronze, iron
Price Range/Horiz. Ft.: $200 - $1,000

GILMORE METALSMITHING STUDIO

GLENN F. GILMORE
PO BOX 57
BRASSTOWN, NC 28902-0057
FAX 704-837-4326
TEL 704-837-4326
Est. 1974
Products: architectural hardware,
fireplace hardware, furniture, gates
and railings, lighting and candelabras
Process: fabricating, hand forging,
machining
Media: bronze, copper, iron
Specialization: visually pleasing work
Price Range/Horiz. Ft.: $150 - $1,000

JOHN GRANEY

JOHN GRANEY METAL DESIGN
7 NORTH AVE
GARWOOD, NJ 07027-1116
FAX 908-789-7606
TEL 908-789-8500
Est. 1978
Products: gates and railings, lighting
and candelabras, grilles and screens
Process: fabricating, hand forging,
repoussé
Media: bronze, copper, iron, brass, mild
steel
Specialization: the difficult or unusual job
Price Range/Horiz. Ft.: $90 - $1,200
Item Price Range: $300 - $25,000 for
furniture

EDWIN R. GROVE

RR 1 BOX 527
BROWNFIELD, ME 04010-9736
TEL 207-935-2262
Est. 1950
Products: architectural hardware,
fireplace hardware, gates and railings,
grilles and screens, weathervanes
Process: fabricating, hand forging
Media: iron, mild steel
Price Range/Horiz. Ft.: $200 - $1,000

ROBB GUNTER "THE FORGERY"

CUSTOM FORGED IRON &
  SCHOOL OF BLACKSMITHING
13 IMNAHA RD
TIJERAS, NM 87059-7830
TEL 505-281-8080
Est. 1980
Products: architectural hardware,
fireplace hardware, furniture, gates
and railings, lighting and candelabras
Process: fabricating, hand forging,
repoussé copper
Media: copper, iron, stainless steel
Price Range/Horiz. Ft.: $80 - $1,600

Peter Fillerup, *Steamboat*, 1990, maquette, bronze, 48"H, reproduced as a monument, 16'H

PETER HAPPNY

PETER HAPNEY, BLACKSMITH
66 ROCK ST
PORTSMOUTH, NH 03801-3915
TEL 603-436-4859
Est. 1972
Products: architectural hardware, doors, fences, fireplace hardware, furniture, others
Process: fabricating, hand forging, repoussé
Media: brass, bronze, copper, others
Specialization: 3-D sculptural lighting
Price Range/Horiz. Ft.: $75 - $1,500

HARMONY FORGE

WARD BRINEGAR/JIM PEPPERL
1240F CALLE DE COMERCIO
SANTA FE, NM 87505-3125
TEL 505-471-3745
Est. 1977
Products: gates and railings, lighting and candelabras, grilles and screens, architectural hardware, fireplace hardware
Process: hand forging, fabricating
Media: iron, mild steel, copper
Price Range/Horiz. Ft.: $250 - $750
Item Price Range: $3,000 - $20,000 for gates

★ HARMONY WIND HARPS

R. SUNDHARA BARRABLE
PO BOX 3039
PAGOSA SPRINGS, CO 81147-3039
FAX 970-264-2962
TEL 970-264-2962
Est. 1980
Products: sculpture, wind harps and sound gardens
Process: casting, fabricating, machining
Media: bronze, stainless steel, titanium
Specialization: sound acoustic sculpture
Item Price Range: $6,000 - $60,000 for outdoor wind-harp sculpture

See page 145 for photographs and additional information.

JACK HASTINGS

HASTINGS + ENDE DESIGN PARTNERS
PO BOX 3333
SEWANEE, TN 37375-3333
TEL 615-598-0660
Products: sculpture, wall pieces, grilles and screens, lighting, mobiles, windvanes
Process: fabricating, machining, painted, permanent colors
Media: stainless steel, aluminum, copper
Specialization: unique works on commission
Item Price Range: $400 - $4,000 for various products

★ HISTORICAL ARTS & CASTING, INC.

RUTH B. EDWARDS
5580 W BAGLEY PARK RD
WEST JORDAN, UT 84088-5697
FAX 801-280-2493
TEL 801-280-2400
Products: gates and railings, lighting and candelabras, grilles and screens, doors, fences
Process: casting, fabricating
Media: iron, bronze, aluminum
Specialization: custom work, restoration
Price Range/Horiz. Ft.: $250 - $2,000
Item Price Range: $400 - $10,000 for lighting (excluding chandeliers)

See page 26 for photographs and additional information.

★ LINDA HOWARD

527 72ND ST
HOLMES BEACH, FL 34217
TEL 813-739-9228
Products: sculpture, wall pieces
Process: fabricating
Media: aluminum
Specialization: outdoor sculpture
Item Price Range: $15,000 - $150,000 for sculpture

See page 242 for photograph.

MILES D. HUFFMAN

UNIONTOWN FORGE
1538 NW WEST UNION RD
TOPEKA, KS 66615
TEL 913-256-4015
Products: lighting and candelabras, grilles and screens, architectural hardware, fireplace hardware, weathervanes
Process: hand forging, repoussé
Media: brass, mild steel, copper
Specialization: traditional design
Item Price Range: $200 - $1,200 for window grilles

BRIAN HUGHES

PO BOX 10033
PRESCOTT, AZ 86304-0033
TEL 602-275-7680
Est. 1976
Products: gates and railings, furniture, lighting and candelabras, sculpture, grilles and screens
Process: hand forging
Media: iron, copper
Specialization: sculpture
Price Range/Horiz. Ft.: $100 - $700
Item Price Range: $100 - $10,000 for sculpture

WALT HULL

WALT HULL IRON WORK
2043 MASSACHUSETTS ST
LAWRENCE, KS 66046-2945
FAX 913-842-2954
TEL 913-865-5771
Est. 1982
Products: gates and railings, furniture, sculpture, grilles and screens, fences
Process: hand forging, fabricating
Media: iron, mild steel, copper
Specialization: forged steel
Price Range/Horiz. Ft.: minimum $25

DANIEL HURWITZ

DANNY HURWITZ METALWORK
20338 BASSWOOD LN
BROWNSVILLE, MD 21715-9999
FAX 301-432-2668
TEL 301-432-2154
Est. 1974
Products: gates and railings, furniture, stairs
Process: hand forging, casting, fabricating
Media: iron, stainless steel, brass, bronze
Specialization: interior foyer railings
Price Range/Horiz. Ft.: $1,000 - $2,000
Item Price Range: $1,500 - $4,000 for coffee tables

J. DONALD FELIX - COPPERSMITH

PO BOX 995
HAMPTON, NH 03842
TEL 603-474-2225
Est. 1983
Products: lighting and candelabras, sculpture, wall pieces, weathervanes
Process: hand forging, repoussé
Media: brass, copper, weathervanes
Specialization: weathervanes
Item Price Range: $29 - $5,000 for custom copper weathervanes

BRUCE JOHNSON

MARSHALL MILLS RD.
ASHBURNHAM, MA 01430
TEL 508-827-4774
Est. 1979
Products: gates and railings, sculpture, grilles and screens, architectural hardware, fireplace hardware
Process: hand forging, fabricating, stone carving
Media: iron, brass, stone
Specialization: stone and iron
Price Range/Horiz. Ft.: $200 - $1,000

CRAIG KAVIAR

KAVIAR FORGE
147 STEVENSON AVE
LOUISVILLE, KY 40206-3124
FAX 502-581-0377
TEL 800-500-3890
Products: gates and railings, furniture, lighting and candelabras, sculpture, grilles and screens
Process: hand forging, casting, fabricating
Media: iron, bronze, all other metals
Price Range/Horiz. Ft.: $300 - $1,000
Item Price Range: $400 - $4,500 for furniture

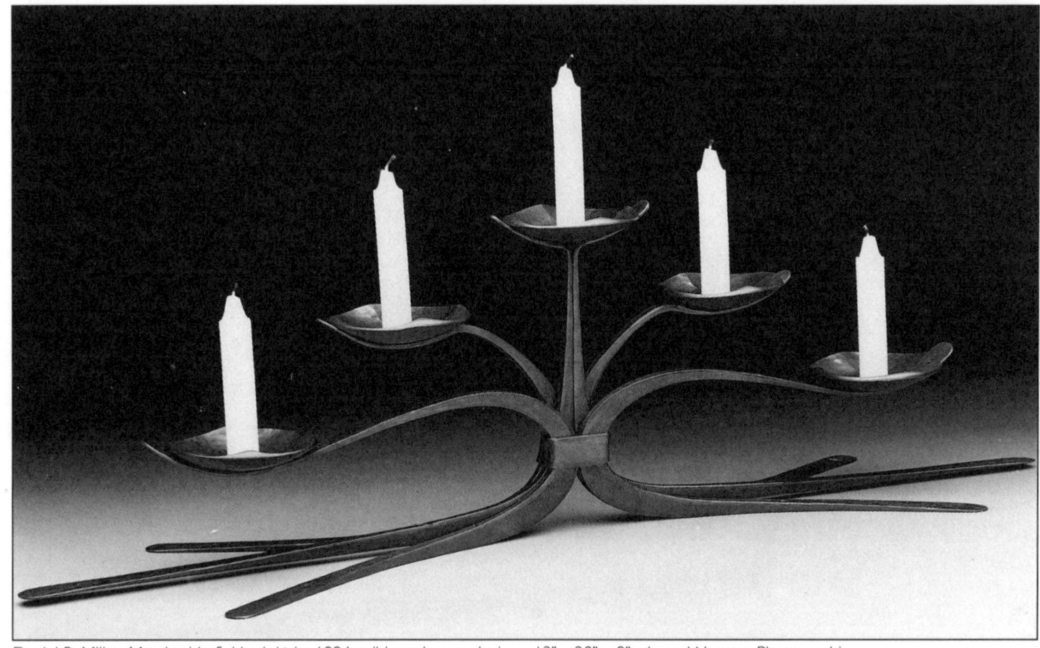

Daniel B. Miller, Metalsmith, *Sabbath Light*, 1994, mild steel, wrought iron, 13" x 28" x 9", photo: Weststar Photographic

PHILIPPE KLINEFELTER

800 GULLETT ST
AUSTIN, TX 78702-4126
TEL 512-389-1920
Est. 1982
Products: architectural hardware, doors,
furniture, grilles and screens, sculpture
Process: fabricating, hand forging
Media: iron, mild steel, stainless steel
Specialization: wood, metal and stone
Item Price Range: $1,000 - $30,000
and up per project

BARBARA KORMAN

B. KORMAN, SCULPTURE
357 E 201 ST
NEW YORK, NY 10458-2205
TEL 718-364-6640
Est. 1962
Products: sculpture, wall pieces
Process: casting, fabricating
Media: stainless steel, bronze
Specialization: abstract sculpture
Item Price Range: $5,000 and up
for freestanding and wall pieces

★ GREG LEAVITT

LEAVITT STUDIOS
476 VALLEY BROOK RD
WAWA, PA 19063
FAX 610-358-1766
TEL 610-358-1766
Est. 1972
Products: gates and railings, furniture,
sculpture, grilles and screens, doors
Process: hand forging, fabricating,
repoussé
Media: iron, bronze, copper
Specialization: architectural metal
sculpture
Price Range/Horiz. Ft.: $300 - $2,000
Item Price Range: $2,500 - $50,000
for gates

**See page 28 for photographs
and additional information.**

LES METALLIERS
CHAMPENOIS CORP.

MR. JEAN WIART
77 2ND AVE
PATERSON, NJ 07514-2005
FAX 201-881-0235
TEL 201-279-3573
Est. 1986
Products: gates and railings
Media: brass, mild steel, copper
Specialization: stair railings
Price Range/Horiz. Ft.: $950 - $3,800

THOMAS R. MARKUSEN

METALSMITHING STUDIO
17218 ROOSEVELT HWY
KENDALL, NY 14476-9762
FAX 716-659-8001
TEL 716-659-8001
Products: furniture, lighting and
candelabras, sculpture, grilles and
screens, wall pieces
Process: hand forging, casting, hot forming
Media: brass, copper, silver
Specialization: table top items
Item Price Range: $125 - $10,000
for candle holders to sculpture

MAUREEN R. WEISS, ARTIST

PO BOX 8615
RANCHO SANTA FE, CA 92067-8615
TEL 619-792-9206
Est. 1991
Products: sculpture, wall pieces
Process: hand building
Media: stainless steel, aluminum, copper
Specialization: metal wall/floor sculpture
Item Price Range: $200 - $4,000 for
metal wall/floor sculpture

KIRK MCNEILL

FREEDOM FORGE
1505 BULB AVE
SANTA CRUZ, CA 95062-3218
FAX 408-439-9024
TEL 408-427-3422
Products: gates and railings, furniture,
sculpture, architectural hardware,
wall pieces
Process: hand forging, repoussé
Media: bronze, mild steel, copper
Price Range/Horiz. Ft.: $200 - $600
Item Price Range: $7,000 - $30,000
for gates

★ DANIEL B. MILLER

DANIEL MILLER, METALSMITH
1181 WALNUT CREEK RD
PO BOX 215
HAZELWOOD, NC 28738-0215
TEL 704-456-9330
Est. 1976
Products: sculpture, furniture, gates and
railings, fireplace hardware, architectural
hardware
Process: fabricating, hand forging
machining
Media: brass, iron, mild steel
Specialization: lighting as sculpture
Price Range/Horiz. Ft.: $200 - $1,000
Item Price Range: $500 - $5,000 for
candelabras, chandeliers

See photograph page 279.

MT. SHARON FORGE

RAYMOND SPILLER
4335 MOUNT SHARON RD
GREENBRIER, TN 37073-5130
TEL 615-382-1464
Est. 1983
Products: furniture, gates and railings,
lighting and candelabras, sculpture,
weathervanes
Process: fabricating, hand forging,
repoussé
Media: iron, mild steel, bronze, copper
Price Range/Horiz. Ft.: $200 - $2,500

★ DIETER MULLER-STACH

1959 PORT CARDIFF PL
NEWPORT BEACH, CA 92660
FAX 310-985-1650
TEL 714-644-5197
Products: gates and railings, furniture,
sculpture, fireplace hardware, wall pieces
Process: hand forging, casting, fabricating
Media: iron, bronze, most metals
Specialization: custom designs/metal
Item Price Range: $8,000 - $120,000
for single, complete gate sets with lights

**See page 29 for photographs
and additional information.**

★ MYERS & COMPANY
ARCHITECTURAL METALS

ROBERT MYERS
555 BASALT AVE BOX 1025
BASALT, CO 81621
FAX 970-927-4610
TEL 970-927-4761
Est. 1975
Products: gates and railings, furniture,
lighting and candelabras, doors, stairs
Process: hand forging, fabricating,
machining
Media: brass, mild steel, copper
Specialization: large complex projects
Price Range/Horiz. Ft.: $300 - $900
Item Price Range: $15,000 - $25,000
for custom, entry doors, turnkey

See photograph this page.

Myers & Company, Architectural Metals, private residence ground entry, cattails and lillies,
forged steel, plate, tubing, Aspen, CO, 6' x 14'

★ DANIEL M. NAUMAN

BIGHORN FORGE, INC.
4190 BADGER RD
KEWASKUM, WI 53040-9484
FAX 414-626-2208
TEL 414-626-2208
Est. 1984
Products: architectural hardware, fireplace hardware, gates and railings, grilles and screens, lighting and candelabras
Process: hand forging, repoussé
Media: iron, mild steel
Specialization: traditionally made work
Price Range/Horiz. Ft.: $150 - $900

See photograph below.

NEW CASTLE IRON, INC.

BO DAVIS & SHARON BLONDET
617 SW 2ND AVE
FT LAUDERDALE, FL 33301
FAX 305-524-6428
TEL 305-524-1441
Products: gates and railings, furniture, lighting and candelabras, accessories, sculpture
Process: hand forging, fabricating, traditional & modern joinery
Media: iron, stainless steel, bronze, aluminum
Specialization: site-specific details
Price Range/Horiz. Ft.: $250 - $1,200

NORTHRIDGE FORGE

BRUCE NORTHRIDGE
12607 HUTTO RD
SMARTVILLE, CA 95977-9605
FAX 916-639-1430
TEL 916-639-1018
Est. 1972
Products: gates and railings, lighting and candelabras, architectural hardware, fireplace hardware, wall pieces
Process: hand forging, fabricating, power hammer forging
Media: iron, bronze, copper mild steel
Specialization: custom price
Price Range/Horiz. Ft.: $150 - $2,000
Item Price Range: $150 - $14,000
for sculpture and wall hangings

OEST METALWORKS

JEFF OESTERLE
1230A E JACKSON ST
PHOENIX, AZ 85034
FAX 602-254-8178
TEL 602-256-7567
Products: gates and railings, furniture, sculpture, architectural hardware, retail fixtures
Process: hand forging, fabricating, spinning
Media: iron, stainless steel, mild steel
Specialization: functional art
Price Range/Horiz. Ft.: $120 - $480
Item Price Range: $420 - $50,000
for chairs to custom artwork

JOHN OKULICK

604 HAMPTON DR
VENICE, CA 90291-2626
FAX 310-392-3092
TEL 310-392-6949
Est. 1972
Products: doors, fences, gates and railings, grilles and screens, sculpture
Process: casting, fabricating
Media: aluminum, bronze, mild steel
Specialization: unique sculptural design

GENE OLSON

THE METTLE WORKS
8600 ODEAN AVE NE
ELK RIVER, MN 55330-7167
FAX 612-441-5846
TEL 612-441-1563
Est. 1970
Products: architectural hardware, furniture, sculpture, wall pieces, custom fabrication
Process: casting, fabricating, machining
Media: aluminum, bronze, stainless steel
Price Range/Horiz. Ft.: $300 - $1,000

Daniel M. Nauman, *Window Grille*, 1990, mild steel, 24" x 34", photo: John Cumming

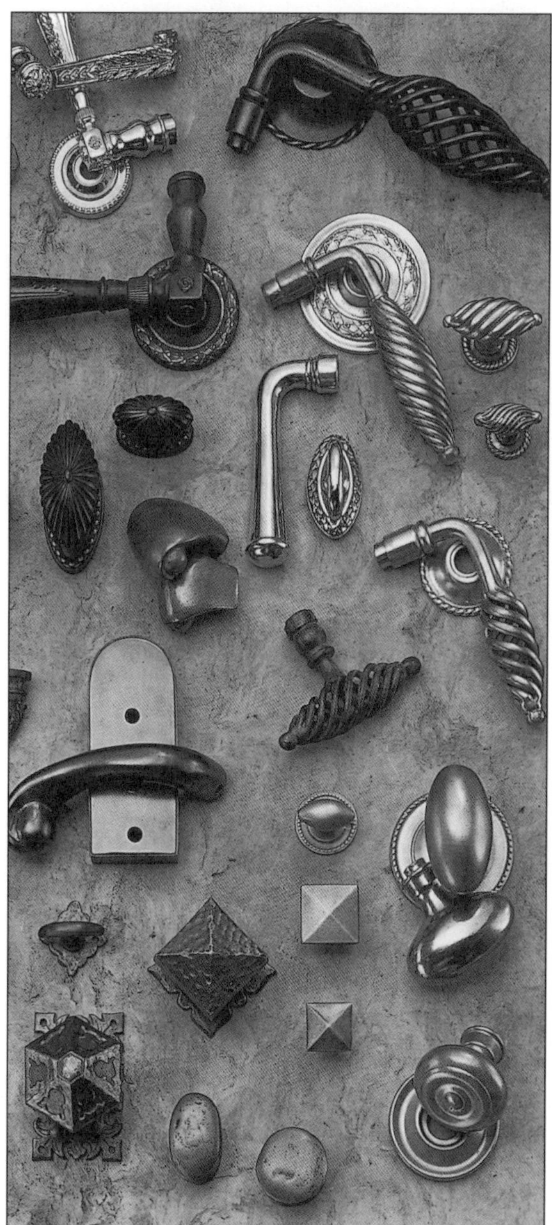

Patten Design, door, cabinet and window hardware, custom architectural castings, brass, bronze, stainless, ¹/₂" to 6"

★ PATTEN DESIGN

THEODORE OR TAYLOR PATTEN
15581 PRODUCT LN #C4
HUNTINGTON BEACH, CA
92649-1344
FAX 714-894-0031
TEL 714-894-0131

Est. 1969
Products: gates and railings, doors, grilles and screens, decorative cast pieces
Process: hand forging, casting, fabricating
Media: bronze, brass, copper, pewter, steel, stainless steel
Specialization: custom-designed hardware
Item Price Range: $20 - $3,500

See photograph 281

★ WILLIAM PERRY

PIÑON FORGE
PO BOX 122
CARBONDALE, CO 81623-0122
FAX 970-963-2390
TEL 970-963-2079

Est. 1980
Products: furniture, lighting and candelabras, sculpture, doors, wineracks
Process: hand forging, repoussé
Media: iron, bronze, copper
Item Price Range: $2,500 - $15,000 for doors

See photograph below.

STAN PLOTNER

L'ATELIER PLOTNER
214 GOAT FARM RD
GLOVERSVILLE, NY 12078
TEL 518-725-3222
Est. 1959
Products: Jewish liturgical
Process: fabricating, raising
Media: brass, copper, sterling silver
Specialization: custom modern designs
Item Price Range: $150 - $5,000

DAVID A. PONSLER

WONDERLAND PRODUCTS, INC.
5772 LENOX AVE
JACKSONVILLE, FL 32205
FAX 904-786-0145
TEL 904-786-0144
Est. 1950
Products: gates and railings, furniture, lighting and candelabras, grilles and screens, fences
Process: hand forging, fabricating, repoussé
Media: iron, bronze, copper
Specialization: design, fabrication
Price Range/Horiz. Ft.: $250 - $1,000
Item Price Range: $9,000 - $25,000 for gates

★ NOL PUTNAM

WHITE OAK FORGE, LTD.
45 MAIN ST
THE PLAINS, VA 22171
FAX 703-253-5173
TEL 703-253-5269

Est. 1973
Products: fireplace hardware, gates and railings, grilles and screens, lighting and candelabras
Process: hand forging, repoussé
Media: brass, iron, copper
Specialization: one-of-a-kind commissions
Price Range/Horiz. Ft.: $300 - $1,500

See page 30 for photographs and additional information.

RELIEF

CAROL MILNE
13529 1ST AVE NE
SEATTLE, WA 98125
TEL 206-368-8743
Est. 1991
Products: sculpture, architectural hardware, wall pieces
Process: casting
Media: bronze, aluminum
Item Price Range: $20 - $800 for architectural hardware

SEBASTIEN RICHER

SEBASTIEN RICHER
PO BOX 1148
BARNSTABLE, MA 02630-2148
TEL 508-362-2559
Est. 1992
Products: fences, furniture, gates and railings, grilles and screens, lighting and candelabras, stairs
Process: fabricating, hand forging, repoussé
Media: aluminum, iron, stainless steel, copper, brass
Price Range/Horiz. Ft.: $200 - $1,600

★ WILLIAM ROAN

1805 E 14TH ST #6
OAKLAND, CA 94606
TEL 510-532-5158

Products: gates and railings, sculpture, architectural hardware, furnishings gargoyles
Process: hand forging, fabricating, repoussé
Media: iron, bronze and copper
Specialization: forged animals
Price Range/Horiz. Ft.: $100 - $500
Item Price Range: $120 - $2,500 for forged iron animals

See photograph page 283.

WILLIAM S. ROGERS

WILLIAM S. ROGERS METALS
487 THISTLE LN
CHRISTIANSBURG, VA 24073-6061
TEL 703-382-3946
Est. 1980
Products: architectural hardware, fences, fireplace hardware, gates and railings, lighting and candelabras
Process: hand forging, repoussé
Media: brass, copper, iron
Specialization: combined metals
Price Range/Horiz. Ft.: $100 - $10,000

SAMUEL YELLIN METALWORKERS

721 MOORE AVE
BRYN MAWR, PA 19010-2208
FAX 610-527-2412
TEL 610-527-2334
Est. 1909
Products: gates and railings, furniture, lighting and candelabras, grilles and screens, fireplace hardware, doors
Process: hand forging, fabricating, repoussé
Media: iron, bronze, copper, monel
Specialization: museum-quality metalwork

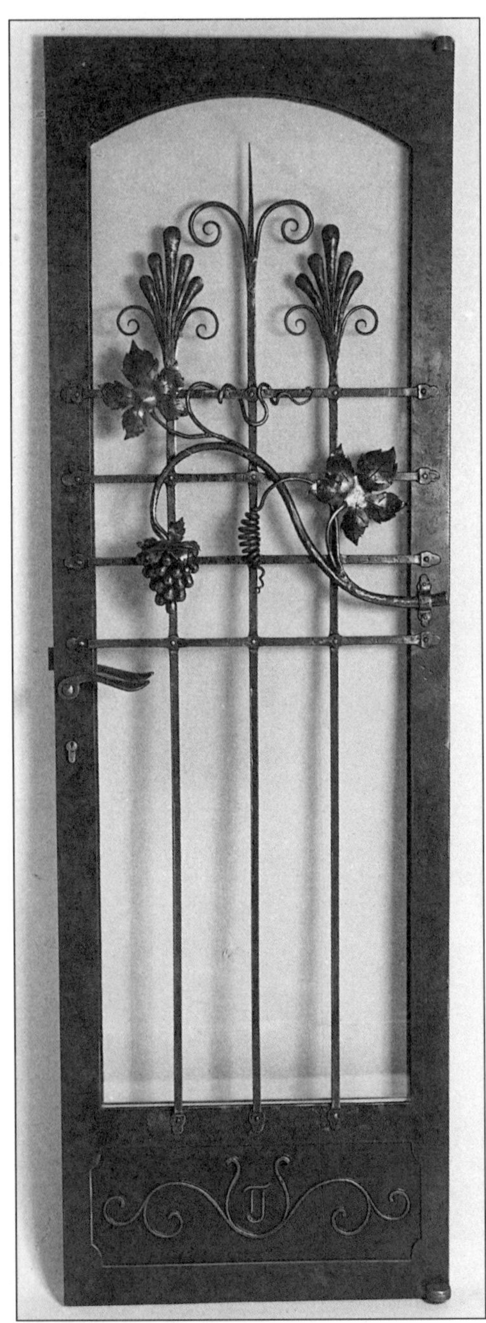

William Perry, wine cellar door, 1993, residence in Wyoming, forged and repoussé steel, 76"H x 25"W

JOEL A. SCHWARTZ

SCHWARTZ'S FORGE AND
  METALWORKS, INC.
PO BOX 205 2695 RT 315
DEANSBORO, NY 13328-0205
FAX 315-841-4694
TEL 315-841-4477
Est. 1977
Products: doors, gates and railings, grilles
and screens, lighting and candelabras, stairs
Process: fabricating, hand forging, machining
Media: bronze, iron, stainless steel
Specialization: stair balustrades,
entry doors
Price Range/Horiz. Ft.: $200 - $1,000

ARNOLD SCHWARZBART

THE STUDIO OF
  ARNOLD SCHWARZBART
5200 BUCKHEAD TR
KNOXVILLE, TN 37919
FAX 423-584-4181
TEL 423-588-6111
Est. 1981
Products: sculpture, wall pieces,
eternal lights
Process: hand forging, casting
Media: bronze, copper, silver
Specialization: Judaica
Item Price Range: $3,000 - $7,000
for eternal lights

LARS STANLEY

ARCHITECTS AND ARTISANS
PO BOX 3095
AUSTIN, TX 78764-3095
FAX 512-445-0444
TEL 512-445-0444
Est. 1984
Products: fireplace hardware, furniture,
gates and railings, grilles and screens,
lighting and candelabras
Process: fabricating, hand forging,
machining
Media: bronze, copper, mild steel
Specialization: custom, site-specific work
Price Range/Horiz. Ft.: $100 - $1,000

STEEL FORGE INC.

TERRY STEEL
3502 CLIPPER RD
BALTIMORE, MD 21211-1402
FAX 410-366-1275
TEL 410-366-1275
Est. 1975
Products: gates and railings, furniture,
grilles and screens, architectural hard-
ware, fences
Process: hand forging, casting, fabricating
Media: bronze, mild steel
Specialization: large gate work
Price Range/Horiz. Ft.: $250 - $1,000
Item Price Range: $1,000 - $60,000
for gates

THE STEWART IRON WORKS CO., INC.

20 W 18TH ST
COVINGTON, KY 41011-3329
FAX 606-431-2035
TEL 606-431-1985
Est. 1886
Products: gates and railings, furniture,
lighting and candelabras, sculpture,
fences
Process: hand forging, casting, fabricating
Media: iron, brass, bronze
Specialization: custom fences and gates
Price Range/Horiz. Ft.: $50 - $500
Item Price Range: $25 - $200 for fences

STEPHEN JOHN STOKES

STOKES OF ENGLAND
4085 KESWICK RD
KESWICK, VA 22947-9329
FAX 804-978-2950
TEL 804-295-9848
Est. 1981
Products: architectural hardware,
fireplace hardware, furniture, gates
and railings, lighting and candelabras
Process: fabricating, hand forging,
machining
Media: bronze, copper, iron
Specialization: hand-forged iron gates
Price Range/Horiz. Ft.: $175 - $1,500
Item Price Range: $300 - $10,000 for
weathervanes

★ TOM TORRENS SCULPTURE DESIGN

PO BOX 1819
GIG HARBOR, WA 98335-3819
FAX 206-265-2404
TEL 206-857-5831
Est. 1984
Products: furniture, gates and railings,
grilles and screens, lighting and cande-
labras, wall pieces fountains, birdbaths
Process: fabricating, spinning
Media: copper, mild steel, stainless steel
Specialization: fountains, recycled material

**See page 146 for photographs
and additional information.**

TRUSO DESIGN

JOHN TRUSO
PO BOX 10788
ASPEN, CO 81612-7351
TEL 303-920-3768
Est. 1989
Products: architectural hardware
Process: hand forging, casting, fabricating,
machining
Media: stainless steel, brass, bronze,
mild steel
Specialization: architectural hardware
Item Price Range: $100 - $500 for
entrance door pulls

ENRIQUE VEGA

E. VEGA STUDIOS
505 LUTHER RD
APEX, NC 27502
FAX 919-362-0543
TEL 919-362-0543
Est. 1980
Products: furniture, gates and railings,
grilles and screens, sculpture, glass
etching
Process: fabricating, hand forging, etching
Media: iron, bronze, nonferrous
Specialization: handcrafted metal, glass
Price Range/Horiz. Ft.: $150 - $1,500
Item Price Range: $1,500 - $20,000
for entry gates

VEGA METALS, INC.

FRANCIS VEGA/NEAL CARLTON/
  DAVID RUSINYAK
214 HUNT ST
DURHAM, NC 27701-2116
FAX 919-688-4462
TEL 919-688-8267
Est. 1984
Products: gates and railings, furniture,
lighting and candelabras, sculpture,
architectural hardware
Process: hand forging, fabricating,
machining
Media: brass, bronze, mild steel
Specialization: railings, furnishings
Price Range/Horiz. Ft.: $150 - $2,500
Item Price Range: $1,500 - $8,500
for tables

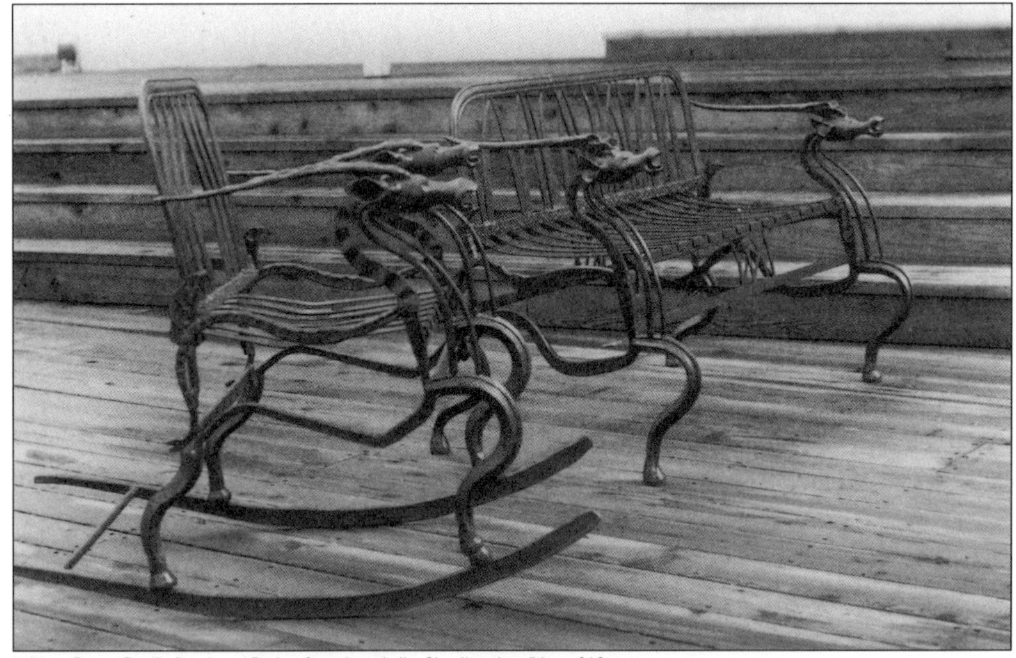

William Roan, *Gazelle Bench and Rocker*, forged steel, 4' x 2' x 4' each, edition of 10

ARCHITECTURAL METAL

★ WAYLAN SMITHY

TOBY HICKMAN, OWNER
6030 ROBLAR RD
PETALUMA, CA 94952-9790
FAX 707-664-1691
TEL 707-664-8910
Est. 1975
Products: gates and railings, furniture, lighting and candelabras, architectural hardware, wall pieces
Process: hand forging, fabricating, machining
Media: stainless steel, bronze, mild steel
Specialization: restaurant interiors, lighting
Price Range/Horiz. Ft.: $250 - $1,200
Item Price Range: $500 - $2,500 for pendant frame

See page 31 for photographs and additional information.

DOUG WEIGEL

STEEL SCULPTURES BY DOUG WEIGEL
4415 ANAHEIM NE
ALBURQUERQUE, NM 87113
FAX 505-822-9696
TEL 505-821-6600
Products: gates and railings, furniture, lighting and candelabras, sculpture, wall pieces
Process: hand forging, fabricating
Media: stainless steel, mild steel, copper
Item Price Range: call for quote

DOUGLAS E. WILSON

WILSON FORGE
PO BOX 225
DEER ISLE, ME 04627-0225
TEL 207-348-6871
Est. 1981
Products: architectural hardware, fireplace hardware, furniture, gates and railings, lighting and candelabras
Process: hand forging
Media: iron, bronze, stone
Specialization: design and forged ironwork
Price Range/Horiz. Ft.: $250 - $1,500

EUGENE WILSON

WILSON METAL SCULPTURE & DESIGN
4589 PEYTONSVILLE RD
FRANKLIN, TN 37064-7608
TEL 615-790-6277
Est. 1990
Products: fireplace hardware, furniture, lighting and candelabras, sculpture
Process: casting, fabricating, hand forging
Media: bronze, copper, iron
Price Range/Horiz. Ft.: $200 - $2,000

SUSAN WOOD

BEAR WALLOW RIDGE STUDIO
RT 2 BOX 142B
LEON, WV 25123
TEL 304-895-3485
Est. 1983
Products: lighting and candelabras, sculpture, architectural hardware, wall pieces
Process: casting, fabricating
Media: bronze, mild steel
Specialization: garden sculpture
Item Price Range: $500 - $20,000 for sculpture

♦

GLOSSARY OF TERMS

Casting	a process of pouring molten metal into a mold.
Etching	a use of chemicals to achieve a surface treatment.
Fabricating	assembling, forming, manufacturing, or otherwise constructing metal products.
Hand-forging	a process of heating and hammering metal into a desired form.
Machining	a cold-process method of shaping material by turning, grinding, or cutting.
Spinning	the process of shaping a sheet metal disk by turning it with pressure against a form.

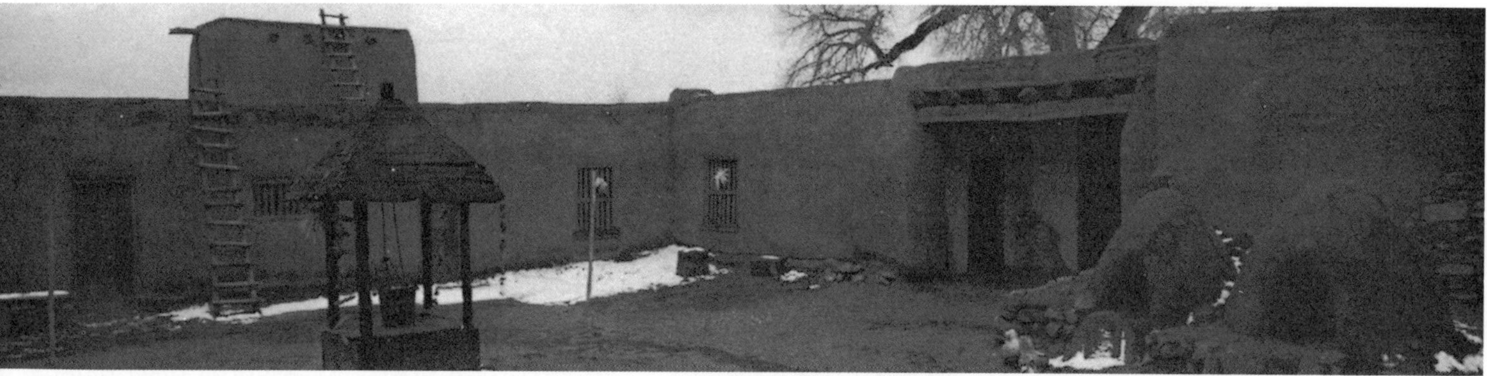

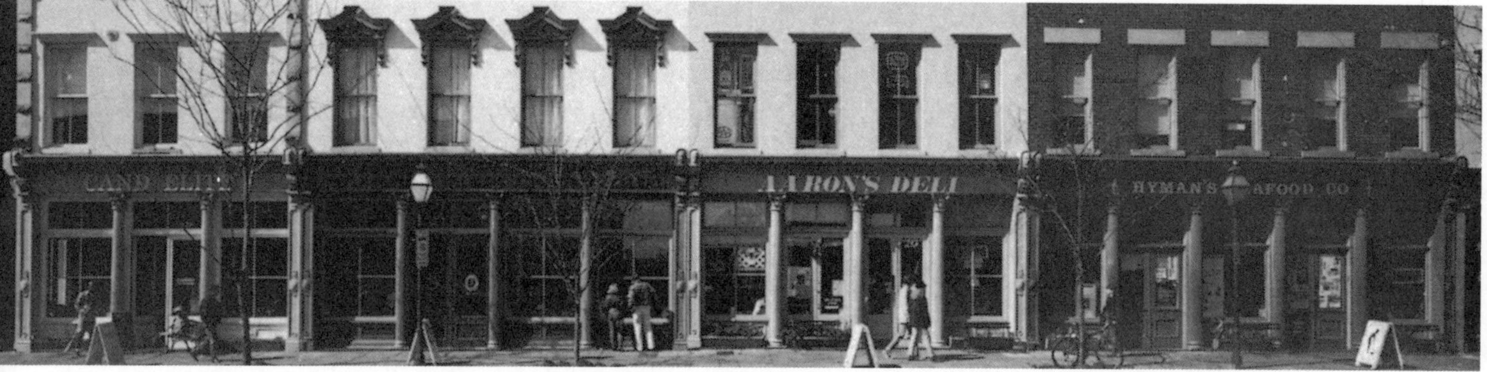

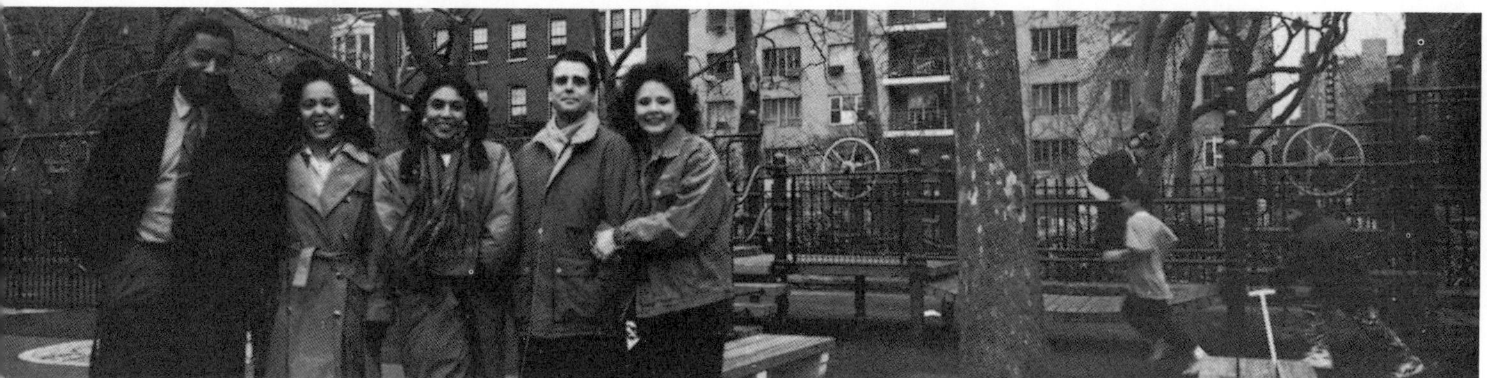

What is historic preservation?

It's your memory. It's our history. It's worth saving.

NATIONAL TRUST FOR HISTORIC PRESERVATION   1 800 289 7091

1785 MASSACHUSETTS AVENUE, N.W. WASHINGTON, DC 20036

THE GUILD REGISTER®
of *Architectural Restoration*

THE GUILD REGISTER® of Architectural Restoration is an inventory of professional artists and artisans working in all areas of architectural restoration and conservation.

SUMMARY OF RESTORATION SERVICES

	ARCHITECTURAL CERAMICS, MOSAICS & WALL RELIEFS						ARCHITECTURAL GLASS						ARCHITECTURAL METAL					
	decorative plaster	flooring	glass mosaics	terra cotta work	tile work	other wall relief	blown/cast work	etched work	leaded work	mirrors	painted work	stained work	cast work	forged work	hardware/lighting fixtures	pressed or formed sheet	streetscape elements	structural elements
ALPINE MOULDING																		
AMERICAN STONECRAFTERS		•			•	•												
ANDERSON BUILDING RESTORATION																		
ARCHICAST	•												•					
ARCHITECTURAL IRON COMPANY													•	•			•	•
ARCHITECTURAL MURALS																		
ARCHITECTURAL RECLAMATION, INC.	•															•		•
ARCHITECTURAL SCULPTURE LTD.	•					•												
ART & METAL LTD.													•	•	•	•	•	•
ART GLASS OF AMERICA									•	•	•	•						
ART HOME SCULPTURE STUDIOS, CO.	•			•														
ART IN ACTION				•		•												
AURORA GLASS STUDIO							•	•	•		•	•						
BAREWOOD																		
BLUE OX MILLWORKS/HISTORIC PARK	•																	
BOVARD STUDIO, INC.								•	•		•	•	•					
BRADBURY & BRADBURY WALLPAPERS																		
RORY BRENNAN	•					•												
CAMBRIDGE SMITHY														•	•			
CARL SCHILLING STONEWORKS																		
CARPENTER & SMITH RESTORATIONS																		
CEDAR GUILD INC.																		
CHRISTOPHER WALBERG LTD.	•			•		•							•		•	•		
COLONIAL RESTORATIONS																		

Please note the two-part format. The Summary of Restoration Services (below) allows you to quickly identify artists and companies providing the specific services you need. The listings that follow (beginning on page 294) include contact and pricing information, as well as detailed service descriptions.

While every effort has been made to provide accurate information from experienced professionals, inclusion in THE GUILD REGISTER of Architectural Restoration does not constitute a referral from THE GUILD. We urge you to contact references from similar projects, as you would when seeking any other professional services.

SUMMARY OF RESTORATION SERVICES

	ARCHITECTURAL WOOD					DECORATIVE FINISHES					MASONRY						
	carved work	casework	flooring	furniture	millwork	wall coverings	decorative painting	gilding	murals	frescos	brick work	cast stone	stucco/cement work	granite/limestone/sandstone	marble work	slate work	
ALPINE MOULDING		•			•												
AMERICAN STONECRAFTERS						•								•	•		
ANDERSON BUILDING RESTORATION											•			•			
ARCHICAST												•					
ARCHITECTURAL IRON COMPANY																	
ARCHITECTURAL MURALS						•	•	•	•	•							
ARCHITECTURAL RECLAMATION, INC.					•						•			•			
ARCHITECTURAL SCULPTURE LTD.																	
ART & METAL LTD.																	
ART GLASS OF AMERICA																	
ART HOME SCULPTURE STUDIOS, CO.												•	•				
ART IN ACTION																	
AURORA GLASS STUDIO																	
BAREWOOD	•	•	•	•	•												
BLUE OX MILLWORKS/HISTORIC PARK	•	•	•	•	•												
BOVARD STUDIO, INC.		•															
BRADBURY & BRADBURY WALLPAPERS						•											
RORY BRENNAN																	
CAMBRIDGE SMITHY																	
CARL SCHILLING STONEWORKS														•	•		
CARPENTER & SMITH RESTORATIONS				•	•												
CEDAR GUILD INC.					•												
CHRISTOPHER WALBERG LTD.	•	•	•	•	•		•	•	•	•	•	•	•	•	•	•	
COLONIAL RESTORATIONS		•			•												

Please see the listings which follow this chart for more complete information about these individuals and companies.

ARCHITECTURAL RESTORATION

SUMMARY OF RESTORATION SERVICES

Column groups: **ARCHITECTURAL CERAMICS, MOSAICS & WALL RELIEFS** (decorative plaster, flooring, glass mosaics, terra cotta work, tile work, other wall relief) · **ARCHITECTURAL GLASS** (blown/cast work, etched work, leaded work, mirrors, painted work, stained work) · **ARCHITECTURAL METAL** (cast work, forged work, hardware/lighting fixtures, pressed or formed sheet, streetscape elements, structural elements)

	decorative plaster	flooring	glass mosaics	terra cotta work	tile work	other wall relief	blown/cast work	etched work	leaded work	mirrors	painted work	stained work	cast work	forged work	hardware/lighting fixtures	pressed or formed sheet	streetscape elements	structural elements
CONRAD SCHMITT STUDIOS, INC.			●					●	●		●	●						
CREATIVE SCULPTURES & RESTORATION																		
CUMMINGS STAINED GLASS STUDIOS									●		●	●						
DANIEL MAHER STAINED GLASS									●		●	●						
DAPRATO RIGALI, INC.			●						●		●	●	●					
TIM DE CHRISTOPHER						●												
DAVID FLAHARTY, SCULPTOR	●												●					
DOWNSTATE RESTORATIONS	●			●													●	●
DURHAN STUDIOS, INC.								●	●		●	●						
FELBER ORNAMENTAL PLASTERING CORP.	●					●												
FEMENELLA & ASSOCIATES, INC.			●				●	●	●	●	●	●						
FERGUSON'S CUT GLASS WORKS, INC.									●	●	●		●					
FINE ART CONSERVATION LAB.																		
THE FINE WOODWORKING CO. INC.																		
FISCHER ARTWORKS													●			●		
FORGING A FUTURE														●	●	●	●	●
LES FOSSEL														●				
PAUL FRIEND								●	●		●	●						●
FULL CIRCLE GLASS COMPANY							●	●	●	●	●	●						
GOLD LEAF STUDIOS	●																	
GREAT PANES ARCHITECTURAL GLASS ART			●	●				●	●	●	●	●						
HISTORICAL ARTS & CASTING INC													●		●		●	●
STACIA A. HUMMEL																		
INT'L. FINE ART CONSERVATION STUDIOS	●					●					●							
J. RING GLASS STUDIO, INC.			●						●	●								
TERI ARTHUR JEFFERSON	●						●	●	●		●	●	●	●	●			
JOHNSON ATLIER-TECH. INST. OF SCULPTURE	●					●							●		●		●	●
ROBERT S. JORDAN					●					●				●	●			
THE JUDSON STUDIOS			●					●	●		●	●						
KAYE RESTORATIONS	●																	
KAYNE & SON CUSTOM HARDWARE													●	●	●	●		
GUY KEMPER								●			●	●						

SUMMARY OF RESTORATION SERVICES

	ARCHITECTURAL WOOD					DECORATIVE FINISHES					MASONRY					
	carved work	casework	flooring	furniture	millwork	wall coverings	decorative painting	gilding	murals	frescos	brick work	cast stone	stucco/cement work	granite/limestone/sandstone	marble work	slate work
CONRAD SCHMITT STUDIOS, INC.							•	•	•	•						
CREATIVE SCULPTURES & RESTORATION												•	•	•	•	•
CUMMINGS STAINED GLASS STUDIOS																
DANIEL MAHER STAINED GLASS																
DAPRATO RIGALI. INC.	•			•			•	•	•						•	
TIM DE CHRISTOPHER														•	•	•
DAVID FLAHARTY, SCULPTOR																
DOWNSTATE RESTORATIONS		•			•	•	•	•	•	•	•	•	•	•	•	•
DURHAN STUDIOS, INC.																
FELBER ORNAMENTAL PASTERING CORP.												•				
FEMENELLA & ASSOCIATES, INC.		•			•											
FERGUSON'S CUT GLASS WORKS., INC.																
FINE ART CONSERVATION LAB.							•	•	•	•						
THE FINE WOODWORKING CO. INC.		•		•	•											
FISCHER ARTWORKS																
FORGING A FUTURE							•	•								
LES FOSSEL	•	•	•		•						•			•		
PAUL FRIEND																
FULL CIRCLE GLASS COMPANY																
GOLD LEAF STUDIOS		•						•								
GREAT PANES ARCHITECTURAL GLASS																
HISTORICAL ARTS & CASTING																
STACIA A. HUMMEL							•	•	•							
INT'L. FINE ART CONSERVATION STUDIOS						•	•	•	•	•						
J. RING GLASS STUDIO, INC.																
TERI ARTHUR JEFFERSON								•								
JOHNSON ATELIER-TECH. INST. OF SCULPTURE							•	•								
ROBERT S. JORDAN																
THE JUDSON STUDIOS																
KAYE RESTORATIONS																
KAYNE & SON CUSTOM HARDWARE																
GUY KEMPER	•	•			•											

Please see the listings which follow this chart for more complete information about these individuals and companies.

ARCHITECTURAL RESTORATION

SUMMARY OF RESTORATION SERVICES

SUMMARY OF RESTORATION SERVICES	ARCHITECTURAL CERAMICS, MOSAICS & WALL RELIEFS						ARCHITECTURAL GLASS						ARCHITECTURAL METAL					
	decorative plaster	flooring	glass mosaics	terra cotta work	tile work	other wall relief	blown/cast work	etched work	leaded work	mirrors	painted work	stained work	cast work	forged work	hardware/lighting fixtures	pressed or formed sheet	streetscape elements	structural elements
PETER KRAMER																		
LAMB STUDIOS									•		•	•						
LANDMARK STUDIOS	•			•	•	•												
JOHN LEEKE																		
LIGHT HAUS INC.							•	•	•	•	•	•						
DAVID LINKER																		
LITTLEWOOD & MAUE													•		•			
M.J. MAY BUILDING RESTORATION																		
MAD RIVER WOODWORKS																		
MARTINO ART GLASS STUDIO							•	•	•		•	•						
CRAIG MCCULLEN								•	•			•						
MEETING HOUSE FURNITURE RESTORATION																		
MELOTTE-MORSE STAINED GLASS, INC.								•	•	•	•	•						
DON MESERVE INC.				•		•			•				•					
MICHAEL DOTZEL & SON INC.													•	•	•	•		
MUSEUM QUALITY RESTORATIONS															•			
NY DECORATIVE ARTS STUDIO																		
NIKO CONTRACTING CO., INC.																	•	
NORTH AMERICAN SLATE, INC.																		
OLD WORLD RESTORATIONS, INC.	•		•	•		•		•	•	•	•	•	•		•			•
THE ORUM SILVER CO. INC.										•					•			
PACE COMPANY																		
PACIFIC STATES CARPENTRY																		
PINSON AND WARE, PAINTED ORNAMENT											•							
PROSTONE RESTORATIONS, INC.		•		•	•													
E.W. PYFER									•			•			•			
R.E. STAHL, STONECARVER						•												
GAIL REDMAN																		
REFLECTION STUDIOS, INC.							•	•	•		•	•						
RICK REALE CO. PAINTING & DECORATING																		
ROBERT BOUCHER & ASSOCIATES	•			•	•	•												
ROBSUN WORLDWIDE GRAINING LTD.																		

SUMMARY OF RESTORATION SERVICES

ARCHITECTURAL WOOD					DECORATIVE FINISHES					MASONRY						
carved work	casework	flooring	furniture	millwork	wall coverings	decorative painting	gilding	murals	frescos	brick work	cast stone	stucco/cement work	granite/limestone/sandstone	marble work	slate work	
	●		●	●												PETER KRAMER
																LAMB STUDIOS
											●	●	●			LANDMARK STUDIOS
●	●	●	●	●						●			●			JOHN LEEKE
																LIGHT HAUS INC.
			●				●									DAVID LINKER
																LITTLEWOOD & MAUE
	●	●	●	●												M.J. MAY BUILDING RESTORATION
				●												MAD RIVER WOODWORKS
																MARTINO ART GLASS STUDIO
																CRAIG MCCULLEN
●			●													MEETING HOUSE FURNITURE RESTORATION
																MELOTTE-MORSE STAINED GLASS, INC.
											●		●	●		DON MESERVE
																MICHAEL DOTZEL & SON INC.
																MUSEUM QUALITY RESTORATIONS
						●	●	●	●			●				NY DECORATIVE ARTS STUDIO
																NIKO CONTRACTING CO., INC.
											●				●	NORTH AMERICAN SLATE, INC.
●			●		●	●	●	●	●					●		OLD WORLD RESTORATIONS, INC.
																THE ORUM SILVER CO. INC.
	●			●												PACE COMPANY
	●	●		●								●				PACIFIC STATES CARPENTRY
						●	●									PINSON AND WARE, PAINTED ORNAMENT
													●	●	●	PROSTONE RESTORATIONS, INC.
																E.W. PYFER
													●	●		R.E. STAHL, STONECARVER
				●												GAIL REDMAN
																REFLECTION STUDIOS, INC.
						●	●	●								RICK REALE CO. PAINTING & DECORATING
											●					ROBERT BOUCHER & ASSOCIATES
						●										ROBSUN WORLDWIDE GRAINING LTD.

Please see the listings which follow this chart for more complete information about these individuals and companies.

SUMMARY OF RESTORATION SERVICES

	ARCHITECTURAL CERAMICS, MOSAICS & WALL RELIEFS						ARCHITECTURAL GLASS						ARCHITECTURAL METAL					
	decorative plaster	flooring	glass mosaics	terra cotta work	tile work	other wall relief	blown/cast work	etched work	leaded work	mirrors	painted work	stained work	cast work	forged work	hardware/lighting fixtures	pressed or formed sheet	streetscape elements	structural elements
ROHLF'S STAINED & LEADED GLASS			•					•	•		•	•						
RUDOLPH N. ROHN ART STUDIOS, LTD.	•		•	•	•	•	•	•	•		•	•	•	•				
RUSSELL RESTORATION	•					•												
ST. LOUIS ANTIQUE LIGHTING CO.													•		•	•		
KENNETH A. SALOWE	•					•												
SCALAMANDRE																		
SHADETREE STUDIO								•	•		•	•						
SIERRA ARCHITECTURAL CAST STONE INC.	•																	
STONE FACES																		
STONELEDGE FINE ARTS CONSERVATION			•	•		•			•		•	•	•	•				
STUDIO ARTS & GLASS, INC.								•	•	•	•	•						
SUNBURST STAINED GLASS CO., INC.								•	•	•	•	•						
TEACO CONSTRUCTION CORP.																		
TIDEWATER RESTORATION CENTER	•	•											•	•				•
TILE RESTORATION CENTER		•		•	•													
DAVID TREZISE						•												
VEGA METALS															•	•		•
WARDELL ART GLASS								•	•		•	•						
FREDERICK WILBUR						•												
WILLIAM R. WRIGHT, AIA, SGAA								•	•									

SUMMARY OF RESTORATION SERVICES

ARCHITECTURAL WOOD					DECORATIVE FINISHES					MASONRY						
carved work	casework	flooring	furniture	millwork	wall coverings	decorative painting	gilding	murals	frescos	brick work	cast stone	stucco/cement work	granite/limestone/sandstone	marble work	slate work	
																ROHLF'S STAINED & LEADED GLASS
●	●	●	●	●		●	●	●	●		●			●		RUDOLPH N. ROHN ART STUDIOS, LTD.
						●			●							RUSSELL RESTORATION
																ST. LOUIS ANTIQUE LIGHTING CO.
						●	●	●	●							KENNETH A. SALOWE
					●											SCALAMANDRE
	●			●												SHADETREE STUDIO
											●					SIERRA ARCHITECTURAL CAST STONE INC.
										●	●	●	●	●	●	STONE FACES
●			●			●	●	●	●					●		STONELEDGE FINE ARTS CONSERVATION
																STUDIO ARTS & GLASS, INC.
																SUNBURST STAINED GLASS CO., INC.
													●			TEACO CONSTRUCTION CORP.
●	●	●		●						●		●	●		●	TIDEWATER RESTORATION, INC.
								●								TILE RESTORATION CENTER
													●	●		DAVID TREZISE
																VEGA METALS
																WARDELL ART GLASS
●			●	●			●									FREDERICK WILBUR
●																WILLIAM R. WRIGHT, AIA, SGAA

Please see the listings which follow this chart for more complete information about these individuals and companies.

ARCHITECTURAL RESTORATION

ALPINE MOULDING

WAYNE S. BOEHME
155 INDUSTRIAL DR
BURLINGTON, WI 53105-2318
FAX 414-767-0411
TEL 414-767-0336
TEL 800-870-0336

Specializing in the reproduction of period moldings. Products: crown, picture and panel molds; chair rails; door and window casings; baseboard and basecaps; rosettes; plinth blocks; many more interior and exterior applications.

Price Range: $15 - $20/inch knife grinding; $100 - $4,500/project
Recent Projects: Millwork, crowns, casings, baseboards for M.J. May Restoration; rosettes, plinth blocks, casings, baseboards for a residence in Lake Geneva, WI

AMERICAN STONECRAFTERS

JOHN KRONBERG
488 WASHINGTON ST
WALLINGFORD, CT 06492-2362
FAX 203-269-7471
TEL 800-877-8663

American Stonecrafters specializes in restoration and replication of interior and exterior stone floors, walls, building components, statuary, turned columns and components carvings, and church altars. We expertly cut, carve, shape and polish marble, granite, limestone soapstone, etc.

Price Range: $6 - $200/sq. ft.; $40 - $70/hour; $1,000 - $300,000/project
Recent Projects: Replicated and installed original marble fireplaces for city hall, New Haven, CT; restored marble for Mystic Noank Library, CT

ANDERSON BUILDING RESTORATION

ROGER ANDERSON
923 MARION AVE
CINCINNATI, OH 45229
FAX 513-281-5258
TEL 513-281-5258

Masonry restoration contractors specializing in tuckpointing and repair of historic masonry structures.

Price Range: $5,000 - $250,000/ project
Recent Projects: Removal of paint from masonry surfaces, extensive tuckpointing, and brick repair for The Hauck House, University of Cincinnati Foundation, OH; extensive tuckpointing and repair of decorative stonework for the Asa Bushnell House, Springfield, OH

ARCHICAST

DAN SPECTOR
2527 BROAD AVE
MEMPHIS, TN 38112-2613
FAX 901-323-8717
TEL 901-323-8717

Custom mold making and casting in plaster (GRG), resins, wax, and cast stone. Sculpting and careful repair. Ten years old.

Price Range: $75/10" Scamozzi capital; $25 - $35/hour; $20,000/large project
Recent Projects: Repaired and made molds of decayed capitals and re-cast for Woodward-White House, Aiken, SC; sculpted molding and medallion from old photos and re-cast for the P.T. Barnum Museum, Bridgeport, CT

ARCHITECTURAL IRON COMPANY, INC.

DONALD QUICK
PO BOX 126
MILFORD, PA 18337-0126
FAX 717-296-4766
TEL 800-442-4766

Architectural Iron Company is engaged in the restoration and reproduction of 18th and 19th century cast and wrought iron. AIC also executes fabrications for artists and sculptors. The company has an on-premises foundry.

Price Range: $200 to $3,600/linear ft.; $6,000 to $500,000/project
Recent Projects: Many diverse wrought and cast iron projects in Central Park, New York, NY; an award-winning fence for Public School 234, New York, NY

ARCHITECTURAL MURALS

JOSHUA WINER
32 SCHOOL ST
ARLINGTON, MA 02174-6122
FAX 617-643-3517
TEL 617-643-3517

Architectural Murals specializes in the design and painting of interior and exterior murals for historic and new buildings. Joshua Winer is a professional muralist and a licensed architect.

Price Range: $10 - $50/sq. ft.; $20 - $100/hour; $15,000 - $250,000/project
Recent Projects: Historic theater facade and interior paint restoration with new murals, John Harms Center for the Arts, Englewood, NJ; paint restoration with new murals at Boston's Old City Hall, Boston, MA

ARCHITECTURAL RECLAMATION, INC.

ANDY BRUCE AND SUSAN STEWART
312 S RIVER ST
FRANKLIN, OH 45005-2240
TEL 513-746-8964

Small family construction firm specializing in historic restoration and rehabilitation. Experienced in structural repairs, log and timber frame work, masonry, custom woodworking sheet metal roofing and box gutters, plastering and more. Serving the southwestern OH area.

Price Range: $25 - $35/hour; $2,000 - $200,000/project
Recent Projects: Restoration of the Cottman and Baker farmhouse (1850s) in public park, Miami Township, OH; major addition to Victorian house, compatible with original Mowry Residence, Wyoming, OH

★ ARCHITECTURAL SCULPTURE LTD.

**EUCLIDES PAGÁN
242 LAFAYETTE ST
NEW YORK, NY 10012-4029
FAX 212-431-5873
TEL 212-431-5873**

Architectural Sculpture Ltd. is an interior ornamental plaster company dedicated to ornamental plaster decoration and restoration. We do custom work and have our own collection of many different historical styles.

Price Range: $3 - $80/sq. ft.; $1,500 - $60,000/project
Recent Projects: Custom ornamental work for a private residence in New York City; restoration of library ceiling for the New York Athletic Club, New York, NY

See photograph this page.

ART & METAL LTD.

MICHAEL DESTEFANO
232 JUPITER ST
JUPITER, FL 33469
FAX 407-745-9403
TEL 407-745-9403
TEL 813-646-1087

Recipients of eight prestigious awards for excellence in architectural metalwork by an international group of peers, Art & Metal Ltd. is a team of artists committed to creating works that consistently surpass their clients' greatest expectations.

Price Range: $100 - $4,000/linear ft. (railings); $45 - $100/hour; $4,000 - $250,000/project
Recent Projects: 1920s-style balconies and lighting for residence in Mountain Lake Estates, Lake Wales, FL; 19th-century lighting and hardware for residence in Boca Raton, FL

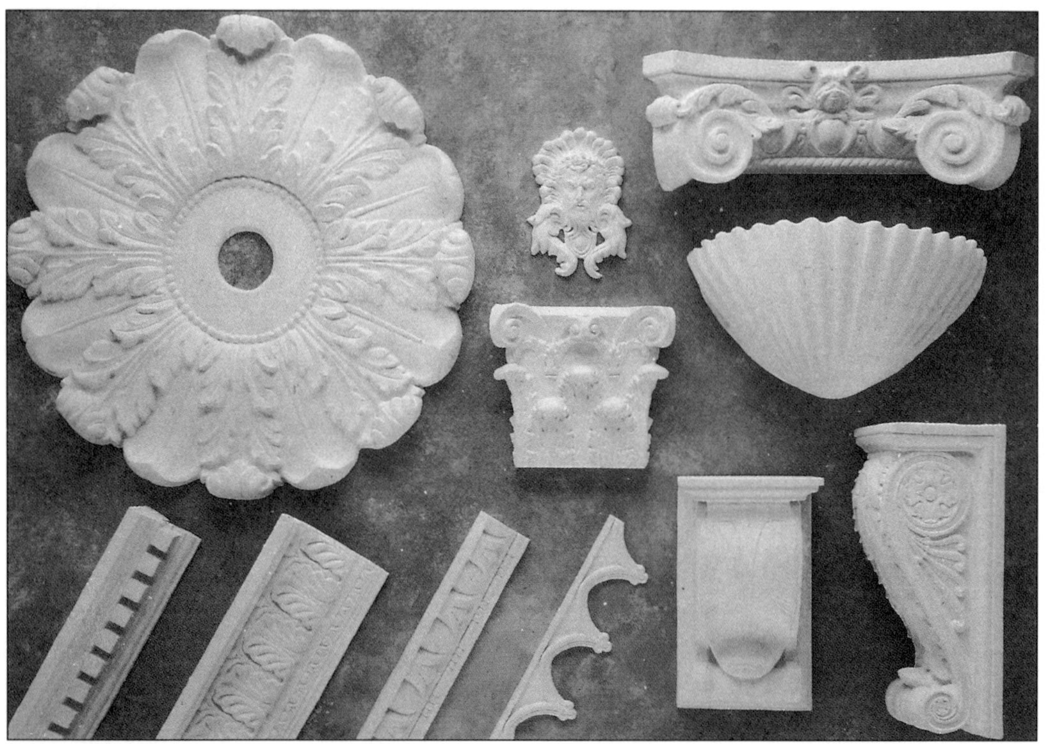

Architectural Sculpture Ltd., samples of ornamental elements

ART GLASS OF AMERICA

ROBERT M. NELSON, JR.
PO BOX 760
NATICK, MA 01760-0007
TEL 800-636-4242

Price Range: $500 - $60,000/project
Recent Projects: Restored rose window and frame for the Baptist Church of Cambridge; removed and restored window in the main stairwell of the Massachusetts State House

★ ART HOME SCULPTURE STUDIOS, CO.

NASSIR RAZZAK
666 MORGAN AVE
BROOKLYN, NY 11222
FAX 718-218-9318
TEL 800-383-0603

Art Home Studios creates and re-creates architectural sculptural elements in glass-fiber reinforced concrete, fiberglass, gypsum and cast stone for historical landmark buildings restoration and new construction; a free brochure is available.

Price Range: $5,000 - $250,000/project
Recent Projects: Glass-fiber reinforced concrete (GFRC) for Public School 217 Brooklyn, NY; extensive decorative plaster restoration for the lobby of an architectural firm, New York, NY

See photograph this page.

ART IN ACTION

BARRY ROSE
1450 LOGAN ST
DENVER, CO 80203-1911
TEL 303-832-3250

Barry Rose offers full design, production and installation services, including sculpted originals, rubber, plaster molds and stonework. He enjoys collaborating or supplying original designs for building facades and smaller architectural details.

Price Range: $20 - $100/hour; $500 - $50,000/project
Recent Projects: New terra cotta to match old and restoration for Denver Museum of Natural History; facade restoration and other work for Oxford Alexis Hotel, Denver, CO

AURORA GLASS STUDIO

SANDRA D. EISMIN
634 MAIN ST
LAFAYETTE, IN 47901-1451
FAX 317-742-2721
TEL 317-742-7387

Restoration of stained and painted leaded-glass panels; also restoration of various slumped glass paneled lamp shades of antique qualities.

Price Range: $75 - $200/sq. ft.; $50 - $100/hour; $300 - $1,000/project
Recent Projects: Restoration and resizing of old windows for new church Evangelical Covenant, Lafayette, IN; residential restoration and reframing of antique glass panel Lafayette, IN

BAREWOOD

LESLIE NEILSON
106 FERRIS ST
BROOKLYN, NY 11231-1018
FAX 718-875-3833
TEL 718-875-9037

Barewood specializes in 18th & 19th century furniture and architectural woodworking, including wood turning and carving. Products include fireplace mantels, doors and windows, paneling columns, and stair parts. We also do prototypes for casting by others.

Price Range: $55 - $175/hour; $100 - $150,000/project
Recent Projects: Column and bracket replacement for Belvedere Castle, Central Park Conservancy, NY; porch components, windows, doors for National Landmarks Conservancy, Astor Row, NY

BLUE OX MILLWORKS AND HISTORIC PARK

#2 X ST
EUREKA, CA 95501
TEL 800-248-4259
TEL 707-444-3437

Historically accurate. Molding and turning patterns matched. 4,000 molded knives. Straight or curved redwood gutter. Design assistance. Your custom woodwork specialists. Quality work at reasonable prices.

Price Range: $35 - $50/hour; $10 - $100,000/project
Recent Projects: All interior and exterior millwork for the Bauriedel home; molding for the historic Waioli Hui'ia church

BOVARD STUDIO, INC.

RONALD BOVARD
52 E BRIGGS AVE
FAIRFIELD, IA 52556-2846
FAX 515-472-0974
TEL 515-472-2824

Have extensive restoration experience. Produce new stained glass, hand-painted glass and faceted glass windows. Complete with wood, aluminum, or steel frames, custom storm windows, and wood or bronze doors.

Price Range: $10,000 - $200,000
Recent Projects: Restored Charles Connicle stained glass, fabricated over 100 new stained glass windows for the Fourth Presbyterian Church, Chicago, IL; stained glass windows for a new chapel, Maxwell Airforce Base, Montgomery, AL

BRADBURY & BRADBURY ART WALLPAPERS

PO BOX 155
BENICIA, CA 94510-0155
FAX 707-745-9417
TEL 707-746-1900

Hand-printed wallpapers from the Victorian and Arts & Crafts periods (1860-1918) including borders, dadoes, friezes, panels and elaborate ceiling ornaments.

Price Range: $39 - $76/roll; $18 - $20,000/project
Recent Projects: Supplied wallpapers for Lumber Baron Inn, Denver, CO; supplied wallpapers for An Elegant Victorian Mansion, Eureka, CA

RORY BRENNAN

PRESERVATION PLASTERING
RFD 1 BOX 772
PUTNEY, VT 05346
TEL 802-387-4623

Plaster preservation and conservations, blending traditional craftsmanship with modern conservation techniques; plaster adhesive reattachments, custom enrichment, run replications and installations, historic formulations, documentation analysis, and consultation.

Price Range: custom work only
Recent Projects: Support brackets rebuilt, including enrichment, bench runs attached, adhesive reattachment, in-kind replacements, United Church of Christ, Keene, NH; adhesive reattachment, bench-run installation, in-kind replacements, Vermont Statehouse, Montpelier, VT

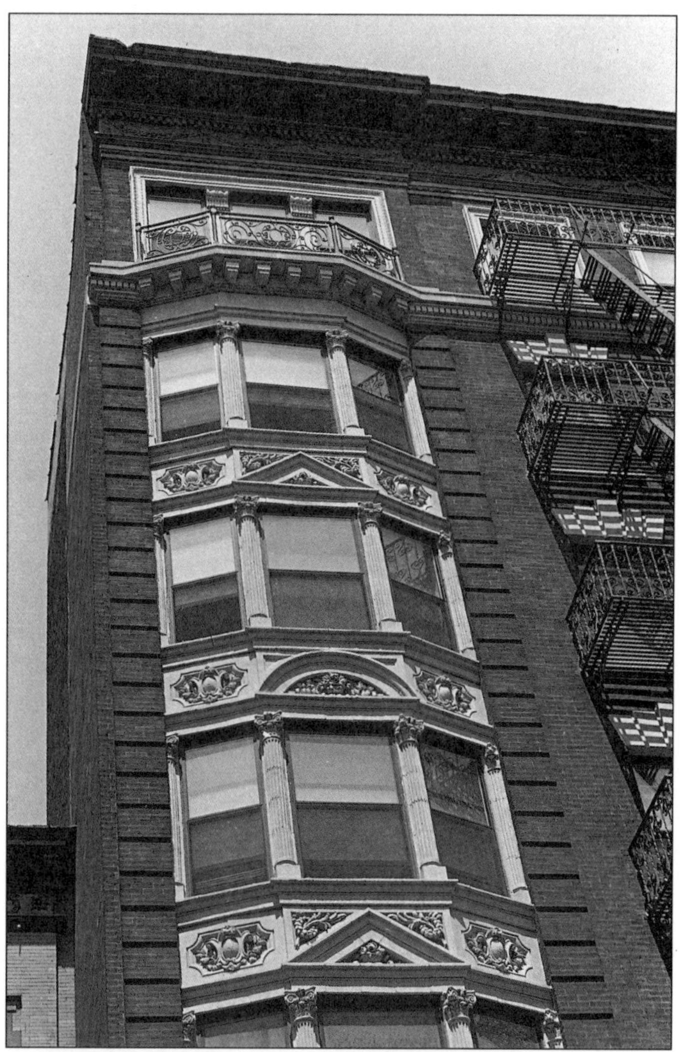

Art Home Sculpture Studios replaced terra cotta architectural elements with glass-fiber-reinforced concrete (GFRC) at Weston House, New York, NY

CAMBRIDGE SMITHY

PETER A. KRUSCH
RR 2 BOX 1280
CAMBRIDGE, VT 05444-9717
TEL   802-644-5358

Cambridge Smithy, a small company founded in 1971, specializes in one-of-a-kind weathervanes (copper and steel, some incorporating stained glass) and special wrought iron lighting fixtures, commissions and repairs.

Price Range: $30 - $50/hour
Recent Projects: Restored weathervanes and wrought iron lighting fixtures for public and private sites

CARL SCHILLING STONEWORKS

PO BOX 607
PROCTOR, VT 05765-0607
FAX   802-459-2948
TEL   802-459-2200

Quarrier and fabricator in marble, granite and sandstone.

Price Range: $10,000 - $2,000,000/project
Recent Projects: Brownstone replacement stone for Jackson Place exterior restoration; brownstone for Hubbard Memorial Library.

CARPENTER & SMITH RESTORATIONS

PETER A. NICOLAZZI, II
33301 GENEVA RD
BURLINGTON, WI 53105-8804
FAX   414-537-2641
TEL   800-728-3653

Preserving our architectural heritage since 1972. Woodworkers expressively involved in restoration, from furniture to buildings. Products, services, workshops and consulting services available to architects, contractors, municipalities, museums and homeowners.

Price Range: $37.50 - $75/hour; $500 - $150,000/project
Recent Projects: Restored curved-corner porch and was recipient of a local preservation award, Kenosha, WI; reproduced and repaired cornice and overhangs of an 1846 Greek Revival private residence in Lake Geneva, WI

CEDAR GUILD INC.

JIM AND NANCY CAREY
PO BOX 249A
LYONS, OR 97358-0249
FAX   503-897-2442
TEL   503-897-2541
TEL   800-270-2541

The Cedar Guild provides custom replication work in cedar and redwood for roofs and sidewalls, 57 patterns available. Did reproduction shake and shingles for Fort Wilderness Lodge at Disneyworld, FL.

Price Range: $58 - $65/fancy patterned shingle
Recent Projects: Replicated circa-1800 patterned roof material for steeple and roof replacement, St. James Episcopal Church, Long Island, NY; Market Street house, Independence Square, Independence National Historic Park, Philadelphia, PA (1994)

CHRISTOPHER WALBERG LTD.

C. WALBERG
1944 W SUPERIOR ST
CHICAGO, IL 60622-5531
TEL   312-738-3256

Contractor and consultant for historic rehabilitation, interior and exterior.

Price Range: $36 - $400/hour; $2,000 - $2,785,000/project
Recent Projects: Total rehabilitation of several sites; total rehabilitation to deconvert monastery to single family residence

COLONIAL RESTORATIONS

THOMAS O. GREEN
26 MAIN ST
BROOKFIELD, MA 01506-1500
TEL   508-867-4400

Colonial Restorations provides structural restoration of early buildings. Replacement of beams involves not only structural integrity, but the aesthetic beauty of the frame itself.

Price Range: $100 - $150/linear ft.;
Recent Projects: Structural and exterior restoration for the Merrifield-Libbey house; structural restoration and new timber-frame addition for a private residence

★ CONRAD SCHMITT STUDIOS, INC.

HEIDI GRUENKE EMERY
2405 S 162ND ST
NEW BERLIN, WI 53151-2805
FAX 414-786-9036
TEL 800-969-3033
TEL 414-786-3030

Since 1889, the Conrad Schmitt Studios has restored and decorated hundreds of interiors across the country. Their scope includes the investigation and documentation of original design schemes, gilding, glazing, marbleizing, stencilling, trompe l'oeil, and graining, as well as the conservation and replication of murals and stained glass.

Price Range: $2,000 - $1,000,000/project
Recent Projects: Restoration of interior, including investigation and documentation of original decorative scheme, gilding, glazing, marbleizing, Wang Center, Boston; artistic replication of aged finishes within the Miller Museum, Miller Brewing Company, Milwaukee, WI

See page 98 for photographs and additional information.

CREATIVE SCULPTURES & RESTORATION

GARY KESHNER
12100 E 67TH ST
KANSAS CITY, MO 64133-6907
TEL   816-353-3385

Restoration work on monuments, sculptures, historic buildings, and fountains. We also provide restoration consulting.

Price Range: $50/hour
Recent Projects: Restored monuments, sculptures, fountains, etc. for parks and museums

CUMMINGS STAINED GLASS STUDIOS, INC.

H.W. CUMMINGS
PO BOX 427
NORTH ADAMS, MA 01247-0427
FAX   413-664-6570
TEL   413-664-6578

Over 70 years of experience in stained glass. Technical expertise and practical business approaches have become our hallmarks. American stained glass of the 1880s to 1920s.

Price Range: $200 - $2,000/sq. ft.; $1,000 - $1,000,000/project
Recent Projects: 12th and 15th Century windows, Gardner Museum; Tillinghost and Booker windows, Grace Church, NY

DANIEL MAHER STAINED GLASS

DANIEL MAHER
266 CONCORD AVE
CAMBRIDGE, MA 02138-1338
TEL   617-661-5771

Extensive experience in the restoration and conservation of fine art glass windows such as those created by Tiffany, La Farge, and Connick. Employing the latest conservation methods for museum-quality restoration.

Price Range: $75 - $1500/sq. ft.; $1,000 - $97,000/project
Recent Projects: Restoration of Miller Memorial Window by Tiffany and 22 ornamental windows, St. Paul's Church, Milwaukee, WI; recreated and restored fire-damaged windows for the Grace Episcopal Church, New Bedford, MA

DAPRATO RIGALI, INC.

ROBERT RIGALI
7956 OAKTON ST
NILES, IL 60714
FAX   708-692-3445
TEL   708-692-6350

Daprato Rigali, Inc. is an interior restoration and decoration company of designers consultants, and craftsmen. We specialize in gilding, stenciling, stained glass and marble work.
Recent Projects: Restoration and gilding of marble for The Rookery Building Chicago, IL; general contractors for interior and stained glass restoration of Sacred Heart Church Winnetka, IL

DAVID FLAHARTY, SCULPTOR

DAVID FLAHARTY
1064 MAGAZINE RD
GREEN LANE, PA 18054-2232
FAX   215-234-8242
TEL   215-234-8242

Specializing in cornices and ceiling medallions, this studio replicates period interiors from the 19th century. Flaharty also undertakes stabilization of ornamented ceilings in danger of falling. Ornamental metal pattern-making is a specialty.

Price Range: $1,000 - $3,000/ceiling medallion; $10,000 - $50,000/project
Recent Projects: Stabilized a parlor and a stairhall ornamental ceiling for the Chase Lloyd House, c. 1770, Annapolis, MD; ornamental plaster and bronze handprints of presidential grandchildren, The White House, Washington, DC

TIM deCHRISTOPHER

NEW ENGLAND STONEWORKS
80 MONTAGUE RD
SHUTESBURY, MA 01072-9709
FAX   413-259-1066
TEL   413-259-1066

New England Stoneworks is uniquely qualified to provide restoration services for any and all aspects of cut stone masonry and ornamental stonework. Highly skilled carving a specialty. Limestone, marble, slate, granite.

Price Range: $1,000 - $10,000/project
Recent Projects: Cleaning and recarving of monumental entryway sculpture for the U.S. Custom House, Battery Park, NY; restoration stonework, dismantled and rebuilt dormer gable for the Jewish Museum, New York, NY

DOWNSTATE RESTORATIONS

1944 W SUPERIOR ST
CHICAGO, IL 60622
TEL   312-738-3256

Restoration contractor and consultant emphasizing facades.

Price Range: $36 - $400/hour; $4,000 - $1,000,000/project
Recent Projects: Masonry restoration, Dwight Library, Dwight, IL; restored roof gutters, and dormers, Lloyd Residence, north suburban Chicago, IL

DURHAN STUDIOS, INC.

PAUL COULAZ
330 EAGLE AVE
WEST HEMPSTEAD, NY 11552-3844
FAX   516-481-7905
TEL   516-481-5656

We are a full service studio, providing all work from design to installation. Repairs and restorations, frames and protective material. Emergency service available.
Recent Projects: Repairs and restoration to stained glass windows for St. Joseph's Roman Catholic Church, Jamaica, NY; repairs and restoration to stained glass windows for St. Joseph's Roman Catholic church, Garden City, NY

FELBER ORNAMENTAL PLASTERING CORP.

JAMES J. KURYLOSKI
PO BOX 57 1000 W WASHINGTON ST
NORRISTOWN, PA 19404
FAX 610-275-6636
TEL 610-275-4713

We are experts in the field of architectural ornamentation with extensive experience in restoring and replicating historic ornament. We have an historic collection of over 5000 models and molds representing all styles and periods.

Price Range: $150 - $100,000/project
Recent Projects: Supplied large quantities of cornice and moldings to match originals, New Jersey State Annex Building, Trenton, NJ; supplied all cornice and moldings to match originals after fire damage, Mead Hall, Drew University, Madison, NJ

FEMENELLA & ASSOCIATES, INC.

ARTHUR J. FEMENELLA
3 BRIGHTON CT
ANNANDALE, NJ 08801-3348
FAX 908-713-1771
TEL 908-735-6840

Stained and decorative glass, and historic wood window restoration consultant. Condition reports, restoration specifications and project quality control. Twenty-two years experience restoring the work of Tiffany, La Farge and other great glass artists.

Price Range: $85 - $110/hour; $3,500 - $100,000/project
Recent Projects: Condition survey, restoration specifications, and supervision for Tiffany window restoration, St. Paul's Episcopal Church, Nantucket, MA; condition reports, restoration specification, and supervision for restoration of 60 stained glass windows, Cadet Chapel, West Point Military Academy

FERGUSON'S CUT GLASS WORKS, INC.

CARY S. FERGUSON
4292 PEARL RD
CLEVELAND, OH 44109
TEL 216-459-2929

Ferguson's specializes in the restoration of hand-cut and beveled glass for Victorian- style entrance ways; restoration services also include hand-cut crystal, chandeliers lamps, Venetian glass and mirrors.

Price Range: $800 - $20,000/project
Recent Projects: Hand-cut glass, polished and etched, Victorian-style door panels for Hower House, the University of Akron, OH; restoration of hand-cut crystal lamps, the Antiquarium, OH

FINE ART CONSERVATION LABORATORIES

SCOTT M. HASKINS
PO BOX 23557
SANTA BARBARA, CA 93121-3557
FAX 805-568-1178
TEL 805-564-3438

FACL specializes in the conservation of murals (affresoes, paint on plaster marouflage) and decorative surfaces. Paint analysis consultations, project management.

Price Range: $10,000 - $400,000/project
Recent Projects: Affresco cleaning, consolidation, repainting, water damage repair for Hearst Castle, San Simeon, CA; earthquake repair damage for the Los Angeles Central Library, CA

THE FINE WOODWORKING COMAPANY INC.

CRISPIN BEROZA
16750 WHITES STORE RD
BOYDS, MD 20841-9673
FAX 301-916-3509
TEL 301-972-8808

Designers, producers and installers of quality architectural freestanding woodwork and furniture; extensively experienced in residential period preservation, restoration, and replication work. Featured in many national trade publications. Brochure available.

Price Range: $300 - $1,250/custom doors; $28.50 - $35.50/hour; $300 - $300,000/project
Recent Projects: Historic renovation and custom woodworking for various residences in Georgetown, Capitol Hill, and Montgomery County, MD; historic renovation custom woodworking and design for an historic residence in Chevy Chase, MD

FISCHER ARTWORKS

BRIAN FISCHER
6530 S WINDERMERE ST
LITTLETON, CO 80120-3202
TEL 303-798-4841
TEL 800-441-6067

Finely crafted roof spires, lightning rods, gable ends, and roof cresting, for replication or restoration. Copper and bronze specializing in custom Victorian designs.

Price Range: $350 - $650/finials; $350 - $1800/project
Recent Projects: Finials for Silverton Town Hall Restoration, Lagoon Park Amusement Center expansion

FORGING A FUTURE

MICHAEL W. CHISHAM
PO BOX 82
PETALUMA, CA 94953
FAX 707-765-9861
TEL 707-765-9861

100% custom-forged ferris and non-ferris metal, specializing in faux-painted iron work. "Your imagination is my limit."

Price Range: $50 - $125/gate, rails, guard rails; $60/hour; $50 - $75,000/project
Recent Projects: Stainless-forged hand rails, door pulls and glass shelves for Hawthorne Street Restaurant, San Francisco, CA; stainless-forged 32'L pot rack with shelf for the Scalas Restaurant, Sir Francis Drake Hotel, San Francisco, CA

LES FOSSEL

RESTORATION RESOURCES
PO BOX 525
ALNA, ME 04535-0525
TEL 207-586-5690

I've been restoring 18th and early 19th century buildings for 20 years. I have a crew of five people. I offer everything from the smallest molding to complete buildings.

Price Range: $7 - $25/hour; $500 - $170,000/project
Recent Projects: Fireplace, paneling, staircase, flooring and plaster restoration, Newcastle, ME; 1780s bow roof cape removed, restored, and re-erected, Woolwich, ME

PAUL FRIEND

PAUL FRIEND ARCHITECTURAL GLASS AND DESIGN, INC.
216 LINCOLN AVE
HADDONFIELD, NJ 08033-1851
FAX 609-428-1199
TEL 609-428-9100

Paul Friend's glass facilities are located under one roof, which allows tight control over each phase of every project. The studio's commitment to professionalism in architectural glass and restoration is apparent with on-time completions and budget requirements.

Price Range: $125 - $175/sq. ft.; $37.50 - $87.50/hour; $2,500 - $60,000/project
Recent Projects: Total restoration of 100-year-old windows, First Baptist Church Haddonfield, NJ; total restoration of chapel windows, St. Mary's Episcopal Church, Haddon Heights, NJ

FULL CIRCLE GLASS COMPANY

FRANK M. QUAGLIA
62 WALTER ST
PEARL RIVER, NY 10965-1722
FAX 914-735-0662
TEL 914-735-4137

Est. 1976. Products include custom stained and beveled glass in lead, zinc, brass wheel engraving, embossing, sand etching and carving, mirrored wall sculptures, experimental windows.

Price Range: $50 - $450/sq. ft.; $50 - $150/hour; $900 - $8,000/project
Recent Projects: Replication of glass for 150 casement windows in the Arts and Crafts style, private residence; restoration of engraved Venetian mirror for a residence, Westport, CT

GOLD LEAF STUDIOS

WILLIAM ADAIR
443 I ST NW PO BOX 50156
WASHINGTON, DC 20091
FAX 202-347-4569
TEL 202-638-4660

Specializing in conservation and fabrication of gilded antiques, frame fabrication quality reproduction of period frames.

Price Range: $45 - $90/hour; $1,000 - $8,500/project
Recent Projects: Re-gilded gates in 23K gold leaf; Dumbarton Oaks, Washington DC; re-gilded architectural elements for the Department of State diplomatic reception rooms

GREAT PANES ARCHITECTURAL GLASS ART

RAYMOND I. CENTANNI
3764 SILVERADO TRL
CALISTOGA, CA 94515-9613
FAX 707-963-9115
TEL 707-963-9115

We have created and restored glass art internationally for over 20 years. From frame structures to highly refined, detailed glass painting and intricate lead work. Large projects our specialty.
Recent Projects: Releaded, repainted and reinstalled 1,500 sq. ft. of windows for the 100-year-old St. Francis of Assisi Catholic Church, Sacramento, CA; releaded, repainted and reinstalled windows, including three 20'Dia rose windows, for the Mission Presbyterian Church, San Francisco, CA

★ HISTORICAL ARTS & CASTING INC.

RUTH B. EDWARDS
5580 BAGLEY PARK RD
WEST JORDAN, UT 84088-5642
FAX 801-280-2493
TEL 801-280-2400

Working with bronze, aluminum, and iron, the craftsmen at Historical Arts design and manufacture a wide variety of cast metal ornament from lighting and railings to fountains and storefronts. We specialize in restoration and restoration projects.

Price Range: $200 - $2,000/linear ft.; Recent Projects: Restored waiting room chandeliers using bronze with nickel and gold plating, Grand Central Terminal, New York, NY; cast iron facade restoration, New York, NY

See page 26 for photographs and additional information.

STACIA A. HUMMEL

CURIO
40 W MARKET ST
MARIETTA, PA 17547-1424
TEL 717-426-2979

Curio specializes in new decorative painting, recreation of authentic treatments for historic interiors, restoration of existing murals, and decorative painting; projects exhibit skill in trompe l'oeil, grisalle, gilding, faux bois, faux marble for any style or period interior.

Price Range: $50 and up for restorations; $30 - $50/hour; $200 - $2,000/project
Recent Projects: Scenic ceiling mural of a tropical sky with grissaille trellis and monkey for the Eisenhart Residence; faux bois and faux marble on raised panel wainscoat and columns, residences, Harrisburg Builders' Show

★ INTERNATIONAL FINE ART CONSERVATION STUDIOS INC.

GEOFFREY M. STEWARD
PO BOX 180098
ATLANTA, GA 30318-0001
FAX 404-794-6229
TEL 404-794-6142

Research, historic and scientific analysis, condition surveys, estimates, conservation and restoration of period interiors, murals and easel paintings. Specialist decoration executed includes gilding, graining, marbleizing, stencilling, glazing, trompe l'oeil and murals.
Recent Projects: Restoration of murals and decorative painting for the Ohio State Capitol, Columbus, OH; conservation and restoration of historic finishes at the Hay House, Macon, GA

See page 99 for photographs and additional information.

J. RING GLASS STUDIO

2724 UNIVERSITY AVE SE
MINNEAPOLIS, MN 55414
FAX 612-379-4252
TEL 612-379-0902

Twenty-five years experience in custom beveled and leaded art glass, stained glass fabrication and restoration, Prairie School art glass using zinc and copper.

Price Range: $50 - $100/sq. ft.; $35 - $55/hour; $500 - $8,000/project
Recent Projects: Stained glass restoration, First Lutheran Church, Columbia Heights, MN; leaded, beveled, stained art glass at multiple sites

TERI ARTHUR JEFFERSON

JEFFERSON ART LIGHTING CO.
1342 N MAIN ST
ANN ARBOR, MI 48104-1008
FAX 313-663-8482
TEL 313-761-8160

Jefferson Art Lighting Co. designs and fabricates lighting fixtures, architectural plaster ornaments and decorative metal castings for private clients, designers and architects throughout the U.S. The firm specializes in historic preservation and restoration of antique lighting fixtures.

Price Range: $5,000 - $8,000/chandelier; $100/hour
Recent Projects: Replicated historic torcheres, using photographs, for main lobby of the Detroit Symphony Orchestra Hall; restored historic lighting fixtures, including chandeliers from the 1870s, for the Michigan State Capitol Building

JOHNSON ATELIER - TECHNICAL INSTITUTE OF SCULPTURE

60 WARD AVE EXTENSION
MERCERVILLE, NJ 08619
FAX 609-890-1816
TEL 609-890-7777

Fine art foundry and school which offers a full range of custom services and supplies for sculptural projects, fabrication or casting in bronze, ductile iron, aluminum, copper and sterling silver.

Price Range: $500 - $300,000/project
Recent Projects: Remodeled, molded and cast in bronze 20 lampposts in Bryant Park, New York, NY; fabricated and finished 19 commemorative bronze plaques and bas-relief for the Fulton Landing Pier Restoration

★ ROBERT S. JORDAN

ROBERT S. JORDAN
ARTIST/BLACKSMITH
13 CAPTAIN DOANES WAY
ORLEANS, MA 02653-2301
FAX 508-255-3198
TEL 508-240-7661

Twenty-four years experience in forged ornamental metal. Worked and studied under American and European masters. Will work with my designs or yours. Commissioned furniture lighting gates, railings a specialty. Work in forged copper, brass, steel, stainless steel, and aluminum. Highest quality work only.

Price Range: $500 - $4,000/furniture; $50/hour; $2,000 - $110,000/project
Recent Projects: Restored 120' of fence, circa 1872, Boston, MA; fabricated gates and restored triangle above gates, Nauticus Marina, Osterville, MA

See photograph this page.

Robert S. Jordan, griffin (one of a pair), exterior light from Spain, 1880s, restored, reglassed and relighted in 1995, 70"H

TTHE JUDSON STUDIOS

WILLIAM JUDSON
200 SOUTH AVE 66
LOS ANGELES, CA 90042
FAX 213-255-8529
TEL 800-445-8376

Stained glass restoration deserves the finest care, craftsmanship and respect. We give your project meticulous attention, backed with 100 years experience. Recent Projects: Complete restoration of stained glass dome, Los Angeles Museum of Natural History; restoration of stained glass windows, Mount St. Mary's College Chapel, Los Angeles, CA

KAYE RESTORATIONS

BOB KAYE
537 9TH ST
BROOKLYN, NY 11215-4205
TEL 718-788-1837

Twenty years experience in straight and ornamental plaster work, can duplicate most cast plaster. Pieces also have a line of ceiling medallions and wall brackets.

Price Range: $25 - $40/hour; varies according to project
Recent Projects: Complete restoration of plaster straight and ornamental three-story brownstone, Brooklyn, NY restoration of Victorian moldings and original plaster ceiling, walls, Brooklyn, NY

KAYNE & SON CUSTOM HARDWARE

STEVE KAYNE
100 DANIEL RIDGE RD
CANDLER, NC 28715-9434
FAX 704-665-8303
TEL 704-667-8868

Repairs, restorations, reproductions; custom hand-forged strap hinges, thumb latches bolts, fireplace accessories, hooks, brackets, shutter dogs, nails, cast brass and bronze exterior thumb latch and lock sets, interior sets, pulls. Catalogs are available for $5.

Price Range: minimum $50/hour
Recent Projects: Hand-forged hinges, pulls, fireplace cranes, trammel hooks colonial lighting, brackets, boot scrapers, for the film, *Nell,* Lost Pond Enterprises, Fontana Dam NC; window hardware restorations in brass and steel, Grove Park Inn, Asheville, NC

★ GUY KEMPER

KEMPER STUDIO
190 N BROADWAY ST
LEXINGTON, KY 40507-1270
FAX 606-254-3507
TEL 606-254-3507

Since 1983, conscientious restorer and repairer of small-scale leaded-glass installations and fixtures.

Price Range: $500 - $5,000/panel; $75/hour; $500 - $3,500/project
Recent Projects: Repaired 3rd Street studio window, Lexington, KY; repaired two glass-domed skylights for the Kentucky Theatre, Lexington, KY

See page 50 for photographs and additional information.

PETER KRAMER

REMARK DESIGN INC.
PO BOX 232
WASHINGTON, VA 22747-0232
TEL 703-675-3625

Peter Kramer has supervised the restoration of a number of structures in the historic district of Washington, VA. He is a furniture designer and cabinetmaker who applies the best traditional methods to his original and reproduction designs.

Price Range: $600 - $1,500/chairs; $38 - $50/hour; $1,200 - $170,000/project
Recent Projects: Restored many homes in Washington, VA; designed and managed major restoration of four buildings at the Shenandoah Country Club

LAMB STUDIOS

DONALD SAMICK
PO BOX 291
PHILMONT, NY 12565
FAX 518-672-7597
TEL 518-672-7267

Established in 1957, Lamb Studios is the oldest studio in America. We work throughout the United States and specialize in restoring Lamb, LaFarge and Tiffany stained glass windows. Zinc came is our speciality.

Price Range: $200 - $300/sq.ft;
Recent Projects: Reconstruction of 8' x 10' leaded-glass window, replaced all lead came for Sleepy Hollow Country Club, Scarborough, NY; restored 2 leaded-glass windows for Nassau County Recreation and Parks in Mineola, NY

★ LANDMARK STUDIOS

LARRY POTTER
59 LOWER KINGTOWN RD
PITTSTOWN, NJ 08867-4147
FAX 908-730-8851
TEL 908-730-8895

Landmark Studios produces and restores architectural sculpture and historic building elements, primarily of stone, plaster and terra cotta. Services include: sculpting, mold-making casting and on-site repairs. Delivery of complete projects spawned from drawings and photos, or from damaged architectural features and conditions.

Price Range: $25 - $25,000/sq. ft.; $35 - $200/hour; $2,000 - $350,000/project
Recent Projects: Replication of 12th Century carved stone sculptural elements from a Spanish chapel, The Cloisters, New York Metropolitan Museum of Art; replication and installation of carved marble comice, frieze and banding sections for the New York Bank for Savings, Park Avenue South, New York, NY

See photograph this page.

JOHN LEEKE

JOHN LEEKE, PRESERVATION
   CONSULTANT
26 HIGGINS ST
PORTLAND, ME 04103
TEL 203-773-2306

Thirty years hands-on experience in preservation woodworking; 12 years consulting and design team work on registered and national landmark buildings. Condition assessments training, problem solving. Practical restoration reports: $10 - $15.

Price Range: $45 - $60/hour; $1,000 - $20,000/project
Recent Projects: Exterior wood and sanded paint maintenance for Morse-Libby Mansion, 1858 National Landmark; masonry investigation and project design for Warner House, 1716 National Landmark

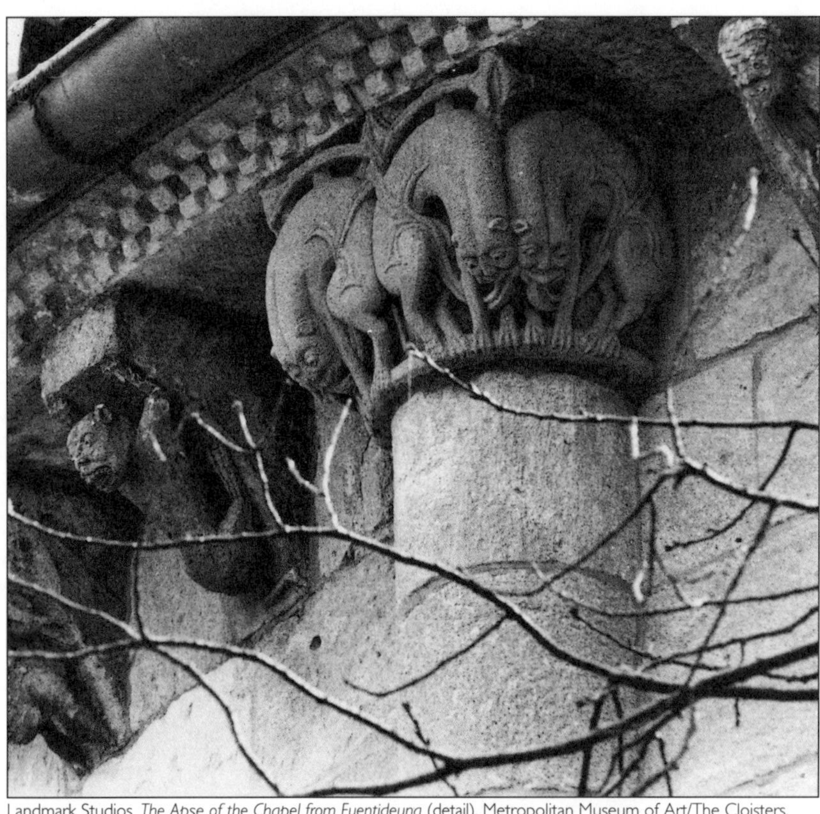

Landmark Studios, *The Apse of the Chapel from Fuentideuna* (detail), Metropolitan Museum of Art/The Cloisters, New York, NY, originally carved in 12th Century Spain, replicated for replacement and record

LIGHT HAUS INC.

STEVEN J. MELAHN
1921 FREEPORT RD
MADISON, WI 53711-3627
FAX 608-274-2403
TEL 608-274-2942

With 16 years experience in complete restoration, Light Haus is able to handle projects requiring repair, removal and installation, painting, custom beveling, metal and wood fabrication.

Price Range: $80 - $175/sq. ft.;
Recent Projects: Extensive restoration of windows, art glass lamp shades and skylight for the Wisconsin State Capitol; removal, restoration and installation of nine windows for St. James Lutheran Church, Verona, WI

DAVID LINKER

DAVID LINKER, LTD.
109 S 5TH ST
BROOKLYN, NY 11211-5501
TEL 718-388-9443

David Linker, master ébéniste, was trained in France and specializes in 17th and 18th century antique furniture restoration, marquetry, French polish, repair and replacement of ormolu mercury gilding, and marble repair.

Price Range: $90/hour;
Recent Projects: Restored Dutch-style marquetry for bureau-plat from 1690's private residence; restored Hudson Valley kas for Gracie Mansion, New York, NY

LITTLEWOOD & MAUE

PO BOX 402
PALMYRA, NJ 08065
TEL 609-829-4615

Restoration specialists of Victorian lighting. Recent Projects: Blair House, the Presidential Guest House, Washington, DC; The Atheneum, Philadelphia, PA

M.J. MAY BUILDING RESTORATION

MICHAEL J. MAY
141 W STATE ST
BURLINGTON, WI 53105-1835
FAX 414-763-8822
TEL 414-763-8822

Established in 1981. Specializing in all phases of interior and exterior building restoration. Strong emphasis on millwork replacement to match, paint removal inside and out followed by precision finishing. Award-winning artisans.

Price Range: $32 - $35/hour;
Recent Projects: Restored exterior, 1858 Hazelo House, 1993 award winner Wisconsin Trust for Historic Preservation; 1994 winner, Wisconsin Trust for Historic Preservation, Issac Ulman House

MAD RIVER WOODWORKS

TIM THORNTON
PO BOX 1067
BLUE LAKE, CA 95525-1067
FAX 707-668-5673
TEL 707-668-5671

Primary focus: replicating millwork with a strong emphasis on the Victorian Era, as well as more contemporary design. Will work from paint scars, photographs, or existing millwork. Established 1981.

Price Range: $2,000 - $18,000/project
Recent Projects: Restored lower facade to original appearance from circa-1905 photo, The Gazebo, Ferndale, CA; restored portions of original architecture and addition to form a complete meld, Eureka, CA

MARTINO ART GLASS STUDIO

NINO MARTINO
839 ELLROSE AVE
WINDSOR, ON N8Y-3W6
CANADA
TEL 519-974-2780

Over 16 years of specialization in restoration. Offers quality and experienced workmanship to suit the most demanding needs. Pricing is competitive. Established 1989.

Price Range: $40 - $150/sq. ft.; $35 - $70/hour;
Recent Projects: Major restoration of 38 windows, 3 rose windows, 8 panels for Sacred Heart Church, Windsor, ON; major restoration of 77 stained glass windows for St. Simon & St. Jude Church, Belle River, ON

CRAIG MCCULLEN

WHOOJOO GLASS STUDIO
PO BOX 2591
LAFAYETTE, LA 70502-2591
FAX 318-269-9310
TEL 318-269-9310

BFA and MFA from the LSU stained glass program in 1979. Owner of WhooJoo Glass Studio since 1979.

Price Range: $15 - $250/sq. ft.;
Recent Projects: Restored glass and replicated windows, St. Margaret Catholic Church, Lake Charles, LA; restored all stained glass, painted glass to replace broken pieces, St. John Berchman Catholic Church, Carkton, LA

MEETING HOUSE FURNITURE RESTORATION

JONATHAN T. SCHECHTMAN
GENERAL DELIVERY
QUECHEE, VT 05059-9999
FAX 802-296-5911
TEL 802-295-1309

We have conserved, repaired, restored and refinished antique and contemporary furniture and architectural woodwork for collectors, antique dealers, historic houses, museums and state buildings. Replication of missing carved or turned elements our specialty.

Price Range: $32 - $48/hour;
Recent Projects: Restored 150 legislators' desks in the House of Representatives, Vermont State House; restored 1858 piano in Summer White House, Calvin Coolidge Historic Birthplace

MELOTTE-MORSE STAINED GLASS, INC.

STEVE BROOKS
213 1/2 S 6TH ST
SPRINGFIELD, IL 62701-1502
FAX 217-789-9518
TEL 217-789-9523

Melotte-Morse Stained Glass, Inc. offers complete restoration services from removal to installation. The studio, as part of a larger architectural firm, brings the experience of architects to the process.

Price Range: $1,000 - $75,000/project
Recent Projects: Complete restoration of 77 stained glass panels for Drake University main auditorium, Des Moines, IA; restoration of approximately 225 art glass pieces for the Frank Lloyd Wright designed Dana-Thomas House, Springfield, IL

DON MESERVE

DON MESERVE INC.
PO BOX 152
ROUND POND, ME 04564-0152
FAX 207-529-5327
TEL 207-529-5327
FAX 914-478-3494
TEL 914-478-3494

Our restoration staff specializes in the reconstruction and installation of large-scale architectural elements (fountains, stairs and statuary), as well as stone and terra cotta restoration on historic structures.

Price Range: $12,000 - $63,000/project
Recent Projects: Restoration and installation of Karl Bitter Pulpit for the Metropolitan Museum, New York, NY; terra cotta restoration, Dexter Library, Dexter, ME

MICHAEL DOTZEL & SON INC.

MICHAEL DOTZEL
402 E 63RD ST
NEW YORK, NY 10021-7901
FAX 212-371-4839
TEL 212-838-2890

Michael Dotzel & Son Inc. specializes in repairing and restoring brass, copper, iron lead, pewter, etc.

Price Range: $65 - $150/hour; $65 - $5,000/project
Recent Projects: Restoration of antiques after fire damage, private residence; restoration for Sotheby's, New York, NY

MUSEUM QUALITY RESTORATIONS

LITTLEWOOD AND MAUE
319 CINNAMINSON AVE
PALMYRA, NJ 08065-1509
TEL 609-829-4615

MQR provides a historic lighting service to museums, the National Parks Service historic buildings and serious collectors. Specialty metal repair and refinishing to recreate original appearance of historic lighting fixtures. Some custom reproductions of glassware from 1825 to 1875 are available.
Recent Projects: Blair House, the guest house for the President, restoration and annual maintenance White House of the Confederacy, Richmond, VA

NY DECORATIVE ARTS STUDIO

MICHAEL GLICKMAN
537 87TH ST #1E
NEW YORK, NY 10028
FAX 212-570-9373
TEL 212-570-9373

Specialists in the design and painting of interior and exterior murals, faux finishes gilding, Italian encaustic, Venetian stucco.

Price Range: $10 - $50/ sq. ft.; $25 - $75/hour; $25,000/project
Recent Projects: Historical murals, gilding, woodgraining, The Barbizon HoTEL New York, NY; exterior paint restoration and window trompe l'oeil, McDonald's Building, New York, NY

NIKO CONTRACTING CO., INC.

NICHOLAS D. LARDAS
3434 PARKVIEW AVE
PITTSBURGH, PA 15213-4304
FAX 412-687-7969
TEL 412-687-1517

NIKO Contracting Co., Inc. is an architectural sheet metal and roofing contractor with over 20 years experience nationwide. Fabricates and installs all types of ornamental sheet metal and metal roofing, including cornices, dormer surrounds, finials, crests, marquees, etc. Extensive experience with historic restoration.

Price Range: $20 - $300/sq. ft.; $35 - $90/hour; $5,000 - $2,500,000/project
Recent Projects: Replaced copper roofing and architectural copper work to replicate original, Cooper-Hewitt Museum, New York, NY; replaced metal roofing and rebuilt skylights, Tariff Building, Washington, DC

NORTH AMERICAN SLATE, INC.

ROBERT L. TATKO
50 COLUMBUS ST
GRANVILLE, NY 12832-1024
FAX 518-642-3255
TEL 518-642-1702

Quarrier and manufacturer of natural slate products including roofing, flooring and dimensional stone.

Price Range: $2 - $15/sq. ft.;
Recent Projects: Slate restoration including roofing and paving, Casedei Compound; paving restoration, Norstar Fleet Financial Bank; complete restoration of roofing slate Historic Preservation Award, Holworthy Hall, Harvard University, MA

OLD WORLD RESTORATIONS, INC.

DOUGLAS A. EISELE
347 STANLEY AVE
CINCINNATI, OH 45226-2100
FAX 513-321-1914
TEL 513-321-1911

Fine conservation and restoration service providing museum-quality treatments to a wide spectrum of artworks. Experienced staff utilizes great care and sensitivity preserving paintings, porcelain, glass, sculpture, murals and gold leaf. On-site surveys, nationwide service.

Price Range: $50 - $85/hour; $50 - $230,000/project
Recent Projects: Restoration and conservation treatment of fire-damaged murals and frescos, Mother of God Church, Covington, KY; restoration of plaster, First United Methodist Church, Lancaster, OH

THE ORUM SILVER CO. INC.

JOE PISTILLI
51 S VINE ST BOX 805
MERIDEN, CT 06450-0805
FAX 203-237-3037
TEL 203-237-3037

Restoration of antiques, old silverware, pewter and brass; gold, silver, nickel, brass and copper plating. All types of metal finishing and repair done in-house.
Recent Projects: Refinished brass altar pieces, St. Marys Church, New Haven CT; restored mirrors in private homes

PACE COMPANY

2901 AXTON LN
GOSHEN, KY 40026-9743
TEL 502-228-1591

Authentic Log Cabin restorations, 18 years experience. Complete design and consulting. We dismantle and relocate authentic log houses using modern, as well as primitive technology and tools.

Price Range: $50,000 - $250,000/project
Recent Projects: Log cabin inside new home construction at the Amos Martin Building; log cabin room attached to federal design house on the Louisville Homearama Sutherland Farms

PACIFIC STATES CARPENTRY

JAMES SPAULDING
3249 BRIGGS AVE
ALAMEDA, CA 94501-4802
TEL 510-523-0906

Long-time member of the National Trust and A.P.T. We concentrate on the repair and replacement of interior and exterior architectural millwork.

Price Range: $750 - $10,000/project
Recent Projects: Repaired and replaced exterior and interior wooden elements at the Camron-Stanford House, Oakland, CA; replaced missing architectural elements for facade Victorian residence, Alameda, CA

PINSON AND WARE, PAINTED ORNAMENT

ED AND DEBRAH PINSON
PO BOX 292
MONROVIA, CA 91017-0292
TEL 818-359-6113

Pinson and Ware, a small group of artists, restores architectural painted ornament and creates new, historically styled, painted ornament. We also make historically styled lampshades. All projects custom.

Price Range: $35 - $50/hour; $3,000 - $20,000/project
Recent Projects: Restored water-damaged frieze, painted ornament for the Lanterman House, Historic Museum; repaired weather-damaged historic, painted signage, restored 3/4 life-size polychrome nativity set of 33 pieces, El Pueblo de Los Angeles

PROSTONE RESTORATIONS, INC.

JAY L. DUNHAM
PO BOX 1355
PATASKALA, OH 43062-1355
FAX 614-927-8502
TEL 614-927-7371

The restoration and conservation of specialty masonry surfaces is the primary focus of the Ohio-based firm. Equally adept at interior and exterior challenges, Prostone has proven its ability to bring together various techniques in order to satisfy their clients' particular objectives. Resurfacing, stain removal, stabilizing and patching are among the remedies expertly provided by the professionals at Prostone Restorations.

Price Range: $50 - $100/hour; $5,000 - $500,000/project
Recent Projects: Interior and exterior work on limestone, marble, sandstone and ceramic mosaic for the Ohio Statehouse; cleaning and refinishing on travertine, Minnesota stone slate and zenitherm for the New Jersey Senate Building

E.W. PYFER

LAMP SERVICE
218 N FOLEY AVE
FREEPORT, IL 61032-3943
FAX 815-232-5195
TEL 815-232-8968

Lamp repair and wiring, brass and metal refurbishing, lamps made from all items replacement of all missing lamp parts, old chandeliers restored, oil and gas lamps converted to electric, all parts and glass for all lamps old or new, chimneys, glass globes and shades, lighting fixtures, all Aladdin lamp parts, leaded foil and clip in shades repaired, old parts for antique kerosene, electric and gas lamps.

Price Range: $5 - $250; $1 - $250/project
Recent Projects: Restored antique lamps and lighting at numerous sites

R.E. STAHL, STONECARVER

RICHARD E. STAHL
290 S 725 W
HEBRON, IN 46341-9711
TEL 219-988-2233

Stahl hand-carves restoration pieces using limestone, marble or selected matching stone. He combines time-tested methods of stone carving, research, and modern technology to accurately match and enhance restoration on classic structures. He also carves stone for new buildings that reflect classic styling.

Price Range: $500 - $7,000/project
Recent Projects: Replicated two existing capitals for cloistered walk, the Cloisters Building, University of Chicago, Hyde Park, IL; researched and carved historical design for Tympanum, Deschamps Eye Care Center, Merrillville, IN;

GAIL REDMAN

GAIL REDMAN, WOODTURNING
77 14TH ST
SAN FRANCISCO, CA 94103-4205
FAX 415-431-1595
TEL 415-431-1595

Gail Redman has done fine custom wood turning for 20 years. She specializes in architectural turnings and furniture components, from small quantities to production.

Price Range: $16 - $19/red cedar baluster
Recent Projects: All woodturning for approximately 12 homes in Preservation Park, Oakland, CA; all woodturning for San Francisco Victorianna

REFLECTION STUDIOS, INC.

ALLEN DRAGGE
1418 62ND ST
EMERYVILLE, CA 94608-2036
FAX 510-658-6138
TEL 510-652-4884

For over 25 years, Reflection Studios has produced works of exceptional quality in the field of stained glass arts.

Price Range: $100 - $1,000/sq. ft.
Recent Projects: Restored 100-year-old windows, Saint Francis de Sales Church; restored dome ceiling, Garden Court of the Sheraton Palace

RICK REALE CO. PAINTING AND DECORATING

MARTIN P. ZEISER AND
   RICHARD REALE
406 PARKER AVE S
MERIDEN, CT 06450-5958
FAX 203-634-3444
TEL 203-238-9021

Est. 1971. Traditional and decorative finishes. Marbling, graining, stenciling, gold and metal leaf, glazing, antique and distressed finishes, trompe l'oeil, restorations and fine residential work.

Price Range: $40 - $60/hour;
Recent Projects: Gilding, murals, stencilling, striping, glazing, graining and wood finishing, Smith Ruzzo Funeral Home, Inc.; exterior restoration of existing studio, fine interior finishes, Mercer Mayer studio

★ ROBERT BOUCHER & ASSOCIATES

RR 2 BOX 21B
HEREFORD, AZ 85615-9802
TEL 602-366-5769

Specializing in custom design and sculpting services ranging from large commercial architectural facades to architectural furniture and murals in cast stone, GFRC and glazed terra cotta.
Recent Projects: Restored four facades on 100' historic watertower, recreating missing elements, Tucson, AZ (1993); recreated historic 3-story Owl's Club facade entirely from photographs, Tucson, AZ (1987 Governor's Award)

See page 96 for photographs and additional information.

ROBSUN WORLDWIDE GRAINING LTD.

MALCOLM ROBSUN
4308 ARGONNE DR
FAIRFAX, VA 22032-1405
TEL 703-978-5331

Fifth and sixth generation of master grainers and marblers specializing in restoration recreation, and contemporary rendering of all woods, marbles, and special wall glazing on architectural surfaces as faux finishes.

Price Range: Individualized quotation
Recent Projects: Recreated original graining for George Washington's Mount Vernon home; graining and marbling recreation for Kappa Kappa Gamma headquarters

ROHLF'S STAINED & LEADED GLASS STUDIO, INC.

PETER ROHLF
783 S 3RD AVE
MOUNT VERNON, NY 10550-4946
FAX 914-699-7091
TEL 800-969-4106

Design, fabricate and install stained, leaded and faceted glass, along with restoration and protective glazing of all previously mentioned glasses.

Price Range: $75 - $500/sq. ft.; $2,500 - $400,000/project
Recent Projects: Stained glass restoration and protective glazing, Church of St. Luke & St. Matthew, Brooklyn, NY; stained glass restoration and protective glazing, Cathedral Church of the Advent, Birmingham, AL

RUDOLPH N. ROHN ART STUDIOS, LTD.

ROLF ROHN
807 CRANE AVE
PITTSBURGH, PA 15216-3049
FAX 412-561-8129
TEL 412-561-1228

Est. 1952. Custom design and fabrication or restoration for secular and religious institutions. Over 2,400 commissions. Works on commission basis, or total budget fees. Design development is included. Initial project review gratis. Portfolio on request.

Price Range: $45 - $300/sq. ft.; $65 - $105/hour;
Recent Projects: Mural restoration, St. Peters Cathedral, Erie, PA; leaded glass restoration, Sacred Heart-St. Mary's, PA

RUSSELL RESTORATION

DEAN M. RUSSELL
5550 BERGEN AVE
MATTITUCK, NY 11952-1429
TEL 516-765-2481

All phases of plastering, from lathing, traditional three-coat plaster, drawn cornices custom moldmaking and casting repair, stabilization and restoration of decorated and ornamental plaster, adhesive reattachment of historic plaster.

Price Range: $36 - $52/hour; $550 - $65,000/project
Recent Projects: Plaster cornices, barrel ceilings, flat plaster for a private residence in New York City; restoration of Tudor ceiling and casting of panels, Buckley Day School, Shearson Estate, Long Island, NY

ST. LOUIS ANTIQUE LIGHTING CO.

GARY H. BEHM
801 N SKINKER BLVD
SAINT LOUIS, MO 63130
FAX 314-863-6702
TEL 314-863-1414

Since 1973, residential and commercial custom design, fabrication and consultation for historic and architectural lighting, restoration and lighting engineering services.

Price Range: $500 - $10,000/ornamental chandeliers; $65 - $100/hour; $5,000 - $300,000/ project
Recent Projects: Silver-plated bronze chandeliers from original photographs for the United States Capitol; reproduction, repair, restoration of pendant chandelier, wall brackets and historic lighting for the Michigan State Capitol

KENNETH A. SALOWE

WONDERFAUX WALLS, INC.
4411 SW FIRST ST
FORT LAUDERDALE, FL 33317
FAX 305-581-5737
TEL 305-581-5737

Extensive background, education, experience in architectural surface finishes, wall glazing, faux finishing, trompe l'oeil, boiserie restoration; principal artist and trained architect Kenneth Salowe, always provides hands-on service.

Price Range: $20 - $60/sq. ft. trompe l'oeil; $1,000 - $70,000/project
Recent Projects: Extensive faux painting, wall glazing, trompe l'oeil, Guatemald, CA; wall glazing, hand-painted and stencilled designs for the Daniels' residence

SCALAMANDRE

300 TRADE ZONE DR
RONKONKOMA, NY 11779
FAX 516-467-9448
TEL 516-467-8800

65 years experience in reproduction techniques, manufacturing of hand-printed wallpapers in company's own facility; hundreds of papers reproduced for many historic sites (list available).

Price Range: $20 - $150/per roll (approx. 36 sq. ft.)
Recent Projects: Several hand-printed side papers and borders for late 18th and early 19th Century interiors, Prestwould Plantation, Clarkesville, VA; reproduction of hand-blocked papers and borders, The Hermitage, home of Andrew Jackson, Nashville, TN

★ SHADETREE STUDIO

JOHN BOWE AND PENNY KRISTO
417 HOWARD ST
PETOSKEY, MI 49770-2621
FAX 616-347-1011
TEL 616-347-1011

The Shadetree Studio is a full-service architectural glass studio specializing in high-quality stained glass restoration. We have over 20 years of experience in residential, commercial, and ecclesiastical glass restoration.

Price Range: $35 - $50/hour; $3,000 - $10,000/project
Recent Projects: Removed, totally restored and reinstalled circa-1890s decorative church window, All Saints Episcopal Church, Newberry, MI; assisted Art Femenella in removal, restoration and reinstallation of signed Tiffany window, Beecher House, Wayne State University, Detroit, MI

See photograph page 271.

SIERRA ARCHITECTURAL CAST STONE INC.

PETER MARROCCA
1580 E. EDDINGER #G
SANTA ANA, CA 92705
FAX 714-550-7385
TEL 800-333-9302

European method of hand casting since 1925. Supplier of stock and custom architectural components and systems in precast concrete. Large-scale residential estates and commercial products.
Recent Projects: Manufactured 12 columns in loggio to original color specs, Scripps College, Claremont, CA; duplication of baluster systems, columns, steps and panels of 50-year-old Von Haussen installation, W. Bell Estate, Bel Air, CA

STONE FACES

LYNETTE STRANGSTAD
PO BOX 21090
CHARLESTON, SC 29413-1090
TEL 803-762-6025

Established in 1984, Stone Faces is a nationally known architectural conservation firm specializing in the preservation of historic burial grounds. Services include consultation workshops, site assessments, master burial ground preservation plans and conservation.

Price Range: $500 - $50,000+/project
Recent Projects: Conservation of eight outdoor statues at New Iberia, LA, National Trust For Historic Preservation; preservation of historic gravemarkers and tombs at the Colonial Park Cemetery, and site assessment of Savannah City Monuments, GA

STONELEDGE FINE ARTS CONSERVATION, INC.

GORDON A. LEWIS, JR.
111 HOWARD BLVD
MOUNT ARLINGTON, NJ 07856-1315
FAX 201-770-0379
TEL 201-770-0303

Conservation and restoration of fine arts and antiques, including paintings, works on paper, sculpture, objects, facility and collection surveys.
Recent Projects: Removed section of wall with Thurber drawings, reinstalled into framing system to inset into new offices, *The New Yorker*, NYC; conservation and restoration of bronze and stone outdoor sculptures for the Franklin D. Roosevelt Library, Hyde Park, NY

STUDIO ARTS & GLASS, INC.

ROBERT L. JOLIET
1132 30TH ST NW
CANTON, OH 44720
FAX 216-492-7751
TEL 216-492-7326

Artist Robert Joliet custom designs art glass, such as ceilings, sky lights, windows entrances, domes, and transoms. Complete service is provided from art to fabrication to installation.

Price Range: $50 - $500; $250 - $300,000/project
Recent Projects: Restoration of leaded glass windows for St. John's Catholic Church, Canton, OH; restoration of leaded glass windows for First Presbyterian Church, Ashland, OH

SUNBURST STAINED GLASS CO., INC.

SUE COLVIN, PRESIDENT
20 W JENNINGS ST
NEWBURGH, IN 47630-1212
TEL 800-982-1521
TEL 812-853-0460

Eighteen years experience in church, residential, and commercial glass restoration.

Price Range: $60 - $150/sq. ft. stained glass; $10 - $100/hour; $3,000 - $40,000/project
Recent Projects: Total tear down and rebuild, painting and firing, storms, Immaculate Conception Church; clean and repair, rebuild, new storms, First United Methodist Church

TEACO CONSTRUCTION CORP.

ROBERT J. TEDALDI
1174 COMMERCE AVE
BRONX, NY 10462-5595
FAX 718-792-6704
TEL 718-792-6703

We furnish, install and restore stone masonry of granite, limestone or bluestone. Our work includes historic buildings, monuments and statues. We also act as consultants on restoration projects.

Price Range: $50 - $500/sq. ft. stone restoration; $500 - $750,000/project
Recent Projects: Restoration of Columbus Monument, D'Auria Square Reconstruction, Bronx, NY; restoration of Central Park West Plaza, Museum of Natural History NYC

TIDEWATER RESTORATION, INC.

FREDERICK H. ECKER, II
PO BOX 7745
FREDERICKSBURG, VA 22404-7745
FAX 703-899-0094
TEL 703-899-8969

Tidewater Restoration, Inc. is an architectural preservation firm specializing in the conservation of 18th and early 19th century building fabric utilizing an in-house staff of skilled masons, carpenters, painters and plasterers.
Recent Projects: Complete restoration of the Octagon Museum (1799), including brick, plaster, wood roof, epoxy consolidation, mechanical, electrical and plumbing; complete conservation of stained glass, decorative plaster, vaulted ceilings, Old St. Paul's Church, 1850s masonry church designed by Upjohn

TILE RESTORATION CENTER, INC.

DELIA TAPP
3511 INTERLAKE AVE N
SEATTLE, WA 98103-8915
FAX 206-633-4866
TEL 206-633-4866

The Tile Restoration Center reproduces and restores historic art tiles from the early 1900s. Our carved relief tiles for fireplaces are popular in Bungalow and Craftsman homes, and are distinguished by their subtle clay and stony matte color.

Price Range: $50 - $250/sq. ft.; $75 - $150/hour; $1,000 - $6,000/project
Recent Projects: Restored two Claycraft fireplaces, repaired and resurfaced painted and badly worn tiles, Los Angeles, CA; recreated fireplace tiles (originals by Batchelder) at a private residence, Pasadena, CA

DAVID TREZISE

2901 PHEASANT BRANCH RD
MIDDLETON, WI 53562-1116
FAX 608-836-8605
TEL 608-836-8605

Trezise combines traditional carving methods with modern techniques. Collaborating with architects and designers, or working directly with individual clients, he uses his sculptural and technical skills and experience to create precise, detailed, structurally sound stonework for indoor and outdoor settings.

Price Range: $35 - $50/hour; $1,000 - $8,000/project
Recent Projects: Four limestone capitals, First National Bank and Trust Company of Baraboo, Baraboo, WI; six pineapple finials, Green Lake Public Library, Green Lake, WI

VEGA METALS, INC.

FRANCIS VEGA, NEAL CARLTON, DAVE RUSINYAK
214 HUNT ST
DURHAM, NC 27701-2116
FAX 919-688-4462
TEL 919-688-8267

Vega Metals, Inc. is a collaborative team of visionary artist-blacksmiths with over 30-years combined experience in working steel, bronze, copper and aluminum. Attention to detail is their trademark.

Price Range: $250 - $2,500/linear ft. of railing; $45 - $60/hour; $900 - $250,000/project
Recent Projects: Renovated ornamental railings for Lilly Library, Duke University; restored large antique fireplace andirons for private residence

WARDELL ART GLASS

JOHN WARDELL CLARK
16 N FIRST AVE
ST. CHARLES, IL 60174
TEL 708-584-4110

Twenty-two years experience in stained glass; studio specializes in repair and restoration for residential, commercial, and church settings; Studio Member, Stained Glass Association of America.
Recent Projects: Restored eleven stained glass windows and wood sashes, Serena Methodist Church, Serena, IL; replication of existing art glass for new addition to historic St. Charles Municipal Building, St. Charles, IL

FREDERICK WILBUR

FREDERICK WILBUR, CARVER
PO BOX 425
LOVINGSTON, VA 22949-0425
FAX 804-263-5958
TEL 804-263-4827

Since 1982 I have specialized in traditional architectural wood carving, including ecclesiastical commissions requiring extensive gold leaf. A working knowledge of historical styles allows me to carve museum-quality furniture.

Price Range: $20 - $40/hour; $500 - $50,000/project
Recent Projects: Moldings, console blocks, rosettes, Blandfield, Caret, VA; reredos and baptismal screen for the Grace and Holy Trinity Cathedral, Kansas City, MO

WILLIAM R. WRIGHT, AIA, SGAA

WRIGHT STUDIOS INC.
RR 2 BOX 250
BLOOMINGTON, IL 61704-9634
FAX 309-378-4651
TEL 309-378-4651

Commission artists specializing in architectural crafts with emphasis on design fabrication and installation of art glass panels, windows and luminaires, as well as restoration of stained and leaded glass windows.

Price Range: $140 - $330/sq. ft.; $10,000 - $22,000/project
Recent Projects: Complete repair, cleaning and restoration of 120-year-old Dove Window, United Methodist Church, Dwight, IL; restoration and releading of 100-year-plus beveled coach house windows, Central Station Restaurant, Bloomington, IL

◆

~~RESTORATION~~
is ON THE MOVE and GROWING!

With New Venues that Span the Continent.

Born in Europe in the mid 80's, and brought to the U.S. in 1993, RESTORATION™ has established itself as the largest trade event in North America for the historic marketplace.

RESTORATION 95 in Boston attracted **275 exhibitors, over 10,000 visitors and 1500 conference participants.**

Now, RESTORATION is on the move to other venues — giving more of North America easier access to this exciting event:

RESTORATION/San Francisco
December 10-12, 1995

RESTORATION 96
Baltimore
March 17-19, 1996

RESTORATION/Chicago
October 18-20, 1996

RESTORATION 97
Atlanta
April 20-22, 1997

RESTORATION/Canada
Toronto
June 22-24, 1997

RESTORATION/San Francisco
Fall 1997
dates to be announced

If you are:

▲ a specialist in the restoration of historical structures and landscapes, art, antiques or other cultural artifacts

▲ or a professional, tradesperson or artisan developing an expertise in preservation or the re-creation of historical places, spaces and objects

RESTORATION should be on your calendar of "must attend" events.

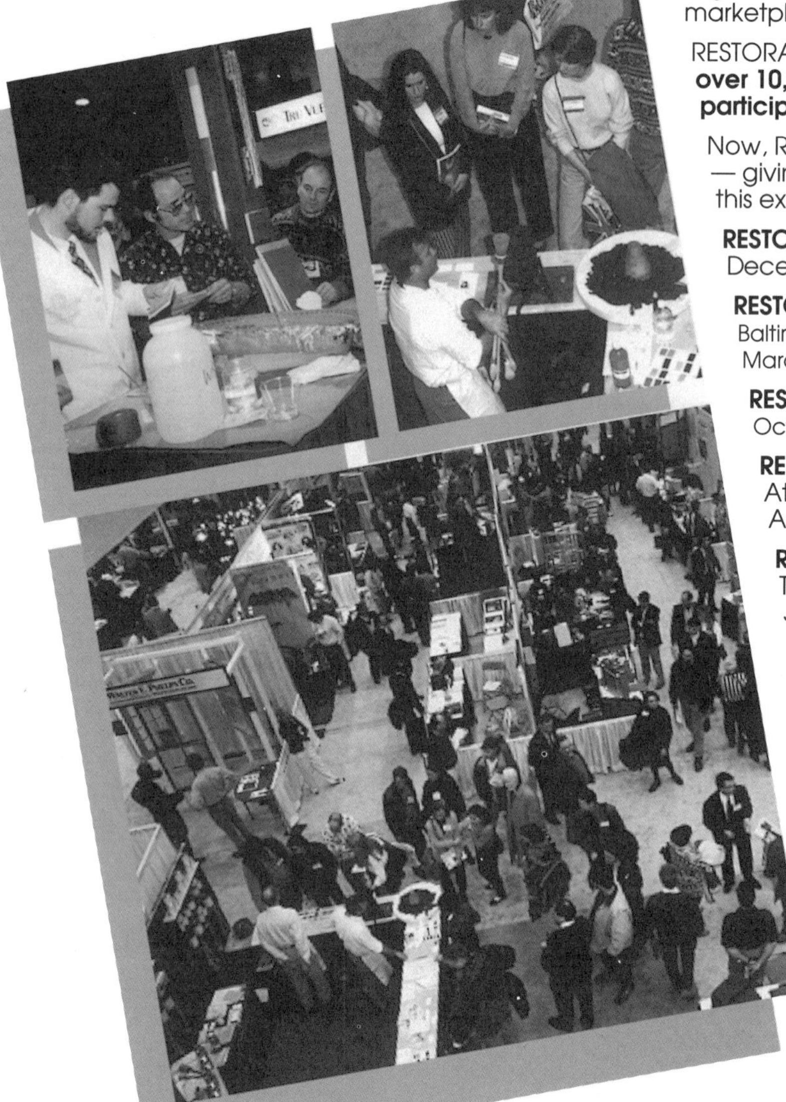

For more information:

RAI/EGI Exhibitions, Inc.
129 Park Street
North Reading, MA 01864 USA
tel 508.664.8066 (visitor hotline)
tel 508.664.6455 (exhibitor info)
fax 508.664.5822

™RESTORATION is a trademark of RAI/EGI Exhibitions, Inc.

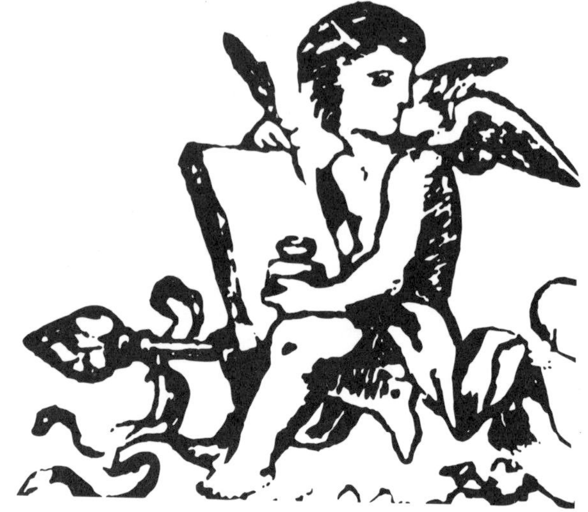

TEN years ago there was no such thing as an art consultant, according to Peter Mistretta, who for 30 years was the senior interior designer for IBM and is now president of Mistretta Design Inc. Art expertise was limited to those associated with universities, museums and galleries. Today, the art consulting profession reflects a decade of experience as well as the diverse backgrounds (art, design, art history, architecture and landscape architecture, to name a few) of its practitioners.

Art consultants have taken the job of matching art to clients and environments, and developed it into a sophisticated profession which incorporates expertise in art, architecture, engineering, lighting, acoustics, law, human relations and aesthetics. This establishes them as yet another professional resource to be relied upon by the design trade in the execution of its projects. Art consultants' enormous files of art resources have expanded options for design professionals and stimulated demand for a wide range of art. This has moved many artists into a whole new realm of commissioned art.

To be sure, there are many instances when architects and designers will continue to specify their own art. But, as the scope of commissioned art has grown—spurred by Percent for Art programs that require art in government projects, along with private corporations' recognition of art's public relations value—so has the need for the technical expertise required to find, select and place art.

It is often a better use of a firm's resources to bring in an outside expert, states Mistretta, who has purchased a great deal of art for projects—enough, he says, to understand the limitations of his own abilities. "An art consultant can do it faster, better and cheaper than a designer," he adds. "The art becomes an investment for the company, and if you're going to invest your money, you'd better do it right. Find the experts to help you with that investment, just as you would hire a stockbroker or an investment advisor if you invest in securities."

Consultants are particularly helpful when the scale of a project or the number of pieces demand assistance, or on large commissioned works that may involve design competitions. Consultants have access to broader art resources that are also useful when changing direction or bringing focus to an existing art collection.

An experienced art consultant brings resources, technical expertise, the ability to interface with artists, and the know-how to orchestrate a project from conception to installation and beyond—to cataloging, management, maintenance and public relations.

As the scope of commissioned art has grown ... so has the need for the technical expertise required to find, select and place art.

INVOLVE THE ART CONSULTANT AS EARLY AS POSSIBLE

Once you decide to hire a consultant, choose the best available to you (see sidebar) and bring her or him into the picture as early as possible. Doing so "increases the opportunities to maximize the impact of the art on the project," says Karen League, director of interior design for Jova Daniels Busby, an Atlanta architectural and interior design firm. "The art can be used much more dramatically: Walls can become art, sculpture can be a major focus, structural features can be reinforced and displayed correctly. The design [more fully] accommodates the art."

ESTABLISH FEES AND PAYMENT SCHEDULES

Establishing up front a fee schedule satisfactory to all is essential. Some consultants work on a percentage of the cost of the art, while others prefer to establish fees based on services rendered, thereby avoiding any conflict of interest or incentive to spend more on the art itself.

The fee may be a percentage of the total art budget, or on a sliding scale that decreases the percentage as the budget increases. Percentages may also be altered to reflect the complexity of the project, including the number of pieces and amount of legwork involved.

Payments can be made monthly (based on the number of hours of work involved) or tied to key points in the progress of the project. It is generally agreed that the artist should contract directly with the client, or be part of a three-party contract that includes the consultant. The art consultant plays a key role in finalizing this, working to protect the rights of both parties— artist and client. The consultant remains with the project as administrator and impartial interpreter for all points of view.

ESTABLISH PROJECT OBJECTIVES

The first step in the consultant/designer/client relationship is to establish the objectives of the art project within the budget and to develop a time-line for the art that meets the client's schedule. On the aesthetic side, the consultant, says Susan Evans, a San Francisco-based former art consultant specializing in sculpture, "studies the physical, as well as spiritual, needs of the site to be able to discuss the desired effect and overall philosophy with the client."

Effective three-way conversations, says Dorothy Solomon, principal of Dorothy Solomon Associates, Inc., "open discussion on issues that have not previously been addressed: Does the project include an entire body of work for office interiors? On one or several floors? Or is it a single major piece? What are its objectives in terms of space? In terms of intangible benefits, such as creating a pleasant environment, conveying a certain image or message to clients or to the outside world?" The art consultant, adds Karen League, can help the client make the most effective use of its budget to meet these objectives.

To fulfill the design objectives, consultants draw on existing resources and research to provide the client with appropriate choices. Sue Wiggins, president of the Philadelphia art research and resource firm ArtSouth, shows clients "every art piece that fits the job's parameters in terms of technical appropriateness (climatic, weight, durability, etc.), style, medium, size and availability." ArtSouth uses a "very democratic review and selection process" that gives equal opportunity to artists and leaves final aesthetic and budgetary decisions up to the client. To preserve the integrity of the art and the artists, Wiggins believes prices for art should be established by each individual artist and not by the consultant.

FINALIZING DETAILS AND MONITORING PROGRESS

Once the artist has been selected, it is the consultant's job to finalize the contractual details, advise on lighting and load considerations, and coordinate delivery. In the case of a commissioned work, the consultant may also supervise production. Throughout the process, the consultant keeps the client informed of the art's progress and the artist informed of the project's progress and needs. She also monitors payment schedules and may make studio visits to ensure that the art is on schedule and conforming to approved sketches. The designer, the client, or the art committee may also be encouraged to visit the work-in-progress.

Final responsibilities may also involve making sure that the art arrives on site and overseeing installation. This often involves details such as insurance, packing, transportation logistics, temporary storage, and arranging the necessary equipment for installation. Once the art is in place, consultants often provide such adjunct services as maintenance, art education for employees, development of public relations materials, and arrangements for traveling exhibits.

As the scope of art has exploded to include forms and materials far beyond a two-dimensional, oil-on-canvas world, so too the range of today's art consultant has become ever more sophisticated and multi-dimensional. What art consultants bring to design professionals is an important combination of technical expertise, aesthetic judgment and sound business management.

What art consultants bring to design professionals is an important combination of technical expertise, aesthetic judgment and sound business management.

CHOOSING AN ART CONSULTANT

ARCHITECTS and designers are accustomed to relying on a variety of professional consultants, and an art consultant is no different.

○ Art consulting is about service as well as selling art. The right person brings you an opportunity to find the most exciting artwork at the best price, through a combination of technical expertise and aesthetic vision.

○ Before you begin your search, define a starting point for the art in the project. This may be the budget, the scope of the collection, the art style or media. Goals need not be fully developed (this is part of the art consultant's role), but establishing parameters will help you match the requirements of your project with the expertise of a particular consultant.

○ Using all available sources—listings in THE GUILD, contact networks, yellow pages, and other published lists—identify several firms or individuals to invite for interviews and presentations.

○ Carefully review qualifications and credentials, following up on references, especially those most relevant to your own project. Talk with consultants' former clients, as well as artists.

○ Request a thorough presentation of past work: slides, a portfolio, or actual on-site visits.

○ Art consultants may place a broad range of work in a variety of environments or they may specialize. Find out the consultant's specialty.

Does he have ample resources among regional artists? Does he have experience with museum-level shows? Folk art? Large, outdoor sculpture? Revolving art programs?

○ Is the consultant experienced with your type of space—atriums, outdoor plazas, boardrooms, office corridors?

○ Does the size (number of pieces, budget) of the consultant's past projects match your own?

○ Does the consultant's experience involve individual or corporate clients? The concerns of each are different, cautions Karen League. Corporate concerns go beyond satisfying individual tastes to fulfilling broader committee-determined aesthetics, and often have public relations goals. "When hiring for a corporate client," League says, "you are hiring a team member. Their personal approach and professionalism need to be compatible with the team's objectives. It's important for the art consultant to understand the overall project and the role of art in it." The design professional, League says, is the team leader orchestrating the contributions of a variety of professional players.

○ Another point to keep in mind: A successful consultant acknowledges and attempts to satisfy the client's needs, instead of pursuing a personal agenda or taste, or promoting the work of favored artists.

○ The consultant must be able to talk comfortably with all involved as an effective interpreter and facilitator

of the art project, according to Dorothy Solomon. And a consultant should be forthright about how he or she derives income from a project.

○ Consider whether a consultant who promotes a stable of artists will serve you as well as one who maintains broad libraries of art resources and/or is willing to do extensive research on your behalf. Does he use resources such as THE GUILD in addition to artists with whom he is familiar?

○ Does the consultant bring in projects within budget?

○ Finally, be sure the art consultants you consider clearly understand the full scope of your project through discussions that include consultant, designer and client. Not only do such interactions provide necessary information for all involved, they clearly indicate the amount of synergy and personal chemistry the project will generate.

Despite the often-abstract, aesthetic nature of their product, selecting an art consultant boils down to the concrete steps of choosing a professional consultant of any kind. Do your homework, match the consultant's experience and expertise with your project's needs, and watch for that personal feeling that tells you *this* is the person you want to work with.

ART CONSULTANTS

A state-by-state directory, including client lists and business descriptions

ARKANSAS

✪ HERR-CHAMBLISS FINE ARTS CORPORATE ART SERVICES

Est. 1988
718 CENTRAL AVE
HOT SPRINGS NATIONAL PARK, AR
 71901-5333

CONTACT:
Melinda Herr-Chambliss
TEL 501-624-7188

CLIENTS INCLUDE:
Corporations
Private Collectors
Healthcare Industry
Hospitality Industry

Herr-Chambliss Corporate Arts advisory services is qualified to provide professional guidance to clients on the purchase, commission, installation, placement and maintenance of two/three dimensional works of art for indoor, outdoor and site specific projects. Herr-Chambliss has overseen the installation of fine art programs in financial institutions, medical facilities, professional offices, and research facilities, many of which have received state awards. We specialize through research, presenting international, national or regional artwork which have a distinct and unitive application to each client's individual needs while also achieving client satisfaction within budgetary guidelines.

CALIFORNIA

✪ ART SOURCE L.A., INC.

Est. 1980
11901 SANTA MONICA BLVD #555
LOS ANGELES, CA 90025

CONTACT:
Francine Ellman, President
FAX (310) 479-3400
TEL 310-479-6649

CLIENTS INCLUDE:
Bentall Development Company
Kintetsu Department Stores
Los Angeles International Airport
American Restaurant Group
Nissan Motor Corporation, U.S.A
R&B Realty Group

Professional art consulting, private, corporate, hospitality and healthcare acquisitions, public art programs, complete curatorial services, traveling exhibitions, exhibitions in alternative spaces and exhibition design. Houses an extensive slide library and on-site inventory of artwork in all fine art media. Art Source L.A. develops projects and maintains relations with artists, galleries, creative sources and clients on a worldwide basis.

CAROL A. DABB, INC. ART CONSULTANTS

Est. 1986
41 SUNKIST LN
LOS ALTOS, CA 94022

CONTACT:
Carol Dabb
FAX (415) 948-4019
TEL 415-941-1907

CLIENTS INCLUDE:
Corporate
Medical
Residential
Municipal
Architects/Designers

CORPORATE FINE ART

Est. 1989
9247 FRANKLIN ST
CHATSWORTH, CA 91311

CONTACT:
Patricia Peden Everett
TEL 818-884-8574

CLIENTS INCLUDE:
Corporations
Developers
Healthcare
Public Art

DORSEY BARR CONTEMPORARY ART CONSULTANT

Est. 1985
333 18TH ST
SANTA MONICA, CA 90402

CONTACT:
TEL 310-393-3345

CLIENTS INCLUDE:
Payden and Rygel, Los Angeles, CA
Nat West Markets, Los Angeles, CA
Merrill Lynch, Los Angeles, CA
Northwestern Mutual Life, Los Angeles, CA

✪ FRESH PAINT, INC.

Est. 1980
2511 CENTINELA AVE
SANTA MONICA, CA 90405-3100

CONTACT:
Josetta Sbeglia
Helene Brown
FAX (310) 399-1585
TEL 310-399-1929

CLIENTS INCLUDE:
Prudential California Realty
Healthnet
Scitex America Corporation
Hyatt Hotel Corporation
Steve Chase Associates

Our goal at Fresh Paint is to create the perfect balance between artistic effort and client need. We interact with architects, designers and art committee members from initial concept to on-site placement. We differ from galleries and other consulting firms in that we have a large reservoir of artwork and are not limited by a need to promote specific individuals. From concept to conclusion, we oversee the entire project to insure its success.

INTERNATIONAL ART SOURCE

Est. 1992
8933 LOMBARD PL #221
SAN DIEGO, CA 92122

CONTACT:
Nancy L. Hogstrom, Principal
FAX (619) 457-2688
TEL 619-457-2688

A complete art source for all art needs.

✪ JOANNA BURKE ART CONSULTANTS, INC.

Est. 1986
685 VENICE BOULEVARD STUDIO 3
VENICE, CA 90291

CONTACT:
Joanna Burke
FAX (310) 305-1556
TEL 310-305-1313

CLIENTS INCLUDE:
Corporations
Healthcare Industry
Financial Institutions
Communications and Media

Joanna Burke Art Consultants has been in the business of art since 1986. Our client base runs the gamut of media and business enterprises in both the national and international arenas. We specialize in custom artwork commissions and installations in all media. A complete roster of services is offered. Joanna Burke Art Consultants maintains an ever-expanding global network of artists and resources. We offer each of our clients the very highest level of quality, experience and commitment to excellence.

✪ MARDINE DAVIS ART CONSULTANT

Est. 1990
850 N POINSETTIA PL
LOS ANGELES, CA 90046

CONTACT:
Mardine Davis
FAX (213) 937-5676
TEL 213-937-9656

CLIENTS INCLUDE:
Steven Bochco Productions, Inc.
Kaiser Permanente Foundation Health Plan
Methodist Hospital of Southern CA
Twentieth Century Fox Film Corp.
Castle Rock Entertainment

Interfaces with architects, designers and clients to develop artwork themes consistent with corporate identity. Selects and acquires artwork working within budgetary and time constraints. Commissions and supervises site-specific and large-scale works. Coordinates and supervises framing, installation and follow-up. Utilizes local and national resources. Offers a variety of media: prints, paintings, photography, paper, fiber, sculpture, ceramics and wall treatments. Offers experience of ten years art consulting to the corporate community.

✪ MICHELLE ISENBERG & ASSOCIATES, INC.

Est. 1982
1440 EAST 17TH ST
LOS ANGELES, CA 90021

CONTACT:
Michelle Isenberg, Director
FAX (213) 388-3989
TEL 310-275-1160

CLIENTS INCLUDE:
Toyota USA
Sony Pictures Entertainment
City of Culver City and Pasadena
St. Vincents Medical Hospital
Litton Industries, Inc.

Michelle Isenberg & Associates Inc. provide professional art advisory services to the public and private sectors for the development of fine art programs. The firm is responsible for the concept, coordination, and management of all aspects of art programs and public art projects. MI&A has served as consultant to many Los Angeles-based developers, architects, and public agencies. The firm acts as liaison between commissioned artists and developers/architects in association with city planners, design and art advisory committees, securing all required approvals for successful project completion.

✪ SELTZ ART CONSULTING

Est. 1987
4223 GLENCOE AVE #A215
MARINA DEL RAY, CA 90292

CONTACT:
Catherine Seltz
Christine Vilim
FAX (310) 577-8224
TEL 310-577-8222

CLIENTS INCLUDE:
Coopers & Lybrand
Price Waterhouse
Dean Witter
Hewlett Packard
Allstate Insurance

Seltz Art Consulting is a California based firm specializing in advising corporate, healthcare and hospitality industries concerning the visual arts and establishing acquisition and installation programs of fine art and major sculpture. As professional art advisors, we provide the client a conduit to the art world and market. We have an extensive art history background, and a comprehensive working knowledge of fine art resources. We will work closely with you to develop a concept, theme and budget for your collection that best suits your objectives. Our emphasis is on proper selection and appropriateness of an art statement within the established guidelines and a firm commitment to quality.

SUZY R. LOCKE & ASSOCIATES

Est. 1975
4254 PIEDMONT AVE
OAKLAND, CA 94611

CONTACT:
Suzy Locke
Bill Fredriksson
FAX (510) 547-5495
TEL 510-547-5455

CLIENTS INCLUDE:
Bank of America
Grubb Ellis
Dreyer's Grand Ice Cream
Chevron USA
Kaiser Permanente

COLORADO

✪ ARTIST SHOWCASE

Est. 1979
1625 LARIMER #601
DENVER, CO 80202

CONTACT:
Nancy Noyes
Rachelle Koster
FAX (303) 825-6414
TEL 303-825-1955

CLIENTS INCLUDE:
US West, Denver, CO
Mercy Medical Center, Denver, CO
Longmont United Hospital, Longmont, CO
Sunrise Health Care Centers
Prudential Healthcare Centers

Full-service art design specializing in healthcare, retirement and corporate facilities in Colorado and around the country. Working with design teams of architects and designers or directly with the end user creating total ambiance of the project. Selection, acquisition, design custom framing and security installation executed with no design fee to the client. Access to artists locally and nationally. Handling all types of art from posters to Salvador Dali at reasonable prices.

CONNECTICUT

✪ ART OVERSEAS, INC.

Est. 1971
443 WEBBS HILL RD
STAMFORD, CT 06903

CONTACT:
Katharine C. Sachs, President
Claudie Gvertz, Sales Director
TEL 203-322-1105

CLIENTS INCLUDE:
The O'Connor Group
The Westchester
Citibank
Wachtell, Lipton, Rosen & Katz
Menlo Park Mall
New York Hospital

(Listing continued)

ART CONSULTANTS

Art Overseas is a private gallery whose professional staff works closely with architects, designers, art advisors and collectors to meet their needs for a wide range of paintings, sculpture, tapestries, works on paper and other artwork which will complement and enhance the project at hand. We offer from our own inventory works by over 100 artists in an extensive range of styles and media. In addition, we undertake commissions with individual artists to produce site-specific pieces for our clients. Our projects include monumental sculpture installations, medical facilities and hospitals, corporate collections and private homes. Our strength lies in our ability to understand and translate our clients' desires and preferences into their desired image, while keeping within economic boundaries.

ARTWORKS FINE ART ADVISORS

Est. 1985
15 POTTER DR
OLD GREENWICH, CT 06870-1507

CONTACT:
Wendy T. Kelley, Director
FAX (203) 637-0417
TEL 203-637-5562

CLIENTS INCLUDE:
Time-Warner Companies
New York Hospital
HBO Entertainment Inc.
Aetna Life Insurance Co.
Intercontinental Hotels

IMAGES SCULPTURAL CONCEPTS

16 AVERY PL
WESTPORT, CT 06880

CONTACT:
Joan Starr
FAX (203) 226-9624
TEL 203-222-0040

CLIENTS INCLUDE:
General Electric Corporation
Hitachi America
Pilot Pen Corporation
U.S. Surgical Corporation
American Skandia, Inc.

MCGREGOR CUTTING ASSOCIATES

Est. 1990
PO BOX 72
GUILFORD, CT 06437

CONTACT:
Jennifer Cutting
FAX (203) 458-7110
TEL 203-458-7142

CLIENTS INCLUDE:
Lehman College
Arts Commission of Greater Toledo
New York Hall of Science
Prospect Park Alliance
Queens College

DISTRICT OF COLUMBIA

HOLLY ROSS ASSOCIATES

Est. 1981
516 C ST NE
WASHINGTON, DC 20002

CONTACT:
Holly Ross
Timothy Lowe
TEL 202-544-0400

CLIENTS INCLUDE:
Oracle, Inc.
Two Lions Antiques & Interiors
Georgetown University Law Center
Weinberg, Bergeson & Neuman
Robert Pahnke

THE ROSENBERG GROUP

Est. 1982
3427 PORTER ST NW
WASHINGTON, DC 20016-3125

CONTACT:
Randy Rosenberg
Joel Makower
FAX (202) 332-3028
TEL 202-332-4700

CLIENTS INCLUDE:
Hospitals & Healthcare
Hotels
Corporations
Law Firms
Architects & Designers

DELAWARE

✪ DESIGN CONSULTANT

Est. 1986
2211 NORTH GRANT AVE
WILMINGTON, DE 19806

CONTACT:
Gina Bosworth
FAX (302) 425-4411
TEL 302-654-0577

CLIENTS INCLUDE:
Delaware River & Bay Authority
Wilmington Trust
Johnson & Johnson
Star Enterprises
Nuclear Electric Insurance Limited

Delaware's only full service art consultant. Ten years in business, serving designers, corporations, financial institutions, law firms, professionals, small business and the healthcare industry. Experienced in working with non-profits and galleries. Access to all media, and to national and international artists (the Internet is ingenious!). Special interest in contemporary craft - textile, clay, metal, wood, glass and paper. Challenged by site-specific commissions. Member, International Furnishings and Design Association.

FLORIDA

✪ ADMINISTRATIVE ARTS, INC.

Est. 1983
PO BOX 547935
ORLANDO, FL 32854-7935

CONTACT:
Ms. Brenda B. Harris
TEL 407-849-9744

CLIENTS INCLUDE:
Budget Rent A Car World Headquarters
Price Waterhouse
Ernst & Young
Deloitte & Touche
Marriott

National arts advisory firm servicing industries such as professional services, development and leasing, health care, hospitality and travel. Professional staffing includes experts in art research and acquisitions, public art, project management, and marketing. Our staff works closely with designers, architects, and end-users to develop totally managed art programs. Services include site analysis, budgeting, art research, art commissions and contract negotiation, framing, installation, documentation and publicity. Specialized services include public art organizational and program development.

✪ THE ART RESOURCE, INC.

Est. 1981
1451 NW 112TH TERRACE
PEMBROKE PINES, FL 33026

CONTACT:
Fran Davidman
FAX (305) 432-4312
TEL 305-432-9242

CLIENTS INCLUDE:
Nations Bank
Jackson Memorial Hospital
Cedars Hospital
Divi Hotels
Coopers & Lybrand

The Art Resource, Inc. has been a leading art dealership and consulting firm in the south Florida, Maryland and Washington, DC, areas for over fourteen years. The Art Resource represents hundreds of artists including painters, printmakers, sculptors, weavers, mixed media, published works and reproductions. Our clients include architects, developers, interior designers, corporations and private collectors. We develop your complete art program, providing artwork to fit a myriad of price ranges, offering custom framing and installation.

GEORGIA

✪ BARKIN-LEEDS, LTD.

Est. 1984
6 HARRIS GLEN
ATLANTA, GA 30327

CONTACT:
Temme Barkin-Leeds, President
Sally Faulkner, Manager
FAX (404) 816-0089
TEL 404-816-9777

CLIENTS INCLUDE:
King & Spalding
Trammell Crow Company
McKinsey & Company, Inc.
Cousins Properties, Inc.
Federal Reserve Bank

Barkin-Leeds Ltd. is a fine art consulting service providing a wide range of services including procurement of art (painting, sculpture, prints, photography, crafts), curatorial services including changing exhibitions and registrarial responsibilities including receiving, condition reports, lighting advice and installation. Barkin-Leeds Ltd.'s work is not limited to Georgia, having worked on collections in Ohio, Florida, Mississippi, Alabama, Tennessee, Kentucky and North Carolina. Barkin-Leeds' strong points include museum experience and access to a wide range of local and national artists.

EDL & ASSOCIATES

Est. 1986
3221B CAINS HILL PL
ATLANTA, GA 30305

CONTACT:
Elizabeth Lynch
Cheryl Hagen
FAX (404) 233-3536
TEL 404-233-3602

CLIENTS INCLUDE:
The Habitat Company
Kaiser Permanente
Holiday Inn Worldwide
Hyatt Regency
Cousins Properties

ILLINOIS

✪ CAROLYN S. HUSEMOLLER FINE ARTS LTD.

Est. 1989
PO BOX 933
BARRINGTON, IL 60011-0933

CONTACT:
Carolyn Husemoller, President
FAX (708) 526-5271
TEL 708-526-3444

Provides quality and distinctive art consultation on original fine art acquisition. Has access to a fine and quality selection of mid-west artists in all media. Works with interior designers as an original fine art source. Has a vendor membership in International Society for Interior Designers. Has an extensive slide registry and two showroom galleries in residence. Specializing in residential and some commercial art acquisition. Hours by appointment.

✪ CORPORATE ARTWORKS, LTD.

Est. 1987
1300 REMINGTON RD #H
SCHAUMBURG, IL 60173

CONTACT:
Denise Rippinger, President
Kathy Sherwin, Coordinator
FAX (708) 843-8047
TEL 708-843-3636

CLIENTS INCLUDE:
United Airlines
Motorola
Kemper Group
OCE-USA
Evangelical Health Systems

Corporate Artworks, Ltd. specializes in providing fine art for corporations, law firms, health care facilities and residential homes. Our showroom houses a large collection of artwork ranging from canvases and watercolors to tapestries and sculpture, as well as limited edition graphics. Experienced art consultants work closely with architects, designers and selection committees in budget development and company image. Our expansive framing facilities enable us to customize our projects to each individual's needs.

✪ EWP ART CONSULTING SERVICES

Est. 1972
593 CHEROKEE RD
HIGHLAND PARK, IL 60035

CONTACT:
Ellen Paushter
FAX (708)266-0778
TEL 708-266-0758

CLIENTS INCLUDE:
McDonald's Corporation
The Kemper Insurance and Financial Co.
Schiff, Hardin & Waite, Attorneys at Law
University Orthopedics Medical
Altschuler, Melvoin and Glasser, CPA

EWP Art Consulting Services offer personalized, comprehensive art consultations for both corporate and residential settings throughout Chicago. We currently represent 250 artists nationwide, with a slide inventory of over 16,000 available works. Media include original paintings, three-dimensional wall pieces, prints, fiber art, sculpture, art furniture, photography and large-scale ceramic objects. Services include custom slide presentations, framing, delivery and installation. Professional discount to the trade.

✪ GRAPHIC RESOURCES CORPORATE ART SERVICE

Est. 1981
465 LAKESIDE PL
HIGHLAND PARK, IL 60035

CONTACT:
Alyson Breuer
Linda Brodson
FAX (708) 433-3688
TEL 708-433-3688

CLIENTS INCLUDE:
Office of The Comptroller of Currency
United Airlines
Bell & Howell
Wheels, Inc.

Graphic Resources is an advisor to corporate clients, architects and designers in developing customized art programs. We specialize in client acquisition of two- and three-dimensional fine art in all price ranges; site-commissions; unique photography programs for fine art and product orientation; all sized projects from corporate headquarters to professional suites; coordination of professional services; framing; installation; valuation; inventory; restoration, etc. Worldwide resources used for on-site presentations.

✪ ROBERT GALITZ FINE ART

Est. 1986
166 HILLTOP
SLEEPY HOLLOW, IL 60118

CONTACT:
Robert Galitz
FAX (708) 426-8846
TEL 708-426-8842

Robert Galitz Fine Art specializes in providing art in all media for architects, designers and corporate collections. Contemporary paintings, works on paper, watercolors, mixed media and prints, both realist and abstract. Over 100 national artists in collection. Works provided out of case or to your specification by commission. Additionally a direct source for many other well-known artists, American and European oil paintings. Home or business presentations.

THE ART SOURCE LTD

Est. 1986
5520 TOUHY AVE #L
SKOKIE, IL 60077

CONTACT:
Kay Mangum, President
FAX (708) 675-9902
TEL 708-675-5800

CLIENTS INCLUDE:
Corporate
Hospitality
Medical
Residential
Architects/Designers

KENTUCKY

PINKERTON HOUSE PORTFOLIO INC.

Est. 1983
1536 LYTLE ST
LOUISVILLE, KY 40203

@CONTACT:CONTACT:
Judith Cobb
Melissa Cobb
FAX (502) 584-1326
TEL 502-584-2568

CLIENTS INCLUDE:
META and Associates
Caritas Healthcare
General Electric
Toyota Motor
Ernst and Young

MARYLAND

✪ ARTEMIS, INC.

Est. 1990
4715 CRESCENT ST
BETHESDA, MD 20816-1720

CONTACT:
Sondra Tropper
FAX (301) 229-2186
TEL 301-229-2058

Artemis, Inc. is an art dealership and appraisal service working with corporate and private collectors in the Washington, DC, area. The firm represents painters, printmakers, sculptors, weavers, craftspeople and mixed-media artists offering works appropriate to clients' budgets, tastes and settings. In addition, Ms. Tropper is an accredited member of the American Society of Appraisers and handles appraisals for insurance, estates and liquidation.

✪ ARTISTS CIRCLE, LTD.

Est. 1972
11544 SPRING RIDGE RD
POTOMAC, MD 20854

CONTACT:
Sharon Buchanan
Jack Devine
FAX (301) 921-9183
TEL 301-921-0572

CLIENTS INCLUDE:
ASEA Brown Bovera/ABB
Airtouch
Arbitron
Heidrick & Struggles
Signet Bank

Comprehensive & professional art consulting services. Distinctive artwork from artists of reputation. Develop and oversee all phases of project: budget, acquisition, shipping, framing, installation, cataloguing. Long standing experience with large and small commissions. Poster projects or budget facilities turnkeyed.

✪ ONTOGENY

Est. 1981
10404 LLOYD RD
POTOMAC, MD 20854

CONTACT:
Phyllis P. Beek
FAX (301) 762-5127
TEL 301-340-0143

Ontogeny provides art consulting services and artwork nationwide to designers and architects, builders and developers, corporate clients and private individuals. We provide art in all media: paintings, drawings, sculpture, glass, ceramics, fiber art, handmade paper art, fine antique and contemporary original graphics of all types. Ontogeny also commissions artists for site specific works and publishes limited edition offset lithographs at modest prices for special projects. We operate our own 5,500 square foot framing facility for production and custom framing. We can also provide for professional installers and for packing and shipping art to final destination.

✪ THE ART RESOURCE, INC.

Est. 1981
902 BRANTFORD AVE
SILVER SPRING, MD 20902

CONTACT:
Laura Kaufman
FAX (301) 622-3094
TEL 301-622-2371

CLIENTS INCLUDE:
McCormick Spice Co.
Union Memorial Hospital
Westinghouse
Price Waterhouse
Gallup
Associated Growth Enterprises

The Art Resource, Inc. has been a leading art dealership and consulting firm in the Maryland, Washington, DC and south Florida areas for over fourteen years. The Art Resource represents hundreds of artists including painters, printmakers, sculptors, weavers, mixed media, published works and reproductions. Our clients include architects, developers, interior designers, corporations and private collectors. We develop your complete art program, providing artwork to fit a myriad of price ranges, offering custom framing and installation.

MASSACHUSETTS

NORTON-SHANEL ART CONSULTANTS

Est. 1980
20 SHEPARD ST
CAMBRIDGE, MA 02138

CONTACT:
Madlyn Shanel
FAX (617) 492-2385
TEL 617-492-2385

CLIENTS INCLUDE:
Sheraton Corporation Hotels USA
Hilton Corp Domestic & Intl Hotels
Hyatt Hotels Domestic & Intl Hotels
Doubletree Guest Quarters Hotels
Marriott Corporation

MICHIGAN

ART CONSULTING SERVICES

Est. 1990
3148 PLAINFIELD NE #140
GRAND RAPIDS, MI 49505

CONTACT:
Kay Tiedt
Jeanine Samuelson
FAX (616) 361-9172
TEL 616-361-9172

CLIENTS INCLUDE:
Blodgett & Butterworth Hospitals
First of America
DOW
Upjohn
Midland Convention Center
Michigan State University

✪ CORPORATE PORTFOLIO

Est. 1984
244 MORNINGSIDE DR SE
GRAND RAPIDS, MI 49506

CONTACT:
Concy Seeley, Partner
Karen Paul, Partner
TEL 616-949-4730

CLIENTS INCLUDE:
McDonald's Corporation, Chicago
Amway Corporation
Citibank, Chicago Headquarters
Butterworth Hospital
Foremost Insurance Company of America
Meijers Corporate Headquarters

Corporate Portfolio specializes in all media of art. Representing artists both nationally and internationally including originals, graphics, ceramics, sculpture, tapestries and drawings. Custom framing, installation, documentation and written contracts are part of our services. All projects are executed to meet our client's needs and budget with an emphasis on service.

NEW JERSEY

ART PLUS

Est. 1984
120 MORRIS AVE
SPRINGFIELD, NJ 07081

CONTACT:
Carol M. Rush
Debbie Jeffrey
FAX (201) 376-0024
TEL 201-376-2400

CLIENTS INCLUDE:
Dean Witter
Merck Pharmaceutical
Hewlett Packard
ADP
Simon & Schuster
Boise Cascade

✪ GALMAN LEPOW ASSOCIATES, INC.

Est. 1979
1879 OLD CUTHBERT RD #12
CHERRY HILL, NJ 08034

CONTACT:
Elaine Galman
Judith Lepow
TEL 609-354-0771

CLIENTS INCLUDE:
Bell Atlantic Corporation
CoreStates Financial Corp.
Deloitte Touche
E.I. DuPont de Nemours & Co.
Subaru of America

Full resource art advisory service assisting in art acquisitions. Clients include corporations, health care facilities, hospitality services, architects, designers and developers. GLA provides a full range of services from budget and space planning to site-specific commissions, through installation.

LEADER ASSOCIATES

Est. 1987
7 NOTTINGHAM RD
WAYNE, NJ 07470-3246

CONTACT:
Bernice K. Leader, Ph.D.
FAX (201) 696-1836
TEL 201-696-1836

CLIENTS INCLUDE:
Hospital/Healthcare
Corporations
Professional Service Firms
Hotels
Residential

NEW YORK

✪ ART ADVISORY SERVICES, INC.

Est. 1970
530 PARK AVE
NEW YORK, NY 10021

CONTACT:
Judith Selkowitz
FAX (212) 755-3924
TEL 212-935-1272

CLIENTS INCLUDE:
Price Waterhouse
Saudi Petroleum
Battle Fowler
Gensler & Associates
Skidmore, Owings & Merrill

We have advised corporations and private clients on the acquisition of millions of dollars of artwork for a quarter of a century. We find splendid 19th and 20th century works not seen in everyone else's spaces. Our excellent resources provide contemporary paintings under $5,000 to $10,000 and many works on paper under $1,000. Because we are constantly in the art market, we know how to negotiate the price most beneficial to the client.

ART CONSULTANTS TO THE TRADE

Est. 1982
60 W 57TH ST
NEW YORK, NY 10019

CONTACT:
January Sarasohn
J. Gold
FAX (212) 446-9008
TEL 212-541-5399

CLIENTS INCLUDE:
Katz Communications Inc.
The Olsten Corporation
GHI Corporation
Vanity Fair Inc.
Englewood Hospital

✪ ART OVERSEAS, INC.

Est. 1971
207 EAST 74TH ST
NEW YORK, NY 10021

CONTACT:
Katharine C. Sachs, President
Claudie Gvertz, Sales Director
TEL 212-472-9426

CLIENTS INCLUDE:
The O'Connor Group
The Westchester
Citibank
Wachtell, Lipton, Rosen & Katz
Stamford Hospital
McDonald's Corporation

ART OVERSEAS is a private gallery whose professional staff works closely with architects, designers, art advisors and collectors to meet their needs for a wide range of paintings, sculpture, tapestries, works on paper and other artwork which will complement and enhance the project at hand. We offer from our own inventory works by over 100 artists in an extensive range of styles and media. In addition, we undertake commissions with individual artists to produce site-specific pieces for our clients. Our projects include monumental sculpture installations, medical facilities and hospitals, corporate collections and private homes. Our strength lies in our ability to understand and translate our clients' desires and preferences into their desired image, while keeping within economic boundaries.

✪ BLUMBERG & HARRIS INC.

Est. 1981
55 E 87TH ST #5D
NEW YORK, NY 10128-1054

CONTACT:
Francis P. Harris
Sandra Blumberg
TEL 212-876-6538

CLIENTS INCLUDE:
Insurance Companies
Law Offices
Financial Institutions
Private Collectors
Architects

As art advisors/consultants, our principals acquired professional expertise through a combination of educational background and many years of work experience. Contacts are maintained with a wide range of sources in the United States as well as Europe. As a result of these contacts, there is a continual awareness of the trends and a sensitivity to private and corporate collectors' requirements. We are, of course, accustomed to working closely with architects and/or interior designers to realize the full potential of each work in a particular setting, new or existing. Offices in New York and Philadelphia.

CORPORATE ART DIRECTIONS

Est. 1978
41 EAST 57TH ST 8TH FL
NEW YORK, NY 10022

CONTACT:
Ms. Betty Levin, President
FAX (212) 758-6332
TEL 212-355-5370

CLIENTS INCLUDE:
The Bank of New York
Banker's Trust
First Boston
Credit Suisse
Stroock & Stroock & Lavan

✪ DANETTE KOKE FINE ART
RAMSCALE ART ASSOCIATES

55 BETHUNE ST
NEW YORK, NY 10014

CONTACT:
Danette Koke
Tracy Brymer
FAX (212) 206-6683
TEL 212-206-6566

CLIENTS INCLUDE:
Large and Small Corporations
Hotels
Restaurants
Hospitals

ART CONSULTANTS

Danette Koke Fine Art and RamScale Art Associates have been working successfully with the architectural and interior design industry for the past decade. We offer an extensive and expert source for collecting art: research, planning, presentation, selection, framing, and installation. Our portfolio includes paintings, sculpture, original works on paper, photography, textiles, antique prints and posters, ranging from representational and traditional to contemporary and abstract.

OHIO

✪ THE ART EXCHANGE

Est. 1979
539 E TOWN ST
COLUMBUS, OH 43215

CONTACT:
Fran Rothman
Marjie Coopersmith
FAX (614) 464-4619
TEL 614-464-4611

CLIENTS INCLUDE:
Chemical Mortgage Bank
State Auto Insurance Companies
Mt. Carmel Medical Centers
Ohio State Bar Association
Wendy's International

An art resource firm providing professional consulting services to architects, interior designers and corporations. Offers creative planning and coordination of each project from concept through completion. Vast selection of art work is available in wide range of media, from traditional to contemporary. Representing an impressive collection of emerging and nationally recognized artists. Committed to high quality service, excellent client relationships, genuine enthusiasm for profession and sharing the vision of art's place in the public eye.

OKLAHOMA

ARTSOURCE, INC.

Est. 1980
320 SOUTH BOSTON AVE
TULSA, OK 74103

CONTACT:
Susan Hammond
FAX (918) 599-7167
TEL 918-585-8718

CLIENTS INCLUDE:
Amoco Corporation
Bank IV
LDDS/Wiltel Corp.
Hillcrest Medical Center
Thrifty Rent A Car

OREGON

ART CONSULTATION SERVICES

Est. 1977
725 SW 84TH AVE #1000
PORTLAND, OR 97225-6311

CONTACT:
Jacqueline Davis
Ted Lehman
FAX (503) 288-3806
TEL 503-292-1988

CLIENTS INCLUDE:
Delta Air Lines
First Interstate Bank
Bonneville Power Administration
Legacy Health Systems
Sheraton Hotels

✪ CORPORATE ART DESIGN

Est. 1989
PO BOX 19432
PORTLAND, OR 97280

CONTACT:
Irene Osborne Snider
TEL 503-246-1648

CLIENTS INCLUDE:
Good Samaritan Hospital
1st Interstate Bank
Rollins Hudig Hall
US Bank
PAC TEL Paging, Inc.
Sun Mark Data, Inc.

We are an established, full-service company, with two galleries in Salem, Oregon. We supply art and framing to corporate clients. Our companies have access to other mediums, including sculpture, tapestries and photography. Serving the art industry, we work with both old and new clients in healthcare, banking, insurance and other facilities. Our aim is to evaluate with designers their total needs in enhancing their environment.

PENNSYLVANIA

✪ ARTSOUTH, INC.

Est. 1978
4401 CRESSON ST
PHILADELPHIA, PA 19127

CONTACT:
Sue Wiggins, President
FAX (215) 482-4572
TEL 215-482-4500

CLIENTS INCLUDE:
Rhone-Poulenc Rorer Inc.
Price Waterhouse
Graphic Packaging Corporation
Sterling Winthrop Inc.
Glaxo Holdings, P.L.C.

ArtSouth, Inc. (ASI) develops corporate art programs for businesses worldwide. ASI designs the fine art program as a source for public relations, marketing and educational purposes. Primary considerations include defining a budget, careful review of the architectural and interior designs, and the placement of the acquired or existing artwork. In addition, the Collections Management Department offers valuable curatorial maintenance services to clients with existing collections.

THE ART BANK

Est. 1985
3028 N WHITEHALL RD
NORRISTOWN, PA 19403

CONTACT:
Phyllis Sunberg
FAX (610) 539-2265
TEL 610-539-2265

CLIENTS INCLUDE:
SmithKline Beecham
US Healthcare/Criterion
Benneton Sportsystems
Holman Motors
Trop World Casino/Hotel

SOUTH CAROLINA

ART FOR BUSINESS

Est. 1981
143 TRADD ST
CHARLESTON, SC 29401

CONTACT:
Barbara K. Stender
FAX (803) 577-6355
TEL 803-577-6355

CLIENTS INCLUDE:
Bank of South Carolina
Hollings Cancer Center
Southern Bell
M.U.S.C. Hospital
Kiawah Island Resort Hotel

TEXAS

✪ AMERICAN ART RESOURCES

Est. 1972
3262 SUL ROSS ST
HOUSTON, TX 77098-1930

CONTACT:
Kathy Hathorn, Principal
FAX (713) 527-9676
TEL 800-282-0204

CLIENTS INCLUDE:
Green Hospital of Scripps Clinic
Vanderbilt Child & Adolescent Hospital
University of Miami Hospital
Shriner's Hospital for Crippled Children
Loma Linda University Medical Center
Health Central

Serving the healthcare industry exclusively. Over 500 projects completed in 41 states. A turnkey, total responsibility vendor emphasizing the use of fine art for therapeutic value. Twenty years experience working with top national architectural and design firms.

GAGNAIRE & GOODE

Est. 1983
9504 SUMMERHILL LN
DALLAS, TX 75238-1040

CONTACT:
Leilani Gagnaire
Dianne Goode
FAX (214) 341-2292
TEL 214-343-8558
CLIENTS INCLUDE:
American Airlines
Northern Telecom
Long Term Credit Bank of Japan
Gerald Hines Interests
Lee Hecht Harrison

KITTRELL/RIFFKIND ART GLASS, INC.

Est. 1979
5100 BELTLINE RD #820
DALLAS, TX 75240

CONTACT:
Barbara Kittrell
Michael Riffkind
FAX (214) 239-7998
TEL 214-239-7957

♦

SELECTED ORGANIZATIONS

AMERICAN CRAFT COUNCIL

72 SPRING ST
NEW YORK, NY 10012-4006
FAX 212-274-0650
TEL 212-274-0630

Hunter Kariher, Executive Director

The American Craft Council (ACC) stimulates public awareness and appreciation of the work of American craftspeople through museum exhibitions and educational programs, visual aids and publications. The American Craft Museum is an affiliate of the ACC; membership is shared.

The ACC consists of four operating units:

1. American Craft Enterprises produces exhibitions of handmade objects made by America's most talented craftspeople to enhance the awareness of American craft and to provide the opportunity for the public to acquire such crafts;

2. American Craft Publishing produces a bimonthly magazine to enhance the understanding and appreciation of American craft;

3. American Craft Association produces educational seminars and audio-visual materials to educate craftspeople, and provides support services for craftspeople;

4. American Craft Information Center provides information on American craft through a book/exhibit catalog collection and unique files on American craftspeople.

ARCHITECTURAL WOODWORK INSTITUTE

13924 BRADDOCK ROAD #100
PO BOX 1550
CENTREVILLE, VA 22020
FAX 703-222-2499
TEL 703-222-1100

The Architectural Woodwork Institute is a non-profit organization devoted to the education and development of the architectural woodwork field. The AWI provides a number of services including brief informational publications and research of various aspects of the industry. It also coordinates meetings of professionals within the woodwork realm. Membership is available to manufacturers and suppliers in the woodworking field interested in helping to further public knowledge.

ARTIST-BLACKSMITHS' ASSOCIATION OF NORTH AMERICA

PO BOX 206
WASHINGTON, MO 63090
FAX 314-390-2133
TEL 314-390-2133

Janelle Gilbert, Executive Secretary

Artist-Blacksmiths' Association of North America (ABANA) is a non-profit organization devoted to promoting the art of blacksmithing. ABANA serves to educate blacksmiths, acts as a resource for blacksmithing information, and publishes *Anvil's Ring*, a quarterly technical journal for blacksmiths.

GLASS ART SOCIETY

1305 FOURTH AVE #711
SEATTLE, WA 98101-2401
FAX 206-382-2630
TEL 206-382-1305

Alice Rooney, Executive Director

The Glass Art Society (GAS), an international non-profit organization, was founded in 1971 to encourage excellence and advance appreciation, understanding and development of the glass arts worldwide. GAS promotes communication among artists, educators, students, collectors, gallery and museum personnel, art critics, manufacturers and others through an annual conference and through the *Glass Art Society Journal* and newsletters.

INTERNATIONAL SCULPTURE CENTER

1050 17TH ST NW #250
WASHINGTON, DC 20036
FAX 202-785-0810
TEL 202-785-1144

David Furchgott, Executive Director

The International Sculpture Center (ISC) is a non-profit membership organization devoted to the advancement of contemporary sculpture. The ISC publishes *Sculpture* magazine, *Maquette*, and *InSite*. Activities include conferences; workshops; Sculpture Source, a computerized referral service and registry; exhibitions; and various other member benefits.

NATIONAL COUNCIL ON EDUCATION FOR THE CERAMIC ARTS

PO BOX 158
BANDON, OR 97411
TEL 503-347-4394
TEL 800-99N-CECA

Regina Brown, Executive Secretary

The National Council on Education for the Ceramic Arts (NCECA) is a professional organization of individuals whose interests, talents, or careers are primarily focused on the ceramic arts. NCECA strives to stimulate, promote and improve education in the ceramic arts, and to gather and disseminate information and ideas that are vital and stimulating to teachers, studio artists and others.

NATIONAL ORNAMENTAL & MISCELLANEOUS METALS ASSOCIATION

804-10 MAIN ST #E
FOREST PARK, GA 30050
FAX 404-366-1852
TEL 404-363-4009

Barbara Cook, Executive Director

The National Ornamental & Miscellaneous Metals Association (NOMMA) is the trade organization for those who produce ornamental gates, railings, furniture, sculpture and other fabricated metal products. NOMMA publishes a professional 'glossy' magazine, newsletter and various sales aids. The association also holds an annual awards competition, trade show and convention. During the convention, NOMMA provides an intensive education program. NOMMA has six chapters, one regional association and 20 committees.

STAINED GLASS ASSOCIATION OF AMERICA

PO BOX 22642
KANSAS CITY, MO 64113
FAX 816-361-9173
TEL 800-888-7422

Kathleen Murdock, Executive Secretary

The Stained Glass Association of America is a non-profit national organization founded to promote the finest in stained and art glass. In addition to publishing *Stained Glass* magazine, it sponsors educational programming and public awareness programs.

TILE HERITAGE FOUNDATION

PO BOX 1850
HEALDSBURG, CA 95448
FAX 707-431-8455
TEL 707-431-8453

Joseph A. Taylor, President

The Tile Heritage Foundation is a national non-profit organization dedicated to promoting awareness and appreciation of ceramic surfaces in the United States. In addition to maintaining a reference and research library, Tile Heritage publishes a biannual magazine and a quarterly newsletter, conducts annual symposiums, and supports research in the field of ceramic history and conservation.

AMERICAN CERAMICS

9 EAST 45 ST #603
NEW YORK, NY 10017
FAX 212-661-2389
TEL 212-661-4397

$28/year

American Ceramics, an art quarterly, was founded to enhance the preservation of ceramics' rich heritage and to document contemporary developments in the field. Articles feature the best and brightest ceramists: rising stars and established luminaries, as well as those early pioneers who transformed ceramics into a genuine art form.

AMERICAN CRAFT

AMERICAN CRAFT COUNCIL
72 SPRING ST
NEW YORK, NY 10012-4019
FAX 212-274-0650
TEL 212-274-0630

$40/year

American Craft, a bimonthly magazine, focuses on contemporary craft through artist profiles, reviews of major shows, a portfolio of emerging artists, a national calendar and news section, and book reviews, as well as illustrated columns reporting on commissions, acquisitions and exhibitions.

CERAMICS MONTHLY

PROFESSIONAL PUBLICATIONS, INC.
1609 NORTHWEST BLVD
PO BOX 12788
COLUMBUS, OH 43212-0788
FAX 614-488-4561
TEL 614-488-8236

$22/year

Ceramics Monthly offers a broad range of articles—including artist profiles, reviews of exhibitions, historical features, and business and technical information—for potters, ceramic sculptors, collectors, gallery and museum personnel, and interested observers.

DESIGN SOLUTIONS

ARCHITECTURAL WOODWORK
INSTITUTE
PO BOX 1550
CENTREVILLE, VA 22020-8550
FAX 703-222-2499
TEL 703-222-1100

$18/year

Design Solutions, a quarterly magazine, focuses on architectural woodwork, including explanations of techniques, materials, installations and restorations.

HISTORIC PRESERVATION

NATIONAL TRUST FOR HISTORIC
PRESERVATION
1785 MASSACHUSETTS AVE NW
WASHINGTON, DC 20036
FAX 202-673-4038
TEL 202-673-4000

$20/year

Historic Preservation, an award-winning magazine published six times a year, is the official journal of the National Trust for Historic Preservation. It includes full-color feature articles on historic people and places, architecture, garden restorations, and a special news section covering the highlights of preservation activity in each region of the country.

MARBLE AND ARCHITECTURAL STONE

DAVID ALLAN GLEN & CO.
PO BOX 4170
LAGUNA BEACH, CA 92652
FAX 714-470-0856
TEL 714-470-1388

$65/year

Six annual issues of *Marble and Architectural Stone* '… open new windows to the world of marble and its terrestrial relatives, illuminating in splendid color the amazing number and diversity of stones available for design and architectural use ….' The magazine features projects throughout the world and includes sourcing information on stone and fabricators.

ORNAMENTAL & MISCELLANEOUS METAL FABRICATOR

NATIONAL ORNAMENTAL & MISCELLANEOUS METALS ASSN.
804-10 MAIN ST #E
FOREST PARK, GA 30050
FAX 404-366-1852
TEL 404-363-4009

$18/year

Printed bimonthly, *Ornamental & Miscellaneous Metal Fabricator* is a resourceful guide to metalwork techniques, business tips, new products and book reviews.

PUBLIC ART REVIEW

FORECAST PUBLIC ARTWORKS
2324 UNIVERSITY AVE W #102
ST PAUL, MN 55114
FAX 612-641-0028
TEL 612-641-1128

$15/year

Public Art Review is a biannual journal exploring the many dimensions of public art. Each issue focuses on an overall theme— such as art in historic places or transit art—and offers listings of recently completed projects and artist opportunities, as well as critical reviews of books, exhibits and conferences.

SCULPTURE

INTERNATIONAL SCULPTURE CENTER
1050 17TH ST NW #250
WASHINGTON, DC 20036
FAX 202-785-0810
TEL 202-785-1144

$32/year

Sculpture, a bimonthly, four-color journal, focuses on established and emerging sculptors from the United States and abroad through profiles, interviews and critical reviews. Each issue also highlights collectors, commissions, opinion pieces, site-specific works and a calendar of exhibitions.

STAINED GLASS MAGAZINE

STAINED GLASS ASSOCIATION
OF AMERICA
CIRCULATION DEPARTMENT
6 SW SECOND ST #7
LEE'S SUMMIT, MO 64063
FAX 816-524-9405
TEL 816-524-9405
TEL 800-438-9581

$30/year

Since 1906, this quarterly publication has focused on expanding use of stained glass as an architectural element. *Stained Glass Magazine* features descriptions of materials and techniques, artist profiles, trade news and source information.

TILE HERITAGE

TILE HERITAGE FOUNDATION
PO BOX 1850
HEALDSBURG, CA 95448
FAX 707-431-8455
TEL 707-431-8453

$20/year

Tile Heritage: A Review of American Tile History, a biannual publication, features informative articles on both historic and contemporary ceramic tiles, written from a humanistic perspective and enhanced with large black-and-white photographs.

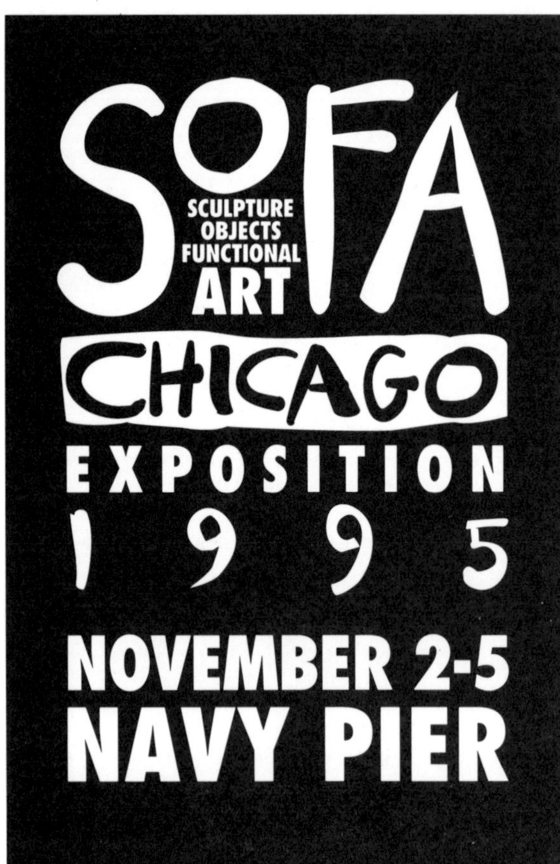

The Second Annual International Exposition of Sculpture, Objects & Functional Art presented by art galleries and dealers. In the new Festival Hall at Navy Pier.

A provocative artist/professional talk series will be held at the Exposition.

For Exposition and hotel/travel information:

Mark Lyman/SOFA CHICAGO 1995
210 West Superior Street
Chicago, IL 60610
T: 1.800.353.SOFA
F: 616.469.6356
E mail: sofa1@aol.com
Visit us on the World Wide Web:
http://www.sofaexpo.com

Opening Night Preview

A benefit for pediatric AIDS/HIV by the John Thomas Graziano Fund of Children's Memorial Hospital Thursday evening, November 2. Call Sarah Hall at 312.880.6860.

A project of Expressions of Culture, Inc.

WE COVER PUBLIC ART

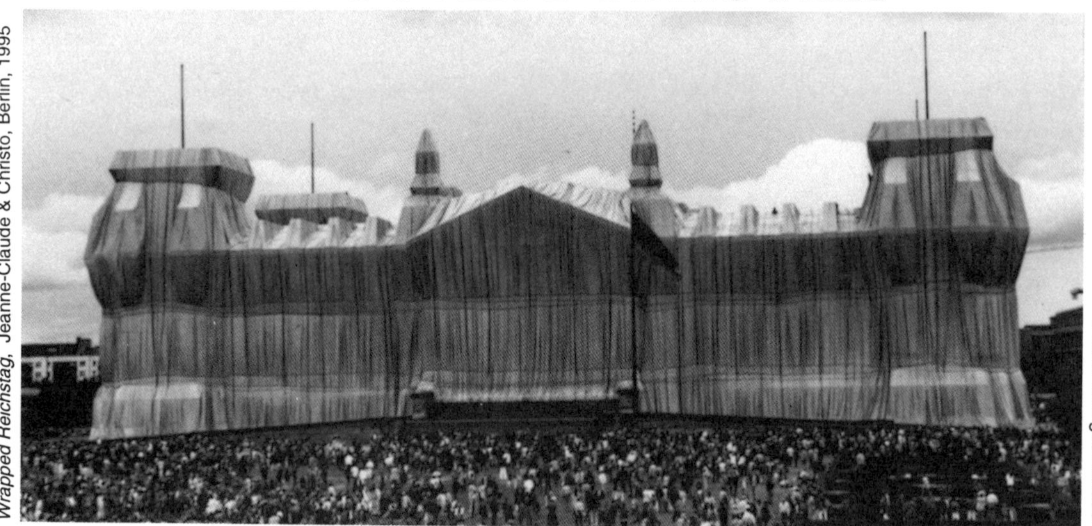

Public **Art** Review

THE ONLY JOURNAL OF ITS KIND

Public Art Review • 2324 University Ave. West, Suite 102 • St. Paul, MN 55114
PHONE 612-641-1128 • FAX 612-641-0028 • E-MAIL forecast@mtn.org

Published in April and October. Subscriptions are $15 a year (U.S. rates). Call for advertising rates.

INDEX OF ARTISTS AND COMPANIES

INDEX OF ARTISTS AND COMPANIES

INDEX OF ARTISTS AND COMPANIES